Psychology

Psychology

Fourth Edition

G. Neil Martin
Middlesex University, UK

Neil R. Carlson
University of Massachusetts, USA

William Buskist
Auburn University, USA

Allyn & Bacon
is an imprint of

PEARSON

Harlow, England • London • New York • Boston • San Francisco • Toronto
Sydney • Tokyo • Singapore • Hong Kong • Seoul • Taipei • New Delhi
Cape Town • Madrid • Mexico City • Amsterdam • Munich • Paris • Milan

PEARSON EDUCATION LIMITED

Edinburgh Gate
Harlow
Essex CM20 2JE
England

and Associated Companies throughout the world

Visit us on the World Wide Web at:
www.pearsoned.co.uk

Original edition published by Allyn and Bacon,
A Pearson Education Company
Needham Heights, Massachusetts, USA
Copyright © 1997 by Allyn and Bacon

First published by
Pearson Education Limited in Great Britain in 2000
Second edition published in 2004
Third edition published in 2007
Fourth edition published in 2010

© Pearson Education Limited 2000, 2004, 2007, 2010

ISBN: 978-0-273-72011-9

British Library Cataloguing-in-Publication Data
A catalogue record for this book is available from the British Library

Library of Congress Cataloging-in-Publication Data
A catalog record for this book is available from the Library of Congress

10 9 8 7 6 5 4 3 2 1
14 13 12 11 10

Typeset in 9.75/12pt Sabon by 30
Printed and bound by Rotolito Lombarda, Italy

The publisher's policy is to use paper manufactured from sustainable forests.

Brief contents

Contents

5 Sensation

6 Perception

7 Learning and behaviour

Preface to the fourth edition

Here's an apparently simple question: What made you pick up this book and read it? You might be a psychology student and spotted this book in your library or bookshop. It might be the recommended text on your course. You may have been at a friend's house, become bored and begun leafing through this book lying on a table. You may have been attracted to the cover. You may even have liked the authors' other books so much that you had to read this one as well.

This simple exercise illustrates the essence of psychology – the scientific study of why and how humans (and animals) behave in the way that they do. Psychology is the science of behaviour and, being a science, it approaches the understanding of behaviour in a specific way. Everyone has an opinion on psychology and on what motivates people and what brings people to react and behave in the way that they do. We are all quasi-psychologists, in a way. Trained psychologists, however, attempt to understand behaviour through careful experimentation and empirical observation. They do this because it is the best method of gaining useful and reliable information about behaviour and the causes of behaviour. This book, the fourth edition of *Psychology*, introduces you to the scientific approach to understanding human behaviour and each chapter reviews the current state of knowledge about behaviour – from intelligence and emotion to child development and prejudice – based on sound scientific study.

Let's go back to the opening paragraph. The reason you are reading this book is probably because it was recommended on your psychology course or because you have spotted it in the library or bookshop and think that it will give you good value for money. As a student of psychology, you are studying the most fascinating and complex subject matter in science – human behaviour. You study not just how individuals develop language, perceive visual images, reason, feel, respond to others and learn, but also the biological bases of these behaviours. You will learn about the various methods that psychologists adopt when studying behaviour and how people evolved to do the things that they do (although scientists do have disagreements over the best method of study to adopt – the one certain fact you will learn in psychology is that no finding is ever 'cut and dried', there is always discussion and controversy).

Psychology is one of the most popular degree courses in Europe and in North America – it is the third most popular degree subject in the UK, based on student applications to study. The subject matter is intrinsically interesting and its study allows students to develop what are called, in management-speak, 'transferable skills' – skills such as operating a computer, writing laboratory reports, producing clear and evaluative written work, performing statistical operations, using statistical software packages, designing projects, communicating,

material to an audience ... all of these, in addition to understanding specific aspects of human behaviour such as how children learn to read, why we perceive in the way that we do, how we influence others, how the brain works, how we reason and so on.

The fourth edition – pedagogical features

The fourth edition of *Psychology* continues where the last three editions left off. It is designed to give you a flavour of what modern psychology is about. It describes every major field of psychology and includes up-to-date information and clear evaluation of controversial findings, theories and models in psychology. One of the best ways to learn about psychology is to keep abreast of new developments in the field. As a beginning student, you clearly need to know and understand the basics, but you also need to know how those basic findings are being modified and challenged. As a result, the new edition has over 430 new references, reflecting the extensive nature of the updated content and its emphasis on presenting you with up-to-date information from the psychology research literature (it also reflects how prolific psychologists are).

This fourth edition, like the previous three, has several features to help you understand the applications and controversies in psychology and to make you think more deeply about psychological issues and psychological research. Here's a brief summary:

Conceptual and Historical Issues in Psychological Science

Understanding the history of a discipline and the context in which research emerged is important for any discipline. Throughout the book, at the relevant point, a CHiPS symbol will appear next to the text which will flag up any issues related to a major conceptual or historical milestone in psychology. When you come across one of these icons, pause and think about issues surrounding the topic being described and evaluated.

An International Perspective

Every chapter has a section headed 'An International Perspective', which allows you to see how psychology is, and has been, studied across nations and cultures. An important issue in psychological research is whether findings are universal or specific to a group being studied. If you find that someone behaves in a particular way in one group in one culture or country, would a similar person behave in the same way, under the same conditions in another culture or country? This section provides an international perspective on topics such as emotion, personality, memory, cannabis use, physical attraction, infidelity, sex bias, language and brain activation, prejudice, eating disorders, mental illness and many others.

MyLab

At various points in the text, you'll find this symbol: .

This will alert you to one of the major interactivities in MyLab, your online course in introductory psychology that helps you test your knowledge and understanding of the material in each chapter. The interactivities come in various forms – multiple choice questions, true or false questions. Most, however, will involve you applying your knowledge and understanding via interactive exercises.

The chapters in MyPsychLab correspond to those in your book. When you are ready to explore the resources for a chapter you will need to log in to MyPsychLab, to the relevant chapter and click on to the study guide. From here, you can watch and work through animations, exercises, interactions, tests and much more to help further and consolidate your understanding.

Cutting Edge

The Cutting Edge feature reviews a recent study or series of studies that are novel, important or make a really significant contribution to our knowledge and understanding of psychology. Some of these include research on: why celebrity worshippers worship (Chapter 1), how stories are more persuasive than statistics (Chapter 2), whether a woman's fertility influences her acceptance of a date (Chapter 3), jealousy and brain activity (Chapter 3), the neurobiological correlates of behaving like James Bond (Chapter 4), predictors of university success (Chapter 7), the effect of chewing gum on memory (Chapter 8), how evening and morning types differ (Chapter 9), the role of the brain in interpreting irony (Chapter 10), the effect of intelligence on wealth and health (Chapter 11), how eBay works (Chapter 11), loneliness and autistic tendency (Chapter 12), how posture influences emotion (Chapter 13), how emotion affects food intake (Chapter 13), whether your email address reflects your personality (Chapter 14), whether different States show different personalities (Chapter 14), whether sexist humour makes us sexist (Chapter 15), how obedience to authority has not changed for decades (Chapter 16), the relationship between ostracism and our perception of our environment (Chapter 16), the relationship between your name and your success (Chapter 16), the role of telomeres in stress (Chapter 17), and the effect of commuting distance on stress (Chapter 17). There are 44 new Cutting Edge sections in this edition.

Controversies in Psychological Science

Each chapter contains at least one section which focuses on a controversy in psychological science. The best advice I was given by one of my tutors as an undergraduate was, 'question everything'. By this, he did not mean criticising studies or theories for the sake of it. He meant that psychology was a live, constantly evolving science which, like all sciences, progresses by contradiction: somebody reports a finding; another refines this finding by showing that it applies only to certain contexts, people, conditions and so on. Most introductory texts can appear biblical: unquestionable towers of knowledge. But, although a great deal of fact is presented in this text, it also shows you how facts can be interpreted in different ways.

The Controversies in Psychological Science sections are made up of three parts. The first part (the issue) outlines the controversy; the second part (the evidence) describes and evaluates the data that give rise to the controversy; finally, the third part (conclusion) briefly suggests what we can conclude from the evidence available. One aim of the Controversies in Psychological Science sections is to engage you in critical thinking by presenting you with a controversial topic, theme or idea in psychology and take you through evidence for and against a topic, theme or idea. Some of these controversies are well known: Is intelligence racially determined? Can primates learn language? Are psychiatric patients violent? Others are not so well known but cast some light on some aspect of psychology and behaviour: Is psychology common sense? Does the weather influence mood and thinking? Do 'smart' drugs work? Can neuroimaging detect deception? And so on. The material covered in the Controversies sections will give you a hint of the liveliness of debate surrounding some issues in psychology and could form the basis of discussion with your fellow students or with colleagues in tutorials or seminars.

Psychology in Action

Research in psychology is aimed at exploring, defining and predicting the causes of behaviour. Some of it is also aimed at using such research in an applied, practical setting. The Psychology in Action sections review the evidence for the application of psychological principles to a 'real-life' issue: for example, using closed-circuit television (CCTV) to identify criminals; jury decision-making; road traffic accident reduction; the use of brain technology to help the seriously ill to communicate; differences between men and women in the ways they use language, and so on. Chapter 18 on mental disorders is almost a whole PiA section in itself because it describes the study and treatment of mental illness. These sections aim to show you how principles from psychology can be used to help us to understand why we behave in the way that we do.

What you should be able to do after reading the chapter

At the beginning of each chapter there is a brief description about what you should be able to do after reading the chapter. This section provides you with a set of goals that you should try to achieve during the course of reading the chapter. The items in these sections are, in essence, your learning objectives.

Questions to think about

The beginning of each chapter also presents you with a series of questions to think about. The Questions to Think About feature has been designed to help you ask questions about your knowledge of psychology and to probe what you have learned from the topic you have read. There are further questions for you to think about embedded throughout each chapter.

Chapter reviews

At the end of each chapter there is a summary of the information that has gone before. The summary has been bullet-pointed to make it easy to read and understand.

Glossary

Important terms that are defined in the text and which appear in bold also appear, alphabetically, in a glossary at the end of the book.

Suggestions for further reading

As an intelligent reader of an introductory textbook you will be hungry for more psychological knowledge after having tasted this starter. The suggestions for further reading are designed to satisfy your appetite. All the recommended readings come with comments and these should help you to decide on what further reading is best for you. Some of the reading is quite advanced; other readings are less demanding. You should try to consult at least a few of these per chapter because the further reading will lead you into more detailed description and discussion of psychological topics.

Journals to consult

In addition to the further reading, we have added a list of journals for you to consult. About 90 per cent of the facts, theories and ideas that you read about in this book have been published in science journals and there are many different types of journals in psychology. This is where original research, theories and methods in psychology are published. If you want to go direct to the source of psychological research then journals are the place to go. You might find much of the material in them deeply unattractive, incomprehensible or abstruse. However, you will also find material that is original and new. Textbook authors are a little like journalists reporting the events and people that they think readers will be interested in. Of course, textbook authors have few of the failings of journalists but they can only give you a brief glimpse of the events that they report. The beauty of psychology is that you can consult the source yourself, and the journals listed should help you do this.

Website addresses

Following the annotated suggested reading, we have included, for each chapter, the internet addresses of some websites which are worth visiting. Some of these give you more information about the general or specific issues raised in the chapter; some provide you with online tutorials, experiments, virtual libraries or bibliographies.

All of these features, together with the extensive revision of the text to make it up-to-date and comprehensive, should provide you with an effective learning tool. To familiarise yourself with these features and how they will benefit your study of this text, they are reproduced and described in the guided tour which follows.

I very much hope that you will learn a lot about psychology from the fourth edition of *Psychology*. I also hope that you enjoy what you learn and that the book will take you to places you had not thought of exploring. This is the beauty of psychology. Opening one door will lead you to several others. If you like what you have read, then please do let me know. One of the joys of teaching and researching is obtaining feedback about the work that you produce. If you have any comment to make or suggestion for improvement, then please write to me, G. Neil Martin, Department of Psychology, School of Health and Social Sciences, Middlesex University, The Burroughs, Hendon, London, NW4 4BT, UK, or email me at: n.martin@mdx.ac.uk. You can also visit my website at: http://www.mdx.ac.uk/hssc/staff/profiles/academic/martinn.htm.

G. Neil Martin, FRSA
London, 2009

Guided tour

This book is accompanied by **MyPsychLab**, which contains a wealth of interactive learning tools to enrich your experience of the text, including a study plan, multiple choice questions, animations, interactions and questions. Log on to **http://www.mypsychlab.co.uk** and follow the registration instructions inside the access card at the back of this book to access these valuable resources.

Each chapter of **Psychology** begins with an extract introducing you to the topic by using a real world example. **Questions to think about** encourage you to reflect on the key issues in the chapter, while the list of **What you should be able to do** helps you to track your learning as you read. The **MyPsychLab feature** also suggests some of the interactive resources available to support your understanding of these topics. [

Throughout the text you'll see this icon, which indicates that there is a relevant resource in MyPsychLab to enable fuller understanding of the topic.

This new edition is richly illustrated with diagrams and photographs.

Psychology in action uses fascinating, real-life examples to show how psychology is applied in the real world.

Cutting edge introduces you to some of the most interesting new subjects of study in contemporary psychology.

An International Perspective allows you to explore global differences in psychological research, attitudes, policies and methods.

To be a true psychologist it is vital to understand the conceptual and historical issues that shape the field. Watch out for this icon as you read, which will help you remember key milestones in the development of psychological science.

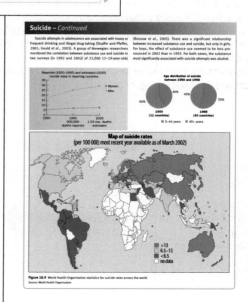

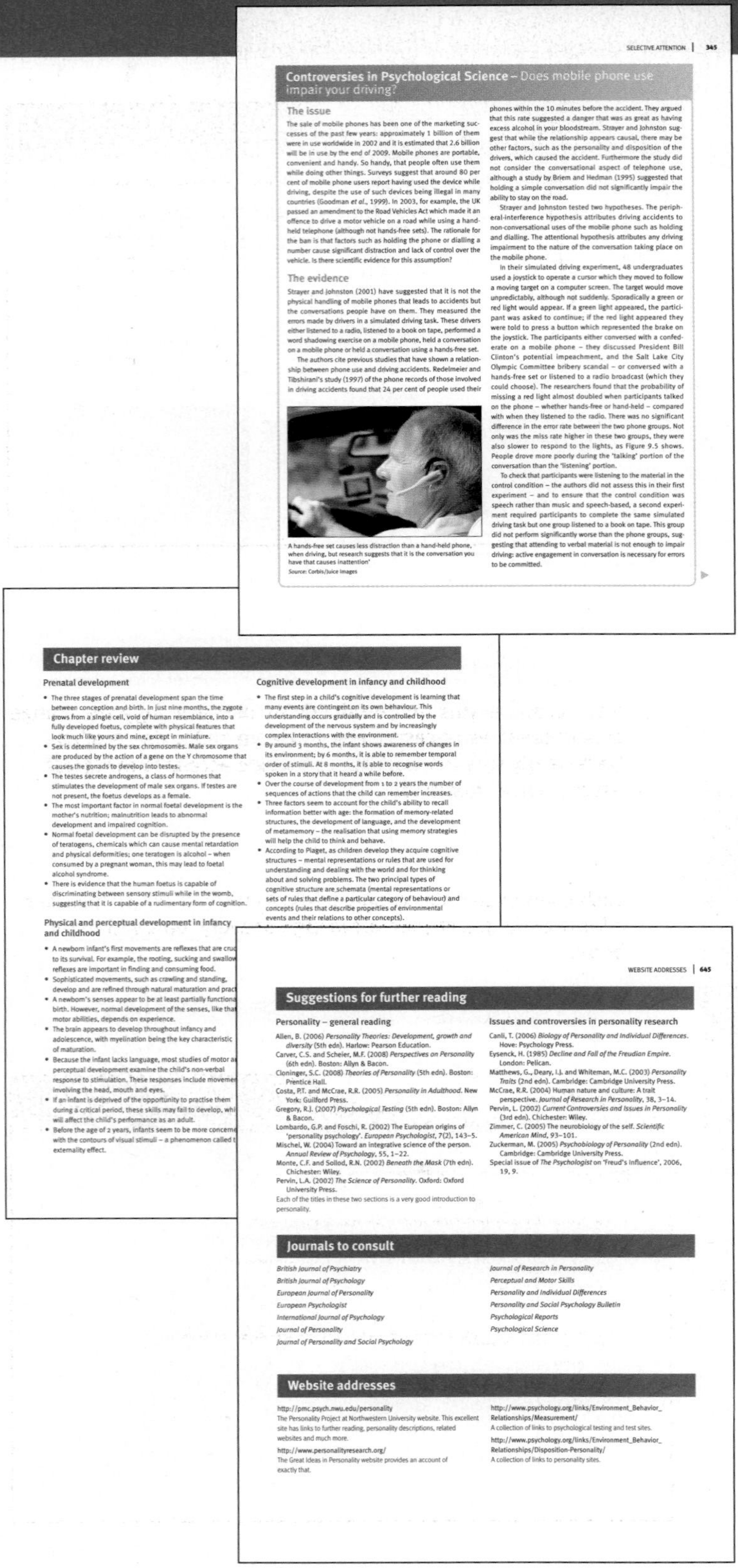

Controversies in Psychological Science – Does mobile phone use impair your driving?

The issue

The sale of mobile phones has been one of the marketing successes of the past few years: approximately 1 billion of them were in use worldwide in 2007 and it is estimated that 2.6 billion will be in use by the end of 2009. Mobile phones are portable, convenient and handy. So handy, that people often use them while doing other things. Surveys suggest that around 80 per cent of mobile phone users report having used the device while driving, despite the use of such devices being illegal in many countries (Goodman et al., 1999). In 2003, for example, the UK passed an amendment to the Road Vehicles Act which made it an offence to drive a motor vehicle on a road while using a hand-held telephone (although not hands-free sets). The rationale for the ban is that factors such as holding the phone or dialling a number cause significant distraction and lack of control over the vehicle. Is there scientific evidence for this assumption?

The evidence

Strayer and Johnston (2001) have suggested that it is not the physical handling of mobile phones that leads to accidents but the conversations people have on them. They measured the errors made by drivers in a simulated driving task. These drivers either listened to a radio, listened to a book on tape, performed a word shadowing exercise on a mobile phone, held a conversation on a mobile phone or held a conversation using a hands-free set.

The authors cite previous studies that have shown a relationship between phone use and driving accidents. Redelmeier and Tibshirani's study (1997) of the phone records of those involved in driving accidents found that 24 per cent of people used their phones within the 10 minutes before the accident. They argued that this rate suggested a danger that was as great as having excess alcohol in your bloodstream. Strayer and Johnston suggest that while the relationship appears causal, there may be other factors, such as the personality and disposition of the drivers, which caused the accident. Furthermore the study did not consider the conversational aspect of telephone use, although a study by Briem and Hedman (1995) suggested that holding a simple conversation did not significantly impair the ability to stay on the road.

Strayer and Johnston tested two hypotheses. The peripheral-interference hypothesis attributes driving accidents to non-conversational uses of the mobile phone such as holding and dialling. The attentional hypothesis attributes any driving impairment to the nature of the conversation taking place on the mobile phone.

In their simulated driving experiment, 48 undergraduates used a joystick to operate a cursor which they moved to follow a moving target on a computer screen. The target would move unpredictably, although not suddenly. Sporadically a green or red light would appear. If a green light appeared, the participant was asked to continue; if the red light appeared they were told to press a button which represented the brake on the joystick. The participants either conversed with a confederate on a mobile phone – they discussed President Bill Clinton's potential impeachment, and the Salt Lake City Olympic Committee bribery scandal – or conversed with a hands-free set or listened to a radio broadcast (which they could choose). The researchers found that the probability of missing a red light almost doubled when participants talked on the phone – whether hands-free or hand-held – compared with when they listened to the radio. There was no significant difference in the error rate between the two phone groups. Not only was the miss rate higher in these two groups, they were also slower to respond to the lights, as Figure 9.5 shows. People drove more poorly during the 'talking' portion of the conversation than the 'listening' portion.

To check that participants were listening to the material in the control condition – the authors did not assess this in their first experiment – and to ensure that the control condition was speech rather than music and speech-based, a second experiment required participants to complete the same simulated driving task but one group listened to a book on tape. This group did not perform significantly worse than the phone groups, suggesting that attending to verbal material is not enough to impair driving: active engagement in conversation is necessary for errors to be committed.

A hands-free set causes less distraction than a hand-held phone, when driving, but research suggests that it is the conversation you have that causes inattention.
Source: Corbis/Juice Images

Chapter review

Prenatal development

- The three stages of prenatal development span the time between conception and birth. In just nine months, the zygote grows from a single cell, void of human resemblance, into a fully developed foetus, complete with physical features that look much like yours and mine, except in miniature.
- Sex is determined by the sex chromosomes. Male sex organs are produced by the action of a gene on the Y chromosome that causes the gonads to develop into testes.
- The testes secrete androgens, a class of hormones that stimulates the development of male sex organs. If testes are not present, the foetus develops as a female.
- The most important factor in normal foetal development is the mother's nutrition; malnutrition leads to abnormal development and impaired cognition.
- Normal foetal development can be disrupted by the presence of teratogens, chemicals which can cause mental retardation and physical deformities; one teratogen is alcohol – when consumed by a pregnant woman, this may lead to foetal alcohol syndrome.
- There is evidence that the human foetus is capable of discriminating between sensory stimuli while in the womb, suggesting that it is capable of a rudimentary form of cognition.

Physical and perceptual development in infancy and childhood

- A newborn infant's first movements are reflexes that are crucial to its survival. For example, the rooting, sucking and swallowing reflexes are important in finding and consuming food.
- Sophisticated movements, such as crawling and standing, develop and are refined through natural maturation and practice.
- A newborn's senses appear to be at least partially functional at birth. However, normal development of the senses, like that of motor abilities, depends on experience.
- The brain appears to develop throughout the key characteristic of maturation.
- Because the infant lacks language, most studies of motor and perceptual development examine the child's non-verbal response to stimulation. These responses include movement involving the head, mouth and eyes.
- If an infant is deprived of the opportunity to practise them during a critical period, these skills may fail to develop, which will affect the child's performance as an adult.
- Before the age of 2 years, infants seem to be more concerned with the contours of visual stimuli – a phenomenon called the externality effect.

Cognitive development in infancy and childhood

- The first step in a child's cognitive development is learning that many events are contingent on its own behaviour. This understanding occurs gradually and is controlled by the development of the nervous system and by increasingly complex interactions with the environment.
- By around 3 months, the infant shows awareness of changes in its environment; by 6 months, it is able to remember temporal order of stimuli. At 8 months, it is able to recognise words spoken in a story that it heard a while before.
- Over the course of development from 1 to 2 years the number of sequences of actions that the child can remember increases.
- Three factors seem to account for the child's ability to recall information better with age: the formation of memory-related structures, the development of language, and the development of metamemory – the realisation that using memory strategies will help the child to think and behave.
- According to Piaget, as children develop they acquire cognitive structures – mental representations or rules that are used for understanding and dealing with the world and for thinking about and solving problems. The two principal types of cognitive structure are schemata (mental representations or sets of rules that define a particular category of behaviour) and concepts (rules that describe properties of environmental events and their relations to other concepts).

Suggestions for further reading

Personality – general reading

Allen, B. (2006) *Personality Theories: Development, growth and diversity* (5th edn). Harlow: Pearson Education.
Carver, C.S. and Scheier, M.F. (2008) *Perspectives on Personality* (6th edn). Boston: Allyn & Bacon.
Cloninger, S.C. (2008) *Theories of Personality* (5th edn). Boston: Prentice Hall.
Costa, P.T. and McCrae, R.R. (2005) *Personality in Adulthood*. New York: Guilford Press.
Gregory, R.J. (2007) *Psychological Testing* (5th edn). Boston: Allyn & Bacon.
Lombardo, G.P. and Foschi, R. (2002) The European origins of 'personality psychology'. *European Psychologist*, 7(2), 143–5.
Mischel, W. (2004) Toward an integrative science of the person. *Annual Review of Psychology*, 55, 1–22.
Monte, C.F. and Sollod, R.N. (2003) *Beneath the Mask* (7th edn). Chichester: Wiley.
Pervin, L.A. (2002) *The Science of Personality*. Oxford: Oxford University Press.

Each of the titles in these two sections is a very good introduction to personality.

Issues and controversies in personality research

Canli, T. (2006) *Biology of Personality and Individual Differences*. Hove: Psychology Press.
Eysenck, H. (1985) *Decline and Fall of the Freudian Empire*. London: Pelican.
Matthews, G., Deary, I.J. and Whiteman, M.C. (2003) *Personality Traits* (2nd edn). Cambridge: Cambridge University Press.
McCrae, R.R. (2004) Human nature and culture: A trait perspective. *Journal of Research in Personality*, 38, 3–14.
Pervin, L. (2002) *Current Controversies and Issues in Personality* (3rd edn). Chichester: Wiley.
Zimmer, C. (2005) The neurobiology of the self. *Scientific American Mind*, 93–101.
Zuckerman, M. (2005) *Psychobiology of Personality* (2nd edn). Cambridge: Cambridge University Press.
Special Issue of *The Psychologist* on 'Freud's Influence', 2006, 19, 9.

Journals to consult

British Journal of Psychiatry
British Journal of Psychology
European Journal of Personality
European Psychologist
International Journal of Psychology
Journal of Personality
Journal of Personality and Social Psychology

Journal of Research in Personality
Perceptual and Motor Skills
Personality and Individual Differences
Personality and Social Psychology Bulletin
Psychological Reports
Psychological Science

Website addresses

http://pmc.psych.nwu.edu/personality
The Personality Project at Northwestern University website. This excellent site has links to further reading, personality descriptions, related websites and much more.

http://www.personalityresearch.org/
The Great Ideas in Personality website provides an account of exactly that.

http://www.psychology.org/links/Environment_Behavior_Relationships/Measurement/
A collection of links to psychological testing and test sites.

http://www.psychology.org/links/Environment_Behavior_Relationships/Disposition-Personality/
A collection of links to personality sites.

New **Controversies in Psychological Science** examine recent reports and beliefs about psychological findings, to help develop your skills in critical analysis.

The extensive **Chapter review** enables you to consolidate what you've just learnt and is a great tool to help you revise.

At the end of each chapter, **Suggestions for further reading, Journals to consult** and **Website addresses** provide links to further sources of information, allowing you to broaden your understanding of the topic and providing a great starting point for your own research.

MyPsychLab walkthrough

Log in to http://www.mypsychlab.co.uk to access all the additional learning materials that accompany *Psychology*, Fourth Edition.

Study Plan

The **Study Plan** section of MyPsychLab is a comprehensive self-test and revision centre. When you log in to **MyPsychLab** you can select any chapter and take a **'pre-test'**, to check how well you understand the topics in that chapter. This identifies any areas you need to work on and generates a **personal study plan** to help you learn. You can then take a **'post-test'** after revising the study materials in more depth, to check your progress. The study plan includes:

- Pre-test and post-test questions
- Learning resources including simulations, animations and video
- 'Quick review' revision questions
- eText

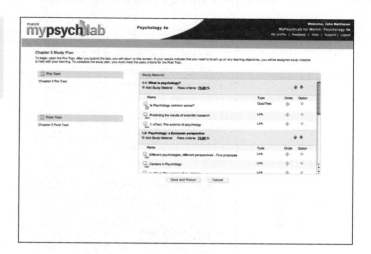

Also accompanying the Fourth Edition of *Psychology* are a range of additional resources to help you learn and revise, such as twice-yearly **research updates** to provide access to the latest psychological literature.

Each chapter contains a large bank of **multiple choice questions** allowing you to test your knowledge of every topic within the book.

Flashcards are available for all key terms in the book, as well as an easy-to-access online glossary.

Media Library

The MyPsychLab **Media Library** contains a wealth of chapter-specific, rich learning resources to help you assess your knowledge and master key concepts.

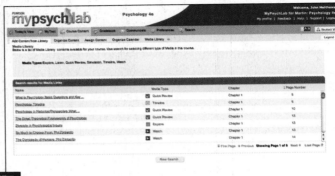

Video

Watch video clips of key experiments and phenomena in psychology and test yourself on what you have observed.

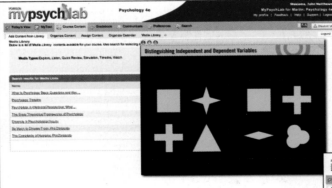

Simulations

Interactive activities that test your understanding in a practical way.

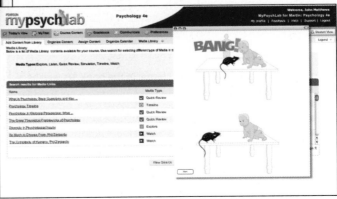

Animations

Fun and interesting animations allow you to watch psychology in action.

The teaching package

For lecturers a range of supplementary materials is available to help you to plan lectures, create customised tests and set additional, tracked assignments for students. This package includes:

Instructor's Manual

PowerPoint® Slides

MyPsychLab with additional assignments

MyTest testbank

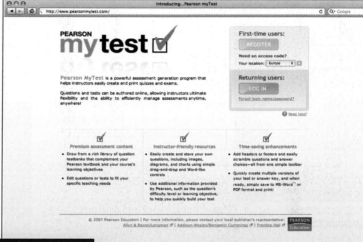

The authors

Dr G. Neil Martin is Reader in Psychology at Middlesex University, UK, a Chartered Scientist, and a Fellow of the Royal Society of Arts. He was educated in Wales, Scotland and England, graduating with a first-class Master of Arts degree in psychology from the University of Aberdeen, where he also won the annual Henry Prize for outstanding undergraduate achievement in psychology. He completed his Ph.D. on psychophysiology and olfactory perception at the University of Warwick, England.

He is the author of *Psychology – A Beginner's Guide* (Oneworld, 2008); *Human Neuropsychology*, the first European textbook in the field now in its second edition (Pearson Education, 2006); *Essential Biological Psychology* (Hodder Arnold, 2003); *Study Guide – Psychology*, with Nicky Brunswick (Pearson Education, 2005); and the 6th and 7th international editions of *Psychology*, with Neil Carlson and colleagues from the US and Canada (Allyn & Bacon, 2006, 2009). With Nicky Brunswick, he wrote the first European online course in introductory psychology (Pearson Education, 2001, 2003), now in its third edition (Pearson Education, 2006). He is the author of over 150 articles on psychology, has contributed to the *Oxford Companion to Food*, and acts as consultant to industry, business and the media on the psychology of olfaction and humour. He has been an editorial board member of *The Psychologist, Journal of Health, Social and Environmental Issues* and the *Annals of Improbable Research* – the satirical journal which awards the annual IgNobel prizes for science that should never be repeated – for which he is also a columnist. He also works as a freelance journalist; his first article for a major national newspaper was entitled 'More than 20 things you needed to know about the nose'.

Dr Neil R. Carlson is Professor of Psychology at the University of Massachusetts, USA. He studied as an undergraduate and postgraduate at the University of Illinois.

He wrote his first textbook, *Physiology of Behavior*, while on sabbatical leave at the University of Victoria in British Columbia. He was the first Allyn & Bacon author to submit a book manuscript on a computer disk.

A few years ago he began to collaborate with Jay Alexander, an artist who works as a laboratory technician at the University of Massachusetts. They prepare all the artwork for Professor Carlson's books.

Dr William Buskist is Professor of Psychology at Auburn University, USA, where he regularly teaches the introductory psychology and the teaching of psychology courses. He has directed Auburn's psychology research laboratories. He also teaches seminars and workshops for undergraduates who are preparing for graduate study in psychology.

He graduated from Brigham Young University in 1981 with a Ph.D. in experimental psychology. Although most of his research has been in the area of human social behaviour, particularly competitive behaviours, Dr Buskist's research now largely focuses on issues in the teaching of psychology.

Dr Michael Hogg is Professor of Social Psychology at Claremont Graduate University, USA, and is a Fellow of the Society for the Psychological Study of Social Issues, the Society for Personality and Social Psychology, and the Academy of the Social Sciences in Australia. He was the foundation director of the Centre for the Study of Group Processes at the University of Queensland, and in 2004 he was a British Academy Visiting Professor at Birmingham University. Educated at Bristol Grammar School and the University of Birmingham, he received his Ph.D. in 1983 from Bristol University, and has held teaching posts at Bristol University, Macquarie University, the University of Melbourne, the University of Queensland, and Princeton University, and visiting appointments at the University of California, Los Angeles, the University of California, Santa Cruz, the University of California, Santa Barbara, City University, Hong Kong, and the University of Kent, UK.

Michael Hogg's research on group processes, intergroup relations, social identity, and self-conception is closely associated with the development of social identity theory. He has published over 200 scientific books, chapters and articles on these topics. With Graham Vaughan he is the author of *Social Psychology* – one of the leading introductory social psychology texts in Europe and the UK, it was first published in 1995 and is now in its fifth edition. An associate editor of the *Journal of Experimental Social Psychology*, Michael Hogg serves on the editorial board of most of the main social psychology journals, and is foundation co-editor with Dominic Abrams of the journal *Group Processes and Intergroup Relations*, and senior consultant editor for the *Sage Social Psychology Program*. This current research focuses on leadership, deviance, uncertainty reduction, extremism, and sub-group relations. Michael Hogg lives in Los Angeles, but spends substantial time each year in the UK, and in Brisbane, Australia.

Dr Dominic Abrams is Professor of Social Psychology and Director of the Centre for the Study of Group Processes at the University of Kent, Canterbury, UK. He is a Chartered Psychologist, Fellow of the Society for the Psychological Study of Social Issues, and of the Academy of Social Sciences. Following his undergraduate degree at Manchester University and a Masters at the London School of Economics and Political Sciences, he received his Ph.D. in 1984 from the University of Kent, and held teaching posts at the universities of Bristol and Dundee before returning to Kent in 1989. He has held visiting appointments at the universities of Melbourne, Queensland and Urbana-Champaign, Illinois.

This research on intergroup relations and the self-concept has concentrated on social identity, and spans childhood to old age, and groups defined by gender, ethnicity, language, faith, sexuality and disability. He has been associate editor for the *British Journal of Social Psychology*, and special issue editor for the *Journal of Community and Applied Psychology* and the *International Journal of Behavioral Development*. He is foundation editor, with Michael Hogg, of *Group Processes and Intergroup Relations*, and serves on the editorial boards of *Journal of Personality and Social Psychology* and the *European Review of Social Psychology*. He has recently been chair of the British Psychological Society Research Board, and now chairs the Joint Committee for Psychology in Higher Education in the UK. His current research focuses on the social psychology of social inclusion and exclusion, societal indices of prejudice, the development of group understanding, and the role of intergroup contact in prejudice reduction.

Dr Nicky Brunswick is Senior Lecturer in Psychology at Middlesex University, UK. She studied for her Ph.D. in the psychophysiology of dyslexia at the University of Warwick and completed her postdoctoral training with Chris and Uta Frith at the Wellcome Department of Cognitive Neurology, Institute of Neurology, London. She researches in the areas of health psychology and developmental dyslexia and her research on reading and dyslexia has appeared in the journals, *Brain*, *Nature Neuroscience* and *Science*. She is the author of *Dyslexia – A Beginner's Guide* (Oneworld, 2009).

Acknowledgements

In the course of writing and revising *Psychology*, I have had the good fortune to call on the expertise and detailed knowledge of a number of people. These include colleagues who reviewed my proposal for a revision of this text, members of Prentice Hall Europe's Special Editorial Board for the first edition of *Psychology*, and my colleagues at Middlesex University and elsewhere. Their contribution is very gratefully acknowledged below. In addition, there are one or two people in particular I would like to thank for contributing to this and previous editions.

From the first and second editions

From Pearson Education, I would like to thank (in chronological order), Christina Wipf-Perry who originally suggested the idea of a European adaptation and who has continued to take an interest in this blossoming pedagogy; Tim Pitts, for his unfailing philosophical outlook; Sue Phillips, development editor for the first edition; Liz Tarrant, production editor for the first edition; Jane Powell, who commissioned the first set of research updates for the website; Matthew Smith, an author's editor; and John Yates, the very tall and charming publisher who helped to launch the first edition. Finally, I would like to thank my current editors and publishers: Ruth Haggerty, Louise Lakey, Karen Mclaren and the incomparable Morten Fuglevand. The second edition was written as *Fame Academy* reached its denouement. I would like to thank the inmates, especially Ainslie and David, for many hours of terpsichorean entertainment.

I would like to thank for the following colleagues who either reviewed draft manuscripts or chapters or assisted in the completion of the book in many other invaluable ways.

From the third edition

Thanks, as ever, go to the indomitable Morten Fuglevand who was the guiding hand in this, and other, projects. His influence was enormous. Thanks, too, to Janey Webb for carrying on the Psychology torch, getting the third edition into shape and for assorted treats; Sarah Wild (for all the sterling help with figure queries); Stephen Jeffrey and Nada Jolic (for all the help with MyLab); Robert Chaundy and Jonathan Price for the punctillious copy-editing and proofing; Sarah Busby, Geoff Chatterton, Georgina Clark-Mazo, Nicola Shortt, Alun Swift, Maggie Wells, and the UK and AU marketing teams for all their hard work.

Thanks to the following for all their feedback and advice on the first, second and third editions.

Dave Alcock	University of Bristol
Bruce Arnow	Stanford University
Jane Barnet	Middlesex University
John H.W. Barrett	University of Bristol
Sarah Beck	University of Birmingham
Joe Boden	University of Plymouth
Glynis Breakwell	University of Surrey
Vicki Bruce	Edinburgh University
Brian Brunswick	
Nicola Brunswick	Middlesex University
Andrew Calder	University of Cambridge
David Carey	University of Aberdeen
Julia Cogan	
Gillian Cohen	Open University
Martin Conway	University of Durham
Neil Cooper	University of East Anglia
Mats Danielsson	Lulea University of Technology
Alyson Davis	Surrey University
Sergia Della Sala	University of Edinburgh
Jan Deregowski	University of Aberdeen
Paul Emmelkamp	Amsterdam University
Ann Erling	Gothenburg University
Anthony Esgate	University of Westminster
Nigel Foreman	Middlesex University
Adrian Furnham	University College London
Peter Garrard	Institute of Cognitive Neuroscience, UCL
Ken Gilhooly	Brunel University
Nitin Gogtay	Child Psychiatry Branch, NIMH
Caroline Green	University of Aberdeen
Ruth Green	Staffordshire University
Sheila Hale	
Peter Halligan	University of Cardiff
Usneeral B. Hamaker	University of Amsterdam
Trevor Harley	University of Dundee
Ronald Henss	University of Saarland
Kenneth Hugdahl	University of Bergen
Dai Jones	University of Glamorgan
Gail Kinman	University of Bedfordshire
Paul Kinnear	University of Aberdeen
Winek Koisor	Pearson Education

Virginia Lam	University of East London
Robert Logie	University of Aberdeen
Monicque M. Lorist	University of Groningen, The Netherlands
Geoff Lowe	University of Hull
Bjorn Lyxell	Linkoping University
Neil MacRae	University of Bristol
Caroline Mansfield	Oxford Brookes University
MarkMcDaniel	University of New Mexico
Maggie McGonigle	University of Edinburgh
Aidan Moran	University College Dublin
Peter Morris	University of Lancaster
David Moxon	Peterborough Regional College
Tom Nugent	Child Psychiatry Branch, NIMH
Rory O'Connor	University of Strathclyde
Michael Oddy	Brain Injury Rehabilitation Trust
Adrian Parker	Gothenburg University
Andy Peart	Blackwell
John Pickering	University of Warwick
Arne Poulsen	University of Roskilde
Jan Pryor	Wellington University
Sandra Read	University of Bedfordshire
Andries F. Sanders	Vrije University
Tony Shelton	Liverpool John Moores University
Dean Keith Simonton	University of California, Davis
Michele Surbey	James Cook University
Frode Svartdal	University of Tromsø
Jaqui Taylor	Bournemouth University
Kevin Thomas	Trinity College Dublin
Jimmie Thomson	University of Strathclyde
Zazie Todd	University of Leeds
Andy Tolmie	University of Strathclyde
Margit Torneus	Umea University
Andy Tramo	Harvard University
Erik Wastlund	Karlstad University
Claire Wells	
Brian Young	University of Exeter
Rob Bell	Queen's University Belfast

From the fourth edition

Thanks to all those who helped by offering feedback and suggestions for this fourth edition of *Psychology*.

Mark Burgess	Oxford Brookes University
Kate Eames	Coventry University
Eddie Edgerton	University of the West of Scotland
Ian Fairholm	Bath University
Nollaig Frost	Middlesex University
Kerry Greer	Mary Immaculate, Limerick
Eilis Hennessy	University College Dublin
Philip A. Higham	University of Southampton
Fay Julal	Southampton Solent University
Maggie McGonigle	Edinburgh University
Paddy O'Donnell	University of Glasgow
Qazi Rahman	Queen Mary University, London
Kevin Silber	University of Derby
Ian Stewart	Galway University
John Turner	University of East London
Lorenzo Vigentini	Edinburgh University

Thanks also to the students from the University of Edinburgh and Southampton Solent University.

And finally, I would like to thank Janey Webb for all her help, support and encouragement during the third transmogrification; Catherine Morissey, redoubtable production-editor-in-waiting, plus Tim Parker, Barbara Massam, Rose James, Jane Ashley, Leo Stanley and John Matthews for all their hard work on the fourth edition of the book and MyPsychLab. Also, thanks to Beth Rix and Robert Chaundy for their help on the Research and Study Guide for the third edition; all of the reps at Pearson for their indefatigable drive and tenacity; Dame Marjorie Scardino, for the coffee, the chat, and the honour of discussing the project with her; the staff at Coffee Bean and Costa in High Barnet for providing the space where the bulk of the research for the fourth edition was written up and the first draft revised; and Niki for her 'how are yous?', her love of leteeoos, and her patience.

Publisher's acknowledgements

We are grateful to the following for permission to reproduce copyright material:

Figures

Figure 1.1 from Psychology's status as a scientific discipline: its empirical placement within an implicit hierarchy of the sciences, *Review of General Psychology*, 8 (1), p. 65, Figure 2 (Simonton, D.K. 2004); Figure 1.2a from Foltveld, P. The psychological profession in Denmark. in Schorr, A. and Saari, S. (eds) Psychology in Europe., ISBN 0-88937-155-5, © 1995, Hogrefe & Huber Publishers, Seattle, Toronto, Göttingen, Bern; Figure 1.2b from Van Drunen, P. Professional psychology in the Netherlands: history and recent trends. In Schorr, A. and Saari, S. (eds) Psychology in Europe., ISBN 0-88937-155-5, © 1995, Hogrefe & Huber Publishers, Seattle, Toronto, Göttingen, Bern; Figure 1.3 from Montin, S. The public image of psychologists in Finland. Reproduced with permission from Psychology in Europe by Schorr, A. and Saari, S. (eds), ISBN 0-88937-155-5, © 1995, Hogrefe & Huber Publishers, Seattle, Toronto, Göttingen, Bern.; Figure 1.4 Stock Montage Inc.; Figure 1.5 by permission of The McGraw-Hill Companies; Figure 1.6a from The return of Phineas Gage: clues about the brain from a famous patient, *Science*, 264, pp. 1102–1105 (Damasio, H., Grabowski, T., Frank, R., Galaburda, A.M. and Damasio, A.R. 1994), Department of Neurology and Image Analysis Facility, University of Iowa; Figure 1.7 from Explicit and implicit processing of words and pseudowords by adult developmental dyslexics: A search for Wernicke's Wortschatz?, *Brain*, 122 (Brunswick, N., McCory, E., Price, C., Frith, C. and Frith, U. 1999); Figure 3.1 from Public acceptance of evolution in 34 countries, *Science*, 313, p. 765 (Miller, J.D., Scott, E. and Okamoto, S. 11 August 2006), Reprinted with permission from AAAS; Figure 3.4 from *Fig. 9.1, p. 241 from MOLECULAR BIOLOGY OF THE GENE, 4th ed. by James D. Watson, Nancy H. Hopkins, Jeffrey W. Roberts, Joan Argetsinger Steitz, and Alan M. Weiner. Copyright (c) 1987 by the Benjamin/Cummings Publishing Company, Inc. Reprinted by permission of Pearson Education, Inc.*; Figure 3.5 CNRI/Science Photo Library Ltd.; Unnumbered figure on page 90 Science Photo Library Ltd: Jacopin; Figure 3.8 Corbis: Outline; Figure 3.10 from *Durante et al, Personality and Social Psychology Bulletin, 34(11), pp. 1451–1460, Changes in women's choice of dress across the ovulatory cycle: Naturalistic and laboratory task-based evidence* (2008) (c) 2008, Sage Publications. Reprinted by permission of Sage Publications; Figure 3.11 from Patterns and universals of mate poaching across 53 nations: the effects of sex, culture and personality on romantically attracting another person's partner, *Journal of Personality and Social Psychology*, 86(4), figure 2 pp. 560–584 (Schmitt, D.P. 2004), reprinted with permission of American Psychological Association and David P. Schmitt; Figure 4.2 Professor Peter Cull/Science Photo Library Ltd.; Figure 4.3 Harvard Medical School/Betty G. Martindale; Figure 4.16(a) BSIP, Astier/Science Photo Library Ltd., (b) Abby Johnston: John Reardon; Figure 4.17 from Coping with severe memory impairment, *Neuropsychological Rehabilitation*, 14(5), pp. 481–94 (Oddy, M. and Cogan, J. 2004), Psychology Press, reprinted by permission of the publisher (Taylor & Francis Group, http://www.informaworld.com); Figure 4.18 (a) University of Florida: Arturo Sinclair, (b) Landov Media: David Kamerman/The Boston Globe; Figure 4.20 Daniel Sambraus/Science Photo Library Ltd.; Figure 4.21a from Imaging cognition II: an empirical review of 275 PET and fMRI studies, *Journal of Cognitive Neuroscience*, 12(1), pp. 1–47 (Cabeza, R. and Nyberg, L. 2000), reprinted by permission of the authors; Figure 4.21b from Anjan Chatterjee, Commentary: A madness to the methods of cognitive neuroscience?, *Journal of Cognitive Neuroscience*, 17:6 (June, 2005), figure 1, pp. 847-9 (2005) (c) 2005 by the Massachusetts Institute of Technology; Figure 4.22 (a) Hank Morgan/Rainbow, (b) Dr J. McA. Jones, Good Samaritan Hospital, Portland, Oregon, USA.; Figure 4.23 Corbis/Owen Franken; Figure 4.24 Scott Camazine/Photo Researchers, Inc; Figure 4.25 Pearson Education/Prentice Hall; Figure 4.26 Reprinted with permission from Elsevier: Reprinted from NeuroImage, Vol. 45, Issue 3, B.A. Parris, G. Kuhn, G.A. Mizen, A.Benattayallah and T.L. Hodgson, Imaging the Impossible: An fMRI study of impossible causal relationships in magic tricks, 1033-39, copyright 2009; Figure 4.27 Reprinted with permission from Elsevier: Reprinted from NeuroImage, vol. 40, issue 3, S.a. Spence, C. Kaylor-Hughes, T.F.D. Farrow and I.D. Wilkinson, Speaking Secrets and Lies: The contribution of ventrolateral prefrontal cortex to vocal deception, pages 1411-18, copyright 2008; Figure 4.28 University of Durham/Simon Fraser/Science Photo Library Ltd.; Figures 4.30a, 4.30b from *Physiology of Behavior*, 6th ed., Ally & Bacon (Carlson, N.R. 1998) p. 235 (c) Allyn & Bacon. Reproduced with permission; Figure 4.31 (b) Tissuepix/Science Photo Library Ltd.; Figure 4.36 from *Pinel, BIOPSYCHOLOGY, Fig. 4.36 © 2003, 2000, 1997 Allyn and Bacon Reproduced by permission of Pearson Education, Inc.*; Figure 4.37 Science Photo Library Ltd.; Figure 4.41 from Mental health of teenagers who use cannabis, *British Journal of Psychiatry*, 150, pp. 216–221 (Rey, J.M., Sawyer, M.G., Raphael,

B., Patton, G.C. and Lynskey, M. 2002), reprinted by permission of the Royal College of Psychiatrists; Figure 5.3 J. Silver/SuperStock; Figure 5.10 Richard Elliot/Stone/Getty; Figure 5.12 Courtesy of Douglas G. Mollerstuen, New England Medical Center; Figure 5.14 adapted from *Proceedings of the Royal Society (London)*, Series B, 166, pp. 80–111 (Dowling, J.E. and Boycott, B.B. 1966), redrawn by permission of the Royal Society; Figure 5.16 from The disappearance of steady fixated visual test objects, *Journal of the Optical Society of America*, 43, pp. 495-501 (Riggs, L.A., Ratliff, F., Cornsweet, J.C. and Cornsweet, T.N. 1953); Figure 5.22 Courtesy of American Optical Corporation; Figure 5.23 Brash, S., Maranto, G., Murphy, W. and Walker, B. (1990) *How Things Work: The brain*. Virginia: Time-Life Books. © 1990 Time-Life Books; Figure 5.26a from *Principles of Behavioral Neuroscience*, McGraw-Hill (Beatty, J. 1995) reprinted with permission of Jackson Beatty; Figures 5.28, 5.30, 5.31, 5.32 (b), 5.39 and 5.40 From GOLDSTEIN. Sensation and Peception, 7E. © 2007 Wadsworth, a part of Cengage learning, Inc. Reproduced by permission. www.cengage.com/ permissions; Figure 5.29 from *Cognitive Psychology*, Houghton Mifflin (Payne, D.G. and Wenger, M. 1998) p. 75 (c) 1998 Houghton Mifflin Company. Used with permission; Figure 5.33 from *Pinel, BIOPSYCHOLOGY BEYOND THE BRAIN & BEHAVIOR CD, fig. 5.33* (c) 2003, 2000, 1997 Allyn & Bacon. Reproduced by permission of Pearson Education, Inc.; Figure 5.35 Whitfield, P. and Stoddart, M. *Pathways of Perception*. New York: Torstar Books; Figure 5.36 Reprinted by permission from MacMillan Publishers Ltd: Nature Neuroscience vol.10. Nr.1, Jan 2007, copyright 2007 (r). Science Faction: Louie Psihoyos (l); Figure 5.38 Louis Psihoyos/Science Faction Images; Figure 6.9 from *Cognitive Psychology*, New York: Appleton-Century-Crofts (Neisser, U. 1967) reprinted with permission; Figure 6.13 adapted from *Osherson, Daniel N., Stephen M. Kosslyn, and John Hollerbach, eds., An Invitation to Cognitive Science, Volume 2: Visual Cognition and Action, figure 2.4, adapted* (c) 1990 Massachusetts Institute of Technology, by permission of the MIT Press; Figure 6.14 adapted from *Osherson, Daniel N., Stephen M. Kosslyn, and John Hollerbach, eds., An Invitation to Cognitive Science, Volume 2: Visual Cognition and Action, figure 2.9, adapted* (c) Massachusetts Institute of Technology, by permission of the MIT Press; Figure 6.17 from The effects of contextual scenes on the identification of objects, *Memory and Cognition*, 3, pp. 519–23 (Palmer, S.E. 1975), reprinted by permission of the Psychonomic Society, Inc.; Figure 6.19 Reproduced with permission from © The British Psychological Society: Journal of Neuropsychology; Figure 6.20 Reprinted with permission from Elsevier: Reprinted from Acta Psychologica, vol. 130, issue 2, R. McBain, D. Norton and Y. Chen, Females excel at basic face perception, pages 168–173, copyright 2009; Figure 6.21 Reproduced with permission from © The British Psychological Society: British Psychological Society; Figure 6.22 from *Matlin/Foley, SENSATION & PERCEPTION, fig. 6.22* (c) 1992. Reproduced by permission of Pearson Education, Inc.; Figure 6.24 from Texture and visual perception, *Scientific American*, 212, pp. 34–38 (Julesz, B. 1965), reprinted with permission of Dr. Bela Julesz; Figure 6.27 Powerstock/SuperStock; Figure 6.30 from

HABER, Psychology of Visual Perception, 1st ed. (c) 1973 Wadsworth, a part of Cengage Learning, Inc. reproduced by permission, www.cengage.com/permissions; Figure 6.38 from *Matlin/Foley, SENSATION & PERCEPTION, FIG. 6.38* (c) 1992. Reproduced by permission of Pearson Education, Inc.; Figure 6.45 Pearson Education Inc.; Figure 6.46 Cengage: Thomson Learning; Figure 6.50 from Human Neuropsychology, 2nd edn, Pearson/Prentice Hall (Martin, G.N., 2006). Image kindly provided by Dr Olaf Blanke; Figure 6.51 Chatterjee, A.A. madness to the methods of cognitive neuroscience? Journal of Cognitive Neuroscience, 2005, 17, 6, 847–9, © by the Massachusetts Institute of Technology; Figure 6.52 Reprinted from *The Lancet*, 350, P. Halligan and J. Marshall, The Art of Visual Neglect, pp. 139–40, Copyright 1997, with permission from Elsevier; Figure 7.4 adapted from *Hill, LEARNING: A SURVEY OF PSYCHOLOGICAL INTERPRETATIONS, fig. 7.4* (c) 2002, 1997, 1990 Allyn & Bacon. Reproduced by permission of Pearson Education, Inc.; Figure 7.5 from *Hill, LEARNING: A SURVEY OF PSYCHOLOGICAL INTERPRETATIONS, fig. 7.5* (c) 2002, 1997, 1990 Allyn & Bacon. Reproduced by permission of Pearson Education, Inc.; Figure 7.6 from Improving spatial awareness in physically disabled children using virtual environments, *Engineering Science and Education Journal*, 8(5), pp. 196–200 (Wilson, P.N. et al. 1999), reprinted by permission of the Institute of Electrical Engineers; Figure 7.10 Powerstock/SuperStock; Figure 7.11 from Insight and problem solving (Dominowski, R.L. and Dallob, P.) in, *The Nature of Insight* (Sternberg, R. and Davidson, J. (eds) 1996), Reproduced with permission from MIT Press; Figure 8.4 adapted from *Visual Spatial Working Memory*, Psychology Press Limited (Logie, R. 1995) p. 127 (c) 1995. Reprinted by permission of Psychology Press Limited, Hove, UK and Professor Robert Logie; Figure 8.15 Schmolck, H., Buffalo, E.A. and Squire, L.R., 'Memory distortions develop over time: recollections of the OJ Simpson trial verdict after 15 and 32 months', *Psychological Science*, 2000, 11(1), 39–45, reprinted by permission of Blackwell Publishers Ltd.; Figure 8.21 Reprinted by permission from Macmillan Publishers Ltd: *NATURE, Place navigation impaired in rats with hippocampal lesions*, 182(297), pp. 681–683 (Morris, R.G.M. et al. 1982), Copyright 1982; Figures 8.22, 8.23 from Recalling routes around London: Activation of the right hippocampus in taxi drivers, *Journal of Neuroscience*, 17, p. 7103 (Maguire, E.A., Frackowiak, R.S.J. and Frith, C.D. 1997) (c) 1997 by the Society for Neuroscience; Figure 8.24 reprinted by permission of Oxford University Press: I.G Dobbins and A.D. Wagner, Domain-general and domain-sensitive prefrontal mechanisms for recollecting events and detecting novelty, Cerebral Cortex November 2005, 15, pages 1768–78; Figure 9.2 from *Hameroff, Stuart, Alfred Kaszniak, and Alwyn Scott, eds., Toward a Science of Consciousness II: The Second Tucson Discussions and Debates, figure 18.1 (c) 1998 Massachusetts Institute of Technology, by permission of the MIT Press;* Figure 9.5 Strayer, D.L. and Johnston, W.A., *Driven to distraction: Dual-task studies of simulated driving and conversing on a cellular telephone*. Psychological Science, 2001, 12 (6), 462–6, reprinted by permission of Blackwell

Publishers Ltd.; Figure 9.7 figure provided by Daniel Simons: Reproduced with kind permission Perception 1999, vol. 28, pages 1059-74, Simons D.J., Chabris C.F., "Gorillas in our midst sustained inattentional blindness for dynamic events."; Figure 9.8 adapted from *Human Neuropsychology*, 2nd ed., Pearson Education (Martin, G.N. 2006), reproduced with permission; Figure 9.9 from *Why We Sleep: The Functions of Sleep in Humans and other Mammals*, Oxford University Press (Horne, J.A. 1988) figure 1.1 p. 10, By permission of Oxford University Press; Figures 9.10, 9.12 from *The Biology of Dreaming*, courtesy of Charles C Thomas, Publisher, Ltd. Springfield, Illinois (Hartmann, E. 1967); Figure 9.11 from Hobson, J.A., *Consciousness*. New York: W.H. Freeman, 1999; Figure 10.1 from The future of language, *Science*, 303, figure 1 p. 1329 (Graddol, D. 27 February 2004), copyright (2004) AAAS, Reprinted with permission from AAAS; Figure 10.2 from The future of language, *Science*, 303, p. 1330 (Graddol, D. 27 February 2004), copyright (2004) AAAS, Reprinted with permission from AAAS; Figure 10.3 from *Cognitive Psychology*, first ed., Houghton Mifflin (Payne, D.G. and Wenger, M.J. 1998) (c) 1998 by Houghton Mifflin Company. Used with permission; Figure 10.4 from *Campbell, Lyle, Historical Linguistics: An Introduction, figure 6.1, redrawn* (c) 1999 Massachusetts Institute of Technology, by permission of the MIT Press; Figure 10.5 from *Just/Carpenter, PSYCHOLOGY OF READING, fig. 10.5* (c) 1987 Allyn & Bacon. Reproduced by permission of Pearson Education, Inc.; Figure 10.6 from An interactive activation model of context effects in letter perception: Part 1: An account of basic findings, *Psychological Review*, 88, pp. 375–407 (McClelland, J.L. and Rumelhart, D.E. 1981), reprinted with permission of The American Psychological Association and James L. McClelland; Figure 10.7 from Principles that are invoked in the acquisition of words, but not facts, *Cognition*, 77, B33-B43 (Waxman, S.R. and Booth, A.E. 2000) (c) 2000, with permission of Elsevier; Figure 10.8 © 1999 Cable News Network, LP, LPP, All rights reserved.; Figure 10.10 from Language deficits and genetic factors, *Trends in Cognitive Sciences*, 1(1), p. 7 (Gopnik, M. 1997) (c) 1997, with permission from Elsevier; Figure 10.11 from On genes, speech and language, *New England Journal of Medicine*, p. 1655 (Fischer, S.E. 20 October 2005), Copyright (c) 2005 Massachusetts Medical Society. All rights reserved; Figure 10.13 PNAS: copyright 2008 National Academy of Sciences, USA; Figure 10.14 from Sound and meaning: how native language affects reading strategies, *Nature Neuroscience*, 3(1), pp. 3-5 (Fiez, J. 2000), reprinted by permission of the author; Figure 11.1 from *Technical Supplement for the Culture Fair Intelligence Test Scales 2 and 3, figure 1, p.7* Originally published by The Institute of Personality and Ability Testing, Inc., Champaign, IL, USA Currently published by Hogrefe Ltd., Oxford, UK (www.hogrefe.co.uk). copyright (c) 1973 (c) 2008, by Hogrefe Ltd. Reproduced with permission. All rights reserved; Figure 11.3 from Decomposing self-estimates of intelligence: Structure and sex differences across 12 nations, © *British Journal of Psychology*, Vol Number:100, figure 1, pp. 429–442 (von Stumm, S., Charmorro-Premuzic, T. and Furnham, A. 2009), Reproduced with permission of The British Psychological Society;

Figure 11.4 from The effects of sex and context on paper and pencil spatial task performance, *Journal of General Psychology*, vol. 116, pp. 133–139 (Kalichman, S.C. 1989), reprinted by permission of the publisher (Taylor & Francis, http://www.informaworld.com); Figure 11.5 from Frequency curve and percent curve *from the Stanford-Binet Intelligence Scales, First-Fourth Editions (SB) by Various,* 1916, 1937, 1960, 1972, 1986, Austin: PRO-ED. Product number: R13376, with permission from Pro-Ed Inc.; Figure 11.7 © Bob Daemmrich/The Image Works. Reproduced with permission.;Figure 11.8 from Rising mean IQ: cognitive demand of mathematics education for young children, population exposure to formal schooling, and the neurobiology of the prefrontal cortex, *Intelligence*, 33, figure 1, p. 94 (Blair, C., Gamson, D., Thorne, S. and Baker, D. 2005), with permission of Elsevier; Figure 11.9 Katherine K. Sulik; Figures 11.10, 11.11 from The genetics of cognitive abilities and disabilities, *Scientific American*, 278(5), pp. 40–7 (Plomin, R. and DeFries, J.C. 1998), reprinted by permission of Dr. Jennifer C. Christiansen; Figure 11.12 from *Reprinted from Neurobiology of Aging, 30(4), T. A. Salthouse, When does age-related cognitive decline begin? figure 2, pp. 507–14, Copyright 2009*, with permission from Elsevier; Figure 11.13 from Beatty, J. (1995). Principles *of Behavioral Neuroscience*. New York: Brown and Benchmark/William C. Brown Communications Inc., Reprinted with permission; Figure 11.14 (a) Alfred Pasieka/Science Photo Library; Figure 11.15 Reprinted with permission from Elsevier: Reprinted from NeuroImage, 45, issue 3, A.D. Leow, I. Yanovsky, N. Parikshak, X. Hua, S. Lee, et al., Alzheimer's Disease Neuroimaging Initiative: A one year follow up study using tensor-based morphometry correlating degenerative rates, biomarkers and cognition, pages 645–55, copyright 2009; Figure 11.16 from Cognitive deficits in the early stages of Alzheimer's disease, *Current Directions in Psychological Science* 17, 3, 198–202. (Storandt, M. 2008), Wiley-Blackwell, reproduced with permission; Figure 11.17 Reprinted with permission from Elsevier: Reprinted from NeuroImage, vol. 45, issue 1, G.C.Schwindt and S.E. Black, Functional imaging studies of episodic memory in Alzheimer's disease: a quantitive meta-analysis, pages 181–91, copyright 2009; Figure 11.18 (a) by permission of Oxford University Press: Oxford University Press, (c) Corbis: Basso uls Sophie/CORBIS Sygma; Figure 11.19 from *Solso, COGNITIVE PSYCHOLOGY, fig. 11.19* (1998) Reproduced by permission of Pearson Education, Inc.; Figure 11.23 from *Pinel, BIOPSYCHOLOGY, fig. 11.23* (c) 2003, 2000, 1997 Allyn & Bacon. Reproduced by permission of Pearson Education, Inc.; Figure 12.1 Neil Harding/Getty Images; Figure 12.3 from *Berk, CHILD DEVELOPMENT, fig. 12.3* (c) 1997 Pearson Education, Inc. Reproduced by permission of Pearson Education, Inc.; Figure 12.4 Images courtesy of P. Ellen Grant, M.D.; Figure 12.5 from The development of the brain, *Scientific American*, 241, pp. 106–17 (Cowan, W.M. 1979), with permission of Nelson H. Prentiss; Figure 12.6 adapted from Pattern perception in early infancy (Salapatek, P.), *Infant Perception: From Sensation to Cognition* (Cohen, L.H. and Salapatek, P. (eds) 1975), Copyright 1975, with permission from Elsevier; Figure 12.9 from Reactions to responsive contingent stimulation in early infancy, *Merrill-Palmer Quarterly*, 18, pp. 219–227 (Watson, J.S. and Ramey, C.T. 1972); Figure 12.10 W.H. Freeman and Company; Figure 12.11 from *Of Children: An introduction to child development*, 4th ed., Wadsworth (Lefrancois, G.R. 1983) with permission of Guy Lefrancois; Figure 12.12 adapted from Development functions for speeds of cognitive processes, *Journal of Experimental Child Psychology*, 45 p. 361 (Krails, R. 1988), Copyright 1988, with permission from Elsevier; Figure 12.13 from Autism: cognitive deficit or cognitive style?, *Trends in Cognitive Sciences*, 3(6), pp. 216–22 (Happé, F. 1999), copyright 1999, with permission of Elsevier; Figure 12.14 from Why may girls persist in smoking?, *Journal of Adolescence*, 22, pp. 657-72 (Crisp, A. et al 1999), copyright 1999, with permission of Elsevier; Figure 12.15 from Up and down in middle age: monotonic and nonmonotonic changes in roles, status and personality, *Journal of Personality and Social Psychology, 89(2), pp. 194–204, APA* (Helson, R. and Soto, C.J. 2005), reprinted with permission; Figure 12.16 National Centre on Health Statistics; Figure 12.17 from Thoughts for today, *British Medical Journal*, 331, p. 1550, unnumbered figure (24-31 December 2005), reproduced with permission from the BMJ Publishing Group; Figure 13.4 from How sensory properties of foods affect human feeding behaviour, *Psychology and Behaviour*, 29, pp. 409–417 (Rolls, B.J., Rolls, E.T. and Rowe, E.A. 1982), © 1982, with permission of Elsevier and Rolls, B.J. and Rolls, E.T.; Figure 13.5 from Obesity: responding to the global epidemic, *Journal of Consulting and Clinical Psychology*, 70(3), pp. 510–525 (Wadden, T.A., Brownell, K.D. and Foster, G.D. 2002), with permission of American Psychological Association and Shape Up America! www.shapeup.org; Figure 13.6 from What predicts weight regain in a group of successful weight losers?, *Journal of Consulting and Clinical Psychology*, 67(2), pp. 177–185 (McGuire, T.M., Wing, R.R., Klem, W., Lang, M.L. and Hill, J.O. 1999), with permission of American Psychological Association; Figure 13.7 Photo courtesy of Dr J. Sholtis, The Rockefeller University. © 1995 Amgen, Inc.; Figure 13.8 Reprinted with permission from Elsevier from *Physiology & Behavior*, vol. 94, issue 1, Walter Kaye, Neurobiology of anorexia and bulimia nervosa, pages 121–35, copyright 2008; Figure 13.9 Reprinted by permission of Oxford University Press and Bruce Arnow; Figures 13.10, 13.11 Paul Ekman Group, LLC; Figure 13.12 Science Photo Library Ltd/CLAUS LUNAU / BONNIER PUBLICATIONS; Figure 13.13 Science Photo Library Ltd.; Figure 13.14 from The return of Phineas Gage: Clues about the brain from a famous patient, *Science* 246, pp. 1102–1105 (Damasio, H. Grabowski, T., Frank, R., Galaburda, A.M. and Damasio, A.R. 1994); Figure 13.15 The Orion Publishing Group Ltd: Reproduced from Emotions Revealed by Paul Ekman, Weidenfeld & Nicolson, London; Figure 13.16 adapted from The repertoire of nonverbal behavior: categories, origins, usage and coding, *Semiotica*, 1, pp. 49-68 (Ekman, P. and Friesen, W. 1969), with permission of Mouton de Gruyter and Dr. Paul Ekman; Figure 13.17 from Inhibiting and facilitating conditions of the human smile: a nonobtrusive test of facial feedback hypothesis, *Journal of Personality and Social Psychology*, 54, pp. 768–777 (Strack, F. et al. 1988), with permission of Prof. Dr. Fritz Strack; Figure 14.2 from *16PF® Fifth Edition Administrator's Manual.* , Copyright © 1993 by the Institute for Personality and Ability Testing, Inc., Champaign, Illinois, USA. All rights reserved. Reproduced with permission . "16PF" is a registered trade mark of IPAT Inc. IPAT is a wholly owned susidiary of OPP Ltd.; Figure 14.3 from Eysenck, H.J., *The Inequality of Man*. London: Temple Smith, 1973; Figure 14.4 from *Human Neuropsychology*, 2nd ed., Pearson Education (Martin, G.N. 2006), reproduced with permission; Figure 16.2 from *Baron/Byrne, SOCIAL PSYCHOLOGY: UNDERSTANDING HUMAN INTERACTION, fig. 16.2 (c)* 2006 Allyn & Bacon. Reproduced by permission of Pearson Education, Inc.; Figure 17.1 from Tackling health inequalities: all agenda for action (Whitehead, M. 1995) in *Tackling Inequalities in Health: An Agenda for Action* (Benzenal et al. (ed)); Figure 17.2 WHO: World health statistics 2007, part 1, 10 statistical highlights in global public health p. 13. www.who.int/whosis/whostat2007/en/ index.html; Figure 17.3 from Annual cigarette consumption per person for 1998, or latest available data, http://www.who.int/ tobacco/statistics/tobacco_atlas/en/, by permission of the World Health Organization; Figure 17.4 from Smoke-free Areas, http://www.who.int/tobacco/statistics/tobacco_atlas/en/, by permission of the World Health Organization; Figure 17.5 from *World Health Statistics 2007*, 1st ed., World Health Organization (2007) p. 15; Figure 17.6 from Countries which now ban tobacco advertising, http://www.who.int/tobacco/statistics/ tobacco_atlas/en/, by permission of the World Health Organization; Figure 17.7 from Health warnings and legislation, http://www.who.int/tobacco/statistics/tobacco_atlas/en/, by permission of the World Health Organization; Figures 17.8a, 17.8b from *IAS Fact Sheet: Alcohol Consumption and Harm in the UK and EU* London: IAS Unnumbered figures, p. 3 and p. 4; Figures 17.9a, 17.9b from *IAS Fact Sheet: Alcohol Consumption and Harm in the UK and EU* London: IAS Unnumbered maps, p. 7 and p. 8; Figure 17.10a from Aids (HIV Disease) Age standardised mortality in males aged 0+64 (1994-6) - NUTS 2 p. 111, *Atlas on Mortality in the European Union*, Map 21.1 Publications Office for the European Union (c) European Communities (2002); Figure 17.10b from Aids (HIV Disease) Age standardised mortality in females aged 0+64 (1994-6) - NUTS 2 p. 112, *Atlas on Mortality in the European Union*, Map 21.2 Publications Office for the European Union (c) European Communities (2002); Figure 17.11 from Seyle, H., *Stress without Distress*, © Lippincott Williams & Wilkins 1974; Figure 17.14 Andrejs Liepins/Science Photo Library/Photo Researchers Inc.; Figure 17.15 Reprinted from *The Lancet, 346, J. K. Kiecolt, P. T. Marucha, W.B. Malarkey, A. M. Mercado, and R. Glaser, Slowing of wound-healing by psychological stress, pp. 1194–96, Copyright 1995* , with permission from Elsevier; Figure 17.17 from Longitudinal study of procrastination, performance, stress and health: the costs and benefits of dawdling, *Psychological Science*, 8(6), pp. 454-8 (Tice, D.M. and Baumeister, R.F. 1997), reprinted by permission of

Blackwell Publishing Ltd.; Figure 17.18 from The impact of work on the psychological health and well-being of older Americans, *Annual Review of Gerontology and Geriatrics*, 26, pp. 153–174 (James, J.B. and Spiro, A. 2007) (c) Springer Publishing Company, Reproduced with the permission of the Springer Publishing Company, LLC, New York, NY 10036; Figure 18.1 Loren McIntyre/Woodfin Camp & Associates, Inc.; Figure 18.2 © Bettman/Corbis; Figure 18.6 from Repeated exposure of flight phobics to flights in virtual reality, *Behaviour Research and Therapy*, 39, pp. 1033–50 (Muhlberger, A. et al.), copyright 2000, with permission from Elsevier; Figure 18.8 from Neuroimaging and neuropathological studies of depressions: Implications for the cognitive-emotional features of mood disorders, *Current Opinion in Neurobiology*, 11 (Drevets, W.C.), copyright 2001, with permission from Elsevier; Figure 18.9 WHO: SUPRE suicide prevention information leaflet "Live Your Life" available online page 2, www.who.int/mental_health/management/en/SUPRE_flyer1.pdf;

Tables

Table 1.2 from Psychological evidence in court, *The Psychologist*, pp. 213–17 (Gudjonsson, G.H. May 1996), © The British Psychological Society, by kind permission of Professor Gudjonsson; Table 1.5 adapted from Friedlmayer, S. and Rossier, E. Professional identity and public image of Austrian psychologists. Reproduced with permission from Psychology in Europe by Schorr, A. and Saari, S. (eds), ISBN 0-88937-155-5, © 1995, Hogrefe & Huber Publishers, Seattle, Toronto, Göttingen, Bern.; Table 1.6 adapted from The 100 most eminent psychologists of the twentieth century, *Review of General Psychology*, 6, pp. 139–52 (Hagbloom, S.J., Warnick, R., Warnick, J.E., Jones, V.K., Yarborough, G.L., Russell, R.M., Borecky, C.M., McGahhey, R., Powell, J.L., Beavers, J. and Monte, E. 2002), with permission of Steve Haggbloom; Table 2.1 from The Barnam effect I: Personnel managers' reactions to their 'personality analysis', *Complementary Therapies in Medicine*, 2, pp. 1–4 (Furnham, A. 1994), copyright 1994, reprinted with permission from Elsevier; Table 2.3 Extract 1 from Emanuel A. Schegloff, "On an Actual Virtual Servo-Mechanism for Guessing Bad News: A Single Case Conjecture", *Social Problems*, Vol. 35, No. 4, 442–457 © 1988, The Society for the Study of Social Problems Inc. Used by permission. All rights reserved.; Table 2.3 Extract 2 from *On clinicians co-implicating recipients' perspectives in the delivery of diagnostic news* (Maynard, D. W. 1992) 337-8, in Drew, P. and Heritage, J. (eds). Talk at Work. Cambridge:Cambridge University Press., reproduced with permission; Table 3.1 from *Concepts of Genetics Scott, Foresman and Company, 1986* 2nd ed. (Klug, W.S. and Cummings, M.R. 1986) Table 7.4 p.161 (c) 1986 Scott Foresman and Company, Reprinted by permission of Pearson Education, Inc.; Table 3.2 adapted from The heritability of attitudes: a study of twins, *Journal of Personality and Social Psychology* 80(6), pp. 845-60 (Olson, J.M., Vernon, P.A., Harris, J.A. and Lang, K.L. 2001), reprinted with permission of American Psychological Association and James M. Olson; Table 8.1 from *Remembering*, Cambridge University Press (Bartlett, F.C. 1932), reproduced with permission;Table 9.1 from *Pharmacology* Churchill Livingstone (Rang, H.P., Dale, M.M. and Ritter, J.M. 1995) with permission of Elsevier; Table 10.5 from *Berko Gleason, DEVELOPMENT OF LANGUAGE* (c) 1997.Reproduced by permission of Pearson Education, Inc.; Tables 10.6, 10.7 adapted from *Psychology and Language: An Introduction to Psycholinguistics*, Wadsworth (Clark, H.H. and Clark, E.V. 1977) reprinted by permission of H.H. Clark & E.V. Clark; Table 10.8 from Savage-Rumbaugh, E.S., Language acquisition in nonhuman species, *Development Psychology*, 1990, 23, 599–620. Copyright © 1990, this material is used by permission of John Wiley & Sons, Inc.; Table 10.9 from *Human Neuropsychology*, 2nd ed., Pearson Education (Martin, G.N. 2006), reproduced with permission; Table 10.12 from Timothy Justus, The cerebellum and English grammatical morphology: evidence from production, comprehension, and grammaticality judgements, *Journal of Cognitive Neuroscience*, 16:7 (September, 2004), pp. 1115-30 (c) 2004 by the Massachusetts Institute of Technology; Table 11.1 adapted from *Multivariate Statistical Methods*, McGraw-Hill (Morrison, D.F. 1967) reprinted with permission of Donald F. Morrison; Table 11.2 adapted from Organization of abilities and the development of intelligence, *Psychological Review*, 75, p. 249 (Horn, J.L. 1968) (c) 1968 by the American Psychological Association. Adapted by permission; Table 11.4 adapted from Sex difference in intelligence, *American Psychologist*, 52(10), pp. 1091–1102 (Halpern, D.F. 1997), adapted with permission from The American Psychological Association and Diane Halpern; Table 11.5 adapted from Scarr, S. in *Intelligence, Heredity and Environments* (Sternberg, R.J. and Grigorenko, E. 1997), Cambridge University Press; Table 11.6 from Extensional versus intuitive reasoning: conjunction fallacy in probability judgement, *Psychological Review*, 90(4), pp. 293–315 (Tversky, A. and Kahneman, D. 1983), reprinted with permission of American Psychological Association and Professor Daniel Kahneman; Table 11.7 from Verbal creativity, depression and alcoholism, *British Journal of Psychiatry*, 168, pp. 545–55 (Post, F. 1996), reproduced with permission of the Royal College of Psychiatrists;Table 12.2 from *Berk, CHILD DEVELOPMENT, table 12.2* (c) 1997 Pearson Education, Inc. Reproduced by permission of Pearson Education, Inc.; Table 12.6 adapted from What is successful ageing and who should define it?, *British Medical Journal*, 331, pp. 1548–51 (Bowling, A. and Dieppe, P. 2005), reproduced with permission from the BMJ Publishing Group; Table 13.1 adapted from The distribution of basic emotions in everyday life: a state and trait perspective from experience sampling data, *Journal of Research in Personality*, 34, pp. 178–97 (Zelenski, J.M. and Larsen, R.J. 2000), © 2000, with permission of Elsevier; Table 13.3 adapted from 'No longer Gage': frontal lobe dysfunction and emotional changes, *Journal of Consulting and Clinical Psychology*, 60(3), pp. 349–59 (Stuss, D.T., Gow, C.A. and Hetherington, C.R. 1992), © American Psychological Association. Adapted with permission of American Psychological Association and Dr. Donald

Stuss; Table 13.4 adapted from Face and voice expression identification in patients with emotional and behavioural changes following ventral frontal lobe damage, *Neuropsychology*, 34(4), pp. 247–61 (Hornak, J., Rolls, E.T. and Wade, D. 1996), © 1996, with permission of Elsevier; Table 14.1 adapted from *Personality and Individual Differences: A Natural Science Approach* New York: Plenum Press (Eysenck, H.J. and Eysenck, M.W. 1985), with kind permission from Springer Science and Business Media; Table 15.4 adapted from Specificity of the attitude as a determinant of attitude–behavior congruence, *Journal of Personality and Social Psychology*, 30, pp. 724–8 (Weigel, R., Vernon, D.T.A. and Tognacci, L.N. 1974), © American Psychological Association, reprinted with permission of American Psychological Association and Dr. Russell Weigel; Table 16.1 from Out of mind but back in sight: stereotypes on the rebound, *Journal of Personality and Social Psychology*, 67, pp. 808–71 (Macrae, C.N., Bodenhausen, G.V., Milne, A.B. and Jetten, J. 1994) (c) American Psychological Association, with permission of American Psychological Association and Professor Neil Macrae; Table 17.1 from No Smoking Day website, www.nosmokingday.org.uk; Table 18.4 from Drugs and the treatment of psychiatric disorders: psychosis and anxiety (Baldessarini, R.J.) in, *Goodman and Gilman's:The Pharmacological Basis of Therapeutics*, 9th ed. (Hardman, J.G. and Limbird, L.E. (eds) 1996), New York: McGraw-Hill, reproduced with permission of The McGraw-Hill Companies; Table 18.7 adapted from *Carson, ABNORMAL PSYCHOLOGY AND MODERN LIFE, Table 18.8* (c) 1996 Pearson Education, Inc. Reproduced by permission of Pearson Education, Inc.; Table 18.8 from Cleckley, H., *The Mask of Sanity*, pp. 337–8. St. Louis: C.V. Mosby,1976; Table 18.9 from Drugs and the treatment of psychiatric disorders: psychosis and anxiety (Baldessarini, R.J.) in, *Goodman and Gilman's: The Pharmacological Basis of Therapeutics* 9th ed. (Hardman, J.G. and Limbird, L.E. (eds) 1996), New York: McGraw-Hill, reproduced with permission of The McGraw-Hill Companies

Text

Extract on page 47 from *All in the Mind: The Essence of the Mind*, Whurr (Furnham, A. 1996) pp. 83-84 (c) John Wiley & Sons Limited. Reproduced with permission; Article on page 75 from Science finds the secret of a hot kiss, *The Sunday Times* 8 February 2009, reproduced with permission; Article on page 113 from Found: the brain's centre of vision, *The Sunday Times* 5 April 2009 (Leake, J.), Reproduced with permission; Article on page 167 from You really can smell fear, say scientists, *The Guardian*, 4 December 2008 (Randeson, J.), Copyright Guardian News & Media Ltd 2008; Extract on page 213 from Bruce, V. (1998). Fleeting images of shade, *The Psychologist*, 11, p. 331–337 For full article, see www.bps.org.uk/fios; Extract on page 257 adapted from *Behavior Principles in Everyday Life*, 3rd ed., Prentice Hall (Baldwin, John. D. and Baldwin, Janice. I. 1998) (c) 1998. Adapted by permission of Pearson Education, Inc., Upper Saddle River, NJ; Extract on page 291 from *Forever Today by Deborah Wearing*, published by Doubleday. Reprinted by permission of The Random House Group Ltd.; Article on page 337 from Court told of sleep deprivation clue in Selby train case, *The Guardian*, 30 November 2001, Copyright Guardian News & Media Ltd 2001; Article on page 431 from Lessons from a tragedy, *The Sunday Times Magazine*, 23 June 2005 (Cornwell, J.), Reproduced with permission; Article on page 493 from Police refute Bridgend suicides linkn, *Times Online*, 19 February 2008 (Hines, N.), Reproduced with permission; Article on page 553 from How happiness can be catching, *The Guardian*, 5 December 2008 (Boseley, S.), Copyright Guardian News & Media Ltd. 2008; Article on page 609 from Mapped out: Britain's personality clusters, *The Sunday Times*, 14 April 2009 (Leake, J. and Brooks, H.), Reproduced with permission; Article on page 647 from 'MI5' fantasy conman faces life sentence for deception, *Times Online*, 23 June 2005 (Freeman, S.), Reproduced with permission; Article on page 727 from Which? Calls for 'fat tax' on unhealthy food, *The Guardian*, 11 March 2009 (Smithers, R.), Copyright Guardian News & Media Ltd 2008

Photographs

The publisher would like to thank the following for their kind permission to reproduce their photographs:

(Key: b-bottom; c-centre; l-left; r-right; t-top)
2 Aldo Sessa/Getty Images; 5 Alamy Images: Tomas de Amo (l), Corbis: Pelaez Inc (r); 11 PA Photos; 13 Getty Images: NYC PD/AFP (a); Simon Frederick (b); 15 Kobal Collection Ltd: 20th Century Fox; 22 Stock Montage Inc.; 27 National. Library of Medicine/ Science Photo Library Ltd (a), AFP/Getty Images (b), Popperphoto /Alamy Images: (c); 29 Corbis: Bettmann/CORBIS (t); Archives of the History of American Psychology (b); 33 Corbis: Lynn Goldsmith (br), Getty Images: Hulton Archive (tr), Robert McCrae (bl), Bo Mathisen (tl); 34 Corbis: Jodi Hilton/Pool/Reuters (l). Copyright UK Medical Research Council (2009) used by kind permission.: (r); 35 Barbara Tversky: (tr). Corbis: Reuters (tl); 56 Getty Images: Popperfoto; 74 James Balog/Getty Images; 77 North Wind Picture Archives: North Wind Picture Archives; 84 Barrington Brown/Science Photo Library; 98 Mitchell Gerber/Corbis; 112 G. Neil Martin; 127 Alamy Images: Mirrorpix; 133 Universal/Everett/Rex Features; 134 Alamy Images/TopFoto/Sony Pictures; 140 Guardian News and Media Ltd/Charles O'Rear/Corbis; 159 Hulton Archive/Getty Images; 160 Ben Martin/Time Life Pictures/Getty Images; 183 Getty Images: Chris Coleman/Manchester United; 232 Metropolitan Police Service; 248 Guardian News and Media Ltd.: Fabio De Paola; 280 Sam Ogden/Science Photo Library Ltd.; 314 Paramount Television/The Kobal Collection Ltd; 318 Press Association Images; 324 Summit Entertainment/The Kobal Collection Ltd (l), W. Disney/Everett/Rex Features (r); 345 Corbis: Juice Images; 354 Bridgeman Art Library Ltd: British Museum; 363 York Post/Corbis Sygma; 365 Debra L. Rothenberg/Rex Features; 410 S. Hale (2002) *The Man Who Lost His Language*. London: Penguin; 415 Frazer Harrison/Getty Images (a); Getty Images: Chris Jackson (b);

Stephen Shugerman/Getty Images (c); Walter Bird (d); 424 Press Association Images: Molly Riley/AP; 437 Press Association Images, Magnum Photos, Bettman/CORBIS; 466 Getty Images: Peter Macdiarmid; 483 Bridgeman Art Library Ltd/Index; 486 Corbis: Hugh Stewart/Corbis Outline (r). Getty Images: WireImage (l); 497 Getty Images: AFP; 503 Andy Crawford @ DK Images; 522 www.eyevinearchive.com: Adam Nadel; 536 Getty Images; 546 Press Association Images; 552 Peter Hince/Getty Images; 564 Copyright © News Group Newspapers Ltd: (r). Corbis: Peter Dench (l). Ross Parry Agency: (c); 571 The Advertising Archives; 608 Darkmatter Photography/Getty Images; 622-624 Wiley-Blackwell, Oxford.: P.J. Rentfrow, S.D. Gosling and J. Potter, A theory of the emergence, persistence, and expression of geographic variation in psychological characteristics, Perspectives on Psychological Science.; 640 Science Photo Library Ltd: Will & Deni McIntyre; 652 Getty Images: (l, r); 682 Reuters: Rick Wilking; 684 TopFoto: The Granger Collection, New York; 686 Press Association Images: Nikos Giakoumidis; 688 Philip G Zimbardo, Ph.D.; 689 Getty Images: Peter Macdiarmid; 701 Press Association Images/Christophe Ena; 730 Marty Chobot/National Geographic Image Collection; 761 Rex Features: OnEdition; 779 Copyright © News Group Newspapers Ltd: The Sun/NI Synd.; 811 Everett Collection/Rex Features; 812 Greater Manchester Police and Press Association Images; 820 Getty Images/Tim Whitby; 821 Getty Images; 822 Courtesy Lewis Wolpert (l), Press Association Ltd. (r); 829 Science & Society Picture Library;

All other images © Pearson Education.

Picture Research by: Debra Weatherley and Alia Rayyan.

In some instances we have been unable to trace the owners of copyright material, and we would appreciate any information that would enable us to do so.

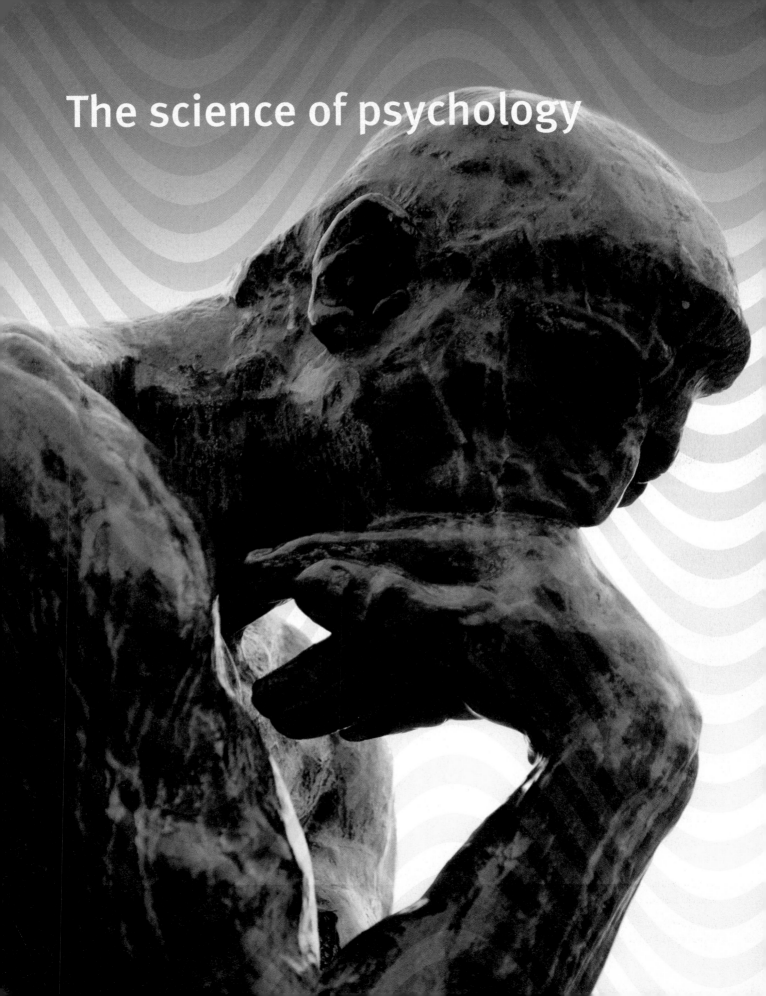

The science of psychology

It appears to be an almost universal belief that anyone is competent to discuss psychological problems, whether he or she has taken the trouble to study the subject or not, and that while everybody's opinion is of equal value, that of the professional psychologist must be excluded at all costs because he might spoil the fun by producing some facts which would completely upset the speculation and the wonderful dream castles so laboriously constructed by the layman.

Source: Eysenck, 1957, p. 13.

Explore the accompanying videos, simulations, and animations on MyPsychLab. This chapter includes activities on: Behaviourism • Little Albert • The Skinnerian learning process • Fixed-interval and Fixed-ratio scheduling • Check your understanding and prepare for your exams using the multiple choice, short answer and essay practice tests also available.

WHAT YOU SHOULD BE ABLE TO DO AFTER READING CHAPTER 1

- Define psychology and trace the history of the discipline.

- Be aware of the different methods psychologists use to study behaviour.

- Distinguish between the branches of psychology and describe them.

- Understand what is meant by the 'common-sense' approach to answering questions about psychology and outline its flaws.

- Describe and understand historical developments in psychology such as structuralism, behaviourism and the cognitive revolution.

- Be aware of how psychology developed in Europe and across the world.

QUESTIONS TO THINK ABOUT

- Before you read this chapter, think about your own definition of psychology. Once you have finished reading Chapter 1, see whether your view has changed.

- What types of behaviour do you think a psychologist studies?

- Are there any behaviours that a psychologist cannot or should not study?

- Can psychologists use data from animal experiments to draw meaningful conclusions about human behaviour?

- What do you think psychologists mean when they say they adopt the 'scientific approach'?

- Should psychological research always be carried out to help people?

- Do you think that much of what we know from psychology is 'common sense'? Why?

- Are some psychological phenomena universal, i.e. they appear across nations and cultures?

- How does psychology differ from other disciplines, such as biology, sociology and physics? Which discipline/subjects do you think it is closest to and why?

What is psychology?

If you asked this question of several people, you would probably receive several, very different answers. In fact, if you asked this question of several psychologists, you would still not receive complete agreement on the answer. Psychologists engage in research, teaching, counselling and psychotherapy; they advise industry and government about personnel matters, the design of products, advertising, marketing and legislation; they devise and administer tests of personality, achievement and ability. And yet psychology is a relatively new discipline; the first modern scientific psychology laboratory was established in 1878 and the first person ever to call himself a psychologist was still alive in 1920. In some European universities the discipline of psychology was known as 'mental philosophy' – not psychology – even as late as the beginning of the twentieth century.

Psychologists study a wide variety of phenomena, including physiological processes within the nervous system, genetics, environmental events, personality characteristics, human development, mental abilities, health, and social interactions. Because of this diversity, it is rare for a person to be described simply as a psychologist; instead, a psychologist is defined by the sub-area in which they work. For example, an individual who measures and treats psychological disorders is called a clinical psychologist; one who studies child development is called a developmental psychologist; a person who explores the relationship between physiology and behaviour might call themselves a neuropsychologist (if they study the brain) or a biopsychologist/physiological psychologist/psychobiologist (if they study the brain and other bodily processes, such as heart rate). Modern psychology has so many branches that it is often impossible to demonstrate expertise in all of these areas. Consequently, and by necessity, psychologists have a highly detailed knowledge of sub-areas of the discipline and the most common are listed in Table 1.1 on p. 9.

Psychology defined

Psychology is the scientific study of behaviour. The word 'psychology' comes from two Greek words, *psukhe*, meaning 'breath' or 'soul', and *logos*, meaning 'word' or 'reason'. The modern meaning of psycho- is 'mind' and the modern meaning of -logy is 'science'; thus, the word 'psychology' literally means 'the science of the mind'. Early in the development of psychology, people conceived of the mind as an independent, free-floating spirit. Later, they described it as a characteristic of a functioning brain whose ultimate function was to control behaviour. Thus, the focus turned from the mind, which cannot be directly observed, to behaviour, which can. And because the brain is the organ that both contains the mind and controls behaviour, psychology very soon incorporated the study of the brain.

The study of physical events such as brain activity has made some psychologists question whether the word 'mind' has any meaning in the study of behaviour. One view holds that the 'mind' is a metaphor for what the brain does; because it is a metaphor it should not be treated as if it actually existed. In his famous book *The Concept of Mind*, the philosopher Gilbert Ryle describes this as the 'ghost in the machine' (Ryle, 1949). One might, for example, determine that the personality trait of extroversion exists and people will fall on different points along a dimension from very introvert to very extrovert. But does this mean that this trait really exists? Or is it a label used to make us understand a complex phenomenon in a simpler way? This is called the problem of **reification** in psychology: the assumption that an event or phenomenon is concrete and exists in substance because it is given a name.

The approach adopted by modern psychology is scientific, that is, it adopts the principles and procedures of science to help answer the questions it asks. Psychologists adopt this approach because they believe that it is the most effective way of determining 'truth' and 'falsity'; the scientific method, they argue, incorporates fewer biases and greater rigour than do other methods. Of course, not all approaches in psychology have this rigorous scientific leaning: early theories of personality, for example, did not rely on the scientific method (these are described in Chapter 14). Recent developments in the methodology of psychology have yielded methods that are not considered to be part of the scientific approach: qualitative approaches to human behaviour, for example, reviewed in next chapter.

For the moment, however, consider the value of this approach in psychology. Imagine that you were allowed to answer any psychological question that you might wish to ask: what is the effect of linguistic deprivation on language development, say, or the effect of personality on the stability of romantic relationships? How would you set about answering such questions? What approach do you think would be the best? And how would you ensure that the outcome of your experiment is determined only by those factors you studied and not by any others? These are the types of problem that psychologists face when they design and conduct studies. Sometimes, the results of scientific studies are denounced as 'common sense': that they were so obvious as to be not worth the bother of setting up an experiment. The view, however, is generally ill-informed because, as you will discover throughout this book, psychological research frequently contradicts common-sense views. As the late, influential

British psychologist Hans Eysenck noted in this chapter's opening quote, most people believe that they are experts in human behaviour. And to some extent we are all lay scientists, of a kind, although generally unreliable ones. Psychological research, however, frequently contradicts people's assumed expertise as the Controversies section below illustrates.

Cutting edge – How much of a science is psychology?

Psychology is a young science and the discipline has tried hard to earn and demonstrate its scientific spurs. Chemistry, physics or biology seem to have no such problems: their history is testament to their status as a science. A new study, however, suggests that psychology is gaining ground.

Simonton (2004) compared the scientific status of psychology with that of physics, chemistry, sociology and biology. He identified a number of characteristics that typified a general science including:

- the number of theories and laws mentioned in introductory textbooks (the higher the ratio of theory to law, the 'softer' – i.e. less scientific – the discipline);
- publication rate (the more frequent, the more scientific the discipline);
- the appearance of graphs in journal papers (the 'harder' the discipline, the greater the number of graphs);
- the impact made by young researchers (the more scientific the discipline, the greater the agreement that a researcher's contribution is significant);
- how peers evaluated 60 of their colleagues in their own disciplines, and how often single papers are cited (referred to in research papers).

Simonton also looked at other measures of scientific standing: 'lecture disfluency' (the number of pause words such as 'uh', 'er' and 'um': these are more common in less formal, less structured and less factual disciplines); the extent to which references in journal articles were recent; the age at which a person received the Nobel prize; and perceived difficulty of the discipline. Simonton combined these measures to provide a composite measure of scientific status.

Based on the first set of indicators, Simonton found that the natural sciences were judged to be more 'scientific' than were the social sciences. Psychology fell right on the mean – at the junction between natural and social sciences, as Figure 1.1 shows. However, psychology's score was much closer to biology than to sociology. The biggest gap in scores was found between psychology and sociology, suggesting that the discipline is closer to its natural science cousins than its social science acquaintances.

The stereotypical image of a psychologist (a) and a traditional scientist (b).

Source: (a) Pelaez Inc./Corbis; (b) Tomas de Arno/Alamy Images.

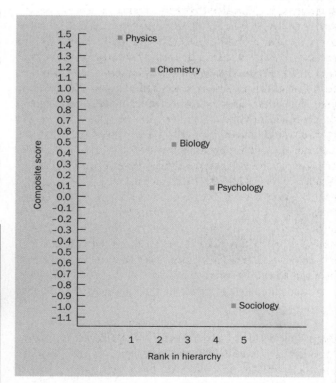

Figure 1.1 According to Simonton's study, psychology's scientific status was more similar to that of biology than other disciplines traditionally associated with it, such as sociology.

Source: D.K. Simonton, 'Psychology's status as a scientific discipline: its empirical placement within an implicit hierarchy of the sciences', *Review of General Psychology*, 2004, 8, 1, p. 65 (Fig. 2).

Cutting edge – *Continued*

A gap also separated chemistry and biology, suggesting that the sciences might be grouped according to three clusters: the physical sciences (chemistry and physics), life sciences (biology and psychology) and social science (sociology).

Simonton concludes with an interesting observation. He argues that psychology's position in this hierarchy does not really reflect its scientific approach but its subject matter: because the subject matter of psychology can be viewed as not directly controllable or manipulable it may be perceived erroneously, despite its adoption of the scientific method, as neither scientific fish nor fowl.

Controversies in Psychological Science – Is psychology common sense?

The issue

Take a look at the following questions on some familiar psychological topics. See how many you can answer correctly.

1 Schizophrenics suffer from a split personality. Is this:
   (a) true most of the time
   (b) true some of the time
   (c) true none of the time, or
   (d) true only when the schizophrenic is undergoing psychotherapy?

2 Under hypnosis, a person will, if asked by a hypnotist:
   (a) recall past life events with a high degree of accuracy
   (b) perform physical feats of strength not possible out of hypnosis
   (c) do (a) and (b), or
   (d) do neither (a) nor (b)?

3 The learning principles applied to birds and fish also apply to:
   (a) humans
   (b) cockroaches
   (c) both (a) and (b), or
   (d) neither (a) nor (b)?

4 Are physically attractive people:
   (a) more likely to be stable than physically unattractive people
   (b) equal in psychological stability
   (c) likely to be less psychologically stable, or
   (d) likely to be much more unstable?

How well do you think you did? In a study published in 1997, these four questions featured in the ten most difficult questions answered by first-year psychology undergraduates who completed a 38-item questionnaire about psychological knowledge (Martin *et al.*, 1997). In fact, when the responses from first- and final-year psychology, engineering, sociology, English and business studies students were analysed, no one group scored more than 50 per cent correct. Perhaps not surprisingly, psychologists did significantly better than the other students, with sociologists following close behind. Why should psychology (and other) students perform so badly on a test of psychological knowledge?

The answer lies in the fact that the questionnaire was not really a test of psychological knowledge but of common-sense attitudes towards psychological research. Common-sense mistakes are those committed when a person chooses what they think is the obvious answer but this answer is incorrect. Some writers suggested that 'a great many of psychology's basic principles are self-evident' (Houston, 1983), and that 'much of what psychology textbooks purport to teach undergraduates about research findings in the area may already be known to them through common, informal experiences' (Barnett, 1986). Houston reported that although introductory psychology students answered 15 out of 21 questions about 'memory and learning' correctly, a collection of 50 individuals found in a city park on a Friday afternoon scored an average of 16. The 21 December 2008 edition of *The Sunday Times* featured a full-page article, boldly headed 'University of the bleedin' obvious', in which the journalist bemoaned what he perceived to be the triviality of (mostly) behavioural research. 'Why are we,' asked the journalist or his sub-editor, 'deluged with academic research "proving" things that we know already?', citing a string of seemingly irritating, self-evident bons mots from various university departments.

Is the common-sense view of psychological research, justified?

The evidence

Not quite. Since the late 1970s, a number of studies have examined individuals' false beliefs about psychology, and students' beliefs in particular. Over 76 per cent of first-year psychology students thought the following statements were true: 'Memory can be likened to a storage chest in the brain into which we deposit

Controversies in Psychological Science – *Continued*

material and from which we can withdraw later', 'Personality tests reveal your basic motives, including those you may not be aware of', and 'Blind people have unusually sensitive organs of touch'. This, despite the fact that course materials directly contradicted some of these statements (Vaughan, 1977).

Furnham (1992, 1993) found that only half of such 'common-sense' questions were answered correctly by 250 prospective psychology students, and only 20 per cent of questions were answered correctly by half or more of a sample of 110 first-year psychology, fine arts, biochemistry and engineering students. In Martin *et al.*'s (1997) study, final-year students answered more questions correctly than did first-year students but there was no significant difference between first- and final-year psychology students. This suggests that misperceptions are slowly dispelled after students undergo the process of higher education and learning, but that studying specific disciplines does nothing to dispel these myths effectively. This is just one explanation.

What, then, is 'common' about 'common sense'? Some have likened common sense to fantastical thinking. This describes ways of reasoning about the world that violate known scientific principles (Woolley, 1997). For example, the beliefs that women can control breast cancer by positive thinking (Taylor, 1983), that walking under a ladder brings bad luck and that touching wood brings good luck (Blum and Blum, 1974) violate known physical laws, but people still believe in doing such things. People often draw erroneous conclusions about psychological knowledge because they rely on small sets of data, sometimes a very small set of data (such as a story in a newspaper or the behaviour of a friend). Take the relationship between a mental disorder such as schizophrenia and murders committed by schizophrenic patients, for example.

Despite the small number of murders committed by schizophrenic patients, the few cases which do receive media attention suggest that people with schizophrenia are uncontrollable murderers who should be put out of harm's way (the role of the media in promoting psychology is returned to in the next chapter). As you will see from the chapter on abnormal psychology (Chapter 18) this thinking is blatantly perverse: the majority of schizophrenic individuals will not cause harm to others. It is an example of what social psychologists call the 'under-utilisation of base rate information' (Fiske and Taylor, 1991; you will find more about this in Chapters 11, 15 and 16). It means that individual, vivid, single or a small number of examples are taken to represent the behaviour of an entire group. The base rate information (the actual incidence of behaviour in such groups in general), however, contradicts these single, vivid examples but is either ignored or dismissed. A similar process may be operating when people misperceive some aspects of psychology. Psychologists have discovered that two determinants of fantastical thinking are lack of information and an inability to explain behaviour. It seems likely that these factors could underpin misperceptions about psychology.

Conclusion

As you work through your psychology course and through this book, discovering new and sometimes complicated ways of analysing and understanding human behaviour, you will realise that many of the beliefs and perceptions you held about certain aspects of psychology are false or only half right. Of course, no science is truly infallible and there are different ways of approaching psychological problems (and perhaps, sometimes, some problems are insoluble or we have no good method of studying them satisfactorily). Psychology, however, attempts to adopt the best of scientific approaches to understanding potentially the most unmanageable of subject matter: behaviour. And, for those of you who were wondering, the answers to the questions at the start of the box are c, d, c and a.

Explaining behaviour

The ultimate goals of research in psychology are to understand, predict and change human behaviour: to explain why people do what they do. Different kinds of psychologists are interested in different kinds of behaviour and different levels of explanation. Not all psychologists study humans; some conduct research using laboratory animals or study the behaviour of wild animals in their natural habitat. Research using animals has provided many insights into the factors that affect human behaviour, such as the effect of sensory deprivation on the development of the senses.

How do psychologists 'explain' behaviour? First, they must describe it accurately and comprehensively. We must become familiar with the things that people (or other animals) do. We must learn how to categorise and measure behaviour so that we can be sure that different psychologists in different places are observing the same phenomena. Next, we must discover the causes of the behaviour we observe – those events responsible for its occurrence. If we can discover the events that caused the behaviour to occur, we have 'explained' it. Events that cause other events (including behaviour) to occur are called **causal events** or **determinants**.

For example, one psychologist might be interested in visual perception and another might be interested in romantic attraction. Even when they are interested in the same behaviour, different psychologists might study different levels of analysis. Some look inside the organism in a literal sense, seeking physiological causes, such as the activity of nerve cells or the secretions of glands. Others look inside the organism in a metaphorical sense, explaining behaviour in terms of hypothetical mental states, such as anger, fear, curiosity or love. Still others look only for events in the environment (including things that other people do) that cause behaviours to occur.

Established and emerging fields of psychology

see activity on mypsychlab Throughout this book you will encounter many types of psychologist and many types of psychology. As you have already seen, very few individuals call themselves psychologists, rather they describe themselves by their specialism – cognitive psychologist, developmental psychologist, social psychologist, and so on. Before describing and defining each branch of psychology however, it is important to distinguish between three general terms: psychology, **psychiatry** and **psychoanalysis**. A psychologist normally holds a university degree in a behaviour-related discipline (such as psychology, zoology, cognitive science) and usually possesses a higher research degree (a Ph.D. or doctorate) if they are teaching or a researcher.

Those not researching but working in applied settings such as hospitals or schools may have other, different qualifications that enable them to practise in those environments. Psychiatrists are physicians who have specialised in the causes and treatment of mental disorder. They are medically qualified (unlike psychologists, who nonetheless do study medical problems and undertake biological research) and have the ability to prescribe medication (which psychologists do not). Much of the work done by psychologists in psychiatric settings is similar to that of the psychiatrist, implementing psychological interventions for patients with mental illness. Psychoanalysts are specific types of counsellor who attempt to understand mental disorder by reference to the workings of the unconscious. There is no formal academic qualification necessary to become a psychoanalyst and, as the definition implies, they deal with a limited range of behaviour.

Most research psychologists are employed by colleges or universities, by private organisations or by government. Research psychologists differ from one another in two principal ways: in the types of behaviour they investigate and in the causal events they analyse. That is, they explain different types of behaviour, and they explain them in terms of different types of cause. For example, two psychologists might both be interested in memory, but they might attempt to explain memory in terms of different causal events – one may focus on physiological events (such as the activation of the brain during memory retrieval) whereas the other may focus on environmental events (such as the effect of noise level on task performance). Professional societies such as the American Psychological Association and the British Psychological Society have numerous subdivisions representing members with an interest in a specific aspect of psychology. This section outlines some of the major branches or subdivisions of psychology. A summary of these can be found in Table 1.1.

Psychobiology/biological psychology is the study of the biological basis of behaviour (G. N. Martin, 2003). Other terms for the same branch include physiological psychology and biopsychology. It investigates the causal events in an organism's physiology, especially in the nervous system and its interaction with glands that secrete hormones. Psychobiologists study almost all behavioural phenomena that can be observed in non-human animals, including learning, memory, sensory processes, emotional behaviour, motivation, sexual behaviour and sleep, using a variety of techniques described in Chapter 4.

Psychophysiology is the measurement of people's physiological reactions, such as heart rate, blood pressure, electrical resistance of the skin, muscle tension and electrical activity of the brain (Andreassi, 2001). These measurements provide an indication of a person's degree of arousal or relaxation. Most psychophysiologists investigate phenomena such as sensory and perceptual responses, sleep, stress, thinking, reasoning and emotion.

Neuropsychology and **neuroscience** examine the relationship between the brain and spinal cord, and behaviour (Martin, 2006). Neuropsychology helps to shed light on the role of these structures in movement, vision, hearing, tasting, sleeping, smelling and touching as well as emotion, thinking, language and object recognition and perception, and others. Neuropsychologists normally (but not always) study patients who have suffered injury to the brain – through accident or disease – which disrupts functions such as speech production or comprehension, object recognition, visual or auditory perception, and so on. **Clinical neuropsychology** involves the identification and treatment of problems arising from nervous system disorders and injuries. Clinical neuropsychologists typically work in a hospital and collaborate closely with neurologists (physicians who specialise in diseases of the nervous system), although some teach or work in private practice.

Modern neuropsychology also relies on sophisticated brain imaging techniques such as positron emission tomography (PET) and functional magnetic resonance imaging (fMRI) which allow researchers to monitor the activity of the brains of individuals while they perform some psycho-

Table 1.1 The major branches of psychology

Branch	Subject of study
Psychobiology/Biological psychology	Biological basis of behaviour
Psychophysiology	Psychophysiological responses such as heart rate, galvanic skin response and brain electrical activity
Neuropsychology	Relationship between brain activity/structure and function
Comparative psychology	Behaviour of species in terms of evolution and adaptation
Ethology	Animal behaviour in natural environments
Sociobiology	Social behaviour in terms of biological inheritance and evolution
Behaviour genetics	Degree of influence of genetics and environment on psychological factors
Cognitive psychology	Mental processes and complex behaviour
Cognitive neuroscience	Brain's involvement in mental processes
Developmental psychology	Physical, cognitive, social and emotional development from birth to senescence
Social psychology	Individuals' and groups' behaviour
Individual differences	Temperament and characteristics of individuals and their effects on behaviour
Cross-cultural psychology	Impact of culture on behaviour
Cultural psychology	Variability of behaviour within cultures
Forensic and criminological psychology	Behaviour in the context of crime and the law
Clinical psychology	Causes and treatment of mental disorder and problems of adjustment
Health psychology	Impact of lifestyle and stress on health and illness
Educational psychology	Social, cognitive and emotional development of children in the context of schooling
Consumer psychology	Motivation, perception and cognition in consumers
Organisational or occupational psychology	Behaviour of groups and individuals in the workplace
Ergonomics	Ways in which humans and machines work together
Sport and exercise psychology	The effects of psychological variables on sport and exercise performance, and vice versa

logical task. This approach combines two approaches in psychology: neuroscience and cognitive psychology (see below). Because of this, the area of study is sometimes described as **cognitive neuroscience** (Gazzaniga, 1995) or behavioural neuroscience. A new development in this area has been the study of the psychobiological processes involved in social behaviour, a sub-branch called social neuroscience. Social neuroscientists examine the role of the brain in behaviours such as empathy, turn-taking, seeing things from another person's point of view, social interaction, political outlook, and so on. We look at the work of cognitive/behavioural/social neuroscientists in more detail in Chapter 4 and throughout this book.

Comparative psychology is the study of the behaviour of members of a variety of species in an attempt to explain behaviour in terms of evolutionary adaptation to the environment. Comparative psychologists study behavioural phenomena similar to those studied by physiological psychologists. They are more likely than most other psychologists to study inherited behavioural patterns, such as courting and mating, predation and aggression, defensive behaviours and parental behaviours.

Closely tied to comparative psychology is **ethology**, the study of the biological basis of behaviour in the context of the evolution of development and function. Ethologists usually make their observations based on studies of animal behaviour in natural conditions and investigate topics such as instinct, social and sexual behaviour and cooperation. A sub-discipline of ethology is **sociobiology** which attempts to explain social behaviour in terms of biological inheritance and evolution. Ethology and sociobiology are described in more detail in Chapter 3, as is evolutionary psychology (an approach which interprets behaviour in terms of evolution).

Behaviour genetics is the branch of psychology that studies the role of genetics in behaviour (Plomin and DeFries, 1998). The genes we inherit from our parents include a blueprint for the construction of a human brain. Each blueprint is a little different, which means that no two brains are exactly alike. Therefore, no two people will act exactly alike, even in an identical situation. Behaviour geneticists study the role of genetics in behaviour by examining similarities in physical and behavioural characteristics of blood relatives, whose genes are more similar than those of unrelated individuals. They also perform breeding experiments with laboratory animals to see what aspects of behaviour can be transmitted to an animal's off-spring. Of course, genetic differences are only one of the causes of individual differences. People have different experiences, too, and these experiences will affect their behaviour. Behavioural geneticists study the degree to which genetics are responsible for specific behaviours such as cognitive ability. We examine the work of behavioural geneticists in Chapter 3 and evaluate the contribution of this research to the study of intelligence (in Chapter 11 (and to other topics, such as personality) and throughout the book).

Cognitive psychology is the study of mental processes and complex behaviours such as perception, attention, learning, memory, concept formation and problem-solving (Eysenck and Keane, 1995). To cognitive psychologists, the events that cause behaviour consist of functions of the human brain that occur in response to environmental events. Their explanations involve characteristics of inferred mental processes, such as imagery, attention, and mechanisms of language. Most cognitive psychologists do not study physiological mechanisms, but recently some have begun collaborating with neurologists and other professionals who utilise neuroimaging. A branch of cognitive psychology involves the modelling of human function using computer simulation or 'neural networks'; this is called **cognitive science** and we briefly

examine the contribution of such computer simulations to our understanding of behaviour in Chapters 7 and 10.

Developmental psychology is the study of physical, cognitive, emotional and social development, especially of children (Berk, 2009) but, more broadly, of humans from foetus to death (these psychologists are sometimes called lifespan developmental psychologists). Some developmental psychologists study the effects of ageing on behaviour and the body (a field called gerontology). Most developmental psychologists restrict their study to a particular period of development, such as infancy, adolescence or old age. This field is described and illustrated in more detail in Chapter 12. The development of children's language is described in Chapter 10, and the effects of ageing on cognitive performance are reviewed in Chapter 11.

Social psychology is the study of the effects of people on people. Social psychologists explore phenomena such as self-perception and the perception of others, cause-and-effect relations in human interactions, attitudes and opinions, interpersonal relationships, group dynamics, and emotional behaviours, including aggression and sexual attraction (Hogg and Vaughan, 2007). Chapters 15 and 16 explore these issues and themes in social psychology and the Psychology in Action section here describes some of the recent, counter-intuitive findings from studies of a behaviour that is perennially fascinating but which also has serious consequences: lying.

Psychology in action – How to detect a liar

Take a look at the following behaviours? Which do you think are characteristic of a person who is lying. Think about the reasons for your choices.

- Averting gaze
- Unnatural posture
- Posture change
- Scratching/touching parts of the body
- Playing with hair or objects
- Placing the hand over the mouth
- Placing the hand over the eyes

Which of these did you think predicted lying? According to a standard manual of police interviewing, these features are all characteristic of a liar (Inbau *et al.*, 1986). A study of participants in 75 countries found that 'averting gaze' was described as the best tell-tale sign of lying (Global Deception Research Team, 2006).

Unfortunately, despite the manual's exhortations and the international guesswork, none of these behaviours is actually reliably associated with deception and several studies have shown that general law enforcement officers are usually as poor as the average undergraduate at detecting truth and fal-

sity. Research by psychologists such as Aldert Vrij, for example, has highlighted how bad people are at detecting whether someone is telling the truth or is lying (Vrij, 2000, 2004b). However, it has also identified behaviours which are reliably associated with lying and suggests that the best way of detecting deception is to do so indirectly.

Studies of police officers' and students' ability to detect deception, all report detection rates of between 40 and 60 per cent – a result no better than we would expect by chance (Vrij and Mann, 2001; Vrij, 2000; DePaulo and Pfeifer, 1986). Police officers and people who operate polygraphs – the so-called lie detector which measures skin conductance responses – generally do no better than students (Ekman and O'Sullivan, 1991). The exception to this generally ignominious performance seems to be Secret Service agents – police officers specifically trained to be sensitive to behaviour during interviewing, and criminals (Ekman *et al.*, 1999). These groups tend to perform better than students and general law enforcement officers.

Perhaps the best detectors of dissembling would be those who routinely lie in order to get out of trouble. Researchers from the University of Goteborg, Sweden (Hartwig *et al.*, 2004) found that criminals were significantly better than students at

Psychology in action – *Continued*

These are images of former American President Bill Clinton, British novelist Jeffrey Archer and former American President Richard Nixon. What features might have revealed that they were lying? Clinton claimed not to have had sexual relations with his intern, Monica Lewinsky, Jeffrey Archer was convicted of perjury, and Richard Nixon authorised but denied the tapping of 17 government officials' and reporters' telephones and those of opponents at the Democratic National Committee headquarters at the Watergate apartments.
Source: PA Photos.

detecting liars. However, this finding was coloured by another – the criminals also detected fewer truth-tellers. The lie bias – that criminals are more likely to judge that someone is lying than telling the truth – might stem from the fact that criminals are naturally suspicious (because they are used to being lied to, whether in prison or in the context of their relationships with others) and because they themselves are practised liars (and, therefore, expect the worst of others).

In another study, adult male offenders from a medium security Canadian prison and a group of undergraduates were asked to recall four emotional events from their lives (Porter *et al.*, 2008) but lie about two of them. The researchers measured the number of illustrators (the use of hands to signify something), self-manipulations (touching/scratching the hand, head or body), frequency of head movement and number of smiles and laughs. Verbal indicators were number of words spoken per minute, filled pauses ('umms' and 'ahs'), self-references and pauses longer than two seconds. Illustrators were higher when lying than not telling the truth in both groups. Offenders, however, used more self-manipulations when lying compared with non-offenders, a finding that seems to contradict previous studies. The authors suggest that this may be due to the specific context in which experiments take place, the type of lie, motivation, the consequences of the lie, and so on. The offenders also smiled less than the students when lying about emotional events.

Of course, deception studies are fairly artificial: they usually involve participants watching a videotape of a person, and basing their judgement about the person's truthfulness on

these data. Interviewing suspects, the police would argue, gives you much more information on which to base a judgement. Sadly, research does not support this view. Studies have shown that observers of an interview are better at discriminating between truth-tellers and liars than are the interviewers themselves (Buller *et al.*, 1991; Granhag and Stromwall, 2001). The interviewers also showed evidence of truth bias – the tendency to declare that someone was saying the truth when they were not. People tend to focus on different behavioural cues when deciding on whether a person is telling the truth or lying, with people relying on verbal cues when judging the truthfulness of a story and on non-verbal cues when the story is deceptive (Anderson *et al.*, 1999).

What, therefore, signals that lying is taking place? Two of the most fairly reliable indicators appear to be a high-pitched voice and a decrease in hand movements. People are also better at identifying deception accurately if they are asked about it indirectly. For example, people are less accurate when asked, 'Is this person lying?' than when asked 'Does the person x sincerely like the person y?' (Vrij, 2001). When people are questioned indirectly they tend to focus on those behavioural cues that have been found to predict deception, such as decreased hand movement, rather than those that do not (Vrij, 2001).

New research on lying is presenting us with some counterintuitive and challenging findings about psychology and human behaviour. Often as you saw in the Controversies in Psychological Science section earlier, these studies contradict 'received wisdom' and 'common sense'.

Individual differences is an area of psychology which examines individual differences in temperament and patterns of behaviour. The primary focus of individual differences research is on how large groups can be further subdivided into more meaningful groups. For example, instead of examining a group's response to the effect of mild alcohol intake on task performance, a psychologist might decide to examine differences between men and women or people who are extraverted or introverted. Some examples of individual differences studied by psychologists include personality, intelligence, hand preference, sex and age. (The Cutting Edge section below looks at the role of personality in a behaviour that some have associated with mental ill-health: celebrity worship.)

Cross-cultural psychology is the study of the impact of culture on behaviour (Segall *et al.*, 1998). The ancestors of people of different racial and ethnic groups lived in different environments which presented them with different problems and opportunities for solving those problems. Different cultures have, therefore, developed different strategies for adapting to their environments. These strategies show themselves in laws, customs, myths, religious beliefs and ethical principles as well as in thinking, health beliefs and approaches to problem-solving.

In each chapter of the book, you'll find a section entitled, '. . . An international perspective'. This takes a topic in psychology and examines how it is has been studied cross-culturally, e.g. Are personality traits universal?, Is the recognition of emotion culture-specific?, Do culture-specific mental illnesses exist?, and so on. But throughout every chapter, you will discover how studies from research laboratories and centres across the world have contributed to our understanding of behaviour.

A similar – but different – term, **cultural psychology**, has been used to describe the study of variations within cultures (not necessarily across cultures). The assumption in cultural psychology is that cultures, and their processes and contents, are variable and not universal (Miller, 1997).

Forensic and **criminological psychology** applies psychological knowledge to the understanding, prediction and nature of crime and behaviour related to crime. There is a distinction between criminological and forensic psychology. Forensic psychologists can be commissioned by courts to prepare reports on the fitness of a defendant to stand trial, on the general psychological state of the defendant, on aspects of psychological research (such as post-traumatic stress disorders), on the behaviour of children involved in custody disputes and so on. Criminological psychology refers to the application of psychological principles to the criminal justice system (Blackburn, 1996). The terms, however, are often used interchangeably. One example of the way in which criminological psychologists can apply their research to crime is in the study of eyewitness testimony. Eyewitness testi-

mony is a highly unreliable source of information and psychologists have helped show how flawed this method of memory retrieval is and have suggested alternative methods of prompting witnesses' memory of crime. We examine some of these methods in Chapter 8.

The Psychology in Action section below also shows you some of the ways in which the work of psychologists has been useful to the criminal justice system, either by improving police detection techniques or by advising on the reliability of testimony. Many psychologists' work can help to solve or understand pressing human problems such as drug and alcohol abuse, stress, susceptibility to illness, mental disorder, developmental disorders, work inefficiency, witness memory, eyewitness testimony, crowd control and so on.

Clinical psychology 'aims to reduce psychological distress and to enhance and promote psychological well-being by the systematic application of knowledge derived from psychological theory and data' (BPS Division of Clinical Psychology, 2001). It is an applied branch of psychology because clinical psychologists do not work in the laboratory under well-controlled experimental conditions but out in the field, applying the knowledge gained from practice and research. Most clinical psychologists are specially trained practitioners who attempt to assess and treat people's psychological problems.

The remainder represent scientists who investigate a wide variety of causal events, including genetic factors, physiological factors and environmental factors such as parental upbringing, interactions with siblings and other social stimuli. Clinical psychologists can work in private practice (on their own or as part of a joint practice), in hospitals and mental health clinics, as part of government services, in work organisations, and sometimes as lecturers in colleges and universities. Chapter 18 describes some of the problems seen by clinical psychologists.

Perhaps two of the greatest bugbears for psychologists have been the misrepresentation of research and the inaccurate reporting of research, such as the portrayal of mental illness. A research team from the University of Auckland, New Zealand, for example, analysed a week's worth of children's programmes on two television stations to see how mental illness was portrayed (Wilson *et al.*, 2000). Forty-six different programmes were analysed representing 128 different episodes: 60 per cent were made in the USA and over 80 per cent were cartoon animations. Characters were defined as mentally ill if they were referred to by other characters as having a mental illness.

Of the 128 episodes, over 45 per cent contained reference to mental illness. Most of these programmes were cartoons. The most common terms for mental illness were 'crazy', 'mad' and 'losing your mind', although 'mad' and 'crazy' were interchangeably used to mean 'angry'. Other terms included 'driven bananas', 'wacko', 'nuts', 'loony',

Cutting edge – I'm your biggest fan... What makes a celebrity worshipper worship?

Shakespeare, in his day, probably had fans whose responses were a little overenthusiastic, but the explosion of media available in the twenty-first century means that people can now gorge themselves on as much information about their favourite celebrities as they want. According to research, fans (or 'celebrity worshippers') tend to be adolescents or young adults and enjoy 'game-playing' in romantic relationships. They appear to be no more or less shy or lonely than is normal but their degree of worship has been associated with psychological disorder. Some fans can cross the conventional line between worshipping at a distance and becoming overly-obsessed by their idol.

Maltby, McCutcheon and their colleagues have described celebrity worship as having three components (Maltby *et al.*, 2001; McCutcheon *et al.*, 2002). Low levels of worship are characterised as having entertainment-social value (e.g. 'My friends and I like to discuss what my favourite celebrity has done'). Intermediate levels are expressed in attitudes such as 'I consider my favourite celebrity to be my soul mate' (intense-personal value). Extreme levels, called borderline-pathological, are expressed in views such as 'If I were lucky enough to meet my celebrity, and he/she asked me to do something illegal as a favour, I would probably do it'. Those expressing low levels of worship tend to be extravert (sociable, lively, active, etc.), those expressing intermediate levels tend to be neurotic (tense, moody, emotional), and those showing evidence of borderline-pathological attitudes express some of the traits seen in the psychoticism scale, such as impulsivity and antisocial behaviour (Maltby *et al.*, 2003).

In a study of the relationship between celebrity worship, personality and mental health, Maltby *et al.* (2004) found that in their sample of over 350 participants, 15 per cent were classified as expressing entertainment-social attitudes; 55 per cent expressed intense-personal attitudes; and 1 per cent expressed pathological attitudes. The researchers found that, as predicted in their previous study, the three levels of

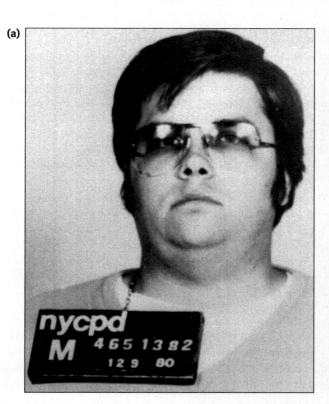
(a)

(b)

The two faces of celebrity. Mark Chapman was obsessed with J.D. Salinger's *The Catcher in the Rye* and assassinated former Beatle John Lennon outside the Dakota Hotel in New York. In 2002, Japanese businessman Masahiko Shizawa was issued with a restraining order because he was 'abnormally obsessed' with Britney Spears.

Source: (a) NYC PD/AFP/Getty Images; (b) Simon Frederick/Getty Images.

Cutting edge – *Continued*

worship were significantly correlated with personality type. Celebrity worshippers who followed their idols for entertainment or social reasons were extravert, sought information and support and were open in showing their emotions. Those who followed their idols for intense or personal reasons were neurotic. Those at the extreme end were more likely to use humour to cope with life, to use drink and drugs and to be non-religious.

Surprisingly, only one level of worship was associated with mental health problems. Those celebrity worshipping for intense-personal reasons had poorer general health (depression, anxiety and social dysfunction), expressed more negative affect (stress and low life satisfaction) and did not cope effectively with everyday life events. The researchers suggest that these problems may be underpinned by personality style (neuroticism) – one that reflects a disengagement from life.

'cuckoo' and 'freak'. Mental illness was frequently portrayed as reflecting a loss of control. Characters at the receiving end of these epithets were routinely and invariably seen as negative, as objects of amusement or derision or as objects of fear. The characters were either comical or villainous. You'll see in the last chapter how psychologists have identified views such as these and proposed ways of changing them.

Psychology in action – Psychology in the witness box

Recent years have seen a surge of interest in forensic or criminological psychology. Forensic psychology refers to the branch of psychology which involves the 'collection, examination and presentation of evidence for judicial purposes' (Haward, 1981; Blackburn, 1996). The British Psychological Society has its own division of criminological and legal psychology and a European Association for Psychology and Law has been established (Blackburn, 1996). Several popular accounts of the forensic psychologist's work have been published (for example, Canter, 1994; Britton, 1997) and the day-to-day work of the profession has been fictionalised (not entirely accurately) in programmes and films such as *Criminal Minds*, *Cracker*, *The Silence of the Lambs* and *Hannibal*.

The application of psychology to law, however, is a recent phenomenon. The first psychologist to give expert testimony in court was the German Albert Schrenk-Notzing in 1896. Schrenk-Notzing became involved in the trial of a Munich man accused of murdering three women (Bartol and Bartol, 1987). His contribution helped the court to understand the concept of retroactive memory falsification – the confusion that arises between what witnesses say they saw and what actually happened. A little later, in the USA, the advice of Hugo Munsterberg, one of the pioneers of forensic psychology, was sought in two murder trials (Colman, 1995). His work on the reaction time between rifle shots was cited in the case relating to the assassination of John F. Kennedy (Haward, 1979; Colman, 1995).

The psychologists most often consulted by lawyers are clinical and educational psychologists (Lloyd-Bostock, 1988;

Gudjonsson, 1996a). Prison psychologists might also be consulted to assess offenders and give supporting evidence in court; occupational psychologists might be called on in cases involving personal injury or discrimination; academic psychologists might be asked to advise on specialised areas of psychology, such as factors which could influence face identification (Lloyd-Bostock, 1988); clinical neuropsychologists might be asked to determine whether a defendant is malingering, i.e. feigning mental disorder or intellectual incompetence (Martin, 2006). See Table 1.2.

Table 1.2 The types of evidence provided by forensic psychologists

Types of evidence provided	Percentage recorded
Interview with client	97
Studying relevant documents	87
Psychometric test results	85
Interview with informants	79
Behavioural assessment	64
Other (e.g. reviewing audio/video material, conducting research reviews/psychophysiological measurements)	20

Source: Based on the responses of 522 psychologists in the UK. Gudjonsson, G.H., Psychological evidence in court. *The Psychologist*, 1996, May, 213–17. © The British Psychological Society.

Psychology in action – *Continued*

At the trial stage of criminal proceedings, psychologists may assess an individual's state of mind and determine whether the offence was intentional. Much of the empirical research in psychology could also be applied at this stage – especially research that can inform jurors' understanding of behaviours such as witness memory and eyewitness identification (Loftus, 1986). In North America, and also in England and Wales in particular, the legal and police systems have taken steps to issue guidelines on, for example, eyewitness testimony and its reliability, such as the *Memorandum of Good Practice on Video-recorded Interviews with Child Witnesses for Criminal Proceedings* (1992) in the UK, and *Eyewitness Evidence: A Guide for Law Enforcement* (1999) in the US (Wells *et al.*, 2000).

One tool associated with criminological psychology, and which has given it some cinematic glamour, is **offender profiling**, a technique that dates back to the 1950s (Brown, 1998). The purpose of offender profiling is to present a composite description of a perpetrator, based on biographical and behavioural cues, that can lead to the apprehension of that perpetrator. It can also be used to narrow the focus of an investigation (by specifying the perpetrator's age or sex, or where he/she lives) or to provide suggestions for interviewing suspects (McCann, 1992). By collating data and evaluating evidence, such techniques have led to the arrest of serious criminals, such as the British criminal, John Duffy, who murdered his victims near railways (Canter, 1989). However, even psychologists who have used – and pioneered – such techniques suggest caution in using this technique. The romantic, insightful detective who uses implicit learning to make his deductions dates back to Sherlock Holmes. In a review of offender profiling, a leading forensic psychologist, David Canter from the University of Liverpool, has argued that, 'Much of what passes for "offender profiling" in practice and as reported in the factual and fictional media has no basis in empirical research' (Canter, 2000). He criticises the 'implicit reasoning' approach, popularised by Conan Doyle in his Holmes stories, using an interesting illustration. Holmes's approach involved using experience or logic to draw inferences about the criminal.

In a real-life example cited by Canter, a victim had noticed that the assailant had short fingernails on the left hand and long ones on the right hand. Someone with information about guitar playing suggested that this was a characteristic of serious guitar players and the search was on for a guitarist. When the offender was eventually arrested, he was found to have no connection with guitars. He had asymmetrical fingernails because of his job as a tyre repairman.

'I can never bring you to realise the importance of sleeves, the suggestiveness of thumbnails, or the great information that may hang from a bootlace,' said the great Sherlock Holmes in *A Case of Identity*. Modern crime detection, however, would suggest that Holmes's strategy would convict more innocent people than guilty.
Source: 20th Century Fox/Kobal Collection Ltd.

Canter also describes a team of northern European profilers who mistakenly assumed that because a murdered woman's face had been severely beaten, the offender knew his/her victim and was exacting some form of revenge (**http://www.liv.ac.uk/ InvestigativePsychology/invpub.htm**).The murdered woman was a teacher and attention was quickly focused on those pupils who may have been ignored or spurned by her. The murderer turned out to be a drug addict who killed the woman when she disturbed him burgling her house.

Canter suggests adopting a more statistical approach to offender profiling: collecting bits of data so that consistencies between crimes can be highlighted. Although an individual crime will differ from crime to crime, there may be a consistent theme running through that series of crimes. Canter argues that this systematic, clinical approach is more likely to be successful in profiling offenders than is that of the lone detective working on hunches.

Health psychology is the study of the ways in which behaviour and lifestyle can affect health and illness (Sarafino, 2002). For example, smoking is associated with a number of illnesses and is a strong risk factor for death. Health psychologists study what makes people initiate and maintain unhealthy behaviour and can help devise strategies to reduce it. Health psychologists are employed in a variety of settings including hospitals, government, universities and private practice. The work of health psychologists is described in Chapter 17.

Educational psychology is another branch of applied psychology. Educational psychologists assess the behavioural problems of children at school and suggest ways in which these problems may be remedied. For example, the educational psychologist might identify a child's early inability to read (dyslexia) and suggest a means by which this may be overcome through special training. The educational psychologist might also deal with all aspects relevant to a child's schooling such as learning, social relations, assessment, disruptive behaviour, substance abuse, bullying and parental neglect.

Consumer psychology is the study of the motivation, perception, learning, cognition and purchasing behaviour of individuals in the marketplace and their use of products once they reach the home. Some consumer psychologists take a marketer's perspective, some take a consumer's perspective, and some adopt a neutral perspective, especially if they work at a university.

Organisational or **occupational psychology** is one of the largest and oldest fields of applied psychology and involves the study of the ways in which individuals and groups perform and behave in the workplace (Huczynski and Buchanan, 2006). Early organisational psychologists concentrated on industrial work processes (such as the most efficient way to shovel coal), but organisational psychologists now spend more effort analysing modern plants and offices. They are involved in the administration and development of personality aptitude tests and can also be involved in stress management. Most are employed by large companies and organisations, but almost one-third are employed in universities.

Ergonomics or **human factors psychology** focuses mainly on the ways in which people and machines work together (Shackel, 1996). They study machines ranging from cockpits to computers, from robots to MP3/4 players, from transportation vehicles for the disabled to telephones. If the machine is well designed, the task can be much easier, more enjoyable and safer. Ergonomists help designers and engineers to design better machines; because of this, the terms ergonomics and engineering psychology are sometimes used interchangeably (Stanton, 1996).

Sport and exercise psychology applies psychological principles to the area of sport. It also involves the study of the effects of sport and exercise on mood, cognition, well-being and physiology. This area is examined in more detail in Chapter 17.

Psychology – An international perspective

Behind almost all research endeavours in psychology is a common aim: to discover a psychological universal. According to Norenzayan and Heine (2005), **psychological universals** are 'core mental attributes shared by humans everywhere'. That is, they are conclusions from psychological research that can be generalised across groups – ways of reasoning, thinking, making decisions, interpreting why people behave in the way that they do, recognising emotions and so on, are all examples of core mental attributes. A sound case for a psychological universal can be made if a phenomenon exists in a large variety of different cultures.

However, as might be obvious to you, some differences may be more obvious in some groups than others – men and women, for example, the young and the old, the mentally ill and the mentally healthy, and so on. At this level of analysis, we cannot say that people in general behave in a particular way, but that a spe-

cific group of people behave in a particular way. Nowhere is this more relevant than when considering the role of culture in psychological studies. A variety of behaviours are absent or are limited in a variety of cultures and nations. Some recent research, for example, has highlighted significant differences between Western and Asian cultures in the types of autobiographical memory they recall, the parts of a landscape and photograph they focus on, and the way in which they draw and take a photograph. Table 1.3 summarises some of these differences.

One approach to demonstrating a psychological universal is to examine a behaviour in three or more cultures, two of which are very different, with a third falling between them, and see how each differs from, or is similar to, the other. The best way, however, is to examine a variety of cultures, as Daly and Wilson (1988) did. Their research examined sex differences in the international rates of homicide and found that men were more

Psychology – *Continued*

Table 1.3 Behaviours which have been reported to vary across cultures, or which may be less evident in certain cultures. Unfamiliar terms are defined in the chapters referred to in brackets

- Memory for and categorisation of focal colours
- Spatial reasoning (see Chapter 8)
- Autobiographical memory
- Perception of the environment
- Appreciation of art
- Some types of category-based inductive reasoning (see Chapter 11)
- Some perceptual illusions
- Some ways of approaching reasoning
- Aspects of numerical reasoning
- Risk preferences in decision-making (see Chapter 11)
- Self-concept (see Chapters 15 and 16)
- Similarity-attraction effect (see Chapters 15 and 16)
- Approach-avoidance motivation (see Chapter 13)
- The fundamental attribution error (see Chapters 15 and 16)
- Predilection for aggression
- Feelings of control
- High subjective well-being and positive affect
- Communication style
- Prevalence of major depression
- Prevalence of eating disorders (see Chapter 13)
- Mental illness (those that appear in some cultures but not others – see the Controversies in Psychological Science section in Chapter 18)
- Noun bias in language learning (see Chapter 10)
- Moral reasoning
- Prevalence of different attachment style (see Chapter 12)
- Disruptive behaviour in adolescence
- Personality types (see Chapter 14)
- Response bias (see Chapter 2)
- Recognition of emotion
- Body shape preference

Source: Adapted from Norenzayan and Heine (2005).

likely to kill men than women were to kill women. Debate then ensues as to why this universal should be (and that debate is often heated, as most in psychology are).

A related approach is to examine the degree to which a psychological phenomenon is present –personality type is a good example of this. As Chapter 14 will show you, the dominant approach in personality views us as differing along five major personality dimensions. Cross-cultural research has highlighted (i) the universality of these five dimensions but also (ii) the differences or 'variation' which exist between and within cultures

within each dimension – so some cultures or states may express more or less of a personality type such as extraversion or conscientiousness, for example.

In the book, examples of universals (and exceptions) are described in the sections: '. . . An international perspective'. These will help you put the findings you read about into some form of cultural or international context. They should also help demonstrate that although studies sometimes report findings as being absolute and generalisable to populations in general, sometimes these findings are not.

Psychology: a European perspective

Psychology is one of the most popular degree courses in Europe. In 2008, psychology was the third most popular UK University degree in terms of applications (70,295, pipped only by law and pre-clinical medicine, see Table 1.4). It is estimated that 1 in 850 people in the Netherlands has a degree in psychology (Van Drunen, 1995), and no course is more popular in Sweden (Persson, 1995).

Modern psychology has its origins in Europe: the first psychological laboratory was established in Europe and some of the first designated university degrees in psychology were established there. Research in North America and Europe accounts for the majority of psychological studies published in the world (Eysenck, 2001) and there continues to be debate over whether these two fairly large 'geographical' areas adopt genuinely different approaches to the study of psychological processes (G. N. Martin, 2001).

Psychology as a discipline occupies a different status in different European countries and each country has established its own degrees and societies at different times, for historical or political reasons. Almost all countries have a professional organisation which regulates the activity of psychologists or provides psychological training or licensing of psychologists. The first such association in Denmark was founded in 1929 (the Psychotechnical Institute in Copenhagen) and what we would now call educational psychology formed the basis of the professional training it provided: the job of the institute was to select apprentices for the printing trade (Foltveld, 1995). The Netherlands' first psychological laboratory was founded in 1892 at Gröningen, Denmark's in 1944 at the University of Copenhagen and Finland's in 1921 by Eino Kaila at the University of Turku (Saari, 1995). Coincidentally, 1921 was also the year in which The Netherlands passed a Higher Education Act allowing philosophy students to specialise in psychology.

Table 1.4 The top ten degree subjects in the UK, as indexed by applications to study at university (2008)

1	Law	77,459
2	Pre-clinical medicine	70,377
3	Psychology	70,295
4	English studies	50,251
5	Management studies	49,447
6	Nursing	47,051
7	Teacher training	43,896
8	Business/admin studies	42,816
9	History	41,917
10	Business studies	41,583

The British Psychological Society (BPS) was formed in 1901, with laboratories established at the University of Cambridge and University College London in 1897, closely followed by the establishment of laboratories in Aberdeen, Edinburgh and Glasgow (Lunt, 1995). Sweden's professional association was founded in 1955 (Sveriges Psykologforbund), with the Netherlands' predating that in 1938 (Nederlandsch Instituut van Practizeerende Psychologen, or NIPP). Portugal is one of the younger psychology nations – the first graduates in psychology left university in 1982 (Pereira, 1995). Because of the history of the country, psychology was not acknowledged as a university subject in Portugal until after the democratic revolution of 1974.

Psychological training and status of psychology in Europe

The types of career that psychology graduates pursue are similar across most European countries. Figures 1.2(a) and (b) show you the employment destination of psychologists in Denmark and The Netherlands. You can see from these figures that most psychologists are employed in the public sector, with the majority of those working in the clinical, educational or organisational fields. Around 90 per cent of psychologists are employed in the public sector in Finland and 70 per cent of these work in health, clinical or social work-related areas (Saari, 1995). A similar pattern is seen in Sweden (Persson, 1995).

Training for psychologists varies between countries and controversy surrounds the licensing or the legalisation of the profession. For example, psychologists in almost all countries wish for formal statutory regulation of the profession (the medical and legal professions are regulated). In Denmark, the title of psychologist was legally protected in 1993 so that no one could call themselves a psychologist unless they had received specified training. In Greece, a law was passed in 1979 licensing psychologists to practise (Georgas, 1995). These enlightened views have not extended to some other countries, however, despite the attempts of professional organisations in lobbying their legislators. Finland and the UK have faced obstacles in legalising the profession.

The BPS has its own regulatory system so that applied psychologists need to undergo an approved route of training (to go on to practise as forensic, clinical, educational, health psychologists, for example) before they are recognised as qualified professional psychologists by the Society. Most of these individuals choose to register themselves as Chartered Psychologists – a person using the services of a psychologist designated chartered can, therefore, be assured that the person is a recognised professional psychologist.

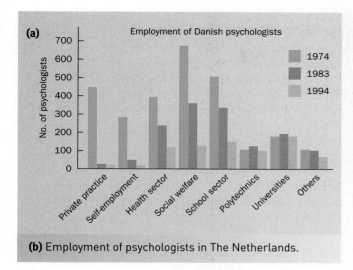

(a)

Employment of Danish psychologists

No. of psychologists

700 / 600 / 500 / 400 / 300 / 200 / 100 / 0

1974 / 1983 / 1994

Private practice / Self-employment / Health sector / Social welfare / School sector / Polytechnics / Universities / Others

(b) Employment of psychologists in The Netherlands.

Setting	Number of members	
	1991	**1995**
General and mental health care		
Psychiatric hospitals and clinics	441	511
Semi-residential mental health care	62	63
Non-residential mental health care	670	681
General and academic hospitals	448	523
Specialised hospitals and clinics	101	125
Psychogeriatric nursing homes	127	175
Institution for alcoholics and drug addicts	58	61
Forensic settings	32	41
Preventive psychology	240	498
Private practice	991	929
Education and youth care		
Schools for special education	68	76
Institutions for educational counselling	140	128
Homes for the mentally handicapped	110	107
Children's homes	44	36
Work		
Consulting firms	308	387
Industrial psychologists	242	206
Vocational guidance	61	69
Other		
School for professional education	124	99
Universities	378	355
Research institutes	32	15

Figure 1.2 (a) Areas of employment taken up by Danish psychologists across three decades; **(b)** employment destinations of members of the Netherlands Institute of Psychology in 1991 and 1995.

Sources: (a) Foltveld, P., The psychological profession in Denmark. In A. Schorr and S. Saari (eds) *Psychology in Europe*; (b) Van Drunen, P., Professional psychology in the Netherlands: history and recent trends. Reproduced with permission from *Psychology in Europe*, by A. Schorr and S. Saari (eds), ISBN 0-88937-155-5, © 1995, Hogrefe & Huber Publishers, Seattle, Toronto, Göttingen, Bern

European views of psychology and psychologists

Non-psychologists' views of what psychology is and what psychologists do are encouragingly positive and generally, accurate although their knowledge of psychological research (as you saw earlier) is flawed. Table 1.5 shows you the responses of an Austrian sample to the question, 'What do you expect a psychologist to do?', and to the sentence, 'Psychologists can . . .' (Friedlmayer and Rossler, 1995).

A Finnish study which asked adults to rate which of a number of professions was more knowledgeable about human nature, found that 53 per cent believed doctors were more knowledgeable, with psychologists following behind in second place (29 per cent) (Montin, 1995). A Norwegian study, however, found the opposite: 49 per cent chose psychologists and 23 per cent chose doctors (Christiansen, 1986). Figures 1.3 (a)–(d) give some of the other illuminating responses to the other questions asked in the Finnish survey. These not only reveal how people

Table 1.5 Austrian views of psychologists (based on a sample of 300 respondents)

Statement/question	%
'Psychologists can . . .'	
See through other people	68
Help other people to change	72
Help others to help themselves	90
Exert influence through reports	57
Release people from mental suffering	62
Listen patiently	88
Direct the attention of social policy-makers	53
Handle children well	55
Cause harm by making mistaken diagnoses	68
Make people happier	54

Statement/question	%
What do you expect a psychologist to do?'	
Talk	97
Testing	90
Filing a report	85
Treatment/therapy	91
Training children	46
Proposing interventions	86
Negotiating conflicts	65
Giving guidance and advice	94
Solving problems	44

Source: Based on Friedlmayer, S. and Rossler, E., Professional identity and public image of Austrian psychologists. Reproduced with permission from *Psychology in Europe* by A. Schorr and S. Saari (eds), ISBN 0-88937-155-5,© 1995, Hogrefe & Huber Publishers, Seattle, Toronto, Göttingen, Bern.

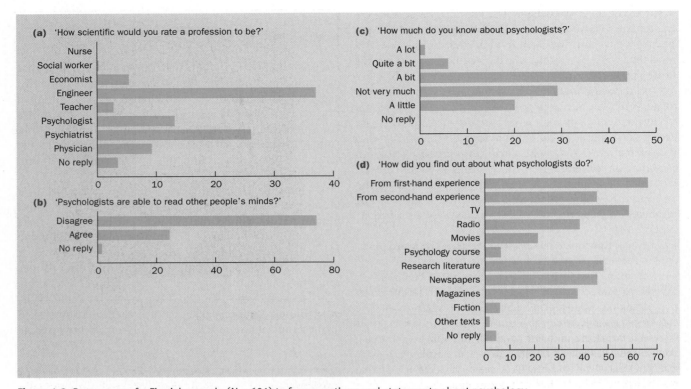

Figure 1.3 Responses of a Finnish sample (*N* = 601) to four questions and statements about psychology.

Source: Montin, S. The public image of psychologists in Finland. Reproduced with permission from *Psychology in Europe* by A. Schorr and S. Saari (eds), ISBN 0-88937-155-5, © 1995, Hogrefe & Huber Publishers, Seattle, Toronto, Göttingen, Bern.

receive or obtain their information about psychology but also show that the discipline is still shrouded in some mystery – 49 per cent declare knowing only 'a little' about psychology. Mercifully, 75 per cent of respondents disagreed that psychologists could read minds.

You will find the addresses of professional associations and organisations of psychology in Europe at the end of the chapter. You can contact them for more information about postgraduate courses and training opportunities in psychology.

Psychology: the development of a science

Although philosophers and other thinkers have been concerned with psychological issues for centuries, the science of psychology is comparatively young. To understand how this science came into being, it is useful to trace its roots back through philosophy and the natural sciences. These disciplines originally provided the methods we use to study human behaviour and took many centuries to develop.

Philosophical roots of psychology

Animism

Each of us is conscious of our own existence. Furthermore, we are aware of this consciousness. Although we often find ourselves doing things that we had not planned to do (or had planned not to do), by and large we feel that we are in control of our behaviour. That is, we have the impression that our conscious mind controls our behaviour. We consider alternatives, make plans, and then act. We get our bodies moving; we engage in behaviour.

Earlier in human history, philosophers attributed a life-giving animus, or spirit, to anything that seemed to move or grow independently. Because they believed that the movements of their own bodies were controlled by their minds or spirits, they inferred that the sun, moon, wind, tides and other moving entities were similarly animated. This primitive philosophy is called **animism** (from the Latin *animare*, 'to quicken, enliven, endow with breath or soul'). Even gravity was explained in animistic terms: rocks fell to the ground because the spirits within them wanted to be reunited with Mother Earth.

Obviously, animism is now of historical interest only. No educated person believes that rocks fall because they 'want to'. Rather, we believe that they fall because of the existence of natural forces inherent in physical matter, even if we do not understand what these forces are. But note that different interpretations can be placed on the same events. Surely, we are just as prone to subjective interpretations of natural phenomena, albeit more sophisticated ones, as our ancestors were. In fact, when we try to explain why people do what they do, we tend to attribute at least some of their behaviour to the action of a motivating spirit – namely, a will. In our daily lives, this explanation of behaviour may often suit our needs. However, on a scientific level, we need to base our explanations on phenomena that can be observed and measured objectively. We cannot objectively and directly observe 'will'.

The best means we have to ensure objectivity is the scientific method, which is described in more detail in the next chapter. Psychology as a science must be based on the assumption that behaviour is strictly subject to physical laws, just as any other natural phenomenon is. The rules of scientific research impose discipline on humans whose natural inclinations might lead them to incorrect conclusions. It seemed natural for our ancestors to believe that rocks had spirits, just as it seems natural for people nowadays to believe that behaviour can be affected by a person's will. In contrast, the idea that feelings, emotions, imagination and other private experiences are the products of physical laws of nature did not come easily; it evolved through many centuries.

Dualism: René Descartes

Although the history of Western philosophy properly begins with the Ancient Greeks, a French philosopher and mathematician, René Descartes (1596–1650), is regarded as the father of modern philosophy. He advocated a sober, impersonal investigation of natural phenomena using sensory experience and human reasoning. He assumed that the world was a purely mechanical entity that, having once been set in motion by God, ran its course without divine interference. Thus, to understand the world, one had only to understand how it was constructed. This stance challenged the established authority of the Church, which believed that the purpose of philosophy was to reconcile human experiences with the truth of God's revelations.

To Descartes, animals were mechanical devices; their behaviour was controlled by environmental stimuli. His view of the human body was much the same: it was a machine. Thus, Descartes was able to describe some movements as automatic and involuntary. For example, the application of a hot object to a finger would cause an almost immediate withdrawal of the arm away from the

René Descartes (1596–1650).

source of stimulation. Reactions like this did not require participation of the mind; they occurred automatically. Descartes called these actions **reflexes** (from the Latin *reflectere*, 'to bend back upon itself'). A stimulus registered by the senses produces a reaction that would be entirely physical and beyond voluntary control. There would be no intention or will to produce this physical reaction. Consider the well-known reflex of sensing the heat of a flame, as seen in Figure 1.4. The body recoils from flame in an involuntary way: we do not intentionally move away from the flame but our body reflexively puts in place a chain of muscle contractions which make us withdraw. The term 'reflex' is still in use today, but, of course, we explain the operation of a reflex differently, as you'll see in Chapter 4.

What set humans apart from the rest of the world, according to Descartes, was their possession of a mind. This was a uniquely human attribute and was not subject to the laws of the universe. Thus, Descartes was a proponent of **dualism**, the belief that all reality can be divided into two distinct entities: mind and matter (this is often referred to as **Cartesian dualism**). He distinguished between 'extended things', or physical bodies, and 'thinking things', or minds. Physical bodies, he believed, do not think, and minds are not made of ordinary matter.

Although Descartes was not the first to propose dualism, his thinking differed from that of his predecessors in one important way: he was the first to suggest that a link exists between the human mind and its purely physical housing. Although later philosophers pointed out that this theoretical link actually contradicted his belief in

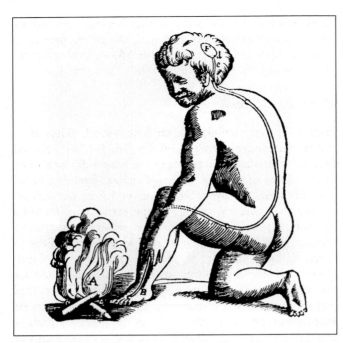

Figure 1.4 Descartes's diagram of a withdrawal reflex.
Source: Image 9902 from Stock Montage, Inc.

dualism, the proposal of an interaction between mind and matter, **interactionism**, was absolutely vital to the development of the science of psychology.

From the time of Plato onwards, philosophers had argued that the mind and the body were different entities. They also suggested that the mind could influence the body but the body could not influence the mind, a little like a puppet and puppeteer with the mind pulling the strings of the body. Not all philosophers adopted this view, however. To some, such as Spinoza (1632–1677), both mental events (thinking) and physical events (such as occupying space) were characteristic of one and the same thing, in the same way that an undulating line can be described as convex or concave – it cannot be described as exclusively one thing or another (this is called **double-aspect theory**).

Descartes hypothesised that this interaction between mind and body took place in the pineal body, a small organ situated on top of the brain stem, buried beneath the large cerebral hemispheres of the brain. When the mind decided to perform an action, it tilted the pineal body in a particular direction, causing fluid to flow from the brain into the proper set of nerves. This flow of fluid caused the appropriate muscles to inflate and move.

How did Descartes come up with this mechanical concept of the body's movements? Western Europe in the seventeenth century was the scene of great advances in the sciences. This was the century, for example, in which William Harvey discovered that blood circulated around the body. It was not just the practical application of science that impressed Europeans, however, it was the beauty, imagination and fun of it as well. Craftsmen constructed many elaborate mechanical toys and devices during this period. The young Descartes was greatly impressed by the moving statues in the Royal Gardens (Jaynes, 1970) and these devices served as models for Descartes as he theorised about how the body worked. He conceived of the muscles as balloons. They became inflated when a fluid passed through the nerves that connected them to the brain and spinal cord, just as water flowed through pipes to activate the statues. This inflation was the basis of the muscular contraction that causes us to move.

This story illustrates one of the first examples of a technological device used to model and explain how the nervous system works. In science, a **model** is a relatively simple system that works on known principles and is able to do at least some of the things that a more complex system can do. For example, when scientists discovered that elements of the nervous system communicate by means of electrical impulses, researchers developed models of the brain based on telephone switchboards and, more recently, computers. Abstract models, which are completely mathematical in their properties, have also been developed. Clinical psychologists may interpret mental disorder according to a medical model which conceives of clinical mental disturbance as an illness.

Although Descartes's model of the human body was mechanical, it was controlled by the non-mechanical (in fact, non-physical) mind. Thus, humans were born with a special capability that made them greater than simply the sum of their physical parts. Their knowledge was more than merely a physical phenomenon.

Descartes's influence on the development of psychology was considerable. He proposed the revolutionary idea that the mind and the body were mutually interacting and suggested a method of studying 'the mind' which was based on reasoning and not metaphysical analysis. Descartes's notion of interactionism gave rise to two very influential but very different schools of thought in psychology at the end of the nineteenth and the beginning of the twentieth centuries: introspectionism and behaviourism. We consider these later in the chapter.

Empiricism: John Locke and David Hume

With the work of the English philosopher John Locke (1632–1704), the mechanisation of the whole world became complete. Locke did not exempt the mind from the mechanical laws of the material universe. Descartes's rationalism – pursuit of truth through reason – was replaced by **empiricism** – pursuit of truth through observation and experience (in Greek, *empeiria* means experience).

A prevalent belief in the seventeenth century was that ideas were innately present in an infant's mind. Locke rejected this belief. Instead, he proposed that all knowledge must come through experience: it is empirically derived. His model of the mind was a tablet of soft clay, a tabula rasa, smooth at birth and ready to accept the writings of experience imprinted upon it. Locke believed that our knowledge of complex experiences was nothing more than links between simple, primary sensations: simple ideas combined to form complex ones.

This notion was developed further by the Scottish philosopher David Hume (1711–76). In his book *A Treatise of Human Nature* (1739), Hume argued that the study of human nature could best be undertaken through experience and observation. Hume's conception of the mind was slightly different from that of Locke. Whereas Locke wrote of ideas, Hume wrote of perceptions which were composed of impressions and ideas. Impressions were what we would consider sensations – seeing print on a paper or hearing a loud bang; ideas were the less vivid recollection of such sense experiences. Impressions, according to Hume, were the most important perceptions because these were derived directly from observation. Any ideas based on content which was not derived empirically were not valuable and not trustworthy. Hume, therefore, espoused what is known as **positivism** – the school of thought which argues that all meaningful ideas can be reduced to observable material.

Perhaps Hume's greatest contribution to psychology was the **doctrine of the association of ideas**. In *An Inquiry Concerning Human Understanding* (1748), Hume argued that there were various types of connection or association between ideas. This was not itself a new idea. Aristotle had proposed the notion of an association of ideas: two stimuli if paired frequently enough would result in the presentation of one event stimulating thoughts of the other. Hume suggested three specific types of association: resemblance (when we look at someone's photograph, for example, this triggers off thoughts about that person), contiguity (thoughts of an object or event will trigger thoughts related to those objects and events), and cause and effect (the idea that actions have identifiable causes). These associations were the 'cement' that helped bind the universe, and all complex human experiences were based on simple ideas derived from impressions. The most important of these associations was cause and effect, and Hume developed this theme by describing behaviour in terms of custom and habit. According to Hume, if one performs an act which produces an effect which makes a repetition of that act likely, this is a habit or custom. For example, think of a simple behaviour such as switching on a light. Your knowledge that switching a light on will illuminate a room will result in your habitually pressing the switch if you need light.

These notions of habit and causality became very important in the twentieth century with the development of behaviourism and the work of the Swiss developmental psychologist Jean Piaget (1896–1980), described later.

Idealism: Bishop Berkeley

In contrast to the empiricists, the Irish bishop, philosopher and mathematician George Berkeley (1685–1753) believed that our knowledge of events in the world did not come simply from direct experience. Instead, Berkeley (who gave his name to the famous university in California) argued that this knowledge is the result of inferences based on the accumulation of past experiences derived through the senses. In other words, we must learn how to perceive. For example, our visual perception of depth involves several elementary sensations, such as observing the relative movements of objects as we move our head and the convergence of our eyes (turning inward towards each other or away) as we focus on near or distant objects. Although our knowledge of visual depth seems to be immediate and direct, it is actually a secondary, complex response constructed from a number of simple elements. Our perceptions of the world can also involve integrating the activity of different sense organs, such as when we see, hear, feel and smell the same object. The aspect of Berkeley's philosophy which argues that all ideas come from the senses (*esse est percipi*) is called **idealism**.

As you can see, the philosophers Locke, Hume and Berkeley were grappling with the workings of the human mind and the way in which people acquire knowledge. They were dealing with the concept of learning. Modern psychologists are still concerned with the issues that Berkeley raised. As philosophers, they were trying to fit a non-quantifiable variable – reason – into the equation.

Materialism: James Mill

With the work of the Scottish philosopher James Mill (1773–1836), the pendulum took its full swing from animism (physical matter animated by spirits) to materialism (mind composed entirely of matter). **Materialism** is the belief that reality can be known only through an understanding of the physical world, of which the mind is a part. Mill worked on the assumption that humans and animals were fundamentally the same. Both humans and animals were thoroughly physical in their make-up and were completely subject to the physical laws of the universe. He agreed in essence with Descartes's approach to understanding the human body but rejected the concept of an immaterial mind. Mind, to Mill, was as passive as the body. It responded to the environment in precisely the same way. The mind, no less than the body, was a machine.

In the nineteenth century, the philosophy of the past began to make way for the experimentation of the future. In the latter part of the century, a part of Germany gave birth to modern psychology as we know it. Its midwife was Wilhelm Wundt.

Modern psychology: from the Leipzig laboratory to the cognitive revolution

Wilhelm Wundt (1832–1920) was the first person to call himself a psychologist and he shared the conviction of other German scientists that all aspects of nature, including the human mind, could be studied scientifically, an approach summarised in his book *Principles of Physiological Psychology*, the first textbook in psychology.

Wundt's approach was experimental in nature and his and his colleagues' work was conducted at the Leipzig laboratory. Over one hundred studies were conducted in the first twenty years of the laboratory's life. Initially, these were studies of the psychological and psychophysiological aspects of vision (seeing), audition (hearing) and somatosensation (feeling and touching). Later work focused on reaction time and the process involved in perceiving and then responding to a stimulus. Wundt also explored the nature of attention and emotional feeling as well as word association.

The fact that Germany was the birthplace of psychology had as much to do with social, political and economic influences as with the abilities of its scientists and scholars. The German university system was well established, and professors were highly respected members of society. The academic tradition in Germany emphasised a scientific approach to a large number of subject areas, such as history, phonetics, archaeology, aesthetics and literature. Thus, in contrast to French and British scholars, who adopted the more traditional, philosophical approach to the study of the human mind, German scholars were open to the possibility that the human mind could be studied scientifically. Experimental physiology, one of the most important roots of **experimental psychology**, was well established there. Eventually, Wundt's influence began to extend to other parts of Europe (especially the UK) and to the USA.

Structuralism: Wilhelm Wundt

Wundt defined psychology as the 'science of immediate experience', and his approach was called **structuralism**, the first proper school of thought to emerge in the history of psychology. Its subject matter was the structure of the mind, built from the elements of consciousness, such as

ideas and sensations. These elements could be constructed into a table of elements similar to a chemical table of elements. Structuralism's raw material was supplied by trained observers who described their own experiences under well-controlled conditions. The observers were taught to engage in introspection (literally, 'looking within'), the use of which was governed by strict rules. Introspectionists observed stimuli and described their experiences. According to Boring (1953), observers participating in reaction time experiments had to produce approximately 10,000 introspective observations before their data were considered valid and they themselves considered to be qualified introspectionists.

Wundt's aims were threefold: to analyse the contents of conscious experience, to determine how the elements of consciousness are connected, and to devise a law which would explain such connections. Wundt and his associates, Edward Tichener (1867–1927) and Gustav Fechner (1801–87), made inferences about the nature of mental processes by seeing how changes in the stimuli caused changes in the verbal reports of their trained observers.

Wundt was particularly interested in the problem that had intrigued Berkeley: how did basic sensory information give rise to complex perceptions? His **doctrine of apperception** attempted to account for the fact that when we perceive, this perception is of a whole object and not separate elements of it. We see wholes, according to Wundt, because of the process of creative synthesis (or law of psy-

Wilhelm Wundt (1832–1920).

chic resultants): a process which combines or synthesises elements to form a whole. Again, this process is very similar to a process in chemistry in which individual chemical elements when combined will form a new, wholly different entity. The whole would not be equivalent to the sum of its parts. Much of Wundt's work, however, aimed to break down and analyse the contents of the mind rather than determine how they are combined.

Wundt was an ambitious and prolific scientist who wrote many books and trained many other scientists in his laboratory. However, his method did not survive the test of time; structuralism died out in the early twentieth century. The major problem with his approach was the difficulty encountered by observers in reporting the raw data of sensation, data unmodified by experience. Although introspectionism aimed to establish well-controlled experimental conditions which would lead to reliable introspective observations, there was often little agreement between observers about their introspections. The method has also been criticised for its reliance on retrospection; the recollection of an experience was frequently elicited some time after the experience itself had occurred and was, therefore, subject to error.

In addition, attention began to shift from study of the human mind to the study of human behaviour. Behaviourism provided a devastating and critical alternative to introspectionism. According to behaviourism's founding father, the American John B. Watson, introspectionism was akin to superstition, an argument considered in detail a little later on. Recently, psychologists have resumed the study of the human mind, but we now have better methods for studying it than were available to Wundt.

Although structuralism has been supplanted, Wundt's contribution must be acknowledged. He was responsible for establishing psychology as a recognised, experimental science that was separate from philosophy. He used methods which involved observation and experimentation and trained a great number of psychologists, many of whom established their own schools and continued the evolution of the new discipline.

Memory: Hermann Ebbinghaus

Most of the pioneers of psychology founded schools, groups of people having a common belief in a particular theory and methodology. In this context, the word school refers to a branch of a particular academic discipline, not a building or institution. Structuralism was a school of psychology. The exception to this trend was Hermann Ebbinghaus (1850–1909). In 1876, after receiving his Ph.D. in philosophy but still unattached to an academic institution, Ebbinghaus came across a second-hand copy of a book by Gustav Fechner describing a mathematical approach to the measurement of human sensation.

Intrigued by Fechner's research, Ebbinghaus decided to attempt to measure human memory: the processes of learning and forgetting.

Working alone, Ebbinghaus devised methods to measure memory and the speed with which forgetting occurred. He realised that he could not compare the learning and forgetting of two prose passages or two poems because some passages would undoubtedly be easier to learn than others. Therefore, he devised a relatively uniform set of materials – nonsense syllables, such as 'juz', 'bul' and 'gof'. He printed the syllables on cards and read through a set of them, with the rate of presentation controlled by the ticking of a watch. After reading the set, he paused a fixed amount of time, then read the cards again. He recorded the number of times he had to read the cards to be able to recite them without error. He measured forgetting by trying to recite the nonsense syllables on a later occasion – minutes, hours or days later. The number of syllables he remembered was an index of the percentage of memory that had been retained.

Ebbinghaus's approach to memory was entirely empirical; he devised no theory of why learning occurs and was interested only in gathering facts through careful, systematic observation. However, despite the lack of theory, his work made important contributions to the development of the science of psychology. He introduced the principle of eliminating **variable errors** by making observations repeatedly on different occasions (using different lists each time) and calculating the average of these observations. Variable errors include errors caused by random differences in the subject's mood or alertness or by uncontrollable changes in the environment. He constructed graphs of the rate at which the memorised lists of nonsense syllables were forgotten, which provided a way to measure mental contents across time. As you will see in Chapter 8, Ebbinghaus's research provided a model of systematic, rigorous experimental procedures that modern psychologists still emulate.

Functionalism: William James and James Angell

After structuralism, the next major trend in psychology was **functionalism**. This approach, which began in the USA, was in large part a protest against the structuralism of Wundt. Structuralists were interested in what they called the components of consciousness (ideas and sensations); functionalists were more interested in the process of conscious activity (perceiving and learning). Functionalism grew from the new perspective on nature provided by Charles Darwin and his followers. Proponents of functionalism stressed the biological significance (the purpose, or function) of natural processes,

William James (1842–1910).

including behaviours. The emphasis was on overt, observable behaviours, not on private mental events.

The most important psychologist to embrace functionalism was William James (1842–1910), brother of novelist Henry. As James said, 'My thinking is first, last, and always for the sake of my doing.' That is, thinking was not an end in itself; its function was to produce useful behaviours. Although James was a champion of experimental psychology, he did not appear to enjoy doing research, instead spending most of his time reading, thinking, teaching and writing during his tenure as professor of philosophy (later, professor of psychology) at Harvard University.

Unlike structuralism, functionalism was not supplanted; instead, its major tenets were absorbed by its successor, behaviourism. One of the last of the functionalists, James Angell (1869–1949), described its basic principles:

- Functional psychology is the study of mental operations and not mental structures. It is not enough to compile a catalogue of what the mind does; one must try to understand what the mind accomplishes by doing this.

- Mental processes are not studied as isolated and independent events but as part of the biological activity of the organism. These processes are aspects of the organism's adaptation to the environment and are a product of its evolutionary history. For example, the fact that we are conscious implies that consciousness has adaptive value for our species.

- Functional psychology studies the relation between the environment and the response of the organism to the environment. There is no meaningful distinction between mind and body, they are part of the same entity.

Evolution and heritability: Charles Darwin and Francis Galton

Charles Darwin (1809–82) proposed the theory of evolution in his book *On the Origin of Species by Means of Natural Selection,* published in 1859. His work, more than that of any other person, revolutionised biology. The concept of natural selection showed how the consequences of an animal's characteristics affect its ability to survive. Instead of simply identifying, describing and naming species, biologists began now to look at the adaptive significance of the ways in which species differed.

Darwin's theory suggested that behaviours, like other biological characteristics, could best be explained by understanding their role in the adaptation of an organism (a human or other animal) to its environment. Thus, behaviour has a biological context. Darwin assembled evidence that behaviours, like body parts, could be inherited. In *The Expression of the Emotions in Man and Animals*, published in 1873, he proposed that the facial gestures that animals make in expressing emotions were descended from movements that previously had other functions. New areas of exploration were opened for psychologists by the ideas that an evolutionary continuity existed among the various species of animals and that behaviours, like parts of the body, had evolutionary histories. Darwin's notion of natural selection has had great impact on the way in which we view the genetic determinants of behaviour (as Chapter 3 will show).

One of the first psychologists to study the influence of genetics on human behaviour was Sir Francis Galton (1822–1911), Darwin's first cousin. Galton was a polymath who made many other contributions to the field of science: he constructed the first weather maps of the British Isles, discovered and named the weather phenomenon we know as anticyclone, invented the term 'correlation' (which describes the statistical relationships between two variables or factors), developed the technique of fingerprinting, founded the discipline of psychometrics, which applies statistical principles to the measurement of individual differences and the construction of psychological tests, and established the Anthropometric Laboratory in London in 1884, the birthplace of intelligence testing.

Galton was interested in discovering whether people's physical features correlated with each other and whether such correlations occurred for psychological features such as sensory capacity, reaction time, intellect and eminence. In fact, Galton did find that features such as height, arm length and weight were highly and positively correlated and argued from this that if one part of the body's dimensions were known then one could construct the rest of the body to scale.

Importantly, Galton was the first to provide statistical evidence for the heritability of psychological variables. In his study of eminent men, published in his book *Hereditary Genius* (Galton, 1869), Galton found that 31 per cent of illustrious men had eminent fathers and 48 per cent of these men had eminent sons. Of course, by today's standards, this study has several methodological shortcomings, not least of which is the collection of data from eminent men only (to make a valid comparison, you would also need to look at non-eminent men and their offspring). There is also the argument that eminence may not have been inherited but had been determined by the environment in which these men were raised (issues discussed in detail in Chapters 3 and 11). However, Galton remains an important figure in the history of psychology. His greatest contribution is the establishment of the study of individual differences as a scientific enterprise.

Psychodynamic theory: Sigmund Freud

While psychology was developing as a fledgling science, Sigmund Freud (1856–1939) was formulating a theory of human behaviour that would greatly affect psychology and psychiatry (not necessarily for the good) and radically influence intellectual thinking of all kinds. Freud began his career as a neurologist, so his work was originally firmly rooted in biology. He soon became interested in behavioural and emotional problems and began formulating his psychodynamic theory of personality, which would evolve over his long career. Although his approach was based on observation of patients and not on scientific experiments, he remained convinced that the biological basis of his theory would eventually be established.

Freud and his theory are discussed in detail in Chapter 14 (Personality) but he is mentioned here to mark his place in the history of psychology. His theory of the mind included structures, but his structuralism was quite different from Wundt's. He devised his concepts of ego, superego, id and other mental structures through talking with his patients, not through laboratory experiments. His hypothetical mental operations included many that were unconscious and hence not available to introspec-

(a)   (b)

(c)

The three most widely cited psychologists of the 20th century: **(a)** Sigmund Freud; **(b)** Jean Piaget; **(c)** Hans J. Eysenck.
Source: (a) National Library of Medicine/Science Photo Library Ltd.; (b) AFP/Getty Images; (c) Popperfoto/Alamy Images.

tion. And unlike Wundt, Freud emphasised function; his mental structures served biological drives and instincts and reflected our animal nature.

For better or worse Freud's name is the one most closely allied to psychology in the mind of the public. In a recent study of the most eminent psychologists, as measured by citations in journals, introductory textbooks and nominations from self-selecting members of the American Psychological Society via an email survey, Hagbloom *et al.* (2002) found that Freud was the most widely cited author in the discipline, as you can see in Tables 1.6 a–c. In second place was Jean Piaget and in third, Hans J. Eysenck.

Table 1.6. The top ten psychologists (a) cited in the professional literature, (b) named as eminent by the American Psychological Society, and (c) most frequently cited in introductory textbooks.

(a)

Rank	Name	Citation frequency
1	Sigmund Freud	13 890
2	Jean Piaget	8 821
3	Hans J. Eysenck	6 821
4	B.J. Winer	6 206
5	Albert Bandura	5 831
6	S. Siegel	4 861
7	Raymond B. Cattell	4 828
8	B.F. Skinner	4 339
9	Charles E. Osgood	4 061
10	J.P. Guilford	4 006

(b)

Rank	Name	Citation frequency
1	B.F. Skinner	58
2	Jean Piaget	33
3	Sigmund Freud	28
4	John B. Watson	24
5	Albert Bandura	23
6.5	William James	21
6.5	Ivan P. Pavlov	21
8	Kurt Lewin/Roger Brown	17
9.5	Carl Rogers	14
9.5	Edward Thorndike	14

(c)

Rank	Name	Citation frequency
1	Sigmund Freud	560
2	B.F. Skinner	310
3	Albert Bandura	303
4	Jean Piaget	240
5	Carl Rogers	202
6	Stanley Schachter	200
7	Harry F. Harlow	175
8	Roger Brown	162
9	Neal E. Miller	154
10	D.C. McClelland	153

Source: Hagbloom, S.J., Warnick, R., Warnick, J.E., Jones, V.K., Yarbrough, G.L., Russell, T.M., Borecky, C.M., McGahhey, R., Powell, J.L., Beavers, J. and Monte, E., The 100 most eminent psychologists of the 20th century. *Review of General Psychology*, 2002, 6, 139–52, copyright © 2002 by the Educational Publishing Foundation, reprinted with permission.

Behaviourism: Edward Thorndike and Ivan Pavlov

The next major trend in psychology, behaviourism, followed directly from functionalism. It went further in its rejection of the special nature of mental events, denying that unobservable and unverifiable mental events were properly the subject matter of psychology. Behaviourists believed that because psychology is the study of observable behaviours, mental events – which cannot be observed – are outside the realm of psychology. **Behaviourism** is thus the study of the relation between people's environments and their behaviour; what occurs within their heads is irrelevant.

One of the first behaviourists was Edward Thorndike (1874–1949), an American psychologist who studied the behaviour of animals. He noticed that some events, usually those that one would expect to be pleasant, seemed to 'stamp in' a response that had just occurred. Noxious events seemed to 'stamp out' the response, or make it less likely to recur. We now call these processes reinforcement and punishment, and they are described in more detail in Chapter 7 (Learning and behaviour). Thorndike defined the law of effect as follows (1905, p. 203):

> Any act which in a given situation produces satisfaction becomes associated with that situation, so that when the situation recurs the act is more likely than before to recur also. Conversely, any act which in a given situation produces discomfort becomes disassociated from that situation, so that when the situation recurs the act is less likely than before to recur.

The **law of effect** is in the functionalist tradition. It observes that the consequences of a behaviour act back upon the organism, affecting the likelihood that the behaviour that just occurred will occur again. An organism does something, and the consequences of this action make that action more likely. This process is very similar to the principle of natural selection. Just as organisms that successfully adapt to their environments are more likely to survive and breed, behaviours that cause useful outcomes are more likely to recur.

Although Thorndike insisted that the subject matter of psychology was behaviour, his explanations contained mentalistic terms. For example, in his law of effect he spoke of 'satisfaction', which is certainly not a phenomenon that can be directly observed. Later behaviourists threw out terms like 'satisfaction' and 'discomfort' and

И. П. Павлов наблюдает за подопытной собакой
(1911 год)

Ivan Pavlov (1849–1936) in his laboratory with some of his collaborators. His research revealed valuable, though unsought, information about the principles of learning.

Source: Bettman/CORBIS, reprinted by permission.

replaced them with more objective terms that reflected the behaviour of the organism rather than any feelings it might have.

Another major figure in the development of behaviourism was not a psychologist but a physiologist: Ivan Pavlov (1849–1936), a Russian who studied the physiology of digestion (for which he later received a Nobel Prize). In the course of studying the stimuli that produce salivation, he discovered that hungry dogs would salivate at the sight of the attendant who brought in their dishes of food. Pavlov found that a dog could be trained to salivate at completely arbitrary stimuli, such as the sound of a bell, if the stimulus was quickly followed by the delivery of a bit of food into the animal's mouth.

Pavlov's discovery had profound significance for psychology. He showed that through experience an animal could learn to make a response to a stimulus that had never caused this response before. This ability, in turn, might explain how organisms learn cause-and-effect relations in the environment. In contrast, Thorndike's law of effect suggested an explanation for the adaptability of an individual's behaviour to its particular environment. So, from Thorndike's and Pavlov's studies two important behavioural principles had been discovered.

Behaviourism: John B. Watson

Behaviourism as a formal school of psychology began with the publication of a book by John B. Watson (1878–1958), *Psychology from the Standpoint of a Behaviorist* (Watson,

1919). Watson was a charismatic professor of psychology at the Johns Hopkins University in the US, a popular teacher and writer and was a very convincing advocate of behaviourism. Even after leaving Johns Hopkins under mysterious circumstances and embarking on a highly successful career in advertising, he continued to lecture and write magazine articles about psychology.

According to Watson, psychology was a natural science whose domain was restricted to observable events: the behaviour of organisms. Watson's behaviourism can be best summed up by his definition published in an article entitled, 'Psychology as the behaviorist views it' (Watson, 1913):

> Psychology as the behaviorist views it is a purely objective experimental branch of natural science. Its theoretical goal is the prediction and control of behavior. Introspectionism forms no essential part of its methods, nor is the scientific value of its data dependent upon the readiness with which they lend themselves to interpretation in terms of consciousness. The behaviorist, in his efforts to get a unitary scheme of animal response, recognises no dividing line between man and brute.

Watson believed that the elements of consciousness studied by structuralists were too subjective to lend themselves to scientific investigation. He defined psychology as the objective study of behaviour and the stimuli which produce such behaviour. The important feature of behaviourism was its reliance only on observable behaviour. Even thinking was reduced to a form of behaviour –

John B. Watson (1878–1958).

Source: Archives of the History of American Psychology.

talking to oneself. Watson described visually observable behaviour as 'explicit behaviour' and those behaviours which could not be directly observed but potentially observed as 'implicit behaviour'. For example, we cannot see the body's cells transmitting electrical signals but we can observe such behaviour by using the correct electrical recording equipment.

Another important feature, tied to observation, was that the brain had very little to do with what was directly observed. What was important to Watson was the concept of stimulus and response, an idea suggested by Descartes and explicitly described by Pavlov. Watson argued that, given the correct stimuli, the organism could learn to behave (give responses) in a specific way (in the same way that Pavlov's dogs had 'learned' to associate the bell with the appearance of food). Watson, however, famously went further. In his book *Behaviorism* (1930), he argued:

> Give me a dozen healthy infants, well-formed, and my own specified world to bring them up in and I'll guarantee to take any one at random and train him to become any type of specialist I might select – doctor, lawyer, artist, merchant-chief and, yes, even beggar-man and thief, regardless of his talents, penchants, tendencies, abilities, vocations and race of his ancestors.

Many of Watson's ideas, such as the notion that reflexes can be conditioned, have been incorporated into the mainstream of psychology, although the central tenet that all behaviour that is studied must be observable, has not. After Watson, a new form of behaviourism emerged which took Watson's ideas and developed them further. This new form became known as **neobehaviourism** or **radical behaviourism**.

Radical behaviourism: Edward Tolman and Clark Leonard Hull

The period 1930–1960 saw a tremendous surge not only in the description of the ways in which organisms behaved but also in the explanations for why they behaved in the way they did. This surge was generated largely by the work of a group of American psychologists, Edward Tolman (1886–1959), Clark Leonard Hull (1884–1952) and B.F. Skinner (1904–1990). Each had a different view on how behaviour occurred but all used animal experiments and the procedures of learning experiments to support their theories. Hull, for example, proposed a highly detailed mathematical model of behaviour, based on his conditioning work with rats in his book *Principles of Behavior* (Hull, 1943), which sought to explain almost all behaviour. The basic feature of Hull's model was that all human (and any organism's) behaviour evolves through interaction with the environment. However, this interaction occurs within a wider frame of reference – the biological adaptation of the organism to the environment. The variable intervening between environment and organism was drive – a bodily need arising from deprivation or desire or another motivational spur. Although one of the more widely cited psychologists of his day, Clark has not made a lasting impact on psychology largely because his extremely detailed mathematical analyses were based on few experiments, the results of which were generalised well beyond the scope of the experimental context.

Tolman suggested that it was important not only to observe the stimulus and response but to take into account intervening variables. To Tolman, these intervening variables were cognitions and demands, and Tolman's theory became known as **purposive behaviourism**, so-called because all behaviour was goal-directed and had a purpose. Tolman's work did not bequeath any major principles or laws, however, although interest in his work continues (Reid and Staddon, 1998). You will find out more about Hull's and Tolman's approaches in Chapter 7.

Radical behaviourism: Burrhus Frederic Skinner

The bequest of a major framework of thinking in psychology was left to B.F. Skinner (1904–1990), one of the most influential psychologists of the twentieth century whose entry into psychology's history was serendipitous (he originally wanted to be a writer, and actually wrote novels using his research ideas). Skinner's work gave birth to the technology of teaching machines (which have since been replaced by computers), the use of behaviour modification in instruction of the mentally retarded, and the use of behaviour therapy to treat mental disorders.

Skinner's work focused on the idea of reinforcement and was based largely on observation of behaviour in pigeons. He found that a certain set of stimulus conditions (such as a box, hunger, food in sight) would elicit certain behaviours (strutting, random pecking). If the animal behaved in a certain way to obtain food then the food became the reinforcing stimulus or the reinforcer – a stimulus which increases the probability that behaviour will occur again. Using his observations of pigeons' behaviour, Skinner found that the pigeons could be trained to behave in a specific way when responding to specific signals from their environment. For example, the pigeon would learn that it would receive food only if it pecked a food-dispensing lever a certain number of times; instead of randomly pecking at this lever it would then peck only the number of times necessary.

B.F. Skinner (1904–90).

This form of learning, instrumental or operant learning, was of three types. Positive reinforcement refers to pleasant reinforcers such as the attention or approval given to a child from a teacher. Punishment refers to a negative stimulus which is presented when a behaviour occurs (for example, a rat receiving an electric shock whenever it presses a lever). Negative reinforcement refers to a behaviour which reduces the likelihood of negative stimulation (for example, a rat pressing a lever to avoid electric shock).

Reinforcement could also occur according to scheduling. For example, fixed-interval reinforcement involved a reinforcer that was given only after a set time; fixed-ratio reinforcement involved a reinforcer that was given only after a predetermined number of responses. Examples of fixed-interval reinforcement include receiving a wage at the end of the week or a salary at the end of the month; an example of fixed-ratio reinforcement would be the delivery of payment after, say, a certain number of items had been produced in a factory or after a specific number of products had been sold. Chapter 7 takes up these ideas.

Unlike Tolman and Hull, however, Skinner did not propose any intervening variables. To him, the behaving person or pigeon or rat was an 'empty organism'. He argued that humans were machines which behaved in lawful and predictable ways and his system was almost entirely descriptive with little in the way of theory emerging from it. In addition to his scientific work, Skinner published a novel, *Walden Two*, in which he described the way in which radical behaviourism could operate (Skinner, 1948).

Psychologists, including modern behaviourists, have moved away from the strict behaviourism of Watson and Skinner; mental processes such as imagery and attention are again considered to be proper subject matter for scientific investigation. But Watson's emphasis on objectivity in psychological research remains. Even those modern psychologists who most vehemently protest against what they see as the narrowness of behaviourism use the same principles of objectivity to guide their research.

Genetic epistemology: Jean Piaget

While American approaches to psychology were dominated by the new behaviourism, a different approach to the study of cognitive function was being espoused in Europe. The Swiss psychologist Jean Piaget (1896–1980) became interested in the question of human knowledge and how we begin to acquire knowledge. He believed that answers to such questions could be obtained by empirical, scientific research and he would measure the development of the acquisition of knowledge in children by presenting them with intellectual tasks at various stages of their lives (in fact, Piaget had worked with Theophile Simon, the collaborator of the man who designed the first IQ test, Alfred Binet). Piaget termed his approach to psychology as **genetic epistemology**: the study of the origin of knowledge in child development.

Apart from Piaget's focus on the acquisition of knowledge in groups of individuals, another difference between his European approach and that of his American counterparts was the lack of interest in the applied nature of research. Questions regarding the possibility of improving or accelerating children's learning did not interest Piaget, nor did it interest other European researchers (Leahey, 2003). Although his work made little impact on psychology at the time, the subsequent circulation of his work – with translations of his books – led to a considerable interest in his research (Smith, 1996), so much so, that few psychologists have dominated the study of child development in the way that Piaget has. Piaget's contribution to our understanding of child cognition is assessed in Chapter 12.

Gestalt psychology: Max Wertheimer

The structuralism of Wilhelm Wundt was not the only German influence on the development of psychology. In 1911, a German psychologist, Max Wertheimer (1880–1943), bought a toy that presented a series of pictures in rapid succession. Each picture was slightly different from the one that preceded it, and the resulting impression was that of continuous motion, like a film. Wundt and his followers insisted that if we want to understand the nature of human consciousness we must analyse it – divide it into its individual elements. But Wertheimer and his colleagues realised that the perception of a motion picture was not that of a series of individual still pictures. Instead, viewers saw continuity in time and space. They saw objects that retained their identity as they moved from place to place. Asking people to study these pictures one at a time and to describe what they saw (the structuralist approach) would never explain the phenomenon of the motion picture.

Wertheimer and his colleagues attempted to discover the organisation of cognitive processes, not their elements. They called their approach **Gestalt psychology**. *Gestalt* is a German word that roughly translates into 'unified form' or 'overall shape'. Gestalt psychologists insisted that perceptions resulted from patterns of interactions among many elements – patterns that could exist across both space and time. For example, a simple melody consists of a pattern of different notes, played one at a time. If the melody is played in different keys, so that the individual notes are different, people can still recognise it. Clearly, they recognise the relations the notes have to each other, not just the notes themselves.

Although the Gestalt school of psychology no longer exists, its insistence that elements of an experience interact – that the whole is not simply the sum of its parts – has had a profound influence on the development of modern psychology. Gestalt psychology did not disappear because of some inherent fatal flaw in its philosophy or methodology. Instead, many of its approaches and ideas were incorporated into other areas of psychology. Gestalt psychology is discussed in more detail in Chapter 6.

Humanistic psychology

Humanistic psychology developed during the 1950s and 1960s as a reaction against both behaviourism and psychoanalysis. Although psychoanalysis certainly dealt with mental phenomena that could not be measured objectively, it saw people as products of their environment and of innate, unconscious forces. Humanistic psychologists insist that human nature goes beyond environmental influences, and that conscious processes, not unconscious ones, are what psychologists should study. In addition, they note that psychoanalysis seems preoccupied with mental disturbance, ignoring positive phenomena such as happiness, satisfaction, love and kindness. **Humanistic psychology** is an approach to the study of human behaviour that emphasises human experience, choice and creativity, self-realisation and positive growth. The father of humanistic psychology, Abraham Maslow (1908–1970), wrote: 'What a man can be, he must be. He must be true to his own nature . . . [to a] desire to become more and more what one idiosyncratically is, to become everything that one is capable of becoming' (1970, p. 46).

Humanistic psychologists emphasise the positive sides of human nature and the potential we all share for personal growth. In general, humanistic psychologists do not believe that we will understand human consciousness and behaviour through scientific research. Thus, the humanistic approach has not had a significant influence on psychology as a science. Its greatest impact has been on the development of methods of psychotherapy based on a positive and optimistic view of human potential.

The personality psychologists: Gordon Allport, Raymond Cattell, Hans Eysenck, Walter Mischel, Paul Costa and Robert McCrae

As the humanist movement was in full swing – or as swinging as it could manage – experimental psychologists had turned their attention to the scientific measurement of another important facet of behaviour: personality. This attention took the form of a search for universal **personality traits** – enduring personal characteristics which form a continuum along which we all fall. The earliest of these theorists was Gordon Allport (1897–1967) who, using dictionary terms as his starting point, suggested that personality comprised between 3 and 16 personality traits. Allport's scheme formed the basis for the model devised by Raymond Cattell (1905–1998). He collected data from interviews and various questionnaires, concluding that 16 personality traits comprised the essence of personality.

A more parsimonious account, based on a statistical technique called factor analysis, was proposed by Hans J. Eysenck (1916–1997). In what was, until recently, one of the most widely accepted views of personality traits, Eysenck proposed that personality comprised three dimensions: neuroticism–stability, extraversion–intraversion and psychoticism–normality, all of which had a biological basis. Each of us scores somewhere along all three dimensions. Meanwhile, influential American psychologists such as Walter Mischel (1930–) argued that traits did not exist and that, when we behave, we are reacting to changes in our environment or situation (this approach is called situationism): that we may respond in a consistent way lulls us into thinking that we possess something called 'personality', characterised by a number of traits. The debate continues, but the situationists seem to be fighting a losing battle. Substantial research supported Eysenck's model but this was usurped in the 1980s by the Five Factor Model of Paul T. Costa and Robert R. McCrae. This, now the most widely accepted view of personality, argues that our personality comprises five traits which we possess to varying degrees: agreeableness, conscientiousness, extraversion, neuroticism and openness to experience. You'll find more information on all of these approaches in Chapter 14.

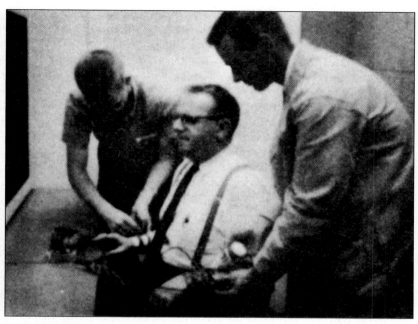

Paul T. Costa.
Source: Bo Mathisen

A photograph of Milgram's experiment.
Source: Getty Images/Hulton Archive

The social psychologists

From the middle of the twentieth century there also appeared a phenomenal body of research into how we view and influence other individuals. Here, there are too many significant figures to mention but some of the most prominent that contributed significant new data and models which helped us understand social behaviour include Leon Festinger, Albert Bandura, Stanley Milgram, Philip Zimbardo, Elliot Aronson, Robert Zajonc, Richard Nisbett and Edward Jones. All Americans or working in the US, these psychologists demonstrated how we could

Robert R. McCrae.
Source: Robert McCrae

Philip Zimbardo.
Source: Corbis: Lynn Goldsmith

hold two seemingly contradictory views (Festinger), how **deindividuation** could strip us of our humanity (Zimbardo), how observation of others makes us imitate them (Bandura), how we become obedient to authority (Milgram), how we interpret the causes of our own behaviour differently from how we interpret that of others (Nisbett, Jones), amongst other things. You'll find descriptions of their research and the impact this has had on our understanding of social behaviour in Chapters 15 and 16.

The cognitive revolution: beyond behaviourism

The emphasis on behaviourism in the first half of the twentieth century restricted the subject matter of psychology to observable behaviours. For many years, concepts such as consciousness were considered to be outside the domain of psychology. As one psychologist put it, 'psychology, having first bargained away its soul and then gone out of its mind, seems now . . . to have lost all consciousness' (Burt, 1962, p. 229).

In the decades that followed many psychologists protested against the restrictions of behaviourism and turned to the study of consciousness, feelings, memory, imagery and other private events (although behaviourism was still a potent force and continues to runs through much of today's experimental psychology like marble).

Much of cognitive psychology uses an approach called **information processing** – information received through the senses is 'processed' by various systems in the brain. Some systems store the information in the form of memory, and other systems control behaviour. Some systems operate automatically and unconsciously, while others are conscious and require effort on the part of the individual. Because the information-processing approach was first devised to describe the operations of complex physical systems such as computers, the modern model of the human brain is, for most cognitive psychologists, the computer. As you will see in Chapter 7, another model (neural networks) is now being used as an alternative to the computer.

Although cognitive psychologists study mental structures and operations, they have not gone back to the introspective methods that structuralists such as Wundt employed. Instead, they use experimental methods, under controlled conditions, to test hypotheses and discover facts about how we think and remember. Cognitive psychologists such as Donald Broadbent, Stanley Schachter, Neal Miller, Don McClelland, Alan Baddeley, Ulric Neisser, Allan Paivio, Stephen Kosslyn, Endel Tulving, Elizabeth Loftus, Daniel Kahneman and Amos Tversky (the last two won the Nobel Prize for economics in 2002) discovered new and important data about how we learn to learn, remember and reason. You'll find their research in Chapters 8 and 11 but also throughout the book.

Elizabeth Loftus.
Source: Jodi Hilton/Pool/Reuters

Alan Baddeley.
Source: Copyright UK Medical Research Council (2009) used by kind permission.

Daniel Kahneman.
Source: Corbis: Reuters

Amos Tversky.
Source: Barbara Tversky

The biological revolution

Biology has always been closely tied to psychology and as psychology began to flourish, it was against a backdrop of some quite staggering discoveries in the physical science. For example, Descartes's hydraulic model of muscular movement was shown to be incorrect by Luigi Galvani (1737–98), an Italian physiologist who discovered that muscles could be made to contract by applying an electrical current directly to them or to the nerves that were attached to them. The muscles themselves contained the energy needed for them to contract. They did not have to be inflated by pressurised fluid. This discovery is the source of a modern-day technique for helping people recover from serious, paralysing illnesses and injury: the use of brain electrical activity to control objects such as a computer cursor or a prosthetic limb. There is a special Psychology in Action section on this technique in Chapter 4.

The brain and sensation: Johannes Müller

The work of the German physiologist Johannes Müller (1801–58) flags a definite transition from the somewhat sporadic, isolated instances of research into human physiology to the progressively more direct and precise exploration of the human body. Müller was a forceful advocate of applying experimental procedures to the study of physiology. He recommended that biologists should do more than observe and classify; they should remove or isolate animals' organs, test their responses to

chemicals, and manipulate other conditions in order to see how the organism worked. His most important contribution to what would become the science of

Johannes Müller (1801–58).

psychology was his **doctrine of specific nerve energies**. He noted that the basic message sent along all nerves was the same – an electrical impulse. And the impulse itself was the same, regardless of whether the message concerned was, for example, a visual perception or an auditory one. What, then, accounts for the brain's ability to distinguish different kinds of sensory information? That is, why do we see what our eyes detect, hear what our ears detect, and so on? After all, both the optic nerves and the auditory nerves send the same kind of message to the brain.

The answer is that the messages are sent over different channels. Because the optic nerves are attached to the eyes, the brain interprets impulses received from these nerves as visual sensations. You have probably already noticed that rubbing your eyes causes sensations of flashes of light. When you rub your eyes, the pressure against them stimulates visual receptors located inside. As a result of this stimulation, messages are sent through the optic nerves to the brain. The brain interprets these messages as sensations of light.

Müller's ideas have endured, forming the basis for investigations into the functions of the nervous system. For centuries, philosophers had identified thinking or consciousness as the distinguishing feature of the human mind and had concluded that the mind was located in the brain. Now the components of the nervous system were being identified and their means of operation were being explored.

Pierre Flourens (1794–1867), a French physiologist, provided experimental evidence for the implications of Müller's doctrine of specific nerve energies. He operated on animals, removing various parts of the nervous system. He found that the resulting effects depended on which parts were removed. He observed what the animal could no longer do and concluded that the missing capacity must have been the function of the part that he had removed. For example, if an animal could not move its leg after part of its brain was removed, then that region must normally control leg movements. This method of removal of part of the brain, called experimental ablation (from the Latin *ablatus*, 'carried away'), was soon adopted by neurologists, and it is still used by scientists today. Through experimental ablation, Flourens claimed to have discovered the regions of the brain that control heart rate and breathing, purposeful movements, and visual and auditory reflexes.

Brain damage and behaviour: Paul Broca and Carl Wernicke

One of the first people to apply the logic of Flourens's method to humans was Paul Broca (1824–80). In 1861, Broca, a French surgeon, reported the results of an autopsy on the brain of a man who had suffered a stroke several years previously. The stroke (damage to the brain caused, in this case, by a blood clot) had caused the man to lose the ability to speak. The patient, whose real name was Leborgne, was called Tan because this was the only word he uttered. Broca discovered that the stroke had damaged part of the brain on the left side, as Figure 1.5 shows, although Marc Dax had reported similar findings earlier that century. Broca suggested that this region of the brain is a centre for speech – this part is now called Broca's area. Broca's work was followed, independently, by Carl Wernicke (1848–1905), who noted that damage to an adjacent part of the brain on the same side impaired his patient's speech comprehension and production. Chapter 10 has more on both of these language disorders and how psychologists still debate the areas which, if damaged, create problems in speech production and comprehension. Recent research, for example, suggests that the brain also needs to be injured outside Broca's area in order to see the deficit reported in his patient (Dronkers *et al.*, 2007).

Studying the effects of accidental brain damage on function has allowed neuroscientists to predict which regions of the brain may be involved in specific functions. One famous example of brain damage leading to speculation about the function of a brain region is that of Phineas Gage. Gage was a railroad construction supervisor who, in the mid-nineteenth century, had an accident at work. An iron rod shot through his face, through the front part of his brain and straight out of the top of his head. A reconstructed image of the trajectory of the rod through his skull can be seen in Figure 1.6a. Figure 1.6b is the only existing image of Gage (with the rod tastefully superimposed).

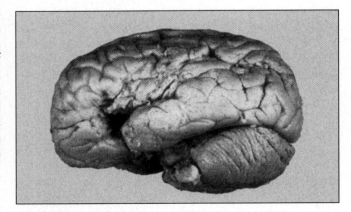

Figure 1.5 A photograph of Tan's brain. Note the egg-shaped cavity – this was thought to be responsible for his inability to speak fluently.

Source: T.E. Feinberg and M.J. Farah (1997) *Behavioral Neurology and Neuropsychology*. © The McGraw-Hill Companies.

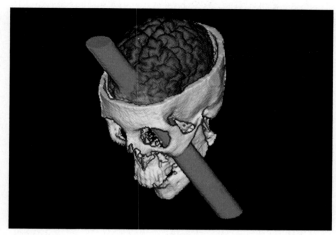

(a)

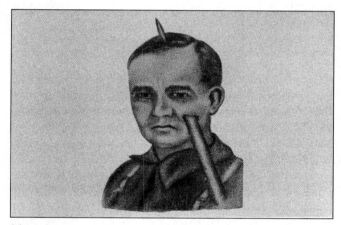

(b)

Figure 1.6 On a September afternoon in 1848, an unusual accident befell a young American railroad worker called Phineas Gage. An iron rod shot through his head as a result of an uncontrolled explosion at work. Almost 150 years later, Hannah Damasio and her colleagues at the University of Iowa took the medical reports of Gage's injury and plotted the course of the rod, using modern computer technology. **(a)** Shows one of the images of the rod's trajectory. **(b)** Shows a depiction of Gage himself.

Source: (a) From H. Damasio, T. Grabowski, R. Frank, A.M. Galaburda and A.R. Damasio, The return of Phineas Gage: Clues about the brain from a famous patient. *Science*, 1994, 264: 1102–05. Department of Neurology and Image Analysis Facility, University of Iowa. (b) From MIT:Bradford Macmillan, *An odd kind of fame*.

Whereas before the injury, Gage had been a hardworking and conscientious individual, after the injury he became boorish, unpleasant and unreliable. The part of the brain damaged seemed to be that responsible for inhibiting inappropriate behaviour. We now know that patients with damage to this part of the brain have difficulty in inhibiting such behaviour (there is more on this phenomenon in Chapter 13).

Localisation of function: Gustav Fritsch and Eduard Hitzig, Franz Gall and Johann Spurzheim

In 1870, the German physiologists Gustav Fritsch and Eduard Hitzig introduced the use of electrical stimulation as a tool for mapping the functions of the brain. For example, Fritsch and Hitzig discovered that applying a small electrical shock to different parts of the cerebral cortex caused movements of different parts of the body. In fact, the body appeared to be 'mapped' on the surface of the brain, so that the feet, hands, fingers and so on, had a part of the brain dedicated to them.

Originally, this work was conducted on dogs on Frau Hitzig's dressing table (because they had no available laboratory space). Such humble conditions gave rise to the first experiment in **localisation of function** in the brain – the goal of neuropsychology. No less elaborate, but ultimately doomed, was the attempt at localising function by Franz Gall (1758–1828) and Johann Spurzheim (1776–1832). Their anatomical personology – or as it is commonly known, phrenology – suggested that if we were very adept at a function the part of the brain responsible would be overactive. This overactivity caused an indentation in the skull. If a person was mathematically gifted, therefore, the part responsible for this would be active and cause a bump in the skull, which the experimenter could palpate. This hypothesis was beautifully testable and it was not long before the edifice came crashing down. It is, however, an attempt at localising function in the brain. Although Gall is best known for this, he also made more worthwhile contributions to neuroscience, such as identifying the importance of the left front part of the brain to speech.

Speed and magnitude of nerve impulses: Hermann von Helmholtz and Ernst Weber

A different and yet essentially physical approach to studying behaviour was also seen in the work of the German physicist and physiologist Hermann von Helmholtz (1821–94), who did much to demonstrate that mental phenomena could be explained by physiological means. This extremely productive scientist made contributions to both physics and physiology. He actively disassociated himself from natural philosophy, from which many assumptions about the nature of the mind had been derived. Müller, under whom Helmholtz had conducted his first research, believed that human organs were endowed with a vital immaterial force that coordinated physiological behaviour, a force that was not subject to experimental investigation. Helmholtz would allow no such assumptions about unproved (and unprovable) phenomena. He advocated a purely scientific approach, with conclusions based on objective investigation and precise measurement.

Hermann von Helmholtz (1821–94).

Until Helmholtz's time, scientists believed that the transmission of impulses through nerves was as fast as the speed of electricity in wires; under this assumption, transmission would be virtually instantaneous, considering the small distances that impulses have to travel within the human body. Helmholtz successfully measured the speed of the nerve impulse and found that it was only about 90 feet per second, which is considerably slower than the speed of electricity in wires. This finding suggested to later researchers that the nerve impulse is more complex than a simple electrical current passing through a wire, which is indeed true.

Helmholtz also attempted to measure the speed of a person's reaction to a physical stimulus, but he abandoned this attempt because there was too much variability from person to person. However, this variability interested scientists who followed him; they tried to explain the reason for individual differences in behaviour. Because both the velocity of nerve impulses and a person's reactions to stimuli could be measured, researchers theorised that mental events themselves could be the subject of scientific investigation. Possibly, if the proper techniques could be developed, one could investigate what went on within the human brain. Thus, Helmholtz's research was important in setting the stage for the science of psychology.

In Germany, a contemporary of von Helmholtz's, Ernst Weber (1795–1878), began work that led to the development of a method for measuring the magnitude of human sensations. Weber, an anatomist and physiologist, found that people's ability to tell the difference between two similar stimuli – such as the brightness of two lights, the heaviness of two objects, or the loudness of two tones – followed orderly laws. This regularity suggested to Weber and his followers that the study of perceptual phenomena could be as scientific as that of physics or biology. In Chapter 6 we consider the study of the relation between the physical characteristics of a stimulus and the perceptions they produce, a field called psychophysics, or the physics of the mind.

Cognitive neuroscience: the future of the biology of the 'mind'?

The cognitive revolution did not lead to a renewed interest in biology. But the extraordinary advances in neurobiology in the late twentieth century have revolutionised psychology. Neurobiologists (biologists who study the nervous system) and scientists and engineers in allied fields have developed ways to study the brain that were unthinkable just a few decades ago. We can study fine details of nerve cells, discover their interconnections, analyse the chemicals they use to communicate with each other, produce drugs that block the action of these chemicals or mimic their effects.

More importantly, using PET or (now, more commonly) fMRI, we can see the internal structure of a living human brain, and measure the activity of different processes of the brain – in regions as small as a few cubic millimetres – while people are thinking, feeling, perceiving, comprehending and moving (Martin, 2006; Raichle, 2008). One application of this technique can be seen in Figure 1.7 (a)–(b).

This combination of cognitive psychology and neuroscience – cognitive neuroscience – provides a different way of studying behaviour and describing its causes. Currently, the endeavours in cognitive neuroscience are, because of the nature of the techniques used, directed towards studying basic, yet essential, behaviour such as rudimentary reading, recognising emotion, remembering and speaking. But this is changing and studies are now using neuroimaging to study how people converse, make moral decisions, appreciate television programmes, react to a lover's face and voice and even understand magic tricks. You'll find a review of many of these studies in Chapter 4.

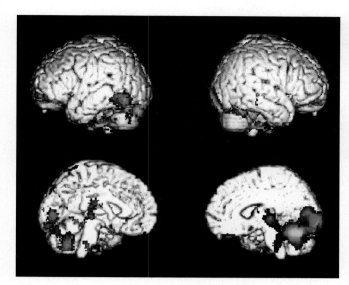

(a) Areas where normal readers show more activation than do dyslexic participants.

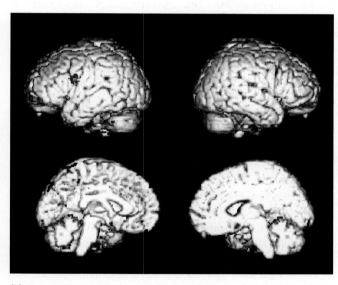

(b) Areas where dyslexic participants shown more activation than do normal readers.

Figure 1.7 Areas of activation in the human brain while it engages in language tasks. In this experiment, the reading performance and brain activation of dyslexic and normal readers are compared.

Source: Brunswick, N., McCory, E., Price, C., Frith, C. and Frith, U., Explicit and implicit processing of words and pseudowords by adult developmental dyslexics: A search for Wernicke's Wortschatz? *Brain*, 1999, 122, 1901–17. Reproduced with permission from Oxford University Press.

Conceptual and historical issues in psychology

As this chapter has shown you, understanding a discipline's past can help you better understand its present and its future. Understanding a discipline's past shows you the stages – usually chaotic, not linear or orderly – that psychology has gone through to reach the status it has attained today and the body of knowledge it has accrued. The shifts in approach and subject matter across its history will be reflected in its future shifts. But these shifts will be gradual. The danger in highlighting stages in history, as is done here, is that that they are seen as discrete and self-contained. They are only discrete and self-contained because the prism of historical retrospection makes them so and we can reflect back, soberly, on some of the momentous conceptual and experimental changes that psychology underwent. We are currently amidst an extraordinary boom in neuroimaging work. In 50 years' time, all of this work may seem quaintly obsolete. We don't know.

Historical milestones are one thing. Conceptual issues are another. The trends and schools described here arose when researchers operated in a different world and context to that in which we operate today. Much – if not most – research conducted in universities is funded by government, and government has priorities. Will these priorities see a shift in the types of topics psychologists study in the future?

On a grander scale, conceptual issues can be virtually synonymous with philosophical issues. For example, the question 'Is the scientific method the best method for establishing truth?' is a philosophical, rather than a psychological question, because it doesn't have an absolute answer. When we have answers to questions, philosophy is dead. In the chapters that follow you should be able to see how the research they describe arose and in what context – how some of the work in social psychology emerged from real-life events, such as the apparent reluctance to assist a person crying for help, or a soldier saying he was only obeying orders, for example. Or how cross-cultural research on facial expression led to a theory of emotion. Or how research on race differences in IQ became controversial. Or how we classify and diagnose mental illness. Or how sociobiology, according to some views, reduces human beings to self-interested savages.

So far, you have seen how psychology is a discipline that comprises a number of different branches. This survey of the history of psychology reveals a number of methodological approaches to the study of behaviour. In the next chapter you will see in more detail how psychologists study behaviour. You will also discover the dominant methodological approach to answering questions about psychology.

Chapter review

What is psychology?

- Psychology is the science of behaviour, and psychologists study a large variety of behaviours in humans and other animals.
- Psychology has many major branches:
  - Psychobiologists study the biological basis of behaviour.
  - Psychophysiologists study people's physiological reactions, such as changes in heart rate and muscle tension.
  - Neuropsychologists study the relationship between central nervous system activity and structure and function.
  - Comparative psychologists study the evolution of behaviour by comparing the behavioural capacities of various species of animals.
  - Ethologists study the biological bases of behaviour through observation of animals in natural environments.
  - Sociobiologists attempt to interpret human and animal behaviour in terms of evolution and biological inheritance.
  - Behaviour geneticists study the degree of influence exerted by heredity and environment on behaviour.
  - Cognitive psychologists study complex human behaviours such as cognition, memory and attention.
  - Cognitive neuroscientists study the role of the human and animal brain in behaviour.
  - Developmental psychologists study the development of behaviour throughout the lifespan.
  - Social psychologists study the effects of people on the behaviour of other people.
  - Individual differences involves the study of the effects of specific characteristics or traits on behaviour.
  - Cross-cultural psychologists study the impact of culture on behaviour.
  - Forensic and criminological psychologists study the ways in which psychological knowledge can be applied in criminal and legal settings.
  - Clinical psychologists study the causes and treatment of mental disorders and problems of adjustment.
  - Health psychologists study the ways in which lifestyle and behaviour affect illness and health.
  - Educational psychologists assess the cognitive, social and emotional development of children in the school environment.
  - Consumer psychologists study what motivates people to consume and how consumers' perceptions are formed.
  - Organisational or occupational psychologists study the behaviour of individuals and groups in the workplace.
  - Ergonomists help to design machines and workplace environments that enhance work performance.

The development of psychology as a science

- Psychology has its modern roots in the thinking of the French philosopher and mathematician René Descartes who argued that the mind and the body were two separate entities which interacted (dualism).
- The mid-nineteenth century gave rise to materialism and empiricism. Materialism maintained that the mind was made of matter; thus all natural phenomena, including human behaviour, could be explained in terms of physical entities: the interaction of matter and energy. Empiricism emphasised that all knowledge was acquired by means of sensory experience; no knowledge was innate. The concept of empiricism was developed by the philosophers John Locke and David Hume.

Modern psychology

- The first laboratory of experimental psychology was established in Leipzig in 1879 by Wilhelm Wundt.
- Wundt and his colleagues' work gave rise to structuralism: the idea that the mind was made up of components which could be broken apart and studied. The method of studying these components was introspection – the observation and recall of experience.
- At about the same time, Ebbinghaus contributed important methods for objectively measuring learning and forgetting.
- Darwin's ground-breaking theory of evolution, or theory of natural selection, argued that traits necessary for survival would be inherited and that only those adaptively useful traits would survive.
- Francis Galton founded the scientific study of individual differences in human behaviour and suggested that certain psychological characteristics could be inherited.
- Functionalism, which grew out of Darwin's theory of evolution, was concerned with the processes of consciousness such as perceiving and learning. Its major advocates were William James and James Angell.
- Functionalism gave rise to behaviourism, founded by John Watson, which still dominates the way we do research. The

subject matter of behaviourism is observable behaviour; according to the behaviourists, mental events – because they were unobservable – should play no part in scientific psychology. Behaviourism developed a radical strain in the 1950s which viewed the organism's behaviour strictly in terms of stimulus and response.

- Humanistic psychology is concerned with the special nature of humanity and emphasises human experience, choice and creativity, and the potential for personal growth.
- The cognitive revolution arose from the belief that behaviourism's emphasis on observable behaviour missed some of the complexity of human cognition and behaviour. The cognitive revolution saw a rekindling of interest in phenomena such as memory, thinking, creativity, imagination and so on, and human behaviour was interpreted in terms of information processing.
- The biological revolution in psychology manifested itself in the increased interest of psychologists in all fields – not just physiological psychology – in the role of biological factors in behaviour. This has given rise to cognitive neuroscience in which the disciplines of neuropsychology and cognitive psychology have combined and used neuroimaging methods to create a greater understanding of the role of the brain in thinking, feeling and perceiving, specifically to localise function in the brain.

Suggestions for further reading

The history of psychology

Crivellato, E. and Ribatti, D. (2007) Soul, mind, brain: Greek philosophy and the birth of neuroscience. *Brain Research Bulletin*, 71, 327–36.

Hock, R. (2009) *Forty studies that changed psychology* (6th edn). Harlow: Pearson Education.

Leahey, T.H. (2003) *A History of Psychology* (6th edn). Englewood Cliffs, NJ: Prentice Hall International.

Mandler, G. (2002) Origins of the cognitive (r)evolution. *Journal of History of the Behavioral Sciences*, 38, 4, 339–53.

Shepard, R.N. (2004) How a cognitive psychologist came to seek universal laws. *Psychonomic Bulletin and Review*, 11, 1, 1–23.

Several sources describe the history of psychology, including its philosophical and biological roots, and these are some very good introductions.

Concepts and controversies in psychology

Furnham, A. (1996) *All in the Mind*. London: Whurr Publishers.

Kassin, S., Briggs, K.H. and Tavris, C. (2008) *Current Directions in Introductory Psychology*. Boston: Allyn & Bacon.

Valentine, E.R. (1992) *Conceptual Issues in Psychology* (2nd edn). London: Routledge.

Excellent introductions to some of the controversial issues and the major concepts in psychology.

Influential psychologists

Cohen, D. (2004) *Psychologists on Psychology*. London: Hodder & Stoughton.

Fancher, R.E. (1996) *Pioneers of Psychology* (3rd edn). New York: W.W. Norton.

Kimble, G.A., Wertheimer, M. and White, C.L. (1991) *Portraits of Pioneers in Psychology*. Hillsdale, NJ: Lawrence Erlbaum Associates/American Psychological Association.

Cohen's book contains an excellent set of interviews with some of the leading psychologists of the time. The books by Kimble et al. and Fancher contain biographical sketches of the major scientists who have contributed to psychology and so provide a good potted introduction to the personalities (and themes, ideas and developments) in psychology.

Reflections on psychology's past and future

Fuller, R., Walsh, P.N. and McGinley, P. (1997) *A Century of Psychology*. London: Routledge.

Solso, R.L. (1997) *Mind and Brain Sciences in the 21st Century*. Cambridge, MA: MIT Press.

British Journal of Psychology, special issue, Supplement 1, April 2009.

The two books comprise a collection of chapters written by some of the last century's outstanding psychologists. Both are good books to read if you are interested in the leading scientists' assessment of psychology's past and their predictions of how psychology will develop in the future. The special issue of the British Journal of Psychology reprints some of the most influential research papers of the past 100 years, with commentaries.

Journals to consult

American Psychologist

Annual Review of Psychology

Australian Psychologist

British Journal of Psychology

Current Directions in Psychological Science

European Psychologist

Psychological Bulletin

Psychological Science

The Psychologist

Website addresses

General psychology

http://www.utoledo.edu/~mcaruso/prolynxnf.html
A massive collection of links to psychology and education-related websites.

http://www.tamiu.edu/coah/psy/directories.htm
A collection of psychological resources web pages.

http://onlinebooks.library.upenn.edu/webbin/book/subjectstart?BF
This is a link to the University of Pennsylvania's collection of online psychology texts. It is frighteningly sub-headed 'Psychology (include. Parapsychology and the occult)' but don't let this put you off.

www.improb.com
A sceptical treatment of the eccentricities in science, including psychology, from the authors and editors of the Annals of Improbable Research.

http://www.psychology.org/links/Resources/Pseudoscience/
A collection of sites critical of pseudoscience.

http://nobelprize.org/nobel_prizes/economics/laureates/2002/kahneman-lecture.html
An online video of Daniel Kahneman's Nobel Prize lecture.

http://www3.uakron.edu/ahap/
The Archives of the History of American Psychology– some interesting video and audio clips in here.

http://www.muskingum.edu/~psych/psycweb/history.htm
A collection of biographies of well-known historical figures in psychology.

From the archive

This is a selective list of some of the outstanding contributions to psychological thinking made by some significant philosophers and psychologists over the centuries. They are available free and online. The psychclassics site has been developed by Christopher Green.

http://psychclassics.asu.edu/Aristotle/De-anima/index.htm
Aristotle's De Anima, 350 BC.

http://psychclassics.asu.edu/Berkeley/vision.htm
Berkeley's An essay towards a new theory of vision, 1732 (4th edn).

http://psychclassics.asu.edu/Wundt/Physio/
Wundt's Principles of Physiological Psychology (1874/1902/1904).

http://psychclassics.asu.edu/Titchener/structuralism.htm

http://psychclassics.asu.edu/Titchener/strucfunc.htm
Titchener's views on structuralism and functionalism, from Philosophical Review (1898).

http://psychclassics.asu.edu/Titchener/brentano-wundt.htm
Titchener's article on Brentano and Wundt from American Journal of Psychology (1921).

http://psychclassics.asu.edu/Angell/functional.htm
James Angell's 'The province of functional psychology' from Psychological Review (1907).

http://psychclassics.asu.edu/Allport/frame.htm
Gordon Allport's 'The psychologist's frame of reference' in Psychological Bulletin (1940).

http://psychclassics.asu.edu/Pavlov/
Pavlov's Conditioned reflexes: An investigation of the physiological activity of the cerebral cortex (1927).

http://psychclassics.asu.edu/Watson/views.htm
Watson's 'Psychology as the behaviourist views it', from Psychological Review (1913).

http://psychclassics.asu.edu/Titchener/watson.htm
Titchener's comments on above (1914) from Proceedings of the American Philosophical Society.

http://psychclassics.asu.edu/Watson/emotion.htm
Watson and Rayner's 'Conditioned emotional reactions' from Journal of Experimental Psychology (1920).

http://psychclassics.asu.edu/Jones/
Jones's 'A laboratory study of fear: the case of Peter' from Pedagogical Seminary (1924).

http://psychclassics.asu.edu/Watson/Battle/
Two papers by Watson and MacDougall on behaviorism (1929).

http://psychclassics.asu.edu/Tolman/formula.htm
Tolman's 'A new formula for behaviorism' from Psychological Review (1922).

http://psychclassics.asu.edu/Tolman/Maps/maps.htm
Tolman's 'Cognitive maps in rats and men' from Psychological Review (1948).

http://psychclassics.asu.edu/Hull/Hierarchy/part1.htm

http://psychclassics.asu.edu/Hull/Hierarchy/part2.htm

Hull's concept of the habit–family hierarchy and maze learning from Psychological Review (1934).

http://psychclassics.asu.edu/Skinner/Twotypes/twotypes.htm

http://psychclassics.asu.edu/Skinner/Konorski/

http://psychclassics.asu.edu/Skinner/ReplytoK/reply.htm

Two papers by Skinner on the conditioned reflex from Journal of General Psychology (1935), plus a reply.

http://psychclassics.asu.edu/Skinner/Pigeon/

Skinner's 'superstition' in the pigeon article from Journal of Experimental Psychology (1948).

http://psychclassics.asu.edu/Skinner/Theories/

Skinner's 'Are theories of learning necessary?' from Psychological Review (1950).

http://psychclassics.asu.edu/Ebbinghaus/index.htm

Ebbinghaus's Memory: A contribution to experimental psychology (1885).

http://psychclassics.asu.edu/Munster/Witness/

Munsterberg's On the witness stand (1908/1925).

http://psychclassics.asu.edu/Terman/terman1.htm

Terman's chapter 'The uses of intelligence tests' (1916).

http://psychclassics.asu.edu/Galton/talent.htm

Galton's 'Hereditary talent and character' from Macmillan's Magazine (1865).

Addresses

Major international professional psychology organisations and societies

Europe

European Federation of Psychologists' Associations
http://www.efpa.be

Australia

Australian Psychological Society, PO Box 38, Flinders Lane Post Office, Melbourne VIC 8009
http://www.psychology.org.au/

Austria

Berufsverband Österreichischer, Psychologen/innen, Möllwaldplatz 4/4/39, A-1040 Vienna, Austria
http://www.boep.or.at

Belgium

Belgische Federatie van Psychologen-Fédération Belge des Psychologues BFP, Agora galerij, Grasmarkt 105/18, B-1000 Brussels, Belgium
http://www.vub.ac.be/gst/bfp

Canada

Canadian Psychological Association, 141 Laurier Avenue West, Suite 702, Ottawa, Ontario K1P 5J3
http://www.cpa.ca/cpasite/splash.asp

Croatia

Croatian Psychological Association, Ivana Lucica 3, HR-10000 Zagreb, Republic of Croatia

Cyprus

Cyprus Psychologists' Association, PO Box 20537, CY-1678 Nicosia, Cyprus

Czech Republic

Unie Psychologickych Asociaci CR, Kladenska 48, CR-16000 Praha 6, Czech Republic

Denmark

Dansk Psykologforening, Stockholmsgade 27, DK-2100 Kobenhavn, Denmark

Estonia

Eesti psühholoogide liit – Union of Estonian Psychologists, c/o Toomas Niit, Department of Psychology, Tallinn Pedagogical University, PO Box 572, EE-0010 Tallinn, Estonia

Finland

Suomen Psykologiliitto, Bulevardi 30 B3, 00120 Helsinki, Finland
http://www.psyli.fi

France

Association Nationale des Organisations de Psychologues – ANOP, 20 bis Grand Rue, Croix Rouge, F-13013 Marseille, France
http://www.club-internet.fr/perso/anop

Germany

Berufsverband Deutscher Psychologinnen und Psychologen e.V. – BDP, Glinkastrasse 5–7, D-10117, Berlin, Germany
http://www.bdp-verband.org

Greece

Association of Greek Psychologists, Avlidos 8, 11527 Athens, Greece

Hungary

Magyar Pszichológiai Társaság, PO Box 220, H-1536 Budapest, Hungary

Iceland

Association of Icelandic Psychology, Lagmuli 7, IS'-108, Reykjavik, Iceland

Ireland

Psychological Society of Ireland, CX House, 2a com Exchange Place, Poolbegstreet, IRL-Dublin 2, Ireland

Italy

Italian Network of Professional Psychologists Association, c/o AUPI, Via Arenula 16, 00186 Roma, Italy
http://www.aupit.it

Latvia

Latvijas Profesionalo Psihologu Asociacija, Latvijas Universitate, abon. kaste 238, LV 1011 Riga, Latvija

Liechtenstein

Berufsverein der Psychologen/innen Liechtensteins, Meierhofstrasse 100, FL-9495 Triesen, Liechtenstein

Lithuania

Lithuanian Psychological Association, Didlaukio 47, Vilnius 2057, Lithuania

Luxembourg

Société Luxembourgeoise de Psychologie, BP 1787, L-1017 Luxembourg, Luxembourg
http://www.slp.lu

Malta

Malta Union of Professional Psychologists, PO Box 341, Valletta, Malta

The Netherlands

Nederlands Instituut van Psychologen, Postbus 9921, 1006 AP Amsterdam, The Netherlands
http://www.psynip.nl

Norway

Norsk Psykologforening (Norwegian Psychological Association), Norsk Psykologforening Postboks 8733 Youngstorget, N-0028 Oslo, Norway
http://www.psykol.no

Poland

Polskie Towarzystwo Psychologow Praktykow (Polish Society of Professional Psychologists), ul. Koszykarska 33, 30717 Krakow, Poland

Portugal

Sindicato Nacinal dos Psicologos, R. Ferreira Lapa 2-B, 3- Dto., P1150-157 Lisbon, Portugal

Slovakia

Slovenska komora psychologov, Zapadna 2, 82102 Bratislava, Slovakia

Slovenia

Drustvo Psihologov Slovenije, Ulica stare pravde 2, SLO-1000 Ljubljana, Slovenia

Spain

Colegio Oficial de Psicologos, C/Conde de Peñalver, num. 45-5°, E-28006 Madrid, Spain

Sweden

Sveriges Psykologforbund, Box 3287, S-10365 Stockholm, Sweden
http://www.psykologforbundet.se

Switzerland

Foderation der Schweizer Psychologinnen und Psychologen FSP, Choisystrasse 11, 3000 Bern 14, Switzerland
http://www.fsp.psy.ch

Turkey

Turkish Psychological Association, P.K., Mesrutiyet Cad. 22/12 Kizilay, 06640, Ankara, Turkey

United Kingdom

The British Psychological Society, St Andrews House, 48 Princess Road East, Leicester LE1 7DR
http://www.bps.org.uk

United States of America

American Psychological Association, 750 First Street, NE, Washington, DC 20002-4242
http://www.apa.org

Research methods in psychology

Explore the accompanying videos, simulations, and animations on MyPsychLab. This chapter includes activities on: Distinguishing independent and dependent variables • Personality testing • Ethics in Psychological Research • Descriptive statistics, finding the average • Check your understanding and prepare for your exams using the multiple choice, short answer and essay practice tests also available.

CHAPTER 2

Clever Hans: A lesson in research methods

Because of his long-lasting fame at the turn of the century many people know about 'Clever Hans', the mind-reading horse. If people gave the owner a question for Hans, he would look directly at the horse and repeat the question in what seemed like a normal tone of voice. Hans would then lift his hoof and tap out the answer. Thus, if asked, 'What is 2 + 2?', Hans would tap the ground four times. After Hans had given the correct answer, the owner would reward the animal by patting it or give it food as a reward.

In 1904, several of the best-known scientists in Germany formed a 'commission' to study the animal. These distinguished scientists stated boldly that they could find no evidence that Hans was responding to external cues from his questioners and perhaps really could read minds. However, the psychologist on the commission, clearly not satisfied, told one of his graduate students to look into the matter.

The student put blinkers on Hans so the animal could not watch the people who were asking him the questions. The horse's ability to respond correctly decreased significantly.

Clever Hans was, indeed, a 'genius of a horse' but was not a mind-reader. The animal was superb at reading 'body language' – cues that questioners almost always give to an animal. But these were so slight and so subtle that most people were completely unaware they were giving them. In this sense, the sceptics were right all along.

Source: Furnham, 1996, pp. 83–5.

WHAT YOU SHOULD BE ABLE TO DO AFTER READING CHAPTER 2

- Define and describe the scientific approach to studying psychological variables.

- Define concepts such as hypotheses, theories and variables.

- Have an awareness of the ethical principles adopted by psychologists.

- Describe the quantitative and qualitative approaches to psychology and be aware of the advantages and disadvantages of each.

- Have an awareness of how psychologists control variables.

QUESTIONS TO THINK ABOUT

- What is the scientific method and why is it so important to psychology?

- What are the goals of psychological research?

- Does following the steps of the scientific method guarantee that the results of a study will be important?

- Does the scientific method apply to all psychological research?

- How would you set up experiments to answer some of the questions you have about behaviour?

- How do the methods of psychology differ from those of other sciences? Do they?

- Why is obtaining informed consent from participants who take part in research important?

- Are some psychological subjects impossible to study? Why?

- What are the dangers in drawing conclusions from studies in which there is only one participant?

The process of discovery in psychology: the scientific method

The goal of psychological research is to discover, describe, explain and change the causes of behaviour. To do this, we need to describe behaviours and the events that are responsible for their occurrence in a language that is both precise enough to be understood by others and general enough to apply to a wide variety of situations. As you saw in Chapter 1, this language takes the form of explanations, which are general statements about the events that cause phenomena to occur. The nature of these general statements will become clear as we see how psychologists use the **scientific method**.

There are three major scientific approaches to research. **Naturalistic observations** – observations of people or animals in their natural environment – are the least formal and are constrained by the fewest rules. Naturalistic observations provide the foundations of the biological and social sciences. As Chapter 3 shows in detail, Charles Darwin's observation and classification of animals, plants and fossils during his voyage around the world provided him with the raw material for his theory of evolution. Jean Piaget collected much of his early data by observing his own children. **Correlational studies** are observational in nature, but they involve more formal measurement – of environmental events, of individuals' physical and social characteristics, and of their behaviour. Researchers examine the relations between these measurements in an attempt to discover the causes of the observed behaviours. **Experiments** go beyond mere measurement. A psychologist performing an experiment makes things happen and observes the results. As you will see, only an experiment can positively identify cause-and-effect relations.

The scientific method consists of a set of rules that dictates the general procedure a scientist must follow in their research. These rules are not arbitrary; they are based on logic. The following five steps summarise the rules of the scientific method that apply to experiments, the most rigorous form of scientific research. As we will see later, many of these rules also apply to observational studies. Some new terms introduced here without definition will be described in detail later in this chapter.

Stages in experimentation

1 *Identify the problem and formulate hypothetical cause-and-effect relations among variables.* This step involves identifying variables (particular behaviours and environmental and physiological events) and describing the relations among them in gen-eral terms. Consider the hypothesis that positive mood increases creativity. This statement describes a relation between two variables – mood and creativity – and states that an increase in one causes an increase in the other.

2 *Design the experiment.* Experiments involve the manipulation of factors called independent variables and the observation of dependent variables (these are defined in detail later in the chapter). For example, if we wanted to test the hypothesis that positive mood (independent variable) increases creativity (dependent variable), each variable would have to be operationally defined. The independent variable must be controlled so that only it, and no other variable, is responsible for any changes in the dependent variable.

3 *Conduct the experiment.* The researcher must organise the material needed to perform the experiment, train the people who will conduct the research, recruit volunteers whose behaviour will be observed, assign each of these volunteers to a treatment group or a control group and arrange the setting for the experiment. The experiment is performed and the observations are recorded.

4 *Evaluate the hypothesis by examining the data from the study.* Do the results support the hypothesis, or do they suggest that it is wrong? This step often involves mathematical procedures used to determine whether the relationship between two variables is statistically significant, i.e. not due to chance.

5 *Communicate the results.* (See next section.)

Following these simple steps decreases the chances that we will be misled by our observations and come to incorrect conclusions from our research. The approach of formulating hypotheses and then setting up experiments to test them is sometimes known as **hypothetico-deductive**. As you saw in Chapter 1, and will see in Chapter 11, people have a tendency to accept some types of evidence even though the rules of logic indicate that they should not. The Cutting Edge box illustrates this, using a new study of the predictors of having the hepatitis B vaccine. This tendency usually serves us well in our daily lives, but it can lead us to draw the wrong conclusions when we try to understand the true causes of natural phenomena, including our own behaviour (the same tendency results in the making of common-sense mistakes when predicting the outcome of psychological research, as you saw in Chapter 1).

Communicating the results of scientific research

Once psychologists have learned something about the causes of a behaviour from an experiment or observational study, they must tell others about their findings. When a piece of research is complete, it is written up in

Cutting edge – Stories conquer statistics

Psychology, like all sciences, uses statistics to determine whether the results it finds are not due to chance. However, humans are less likely to believe statistics than they are convincing narratives: we find words more persuasive. There may be no evidence for a therapy working but a friend's positive experience of it may convince you to give it a go; there may be no statistical evidence that a multiple vaccination can cause autism, but parents will refuse to allow their children to become so vaccinated because of harrowing case studies allegedly demonstrating this link. Chapter 15 describes a few more of these errors in reasoning.

A study in *Health Psychology* has extended this phenomenon to the area of ill-health prevention (DeWit *et al.*, 2008). An online study examined the effects of narrative evidence and statistical evidence on men's perception of risk of contracting the hepatitis B virus and whether they would seek vaccination. All the participants were homosexual. As predicted, narrative evidence was more persuasive than statistical evidence in heightening awareness of the risk of contracting the illness and in predicting participants' intention to get vaccination.

the form of a journal paper and sent to an academic, peer-reviewed scientific journal. This means that the paper will be critically evaluated, usually anonymously, by two or three of the author's peers (the process is called 'peer review'). The editor and reviewer will be individuals with expertise in the author's field.

The scientific method insists that scientists report the details of their research so that other investigators can repeat, or replicate, the study. **Replication** is one of the great strengths of science; it ensures that erroneous results and incorrect conclusions are weeded out. When scientists publish a study, they know that if the findings are important enough, their colleagues will try to replicate it (perhaps with some variation) to be sure that the results were not just a statistical fluke, specific to the sample studied or the methods used, or the result of some unsuspected errors in the design or execution of the study.

The types of article that scientists will write fall broadly into four categories. First, there are empirical papers that report the conduct and results of an experiment. Most scientific journals publish papers of this kind (such as *Nature, Psychological Science, British Journal of Psychology*, etc.) and most follow a format. They will invariably comprise sections and these sections will include a title, an abstract, an introduction, the method, the results, a discussion, references and an appendix. There are deviations from this format: *Science* and the *Journal of Cognitive Neuroscience*, to name only two, do not adopt this structure (the study's methods are reported either at the end of the paper or on the journal's website). But, by and large, papers follow this structure:

- **Title (and affiliations)**. The title describes the general thrust of the article. It is normally followed by the full names of all authors together with their affiliation (who they work for/on behalf of, e.g., 'Department of Psychology, Middlesex University, UK').

- **Abstract**. This is usually a 150–200 word paragraph that summarises ('abstracts' the information from) the article. It has a statement of intent, a brief description of the study and results and a general conclusion. Some abstracts have a different format and are sectioned in the same way as the paper: research suggests that this is a more informative way of summarising a paper.

- **Introduction**. This is the first of the four major sections of a paper. It reviews the literature pertaining to the subject of the paper and presents a set of hypotheses which the study aims to test.

- **Method**. This section describes what the experimenters did and who took part. Conventionally, this is divided into these subsections: participants, apparatus/materials and procedure. Under participants, all of the important information about the study's sample is included: age, sex, race, education and any other variable that the study is interested in. The apparatus/materials section includes details of any specialist technology or materials used. The procedure section describes what the experimenters did. Anyone reading this section should be able to conduct an identical experiment – facilities and time willing – on the basis of reading this section.

- **Results**. This section reports the results of the study. At this stage of your degree, reading the results section of a paper can seem like reading a foreign language because it is replete with impenetrable statistics.

- **Discussion**. The final major section, the discussion, discusses the results found and their implications for the field. If interprets findings in light of previously published data and suggests future avenues of enquiry.

- **References**. This section lists, usually in alphabetical order, all the studies cited in the text. Any study cited in the text should appear here and every item in the reference list should have been cited.

- **Appendix (optional).** Sometimes papers include appendices providing additional information such as word lists or questionnaires.

Secondly, in addition to journals that publish the results of experiments, there are also those that publish methodological papers reporting a new technique, questionnaire, procedure or new piece of equipment for use in psychological research. Thirdly, there are journals for theoretical papers that formulate a new theory arising from reviewed data. The journal *Psychological Review* is devoted to articles of this kind, for example. Finally, there are review papers that synthesise a number of articles on a given topic. *Psychological Bulletin* and *Current Direction in Psychological Science* publish papers exclusively of this kind and are good journals for keeping abreast of general topics in psychology.

Most journals in psychology, however, tend to focus on the sub-areas of psychology. The *European Journal of Social Psychology, Memory and Cognition, Journal of Applied Psychology, Neuropsychologia, Child Development, Personality and Individual Differences, Health Psychology, Emotion*, and so on, are examples of this kind. Some journals publish even more specialised research (e.g. *Social Neuroscience, Laterality*).

Researchers also present their findings at conferences or professional conventions.

As a result of their research being disseminated, other psychologists can incorporate these findings in their own thinking and hypothesising.

Controversies in Psychological Science – Psychology and the media

The issue

The media are voracious beasts. Newspapers, television, radio and online sites all have space and air to fill, often with few resources. Psychology's asset, but also its Achilles heel, is that it studies a topic that most people think they know something about (human behaviour) and produces data that are fascinating and stimulate human interest. The BPS's Press Office has a media database of over 1,000 members, and receives around 350 queries a month. But how accurately is psychological and other research presented in the media and is this portrayal – skewed or otherwise – important?

The evidence

First, let's start with the source of the research. Simply because a paper is published in a science journal does not mean that its method or results are unassailable. At the extreme end, journals can publish data that turn out to be fraudulent. In 2005, the journal *Nature* found that 0.3 per cent of the 3,247 scientists who participated in their confidential study claimed to have published bogus data and 6 per cent admitted failing to publish data that contradicted their own theoretical positions. In the same year, *Science*, one of the two premier general science journals in the world, withdrew a paper by the Korean scientist Hwang Wo-suk because the stem cell lines he had created (and wrote about in *Science*) did not exist.

Another scandal broke in 2004 when the *Journal of Reproductive Medicine* published a physics-defying article on the effect of prayer on *in vitro* fertilisation which was generally agreed to be flawed and possibly fabricated. The author was later convicted of criminal fraud. In 2009, an anaesthesiologist was found to have made up most of the data in his 10-year publishing career, and, at the time of writing, editors are being requested to withdraw 21 of his papers. This man researched the nature of pain management after operations – it was not a frivolous topic of little consequence. Even more seriously, flawed research claiming a link between the MMR vaccine and autism – and, more importantly, the enormously tendentious publicity this generated in 2002–3 – has caused completely avoidable harm to children, given the dramatic increase in measles and mumps following this hoo-hah.

Psychology is not immune. There continues to be debate over whether the British psychologist, Cyril Burt, invented his data concerning twins and intelligence. And, of course, there is the famous Sokal Hoax, in which a scientist submitted an utterly nonsensical anti-science article to a famously anti-objectivity social science journal and not only had it accepted but praised by the organ's clueless reviewers.

In experiments to examine whether the peer-review process works, researchers found that there is large variation in what reviewers judge to be quality research – reviewers can normally agree on the really bad studies, but there is more disagreement about the average-to-good ones. Science progresses by contradiction, and new articles develop ideas generated by previous publications or take into account variables that the previous studies had not. Although there are checks in place to weed out 'bad' research, it is common to see a lot of it published. This is why you should adopt an inquisitive but informed approach when reading research papers: do not be afraid to question an aspect of procedure or an analysis of logical thinking if you think it is wrong or misguided. You might be right.

While some of the stories you see reported or hear broadcast are well researched, balanced and informed it is generally the case that most are not. Journals are intended primarily for other scientists. Journals, however, are also consulted by medical or

Controversies in Psychological Science – *Continued*

science (or non-specialist) journalists interested in writing about innovative psychological breakthroughs. Conferences at which psychologists present the results of their studies are also extensively reported by specialist reporters in the media and some psychological societies have effective press offices which proactively publicise society conference papers.

However, never take any report you read in a newspaper or magazine or see or hear on the television or radio of a published study at face value. If you read the articles on the excellent website **www.badscience.net**, you will see why: journalists sometimes try to make a study more exciting than it is and make wild claims about the results that the researchers would never dream of doing. According to Goldacre (2008), 'Science stories generally fall into one of three categories: the wacky stories, the "breakthrough" stories, and the scare stories. Each undermines and distorts science in its own idiosyncratic way' (p. 208). Stories with headlines such as – and these are genuine – 'Infidelity is genetic', 'Electricity allergy real', 'Scans that spot killer babies' and 'In future, all men will have big willies' reflect a tenous relationship with the data (if the data exist) they claim to report. Similarly, newspaper articles claiming to report the mathematical formula for (and, again, all of these are real) the perfect way to eat ice cream ($A \times Tp \times Tm/Pt \times At + V \times LT \times SP \times W/Tt = 3d20$, if you're interested), the best sitcom, the best way to boil an egg, the best joke, the most depressing day of the year, are all bogus – they are not based on any real research or any real science. Most are commissioned by companies keen to harness the solid appeal of science to market their products.

The journalist Nick Davies, in his book *Flat Earth News*, describes the stories that boast none of the good features of journalism as 'churnalism': the writers parrot what is given to them by PR agencies or wire services, often unedited (Davies, 2008). In one survey, 80 per cent of British broadsheet news stories were 'wholly, mainly or partially' based on 'material provided by news agencies and the PR industry'. This is not a trivial issue because most of us will have our first encounter with new studies, not from a studious acquaintance with Web of Knowledge or Science Direct, but from magazines, newspapers, television or radio. We rely on journalists – the conduit between us and the research – to present findings lucidly, accurately, interestingly and not to oversimplify the data or

misrepresent it. And the media has influence, through selecting what it exposes. After Kylie Minogue's well-documented cancer, the *Medical Journal of Australia* reported a 40 per cent increase in mammogram bookings; in 2009, in the UK, stories reporting the terminal cancer of a female reality TV contestant appeared to coincide with an increase in cervical cancer checks. More self-servingly, the American Association for the Advancement of Science found that a mention of a researcher's study in the *New York Times* increased the number of times his or her paper was referred to by other colleagues in their papers (this is an important indicator of impact in the science world). Television and radio exposure increased this still further.

One new field that gets both journalists and readers excited is neuroimaging. And the fact that you can illustrate a story involving the brain's role in behaviour with a screen- and print-friendly brain scan makes the research even more appealing. But neuroimaging technology, and its data analysis, are complex and the studies using it very detailed in their method. Sometimes the details are sacrificed for a headline. Hence, stories screaming: 'Scary or sensational? A machine that can look into the mind' (genuine). Chapter 4 will take a further look at the role of brain scans and the way in which they make research more persuasive than a story with just words.

In rare circumstances, the authors (researchers and journalists) can collude. An excellent example of this was the so-called study reported in December 2005 – 2005 was clearly a good year for hoaxes – claiming that the success of Agatha Christie was attributable to her use of words and phrases that raised levels of chemicals in the brain ('Agatha Christie grey cells mystery' teased *The Sunday Times*). You would have thought that this study involved neuroimaging or analysis of readers' brains. In fact, no. You would be hard pushed to find any brain research at all. The study – actually, an examination of the types of words used in Christie's novels – was used to publicise a television documentary on Christie's success. The only reference to brain activity in that programme came from a hypnotist and a self-help guru.

Conclusion

The important message of this story, and this section, is less complex than a Christie plot but as easy to understand as her prose: question everything.

Identifying the problem: getting an idea for research

According to Bausell (1993), psychologists undertake research for a wide variety of reasons – some sensible, some impracticable. Some of these include:

- changing distasteful professional practice;
- learning everything there is to know about a subject;
- discrediting a theory that is archaic or wrong;
- testing a theory to see if it is valid;
- lending credence to the experimenter's own theory;

- furthering a career by producing a seminal study;
- furthering a career by obtaining a publication;
- obtaining a doctorate for professional gain;
- becoming famous;
- furthering scientific progress;
- discovering something of intellectual interest.

Which of these do you think makes the best, most realistic goal? Although scientists may undertake study for some or all of these reasons, it is unlikely that they will become famous through their scientific work. Very few scientists attract the fame (and pay) of members from more alluring professions. There are millionaires in psychology, but more in pop music.

Publishing a paper for personal gain is also a poor reason. Perhaps the two most important spurs to scientific research are the desires to further science and, more importantly, to discover something of intellectual interest. What do you need to become a good scientist? A great scientist certainly needs to be curious, hard working and dedicated – perhaps even obstinate and relentless. They need to be sceptical, open-minded and methodical. But above all, a successful scientist needs to have good ideas. Where do those ideas come from?

Constructing a hypothesis

A hypothesis is the starting point of any study. It is an idea, phrased as a general statement, that a scientist wishes to test through scientific research. In the original Greek, *hypothesis* means 'suggestion', and the word still conveys the same meaning. When scientists form a hypothesis, they are simply suggesting that a relation exists among various phenomena (like the one that might exist between increased positive mood and increased risk-taking). Thus, a **hypothesis** is a tentative statement about a cause-and-effect relation between two or more events. Productive and creative scientists formulate new hypotheses by thinking about the implications of studies that they have performed or that have been performed by others.

At other times, however, researchers may not know exactly what they expect to find. Such research endeavours are called 'fishing expeditions'. In the same way that an angler may not know whether they will catch a trout or an old car seat, the researcher does not know whether they will find result X or result Y. An example of such research would be the measurement of people's attitudes towards a particular subject such as animal experimentation or alternative medicine. In such cases, an experimenter would not be able to make an absolute prediction based on hypothetico-deductive reasoning (unless, for example, they compared attitudes among two groups such as vegans and meat-eaters, or users of conventional medicine and users of homoeopathic remedies).

Creating a theory

A **theory**, a set of statements designed to explain a set of phenomena, is an elaborate form of hypothesis. In fact, a theory can be a way of organising a system of related hypotheses to explain some larger aspect of nature. A good theory fuels the creation of new hypotheses. More accurately, a good scientist, contemplating a good theory, thinks of more good hypotheses to test. For example, Albert Einstein's theory of relativity states that time, matter and energy are interdependent. Changes in any one will produce changes in the others. The hypotheses suggested by this theory revolutionised science; the field of nuclear physics rests largely on experiments arising from Einstein's theory.

A good theory is one that generates testable hypotheses – hypotheses that can potentially be supported or proved wrong by scientific research. Some theories are so general or so abstract that they do not produce testable hypotheses and hence cannot be subjected to scientific rigour. The framework for most psychological research is larger in scope than a hypothesis but smaller in scope than a fully-fledged theory. For example, the frustration–aggression hypothesis in social psychology suggests that people (or other animals) tend to become aggressive when they do not achieve a goal that they have been accustomed to achieving. This hypothesis makes a prediction that might fit many different situations. Indeed, many experiments have been performed to test this hypothesis under different conditions.

Even though the frameworks that most psychologists construct fall short of constituting theories, they serve a similar function by stimulating researchers to think about old problems in new ways and by showing how findings that did not appear to be related to each other can be explained by a single concept. One recent theory of emotional experience, for example, suggests that increases or decreases in the left and right front part of the brain are associated with positive and negative emotions, reflecting a tendency to 'withdraw' or 'approach' a stimulus (Davidson and Sutton, 1995). Such a theory can be used to test a number of hypotheses such as, 'depressed individuals will show less left frontal brain activity' and research on frontal lobe activation and emotion has resulted in a modification of thinking on the relationship between the two (Peters and Harmon-Jones, 2009), as you'll see in Chapter 13.

Quantitative research methods: designing an experiment

Although naturalistic observations enable a psychologist to classify behaviours into categories and provide hypothetical explanations for these behaviours, only an experiment can determine whether these explanations are correct. This approach is known as **quantitative research** because behaviours are reduced to quantities or can at least be seen as quantifiable. Personality or visuospatial ability may be quantified by a score on a questionnaire, for example, or the ability to react correctly and quickly on a reaction time task may be quantified by the number of correct decisions and the speed of responding.

There are various types of experiment we can design. We could conduct an experiment in which we looked at the effect of sleep deprivation on mental arithmetic ability; one group might be deprived of sleep for 24 hours, another for 36 hours and another would be allowed to sleep normally. In a more elaborate study, we could use neuroimaging techniques to monitor changes in brain activation at each stage. In the neuroimaging study this would be the **control group** because it is unaffected by the features of the experiment that we are interested in looking at and can, therefore, be used as a comparison group. The others are called **experimental groups**. Because the individuals in one group are not the same people as the ones in another group, the design of the experiment is called **independent groups** or **between-groups**.

A slightly different experiment might involve people performing different levels of the same experiment. For example, we may be interested in finding out if people recognise real English words more quickly than they do pseudowords (words which follow the same rules of English but have no meaning) or non-words (words which do not follow the rules of English). This is called a lexical decision task. Here, every individual would respond to each type of word (but might be quicker responding to some types of word than others). Because each individual is exposed to the same condition of the experiment (each type of word), the design is called **repeated measures** or **within-groups**.

There are advantages to using both types of design: independent groups and repeated measures. For statistical reasons, it may be easier to obtain significant results by employing a repeated measures design because this approach eliminates the amount of variability that exists between data from different individuals. Because each participant acts as his or her control (that is, completes each condition in the experiment), there is less variability in the data (such as sex, age and personality differences or the ability to respond quickly to visual stimuli or the tendency to think better in the morning than in the afternoon, etc.).

Independent groups designs are advantageous when you do not want to expose the same individuals to the same conditions. For example, if we wanted to compare the effect of fat, carbohydrate and protein intake on people's ability to react quickly to visual stimuli (because

we hypothesised that certain foods made you drowsy), there would be disadvantages to having them all eat each different type of food (to begin with, if they were tested on different days, they may get better on the reaction time tasks because of practice; secondly, because different food is presented on each occasion, they may become suspicious). An independent groups design would help to eliminate these problems. Such designs are useful to medicine and the study of treatment for mental illness (as you will see in Chapter 18). A mentally ill group would take treatment A, another group treatment B, another group a placebo (we will come on to this later) and a final group would receive no treatment. If treatment A is successful, there should be a difference in outcome between this group and others in the study.

Imagine that you were a researcher who was interested in discovering whether people's cognitive ability declined with age. You take five groups of adults: 20–30-year-olds, 31–40-year-olds, 41–50-year-olds, 51–60-year-olds and the over-61-year-olds. You administer a series of tests which measures a range of cognitive abilities such as verbal and visuospatial ability. You find that whereas most of the over-61 group perform more poorly at most of the tests than do the other groups, they do better at some of the verbal tests such as vocabulary. What do you conclude from this study? If you conclude that verbal ability does not decline as rapidly as other abilities with age, you would be wrong. Can you think why? (The answer appears in Chapter 11.) Using the same example, what would be the theory and what would be the hypothesis in this experiment? What would be the independent and dependent variables?

Another approach to studying behaviour might be to conduct an experiment under laboratory or naturalistic conditions. In a laboratory experiment, the experimenter has control over most of the variables that they think will affect the outcome of the experiment. For example, we could design an experiment in which the effect of ambient noise on work performance was measured. We could expose individuals to specific noises at specific levels at specific times while they completed specific tasks and questionnaires assessing mood. Alternatively, we could set up a **field experiment** in which participants would be observed under fairly 'natural' conditions. For example, we might compare the effects of different office lighting conditions, or the weather, on individuals' mood and productivity.

The important feature of naturalistic observations is that the observer remains in the background and does not interfere with the people (or animals) being observed. In some cases, psychologists do interfere with a situation in a natural setting. For example, Chapters 15 and 16 describe some experiments designed to discover what factors determine whether bystanders come to the aid of people who have been hurt or who are in distress. An 'accident' is

see activity on mypsychlab

staged, and the behaviour of passers-by is surreptitiously observed. Although studies such as these take place outside the laboratory – at job sites or on the street – they are experiments, not naturalistic observations. Such experiments might be called quasi-field studies.

Variables: what is studied and measured

Variables are things that have a particular value but which can vary. Scientists either measure or manipulate the values of variables. Manipulate literally means 'to handle' (from *manus*, 'hand'). Psychologists use the word 'manipulate' to refer to setting the value of a variable for experimental purposes. The results of this manipulation determine whether the hypothesis is true or false. Direct manipulation of an independent variable, for example, would involve placing individuals into different treatment groups, such as drug A, drug B, a placebo and no drug. Indirect manipulation would involve differentiating individuals with different personality types. For example, we might be interested in whether individuals low, medium or high in trait anxiety (the degree of anxiety they habitually feel) selectively attend to anxiety-related stimuli (such as pictures of snakes, spiders, blood and so on).

Or we might look at the effect of positive mood on risk-taking. We would assemble four groups of volunteers to serve as participants. We manipulate mood by having participants watch a comedy film (which would put participants in a positive mood), an unpleasant film (which would put participants in a negative mood) or a neutral film (which would not be expected to influence participants' mood negatively or positively). We would have a fourth group which would watch no film (the control group). We would then examine the effect of this measure (mood) on risk-taking, such as the amount spent gambling at roulette (taking care, of course, to ensure that our 'manipulation' worked).

This experiment examines the effect of one variable on another. Here, the variable that we manipulate (mood) is called the **independent variable**. We could also have a second independent variable, such as the sex of the gambler (Do men or women gamble more? Would we have a good reason for hypothesising a sex difference?) The variable that we measure (risk-taking) is the **dependent variable**. An easy way to keep the names of these variables straight is to remember that a hypothesis describes how the value of a dependent variable depends on the value of an independent variable. Our hypothesis proposes that increased gambling depends on the individual's level of mood. Suppose that you were interested in studying the effects of sleep deprivation on learning ability. Which of these two variables would be the independent variable and which would be the dependent variable? How might you define these variables operationally? You can see the relationship between the two variables illustrated in Figure 2.1.

Sometimes, we want to understand the causes of behaviour in more than one specific situation. Thus, the variables that hypotheses deal with are expressed in general terms. Independent and dependent variables are categories into which various behaviours are classified. For example, we would probably label all of the following behaviours as 'interpersonal aggression': hitting, kicking, throwing something at someone. Presumably, these behaviours would have similar causes. A psychologist must know enough about a particular type of behaviour to be able to classify it correctly.

Although one of the first steps in psychological investigation involves naming and classifying behaviours, we must be careful to avoid committing the nominal fallacy or reification. The **nominal fallacy** refers to the erroneous belief that one has explained an event simply by naming it (*nomen* means 'name'). Classifying a behaviour does not explain it; classifying only prepares us to examine and discover events that cause a behaviour. For example, suppose that we see a man frown and shout at other people without provocation, criticise their work when really it is acceptable, and generally act unpleasantly towards everyone around him. Someone says, 'He's really angry today.' Does this statement explain his behaviour?

It does not; it only describes the behaviour. To say that he is angry suggests that an internal state is responsible for his behaviour – that anger is causing his behaviour. But all we have observed is his behaviour, not his internal state. Even if he is experiencing feelings of anger, these feelings still do not explain his behaviour. What we really need to know is what events made him act the way he did. Perhaps he has a painful toothache. Perhaps he had just learned that he was passed over for a promotion. Perhaps he had a terrible fight with his wife. Perhaps he had just read a book that advised him to be more assertive. Events like these are causes of both the behaviour and the feelings. Unless they are discovered, we cannot say that we have explained his behaviour. The

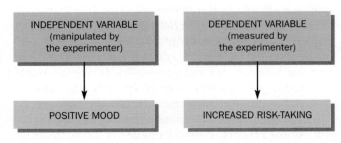

Figure 2.1 Independent and dependent variables described in the mood and risk-taking experiment.

task of a psychologist is to determine which of the many events that occurred before a particular behaviour caused that behaviour to happen.

Operational definitions

This translation of generalities into specific operations is called an **operational definition**: independent variables and dependent variables are defined in terms of the operations an experimenter performs to set their values or to measure them. In our proposed experiment, for example, the operational definition of the independent and dependent variables might be:

- Independent variable: participants' mood was induced by watching pleasant, neutral or unpleasant video films; a control group watched none of the films.
- Dependent variable: participants' risk-taking behaviour was measured by monitoring the amount of money spent betting on the outcome of a roulette wheel when the probability of winning was high and when it was low.

Providing an operational definition of variables is a hall-mark of well-conducted research. If research is to be understood, evaluated and replicated by other people (step 5 of the scientific method described at the beginning of this chapter), the investigator must provide others with a thorough and adequate description of the procedures used to manipulate the independent variable and to measure the dependent variable. For example, a complete definition of the dependent variable (risk-taking) would have to include a detailed description of the type of gambling task and the probability of winning.

There are many ways to translate a general concept into a set of operations. We might decide to adopt a different measure of mood, such as having participants complete a mental arithmetic task and inform them that they did well or badly (regardless of how they actually performed). This might also be expected to increase or decrease mood. We might choose a different measure of risk-taking such as asking participants to make decisions about a hypothetical risky treatment for a disease that they have (hypothetically) developed. Which operational definition of mood and risk-taking do you think is correct? Is there only one correct definition in this case? What these questions address is the issue of validity.

Validity

The **validity** of an operational definition refers to how appropriate it is – how accurately it represents the variable whose value has been manipulated or measured. You'll sometimes find the term 'ecological validity' being used: this refers to the degree to which the experimental context accurately presents that which the experimenter wants to reproduce. If you set up an experiment to monitor how much people laughed at a comedy, for example, and also measured their brain electrical activity and heart rate, which means attaching wires with electrodes to the head, fingers and chest, would this accurately represent the context in which a person would normally laugh at a comedy programme? The experience could be reasonably said to lack ecological validity.

Given enough time, the validity of an operational definition will emerge (or so we hope). If different investigators define the variable in slightly different ways but their experiments yield similar results, we become more confident that the research is leading to an understanding of the phenomena we are studying.

The issue of validity is illustrated, famously, by the Barnum effect. The Psychology in Action box tells you more.

Psychology in action – The Barnum effect

Research has shown that highly intelligent readers who are attracted to the boxed off sections of introductory psychology textbooks, have certain personalities. This personality evaluation is presented below – see how much or how little you disagree with it.

see activity on mypsychlab

You are the type of person who has a tendency to be critical of yourself. You have a great need for other people to like and admire you but you pride yourself on being an independent thinker and do not accept others' statements without satisfactory proof. You have a great deal of unused capacity which you have not turned to your advantage. While you have some personality weaknesses, you are generally able to compensate for them. You prefer a certain amount of change and variety and become dissatisfied when hemmed in by restrictions and limitations.

Does this description accurately reflect your own personality? It probably does. More than that, it probably applies to the majority of the population. These are universally valid statements which refer to nothing specific but to general feelings and beliefs that could apply to almost everyone. That most people believe that these vague personality descriptions accurately reflect their own personality is called the **Barnum effect** (Meehl, 1956). The phenomenon is named after Phineas T. Barnum, the great American circus showman, who declared

▶

Psychology in action – *Continued*

The circus showman, P.T. Barnum, who gave his name to the Barnum effect.

Source: Popperfoto/Getty Images.

that there was a 'sucker born every minute' and believed that his entertainments provided 'a little something for everybody'. The Barnum effect is seen clearly when individuals accept that 'generalized, vague, bogus descriptions of themselves which have high base-rate occurrence in the general population' are correct (Furnham and Schofield, 1987).

The phenomenon has a long history in psychology and a less honourable one among proponents of pseudoscience and pseudotherapy. Any clairvoyant or fortune-teller will make cunning use of the Barnum effect to dupe credulous punters. This is not surprising: people have been found to be more accepting of generalised feedback than actual, factual feedback (Merrens and Richards, 1970). A study of 68 personnel managers in the 1950s highlights the way in which we can accept the most vague statements about our personality as reflecting reality. Stagner (1958) administered personality tests to these managers and gave them 13 bogus statements that were assumed to represent actual feedback about their personality from the tests. The statements are listed in Table 2.1. See how many you agree with.

Table 2.1 The Barnum effect 1: personnel managers' reactions to their 'personality analysis

	Judgements as to accuracy of item (% choosing)				
	Amazingly accurate	Rather good	About half and half	More wrong than right	Almost entirely wrong
You have a great need for other people to like and admire you	39	46	13	1	1
You have a tendency to be critical of yourself	46	36	15	3	0
You have a great deal of unused capacity wihch you have not turned to your advantage	37	36	18	1	4
While you have some personality weaknesses, you are generally able to compensate for them	34	55	9	0	0
Your sexual adjustment has presented problems for you	15	16	16	33	19
Disciplined and self-controled outside, you tend to be worrisome and insecure inside	40	21	22	10	4
At times you have serious doubts as to whether you have made the right decision or done the right thing	27	31	19	18	4
You prefer a certain amount of change and variety and become dissatisfied when hemmed in by restrictions and limitations	63	28	7	1	1
You pride yourself as an independent thinker and do not accept others statements without satisfactory proof	49	31	12	4	4
You have found it unwise to be too frank in revealing yourself to others	31	37	22	6	4
At times you are extroverted, affable, sociable, while at other times you are introverted, wary and reserved	43	25	18	9	5
Some of your aspriations tend to be pretty unrealistic	12	16	22	43	7
Security is one of your major goals in life	40	31	15	9	5

Psychology in action – *Continued*

When asked to rate how strongly the participants agreed with these statements, almost all indicated that they believed them to some extent and one-third regarded their profile as a 'good' reflection of their character. For some statements such as, 'You prefer a certain amount of change and variety . . .', and 'While you have some personality weaknesses . . .', over 80 per cent of participants expressed agreement with them.

In an ingenious spin on the Barnum phenomenon, Furnham (1994) set up an experiment in which undergraduates gave samples of their hair to an experimenter. A week later the participants were given a 'trichological analysis' – 24 bland statements regarding their health based on the hair sample – that was totally bogus. Most students thought that these randomly applied statements were very accurate.

What does research on the Barnum effect tell us? First, it shows us that most individuals are inclined to accept bland feedback about themselves. Secondly, it shows us that the validity of a test involves more than intuitively 'knowing' that a test measures something. Most individuals – unless they knew about the Barnum effect – would have regarded the statements at the beginning of this section as true and might have accepted the statement that intelligent but sceptical readers are drawn to boxed-off areas of textbooks. This statement is, of course, nonsense. Thirdly, and perhaps most importantly, the Barnum effect shows us that we should always adopt a sceptical and questioning approach to statements made about human behaviour – even to this last statement.

Control of independent variables

If a scientist performs an experiment and finds that manipulating the value of the independent variable changes the dependent variable, the scientist can conclude that there is a cause-and-effect relation between the variables. That is, changes in the value of the independent variable cause changes in the value of the dependent variable.

In designing an experiment, the experimenter must manipulate the value of the independent variable and only the independent variable. For example, if we want to determine whether noise has an effect on people's reading speed, we must choose our source of noise carefully. If we use the sound from a television set to supply the noise and find that it slows people's reading speed, we cannot conclude that the effect was caused purely by noise. We might have selected an interesting programme, thus distracting the participants' attention from the material they were reading. If we want to do this experiment properly, we should use noise that is neutral and not a source of interest by itself, for example, noise like the 'sssh' sound that is heard when an FM radio is tuned between stations.

In this example, we intended to test the effects of an independent variable (noise) on a dependent variable (reading speed). By using a television to provide the noise, we were inadvertently testing the effects of other variables besides noise on reading speed. We introduced unwanted variables in addition to the independent variable.

Schwartz (1999) cites a study showing that when respondents were asked to determine the causes of mass murder reported in newspapers, those doing so on notepaper headed 'Institute of Personality' cited more reasons related to personality whereas those doing so on notepaper headed 'Institute of Social Science' gave more context-social related reasons for the crime. This example, and others in the review, shows that even small details in the conduct of research can influence respondents' answers and thus affect validity.

Confounding and counterbalancing

One of the meanings of the word 'confound' is to fail to distinguish. If an experimenter inadvertently introduces one or more unwanted independent variables, they cannot distinguish the effects of any one of them on the dependent variable. That is, the effects of the variables will be confounded and this is called the **confounding of variables**. It is often difficult to be sure that independent variables are not confounded. We must be certain that when we manipulate the independent variable that variable only, and no other variable, is affected.

One method of addressing confounding variables is called **counterbalancing**, which means to 'weigh evenly'. Imagine that an experimenter decided to investigate the effect of a memory-enhancing drug on people's ability to remember concrete and abstract nouns. An experiment is designed in which three groups of people – one taking the drug, another taking a harmless pill and a control group which takes nothing – complete a word recognition experiment. For all groups, the concrete words are presented in the first part of the experiment and the abstract words are presented in the second half. To the experimenter's surprise, although the drug group's performance is better than the others', all groups have more difficulty in remembering the abstract nouns. Does this finding mean that individuals find abstract nouns less memorable?

The answer is that, on the basis of the design of the experiment, we cannot know. Because the abstract words always appeared in the second half of the experiment, it is possible that the groups simply felt more tired towards the end of the experiment and that their fatigue influenced their recognition scores; they may even have become more bored towards the end of the experiment. Perhaps, having been used to memorising concrete nouns, the shift to a different type of word interfered with the individuals' memory strategy. A solution would be to counterbalance the presentation of the types of word so that some individuals received the abstract nouns first followed by the concrete nouns whereas others received the concrete nouns first. If the original results were attributable to tiredness or fatigue then the same decrease in recall should be seen in the second half of the experiment. If individuals continue to recall abstract nouns less frequently than concrete nouns, then the result is not due to the effects of the confounding variables of tiredness and fatigue.

Having carefully designed a study, we must then decide how best to conduct it. This brings us to step 3 of the scientific method: performing the experiment. We must decide what participants will be used, what instructions will be given, and what equipment and materials will be used. We must ensure that the data collected will be accurate.

Reliability

If the procedure described by an operational definition gives consistent results under consistent conditions, the procedure is said to have high **reliability**. For example, measurements of people's height and weight are extremely reliable. Measurements of their academic aptitude (by means of standard, commercial tests) are also reliable, but less so.

Achieving reliability is usually much easier than achieving validity. Reliability is mostly a result of care and diligence on the part of researchers in the planning and execution of their studies. Alert, careful experimenters can control most of the extraneous factors that might affect the reliability of their measurements. Conditions throughout the experiment should always be as consistent as possible. For example, the same instructions should be given to each person who participates in the experiment, all mechanical devices should be in good repair, and all assistants hired by the experimenter should be well trained in performing their tasks. Noise and other sources of distraction should be kept to a minimum.

Another issue that affects reliability is the degree of subjectivity involved in making a measurement. In the experiment described above – the investigation of the effects of mood on creativity – our definition of mood was objective; even a non-expert could follow our procedure and obtain the same results. But researchers often attempt to study variables whose measurement is subjective, that is, it requires practical judgement and expertise.

For example, suppose that a psychologist wants to count the number of friendly interactions that a child makes with other children in a group. This measurement requires someone to watch the child and count the number of times a friendly interaction occurs. But it is difficult to be absolutely specific about what constitutes a friendly interaction and what does not. What if the child looks at another child and their gazes meet? One observer may say that the look conveyed interest in what the other child was doing and so should be scored as a friendly interaction. Another observer may disagree.

The solution in this case is, first, to try to specify as precisely as possible the criteria to be used for defining an interaction as friendly in order to make the measurement as objective as possible. Then, two or more people should watch the child's behaviour and score it independently, that is, neither person should be aware of the other person's ratings. If their ratings agree, we can say that the scoring system has high **interrater reliability**. If they disagree, interrater reliability is low, and there is no point in continuing the study. Instead, the rating system should be refined and the raters should be trained to apply it consistently. Any investigator who performs a study that requires some degree of skill and judgement in measuring the dependent variables must do what is necessary to produce high interrater reliability.

There are other ways in which a researcher can test the reliability of their data. For example, say that we wanted to examine whether an individual's responses on a personality questionnaire were reliable. One method of determining this might be to divide the questionnaire and compare the responses of the participant in each of the two sections of the questionnaire. If there is strong agreement between scores from each half, the questionnaire results are said to be reliable. This is called **split-half reliability** because the measure (the personality questionnaire) is split and responses to the two split parts compared.

But what if the questionnaire is too short for split-half reliability to be tested or the test measures many different factors (as an intelligence test does)? One way of testing reliability in such circumstances might be to administer the test at one session and then again at another session, some time apart. If the test is reliable, it should yield the same scores at the first as at the second session. This is called **test–retest reliability**. However, can you see a possible confound here? Imagine if you were to examine the test–retest reliability of an IQ test. The scores at the second session may be better because the participant has already undertaken the same test once. So, the test may be reliable but the data obtained from the test suggest that it is not. Can you think of a way of circumventing this problem? (Chapter 11, Intelligence and thinking, takes up this issue in more detail.)

Selecting participants

So far, we have dealt with what we, as researchers, would do – what hypothesis we would test, how we would design the experiment, and how we would obtain valid and reliable measurements. Now let us turn to the people who will participate in our experiment: our participants. How do we choose them? How do we assign them to the experimental or control group? These decisions must be carefully considered because, just as independent variables can be confounded, so can variables that are inherent in participants whose behaviour is being observed.

Consider the following example. A lecturer wants to determine which of two teaching methods works best. She teaches two courses in introductory psychology, one that meets at 9.30 a.m. and another that meets at 4 p.m. She uses one teaching method for the morning class and another for the afternoon class. At the end of the term she finds that the final examination scores were higher for her morning class. She concludes that from now on she will use that particular teaching method for all of her classes. However, there is a problem. Think about what this might be before you read the next sentence.

The two groups of participants for the experiment are not equivalent. People who sign up for a class that meets at 9.30 a.m. are likely to differ in some ways from those who sign up for a 4 p.m. class. Some people prefer to get up early whereas others prefer to sleep late. Perhaps the university sports department schedules some kinds of activity late in the afternoon, which means that students interested in participating in these activities will not be able to register for the 4 p.m. class. For many reasons, the students in the two classes will probably not be equivalent. Therefore, we cannot conclude that the differences in their final examination scores were caused solely by the differences in the teaching methods.

Of course, in the past ten years or so, researchers have also been exploiting the internet as a source of participants. It can be a quick and very effective way of recruiting large numbers of participants. It has advantages over paper-and-pencil (PP) versions of tests – the error rate is lower (electronic responses are more legible than written ones) and the response/take-up rate is higher. However, there is evidence that internet participants leave out more items on test inventories and choose the extreme ends of responding, selecting strongly agree/disagree more often than do PP participants.

All psychological experiments use samples – human or animal – and researchers usually know the type of sample they need. If they are testing the efficacy of a drug or the effectiveness of a type of rehabilitation following brain injury, for example, they include samples with specific characteristics. Most psychological researchers, however, recruit opportunity samples: people willing to give up their time and participate in research. But how representative are these opportunity samples? The Controversies in Psychological Science section takes up this topic.

Participants must be carefully assigned to the various groups used in an experiment. The usual way to assign them is by **random assignment**. One way to accomplish random assignment is to list the names of the available participants and then to toss a coin for each one to determine the participant's assignment to one of two groups. More typically, the assignment is made by computer or by consulting a list of random numbers. We can expect people to have different abilities, personality traits and other characteristics that may affect the outcome of the experiment, but if people are randomly assigned to the experimental conditions, these differences should – according to the principle of random sampling – be equally distributed across the groups.

Controversies in Psychological Science – How representative are samples in psychological research?

The issue

As a psychology student, you will inevitably be asked to participate in a psychology experiment. This may be part of your research methods or other course; or it may be an experiment run by your tutor or department. In fact, if you look at the method sections of scientific articles published in psychology, you will find that the majority of these reports recruit participants just like you: psychology students. This is a source of concern for some psychologists because the findings from such a group may not be representative of the behaviour of other sections of the population. How representative, therefore, are examples in psychological research?

The evidence

In a study of recruits from undergraduate psychology classes who participate in psychology experiments, Quinones-Vidal *et al.* (2004) found that of all papers in the prestigious *Journal of Personality and Social Psychology* (a leader in its field) 92 per cent originated in the US and Canada and 99 per cent from Western countries.

▶

Controversies in Psychological Science – *Continued*

Another study, which investigated the degree of over-representation of psychology students in psychology research published in the *British Journal of Social Psychology* (*BJSP*) and the *British Journal of Psychology* (*BJP*) in 1995 and 1996, found that of 107 studies 29 per cent used non-student adults and 15.9 per cent of the experiments were in a real-life environment (Banyard and Hunt, 2000). Twenty-eight per cent were based in a laboratory and 26.2 per cent were conducted in other parts of a university such as a lecture hall. Pressure to participate was evident in 58 per cent of the studies (students would take part to obtain course credit or because experiments were a course requirement).

Volunteers were used in 17.8 per cent of the studies. Over 70 per cent of papers in *BJSP* used self-report measures whereas over 50 per cent of *BJP* studies used laboratory-based measures. One-third of studies did not record how the sample was recruited and only 33 per cent of the 18,635 people who participated in the experiments were coded for their sex. Ethnicity was considered in only one study.

The study highlights some important points to remember when reading and explaining the findings of research (although this analysis was based on two journals published in two years). The authors state that using students for research is acceptable but they query how representative this sample is.

The view is echoed in another study of ethnic representation among samples in applied psychology studies (Case and Smith, 2000). Case and Smith found that in 2,536 articles from 14 applied psychology journals taken in a 5-year period, almost 40 per cent indicated the ethnicity of the participant. In the articles that did include details of ethnicity, there was an over-representation of African Americans and an under-representation of Hispanic Americans (compared with the actual number of Hispanic people in the population).

Conclusion

'Because psychological research must be relevant and appropriate for individuals from diverse ethnic backgrounds,' the authors argue, 'researchers must use samples that adequately represent diverse populations.' They go on to argue that if we are to find out what works for whom, then we must include factors such as ethnicity in studies of psychological processes. When you read primary sources in psychology – journal articles – take some time to study the sample used and think of why the authors chose this sample.

Response bias... – An international perspective

Response bias – responding to a questionnaire in a way that is not genuine or honest but in an irrelevant way such as always responding 'yes' to a series of questions – is an important concept in research methods because it can skew results and tell researchers something which is not very meaningful. A Dutch study of six European countries has found that response bias varies by cultures.

Researchers used existing data from a multinational marketing survey to examine response bias in participants from Greece, Italy, Spain, France, Germany and the UK (Van Herk *et al.*, 2005). They found that unlike participants from north-western European countries, those from Mediterranean countries showed an abnormally high tendency to agree than disagree with answers (acquiescence), and a greater likelihood to chose extreme response categories (e.g. selecting 1 or 5 on a 5-point scale). Greek participants, in particular, significantly exhibited these response biases. Spain and Italy scored higher on these two biases than did the UK, France and Germany. The British were the least acquiescent.

The authors suggest that such differences might reflect the different types of cultures in these countries: collectivistic versus individualistic. The more individualistic the societies were, the less acquiescent they seemed.

Researchers must remain alert to the problem of confounding subject variables even after they have designed an experiment and randomly assigned participants to the groups. Some problems will not emerge until the investigation is actually performed. Suppose that an experimenter was interested in learning whether anger decreases a person's ability to concentrate. The experimenter acts rudely towards the participants in the experimental group, which presumably makes them angry, but treats the participants in the control group politely. After the rude or polite treatment, the participants watch a video screen that shows a constantly changing display of patterns of letters. Participants are instructed to press a button whenever a particular letter appears. This vigilance test is designed to reveal how carefully participants are paying attention to the letters.

The design of this experiment is sound. Assuming that the participants in the experimental group are really angry and that our test is a valid measure of concentration, we should be able to make conclusions about the effects of anger on concentration. However, the experiment, as performed under real conditions, may not work out the way it was designed. Suppose that some of our 'angry' participants simply walk away. All experimenters are required to tell participants that they are free to leave at any time (and the section on ethics later in this chapter will tell you why); some angry participants might well do so. If they do, we will now be comparing the behaviour of two groups of participants of somewhat different character – a group of people who are willing to submit to the experimenter's rude behaviour and a group of randomly selected people, some of whom would have left had they been subjected to the rude treatment. Now the experimental group and control group are no longer equivalent. Figure 2.2 illustrates this.

The moral of this example is that an experimenter must continue to attend to the possibility of confounded variables even after the experiment is under way. The solution in this case? There probably is none. Because we cannot force participants to continue to participate, there is a strong possibility that some of them will leave. There is also the flip side to this problem, where participants will respond in an unnaturally positive way because this is what they believe the experimenter wants. For example, they may give answers on personality or other questionnaires that portrays them in the best light. This is called **social desirability**. As you will see in Chapters 15 and 16 (on social psychology), the relationship between experimenter and participant is sometimes a complex one. Some psychological variables are, by their nature, difficult to investigate.

Participants' expectations

Participants in a psychology experiment are not simply passive participants whose behaviour is controlled solely by the independent variables manipulated by the experimenter. Participants know that they are being observed, and this knowledge is certain to affect their behaviour. This is sometimes known as the Hawthorne effect: the notion that the act of observation can change what it is you are observing. It derives from, ostensibly, a phenomenon that occurred in the Hawthorne Works of the Western Electric Company in Chicago in the 1902s and 1930s. The managers hypothesised that increasing the lighting conditions would increase productivity, which it did but this effect was short-lived. Productivity increases were seen when the lighting conditions changed, as if the workers were aware of the manipulation and worked harder (Adair, 1984). While the Hawthorne effect is not that well established (the name was given to the effect in a book published in 1953 and the original studies were never published; Chiesa and Hobbs, 2008), participants will behave as if an hypothesis is true if they find out the hypothesis. For example, Young *et al.* (2007) found that if people were given questionnaires on motion sickness to complete before they were exposed to virtual reality displays (which they were told might induce motion sickness), they reported more motion sickness than those who did not complete such questionnaires.

Because the study is being run by a psychologist, some participants are unlikely to take what they say at face value and will look for motives hidden behind an apparently simple task. Actually, most experiments are not deceptive at all; they are what they appear to be and 'deceptive' studies do not always succeed in fooling the participants. For example, suppose you are a participant in an experiment that was represented as being a learning study. On the table in front of you is an assortment of knives and pistols. The experimenter says, 'Oh, ignore them. Someone else left them here. They have nothing to do with this study.' Do you believe her? Probably not, and you will undoubtedly try to figure out how the presence of these weapons is supposed to affect your behaviour. You may suspect that the psychologist is trying to determine whether the presence of weapons will increase your hostility. With this suspicion in mind, you may (1) act naturally, so that you will not spoil the experiment; (2) act aggressively, to help the experimenter get the results you think she wants; or (3) act non-aggressively, to prove that you are immune to the effects of

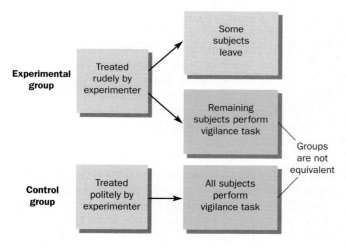

Figure 2.2 A possible problem with the anger and concentration experiment: loss of subjects from the experimental group.

objects associated with violence. The results of this study may not show the effects of the presence of weapons on aggression but, rather, show the relative numbers of people who select strategy 1, 2 or 3 in response to the knowledge that they are being observed.

Experimenters must always remember that their participants do not merely react to the independent variable in a simple-minded way. As Chapters 15 and 16 show, these considerations are especially important in social psychology experiments. In some of these studies, the experimenter or the experimenter's assistants act out roles designed to provide a particular kind of social situation to which the participants are exposed. Obviously, the participants' interpretation of these situations affects their behaviour.

Single-blind experiments

A special problem is posed by experiments in which participants' behaviour might be affected by their knowledge of the independent variable. Two methods of circumventing this problem are single- and double-blind experiments. For example, suppose that we want to study the effects of a stimulant drug, such as amphetamine, on a person's ability to perform a task that requires fine manual dexterity. We will administer the drug to one group of participants and leave another group untreated. We will count how many times each participant can thread a needle in a 10-minute period (our operational definition of fine manual dexterity). We will then see whether taking the drug had any effect on the number of needle threadings.

But there is a problem in our design. For us to conclude that a cause-and-effect relation exists, the treatment of the two groups must be identical except for the single variable that is being manipulated. In this case the mere administration of a drug may have effects on behaviour, independent of its pharmacological effects. The behaviour of participants who know that they have just taken amphetamine is very likely to be affected by this knowledge as well as by the drug circulating in their bloodstream. To solve this problem, we should give pills to the members of both groups. People in one group will receive amphetamine, and those in the other group will receive an inert pill – **a placebo**, from the Latin *placere*, 'to please'. A physician sometimes gives a placebo to anxious patients to placate them. Participants will not be told which pill they receive. By using this improved experimental procedure called a **single-blind study**, we can infer that any observed differences in needle-threading ability of the two groups were produced solely by the pharmacological effects of amphetamine. The placebo effect is a strong one – brain imaging studies have found that when people are given a placebo 'treatment' for pain, there is a reduction in the activation of brain areas involved in pain (Wager *et al.*, 2004).

Double-blind experiments

In a single-blind experiment, only the participants are kept ignorant of their assignment to a particular experimental group; the experimenter knows which treatment each participant receives. Now let us look at an example in which it is important to keep both the experimenter and the participants in the dark. Suppose we believe that if patients with mental disorders take a particular drug, they will be more willing to engage in conversation. The drug is given to some patients and a placebo is administered to others. We talk with all the patients afterwards and rate the quality of the conversation. But 'quality of conversation' is a difficult dependent variable to measure, and the rating is therefore likely to be subjective. The fact that the experimenters know which patients received the drug means that we may tend to give higher ratings to the quality of conversation with those patients. Of course, we would not intentionally cheat, but even honest people tend to perceive results in a way that favours their own preconceptions.

The solution to this problem is simple. Just as the patients should not know whether they are receiving a drug or a placebo, neither should the experimenter. That is, we should carry out a **double-blind study**. Someone else should administer the pill, or the experimenter should be given a set of identical-looking pills in coded containers so that both experimenter and patient are unaware of the nature of the contents. Now the ratings cannot be affected by any preconceived ideas the experimenter may have. The double-blind procedure does not apply only to experiments that use drugs as the independent variable. Suppose that the experiment just described attempted to evaluate the effects of a particular kind of psychotherapy, not a drug, on the willingness of a patient to talk. If the same person does both the psychotherapy and the rating, that person might tend to see the results in a light that is most favourable to their own expectations. In this case, then, one person should perform the psychotherapy and another person should evaluate the quality of conversation with the patients. The evaluator will not know whether a particular patient has just received psychotherapy or is a member of the control (untreated) group.

The expectations of experimenters can influence results in studies with laboratory animals as much as in studies with human participants. Rosenthal and Fode (1963) demonstrated the influence of expectations by having students train rats to learn the way through a maze. They told half the students that they had 'stupid' rats and the other half that they had 'smart' rats. In fact, there were no differences in the animals' abilities. However, an analysis of the results indicated that the 'smart' animals learned faster than the 'stupid' ones. The students' expectations clearly affected their rats' performances.

Presumably, the students who had 'smart' rats took better care of them, which affected the animals' performances.

Correlational studies

To be certain that a cause-and-effect relation exists, we must perform an experiment in which we manipulate the independent variable and measure its effects on the dependent variable. But there are some variables, especially participant variables, that a psychologist cannot manipulate. For example, a person's sex, genetic history, income, social class, family environment and personality are obviously not under the psychologist's control. Nevertheless, these variables are important and interesting because they often affect people's behaviour. Because they cannot be manipulated, they cannot be investigated in an experiment. A different method must, therefore, be used to study them: a correlational study.

The basic principle of a correlational study is simple: for each member of a group of people we measure two or more variables as they are found to exist, and we determine whether the variables are related by using a statistical procedure called correlation. Correlational studies are often done to investigate the effects of personality variables on behaviour. For example, we may ask whether shyness is related to daydreaming. Our hypothesis is that shy people tend to daydream more than people who are less shy. We decide how to assess a person's shyness and the amount of daydreaming that they engage in each day, and we then take the measure of these two variables for a group of people. If shy people tend to daydream more (or less) than people who are not shy, we can conclude that the variables are related.

Imagine that we do find that shy people spend more time daydreaming. Such a finding tells us that the variables are related – we say they are correlated – but it does not permit us to make any conclusions about cause and effect. Shyness may have caused the daydreaming, or daydreaming may have caused the shyness, or perhaps some other variable that we did not measure caused both shyness and an increase in daydreaming. In other words, correlations do not necessarily indicate cause-and-effect relations.

A good illustration of this principle is provided by a correlational study that attempted to determine whether membership in the boy scouts would affect a person's subsequent participation in community affairs (Chapin, 1938). The investigator compared a group of men who had once been boy scouts with a group of men who had not. He found that the men who had been boy scouts tended to join more community affairs groups later in life. The investigator concluded that the experience of being a boy scout increased a person's tendency to join community organisations. However, this conclusion is not warranted. Can you see why? All we can say is that people who join the boy scouts in their youth tend to join community organisations later in life. It could be that people who, for one reason or another, are 'joiners' tend to join the boy scouts when they are young and community organisations when they are older. To determine cause and effect, we would have to perform an experiment. For example, we would make some boys join the boy scouts and prevent others from doing so, and then see how many organisations they voluntarily joined later in life. Because we cannot interfere in people's lives in such a way, we can never be certain that being a boy scout increases a person's tendency to join community organisations later.

The news media often report the results of correlational studies. We are led to believe that because two variables are correlated, one event causes another. But this conclusion may not be true. For example, a news magazine reported a study in which small companies that make heavy use of computers were found to have productivity levels 2.5 times greater than companies that did not. Can we conclude that the heavy use of computers is the cause of the increased productivity? No, we cannot; correlation does not prove causation. Is it likely that the two types of small company (those that make heavy use of computers and those that do not) are identical in all other ways? Probably not. For example, companies that make heavy use of computers can afford to do so, and they can probably afford to make other investments that might increase productivity. In addition, these companies may also have managers who are up to date in other respects, and having modern ideas about other aspects of running a company may also improve productivity. The use of computers may indeed increase productivity, but the information presented does not permit us to come to this conclusion.

Can anything be done to reduce some of the uncertainty inherent in correlational studies? The answer is yes. When attempting to study the effects of a variable that cannot be altered (such as sex, age, socio-economic status or personality characteristics) we can use a procedure called **matching**. Rather than selecting participants randomly, we match the participants in each of the groups on all of the relevant variables except the one being studied. For instance, if we want to study the effects of shyness on daydreaming, we may gather two groups of participants, shy and non-shy. We select the participants in each group in such a way that the effects of other variables are minimised. We make sure that the average age, intelligence, income and personality characteristics (other than shyness) of the two groups are the same. If we find that, for example, the shy group is, on average, younger than the non-shy group, we will replace some of the people in the shy group with older shy people until the average age is the same.

If, after following this matching procedure, we find that shyness is still related to daydreaming, we can be more confident that the relation is one of cause and effect and that the differences between the two variables are not caused by a third variable. The limitation of the matching procedure is that we may not know all the variables that should be held constant. If, unknown to us, the two groups are not matched on an important variable, then the results will be misleading. In any case, even the matching procedure does not permit us to decide which variable is the cause and which is the effect; we still do not know whether shyness causes daydreaming or daydreaming causes shyness.

The strengths and limitations of correlational studies will become evident in subsequent chapters in this book. For example, almost all studies that attempt to discover the environmental factors that influence personality characteristics or the relation between these characteristics and people's behaviour are correlational.

Single-case studies

Not all investigations in psychology use groups of participants. **Single-case study research** explores the behaviour of individuals, and for some phenomena this method is very effective. Single-case study research can involve either experiments or correlational studies. Ebbinghaus's studies of memory, for example, were based on studies of individuals (usually, Ebbinghaus himself). Similarly, much of B.F. Skinner's work was based on small numbers of participants.

In a single-case study, psychologists can take advantage of events that have occurred outside their control and the most common of these are found in the field of neuropsychology. For example, a patient known as HJA was a businessman who had suffered a stroke and had consequently sustained damage to specific regions of his brain. HJA's behaviour after the damage was perceptually unusual. Although some aspects of his visual perception were preserved, he would have difficulty in recognising objects. For example, he would spend up to six hours making painstaking drawings of objects which he would be unable to name (Humphreys and Riddoch, 1987a, b). This is a disorder called **visual agnosia**, a specific deficit in the ability to perceive objects, described in more detail in Chapter 6. By conducting single-case studies of patients like HJA, psychologists can explore the behavioural consequences of unusual events or actions that the patient has suffered.

Single-case studies have contributed substantially to our knowledge of neuropsychology, the study of the relationship between the activity of the brain and its function, although this method has been criticised. For example, there is frequently no way of knowing for certain how an individual behaved before the accident; there is no control over the degree and type of injury; and there is the possibility that personal characteristics (such as medication use, sex, age, socio-economic status, IQ) could influence results (Shallice, 1988; Martin, 2006).

The single-participant research design (SPRD) does have advantages, however. One is that by continuously studying a participant over an extended period, we can be sure that the sample of behaviour that is measured is representative of the participant's typical behaviour. This also allows for easy replication although there are some studies which cannot be properly replicated – a learning intervention, for example, cannot be easily unlearned. The SPRD approach allows us to see the natural variability in the participant's behaviour – marked changes in behaviour that are not attributable to experimental manipulation. SPRDs also involve participants as their own controls, thereby reducing the individual difference that could account for differences between (and within) large groups.

Generalising from data

When we carry out an experiment or a correlational study, we probably assume that our participants are representative of the larger population. In fact, a representative group of participants is usually referred to as a **sample** of the larger population. If we study the behaviour of a group of 5-year-old children, we want to make conclusions about 5-year-olds in general. We want to be able to **generalise** our specific results to the population as a whole – to conclude that the results tell us something about human nature in general, not simply about our participants.

Many researchers recruit their participants from introductory courses in psychology because this is a convenient way of obtaining participants. The results of studies that use these students as participants can be generalised only to other groups of students who are similarly recruited. In the strictest sense, the results cannot be generalised to students in other courses, to adults in general, or even to all students enrolled in introductory psychology – after all, students who volunteer to serve as participants may be different from those who do not. Even if we used truly random samples of all age groups of adults in our area, we could not generalise the results to people who live in other geographical regions. If our ability to generalise is really so limited, is it worthwhile doing psychological research?

In reality we are not so strictly limited. Most psychologists assume that a relation among variables that is observed in one group of humans will also be seen in other groups as long as the sample of participants is not especially unusual. For example, we may expect data obtained from prisoners to have less generality than data obtained from college students.

Application of psychological research

There is sometimes a distinction made in the sciences between applied and pure aspects of research. Pure research is research carried out for its own ends; the implications or consequences of such research are not known but it is designed simply to find out how something works or behaves (or does not). Applied research, on the other hand, is designed to have a practical application. Often in psychology (as in most other sciences), this dichotomy is false. Pure research can often have surprising practical applications: it depends on how creative the scientist is in finding such applications. Throughout this book, you will find examples of research that seems to fall into these categories. When you do, reflect on what you have read and try to see the point of having conducted that piece of research. The Psychology in Action sections in this book show how dry, academic, laboratory-based research can tell us much about how we behave 'outside' the laboratory. Should psychological research always have a practical outcome?

Qualitative analysis

The majority of research undertaken in psychology is empirical and quantitative. Another approach relies less on these types of data. Some researchers have argued that traditional quantitative techniques do not allow psychologists to explore the richness of human experience, feeling, thought and social interaction. They suggest that this richness is better measured by paying close attention to the ways in which people use words, express feelings and arguments and by allowing individuals to explore ideas in discussion. Themes and ideas can then be interpreted from transcripts of these discussions. This approach is called **qualitative analysis** and is concerned with 'meanings, context and a holistic approach to material' (Hayes, 1997). It is more popular in European research centres than in North America. The BPS's Qualitative Methods Section was formed in 2006, for example, but a proposal for a new Division of Qualitative Inquiry was rejected by the American Psychological Association in 2008.

This approach is called phenomenological because the experience, reactions and feelings of the individual are considered to be of paramount importance. Originally, qualitative analysis emerged as a new paradigm in the 1970s called ethogenics which sought to provide a better method of investigation in psychology (Harré and Secord, 1972). The new approach placed great emphasis on people's use of language, especially the ways in which people accounted for their behaviour, thoughts and feelings: to understand real psychology meant analysing real talk (Foster and Parker, 1995) and this talk is, itself, 'action'; we use words to convey some action (blame, sorrow, anger, etc.). The approach has been used to study the impact of a child's serious illness on the family (Hopi *et al.*, 2005), how dietary regimes are viewed in people with type 2 diabetes (Peel *et al.*, 2005), and how doctor and patient interact with each other (McCabe *et al.*, 2002).

The emphasis in the qualitative approach is not on quantifying data (in many cases this is actively discouraged) but in exploring the quality of data in depth. Some qualitative analysts have insisted that this form of analysis should not involve any numbers or counting at all (Strauss and Corbin, 1990), although this strict criterion is not often adhered to. Many qualitative analyses draw attention to concepts involving quantity such as frequency of utterances. Another important distinction between qualitative and quantitative analysis is that the former views the researcher as being central to the analysis and the process of data collection: they may participate in or facilitate discussion and will analyse the data obtained from their research. The interpretation of the data is also undertaken by the researcher/interviewer.

The data for qualitative analysis usually come from group discussions or interviews and there are various methods for conducting qualitative analysis. Some of these are outlined below.

Structured and semi-structured interviews

Using the format of an interview to obtain information in psychology is not unusual. Many neuropsychological tests are administered by experimenters in an interview-type context. When such tests are administered, the researcher keeps to a strict 'script' in order to avoid influencing the performance of the respondent. In a sense, this is something like the format of a structured interview. The **structured interview** is conducted along predefined and predetermined lines with little scope for deviation from a script. The experimenter decides what they want to explore, with little variation between interviews. Many structured interviews may comprise an interviewer reading questions from a questionnaire and soliciting responses from an interviewee.

Sometimes, however, it may be interesting and informative to explore interviewees' responses more deeply while keeping to some overall plan or structure. Semi-structured interviews provide such a possibility. The **semi-structured interview** allows the establishment of rapport with the interviewee by placing less emphasis on the order of questions, where the interviewer is free to develop themes and issues raised by the interviewee and where open-ended questions are used. For example, whereas a structured interview might ask, 'Do you think that racism is caused by a, b, c or d?', a semi-structured interview might ask, 'What do you think are the causes of racism?' It is suggested that funnelling is a useful approach to semi-structured interviews: the interviewer elicits a general opinion and then probes more specific issues relating to this general view.

The semi-structured interview has proved to be useful to some qualitative analysts. Others, however, would argue that even a semi-structured format is too restrictive and that in order to elicit and understand genuine thoughts and feelings, you must allow discussion to occur freely (Hammersley, 2008). Such an approach is taken by discourse analysis.

Discourse analysis

Discourse analysis is a method which was developed in the mid-1980s to identify thoughts, feelings and themes from transcripts of data derived from conversations involving two or more individuals. Discourse analysis examines what people do with conversation and writing (Potter and Wetherell, 1995). Discourses themselves are linguistic repertoires (Potter and Wetherell, 1987) which vary according to context. The most detailed analysis of discourses would examine the use of sound and verbal devices in conversation as well as mechanisms of persuasion and argument (Edwards and Potter, 1992).

Discourse analysis places importance on the use of language and what people mean when they express themselves verbally (Billig, 1997). Such speech acts could be complicated and would require careful analysis in order to discover what was meant. Discourse analysis does not assume that attitudes are stable; in fact, it assumes that 'giving views' is relatively unstable and that a person can give one view to one person and a contrary view to another: context, therefore, is important to the interpretation of attitude. A teenage girl's attitudes towards social issues might be expressed differently to a parent and to a member of her peer group, for example (Billig, 1997). In Table 2.2, Billig outlines the typical discourse analysis which could be performed on these transcripts.

Transcripts should be read and reread; the analyst should begin to develop 'hunches' or intuitive understanding and they should, after rereading, create index categories of themes and major issues and of conversational details such as interruption or non-verbal agreement.

Conversation analysis

As the name suggests, **conversation analysis** involves the analysis of the content and use of conversation. The

---

Table 2.2 Suggested procedure for qualitative analysis

- Read background material about discursive psychology and topic of interest
- Decide on type of data to be studied
- Collect data
- Collect, listen to and transcribe tape-recordings
- Check the transcriptions against the tapes
- Read transcriptions
- Look for interesting features and develop 'intuitive hunches'
- Begin indexing themes and discursive features
- Write preliminary analysis, testing 'hunches' against data
- Draft and redraft analyses, making note of counter examples

Source: Adapted from M. Billig, Rhetorical and discursive analysis. In N. Hayes (ed.) *Doing Qualitative Analysis in Psychology*. Hove: Psychology Press, 1997. © 1997. Reprinted by permission of Psychology Press Limited, Hove, UK.

---

assumption behind conversational analysis (CA) is that talk is action and that it is structurally organised. The focus is less on the content of the talk but on what people do with it – complaining, complementing, news-telling, turn-taking, and so on (Wilkinson and Kitzinger, 2008). Data are collected in 'naturalistic' environments – the researcher is not present and the participant is audio- or video-recorded. These data take the form of transcripts, complete with inbreaths, sound stretches, pauses and other example of oral punctuation. An example of how CA has been used to analyse how people use talk is seen in Table 2.3. This is a transcript of an exchange between two friends, Belle and Fanny, one of whom (Belle) has some bad news to break. Take a look at this exchange before reading on. Did you notice something unusual in the conversation? Although it was Belle who had bad news to break, it was Fanny who 'announced' the news. CA has revealed that we often do this – the recipient of bad news tends to be the one who raises the matter of bad news, whether it is a cancelled trip or a medical diagnosis (Drew, 1984; Maynard, 1992). In another example of the use of CA, Clayman and Heritage (2002) analysed 4,000 questions asked by journalists in US Presidential Conferences from 1950 to 2000, and found that the questions became less deferential and more combative over time.

Grounded theory

Grounded theory was one of the earliest attempts at qualitative analysis and involves establishing a set of strategies for the analysis of data and the construction of theory (Glaser and Strauss, 1967; Charmaz and Henwood, 2008). Individual cases, incidents or experiences are analysed and theories are derived from such analysis (Charmaz, 1990). Unlike discourse analysis, grounded theory actively attempts to develop theory from information obtained

Table 2.3 The format in which conversation is transcribed in conversation analysis. The first extract shows you a conversation between two friends, one of whom had bad news to break. The second is an exchange between a doctor and a patient which, again, involves the breaking of unwelcome news.

```
Extract 1
(DA: 2 : 10.  from Schegloff (1988: 443)
The audio file for this data
extract can be accessed at:
<http://www.sscnet. ucla.edu/soc/
faculty/schegloff/RealSoundFiles/
Servo-Mechanism/page443.ram>}
01 Bel: ...  I,  I-I had something
02      (.) terrible t'tell you.=
03      =So {uh:  }
04 Fan:    {How t}errible {is it.}
05 Bel:                    {.hhhhh}
06      (.)
07 Bel: Uh: en worse it could be:.
08      (0.7)
09 Fan: W'y'mean 1da?
10      (.)
11 missing line from photocopy
12 Fan: Wud she do die:?=
13 Bel: = Mm:hm.

Extract 2
(8.013), from Maynard (1992: 337-8)
01 Dr: What do you see? as- as his
02     (0.5) difficulty.
03     (1.2)
04 Mo: Mainly his uhm: (1.2) the
05     fact that he doesn't
06     understand everything.
07     (0.6) and also the fact
08     that his speech (0.7) is
09     very hard to understand
10     what he's saying (0.3)
11     lot{s of ti}me
12 Dr:     { right }
13     (0.2)
14 Dr: Do you have any ideas wh:y it
15     is: are you: d}o yo}u?h
16 Mo:              { No }
17     (2.1)
18 Dr: .h okay I (0.2) you know I
19     think we basically (.) in
20     some ways agree with you:
21     (0.6) .hh insofar as we think
22     that (0.3) Dan's main problem
23     (0.4) .h you know does:
24     involves you know language.
26 Mo: Mm hmm
27     (0.3)
28 Dr: you know both (0.2) you know
29     his- (0.4) being able to
30     understand you know what is
31     said to him (0.4) .h and
32     also certainly also to be
33     able to express:: (1.3) you
34     know his uh his thoughts
35     (1.1)
36 Dr: .hh uh:m (0.6) .hhh in
37     general his development...
```

Source: Wilkinson, S. and Kitzinger, C. (2008) Conversation analysis. In C. Willig and W. Stainton-Rogers (eds) *The Sage Handbook of Qualitative Research in Psychology*. London: Sage.

from transcripts of conversations. Theorising is made possible by painstaking line-by-line coding of transcripts, by memo-taking and by constructing categories (themes/patterns) from responses. The theory is therefore grounded in what the respondents have had to say. An example of the approach would be the exploration of the loss of self/the expression of self in patients who have suffered traumatic brain injury (Nochi, 1998).

Q methodology

One of the more complex of the qualitative techniques, Q methodology is also one of the most numerical and was first developed in the 1930s. It has been described as the systematic study of subjectivity and used to 'explore the subjective dimension of any issue towards which different points of view can be expressed' (Stenner *et al.*, 2008, p. 215). In this approach, data are collected in the form of Q-sorts: a collection of statements with which a participant agrees, disagrees or has no opinion about. A researcher might start with a clear question, such as 'What is your understanding of qualitative research?' and a number of items that represent this issue are devised (say around 100) and are given to students, qualitative practitioners and so on who sort them according to level of dis/agreement. A reduced number of around 60 will then be given to participants and each is rated on a 13-point scale for dis/agreement. The unique feature of Q methodology is that the person becomes the variable. Q methodology has been used in a number of contexts. One study found that the greater the disagreement about the causes of irritable bowel syndrome between the doctors and patients, the greater the patient's antagonism; the greater the agreement, the more positive the relationship (Stenner *et al.*, 2000).

Limitations of qualitative analysis

Qualitative analysis, although not widely used, has become a popular research tool in many areas of psychology where analysis can be used to explore issues such as attitudes to death, racism, the monarchy, sexual identity, chronic illness, work relationships and so on. Currently, qualitative analysis has had little impact outside these areas because of several perceived shortcomings. The most obvious, and difficult to reject, is that the process of qualitative analysis is subjective: the selection, analysis and interpretation of the material is made by the analyst. This introduces an element of bias into the study which could cloud an 'objective' analysis of the data. This argument is difficult to challenge effectively, although Hayes (1997) has suggested a 'halfway house' solution whereby a theory determined prior to the study may be used to guide later analysis. In this way, the study has a pre-stated focus and direction but it also allows for unpredicted insights.

Hammersley (1992) has identified several examples of the perceived differences between qualitative and quantitative analysis. For example, it is assumed that the types of data analysed by the two methods are totally different; the environments in which studies take place are different; one focuses on meaning (qualitative), the other on behaviour; quantitative methods adopt natural science as a model whereas qualitative analysis rejects it; one is inductive, the other deductive; one seeks patterns, the other seeks laws and so on. Hayes (1997) has given an excellent account of how this dichotomy may be more imagined than real. For example, she argues that qualitative researchers do sometimes use measures of quantity and that quantitative methods are often applied in naturalistic settings. Qualitative analysts do use conversational analysis to study behaviour as well as meaning. Furthermore, the rejection of the natural science model assumes that all of the natural sciences adopt the same experimental approach. Of course, they do not. Hayes, therefore, argues that the dichotomy between the two types of research methods is not as great as it would appear. If you were to set up a study in which you wanted to explore people's attitudes to animal experimentation, say, which approach – qualitative or quantitative – would you think is best?

Ethics

Because psychologists must study living participants, they must obey ethical rules as well as scientific rules. Great care is needed in the treatment of human participants because we can hurt people in very subtle ways. The rules that govern psychologists' conduct during experiments have been set by governments, institutions or professional societies and all psychologists engaged in research must abide by them.

Research with human participants

In Europe, North America and elsewhere, research undertaken by hospitals and universities will have been vetted by an ethics committee, which decides on whether the proposed research meets the institution's ethical criteria regarding the welfare of human and animal participants in scientific research. Various professional societies such as the British Psychological Society (2006) and American Psychological Association (2002) issue guidelines for the treatment of humans and animals participating in research. In some countries, data may also fall within the remit of a data protection Act which, in its most general

form, allows an individual access to any information held electronically about them and, in research, allows the participant control over the use of such material.

The BPS lists a number of recommendations which its members should follow (British Psychological Society, 2006). These recommendations fall into the general categories of consent, deception, debriefing, withdrawal, confidentiality and protection of participants.

In general terms, a psychologist must treat participants with respect and must have taken all conceivable and practicable precautions to ensure that participants are not harmed. Threats to health, well-being, values and dignity should be eliminated.

Informed consent

An important part of any procedure designed to ensure the proper treatment of participants is informed consent. When possible, a psychologist should always inform the participant of the nature of the experiment and, having been told the detail of this research, the participant – if willing – will consent to take part. This represents **informed consent**. Of course, it is not always possible to secure informed consent because divulging all aspects of the experiment will influence the decisions, thoughts, feelings and behaviours of the participant. This is considered in more detail in the section on deception.

Usually, the potential participant reads a written statement prepared by the researcher. This discloses aspects of the research that might affect a person's willingness to participate in the study. The informed consent statement constitutes a contract between participant and researcher and is normally signed by both of them. Examples of these appear in Figure 2.3.

If participants are children, informed consent should be obtained from parents or guardians. The issue of child participation in research is an interesting one because, as you will see in Chapter 12, a child begins to grasp concepts and understand abstract ideas at certain periods in its development. This is the principal reason why parents or guardians consent to their children's participation on their behalf. A study from the University of Texas suggests that this is sensible because children often do not understand the purpose of an experiment or may not understand what confidentiality of a person's data means (Hurley and Underwood, 2002). Although the children understand some aspects better than others, they may continue to extend their trust to the experimenter.

As with healthy, normally developing child participants, if a child or an adult participant is mentally ill, is unable to communicate or is mentally retarded, then a parent, healthcare worker or guardian should be informed and consent obtained from disinterested independent advisers.

Attitudes of Mental Illness Study
Informed Consent Form

Please read the following information carefully and before you sign this form please ask questions you may have about the 'attitudes to mental illness'study and your participation in it.

In this study you will be asked to rate your agreement/disagreement with a series of statements about mental illness, along a 7-point scale with 1 representing strong agreement and 7 representing strong disagreement. For example, if you strongly agreed with the statement 'I think that all mental illness is biological in origin', you would circle '1'. The study will take approximately 30 minutes to complete.

I fully understand the nature of the 'attitudes to mental illness study', that my participation is voluntary and that at any time I can terminate my participation without penalty. I am also aware that all my personal details and any information gathered about me will be kept confidential and will not be used for any purpose that is unrelated to the study. I understand that my data may be used to conduct analysis that may later be used for publication but that I will not be personally identifiable from these data

Signed _____ Date _____ (participant)

Figure 2.3 (a) An example of a consent form used in research.

HIGHFLYER UNIVERSITY
DEPARTMENT OF PSYCHOLOGY
Psychology of Learning Experiment

I confirm that I give my full and informed consent to participate in the above experiment. I understand that the information I provide will remain anonymous and disguised so that I may not be identified. I therefore give my permission for the results of this study to be published.

(a) I understand that as part of this study I will be required to learn the works of Shakespeare.
(b) I have been informed that the general aim of the study is to investigate learning strategies.
(c) I have been informed that my general participation in this study will not involve unexpected discomforts or risks.
(d) I have been informed that there are no disguised procedures in this experiment. The instructions can be taken at face value.
(e) I understand that the experimenter will answer any questions that I have regarding the study once I have participated.
(f) I understand that I am free to withdraw from the study at any time without penalty.

Concerns about the study may be directed to the Chair of the Ethics Committee, School of Psychology, HighFlyer University

Experimenter _____ Date _____

Participant _____ Date _____

Figure 2.3 (b) A second example, suggested by R.J. Sternberg (1988a).

If a researcher is undertaking observational research then the privacy and psychological well-being of the participant must be accounted for. Unless consent to being observed is obtained, participants should normally be observed only under conditions where they would expect to be observed by strangers.

Deception

Psychologists are advised never to withhold information or mislead participants if an individual is likely to be uneasy when eventually told the purpose of the experiment. Sometimes, however, withholding information or using misleading information is necessary for good scientific reasons. When this occurs, it must be undertaken after obtaining the sound advice and approval of an ethics committee and colleagues.

Debriefing

When participants take part in an experiment, the experimenter is obliged to disclose to the participant the real and actual nature of the experiment and to answer any questions that the participant may ask about the experiment. This is called **debriefing**.

Withdrawal

If a participant feels that they have been unfairly misled or improperly treated, the participant has the absolute right to withdraw from the experiment. In fact, it should be made clear to all participants from the outset of the experiment that they are free to withdraw at any time, for whatever reason. The participant has the right to withdraw consent following the experiment or debriefing and request that their data be discarded or destroyed, or both.

Confidentiality

Laws of the land notwithstanding, information and data provided by the participant in research are confidential. If data are published then those of individuals should not be identifiable, unless consent has been obtained.

Protection of participants

Tied to the recommendations concerning consent and deception are those governing the protection of the partici-pant, which are very similar. Psychologists have a primary responsibility to their participants to avoid harm (physical or mental) and if harm is identified, to remove it.

Controversies in Psychological Science – Can research with animals help us to understand human behaviour?

The issue

Although most psychologists study the behaviour of humans, some study the behaviour of other animals. When we use another species of animal for our own purposes, we should be sure that what we are doing is both humane and worthwhile. Evidence suggests that whereas students regard the use of animals in medical testing as being warranted, they are less likely to agree that animals should be used in psychological experiments (Furnham and Heyes, 1993). Can animal research in psychology, therefore, be humane and worthwhile?

The evidence

Humane treatment is a matter of procedure. We know how to maintain laboratory animals in good health in comfortable, sanitary conditions. For experiments that involve surgery, we know how to administer anaesthetics and analgesics so that animals do not suffer. Most industrially developed societies have strict regulations about the care of animals and require approval of the procedures that will be used in the experi-ments in which they participate. There is no excuse for mistreating animals in our care. In fact, the vast majority of laboratory animals are treated humanely because government departments ensure it.

Whether an experiment is worthwhile is more difficult to say. We use animals for many purposes. We eat their meat and their eggs and drink their milk; we turn their hides into leather; we extract insulin and other hormones from their organs to treat people with diseases; we train them to do useful work on farms or to entertain us. These are all forms of exploitation. Even having a pet is a form of exploitation: it is we – not they – who decide that they will live in our homes. The fact is, we have been using other animals throughout the history of our species.

Pet-owning causes much more suffering among animals than scientific research does. As Miller (1983) notes, pet owners are not required to receive permission to house their pets from boards of experts that include veterinarians, nor are they subject to periodic inspections to ensure that their homes are clean and sanitary, that their pets have enough space to exercise, and that their diets are appropriate. Scientific researchers are. Miller also notes that 50 times more dogs and cats are killed by humane societies each year because they have been abandoned by their former owners than are used in scientific research.

The use of animals in research and teaching is a special target of animal rights activists. Nicholl and Russell (1990) examined 21 books written by activists and calculated the number of pages devoted to concern for different uses of ani-mals. Next, they compared the relative concern the authors showed for these uses to the numbers of animals involved in each of these categories. The authors showed relatively little concern for animals used for food, hunting or furs or for those killed in pounds. However, although only 0.3 per cent of the animals were used for research and education, 63.3 per cent of the pages were devoted to this use. In terms of pages per million animals used, the authors showed 665 times more concern for research and education than for food and 231 times more than for hunting. Even the use of animals for furs (which consumes two-thirds as many animals as research and education) attracted 41.9 times less attention per animal.

Conclusion

Our species is beset by medical, mental and behavioural prob-lems, many of which can be solved only through research involving animals. In fact, research with laboratory animals has produced important discoveries about the possible causes or potential treatments of neurological and mental dis-orders, including Parkinson's disease, schizophrenia, manic-depressive illness, anxiety disorders, obsessive-compulsive disorders, anorexia nervosa, obesity and drug addictions. Although much progress has been made, these problems are still with us and cause much human suffering. Unless we continue our research with laboratory animals, these problems will not be solved. Some people have sug-gested that instead of using laboratory animals in our research, we could use tissue cultures or computer simula-tions. Unfortunately, tissue cultures or computer simulations are not substitutes for living organisms. We have no way to study behavioural problems such as addictions in tissue cul-tures, nor can we program a computer to simulate the workings of an animal's nervous system. If we could, we would already have all the answers.

Chapter review

The scientific method in psychology

- The scientific method allows us to determine the causes of natural phenomena.
- There are three basic forms of scientific research: naturalistic observations, experiments and correlational studies.
- Hypotheses are statements or predictions made on the basis of naturalistic observations, previous experiments or from formal theories.
- Psychologists might conduct experiments in which groups are independent of each other, the individuals in one group are not the same as those in the other (independent groups design); or experiments in which the same individuals take part in all conditions of the experiment (repeated measures design).
- An independent variable is an event, factor or action that is manipulated by the experimenter; the dependent variable is the quantity measured in an experiment (and is hypothesised to be influenced by the independent variable). To perform an experiment, a scientist alters the value of the independent variable and measures changes in the dependent variable.
- A psychologist must specify the particular operations that they will perform to manipulate the independent variable and to measure the dependent variable.
- Operational definitions are a necessary part of the procedure by which a hypothesis is tested; they can also eliminate confusion by giving concrete form to the hypothesis, making its meaning absolutely clear to other scientists.
- Validity is the degree to which an operational definition produces a particular value of an independent variable or measures the value of a dependent variable.
- Reliability refers to the consistency and precision of an operational definition.
- Researchers achieve high reliability by carefully controlling the conditions of their studies and by ensuring that procedures are followed correctly. Measurement involving subjectivity requires researchers to seek high interrater reliability.
- When designing an experiment, experimenters ensure that they control extraneous variables that may confound their results. If an extra variable is inadvertently manipulated and if this extra variable has an effect on the dependent variable, then the results of the experiment will be invalid. Confounding of subject variables can be caused by improperly assigning participants to groups or by treatments that cause some participants to leave the experiment.
- Most participants in psychological research try to guess what the experimenter is trying to accomplish, and their conclusions can affect their behaviour. If knowledge of the experimental condition could alter the participants' behaviour, the experiment should be conducted with a single-blind procedure (where the participant is unaware of the condition they are in). If that knowledge might also alter the experimenter's assessment of the participants' behaviour, a double-blind procedure should be used (where the participant and experimenter are unaware of the condition that the participant is in).
- Correlational studies involve assessing relations among variables that the researcher cannot readily manipulate, such as personality characteristics, age and sex. The investigator attempts to hold these variables constant by matching members in each of the groups on all relevant variables except for the one being studied. Correlational studies cannot determine which variable is the cause and which is the effect.
- Single-subject research consists of the detailed observation of individual participants under different conditions. Case studies involve careful observations of the behaviour of specific people, such as those with psychological or neurological disorders.
- Researchers are seldom interested only in the particular participants they study; they want to be able to generalise their results to a larger population. The confidence that researchers can have in their generalisations depends on the nature of the variables being studied and on the composition of the sample group of participants.
- Qualitative analysis involves the examination of individuals' expression of ideas, thoughts and feelings and is usually based on transcripts of discussion between individuals or between the experimenter and an individual/individuals.

Ethics

- Because psychologists study living organisms, they must follow ethical principles in the treatment of their participants. Professional societies run by and for psychologists develop ethical guidelines that require informed consent, confidentiality and a post-experiment debriefing.
- Participants may withdraw their consent to participate at any time before or during an experiment without any penalty. If deception is necessary, the experimenter must be certain that the participants will not be harmed psychologically or physically and that their dignity will be maintained.
- Committees review all psychological research before giving their consent for it to be carried out to ensure that these guidelines are met.
- Research that involves the use of laboratory animals is also guided by ethical principles. It is incumbent on all scientists using these animals to see that they are housed comfortably and treated humanely, and laws have been enacted to ensure that they are. Such research has already produced many benefits to humankind and promises to continue to do so.

Suggestions for further reading

Research methods: general reading

There are many books about research methods, design and analysis available. Some of them you probably would not want to read – they aren't the most riveting reads – but they serve a purpose in explaining how to do things. The best of research methods books, however, manage to engage you in the process of finding out how people behave. Some of these include the following:

Bausell, R.B. (1993) *Conducting Meaningful Experiments: 40 steps to becoming a scientist*. London: Sage.

Bausell's short book is a very well-written, straightforward account of what you need to know and to do in order to become a scientist. It is laid out in the form of principles (40 of them) which the author describes, explains and illustrates.

Foster, J.J. and Parker, I. (1995) *Carrying Out Investigations in Psychology*. Leicester: BPS Books.

Another text which approaches research methods from the psychologist's perspective and considers aspects of design not considered in more quantitative texts.

Robson, C. (2002) *Real World Research* (2nd edn). Oxford: Blackwell.

Robson's excellent, well-written book delivers a comprehensive account of how to conduct 'difficult' research (i.e. out of the laboratory).

Solso, R.L., Johnson, H.H. and Beal, M.K. (1998) *Experimental Psychology* (6th edn). Harlow: Longman.

Solso et al.'s text provides a lot of very useful information about tracking down materials and writing up research as well as analysing some real, published research section by section.

Critical thinking

Gabennesch, H. (2006) Critical thinking: What is it good for? *Skeptical Inquirer*, 30, 2, 36–41.

Martin, G. N. (2009) *Research and Study Update for Psychology* (3rd edn). Harlow: Pearson Education.

Matthies, B. (2005) The psychologist, the philosopher, and the librarian: The information-literacy version of CRITIC. *Skeptical Inquirer*, May/June, 49–52.

Meltzoff, J. (1998) *Critical Thinking about Research: Psychology and related fields*. Washington, DC: American Psychological Association.

Melzoff's is an extraordinary book because instead of analysing real research articles for quality, the author has composed several fictitious ones to highlight flaws in the ways in which studies are conducted, analysed and reported. The first half of the book is an excellent introduction to research methods; the second half consists of the research articles with a critical analysis of each. Superb for helping you develop critical thinking skills. The papers by Matthies and Gabennesch give some sound advice on critical thinking, as does the Martin title.

Qualitative research

Smith, J.A. (2008) *Qualitative Psychology* (2nd edn). London: Sage.

Willig, C. and Stainton-Rogers, W. (2008) *The Sage Handbook of Qualitative Research in Psychology*. London: Sage.

Two relatively accessible texts on qualitative analysis.

Ethical issues in psychological testing

Francis, R.D. (2009) *Ethics for psychologists*. Oxford: Wiley-Blackwell

Gale, A. (1995) Ethical issues in psychological research. In A.M. Coleman (ed.), *Psychological Research Methods and Statistics*. London: Longman.

Hurley, J.C. and Underwood, M.K. (2002) Children's understanding of their research rights before and after debriefing: Informed assent, confidentiality and stopping participation. *Child Development*, 73, 132–43.

Lindsay, G. (1996) Psychology as an ethical discipline and profession. *European Psychologist*, 1, 2, 79–88.

Wilhelm, K. (2006) Do animals have feelings? *Scientific American Mind*, 17, 1, 24–9.

Gale's succinct chapter is a good introduction to ethics and psychological research. Lindsay's article considers the ethical basis for the development of 'ethical codes' in psychology (such as those adopted by the British, American and European psychologists' associations). Hurley and Underwood's paper considers the implications of child development for obtaining ethical consent and for testing with children.

Journals to consult

American Psychologist

Behavior Research, Instruments and Design

British Journal of Mathematical and Statistical Psychology

Current Directions in Psychological Science

Educational Measurement and Assessment

Neurocase

Psychological Bulletin

Psychological Methods

Skeptical Inquirer

Website addresses

http://www.apa.org/psycinfo/

http://wok.mimas.ac.uk/

http://www.ncbi.nlm.nih.gov/entrez/query.fcgi/

http://www.csa.com

http://cogprints.org/

http://www.psycline.org/journals/psycline.html
A collection of links to resources in psychology, especially journals. Web of Knowledge (the second link) is particularly good.

http://trochim.human.cornell.edu/tutorial/tutorial.htm

http://www.socialresearchmethods.net/

http://davidmlane.com/hyperstat/

http://glass.ed.asu.edu/stats/

http://spsp.clarion.edu/RDE3/start/
A collection of links to sites and papers on research methods and statistics tutorials, including some online texts in research methods.

http://www.psychology.org/links/Resources/Doing_Research/
A good site with links to sites featuring basic information about doing research.

http://psych.hanover.edu/research/exponnet.html
This is a link to an enormous collection of online psychology experiments. Many psychologists are now conducting international and cross-cultural experiments in this way.

http://psychexps.olemiss.edu/

http://epsych.msstate.edu/

http://kenstange.com/psycsite/
A few more links to online experiments and demonstrations in psychology.

http://www.psychology.org/links/Resources/Ethical_Issues/
An excellent collection of links to sites on the psychology and ethics.

http://www.badscience.net
Ben Goldacre's excellent debunking of pseudoscience and bad science reporting.

Evolution, genetics and behaviour

CHAPTER 3

Science finds the secret of a hot kiss

If you always thought you had a special chemistry with your loved one, you may finally have been proved right.

Researchers have found that a passionate kiss unleashes a complex surge into the brain which makes a lover feel excited, happy or relaxed.

There is also speculation that this hormone release may be triggered directly by an exchange of sexually stimulating pheromones in the saliva.

[The] research looked at the impact of kissing on levels of two hormones, oxytocin and cortisol, in 15 male–female couples before and after holding hands and before and after kissing.

Source: *The Sunday Times*, 8 February, 2009.

Explore the accompanying videos, simulations, and animations on MyPsychLab. This chapter includes activities on: Chromosomes • Dominant and recessive traits • Twin studies and adoption studies of heritability • The inheritance of Huntington's disease and Phenylketonuria • Check your understanding and prepare for your exams using the multiple choice, short answer and essay practice tests also available.

WHAT YOU SHOULD BE ABLE TO DO AFTER READING CHAPTER 3

- Describe Darwin's theory of evolution.
- Outline the principles of genetic inheritance.
- Evaluate the contribution of genetics to psychology.
- Describe and evaluate sociobiology and evolutionary psychology's contribution to our understanding of behaviour.
- Discuss some of the reasons why we are sexually attracted to certain body types.
- Describe the psychological and evolutionary significance of altruism.

QUESTIONS TO THINK ABOUT

- What do you think is meant by the term 'evolution of behaviour'?
- When did the modern human being evolve?
- What are the implications of the theory of evolution for psychology?
- How do you think the process of evolution could explain modern behaviour such as romantic attraction, jealousy, language and marriage?
- Are we attracted to certain body types? If so, why?
- Why do you think that we have become more intelligent and sophisticated than our ancestors?
- What do you understand by the terms 'genetics' and 'heredity'?
- Does culture or genetics have the greater influence on behaviour? Is the question an important one to ask?
- Are there any behaviours that can be unaffected by genetics?
- Why can we be altruistic and are we more altruistic to certain people than others?

The development of evolutionary theory

From my early youth I have had the strongest desire to understand and explain whatever I observed, that is, to group all facts under some general laws. . . Therefore, my success as a man of science, whatever this may have amounted to, has been determined, as far as I can judge, by complex and diversified mental qualities and conditions. Of these, the most important have been – the love of science – unbounded patience in long reflecting over any subject – industry in observing and collecting facts – and a fair share of invention and common sense. With such moderate abilities as I possess, it is truly surprising that I should have influenced to a considerable extent the belief of scientific men on some important points.

Source: Darwin, 1887, pp. 67–71.

These fairly humble words were written by a man who has influenced the course of scientific thought more than any other individual since Copernicus (who, in 1543, proposed that the sun, not the earth, was at the centre of the universe). Charles Darwin argued that, over time, organisms originate and become adapted to their environments by biological means. This concept is referred to as **biological evolution** – changes that take place in the genetic and physical characteristics of a population or group of organisms over time – and it stands as the primary explanation of the origin of life (Dawkins, 1986). The bicentenary of Darwin's birth was marked in 2009, together with the 150th anniversary of the publication of one of the most important books published in the past 300 years – *On the Origin of Species by Means of Natural Selection*. In this book, Darwin distilled his theory of evolution.

There is evidence of life on earth a billion years after the formation of the earth 4.5 billion years ago (Eiler, 2007) and the human race has existed, in various forms, for over 10 million years. This time-span has seen a tremendous change in our physical appearance, our biology and our behaviour. Our brains have developed, our societies have become more sophisticated, our intelligence has increased, our ability to communicate has improved, we have developed language systems. These processes illustrate the ways in which we have evolved and evolutionary theory seeks to explain why we have evolved in the way that we have. Why do birds have wings, giraffes have long necks, humans have bigger brains than other higher primates? How do changes in organic structure

occur and how does this happen? The answers to questions such as these have important implications for the topics discussed in other chapters in this book: intelligence, personality, social interaction, the use of language, the perception and expression of emotion, sex, hunger, mental disorder and so on.

Although it has its roots in biology, Darwin's work transcends biology and has influenced all the natural sciences, especially psychology (Dewsbury, 2009). In fact, Darwin himself had some aspirations for the young science. He wrote in 1859.

In the distant future, I see open fields for more important researches. Psychology will be based on a new foundation, that of the necessary acquirement of each mental power and capacity by gradation. Much light will be thrown on the origin of man and his history.

Since the 1970s, some psychologists have become increasingly aware of the various ways in which biology can influence behaviour. As you will see later in the chapter, many behavioural differences among organisms, both within and across species, correspond to genetic and other biological differences. Understanding these differences and their evolution allows psychologists to understand behaviour in terms of its possible origins and **adaptive significance** – its effectiveness in aiding the organism to adapt to changing environmental conditions.

For example, gregariousness is the tendency to form groups or to be sociable; people tend to form social units. We live in families, have circles of friends, and join groups, such as churches, clubs or professional or recreational societies and political organisations. To understand the adaptive significance of gregariousness, we need to consider two questions. First, what events and conditions in a person's lifetime might contribute to an individual's gregariousness – what function does gregariousness serve in helping people adapt to the changing circumstances of life? Secondly, what events and conditions in the evolution of our species favoured gregariousness – what functions has gregariousness served in the history of humankind? These are important questions because a complete understanding of gregariousness, like any behaviour, requires that we understand both the past and present conditions that influence it.

In other words, psychologists might research how past environmental conditions favoured gregariousness over a more solitary existence as a means of organising human culture and how the immediate environment influenced day-to-day sociability. They are interested in understanding both **ultimate causes** (from the Latin *ultimatus*, 'to come to an end') of behaviour – events and conditions that, over successive generations, have slowly shaped the behaviour of our species – and **proximate causes** (from the Latin *proximus*, 'near'), namely immediate environmental variables that affect behaviour.

By understanding how adaptive behaviour developed through the long-term process of evolution, psychologists are able to gain a more thorough understanding of our ability to adjust to changes in our immediate environment. To understand the present, we must understand the past – the history of the individual and the history of our species. We behave as we do because we are members of the human species – an ultimate cause – and because we have learned to act in special ways – a proximate cause. Both biology and environment contribute to our personal development.

Relatively recently, a field of psychology has emerged, **evolutionary psychology** (Tooby and Cosmides, 1989; Buss, 1995), which attempts to describe and explain how an organism's evolutionary history contributes to the behaviour patterns and cognitive strategies it uses for reproduction and survival during its lifetime. Evolutionary psychology's contribution to our understanding of human behaviour is assessed later in the chapter. First, however, we describe Darwin's theory of evolution. An understanding of this complex theory will help shed light on how behaviour has been interpreted, by some psychologists, in terms of evolution.

In the beginning: the voyage of the *Beagle*

The story of how Charles Darwin developed his theory illustrates the mix of hard work, intellect and good fortune that often makes scientific discovery possible. In fact, Darwin's work is an excellent example of how observation and experimentation can lead to scientific breakthroughs.

After receiving a degree in theology from the University of Cambridge, England, in 1831, Darwin met a Captain Robert FitzRoy who was looking for someone to serve as an unpaid naturalist and travelling companion during a five-year voyage on board HMS *Beagle*. The Beagle's mission was to explore and survey the coast of South America and to make longitudinal measurements worldwide.

During the voyage, Darwin observed the flora and fauna of South America, Australia, South Africa and the islands of the Pacific, South Atlantic and Indian Oceans. He collected creatures and objects of every sort: marine animals, reptiles, amphibians, land mammals, birds, insects, plants, rocks, minerals, fossils and seashells. These specimens, which were sent back to England at various stages of the trip, were later examined by naturalists from all over Europe.

Darwin did not form his theory of evolution while at sea. Although he was impressed by the tremendous amount of diversity among seemingly related animals, he believed in creationism, the view that all living things were designed by God and are non-evolving (Gould, 1985).

Charles Darwin (1809–82).
Source: Northwind Photo Library.

The Origin of Species

Upon his return home to England in 1836, Darwin continued to marvel at the many ways animals and plants adapt to their environments. He sifted through his collections, often discussing his findings and ideas with other scientists. He carefully reviewed the work of earlier naturalists who had developed their own theories on evolution. Darwin was not the first person to propose a theory of evolution, but he was the first to amass considerable evidence in its favour. He became interested in artificial selection, a procedure in which particular animals are mated to produce offspring that possess desirable characteristics. For example, if a farmer wished to develop cattle that yielded the largest steaks, then they would examine the available breeding stock and permit only the 'beefiest' ones to reproduce. If this process is repeated over many generations of animals, the cattle should become beefier. In other words, in artificial selection, people select which animals will breed and which will not based on specific, desirable characteristics of the animals.

As he pondered on whether there might be a natural process corresponding to the role that humans play in artificial selection, Darwin's views on evolution began slowly to change. He believed that 'selection was the keystone of man's success in making useful races of animals and plants. But how selection could be applied to organisms living in a state of nature remained for some time a mystery to me' (Darwin, 1887, p. 53).

A year-and-a-half later, on reading Malthus's *Population*, Darwin proposed that because the 'struggle for existence' continued in plants and animals, then favourable variations would be preserved and unfavourable ones would die out. The result of such 'selection' would be the development of new species (Darwin, 1887).

This proposal contains the idea of natural selection: within any given population, some members of a species will produce more offspring than will others. Any animal that possesses a characteristic that helps it to survive or adapt to changes in its environment is likely to live longer and to produce more offspring than are animals that do not have this characteristic.

Darwin was well aware of the significance of his discovery but did not publish his theory until 20 years later, taking great pains to develop a clear, coherent and accurate case for his theory.

Darwin might have been even slower in publishing his theory had it not been for an intriguing coincidence. In 1858, he received a manuscript from the Welshman, Alfred Russell Wallace, another naturalist, outlining a theory of natural selection identical to his own. Darwin's colleagues suggested that he and Wallace make a joint presentation of their separate works before a learned society – the Linnean Society – so that each might lay equal claim to the theory of natural selection. This was done, and a year later Darwin published his 'abstract', which we know today as *The Origin of Species*. The book sold out on its first day of publication and has been selling steadily ever since. And although theories of evolution had existed before Darwin, he was the first to offer a systematic explanation for how evolution worked.

Natural selection and evolution

Two concepts are central to Darwin's theory of evolution: adaptation and natural selection. **Adaptation** refers to the ability of generations of species to adapt effectively to changes in the environment. **Natural selection** refers to the process whereby some variations in species will be transferred from one generation to the next but others will not. The Oxford zoologist, Richard Dawkins, has likened the process of natural selection to a sieve because it leaves out what is unimportant (Dawkins, 1996).

Darwin's theory has four basic premises:

1 The world's animal and plant communities are dynamic, not static: they change over time with new forms originating and others becoming extinct.

2 The evolutionary process is gradual and continuous. New species arise through slow and steady environmental changes that gradually 'perfect' each species to its surroundings. When sudden and dramatic changes occur in the environment, a species' ability to adapt is usually challenged. Some species adapt and live; others become extinct.

3 All organisms are descended from an original and common ancestor. Over time, the process of natural selection has created different species, each specifically adapted to its ecological niche.

4 Natural selection not only causes changes within populations during changing environmental conditions but also acts to maintain the status quo under relatively constant environmental conditions.

According to Jacob (1977), natural selection results from two characteristics of life. First, reproduction produces offspring that are slightly different from their parents. Secondly, interaction with a changing environment requires that living things adapt behaviourally to its vagaries, otherwise they will risk injury, illness or death. The interaction of these factors causes differential reproduction, and, ultimately, evolution. Evolution, in this sense, is a process that is strongly influenced by behavioural adaptations to changing environments (Buss *et al.*, 1998).

Natural selection

The essence of Malthus's essay, which Darwin was reading when the idea of natural selection first occurred to him, was that the earth's food supply grows more slowly than populations of living things. The resulting scarcity of food produces competition among animals, with the less fit individuals losing the struggle for life. For example, wolves who are agile are better able to capture prey than are slower packmates. Fast wolves will therefore tend to outlive and out-reproduce slower wolves. If a wolf's tendency to run fast is a genetically controlled trait, it will be passed on to its offspring. These offspring will be more likely to catch prey and will therefore live longer and have more opportunities to reproduce.

The ability of an individual to produce offspring defines that individual's reproductive success – the number of viable offspring it produces relative to the number of viable offspring produced by other members of the same species. Contrary to popular interpretation, 'survival of the fittest' does not always mean survival of the most physically fit or of the strongest. The evolutionary 'bottom line' is not physical strength but reproductive success. Physical strength is only one factor that might contribute to such success. In humans, for example, good looks, charm and intelligence play an important role in an individual's ability to attract a mate and reproduce. What is more, natural selection is not 'intentional'. Giraffes did not grow long necks in order to eat leaves from trees, but those with longer necks who were able to reach the leaves successfully reproduced while the others died out.

Two aspects of natural selection – variation and competition – are the critical factors that determine whether any particular animal and its offspring will enjoy reproductive success.

Variation

Variation includes differences among members of a species, such as physical characteristics (size, strength or physiology) and behavioural characteristics (intelligence or sociability). What factors are responsible for these sorts of variation?

First, an individual organism's genetic make-up – or its **genotype** – differs from that of all other individuals (except in the case of identical twins). As a result of these genetic differences, an individual organism's physical characteristics and behaviour, or its **phenotype**, also differs from that of every other individual.

Every individual's phenotype is produced by the interaction of its genotype with the environment. In essence, the genotype determines how much the environment can influence an organism's development and behaviour. For instance, identical twins have exactly the same genotype. If they are separated at birth and one twin has a better diet than the other, their phenotypes will be different: the better-fed twin is likely to be taller and stronger. However, regardless of diet, neither twin will ever become extremely tall or very muscular if they do not possess the genes for tallness and muscularity. Likewise, neither twin will realise their full potential for tallness and muscularity if they do not eat a nourishing diet. In this example, both the genotype (the genes related to tallness and muscularity) and a favourable environment (a well-balanced, nourishing diet) must be present for either twin to reach their full growth potential.

Phenotypes and the genotypes responsible for them may or may not be selected, depending on the particular advantage they confer. Consider, for example, the thirteen species of finch that Darwin discovered in the Galapagos Islands, located off the west coast of South America. A striking physical difference among these birds is beak size. Some finches have a small, thin beak phenotype and others have a large, thick beak phenotype. Birds having small, thin beaks feed on small seeds covered by weak shells, and birds having large, thick beaks feed on large seeds covered by tough shells.

In a study that investigated the relationship between rainfall, food supply and finch population on one island, Grant (1986) discovered that the amount of rainfall and the size of the food supply directly affected the mortality of finches having certain kinds of beak. During droughts, small seeds became scarce. As a result, the finches having small, thin beaks died at a higher rate than finches having bigger, thicker beaks. During the next few years, the number of finches having bigger, thicker beaks increased – just as the principle of natural selection would predict. During times of plentiful rain, small seeds became abundant, and the number of finches having small, thin beaks became more plentiful in subsequent years.

Grant's study makes two important points. First, although evolution occurs over the long run, natural selection can produce important changes in the short run – in the space of only a few years. Secondly, phenotypic variation, in this case differences in beak size, can produce important selective advantages that affect survival. Imagine if all the finches had small, thin beaks: during the drought, most, if not all, of these finches might have died. None would be left to reproduce and these finches would have become extinct on this island. Fortunately, there was phenotypic variation in beak size among the finches, and because phenotypic variation is caused by genetic variation (different genotypes give rise to different phenotypes), some finches – those having large, thick beaks – had an advantage. Their food supply (the larger seeds) was relatively unaffected by the drought, enabling them to out-survive and out-reproduce the finches with small, thin beaks.

On the basis of this evidence, one might reasonably assume that all finches should have developed large, thick beaks. However, when rain is plentiful and small seeds are abundant, birds with small, thin beaks find it easier to feed. Under these environmental conditions, these birds have a phenotypic (and genotypic) advantage.

Competition

The second aspect of natural selection is **competition**. Individuals of a given species share a similar environment. Because of this, competition within a species for food, mates and territory is inevitable. Every fish captured and eaten by one bald eagle is a fish that cannot be captured and eaten by another bald eagle. If one bald eagle finds a suitable mate, then there is one fewer potential mates for other bald eagles and so on.

Competition also occurs between species when members of different species vie for similar ecological resources, such as food and territory. For example, yellow-headed blackbirds and red-winged blackbirds eat the same foods and occupy the same types of breeding territory; thus, they compete for these resources. Such competition does not involve competition for mates (yellow-headed blackbirds do not court red-winged blackbirds and vice versa). However, although these species do not compete for mates, their competition for other resources indirectly influences reproductive success because the ability to find and court a suitable mate depends on the ability to stake out and defend a territory having an adequate food supply. The probability of a yellow-headed blackbird finding a mate and successfully rearing a family depends not only on its success in competing against other yellow-headed blackbirds, but also on its success in competing against red-winged blackbirds.

Natural selection works because the members of any species have different phenotypes. Because these phenotypes are caused by different genotypes, successful individuals will pass on their genes to the next generation. Over time, competition for food and other resources will allow only the best-adapted phenotypes (and their corresponding genotypes) to survive, thereby producing evolutionary change. This is what the theory would predict.

Knowledge and acceptance of evolution

How widespread do you think the acceptance of the theory of evolution is? In the United States, it is law that science and religion are taught separately and that banning the teaching of evolution is unconstitutional (Scott and Matzke, 2007). In 2007, the Council of Europe's Parliamentary Assembly passed a resolution recommending that member states do not teach creationism as if it were the equivalent of science. One survey of over a thousand students at a large American university, however, found that 25 per cent reported that their biology teacher had taught them creationism and 20 per cent were taught neither biology nor creationism (Moore, 2007). Creationism – the rejection of the theory of evolution in favour of the belief that the world was originated by a Creator – has gained some momentum in the US, although recent legal rulings suggest that evolution is fighting back. Creationism's new incarnation is Intelligent Design but, to all intents and purposes, the terms are synonymous. The fierce and often acrimonious debate that exists between scientists and intelligent design advocates – see Dawkins's excoriating *The God Delusion* – could probably make a Controversies in Psychological Science section in itself.

Since 1985, American adults at various time intervals have been asked if the following statement is true or false: 'Human beings, as we know them, developed from earlier species of animals'. In 2002, US data were compared with those from 9 European countries, with 32 countries in 2005 and with a survey of Japanese respondents in 2001 (Miller *et al.*, 2006). Figure 3.1 illustrates agreement/disagreement with the statement by nation.

Miller *et al.* found that over 20 years the percentage of Americans agreeing with the statement fell from 45 per cent to 40 per cent. Those who completely rejected the statement also fell from 48 per cent to 39 per cent. Those who were unsure jumped from 7 per cent in 1985 to 21 per cent in 2005. In later surveys, respondents were given the option of responding in a different way. They were asked whether the statement was definitely true, probably true, probably false, definitely false or don't know. A third of Americans considered the statement to be false and only 14 per cent regarded it as definitely true. European and Japanese respondents were more likely to accept the statement as true. In fact, the only country which was more sceptical than the US was Turkey. Eighty per cent of Iceland, Denmark, Sweden and France agreed; 78 per cent of the

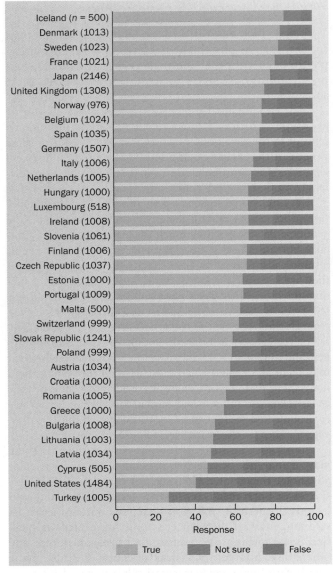

Figure 3.1 This graph shows 34 nations' degree of agreement with the statement 'Human beings, as we know them, developed from earlier species of animals'. The survey was undertaken in 2005.

Source: Miller, J.D., Scott, E. & Okamoto, S. (2006) Public acceptance of evolution. *Science*, 313, 765–6. Reprinted with permission from AAAS.

Japanese did. In European countries, the percentage absolutely disagreeing ranged from 7 per cent (Denmark, France, United Kingdom) to 15 per cent (The Netherlands).

Those who strongly believed in God, who prayed often and held pro-life beliefs were the most rejecting of the statement. All of these were more common in the US. Miller *et al.* explains the geographic disparity by suggesting that biblical fundamentalism – Genesis is to be read literally – is greater in the US, whereas in Europe Genesis is regarded as being more of a metaphor. A third of US respondents also agreed that half of the genes of mice and humans are identical and 38 per cent believed that we have half in common with chimps (as you'll see later, the percentage we share is a lot higher). Even if respondents disagreed with evolution, you might expect them to have a reasonable knowledge of the building blocks of life. Fewer than half of Americans surveyed were able to provide a passable definition of DNA.

Human evolution

Reconstruction of human evolution is a difficult job, something akin to assembling a giant jigsaw puzzle whose pieces have been scattered throughout the world. Some of the pieces may have been lost for ever; others have become damaged beyond recognition; and those few that are found force continual reinterpretation of how the other pieces might fit the puzzle. Another way in which we can date our remains is via carbon dating. Animals breathe a form of (naturally occurring) radioactive carbon called C14. When an animal dies, this carbon decays but at a constant rate. By examining the content of the carbon in the fossil or surrounding material, therefore, we can estimate the date of its existence. One problem here is that the amount of carbon found can be influenced by the amount in the air at the time.

We can also analyse the changes in DNA between similar fossils – the less the change in DNA, the closer the two fossils are in time. But the best we can do is make an educated guess about the evolution and lifestyles of our ancestors.

Many biologists and natural historians of Darwin's time believed that natural selection applied to all animals, including humans. Others insisted that although natural selection applied to other animals, it did not apply to humans. However, through study of the fossil record and recent developments in genetic research, we now know that our species is related genetically to other mammals. The gorilla and the chimpanzee are our closest living relatives, and together we appear to have descended from a common ancestor. You may have heard it said that we share 99 per cent of our genes with chimps. In fact, what we share is DNA involved in the production of proteins. Ninety-nine per cent of our DNA in this regard is identical (King and Wilson, 1975). Why, then, are we not exactly hirsute, whooping, tyre-swinging, banana-eaters? The reason is that 98 per cent of the human genome is not involved in the production of proteins. The remainder is involved in the timing of production and how much is produced (these are called regulatory genes – there is a more detailed description of genetics later in the chapter). It is this percentage which causes the great difference between the species (Demuth *et al.*, 2006; Cohen, 2007). Humans also have multiple copies of genes that chimps

do not (Pennisi, 2006). Therefore, while we have proteins in common, it is the way in which these proteins are organised which determines the differences between us.

Our dependence on information from fossil remains and other archaeological artefacts is problematic. As Byrne (1995) has colourfully pointed out, much of what we conclude about our ancestors' behaviour from archaeological findings is speculative; some is sensible speculation but it is speculation nonetheless. There is no way of empirically or conclusively demonstrating that artefacts were used in the way in which we suggest or that they indicate a specific way of living or behaving. In this sense, **paleoanthropology** – the study of human behaviour using information from fossil remains – is more like detective work than scientific work. 'The reality', Byrne argues, 'is that we will never know with confidence the answers to many of the most important questions we would like to ask about what happened in the past five million years' (1995, p. 6).

With this caveat in mind, the general pattern of evolution is thought to occur something like this. Our evolution from a common ancestor appears to have begun in Africa about 2 to 4 million years ago (Clark, 1993).

The earliest humans have been labelled *Homo habilis* (literally 'handy man'). *Homo habilis* was small (only about 1.3 m tall and about 40 kg in weight), but was bipedal (able to walk upright on two feet). Compared with its predecessor – a species called *Australopithecus* ('apes from the South') – *Homo habilis* had a larger brain and more powerful hands. The strong hands were well suited to making simple stone tools; hence the name 'handy man'. A natural selection interpretation of such adaptively significant traits would argue that these early humans adapted to the environment in terms of creating shelter against the elements, catching and preparing food, and making weapons for self-defence.

Homo habilis was succeeded, about 400,000 years later, by *Homo erectus* ('upright man'). *Homo erectus* had a much larger brain and stood more erect than *Homo habilis* and had a more complex lifestyle. *Homo erectus* was the first of our ancestors to establish regular base camps, which probably served as centres for social activities, including the preparation and eating of food. We cannot be absolutely sure that these interpretations are the correct ones, however. *Homo erectus* created more efficient and stronger tools than did *Homo habilis*, successfully hunted big game, and discovered and used fire. Fire enabled these early humans to cook food, remain warm in cold weather and protect themselves from predators. *Homo erectus*'s use of fire, coupled with its apparent social nature and its ability to hunt and/or scavenge big game, permitted it to explore and settle new environments, including Europe, Asia, America and other parts of Africa (Spoor *et al.*, 2007).

The earliest known *Homo sapiens* ('intelligent man') appears to have arisen about 500,000 years ago. The best known of the early *Homo sapiens*, *Homo sapiens neanderthalensis* (so-called Neanderthals, named after the German valley in which the fossils were discovered), lived throughout Europe and Central Asia between approximately 300,000 and 35,000 years ago. Neanderthals constructed small huts from bones and animal skins and sometimes burned bones as fuel. They were skilled big game hunters, tool makers and clothiers, and they had cultural rituals for burying their dead. In one Neanderthal burial site unearthed in France, a small boy was found positioned on his left side with a small pillow of flints under his head and an axe positioned by his right hand. Similar Neanderthal burial sites have been discovered, suggesting that these humans possessed cultural traditions not previously found in the prehistoric record.

Informed speculation suggests that Neanderthals and modern humans (*Homo sapiens sapiens*) overlapped each other, although the origin of *Homo sapiens sapiens* is unclear. It seems to have arisen between 200,000 and 100,000 years ago. The Neanderthals became extinct around 25,000 years ago, with last evidence of their existence found in Gibraltar (Finlayson *et al.*, 2006). What is clear, though, is that the *Homo sapiens sapiens* line has survived to flourish in all parts of the world, despite the presence of hostile climate, terrain and predators. Figure 3.2 charts the suspected development of *Homo sapiens sapiens*. Some theorists have suggested that the variety of species is greater nearer the equator (Hillebrand, 2004) and that tropical environments create a museum and a cradle for species to flourish (McKenna and Farrell, 2006).

Natural selection and human evolution

The apparent success of the human species in adapting to a variety of ecological niches stems from the fact that natural selection has favoured two important human characteristics: **bipedalism**, the ability to move about the environment on two feet, and **encephalisation**, increased brain size. The ability to walk upright, which appears to have evolved in our early hominid ancestors over 4 million years ago (Boaz, 1993; Ruff *et al.*, 1997), may have arisen from the need to stand on branches to reach food on other branches above (Thorpe *et al.*, 2007). Bipedalism allowed not only greater mobility, but also freed the hands for grabbing, holding and throwing objects. The ability to grasp

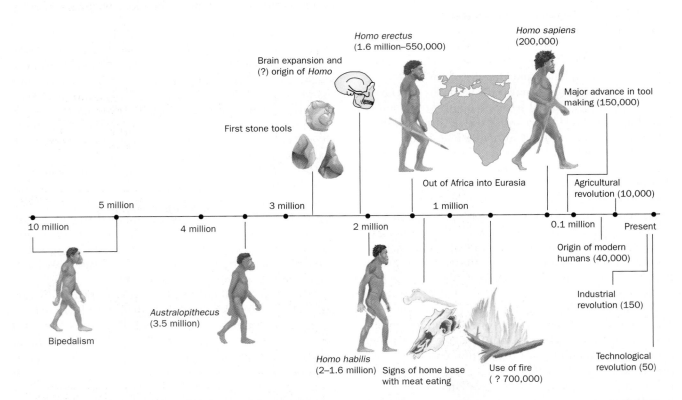

Figure 3.2 Major milestones in human evolution. The ability to walk upright freed the hands for tool use and other manipulative skills. Increased brain size accompanied increased intelligence. These two adaptations combined probably contributed significantly to all other major adaptations in human evolution.

Source: Adapted from Lewin, R., *Human Evolution: An illustrated introduction*. Cambridge, MA: Blackwell Scientific Publications, Inc., 1984.

objects, in combination with an expanding capacity for learning and remembering new skills provided by a larger brain, led to advances in tool making, food gathering, hunting and escaping predators (Eccles, 1989).

Early hominids had a brain volume of 650 cm³ (and they were about 155cm tall). Current humans have a brain size of 1,500 cm³ and are, on average, 175 cm tall. It used to be thought that there was a relationship between body size and brain volume. However, the relationship is between relative size and brain volume and Figure 3.3 (a)–(c) shows the differences in brain and body size between various species. The increase in our brain relative to our size is called **positive brain allometry**. This began around 2 million years ago and has increased, more or less, since – from 450 cm³ (*Homo habilis*) to

1,000 cm³ (*Homo erectus*) to 1,350 cm³ 100,000 years ago (*Homo sapiens*). The increase may be attributable to better diet, better defence and, therefore, better survival. Children began to live longer, thus enabling the brain to be more fully developed when they conceived.

As the brain became larger, more of its volume – especially the front part which is the most recently evolved – appeared to become devoted to thinking, reasoning, decision-making and other complex cognitive, 'higher' functions. We will return to the role of this part of the brain in thinking in Chapter 11.

Another important ability that emerged from encephalisation was planning: the ability to anticipate future events and to consider the effects of these events on an individual or group of individuals. Such planning might have involved the organisation of hunts, the institution of social customs and events (such as weddings and funerals), and the planting and harvesting of crops. Over time, the interaction between bipedalism and encephalisation allowed humans to exploit new environments and establish well-organised communities.

Advances in tool making and hunting, combined with the use of fire for cooking, protection and warmth, were adaptive: they helped humans to live longer. The increased lifespan of humans may have aided the gradual accumulation of wisdom as the older members of early

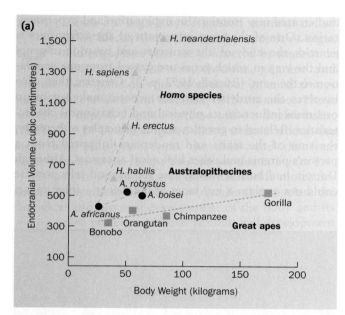

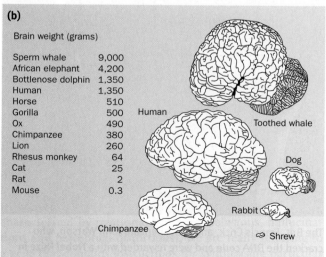

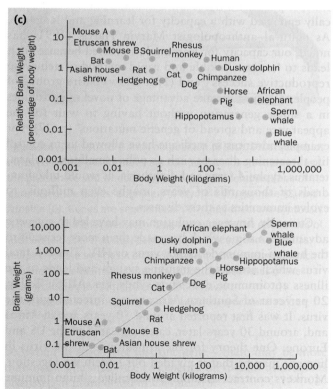

Figure 3.3 These three figures show the relationship between brain size and body weight in our human ancestors and non-human primates **(a)**; the weight of various species brains **(b)**; and the relationship between body weight and brain size in a variety of different species **(c)**.

Source: Dicke, U. and Roth, G. (2008). Intelligence evolved. *Scientific American Mind*.

tion. As we will see later, a faulty gene may contain instructions for synthesis of faulty enzymes, which produces serious physiological and behavioural problems.

Chromosomes and meiosis

Genes are located on **chromosomes**, the rod-like structures made of DNA found in the nucleus of every cell. In essence, genes are particular regions of chromosomes that contain the recipes for particular proteins. Each set of chromosomes contains a different sequence of genes. We inherit 23 individual chromosomes from each of our parents, giving us 23 pairs – 46 individual chromosomes – in most cells of the body. One pair of chromosomes, the **sex chromosomes**, contains the instructions for the development of male or female sex characteristics – those characteristics that distinguish males from females.

Sexual reproduction involves the union of a sperm, which carries genetic instructions from the male, with an ovum (egg), which carries genetic instructions from the female. Sperms and ova differ from the other bodily cells in at least two important ways. First, new bodily cells are created by simple division of existing cells. Secondly, all 23 pairs of chromosomes divide in two, making copies of themselves. The copies pull apart, and the cell splits into two cells, each having a complete set of 23 pairs of chromosomes. Sperms and ova are formed by a special form of cell division called **meiosis**. The 23 pairs of chromosomes break apart into two groups, with one member of each pair joining one of the groups. The cell splits into two cells, each of which contains 23 individual chromosomes. The assignment of the members of each pair of chromosomes to a particular group is a random process; thus, a single individual can produce 223 (8,388,608) different ova or sperms.

Although brothers and sisters may resemble each other, they are not exact copies. Because the union of a particular sperm with an ovum is apparently random, a couple can produce 8,388,608 × 8,388,608, or 70,368,774,177,664 different children. Only identical twins are genetically identical. Identical twins occur when a fertilised ovum divides, giving rise to two identical individuals. Fraternal twins are no more similar than any two siblings. They occur when a woman produces two ova, both of which are fertilised (by different sperms).

Sex is determined by the twenty-third pair of chromosomes: the sex chromosomes. There are two different kinds of sex chromosomes, X chromosomes and Y chromosomes. Females have a pair of X chromosomes (XX); males have one of each type (XY). Because women's cells contain only X chromosomes, each of their ova contains a single X chromosome (along with 22 other single chromosomes). Because men's cells contain both an X chromosome and a Y chromosome, half of the sperm they produce contain an X chromosome and half contain a Y chromosome. Thus, the sex of a couple's offspring

depends on which type of sperm fertilises the ovum. A Y-bearing sperm produces a boy, and an X-bearing sperm produces a girl. Figure 3.5(a) illustrates this process; Figure 3.5(b) shows the human chromosomes.

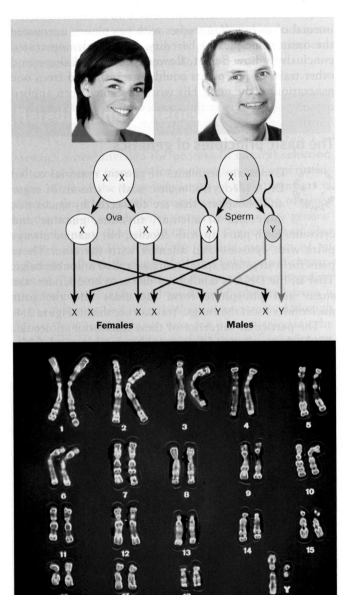

Figure 3.5 **(a)** Determination of sex: the sex of human offspring depends on whether the sperm that fertilises the ovum carries an X or a Y chromosome.
(b) Human chromosomes: the presence of a Y chromosome indicates that this sample came from a male. A sample from a female would include two X chromosomes.
Source: CNRI/Science Photo Library Ltd.

Dominant and recessive alleles

see activity on mypsychlab

Each pair of chromosomes contains pairs of genes: one gene in each pair is contributed by each parent. Individual genes in each pair can be identical or different. Alternative forms of genes are called **alleles** (from the Greek *allos*, 'other'). Consider eye colour, for example. The pigment found in the iris of the eye is produced by a particular gene. If parents each contribute the same allele for eye colour to their child, the gene combination is called homozygous (from the Greek *homo*, 'same', and *zygon*, 'yolk'). However, if the parents contribute different alleles, the gene combination is said to be heterozygous (from the Greek *hetero*, 'different'). Heterozygous gene combinations produce phenotypes controlled by the **dominant allele** – the allele that has a more powerful influence on the expression of the trait. The allele for brown eyes is dominant. When a child inherits the allele for brown eye colour from one parent and the allele for blue eye colour from the other parent, the child will have brown eyes. Brown eye colour is said to be a dominant trait. The blue eye colour controlled by the **recessive allele** – the allele that has a weaker effect on the expression of a trait – is not expressed. Only if both of a child's alleles for eye colour are of the blue type will the child have blue eyes. Thus, having blue eyes is said to be a recessive trait. Inheritance of two alleles for brown eyes will, of course, result in brown eyes. You can see this in Figure 3.6.

Other eye colours, such as hazel or black, are produced by the effects of other genes, which influence the dominant brown allele to code for more (black) or less (hazel) pigment in the iris.

It is important to remember that the genetic contributions to our personal development and behaviour are extremely complex. One reason for this complexity is that protein synthesis is often under polygenic control, that is, it is influenced by many pairs of genes, not just a single pair. The inheritance of behaviour is even more complicated, because different environments influence the expression of polygenic traits. Consider, for example, the ability to run. Running speed for any individual is the joint product of genetic factors that produce proteins for muscle, bone, blood, oxygen metabolism and motor coordination (to name but a few) and environmental factors such as exercise patterns, age, nutrition, accidents and so on.

Genetic diversity

No two individuals, except identical twins, are genetically identical. Such genetic diversity is a characteristic of all species that reproduce sexually. Some organisms, however, reproduce asexually, such as yeast and fungi. Nurseries often reproduce plants and trees through grafting, which is an asexual process. But when we examine the world around us, we find that the overwhelming majority of species reproduce sexually. Why?

One answer is that sexual reproduction increases a species' ability to adapt to environmental changes. Sexual reproduction leads to genetic diversity, and genetically diverse species have a better chance of adapting to a changing environment. When the environment changes, some members of a genetically diverse species may have genes that enable them to survive in the new environment. These genes manufacture proteins that give rise to physical structures, physiological processes, and, ultimately, adaptively significant behaviour that can withstand particular changes in the environment.

This reasoning explains why so many insects, such as cockroaches, have survived our species' best efforts to exterminate them. The lifespan of insects is very short, so that even in a short period of time, many generations are born and die. When we attempt to alter their environment, as we do when we apply an insecticide to their habitat, we may kill many of them. However, some survive because they had the right combination of genes (and hence, the necessary physiological processes and behaviour patterns) to resist the toxic effects of the poison. The survivors then reproduce. Our reaction is to attempt to develop a new poison to which this generation of insects is not resistant. The result is a sort of evolutionary 'arms race' in which both insects and humans produce newer and more powerful adaptations in response to each other (Dawkins, 1986).

Influences of sex on heredity

An individual's sex plays a crucial role in influencing the expression of certain traits. A good example is haemophilia, an increased tendency to bleed seriously from even minor injuries. The blood of people who do not have haemophilia will begin to clot in the first few minutes after they sustain a cut. In contrast, the blood of people who have haemophilia may not do so for 30 minutes or even several hours. Haemophilia is caused by a recessive gene on the X chromosome that fails to produce a protein necessary for normal blood clotting. Because females have two X chromosomes, they can carry an allele for haemophilia but still have normal blood clotting if the other allele is normal. Males, however, have only a single X chromosome, which they receive from their mothers. If the gene for blood clotting carried on this chromosome is faulty, they develop haemophilia.

The gene for haemophilia is an example of a **sex-linked gene**, so named because this gene resides only on the sex chromosomes. There are also sex-related genes that express themselves in both sexes, although the phenotype appears more frequently in one sex than in the other. These genes are called **sex-influenced genes**. For example, pattern baldness (thin hair across the top of the head)

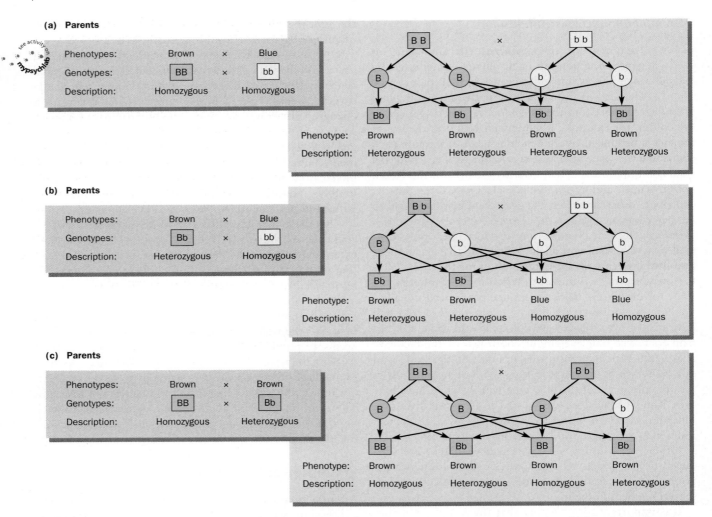

Figure 3.6 Patterns of inheritance for eye colour. **(a)** If one parent is homozygous for the dominant eye colour (BB), and the other parent is homozygous for the recessive eye colour (bb), then all their children will be heterozygous for eye colour (Bb) and will have brown eyes. **(b)** If one parent is heterozygous (Bb), and the other parent is homozygous recessive (bb), then their children will have a 50 per cent chance of being heterozygous (brown eyes) and a 50 per cent chance of being homozygous recessive (blue eyes). **(c)** If one parent is homozygous dominant (BB), and the other parent is heterozygous (Bb), then their children will have a 50 per cent chance of being homozygous for the dominant eye colour (BB) and will have brown eyes, and a 50 per cent chance of being heterozygous (Bb) for the trait and will have brown eyes.

Source: Based on Klug, W.S. and Cummings, M.R., *Concepts of Genetics* (2nd edn). Glenview, IL: Scott, Foresman, 1986. © 1986 Scott, Foresman & Co. Reprinted by permission of Addison Wesley Educational Publishers, Inc.

develops in men if they inherit either or both alleles for baldness, but this trait is not seen in women, even when they inherit both alleles. The expression of pattern baldness is influenced by an individual's sex hormones, which are different for men and women. The effects of these hormones on expression of pattern baldness explains why it is much more common among men than women.

Sex-related chromosomes may be responsible for social cognition in humans (Skuse *et al.*, 1997). Skuse and his colleagues examined a group of females aged between 6 and 25 years who had Turner's syndrome. **Turner's syn-**

drome is a genetic disorder in which all or part of one X chromosome in females is absent. These individuals are within the normal range of intelligence but they do have problems with social adjustment. In 70 per cent of Turner's individuals, the remaining X chromosome is maternal in origin (Xm); in the rest it is paternal (Xp). Skuse and his group examined whether there were any differences between those individuals with an X chromosome that was maternal or paternal in origin.

The researchers found that those with the maternally derived chromosome were less well adjusted than the 45,

Xp individuals. The 45, Xm individuals were also less skilled in verbal ability and in reasoning, two functions which are essential to social cognition. The authors of the study suggest that these results indicate a genetic locus for social cognition. They also suggest that because the social cognition chromosome is derived from the father, this might explain why certain 46, XY males (whose X chromosome is derived from the mother) are more susceptible to developmental disorders such as autism (a disorder of social communication, language and emotion) than are 46, XX females. Developmental disorders such as autism are described in more detail in Chapter 12.

Mutations and chromosomal aberrations

Changes in genetic material are caused by **mutations** or **chromosomal aberrations**. Mutations are accidental alterations in the DNA code within a single gene. Mutations are the original source of genetic diversity. Although most mutations have harmful effects, some may produce characteristics that are beneficial in certain environments. Mutations can be either spontaneous, occurring naturally, or the result of human-made factors such as high-energy radiation.

Haemophilia provides one of the most famous examples of mutation. Although haemophilia has appeared many times in human history, no other case of haemophilia has had as far-reaching effects as the spontaneous mutation that was passed among the royal families of nineteenth-century Europe. Through genealogical analysis, researchers have discovered that this particular mutant gene arose with Queen Victoria (1819–1901). She was the first in her family line to bear affected children – two female carriers and an afflicted son. The tradition that dictates that nobility marry only other nobility caused the mutant gene to spread rapidly throughout the royal families, as you can see from Figure 3.7.

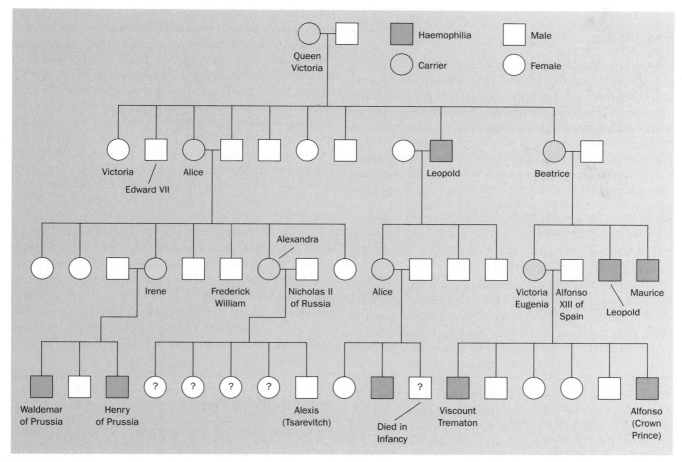

Figure 3.7 Genealogical analysis of the inheritance of haemophilia among European royal families. The gene for this disorder most likely originated with Queen Victoria of England. She was the first woman in the English royal family to bear an afflicted son or a carrier daughter. Circles represent females; squares represent males; a question mark indicates that carrier/afflicted status is unknown for that individual.

Source: Adapted from Winchester, A.M., *Genetics: A survey of the principles of heredity*. Boston: Houghton-Mifflin, 1972.

The second type of genetic change, chromosomal aberration, involves either changes in parts of chromosomes or a change in the total number of chromosomes. An example of a disorder caused by a chromosomal aberration – in this case, a partial deletion of the genetic material in chromosome 5 – is the **cri-du-chat syndrome**. Infants who have this syndrome have gastrointestinal and cardiac problems, are severely mentally retarded, and make crying sounds resembling a cat's mewing (hence its name, 'cry of the cat'). In general, the syndrome's severity appears to be directly related to the amount of genetic material that is missing. Psychologists and developmental disability specialists have discovered that early special education training permits many individuals having this syndrome to learn self-care and communication skills. This fact highlights an important point about genetics and behaviour: even behaviour that has a genetic basis can often be modified through training or experience, a notion called **epigenetics**.

Epigenetics

External events like trauma, drug abuse, lack of affection can affect the functioning of DNA. When these happen, the DNA does not alter, but is coated with molecules. These molecules alter the expression of the gene in two ways – either by preventing protein being constructed or by accelerating it. As you have seen, protein is essential to maintain the body and the brain. In the body, there is selective gene expression – each cell in the body may have the same gene but different cells use different types of gene. It does this via a molecule called ribonucleic acid (RNA), an intermediate molecule which is used by proteins attached to DNA to convert into other proteins. This is why a cell from the lung, for example, is different from one from the brain or the heart.

A gene can be silenced; molecules can be prevented from accessing it and this is what epigenetic mechanisms do. They either facilitate or block access to the genes in cells. This, consequently, affects gene expression. In one experiment, the stress response of rats whose mothers had licked or groomed them consistently for up to 10 days after birth was compared with those who had not. The first group showed less anxiety and stress. The gene that allows the release of a hormone called corticosterone was examined in these pups and those who had not been licked had fewer corticosterone receptors in their brain (Meaney, 2004). One proposed mechanism for this is that the hormone interacts with a structure in the brain called the hypothalamus to prevent it from overreacting to stressful events.

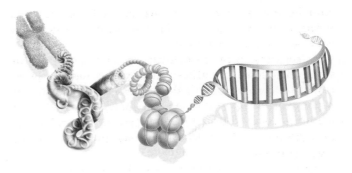

A chromosome unravelled
Source: Science Photo Library Ltd: Jacopin

Another protein, brain-derived neurotrophic factor (BDNF), which is important for the growth, integrity and functioning of cells, is lower in women with depression and it has been suggested that distressing events or experiences can alter the DNA that encodes this protein. In one experiment, 'bully' mice and smaller, normal mice were placed in a cage together for 5 minutes and then separated by a mesh for 10 days (Berton *et al.*, 2006). As you might predict, the smaller mice showed the typical stress reaction – they would become submissive and anxious. However, when their brains were examined for levels of BDNF, these were lower in the bullied mice. More importantly, the molecule known to affect the expression of this protein was found in one region of the mice's brains. This molecule had shut off the BDNF protein. A course of antidepressants raised the levels of BDNF.

Similar to these genes are 'knockout genes', which work in a similar way. The animal is exposed to radiation which damages a gene. This inserts nucleotides in the gene which prevent it from expressing itself, hence, the gene has been 'knocked out'. When the gene which encodes for spatial learning had been knocked out in rats, their ability to learn to swim to a platform that was not visible underneath a pool of water was impaired (Nakazawa, 2003).

Genetic disorders

Many genes decrease an organism's viability – its ability to survive. These 'killer genes' are actually quite common. On average, each of us has two to four of them. Fortunately, these lethal genes are usually recessive, and there are so many different types that most couples do not carry the same ones. When a child inherits the dominant healthy gene from one parent and the recessive lethal gene from the other, the destructive effects of the lethal gene are not expressed.

A few lethal **genetic disorders** are caused by a dominant gene, however. Different dominant lethal genes express themselves at different times in the lifespan. A foetus may die and be spontaneously aborted before a woman even realises that she is pregnant; a baby may be stillborn, or the lethal genes may not be expressed until adulthood.

There are many human genetic disorders. Those described below are some of the more common ones that impair mental functioning and behaviour and so are of special interest to psychologists.

Down syndrome

Down syndrome is caused by a chromosomal aberration consisting of an extra twenty-first chromosome (Simonoff *et al.*, 1996). People having Down syndrome are generally short, have broad skulls and round faces, and show impaired physical, psychomotor and cognitive development. It occurs in around 1 in 1,000 births (DeGrouchy and Turleau, 1990) and about 15 per cent of children born with this condition die before their first birthday, usually from heart and respiratory complications. The frequency of Down syndrome increases with the age of the mother: about 40 per cent of all Down syndrome children are born to women over 40 years old. To a lesser extent, the age of the father also increases the chances of Down syndrome. Although people having Down syndrome are mentally retarded, special educational training permits many of them to hold jobs involving simple tasks. Despite the fact that Down syndrome is caused by a chromosomal aberration, it is not a hereditary disorder.

Huntington's disease

Huntington's disease is a disorder of movement involving involuntary dance-like (choreiform), jerky movement. It does not emerge until the afflicted person is between 30 and 40 years old and is caused by a dominant lethal gene on the arm of chromosome 4 that results in degeneration in certain parts of the brain. Before the onset of this disease, an individual may be healthy in every respect. After onset, however, the individual experiences slow but progressive mental and physical deterioration, including loss of coordination and motor ability. Death generally occurs 5–15 years after onset. Because the age of onset for Huntington's disease is long after sexual maturity, this lethal gene can be passed from parent to child before the parent even knows that he or she has the gene. The disease is rare (the prevalence is 2–7 individuals per 1,000) but because it is autosomal dominant, the child of a parent with Huntington's disease has a 50 per cent chance of developing the disease. If the gene is present in the carrier, it will be expressed. There are genetic tests which help identify those individuals who carry the gene but this may present a horrible dilemma: if a person takes the test and is found not to carry the gene, then all well and good. If, however, the person is identified as a carrier, then this person will develop the disease and die from it because there is currently no cure. The Psychology in Action section describes some of the psychological consequences of this disclosure.

Phenylketonuria

Individuals with **phenylketonuria** (PKU) are homozygous for a recessive gene on chromosome 12 responsible for synthesis of a faulty enzyme (called phenylalamine hydroxylase – around 500 mutations of the enzyme's gene have been identified; see Widaman, 2009). This renders them unable to break down phenylalanine, an amino acid found in many foods. As a result, blood levels of phenylalanine increase, causing severe brain damage and mental retardation. Greater than 10 mg phenylalamine can be dangerous; a diet low in phenylalanine three weeks after birth can reduce this to between 3 and 10 mg. PKU is one of the many diseases for which infants are routinely tested before they leave the hospital. It occurs in 1 in 10,000–15,000 infants and those diagnosed as having PKU are placed on a low-phenylalanine diet shortly after birth.

The disorder was originally reported by a Norwegian dentist who noticed that his two retarded children had a peculiar odour. This odour aggravated his asthma so badly that he could not stay in the same room with them (Plomin, 1997). Folling, the physician who examined the children, found excess amounts of phenylpyruvic acid in their urine because of disturbed phenylalanine metabolism. If diet is unrestricted, intellectual ability plummets and mental retardation can occur by the age of 2 (the child's IQ would be around 50 or less, compared with the average 100). This decline is irreversible if there is no change in diet, which highlights the importance of altering diet quickly. Children who have been placed on a low phenylalanine diet for 20 years achieve normal development but if the diet is discontinued there is a drop in IQ performance (Koch *et al.*, 2002). When the diet is restarted, the points are regained. It is estimated that for every mg of phenylala- nine above 6.6, there is a 4.7 point loss in IQ (Koch *et al.*, 2003).

The mechanism for the illness is unclear but two candi- dates are the deficiency of a brain chemical called dopamine (described in the next chapter) or the slowing of myelination, the process whereby parts of a nerve cell are coated (this coating makes cells communicate more effectively) (Widaman, 2009).

Fragile X

Fragile X is the most important cause of mental retardation after Down syndrome and is the most common inherited cause of mental retardation (Simonoff *et al.*, 1996). It affects twice as many boys as girls (Kahkonen *et al.*, 1987) and is so called because the X chromosome is fragile and easily broken. Children with fragile X tend to have large fore- heads, prominent jaws and brow, and protruding ears.

Psychology in action – The psychological consequences of genetic counselling

Genetic testing of susceptibility to disease has brought with it many remarkable psychological benefits, certainty and relief following a negative outcome being two of the more obvious. Positive outcomes appear to present an entirely different pic- ture and one which may not be beneficial. Many anecdotal sources suggest that knowing the positive outcome of a genetic test for disease is associated with a decline in self- esteem and psychological well-being. There may also be health impairments that are unrelated to the disease.

Couples having a family history of genetic disorders often seek genetic counselling, the process of determining the like- lihood that a couple may produce a child having a genetic disorder. Individuals who suspect that they may have a genetic disorder may also seek such counselling. In women who might be carriers of the breast cancer gene (*BRCA1/2*), they do so for the sake of their children (d'Agincourt-Canning, 2006). Similar reasons, plus a feeling of responsibility to their families, are behind reasons for genetic testing for colon cancer and Huntington's disease (Warner *et al.*, 2006; Etchary, 2006).

In instances where the woman is already pregnant, the foetus can be tested for genetic disorders. In fact, such testing is often recommended for pregnant women over 35 years of age or for those whose family pedigrees reveal a genetic problem. The most common prenatal detection method is amniocentesis, which involves removal and examination of foetal cells found in the amniotic fluid surrounding the foetus, usually during the sixteenth week of pregnancy. The chromosomes in the foetal cells are examined for incomplete, missing or extra chromo- somes. In addition, amniocentesis allows parents to know the sex of their unborn child, which may be relevant in the case of sex-linked disorders.

The first step in genetic counselling is generally a pedigree analysis of the family or families involved. This analysis identi- fies any family history of genetic disorders and provides an estimate of the likelihood that a genetic disorder is present. If a family history of genetic disorders is discovered, the genetic counsellor discusses the probability of the couple having a child who has a disorder. In the case of an individual, the counsellor may recommend screening for the disorder.

A group of researchers from the Netherlands (Tibben *et al.*, 1997) examined levels of psychological distress in carriers and non-carriers of Huntington's disease at four testing points: before knowing the results, one week after, six months after and three years after. They found that although helpless- ness increased in carriers and decreased in non-carriers at one week, the difference disappeared after six months. Those carriers with children reported greater distress than those without, and the partners of non-carriers were less distressed than those of carriers at three years. A study from the USA sug- gests a similar response but one which may be mediated by people's approaches to coping with the illness (Codori *et al.*, 1997). Codori *et al.* examined levels of hopelessness and depressive symptoms in patients tested positive for Huntington's disease and those tested negative. They found that those who were least well adjusted were likely to have been positively diagnosed, were married with no children and were closer to their estimated age of onset.

Men and women can differ in how they respond to the results of genetic testing (Marteau *et al.*, 1997). Women carry- ing the cystic fibrosis gene mutation, for example, have been found to be more likely than men to be more relieved when told they were non-carriers but were also more likely to be less relieved than men when informed that they were carriers.

These studies highlight a number of important questions in the area of genetic testing: which individual differences are risk factors for the anxiety and distress experienced following a positive test? Does the degree of distress change depending on the type of disease diagnosed? What are the long-term con- sequences of knowing the results of genetic testing? Studies such as those above present a fairly coherent beginning to finding answers to such questions.

Heredity and behaviour genetics

see activity on mypsychlab

Each of us is born into a different environment and each of us possesses a unique combination of genetic instructions. As a result, we differ from one another. Consider your fellow undergraduates, for example. They come in different sizes and shapes, they vary in personality and intelligence, and they possess unequal artistic and athletic abilities. To what extent are these sorts of differences attributable to heredity or to the environment? If all your classmates had been reared in identical environments, any differences between them would necessarily be due to genetics. Conversely, if all your classmates had come from the same fertilised egg but were subsequently raised in different environments, any differences in their personal characteristics would necessarily be due only to the environment.

Heritability is a statistical term that refers to the amount of variability in a trait in a given population that is due to genetic differences among the individuals in that population. Heritability is sometimes confused with inheritance, the tendency of a given trait to be passed from parent to individual offspring. But heritability does not apply to individuals, it pertains only to the variation of a trait in a specific population. The more that a trait in a given population is influenced by genetic factors, the greater its heritability. The scientific study of heritability – of the effects of genetic influences on behaviour – is called **behaviour genetics**. As noted by one of this field's most prolific researchers, Robert Plomin, behaviour genetics is intimately involved with providing an explanation of why people differ (Plomin, 2008). As we will see below, behaviour geneticists attempt to account for the roles that both heredity and the environment play in individual differences in a wide variety of physical and mental abilities. The contribution of behaviour genetics to our understanding of the determinants of intelligence and personality are considered in more detail in Chapters 11 and 14.

Studying genetic influences

Although farmers and animal breeders had experimented with artificial selection for thousands of years, only within the past 150 years has the relation between heredity and behaviour been formally studied in the laboratory. Mendel's careful analysis of genetic influences on specific characteristics gave us the first good clue that traits were actually heritable. As you saw in Chapter 1, Galton (1869) stimulated further interest in this field with his studies showing that intelligence tends to run in families: if parents are intelligent then, in general, so are their children. The search for genetic bases of behaviour has been active ever since. In fact, the search to understand the relative contributions of heredity and environment to human behaviour is among the most heavily researched areas in psychology.

Artificial selection in animals

Any heritable trait can be selected in a breeding programme. The heritability of many traits in animals, such as aggression, docility, preference for alcohol, running speed, and mating behaviours, can be studied by means of artificial selection.

Consider, for example, Tryon's (1940) study of maze learning in rats. Tryon wished to determine whether genetic variables influenced learning. He began his study with a large sample of genetically diverse rats. He trained them to learn a maze and recorded the number of errors each rat made in the process. He then selected two groups of rats – those that learned the fastest (bright) and those that learned the slowest (dull). He mated 'bright' rats with other 'bright' rats and 'dull' rats with other 'dull' rats. To ensure that the rats were not somehow learning the maze from their mothers, he 'adopted out' some of the pups: some of the bright pups were reared by dull mothers and some of the dull pups were reared by bright mothers. He found that parenting made little difference in his results, so this factor can be discounted.

Tryon continued this sequence of having rats learn the maze and selectively breeding the best with the best (bright) and the worst with the worst (dull) over many generations. Soon, the maze performance of each group was completely different. He concluded that maze learning in rats could be manipulated through artificial selection.

Later studies showed that Tryon's results were limited by the standard laboratory cage environment in which rats lived when they were not running the maze. For example, Cooper and Zubek (1958) demonstrated that differences in maze ability were virtually eliminated when bright and dull strains of rats were reared in either enriched environments designed to stimulate learning (cages containing geometric objects, such as tunnels, ramps and blocks) or impoverished environments designed to inhibit learning (cages containing only food and water dishes).

However, Cooper and Zubek's rats that were reared in the standard laboratory cage performed similarly to Tryon's rats: the bright rats outperformed the dull rats. Thus, changing the environmental conditions in which the rats lived had an important result – reducing the effects of genetic differences between the bright and dull rats. This finding makes good sense when you consider the fact that genes are not expressed in the absence of an environment.

Tryon's research demonstrated that over successive generations a trait can be made to become more or less likely in a given population, but we do not know precisely why. We do not know whether genes related to learning or genes related to other traits were selected. Tryon's rats may have been neither especially bright nor especially dull. Perhaps each of these strains differed in its capacity to be motivated by the food reward that awaited it at the end of the maze.

Can gene manipulation ever occur in humans? Recent experiments involving the cloning of sheep illustrate the power of molecular genetics in radically altering nature's forms. Gene mapping may help us to understand how specific DNA sequences can influence physiological processes that affect behaviour, emotion, remembering and thinking and play a crucial role in identifying specific genes involved in psychological disorders (Plomin and DeFries, 1998). Some of these issues are discussed in the chapters on memory, intelligence and mental disorders (Chapters 8, 11 and 18).

Twin studies

There are two barriers to studying the effects of heredity on behavioural traits in humans. First, ethical considerations prevent psychologists and geneticists from manipulating people's genetic history or restricting the type of environment in which they are reared. For example, we cannot artificially breed people to learn the extent to which shyness, extraversion or any other personality characteristics are inherited or deprive the offspring of intelligent people of a good education to see if their intelligence will be affected. Secondly, in most cases, the enormous variability in human environments effectively masks any correlation that might exist between genetics and trait expression.

Psychologists have been able to circumvent these barriers by taking advantage of an important quirk of nature – multiple births. Recall that identical twins, also called **monozygotic (MZ) twins**, arise from a single fertilised ovum, called a zygote, that splits into two genetically identical cells. **Fraternal** or **dizygotic (DZ)** twins develop from the separate fertilisation of two ova. DZ twins are no more alike genetically than any two siblings. Because MZ twins are genetically identical, they should be more similar to one another in terms of their psychological characteristics (such as personality or intelligence) than either DZ twins or non-twin siblings (see Figure 3.8).

Concordance research examines the degree of similarity in traits expressed between twins. Twins are concordant for a trait if both of them express it or if neither does, and they are discordant if only one expresses it. If concordance rates (which can range from 0 to 100 per cent) of any given trait are substantially higher for MZ twins than for DZ twins, heredity is likely involved in the expression of that trait. Table 3.1 compares concordance values between MZ and DZ twins for several traits.

When we observe a trait exhibiting a high concordance for MZ twins but a low one for DZ twins, we can conclude that the trait may be strongly affected by genetics. This is especially true for a trait such as blood type, which has a heritability of 100 per cent. If the concordance rates are similar, the effect of heredity is low. For

Figure 3.8 Monozygotic twins.
Source: Corbis: Outline.

example, consider the characteristic of religious beliefs. In this case, a high concordance value (that is, both twins having similar beliefs) probably reflects the fact that they acquired their beliefs from their parents. In fact, the concordance rate for religious beliefs of DZ twins is generally just as high as that of MZ twins (Loehlin and Nichols, 1976). Thus, religious beliefs are not inherited.

Twin studies have been used to study a wide range of psychological phenomena. This research has shown that genetic factors affect cognitive abilities such as language ability, mathematical ability and vocabulary skills; personality traits such as extraversion (the tendency to be outgoing) and emotional stability; personality development; psychological disorders such as schizophrenia and mental retardation; and attitudes (Plomin *et al.*, 1994b; Bouchard and Propping, 1993).

Table 3.1 Comparison of concordance rates between monozygotic (MZ) and dizygotic (DZ) twins for various traits

Trait	Concordance %	
	MZ	DZ
Bood types	100	66
Eye colour	99	28
Mental retardation	97	37
Measles	95	87
Idiopathic epilepsy	72	15
Schizophrenia	69	10
Diabetes	65	18
Identical allergy	59	5
Tuberculosis	57	23

Source: Table 7.4, p. 161 from *Concepts of Genetics*, 2nd edn, by William S. Klug and Michael R. Cummings. Copyright © 1986 by Scott, Foresman and Company, Reprinted by permission of Pearson Education, Inc.

Controversies in Psychological Science – Are attitudes genetically inherited?

The issue

Although social psychologists have explored why people hold the attitudes that they do, little research has considered the role of genetics in how these attitudes are formed. The general view is that our attitudes are shaped by our learning and by our experience. However, there are studies of dizygotic and monozygotic twins which suggest that pairs of identical twins hold more similar views on subjects such as religion, crime, punishment and so on than do pairs of dizygotic twins (Eaves et al., 1989).

The evidence

In a study of the attitudes of 195 pairs of monozygotic twins and 141 pairs of dizygotic twins, Olson and his colleagues asked participants for their views on 30 diverse topics such as crossword puzzles, the death penalty for murder, sweets, immigration, loud music, making racial discrimination illegal, exercising and so on (Olson et al., 2001). Participants also rated themselves according to 20 personality traits, were asked how athletic, strong and physically attractive they thought they were and whether people considered them to be good-looking. The twins were recruited via newspaper advertisements.

Identical twins were more likely to share similar attitudes on 26 of 30 attitude items than were dizygotic twins. Table 3.2 illustrates the concordance rates for the twins' attitudes and personality traits.

Does this suggest that there are genes for such attitudes? This is highly unlikely. Instead, the authors suggest that there may be more general traits of factors which reflect specific attitudes. For example, when they took personality into account, they found that the trait of sociability was highly associated with five of the six attitude factors, perhaps suggesting that sociability may be the underlying 'cause' of such attitudes and which may be the heritable factor. Participants' attitudes towards leadership correlated with self-reported physical attractiveness, sociability and aggressiveness, but interpreting this relationship is difficult. For example, it could be argued that very attractive, sociable or aggressive people achieve leadership more easily and readily than do their less attractive, less sociable and less aggressive counterparts and that attitudes to leadership became more positive as a consequence. Conversely, participants may have been favourable towards leadership and made themselves more attractive, sociable or aggressive in order to achieve the status of leader.

The researchers note that while their study showed a high degree of heritability of attitudes, the greatest predictor of variability in the attitude scores was variation in the experiences of individual pair members. For example, having a good football coach might make a physically able person more posi-

Table 3.2 Similarities in attitudes of monozygotic and dizygotic twins

Attitude	Correlations	
	MZ	DZ
Doing crossword puzzles	0.46	0.11
Death penalty for murder	0.45	0.33
Sweets	0.36	0.23
Open-door immigration	0.47	0.20
Doing athletic activities	0.41	0.26
Voluntary euthanasia	0.45	0.21
Smoking	0.49	0.38
Being the centre of attention	0.31	0.14
Separate roles for men and women	0.27	0.26
Education	0.30	0.14
Making racial discrimination illegal	0.37	−0.01
Loud music	0.53	0.49
Getting along well with other people	0.20	0.19
Capitalism	0.41	0.19
Playing organised sports	0.52	0.10
Big parties	0.44	0.30
Playing chess	0.38	0.22
Looking my best all the time	0.42	0.14
Abortion on demand	0.53	0.28
Public speaking	0.34	0.26
Playing bingo	0.37	0.33
Wearing clothes that draw attention	0.38	0.28
Easy access to birth control	0.24	0.27
Exercising	0.35	0.17
Organised religion	0.43	0.21
Being the leader of groups	0.40	0.08
Reading books	0.55	0.24
Castration as punishment for sex crimes	0.39	0.29
Being assertive	0.28	0.27
Roller coaster rides	0.50	0.31

Source: Adapted from Olson, J.M., Vernon, P.A., Harris, J.A. and Jang, K.L. The heritability of attitudes: A study of twins. Journal of Personality and Social Psychology, 2001, 80(6) 845–60, copyright 2001 by the American Psychological Association, reprinted with permission.

tive about their physical strength and help them develop more positive attitudes towards sports; similarly, poor reinforcement from teachers or criticism of performance might lead to a child's withdrawal into shyness and subsequent negative attitudes towards leadership.

Conclusion

While there is a strong relationship between the attitudes of each of a pair of identical twins, there are events that both twins experience which could shape such attitudes.

Sociobiology

Sociobiology has been defined as 'the systematic study of the biological basis of all social behaviour' (Wilson, 1975). It represents the synthesis of research findings regarding social behaviour from many other fields of science, including those from evolutionary psychology, anthropology and behaviour genetics. Evolutionary psychology and behaviour genetics are more specific fields than sociobiology in the sense that both are concerned with phenomena such as intelligence and cognition, in addition to social behaviour.

Sociobiologists are especially interested in understanding the evolutionary roots of our modern-day social actions. More often than not, sociobiologists study the evolutionary bases of social behaviour in non-human animals and then extrapolate from those species to humans (Barash, 1982). Sociobiology represents an interface between the biological sciences and psychology. However, not all psychologists are convinced of the sociobiologists' claims, arguing that sociobiology is too simplistic and that its emphasis on genetics inadequately explains the complexities of human behaviour.

Reproductive strategies and the biological basis of parenting

Perhaps the most important social behaviours related to the survival of a species are those related to reproduction and parenting. A focal point of sociobiological research and theory has been understanding more about the different kinds of social organisation that result from particular **reproductive strategies** – systems of mating and rearing offspring.

We assume that most Western sexual relationships are monogamous: the mating of one female and one male. If mating is successful, the individuals share in the raising of the child or children. But **monogamy** is just one of several reproductive strategies sexual creatures employ in mating and rearing of offspring (Barash, 1982). Three other major classes of reproductive strategy are also possible:

- **Polygyny**: one male mates with more than one female.
- **Polyandry**: one female mates with more than one male.
- **Polygynandry**: several females mate with several males.

Figure 3.9 illustrates the combinations of partners that give rise to these classes.

According to Trivers (1972), these four reproductive strategies evolved because of important sex differences in the resources that parents invest in conceiving and rearing their offspring. **Parental investment** is the time, physical

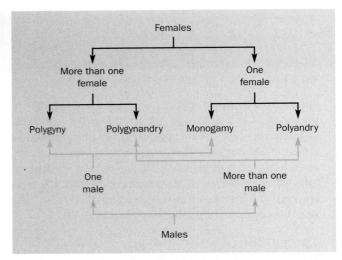

Figure 3.9 Reproductive strategies. Different numbers of males mating with different numbers of females yields the four reproductive strategies of monogamy, polygyny, polyandry and polygynandry.

effort and risks to life involved in procreation and in the feeding, nurturing and protecting of offspring. According to sociobiologists, parental investment is a critical factor in mate selection. An individual who is willing and able to make a greater investment is generally more sought after as a mate and is often more selective or discriminating when selecting a mate (Trivers, 1972). Given that a human female will gestate for nine months, she should be highly selective about choosing a mate. On the basis of Trivers's theory, it is possible to predict that women will express an (evolved) preference for men who have high status and will divorce those who do not contribute the expected resources or who divert them to other women and children (Buss, 1995).

In some species, competition for mates leads to **sexual selection** – selection for traits specific to sex, such as body size or particular patterns of behaviour. For example, in some animals, such as buffalo, females select mates based on the male's ability to survive the skirmishes of the rutting (mating) season. In general, the larger and more aggressive males win these battles and gain access to more females and enjoy greater reproductive success.

Polygyny is by far the most common reproductive strategy among humans. Eighty-four per cent of human societies practise polygyny or allow men who are either wealthy or powerful to practise it (Badcock, 1991). Monogamy is the next most popular reproductive strategy, with about 15 per cent of all human cultures practising it. Polyandry and polygynandry are both rare: combined, these two reproductive strategies dominate in fewer than 1 per cent of all human cultures.

Polygyny: high female and low male parental investment

In many species, the female makes the greater parental investment. According to sociobiological theory, whether one is an ova producer or a sperm producer defines the nature of one's parental investment. The fundamental asymmetry between the sexes has been aptly captured by sociobiologists Daly and Wilson (1978, p. 48):

> Although each parent contributes almost equally to the genetic resources of the new creature they create, not all contributions are equitable. The female provides the raw materials for the early differentiation and growth of their progeny. Here at the very fundament of sexuality, is love's labour divided, and it is the female who contributes the most.

Among most mammals (including humans), the costs associated with reproduction are higher for females than for males. First, females have fewer opportunities than males to reproduce. Generally, females produce only one ovum or a few ova periodically, whereas males produce vast quantities of sperm over substantially shorter time intervals. Secondly, females carry the fertilised ovum in their bodies during a long gestation period, continuously diverting a major portion of their own metabolic resources to nourish the rapidly growing foetus. Females also assume all the risks that accompany pregnancy and childbirth, including physical discomfort and possible death. The male's contributions to reproduction are, at a minimum, the sperm and the time needed for intercourse. Thirdly, after the offspring is born, females may continue to devote some of their metabolic resources to the infant by nursing it. Just as important, they usually devote more time and physical energy than males to caring for the newborn.

In addition, a female can only bear a certain number of offspring in a lifetime, regardless of the number of males with whom she mates. In contrast, a male is limited in his reproductive success only by the number of females he can impregnate. For example, consider the differences between females and males in our species. If a woman became pregnant once a year for ten years, she would have ten children – only a fraction of the number of children that a man is capable of fathering over the same interval. If a man impregnated a different woman every month for ten years, he would have fathered 120 children. This example is hardly an exaggeration. According to the *Guinness Book of World Records*, the largest number of live births to one woman is 69 (she had several multiple births). In contrast, King Ismail of Morocco is reported to have fathered 1,056 children.

In many polygynous species, intense competition for the opportunity to mate occurs among males. The competition almost always involves some sort of physical confrontation: that is, males fight among themselves for the opportunity to mate. Usually, the larger, stronger and more aggressive male wins, which means that only he will mate with the available females in the vicinity. If one of the smaller, weaker males attempts to mate with a female, he is generally chased away by the victorious male.

Because females in polygynous species invest so heavily in their offspring, they are – according to sociobiologists – usually highly selective of their mates, choosing to mate only with those males who possess specific attributes, such as physical size, strength and aggressiveness. Such selectivity makes adaptive sense for both the female and her progeny. After all, bearing the offspring of the victor means that her male offspring will tend to possess the same adaptively significant attributes as their father and thus be more likely to win their own quests for mating privileges. And, as a result, genes for large size, increased strength and aggressiveness will continue to have greater representation in future generations than will genes for less adaptive attributes. The theory also works the other way – the male will select a female that he considers attractive and healthy and would, therefore, be a fit mother for a child. This interpretation, however, rests on the assumption that mate selection is governed by the perceived ability to reproduce successfully. In essence, it is, like the assumptions made about the evolution of our ancestors: speculative. This view does not explain why some couples decide to forgo the opportunity to have children. Physical attraction is also heavily culture-bound, as the International Perspective section shows.

Facial and bodily attractiveness

As the International Perspective section below shows, some studies find that body mass index (BMI) is more important than shape to ratings of physical attractiveness, especially when full-frontal figures are rated. Shape may be more important if a figure is seen in profile.

To test this hypothesis, Tovee and Cornelissen (2001) asked 40 male and 40 female undergraduates in the UK to rate a set of photographs of real women with obscured faces. The authors criticise previous studies for using unrealistic stimuli, such as (poor) line drawings of female figures presented in front view only, hence the use of real photographs and two views. There were 50 front-view figures and 50 in profile. BMI, not waist-to-hip ratio, was the best predictor of attractiveness for figures seen from the front or in profile. Both men and women gave similar ratings, thus supporting the second hypothesis, and both sexes preferred the figures with the lowest waist-to-hip ratio (a curvaceous figure).

Physical attraction – An international perspective

see activity on mypsychlab

In the developed world, physically attractive women are considered to be those with a low **waist-to-hip ratio (WHR)**; this WHR is achieved because more fat is deposited on the buttocks and hips than the waist (this, in turn, is the result of women having higher levels of oestrogen than testosterone) (Singh, 1995).

This apparent universal preference for women with low WHR would seem to bolster the sociobiologist's argument that mates are selected for their health and fitness. However, these preferences are not universal. Yu and Shepard (1998) compared the body shape preferences of American men and men from the Matsigenka people in south-east Peru. The Matsigenka's culture is basically agrarian: they engage in slash and burn agriculture and supplement this food production with game and fruit gathered using traditional tools. Only scientists and official visitors are allowed to visit the village. The men had lived in the village since birth and would not, therefore, have been exposed to Western civilisation (no television, film, newspapers and so on).

Whereas the Western sample predictably preferred those females with low WHR, the Matsigenka men preferred overweight females and those with high WHR, rating these as the more attractive, healthy and more desirable as a spouse. The authors repeated the experiment on two other groups living outside the Matsigenka's village and who had been exposed to more Western influences. Here, the findings were mixed. One group showed the same pattern whereas the other gave comparable ratings to the Americans. These findings cannot be explained in terms of individuals selecting the fittest, most convincing-looking baby-producing machines. The non-Westernised group regarded a high WHR as healthier than a low WHR; the opposite effect was seen in the American group.

In a similar study, Frank Marlowe and Adam Wetsman, two American anthropologists, presented a series of frontal drawings of women which varied in their WHR to the Hazda group of hunter-gatherers who inhabit mixed savannah woodland in Tanzania (Marlowe and Wetsman, 2001). A previous study had shown that the men in this group were more swayed by women's weight than their WHR and strongly disliked thin women. In their new study, the images varied only by WHR, not weight. The group's responses were compared with those of a group of American men.

The researchers found that whereas the American men preferred a low WHR and especially liked the intermediate image showing a WHR of 0.7, the Hazda men preferred a higher WHR. The authors argue that this choice reflects a preference for heavier women and further speculate that 'the more subsistence-oriented a society is, and the more energetically expansive women's work, the more men will find fatter women attractive. Among foragers, thinness probably indicates poorer health.'

A study of physical attraction in Britain and Malaysia has found that participants in both countries consider body mass index (BMI), weight adjusted for height (see Chapter 13 to see how you calculate this), to be a better index of female attractiveness than waist-to-hip ratio (Swami and Tovee, 2005a). The researchers asked 682 participants to rate the photographs of real women. The study found that those who lived in urban areas preferred lower BMIs than did those living in the country, perhaps reflecting the greater exposure of urbanites to slimmer women. Geographical differences were also found when British and Malaysian people rated photographs of men (Swami and Tovee, 2005b). People who lived in urban areas preferred men with low **waist-to-chest ratio** (BMI or waist-to-hip ratio were not good predictors). In rural areas, however, BMI was the primary predictor of attractiveness. Urban raters preferred a men with an 'inverted triangle' shaped torso, whereas rural raters preferred heavier men with a less triangular shape. Swami and colleagues have also reported an interaction between WHR and breast size. South African men preferred high-WHR black figures with large breasts and high-WHR white figures with small breasts, whereas white British men and British Africans preferred high-WHR black figures with small breasts and high-WHR white figures with large breasts (Swami *et al.*, 2009).

Is women's waist-to-hip ratio and men's waist-to-chest ratio the key to physical attractiveness?
Source: © Mitchell Gerber/Corbis.

What this might suggest is that BMI and WHR reflect different aspects of female health and fitness. BMI may reflect general fitness and fertility whereas WHR is a 'more specific cue to fertility and pubertal status' although the authors acknowledge that this cue has its limitations. The WHR of anorexic and healthy women is similar, for example, although the anorexic group (which is amenorrheic, i.e. not menstruating) is not fertile whereas the healthy group is.

The same research group has also investigated what makes the ideal male body shape (Maisey *et al.*, 1999). They asked 30 female undergraduates to rate the attractiveness of 50 men. Each man was measured for waist-to-chest ratio (WCR), WHR and BMI. They found that the best predictor of a man's attractiveness was his waist-to-chest ratio. Unlike men, who prefer a certain body size, women prefer a certain shape. This is the 'inverted triangle' (narrow waist, broad shoulders). The researchers suggest that if the desirable WHR in women signifies health and reproductive potential, then a desirable WCR in men signifies physical strength.

The preference for the triangular shape in urban dwellers is probably influenced, in part, by the muscular quality that the shape presents. If men believe that a muscular body is attractive, then attaining a muscular torso should improve their body image. In a study where men and women engaged in a 12-week muscular training exercise programme, men who trained were significantly happier with their body image at the end than at the beginning (Ginis *et al.*, 2005). Interestingly, this improvement correlated with physical improvements in strength in men but with both physical improvements and subjective ratings of physical improvement in women.

Homosexual men also judge muscularity to be more important than weight when they rate their own attractiveness (Levesque and Vichesky, 2006). Men's weight, however, can influence people's judgement of their personality. Wade *et al.* (2007) found that thinner men were rated as more socially desirable than overweight men. Thin men and men of normal weight also received higher ratings for friendliness, trustworthiness, intelligence and mate potential.

Bodies are often covered and we may not be able to perceive their exact shape; faces, however, are almost always exposed and offer an immediate source of information about physical attractiveness. Furnham *et al.* (2001) asked 100 young men to rate the images of women for attractiveness, sexiness, and health. The images had been morphed so that bodies varying in WHR either featured an attractive or unattractive face (as determined in a pilot study).

Contrary to what one might expect, images with attractive faces were rated as healthier, sexier, more attractive and more fertile regardless of WHR. The evidence is contrary to what we would expect from the 'first pass filter' theory of mate selection. This refers to the notion that WHR is the first feature we focus on to determine our attraction to a partner; if it is acceptable, we then focus on other features and behaviours to further refine our choice.

People also find facial symmetry (where the left and right sides are almost totally symmetrical) attractive and healthy. Men with more symmetrical bodies have been reported to display more direct, sexual, competitive tactics when trying to win their date (Simpson *et al.*, 1999) and symmetrical movers are judged to be significantly better dancers than are asymmetrical ones (Brown *et al.*, 2005b).

Of course, physical beauty is stereotypically (and self-evidently) skin-deep. A study by Swami *et al.* (2007) asked participants to rate line drawings of women which varied in body weight, waist-to-hip-ratio and personality (extravert, introvert). Extraverted 'women' were judged to be more attractive and sociable than introverted ones, indicating that non-physical features are also an important determinant of attractiveness.

The perils of being beautiful

Is there a disadvantage to being very attractive? Research suggests that there is. When female students were asked to judge the suitability of an attractive, average and unattractive man as a long-term partner in tandem with a lonely heart advertisement implying high, medium or low socio-economic status, who do you think the women chose? If you said high-status, attractive men, you'd be wrong. If you'd said attractive men of medium status, you'd be right. Why? According to the authors (Chu *et al.*, 2007) the women regarded attractive, high-status men as pursuing a mating strategy (simply put, they were after sex), rather than a parenting strategy (wanting to settle down). High-status, attractive men would, therefore, be far more likely to be the recipient of other women's attention (and, therefore, be at greatest risk of yielding to this attention). Women – well, UK undergraduates – it seems, don't want Mr Perfect, just Mr Almost Perfect.

They might also settle for Mr Average. In one study women engaged in speed-dating were asked how important they thought a man's physical attractiveness and earning prospects were (Eastwick and Finkel, 2008). In an ideal partner, these were considered to be important. However, this preference did not predict their mate choice at the dating evening, neither did it predict their choice of real-life partners when the researchers contacted them after the study.

One theory of attractiveness (the topic of romantic attraction is considered further in Chapter 16) suggests that we choose a mate who is similar in attractiveness to ourselves (even if we prefer busty blondes or six-packed hunks). This is called the matching phenomenon (Walster *et al.*, 1966), but no model can explain this satisfactorily – is it because we are more anxious or insecure, or fear rejection, or have low self-esteem? Some social psychologists argue that we view others through our own egotistical lens. 'The self provides the frame of reference from which all else is observed', state Combs and Snygg (1959), 'People are not really fat unless they are fatter than we.' This would suggest that our ratings of others' physical attractiveness is affected by our assessment of our own physical attractiveness (whether this view is shared by others or not). Montoya (2008) found that people don't seem to settle. In their study, participants' ratings of

another person's attractiveness decreased with the increasing, objective, physical attractiveness of the rater. People rating themselves moderate in attractiveness paired themselves with people they thought were attractive. There is support for his finding. A recent study found that people rated their partners as being significantly more attractive than themselves – there was no difference between men or women (Swami *et al.*, 2009). Are these people deluding themselves? Or are we all physically attractive and beauty is in the eye of the beholder? Remember that these studies focused on physical attractiveness, not the attractiveness of a partner's personality or outlook or love of cats or helping old ladies with their shopping. Why do you think these percentages are so high?

Cutting edge – Can I have your number?

Can times of high and low fertility influence a woman's acceptance of a romantic overture? Nicolas Guegen, from the University of Bretagne-Sud, set up an experiment in which a 20-year-old confederate approached women in a pedestrianised zone of the city of Vannes and said: 'Hello. My name's Antoine. I just want to say that I think you're really pretty. I have to go to work this afternoon, and I was wondering if you would give me your phone number.' (Guegen, 2008)

He then waited for 10 seconds, gazed at his prey, smiled and waited for a response. Thirty to forty seconds after the woman departed, she was approached by a researcher who explained that the man was part of study and that they were interested in her responses to certain questions: 455 women participated.

The preference for Gallic *fromage* aside, did women's menstrual cycle influence their likelihood of accepting the overture? Yes, it did. Those in the fertile phase of their cycle were more likely to furnish their number, but only if they were not taking oral contraceptives. Guegen (2008) suggests that this might be explained by the fact that young French women are likely to use the pill when in a relationship, but stop when this ends. The combination of availability and high fertility may have led to the increased willingness to give a strange, attractive man their number.

This research is one in a line of studies exploring the effects of point of menses on women's feelings of sexual attractiveness. Women are judged to be more attractive when they are in the follicular stage of their cycle and men find their body odour more attractive. Women's appetite decreases during ovulation. They also make themselves look more attractive during this period. For example, Haselton *et al.* (2007) asked men and women to judge the attractiveness of 30 women who had partners and who were in the luteal or follicular stage of their cycle. More women in the follicular stage were judged as 'trying to

look more attractive'. The closer the women were to ovulation (when the photograph was taken), the more likely the photograph was chosen as signifying someone attractive. These women were judged to wear more fashionable clothes, nicer clothes and show more upper body skin.

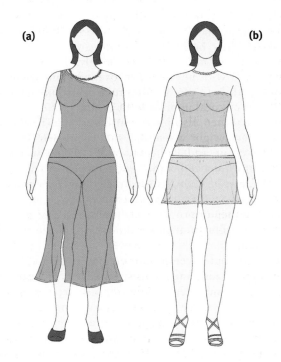

Figure 3.10 Example of an outfit illustration drawn by the same participant at low fertility **(a)** and high fertility **(b)**.

Source: Durante. K.M., Li, N.P. and Haselton, M.G. (2008) Changes in women's choice of dress across the ovulatory cycle: Naturalistic and laboratory task-based evidence. *Personality and Social Psychology Bulletin*, 34, 11, 1451–60.

Cutting edge – *Continued*

This perception is mirrored in women's own behaviour. Women were asked to report to a laboratory on high or low fertility days (confirmed by a hormone test) and to pose for photographs and draw an outfit that they would prefer to wear that evening (Durante *et al.*, 2008). Women were more likely to sketch sexier outfits during the high fertility period – they drew more revealing outfits, as the example in Figure 3.10 shows. The more sexually experienced the woman, the skimpier the outfit. Single women drew more revealing outfits than those who had partners but the more satisfied the women were with their partners, the more revealing the outfit they drew (suggesting that they were confident to express their sexuality in the context of a secure relationship).

Psychologists from the University of Tromsø, Norway, have also recorded the way in which women's pupils reacted as they watched photographs of either their boyfriends or celebrities (Laeng and Falkenberg, 2007). Fourteen women participated during three menstrual periods – luteal, ovulatory and menstrual. An eye-tracking device measured pupil size. (Pupil diameter increases when people are sexually aroused.)

Women during the fertile phase of their cycle showed larger pupil diameter when viewing photographs of their boyfriends, but this effect was found only on those who did not use oral contraceptives.

Monogamy: shared, but not always equal, parental investment

Around 3 per cent of the relationships in mammals are monogamous. Monogamy has evolved in those species whose environments have favoured the contributions of both parents to the survival and reproductive success of their offspring. In other words, under some conditions, two individuals sharing parental duties enjoy more reproductive success than does one individual who must do it all alone.

Although both parents in monogamous species share offspring-rearing duties, each parent may not make an equal contribution towards that end. Like females in polygynous species, females in monogamous species generally have greater parental investment in the offspring, for many of the same reasons: the limited opportunity for mating relative to that for males, pregnancy and its accompanying risks, providing milk to the newborns, and the time and energy spent in caring for them. As a result, very few monogamous species, including our own, are exclusively monogamous. In fact, there is a strong tendency in most monogamous species towards patterns of reproductive behaviour and parental investment that resemble those of polygynous species.

For example, in monogamous species, females tend to be more careful than males in selecting a mate, and males tend to be more sexually promiscuous than females (Badcock, 1991). In our own species, men tend to engage in premarital sexual intercourse more often than do females (Kinsey *et al.*, 1948, 1953; Hunt, 1974), although this gap appears to be decreasing. Men also tend to have more premarital and extramarital sexual partners (Symons, 1979), although recent studies show that over 90 per cent of male and female undergraduate respondents want to settle down with one partner exclusively at some point (Pedersen *et al.*, 2002).

Reproductive success today may not be thought of in terms merely of the number of children we have (although among some religious subcultures this is still an important measure of success), but in terms of how well individuals raise healthy, happy and well-adjusted children. Although most people have the biological capacity to produce a large number of children, many do not have the psychological or financial wherewithal to do so. Some people fear that a large family will reduce the amount of money they can make and will therefore lower their quality of life. Others see a large family as an impediment to obtaining career goals and other life aspirations. And still others simply have no desire to have any children at all.

Monogamy and hormones

Some scientists have hypothesised that monogamy may be attributable to chemicals called hormones, described in detail in the next chapter (Young *et al.*, 1998). These are generated by a region in the brain which sends signals to organs of the body to react in a certain way. The proposed relationship between hormones and monogamy has been based on studies of a type of rodent, the vole. Researchers have found that two types of vole show very different patterns of mating: the prairie vole is largely monogamous, forming lasting partnerships; the montane vole, however, is promiscuous and not a particularly social species. The male montane vole is not parental and does not form a bond with its partner; the female montane vole abandons its offspring around two to three weeks after birth (Young *et al.*, 1998).

Two key hormones have been identified that could underpin these behaviours: oxytocin (OT) and vasopressin (AVP). In prairie voles, vaginal-cervical copulation leads to an increase in the release of OT. This release may promote intense mating in females but has little effect on males. Vasopressin, however, does affect male prairie voles. Administering this hormone in these male voles leads to a preference for an exclusive partner, aggression towards strangers and an increase in paternal care (Young *et al.*, 1998). In the montane male vole, the effect of the hormones is not aggression but self-grooming. The receptor distribution for these hormones in the brain of the prairie vole is similar to that in other monogamous types of vole; conversely, the distribution of receptors in montane voles is similar to other promiscuous vole types. Levels of oxytocin have recently been associated with trustworthiness and trustworthy behaviour in humans (Zak *et al.*, 2005).

Together, these findings suggest that there may be some hormonal basis to the monogamy seen in certain species and that this hormonal basis arises from receptor distributions which, in turn, arise from the expression of a gene. The idea is controversial and provocative but interesting. It is unclear, with primates' high degree of (largely) sophisticated social interaction, whether such endocrinal expressions could explain monogamy and promiscuity in humans.

Infidelity

It has been estimated that between 20 and 50 per cent of people who are married will be unfaithful to each other at some point (Thompson, 1983; Wiederman, 1997), and men claim to want a greater number of sexual partners across a lifetime than do women.

For various evolutionary reasons, evolutionary psychologists suggest that men and women respond differently to different types of infidelity. Heterosexual men, for example, are more likely to show jealousy in response to sexual infidelity (a partner having sex with another man), whereas heterosexual women are more likely to show jealousy in response to emotional infidelity (a partner having a very deep, loving, yet non-sexual, relationship with another woman). A study in which male and female undergraduates were asked whether they would forgive the two types if infidelity in their partner conformed to the expected pattern and found that men were less likely to forgive sexual than emotional infidelity whereas women showed the opposite pattern (Shackelford *et al.*, 2002). Men were also more likely to terminate a relationship if their partner committed sexual infidelity.

Harris (2002) examined men's and women's responses to infidelity by giving them a scenario to respond to. As in most other studies, participants were asked whether they would be more upset if they found out that their partner was trying different sexual positions with another or if their partner was falling in love with another. Some 196 participants, with a mean age of 37, were recruited via newspaper advertisements and flyers. Harris was also interested in whether responses would be similar in

homosexual and heterosexual men and women and so recruited roughly equal numbers of each. Participants were asked if they had been 'cheated' on, whether they focused on the emotional or sexual consequences of the cheating and whether the relationship ended as a result.

As predicted by evolutionary psychology, heterosexual men were more likely to find sexual infidelity more upsetting than they would emotional infidelity when responding to the forced-choice question. The reverse pattern was found for women. When participants recalled actual examples of infidelity, however, no sex differences were found. Regardless of sexual orientation, both men and women were more likely to focus on a partner's emotional than sexual infidelity as the source of distress. No relationship was found between participants' responses to hypothetical and actual infidelity.

Harris (2002) concludes:

> If emotional jealousy was selected for because it helps women prevent loss of a mate's resources, then how did men come by such a mechanism?. . . the farther one moves away from asking college students the forced-choice question regarding hypothetical infidelity toward assessing real infidelity with adults, the less support one finds for the [evolutionary] hypothesis.

People who are married to disagreeable, undependable and emotionally unstable partners are less satisfied with their marriage (Shackelford and Buss, 2000). Low agreeableness, low emotional stability and low conscientiousness in women is associated with low marital satisfaction in men. Disagreeable, emotionally unstable men were also more likely to abuse their wives than their agreeable, emotionally stable counterparts. Furthermore, mate-guarding tactics such as threatening infidelity, threatening to punish infidelity and emotional manipulation (i.e. the factors which inflict costs on a relationship) were associated with lower marital satisfaction in the people at the receiving end of these tactics.

What makes a mate poacher? When infidelity occurs, are there factors that can dispose a person to being unfaithful and to wanting to have a relationship with a person who already has a partner? One study found that 84 per cent of undergraduates reported that attempts had been made to poach them from their partners (Schmitt and Buss, 2001). Of those who were romantically linked (just over 55 per cent), 20 per cent of men and 28 per cent of women stated that their partners had been poached from someone else. In terms of personality, agreeable and conscientious people were least likely to be mate poachers, a finding that is found internationally (Schmitt, 2004). Those who did not regard relationships

Cutting edge – Jealousy, infidelity and the brain

Although romantic jealousy seems more common in men than women, the sexes may also differ in what they become jealous about. Men are more likely to be jealous, angry and upset about sexual infidelity whereas women are more likely to be upset by emotional infidelity (their partner engaging in a warm and fulfilling friendship with another woman). These differences might have a neural basis (Takahashi *et al.*, 2006).

Twenty-one men and women read the statements in Table 3.3 silently as brain activation was recorded. They read the statements again after scanning and were asked how they would feel if their boyfriend or girlfriend was the protagonist.

Men and women did not differ significantly in terms of the types of infidelity they felt jealous about – both sexes became equally jealous under both conditions (emotional or sexual infidelity). However, brain activation did differ by sex. Men showed greater activation in the amygdala during sexual jealousy and in the hypothalamus during emotional infidelity. These are structures involved in sexuality and reproduction, amongst other functions. Women showed greater activation in the posterior superior temporal sulcus, an area the authors suggest is implicated in 'the detection of others' intention or violation of social norms'.

The data from this small group of healthy young adults suggest that subtle neural differences might underlie jealous responses to certain types of infidelity.

Table 3.3 Examples of the jealousy-arousing sentences used in Takahashi *et al.*'s study

Neutral

My girlfriend stayed in a twin-bed room in a hotel with her female friend
My girlfriend wrote a new year's card to her female friend
My girlfriend spent a night in her female friend's room
My girlfriend meets her best female friend frequently
My girlfriend had her coat taken off by her female friend
My girlfriend telephones her parents on the weekend
My girlfriend e-mailed her mother yesterday.

Sexual infidelity

My girlfriend stayed in a double-bed room in a hotel with her ex-boyfriend
My girlfriend took a bath with another man
My girlfriend had her underwear taken off by another man
My girlfriend spent a night in her ex-boyfriend's room
My girlfriend kissed another man deeply
My girlfriend passionately embraced another man
My girlfriend took an overnight trip with another man
My girlfriend was naked with her ex-boyfriend in his bed.

Emotional infidelity

My girlfriend wrote a love letter to another man
My girlfriend had dinner with another man on my birthday
My girlfriend supplied another man with all the money she had saved
My girlfriend telephones her ex-boyfriend every day
My girlfriend always talks with delight about her ex-boyfriend in front of me
My girlfriend emails to her ex-boyfriend every night
My girlfriend gave gorgeous birthday presents to her ex-boyfriend
My girlfriend meets another man more frequently than she does me

as exclusive and described themselves as having erotophilic tendencies – a constant desire to satisfy sexual needs – were more likely to poach. These individuals also scored high on sexual attractiveness: it appears that the poacher may have to be sexy, as well as adulterous.

Extraverts were more likely than introverts to be recipients of poaching attempts. Those who rated themselves as sexually attractive, as not relationship exclusive and as emotionally investing (loving) were those who were most likely to be poached.

Physical attractiveness was more important for men than it was for women. Women, conversely, were more likely to view resource acquisition as a benefit of poaching, especially in short-term relationships. Because men value physical attractiveness in women, women pay greater attention to using physical characteristics as cues to attraction. Women, on the other hand, placed greater value on resources. Men, consequently, emphasised cues that indicate that they are resource-laden (such as expensive clothes, cars, jewellery and so on). Women who thought they could make themselves more attractive by disparaging the partner of the person they wanted to poach were not as effective as enhancing physical attractiveness.

As predicted, men were found to be more successful than women at poaching when they displayed resources. Men who showed displays of dominance were also more likely to be effective at poaching in the short term, but this factor was not rated very highly. Getting a mate drunk was an ineffective poaching cue in the long term but one with moderate success in the short term, especially when used by women. Men were more effective at using humour as a poaching cue than were women in the short and long term. Women employed a tactic that was significantly more effective when used by them than by men: boosting the partner's ego.

When the relationship of the person who was being poached was long-distance, not committed or about to end, poaching was effective; when the relationship involved marriage, great commitment, living together or just beginning, poaching was seen as ineffective.

Although based on a sample of undergraduates, and assessing perceived effectiveness rather than actual effectiveness of poaching, this series of studies shows that poaching is a common phenomenon and that men and women use different cues with varying degrees of success to poach a mate from their existing partner.

Promiscuity

Promiscuity – the tendency to engage in sexual activity with multiple partners (not necessarily at the same time) – has been associated with specific personality types. Sensation-seekers, for example, have more partners than

low sensation-seekers; and the unconscientious, extravert, the less agreeable and more antagonistic similarly report having more sexual partners than the conscientious, the less extravert and the more agreeable/less antagonistic. A new study has associated two other factors with this behaviour (Markey and Markey, 2007). In a study of 105 young men and 105 young women, people who were dominant had significantly more sexual partners than did those who were less so. Curiously, people who were personally warm were also more likely to have had more sexual partners than the less warm. 'This indiscriminate behaviour [promiscuity]', the authors conclude, 'may not always be ill-intentioned but, in some cases, may be an expression of warmth.' Commenting on the findings regarding dominance, the authors suggest that 'selective participation in sexual behaviours may be a reflection of an individual's submissiveness, not their "moral piety"'.

A related study examined whether men who engaged in unrestricted sexual activity – engaging in transient sexual relations – perceived women's attractiveness differently from men who were more restricted (Swami *et al.*, 2008). Men self-described as restricted or unrestricted rated the attractiveness of drawings of women who differed according to Body Mass Index and waist-to-hip ratio. The men, regardless of type, used BMI rather than WHR as the basis of their judgement but unrestricted men found women with lower BMI to be more attractive and healthy than did restricted men. The unrestricted men also preferred women with a low WHR.

Polyandry: high male and low female parental investment

Polyandry is a rare reproductive strategy among humans and non-existent in other mammals. It is more prevalent among species that lay eggs. Once the eggs are laid, then either the male or the female may take care of them, although in many instances the male makes the greater investment of time and effort.

An example of polyandry in humans is found among some of the people who live in remote Himalayan villages. These people are extremely poor and live in a harsh environment, which makes their primary livelihood, farming, difficult. In order to prevent the dissolution of family farms through marriage, families that have more than one son limit the number of marriages to only one per generation – several brothers may share the same wife. A female tends to marry more than one man (most often brothers) to guarantee that she will be adequately supported. In other words, the male's primary investment – the farm, which is the source of food and some income for the family – is guarded jealously through polyandry.

Infidelity – An international perspective

While some of the psychological characteristics of mate poachers and mate poaching are well documented, the extent of the behaviour cross-culturally is less well documented. Evolutionary psychologists argue that the nature and degree of mate poaching/poachers should be similar across cultures but with some provisos. Studies show that men are more likely than women to engage in short-term mate poaching and so we might expect this finding across cultures.

However, we might also expect cultures which observe traditional sex roles to show a bigger difference between men and women than cultures that are more liberal and egalitarian. In demanding environments (those that afford fewest resources), there may be less of an opportunity or a desire for mate poaching because the difficulties involved in raising a family require commitment from both partners. These predictions were tested by Schmitt and colleagues (Schmitt *et al.*, 2004) in a study of 16,954 individuals from 53 nations, divided into 10 world regions (North America, South America, western Europe, eastern Europe, southern Europe, the Middle East, Africa, Oceania, South/Southeast Asia, and East Asia).

Mate poaching overall was very common – 70 per cent reported that they had been the object of a poaching attempt. Eighty per cent of poaching attempts were apparently successful with 10 per cent of such attempts leading to a long-term relationship. Mate poaching was most common in southern Europe, South America and western Europe and was least common in Africa, South/Southeast Asia and East Asia, a finding that is consistent with the prediction regarding demanding environments. The number of attempts at mate poaching by members of various cultures can be seen in Figure 3.11.

Also consistent with the study's predictions, men were more vigorous mate poachers than were women, with 60 per cent of men reporting that they had attempted to mate poach and 40 per cent of women reporting so. In cultures where men and women were regarded as equals, this sex difference was smaller.

In keeping with previous studies, the personality measures showed that poachers were extraverted, disagreeable, uncon-

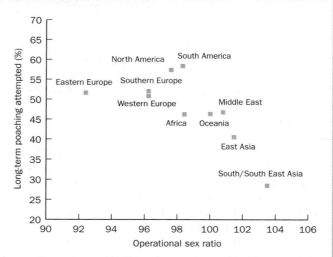

Figure 3.11 The degree of mate-poaching across nations and cultures. Euopeans and Americans seem especially keen on it.

Source: D.P. Schmitt, Patterns and universals of mate poaching across 53 nations: The effects of sex, culture and personality on romantically attracting another person's partner, *Journal of Personality and Social Psychology*, 2004, 86 (4), 560–84, Figure 2.

scientious, slightly narcissistic and (no surprise here) unfaithful. The poached were likely to be extraverted, open, attractive and disagreeable. Both groups were likely to be highly sexual.

Of course, the majority of the study's participants were young undergraduates and the authors note that mate poaching may be more common in this younger group than in an older sample. They also note that studying young married couples would be informative because men are reported to be highly jealous if an attempt is made to woo their wives. These men also appear to be more vigilant in observing such attempts. It would also be useful to measure the degree of satisfaction with a poacher's current relationship and whether this, rather than some personality profile, is the key predictor of poaching.

Polygynandry: group parental investment

Many primates, such as chimpanzees, live in colonies in which few or no barriers are placed on which female mates with which male. In other words, the colonies are promiscuous – during periods of mating, intercourse is frequent and indiscriminate. What is the advantage of such a reproductive strategy?

The primary advantage seems to be the cooperation of males and females in the colony with respect to rearing offspring. Because the males in the colony are not sure which

offspring belong to them, it is in their best interest to help rear and protect all the offspring and defend their mothers. The unity in the colony and the lack of aggression among the males contributes directly to the general welfare of all colony members. Females and males have access to many mates, and the offspring are well cared for.

However, a form of monogamy called a consortship is sometimes observed in polygynandrous species. For instance, a particular male chimpanzee may ward off other male suitors from a particular female, resulting in an exclusive sexual union. If successful, he is guaranteed the certainty of which offspring are his, albeit at some cost. There is a chance that he could be seriously injured in protecting his mate from other males, and therefore he becomes less useful as a parental investor in his offspring or those of the colony.

Incestuous relationships: a universal taboo

All reproductive strategies seem to have one element in common: avoidance of incest. Incest is the mating of kin who share many of the same genes. Avoidance of incest appears to have evolved for a very good reason: closely related relatives are likely to share the same recessive genes that cause genetic disorders. Thus, animals that avoid incestuous matings have an evolutionary advantage over those that do not; they produce healthier offspring who themselves are more likely to live to sexual maturity and produce offspring of their own.

All human cultures have taboos against incest. A taboo is a societal rule prohibiting the members of a given culture from engaging in specific behaviours – in this case, mating with a genetically related individual. Taboos are products of cultural evolution and are socially transmitted through language from one generation to the next.

Incest taboos are probably of secondary importance, serving to reinforce the aversion we have towards incest or mating with non-relatives with whom we were raised. For example, in one study (Shepherd, 1983), the elders actually encouraged the children of the kibbutz to marry so that the children would not end up living far from home. Despite the absence of a taboo and the encouragement of the elders, none of the children married each other.

Altruism and kin selection

A particularly interesting and important social behaviour in terms of evolution is **altruism**, the unselfish concern of one individual for the welfare of another. Examples of altruistic behaviour abound and its most extreme form is when one person risks their life to save the life of another. Examples of altruism are also common throughout the animal kingdom. The honey bee, for example, sacrifices its life on behalf of its hivemates by stinging an intruder. Here, the altruist's chances of survival and reproductive success are lowered while that of the other individuals are raised.

Sociobiologists seek out ultimate causes, especially the consequences of natural selection, to explain altruism. They assert that natural selection has favoured the evolution of organisms that show altruistic tendencies. However, there is an important problem here. On the surface, altruism poses an enigma to evolutionary theory. Recall that according to natural selection only phenotypes that enhance one's reproductive success are

favoured. How could altruistic behaviour have evolved given that, by definition, it is less adaptive than selfish or competitive behaviour?

The geneticist William D. Hamilton (1964, 1970) suggested an answer to this question in a series of mathematical papers. Hamilton's ideas stemmed from examining natural selection from the perspective of the gene instead of from the perspective of the whole, living organism. He argued that natural selection does not favour mere reproductive success but rather **inclusive fitness**, or the reproductive success of those individuals who share many of the same genes. Altruistic acts are generally aimed at close relatives such as parents, siblings, grandparents and grandchildren. The closer the family relation is, the more likely the genetic similarity among the individuals involved. Such biological favouritism towards relatives is called **kin selection** (Maynard Smith, 1964).

The message here is clear: under the proper circumstances, individuals behave altruistically towards others with whom they share a genetic history, with the willingness to do so decreasing as the relative becomes more distant. In this view, altruism is not necessarily a conscious act but rather an act driven by a biological prompt that has been favoured by natural selection. Natural selection would favour this kind of altruism simply because organisms who share genes also help each other to survive.

Parenting is a special case of kin selection and an important contributor to one's survival and reproductive success. In the short run, parents' altruistic actions promote the continued survival of their offspring. In the long run, these actions increase the likelihood that the offspring, too, will become parents and that their genes will survive in successive generations. Such cycles continue according to biological schedule, generation after generation. In the words of sociobiologist, David Barash (1982, pp. 69–70):

> It is obvious why genes for parenting have been selected: all living things are the offspring of parents who themselves were [the offspring of] parents! It is a guaranteed, unbroken line stretching back into time. [Genes] that inclined their bearers to be less successful parents left fewer copies of themselves than did those [genes] that were more successful.

What is at stake is not the survival of individual organisms but the survival of the genes carried by those organisms. Genes allow organisms to maximise their inclusive fitness through altruistic behaviour directed at other organisms sharing the same genes (Dawkins, 1986). Inclusive fitness refers to the idea that reproduction and natural selection occurs because a species' success is measured through the production of offspring. You carry copies of genes that have been in your family line for thousands of years. When the opportunity presents itself, you will most likely carry on the tradition – reproducing and thus projecting your biological endowment into yet another generation. But you did not reach sexual maturity on your own; the concern for your welfare by your parents, brothers, sisters, grandparents and perhaps an aunt or uncle has contributed to your chances of being reproductively successful. Genes not projected into the next generation simply disappear.

Another variable may mediate altruism, however: emotional closeness. Emotional closeness is defined as having a sense of concern and caring for another and enjoying a comforting, emotional relationship with them. One study asked participants to rate how willing they would be to behave altruistically towards members of their family when the family member could live or die, and when helping would be at a cost to the participant (Korchmaros and Kenny, 2001). Participants also indicated how emotionally close they were to these family members.

People were more likely to help family members with whom they shared a close relationship, regardless of the genetic closeness of the relationship, than with those with whom they shared a less close relationship. The findings suggest that emotional closeness may be a mediating cause of altruistic behaviour.

Evidence from step-relations' behaviour supports the idea of inclusive fitness. It has been reported, for example, that a disproportionate number of children in stepfamilies suffer physical harm, especially assault (Daly and Wilson, 1988). Child battering is more common in stepfamilies, as is the incidence of child abuse (Daly and Wilson, 1996). This evidence, the sociobiologists argue, supports the notion than non-genetic relatives are not disposed to invest resources in offspring that are genetically unrelated.

There is also evidence to suggest that cohabitation is a greater risk factor for spousal murder than is marriage. Canadian research published at the beginning of the 1990s suggested that women in cohabiting relationships were more likely than married women to be murdered by their partner (Wilson *et al.*, 1993, 1995). Data from specific US cities show the same pattern (e.g. Wilbanks, 1984). According to the Wilson *et al.* studies, women in their early twenties were at greater risk of homicide if they were married; for cohabiting women, women in their mid-thirties to forties were at greatest risk. A national study of over 400,000 US homicides committed between 1976 and 1994 found that women in cohabiting relationships were nine times more likely than married women to be murdered by their partner (Shackelford, 2001). The risk for married women decreased as they became older. Middle-aged women, however, were at greatest risk if they were in a cohabiting relationship.

Young men were more likely to murder their wives whereas middle-aged men were more likely to murder their cohabiting partners.

One explanation for these findings is that men may tend to feel significantly and abnormally proprietorial about their partners, especially about their partner's sexuality. A man in a cohabiting relationship is more insecure than is a married man because the possibility of either partner leaving the relationship is more likely and is easier to do. The cohabiting man may, therefore, go to more extreme lengths to prevent his partner from leaving him than would a married man because cohabiting relationships are more likely to break than are marriages. There is some evidence in support of this interpretation. Daly and Wilson (1988), for example, cite their partner data showing that men who kill their partners are more likely to do so because they suspect that their partner has been unfaithful or may be about to terminate their relationship.

Reciprocal altruism

Kin selection explains altruism towards relatives, but what about altruism directed towards non-relatives? According to Trivers (1971), this kind of altruism, called **reciprocal altruism**, exists because humans (and other organisms) can function more effectively if they work together. Human groups are hierarchical and cooperative (Buss, 1995), whether at the level of the family, canoe club or workplace. There is also evidence that kindness, dependability, emotional stability and intelligence (all traits one would associate with altruism) are the most valued personality characteristics in potential mates (Buss, 1995). Cooperation between groups is a fundamental survival strategy (Brewer and Caporael, 1990), and is seen in many higher primates (Byrne, 1995). For example, in order to win a mate from a dominant male savannah baboon, a male will engage the help of another baboon who will distract the dominant male and enter into a fight with him. This leaves the other, non-dominant male free to mate with the female. The altruism is reciprocal because the favour will be reciprocated by the successfully paired male in the future (Haufstater, cited in Byrne, 1995). Another primate example where reciprocal altruism can be seen is in food sharing and also in a task called the prisoner's dilemma.

The prisoner's dilemma

An illustration of the way in which reciprocal altruism can work is provided by the 'prisoner's dilemma' (Axelrod and Hamilton, 1981). The **prisoner's dilemma** is a scenario in which individuals are allowed to cooperate or not cooperate. Two suspects are imprisoned separately and are asked to consider being silent (to cooperate) or sing (to defect).

If both prisoners cooperate then they both get lighter sentences; but if one sings then that prisoner gets off still more lightly. If the game is played once, defection is the best strategy; however, if the game is played repeatedly then staying silent might be the best option because the other player can return the favour or punish the defection. Nowak and Sigmund (1998) have suggested that cooperation can still be established even if there is no chance for the cooperation to be reciprocated. The reason for this is that an individual seen to be cooperative or having a reputation for being cooperative will be more likely to experience reciprocal behaviour from others in future. In short, helping will be rewarded by someone who acknowledges your good reputation.

The prisoner's dilemma may not be the most effective test of cooperation because it allows only cooperation or defection. In real life, however, cooperation is not an all-or-nothing behaviour. Some individuals may invest slightly less in cooperation, some slightly more, but they may all cooperate in some form. Imagine two individuals giving to charity: one gives £10, the other gives £100. Both are cooperating (being altruistic), but one is more altruistic than the other (one may be able to afford the £100 but the other is making a financial sacrifice by donating £10). Because of this variation in altruism, Roberts and Sheratt (1998) have suggested a 'raise the stakes' model of altruistic behaviour. This model argues that individuals would offer a small amount at the first meeting and if this amount is reciprocated, then more will be offered at the next opportunity. This model suggests that behaviour cannot be effectively exploited and so cooperation would be enhanced.

Sociobiology and evolutionary psychology as an explanation for human behaviour?

So far in this chapter you have seen that sociobiologists attempt to explain social behaviour by reference to natural selection and genetic inheritance. Evolutionary psychologists 'develop hypotheses about the psychological mechanisms that have evolved in humans to solve the particular adaptive problems that humans have faced under ancestral conditions' (Buss, 1995, p. 4).

Sociobiology has been at the centre of a fierce scientific controversy ever since E.O. Wilson published *Sociobiology: The new synthesis* in 1975, the official birth date of this discipline. Although Wilson's work, which is based chiefly on studies of non-human animal behaviour, has generated an enormous outpouring of scientific research, it has also roused a number of serious charges (Montagu, 1980). Wilson's *On Human Nature* (1978), which extended sociobiological theory to human affairs, ignited even more

criticism. Most of the criticism focuses on the extension of the theory to human behaviour. Two issues which have caused greatest controversy are inclusive fitness and the mechanisms of adaptation.

Recall that inclusive fitness theory argues that reproduction and natural selection occur because species' survival success is measured through the production of offspring. Those characteristics which help promote the transmission of genes (either directly or indirectly) will be naturally selected, akin to Dawkins's sieve mentioned at the beginning of the chapter. Sociobiologists see humans as 'fitness maximisers', or 'fitness strivers' (Alexander, 1979), constantly applying the mechanisms for maximising inclusive fitness. The evolutionary psychologists, however, call this the 'sociobiological fallacy' (Buss, 1991, 1995) because it confuses the theory of origins of mechanisms with the theory of the nature of mechanisms. As Buss argues, if humans were 'fitness maximising blobs', why are men not queuing up at sperm banks to donate their sperm? Why do some couples forgo reproduction? We have developed a preference for fatty foods but this is known to be detrimental to us. If we know this food is unhealthy, why do we eat it? More to the point, we can look at individuals or their behaviour and easily find maximising fitness reasons for this behaviour. The inclusive fitness theory, therefore, cannot account for natural selection and, because of its breadth (one can interpret almost any behaviour in terms of maximising fitness), is virtually limitless in its application.

Instead of seeing humans as fitness maximisers, evolutionary psychologists see humans as 'adaptation executors' or 'mechanism activators' (Tooby and Cosmides, 1990). That is, humans apply evolved solutions to adaptive problems (Buss, 1995). These solutions are domain-specific. That is, the types of solution one would need to reach to select a mate are different from those one needs to obtain food or to parent children. Adaptive problems are large, complex and varied; the success of individuals in solving these problems depends on sex, species, age, context and individual circumstances (Buss *et al.*, 1998). Sociobiology, however, seems to ignore this psychological level of interpretation and goes from evolution straight to patterns of social organisation.

The most intense criticism of sociobiology is political, not scientific. Opponents argue that sociobiology sanctions the superiority of one group over another, be it a race, a gender, or a political organisation. After all, they argue, if one group of individuals is genetically superior to another, then there are 'natural' grounds for justifying the 'survival of the fittest' and one group's unethical and immoral domination of another. An example is Hitler's quest for world domination in the name of Aryan superiority. Sociobiologists flatly deny such allegations and argue that it is the critics and not they who have confused the term 'natural' with the terms 'good' and 'superior'. Are political objections to sociobiology scientifically acceptable ones? Do you think that psychologists should be concerned with political objections to their findings or theories?

Given the broad-sweep nature of sociobiological theory, it is not surprising that the theory fails to account adequately for natural selection. Although kin selection and familial altruism could be interpreted as supporting the inclusive fitness theory, it is true that one could explain away a lot of behaviour by describing it as maximising fitness.

Chapter review

Natural selection and evolution

- Understanding behaviour requires that psychologists learn more about both proximate causes of behaviour – how animals adapt to environmental changes through learning – and ultimate causes of behaviour – historical events and conditions in the evolution of a species that have shaped its behaviour.
- Darwin's voyage on the *Beagle* and his subsequent thinking and research in artificial selection led him to develop the idea of biological evolution, which explains how genetic and physical changes occur in groups of animals over time.
- The primary element of biological evolution is natural selection: the tendency of some members of a species to produce more offspring than other members do. Members of a species vary genetically; some possess specific traits to a greater or lesser extent than other individuals do. If any of these traits gives an animal a competitive advantage over other members of the species then that animal is also more likely to have greater reproductive success. Its offspring will then carry its genes into future generations.
- Two important adaptations during the course of human evolution are bipedalism – the ability to walk upright – and encephalisation – an increase in brain size. The combination of these two factors allowed early humans to explore and settle new environments and led to advances in tool making, hunting, food gathering and self-defence.
- Encephalisation appears to have been associated with language development and cultural evolution. The study of the evolution of our species suggests the nature of the circumstances under which adaptive behaviour first emerged and those circumstances that have been important for its continued expression to the present time.

Heredity and genetics

- The instructions for the synthesis of protein molecules, which oversee the development of the body and all of its processes, are contained in genes. Genes are found on chromosomes, which consist of DNA and are found in every cell.
- Humans inherit 23 individual chromosomes, each of which contains thousands of genes, from each parent. This means that our genetic blueprint represents a recombination of the genetic instructions that our parents inherited from their parents.

- Such recombination makes for tremendous genetic diversity. Genetically diverse species have a better chance of adapting to a changing environment than do genetically non-diverse species because some members of the species may have genes that enable them to survive in a new environment.
- The expression of a gene depends on several factors, including its interaction with other genes (polygenic traits), the sex of the individual carrying the particular gene, and the environmental conditions under which that individual lives. Changes in genetic material caused by mutations or chromosomal aberrations lead to changes in the expression of a particular gene. For example, haemophilia, an increased tendency to bleed from even minor injuries, is the result of a mutation, and Down syndrome, which involves impaired mental, physical and psychomotor development, is the result of a chromosomal aberration.
- Behaviour genetics is the study of how genes influence behaviour. Psychologists and other scientists use artificial selection studies of animals, twin studies, and adoption studies to investigate the possible relationship between genes and behaviour in humans.
- Recent studies suggest that the attitudes and personalities of identical twins are more closely related than are those of fraternal twins.

Sociobiology

- The discovery of the biological basis for social behaviour is the primary goal of sociobiology. Sociobiologists have been especially interested in studying social behaviour related to reproduction and the rearing of offspring.
- Evolutionary psychology is a relatively new sub-field of psychology (and sociobiology) that is devoted to the study of how evolution and genetic variables influence adaptive behaviour.
- Different reproductive strategies are believed to have evolved because of sex differences in the resources that parents invest in procreative and child-rearing activities. These resources include the time, physical efforts and risks to life involved in procreation and in the feeding, nurturing and protection of offspring.
- A low waist-to-hip ratio appears to be preferred by Western heterosexual men; a waist-to-chest ratio that emphasises narrow hips and broad shoulders is preferred by Western heterosexual women. In some cultures, however, there is a

preference for heavier, larger women. One reason for this is that these cultures may not have been exposed to the Western ideals of physical beauty, those which emphasise the curvaceousness of women.

- Recent research suggests that facial attractiveness may be a more important determinant of mate selection than is waist-to-hip ratio.
- Polygynous and monogamous strategies tend to require greater female investment, polyandrous strategies tend to require greater male investment, and polygynandrous strategies tend to require investment on the part of members of a large group, such as a colony of chimpanzees. Despite these differences, all reproductive strategies entail avoidance of incest, either through migration or the recognition of closely related genetic kin or those individuals with whom one was raised. All human cultures have taboos about incest.
- Altruism is difficult to explain by appealing to natural selection. Altruistic behaviour generally involves one organism risking its life for others with whom it shares some genes (kin selection) or who are likely subsequently to be in a position to return the favour (reciprocal altruism).
- Inclusive fitness theory argues that reproduction and natural selection occur because species' survival success is measured through the production of offspring. Those characteristics which help promote the transmission of genes (either directly or indirectly) will be naturally selected.
- Sociobiology has been criticised on the grounds that natural selection is no longer a factor in human evolution, that research on animal social behaviour is not relevant to understanding human social behaviour, that environmental factors play a greater role in shaping human behaviour than genetic factors, and that sociobiology is simply a way to justify the superiority of one group over another. Sociobiologists reply that natural selection has shaped and continues to shape the evolution of culture, that findings from animal research can be generalised to humans, that genes and environment interact to determine behaviour, and, finally, that sociobiology is an attempt to understand human behaviour, not to justify it.

Suggestions for further reading

Evolution: Popular accounts

Brown, A. (2000) *The Darwin Wars*. London: Simon & Schuster.

Darwin, C. (1859) *The Origin of Species by Means of Natural Selection*. London: Murray.

Dawkins, R. (1986) *The Blind Watchmaker*. London: Penguin.

Dawkins, R. (1989) *The Selfish Gene*. London: Penguin.

Dawkins, R. (2003) *A Devil's Chaplain*. London: Weidenfeld & Nicolson.

Dawkins, R. (2009). *The Greatest Show on Earth: The Evidence for Evolution*. Bantam Press

Dennett, D.C. (1995) *Darwin's Dangerous Idea*. London: Penguin.

Scientific American Mind, special edition on 'Becoming Human: evolution and the rise of intelligence', 2006, 16, 2.

Some good introductions to evolutionary theory.

Evolution and the brain

Duchaine, B., Cosmides, L. and Tooby, J. (2001) Evolutionary psychology and the brain. *Current Opinion in Neurobiology*, 11, 225–30.

Roth, G. and Dicke, U. (2005) Evolution of the brain and intelligence. *Trends in Cognitive Sciences*, 9, 5, 250–57.

Both items provide a good grounding in the evolution of the brain.

Behavioural genetics

Eley, T.C. and Craig, I.W. (2005) Introductory guide to the language of molecular genetics. *Journal of Child Psychology and Psychiatry*, 46, 10, 1039–41.

Plomin, R. (2008) *Behavioural Genetics*. London: Palgrave.

Plomin, R. (2005) Finding genes in child psychology and psychiatry: When are we going to be there? *Journal of Child Psychology and Psychiatry*, 46, 10, 1030–38.

Plomin, R. and Colledge, E. (2001) Genetics and psychology: Beyond heritability. *European Psychologist*, 6, 4, 229–40.

Scerif, G. and Karmiloff-Smith, A. (2005) The dawn of cognitive genetics? Critical developmental caveats. *Trends in Cognitive Sciences*, 9, 3, 126–36.

These items give a useful introduction to behavioural genetics (and objections to behavioural genetics).

Evolutionary psychology and sociobiology

Buss, D.M. (2008) *Evolutionary psychology: The new science of mind* (3rd edn). Boston: Allyn & Bacon.

Matsuzawa, T. (2008) *Primate origins of human cognition and behaviour*. New York: Springer.

Pigliucci, M. (2006) Is evolutionary psychology a pseudoscience? *Skeptical Inquirer*, 30, 2, 23–4.

Rose, H. and Rose, S. (2000) *Alas, Poor Darwin*. London: Jonathan Cape.

Wilson, E.O. (1975) *Sociobiology: The new synthesis*. Cambridge, MA: Harvard University Press.

Workman, L. and Reader, W. (2004) *Evolutionary psychology*. Cambridge: Cambridge University Press.

These selected readings are a good introduction to sociobiology and evolutionary psychology. Donald Buss is a highly active researcher and thinker in evolutionary psychology; his book is a very good review of the limits and frontiers of this controversial sub-area. The Workman and Reader book is similar. Wilson's book is a classic in this area. The Roses' edited book is a collection of tendentious essays on evolutionary psychology, with Pigliucci also providing a critical perspective.

Comparative evolution

Byrne, R. (1995) *The Thinking Ape: Evolutionary origins of intelligence*. Oxford: Oxford University Press.
Richard Byrne's excellent little book is a provocative and detailed account of the evolution of intelligence in primates from the perspective of evolutionary psychology.

Journals to consult

American Psychologist

Behavior Genetics

Child Development

Developmental Psychology

Ethology and Sociobiology

Human Nature, Motivation and Emotion

Journal of Evolutionary Psychology

Journal of Personality and Social Psychology

Nature

Personality and Individual Differences

Science

Website addresses

http://www.darinday.org/englishL/home/index.html
A website celebrating the 200th anniversary of Darwin's birth.

http://darwin-online.org.uk/
An online collection of Darwin's manuscripts and other materials.

http://www.pbs.org/wgbh/evolution/
A general, non-specialist introduction to evolution.

http://cogweb.ucla.edu/EP/
A large collection of links to evolutionary psychology, adaptation, paleoanthropology and evolution topics.

http://www.arts.uwaterloo.ca/~acheyne/pce.html
You'll find more links to evolution sites here.

http://www.uni-saarland.de/fak5/ronald/
A link to Ronald Henss's website which allows you to participate in online experiments on physical attractiveness.

http://www.envoyage.com/
A site dedicated to evolutionary psychology.

http://www.georgetown.edu/research/gucdc/hugem/Wfacts.htm
A collection of genetics fact sheets from the University of Georgetown.

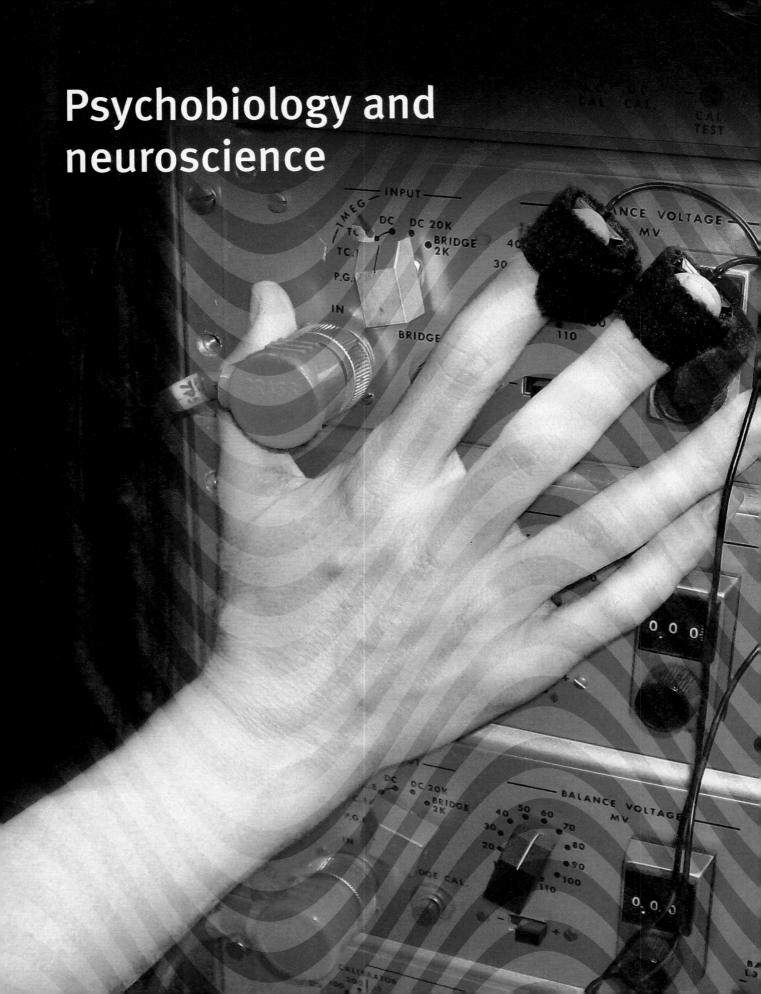

Psychobiology and neuroscience

CHAPTER 4

Found: the brain's centre of wisdom

Jonathan Leake, Science Editor

Scientists have identified the seat of human wisdom by pinpointing parts of the brain that guide us when we face difficult moral dilemmas.

Sophisticated brain scanning techniques have found that humans respond by activating areas associated with the primitive emotions of sex, fear and anger as well as our capability for abstract thought.

The findings, to be published in the *Archives of General Psychiatry*, represent a significant incursion into territory once regarded as the domain of religion and philosophy.

Source: The Sunday Times, 5 April 2009

Explore the accompanying videos, simulations, and animations on MyPsychLab. This chapter includes activities on: Brain structure and function • Brain damage • The autonomic nervous system • The endocrine system • Check your understanding and prepare for your exams using the multiple choice, short answer and essay practice tests also available.

WHAT YOU SHOULD BE ABLE TO DO AFTER READING CHAPTER 4

- Describe the major parts of the nervous system and its principal components.

- Describe and understand the most important functions of these components.

- Describe the parts of a nerve cell and how it functions.

- Understand how nerve cells communicate with each other.

- Describe the various techniques used in neuroscience and psychobiology to study behaviour, from lesioning to heart rate recording to neuroimaging.

- Describe the lobes of the brain and their function.

- Be aware of the effects of drugs on behaviour and how they act on the brain to produce these behaviours.

- Be able to understand some of the psychobiological causes and correlates of behaviour.

QUESTIONS TO THINK ABOUT

- Are two human brains exactly alike?

- Do psychological functions such as language, memory or visual perception reside in specific parts of the brain?

- Do different sides of the brain undertake different functions? If they do, what purpose would this serve?

- What do you think scientists mean by 'nature v. nurture' explanations? Is this concept a sensible one?

- How can we measure the brain and body's responses to external and internal stimuli?

- Is any chemical that has an effect on our body and brain 'a drug'?

- Why do certain drugs have different effects on our behaviour?

- If a person needs a drug to function efficiently, in what way could he or she be said to 'abuse' it?

Psychobiology and neuroscience

In Chapter 1 you saw that psychology is a discipline with many subdivisions. Sometimes these subdivisions are further subdivided into more specific areas of study. Psychologists who study the role of physiology in behaviour, for example, may be interested only in specific behaviours, organisms and techniques. Consequently, psychologists who specialise in researching the role of the brain and body in behaviour are known by different names.

Psychobiology is the study of the role of physiology and anatomy in the regulation and execution of behaviour – these topics can range from the role of hormones in sexual reproduction, the effect of glucose deprivation on hunger, the relationship between hormone secretion and stress, the effect of relaxing music on heart rate, or the activation of the brain while a person is engaged in a particular task. Neuroscientists study similar processes but limit themselves to studying certain parts of the body – the brain and spinal cord. Together these parts are known as the **central nervous system (CNS)**, so called because not only do they occupy the central position of the body but they are also the most important part of the nervous system for maintaining and producing behaviour. Neuroscientists study the CNS of any organism that possesses one.

Neuropsychologists, as you saw in Chapter 1, study the relationship between the brain and its function. A goal of neuropsychology is localisation of function – the idea that parts of the brain perform specific functions. Although much of the research in neuropsychology derives from the effects of brain damage on behaviour, neuropsychologists also study psychological function in healthy individuals by using modern neuroimaging techniques (described later on). Psychophysiologists study physiological processes such as heart rate, hormone secretion, brain electrical activity and skin conductance and the conditions in which changes to these processes arise.

The nervous system: the brain and its components

The brain looks like a lump of porridge and has the consistency of blancmange. This organ, weighing an average 1400 g in an adult human, is the most important part of the body (it was not always so – Aristotle, for example, believed that the heart was more important to behaviour). It contains an estimated 10 to 100 billion nerve cells and about as many supporting cells, which take care of important support and 'housekeeping' functions. The brain contains many different types of nerve cell which differ in shape, size and the kinds of chemicals they produce.

Although nerve cells of the brain are organised in modules – clusters of nerve cells that communicate with each other – individual modules do not stand alone. They are connected to other neural circuits, receiving information from some of them, processing this information and sending the results on to other modules. In his famous book *The Modularity of Mind*, the philosopher Jerry Fodor (Fodor, 1983) argues that particular modules have particular functions – just as the transistors, resistors and capacitors in a computer chip do – and are relatively independent of each other. Although this idea – **modularity** – is still controversial, the evidence broadly supports some degree of modularity in the brain. The aim of psychobiology and neuroscience is to understand how individual nerve cells work, how they connect with each other to form modules, and just what these modules do.

The central nervous system

see activity on mypsychlab

The brain has two primary functions: the control of behaviour and the regulation of the body's physiological processes. The brain cannot act alone – it needs to receive information from the body's sense receptors and it must be connected with the muscles and glands of the body if it is to affect behaviour and physiological processes. The spinal cord is a long, thin collection of nerve cells attached to the base of the brain and running the length of the spinal column (see Figure 4.1). It contains circuits of nerve cells that control some simple reflexes, such as automatically pulling away from a painfully hot object. The central nervous system communicates with the rest of the body through the nerves – bundles of fibres that transmit information in and out of the central nervous system. The nerves, which are attached to the spinal cord and to the base of the brain, make up the **peripheral nervous system**.

The human brain has three major parts: the brain stem, the cerebellum and the cerebral hemispheres. Figure 4.2 shows photographs of the side (a), top (b), cross-section (c) and bottom/underneath (d) of the human cerebral hemispheres. The lower part of the cerebellum and brain stem projects beneath the cerebral hemisphere (see the bottom left of Figure 4.2 (a)); the upper part is normally hidden. If the human brain is removed from the skull, it looks as if it has a handle or stem. The brain stem is one of the most primitive regions of the brain, and its functions are correspondingly basic – primarily control of physiological functions and automatic behaviours such as swallowing and breathing. The brains of some animals, such as amphibians, consist primarily of a brain stem and a simple cerebellum.

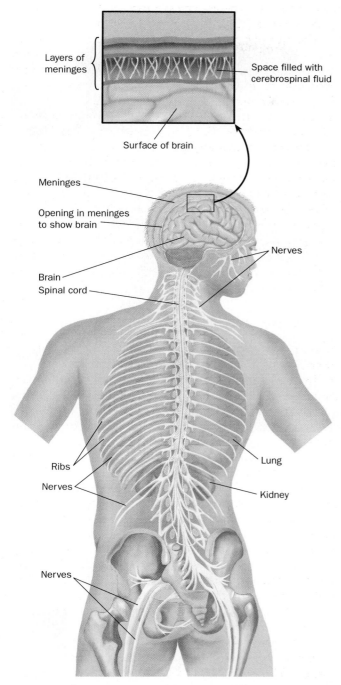

Layers of meninges

Space filled with cerebrospinal fluid

Surface of brain

Meninges

Opening in meninges to show brain

Nerves

Brain

Spinal cord

Ribs

Lung

Nerves

Kidney

Nerves

Figure 4.1 The central nervous system (brain and spinal cord) and the peripheral nervous system (cranial nerves and spinal nerves).

The two **cerebral hemispheres** constitute the largest, and most recently developed, part of the human brain. The cerebellum, attached to the back of the brain stem, looks like a miniature version of the cerebral hemispheres. Its primary function is to control and coordinate movements, although recent research has highlighted its role in language

and thinking, too. The cerebellum in cross-section is on the bottom right of Figure 4.2 (c).

Because the central nervous system is vital to an organism's survival, it is exceptionally well protected. The brain is encased by the skull, and the spinal cord runs through the middle of a column of hollow bones known as **vertebrae**. Both the brain and the spinal cord are enclosed by a three-layered set of membranes called the **meninges** (meninges is the plural of *meninx*, the Greek word for 'membrane'; meningitis is an inflammation of the meninges). The brain and spinal cord do not come into direct contact with the bones of the skull and vertebrae. Instead, they float in a clear liquid called **cerebrospinal fluid (CSF)**. This liquid fills the space between two of the meninges, thus providing a liquid cushion surrounding the brain and spinal cord and protecting them from being bruised by the bones that encase them.

The surface of the cerebral hemispheres is covered by the cerebral cortex (the word cortex means 'bark' or 'rind'). The **cerebral cortex** consists of a thin layer of tissue approximately 3 mm thick. It is often referred to as **grey matter** because of its appearance. It contains billions of nerve cells and is the structure where perceptions take place, memories are stored and plans are formulated and executed. The nerve cells in the cerebral cortex are connected to other parts of the brain by a layer of nerve fibres called the **white matter** because of the shiny white appearance of the substance that coats and insulates them. Figure 4.3 shows a slice of the brain. As you can see, the grey matter and white matter are distinctly different.

The human cerebral cortex is wrinkled in appearance; it is full of bulges separated by grooves. The bulges are called **gyri** (singular 'gyrus'), and the large grooves are called **fissures**. Fissures and gyri expand the amount of surface area of the cortex and greatly increase the number of nerve cells it can contain. Animals with the largest and most complex brains, including humans and the higher primates, have the most wrinkled brains and, thus, the largest cerebral cortices.

The peripheral nervous system

The peripheral nervous system consists of the nerves that connect the central nervous system with sense organs, muscles and glands. Nerves carry both incoming and outgoing information. The sense organs detect changes in the environment and send signals through the nerves to the CNS. The brain sends signals through the nerves to the muscles (causing behaviour) and the glands (producing adjustments in internal physiological processes).

Nerves are bundles of many thousands of individual fibres, all wrapped in a tough, protective membrane. Nerve fibres transmit messages through the nerve, from a sense organ to the brain or from the brain to a muscle or gland.

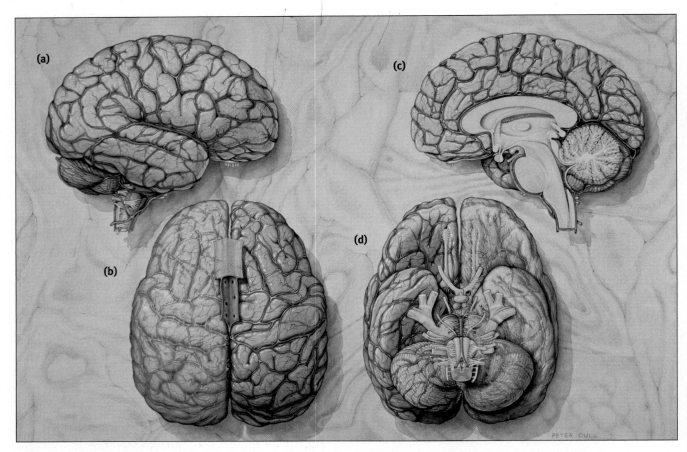

Figure 4.2 The external features of the brain from four angles: **(a)** the side (sagittal), **(b)** top, **(c)** cross-section (lateral) **(d)** bottom/underneath.

Source: Professor Peter Cull/Science Photo Library Ltd

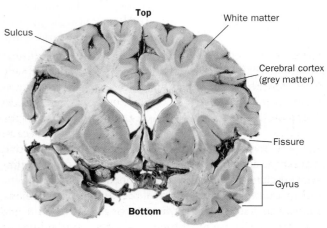

Figure 4.3 A coronal slice of a human brain showing fissures and gyri, the layer of cerebral cortex that follows these convolutions and the white and grey matter.

Source: Harvard Medical School/Betty G. Martindale.

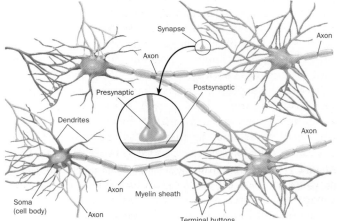

Figure 4.4 The principal parts of a neuron and its connections with other neurons (synapses).

As we saw earlier, some nerves are attached to the spinal cord and others are attached directly to the brain. The spinal nerves, attached to the spinal cord, serve all of the body below the neck, conveying sensory information from the body and carrying messages to muscles and glands. The twelve pairs of **cranial nerves**, attached to the brain, serve primarily muscles and sense receptors in the neck and head. For example, when you taste food, the sensory information gets from your tongue to your brain through one set of cranial nerves. Other sets of cranial nerves bring sensory information to the brain from the eyes, ears and nose. When you chew food, the command to chew reaches your jaw muscles through another set of cranial nerves. Still other cranial nerves control the eye muscles, the tongue, the neck muscles and the muscles we use for speech.

Cells of the nervous system

Neurons, or nerve cells, are the elements of the nervous system that bring sensory information to the brain, store memories, reach decisions and control the activity of the muscles. They are assisted in their task by another kind of cell: the glia. **Glia** (or **glial cells**) get their name from the Greek word for glue and 90 per cent of cells in the brain are glial cells. At one time, scientists thought that glia simply held neurons – the important elements of the nervous system – in place. They do not, however, literally stick neurons together but they do provide important physical support to neurons as well as providing other forms of mechanical support. During development of the brain, some types of glial cells form long fibres that guide developing neurons from their place of birth to their final resting place. Other types of glia manufacture chemicals that neurons need to perform their tasks and absorb chemicals that might impair neurons' functioning. Others form protective insulating sheaths around nerve fibres. Still others serve as the brain's immune system, protecting it from invading micro-organisms that might infect it.

Research suggests that they may play a more important part in brain development than was originally thought. For example, one study has shown that glial cells may determine the number of junctions between neurons – called synapses – generated in the brain (Ullian *et al.*, 2001). This finding followed an experiment by researchers from the same laboratory which found that synapses of neurons grown with a certain type of glial cell were ten times more active than those grown without. The mere proximity of glial cells to neurons made the neurons more responsive. In their most recent experiment, neurons that were exposed to glial cells formed seven times as many synapses as those that were not exposed. This is important because it indicates that glial cells have a much greater role to play in the formation of

synapses in the CNS than had previously been thought. The next step is to identify how the glial cells produce this increase.

The four principal parts of a neuron are shown in Figure 4.4.

1 The **soma**, or cell body, is the largest part of the neuron and contains the mechanisms that control the metabolism and maintenance of the cell. The soma also receives messages from other neurons.

2 The **dendrites**, the tree-like growths attached to the soma, function principally to receive messages from other neurons (dendron means 'tree'). They transmit the information they receive down their 'trunks' to the soma.

3 The nerve fibre, or **axon**, carries messages away from the soma towards the cells with which the neuron communicates. These messages, called action potentials, consist of brief changes in the electrical charge of the axon. For convenience, an action potential is usually referred to as the firing of an axon.

4 The **terminal buttons** are located at the ends of the 'twigs' that branch off the ends of axons. Terminal buttons secrete a chemical called a transmitter substance whenever an action potential travels down the axon, i.e. whenever the axon fires. These chemicals are called **neurotransmitters**. The transmitter substance affects the activity of the other cells with which the neuron communicates. Thus, the message is conveyed chemically from one neuron to another. Most drugs that affect the nervous system and hence alter a person's behaviour do so by affecting the chemical transmission of messages between cells.

Neurotransmitters

There are currently around 50 or so identifiable neurotransmitters and all are important to behaviour in some way. Some, however, play a greater role than others. The amine group of neurotransmitters, for example, which includes dopamine, noradrenaline and serotonin (5-hydroxytryptamine), appears especially important to psychologists because they are involved in a range of behaviours – emotional expression, decision-making, response to reward, inhibiting inappropriate actions, drug-taking and many others.

A part of the brain, called the nucleus accumbens, appears to be part of a reward system in the front and midpart of the brain, which evaluates how salient or important events in the outside world are. It and the system it belongs to are also implicated in impulsive behaviour – the inability to delay reward and to be aware of the consequences of actions, and so on (Pothuizen *et al.*, 2005). Drugs which act on serotonin receptors here, for example, increase impulsivity (Pattij and Vanderschuren,

2008). Such impulsivity, according to some scientists, is linked to the initiation and maintenance of drug-seeking (Krishnan-Sarin *et al.*, 2007).

The events the nucleus accumbens responds to can include rewarding stimuli (food, water, sex), aversive stimuli (ice, shock) and novel stimuli. Dopamine release increases here, as does the firing of dopamine receptors when an organism is rewarded with food or water (Schultz, 2007; Iversen and Iversen, 2007). Dopamine can increase by as much as 20–100 per cent and last for up to 100 minutes (Schultz, 2007). If an organism expects a reward there is a release of dopamine in these regions, but if an organism is completely rewarded there seems to be little dopamine activation. Dopamine is also released in freely moving organisms, which suggests that it is important for motor movement and the motivation to move. Of course, the movement disorder Parkinson's disease, discussed a little later, is treated by a dopamine precursor (called Levodopa), and excessive dopamine is thought to be implicated in some of the symptoms of schizophrenia (described in Chapter 18).

Like all the amines, dopamine receptors begin projecting from the brain stem and certain dopamine receptors terminate (end their projections) in the front part of the brain (called the prefrontal cortex, described below). These receptors, called D1 receptors, appear to be very important to cognitive performance and influence tasks such as our ability to store and manipulate non-verbal information over very short periods of time (a type of memory called working memory, described in Chapter 8). Some people have a mutation of an allele which directly affects dopamine (by inactivating it) with the consequence that their cognitive function is impaired (Turbridge *et al.*, 2006). Another type of dopamine receptor, D2, seems to be reduced in the striatum of drug addicts (Kalivas and Volkow, 2005).

Myelination

Many axons, especially long ones, are insulated with a substance called **myelin**. The white matter located beneath the cerebral cortex gets its colour from the myelin sheaths around the axons that travel through these areas. Myelin, which is part protein, part fat, is produced by special cells that individually wrap themselves around segments of the axon, leaving small bare patches of the axon between them. The principal function of myelin is to insulate axons from each other and thus to prevent the scrambling of messages. It also increases the speed of the action potential.

In some cases, people's immune systems go awry and begin to attack parts of their own bodies. One of these disorders is called multiple sclerosis – an autopsy of the brain and spinal cord will show numerous patches of hardened, damaged tissue (*skleros* is Greek for 'hard'). The immune systems of people who have multiple sclero-

sis attack a protein in the myelin sheath of axons in the central nervous system, stripping it away. Although most of the axons survive this assault, they can no longer function normally, and so, depending on where the damage occurs, people who have multiple sclerosis suffer from various sensory and motor impairments.

There is also evidence to suggest that the central nervous system becomes fully mature when myelination is complete; speed of information processing in children, for example, seems to mirror cortical development and ongoing myelination (Travis, 1998).

The action potential

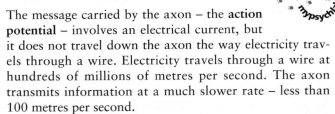

The message carried by the axon – the **action potential** – involves an electrical current, but it does not travel down the axon the way electricity travels through a wire. Electricity travels through a wire at hundreds of millions of metres per second. The axon transmits information at a much slower rate – less than 100 metres per second.

The membrane of an axon is electrically charged. When the axon is resting (that is, when no action potential is occurring), the outside is charged at +70 millivolts (mV, thousandths of a volt) with respect to the inside. An action potential is an abrupt, short-lived reversal in the electrical charge of an axon. This temporary reversal begins at the end of the axon that attaches to the soma and is transmitted to the end that divides into small branches capped with terminal buttons.

The electrical charge of the axon occurs because of an unequal distribution of positively and negatively charged particles inside the axon and in the fluid that surrounds it. These particles, called **ions**, are produced when various substances – including ordinary table salt – are dissolved in water. Normally, ions cannot penetrate the membrane that surrounds axons. However, the axonal membrane contains special submicroscopic proteins that serve as **ion channels** or **ion transporters**. Ion channels can open or close; when they are open, a particular ion can enter or leave the axon. Ion transporters work like pumps. They use the energy resources of the cell to transport particular ions into or out of the axon, as seen in Figure 4.5.

The outside of the membrane is positively charged (and the inside is negatively charged) because the axon contains more negatively charged ions and fewer positively charged ions. When an axon is resting, its ion channels are closed, so ions cannot move into or out of the axon. An action potential is caused by the opening of some ion channels in the membrane at the end of the axon nearest the soma. The opening of these ion channels permits positively charged sodium ions to enter, which reverses the membrane potential at that location. This reversal causes nearby ion channels to open, which produces another reversal at that point. The process continues all the way to the terminal buttons located at the other end of the axon.

Note that an action potential is a brief reversal of the membrane's electrical charge. As soon as the charge reverses, the ion channels close and another set of ion channels opens for a short time, letting positively charged potassium ions out of the axon. This outflow of positive ions restores the normal electrical charge. Thus, an action potential resembles the 'Mexican wave' that football fans often make in a stadium. People in one part of the stadium stand up, raise their arms over their heads, and sit down again. People seated next to them see that a wave is starting, so they do the same – and the wave travels around the stadium. Everyone remains at the same place, but the effect is that of something circling in the stands around the playing field. Similarly, electricity does not really travel down the length of an axon. Instead, the entry of positive ions in one location reverses the charge at that point and causes ion channels in the adjacent region to open, and so on, as seen in Figure 4.6. The ion transporters pump sodium ions out of the axon and pump potassium ions back in, restoring the normal balance.

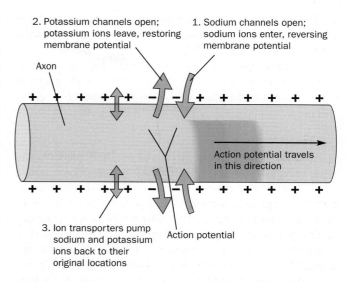

Figure 4.6 Movement of sodium and potassium ions during the action potential. Sodium ions are represented by orange arrows, potassium ions by green arrows.

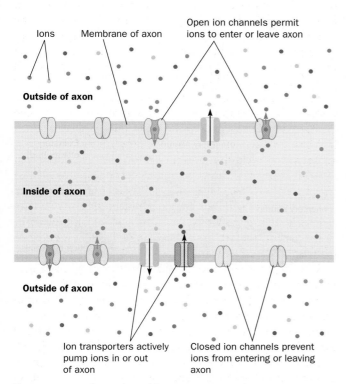

Figure 4.5 Ion channels and ion transporters. These structures regulate the number of ions found inside and outside the axon. An unequal distribution of positively and negatively charged ions is responsible for the axon's electrical charge.

Synapses

Neurons communicate with other cells by means of synapses. A **synapse** is the conjunction of a terminal button of one neuron and the membrane of another cell – neuron, muscle cell or gland cell. The terminal button belongs to the **presynaptic neuron** – the neuron that sends the message. When terminal buttons become active, they release a chemical called a transmitter substance. The neuron that receives the message (detects the transmitter substance) is called the **postsynaptic neuron**. A neuron receives messages from many terminal buttons, and in turn its terminal buttons form synapses with many other neurons. The drawing in Figure 4.4 is much simplified; thousands of terminal buttons can form synapses with a single neuron.

Figure 4.7 illustrates the relation between a motor neuron and a muscle. A **motor neuron** is one that forms synapses with a muscle and controls its contractions. When the axon of a motor neuron fires, all the muscle fibres with which it forms synapses will contract with a brief twitch. A muscle consists of thousands of individual muscle fibres. It is controlled by a large number of motor neurons, each of which forms synapses with different groups of muscle fibres. The strength of a muscular contraction, then, depends on the rate of firing of the axons that control it. If they fire at a high rate, the muscle contracts forcefully; if they fire at a low rate, the muscle contracts weakly.

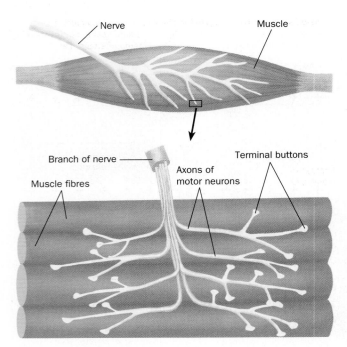

Figure 4.7 Synapses between terminal buttons of the axon of a motor neuron and a muscle.

Excitation and inhibition

There are broadly two types of synapse: excitatory synapses and inhibitory synapses. Excitatory synapses do just what their name implies. When the axon fires, the terminal buttons release a transmitter substance that excites the postsynaptic neurons with which they form synapses. The effect of this excitation is to make it more likely that the axons of the postsynaptic neurons will fire. Inhibitory synapses do just the opposite. When they are activated, they lower the likelihood that the axons of the postsynaptic neurons will fire.

The rate at which a particular axon fires is determined by the activity of the synapses on the dendrites and soma of the cell. If the excitatory synapses are the more active, the axon will fire at a high rate. If the inhibitory synapses are the more active, the axon will fire at a low rate or perhaps not at all, as seen in Figure 4.8.

How do molecules of transmitter substance exert their excitatory or inhibitory effect on the postsynaptic neuron? When an action potential reaches a terminal button, it causes the terminal button to release a small amount of transmitter substance into the **synaptic cleft**, a fluid-filled space between the terminal button and the membrane of the postsynaptic neuron. The transmitter substance causes

reactions in the postsynaptic neuron that either excite or inhibit it. These reactions are triggered by special submicroscopic protein molecules embedded in the postsynaptic membrane called **receptor molecules** (see Figure 4.9).

A molecule of a transmitter substance attaches to a receptor molecule the way a key fits in a lock. After their release from a terminal button, molecules of transmitter substance find their way to the receptor molecules, attach to them and activate them. Once they are activated, the receptor molecules produce excitatory or inhibitory effects on the postsynaptic neuron. They do so by opening ion channels. The ion channels found at excitatory synapses permit sodium ions to enter the neuron; those found at inhibitory synapses permit potassium ions to leave it (see Figure 4.10).

The excitation or inhibition produced by a synapse is short-lived; the effects soon pass away, usually in a fraction of a second. At most synapses, the effects are terminated by a process called **reuptake**. The transmitter substance is released by the terminal button and is quickly taken up again. It has, therefore, only a short time to stimulate the postsynaptic receptor molecules, as you can see from Figure 4.11. The rate at which the terminal button takes back the transmitter substance determines how prolonged the effects of the chemical on the postsynaptic neuron will be. The faster the transmitter substance is taken back, the shorter its effects will be on the postsynaptic neuron. As we will see, some drugs affect the nervous system by slowing down the rate of reuptake, thus prolonging the effects of the transmitter substance.

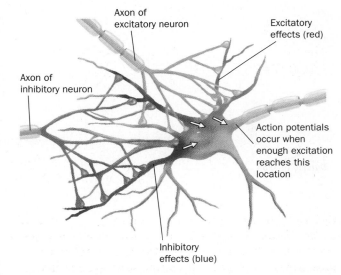

Figure 4.8 Interaction between the effects of excitatory and inhibitory synapses. The rate of firing of the axon of the neuron is controlled by these two factors.

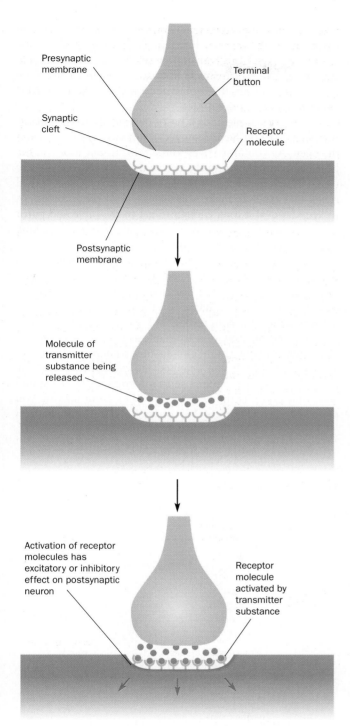

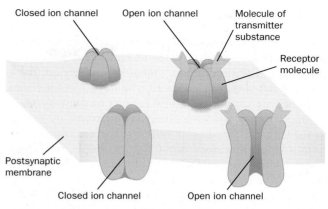

Figure 4.10 Detailed view of receptor molecules in the postsynaptic neuron. When activated by molecules of a transmitter substance, the receptor molecules allow sodium ions to enter the postsynaptic neuron, causing excitation, or allow potassium ions to leave, causing inhibition.

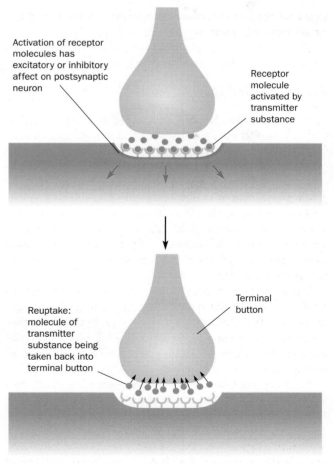

Figure 4.9 The release of a transmitter substance from a terminal button. *Top*: Before the arrival of an action potential. *Middle*: Just after the arrival of an action potential. Molecules of transmitter substance have been released. *Bottom*: Activation of receptor molecules. The molecules of transmitter substance diffuse across the synaptic cleft and some of them activate receptor molecules in the postsynaptic membrane.

Figure 4.11 Reuptake of molecules of transmitter substance.

A simple neural circuit

The interconnections of the billions of neurons in our central nervous system provide us with the capacities for perception, decision-making, memory and action. It has been estimated that there are 13 trillion such connections. Although we do not yet know enough to draw a 'neural wiring diagram' for such complex functions, we can do so for some of the simpler reflexes that are triggered by certain kinds of sensory stimuli. For example, when your finger touches a painfully hot object, your hand withdraws. When your eye is touched, your eyes close and your head draws back. When a baby's cheek is touched, it turns its mouth towards the object, and if the object is of the appropriate size and texture, the baby begins to suck. All these activities occur quickly, without thought.

A simple withdrawal reflex, which is triggered by a noxious stimulus (such as contact with a hot object), requires three types of neuron. **Sensory neurons** detect the noxious stimulus and convey this information to the spinal cord. **Interneurons**, located entirely within the brain or spinal cord, receive the sensory information and in turn stimulate the motor neurons that cause the appropriate muscle to contract, as seen in Figure 4.12.

The sequence is simple and straightforward. A noxious stimulus applied to the skin produces a burst of action potentials in the sensory neurons. Their axons fire, and their terminal buttons, located within the spinal cord, release an excitatory transmitter substance. The chemical stimulates the interneurons and causes them to fire. The interneurons excite the motor neurons, and these neurons cause the muscle to contract.

The next example adds a bit of complexity to the circuit. Imagine that you have removed a hot casserole dish from the oven. As you move over to the table to put it down, the heat begins to penetrate the rather thin ovengloves you are using. The pain caused by the hot dish triggers a withdrawal reflex that tends to make you drop it. And yet you manage to keep hold of it long enough to get to the table and put it down. What prevented your withdrawal reflex from making you drop the dish on the floor?

As you saw earlier, the activity of a neuron depends on the relative activity of the excitatory and inhibitory synapses on it. The pain from the hot casserole dish increases the activity of excitatory synapses on the motor neurons, which tends to cause the hand to open. However, this excitation is counteracted by inhibition from another source – the brain. The brain contains neural circuits that recognise what a disaster it would be if you dropped the casserole dish on the floor. These neural circuits send information to the spinal cord that prevents the withdrawal reflex from making you drop the dish. Figure 4.13 shows how this information

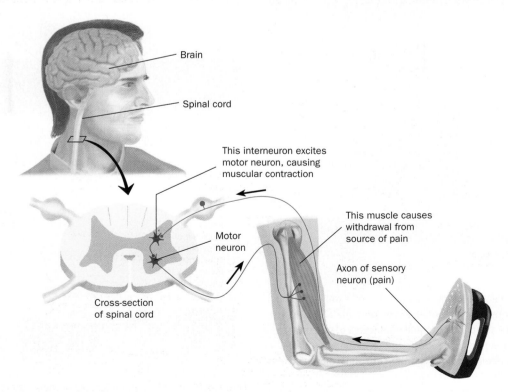

Figure 4.12 Schematic representation of the elements of a withdrawal reflex. Although this figure shows just one sensory neuron, one interneuron and one motor neuron, in reality many thousands of each type of neuron are involved.

reaches the spinal cord. As you can see, an axon from a neuron in the brain reaches the spinal cord, where it forms a synapse with an inhibitory interneuron. When the neuron in the brain becomes active, it excites this inhibitory interneuron. The interneuron releases an inhibitory transmitter substance, which decreases the rate of firing of the motor neuron, preventing your hand from opening. This circuit provides an example of a contest between two competing tendencies: to drop the casserole dish and to hold onto it. Complex decisions about behaviour are made within the brain by much more complicated circuits of neurons, but the basic principles remain the same.

Neuromodulators: action at a distance

Terminal buttons excite or inhibit postsynaptic neurons by releasing transmitter substances. These chemicals travel a very short distance and affect receptor molecules located on a small patch of the postsynaptic membrane. But some neurons release chemicals that get into the general circulation of the brain and stimulate receptor molecules on many thousands of neurons, some located a considerable distance away. The chemicals these neurons release are called **neuromodulators**, because they modulate the activity of the neurons they affect.

We can think of neuromodulators as the brain's own 'drugs'. Because these chemicals diffuse widely in the brain, they can activate or inhibit many different circuits of neurons, thus exerting several behavioural and physiological effects. These effects act together to help achieve a particular goal.

The best-known neuromodulator is a category of chemicals called endorphins, or opioids ('opium-like substances'). **Opioids** are neuromodulators that stimulate special receptor molecules (opioid receptors) located on neurons in several parts of the brain. Their behavioural effects include decreased sensitivity to pain and a tendency to persist in ongoing behaviour. Opioids are released while an animal is engaging in important species-typical behaviours, such as mating or fighting. The behavioural effects of opioids ensure that a mating animal or an animal fighting to defend itself is less likely to be deterred by pain; thus, conception is more likely to occur and a defence is more likely to be successful.

Many years ago, people discovered that eating or smoking the sap of the opium poppy decreased their sensitivity to pain, so they began using it for this purpose. They also discovered that the sap produced pleasurable effects: people who took it enjoyed the experience and wanted to take more. In recent times, chemists have discovered that the sap of the opium poppy contains a class of chemicals called opiates. They also learned how to extract and concentrate them and to produce synthetic versions with even greater potency. In the mid-1970s, neurobiologists learned that opiates produce their effect

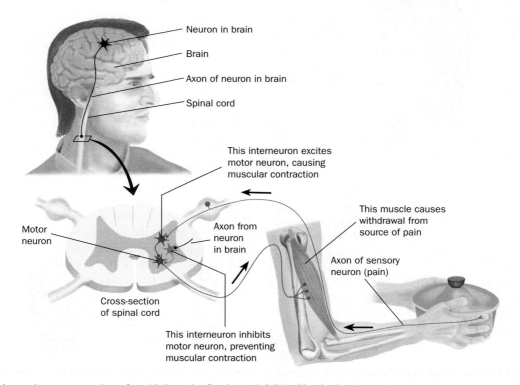

Figure 4.13 Schematic representation of a withdrawal reflex being inhibited by the brain.

by stimulating special opioid receptor molecules located on neurons in the brain (Pert *et al.*, 1974). Soon after that, they discovered the brain's opioids (Terenius and Wahlström, 1975). Thus, opiates mimic the effects of a special category of neuromodulators that the brain uses to regulate some types of species-typical behaviours.

The brain produces other neuromodulators. Some help organise the body's response to stress, while others reduce anxiety and promote sleep. Some promote eating, while others help end a meal.

Techniques in psychobiology and neuroscience

Until relatively recently, most of our knowledge of the functions of the nervous system was obtained through research using laboratory animals. This research produced important discoveries about the causes and treatments of neurological and mental disorders, many of which are discussed in this book. It led to the development of drugs and surgical techniques that help people with neurological disorders, such as Parkinson's disease, and mental disorders, such as schizophrenia, depression and obsessive-compulsive disorders.

Physiological psychologists now have at their disposal a range of research methods to study the function of the brain and body that would have been impossible to imagine just a few decades ago. We have ways to identify neurons that contain particular chemicals. We have ways to take photographs of particular ions entering neurons when the appropriate ion channels open. We have ways to inactivate individual genes to see what happens to behaviour when they no longer function. We can also witness the activity of the brain as it behaves, through the technique of neuroimaging.

Lesioning

The earliest of research methods in psychobiology – and one that is still the most commonly used – involves correlating a behavioural deficit with damage to a specific part of the nervous system. The damage can be studied in one of two ways. For example, a neuropsychologist may examine the effects of brain damage on function, such as the effect of damage to the front part of the brain on a person's ability to create and adhere to plans.

The second way involves the investigator producing an **experimental brain lesion**, an injury to a particular part of the brain, but only in an animal's brain. Of course, neurosurgeons do lesion parts of the brain to alleviate some forms of suffering. One recent, successful treatment for the movement disorder Parkinson's disease, for example, has

involved lesioning a small structure deep within the brain. A similar technique 'lesions' in another way (the procedure is called deep brain stimulation, DBS). In Parkinson's disease, a person may behave rigidly or be unable to walk properly or exhibit tremors or engage in excessive, repetitive, involuntary motor behaviour. Treatment by Levodopa (mentioned earlier) provides some respite but there are off periods when the drug does not work. DBS overstimulates parts of a collection of structures called the basal ganglia, described below. This has been found to be more successful than lesioning the parts directly (Liu *et al.*, 2008). Why lesioning *and* overstimulation seem to work (i.e. produce the same effect) is still a mystery. One theory is that surgery reduces the inhibitory effects of neurons in the basal ganglia and increases them in another structure, the thalamus and cortex (Liu *et al.*, 2008).

When an animal's brain is experimentally lesioned, the investigator hypothesises that this lesion might have specific consequences; they then study the effects of the lesion on the animal's behaviour. If particular behaviours are disrupted, the reasoning suggests, the damaged part of the brain must be involved in those behaviours.

Some lesioning techniques are used in both experimental and neurosurgical work. For example, to reach the region to be lesioned, the experimenter or surgeon uses a device called a **stereotaxic apparatus** to insert a fine wire (called an electrode) into a particular location in the brain, as Figures 4.14 and 4.15 show. The term 'stereotaxic' refers to the ability to manipulate an object in three-dimensional space. The researcher passes an electrical current through the electrode, which produces heat that destroys a small portion of the brain around the tip of the electrode. After a few days, the animal recovers from the operation, and the researcher can assess its behaviour.

A stereotaxic apparatus can also be used to insert wires for recording the electrical activity of neurons in particular regions of the brain. But an electrode placed in an animal's brain can also be used to lead electrical current into the brain as well as out of it. If an electrical connector on the animal's skull is attached to an electrical stimulator, current can be sent to a portion of the animal's brain. This current activates neurons located near the tip of the electrode. The experimenter can then see how this artificial stimulation affects the animal's behaviour.

Neurosurgeons sometimes use stereotaxic apparatus to operate on humans. For example, as you read earlier, destruction of a particular region near the centre of the cerebral hemispheres can alleviate the tremors (trembling) that occur in some cases of Parkinson's disease (Krack *et al.*, 1998; Samuel *et al.*, 1998) (see Figure 4.16). Neurosurgeons can also insert electrodes into the human brain and record the electrical activity of particular regions to try to find locations that might be responsible for triggering epileptic seizures.

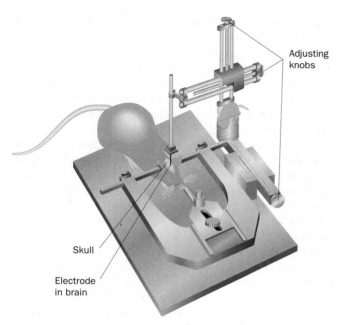

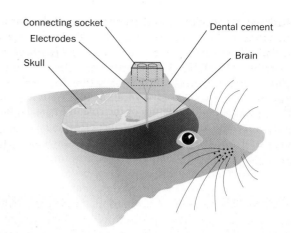

Figure 4.15 A permanently attached set of electrodes in an animal's brain and a connecting socket cemented to the skull.

Figure 4.14 A stereotaxic apparatus, used to insert a wire into a specific portion of an animal's brain.

(a)

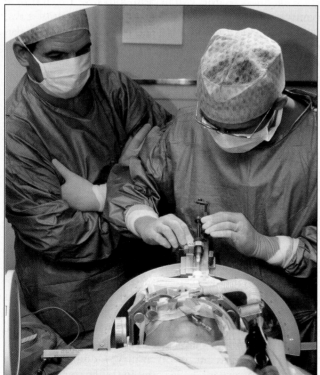

(b)

Figure 4.16 (a) Shows the typical stereotaxic set-up in surgery designed to reduce symptoms of Parkinson's disease. **(b)** Fergus Henderson, celebrated chef of the St John restaurant in London. Henderson suffered from Parkinson's disease until he received surgery to control the symptoms. His hands are in his pockets because he could not keep them still when this photograph was taken.

Source: (a) BSIP, Astier/Science Photo Library Ltd.; (b) © John Reardon, www.abbyjohnston.com.

Studying brain injury: clinical neuropsychology

Although we can, under very careful conditions, experimentally lesion the brains of non-humans, we cannot do this in humans, for very obvious reasons. We have, therefore, relied on studies of accidental brain injury to help us build a picture of the role of damaged brain regions in specific functional impairments.

This approach usually utilises the single-case study design, described in Chapter 2. Brain injury usually results from accident or disease and, because it is more difficult to obtain information of this kind, scientists have studied a small number of individuals intensively over a long period of time. The approach allows neuroscientists to observe how fairly localised brain damage can impair intellectual or emotional function.

Most human brain lesions are the result of natural causes, such as a stroke. A stroke (also known as a cerebrovascular accident, or CVA) occurs when a blood clot obstructs an artery in the brain or when a blood vessel in the brain bursts open. In the first case, the clot blocks the supply of oxygen and nutrients to a particular region and causes that region to die. In the second case, the blood that accumulates in the brain directly damages neural tissue, partly by exerting pressure on the tissue and partly through its toxic effects on cells. The most common causes of strokes are high blood pressure and high levels of cholesterol in the blood. We consider these factors and their effect on health in Chapter 17.

The brain injury in such patients has given rise to a large number of neuropsychological disorders which have helped shape theories of cognitive function. These disorders include the inability to produce or comprehend speech (aphasia), inability to produce speech (fluent or Broca's aphasia), inability to comprehend speech, specifically (Wernicke's aphasia), inability to recognise objects (agnosia), inability to follow motor commands (apraxia), reading impairment (acquired dyslexia), inability to recognise familiar faces (prosopagnosia), inability to attend to stimuli in one half of the visual field (spatial neglect), and a lack of awareness of visual objects, among many others (and you will read more about them in later chapters). Other impairments have no specific name but involve an inability to perform a specific function, such as recognising specific emotions in faces and voices; placing events in sequence; planning; learning new material or retrieving old material from memory.

One of the most famous – if not the most famous – single-case study in neuropsychology is HM. You will find more about HM in the chapter on memory but, briefly, HM underwent surgery for uncontrollable epilepsy in the late 1950s. The surgery involved removal of a part of the brain called the temporal lobe which includes a structure called the hippocampus (this has been implicated in various memory functions). After the surgery and beyond, HM exhibited a form of memory impairment called anterograde amnesia – he was unable to learn new material. The intensive study of HM led to a neurobiological theory of human memory which involved the temporal lobe and the hippocampus and the study has since been supplemented by other case studies and neuroimaging studies of memory in healthy participants.

There have been arguments for and against the single-case study approach in neuropsychology. Some researchers argue that damage to a brain region does not necessarily demonstrate that this region is responsible for any function that is disrupted following injury. Other areas connected to the damaged region may be responsible for the specific function but connections to the intact areas from the lesioned area have been disrupted. There is also the need to specify exactly what function is being measured (this is a problem for psychology in general, rather than neuropsychology in particular). When we say that a region may be 'responsible' for phonological processing, what exactly is meant by phonological processing? Could the region be responsible for some other function which allows phonological processing, rather than being responsible for phonological processing itself?

There are also obvious methodological and practical problems such as the extent and locus of the lesion – because the brain injury is accidental or the result of a disease, the extent of damage is uncontrollable. There is also great variation in regional brain structure between individuals. Amunts *et al.* (1999), for example, found that the size of Broca's area varied enormously in a group of ten individuals: there was a tenfold difference between participants in some cases. When such injury occurs it is also unlikely to be limited to one specific region or structure; it may extend to more than one and so conclusions drawn about the significance of findings in studies such as these need to be done circumspectly. There are also other factors such as sex, personality, handedness and intellectual ability which may need to be taken into account.

Rehabilitation after brain damage

Rehabilitation is an 'active process whereby people who are disabled by injury or disease work together with professional staff, relatives and members of the wider community to achieve their optimum physical, psychological, social and vocational well-being' (McLellan, 1991, p. 785) and programmes have been designed for reading disorders resulting from brain injury (acquired reading disorders) (Patterson, 1994), the inability to produce or understand speech (aphasia) (Berndt and Mitchum, 1995), an inability to attend to or 'see' one half of the world (spatial neglect) (Robertson *et al.*, 1993) and memory disorders (Wilson and Powell, 1994; Glisky, 1997).

The *Top Gear* television presenter Richard Hammond, crashed his car while attempting to break the British land-speed record. His jet-powered vehicle was travelling at 314 mph when a tyre burst. Hammond was hospitalised with brain injury. Although he made a good physical recovery, he still reports periods of severe depression, emotional problems such as becoming angry or scared and not knowing how to cope with these states, and short-term memory loss, including forgetting the PINs of his credit cards.

Source: Alamy Images/Mirrorpix

The most common type of rehabilitation programme is cognitive rehabilitation (Parente and Stapleton, 1997). In this, the patient is encouraged to engage in two types of activity: (1) 'the reinforcing, strengthening or establishing of previously learned behaviour', and (2) the establishment of 'new patterns of cognitive activity or mechanisms to compensate' for the impairment (Bergqvist and Malec, 1997). It shows consistently successful results in the majority of cases of mild to severe brain injury (Ho and Bennett, 1997).

A common form of impairment following brain injury is memory disorder. Specific problems include deficits in learning new material and in retaining other kinds of information (Wilson and Powell, 1994). Some techniques of rehabilitation used to improve memory include exercises and drills, use of external aids, and the use of mnemonic strategies. The patients 'JC' and Julia Cogan are good examples of how rehabilitation strategies can work effectively in reducing problems in everyday life in individuals with severe memory impairment (Wilson, 1991, 1995; Wilson *et al.*, 1997; Oddy and Cogan, 2005). JC, for example, is a self-employed French-polisher who, during the second year at university, suffered an epileptic seizure and collapsed during a tutorial. Doctors, family and friends noted that JC showed severe loss of memory and could not remember anything 'from one minute to the next'.

JC used external aids, such as a diary or notebook, mnemonics and chaining – where tasks are broken down into smaller steps or stages and which can, for example, help patients to find their way around when planning short journeys. These benefited JC but were developed by him into a more elaborate strategy: he has been using and refining this strategy for at least 10 years following his impairment. During the early stages, he began to use a pocketbook kept in his shirt and used a watch with an alarm that sounded every hour – he would note what he was doing in his notebook when this sounded (Wilson *et al.*, 1997). He would create weekly and daily sheets on which he would write down all appointments and lists of things to do or done. He bought a Dictaphone whose content he would transcribe at the end of everyday. His aunt noted how a new watch helped him because it was capable of 15 programmed weekly alarms and 15 one-off alarms. He would use the one-off alarms for reminding him of individual events. He would role-play some social situations to avoid the embarrassment of not being able to remember in public. He would make a log of all phone calls so that he didn't ring someone twice with the same message.

JC's success is mirrored by that of Julia Cogan, a 23-year-old first class graduate in physics who was studying for a Ph.D. in neuroimaging and oncology when she suffered brain injury (Oddy and Cogan, 2005). She made a full physical recovery but her memory was severely impaired. Her everyday problems are familiar ones; she is unable to remember what she had for breakfast, for example, and relies on the strategies she has developed so that she can lead as normal a life as possible. Like JC, she makes extremely good use of her Filofax and if she cannot remember a piece of information, she can find it quickly in her pad. The pad has extensive notes on people she's met, her travel arrangements, recipes and so on (you can see an example in Figure 4.17). If she is asked how work is going, she can flick to a page which describes her last assignment and her next.

Julia is young, well motivated, intelligent and very well organised. All of these characteristics can make rehabilitation easier.

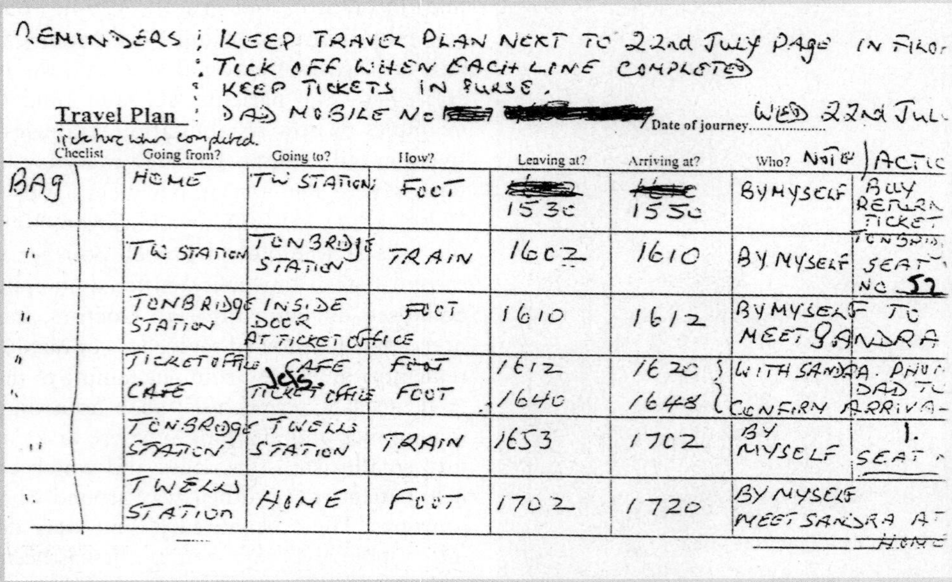

Figure 4.17 An example of the detailed timetable constructed by Julia Cogan to help her remember her travel arrangements.
Source: Figure provided by kind permission of Julia Cogan and Professor Michael Oddy.

Psychology in action – Using brain activity to overcome physical disability

A man in a wheelchair looks at a computer monitor. His arms and legs are still. He cannot speak. Without moving a limb, limbs which cannot move, he is able to move a cursor – not quickly, not effortlessly, but demonstrably – on the screen in front of him. Laboriously, but not without motivation, he spells out a word.

In what seems like a vignette from the most trite science fiction fantasy, he is using the electrical potentials generated by his brain to guide the cursor. This, however, is no third-rate SF make-believe. It is an example of real technology in action: brain–computer interface (BCI).

BCI is a method of controlling electronic or mechanical devices using brain activity. This is useful for people who have suffered illnesses which render them incapable of basic motor behaviour and for whom traditional types of assistive technology are inappropriate because they rely on voluntary motor movement. People who are paralysed, for example, might restore very basic movement through the manipulation of muscles or external devices via signals generated by the brain (Birbaumer, 2006). Those who might benefit include people with amyotrophic lateral sclerosis (ALS) who require artificial respiration and live in a completely 'locked in' state, multiple sclerosis, cerebral palsy, stroke, muscular dystrophy and brain injury who have a severe motor disability/paralysis. The first

of these 'neural prostheses' was inserted into the brain of a patient by US surgeon, Philip R. Kennedy, and his team in 1996. The patient was a teacher and artist who had been paralysed (Kennedy and Bakay, 1998). Two months after the surgery, he had learned how to turn lights on and off (Brown, 2008). A second patient eventually learned to pick out icons on a computer screen and to spell out a small number of words. Figures 4.18 a and b show you a patient in receipt of BCI and a schematic representation of the process.

It is based on the the non-invasive recording of electrical activity (EEG) from the brain's neurons. A person can be trained to use and alter this EEG activity to effect simple changes in motor behaviour. The EEG is 'translated' into output such as moving a cursor around a monitor to indicate 'yes' or 'no' to produce a certain change in the environment, such as switching a light on or off or turning the temperature up or down, spelling out the letters of a word on a monitor, sending an email, accessing the internet, opening and closing a prosthetic hand, or operating a wheelchair (Birbaumer *et al.*, 2007; Daly and Wolpaw, 2008; Pfurtscheller *et al.*, 2003a, b). Research has also found that by changing the appearance of certain types of EEG rhythm, patients can control their epileptic seizures (Sterman, 1981). According to Birbaumer (2006), extensive training can lead to almost 100 per cent control over these seizures.

▶

Psychology in action – *Continued*

Figure 4.18 (a) Dr Phil Kennedy, one of the pioneers of BCI technology, with one of his patients (Kennedy is in the blue shirt).
Source: Landor Media: David Kamerman/The Boston Globe

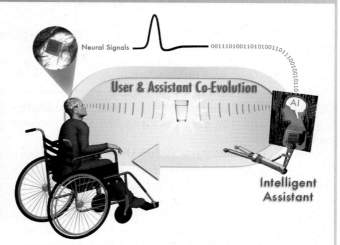

Figure 4.18 (b) A diagram showing the stages and processes involved in brain computer interface.
Source: University of Florida: Arturo Sinclair

The process involves two stages. The first is feature extraction and this involves the identification of the type of signal – its rhythm and amplitude, the neuron's firing rate – that will influence output. The second involves using an algorithm which translates these signals into commands which specify outputs – the selection of letters, the movement of a cursor, etc. The patient might use the beta rhythm recorded over the sensorimotor cortex to make a movement. The algorithm takes into account that activity in a certain EEG frequency range should enable the person to move a cursor to left or right of a monitor. With repeated training and practice, the process becomes less

'effortful' and becomes automatic, in the way that many initially difficult behaviours become automatic with practice.

That said, despite advances in technology and research, the advances are impressive but modest – typing on screen amounts to three to four words per minute, for example. Currently, these techniques are also vision-based: people must be able to see and need to maintain gaze for the technology to work but auditory versions are now being investigated (Nijboer *et al.*, 2008). It is an unusual and innovate way of harnessing the power of the brain.

Psychophysiology: measuring CNS activity

When psychobiologists record brain electrical activity from deep inside the structure, the technique is invasive, i.e. it invades some part of the body (in this case, the brain). Recording the electrical activity of neurons, for example, may involve inserting electrodes into the brain. However, electrical activity of neurons can also be recorded from the scalp non-invasively. Both methods involve a technique called **electroencephalography** (EEG), the recording of the brain's electrical impulses. Electrodes attached to the scalp can record the activity of groups of millions of neurons (Andreassi, 2001; Martin, 2006). The number of electrodes used in brain research tends to be at the discretion of the experimenter. Some use two or three, others use a lot more (over one hundred in some cases), but in all cases researchers use a map showing where each electrode should be placed on the scalp. This avoids errors and inconsistencies in the application of electrodes.

EEG activity is seen in the form of a line-tracing or **electroencephalogram** (**EEG** or 'brainwave'), although some modern EEG recording machines allow the conversion of EEG data into 'brainmaps' – these are two-dimensional representations of the EEG activity. They can be coloured or in greyscale which means that areas of high and low activity can be represented by darker or lighter colours. There are different types of EEG waves – called frequencies – and these are thought to represent different psychological states. Some large, slow EEG waves, for example, are characteristic of deep sleep. One type of activity, called alpha, is the resting adult EEG; when we are engaged in thinking or making rapid movements, alpha activity changes to another type of activity (Andreassi, 2001). In Chapter 9, you will see how different types of EEG brain activity occur during different stages of sleep and wakefulness.

One benefit of the EEG technique is that, as well as being non-invasive, it provides a measure of the brain's activity in real time, as it happens. We can, therefore, match the presentation of a stimulus or a task with the brain activity associated with it. In this way, we can measure how the brain responds while it is engaged in tasks such as deciding whether two figures rotated in three-dimensional space are the same or different (Williams *et al.*, 1995), watching pleasant or unpleasant visual stimuli (Davidson, 1992), smelling food odour (Martin, 1998) or recognising faces and words (Burgess and Gruzelier, 1997), among many other behaviours.

Sometimes, however, this electrical signal can be messy or noisy: it is difficult to distinguish between the brain's normal background activity and the activity produced by the perception of, or response to, a stimulus. The effect of perceiving a sound, for example, may be so small as to be invisible in an EEG tracing. To overcome this, psychophysiologists have devised the technique of averaging signals across trials. They can do this by recording **event-related potentials** or ERPs (these are sometimes also called evoked potentials). These are electrical signals recorded to a repeatedly presented stimulus (or set of stimuli). Each EEG response to a stimulus is added and averaged to produce one clearer signal or evoked potential. The potentials are event-related because they are related to a specific event that is external or internal to the individual such as decision-making (internal stimulus) or perceiving a flash of light (external stimulus). The point of averaging is to make the effect of a stimulus on the EEG clearer; background noise is reduced and the effect of the stimulus becomes more obvious.

Some ERPs measure sensory responses to stimuli (this is called the N100 (or N1), so called because it appears 100 milliseconds after the onset of a stimulus), others are thought to be associated with more cognitive functions such as understanding words or being able to distinguish one type of visual or auditory stimulus from another. These ERPs occur later, at around 300 or 400 milliseconds after stimulus onset (the P300 or P3 and N400 or N4), perhaps reflecting the time the brain takes to undertake these cognitive operations (Polich and Kok, 1995).

The N400, for example, was the first ERP to be specifically linked with language processing and is elicited when participants read sentences in which the last word is semantically surprising or inappropriate, although linguistically legal (Kutas and Hillyard, 1980). For example, the sentence, 'A man who has lost ninety per cent of his brain is called a widower' is legal but surprising whereas the sentence, 'A man who has lost ninety per cent of his brain is called a zombie' is legal but not surprising. The amplitude of the N400 is associated with processing difficulty such that the more difficult the task, the greater the amplitude of the N400 (Kutas and Van Petten, 1994). The N400

declines when congruous sentences are presented – the last word is predictable – but not when incongruous ones are presented (Van Petten and Kutas, 1990). Some researchers have suggested that the N400 reflects a difficulty in integrating words into a sentence (Kutas *et al.*, 2000): the greater the difficulty, the larger the N400.

ERPs have been used to investigate a number of psychological functions such as decision-making, sentence comprehension, recognition memory and visual, tactile and auditory perception. They are not as good as other techniques at localising activity to a specific brain area but they are good at measuring responses to stimuli in real time. The absence of an evoked potential indicates an impairment in function or a failure to attend to stimuli. Figure 4.19 shows the difference between ERPs evoked by a decision-making task in healthy volunteers and individuals with dementia. Note the reduction in the amplitude (size) of the wave in the demented group.

Psychophysiology: measuring activity outside the CNS

Psychophysiologists can also record electrical activity in the peripheral (or autonomic) nervous system – from the heart, muscles and skin. Some of the most common techniques are EMG, ECG and GSR.

Electromyography (EMG)

The body possesses three types of muscles – skeletal, smooth and cardiac. Skeletal muscles are those such as biceps, triceps and flexor muscles of the upper arm and forearm. These are usually under voluntary control – they make up the voluntary motor system; we decide when to flex and tense our arms (such as when picking up a cup), legs (kicking a ball) or fingers (writing or typing at a keyboard). There are other muscles which are not under voluntary control. Smooth muscles are those over which we have little or no voluntary control – the constriction and dilation of blood vessels, for example. The third type of muscle is cardiac and, as the name suggests, this muscle makes up the heart and its valves. Smooth and cardiac muscles comprise about 10 per cent of total body weight; the skeletal muscles make up around 40 per cent of this weight.

When the muscles of the body contract, they generate electrical potentials. Often, muscles contract for psychological reasons – responding to stress, emotional stimuli, pictures, sounds, faces, and so on – and they sometimes contract for these reasons in ways that are undetectable to the eye. The technique used for measuring skeletal muscles' electrical activity is **electromyography (EMG)**. EMG activity is recorded by electrodes – circular disks of around 10 mm in diameter – from the surface of the skin. The greater the muscle contraction and the closer the elec-

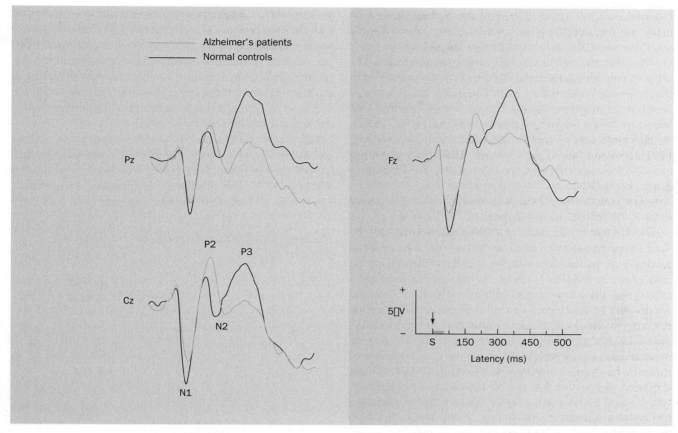

Figure 4.19 Examples of EPs measured in healthy individuals and those with Alzheimer's disease. When a participant is asked to undertake a task such as detecting the number of low tones in a series of high and low tones (where there are always fewer low tones), the ERPs illustrated here are found. The waves on the right show the brain's response to the high tones (the common ones); the N1 sensory and P2 components can be clearly seen. However, when the participant has to make a decision (discriminating between high and low tones) a late wave – the P3 – appears in response to the low tones (the rarer ones). This wave is thought to reflect the brain's decision-making processes. Note how the amplitude (height) of the P3 is lower than that seen in healthy individuals.

trode is to the skin, the greater the electrical activity generated (in fact, EMG records activity from motor units just prior to muscle contraction). For example, imagine a simple behaviour such as gripping an object like a hammer or a handle. The harder you grip the object, the greater the electrical activity produced by musculature and this activity can be picked up as EMG activity from the recording electrode.

Imagining pleasant thoughts results in increased muscle activity in the cheek area responsible for smiling (the zygomatic muscle). A different set of muscles at the eyebrows – called corrugator muscles – are more active during the imagining of unpleasant thoughts (Schwartz, Brown and Ahern, 1980). Activity in the zygomatic muscles has also been found to increase when participants listen to stories with a sexual content rather than a non-sexual content but that corrugator activity is greater when the stories were sexual and unpleasant (Sullivan and Brender, 1986).

Electrocardiography (ECG/EKG)

Cardiac muscle activity is recorded in a similar way to that of skeletal muscle but the differences between the recordings are greater than the similarities. **Electrocardiography (ECG)** refers to the study of the electrical potentials generated by the working of the heart. Before understanding how biological psychologists measure heart activity, it's useful to know a little about how the heart works.

When the heart contracts, it produces an electrical current (as do all other muscular contractions). By placing electrodes near the source of the current, scientists can measure the electrical activity of the heart. The contraction of the heart is the consequence of the organ's chief function – to pump blood around the body. The heart is made up of four chambers which pump blood to the body's tissues. The two chambers at the top of the heart are the atria; the two at the bottom are the ventricles. The atria receive blood returned by the body's veins; the ventricles pump blood away from the heart via arteries (a useful way of remembering the direction in which the blood goes is to think of arteries taking blood away). When you feel – or record – your heartbeat, you are feeling or recording the contraction of the heart as it pumps blood. It beats, on average, 72 times a minute (72 bpm or beats per minute) and, therefore, about 100,000 times a day. The contraction phase of the heart's activity is called systole; the relaxation phase is called the diastole.

The activity of the heart recorded by electrodes can be seen in a typical type of electrical wave. The wave is made up of various characteristic deflections (the direction of the wave characterises various points leading to and during the contraction) – these are the P, Q, R, S and T waves. The P wave is a small deflection produced by the current generated before contraction of the atria; the QRS complex of waves is produced by what is known as depolarisation (more on this later in the chapter) prior to the contraction of the ventricles. The R wave is the largest, most prominent wave. The T wave is the next, small blip-like, deflection after the large R wave and occurs as a result of activity in the ventricles. The P–Q interval lasts about 160 milliseconds; the Q–T interval lasts around 300 milliseconds. It takes around 370 milliseconds to go from the T wave to the next contraction. Figure 4.20 illustrates a typical ECG.

In a study of cardiovascular activity and competitiveness, Harrison *et al.* (2001) asked male and female undergraduates to play a motor racing game either alone, in competition with the experimenter or in cooperation with the experimenter. The competitive condition was associated with significant increases in blood pressure and heart rate whereas the cooperative condition produced barely discernible changes in activity, a finding that echoes reports in the literature of reduced or stable cardiovascular activity in response to stress in the presence of a supportive person (what is known as social affiliation).

Heart rate changes can be seen in response to a number of psychological variables. The promise of financial reward for persuading others (Smith *et al.*, 1990), fear of needles (Shapiro, 1975) and playing Space Invaders (Turner *et al.*, 1983) have all been found to increase heart rate.

Electrodermal response (EDR)/galvanic skin response (GSR)

The measurement of electrical activity of the skin – **electrodermal response** (EDR) or **galvanic skin response** (GSR) – may seem to be completely irrelevant to the study of psychology. The technique, however, is surprisingly useful because skin conductance changes can be influenced by experience of positive and negative emotion, the degree of thinking that goes into the processing of information, and in perceptual awareness. In fact, a French neurologist, Charles Fere, was the first to note in 1888 that changes in a person's mood and environment could lead to changes in the electrical activity recorded from the skin.

The recording of electrodermal activity is based on the properties of skin and what skin does. Human skin has two layers – the epidermis, the outer layer which is about 1 mm thick, and the dermis, the inner layer which varies in thickness depending on the part of the body; it is thinner in the eyelids than the palms of the hands or soles of the feet, for example. The dermis contains blood vessels, hair follicles, sensory nerves and, importantly for EDR, the secretory part of sweat glands. It is sweat which allows conductance to occur on the skin.

The body has two types of sweat glands – apocrine and eccrine. The larger of the two are the apocrine glands which are found in especially hirsute regions such as the armpits and genitals. Sweat is odourless and the odour we associate with it is the result of the reaction between sweat and bacteria on the skin. The eccrine glands are distributed widely and cover most of the skin, with some exceptions (such as lips, outer ear and glans penis, amongst others). Sweat glands are most numerous on the palms of the hands and soles of the feet with around one inch squared of skin having about 3,000 glands (Fowles, 1986). EDR recorded from fingers and palms responds more strongly to sensory stimulation than to physical stimuli such as heat; the opposite pattern is found for EDR recorded from the forehead, neck and back of the

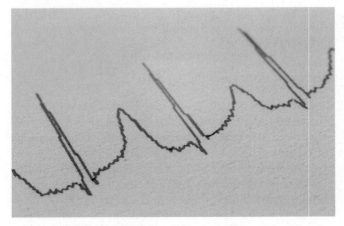

Figure 4.20 This is the PQRST complex of the ECG which represents a heartbeat. Each peak and trough of this complex represents some activity of the heart as it contracts and relaxes.
Source: Daniel Sambraus/Science Photo Library Ltd.

hands which dictates the position of electrodes in EDR recording. Skin conductance increases with increased stress, arousal and cognitive activity and reduces when the organism's level of activity is low. During states of anxiety, for example, there is a great deal of sweating, especially in the palms.

To show how the EDR measure can record changes in behaviour that are not immediately visible, some studies have reported increases in arousal to stimuli that are familiar. For example, Tranel *et al.* (1985) found that when students viewed slides of familiar and unfamiliar faces, skin conductance response was higher when they viewed the familiar faces (even when the participants themselves reported not having seen the face before; they had, in fact, viewed the faces in a previous slide show, which suggests that the body can reveal more than can self-reports). In an intriguing study, Tranel and Damasio (1985) measured skin conductance response in prosopagnosics (remember from an earlier section that these patients are unable to recognise familiar faces such as those of family members). They found that although the patients could not recognise familiar faces, galvanic skin response (GSR) would increase during the presentation of familiar faces, perhaps suggesting a degree of unconscious processing in these patients.

Perhaps one of the more well-known, although poorly validated uses of GSR, is the polygraph, the so-called lie-detector. While its ability to detect actual liars is abysmal, GSR has been found to be a very useful technique when measuring the responses of some criminals – specifically, psychopaths – to emotional stimuli. Psychopaths are people who are utterly remorseless, superficially charming,

In *Meet the Parents*, Robert De Niro's character makes good use of the polygraph to intimidate his son-in-law, played by Ben Stiller. Research, however, indicates that the polygraph is a poor measure of deception.
Source: Universal/Everett/Rex Features.

manipulative and socially deviant. Jailed psychopaths have been found to show little GSR in response to emotional stimulation, a result that has also been found in studies of patients with damage to the front part of the brain (Raine, 1997). This is explored in the personality disorders section of Chapter 18.

Cutting edge – James Bond and the bloody consequences of Mortal Kombat

What man has not thought of spending a day in James Bond's shoes (and what woman has not guffawed at the thought that this is what men would like to do)? A recent study has investigated people's psychophysiological responses while they played James Bond in the game, *JB007: Nightfire* (Ravaja *et al.*, 2008). In the experiment, GSR and EMG were recorded while people either killed or wounded ne'er-do-wells, or were wounded and killed themselves. The aim was to discover the psychophysiological responses generated by different emotional and moral perspectives.

When an opponent was wounded or killed, participants' skin conductance increased but some of the muscles in the face (zygomatic, orbicularis occuli and corrugator mucles, all found around the eyes and mouth) decreased. The more psychotic the

participant, the less pronounced these changes were. When the protagonist was wounded or killed, there was a similar GSR increase but also an increase in two sets of facial muscles and a decrease in another set. These results suggest that the emotional consequences of attacking another or of being attacked can be characterised by subtle, facial muscle changes.

Continuing this theme, blood (or its appearance) can also elicit strong psychophysiological reactions. Bartlett *et al.* (2008) asked 65 men to play the *Mortal Kombat: Deadly Alliance* game as their heart rate was measured. The game differed in the amount of blood that was present in the game – a lot, a moderate amount, a low amount or none. Men in the high and moderate quantity conditions showed the greatest amount of heart rate and also the greatest levels of hostility.

Cutting edge – *Continued*

Men in the low or no-blood condition did not produce these increases. Moreover, in the high/moderate condition, the players were more likely to use their character's weapon more often.

Playing at being James Bond. Putting yourself in the position of another, especially when this position is not normally encountered in real life, produces changes in physiology that are invisible to the human eye but can be recorded by psychophysiologists. Subtle and not-so-subtle cues in the environment – such as the presence of blood – can influence the degree to which we become aggressive. Men playing a game with blood visible show a faster heart rate and greater hostility than do those who saw no blood.

Source: Alamy Images. Top Foto: Sony Pictures

Neuroimaging techniques

The development of machines which can be used to investigate the brain's structure and activity has revolutionised neuroscience. These sophisticated techniques, more than any of the others, have provided neuroscientists with the opportunity of measuring how the whole, living, healthy brain functions. They are called **neuroimaging** techniques because they allow us to visualise and obtain images of brain function and structure. These techniques include CT, MEG, PET, MRI and fMRI. PET and fMRI are measures of brain activity; CT and MRI are measures of brain structure. Figures 4.21 (a) and (b) show how studies using these techniques have increased during the period 1988 to 1998.

Computerised tomography (CT)

Computerised tomography (CT) is a technique used to display the structure of the brain (*tomos*, meaning 'cut', describes the CT scanner's ability to produce a picture that looks like a slice of the brain). The scanner sends a narrow beam of X-rays through a person's head (see Figure 4.22(a)). The beam is moved around the patient's head, and a computer calculates the amount of radiation that passes through it at various points along each angle. The result is a two-dimensional image of a 'slice' of the person's head, parallel to the top of the skull.

Using the CT scanner, an investigator can determine the approximate location of a brain lesion in a living patient. Knowing the results of behavioural testing and the location of the brain damage, the neuropsychologist can compare them and make inferences about the normal function of the damaged brain tissue. Figure 4.22(b) shows CT scans of the brain of a patient with a lesion caused by a stroke.

Magnetoencephalography (MEG)

A more recently developed electrophysiological technique is **magnetoencephalography**. Neurons can generate magnetic as well as electrical currents and these magnetic fields can be measured from the surface of the head via a machine called a superconducting quantum interference

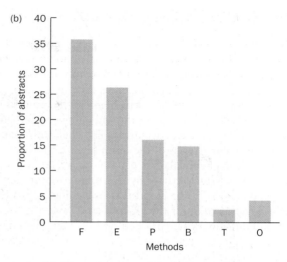

(a)

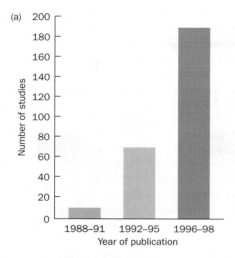

Figure 4.21 (a) The number of PET and fMRI studies of behaviour has increased significantly since 1988.

Source: Cabeza, R. and Nyberg, L. Imaging cognition II: An empirical review of 275 PET and fMRI studies, 2. *Journal of Cognitive Neuroscience*, 2000, 12(1), 1–47. Reprinted by permission of the authors.

Figure 4.21 (b) Shows the proportion of the methods used in abstracts submitted to the 2005 Annual Meeting of the Cognitive Neuroscience Society. F = functional imaging; E = electrophysiological; P = patient; B = behavioural; T = TMS; O = Other.

Source: Chatterjee, A. A madness to the methods of cognitive neuroscience? *Journal of Cognitive Neuroscience*, 2005, 17, 6, 847–9, Figure 1. © by the Massachusetts Institute of Technology.

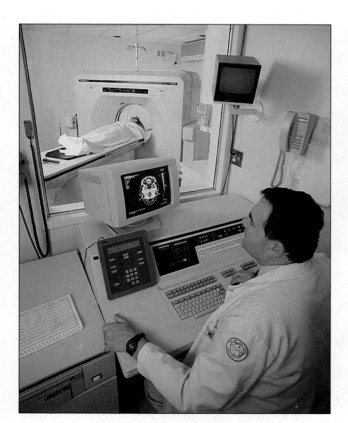

Figure 4.22 (a) A patient being placed in a computerised tomography (CT) scanner.

Source: Hank Morgan/Rainbow. Reproduced with permission.

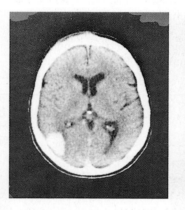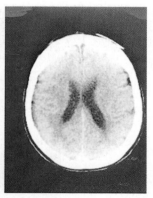

Figure 4.22 (b) A set of CT scans from a patient with a brain lesion caused by a stroke; left and right are traditionally reversed on CT scans, the brain lesion is actually in the right hemisphere.

Source: Courtesy of Dr J. McA. Jones, Good Samaritan Hospital, Portland, Oregon, USA.

device (SQUID) which is immersed in liquid helium. The machine detects the activity of magnetic fields from a large number of neurons because the magnetic fields generated by single neurons are very weak. The subsequent recording is called the magnetoencephalograph or MEG. Unlike the EEG, MEG can be used to localise sources of activity fairly well and these sources can be plotted on a three-dimensional image of the participant's head. MEG has been used to study various functions from language to olfaction.

Positron Emission Tomography (PET)

Positron emission tomography (PET) is an invasive measure of brain metabolism, glucose consumption and blood flow. The procedure for undergoing a PET scan goes something like this. A person is given a harmless dose of a radioactive substance (a form of glucose) which enters the brain (this is why the technique is invasive; the radioactive substance is injected into the participant's arm). The chemical accumulates in particular regions of the brain (the location depends on the specific chemical) but usually goes to active cells. PET measures brain activity by examining the amount of oxygen consumed by, or blood flow travelling to, neurons. The radioactive parts of the glucose emit positrons (hence positron emission) which are detected by a PET scanner, a large, doughnut-shaped piece of equipment which accommodates the prostrate participant's head. This activity is then represented in the form of coloured maps. Because of the radioactivity involved, only certain participants are allowed to take part in PET research. Premenopausal women and children, for example, cannot take part, which limits the use of PET when investigating how brain function develops during the early years. See Figure 4.23.

It is difficult to overestimate the early contribution of PET research to the study of brain function, however. PET has allowed researchers to undertake investigations of the workings of the brain that were thought unrealisable 30 years ago. It is an expensive technique (the scanner's costs run into millions) but a number of PET laboratories now exist around the world and the results from these laboratories have allowed us to see whether the technique shows a consistent pattern of findings (Cabeza and Nyberg, 2000). In later chapters, you will see how PET research has helped us to understand the neural basis of functions such as speech perception, speech comprehension, memory, reading, attention and many others. It has been used to localise the parts of the brain active during word and speech recognition (Petersen *et al.*, 1988; Zatorre *et al.*, 1992; Castro-Caldas *et al.*, 1998; Karbe *et al.*, 1998), face perception (Sergent *et al.*, 1992), language tasks performed by dyslexic individuals (Rumsey *et al.*, 1997; Brunswick *et al.*, 1999), problem-solving (Baker *et al.*, 1996; Nagahama *et al.*, 1996) and remembering events (Fletcher *et al.*, 1998 a, b), among others.

Magnetic Resonance Imaging (MRI) and functional Magnetic Resonance Imaging (fMRI)

A **magnetic resonance imaging (MRI)** scanner provides more detailed images of the structure of the brain than does CT (see Figure 4.24). It does so with the use of magnetic fields and radio waves rather than with X-rays. When a magnetic field is passed over the head, reverberations are produced by hydrogen molecules. These reverberations are picked up by the scanner which can convert the activity into a structural image. This image appears in a form like that seen in Figure 4.25.

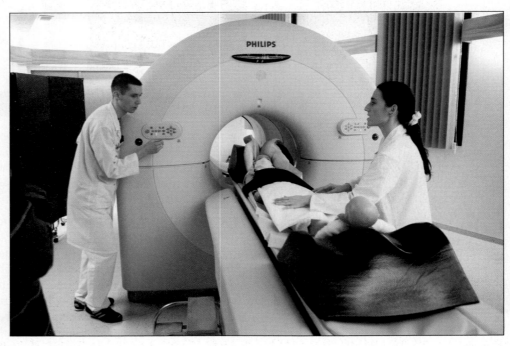

Figure 4.23 A PET scanner.
Source: Corbis/Owen Franken

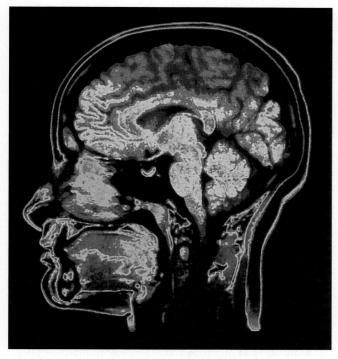

Figure 4.24 A colour-enhanced sagittal MRI scan.
Source: Scott Camazine/Photo Researchers Inc.

It is also possible to use MRI in a functional capacity, to examine the brain's function as well as its structure (Frackowiak *et al.*, 1997). This is called **functional magnetic resonance imaging (fMRI)** and the technique is a measure of the amount of deoxygenated blood in parts of the brain (giving what is called the BOLD signal). The BOLD signals are converted into a form of pixel (in fMRI they are called voxels). Each image contains between 40,000 and 500,000 voxels and each voxel covers between 1 and 123 mm^3 of brain tissue (Vul *et al.*, 2009). Unlike PET, which is invasive (radioactively labelled substances are introduced into the body), MRI and functional MRI are non-invasive, which means that they can be used to investigate the development of function (in, for example, children). fMRI has been used to investigate similar functions to those investigated using PET: language, attention, vision, memory and so on. Both PET and MRI can be used in combination. However, while both have the advantage of good spatial resolution (you can see images and structures more precisely), they also have the disadvantage of poor temporal resolution – it is difficult to match the psychological and neural event in time precisely. The reason for this is that in PET and fMRI a number of scans are recorded and then averaged (see Caveats below).

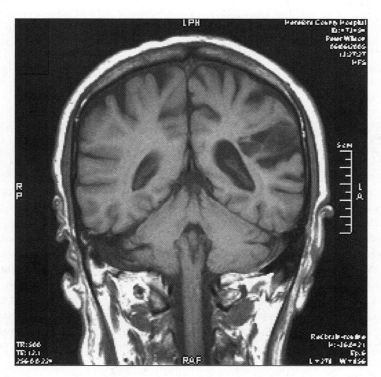

Figure 4.25 An MRI scan taken from a patient with damage to Wernicke's area, following a stroke (the right side of the image represents the left side of the brain).
Source: Figure 4.27 from *Human Neuropsychology*, 2nd edn, p. 36, Pearson/Prentice Hall (Martin, G.N., 2006).

Functional MRI has been used to understand the cerebral correlates of a variety of topics, from being in love (Bartels and Zeki, 2000), to naming animate and inanimate objects (Martin and Chao, 2001), to driving (Horikawa *et al.*, 2005), to navigating a virtual London (Spiers and Maguire, 2007), to friendship and the understanding of magic. The last two in this list form the two Cutting Edge sections.

Cutting edge – Love, friendship and neuroscience

Researchers from the US and Switzerland used fMRI to see how quickly people would respond to words when the name of a loved one, a friend or a 'passionate hobby' (e.g. dance) was subliminally presented before the words (Ortigue *et al.*, 2007). When the word was preceded by a loved one's name or a favoured hobby, reaction time was faster – and activation was greater in areas near the frontal lobe, called the fusiform gyrus and angular gyri. The results suggest that a photograph of a loved one acts as a motivating prime but that it activates a network of brain regions not normally associated with reward.

This motivated attention is also seen in ERP studies. Psychologists from the Netherlands used event-related potentials to see whether stimuli related to a loved one would elicit a late, positive-going brainwave normally found when people are exposed to emotional stimuli (Langeslag *et al.*, 2007). This is what they found – the wave was larger to the face of a loved one than to a friend or that of an unknown, beautiful person.

Friendship, of course, is one aspect of love. In another study, also from researchers in the Netherlands, participants were asked to approach or withdraw from photographs of faces of liked and disliked peers, friends and familiar celebrities, as fMRI measured brain activation (Guroglu *et al.*, 2008). In the task, a face was presented on screen and, using a joystick, participants moved a stimulus on screen towards instructions that read 'I want to approach', 'neutral' and 'I want to go away'. Liked stimuli were approached more than disliked ones and peers more than celebrities. During interaction with friends, four regions were especially activated (the amygdala, hippocampus, nucleus accumbens and ventromedial prefrontal cortex; see below), regions known to be implicated in empathy.

Two of these regions were also activated in a study from the UK and US where people played a videogame in which they either (i) shot an aggressive humanoid or healed a passive, wounded person or (ii) shot the wounded and helped the assailant (King *et al.*, 2006). The aim was to discover the neural substrates of compassionate and violent behaviour, or 'doing the right thing'.

Activation was found in the amygdala and the ventromedial prefrontal cortex regardless of whether the participants helped the wounded or attacked an assailant, suggesting that both regions are implicated in our ability to 'do the right thing' and our understanding of what it is to behave appropriately.

Cutting edge – The magic of neuroimaging or 'You'll like this, not a lot, but you'll like this'

How do we and our brains cope with a violation of what we consider to be normal? Psychologists from the Universities of Durham and Exeter used fMRI to measure how the brain responded to these violations (Parris *et al.*, 2009). A group of young men and women watched video clips of various elementary magic tricks – such as the disappearing coin, where the magician leaves a coin on the table, covers it, and lifts the cover to reveal it has disappeared; a levitation trick where a paper cup is made to levitate, and a cigarette torn and then restored to its intact state. They also watched clips of sequences that were similar but which did not violate expectations.

When they saw the the magic trick, there was significant activation in a part of the frontal lobe, called the dorsolateral prefrontal cortex, and a nearby area, the anterior cingulate cortex. Activity was also greater here than when a person watched a clip of something that was surprising – activity seemed to be dependent on the unfathomable nature of the trick rather than on its surprise value. (See Figure 4.26). The unusual study highlights a part of the brain that may be involved in the understanding of causal relations in what we perceive. Chapter 11 has more on the role of this region during reasoning.

Cutting edge – *Continued*

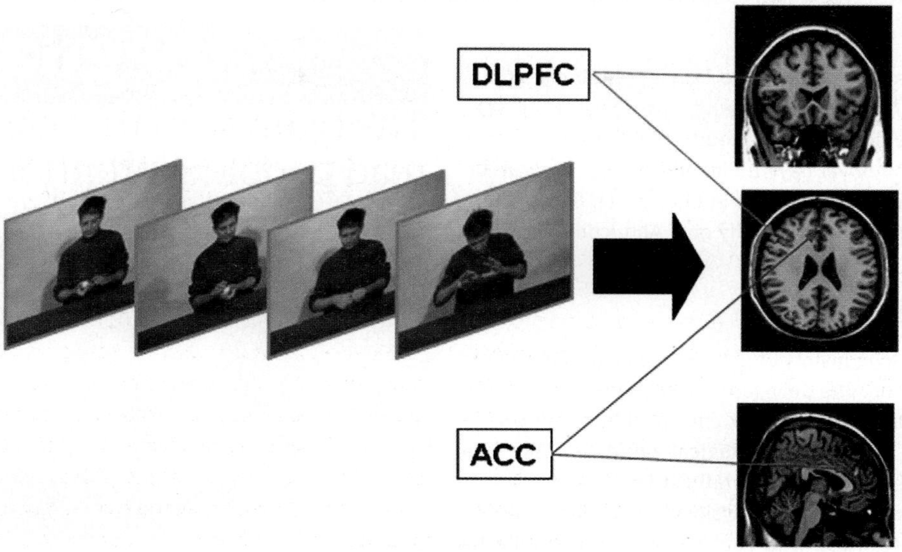

Figure 4.26 Changes in various parts of the frontal lobe as people watch a magic trick.

Source: Parris, B.A., Kuhn, G., Mizon, G.A., Benattayallah, A. and Hodgson, T.L. (2009). Imaging the impossible: An fMRI study of impossible causal relationships in magic tricks. *Neuroimage*, 45, 1033–39.

Caveats

Of course, neuroimaging techniques, although providing us with a new way of viewing brain activation, are not measures of actual neural functioning. Instead, they measure the processes associated with neural function – such as blood flow or oxygen and glucose consumption. They also provide data that are correlational. Researchers draw associations between the stimulus or task they present and the differences in activation in the brain they observe that are not seen at baseline. These data are not particularly time-sensitive because fMRI and PET use the technique of averaging and subtraction – several experimental scans are taken, usually in a mixed order, and then averaged to produce a scan for this condition/group. A scan is taken approximately every three seconds. The average experimental condition is subtracted from the control scan. This means that you cannot associate a scan with a specific event in time. Also, because any task will activate all of the brain to some extent, researchers focus on a region of interest (ROI) and compare activation between two tasks in this area.

These scans are also very persuasive tools. Examine any newspaper report involving the brain and the chances are that the story either involves some new ground-breaking drug or neuroimaging (see the opening vignette for an example). The appeal of neuroimaging is seductive. It is immediate, visual and allows us to see something that was previously unattainable: a pictorial, anatomically correct representation of the living brain. And, as humans, we are very swayed by visual seduction, as McCabe and Castel (2008) have demonstrated in their study.

They asked people to judge the degree of scientific reasoning in three articles about cognitive neuroscience. The articles were accompanied by either bar graphs, topographical maps (brain scans) or no image. Despite there being no difference between the content of the articles, the piece accompanied by a brain map was judged to be more scientific. These images, say McCabe and Castel, 'provide a physical basis for abstract cognitive processes, appealing to people's affinity for reductionistic explanations for cognitive phenomena' (p. 343).

Neuroimaging is being applied to some novel areas of behaviour. A new line of research has examined a particularly controversial topic: the use of neuroimaging to predict lying. The evidence is reviewed in the Controversies in Psychological Science section.

Controversies in Psychological Science – Can brain scanners detect deception?

The issue

If all it took to identify a liar was to examine their extending, Pinnochio-like proboscis, we would encounter a lot less deception and the police and the courts could probably take a day off. But we do not yet have a Pinnochian 'tell' that can do this (you read about the evidence in Chapter 1). Some scientists, however, have tried to identify one. And, controversially, it involves the brain.

The evidence

Psychology has a long history of using physiological measures to identify deception. The polygraph, described in the section earlier, is one measure. This has its critics – it has rightly been taken to task for being methodologically questionable (the polygraph is a measure of arousal, rather than deception).

The key to identifying a neurophysiological marker of deception is attractive to those who could exploit it. This tell-tale activation may not be under conscious control – the liar may not be able to control their brain activation – and it may be present only when a person is lying. It is almost like using neuroimaging as a mind-reading tool, where the observation of a scan would reveal your innermost thoughts and predict your thinking and behaviour. This, however, is currently pie in the sky – the *Eternal Sunshine of the Spotless Mind* is a long way off, if possible at all – but psychologists and neuroscientists have worked at constructing ways in which the brain's behaviour can be measured during acts of deception (Langleben, 2008; Spence, 2008; Sip, Roepstorff, McGregor and Frith, 2007).

According to Vrij (2004a, b), deception involves 'a deliberate attempt, without forewarning, to create in another a belief which the communicator considers to be untrue'. This definition embodies two important points: (i) a liar deliberately and purposefully intends to deceive another person and (ii) deception does not involve instructing the liar to lie – he or she will do this spontaneously.

Around 16 peer-reviewed studies using fMRI to study deception had been published by 2007 (Spence, 2008). Almost all of these studies have implicated one particular part of the brain in deception – the frontal lobes. The majority of the reports specifically find activation in certain areas of the frontal lobes: the ventromedial prefrontal cortex (VPC), dorsolateral prefrontal cortex (DFC) and the anterior cingulate cortex (ACC). For example, researchers have asked participants to lie to the experimenter (Abe *et al.*, 2007). or given them two cards and asked to lie about having one of them (Gamer *et al.*, 2007) or asked volunteers to malinger – feign a memory impairment (Lee *et al.*, 2002; 2005), or instructed them to 'steal' a watch or ring and then reward them for successfully lying about it (Kozel

Headlines such as these are becoming more common (but no more accurate)
Source: Guardian News and Media Ltd.: Charles O'Rear/Corbis

et al., 2005), or asked them to lie about autobiographical events (Spence *et al.*, 2001; Nunez *et al.*, 2005). All activated the prefrontal cortex and some activated the medial temporal gyrus. These activations were not observed when the person was telling the truth or when baseline recordings were taken. According to Spence *et al.* (2008), the VPC may support deceptive behaviour by suppressing a person's ability to tell the truth.

It seems that deception can, therefore, be measured by fMRI. Or can it?

According to Sip *et al.* (2007), fMRI studies of deception are hamstrung by several methodological problems or confounds. They argue that what deception experiments primarily measure are the functions needed for lying, such as inhibiting behaviour (telling the truth), mentalising (reading others' states of mind or intentions) and relating action or behaviour to the outcome (monitoring behaviour). The authors suggest that deception involves keeping track of the lies and truth being told (information management), building trust with the deceived (impression management), appreciating that the gains from lying are greater than the losses and the risks of being found out (risk management) and an intention that lying is done for some good or can be justified in some way (reputation management). All of these behaviours recruit the areas found to be active during deception. See Figure 4.27.

Controversies in Psychological Science – *Continued*

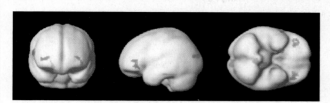

Figure 4.27 Some of the areas of the brain, principally involving the frontal lobe, which become active during the act of lying.
Source: Spence, S.A., Kaylor-Hughes, C., Farrow, T.F.D. and Wilkinson, I.D. (2008). *Neuroimage*, 40, 1411–18.

The problem, however, is that in all fMRI experiments, the participants are instructed to lie by the experimenter. That is, they do not spontaneously lie and, furthermore, do not lie about anything significant (lying about having a playing card is in a different order to lying about running someone over in a car). These participants lack one of the key features of deception – the intention to lie, although it is possible that a person can be instructed to lie on someone's behalf (i.e. provide a false alibi for a criminal). But, then again, the person is motivated to do this – it has a purpose.

The protocols used also neglect the context in which lying occurs and the negative consequences of lying – a person who lies faces no punishment or no censure at all in these experiments. Again, the paradigms used can be regarded as basic and artificial.

Because of these problems, Sip *et al.* have identified a number of related problems in the interpretation of fMRI studies. The first is that although a characteristic of mentalising, emotion and risk-taking is activation in a particular part of the brain, the presence of such activation does not mean that a person is lying. The second is that fMRI deception studies are based on groups – individual responses may vary greatly (depending on the seriousness of the wrongdoing and the individual's predisposition to lie or intention to lie). A third is that instructions to lie 'lift moral sanctions against lying' – there are no real consequences of lying. The fourth is that different people will have different attitudes to deception. At the extreme, think of the psychopath (described in detail in Chapter 18). A psychopath lies effortlessly and shows no empathy – he (and it is usually a he) shows reduced frontal lobe volume and activation, not more. Psychopaths' behaviour stems from their attitude to their victim – they do not regard what they say as wrong when they lie.

Conclusion

In the US, some scientists, entrepreneurs and patent specialists are busying themselves setting up and protecting companies that they claim will use fMRI to detect deception (for example, NoLieMRI in San Diego). However, what the studies to date have done is not so much measure deception but the cognitive processes involved in deception.

Importantly, these studies have a flaw – the liar does not spontaneously lie or has the intention of lying, unlike genuine deception. Future studies, therefore, need a way of allowing a person to decide whether to lie. Of course, these studies will be so tightly straightjacketed that another important element will still be missing – the belief that lying will spare some punishment or will achieve some other, very significant goal. As Sip *et al.* conclude, 'paradigms are still inadequate. The problems that bedevilled old techniques have not been eliminated by the new'. It seems as if there is still no room for Pinnochio's nose inside the scanner.

Modern brain stimulation: transcranial magnetic stimulation (TMS)

Despite having its origins in the nineteenth century, a relatively new, non-invasive, technique for studying localisation is **transcranial magnetic stimulation (TMS)**. TMS involves modulating cortical activity by passing alternating magnetic fields across the scalp (Burt *et al.*, 2002). The consequence of exposure to these fields is that electrical currents are induced in the cortex and the excitability of the cortex is subsequently increased or decreased. These effects can last a few seconds or minutes to a few weeks. The technique's benefits to neuropsychology are that it can produce transient impairment or improvements in cognition non-invasively.

In practice, a metal coil is placed on a participant's scalp, as you can see in Figure 4.28. The alternating electrical current in the coil produces an alternating magnetic field at right angles to the current generated in the coil. This alternating magnetic field then passes through to the cortex and creates an electrical current in the part of the brain (around 1 to 2 cms worth) beneath the coil. The technique is apparently safe – the most likely danger, if a danger occurs, is of a seizure being generated during repeated stimulation. Sometimes headaches can follow and slight periods of mania; scalp facial muscles might twitch.

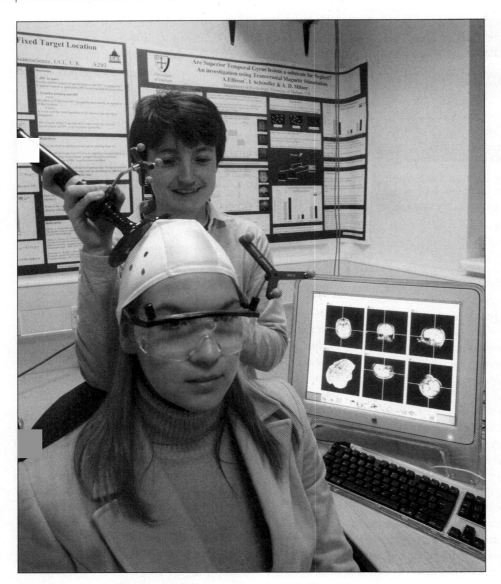

Figure 4.28 A typical rTMS procedure.

Source: University of Durham/Simon Fraser/Science Photo Library Ltd.

In TMS, the magnetic fields – or 'pulses' – can be presented either singly, in pairs a few seconds apart or in quick succession over a period of minutes. These are called single-pulse TMS, paired-pulse TMS and repetitive (r)TMS, respectively. Testing sessions normally last between 20 minutes and an hour. If the stimulation is high frequency, an increase in blood flow is observed; if stimulation is low, excitability is reduced (Chen *et al.*, 1997). Blood flow and cortical excitability are thought to be correlates in this sense although the change in blood flow may occur away from the region that is cortically excited.

The effect of TMS in normal, healthy individuals is analogous to the effect of a lesion – the transient stimulation produces a transient brain disruption of function (although, obviously, with no damage, permanent or otherwise). Unlike neuroimaging, where activation is correlated with behaviour and may not be necessary to produce it, TMS directly stimulates brain regions and the consequences can be observed. The technique has been found to disrupt verbal working memory (Mottaghy *et al.*, 2002), verb generation (Shapiro *et al.*, 2001) and speech (Stewart *et al.*, 2001). Other studies have reported improvements in picture naming following TMS stimulation of Wernicke's area (Topper *et al.*, 1998).

Repetitive TMS has been used in a very novel way. Fregni *et al.* (2008) used it to stimulate a part of the front region of the brain – the dorsolateral prefrontal cortex (DPFC) – while participants were exposed to foods such as chocolate cake, toast and sweets, or a film of foods that strongly induced craving. Participants rated how much they desired food before and after stimulation.

Right-sided stimulation reduced craving after watching food whereas stimulation of the left side reduced the time that participants fixated on the food. Stimulation on both sides of the brain reduced the amount of food that people ate afterwards, compared to a sham condition (in which participants thought they were receiving brain stimulation but did not).

This part of the brain is associated with cravings for other types of substances – such as nicotine. Smokers watching a video involving smoking showed increased activation in several brain regions, including the prefrontal cortex (McBride *et al.*, 2006) and stimulating the right DPFC reduces risk-taking behaviour (Knoch *et al.*, 2006). Perhaps, the authors suggest, modulating activity in this part of the brain inhibits neural circuits involved in reward.

Control of behaviour

The brain has two roles: controlling the movements of the muscles and regulating the physiological functions of the body. The first role looks outwards towards the environment and the second looks inwards. The outward-looking role includes several functions: perceiving events in the environment, learning about them, making plans, and acting. The inward-looking role requires the brain to measure and regulate internal characteristics such as body temperature, blood pressure and nutrient levels.

Organisation of the cerebral cortex

We become aware of events in our environment by means of the five major senses: vision, audition, olfaction (smell), gustation (taste) and the somatosenses ('body' senses: touch, pain and temperature). Three areas of the cerebral cortex receive information from the sensory organs. The **primary visual cortex (V1)**, which receives visual information, is located at the back of the brain, on the inner surfaces of the cerebral hemispheres. The **primary auditory cortex**, which receives auditory information, is located on the inner surface of a deep fissure in the side of the brain. The **primary somatosensory cortex**, a vertical strip near the middle of the cerebral hemispheres, receives informa-

tion from the body senses. Different regions of the primary somatosensory cortex receive information from different regions of the body. In addition, the base of the somatosensory cortex receives information concerning taste. See Figure 4.29.

Primary sensory and motor cortex

The three regions of primary sensory cortex in each hemisphere receive information from the opposite side of the body. Thus, the primary somatosensory cortex of the left hemisphere learns what the right hand is holding, the left primary visual cortex learns what is happening towards the person's right, and so on. The connections between the sensory organs and the cerebral cortex are said to be contralateral (contra 'opposite', lateral 'side').

The region of the cerebral cortex most directly involved in the control of movement is the primary motor cortex (MI), located just in front of the primary somatosensory cortex. Neurons in different parts of the primary motor cortex are connected to muscles in different parts of the body. The connections, like those of the sensory regions of the cerebral cortex, are contralateral; the left primary motor cortex controls the right side of the body and vice versa. Thus, for example, damage to the left primary motor cortex will result in paralysis in

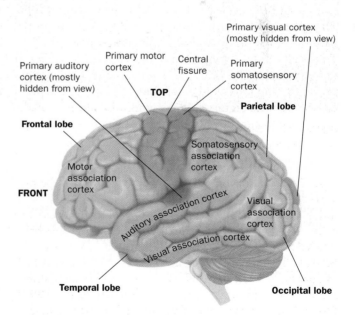

Figure 4.29 The lobes of the brain and the association areas of the cortex, together with the primary functions undertaken by these areas.

the contralateral hand and sometimes in the left hand (Haaland and Harrington, 1989). The hand that one predominantly uses (and this usually means to write with) appears to be related to the side of the brain that is involved in speech production (we'll discuss handedness more in Chapter 10).

Association cortex

The regions of primary sensory and motor cortex occupy only a small part of the cerebral cortex. The rest of the cerebral cortex accomplishes what is done between sensation and action: perceiving, learning and remembering, planning, and acting. These processes take place in the association areas of the cerebral cortex. The central fissure provides an important dividing line between the **anterior** (front) part of the cerebral cortex and the **posterior** (back) regions. The anterior region is involved in movement-related activities, such as planning and executing behaviours. The posterior part is involved in perceiving and learning.

The cerebral cortex is divided into four areas, or lobes, named after the bones of the skull that cover them: the frontal lobe, parietal lobe, temporal lobe and occipital lobe. The brain contains two of each lobe, one in each hemisphere. The **frontal lobe** (the 'front') includes everything in front of the central fissure. The **parietal lobe** (the 'wall') is located on the side of the cerebral hemisphere, just behind the central fissure, behind the frontal lobe. The **temporal lobe** (the 'temple') juts forward from the base of the brain, beneath the frontal and parietal lobes. The **occipital lobe** (*ob* 'in back of', *caput* 'head') lies at the very back of the brain, behind the parietal and temporal lobes. The lobes and association regions of the brain can be seen in Figure 4.30 (a) and an overview of the brain's motor functions can be seen in Figure 4.30 (b).

Temporal sequencing of events

Each primary sensory area of the cerebral cortex sends information to adjacent regions, called the **sensory association cortex**. Circuits of neurons in the sensory association cortex analyse the information received from the primary sensory cortex; perception takes place there, and memories are stored there. The regions of the sensory association cortex located closest to the primary sensory areas receive information from only one sensory system. For example, the region closest to the primary visual cortex analyses visual information and stores visual memories. Regions of the sensory association cortex located far from the primary sensory areas receive information from more than one sensory system; thus, they are involved in several kinds of perception and memory. These regions make it possible to integrate information from more than one sensory system. For example, we can learn the connection between the sight of a particular face and the sound of a particular voice.

Just as regions of the sensory association cortex of the posterior part of the brain are involved in perceiving and remembering, the frontal association cortex is involved in the planning and execution of movements. The anterior part of the frontal lobe – known as the prefrontal cortex – contains the motor association cortex. The motor association cortex controls the primary motor cortex; thus, it directly controls behaviour. Obviously, we behave in response to events happening in the world around us. Therefore, the sensory association cortex of the posterior part of the brain sends information about the environment to the **motor association cortex** (prefrontal cortex), which translates the information into plans and actions (see Figure 4.30).

Lateralisation of function

Although the two cerebral hemispheres cooperate with each other, they do not perform identical functions. Some functions show evidence of **lateralisation**, that is, they are located primarily on one side of the brain (this is also called **functional hemispheric asymmetry**). It is commonly suggested that the left hemisphere participates in the analysis of information (making it good at recognising series of events) whereas the right hemisphere is good at putting items together (making it good at 'holistic' activities). This distinction may, however, be too simplistic. The left hemisphere does appear to be significantly more involved in aspects of language processing such as speech production and comprehension and the appreciation of the sounds in speech than is the right hemisphere. However, as you will see in more detail in Chapter 10 (Language), the right hemisphere is better than the left hemisphere at comprehending metaphors and may undertake the linguistic duties of the left hemisphere when the left is damaged. The right hemisphere also appears to be superior to the left at recognising faces, perceiving emotion and mentally rotating three-dimensional images in space. In the following chapters you will read about these and other examples of function that are lateralised in the brain; you will see that lateralisation of function does not occur in the whole of one hemisphere but in specific parts of it.

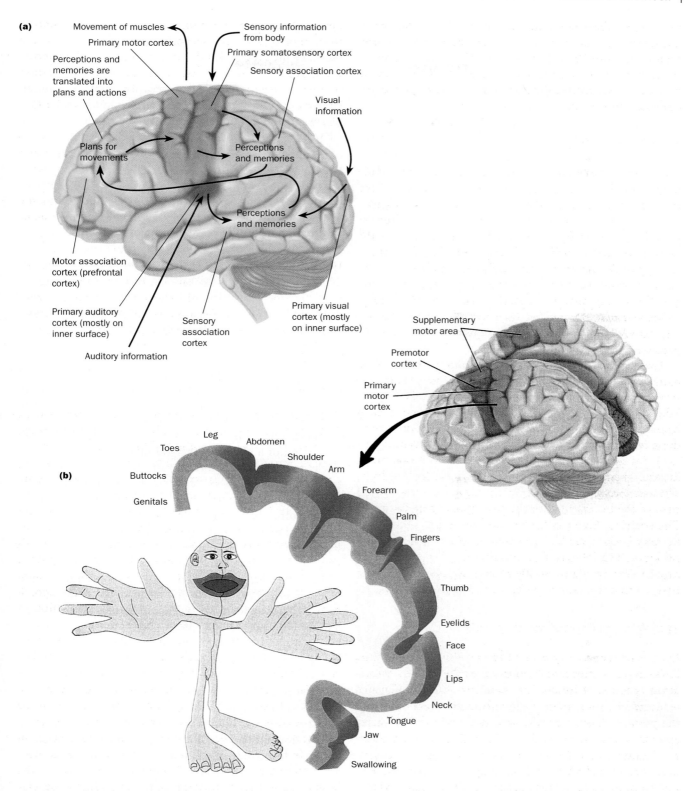

Figure 4.30 (a) The relation between the association cortex and the regions of primary sensory and motor cortex. Arrows refer to the flow of information. **(b)** A motor homunculus. This shows how some parts of the brain are disproportionately involved in certain bodily movements, such as those involving the lips and hands. This little figure illustrates the relative amount of cortex devoted to each body part's movement.

Source: Carlson, N.R., *Physiology of Behavior* (6th edn), p. 235. Boston: Allyn & Bacon, 1988. © Allyn & Bacon. Reproduced with permission.

The two cerebral hemispheres are connected by the **corpus callosum**, a large band of axons, seen in Figures 4.31 (a) and (b). In fact, it is the brain's largest collection of connective fibre. The corpus callosum connects corresponding parts of the left and right hemispheres: the left and right temporal lobes are connected, the left and right parietal lobes are connected, and so on. Because of the corpus callosum, each region of the association cortex knows what is happening in the corresponding region of the opposite side of the brain. Some people have the corpus callosum surgically cut in order to alleviate the symptoms of epilepsy. So-called split-brain patients are interesting to psychologists because their two hemispheres do not appear to be able to communicate. We discuss the effects of split-brain surgery in more detail in Chapter 9 (Consciousness).

Vision: the occipital lobe

The primary business of the occipital lobe – and the lower part of the temporal lobe – is seeing. Total damage to the primary visual cortex, located in the inner surface of the posterior occipital lobe, produces cortical blindness (to distinguish it from other forms of blindness such as congenital blindness). Because the visual field is 'mapped' onto the surface of the primary visual cortex, a small lesion in the primary visual cortex produces a 'hole' in a specific part of the field of vision.

The visual association cortex is located in the rest of the occipital lobe and in the lower portion of the temporal lobe. Damage to the visual association cortex will not cause blindness. In fact, visual acuity may be very good; the person may be able to see small objects and may even be able to read. However, the person will not be able to recognise objects by sight. For example, when looking at a drawing of a clock, the person may say that they see a circle, two short lines forming an angle in the centre of a circle, and some dots spaced along the inside of the circle, but will not be able to recognise what the picture shows. On the other hand, if the person is handed a real clock, they will immediately recognise it by touch. This fact tells us that the person has not simply forgotten what clocks are. Similarly, the person may fail to recognise their spouse by sight but will be able to do so from the sound of the spouse's voice. This deficit in visual perception is called **visual agnosia** (*a-* 'without', *gnosis* 'knowledge') and we return to it in Chapter 6 (Perception).

Audition: the temporal lobe

The temporal lobe contains both the primary auditory cortex and the auditory association cortex. The primary auditory cortex is hidden from view on the inner surface of the upper temporal lobe. The auditory association cortex is located on the lateral surface of the upper temporal lobe. Damage to the primary auditory cortex leads to hearing losses, while damage to the auditory association cortex produces more complex deficits. Damage to the left auditory association cortex causes severe language deficits. People with such damage are no longer able to

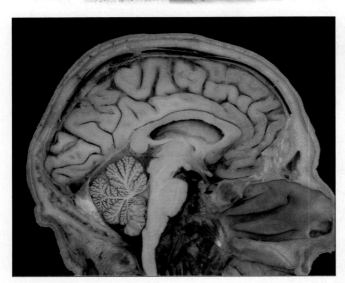

Figure 4.31 (a) A view of the brain that has been sliced through the midline (this is called a sagittal view). The corpus callosum unites the cerebral cortex of the two hemispheres. **(b)** A cross-section of a human head. You can clearly see the general structures of the brain: the neocortex, the corpus callosum, the cerebellum, the pons and the medulla.

Source: (b) Image P330/382 Tissuepix/Science Photo Library Ltd.

comprehend speech, presumably because they have lost the circuits of neurons that decode speech sounds. However, the deficit is more severe than that. They also lose the ability to produce meaningful speech; their speech becomes a jumble of words. Language deficits produced by brain damage are described in more detail in Chapter 10 (Language). See Figure 4.32.

Damage to the right auditory association cortex does not seriously affect speech perception or production, but it does affect the ability to recognise non-speech sounds, including patterns of tones and rhythms. The damage can also impair the ability to perceive the location of sounds in the environment. As we will see later, the right hemisphere is important in the perception of space. The contribution of the right temporal lobe to this function is to participate in perceiving the placement of sounds.

Somatosensation and spatial perception: the parietal lobe

The primary sensory function of the parietal lobe is perception of the body. However, the association cortex of the parietal lobe is involved in much more than somatosensation. Damage to a particular region of the association cortex of the left parietal lobe can disrupt the ability to read or write without causing serious impairment in the ability to talk and understand the speech of other people. Damage to another part of the parietal lobe impairs a person's ability to draw. When the left parietal lobe is damaged, the primary deficit seems to be in the person's ability to make precise hand movements; their drawing looks shaky and sloppy. In contrast, the primary deficit produced by damage to the right parietal lobe is perceptual. The person can analyse a picture into its parts but has trouble integrating these parts into a consistent whole. Thus, they have difficulty drawing a coherent picture. We will look at disorders such as these in Chapter 6 (Perception).

Most neuropsychologists believe that the left parietal lobe plays an important role in our ability to keep track of the location of the moving parts of our own body, whereas the right parietal lobe helps us to keep track of the space around us. People with right parietal lobe damage usually have difficulty with spatial tasks, such as reading a map. People with left parietal lobe damage usually have difficulty identifying parts of their own bodies by name. For example, when asked to point to their elbows, they may actually point to their shoulders. There is also evidence showing that this region of the brain, together with the frontal lobe, is involved in our ability to perform mental arithmetic (Menon *et al.*, 2000; Cowell *et al.*, 2000). This region is smaller in children with mathematical deficits when compared with children with normal maths performance (Isaacs *et al.*, 2001).

The **posterior part of the parietal cortex (PPC)** appears to be specialised for storing representations of motor actions (Milner, 1998). Snyder *et al.* (1997) found that some neurons in the PPC of two adult macaque monkeys were active before and during visually guided arm movements whereas others were active during eye movements. However, rather than directing attention to objects in space, the PPC seems to be responsible for the intention

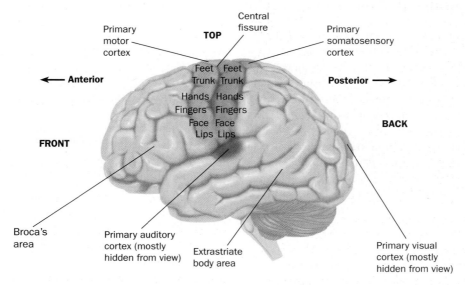

Figure 4.32 Broca's area, located just in front of the face region of the primary motor cortex. This region is involved in the control of speech.

to move. There may be visual neurons in the PPC which are responsible for visually guided movement (Sakata, 1997). Manipulation of body part information appears to involve the left frontal and parietal lobes whereas manipulation of numbers appears to involve the right parietal lobe (Le Clec'H *et al.*, 2000).

Neurons in a part of the brain called the superior temporal sulcus become active when an animal detects head and body movement. In humans, a similar area on the right side of the brain becomes activated when watching the movement of living things – whether in films, or of animals or schematic versions of human beings. One particular area, the extrastriate body area (EBA) seen in Figure 4.32 appears to become active selectively to the sight of human bodies and body parts and is also activated when we imitate the body actions of others (Jackson *et al.*, 2006). Does this region integrate information from a moving human image and process the dynamic elements of human movement, or does it simply process static images?

Researchers from the University of Bangor in North Wales used fMRI to measure brain activation while people watched single frames presented in the correct order from one whole body action (e.g. punching, kicking) or a series of frames involving several actions that were unrelated (Downing *et al.*, 2006). They found that the EBA responded more strongly to the second set of images than the first, suggesting that this region may not be responsible for the representation of dynamic movement/biological motion but, instead, is involved in processing static images of movement.

Planning and moving: the frontal lobe

Because it contains the motor cortex, the principal function of the frontal lobe is to mediate motor activity (it also includes the area responsible for speech perception, Broca's area, seen in Figure 4.32). There is also evidence that the premotor area of the frontal lobes (and a part of the parietal lobe) contains **mirror neurons** (Rizzolatti *et al.*, 1988). Mirror neurons are those which fire when we watch someone perform an action and also fire when we execute that action; they seem to mirror the activity of neurons that are involved in 'doing'. For example, neurons in one part of this area are activated in monkeys when they make a grasping movement with their hand. However, a different set in the same region is also activated when the monkey sees another making reaching movements (Ferrari *et al.*, 2003). Some people have associated dysfunction in these mirror neurons with autism, and the evidence for this is considered in Chapter 12. The frontal lobes are involved in a variety of 'higher' functions including planning, changing strategies, being aware of oneself, empathising with others, evaluating emotional stimuli, inhibiting inappropriate behaviour and behaving spontaneously (some of these are called executive functions).

Damage to the primary motor cortex produces a very specific effect: paralysis of the side of the body opposite to the brain damage. If a portion of the region is damaged, then only the corresponding parts of the body will be paralysed (Passingham, 1995). However, damage to the prefrontal cortex produces more complex behavioural deficits. For example, the person with frontal lobe damage will react to events in the environment but show deficits in initiating behaviour. When a person with damage to the prefrontal cortex is asked to say or write as many words as possible or is asked to describe as many uses for an object as possible, they will have great difficulty in coming up with more than a few, even though they have no problem understanding words or identifying objects by name (Eslinger and Grattan, 1993).

People with damage to the frontal lobe also tend to have difficulty changing strategies. If given a task to solve, they may solve it readily. However, if the problem is changed, they will fail to abandon the old strategy and learn a new one. The Wisconsin Card Sorting Task, for example, presents patients with packs of cards on which are printed symbols of different shape, colour or number (see page 474, Chapter 11). The experimenter decides on a sorting criterion (shape, for example) and the patient has to detect which criterion it is by sorting the cards into piles, receiving feedback from the experimenter. When the criterion unexpectedly shifts, some patients are unable to detect this shift and carry on responding as if the previous criterion still applied. This is called **perseveration**. However, not all frontal lobe patients will exhibit this behaviour (Anderson *et al.*, 1991), only those with damage to a specific region of the frontal lobe.

People with damage to certain areas of the frontal lobe often have rather bland personalities. They seem indifferent to events that would normally be expected to affect them emotionally (Stuss *et al.*, 1992). For example, they may show no signs of distress at the death of a close relative and do not show the typical physiological response to stress (see Martin 2006 for a comprehensive description). They have little insight into their own problems and are uncritical of their performance on various tasks (Stuss *et al.*, 1992; Brazzelli *et al.*, 1994; Hornak *et al.*, 1996; Cicerone and Tanenbaum, 1997). The most famous case study of frontal lobe damage resulting in shifts in emotional and social behaviour is that of Phineas Gage, a man you read about in Chapter 1 and to whom we return in Chapter 13.

In terms of daily living, the most important consequences of damage to the frontal lobe are probably lack of foresight and difficulty in planning. A person with injury to part of the frontal lobe might perform fairly well on tests of intelligence but be unable to hold down a job or organise their day (Eslinger and Damasio, 1985; Wood and Rutterford, 2004). Sequencing – the organisation of material in logical, correct or learned order – is grossly impaired in frontal patients (Sirigu *et al.*, 1995). Often, when given tasks that tap everyday activities (such as undertaking an errand or following a recipe), patients with frontal lobe damage perform poorly (Shallice and Burgess, 1991; Fortin *et al.*, 2003) and may engage in obsessive collecting behaviour (Anderson *et al.*, 2005).

Patients with damage to different regions of the frontal lobe exhibit different symptoms. For example, patients with damage to the orbitofrontal cortex (the tip of the frontal lobes) tend to exhibit impairments in social behaviour, personality and emotional expression but have relatively intact intellect. They are impulsive and don't care what others think or feel. Eslinger and Damasio's (1985) patient, EVR, is a good example. EVR, an ex-accountant who had a tumour removed from the same part of the brain injured in Phineas Gage, has superior intellect but an impaired ability to plan and organise his daily life. He performs at normal levels on tests such as the Wisconsin Card Sorting Task and he has superior IQ. However, his ability to maintain close relationships and a job and his ability to plan and organise his life are grossly impaired. Chapter 13 looks at EVR's case in greater depth.

Control of internal functions and automatic behaviour

The cortex consists of only the outer 3 mm of the surface of the cerebral hemispheres. There are other structures such as the brain stem, the cerebellum and the interior of the cerebral hemispheres which are important to the regulation of behaviour. The cerebellum helps the cerebral hemispheres to control movement and to initiate some automatic movements, such as postural adjustment, on its own. The brain stem and much of the interior of the cerebral hemispheres are involved in homeostasis and control of species-typical behaviours. **Homeostasis** (from the root words *homoios* 'similar', and *stasis* 'standstill') refers to maintaining a proper balance of physiological variables such as temperature, concentration of fluids, and the amount of nutrients stored within the body. **Species-typical behaviours** are the more-or-less automatic behaviours exhibited by most members of a species that are important to survival, such as eating, drinking, fighting, courting, mating and caring for offspring.

The brain stem

The brain stem contains three structures: the medulla, the pons and the midbrain. Figure 4.33 shows a view of the left side of the brain. The brain has been rotated slightly so that we can see some of the front of the brain stem, and the cerebral hemispheres are shown lightly so that the details of the brain stem can be seen. We also see the thalamus, the hypothalamus and the pituitary gland.

The brain stem contains circuits of neurons that control functions vital to the survival of the organism in particular and of the species in general. For example, circuits of neurons in the **medulla**, the part of the brain stem closest to the spinal cord, control heart rate, blood pressure, rate of respiration, and – especially in simpler animals – crawling or swimming motions. Circuits of neurons in the **pons**, the part of the brain just above the medulla, control some of the stages of sleep, and circuits of neurons in the **midbrain** control movements used in fighting and sexual behaviour and decrease sensitivity to pain while engaged in these activities.

The cerebellum

The **cerebellum** plays an important role in the control of movement. It receives sensory information, especially about the position of body parts, so it knows what the parts of the body are doing. It also receives information from the cortex of the frontal lobes, so it knows what

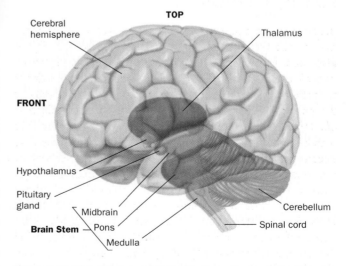

Figure 4.33 The divisions of the brain stem: the medulla, the pons and the midbrain. The thalamus, hypothalamus and pituitary gland are attached to the end of the brain stem.

movements the frontal lobes intend to accomplish. The cerebellum is basically a computer that compares the location of the body parts with the intended movements and assists the frontal lobes in executing these movements. Without the cerebellum, the frontal lobes would produce jerky, uncoordinated, inaccurate movements – which is exactly what happens when a person's cerebellum is damaged. Besides helping the frontal lobes to accomplish their tasks, the cerebellum monitors information regarding posture and balance, to keep us from falling down when we stand or walk, and produces eye movements that compensate for changes in the position of the head.

Some studies have suggested that the cerebellum may also be involved in a variety of other functions such as cognition and language (Schmahmann and Sherman, 1998). The ability to produce words fluently and to solve problems are impaired in patients whose cerebellum has been damaged (Grafman *et al*., 1992; Appollonio *et al*., 1993). Neuroimaging studies show that various parts of the cerebellum become active during tasks involving movement and touch, language and verbal memory, spatial memory, executive function and emotional processing (Stoodley and Schmahmann, 2009). Language has been associated with activation on the right and spatial awareness with the left, which is opposite to that pattern seen at the cortical level presumably because projections to it are crossed. Some psychologists have also implicated the cerebellum in the reading disorder, developmental dyslexia, (see Chapter 10, page 417).

Subcortical structures

The thalamus

If you stripped away the cerebral cortex and the white matter that lies under it, you would find a collection of brain structures. These are called subcortical brain structures and are some of the oldest in the brain. One of the most important is the **thalamus**, located in the heart of the cerebral hemispheres (*thalamos* is Greek for 'inner chamber'). The thalamus is divided into two parts, one in each cerebral hemisphere. Each part looks rather like a football, with the long axis oriented from front to back.

The thalamus performs two basic functions. The first, and most primitive, is similar to that of the cerebral cortex. Parts of the thalamus receive sensory information, other parts integrate the information, and still other parts assist in the control of movements through their influence on circuits of neurons in the brain stem. However, the second role of the thalamus, that of a relay station for the cortex, is even more important. As the cerebral hemispheres

evolved, the cerebral cortex grew in size and its significance for behavioural functions increased. The thalamus took on the function of receiving sensory information from the sensory organs, performing some simple analyses, and passing the results on to the primary sensory cortex. Thus, all sensory information (except for olfaction, which is the most primitive of all sensory systems) is sent to the thalamus before it reaches the cerebral cortex.

The hypothalamus

Hypo- means 'less than' or 'beneath', and, as its name suggests, the **hypothalamus** is located below the thalamus, at the base of the brain. The hypothalamus is a small region, consisting of less than 1 cubic centimetre of tissue (smaller than a grape). Its relative importance far exceeds its relative size.

The hypothalamus, like the brain stem, participates in homeostasis and species-typical behaviours. It receives sensory information, including information from receptors inside the organs of the body; thus, it is informed about changes in the organism's physiological status. It also contains specialised sensors that monitor various characteristics of the blood that flows through the brain, such as temperature, nutrient content and amount of dissolved salts. In turn, the hypothalamus controls the **pituitary gland**, an endocrine gland attached by a stalk to the base of the hypothalamus.

Hormones are chemicals produced by endocrine glands (from the Greek *endo-* 'within', and *krinein* 'to secrete'). **Endocrine glands** secrete hormones into the blood supply, which carries them to all parts of the body. Hormones are similar to transmitter substances or neuromodulators, except that they act over much longer distances. Like transmitter substances and neuromodulators, they produce their effects by stimulating receptor molecules. These receptor molecules are located on (or in) particular cells. The presence of a hormone causes physiological reactions in these cells, which are known as **target cells**. Almost every cell of the body contains hormone receptors of one kind or other. This includes neurons; hormones that affect behaviour do so by altering the activity of particular groups of neurons in the brain. For example, the sex hormones have important effects on behaviour and are discussed in later chapters.

The pituitary gland has been called the 'master gland' because the hormones it secretes act on target cells in other endocrine glands; thus, the pituitary gland controls the activity of other endocrine glands. By controlling the pituitary gland, the hypothalamus controls the entire endocrine system. Figure 4.34 shows some of the endocrine glands and the functions they regulate.

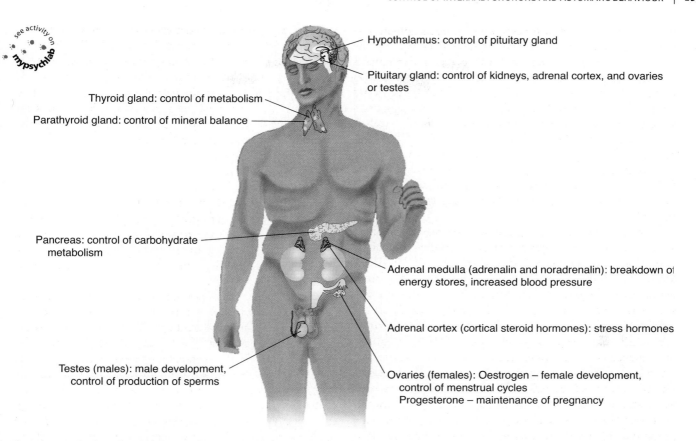

Hypothalamus: control of pituitary gland

Pituitary gland: control of kidneys, adrenal cortex, and ovaries or testes

Thyroid gland: control of metabolism

Parathyroid gland: control of mineral balance

Pancreas: control of carbohydrate metabolism

Adrenal medulla (adrenalin and noradrenalin): breakdown of energy stores, increased blood pressure

Adrenal cortex (cortical steroid hormones): stress hormones

Testes (males): male development, control of production of sperms

Ovaries (females): Oestrogen – female development, control of menstrual cycles
Progesterone – maintenance of pregnancy

Figure 4.34 The location and primary functions of the principal endocrine glands.

The hypothalamus also controls much of the activity of the **autonomic nervous system (ANS)**, which consists of nerves that control the functions of the glands and internal organs. The nerves of the autonomic nervous system control activities such as sweating, shedding tears, salivating, secreting digestive juices, changing the size of blood vessels (which alters blood pressure) and secreting some hormones. The autonomic nervous system has two branches. The **sympathetic branch** directs activities that involve the expenditure of energy. For example, activity of the sympathetic branch can increase the flow of blood to the muscles when we are about to fight someone or run away from a dangerous situation. The **parasympathetic branch** controls quiet activities, such as digestion of food. Activity of the parasympathetic branch stimulates the secretion of digestive enzymes and increases the flow of blood to the digestive system, as seen in Figure 4.35.

The homeostatic functions of the hypothalamus can involve either internal physiological changes or behaviour. For example, the hypothalamus is involved in the control of body temperature. It can directly lower body temperature by causing sweating to occur, or it can raise it by causing shivering to occur. If these measures are inadequate, it can send messages to the cerebral cortex that will cause the person to engage in a learned behaviour, such as turning on an air conditioner or putting another log on the fire. Damage to the hypothalamus can cause impaired regulation of body temperature, changes in food intake, sterility and stunting of growth.

The limbic system

The **limbic system**, a set of structures located in the cerebral hemispheres, plays an important role in learning and in the expression of emotion. Originally, this area was termed rhinencephalon (or 'smell brain') because the areas within it were thought to be involved primarily in the sense of smell.

The limbic system consists of several regions of the **limbic cortex** – the cerebral cortex located around the edge of the cerebral hemispheres where they join with the brain stem (*limbus* means 'border'; hence the term 'limbic system'). Besides the limbic cortex, the most important

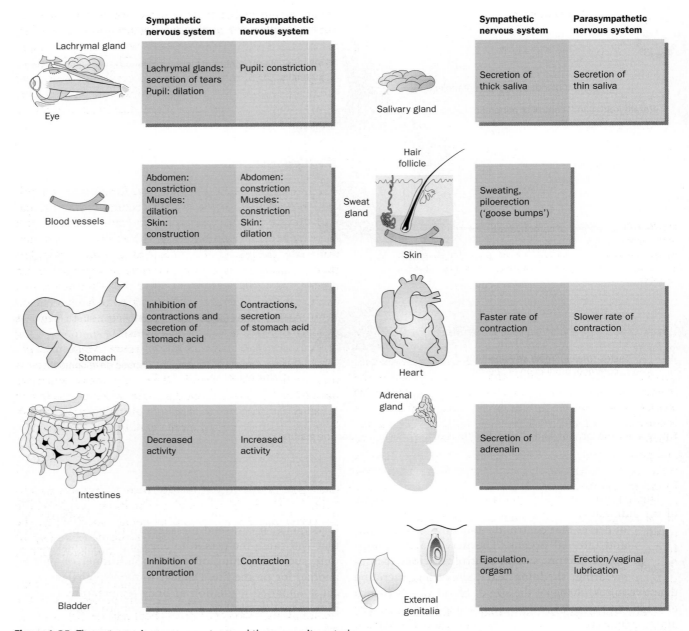

Figure 4.35 The autonomic nervous system and the organs it controls.

components of the limbic system are the amygdala and the hippocampus. The amygdala and the hippocampus get their names from their shapes; amygdala means 'almond' and hippocampus means 'sea horse'.

Figure 4.36 shows a view of the limbic cortex, located on the inner surface of the cerebral hemisphere. The left hippocampus and amygdala, located in the middle of the temporal lobe, are shown projecting out into the place where the missing left hemisphere would be. You can also see the right hippocampus and amygdala, 'ghosted in'.

The amygdala

Damage to the **amygdala**, a cluster of neurons located deep in the temporal lobe, affects emotional behaviour, especially negative emotions such as those caused by painful, threatening or stressful events. Some patients are unable to recognise fear in a person's voice or face (Adolphs *et al.*, 1995, 1999; Morris *et al.*, 1996). In a review of neuroimaging studies, however, Sergerie (2008) found that the amygdala responded to positive and nega-

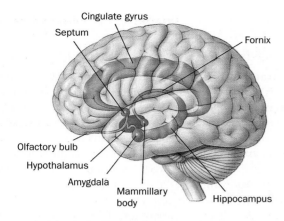

Figure 4.36 Schematic drawing illustrating the structures of the limbic system.

Source: From Pinel, J., *Biopsychology*, 3rd edn, © 1997. Published by Allyn and Bacon, Boston, MA. Copyright © by Pearson Education. By permission of the publisher.

tive emotional visual stimuli and responded more strongly to faces showing emotion than other emotional stimuli that were visual in nature. When the researchers looked at the data closely, they found that the effect sizes – the strength of the phenomenon under study – were larger for studies using positive than negative stimuli, a finding that is consistent with recent studies showing that although the neurons in the amygdala of monkeys respond to negative and positive stimuli, a greater number respond to positive than negative ones (Paton *et al.*, 2006). While the review found no evidence of sex differences in this structure, another single study has found that, at rest, the right side of the amygdala showed greater connectivity with the rest of the brain in men; for women, the same pattern was found for the left side (Kilpatrick *et al.*, 2006). Interestingly, the regions with which the right hemisphere showed connections were different from those with which the left hemisphere showed connections.

Grezes *et al.* (2006) found that the amygdala (and a region called the human face area, described in Chapter 6) showed increased activity when people watched themselves being deceived. The authors attribute the increase to greater personal involvement by the participants when they make 'emotional' judgements that involve them – in this example, deceit is seen as a personal threat.

The amygdala also controls physiological reactions that help provide energy for short-term activities such as fighting or fleeing (LeDoux, 1996). However, if these reactions are prolonged, they can lead to stress-related illnesses. If an animal's amygdala is destroyed, the animal no longer reacts emotionally to events that normally produce stress and anxiety. We might think that an animal would be better off if it did not become 'stressed out' by unpleasant or threatening situations. However, research has shown that animals with damaged amygdalae cannot survive in the wild. The animals fail to compete successfully for food and other resources, and often act in ways that provoke attacks by other animals. The functions of amygdala are discussed further in Chapters 13 and 17.

The hippocampus

The **hippocampus** (or hippocampal formation) is a collection of structures located just behind the amygdala, and plays an important role in memory. People with lesions of the hippocampus lose the ability to learn anything new (Milner *et al.*, 1968; Keane *et al.*, 1995). For them, 'yesterday' is always the time before their brain damage occurred; everything after that slips away, just as the memory of dreams often slips away from a person soon after awakening. The hippocampus and regions around it also seems to be responsible for navigating one's way around certain types of route (Maguire *et al.*, 1997, 1998). In healthy people whose brain activation is measured, this structure is selectively active when we have to find our way around a route, whether it is in our mind or in virtual space. The role of the hippocampus in memory is considered in more detail in Chapter 8.

The basal ganglia

One final group of subcortical structures that is crucial to behaviour is the **basal ganglia**. The basal ganglia is the collective name for a group of nuclei, specifically, the globus pallidus, substantia nigra, striatum (made up of the caudate nucleus and putamen) and subthalamic nucleus (see Figure 4.37).

Some of these receive inputs; some deliver output. The output nuclei, for example, send projections to the thalamus and two other subcortical regions (Utter *et al.*, 2008) and these influence sensory and cognitive behaviour, the movement of the head and the eyes and some aspects of locomotion and posture. (And, as you've seen, deep brain stimulation in Parkinson's disease targets these nuclei.) When the nuclei become dysfunctional, they can produce Parkinson's (the dopamine neurons degenerate in the substantia nigra); the motor disorder, Huntington's disease (remember this from the genetic counselling section from the last chapter) where the defective gene produces degeneration in neurotransmitter-specific neurons in the striatum; extreme of convoluted posture (dystonia); Tourette's syndome (uncontrollable blinking and facial grimacing, plus

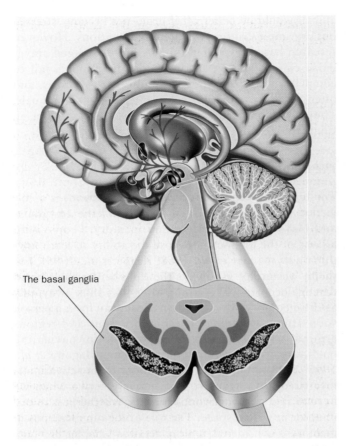

Figure 4.37 The location of the basal ganglia.
Source: Science Photo Library Ltd.

coprolalia – vigorous, unpredictable and involuntary swearing); and obsessive-compulsive disorder (described in Chapter 18), possibly because of dysfunctional loops linking the striatum with the tip of the frontal lobe.

Drugs and behaviour

Communication between neurons involves the release of transmitter substances. Neurons release many different kinds of transmitter substance, and various drugs can affect the production or release of one or more of these chemicals. Drugs can also mimic the effects of transmitter substances on receptor molecules, block these effects, or interfere with the reuptake of a transmitter substance once it is released. Via these mechanisms, a drug can alter the perceptions, thoughts and behaviours controlled by particular transmitter substances.

Stimulating or inhibiting the release of transmitter substances

Some drugs stimulate certain terminal buttons to release their transmitter substance continuously, even when the axon is not firing. Other drugs prevent certain terminal buttons from releasing their transmitter substance when the axon fires. The effects of most of these drugs are more or less specific to one transmitter substance. Because different classes of neuron release different transmitter substances, these drugs affect only a selected set of neurons. An example of a stimulating drug is the venom of the black widow spider, which causes the release of a transmitter substance called acetylcholine, as illustrated by Figure 4.38. In contrast, botulinum toxin, a poison that is sometimes present in improperly canned food, prevents the release of acetylcholine. An adult will almost certainly survive the bite of a black widow spider; the symptoms are severe abdominal cramps. However, an extremely small amount of botulinum toxin – less than one-millionth of a gram – is fatal. The victim becomes paralysed and suffocates to death.

Stimulating or blocking postsynaptic receptor molecules

Transmitter substances produce their effects by stimulating postsynaptic receptor molecules, which excite or inhibit postsynaptic neurons by opening ion channels and permitting ions to enter or leave the neurons. Some drugs duplicate the effects of particular transmitter substances by directly stimulating particular kinds of receptor mole-

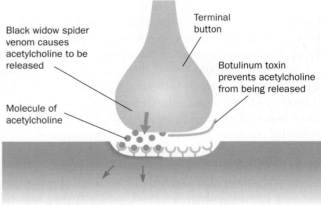

Figure 4.38 Drugs that affect the release of a neurotransmitter, acetylcholine. Black widow spider venom causes acetylcholine to be released. Botulinum toxin prevents the release of acetylcholine from the terminal buttons.

cules. If we use the lock-and-key analogy to describe the effects of a transmitter substance on a receptor molecule, then a drug that stimulates receptor molecules works like a master key, turning the receptor molecules on even when the transmitter substance is not present. For example, nicotine stimulates acetylcholine receptors located on neurons in certain regions of the brain (see Figure 4.39). In low doses, this stimulation has a pleasurable (and addictive) excitatory effect; in high doses, it can cause convulsions and death.

Some drugs block receptor molecules, making them inaccessible to the transmitter substance and thus inhibiting synaptic transmission. A drug that blocks receptor molecules 'plugs up' the lock so that the key will no longer fit into it. A poison called curare, discovered by South American Indians, was used on the darts of their blowguns. This drug blocks the acetylcholine receptors that are located on muscle fibres. The curare prevents synaptic transmission in muscles. The paralysed victim is unable to breathe and consequently suffocates.

Some medically useful chemicals work by blocking receptor molecules. For example, antipsychotic drugs alleviate the symptoms of schizophrenia, a serious mental disorder, by blocking receptor molecules in the brain that are normally stimulated by a transmitter substance called dopamine. This fact has led some investigators to suggest that the symptoms of schizophrenia may be caused by malfunctions of neurons that release dopamine. We dis-cuss antipsychotic drugs later in this chapter and in Chapter 18 (Abnormal psychology).

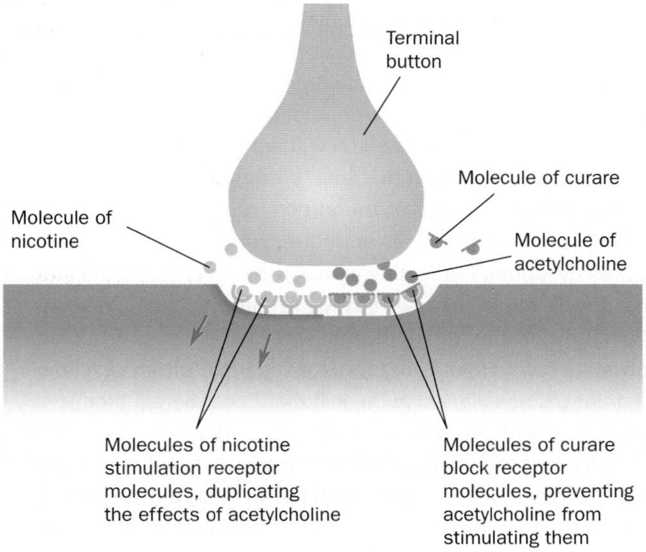

Inhibiting reuptake

The effects of most transmitter substances are kept brief by the process of reuptake. Molecules of the transmitter substance are released by a terminal button, they stimulate the receptor molecules in the postsynaptic membrane for a fraction of a second, and then they are pumped back into the terminal button. Some drugs inhibit the process of reuptake so that molecules of the transmitter substance continue to stimulate the postsynaptic receptor molecules for a long time. Therefore, inhibition of reuptake increases the effect of the transmitter substance. The excitatory effects of cocaine and amphetamine are produced by their ability to inhibit the reuptake of certain transmitter substances, including dopamine (see Figure 4.40).

Sedatives

Some drugs depress behaviour, causing relaxation, sedation, or even loss of consciousness. These are called **anti-anxiety** or **anxiolytic drugs**. In most cases, the depression is caused by stimulation of a class of receptor molecules that is normally activated by neuromodulators produced by the brain. **Barbiturates** depress the brain's activity by stimulating a particular category of neuromodulator receptors. In low doses, barbiturates have a calming effect. In progressively higher doses, they produce difficulty in walking and talking, unconsciousness, coma and death. Barbiturates are abused by people who want to achieve the relaxing, calming effect

Terminal button

Molecule of curare

Molecule of nicotine

Molecule of acetylcholine

Molecules of nicotine stimulation receptor molecules, duplicating the effects of acetylcholine

Molecules of curare block receptor molecules, preventing acetylcholine from stimulating them

Figure 4.39 Drugs that interact with receptor molecules in the postsynaptic membrane. Nicotine directly stimulates the receptor molecules. Curare blocks receptor molecules and thus prevents acetylcholine from activating them.

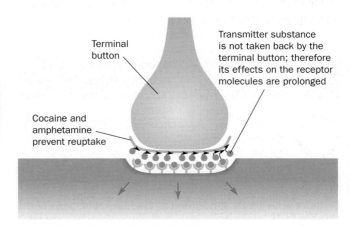

Terminal button

Transmitter substance is not taken back by the terminal button; therefore its effects on the receptor molecules are prolonged

Cocaine and amphetamine prevent reuptake

Figure 4.40 Drugs that block reuptake. Cocaine and amphetamine block the reuptake of certain transmitter substances, thus prolonging their effects on the receptor molecules in the postsynaptic membrane.

of the drugs, especially to counteract the anxiety and irritability that can be produced by stimulants. They are occasionally prescribed as medication for sleep, but they are a poor choice for this purpose because they suppress dreaming and produce a particularly unrefreshing sleep. In addition, a dose of a barbiturate sufficient to induce sleep is not that much lower than a fatal dose. Ideally, the therapeutic dose of a drug is much lower than a fatal dose.

Many anti-anxiety drugs are members of a family known as the **benzodiazepines**, which include the well-known tranquilliser Valium (diazepam). These drugs, too, stimulate some sort of neuromodulator receptors located on neurons in various parts of the brain, including the amygdala. The benzodiazepines are effective in reducing anxiety and are sometimes used to treat people who are afflicted by periodic attacks of severe anxiety. In addition, some benzodiazepines serve as sleep medications. These behavioural effects suggest that they mimic the effects of neuromodulators involved in the regulation of mood and the control of sleep.

By far the most commonly used depressant drug is ethyl alcohol, the active ingredient in alcoholic beverages. This drug has effects similar to those of the barbiturates: larger and larger doses of alcohol reduce anxiety, disrupt motor coordination and then cause unconsciousness, coma and finally death. The effects of alcohol and barbiturates are additive: a moderate dose of alcohol plus a moderate dose of barbiturates can be fatal.

The primary effect of alcohol appears to be similar to that of the benzodiazepines: it stimulates some type of neuromodulator receptor. Suzdak *et al.* (1986) discovered a drug that reverses alcohol intoxication, presumably by blocking some type of neuromodulator receptor. Although the behavioural effects of alcohol may be mediated by neuromodulator receptors, alcohol has other, potentially fatal effects on all cells of the body. Alcohol destabilises the membrane of cells, interfering with their functions. Thus, a person who takes some of the anti-alcohol drug could go on to drink themselves to death without becoming drunk in the process.

Controversies in Psychological Science – What is drug addiction?

The issue

Some drugs have very potent reinforcing effects, which lead some people to abuse them or even to become addicted to them. Robbins and Everitt (1999) report that the annual costs of drug addiction in the USA alone stand at around $80 billion. Many people – psychologists, health professionals and lay people – believe that 'true' addiction is caused by the unpleasant physiological effects that occur when an addict tries to stop taking the drug. For example, Eddy *et al.* (1965) defined physical dependence as 'an adaptive state that manifests itself by intense physical disturbances when the administration of a drug is suspended' (p. 723). In contrast, they defined psychic dependence as a condition in which a drug produces 'a feeling of satisfaction and a psychic drive that requires periodic or continuous administration of the drug to produce pleasure or to avoid discomfort' (p. 723). Most people regard the latter as less important than the former. But, as we shall see, the reverse is true.

The evidence

Robbins and Everitt suggest that 'drug dependence and addiction can be partly understood as gradual adaptations of the brain to chronic drug exposure'. But other psychological factors also influence drug-taking, from finding the drugs, to the motivation for using them, to being able to live without them.

For many years, heroin addiction has been considered as the prototype for all drug addictions. People who habitually take heroin (or other opiates) become physically dependent on the drug, that is, they show tolerance and withdrawal symptoms. **Tolerance** is the decreased sensitivity to a drug that comes from its continued use; the drug user must take larger and larger amounts of the drug in order for it to be effective. Once a person has taken an opiate regularly enough to develop tolerance, that person will suffer withdrawal symptoms if they stop taking the drug. **Withdrawal symptoms** are primarily the opposite of the effects of the drug itself. For example, heroin produces euphoria; withdrawal from it produces dysphoria – a feeling of anxious misery (euphoria and dysphoria mean 'easy to bear' and 'hard to bear', respectively). According to Freud, this was 'agony beyond human power to bear'. Heroin produces constipation; withdrawal from it produces nausea, cramping and diarrhoea. Heroin produces relaxation; withdrawal from it produces agitation.

Most investigators believe that the withdrawal symptoms are produced by the body's attempt to compensate for the unusual condition of heroin intoxication. That is, most systems of the body, including those controlled by the brain, are regulated so that they stay at an optimal value. When a drug artificially changes these systems for a prolonged time, home-

Controversies in Psychological Science – *Continued*

ostatic mechanisms begin to produce the opposite reaction, which partially compensates for the disturbance from the optimal value. These compensatory mechanisms account for the fact that more and more heroin must be taken in order to achieve the effects that were produced when the person first started taking the drug. They also account for the symptoms of withdrawal: when the person stops taking the drug, the compensatory mechanisms make themselves felt, unopposed by the action of the drug.

Heroin addiction has provided such a striking example of drug dependence that some authorities have concluded that 'real' addiction does not occur unless a drug causes tolerance and withdrawal. Withdrawal symptoms make it difficult for a person to stop taking heroin – they help keep the person hooked. But withdrawal symptoms do not explain why a person becomes a heroin addict in the first place; that fact is explained by the drug's reinforcing effect. Certainly, people do not start taking heroin so that they will become physically dependent on it and feel miserable when they go without it. Instead, they begin taking it because it makes them feel good.

Even though the withdrawal effects of heroin make it difficult to stop taking the drug, these effects alone are not sufficient to keep most people hooked (Baker *et al.*, 2006). In fact, when the cost of the habit gets too high, some addicts who stop taking heroin experience 'cold turkey'. Doing so is not as painful as most people believe; withdrawal symptoms have been described as similar to a bad case of influenza – unpleasant, but survivable. Mood declines – people feel unstable, stressed, anxious and depressed (Baker *et al.*, 2006). After a week or two, when their nervous systems adapt to the absence of the drug, these addicts recommence their habit, which now costs less to sustain. However, addicts do cite a fear of withdrawal symptoms as being one reason why they are motivated to continue taking drugs (the effects of withdrawal from a drug like ethanol, for example, include tremors and convulsions). The strength of withdrawal is not related to the strength of relapse. The reason why people take – and continue to take – drugs such as heroin is that the drugs give them a pleasurable 'rush'; in other words, the drugs have a reinforcing effect on their behaviour.

There are two other lines of evidence that contradict the assertion that drug addiction is caused by physical dependence. First, some potent drugs, including cocaine, do not produce physical dependence. That is, people who take the drug do not show tolerance; and if they stop, they do not show any withdrawal symptoms. As a result, experts believed for many years that cocaine was a relatively innocu-

ous drug, not in the same league as heroin. Obviously, they were wrong; cocaine is even more addictive than heroin. As a matter of fact, laboratory animals who can press a lever and give themselves injections of cocaine are more likely to die than are those who can give themselves injections of heroin. Secondly, some drugs produce physical dependence (tolerance and withdrawal symptoms) but are not abused (Jaffe, 1985).

The reason why they are not abused is that they do not have reinforcing effects on behaviour – they are just not any fun to take. People take drugs because they enjoy them. And the more they like them, the more excessive their drug-taking (Ahmed, 2005). Studies in rodents suggest that the greater the access to cocaine, the greater the rat's drug-seeking behaviour (Vanderschuren and Everitt, 2004). A three month exposure to a drug led to rats being unable *not* to seek drugs, even when they were punished for doing so (Deroche-Gamonet *et al.*, 2004). Rats exposed to heroin daily had lower and more stable levels of drug intake than those who were exposed to it for 24 hours (Kenny *et al.*, 2006). As the drug-taking increases, the excitability of the reward systems, reflected in brain activation and neurotransmitter release, decreases. Therefore, more of the drug is needed to resume this level of excitability (Kenny, 2007). Similarly, neuroimaging data from adults has shown that activation in the insula, prefrontal cortex and anterior cingulate cortex is associated with urges to take a drug, whether cigarettes, heroin, alcohol or cocaine (Naqvi and Bechara, 2008). Ultimately drugs 'work' by stimulating the release of dopamine from the brain stem tegmental area (Naqvi and Bechara, 2008).

A study by Kirby *et al.* (1999) tested a specific model of substance abuse which suggests that the value of a reward is affected by the length of time between the promise of that reward and actually obtaining it. For example, if a reward was promised a long time in the future, then its present value would be small. If a competing reward was made available sooner, this would be chosen over the other. This is called delay-discounting. This is relevant to drug use because the delay-discounting model of impulsive behaviour would suggest that impulsive individuals would choose a smaller, immediate reward rather than wait for a larger reward promised after a longer delay.

Kirby *et al.* put this hypothesis to the test in an experiment in which 56 heroin addicts and 60 drug-free controls had to make a choice between either receiving an $11–80 reward available immediately, or receiving a larger reward ($25–85) after a delay from one week to six months. There was a one in

▶

Controversies in Psychological Science – *Continued*

six chance of winning the reward in each trial. The researchers found that heroin addicts were twice as likely as controls to discount delayed rewards in favour of immediate ones. They suggest that these findings are important for treatment interventions that focus on the consequences of drug abuse (such as going to jail, losing a family, failing to get a job, developing HIV) because such consequences may not be particularly salient to the addict. Programmes which provide rewards after short periods of abstinence, Kirby *et al.* argue, should be more effective in preventing drug use because the reward would be immediate and not delayed.

Conclusion

The most important lesson we can learn from the misguided distinction between 'physiological' and 'psychological' addiction is that we should never underestimate the importance of psychological factors. Given that behaviour is controlled by circuits of neurons in the brain, even psychological factors involve physiological mechanisms. People often pay more attention to physiological symptoms than psychological ones – they consider them more real. But behavioural research indicates that an exclusive preoccupation with physiology can hinder our understanding of the causes of addiction.

Stimulants

Several categories of drugs stimulate the central nervous system and thus activate behaviour. Because of the effects some of these drugs have on the neural circuits involved in reinforcement (reward), they tend to be abused. Two popular stimulant drugs, amphetamine and cocaine, have almost identical effects: they inhibit the reuptake of dopamine and thus strengthen the effectiveness of synapses that use this transmitter substance. As you will see in Chapter 13, reinforcing stimuli – such as food for a hungry animal, water for a thirsty one, or sexual contact for a sexually aroused one – exert their behavioural effects largely by increasing the activity of a circuit of dopamine-secreting neurons. Thus, amphetamine and cocaine mimic the effects of reinforcing stimuli. Free-base cocaine (crack) is particularly addictive. The drug has an immediate effect on the reuptake of dopamine and produces such a profound feeling of euphoria and pleasure that the person wants to repeat the experience again and again.

Cocaine and amphetamine, if taken in large enough doses for a few days, can produce the symptoms of paranoid schizophrenia – a serious mental disorder described in Chapter 18. Heavy users of these drugs suffer from hallucinations and their thoughts become confused and difficult to control. They may come to believe that they are being attacked or plotted against. In fact, an experienced clinician cannot distinguish the drug-induced symptoms from those that occur in people who really have the psychosis. This fact has suggested to some investigators that schizophrenia may be caused by overactivity of dopamine-secreting synapses.

Opiate drugs have both excitatory and inhibitory effects on behaviour. All of these effects occur because these drugs mimic the effects of the body's own opioid neuromodulators: they stimulate opioid receptors located on neurons in various parts of the brain. The inhibitory effects include analgesia (reduced sensitivity to pain), hypothermia (lowering of body temperature) and sedation. The pain reduction is accomplished by neurons in the midbrain, the hypothermia by neurons in the hypothalamus and the sedation by neurons in the medulla. A fatal overdose of an opiate kills its victim by inhibiting the activity of circuits of neurons in the medulla that control breathing, heart rate and blood pressure. But it is the excitatory effects of opiates that induce people to abuse them. Some opioid receptors are located on dopamine-secreting neurons involved in reinforcement (reward). When a person takes an opiate such as heroin, the activity of these neurons produces feelings of euphoria and pleasure, similar to those produced by cocaine or amphetamine. These excitatory effects, and not the inhibitory ones, are responsible for addiction.

Drugs and altered states of consciousness

Throughout history, people have enjoyed changing their consciousness now and then by taking drugs, fasting, meditating or chanting. Even children enjoy spinning around and making themselves dizzy – presumably for the same reasons. Chemicals found in several different plants produce profound changes in consciousness. Behaviourally, these changes are difficult to specify. Large doses of drugs such as marijuana or LSD tend to sedate laboratory animals, but the animals give no sign of having their consciousness altered. Only humans can describe the consciousness-altering effects of the drugs. In *Doors of*

Perception, Aldous Huxley described the intense vision he experienced on looking at a bowl of flowers. The experience was induced by a synthetic form of the drug mescaline (derived from cactus peyote), which has been used by shamans for centuries as religious communion.

> [Plato] could never, poor fellow, have seen a bunch of flowers shining with their own inner light and all but quivering under the pressure of the significance with which they were charged; could never have perceived that what rose and iris and carnation so intensely signified was nothing more, and nothing less, than what they were – a transience that was yet eternal life, a perpetual perishing that was at the same time pure Being, a bundle of minute, unique particulars in which, by some unspeakable and yet self-evident paradox, was to be seen the divine source of all existence. I continued to look at the flowers, and in their living light I seemed to detect the qualitative equivalent of breathing – but of a breathing without returns to a starting point, with no recurrent ebbs but only a repeated flow from beauty to heightened beauty, from deeper to ever deeper meaning.
>
> Source: Aldous Huxley (1954), *The Doors of Perception*.

More famously, Samuel Taylor Coleridge wrote *Kubla Khan* after a drug-taking session:

> In the Summer of the year 1797, the Author... had retired to a lonely farmhouse between Porlock and Linton, on the Exmoor confines of Somerset and Devonshire. In consequence of a slight indisposition, an anodyne had been prescribed, from the effects of which he fell asleep in his chair at the moment he was reading. The Author continued for about three hours in a profound sleep, at least of the external senses, during which time he has the most vivid confidence, that he could not have composed less than from two hundred to three hundred lines... on awaking he appeared to himself to have a distinct recollection of the whole, and ... instantly and eagerly wrote down the lines that are here preserved.
>
> Source: Samuel Taylor Coleridge, prefatory note to *Kubla Khan* (1797).

Drugs can affect consciousness in several different ways. We have the clearest understanding of one category of drugs: those that affect synapses that use a transmitter substance called serotonin. Serotonin plays an important role in the control of dreaming. Normally, we dream only when we are asleep, in a particular stage called REM sleep (because of the rapid eye movements that occur then). During the rest of the day, circuits of serotonin-secreting neurons inhibit the mechanisms responsible for dreaming, thus preventing them from becoming active. Drugs such as LSD, psilocybin and dimethyltryptamine (DMT) suppress the activity of serotonin-secreting neurons, permitting dream mechanisms to become active. As a result, hallucinations occur. These hallucinations are often interesting and even awe-inspiring, but sometimes produce intense fear and anxiety.

Not all hallucinogenic drugs interfere with serotonin-secreting synapses. Cocaine and amphetamine, which affect dopamine-secreting synapses, also produce hallucinations. However, the hallucinations produced by cocaine and amphetamine take some time to develop, and they are primarily auditory. LSD-induced hallucinations take place immediately and are primarily visual, as dreams are. The two types of hallucination undoubtedly occur for different reasons.

Aldous Huxley.
Source: Hulton Archive/Getty Images.

On the advice of the novelist Aldous Huxley, Timothy Leary, then a clinical psychologist at Harvard, took his first acid trip and reported its effect. He took lysergic acid (LSD), a powerful psychotropic drug derived from a fungus (ergot) and synthesised in the laboratory in 1930.

Source: Ben Martin/Time Life Pictures/Getty Images.

Tetrahydrocannabinol (THC), the active ingredient in marijuana, exerts its behavioural effects by stimulating THC receptors, specific neuromodulator receptors present in particular regions of the brain. THC produces analgesia and sedation, stimulates appetite, reduces nausea caused by drugs used to treat cancer, relieves asthma attacks, decreases pressure within the eyes in patients with glaucoma, and reduces the symptoms of certain motor disorders. On the other hand, THC interferes with concentration and memory, alters visual and auditory perception, and distorts perceptions of the passage of time (Howlett, 1990).

Drug classification

In the UK, controlled susbstances (drugs) are classified as either A, B or C. Class A drugs are those most likely to cause harm and include LSD, heroin and cocaine. Class B drugs are considered to be not as harmful and include amphetamines, Ritalin and cannabis. In the US, cannabis is deemed a Schedule 1 substance – it has the potential to be 'abused' and has no medical use. Class C drugs include ketamine, painkillers and various other drugs that require a prescription. Cannabis or marijuana is one of the most commonly used, if not the most commonly used prohibited drug in existence. According to one recent UK survey, marijuana was the most commonly experienced drug (87 per cent), followed by cocaine at 35 per cent (Observer Drugs, 2008). The 2006 *National Survey on Drug Use and Health* in the US estimated that 98 million Americans over 12 years of age had tried it at least once (the figure represents 40 per cent of the population). Between 71 and 77 per cent of US prisoners claimed to have used the drug at some point (Bureau of Justice Statistics, 2006). As the International Perspective below shows, it is also commonly used by 18–25-year-olds.

The psychology of cannabis use – An international perspective

Cannabis is a drug derived from the plant genus *Cannabis* and comprises around 400 compounds. The most potent of these is tetrahydrocannabinol (THC), one of the 60 cannabinoids the plant contains, and a typical joint will contain between 150 and 300 mg of THC. Surveys of UK universities show that around 50–60 per cent of respondents report having used cannabis (Ashton, 2001). A study of 1,261 Australian adolescents aged between 13 and 17 years found that a quarter of the sample reported having used cannabis and this use increased with age (Rey *et al.*, 2002). A glance at Figure 4.41 shows that people who are heavy users of cannabis also report higher levels of depression than do light users (Rey *et al.*, 2002). While cannabis has been used recreationally for centuries to elevate mood, recent controversy has surrounded the use of cannabis to alleviate pain. One reason why the drug may be inappropriate is that it may have psychological consequences that could be either harmful or dangerous.

About 50 per cent of THC in a joint of cannabis is inhaled through smoke (the amount is less when taken orally). Because THC has a half-life of seven days, it can remain vital for up to 30 days which means that traces of cannabis can be detected in the body up to a month after inhalation/ingestion.

The psychology of cannabis use – *Continued*

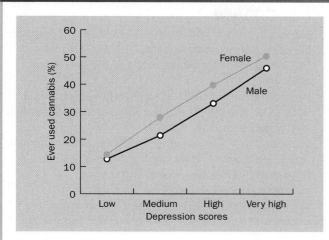

Figure 4.41 The relationship between cannabis use and depression scores in over 4,000 Australian adolescents.

Source: Rey, J.M., Sawyer, M.G., Raphael, B., Patton, G.C. and Lynskey, M., Mental health of teenagers who use cannabis. *British Journal of Psychiatry*, 2002, 150, 216–21, reprinted by permission of the Royal College of Psychiatrists.

The behavioural effects of cannabis are varied. It can stimulate appetite, reduce anxiety and create psychedelic experiences. Doses of THC as low as 2.5 g in herbal cigarettes can produce a feeling of intoxication and a reduction in anxiety (Ashton, 2001). It can also produce panic attacks and paranoia. Its effects on psychomotor performance are similar to those of alcohol: behaviour becomes uncoordinated and reaction time slows. In many European countries, the second most common substance found in the bodies of drivers involved in fatal accidents or in drivers who drive poorly is cannabis. The majority of those who use cannabis show no evidence of excessive or illegal alcohol consumption. Similar performance decrements are seen in pilots (even pilots who are regular cannabis users) 24 hours after cannabis intake.

The association between cannabis use and the development of psychotic disorders, such as schizophrenia, is a controversial one. Many studies have reported that psychotic symptoms can occur but that these are short-lived; few studies have followed up such patients, however, to examine the long-term consequences of cannabis use. A study of 535 Danish patients who had been treated for cannabis-induced psychotic symptoms (Arendt *et al.*, 2005) found that 44 per cent of cases showed schizophrenia-type symptoms. Some 77 per cent of the sample reported new psychotic symptoms. Approximately 47 per cent of the sample received a diagnosis of cannabis-induced schizophrenia a year after seeking treatment for cannabis-related psychosis.

The authors caution, however, that there was a significant delay in the majority of patients in the development of schizophrenia-type symptoms. They also note that they were unable to control for any other type of substance use during the follow-up period. Between 40–51 per cent of patients with schizophrenia have used cannabis (Borsani *et al.*, 2002; Barnett *et al.*, 2007) and there appears to be an association between decreased grey matter and cannabis use in schizophrenia patients who are cannabis users and have had their first episode (Bangalore *et al.*, 2008). (In psychiatry, an episode is one serious experience or appearance of a disorder.)

Recent debate in some European countries has centred on the therapeutic effects of cannabis. Cannabis was a drug recommended for various ills as long as 5,000 years ago in China. A review by Robson (2001) describes how, historically, cannabis mixed with wine was recommended as a surgical analgesic. In nineteenth-century Britain, the use of cannabis for the alleviation of illness was common. Even Queen Victoria's physician lauded cannabis's ability to relieve physical ailments.

There is some evidence for cannabis's therapeutic effects. Patients with cancer frequently report a reduction in the feeling of nausea that is induced by chemotherapy (Robson, 2001). Questionnaire studies of British and American multiple sclerosis sufferers show that cannabis smokers report reduced muscle spasm, increased pain relief, improvement in balance and an improvement in memory. Since 2001, however, the US Congress has ruled that the drug has no medical value.

Cannabis use is legal in some European countries but in restricted contexts. Danish law states that cannabis is illegal but has a provision that condones possession or sale of up to 30 g of cannabis (MacCoun and Reuter, 2001). This level, set in 1976, was reduced to 5 g in 1985. Around 1,200 coffee shops sell cannabis in the Netherlands and operate according to strict guidelines (such as no advertising, no public disturbances, no sales to minors, and so on).

Because of cannabis's status as an illegal drug in some European countries, especially the United Kingdom, much debate has surrounded the legitimacy of this position, with a number of doctors and patients questioning the decision to restrict or prohibit its use.

Chapter review

The brain and its components

- The brain has two major functions: to control behaviour and to regulate the body's physiological processes.
- The central nervous system (CNS) consists of the spinal cord and the three major divisions of the brain: the brain stem, the cerebellum and the cerebral hemispheres. The cerebral cortex, which covers the cerebral hemispheres, is wrinkled by fissures and gyri.
- The brain communicates with the rest of the body through the peripheral nervous system, which includes the spinal nerves and cranial nerves.
- The basic element of the nervous system is the neuron. Neurons are assisted in their tasks by glia, which provide physical support, aid in the development of the nervous system, provide neurons with chemicals they need, remove unwanted chemicals, provide myelin sheaths for axons and protect neurons from infection.
- One neuron communicates with another (or with muscle or gland cells) by means of synapses. A synapse is the junction of the terminal button of the presynaptic neuron with the membrane of the postsynaptic neuron.
- Synaptic communication is chemical; when an action potential travels down an axon, it causes a transmitter substance to be released by the terminal buttons.
- An action potential consists of a brief change in the electrical charge of the axon, produced by a brief entry of positively charged sodium ions into the axon followed by a brief exit of positively charged potassium ions.
- Ions enter the axon through ion channels, and ion transporters eventually restore the proper concentrations of ions inside and outside the cell.
- Molecules of the transmitter substance released by terminal buttons either excite or inhibit the firing of the postsynaptic neuron. The combined effects of excitatory and inhibitory synapses on a particular neuron determine the rate of firing of that neuron.
- Neuromodulators resemble transmitter substances but travel further and are dispersed more widely. They are released by terminal buttons and modulate the activity of many neurons. The best-known neuromodulators are the opioids, which are released when an animal is engaged in essential, meaningful behaviour. The opiates, extracted from the sap of the opium poppy or produced in a laboratory, stimulate the brain's opioid receptors.

Techniques for studying the brain

- Various techniques are available for neuroscientists to investigate brain function. These include experimental lesion, observing the effects of natural or accidental brain damage, recording the electrical activity of the brain or observing its structure or metabolic activity.

- Neuropsychologists study the effects of brain damage on people's behaviour, correlating their behavioural deficits with the location of their lesions. The assessment of cognitive impairment after brain injury is called neuropsychological assessment.
- Neuropsychological rehabilitation refers to a programme of remediation that helps the patient regain some of the function lost through brain injury.
- Techniques used to measure activity of the peripheral nervous system or autonomic nervous system included galvanic skin response (GSR), electrocardiography (ECG) and electromyography (EMG).
- GSR is a measure of arousal indexed by electrodermal response; ECG is a measure of heart rate; EMG is a measure of muscle activity.
- Sophisticated methods of observing brain structure and activity in healthy individuals include computerised tomography (CT), positron emission tomography (PET), magnetic resonance imaging (MRI) and functional magnetic resonance imaging (fMRI).
- CT allows us to view the brain's structure; PET permits researchers to study the neural activity of specific regions of the living human brain. MRI is a measure of brain structure and provides clearer images of the brain's structure than does CT; fMRI is a measure of brain activity.
- Psychophysiologists measure the brain's electrical activity using electroencephalography (EEG) and event-related potentials (ERP). Magnetoencephalography (MEG) records changes in magnetic fields generated by neurons.
- Repetitive transcranial magnetic stimulation (rTMS) involves passing a magnetic current over the head and exciting the cortex; this often results in temporary impairment of cognitive function or an alleviation of depressive symptoms.

Control of behaviour

- Anatomically, the cerebral cortex is divided into four lobes: frontal, parietal, occipital and temporal.
- Functionally, the cerebral cortex is organised into five major regions: the three regions of the primary sensory cortex (visual, auditory and somatosensory), the primary motor cortex and the association cortex.
- The association cortex consists of sensory regions that are responsible for perceiving and learning and motor regions that are responsible for planning and acting.
- Visual stimulation is transmitted from the eyes to the brain through the optic nerves, one of the pairs of cranial nerves. The information is sent to the primary visual cortex in the occipital lobe.
- The motor association cortex in the frontal lobe is responsible for planning activity; the primary motor cortex is responsible for initiating movement.

- Somatosensory information is transmitted from the skin to the spinal cord by means of a spinal nerve. It is then sent up through the spinal cord and is relayed to the primary somatosensory cortex.
- Lateralisation refers to whether a function is localised in the left or right hemisphere. The right and left hemispheres are involved with somewhat different functions: the left is superior at reading, speech production and speech comprehension; the right hemisphere is superior for visuospatial ability and recognition of emotion.
- The two cerebral hemispheres are connected by a large bundle of axons called the corpus callosum which allows the hemispheres to transfer information to one another.
- The frontal lobe is concerned with motor functions, planning strategies for action, working memory, emotion and problem-solving. A region of the left frontal cortex (Broca's area) is specialised for the control of speech.
- Somatosensory information is processed by the parietal lobe, visual information by the occipital and lower temporal lobes, and auditory information by the upper temporal lobe. Other functions of these lobes are related to these perceptual processes; for example, the parietal lobes are concerned with perception of space and knowledge about the body as well as mental arithmetic.

Control of internal functions and automatic behaviour

- The more primitive parts of the brain control homeostasis and species-typical behaviours. The brain stem, which consists of the medulla, the pons and the midbrain, contains neural circuits that control vital physiological functions and produce automatic movements such as those used in locomotion, fighting and sexual behaviour.
- The cerebellum assists the cerebral cortex in carrying out movements; it coordinates the control of muscles, resulting in smooth movements. It also regulates postural adjustments and appears to play some role in cognition and reading impairment.
- The thalamus participates in the control of movement and relays sensory information to the cerebral cortex.
- The hypothalamus receives sensory information from sense receptors elsewhere in the body and also contains its own specialised receptors, such as those used to monitor body temperature. It controls the pituitary gland, which, in turn, controls most of the endocrine glands of the body, and it also controls the internal organs through the autonomic nervous system.
- Hormones, secreted by endocrine glands, are chemicals that act on hormone receptors in target cells and produce physiological reactions in these cells. The hypothalamus can control homeostatic processes directly and automatically through its control of the pituitary gland and the autonomic

nervous system, or it can cause neural circuits in the cerebral cortex to execute more complex, learned behaviour.
- The amygdala and the hippocampus are both located within the temporal lobe, specifically within the limbic system. The amygdala is involved in various emotional processes including fear conditioning.
- The hippocampus is involved in learning and memory; people with damage to this structure can recall old memories but are unable to learn anything new.

Drugs and behaviour

- Many chemicals found in nature have behavioural effects, and many more have been synthesised in the laboratory.
- Drugs can facilitate or interfere with synaptic activity. Facilitators include drugs that cause the release of a transmitter substance (such as the venom of the black widow spider); drugs that directly stimulate postsynaptic receptor molecules, thus duplicating the effects of the transmitter substance itself (such as nicotine); and drugs that inhibit the reuptake of a transmitter substance (such as amphetamine and cocaine).
- Drugs that interfere with synaptic activity include those that inhibit the release of a transmitter substance (such as botulinum toxin) and those that block receptor molecules (such as curare).
- There are several major categories of drugs that affect behaviour. Alcohol, barbiturates and tranquillisers depress the activity of the brain by stimulating various types of receptor molecule.
- Amphetamine and cocaine stimulate the brain primarily by retarding the reuptake of dopamine. The opiates duplicate the effects of the brain's opioids, decreasing sensitivity to pain and producing intensely enjoyable feelings of euphoria and pleasure. LSD, psilocybin and related drugs inhibit the activity of synapses that use serotonin.
- The hallucinogenic effects of these drugs may be related to dreaming, which is controlled by circuits of serotonin-secreting neurons.
- The physiological effects of marijuana are produced by a compound called THC which stimulates receptors that are normally activated by a natural neuromodulator called anandamide.
- Psychotherapeutic drugs include those that reduce the symptoms of schizophrenia and those that relieve depression. Anti-schizophrenic drugs block dopamine receptors, and antidepressant drugs generally facilitate the action of serotonin.
- Opiates produce tolerance and withdrawal symptoms, which make their habitual use increasingly expensive and make quitting more difficult.
- The primary reason for addiction is the reinforcing effect, not the unpleasant symptoms produced when an addict tries to quit. Tolerance appears to be produced by homeostatic mechanisms that counteract the effects of the drug.

Suggestions for further reading

Psychobiology and neuroscience – general reading

Carlson, N.R. (2010) *Physiology of Behaviour* (10th edn). Boston: Allyn & Bacon.

DeVries, A.C. and Nelson, R.J. (2009) *Current Directions in Biological Psychology*. Boston: Allyn & Bacon.

Martin, G.N. (2003) *Essential Biological Psychology*. London: Arnold.

Martin, G.N. (2006) *Human Neuropsychology* (2nd edn). Harlow: Pearson Education.

Toates, F. (2006) *Biological Psychology* (2nd edn). Harlow: Pearson Education.

Wickens, A. (2009) *Introduction to Biopsychology* (3rd edn). Harlow: Pearson Education.

These are good, comprehensive introductions to the physiology of behaviour, the relationship between human brain activity, structure and function, and general psychobiology.

The development of neuroscience

Finger, S. (2000) *Minds behind the brain*. Oxford: Oxford University Press.

Kandel, E.R. and Squire, L.R. (2000) Neuroscience: Breaking down scientific barriers to the study of brain and mind. *Science*, 290, 1113–20.

Two very good items on the history of neuroscience.

Localisation and lateralisation of function

Cowey, A. (2001) Functional lateralization of the brain. *The Psychologist*, 14, 5, 250–54.

Springer, S.P. and Deutsch, G. (2001) *Left Brain, Right Brain* (5th edn). New York: W.H. Freeman.

Excellent accounts of lateralisation of function. Springer and Deutsch's book is probably the best book reviewing functional lateralisation.

Basic neuroanatomy and neurophysiology

England, M.A. and Wakeley, J. (1991) *A Colour Atlas of the Brain and Spinal Cord*. Aylesbury: Wolfe.

Kosslyn, S.M., Cacioppo, J.T., Davidson, R.J., Hugdahl, K., Lovallo, W.R., Spiegel, D. and Rose, R. (2002) Bridging psychology and biology. *American Psychologist*, 57, 5, 341–51.

Swanson, L.W. (2002) *Brain Architecture: Understanding the basic plan*. Oxford: Oxford University Press.

A number of books cover the neuroanatomy and neurophysiology of the brain and the items listed here cover most of these two topics and do it well.

Methods

Andreassi, J.L. (2001) *Psychophysiology* (4th edn). Hillsdale, NJ: Lawrence Erlbaum Associates.

Beaulieu, A. (2002) A space for measuring mind and brain: Interdisciplinarity and digital tools in the development of brain mapping and functional imaging, 1980–1990. *Brain and Cognition*, 49, 13–33.

Cabeza, R. and Nyberg, L. (1997) Imaging cognition: An empirical review of PET studies with normal subjects. *Journal of Cognitive Neuroscience*, 9, 1, 1–26.

Cabeza, R. and Nyberg, L. (2000) Imaging cognition II: An empirical review of 275 PET and fMRI studies. *Journal of Cognitive Neuroscience*, 12, 1, 1–47.

Grafton, S.T., Sinnott-Armstrong, W.P., Gazzaniga, S.I. and Gazzaniga, M.S. (2007) Brain scans go legal. *Scientific American Mind*, 17, 6, 30–37.

Raichle, M.E. (2008) A brief history of human brain mapping. *Trends in Neurosciences*, 32, 2, 118–26.

Andreassi's book is the most well-known general introduction to psychophysiology. Raichle and Beaulieu's articles review the development of the techniques. The Cabeza and Nyberg articles review, and give a more critical account of, the contribution of PET and fMRI studies to neuropsychology.

Drugs and behaviour

Baker, T.B., Japuntich, S.J., Hogle, J.M., McCarthy, D.E. and Curtin, J.J. (2006) Pharmacologic and behavioural withdrawal from addictive drugs. *Current Directions in Psychological Science*, 15, 5, 232–36.

Crombag, H.S. and Robinson, T.E. (2004) Drugs, environment, brain and behavior. *Current Directions in Psychological Science*, 13, 3, 107–11.

Grilly, D.M. (2006) *Drugs and Human Behaviour* (5th edn). Boston: Allyn & Bacon.

Hobson, J.A. (2005) *The Dream Drugstore: Chemically altered states of consciousness*. Cambridge, MA: MIT Press.

Julien, R.M.A. (2007) *A Primer of Drug Action* (11th edn). San Francisco: W.H. Freeman.

Naqvi, N.H. and Bechara, A. (2008) The hidden island of addiction: the insula. *Trends in Neurosciences*, 32, 1, 56–67.

Parrott, A., Morinian, A., Moss, M. and Scholey, A. (2003) *Understanding Drugs and Behaviour*. Chichester: Wiley.

Robinson, T.E. and Berridge, K.C. (2003) Addiction. *Annual Review of Psychology*, 54, 25–54.

Julien's book is probably the best introductory book on drugs and the biochemistry of drug use available. Parrott et al.'s book focuses not only on the psychopharmacology of drug use – from tobacco to ecstasy – but on the health and social consequences of drug use. The other items give very good overviews of drugs and addiction.

Journals to consult

Addiction

Biological Psychology

Brain

Brain and Cognition

Brain and Language

British Journal of Neuropsychology

British Medical Journal

Cerebral Cortex

Cognitive Neuropsychology

Cortex

Current Opinion in Neurobiology

International Journal of Neuroscience

International Journal of Psychophysiology

Journal of Cognitive Neuroscience

Journal of Psychopharmacology

Nature Neuroscience

Neuroimage

Neuropsychologia

Neuropsychology

Psychobiology

Psychoneuroendocrinology

Psychophysiology

Science

Trends in Neuroscience

Trends in Pharmacological Sciences

Website addresses

http://www.psychology.org/links/Paradigms_and_Theories/Neuroscience/
An excellent collection of links to neuroscience sites.

http::/www.functionalmri.org/
A collection of links to fMRI sites and other neuroscience-related topics.

http://pegasus.cc.ucf.edu/~Brainmd1/brain.html
An internet tutorial on parts of the brain and what they do.

http://www.med.harvard.edu/AANLIB/home.html
An excellent brain atlas site from the University of Harvard Medical School.

http://www.psychologie.uni-bonn.de/online-documents/lit_pp.htm
Allows you access to full-text versions of articles on psychophysiology.

http://www.neuropsychologycentral.com
A link to an excellent collection of neuroscience links.

http://www.bigbluedesign.com/quest/addgene.html
A site which considers evidence for an 'alcoholic' gene.

http://www.rci.rutgers.edu/~lwh/drugs/
A link to an online book, Drugs, Brains and Behaviour, by Robin Timmons and Leonard Hamilton.

Sensation

CHAPTER 5

You really can smell fear, say scientists

James Randerson, Science correspondent

The smell of fear, one of the most terrible clichés of pulp fiction, is actually founded in fact, scientists claim today.

People can unconsciously detect whether someone is stressed or scared by smelling a chemical pheromone released into their sweat, according to researchers who have investigated the underarm secretions of petrified skydivers.

The team found that the smell of fear triggered a heightened response in brain regions associated with fear when inhaled by volunteers in a brain scanner. The research suggests that, like many animal species, humans can detect and subconsciously respond to pheromones released by other people.

Source: from 'You really can smell fear, say scientists', *The Guardian*, 4 December 2008 (Randeson, J.),
Copyright Guardian News & Media Ltd 2008.

WHAT YOU SHOULD BE ABLE TO DO AFTER READING CHAPTER 5

- Be aware of the difference between sensation and perception.
- Describe the processes involved in sensation, such as transduction and sensory coding.
- Describe each of the sense organs and how they function.
- Think of reasons why such senses have evolved.

QUESTIONS TO THINK ABOUT

- How many senses do we have?
- Why did the senses evolve?
- Are some senses more important to us than others?
- Which sense do we use least (or think we do) and why?
- Do the different senses function along similar lines, using similar mechanisms?

- Is the importance of a sense reflected in the amount of brain capacity needed to support it?
- Why are some animals more reliant on some senses than others?
- Are there some stimuli that we sense, even though we are not consciously aware of sensing them?
- How can we tell the difference between the sight (and sound) of a bird and a plane, or between the smell of chocolate and gas?

mypsychlab where learning comes to life!

Explore the accompanying videos, simulations, and animations on MyPsychLab. This chapter includes activites on: Normal vision, nearsightedness, farsightedness • Perceiving sound • The olfactory system • Manipulating your sense of smell • Check your understanding and prepare for your exams using the multiple choice, short answer and essay practice tests also available.

Sensation and behaviour

Our senses are the means by which we experience the world; everything we learn is detected by sense organs and transmitted to our brains by sensory nerves. Without sensory input, a human brain would be utterly useless; it would learn nothing, think no thoughts, have no experiences and control no behaviours.

Vision, to most people, is the most important sense modality. Through it we recognise family and friends, see their facial expressions and gestures, learn to read, perceive objects that are beyond our reach, and find our way around our environment. It provides us with information about the size, shape, colour and movement of objects nearby and at a distance. Through vision, we receive some of our most powerful aesthetic experiences, in the form of art, a sexual partner and other beautiful images.

The other senses also contribute to the richness of experience. Because of the role that speech plays in human culture, audition is important for social behaviour and communication. Audition and vision provide information about distant events, as does the sense of smell, which can tell us about sources of aromatic molecules before we can see or hear that source. The other senses deal with immediate and proximal events such as the taste of our favourite food or the touch of someone we love. The body senses are closely tied to our own movements. When we feel an object, the experience is active, not passive; we move our hands over it to determine its shape, texture and temperature. And information from specialised organs in the inner ear and from receptors in the muscles and joints is generated by our own movements. This information helps us to maintain our balance as we engage in our everyday activities.

Sensory processing

Experience is traditionally divided into two classes: sensation and perception. Most psychologists define **sensation** as the detection of simple properties of stimuli, such as brightness, colour, warmth and sweetness. **Perception** is the detection of objects (both animate and inanimate), their locations, their movements and their backgrounds. According to these definitions, seeing the colour red is a sensation, but seeing a red apple is a perception. Similarly, seeing a movement is a sensation, but seeing a cricket ball coming towards us and realising that we will have to move to the left to catch it is a perception. Psychologists used to believe that perceptions depended heavily on learning whereas pure sensations involved innate, 'prewired' physiological mechanisms. However, neither behavioural nor physiological research has been able to establish a clear boundary between 'simple' sensations and 'complex' perceptions. Research indicates that experience is essential to the development of some of the most elementary features of sensory systems (Blakemore and Mitchell, 1973). This is called 'functional validation' – the notion whereby the nervous system needs to be stimulated during development in order for it to develop properly.

According to tradition, we have five senses: vision (seeing), audition (hearing), gustation (tasting), olfaction (smelling) and somatosensation (touching). In fact, we have several more. The somatosensory system, for example, includes separate components that are able to detect touch, warmth, coolness, vibration, physical damage (pain), head tilt, head movement, limb movement, muscular contraction and various events occurring within our bodies (Kandel *et al.*, 1995). Whether we choose to call each of these components 'senses' is a matter of terminology.

Transduction

Sense organs detect the presence of environmental stimuli provided by light, sound, odour, taste or mechanical contact. This information is transmitted to the brain through neural impulses – action potentials carried by the axons in sensory nerves. The task of the sense organs is to transmit signals to the brain that are coded in such a way as to faithfully represent the events that have occurred in the environment. The task of the brain is to analyse this information and reconstruct what has occurred.

Transduction (literally, 'leading across') is the process by which the sense organs convert energy from environmental events into neural activity. Each sense organ responds to a particular form of energy given off by an environmental stimulus and translates that energy into neural firing to which the brain can respond. The means of transduction are as diverse as the kinds of stimuli we can perceive. In most senses, specialised neurons called receptor cells release chemical transmitter substances that stimulate other neurons, thus altering the rate of firing of their axons. In the somatosenses ('body senses'), dendrites of neurons respond directly to physical stimuli without the intervention of specialised **receptor cells**. However, some of these neurons do have specialised endings that enable them to respond to particular kinds of sensory information. Table 5.1 summarises the types of transduction accomplished by our sense organs.

Sensory coding

As you saw in Chapter 4, nerves are bundles of axons which can do no more than transmit action potentials. These action potentials are fixed in size and duration; they

Specialized neurons = Receptor cells

Table 5.1 The types of transduction accomplished by the sense organs

Location of sense organ	Environmental stimuli	Energy transduced
Eye	Light	Radiant energy
Ear	Sound	Mechanical energy
Vestibular system	Tilt and rotation of head	Mechanical energy
Tongue	Taste	Recognition of molecular shape
Nose	Odour	Recognition of molecular shape
Skin, internal organs	Touch	Mechanical energy
	Temperature	Thermal energy
	Vibration	Mechanical energy
	Pain	Chemical reaction
Muscle	Stretch	Mechanical energy

cannot be altered. Thus, different stimuli cannot be translated into different types of action potential. Yet we can detect an enormous number of different stimuli with each of our sense organs. For example, we are capable of discriminating among approximately 7.5 million different colours. We can also recognise touches to different parts of the body, and we can further discriminate the degree of pressure involved and the sharpness or bluntness, softness or hardness, and the temperature of the object touching us. We can detect over 10,000 different odours. If action potentials cannot be altered, how do the sense organs tell the brain that a red apple or a yellow lemon has been seen or that the right hand is holding a small, cold object or a large, warm one? The answer is that the information from the sense organs must be coded in the activity of axons carrying information from the sense organs to the brain.

A code is a system of symbols or signals representing information. Spoken English, written French, semaphore signals, magnetic fields on a recording tape, and the electrical zeros and ones in the memory of a computer are all examples of codes. As long as we know the rules of a code, we can convert a message from one medium to another without losing any information. Although we do not know the precise rules by which the sensory systems transmit information to the brain, we do know that they take two general forms: anatomical coding and temporal coding.

Anatomical coding

Since the early 1800s, when Johannes Müller formulated his doctrine of specific nerve energies (discussed in Chapter 1), we have known that the brain learns what is happening through the activity of specific sets of neurons. Sensory organs located in different places in the body send their information to the brain through different nerves. Because the brain has no direct information about the physical energy impinging on a given sense organ, it uses **anatomical coding** to interpret the location and type of sensory stimulus according to which incoming nerve fibres are active. For example, if you rub your eyes, you will mechanically stimulate the light-sensitive receptors located there. This stimulation produces action potentials in the axons of the nerves that connect the eyes with the brain (the optic nerves). The visual system of the brain has no way of knowing that the light-sensitive receptors of the eyes have been activated by an unnatural stimulus. As a result, the brain acts as if the neural activity in the optic nerves was produced by light – so you see stars and flashes. Experiments performed during surgery have shown that artificial stimulation of the nerves that convey taste produces a sensation of taste, electrical stimulation of the auditory nerve produces a sensation of a buzzing noise, and so forth (Calvin and Ojemann, 1994).

Forms of anatomical coding distinguish not only between the sense modalities themselves, but also between stimuli of the same sense modality. Sensory coding for the body surface is anatomical: different nerve fibres serve different parts of the skin. Thus, we can easily discriminate between a touch on the arm and a touch on the knee. As you saw in Chapter 4, the primary somatosensory cortex contains a neural map of the skin. Receptors in the skin in different parts of the body send information to different parts of the primary somatosensory cortex. Similarly, the primary visual cortex maintains a map of the visual field.

Temporal coding

Temporal coding is the coding of information in terms of time. The simplest form of temporal code is rate. By firing at a faster or slower rate according to the intensity of a stimulus, an axon can communicate quantitative information to the brain. For example, a light touch to the skin can be encoded by a low rate of firing, and a more forceful touch by a high rate. Thus, the firing of a particular set of neurons (an anatomical code) tells where the body is being touched; the rate at which these neurons fire (a temporal code) tells how intense that touch is. As far as we know, all sensory systems use rate of firing to encode the intensity of stimulation.

Psychophysics

Psychophysics is the systematic study of the relation between the physical characteristics of stimuli and the sensations they produce (the 'physics of the mind'). To study perceptual phenomena, scientists had to find reliable ways to measure people's sensations. Two of these methods are the just-noticeable difference and the procedures of signal detection theory.

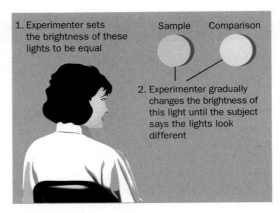

Figure 5.1 The method for determining a just-noticeable difference.

The principle of the just-noticeable difference

Ernst Weber (1795–1878), a German anatomist and physiologist, investigated the ability of humans to discriminate between various stimuli. He measured the **just-noticeable difference (jnd)** – the smallest change in the magnitude of a stimulus that a person can detect. He discovered a principle that held true for all sensory systems: the jnd is directly related to the magnitude of that stimulus. For example, when he presented subjects with two metal objects and asked them to say whether they differed in weight, the subjects reported that the two weights felt the same unless they differed by a factor of 1 in 40. That is, a person could just barely distinguish a 40 g weight from a 41 g weight, an 80 g weight from an 82 g weight, or a 400 g weight from a 410 g weight. Psychologically, the difference between a 40 g weight and a 41 g weight is equivalent to the difference between an 80 g weight and an 82 g weight: 1 jnd. Different senses had different ratios. For example, the ratio for detecting differences in the brightness of white light is approximately 1 in 60. These ratios are called **Weber fractions**.

Gustav Fechner (1801–87), another German physiologist, used Weber's concept of the just-noticeable difference to measure people's sensations. Assuming that the jnd was the basic unit of a sensory experience, he measured the absolute magnitude of a sensation in jnds. Imagine that we want to measure the strength of a person's sensation of light of a particular intensity. We seat the subject in a darkened room facing two discs of frosted glass, each having a light bulb behind it; the brightness of the light bulb is adjustable. One of the discs serves as the sample stimulus, the other as the comparison stimulus, as seen in Figure 5.1.

We start with the sample stimulus and the comparison stimulus turned off completely and increase the brightness of the comparison stimulus until our subject can just

detect a difference. That value is 1 jnd. Then we set the sample stimulus to that intensity (1 jnd) and again increase the brightness of the comparison stimulus just until our subject can again tell them apart. The new value of the comparison stimulus is 2 jnds. We continue making these measurements until our stimuli are as bright as we can make them or until they become uncomfortably bright for our subject. Finally, we construct a graph indicating the strength of a sensation of brightness (in jnds) in relation to the intensity of a stimulus. See Figure 5.2.

Signal detection theory

Psychophysical methods rely heavily on the concept of a **threshold**, the line between not

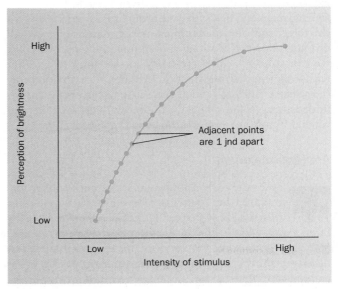

Figure 5.2 A hypothetical range of perceived brightness (in jnds) as a function of intensity.

perceiving and perceiving. The just-noticeable difference can also be called a **difference threshold**, the minimum detectable difference between two stimuli. An **absolute threshold** is the minimum value of a stimulus that can be detected, that is, discriminated from no stimulus at all. Thus, the first comparison in the experiment just described – using a dark disc as the sample stimulus – measured an absolute threshold. The subsequent comparisons measured difference thresholds.

Even early psychophysicists realised that a threshold was not an absolutely fixed value. When an experimenter flashes a very dim light, a subject may report seeing it on some trials but not on others. By convention, the threshold is the point at which a subject detects the stimulus 50 per cent of the time. This definition is necessary because of the inherent variability of the activity in the nervous system. Even when they are not being stimulated, neurons are never absolutely still; they continue to fire. If a very weak stimulus occurs when neurons in the visual system happen to be quiet, the brain is likely to detect it. But if the neurons happen to be firing, the effects of the stimulus are likely to be lost in the 'noise'. Work such as that involved in air traffic control illustrates this point, as seen in Figure 5.3. The worker must select only the most relevant information from a background of competing information.

An alternative method of measuring a person's sensitivity to changes in physical stimuli takes account of random changes in the nervous system (Green and Swets, 1974). According to **signal detection theory**, every stimulus event requires discrimination between signal (stimulus) and noise (consisting of both background stimuli and random activity of the nervous system).

An example of this might involve an individual seated in a quiet room, facing a small warning light. The experimenter informs the individual that when the light flashes, he or she hears a faint tone one second later. The person's task is to say yes or no after each flash of the warning light, according to whether or not they hear the tone. At first, the task is easy: some flashes are followed by an easily heard tone; others are followed by silence. As the experiment progresses, however, the tone gets fainter and fainter, until it is so soft that the individual has doubts about how to respond. The light flashes but did the individual really hear a tone or was it just imagined?

Response bias – which, as you read about in Chapter 2, is the tendency to say yes or no when unsure of detecting a stimulus and can have a considerable effect on signal detection. According to the terminology of signal detection theory, hits are saying 'yes' when the stimulus is presented; misses are saying 'no' when it is presented; correct rejections are saying 'no' when the stimulus is not presented; and false alarms are saying 'yes' when the stimulus is not presented. Hits and correct rejections are correct responses; misses and false alarms are incorrect responses. Figure 5.4 shows the relationship between these responses. If a person wants to ensure that they are correct when they say yes (because they would feel foolish saying they have

Figure 5.3 According to signal detection theory, we must discriminate between the signal, conveying information, and noise, contributed by background stimuli and random activity of our own nervous systems.
Source: J. Silver/SuperStock.

Judgement

	'Yes'	'No'
Light *did* flash	Hit	Miss
Light *did not* flash	False alarm	Correct rejection

Event

Figure 5.4 Four possibilities in judging the presence or absence of a stimulus.

heard something that is not there), the response bias is to err in favour of making hits and avoiding false alarms, even at the risk of making misses. Alternatively, a response bias might be to err in favour of detecting all stimuli, even at the risk of making false alarms.

This response bias can seriously affect an investigator's estimate of the threshold of detection. A conservative person will appear to have a higher threshold than will someone who does not want to let a tone go by without saying yes. Therefore, signal detection theorists have developed a method of assessing people's sensitivity, regardless of their initial response bias. They deliberately manipulate the response biases and observe the results of these manipulations on the people's judgements.

Imagine, for example, that you are a participant in an experiment and the experimenter promises you a sum of money every time you make a hit (correctly report hearing a tone), with no penalty for false alarms. You would undoubtedly tend to say yes on every trial, even if you were not sure you had heard the tone; after all, you have nothing to lose and everything to gain. In contrast, imagine that the experimenter announced that she would fine you the same amount of money every time you made a false alarm and would give you nothing for making hits. You would undoubtedly say no every time, because you would have everything to lose and nothing to gain: you would be extremely conservative in your judgements.

Now consider your response bias under a number of intermediate conditions. If you receive money for every hit but are also fined half that amount for every miss, you will say yes whenever you are reasonably sure you heard the tone. If you receive a sum of money for every hit but are fined twice as much for each false alarm, you will be more conservative. But if you are sure you heard the tone, you will say yes.

The graph in Figure 5.5 is a **receiver operating characteristic (ROC) curve**, named for its original use in research at the Bell Laboratories to measure the intelligibility of speech transmitted through a telephone system. The curve shows performance when the sound is difficult to detect. If the sound were louder, so that you rarely doubted whether you heard it, you would make almost every possible hit and very few false alarms. The few misses you made would be under the low pay-off condition, when you wanted to be absolutely certain you heard the tone. The few false alarms would occur when guessing did not matter because the fine for being wrong was low or non-existent. The difference between the two curves seen in Figure 5.6 demonstrates that the louder tone is easier to detect. Detectability is measured by the relative distances of the curves from a 45-degree line.

The signal detection method is the best way to determine an individual's sensitivity to the occurrence of a particular stimulus. Note that the concept of threshold is

not used. Instead, a stimulus is more or less detectable. The person decides whether a stimulus occurred, and the consequences of making hits or false alarms can bias this decision: for example, missing the sound of an alarm clock may be more important than missing a telephone

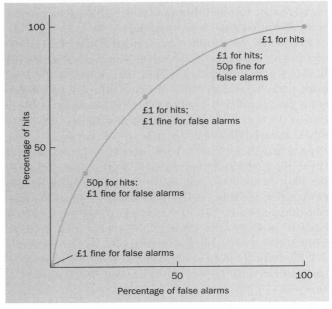

Figure 5.5 A receiver operating characteristic (ROC) curve. The percentage of hits and false alarms in judging the presence of a stimulus under several pay-off conditions.

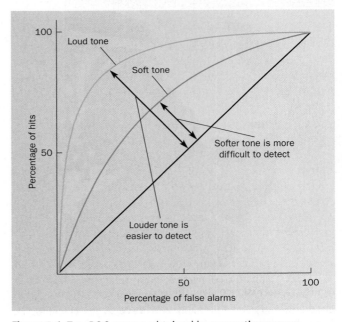

Figure 5.6 Two ROC curves, obtained by presenting a more discriminable stimulus (orange curve) and a less discriminable stimulus (red curve).

call. Signal detection theory emphasises that sensory experience involves factors other than the activity of the sensory systems, such as motivation and prior experience. Sensitivity to a signal can be influenced by these factors. The fact that you know that you will either be rewarded or financially penalised for making false alarms will influence the care with which you make decisions.

You can see signal detection theory applied in a number of important ways. For example, a radiologist who takes an X-ray has to discriminate between shadows on an X-ray image that indicate disease – the signal – and those that just show differences in the anatomy of the patient – the noise (Parasuraman, 1985). Response bias can occur if the radiologist knows whether the patient has a history of disease or not. The likelihood of detecting a tumour increases or decreases, respectively.

There is a quasi-experiment reported in the literature of factory workers complaining about the weight of large boxes that they had to shift. Carrying these heavy boxes made their backs ache. All the boxes were black. The supervisor, for reasons that you can imagine, decided to replace the black boxes with lighter-coloured ones. When the workers returned to the factory after the weekend and had to move the new boxes, they remarked on how much lighter they were than the black boxes even though the new boxes weighed the same as the old boxes. Why do you think this was?

Vision

The visual system allows us to do many activities that we take for granted: in a quick glance we can recognise what there is to see – people, objects and landscapes – in depth and full colour. Because of the dominance of visual information in our lives, it is perhaps not surprising that vision is our dominant sense.

Light

The eye is sensitive to light. Light consists of radiant energy similar to radio waves. As the radiant energy is transmitted from its source, it oscillates. For example, the antenna that broadcasts the programmes of your favourite FM station may transmit radio waves that oscillate at 88.5 MHz (megahertz, or million times per second). Because radiant energy travels at 297,600 km/s, the waves transmitted by this antenna are approximately 3.3 m apart (297,600 km divided by 88.5 million equals approximately 3.3 m). Thus, the **wavelength** of the signal from the station – the distance between the waves of radiant energy – is 3.3 m (see Figure 5.7).

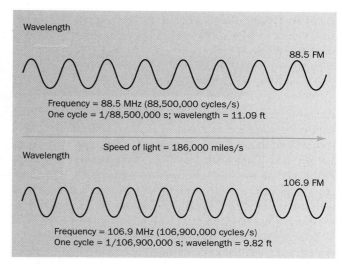

Figure 5.7 Wavelength versus vibration. Because the speed of light is constant, faster vibrations produce shorter wavelengths.

The wavelength of visible light is much shorter, ranging from 380 to 760 nanometres (a nanometre, nm, is one-billionth of a metre). When viewed by a human eye, different wavelengths of visible light have different colours: for instance, 380 nm light looks violet and 760 nm light looks red.

All other radiant energy is invisible to our eyes. Ultraviolet radiation, X-rays and gamma rays have shorter wavelengths than visible light has, whereas infrared radiation, radar and radio waves have longer wavelengths. The entire range of wavelengths is known as the electromagnetic spectrum; the part our eyes can detect – the part we see as light – is referred to as the visible spectrum, as seen in Figure 5.8.

The definition of the visible spectrum is based on the human visual system. Some other species of animals would define the visible spectrum differently. Bees, for example, can see ultraviolet radiation that is invisible to us. Some plants have taken advantage of this fact and produce flowers that contain dyes that reflect ultraviolet radiation, presenting patterns that attract bees to them. Some snakes (notably, pit vipers such as the rattlesnake) have special organs that detect infrared radiation. This ability enables them to find their prey in the dark by detecting the heat emitted by small mammals in the form of infrared radiation.

The eye and its functions

The eyes are important and delicate sense organs – and they are well protected. Each eye is housed in a bony socket and can be covered by the eyelid to keep out dust and dirt. The eyelids are edged by

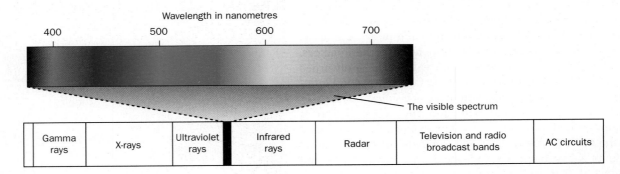

Figure 5.8 The electromagnetic spectrum.

eyelashes, which help keep foreign matter from falling into the open eye. The eyebrows prevent sweat on the forehead from dripping into the eyes. Reflex mechanisms provide additional protection: the sudden approach of an object towards the face or a touch on the surface of the eye causes automatic eyelid closure and withdrawal of the head.

Figure 5.9 shows a cross-section of a human eye. The transparent **cornea** forms a bulge at the front of the eye and admits light. The rest of the eye is coated by a tough white membrane called the **sclera** (from the Greek *skleros*, 'hard'). The **iris** consists of two bands of muscle that control the amount of light admitted into the eye. The brain controls these muscles and thus regulates the size of the pupil, constricting it in bright light and dilating it in dim light. The space immediately behind the cornea is filled with aqueous humour, which simply means 'watery fluid'. This fluid is constantly produced by tissue behind the cornea that filters the fluid from the blood. In place of blood vessels, the aqueous humour nourishes the

cornea and other portions of the front of the eye; this fluid must circulate and be renewed. If aqueous humour is produced too quickly or if the passage that returns it to the blood becomes blocked, the pressure within the eye can increase and cause damage to vision – a disorder known as glaucoma. Because of its transparency, the cornea must be nourished in this unusual manner. Our vision would be less clear if we had a set of blood vessels across the front of our eyes.

The curvature of the cornea and of the **lens**, which lies immediately behind the iris, causes images to be focused on the inner surface of the back of the eye. Although this image is upside-down and reversed from left to right, the brain interprets this information appropriately. The shape of the cornea is fixed, but the lens is flexible; a special set of muscles can alter its shape so that the eye can obtain focused images of either nearby or distant objects. This change in the shape of the lens to adjust for distance is called **accommodation**.

Normally, the length of the eye matches the refractive power of the cornea and the lens so that the image of the visual scene is sharply focused on the retina. However, for some people these two factors are not matched, and the image on the retina is therefore out of focus. There is a problem with sensing objects at various distances: some have difficulty in focusing on objects in the distance; others have difficulty in focusing on near objects. These people need an extra lens in front of their eyes (in the form of spectacles or contact lenses) to correct the discrepancy and bring the image into focus. People whose eyes are too long (front to back) are said to be nearsighted; they need a concave lens to correct the focus. The image on the right of Figure 5.10 shows what a nearsighted person would see.

People whose eyes are too short are said to be farsighted; they need a convex lens. As people get older, not only does the cornea of the eye begin to yellow and the sensitivity of the rods to decline (Sturr *et al.*, 1997), but the lenses of their

Figure 5.9 A cross-section of the human eye.

Figure 5.10 To a nearsighted person, distant objects are blurry and out of focus.
Source: Image 312427-003 Richard Elliot/Stone/Getty.

eyes also become less flexible and it becomes difficult for them to focus on objects close to them. These people need reading glasses with convex lenses (or varifocals, if they already wear glasses) (see Figure 5.11).

The **retina**, which lines the inner surface of the back of the eye, performs the sensory functions of the eye. Embedded in the retina are over 130 million **photorecep-** tors – specialised neurons that transduce light into neural activity. The information from the photoreceptors is transmitted to neurons that send axons towards one point at the back of the eye – the **optic disc**. All axons leave the eye at this point and join the optic nerve, which travels to the brain (see Figure 5.12).

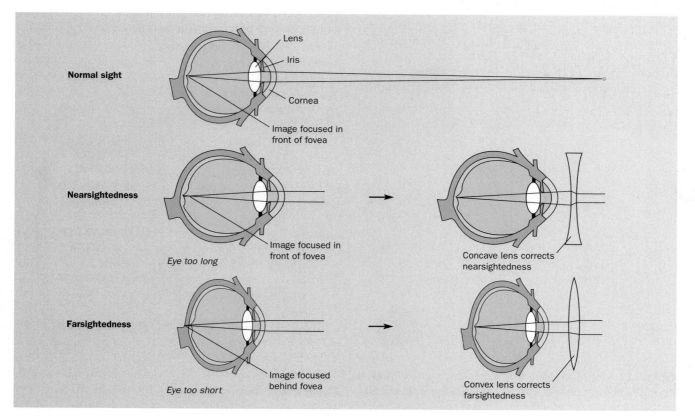

Figure 5.11 Lenses used to correct nearsightedness and farsightedness.

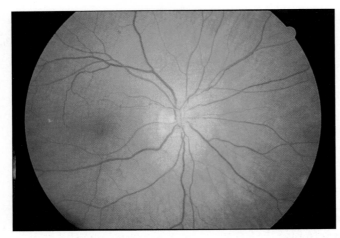

Figure 5.12 A view of the back of the eye. The photograph shows the retina, the optic disc and blood vessels.

Source: Courtesy of Douglas G. Mollerstuen, New England Medical Center.

Because there are no photoreceptors directly in front of the optic disc, this portion of the retina is blind. If you have not located your own blind spot, try the demonstration shown in Figure 5.13.

Before the seventeenth century, scientists thought that the lens sensed the presence of light. Johannes Kepler (1571–1630), the astronomer who discovered the true shape of the planets' orbits around the sun, is credited with the suggestion that the retina, not the lens, contained the receptive tissue of the eye. It remained for Christoph Scheiner (another German astronomer) to demonstrate in 1625 that the lens is simply a focusing device. Scheiner obtained an ox's eye from a slaughter-house. After carefully peeling the sclera away from the back of the eye, he was able to see an upside-down image of the world through the thin, translucent membrane that remained. As an astronomer, he was familiar with the fact that convex glass lenses could cast images, so he recognised the function of the lens of the eye.

Figure 5.14 shows a cross-section of the retina. The retina has three principal layers. Light passes successively through the ganglion cell layer (front), the bipolar cell layer (middle) and the photoreceptor layer (back). Early anatomists were surprised to find the photoreceptors in the deepest layer of the retina. As you might expect, the cells that are located above the photoreceptors are transparent.

Photoreceptors respond to light and pass the information on by means of a transmitter substance to the bipolar cells, the neurons with which they form synapses. **Bipolar cells** transmit this information to the **ganglion cells**, neurons whose axons travel across the retina and through the optic nerves. Thus, visual information passes through a three-cell chain to the brain: photoreceptor–bipolar; cell–ganglion; and cell–brain.

A single photoreceptor responds only to light that reaches its immediate vicinity, but a ganglion cell can receive information from many different photoreceptors. The retina also contains neurons that interconnect both adjacent photoreceptors and adjacent ganglion cells. The existence of this neural circuitry indicates that some kinds of information processing are performed in the retina.

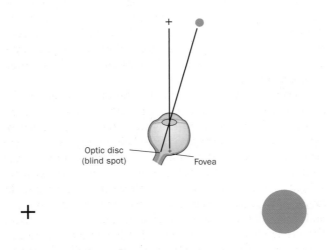

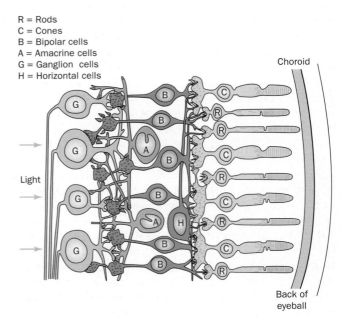

R = Rods
C = Cones
B = Bipolar cells
A = Amacrine cells
G = Ganglion cells
H = Horizontal cells

Figure 5.13 A test for the blind spot. With the left eye closed, look at the + with your right eye and move the page back and forth, towards and away from yourself. At about 20 cm, the coloured circle disappears from your vision because its image falls on your blind spot.

Figure 5.14 The cells of the retina.

Source: Adapted from J.E. Dowling and B.B. Boycott (1996) *Proceedings of the Royal Society of London*, 166, 80–111.

The human retina contains two general types of photoreceptors: 125 million rods and 6 million cones, so called because of their shapes. **Rods** function mainly in dim light; they are very sensitive to light. **Cones** function when the level of illumination is bright enough to see things clearly. They are also responsible for colour vision. The **fovea**, a small pit in the back of the retina approximately 1 mm in diameter, contains only cones and is responsible for our most detailed vision. When we look at a point in our visual field, we move our eyes so that the image of that point falls directly on the cone-packed fovea.

Farther away from the fovea, the number of cones decreases and the number of rods increases. Up to 100 rods may converge on a single ganglion cell. A ganglion cell that receives information from so many rods is sensitive to very low levels of light. Rods are therefore responsible for our sensitivity to very dim light, but they provide poor acuity.

Transduction of light by photoreceptors

Although light-sensitive sensory organs have evolved independently in a wide variety of animals – from insects to fish to mammals – the chemistry is in essence the same in all species: a molecule derived from vitamin A is the central ingredient in the transduction of the energy of light into neural activity (carrots are said to be good for vision because they contain a substance that the body easily converts to vitamin A). In the absence of light, this molecule is attached to another molecule, a protein. The two molecules together form a **photopigment**. The photoreceptors of the human eye contain four kinds of photopigment (one for rods and three for cones), but their basic mechanism is the same. When a photon (a particle of light) strikes a photopigment, the photopigment splits apart into its two constituent molecules. This event starts the process of transduction. The splitting of the photopigment causes a series of chemical reactions that stimulate the photoreceptor and cause it to send a message to the bipolar cell with which it forms a synapse. The bipolar cell sends a message to the ganglion cell, which then sends one on to the brain, as seen in Figure 5.15.

Intact photopigments have a characteristic colour. **Rhodopsin**, the photopigment of rods, is pink (*rhodon* means 'rose' in Greek). However, once the photopigments are split apart by the action of light, they lose their colour – they become bleached. Franz Boll discovered this phenomenon in 1876 when he removed an eye from an animal and pointed it towards a window that opened out onto a brightly lit scene. He then examined the retina under dim light and found that the image of the scene was still there. The retina was pink where little light had fallen and pale where the image had been bright. It was Boll's discovery that led investigators to suspect that a chemical reaction was responsible for the transduction of light into neural activity.

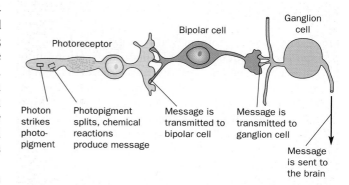

Figure 5.15 Transduction of light into neural activity. A photon strikes a photoreceptor and causes the photopigment to split apart. This event initiates the transmission of information to the brain.

After light has caused a molecule of photopigment to split and become bleached, energy from the photoreceptor's metabolism causes the two molecules to recombine. The photopigment is then ready to be bleached by light again. Each photoreceptor contains many thousands of molecules of photopigment. The number of intact, unbleached molecules of photopigment in a given cell depends on the relative rates at which they are being split by light and being put back together by the cell's energy. The brighter the light, the more bleached photopigment there is.

Adaptation to light and dark

Think, for a moment, about how difficult it can be to find a seat in a darkened cinema. Another example: if you have just come in from the bright sun, your eyes do not respond well to the low level of illumination. However, after a few minutes, you can see rather well – your eyes have adapted to the dark. This phenomenon is called **dark adaptation**.

In order for light to be detected, photons must split molecules of rhodopsin or one of the other photopigments. When high levels of illumination strike the retina, the rate of regeneration of rhodopsin falls behind the rate of the bleaching process. With only a small percentage of the rhodopsin molecules intact, the rods are not very sensitive to light. If you enter a dark room after being in a brightly lit room or in sunlight, there are too few intact rhodopsin molecules for your eyes to respond immediately to dim light. The probability that a photon will strike an intact molecule of rhodopsin is very low. However, after a while, the regeneration of rhodopsin overcomes the bleaching effects of the light energy. The rods become full of unbleached rhodopsin, and a photon passing through a rod is likely to find a target. The eye has become dark adapted.

Eye movements

Our eyes are never completely at rest, even when our gaze is fixed on a particular place called the **fixation point**. Our eyes make fast, aimless, jittering movements, similar to the fine tremors our hands and fingers make when we try to keep them still. They also make occasional slow movements away from the target they are fixed on, which are terminated by quick movements that bring the image of the fixation point back to the fovea.

Although the small, jerky movements that the eyes make when at rest are random, they appear to serve a useful function. Riggs *et al.* (1953) devised a way to project stabilised images on the retina – images that remain in the same location on the retina. They mounted a small mirror in a contact lens worn by the participant and bounced a beam of light off it. They then projected the image onto a white screen in front of the participant, bounced it off several more mirrors, and finally directed it towards the participant's eye, as illustrated by Figure 5.16.

The path of the light was arranged so that the image on the screen moved in perfect synchrony with the eye movements. If the eye moved, so did the image; thus, the image that the experimenters projected always fell on precisely the same part of the retina despite the subject's eye

movements. Under these conditions, details of visual stimuli began to disappear. At first, the image was clear, but then a 'fog' drifted over the subject's field of view, obscuring the image. After a while, some images could not be seen at all. All of this occurred within seconds.

These results suggest that elements of the visual system are not responsive to an unchanging stimulus. The photoreceptors or the ganglion cells, or perhaps both, apparently cease to respond to a constant stimulus. The small, involuntary movements of our eyes keep the image moving and thus keep the visual system responsive to the details of the scene before us. Without these involuntary movements, our vision would become blurry soon after we fixed our gaze on a single point and our eyes became still.

The eyes also make three types of 'purposive' movement: conjugate movements, saccadic movements and pursuit movements. **Conjugate movements** are cooperative movements that keep both eyes fixed on the same target, or, more precisely, that keep the image of the target object on corresponding parts of the two retinas. If you hold up a finger in front of your face, look at it, and then bring your finger closer to your face, your eyes will make conjugate movements towards your nose. If you then look at an object on the other side of the room, your eyes will rotate outward, and you will see two separate blurry images of your finger. As you will learn in Chapter 6, conjugate eye movements assist in the perception of distance.

When you scan the scene in front of you, your gaze travels from point to point as you examine important or interesting features. As you do so, your eyes make jerky **saccadic movements** – you shift your gaze abruptly from one point to another. For example, when you read a line in this book, your eyes stop several times, moving quickly between each stop. You cannot consciously control the speed of movement between stops; during each saccade the eyes move as fast as they can.

Much of the time, the scene in front of us contains moving objects: objects blown by the wind, cars, aeroplanes, animals, other people. When we concentrate on one of these objects, we fix our gaze on it and track its movements with our eyes. These tracking movements, which follow the object we are watching, are called **pursuit movements**.

Colour vision

Light consists of radiant energy having wavelengths between 380 and 760 nm. Light of different wavelengths gives rise to sensations of different colours. How can we tell the difference between different wavelengths of light?

Experiments have shown that there are three types of cone in the human eye, each containing a different type of photopigment. Each type of photopigment is most sensitive to light of a particular wavelength. That is, light of a particular wavelength most readily causes a particular photo-

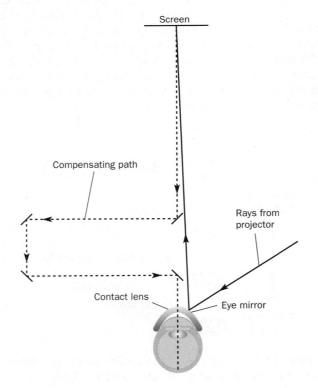

Figure 5.16 A procedure for stabilising an image on the retina.

Source: Riggs, L.A., Ratliff, F., Cornsweet, J.C. and Cornsweet, T.N., *Journal of the Optical Society of America*, 1953, 43, 495–501.

pigment to split. Thus, different types of cone are stimulated by different wavelengths of light. Information from the three types of cone enables us to perceive colours.

Wavelength is related to colour, but the terms are not synonymous. For example, the spectral colours (the colours we see in a rainbow, which contains the entire spectrum of visible radiant energy) do not include all the colours that we can see, such as brown, pink, and the metallic colours silver and gold. The fact that not all colours are found in the spectrum means that differences in wavelength alone do not account for the differences in the colours we can perceive.

The dimensions of colour

Most colours can be described in terms of three physical dimensions: wavelength, intensity and purity. Three perceptual dimensions – hue, brightness and saturation – corresponding to these physical dimensions describe what we see. The **hue** of most colours is determined by wavelength; for example, light having a wavelength of 540 nm is perceived as green. A colour's **brightness** is determined by the intensity, or amount of energy, of the light that is being perceived, all other factors being equal. A colour of maximum brightness dazzles us with a lot of light. A colour of minimum brightness is simply black. The third perceptual dimension of colour, **saturation**, is roughly equivalent to purity. A fully saturated colour consists of light of only one wavelength, for example pure red or pure blue. Desaturated colours look pastel or washed out. See Table 5.2 for a summary of the dimensions of colour.

Saturation is probably the most difficult dimension of colour to understand. White light consists of a mixture of all wavelengths of light. Although its components consist of light of all possible hues, we perceive it as being colourless. White light is completely desaturated; no single wavelength is dominant. If we begin with light of a single wavelength (a pure, completely saturated colour) and then mix in some white light, the result will be a less saturated colour. For example, when white light is added to red light (700 nm), the result is pink light. The dominant wavelength of 700 nm gives the colour a reddish hue, but the addition of white light to the mixture decreases the colour's saturation. In other words, pink is a less saturated version of red. Figure 5.17 illustrates how a colour having a particular dominant wavelength (hue) can vary in its brightness and saturation.

Colour mixing

Vision is a synthetic sensory modality. It synthesises (puts together) rather than analyses (takes apart). When two wavelengths of light are present, we see an intermediate colour rather than the two components. In contrast, the auditory system is analytical. If a high note and a low note are played together on a piano, we hear both notes instead of a single, intermediate tone. The addition of two or more lights of different wavelengths is called **colour mixing**. Colour mixing is an additive process and is very different from paint mixing. So are its results. If we pass a beam of white light through a prism, we break it into the spectrum of the different wavelengths it contains. If we recombine these colours by passing them through another prism, we obtain white light again (see Figure 5.18).

Colour mixing must not be confused with pigment mixing – what we do when we mix paints. An object has a particular colour because it contains pigments that absorb some wavelengths of light (converting them into heat) and reflect other wavelengths. For example, the chlorophyll found in the leaves of plants absorbs less green light than light of other wavelengths. When a leaf is illuminated by white light, it reflects a high proportion of green light and appears green to us.

see activity on mypsychlab

Table 5.2 Physical and perceptual dimensions of colour

Perceptual dimension	Physical dimension	Physical characteristics
Hue	Wavelength	Frequency of oscillation of light radiation
Brightness	Intensity	Amount of energy of light radiation
Saturation	Purity	Intensity of dominant wavelength relative to total radiant energy

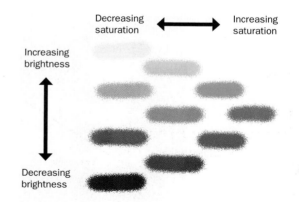

Figure 5.17 Hue, brightness and saturation. The colours shown have the same dominant wavelength (hue) but different saturation and brightness.

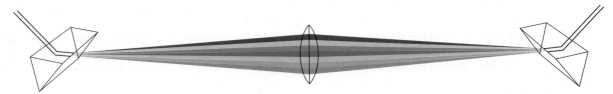

Figure 5.18 Colour mixing. White light can be split into a spectrum of colours with a prism and recombined through another prism.

When we mix paints, we are subtracting colours, not adding them. Mixing two paints yields a darker result. For example, adding blue paint to yellow paint yields green paint, which certainly looks darker than yellow. But mixing two beams of light of different wavelengths always yields a brighter colour. For example, when red and green light are shone together on a piece of white paper, we see yellow. In fact, we cannot tell a pure yellow light from a synthesised one made of the proper intensities of red and green light. To our eyes, both yellows appear identical.

To reconstitute white light, we do not even have to recombine all the wavelengths in the spectrum. If we shine a blue light, a green light and a red light together on a sheet of white paper and properly adjust their intensities, the place where all three beams overlap will look perfectly white. A colour television or a computer display screen uses this system. When white appears on the screen, it actually consists of tiny dots of red, blue and green light (see Figure 5.19).

Colour-coding in the retina

In 1802, Thomas Young, a British physicist and physician, noted that the human visual system can synthesise any colour from various amounts of almost any set of three colours of different wavelengths. Young proposed a **trichromatic theory** ('three colour' theory) of colour vision. He hypothesised that the eye contains three types of colour receptor, each sensitive to a different hue, and that the brain synthesises colours by combining the information received by each type of receptor. He suggested that these receptors were sensitive to three of the colours that people perceive as 'pure': blue, green and red. Young's suggestion was incorporated into a more elaborate theory of colour vision by Hermann von Helmholtz. (We'll return to Young in the section on creativity in Chapter 11.)

Experiments in recent years have shown that the cones in the human eye do contain three types of photopigment, each of which preferentially absorbs light of a particular wavelength: 420, 530 and 560 nm. Although these wavelengths actually correspond to blue-violet, green and yellow-green, most investigators refer to these receptors as blue, green and red cones. To simplify the discussion here, we will assume that the three types of cone respond to these three pure hues. Red and green cones are present in about equal proportions. There are far fewer blue cones.

Several scientists after Young and Helmholtz devised theories that took account of the fact that people also perceive yellow as a psychologically pure hue. Late in the nineteenth century, Ewald Hering, a German physiologist,

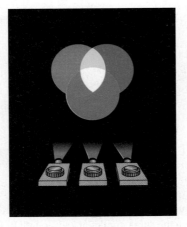

Figure 5.19 Additive colour mixing and paint mixing. When blue, red and green light of the proper intensity are all shone together, the result is white light. When red, blue and yellow paints are mixed together, the result is a dark grey.

noted that the four primary hues appeared to belong to pairs of opposing colours: red/green and yellow/blue. We can imagine a bluish green or a yellowish green, or a bluish red or a yellowish red. However, we cannot imagine a greenish red or a yellowish blue. Hering originally suggested that we cannot imagine these blends because there are two types of photoreceptor, one kind responding to green and red and the other kind responding to yellow and blue.

Hering's hypothesis about the nature of photoreceptors was wrong, but his principle describes the characteristics of the information the retinal ganglion cells send to the brain. Two types of ganglion cell encode colour vision: red/green cells and yellow/blue cells. Both types of ganglion cell fire at a steady rate when they are not stimulated. If a spot of red light shines on the retina, exci-

tation of the red cones causes the red/green ganglion cells to begin to fire at a high rate.

Conversely, if a spot of green light shines on the retina, excitation of the green cones causes the red/green ganglion cells to begin to fire at a slow rate. Thus, the brain learns about the presence of red or green light by the increased or decreased rate of firing of axons attached to red/green ganglion cells. Similarly, yellow/blue ganglion cells are excited by yellow light and inhibited by blue light. Because red and green light, and yellow and blue light, have opposite effects on the rate of axon firing, this coding scheme is called an **opponent process**.

Figure 5.20 provides a schematic explanation of the opponent-process coding that takes place in the retina. Stimulation of a red cone by red light excites the red/green ganglion cell, whereas stimulation of a green

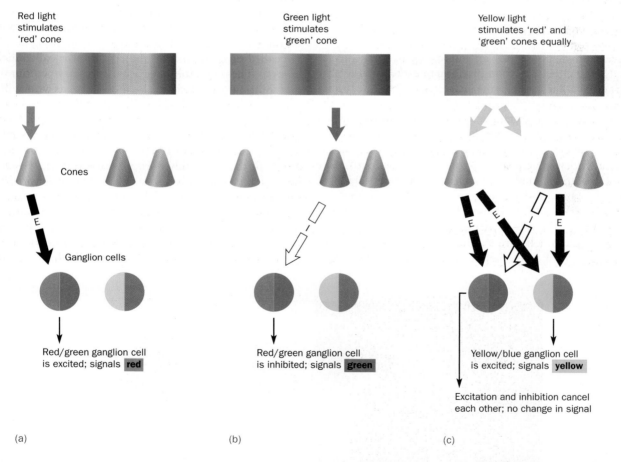

(a)   (b)   (c)

Figure 5.20 Colour coding in the retina. **(a)** Red light stimulating a 'red' cone, which causes excitation of a red/green ganglion cell. **(b)** Green light stimulating a 'green' cone, which causes inhibition of a red/green ganglion cell. (c) Yellow light stimulating 'red' and 'green' cones equally. The stimulation of 'red' and 'green' cones causes excitation of a yellow/blue ganglion cell. The arrows labelled E and I represent neural circuitry within the retina that translates excitation of a cone into excitation or inhibition of a ganglion cell, respectively. For clarity, only some of the circuits are shown.

cone by green light inhibits the red/green ganglion cell (Figure 5.20 (a) and (b)). If the photoreceptors are stimulated by yellow light, both the red and green cones are stimulated equally. Because of the neural circuitry between the photoreceptors and the ganglion cells, the result is that the yellow/blue ganglion cell is excited, signalling yellow (Figure 5.20 (c)).

The retina contains red/green and yellow/blue ganglion cells because of the nature of the connections between the cones, bipolar cells and ganglion cells. The brain detects various colours by comparing the rates of firing of the axons in the optic nerve that signal red or green and yellow or blue. Now you can see why we cannot perceive a reddish green or a bluish yellow: an axon that signals red or green (or yellow or blue) can either increase or decrease its rate of firing. It cannot do both at the same time. A reddish green would have to be signalled by a ganglion cell firing slowly and rapidly at the same time, which is impossible.

Negative after-images

Figure 5.21 demonstrates an interesting property of the visual system: the formation of a **negative after-image**. Stare at the cross in the centre of the image on the left for approximately 30 seconds. Then quickly look at the cross in the centre of the white rectangle to the right. You will have a fleeting experience of seeing the red and green colours of a radish – colours that are complementary, or opposite, to the ones on the left. Complementary items go together to make up a whole. In this context, complementary colours are those that make white (or shades of grey) when added together.

The most important cause of negative after-images is adaptation in the rate of firing of retinal ganglion cells. When ganglion cells are excited or inhibited for a prolonged period of time, they later show a rebound effect,

firing faster or slower than normal. For example, the green of the radish in Figure 5.21 inhibits some red/green ganglion cells. When this region of the retina is then stimulated with the neutral-coloured light reflected off the white rectangle, the red/green ganglion cells – no longer inhibited by the green light – fire faster than normal. Thus, we see a red after-image of the radish.

Defects in colour vision

Approximately one in 12 men has some form of defective colour vision. These defects are sometimes called colour-blindness, but this term should probably be reserved for the very few people who cannot see any colour at all. Men are affected more than women because many of the genes for producing photopigments are located on the X chromosome. Because males have only one X chromosome (females have two), a defective gene there will always be expressed.

There are many different types of defective colour vision. Some individuals are missing a photopigment and are called dichromats (and the condition is called **dichromacy**). These people use two primary colours for matching and confuse various colours, as you will see below. Other individuals, called anomalous trichromats (the condition is called **anomalous trichromacy**), have an altered – not missing – photopigment. These people account for the majority of men with colour defects although they probably do not realise they have a deficit because they may only show a slight loss of sensitivity for the reds, greens and blues, but generally good colour discrimination. Extreme cases, however, will show greater loss of sensitivity and poorer colour discrimination. In rare cases, some people may express more than three photopigments and should, theoretically, have an added

Figure 5.21 A negative after-image. Stare for approximately 30 seconds at the cross in the centre of the left figure; then quickly transfer your gaze to the cross in the centre of the right figure. You will see colours that are complementary to the originals.

Psychology in action – Red light = danger?

According to some anthropologists, the colour red is seen as a sign of dominance in non-human species. Of course, what applies in the animal kingdom does not necessarily apply to the human kingdom. A study from researchers at the University of Durham, UK, however, suggests that it might.

In a novel study, the researchers examined the success and failure of sportsmen and women who wore red or blue costumes (Hill and Barton, 2005). In the 2004 Olympic Games, contestants in the combat sports, boxing, tae kwon do, Greco-Roman wrestling and freestyle wrestling, were randomly given either red or blue costumes to wear. When Hill and Barton (2005) analysed the win rate of contestants, those in red costumes won more fights than those in blue costumes.

They then further extended this research by examining the win rate of players in the Euro 2004 international football competition. The performance of five teams that wore red was compared with the performance of the same teams when they wore a different colour. Again, the study's finding was novel: the team won more often when wearing red shirts.

According to the authors, 'given the ubiquity of aggressive competition throughout human societies and history, our results suggest that the evolutionary psychology of colour is likely to be a fertile field for further investigation'.

The effect of the colour red even seems to extend to cognitive test performance. Researchers exposed students to either the colour red, green or black before giving them a test. Participants who were exposed to red – even if participants were not consciously aware of it – performed less well on a test than did those who were not (Elliot *et al.*, 2007). The effect was found even when a number was written in red ink at the top of a sheet of paper. When participants' brain activation was examined, there was greater activation in the right side of the frontal lobe when seeing the colour red (a theory, described in Chapter 13, argues that the left and right front parts of the brain mediate different kinds of emotional experiences, positive and negative respectively).

But some psychologists have questioned this influence of red, especially that seen in the sport studies. For example, it could be argued that the colour itself did not influence the chances of winning but that fact that red was more highly visible in the sports studied (Rowe *et al*, 2005). Some have also questioned the bias of the referee. The colour might influence the perception of performance, regardless of actual performance.

In an ingenious test of this hypothesis, Hagemann *et al.*, (2008) asked 42 experience tae kwon do referees to watch a videotape of five different sparring competitions. The competitors's heads and trunk were covered in red or blue material. When asked to award points to these competitors, the red ones were given 13 per cent more points (as previous research would predict). Then, and this is the ingenious twist, the experimenters electronically switched the colours of the competitors – the actual competitors remained the same, as did their performance, but the colour they wore changed. When this happened, the points awarded to the red competitors increased. Those who had been given the points in the previous study (and were now dressed in blue) were awarded fewer. These results, according to the authors, suggest 'need a change to the rules (i.e., to forbid red sports attire) and support referees by providing electronic-decision making only'.

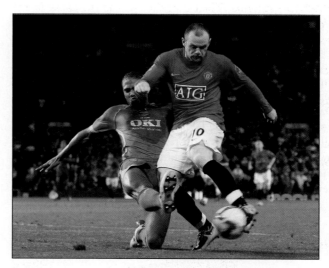

Does the colour of a team's kit influence their success?
Source: Chris Coleman / Manchester United

dimension to their colour vision. A study of women with a phenotype expressing four photopigments found that this was the case: these people perceived more chromatic appearances than did male or female trichromats (Jameson *et al.*, 2001).

Two of the three colour defects described below involve the red/green system. People with these defects confuse red and green. Their primary colour sensations are yellow and blue; red and green both look yellowish. Figure 5.22 shows one of the figures from a commonly used test for defective colour vision. A person who confuses red and green will not be able to see the '5'.

The most serious defect, called **protanopia** (literally, 'first-colour defect'), appears to result from a lack of the photopigment for red cones. The fact that people with protanopia have relatively normal acuity suggests that

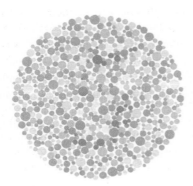

Figure 5.22 A figure commonly used to test for defective colour vision. People with red/green colour blindness will fail to see the 5.

Source: Courtesy of American Optical Corporation.

they have red cones but that these cones are filled with green photopigment (Boynton, 1979). If red cones were missing, almost half of the cones would be gone from the retina, and vision would be less acute. To a protanope, red looks much darker than green, and reds and oranges generally appear very dark because the red end of the spectrum cannot be seen. Around 1 per cent of men suffer from this defect.

The second form of red/green defect, called **deuteranopia** ('second-colour defect'), appears to result from the opposite kind of substitution: green cones are filled with red photopigment. Around 8 per cent of European men and 0.5 per cent of European women have the inherited colour defect, Daltonism (protanopia and deuteranopia) (Fletcher and Voke, 1985) and there is evidence of other culture-related differences in colour vision impairment although whether such differences are due to cultural or physiological differences is unclear (Davies *et al.*, 1998). The topic of colour perception and the use of colour terms across cultures is discussed in more detail in the next chapter.

The third form of colour defect, called **tritanopia** ('third-colour defect'), involves the blue cones and is much rarer: it affects fewer than 1 in 10,000 people. Tritanopes see the world in greens and reds; to them, a clear blue sky is a bright green, and yellow looks pink. The faulty gene that causes tritanopia is not carried on a sex chromosome, therefore it is equally common in males and females. This defect appears to involve loss of blue cones, but because there are far fewer of these than of red and green cones to begin with, investigators have not yet determined whether the cones are missing or are filled with one of the other photopigments.

Synaesthesia

There are some individuals who claim to be able to sense colours when hearing words (and there are others who claim that tastes elicit sensations of shapes). This phenomenon is called **synaesthesia** (from the Greek *syn*, meaning 'union' and *aisthesis* meaning 'sensation'): a sensation in one modality produces an inexorable sensation in another (Harrison and Baron-Cohen, 1996). It affects about 1 in 100,000 and cases of 'coloured hearing' were reported as early as the nineteenth century (Galton, 1883). One very famous composer, Liszt, claimed synaesthetic ability, see Figure 5.23.

The phenomenon seems to be reliable. Baron-Cohen *et al.* (1987) investigated the synaesthetic ability of a 78-year-old woman (EP) who claimed to see colours when she heard words. Her responses were 100 per cent consistent at 10 weeks whereas an IQ-matched control was only 17 per cent consistent at two weeks. Another example, recently reported in the literature, is that of a 20-year old undergraduate who consistently experienced tastes when hearing words (Gendle, 2007). Beeli *et al.* (2005) report the case of a right-handed musician (ES) who, when she hears a musical interval, reports a taste sensation on her tongue that is always associated with that

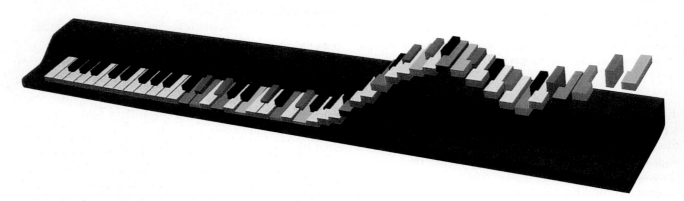

Figure 5.23 Some people claim to 'see' colours when they hear specific musical notes. The composer Liszt was one such person.

Source: Brash, S., Maranto, G., Murphy, W. and Walker, B. (1990) *How Things Work: The brain*. Virginia: Time-Life Books. © 1990 Time-Life Books.

specific interval. (The types of taste sensations evoked by the notes can be seen in Table 5.3).

Baron-Cohen *et al.* (1993) studied nine individuals who claimed to sense colours when hearing speech. The participants were tested at two points, one year apart. The researchers found that identical responses were reported in 92.3 per cent of cases over one year. For a control group, the response rate was 37.6 per cent after only one week. Some colours were specifically elicited by vowels. For example, the same colours were consistently associated with 'i', 'o' and 'u' (88.9 per cent of the time).

One hypothesis suggests that **synaesthetes** show a breakdown in modularity, that is, there are links between the colour and language regions that have either disappeared or never even existed in non-synaesthetes. In synaesthetes, however, these links are intact. Alternatively, non-synaesthetes can inhibit the activity of these modules but this inhibition is dysfunctional in synaesthetes. Paulesu *et al.* (1996) used PET technology to study six synaesthete women who were asked to indicate which colours they sensed when hearing words and tones. The experimenters found that synaesthesia was elicited by words but not by tones. While both synaesthetes and controls activated the perisylvian regions of the brain, the synaesthetes showed activation of other visual association areas including the posterior inferior temporal cortex and the junction between the parietal and occipital cortex. No activation was observed in the major visual areas such as the primary visual cortex (V1) suggesting that it is possible to experience conscious visual perception without activating V1. This lack of V1 activation suggests to the researchers that synaesthesia involves an interaction between the areas of the brain responsible for higher visual function and the areas responsible for aspects of language processing.

Table 5.3 The taste sensations in ES triggered by different notes

Tone interval	Taste experienced
Minor second	Sour
Major second	Bitter
Minor third	Salty
Major third	Sweet
Fourth	(Mown grass)
Tritone	(Disgust)
Fifth	Pure water
Minor sixth	Cream
Major sixth	Low-fat cream
Minor seventh	Bitter
Major seventh	Sour
Octave	No taste

Synaesthesia highlights one of the problems of studying sensation. The problem is as old as psychology and philosophy: how do we really know that the person is experiencing what they say they are experiencing? Baron-Cohen's studies suggest two ways of circumventing this problem: (1) look for consistency of responses in an experimental group over time and compare these with control responses, and (2) compare brain activation in these two groups, working under the assumption that synaesthesia activates different areas of the brain when compared with a resting state and with a non-synaesthete control group.

Audition

Vision involves the perception of objects in three dimensions, at a variety of distances, and with a multitude of colours and textures. These complex stimuli may occur at a single point in time or over an extended period. They may also involve an unchanging scene or a rapidly changing one. The other senses analyse much simpler stimuli (such as an odour or a taste) or depend on time and stimulus change for the development of a complex perception. For example, to perceive a solid object in three dimensions by means of touch, we must manipulate it – turn it over in our hands or move our hands over its surface. The stimulus must change over time for a fully-fledged perception of form to emerge. The same is true for audition: we hear nothing meaningful in an instant.

Most people consider the sense of hearing second in importance only to vision. In some ways it is more important. A blind person can converse and communicate with other people almost as well as a sighted person. Deafness is much more likely to produce social isolation. A deaf person cannot easily join in the conversation of a group of people who do not know sign language. Although our eyes can transmit much more information to the brain, our ears are used for some of our most important forms of social communication.

Sound

Sound consists of pressure changes in air. As an object vibrates, it causes the air around it to move. The surface of a vibrating object moves back and forth. As the surface moves towards you, it compresses molecules of air; as it moves away, it pulls the molecules of air farther apart. These successive waves of compression and 'rarefaction' flow away from the surface as sound. As a pressure wave arrives at your ear, it pushes your eardrum inward. The following wave of negative pressure (when the molecules are pulled farther apart) sucks your eardrum outward.

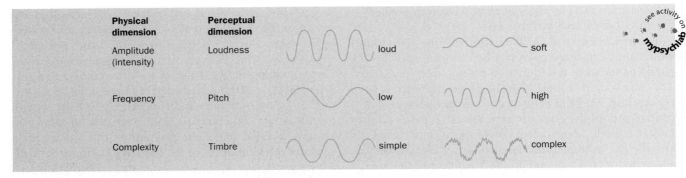

Figure 5.24 The physical and perceptual dimensions of sound waves.

Sound waves are measured in frequency units of cycles per second called **hertz (Hz)**. The human ear perceives vibrations between approximately 30 Hz and 20,000 Hz. Sound waves can vary in intensity and frequency. These variations produce corresponding changes in sensations of loudness and pitch. Consider a loudspeaker. Alternations in the electrical current transmitted from an amplifier cause the loudspeaker cone to move back and forth. If the cone begins vibrating more rapidly, the pitch of the sound increases. If the vibrations become more intense (that is, if the cone moves in and out over a greater distance), the loudness of the sound increases. A third perceptual dimension, timbre, corresponds to the complexity of the sound vibration. See Figure 5.24.

The ear and its functions

When people refer to the ear, they usually mean what anatomists call the pinna – the flesh-covered cartilage attached to the side of the head (*pinna* means 'wing' in Latin). But the pinna performs only a small role in audition: it helps us to determine the direction of sound. The real business of hearing is done in the inner ear (see Figure 5.25).

The eardrum is a thin, flexible membrane that vibrates back and forth in response to sound waves. It passes these vibrations, via the bones of the middle ear, to the inner ear, a 2 cm cavity which separates the outer and middle ear. The eardrum is attached to the first of three middle ear bones called the **ossicles** (literally, 'little bones'). The three ossicles are known as the malleus, incus and stapes (from Latin: hammer, anvil and stirrup) because of their shapes. These bones act together, in lever fashion, to transmit the vibrations of the eardrum to the fluid-filled structure of the inner ear that contains the receptive organ.

The part of the ear that contains the receptive organ of hearing is called the **cochlea** (*kokhlos* means 'snail', which also describes its shape). Uncoiled, this would reach 35 mm and is 2 mm in diameter (Goldstein, 2007). It is filled with liquid and a bony chamber attached to the cochlea (the vestibule) contains two openings, the oval window and the round window. The last of the three ossicles (the stapes) presses against a membrane behind an opening in the bone surrounding the cochlea called the **oval window**, thus transmitting sound waves into the liquid inside the cochlea, where it can reach the receptive organ of hearing. The cochlea is divided along its length into three cavities by the **basilar membrane** and Reissner's membrane. The auditory receptor cells sit on the surface of the basilar membrane. As the footplate of the stapes presses back and forth against the membrane behind the oval window, pressure changes in the fluid above the basilar membrane cause the basilar membrane to vibrate up and down. Because the basilar membrane varies in width and flexibility along its length, different frequencies of sound cause different parts of the basilar membrane to vibrate. High-frequency sounds cause the end near the oval window to vibrate, medium-frequency sounds cause the middle to vibrate, and low-frequency sounds cause the tip to vibrate. Figure 5.26 shows a schematic drawing and the corresponding photographic image of the cochlea.

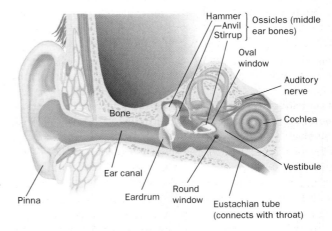

Figure 5.25 Anatomy of the auditory system.

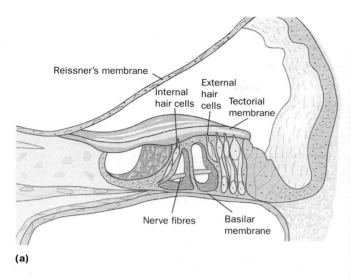

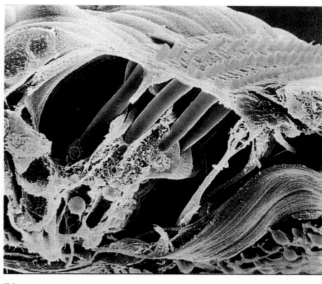

(a)

(b)

Figure 5.26 (a) A schematic image of the cochlea. **(b)** A photographic image of the cochlea.
Source: Beatty, J., *Principles of Behavioral Neuroscience*. Madison: Wm C. Brown Communications, Inc. Reprinted with permission.

In order for the basilar membrane to vibrate freely, the fluid in the lower chamber of the cochlea must have somewhere to go. Free space is provided by the **round window**. When the basilar membrane flexes down, the displacement of the fluid causes the membrane behind the round window to bulge out. In turn, when the basilar membrane flexes up, the membrane behind the round window bulges in.

Some people suffer from a middle ear disease that causes bone to grow over the round window. Because their basilar membrane cannot easily flex back and forth, these people have a severe hearing loss. However, their hearing can be restored by a surgical procedure called fenestration ('window making') in which a tiny hole is drilled in the bone where the round window should be.

Sounds are detected by special neurons known as **auditory hair cells**, located on the basilar membrane. Auditory hair cells transduce mechanical energy caused by the flexing of the basilar membrane into neural activity. These cells possess hair-like protrusions called **cilia** ('eyelashes'). The ends of the cilia are embedded in a fairly rigid shelf (the **tectorial membrane**) that hangs over the basilar membrane like a balcony. When sound vibrations cause the basilar membrane to flex back and forth, the cilia are stretched. This pull on the cilia is translated into neural activity (see Figure 5.27). The threshold for hearing in humans is 100 trillionth of a metre – we can detect a sound that is as little in strength as 100 picometres. See Figure 5.28, which compares the movement of a hair cell with the equivalent necessary to move 10 mm of the Eiffel Tower.

When a mechanical force is exerted on the cilia of the auditory hair cells, the electrical charge across their membrane is altered. The change in the electrical charge causes a transmitter substance to be released at a synapse between the auditory hair cell and the dendrite of a neuron of the auditory nerve. The release of the transmitter substance excites the neuron, which transmits messages through the auditory nerve to the brain.

Detecting and localising sounds in the environment

As we saw, sounds can differ in loudness, pitch and timbre. They also have sources; they come from particular locations. How does the ear distinguish these characteristics? The ear's ability to distinguish sounds by their timbre depends on its ability to distinguish loudness and pitch. Some common auditory stimuli and their loudness levels are presented in Figure 5.29.

Loudness and pitch

Scientists have long debated how the auditory system represents pitch on the auditory nerve. Some think that pitch is represented by axons firing in synchrony with the vibrations of the basilar membrane. However, axons cannot fire rapidly enough to represent the high pitches that we can hear. A good, young ear can distinguish frequencies of more than 20,000 Hz, but axons cannot fire more than 1,000 times per second. Therefore, high-frequency sounds, at least, must be encoded in some other way.

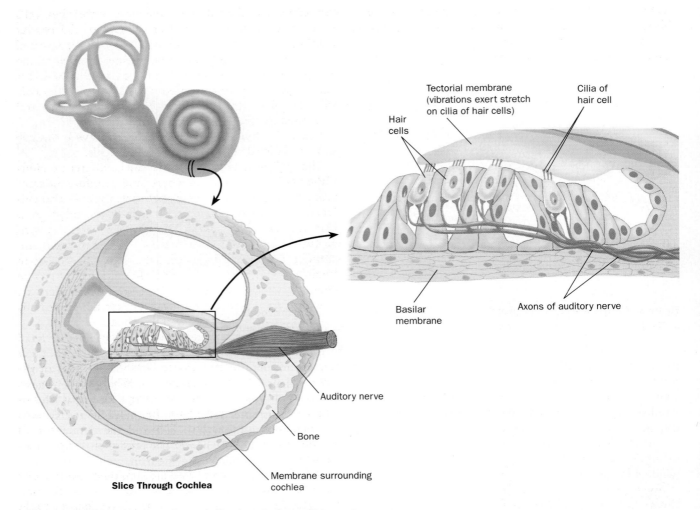

Hair
cells

Tectorial membrane
(vibrations exert stretch
on cilia of hair cells)

Cilia of
hair cell

Basilar
membrane

Axons of auditory nerve

Auditory nerve

Bone

Membrane surrounding
cochlea

Slice Through Cochlea

Figure 5.27 The transduction of sound vibrations in the auditory system.

As we saw, sounds of different frequency cause different parts of the basilar membrane to vibrate. Thus, sounds of different frequencies stimulate different groups of auditory hair cells located along the basilar membrane. So, the brain can be informed of the pitch of a sound by the activity of different sets of axons from the auditory nerve. When low-frequency sound waves reach the ear, the top of the basilar membrane vibrates, and auditory hair cells located in this region are activated. In contrast, high-frequency sounds activate auditory hair cells located at the base of the basilar membrane, near the oval window. Therefore, the brain can tell the frequency from the set of axons which is firing.

Two kinds of evidence indicate that pitch is detected in this way. First, direct observation of the basilar membrane has shown that the region of maximum vibration depends on the frequency of the stimulating tone (von

Békésy, 1960). Van Békésy's place theory of hearing argued that the frequency of a sound is indicated by the place along the organ of Corti where the firing of nerves is strongest. The vibration of the basilar membrane is a little like the snapping of a whip, creating a travelling wave. When electrodes are placed along the cochlea, a map of frequencies can be plotted out along the cochlea (this is called a tonotopic map). Frequencies are higher at the base and lower at the apex of the cochlea.

Secondly, experiments have found that damage to specific regions of the basilar membrane causes loss of the ability to perceive specific frequencies. The discovery that some antibiotics damage hearing (for example, deafness is one of the possible side effects of an antibiotic used to treat tuberculosis) has helped auditory researchers to investigate the anatomical coding of pitch. Stebbins *et al.* (1969) administered an antibiotic to different groups of animals for varying times. Next, they tested the animals' ability to perceive tones of different frequencies. Afterwards, they removed the animals' cochleas and examined them. They found that the longer the animals

10 millimeters   **100 picometers**

Figure 5.28 Comparison of the movement of the cillia of a hair cell with the Eiffel Tower.
Source: Goldstein, E. B. (2007) *Sensation and Perception* (7th edn). California: Thompson.

were exposed to the antibiotic, the more of their hair cells were killed. Damage started at the end of the basilar membrane nearest the oval window and progressed towards the other end. The experimenters compared the various groups of animals and found that the hearing loss was proportional to the amount of damage to the hair cells. The loss began with the highest frequencies and progressed towards the lower frequencies.

Thus, the hair cells nearest the oval window are responsible for detecting high-pitched sounds.

Although different frequencies cause different regions of the basilar membrane to vibrate and therefore different axons from the auditory nerve to fire, there is also evidence that pitch information can be encoded in a different way. The basilar membrane vibrates in synchrony with the sound waves. Neurons that are stimulated by hair cells located there are able to fire in synchrony with these vibrations, thus firing at the same frequency as the sound. The brain times the intervals between these responses and thus detects the pitch. This process is an example of temporal coding.

One piece of evidence that low frequencies are detected in this way comes from an experiment performed many years ago by Miller and Taylor (1948). These investigators used white noise as a stimulus. White noise consists of a random mixture of all the perceptible frequencies of sound – it sounds like the 'sssh' heard when an FM radio is tuned between stations. White noise stimulates all regions of the basilar membrane because it contains all frequencies of sound.

Miller and Taylor presented participants with white noise that passed through a hole in a rotating disc. By spinning the disc at various speeds, the investigators could divide the noise into extremely brief pulses, which could be presented at various rates. Thus, a 'pitch' was artificially created by setting the pulse rate of the white noise. When the frequency of the pulsation was less than 250 Hz, the participants could accurately identify its pitch. However,

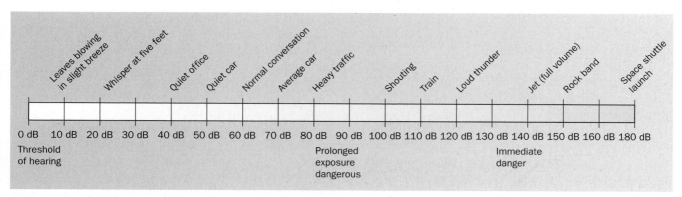

Figure 5.29 The average decibel level of some common (and uncommon) noises.
Source: Payne, D.G. and Wenger, M., *Cognitive Psychology*, 1998, p. 75. © 1998 Houghton Mifflin Company. Used with permission.

above 250 Hz, the perception of pitch disappeared. Because the white noise stimulated all parts of the basilar membrane, the sounds must have been detected by neurons that fired in synchrony with the pulsations.

What about loudness? The axons of the cochlear nerve appear to inform the brain of the loudness of a stimulus by altering their rate of firing. More intense vibrations stimulate the auditory hair cells more intensely. This stimulation causes them to release more transmitter substance, which results in a higher rate of firing by the axons in the auditory nerve. The code is therefore similar to that used in other senses.

However, there is a problem. If they fire more frequently with sound intensity, why does that not signal a higher pitch according to the temporal code described above? Obviously, they cannot signal both loudness and pitch by the same means. The answer is that loudness is signalled by the number of auditory hair cells that are active at a given time. A louder sound excites a larger number of hair cells.

Timbre

You can easily distinguish between the sounds of a violin and a clarinet, even if they are playing tones of the same pitch and loudness. So, clearly, pitch and loudness are not the only characteristics of a sound. Sounds can vary greatly in complexity. They can start suddenly or gradually increase in loudness, be short or long, and seem thin and reedy or full and vibrant. The enormous variety of sounds that we can distinguish is in large part owing to an important characteristic of sound called timbre.

The combining, or synthesis, of two or more simple tones, each consisting of a single frequency, can produce a complex tone. For example, an electronic synthesiser produces a mixture of sounds of different frequencies, each of which can be varied in amplitude (intensity). Thus, it can synthesise the complex sounds of a clarinet or violin or can assemble completely new sounds not produced by any other source. Conversely, complex sounds that have a regular sequence of waves can be reduced by means of analysis into several simple tones.

We can tell a clarinet from another instrument because each instrument produces sounds consisting of a unique set of simple tones called **overtones**. Their frequencies are multiples of the **fundamental frequency**, or the basic pitch of the sound. **Timbre** is the distinctive combination of overtones with the fundamental frequency. The fundamental frequency causes one part of the basilar membrane to vibrate, while each of the overtones causes another portion to vibrate. During a complex sound many different portions of the basilar membrane are vibrating simultaneously. Thus, the ear

analyses a complex sound. Information about the fundamental frequency and each of the overtones is sent to the brain through the auditory nerve, and the person hears a complex tone having a particular timbre. When you consider that we can listen to an orchestra and identify several instruments playing simultaneously, you can appreciate the complexity of the analysis performed by the auditory system.

Locating the source of a sound

When we hear an unexpected sound, we usually turn our heads quickly to face its source. Even newborn infants can make this response with reasonably good accuracy. And once our faces are oriented towards the source of the sound, we can detect changes in its location of as little as 1 degree. To do so, we make use of two qualities of sound: relative loudness and difference in arrival time.

Relative loudness is the most effective means of perceiving the side from which a high-frequency sound comes. Low-frequency sounds can bend around a solid object but high-frequency sounds bounce off. Thus, objects, such as the human head, cast an 'acoustic shadow' (at least for high-frequency sounds), rather as opaque objects cast a shadow in the sunlight. The head reflects high-frequency sounds so that they are made louder to the ear nearer the source of the sound and less loud at the more distant ear which is in the acoustic shadow cast by the head. Thus, if a source on your right produces a high-frequency sound, your right ear will receive more intense stimulation than your left ear will. The brain uses this difference to calculate the location of the source of the sound.

The second method involves detecting differences in the arrival time of sound pressure waves at each eardrum. This method works best for frequencies below approximately 1,500 Hz. A 1,000 Hz tone produces pressure waves approximately 0.3 m apart. Because the distance between a person's eardrums is about half that, a source of 1,000 Hz sound located to one side of the head will cause one eardrum to be pushed in while the other eardrum is being pulled out. In contrast, if the source of the sound is directly in front of the listener, both eardrums will move in synchrony.

Researchers have found that when the source of a sound is located to the side of the head, axons in the right and left auditory nerves will fire at different times. The brain is able to detect this disparity, which causes the sound to be perceived as being off to one side. In fact, the brain can detect differences in firing times of a fraction of a millisecond (ms, one-thousandth of a second). The easiest stimuli to locate are those that produce brief clicks, which cause brief bursts of neural activity. Apparently, it is easiest for the brain to compare the arrival times of single bursts of incoming information.

Each of these cues, the difference in the loudness and the difference in the timing across the ears, allows one to discriminate between left and right. However, humans are also able to tell whether sounds come from in front or behind, above or below. This information cannot be encoded by differences across the ears. This is where the role of the pinna (mentioned above) comes to the fore. The pinna has a very distinctive shape and for humans its usefulness is far from obvious from its appearance – contrast the obvious funnel shape of a horse's ears which has plainly evolved to gather sound from a particular direction. The various ridges and folds of the human ear cause sound to interact with the surface in a process called acoustic interference. The result is that the timbre of the sound changes according to the sound direction. The importance of the pinna's corrugations in sound localisation can be demonstrated by filling up the folds with plastic material and showing that localisation becomes much poorer.

The interaction between audition and vision

The brain can also be 'persuaded' to believe that sounds can enhance the perception of visual stimuli. How senses interact is important because in real life we usually do not experience stimuli in only one sensory modality. In one study, eight observers watched a single flash, which was accompanied by multiple auditory beeps, spaced 57 ms apart (Shams *et al.*, 2000). In this condition, observers reported having seen several flashes and not the one actually presented. Multiple flashes were consistently seen when multiple beeps were presented. When beeps were presented over 70 ms apart, however, the illusion was diminished and observers reported seeing single flashes. When a single beep was presented with multiple flashes, observers correctly reported seeing multiple flashes. The

study highlights how manipulable our senses can be: in this case, simply increasing the number of presentations of stimuli in one modality (vision) while presenting single instances of a stimulus in another modality (audition) made people believe they had been presented with more stimuli in the second of these senses than they had.

A similar study explored the phenomenon whereby the introduction of a sound at the point when two identical visual targets pass 'through' each other leads people to report that they thought the two stimuli collided (Watanabe and Shimojo, 2001). Without the sound, people reported that the stimuli just seemed to stream through each other. Watanabe and Shimojo found that this collision effect could be weakened under certain conditions. For example, when identical auditory stimuli were presented 300 ms before and after the visual targets passed through each other, the collision effect did not occur. However, when the preceding and following sounds were different from the target sound, the collision effect remained. The context and the salience of the target sound, therefore, was important to preserving the effect.

The effect may exist because when two real objects collide they usually make a transient sound. The inclusion of the target noise in these experiments seemed to provide the 'missing' sound that you would expect to hear when two objects collided. But if a target noise is preceded or followed by a similar noise, it will be difficult for the viewer/listener to draw a cause-and-effect relationship between the contact of the two images and the simultaneous noise because the simultaneous noise is the same as that which preceded and followed the collision.

Audition and the temporal cortex

The cortical areas which mediate our perception of sound are located in the temporal cortex. One of the key features of the visual system is that it is organised hierarchically at the neural level. That is, sensory input is broken down and

Cutting edge – Hearing voices

We know that when we hear our own voice on some recording device, it sounds different. We also seem to orient towards our own name, more than that of others – the cocktail party effect described later in Chapter 9.

A group of researchers at the Institute for the Study of Child Development in New Jersey has recently reported that the brain regions activated when we hear our own name are different to those activated when we hear the names of others (Carmody and Lewis, 2006). They scanned four right-handed

young men, using fMRI, and found that areas of the left hemisphere – middle frontal cortex and middle and superior temporal cortex – were more active when the men heard their own names than others.

The researchers note that these regions are also those which become active when people make judgements about themselves or their personal qualities, suggesting that they have a role in mediating our perception of ourselves and of stimuli personally relevant to us as individuals.

then put together to form complex stimuli in various regions of the brain. This means that different regions of neurons are responsible for processing different types of visual stimuli. A similar phenomenon has also been demonstrated for the auditory sense: tones, non-speech stimuli, meaningless speech sounds and other types of auditory stimuli have been found to generate specific areas of the cortex (as well as areas they seem to have in common).

For example, a recent study investigated whether certain types of stimuli activated 'core' auditory areas or a 'belt' region outside this core area (Wessinger *et al.*, 2001). In an fMRI study, Wessinger *et al.*, presented pure tones and complex auditory stimuli to 12 healthy, right-handed men and women. They found that pure tones activated a core area – areas that surrounded Heschl's gyrus – but more complex stimuli activated areas outside this core (the pure tones did not). The authors propose that this hierarchical system of sound analysis participates in the early processing of many sounds including those for speech.

Perry *et al.* (1999) found greater right-sided activation in the temporal cortex (the primary auditory cortex) when people sang than when they passively listened to singing. This region may be responsible for the processing of complex pitches. In an ingenious experiment, Halpern and Zatorre (1999) asked people to imagine the rest of a musical excerpt (the theme to the television series *Dallas*) after being cued with the first few notes. Blood flow was measured while participants imagined the piece of music. In the recruiting session, and prior to the scanning, the tune was played in order to familiarise participants with it. During scanning, the first five notes were played and participants were asked to imagine the rest of the sequence. When people imagined the rest of the tune, the right auditory association cortex and supplementary motor area were activated, suggesting that these regions are recruited in the imagination of meaningful complex auditory stimuli. Pantev *et al.* (1998) also found that musical training increased activation in those parts of the cortex involved in musical processing. In piano players who had played from age 12 to 28 years there was 25 per cent more activation in this region than there was in non-players.

The current view of the auditory cortex's contribution to sound processing, therefore, sees it as a region that is made up of a core (comprising the auditory cortex and nearby areas) and a parabelt (Tramo, 2001; Zattore et al., 2002), both of which contribute the hierarchical processing of sound. The core area extracts and analyses information about the pitch of tones (Zatorre et al., 2002). The belt and the parabelt in the right hemisphere appear to be areas which detect changes in the duration of notes and in the patterns of music; the parabelt in both hemispheres may be involved in grouping sounds by metre (Tramo, 2001). An area beyond the auditory cortex, the frontal cortex, may be involved in organising sounds in time and keeping them 'in mind'.

The where and what aspects of hearing have been likened to those for sight. That is, there are two streams in the brain that allow us to locate a sound and another to identify it (Kaas and Hackett, 1999). The what, or ventral, stream is found anterior to the core of the belt and extends to the prefrontal cortex. The where, or dorsal, stream is found in posterior areas and extends to the parietal lobe. See Figure 5.30. Neurons in the anterior belt area fire more actively when responding to the pattern of sounds but weakly when trying to locate them. This neurophysiological finding is supported by research on a double dissociation in two patients with brain injury. Patient ES, for example, can recognise sounds but the ability to localise is poor (Clarke *et al.*, 2002), whereas another patient is poor at recognising but good at localising sound. Figure 5.31 shows their responses and the brain regions damaged.

Given what you now know about the auditory system, how would you describe the physiological basis of listening to a favourite piece of music, from initial sensation to recognition?

Deafness

Deafness profoundly affects a person's ability to communicate with others but hearing difficulties disappear in the company of other deaf people because they can sign read; it is only in the company of people who have normal hearing that deafness hinders a person's ability to communicate (Sachs, 1989). People who are postlingually deaf – people who become deaf late in life, after they have learned oral and written language – are unlikely to

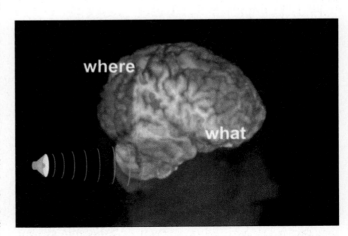

Figure 5.30 Areas associated with what (yellow) and where (blue) auditory functions, as determined by brain imaging.

Source: Goldstein, E. B. (2007) *Sensation and Perception* (7th edn). California: Thompson.

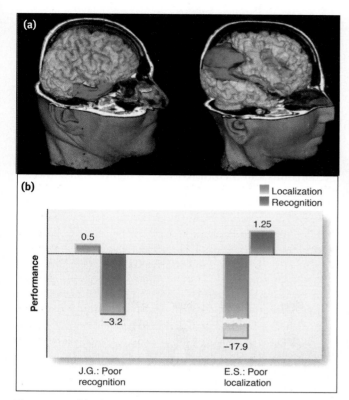

tive. In very rare cases, individuals who have damage to the auditory cortex and should, therefore, be 'cortically' deaf, appear to show evidence of hearing.

If you had a child who was born deaf, would you send your child to a school that taught sign language or to one that emphasised speaking and lip-reading? Why? Now imagine that you are deaf (or, if you are deaf, that you are hearing). Would your answer change?

Gustation

We have two senses specialised for detecting chemicals in our environment: taste and smell. Together, they are referred to as the **chemosenses** and the process by which they sense chemicals is called **chemosensation**. Taste, or **gustation**, is the simplest of the sense modalities. We can perceive four, possibly five, qualities of taste: sourness, sweetness, saltiness, bitterness and umami (which produces a savoury sensation, like monosodium glutamate). Taste is not the same as flavour; the flavour of a food includes its odour, texture, temperature, shape as well as its taste: these are called head factors. You have probably noticed that the flavours of foods are diminished when you have a head cold. This loss of flavour occurs not because your taste buds are ineffective (you can actually tell whether a food is sweet or salty) but because congestion with mucus makes it difficult for odour-laden air to reach your sense of smell receptors. Without their characteristic odours to serve as cues, onions taste much like apples (although apples do not make your eyes water).

Figure 5.31 (a) Coloured areas indicate brain damage for J.G (left) and E.S. (right). **(b)** Performance on recognition test (green bar) and localisation test (red bar). The horizontal line indicates normal performance.

Source: Goldstein, E.B. (2007) *Sensation and Perception* (7th edn). California: Thompson.

learn sign language. (In this context, lingual, from the word for 'tongue', refers to the acquisition of spoken language.) Some prelingually deaf people – people who are born deaf or who become deaf during infancy – never learn sign language, primarily because they are 'main-streamed' in community schools or attend a school for the deaf that teaches oral communication.

A recent technological development, the cochlear implant, is an electronic device surgically implanted in the inner ear that can enable deaf people to hear. Over 120,000 people had received such implants (Moore and Shannon, 2009) and the procedure is very sucessful (Krueger *et al.*, 2008). It is most useful for two groups: people who become deaf in adulthood and very young children who can produce speech more easily if the implant occurs before the age of five (Tye-Murray *et al.*, 1995). Putting a cochlear implant in a young child means that the child's early education will be committed to the oralist approach. Many deaf people, however, resent the implication that deafness is something that needs to be repaired, seeing themselves as different but not at all defec-

Taste receptors and the sensory pathway

The purpose of the sense of taste appears to be to provide guidance or warning to the gastrointestinal system: it will reject tastes it does not like and will accept those it does. This benefits us by allowing us to avoid ingesting potentially harmful substances (most poisons, for example, tend to be very bitter).

Our ability to taste depends on the tongue, mouth and the receptors in them. The tongue has a corrugated appearance, being marked by creases and bumps. The bumps are called **papillae** (from the Latin, meaning 'nipple'). Each papilla contains a number of taste buds (in some cases as many as 200) (see Figure 5.32(a) and (b) for an illustration).

A **taste bud** is a small organ that contains a number of receptor cells, each of which is shaped rather like a segment of an orange. The cells have hairlike projections

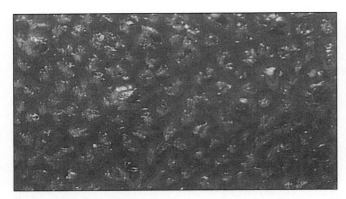

Figure 5.32 (a) The taste buds

called microvilli that protrude through the pore of the taste bud into the saliva that coats the tongue and fills the trenches of the papillae. Molecules of chemicals dissolved in the saliva stimulate the receptor cells, probably by interacting with special receptors on the microvilli that are similar to the postsynaptic receptors found on other neurons. The receptor cells form synapses with dendrites of neurons that send axons to the brain through three different cranial nerves, the vagus, cranial and facial nerves. Information is sent from the nerves to the medulla, then the thalamus and then the cortex, as Figure 5.33 shows.

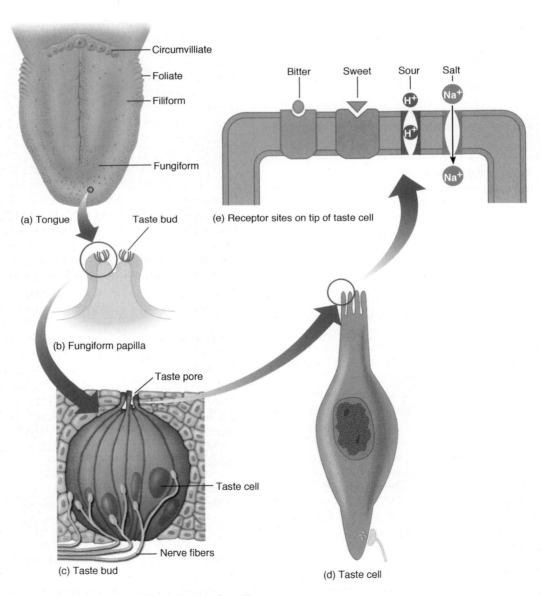

Figure 5.32 (b) The tongue, showing the four different types of papillae
Source: Goldstein, E.B. (2007) *Sensation and Perception* (7th edn) California: Thompson.

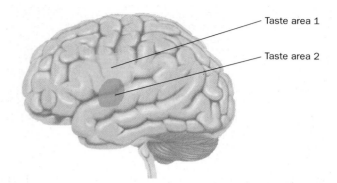

Figure 5.34 The brain seems to have two taste areas – a primary and a secondary – located near the frontal lobe.

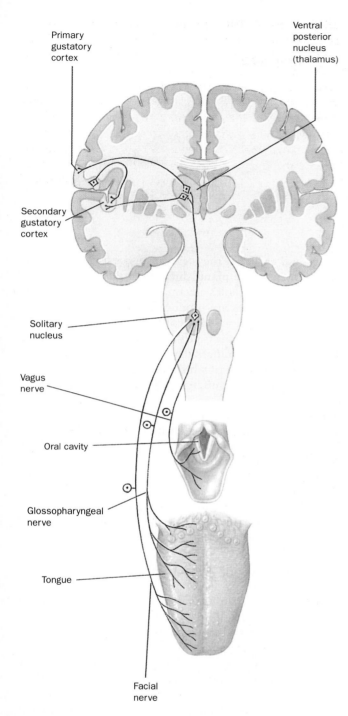

Figure 5.33 The neural pathway from tongue to brain.

Source: Pinel, P.J., *Biopsychology*, 5th edn. Published by Allyn & Bacon, Boston, MA. Copyright © Pearson Education. By permission of the publisher.

Taste and the cortex

There also appear to be primary and secondary taste cortices in the brain, as Figure 5.34 illustrates (Rolls and Baylis, 1994). The primary taste (gustatory) area is found near the front of the brain in regions called the insula or frontal operculum and further back in part of the parietal cortex; the location of the secondary taste cortex is not as well documented but appears to be principally in the orbitofrontal cortex. This is where flavour is thought to be processed (see page 560 in Chapter 13 on flavour).

Other brain structures, such as the amygdala, contain cells that are responsive to taste and these cells may be partly responsible for determining the hedonic quality of taste – whether the food is palatable. The amygdala forms part of an area which Small *et al.* (1997) describe as the anteromedial temporal lobe (AMTL). Patients who have had this removed or damaged report increased sensitivity to bitter tastes and an elevated ability to recognise, but not detect, citric acid. Small *et al.* (2001a) have proposed that this region may play an important role in perceiving the intensity of tastes, especially aversive taste. One reason for the increase in intensity, may be that the damage to the AMTL disinhibited cells in the cortex that are sensitive to taste concentration or palatability.

In a recent experiment, participants who were hungry or sated were asked to taste sucrose, caffeine, saccharine and citric acid (Haase *et al.*, 2009). Hungry people activated different brain regions from those activated in satisfied ones. (Specifically, the insula, thalamus and substantia nigra). The sated participants showed less activation in the hippocampus and an area near the prefrontal lobe.

The four or more qualities of taste

The surface of the tongue was once thought to be differentially sensitive to taste. The tip was considered most sensitive to sweet and salty substances; the sides to sour substances; and the back of the tongue, the back of the throat, and the soft palate overhanging the back of the tongue to bitter substances, as Figure 5.35 illustrates.

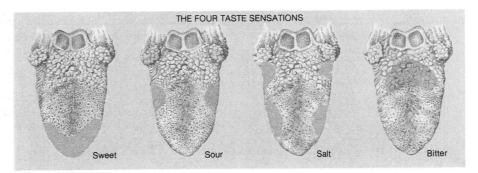

THE FOUR TASTE SENSATIONS

Sweet   Sour   Salt   Bitter

Figure 5.35 It is commonly thought that different parts of the tongue allow the experience of different tastes; the figure seen here, and in many other textbooks, is inaccurate.
Source: Whitfield, P. and Stoddart, M., *Pathways of Perception*. New York: Torstar Books.

This description, however, is largely mythical: the tongue is not this taste-specific and more than one region can detect the same sensation. There is also evidence that there may exist a fifth taste sensation, umami first reported at the beginning of the 20th century. This is difficult to describe accurately but appears to reflect the sensation we get when ingesting monosodium glutamate or very savoury foods (such as Chinese meals).

The physical properties of the molecules that we taste determine the nature of the taste sensations. Different molecules stimulate different types of receptor. For example, all substances that taste salty ionise (break into charged particles) when they dissolve. The most important salty substance is table salt – sodium chloride (NaCl). Other chlorides, such as lithium or potassium chloride, and some other salts, such as bromides or sulphates, are also salty in taste, but none tastes quite as salty as sodium chloride. This finding suggests that the specific function of salt-tasting receptors is to identify sodium chloride. Sodium plays a unique role in the regulation of our body fluid. If the body's store of sodium falls, we cannot retain water and our blood volume will fall. The result can be heart failure. Loss of sodium stimulates a strong craving for the salty taste of sodium chloride.

Both bitter and sweet substances seem to consist of large, non-ionising molecules. Scientists cannot predict, merely on the basis of shape, whether a molecule will taste bitter or sweet (or neither). Some molecules (such as saccharin) stimulate both sweet and bitter receptors; they taste sweet at the front of the tongue and bitter at the back of the palate and throat. Most likely, the function of the bitterness receptor is to avoid ingesting poisons. Many plants produce alkaloids that serve to protect them against being eaten by insects or browsing animals. Some of these alkaloids are poisonous to humans, and most of them taste bitter. In contrast, the sweetness receptor enables us to recognise the sugar content of fruits and other nutritive plant foods. When sweet-loving animals gather and eat fruit, they tend to disperse the seeds and help propagate the plant; thus, the presence of sugar in the fruit is to the plant's advantage as well.

Most sour tastes are produced by acids, in particular, by the hydrogen ion (H+) contained in acid solutions. The sourness receptor probably serves as a warning device against substances that have undergone bacterial decomposition, most of which become acidic.

People who have suffered head injury or experienced certain types of medical treatment, such as radiotherapy, sometimes experience disorders of taste. These can vary from complete loss of taste (ageusia), decreased sensitivity (hypogeusia) and distorted taste sensations, especially those for meats, eggs, fruits, coffee and carbonated drinks (dysgeusia). Patients with these symptoms, however, are rare; only around 1 per cent of patients are ageusic, for example. A common complaint among those who suffer from one of these disorders is the lack of enjoyment of food and a loss of appetite.

The development of taste preference

Newborns seem to respond in a characteristic way to some tastes, especially if these tastes are strong. When babies are given a sweet stimulus to ingest, they typically lick their lips, suck and look relaxed; when given bitter substances, the corners of their mouths depress, they tighten their eyes, flatten their tongues and shake their heads. Many adults who experience unfamiliar, strong bitter tastes do the same. Sour substances tend to elicit similar responses to those elicited by bitter ones but in a more diminished way.

The development of taste preference appears to be highly malleable. For example, if a newborn is given sweetened water at 6 months of age, it will prefer sweetened water a year later; those fed normally will not show this preference for sweetened water. A similar finding is found when the newborn's diet contains additional salt

(Beauchamp and Moran, 1982; Harris and Booth, 1987). This learned response is also illustrated by adults' food preferences. Our liking for foods such as lima beans, coffee, whisky and chillies, for example, grows from late childhood; children tend to find these foods too bitter (or hot in the case of chillies) to ingest.

Olfaction

The sense of smell – **olfaction** – is one of the most interesting and puzzling of the sense modalities. It is unlike other sense modalities in two important ways. First, it is the only sense whose receptors are directly exposed to the environment. Secondly, people have difficulty identifying even familiar odours (Engen, 1987) although they can describe their properties very well (such as how nice smelling they are or what they remind them of). Odours have a powerful ability to evoke memories and feelings, even many years after an event, although they do not appear to be more effective than stimuli in other sensory modalities at doing this (Herz and Cupchik, 1992; Herz and Engen, 1996). At some time in their lives, most people encounter an odour that they recognise as having some childhood association, even though they cannot identify it. One of the most widely quoted examples is the experience of the French novelist Marcel Proust, whose mammoth series of autobiographical adventures, *À la recherche du temps perdu* (*Remembrance of Things Past*), was provoked by the odour of a madeleine cake dipped in tea which transported him back to his childhood. It is also a sense which we think we can do without; if asked which of the senses is least important to us or which we would be willing to relinquish if we had to, people usually nominate the sense of smell (Martin *et al.*, 2001).

Olfaction, like audition, seems to be an analytical sense modality. That is, when humans sniff air that contains a mixture of familiar odours, we usually identify the individual components. The molecules do not blend together and produce a single odour in the same way that lights of different wavelengths produce a single colour.

Other animals, such as dogs, have more sensitive olfactory systems than humans do because they have a great many more olfactory receptors (described below). The difference in sensitivity between our olfactory system and those of other mammals may be that other mammals put their noses where odours are the strongest – just above ground level. Even a bloodhound's nose would not be very useful if it were located five feet above the ground, as ours is. You can see how effective a hound's olfactory system is at tracking other animals from Figure 5.36. However, we should not underrate our own. We can smell some substances at lower concentrations than can the most sensitive instruments (the human nose is actually more sensitive than a smoke detector) and a recent study has found that we can follow a 10 cm trail of chocolate essential oil in an open grass field while wearing a blindfold (Porter *et al.*, 2007). This study also found that both nostrils were better than one at the task but, more specifically, that the velocity of air into the right nostril was 0.45 ms and in the left 0.3 ms. This gives a spatial reach of 1.5–2 cm in the left nostril and 1–1.5 cm in the right. There is also evidence of circadian asymmetry in sniffing. The velocity of inhalation is greater in one nostril than the other and the side changes throughout the day (Sobel *et al.*, 1999).

Odours interact with other senses in very peculiar ways. Djordjevic *et al.* (2004) asked participants to smell or imagine smelling the odours of either strawberry or ham as they took part in a taste detection task – the participants had to indicate at which point they detected the sweet taste of sucrose. People detected the taste of sucrose better when they smelled or imagined smelling strawberry than when they smelled/imagined smelling ham. The imagery of pleasant and unpleasant scents activates similar brain areas to those activated during the actual inhalation of those odours (Bensafi *et al.*, 2007). People exposed to a pleasant odour they were not consciously aware of, have been found to rate photographs of neutral faces as more likeable (Li *et al.*, 2007). The Cutting Edge section gives a more startling illustration.

Figure 5.36 Human's path following a scent trial, as compared to a dog's path. **(a)** Path of a dog following the scent trail of a pheasant dragged through a field (scent trail in yellow, dog's path in red.) **(b)** Path of a human following a scent trail of chocolate essential oil through a field (scent trail in yellow, human's path in red).

Source: Reprinted by permission from MacMillan Publishers Ltd: Nature Neuroscience vol. 10. Nr 1, Jan 2007, copyright 2007 (r). Science Faction: Louie Psihoyos (L).

Odours play an important role in the lives of most mammals. Although we do not make use of olfaction in identifying one another, we do use it to avoid some dangers, such as food that has spoiled, or gas. In fact, the odour of rotting meat will trigger withdrawal – a useful response if some of the rotten meat has been swallowed. Other animals recognise friends and enemies by means of smell and use odours to attract mates and repel rivals. And the reproductive behaviour of laboratory mammals – and even the menstrual cycles of women – may be influenced by the odours emitted by other animals of the same species, a controversial topic taken up in the Controversies in Psychological Science section on p.200.

Cutting edge – Cheese, body odour and the orbitofrontal cortex

Our sense of smell is one of the most manipulable. People can be convinced that a neutral odour has a scent and, when told that an odour has a particular quality, judge that odour accordingly (regardless of whether it has that quality). Researchers at Oxford University presented the odour of isovaleric acid (which has a cheesy odour) to 12 healthy young men and told them it was either 'body odour' or 'cheddar cheese' (de Araujo *et al.*, 2005). Participant's ratings of the odours' pleasantness under each label condition, and their brain activation, was measured.

The odour was rated as significantly more unpleasant when labelled body odour than cheese, and activation in the anterior cingulate cortex and medial orbitofrontal cortex was greater when participants smelled clean air and the odour labelled cheese than body odour.

The experiment demonstrates neatly how semantic information can influence hedonic judgement.

Odour perception – An international perspective

Perfumery is a universal art and few of us have not received or bought a gift of scent or cologne, but do all cultures and nations respond to the same smells in the same way? As you might expect, the answer is no. In general, there are cross-cultural similarities in people's responses to odour: there is a universal correlation between odour familiarity and pleasantness, for example. The more familiar a person thinks an odour is, the more likeable it is judged. A study of Japanese and German participants found that the number of memories evoked by pleasant and unpleasant odours was similar (Schleidt *et al.*, 1988). But different cultures do rate the pleasantness of some odours differently.

In one study, Haller *et al.* (1999) found that exposure to vanilla in childhood affected a German participant's food preferences later in life (Germans, at one time, received bottled milk flavoured with vanilla). When German participants were asked to rate ketchup or ketchup scented with vanilla, those who had been bottle-fed preferred the vanilla ketchup, compared with those who were breast-fed.

More directly, Doty *et al.* (1985) compared the ability of American Korean, Caucasian, African American and Japanese participants to identify odours on a brief scratch and sniff test called the University of Pennsylvania Smell Identification Test (the UPSIT). The Koreans were better at identification than were the Caucasians and African Americans; the last two groups were better than the Japanese, probably because the US-validated odours were more familiar to the Westerners than to the Japanese. A study of odour detection thresholds (the lowest concentration at which a person can detect an odour) reported lower detection thresholds for Japanese ink and aniseed (Hübener *et al.*, in press).

Cultures also differ in the way they classify odour. For example, when Japanese and Sherpa people were asked to classify 20 artificial scents into perceptually similar categories, there was agreement on most but the Japanese classified some odours as 'fishy': Sherpa are not used to eating fish but the Japanese are famously fish-friendly (Ueno, 1993). Americans and French people are more likely to describe fruit odorants as sweets or flowers and flower odorants as cleaning products than are Vietnamese raters (Chrea *et al.*, 2004).

One comprehensive study asked a sample of Japanese and German participants to rate the pleasantness and 'edibility' of three classes of odours which the authors described as 'European', 'Japanese' and 'International' (Ayabe-Kanamura *et al.*, 1998). Table 5.4 shows examples of each. Of the European odours, the Japanese sample rated the odours of church incense, anise and almond as less pleasant than did the

Odour perception – *Continued*

Table 5.4 The odorants used in Ayabe-Kanamura et al. (1998), together with participants' descriptions of them

Odorants	Descriptors
Japanese	
Dried bonito flakes	dried fish
Soy sauce	soy sauce, soy
Roasted tea	Japanese tea
Dried fermented soybeans	fermented soybeans
India ink	India ink
Japanese cypress wood flakes	wood, furniture
International	
Ground coffee	coffee
Grated dark chocolate	chocolate, cacao
Chopped, roasted peanuts	peanuts
Lowenbrau	beer
Vick's Vaporub	ointment with menthol
Angel	perfume
European	
Marzipan	almond, marzipan
Blue cheese	cheese
Pernod	anise
Italian salami	salami
Sawdust of pinewood	wood, furniture
Catholic church incense	incense

Germans, but rated the odour of cheese and pinewood as more pleasant. Of the international odours, the German sample rated perfume to be more pleasant and the odours of beer and peanuts to be less pleasant than did the Japanese. When asked whether the substance represented by an odour was edible, the Japanese rated the Japanese food odours to be more edible than did the Germans; the Germans found anise and almond to be more edible. The odours of cheese and peanuts were rated as more edible by the Japanese than the Germans.

A coda, however. The sense of smell is notoriously duplicitous and deceitful – think of trying to put a name to a familiar or unfamiliar odour. It is difficult and is summed up by the term 'tip-of-the-nose' phenomenon. In the study above, 25 per cent of the Japanese sample thought that India ink represented an edible substance; 40 per cent of Germans thought that Vick's Vaporub did.

Anatomy of the olfactory system

Figure 5.37 shows the anatomy of the olfactory system. The receptor cells for the olfactory system lie in the **olfactory mucosa**, one-inch square patches of mucous membrane located on the roof of the nasal sinuses, just under the base of the brain. The receptor cells have cilia that are embedded in the olfactory mucosa. They also have axons that pass through small holes in the bone above the olfactory mucosa and form synapses with neurons in the olfactory bulbs. The **olfactory bulbs** are stalk-like structures located at the base of the brain that contain neural circuits that perform the first analysis of olfactory information. There is evidence that the cortex also processes aspects of olfactory sensation and perception (Lorig, 1989; Small *et al.*, 1997; Martin, 1998).

For example, Martin (1998) recorded EEG from healthy individuals while they were exposed to a series of synthetic and real food odours. The odours included chocolate, spearmint, baked beans, strawberry, coffee and rotting pork. The odours of spearmint and chocolate (but primarily chocolate) were associated with significant reductions in one type of brain activity, theta (which we will consider at greater length in Chapter 9). Increases in this EEG waveband are thought to be associated with increased attention; it is plausible that the change in response to chocolate may reflect this pleasant odour's ability to distract a person's attention and make them feel relaxed.

In a novel neuroimaging experiment, Small *et al.* (1997) compared neural activation while people smelled substances, tasted them or did both (that is, perceived flavour). In some conditions, the odours and the tastes did not match. Using soy sauce, water, coffee, grapefruit and strawberry as stimuli, the experimenters found that when the odours and tastes were presented simultaneously, there was a decrease in activation at the primary taste cortex and the primary and secondary olfactory cortex. When tastes and smells did not match, increases in the amygdala were found, suggesting a role for the amygdala in the processing of novel or unpleasant stimuli. (We return to this role of the amygdala in emotion in Chapter 13.)

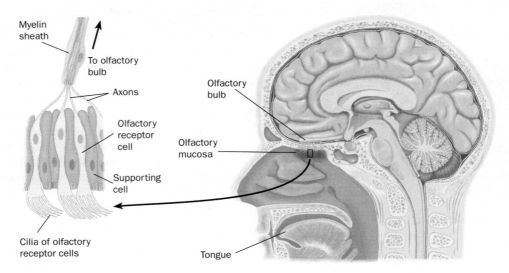

Figure 5.37 The olfactory system.

The interaction between odour molecule and receptor appears to be similar to that of transmitter substance and postsynaptic receptor on a neuron. That is, when a molecule of an odorous substance fits a receptor molecule located on the cilia of a receptor cell, the cell becomes excited. This excitation is passed on to the brain by the axon of the receptor cell. Thus, similar mechanisms may detect the stimuli for taste and olfaction. However, the mechanism for olfactory reception continues to be one of science's mysteries.

Unlike information from all other sensory modalities, olfactory information is not sent to the thalamus and then relayed to a specialised region of the cerebral cortex. Instead, olfactory information is sent directly to several regions of the limbic system, in particular to the amygdala and to the limbic cortex of the frontal lobe.

Controversies in Psychological Science – Do human pheromones exist?

The issue

Some species in the animal kingdom have a terrifically efficient sense of smell. Dogs have a remarkable ability to detect and discriminate between odours, hence their use in drug-sniffing operations. The odour of vaginal copulins can arouse male monkeys. Scents which produce stereotypical responses in a receiving organism without the scent being overtly detected are called **pheromones**. A well-known example is **androstenone** (its full, chemical name is 5-alpha-16-androst-16-en-3-one), a steroid developed in the testes of pigs which has a musk-like odour and is secreted in the saliva of male pigs during mating.

The unusual feature of androstenone is that it can induce a sow to adopt the mating position when it is sprayed on her. Farmers and vets can even buy the chemical in aerosol form, Boarmate, so that the sow can be prepared for mating (Figure 5.38). (In fact, truffle hunters use sows to detect the delicacy because it contains androstenone.) Pigs are not the only species to secrete androstenone. It is also present in men's sweat glands and in the urine of men and women, although at stronger concentrations in men (Brooksbank *et al.*, 1974).

Does a human pheromone exist?

The evidence

One of the earliest studies of the pheromone effect in humans was conducted by Martha McClintock in the 1970s (McClintock, 1971). She found that 17–22-year-old women students who lived and slept in the same halls of residence reported menstrual synchrony. That is, their menstrual cycles began on or about the same time. The effect was unrelated to food intake, lifestyle pattern or stress. The result is difficult to explain because no mechanism that we know of can account for the finding. McClintock suggested that the mechanism might be pheromonal or mediated by an awareness of another's menstrual cycle. To explain the result, replications would be needed. If the effect was pheromonal then a controlled

Controversies in Psychological Science – *Continued*

Figure 5.38 Farmers and veterinary surgeons sometimes spray Boarmate onto a sow to get her to adopt the mating position (Boarmate contains a variant of the pheromone, andro stenone).

Source: National Geographic, September 1986; © Louie Psihoyos/ Science Faction.

experiment in which menstrual cycles were deliberately manipulated would show this. This is what Russell *et al.* (1980) did.

They applied the sweaty secretions of a woman who had a history of 28-day cycles and experience of 'driving' (that is influencing) other women's cycles, on the upper lips of 5 women, 3 times a week for 4 months. Six individuals wore odourless alcohol (the control group). The mean difference in cycle onset for the experimental group was 3–9 days before the experiment; 3–4 days during driving. Controls' figures were 8 days and 9.2 days, respectively. A significant difference, therefore, was found between the experimental group's cycle onset and that of controls. However, there were some important limitations to the study. The experiment was not single- or double-blind, which means (as you will recall from Chapter 2) that the experimenters knew which participant was in each condition and each participant knew the purpose of the experiment. The woman who provided the samples was also one of the experimenters.

A similar experiment found that women reported shorter menstrual cycles when compounds from the follicular (late) stage of another woman's cycle were placed on the upper lip; longer cycles were reported when receiving ovulatory compounds (Stern and McClintock, 1998). A group from the

Monell Chemical Senses Center and Chicago University also found that chemical substances collected from lactating women increased the 'sexual motivation' of other women (such as sexual desire and fantasy) (Spencer *et al.*, 2004). Women with partners experienced more sexual desire whereas women without partners experienced more sexual fantasies. Does this suggest that 'pheromones' can modulate ovulation? Or are the effects limited to healthy young women? Would the same effect occur in women on various types of oral contraceptive? And are there alternative explanations, other than pheromonal ones, for the results?

Questions such as these crop up quite often in pheromone research in humans. They become even more pertinent when examining the results of studies investigating the effect of 'pheromones' on sexual attractiveness. The majority of experiments, for example, have tended to expose subjects to volatile chemicals in contexts which are not generally appropriate. For example, participants have rated imaginary verbal descriptions of people (Filsinger *et al.*, 1984), pictures and slides of buildings, people and animals (Kirk-Smith and Booth, 1977; Kirk-Smith *et al.*, 1978) or have indicated the number of sexual partners they have recently had (Filsinger and Monte, 1986). They have worn masks impregnated with an odour (Cowley *et al.*, 1980), a necklace impregnated with the odour (Cowley and Brooksbank, 1991), worn the odour on the top lip (Benton, 1982), sat on a chair impregnated with the odour (Kirk-Smith and Booth, 1980; Pause, 2004), or used a doctored changing room cubicle (Gustavson *et al.*, 1987). A recent study has even found that the presence of androstadienone increased the perception of pain (Villemure and Bushnell, 2007). As you can see, none of these conditions reflects the behaviour and contexts normally seen when physical attraction might occur.

In the most ecologically valid experiment, Black and Biron (1982) required participants to interact with a confederate of the opposite sex who wore either androstenone or a control odour. The participant was later asked to rate the confederate for attractiveness. The experimenters found no effect of these chemicals on the rated attractiveness of the confederate.

Another investigation examined the effect of male and female fragrances on women's genital arousal during the follicular and periovulatory stages as participants watched a hardcore video or sexually fantasised (Graham *et al.*, 2000). During the follicular stage only, genital arousal was greater during exposure to male fragrance when women were fantasising. One study found that exposure to 4, 16-androstadien-3-one made women feel more focused – although leaving other mood-related states unaffected (Lundstrom *et al.*, 2003) while another found that fertile women were more sensitive to the odour of this chemical than the odour of rose, whereas the opposite was true of women using oral contraceptives (Lundstrom *et al.*, 2006a).

Controversies in Psychological Science – *Continued*

When brain electrical activity in relation to this odour was measured in women, the brain responded more quickly to it than it did to control odours (Lundstrom *et al.*, 2006b). There may be reasons for this beyond pheromonal ones: androstenone can be perceived as unpleasant (smelling like a gents' lavatory) by some people and as a 'chemical' smell in those who can detect it but are not repulsed by it. Both reactions could have made the brain respond to this odour more quickly.

Curiously, homosexual men, like heterosexual women, show increased activation in the hypothalamus when smelling 4, 16-androstadien-3-one (Savic *et al.*, 2005). Common odours were found to activate similar areas in homosexual men and heterosexual men and women, suggesting that the response to the chemical can depend on sexual orientation more than sex.

In a related study in which the body odour preferences of homosexual and heterosexual men and women was measured, researchers found that heterosexual men and women and lesbians preferred the body odour of homosexual men to

gay men; gay men preferred the body odour of gay men (Martins *et al.*, 2005). None of the participants knew the sex or sexual orientation of the person who donated the body odour. All participants over 25, apart from gay men, preferred the body odour of lesbians to that of gay men. Gay men preferred the body odour of heterosexual women to that of heterosexual men. The results suggest that attraction to body odour can be sex- and sexual orientation- specific.

Conclusion

There is some evidence that the organ in the brain responsible for detecting and acting on pheromones (the vomeronasal organ) may be absent in humans (Moran et al., 1995). If this organ is important for sensing pheromones then humans will have difficulty sensing pheromones. Meanwhile, however, the evidence suggests that if you want to attract a member of the opposite sex, a bottle of good perfume or cologne would be a better option than would exposing your armpits, or investing in a can of Boarmate.

The dimensions of odour

Although we know that there are at least four qualities of taste and that a colour can be specified by hue, brightness and saturation, the several attempts at classifying odour have not been particularly successful. It seems to be a slippery sense to make sense of. One of the most famous systems, Henning's odour prism (1916), seen in Figure 5.39, plotted different categories of odour qualities at six corners of a prism.

Recent research in molecular biology suggests that the olfactory system uses up to 1,000 different receptor molecules, located in the membrane of the receptor cells, to detect different categories of odours (Jones and Reed, 1989; Buck and Axel, 1991; Axel, 1995). Linda Buck and Michael Axel won the Nobel Prize in 2004 for their discovery – that a family of genes was responsible for coding olfactory receptors. There are around 1000 different receptors in mice and around 350 in humans (Buck, 2004). Presumably, the presence of molecules of a substance with a particular odour produces a particular pattern of activity in the olfactory system. That is, the molecules will strongly stimulate some receptors, weakly stimulate others, and stimulate still others not at all. This pattern of stimulation is transmitted to the brain, where it is recognised as belonging to a particular odour. Malnic *et al.* (1999) found that some odorants generated weak firing at some receptors and strong firing at others, as the large and

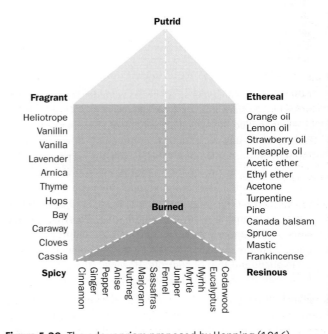

Figure 5.39 The odour prism proposed by Henning (1916).

Source: from Goldstein. *Sensation and Perception, International Edition, 7E.* (c) 2007, Wadsworth, a part of Cengage Learning, Inc. Reproduced by permission. www.cengage.com/permissions

small dots show in Figure 5.40 (a) and (b). It may be that different odorants are coded by different combinations of receptors so that one receptor could respond to more than one odorant. Researchers do not yet know exactly

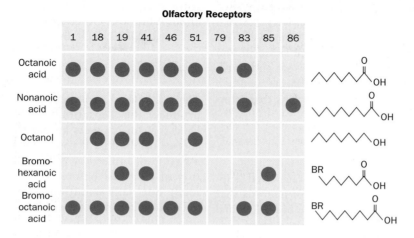

Figure 5.40 (a) Recognition profiles for some odorants. Large dots indicate that the odorant causes a high firing rate for the receptor listed along the top; small dots indicate lower firing rates for the receptor. The structure of the compounds are shown on the right.
Source: Goldstein, E.B. (2007) *Sensation and Perception* (7th edn). California: Thompson.

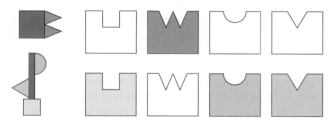

Figure 5.40 (b) The combination code for odour. The receptors that are shown in colour are the ones that respond to the odourant on the left. Notice that each odorant activates a different pattern of receptors, but that a given receptor responds to a number of different odorants.

Source: from Goldstein. *Sensation and Perception, International Edition, 7E.* (c) 2007, Wadsworth, a part of Cengage Learning, Inc. Reproduced by permission. www.cengage.com/permissions

which molecules stimulate which receptors; nor do they know how the information from individual olfactory receptor cells is put together.

Sex differences

Research suggests that women are, on average, better at identifying, recognising and detecting odours than are men (Doty *et al.*, 1985) and give more positive and less negative hedonic emotional responses to some odours (Seubert *et al.*, 2008). This sex difference may have important implications for any study of the neural basis of olfactory processing. If individual differences exist at the behavioural level (for example, detecting, recognising, identifying), then neural activation may be different in men and women when they both smell the same odours. To test this hypothesis, Yousem and his colleagues carried

out an fMRI study of the brain activation of eight right-handed men and eight right-handed women as they smelled pleasant, neutral and unpleasant odours (Yousem *et al.*, 1999). Activation was greater in women, especially in the left and right frontal and perisylvian regions.

The somatosenses

The body senses, or **somatosenses**, include our ability to respond to touch, vibration, pain, warmth, coolness, limb position, muscle length and stretch, tilt of the head and changes in the speed of head rotation. The number of sense modalities represented in this list depends on one's definition of a sense modality. However, it does not really matter whether we say that we respond to warmth and coolness by means of one sense modality or two different ones; the important thing is to understand how our bodies are able to detect changes in temperature.

Many experiences require simultaneous stimulation of several different sense modalities. For example, taste and odour alone do not determine the flavour of spicy food; mild (or sometimes not-so-mild) stimulation of pain detectors in the mouth and throat gives Mexican food its special characteristic. Sensations such as tickle and itch are apparently mixtures of varying amounts of touch and pain. Similarly, our perception of the texture and three-dimensional shape of an object that we touch involves cooperation among our senses of pressure, muscle and joint sensitivity, and motor control (to manipulate the object). If we handle an object and find that it moves smoothly in our hand, we conclude that it is slippery. If, after handling this object, our fingers subsequently slide across each other without much resistance, we perceive a feeling of oiliness. If we sense vibrations when we move our fingers over an object, it is rough. And so on. If you close your eyes as you manipulate some soft and hard, warm and cold, and smooth and rough objects, you can make yourself aware of the separate sensations that interact and give rise to a complex perception.

The skin senses

The entire surface of the human body is innervated (supplied with nerve fibres) by the dendrites of neurons that transmit somatosensory information to the brain. Cranial nerves convey information from the face and front portion of the head (including the teeth and the inside of the mouth and throat); spinal nerves convey information from the rest of the body's surface. All somatosensory information is detected by the dendrites of neurons; the system uses no separate receptor cells. However, some of these dendrites have specialised endings that modify the way they transduce energy into neural activity.

Figure 5.41 shows the sensory receptors found in hairy skin and in smooth, hairless skin (such as skin on the palms of the hands or the soles of the feet). The most common type of skin sensory receptor is the free nerve ending, which resembles the fine roots of a plant. **Free nerve endings** infiltrate the middle layers of both smooth and hairy skin and surround the hair follicles in hairy skin. If you bend a single hair on your forearm, you will see how sensitive the free nerve endings are.

The largest of the special receptive endings, called the Pacinian corpuscle, is visible to the naked eye. **Pacinian corpuscles** are very sensitive to touch. When they are moved, their axons fire a brief burst of impulses. Pacinian

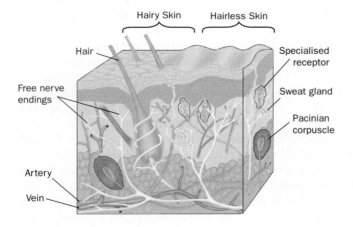

Figure 5.41 Sensory receptors in hairy skin (left) and in hairless skin (right).

corpuscles are thought to be the receptors that inform us about vibration. Other specialised receptors detect other sensory qualities, including warmth, coolness and pain.

Temperature

There is general agreement that different sensory endings produce the sensations of warmth and coolness. Detectors for coolness appear to be located closer to the surface of the skin. If you suddenly place your foot under a stream of rather hot water, you may feel a brief sensation of cold just before you perceive that the water is really hot. This sensation probably results from short-lived stimulation of the coolness detectors located in the upper layers of the skin.

Our temperature detectors respond best to changes in temperature. Within reasonable limits, the air temperature of our environment comes to feel 'normal'. Temporary changes in temperature are perceived as warmth or coolness. Thus, our temperature detectors adapt to the temperature of our environment. This adaptation can be easily demonstrated. If you place one hand in a pail of hot water and the other in a pail of cold water, the intensity of the sensations of heat and cold will decrease after a few minutes. If you then plunge both hands into a bucket of water that is at room temperature, it will feel hot to the cold-adapted hand and cold to the hot-adapted hand. It is mainly the change in temperature that is signalled to the brain. Of course, there are limits to the process of adaptation. Extreme heat or cold will continue to feel hot or cold, however long we experience it.

Pressure

Sensory psychologists speak of touch and pressure as two separate senses. They define touch as the sensation of very light contact of an object with the skin and pressure as the sensation produced by more forceful contact. Sensations of pressure occur only when the skin is actually moving, which means that the pressure detectors respond only while they are being bent. Just how the motion stimulates the neurons is not known. If you rest your forearm on a table and place a small weight on your skin, you will feel the pressure at first, but eventually you will feel nothing at all, if you keep your arm still. You fail to feel the pressure not because your brain 'ignores' incoming stimulation but because your sensory endings actually cease sending impulses to your brain. Studies that have measured the very slow, very minute movements of a weight sinking down into the skin have shown that sensations of pressure cease when the movements stop. With the addition of another weight on top of the first one, movement and sensations of pressure begin again (Nafe and Wagoner, 1941). A person will feel a very heavy weight indefinitely, but the sensation is probably one of pain rather than pressure. In terms of the perception of a person's touch, we judge others' skin to be more pleasant than our own and their forearms as smoother, softer and less sticky (Guest *et al.*, 2009).

Sensitivity to subtle differences in touch and pressure varies widely across the surface of the body. The most sensitive regions are the lips and the fingertips. The most common measure of the tactile discrimination of a region of skin is the **two-point discrimination threshold**. To determine this measure, an experimenter touches a person with one or both legs of a pair of dividers and asks the person to say whether the sensation is coming from one or two points. The further apart the legs of the dividers must be before the person reports feeling two separate sensations, the lower the sensitivity of that region of skin, as seen in Figure 5.42.

Studies have also shown that the brain regions responsible for somatosensation may also be involved in the imagination of somatosensation. Data from neuroimaging studies of visual imagery and the imagination of movement, show that similar brain regions are activated during the actual perception of visual stimuli/the execution of an action and during the imagination of these visual stimuli/imagining making movements. You will find more on this phenomenon in the next chapter.

Pain

Pain is a complex sensation involving not only intense sensory stimulation but also an emotional component. That is, a given sensory input to the brain might be interpreted as pain in one situation and as pleasure in another. For example, when people are sexually aroused, they become less sensitive to many forms of pain and may even find such intense stimulation pleasurable.

Physiological evidence suggests that the sensation of pain is quite different from the emotional reaction to pain. Opiates such as morphine diminish the sensation of pain by stimulating opioid receptors on neurons in the brain; these neurons block the transmission of pain information to the brain. In contrast, some tranquillisers (such as Valium) depress neural systems that are responsible for the emotional reaction to pain but do not diminish the intensity of the sensation. Thus, people who have received a drug like Valium will report that they feel the pain just as much as they did before but that it does not bother them much.

Many noxious stimuli elicit two kinds of pain: an immediate sharp, or 'bright', pain followed by a deep, dull, sometimes throbbing, pain. Some stimuli elicit only one of these two kinds of pain. For example, a pinprick will produce only the superficial 'bright' pain, whereas a hard blow from a blunt object to a large muscle will produce only the deep, dull pain. Different sets of axons mediate these two types of pain. Pain – or the fear of pain – is one of the most effective motivators of human behaviour. However, it also serves us well in the normal course of living. As unpleasant as pain is, we would have difficulty surviving without it. For example, pain tells us if we have sprained an ankle, broken a bone or have an inflamed appendix.

Neuroimaging studies have highlighted how the control of pain is related to different degrees of brain activation. Controlling this activation may reduce pain. For example, Koyama *et al.* (2005) administered thermal pain to 10 healthy volunteers as fMRI measured brain activation. As the pain became more intense, so did activation in the thalamus, prefrontal cortex and anterior cingulate cortex, areas of the brain known to respond to pain. When participants were told that they could expect a reduction in pain, however, there was a decrease in activation in these areas as well as a decrease in self-reported pain.

Taking this finding a step further, deCharms *et al.* (2005) speculated on what might happen if activity in the anterior cingulate cortex (ACC) could be manipulated. If it could be reduced, would participants experience less pain? Hypnosis, for example, has been associated with reduced pain and, in turn, less activation in the ACC. The researchers studied 36 healthy volunteers, some of whom undertook a training course in increasing/decreasing brain activation and pain. These included instructions either to pay attention to the pain or to direct attention away from it; to perceive the stimulus as tissue-damaging, or as a neutral sensory stimulus; to perceive the stimulus as being either very or not very intense; and to control the experience or to be controlled by it. The pain stimulus was heat.

When participants used these instructions to increase or decrease activation in the ACC, the perception of pain changed: those who were instructed to increase ACC activation, experienced more pain. When patients experiencing pain were given the same instructions, decreases in self-reported pain were found after training.

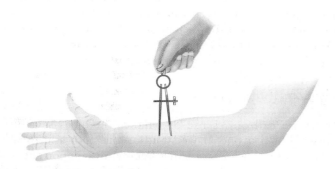

Figure 5.42 The method for determining the two-point discrimination threshold.

The results suggest that when healthy people exposed to pain, and patients experiencing pain, follow instructions designed to reduce activation in a part of the brain known to respond during painful experiences, then such experiences are reduced.

Phantom limbs

A particularly interesting form of pain sensation occurs after a limb has been amputated. After their limbs are gone, up to 70 per cent of amputees report that they feel as though their missing limbs still exist, and that they often hurt. This phenomenon is referred to as the **phantom limb** (Melzak, 1992). People who have phantom limbs report that the limbs feel very real, and they often say that if they try to reach out with their missing limbs, it feels as if they were responding. Sometimes, they perceive the limbs as sticking out, and they may feel compelled to avoid knocking them against the side of a door frame or sleeping in a position that would make the limbs come between them and the mattress. People have reported all sorts of sensations in phantom limbs, including pain, pressure, warmth, cold, wetness, itching, sweatiness and prickliness.

The classic explanation for phantom limbs has been activity of the sensory axons belonging to the amputated limbs. Presumably, this activity is interpreted by the nervous system as coming from the missing limbs. When nerves are cut and connections cannot be re-established between the proximal and distal portions, the cut ends of the proximal portions form nodules known as neuromas. The treatment for phantom pain has been to cut the nerves above these neuromas, to cut the bundles of nerve fibres that bring the information from these nerves into the spinal cord, or to make lesions in somatosensory pathways in the spinal cord, thalamus or cerebral cortex. Sometimes these procedures work for a while, but, unfortunately, the pain often returns.

Melzak (1992) suggests that the phantom limb sensation is inherent in the organisation of the parietal cortex. The parietal cortex is involved in our awareness of our own bodies. Indeed, people who have sensory neglect, caused by lesions of the right parietal lobe, have been known to push their own legs out of bed, believing that they actually belong to someone else. Melzak reports that some people who were born with missing limbs nevertheless experience phantom limb sensations, which would suggest that our brains are genetically programmed to provide sensations for all four limbs even if we do not have them.

The internal senses

Sensory endings located in our internal organs, bones and joints, and muscles convey painful, neutral, and in some cases pleasurable sensory information. For example, the internal senses convey the pain of arthritis, the perception of the location of our limbs, and the pleasure of a warm drink descending to our stomachs.

Muscles contain special sensory endings. One class of receptors, located at the junction between muscles and the tendons that connect them to the bones, provides information about the amount of force the muscle is exerting. These receptors protect the body by inhibiting muscular contractions when they become too forceful. During competition, some weightlifters have received injections of a local anaesthetic near the tendons of some muscles to eliminate this protective mechanism. As a result, they are able to lift even heavier weights. Unfortunately, if they use this tactic, some tendons may snap or some bones may break.

Another set of stretch detectors consists of spindle-shaped receptors distributed throughout the muscle. These receptors, appropriately called **muscle spindles**, inform the brain about changes in muscle length. People are not conscious of the specific information provided by the muscle spindles, but the brain uses the information from these receptors and from joint receptors to keep track of the location of parts of the body and to control muscular contractions.

Together these sensations are called **proprioception** – our sense of bodily position and movement – and the receptors for this sense, as the examples above show, are found in the joints of skeletons and skeletal muscles. Receptors at joints are called mechanoreceptors and these are essential for allowing us to sense the angle of a joint. There are four types of mechanoreceptors, most of which have specific functions such as responding to rapid movement of limbs or maintaining the position of limbs and so on. However, as studies of limb amputation and even hip replacements show, these receptors may take some time to adapt to changing bodily structure or function. People who have had hip replacement surgery, for example, can sense limb position, but they do not sense it very well.

Unlike somatosensation, proprioceptive information seems to recruit different cortical regions so that data about tactile sensation are sent to specific areas of the somatosensory cortex and data from muscle afferents and from joints are sent to different ones. More complex proprioception and tactile sensation most probably involves posterior regions of the parietal lobes.

The vestibular senses

What we call our 'sense of balance' involves several senses, not just one. If we stand on one foot and then close our eyes, we immediately realise how important a role vision plays in balance. The **vestibular apparatus** of the inner ear provides only part of the sensory input that helps us remain upright.

The three **semicircular canals**, located in the inner ear and oriented at right angles to one another, detect changes in rotation of the head in any direction (see Figure 5.43). These canals contain a liquid. Rotation of the head makes the liquid flow, stimulating the receptor cells located in the canals.

Another set of inner ear organs, the **vestibular sacs**, contain crystals of calcium carbonate that are embedded in a gelatin-like substance attached to receptive hair cells. In one sac, the receptive tissue is on the wall; in the other, it is on the floor. When the head tilts, the weight of the calcium carbonate crystals shifts, producing different forces on the cilia of the hair cells. These forces change the activity of the hair cells, and the information is transmitted to the brain.

The vestibular sacs are very useful in maintaining an upright head position. They also participate in a reflex that enables us to see clearly even when the head is being jarred. When we walk, our eyes are jostled back and forth. The jarring of the head stimulates the vestibular sacs to cause reflex

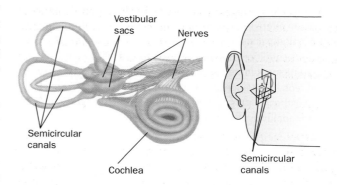

Figure 5.43 The three semicircular canals and two vestibular sacs located in the inner ear.

movements of the eyes that partially compensate for the head movements. People who lack this reflex because of localised brain damage must stop walking in order to see things clearly, for example to read a street sign.

Chapter review

Sensory processing

- We experience the world through our senses. Our knowledge of the world stems from the accumulation of sensory experience and subsequent learning.
- All sensory experiences are the result of energy from events that is transduced into activity of receptors, which are specialised neurons. Transduction causes changes in the activity of axons of sensory nerves, and these changes in activity inform the sensory mechanisms of the brain about the environmental event. The information received from the receptors is transmitted to the brain by means of two coding schemes: anatomical coding and temporal coding.
- In nineteenth-century Germany, Weber devised the concept of the just-noticeable difference (jnd), and Fechner used the jnd to measure the magnitude of sensations.
- The methods of psychophysics apply to all sensory modalities, including sight, smell, taste, hearing and touch.

Vision

- The cornea and lens of the eyes cast an image of the scene on the retina, which contains photoreceptors: rods and cones. Cones gather visual information under illuminated conditions; rods work only when the light is very dim.
- The energy from the light that reaches cones is transduced into neural activity when photons strike molecules of photopigment, splitting them into their two constituents. This

event causes the cones to send information through the bipolar cells to the ganglion cells. The axons of the ganglion cells travel through the optic nerves and form synapses with neurons in the brain.

- Vision requires the behaviour of looking, which consists of moving our eyes and head. Small, involuntary movements keep an image moving across the photoreceptors, thus preventing them from adapting to a constant stimulus.
- Saccadic eye movements are rapid ocular movements that are conjugate in nature; each eye is fixed on the same point.
- The focus of the lenses of the eyes is adjusted when looking from near to distant objects (and vice versa).
- When an image of the visual scene is cast upon the retina, each part of the image has a different colour, which can be specified in terms of its hue (dominant wavelength), brightness (intensity) and saturation (purity).
- Information about colour is encoded trichromatically by your cones; the red, green and blue cones respond in proportion to the amount of the appropriate wavelength contained in the light striking them. This information is transformed into an opponent-process coding, signalled by the firing rates of red/green and yellow/blue ganglion cells, and is transmitted to the brain.
- There are many different types of defective colour vision. Individuals missing a photopigment are called dichromats (and the condition is called dichromacy) and use two primary colours for matching and confuse various colours; anomalous

trichromats (the condition is called anomalous trichromacy) have an altered – not missing – photopigment, and comprise the majority of men with colour defects; protanopia, the most serious condition, appears to result from a lack of the photopigment for red cones: red looks much darker than green, and reds and oranges generally appear very dark.

- Synaesthesia refers to the phenomenon whereby a stimulus in one modality evokes a sensation in another.

Audition

- The physical dimensions of sound – amplitude, frequency and complexity – can be translated into the perceptual dimensions of loudness, pitch and timbre for sounds ranging from 30 Hz to 20,000 Hz.
- Sound pressure waves put the process in motion by setting up vibrations in the eardrum, which are passed on to the ossicles. Vibrations of the stirrup against the membrane behind the oval window create pressure changes in the fluid within the cochlea that cause the basilar membrane to flex back and forth. This vibration causes the auditory hair cells on the basilar membrane to move relative to the tectorial membrane. The resulting pull on the cilia of the hair cells stimulates them to secrete a transmitter substance that excites neurons of the auditory nerve. This process informs the brain of the presence of a sound.
- Two different methods of detection enable the brain to recognise the pitch of a sound. Different high-frequency and medium-frequency sounds are perceived when different parts of the basilar membrane vibrate in response to these frequencies. Low-frequency vibrations are detected when the tip of the basilar membrane vibrates in synchrony with the sound, which causes some axons in the auditory nerve to fire at the same frequency.
- Low-frequency sounds are located by differences in the arrival time of the sound waves in each ear. High-frequency sounds are located by differences in intensity caused by the 'sound shadow' cast by the head.
- The auditory system will analyse sounds of complex timbre into their constituent frequencies, each of which causes a particular part of the basilar membrane to vibrate. All these functions proceed automatically.
- The temporal lobe contains the primary auditory cortex and is active during the comprehension of the phonological aspects of language tasks, and when listening to music.

Gustation and olfaction

- Gustation and olfaction refer to the senses of taste and smell, respectively, and are called chemical senses. Both are served by cells having receptors that respond selectively to various kinds of molecule.
- We can perceive sweet, salty, sour or bitter tastes and a fifth, umami (which delivers a savoury sensation). To most organisms, sweet and moderately salty substances taste pleasant, whereas sour or bitter substances taste unpleasant.
- Sweetness and saltiness receptors permit us to detect nutritious foods and sodium chloride. Sourness and bitterness receptors help us avoid substances that might be poisonous.
- Olfactory information combines with information about taste to provide us with the flavour of a food present in our mouths. We can distinguish countless different odours and can recognise smells encountered in childhood. Women tend to be better detectors of odours than men.
- Unlike visual stimuli, odours do not easily blend. The detection of different odours appears to be accomplished by up to 1,000 different receptor molecules located in the membrane of the olfactory receptor cells.
- Pheromones are chemicals produced by the body which generate a stereotypical behavioural or physiological response without necessarily being detected. The evidence for human pheromones is weak, probably because humans lack the vomeronasal organ necessary to respond to such stimuli.

The somatosenses

- The somatosenses gather several different kinds of information from different parts of the body.
- The skin senses of temperature, touch and pressure, vibration and pain inform us about the nature of objects that come in contact with our skin.
- Pacinian corpuscles in fingers can detect vibration caused by movement which helps us to determine the texture of surfaces.
- Temperature receptors detect hot and cold; free nerve endings can give rise to sensations of pain.
- Sensory receptors in muscles and joints inform the brain of the movement and location of arms and legs. This is called proprioception.
- The vestibular senses help an organism to keep balance.

Suggestions for further reading

Sensation – general reading

Coren, S., Ward, L.M. and Enns, J.T. (2003) *Sensation and perception* (6th edn). Chichester: Wiley.

Goldstein, E.B. (2004) *Blackwell Handbook of Sensation and Perception*. Oxford: Blackwell.

Goldstein, E.B. (2007) *Sensation and Perception*. (7th edn). California: Thompson.

Levine, M.W. and Shefner, J.M. (2000) *Fundamentals of Sensation and Perception*. Oxford: Oxford University Press.

Schiffman, H.R. (2000) *Sensation and Perception: An integrated approach* (5th edn). Chichester: Wiley.

Scientific American, 2006, 16, 3.

Some excellent texts on sensation – and the Goldstein (2007) book is one of the very best on the subject. The special issue of the magazine focuses on the senses and includes excellent articles on the relationship between vision and consciousness, visual microchips, music and the brain, phantom limbs, how the blind draw, the chemistry of smell, and making sense of taste.

Vision

Bruce, V., Green, P. and Georgeson, M. (2003) *Visual Perception: Physiology, psychology and ecology* (4th edn). Hove: Psychology Press.

Gregory, R.L. (1998) *Eye and Brain: The psychology of seeing* (5th edn). New York: Oxford University Press.

Zeki, S. (1993) *A Vision of the Brain*. Oxford: Blackwell Scientific.

These three texts provide an excellent introduction to visual perception. Bruce et al.'s book is a good, solid undergraduate textbook covering most aspects of vision. Gregory's and Zeki's books provide a neurophysiological account of vision: these are exemplary texts of their kind and you should try to consult these.

Audition

King, A.J. and Nelken, I. (2009) Unravelling the principles of auditory cortical processing. *Nature Neuroscience*, 12, 698–701

Moore, D.R. and Shannon, R.V. (2009) Beyond cochlear implants. *Nature Neuroscience*, 12, 6, 686–691

Schnupp, J.W.H. and Carr, C.E. (2009) On hearing with more than one ear. *Nature Neuroscience*, 12, 692–697.

Yost, W.A. (1994) *Fundamentals of Hearing: An introduction* (3rd edn). San Diego: Academic Press.

Zattore, R.J., Berlin, P. and Penhune, V.B. (2002) Structure and function of auditory cortex: Music and speech. *Trends in Cognitive Sciences*, 6, 1, 37–46.

There are many excellent books on hearing. These two are recommended for their thoroughness and accuracy. The Zatorre et al. article is a good review of the role of the cortex in the processing of sound.

Sensory interaction

Kayser, C. (2007) Listening with your eyes. *Scientific American Mind*, 18, 2, 24–29.

A nice article on the interaction between audition and vision.

Somatosensation

Romo, R. and Salinas, E. (2001) Touch and go: Decision-making mechanisms in somatosensation. *Annual Review of Neuroscience*, 24, 107–37.

Dobbs, D. (2007) The pain gate. *Scientific American Mind*, 18, 2, 48–55.

A detailed but informative review of somatosensation and a provocative article on how a rare disorder can shed some light on how we experience pain.

Olfaction and gustation

Doty, R.L. (2003) *Handbook of Olfaction and Gustation* (2nd edn). New York: Dekker.

Martin, G.N. (2004) A neuro-anatomy of flavour. *Petits Propos Culinaires*, 76, 58–82.

Smith, D.V. and Margolskee, R.F. (2001) Making sense of taste. *Scientific American Mind*, March, 26–33.

Doty's edited book covers a broad range of topics related to olfaction and gustation, with a particularly good introductory chapter. The article by Smith and Margolskee provides a very good review of our current understanding of the sense of taste. Martin's article is a good review of the neuro-anatomy of smell and taste.

Journals to consult

Brain

Chemical Senses

Journal of Experimental Psychology: Human perception and performance

Journal of Neuroscience

Nature

Neuroreport

Pain

Perception

Perception and Psychophysics

Psychological Science

Quarterly Journal of Experimental Psychology

Science

Trends in Neurosciences

Vision Research

Website addresses

http://psych.hanover.edu/Krantz/sen_tut.html
A range of sensation and perception demonstrations.

http://krantzj.hanover.edu/classes/Sensation/
John Krantz's page on sensation.

http://ear.berkeley.edu/~ear/
The University of Berkeley's Hearing Sciences web pages; they include demonstrations and links.

http://www.biols.susx.ac.uk/home/Chris_Darwin/Perception/Lecture_Notes/Hearing_Index.html
A large course on auditory perception from the University of Sussex.

http://www.cbn-atl.org/edu_resources/classroom_activities/senses/somatosensation.pdf
A very nice web page illustrating various aspects of somatosensation.

http://online.sfsu.edu/~swilson/emerging/artre325.smelltaste.html
A large collection of gustation and olfaction links.

Perception

In 1988, police raided the home of Cherry Groce, searching for her son, Michael, who was suspected of a robbery at a building society. A police officer shot Mrs Groce in the raid and the incident attracted considerable publicity. Subsequently, the son was apprehended and prosecuted for the robbery, a prosecution based entirely on the evidence of a CCTV (closed circuit television) image which showed a young black man, alleged to be Groce. One witness for the prosecution claimed that he was able to prove that the identities matched by comparing the precise numbers of pixels (the elements which make up a picture) separating key features of the face.

Now this was impressive technical stuff for a jury, until the defence called an expert in facial movement. Alf Linney, a medical physicist from University College London, pointed out that if any of his students had committed such elementary mistakes in face comparison and measurement (not correcting for viewpoint and resolution), they would certainly fail.

Michael Groce was acquitted.

Source: Bruce, 1998, p. 332.

Explore the accompanying videos, simulations, and animations on MyPsychLab. This chapter includes activities on: Facial perception • Recognising the sex of a face • Cues to depth • The phi phenomenon • Check your understanding and prepare for your exams using the multiple choice, short answer and essay practice tests also available.

WHAT YOU SHOULD BE ABLE TO DO AFTER READING CHAPTER 6

- Define perception.
- Describe and understand how form, motion and space might be perceived.
- Describe the way in which the brain processes different types of visual information.
- Describe and understand the way in which we recognise faces and other types of stimuli.
- Understand the consequences of brain damage on visual perception and be aware of how these might help us to understand how the brain normally perceives.

QUESTIONS TO THINK ABOUT

- How do we assemble sensory cues from the environment and turn them into something meaningful?
- What is it about a face that makes it recognisable?
- How can we perceive a moving object as moving?
- How can we tell a moving car from a moving bus or train?
- Damage to which parts of the brain do you think would impair perception?
- Does the brain process different types of perception – form, space, motion, colour – differently?
- Are there stimulus-specific brain regions, ones that respond to specific classes of stimuli but not to others?

The nature of perception

Take a look around you – around the room or out the window. What do you see as you and your eyes move around? Shapes? Figures? Background? Shadows? Areas of light and dark? Your knowledge of the objects you see and their relative location is extensive, and you have a good idea of what they will feel like, even if you have not touched them. If the lighting suddenly changes (if lamps are turned on or off or if a cloud passes in front of the sun), the amount of light reflected by the objects in the scene changes too, but your perception of the objects remains the same – you see them as having the same shape, colour and texture as before. Similarly, you do not perceive an object as increasing in size as you approach it, even though the image it casts upon your retina does get larger. Form, movement and space are the essential elements of perception.

The brain receives fragments of information from approximately 1 million axons in each of the optic nerves. It combines and organises these fragments into the perception of a scene – objects having different forms, colours and textures, residing at different locations in three-dimensional space. Even when our bodies or our eyes move, exposing the photoreceptors to entirely new patterns of visual information, our perception of the scene before us does not change. We see a stable world, not a moving one, because the brain keeps track of our own movements and those of our eyes and compensates for the constantly changing patterns of neural firing that these movements cause.

Definition of perception

Perception is the process by which we recognise what is represented by the information provided by our sense organs. This process gives unity and coherence to this input. Perception is a rapid, automatic, unconscious process; it is not a deliberate one in which we puzzle out the meaning of what we see. We do not first see an object and then perceive it; we simply perceive the object. Occasionally we do see something ambiguous and must reflect about what it might be or gather further evidence to determine what it is, but this situation is more problem-solving than perception. If we look at a scene carefully, we can describe the elementary sensations that are present, but we do not become aware of the elements before we perceive the objects and the background of which they are a part. Our awareness of the process of visual perception comes only after it is com-

plete; we are presented with a finished product, not the details of the process.

The distinction between sensation and perception is not easy to make; in some respects, the distinction is arbitrary. Probably because of the importance we give to vision and because of the richness of the information provided by our visual system, psychologists make a more explicit distinction between visual sensation and perception than they do for any other sensory system.

Perception of form

When we look at the world, we do not see patches of colours and shades of brightness. We see things – cars, streets, people, books, trees, dogs, chairs, walls, flowers, clouds, televisions. We see where each object is located, how large it is, and whether it is moving. We recognise familiar objects and also recognise when we see something we have never seen before. The visual system is able to perceive shapes, determine distances and detect movements; it tells us what something is, where it is located, and what it is doing.

Figure and ground

Most of what we see can be classified as either object or background. Objects are things having particular shapes and particular locations in space. Backgrounds are in essence formless and serve mostly to help us judge the location of objects we see in front of them. Psychologists use the terms **figure** and **ground** to label an object and its background, respectively. The classification of an item as a figure or as a part of the background is not an intrinsic property of the item. Rather, it depends on the behaviour of the observer. If you are watching some birds fly overhead, they are figures and the blue sky and the clouds behind them are part of the background. If, instead, you are watching the clouds move, then the birds become background. If you are looking at a picture hanging on a wall, it is an object. Sometimes, we receive ambiguous clues about what is object and what is background. For example, do you think that Figure 6.1 illustrates two faces or a wine goblet?

What are the characteristics of the complex patterns of light – varying in brightness, saturation and hue – that give rise to perceptions of figures, of things? One of the most important aspects of form perception is the existence of a boundary. If the visual field contains a sharp and distinct change in brightness, colour or texture, we

Figure 6.1 A drawing in which figure and ground can be reversed. You can see either two faces against a white background or a goblet against a dark background.

perceive an edge. If this edge forms a continuous boundary, we will probably perceive the space enclosed by the boundary as a figure, as Figure 6.2 illustrates.

Organisation of elements: the principles of Gestalt

Most figures are defined by a boundary. But the presence of a boundary is not necessary for the perception of form. Figure 6.3 shows that when small elements are arranged in groups, we tend to perceive them as larger figures. Figure 6.4 demonstrates illusory contours – lines that do not exist.

Figure 6.3 Grouping. We tend to perceive a group of smaller elements as a larger figure.

In this figure, the orientation of the pie-shaped objects and the three 45-degree segments makes us perceive two triangles, one on top of the other. The one that looks like it is superimposed on the three black circles even appears to be brighter than the background.

As you saw in Chapter 1, in the early twentieth century, a group of psychologists, Max Wertheimer (1880–1943), Wolfgang Kohler (1887–1967) and Kurt Koffka (1886–1941), devised a theory of perception called **Gestalt psychology**. *Gestalt* is

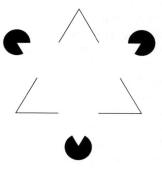

Figure 6.4 Illusory contours. Even when boundaries are not present, we can be fooled into seeing them. The triangle with its point down looks brighter than the surrounding area.

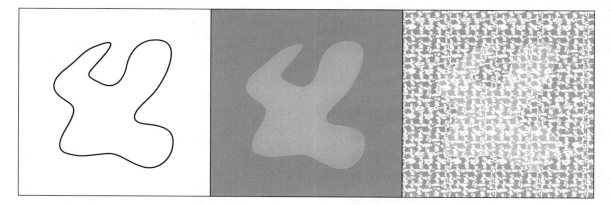

Figure 6.2 Form perception and boundaries. We immediately perceive even an unfamiliar figure when its outline is closed.

the German word for 'form'. They maintained that the task of perception was to recognise objects in the environment according to the organisation of their elements. They argued that in perception the whole is more than the sum of its parts. Because of the characteristics of the visual system of the brain, visual perception cannot be understood simply by analysing the scene into its elements. Instead, what we see depends on the relations of these elements to one another (Wertheimer, 1912).

Elements of a visual scene can combine in various ways to produce different forms. Gestalt psychologists have observed that several principles of grouping can predict the combination of these elements. The fact that our visual system groups and combines elements is useful because we can then perceive forms even if they are fuzzy and incomplete. The real world presents us with objects partly obscured by other objects and with backgrounds that are the same colour as parts of the objects in front of them. The laws of grouping discovered by Gestalt psychologists describe the ability to distinguish a figure from its background.

The **adjacency/proximity principle** states that elements that are closest together will be perceived as belonging together (Wertheimer, 1912). Figure 6.5 demonstrates this principle. The pattern on the left looks like five vertical columns because the dots are closer to their neighbours above and below them than to those located to the right and to the left. The pattern on the right looks like five horizontal rows.

The **similarity principle** states that elements that look similar will be perceived as part of the same form. You can easily see the diamond inside the square in Figure 6.6.

Good continuation is another Gestalt principle and refers to predictability or simplicity. For example, in Figure 6.7 it is simpler to perceive the line as following a smooth course than as suddenly making a sharp bend.

Often, one object partially hides another, but an incomplete image is perceived. The **law of closure** states that our visual system often supplies missing information and 'closes' the outline of an incomplete figure. For example, Figure 6.8 looks a bit like a triangle, but if you

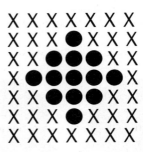

Figure 6.6 The Gestalt principle of similarity. Similar elements are perceived as belonging to the same form.

place a pencil on the page so that it covers the gaps, the figure undeniably looks like a triangle.

The final Gestalt principle of organisation relies on movement. The **principle of common fate** states that elements that move in the same direction will be perceived as belonging together and forming a figure. In the forest, an animal is camouflaged if its surface is covered with the same elements found in the background – spots of brown, tan and green – because its boundary is obscured. There is no basis for grouping the elements on the animal. As long as the animal is stationary, it remains well hidden. However, once it moves, the elements on its surface will move together, and the animal's form will quickly be perceived.

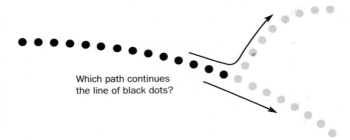

Which path continues the line of black dots?

Figure 6.7 The Gestalt principle of good continuation. It is easier to perceive a smooth continuation than an abrupt shift.

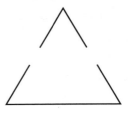

Figure 6.8 The Gestalt principle of closure. We tend to supply missing information to close a figure and separate it from its background. Lay a pencil across the gaps and see how strong the perception of a complete triangle becomes.

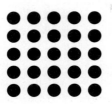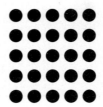

Figure 6.5 The Gestalt principle of proximity. Different spacing of the dots produces five vertical or five horizontal lines.

Models of pattern perception

Templates and prototypes

One explanation for our ability to recognise shapes of objects is that as we gain experience looking at things, we acquire templates, which are special kinds of visual memories stored by the visual system. A **template** is a type of pattern used to manufacture a series of objects (Selfridge and Neisser, 1960). When a particular pattern of visual stimulation is encountered, the visual system searches through its set of templates and compares each of them with the pattern provided by the stimulus. If it finds a match, it knows that the pattern is a familiar one. Connections between the appropriate template and memories in other parts of the brain could provide the name of the object and other information about it, such as its function, when it was seen before, and so forth.

The template model of pattern recognition has the virtue of simplicity. However, it is unlikely that it could actually work because the visual system would have to store an unreasonably large number of templates. Despite the fact that you may look at your hand and watch your fingers wiggling about, you continue to recognise the pattern as belonging to your hand. How many different templates would your visual memory have to contain just to recognise a hand? Figure 6.9 illustrates this problem using the letter A.

A more flexible model of pattern perception suggests that patterns of visual stimulation are compared with prototypes rather than templates. **Prototypes** (Greek for 'original model') are idealised patterns of a particular shape; they resemble templates but are used in a much more flexible way. The visual system does not look for exact matches between the pattern being perceived and the memories of shapes of objects but accepts a degree of disparity; for instance, it accepts the various patterns produced when we look at a particular object from different viewpoints.

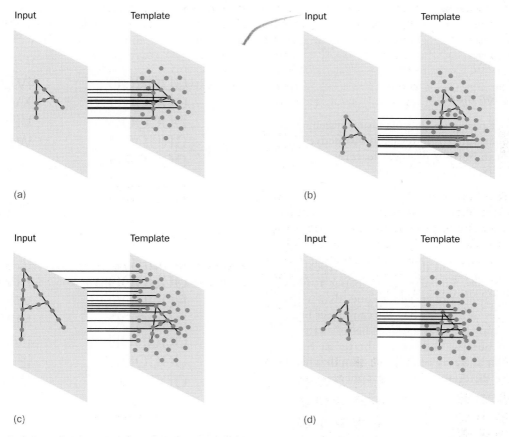

Figure 6.9 These four figures illustrate how template matching can fail. The position of the input may change **(b)**, its size may change **(c)** or its orientation may change **(d)**.

Source: Neisser, U., *Cognitive Psychology*. New York: Appleton-Century-Crofts, 1967. Reprinted with permission.

Most psychologists believe that pattern recognition by the visual system does involve prototypes, at least in some form. For example, you can probably identify maple trees, fir trees and palm trees when you see them. In nature, each tree looks different from all the others, but maples resemble other maples more than they resemble firs, and so on. A reasonable assumption is that your visual system has memories of the prototypical visual patterns that represent these objects. Recognising particular types of tree, then, is a matter of finding the best fit between stimulus and prototype.

The visual system of the brain may indeed contain generic prototypes that help us recognise objects we have never seen before: coffee cups, maple trees, human faces. But we do more than recognise categories of objects; we can recognise particular coffee cups, maple trees or human faces. In fact, we can learn to recognise enormous numbers of objects. Think of how many different people you can recognise by sight, how many buildings in your town you can recognise, how many pieces of furniture in your house and in your friends' houses you are familiar with – the list will be very long. Standing (1973) showed people 10,000 colour slides and found that they could recognise most of them weeks later, even though they had seen them just once.

Feature detection models

Some psychologists suggest that the visual system encodes images of familiar patterns in terms of **distinctive features** – collections of important physical features that specify particular items (Selfridge, 1959). We are better at distinguishing some stimuli from others. We are better at searching for the letter A among a series of Bs than we are searching for the letter B among a series of As; we are better at finding orange-coloured objects in a series of red ones than vice versa; we find it easier to find a tilted item in a series of vertical items than finding a vertical item in a series of tilted ones. Similarly, we are better at finding a mobile object in a series of stationary ones than a stationary one in a series of mobile ones, we can detect bumps in a display of bumpy and flat surfaces better than we can the absence of bumps, and we are better at finding a single stimulus in an array of different stimuli when there are many more different stimuli. It appears, then, that some stimuli have more distinctive features than others and this enhances discrimination.

Figure 6.10 contains several examples of the letter N. Although the examples vary in size and style, recognising them is not problematic because your visual system contains a specification of the distinctive features that fit the criterion for an N: two parallel vertical lines connected by

Figure 6.10 Distinctive features. We easily recognise all of these items as the letter N.

a diagonal line sloping downward from the top of the left one to the bottom of the right one.

An experiment by Neisser (1964) supports the hypothesis that perception involves analysis of distinctive features. Figure 6.11 shows one of the tasks he asked people to do. The figure shows two columns of letters. The task is to scan through them until you find the letter Z, which occurs once in each column.

You probably found the letter in the left column much faster than you did the one in the right column. Why? The letters in the left column share few features with those found in the letter Z, so the Z stands out from the others. In contrast, the letters in the right column have

GDOROC	IVEMXW
COQUCD	XVIWME
DUCOQG	VEMIXW
GRUDQO	WEKMVI
OCDURQ	XIMVWE
DUCGRO	IVMWEX
ODUCQG	VWEMXI
CQOGRD	IMEWXV
DUZORQ	EXMZWI
UCGROD	IEMWVX
QCUDOG	EIVXWM
RQGUDO	WXEMIV
DRGOQC	MIWVXE
OQGDRU	IMEVXW
UGCODQ	IEMWVX
ODRUCQ	IMWVEX
UDQRGC	XWMVEI
ORGCUD	IWEVXM

Figure 6.11 A letter-search task. Look for the letter Z hidden in each column.

Source: Adapted from Neisser, J., Visual search. *Scientific American Mind*, 1964, 210, 94–102.

many features in common with the target letter, and thus the Z is 'camouflaged'.

There are some phenomena that cannot easily be explained by the distinctive-features model. The model suggests that the perception of an object consists of analysis and synthesis; the visual system first identifies the component features of an object and then adds up the features to determine what the object is. We might expect, then, that more complex objects, having more distinctive features, would take longer to perceive. But often, the addition of more features, in the form of contextual cues, speeds up the process of perception. Figure 6.12 contains two sets of four items. One item in each is different from the other three.

The patterns in both sets differ with respect to only one feature: the tilt of the diagonal line. But the addition of the horizontal and vertical lines in Figure 6.12 (b) makes the perceptual task much easier. We see a triangle and three right angles bisected by a diagonal line; the triangle just pops out as being different. If we perceived individual features (such as the diagonal lines) before perceiving more complex figures (such as triangles and bisected right angles) that are composed of these features, then we should perceive simpler figures faster than we perceive more complex ones. The fact that we do not means that a perception is not simply an assembly of individual features.

The distinctive-features model appears to be a reasonable explanation for the perception of letters, but what about

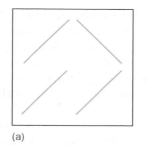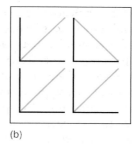

(a) (b)

Figure 6.12 Contextual cues. Perceiving a simple stimulus is facilitated by contextual cues. The line that does not match the other three is more easily recognised in (b).

more natural stimuli, which we encounter in places other than the written page? Biederman (1987, 1990) suggests a model of pattern recognition that combines some aspects of prototypes and distinctive features. He suggests that the shapes of objects that we encounter can be constructed from a set of 36 different shapes that he refers to as **geons**. Figure 6.13 illustrates a few geons and some objects that can be constructed from them. Perhaps, Biederman suggests, the visual system recognises objects by identifying the particular sets and arrangements of geons that they contain.

Even if Biederman is correct that our ability to perceive categories of common objects involves recognition of geons, it seems unlikely that the geons are involved in

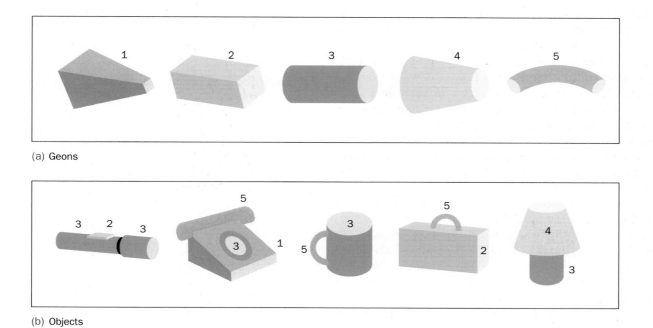

(a) Geons

(b) Objects

Figure 6.13 Geons for perception. **(a)** Several different geons. **(b)** The combination of two or three geons (indicated by the numbers) into common three-dimensional objects.

Source: Adapted from Biederman, I., Higher-level vision. In *An Invitation to Cognitive Science. Vol. 2: Visual Cognition and Action*, edited by D.N. Osherson, S.M. Kosslyn and J. Hollerbach. Cambridge, MA: MIT Press, 1990.

perception of particular objects. For example, it is difficult to imagine how we could perceive faces of different people as assemblies of different sets of geons. The geon hypothesis appears to work best for the recognition of prototypes of generic categories: telephones or torches in general rather than the telephone on your desk or the torch a friend lent you.

Biederman points out that particular features of figures – cusps and joints formed by the ends of line segments – are of critical importance in recognising drawings of objects, presumably because the presence of these joints enables the viewer to recognise the constituent geons. Figure 6.14 shows two sets of degraded images of drawings of five common objects. One set, (a), shows the locations of cusps and joints; the other, (b), does not.

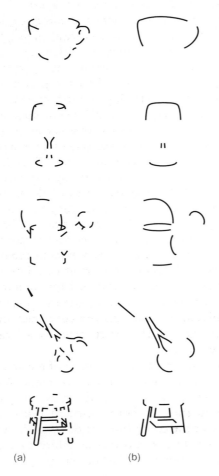

(a)   (b)

Figure 6.14 Incomplete figures. **(a)** With cusps and joints. **(b)** Without cusps and joints. Which set is easier to recognise?

Source: Adapted from Biederman, I., Higher-level vision. In *An Invitation to Cognitive Science. Vol. 2: Visual Cognition and Action*, edited by D.N. Osherson, S.M. Kosslyn and J. Hollerbach. Cambridge, MA: MIT Press, 1990.

Biederman (1990) observed that people found the items with cusps and joints much easier to recognise.

Top-down processing: the role of context

We often perceive objects under conditions that are less than optimum; the object is in a shadow, camouflaged against a similar background or obscured by fog. Nevertheless, we usually manage to recognise the item correctly. We are often helped in our endeavour by the context in which we see the object. For example, look at Figure 6.15. What do you see? Can you tell what they are? Now look at Figure 6.16. With the elements put in context it is quite easy to see what they are.

Palmer (1975b) showed that even more general forms of context can aid in the perception of objects. He first showed his participants familiar scenes, such as a kitchen. Next, he used a tachistoscope to show them drawings of individual items and asked the participants to identify them. A **tachistoscope** can present visual stimuli very briefly so that they are difficult to perceive (nowadays we would use a computer to perform the same function). Sometimes, participants saw an object that was appropriate to the scene, such as a loaf of bread. At other times, they saw an inappropriate but similarly shaped object, such as a letterbox (see Figure 6.17).

Figure 6.15 Simple elements that are difficult to recognise without a context.

Figure 6.16 An example of top-down processing. The context facilitates our recognition of the items shown in Figure 6.15.

Source: Adapted from Palmer, S.E., in *Explorations in Cognition*, D.A. Norman, D.E. Rumelhart and the LNR Research Group. San Francisco: W.H. Freeman, 1975.

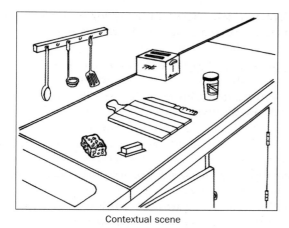

Contextual scene

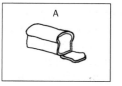 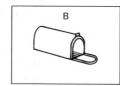

A   B

Target object (presented very briefly)

Figure 6.17 Stimuli from the experiment by Palmer (1975b). After looking at the contextual scene, participants were shown one of the stimuli below it very briefly, by means of a tachistoscope.

Source: Palmer, S.E., The effects of contextual scenes on the identification of objects. *Memory and Cognition*, 1975, 3, 519–26. Reprinted by permission of the Psychonomic Society, Inc.

Palmer found that when the objects fitted the context that had been set by the scene, participants correctly identified about 84 per cent of them. But when they did not, performance fell to about 50 per cent. Performance was intermediate in the no-context control condition, under which subjects did not first see a scene. Thus, compared with the no-context control condition, an appropriate context facilitated recognition and an inappropriate one interfered with it.

The context effects demonstrated by experiments such as Palmer's are not simply examples of guessing. That is, people do not think to themselves, 'Let's see, that shape could be either a letterbox or a loaf of bread. I saw a picture of a kitchen, so I suppose it's a loaf of bread.' The process is rapid, unconscious and automatic; thus, it belongs to the category of perception rather than to problem-solving, which is much slower and more deliberate. Somehow, seeing a kitchen scene sensitises the neural circuits responsible for the perception of loaves of bread and other items we have previously seen in that context.

Psychologists distinguish between two categories of information-processing models of pattern recognition: bottom-up processing and top-down processing. In **bottom-up processing**, also called data-driven processing, the perception is constructed out of the elements – the bits and pieces – of the stimulus, beginning with the image that falls on the retina. The information is processed by successive levels of the visual system until the highest levels (the 'top' of the system) are reached, and the object is perceived. **Top-down processing** refers to the use of contextual information – to the use of the 'big picture'. Presumably, once the kitchen scene is perceived, information is sent from the 'top' of the system down through lower levels. This information excites neural circuits responsible for perceiving those objects normally found in kitchens and inhibits others. Then, when the subject sees a drawing of a loaf of bread, information starts coming up through the successive levels of the system and finds the appropriate circuits already warmed up, so to speak.

Haenny *et al.* (1988) obtained direct evidence that watching for a particular stimulus can, indeed, 'warm up' neural circuits in the visual system. They trained monkeys to look at a pattern of lines oriented at a particular angle, to remember that pattern, and then to pick it out from a series of different patterns presented immediately afterwards. A correct response would be rewarded by a sip of fruit juice. While the animals were performing the task, the experimenters recorded the activity of individual neurons in the visual association cortex. They found that watching for a pattern of lines having a particular orientation affected the responsiveness of the neurons. For example, if the monkeys were watching for a pattern containing lines oriented at 45 degrees, neurons that detected lines of that orientation responded more vigorously than normal when that pattern was presented again. Haenny *et al.* found that this enhancement could even be produced by letting the monkeys feel the orientation of a pattern of grooves in a metal plate they could not see; when a subsequent visual pattern contained lines whose orientation matched that of the grooves, a larger neural response was seen.

In most cases, perception consists of a combination of top-down and bottom-up processing. Figure 6.18 shows several examples of objects that can be recognised only by a combination of both forms of processing. Our knowledge of the configurations of letters in words provides us with the contexts that permit us to organise the flow of information from the bottom up.

Direct perception: Gibson's affordances

In the chapter so far we have considered some of the mechanisms that underlie visual perception. But is this perception a response or a process? That is, is visual perception an

TAE CAT RED SPOT FISH

Figure 6.18 Examples of combined top-down/bottom-up processing. The effect of context enables us to perceive the letters despite the missing or ambiguous features. Note that a given letter may be perceived in more than one way, depending on the letters surrounding it.

Source: Adapted from McClelland, J.J., Rumelhart, D.E. and Hinton G.E., in *Parallel Distributed Processing*. Vol. 1: *Foundations*, edited by D.E. Rumelhart, J.L. McClelland and the PDP Research Group. © 1986 the Massachusetts Institute of Technology; published by the MIT Press, Cambridge, MA.

active or passive process? We saw in an earlier section on cross-cultural differences that context is important for visual perception. The psychologist J.J. Gibson took this notion a step further. Over a period of 35 years, Gibson proposed a theory of perception which argued that perception was direct and did not depend on cognitive processes to bring together fragmented data (Gibson, 1950, 1966, 1979). Because of this, it is considered a direct theory of perception. Originally, Gibson was interested in distinguishing between unsuccessful and successful Second World War pilots. Some of the unsuccessful pilots were unable to land accurately and seemed unable to appreciate distance. However, Gibson found that even when these pilots were given training in depth perception – which may have remedied the problem – they continued to have difficulty.

According to Gibson, 'perceiving is an act, not a response; an act of attention, not a triggered impression; an achievement, not a reflex' (Gibson, 1979). Gibson's view of perception was that classical optical

science ignored the complexity of real events. For example, it would focus on the effects of trivial, basic or simple stimuli on perceptual response. Gibson abandoned the depth/space perception view of the world and, instead, suggested that our perception of surfaces was more important. Surfaces comprised ground (which we discussed earlier) and texture elements in surfaces that would be attached or detached. Attached features would include bumps and indentations in the surface, such as rocks or trees; detached features would include items such as animals (which are detached from the surface).

Given the complex world in which we live, we must be able to perceive not just simple stimuli but stimuli which mean something more to us. We must decide whether an object is throwable or graspable, whether a surface can be sat upon and so on. We ask ourselves what can this object furnish us with, what does it afford us (Gibson, 1982)? These are the meanings that the environment has and Gibson called them **affordances**. Thus, Gibson highlighted the ecological nature of perception: we do not simply perceive simple stimuli but these stimuli mean something more in a wider, more complex context. This was a radical departure in visual perception because it implied that the perception of object meaning is direct. Perception involves determining whether something is capable of being sat upon or is throwable.

However, the theory is not without its problems. Costall (1995), for example, suggests that some affordances may not be able to afford. Imagine the ground covered in frost and a frozen lake. According to Gibson, the ground afforded walking. However, although the frosty ground does, the frozen lake may not. Similarly, although we might agree with Gibson that some surfaces are graspable or supporting we might disagree quite reasonably with the notion that surfaces are edible, for example, that they afford eating. Our decision that something is edible appears to rely on more than direct perception of surfaces.

Face perception

Although object perception is important to us, the perception of specific categories of stimuli may be even more important. One such category is 'faces'. Being able to recognise and identify faces is one of the most important social functions human beings can perform (Bruce, 1994). It helps us form relationships with people, spot faces in a crowd and provides us with potential non-verbal cues as to what a person is thinking or feeling (the role of emotion in facial expression is returned to in Chapter 13).

see activity on **mypsychlab**

Psychologists in the nineteenth century were interested in what makes a face attractive and constructed composites – averages of several different images – to produce a face which they believed was attractive (Galton, 1878; Stoddard, 1886). Recent work has provided a clearer account of what makes an attractive face; it has also helped to indicate which features of the face best allow us to remember a face or which make a face distinctive.

We can identify people better on the basis of the eyes than the mouth and both are more important than the nose (Bruce *et al.*, 1993), even when hairstyle, make-up and facial hair are removed or minimised. A three-dimensional image of a face – such as that seen in three-quarter profile – is better recognised than is a full-frontal photograph. Upright faces are better recognised and identified than are those upside down but there is a curious phenomenon called the 'Thatcher effect', first described by the British psychologist, Peter Thompson (1980). Take a look at the faces in Figure 6.19. They look fairly normal – you can easily identify the image as a face and, while you can see that the faces are inverted, the features appear to be in the right place, and are identifiable.

Now, turn the book upside down and look at the photographs again. It is a grotesque image, but only eyes and the mouth have been turned around (inverted) to create this effect. This is the Thatcher effect (so-called because

Thompson created his stimuli using the face of the British Prime Minister).

Women and girls tend to be better than men and boys at decoding people's facial expression of emotion (McClure, 2000). Women are better at identifying upright faces even when they are masked by visual noise or when there is a delay between the presentation of the face and recall (McBain *et al*; 2009). Figure 6.20 illustrates some of the stimuli in McBain *et al*'s experiment.

Sex of the face

We can usually discriminate between faces more quickly on the basis of their users' sex than familiarity (Bruce *et al.*, 1987). Enlow (1982) and Moss *et al.* (1987), for example, have suggested that men have larger noses and nasopharynxes, more prominent brows, a more sloping forehead and more deeply set eyes than do women. Shepherd (1989) noted that women had fuller cheeks and less facial hair (including eyebrows). Women are also thought to have smaller noses, a more depressed bridge of the nose, a shorter upper lip, and larger eyes with darker shadows, especially young women (Liggett, 1974).

When facial features are presented in isolation, eyes are the most reliable indicator of sex and the nose is the least reliable. With hair concealed, 96 per cent of partici-

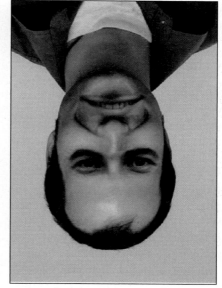

Figure 6.19 The Thatcher effect – turn the page upside down to experience the effect.

Source: Grüter, T., Grüter, M. and Carbon, C-C. Neural and genetic foundations of face recognition and prosopagnosia. *Journal of Neuropsychology* (2008), 2, 79–97, figure 3.

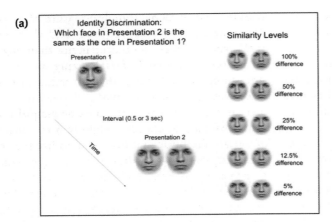

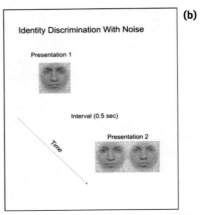

Figure 6.20 **(a)** Face images utilised in the standard and delayed conditions of the facial identity discrimination task. **(b)** Face images utilised in the visual noise condition of the facial identity discrimination task.

Source: McBain, R, Norton, D. and Chen, Y. Females excel at basic face perception. *Acta Psychologica* (2009), 130, 168–73, figure 3.

pants were able to distinguish between faces based on sex (Burton *et al.*, 1993). When individual facial features or pairs of features (such as brow and eyes, nose and mouth) were presented to participants, the features which afforded the best opportunity to make sex discriminations were, in this order: brow and eyes, brow alone, eyes alone, whole jaw, chin, nose and mouth, and mouth alone (Brown and Perrett, 1993). These findings suggest that all facial features carry some information about sex (except the nose) but suggest that it is difficult to find even one or two features which distinguish absolutely between men's and women's faces. Some features, however, provide better clues than others.

Distinctiveness and attractiveness

Each of us finds different faces attractive: some of us find faces friendlier than others, some meaner and others more sexually alluring. Although individual differences exist at this, what seems like, subjective level, studies have shown that some features of the face are generally regarded as more attractive than others. The distinctiveness of the face – defined as the deviation from the norm – is unrelated to attractiveness (Bruce *et al.*, 1994). Galton had hypothesised that averageness was attractiveness. That is, the more average-looking the face, the more attractive it was likely to be. This hypothesis was tested and challenged by Perrett *et al.* (1994), who compared the attractiveness ratings for average, attractive and highly attractive Caucasian female faces.

Perrett *et al.*, using special computer technology, constructed an average composite of photographs of 60 female faces. The 15 faces rated as most attractive from the original 60 were then averaged. Finally, the attractiveness of this average was enhanced by 50 per cent to provide a 'highly attractive' composite. Composites similar to those used in the experiment can be seen in Figure 6.21.

Caucasian raters found the 'attractive' composite more attractive than the average composite and the highly attractive composite more attractive than the 'attractive' composite, thus disconfirming Galton's hypothesis. Furthermore, when similar composites were made of Japanese women, the same results were obtained: both Caucasian and Japanese raters found the enhanced composite more attractive. What distinguished an average face from an attractive one?

Analysis of the composites showed that the more attractive faces had higher cheek bones, a thinner jaw and larger eyes relative to the size of the face. There was also a shorter distance between mouth and chin and between nose and mouth in the attractive faces.

Evolutionary psychologists argue that we are attracted to average faces because this behaviour evolved as a solution to attracting healthy mates – best to stick with what you know and can trust. An alternative view is that we are simply attracted to the familiar – a well-known psychological phenomenon. If this were true, we should be attracted to average-looking stimuli that are non-faces too. This is what Halberstadt and Rhodes (2000) found. They asked people to rate a selection of watches, birds and dogs for attractiveness and

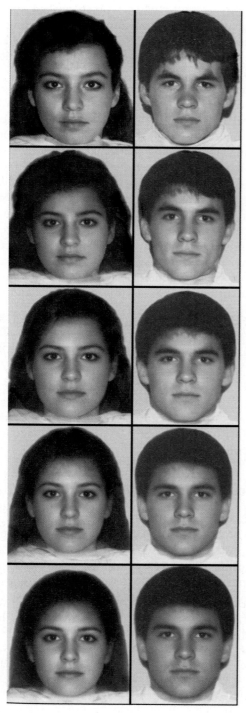

Figure 6.21 Faces similar to those used in Perrett *et al.*'s (1994) experiment. The faces are 'morphed' from averagely attractive (top two faces) to very attractive (bottom two faces). Most people rate the last two faces as most attractive.

Source: From Young, A.W. and Bruce, V., Pictures at an exhibition: The science of the face. *The Psychologist*, 1998, 11(3), 120–5 (see www.thepsychologist.org.uk).

prototypicality (how typical they were of a category), or averageness. The researchers found that participants rated the average-looking stimuli as being the most attractive. One reason for this may be that we have a preference for averageness which 'reflects a more general preference for familiar stimuli'.

In one experiment, Caucasian participants rated their own-race face-composites as more attractive than those of other races but this finding was limited to the male faces (Rhodes *et al.*, 2005). When average composites of Caucasian and Japanese faces were judged, Caucasians preferred the mixed race composite, especially if the face was of the opposite sex. Japanese and Caucasian participants, asked to judge the attractiveness of Caucasian and Japanese faces (from extremely Caucasian and Japanese, to the other end of the continuum) rated the mixed-race composite as most attractive.

Does the attractiveness of a face actually have consequences for us, beyond immediate physical liking for a person? Langlois *et al.* (2000) analysed over 900 studies of people's behaviour towards attractive and unattractive individuals. They found that not only was there agreement between people and cultures about who is attractive and who is not, but also that attractive children and adults were treated and judged more positively than were unattractive children and adults (even when people knew the unattractive individuals).

Although turning hoary maxims such as 'beauty is in the eye of the beholder' on its head, Langlois *et al.* note that the studies they reviewed categorised people into either attractive or unattractive only. Gradations of attractiveness may have elicited different responses in people so that averagely attractive people may have elicited more positive responses than their excessively attractive or unattractive counterparts.

There is also mixed evidence regarding the type of 'sexual' face that we like: some studies suggest that we prefer more feminised faces; others that we like masculinised ones (Johnston, 2006). The explanation for our preference for feminised faces is that they are more youthful, warm and honest; masculinised faces are more cold, dominant, dishonest. Faces morphed to look younger are rated as significantly more attractive (Ishi *et al.*, 2004).

Attractive faces whose gaze is direct can have a knock-on positive effect on our judgements of unrelated objects (Strick *et al.*, 2008). A directly gazing face is considered significantly more attractive than an indirectly gazing one. We also like objects more if we see a person smiling at them than if they show disgust. Furthermore, we are more likely to engage socially with people if they look at us directly. Strick *et al.* paired novel objects – pictures of unknown peppermint brands – with an attractive or unattractive face which looked straight at the participant or which averted its gaze. Participants rated the attractiveness of these objects.

As predicted, objects paired with a directly gazing attractive face were more positively evaluated than were objects paired with an indirectly gazing attractive face or an unattractive face.

We also, naturally, spend more time looking at beautiful faces than unattractive ones, but a study from a group of US researchers has found that although women spend more time looking at beautiful male and female faces than they do unattractive ones, men spend longer than women looking at beautiful female faces (Levy *et al.*, 2008).

What do you find attractive in an attractive face? Do your preferences match those found in experimental studies? Do you think that some facial features we find attractive are so subtle that we cannot consiously detect them?

Face preference and menstrual cycle

When we see faces, we normally make judgements about them – some studies show that women prefer exaggeratedly masculine male faces whereas some studies show that men and women prefer 'average-looking' faces. Women's preference for men's faces can change across the menstrual cycle. Penton-Voak and Perrett (2000) found that women in the follicular phase of their cycle were significantly more likely to prefer a masculine face than those in menses or in the luteal phase. This, the authors provocatively suggest, shows that 'women are attracted to relatively exaggerated male traits when conception following coitus is more likely (days 6–14 of the follicular phase) and not at other times in the menstrual cycle'.

One explanation for the preference is that during this fertile phase of the cycle, women are more likely to seek a sexual partner (and, potentially, a father for their child) who shows evidence of 'genetic benefits' (strength, assertiveness, etc.). This explanation is based on limited experimental data, however, and more direct behaviour – such as the interaction between men and women – has not been studied.

Gangestad *et al.* (2004) found that women during the high fertility portion of their menstrual cycle were more attracted to men who showed social presence and 'intra-sexual competitiveness' than in their low fertility days. Social presence was characterised by composure, having an athletic presence, maintaining eye contact, lack of self-deprecation, lack of downward gaze and 'lack of nice-guy self-presentation'. Direct intrasexual competitiveness was defined by behaviours that derogated competitors, lacked laughter and were directly sexually competitive. This pref-

erence only emerged when women wished short-term rather than long-term relationships, suggesting that a man's demeanour can significantly alter perceived attractiveness by women high in fertility, but this attraction may be short-lived.

A study of 70 young women has found that their level of a hormone called testosterone (described in Chapter 13) is related to how attractive they found others: the greater the testosterone, the greater their attraction to masculine faces (Welling *et al.*, 2007). Another study has found that although very masculine male faces are judged to be dominant, their owners are less likely to be judged suitable as a long-term partner by women than are owners of less masculine faces (Boothroyd *et al.*, 2007).

The group also measured women's judgements of the attractiveness of men's faces across various points of their menstrual cycle. Symmetrical faces are usually judged to be more attractive than asymmetrical ones and there is evidence that facial symmetry in men and women is associated with perceived healthiness (Rhodes *et al.*, 2007) and self-reported extraversion (Pound *et al.*, 2007). The researchers found that women preferred more symmetrical faces when the women were at their most fertile but this preference was found only when the women were seeking a short-term partner or if the women already had a partner (Little *et al.*, 2007). The results suggest that this facial feature may maximise mating by encouraging short-term relationships.

Theories of face perception

The mechanisms that allow us to perceive faces are considered to be different from those that allow us to perceive objects; face perception has been thought of as 'special' (Farah *et al.*, 1998). Face perception involves a number of operations. We can perceive general characteristics such as the colour, sex and age of a face; we can perceive whether a face expresses anger, sadness or joy; we can distinguish familiar from unfamiliar faces. What model of face processing can account for these operations?

Bruce and Young (1986) have suggested that face processing is made up of three functions: perception of facial expression, perception of familiar faces and perception of unfamiliar faces. Why does the model separate these functions? Bruce and Young reviewed extensive evidence which suggested that each of these functions is dependent on different cognitive abilities. Evidence from neuropsychology also supports such a model.

Some patients with right hemisphere damage, as we will see later in the chapter, can perceive and correctly identify emotion in facial expressions, and the sex and age of faces, but they cannot identify faces (Tranel *et al.*, 1988). In a classic study, Young *et al.* (1993) studied face perception in ex-servicemen who had sustained missile wounds to the posterior left and right hemispheres. They administered a series of face perception tests which included tests of familiar face identification, matching unfamiliar faces and facial expression identification. The experimenters found that one patient was poor at identifying familiar faces only, another was selectively poor at matching unfamiliar faces and a group of men was impaired at analysing facial expressions.

Current views of face processing argue that we exploit three strategies when we recognise faces. One strategy involves recognising the features of a face, a second involves recognising the relations between features in a face (configural processing) and a third suggests that we recognise the whole face (the holistic approach) (Gruter *et al.*, 2008). Configural processing works when faces are upright, but fails when they are inverted, à la the Thatcher effect.

Perception of space and motion

In addition to being able to perceive the forms of objects in our environment, we are able to judge quite accurately their relative location in space and their movements. Perceiving where things are and perceiving what they are

doing are obviously important functions of the visual system (Decety *et al.*, 1997; Jeannerod, 1997).

Depth perception

Depth perception requires that we perceive the distance of objects in the environment from us and from each other. We do so by means of two kinds of cues: binocular ('two-eye') and monocular ('one-eye'). Binocular cues arise from the fact that the visual fields of both eyes overlap. Only animals that have eyes on the front of the head (such as primates, cats and some birds) can obtain binocular cues. Animals that have eyes on the sides of their heads (such as rabbits and fish) can obtain only monocular cues.

One monocular cue involves movement and thus must be experienced in the natural environment or in a motion picture. The other monocular cues can be represented in a drawing or a photograph. Most of these cues were originally discovered by artists and only later studied by psychologists (Zeki, 1998). Figure 6.22 shows the most important sources of depth cues.

Binocular cues

Convergence provides an important cue about distance. The eyes make conjugate movements so that both look at (converge on) the same point of the

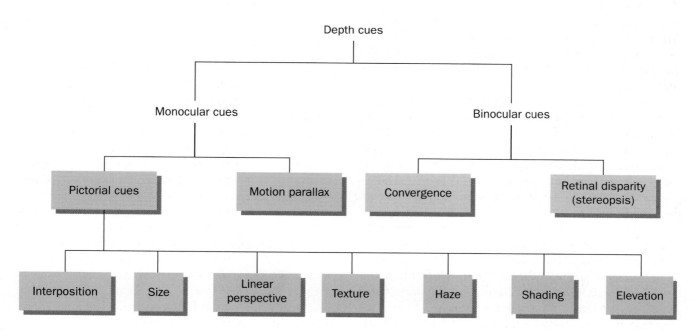

Figure 6.22 The principal monocular and binocular depth cues.

Source: From Margaret W. Matlin and Hugh H.J. Foley, *Sensation and Perception*, 3rd edn © 1992. Published by Allyn & Bacon, Boston, MA. Copyright © by Pearson Education. By permission of the publisher.

visual scene. If an object is very close to your face, your eyes are turned inwards. If it is farther away, they look more nearly straight ahead. Thus, the eyes can be used like range finders. The brain controls the extraocular muscles, so it knows the angle between them, which is related to the distance between the object and the eyes. Convergence is most important for perceiving the distance of objects located close to us, especially those we can reach with our hands (see Figure 6.23).

Another important factor in the perception of distance is the information provided by **retinal disparity** ('unlikeness' or 'dissimilarity'). Hold up a finger of one hand at arm's length and then hold up a finger of the other hand midway between your nose and the distant finger. If you look at one of the fingers, you will see a double image of the other one. Whenever your eyes are pointed towards a particular point, the images of objects at different dis-

tances will fall on different portions of the retina in each eye. The amount of disparity produced by the images of an object on the two retinas provides an important clue about its distance from us.

The perception of depth resulting from retinal disparity is called **stereopsis**. A stereoscope is a device that shows two slightly different pictures, one for each eye. The pictures are taken by a camera equipped with two lenses, located a few inches apart, just as our eyes are. When you look through a stereoscope, you see a three-dimensional image. An experiment by Julesz (1965) demonstrated that retinal disparity is what produces the effect of depth. Using a computer, he produced two displays of randomly positioned dots in which the location of some dots differed slightly. If some of the dots in one of the displays were displaced slightly to the right or the left, the two displays gave the impression of depth when viewed through a stereoscope.

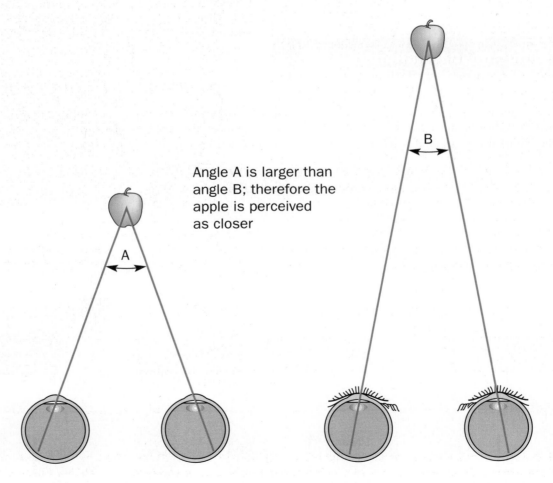

Angle A is larger than angle B; therefore the apple is perceived as closer

Figure 6.23 Convergence. When the eyes converge on a nearby object, the angle between them is greater than when they converge on a distant object. The brain uses this information in perceiving the distance of an object.

Figure 6.24 shows a pair of these random-dot stereograms. If you look at them very carefully, you will see that some of the dots near the centre have been moved slightly to the left. Some people can look at these figures without using a stereoscope and see depth. If you want to try this, hold the book at arm's length and look at the space between the figures. Now pretend you are looking 'through' the book, into the distance. Each image will become double, since your eyes are no longer converged properly. If you keep looking, you might make two of these images fuse into one, located right in the middle. Eventually, you might see a small square in the centre of the image, raised above the background.

Monocular cues

One of the most important sources of information about the relative distance of objects is **interposition** (meaning 'placed between'). If one object is placed between us and another object so that the closer object partially obscures our view of the more distant one, we can immediately perceive which object is closer to us.

Obviously, interposition works best when we are familiar with the objects and know what their shapes should look like. Just as the Gestalt law of good continuation plays a role in form perception, the principle of good form affects our perception of the relative location of objects: we perceive the object having the simpler border as being closer. Figure 6.25 (a) can be seen either as two rectangles, located one in front of the other (Figure 6.25 (b)), or as a rectangle nestled against an L-shaped object (Figure 6.25 (c)). Because we tend to perceive an ambiguous drawing according to the principle of good form, we are more likely to perceive Figure 6.25 (a) as two simple shapes – rectangles – one partly hiding the other.

Figure 6.24 A pair of random-dot stereograms.

Source: Julesz, B., Texture and visual perception. *Scientific American*, 212, 1965, 12, 38–48. © 1965 Scientific American, Inc. Reprinted with permission of Dr. Bela Julesz.

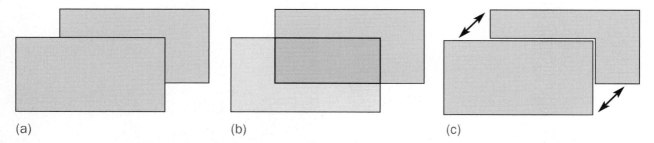

(a)   (b)   (c)

Figure 6.25 Use of the principle of good form in the perception of depth. The two objects shown in **(a)** could be two identical rectangles, one in front of the other, as shown in **(b)** or a rectangle and an L-shaped object, as shown in **(c)**. The principle of good form states that we will see the ambiguous object in its simplest (best) form – in this case a rectangle. As a result, the shape to the right is perceived as being partly hidden and thus further away from us.

Another important monocular distance cue is provided by our familiarity with the sizes of objects. For example, if a car casts a very small image on our retinas, we will perceive it as being far away. Knowing how large cars are, our visual system can automatically compute the approximate distance from the size of the retinal image.

Figure 6.26 shows two columns located at different distances. The drawing shows **linear perspective**: the tendency for parallel lines that recede from us to appear to converge at a single point. Because of perspective, we perceive the columns as being the same size even though they produce retinal images of different sizes. We also perceive the segments of the wall between the columns as rectangular, even though the image they cast on the retina does not contain any right angles.

Texture, especially the texture of the ground, provides another cue we use to perceive the distance of objects sitting on the ground. A coarser texture looks closer, and a finer texture looks more distant. The earth's atmosphere, which always contains a certain amount of haze, can also supply cues about the relative distance of objects or parts of the landscape. Parts of the landscape that are further away become less distinct because of haze in the air. Thus, **haze** provides a monocular distance cue (see Figure 6.27).

The patterns of light and shadow in a scene – its **shading** – can provide us with cues about the three-dimensional shapes of objects. Although the cues that shading provides do not usually tell us much about the absolute distances of objects from us, they can tell us which parts of objects are closer and which are further away. Figure 6.28 illustrates the power of this phenomenon. Some of the circles look as

Figure 6.26 Principle of perspective. Perspective gives the appearance of distance and makes the two columns look similar in size.

Figure 6.27 Cues from atmospheric haze. Variation in detail, owing to haze, produces an appearance of distance.
Source: Powerstock SuperStock, reprinted by permission.

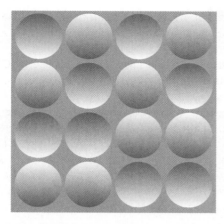

Figure 6.28 Depth cues supplied by shading. If the tops of the circles are dark, they look like depressions. If the bottoms are dark, they appear as bumps.

if they bulge out towards us; others look as if they were hollowed out (dimpled). The only difference is the direction of the shading. Our visual system appears to interpret such stimuli as if they were illuminated from above. Thus, the top of a convex (bulging) object will be light and the bottom will be in shadow. If you turn the book upside-down, the bulges and dimples will reverse.

These features are important to practical aspects of our lives, an example of which appears in the Psychology in Action section below.

Psychology in action – CCTV and face perception

Imagine that you are spending your Saturday afternoon in a busy shopping centre. Browsing in a store, you spot a particularly attractive shirt and take it to the sales counter. When you place the shirt and your wallet/purse on the counter, you feel someone nudge you from behind. You turn around but when you return to the shirt on the counter, you notice that your wallet/purse has disappeared. A person whose face you partly see is running out of the store. Fortunately, the police manage to apprehend a suspect and the store detective informs you that he has video surveillance footage of a man who might be the thief. The suspect does not have your wallet but the image on the surveillance camera looks like the suspect. How accurately would you be able to match the suspect to the image on the video screen?

The increasing use of CCTV has led to an increase in the reliance on CCTV evidence in prosecutions but CCTV footage is usually variable in quality with camera angles and lighting conditions producing an unclear image of the top or back of the head (Bruce, 1998). Changing the lighting conditions reduced performance in a task which required individuals to match the face they had seen with a photograph (Hill and Bruce, 1996). Changing the viewpoint also impaired recognition accuracy but changing both lighting and viewpoint did not make performance any worse. According to a 2009 UK Home Office and police report, around 80 per cent of CCTV images are of no practical use because they are of such poor quality.

Matching faces (and even recognising familiar surfaces) was more accurate when lighting was from above. Why? One explanation is that light from above provides more information by casting fewer shadows. Hill and Bruce (1996) suggest that lighting a face from the bottom reverses the brightness of

facial areas such as the eye sockets and nostrils. In fact, lighting of this sort makes the face look like a negative. This study highlights an important point about face perception (and about the erroneous testimony described at the opening of the chapter). Our recognition of faces is not simply based on 'edge' information, that is, on contour. The shape of the face (viewpoint) and shading are crucial in enabling us to make accurate recognition judgements.

Is recognition improved if the face is moving? After all, a moving image might give more information about shading, shape and contour than would a static one. Some researchers have reported that a moving image is more advantageous to accurate recognition than is a static one (Pike *et al.*, 1997; Knight and Johnston, 1997). Others have found little improvement in recognition when moving and static images are compared (Christie and Bruce, 1998).

Recognition is also enhanced by familiarity. Burton *et al.* (1999) took video footage of male and female university psychology lecturers caught on security cameras at the entrance to the psychology department. They then asked psychology and non-psychology students, as well as experienced police officers, to view this footage and then asked them to indicate which of the people in a set of high-quality photographs they had seen on tape. Psychology students made more correct identifications than did the non-psychology students or police officers, suggesting that previous familiarity with the target helps with recognition.

In the second experiment, the researchers looked at which specific bits of information the participants used to identify the target. They took the same video footage, but this time they either obscured the head, the body or the gait.

Psychology in action – *Continued*

Participants performed quite inaccurately when gait and body were obscured but were significantly worse at identifying the target when the head was obscured. Thus the advantage of familiarity – at least, in this experiment – was due to recognition of facial features rather than the way in which people walk or their body shape. Unusual gaits or shapes may produce different results.

When people watched CCTV footage of a person and then tried to match the image in the footage with either a single snapshot or an array of snapshots, people performed the task poorly (Bruce *et al.*, 2001). However, when the participants knew the person in the footage – the targets were the participants' teachers or colleagues – they were significantly better at the task. Even in experiments where participants were made briefly familiar with the image they were exposed to, this period of familiarisation did not help the participant recognise the face.

According to Bruce *et al.* (2001), 'where a person is recognised on a CCTV image by someone familiar to them, these identifications should be taken very seriously, even if the CCTV image is of low quality'. They refer to the case of the London nail bomber, David Copeland, as an illustration of this finding. Copeland was responsible for killing three people and injuring 129 others in nail bomb explosions in three areas of London – Soho, Brick Lane and Brixton – in the spring of 1999. Copeland's final crime was committed in the Admiral Duncan pub in Soho, Central London. He left the pub at 6.05 p.m. The bomb exploded as Copeland made his way back to his hotel. Three people were killed, four required amputations and 26 suffered burns (Hopkins and Hall, 2000). Eighty minutes before the bomb was detonated Copeland's colleague had telephoned the police and told them that he thought the bomber identified on CCTV and publicised on television looked like his workmate. By that evening, police were planning a raid on Copeland's house.

Bruce *et al.*'s research suggests that this use of CCTV may be one of its most effective.

The site of the bomb placed by David Copeland. Copeland was apprehended after a colleague recognised his face from CCTV footage shown on television. Research suggests that recognition of people seen in CCTV footage is significantly more accurate if these people are familiar. If the target person is not familiar, the likelihood of false positives (making an incorrect identification) increases.

Source: Metropolitan Police Service

Distance and location

When we are able to see the horizon, we perceive objects near it as being distant and those above or below it as being nearer to us. Thus, **elevation** provides an important monocular depth cue. For example, cloud B and triangle B in Figure 6.29 appear further away from us than do cloud A and triangle A.

So far, all the monocular distance cues discussed have been those that can be rendered in a drawing or captured by a camera. However, another important source of distance information depends on our own movement. Try

the following demonstrations. If you focus your eyes on an object close to you and move your head from side to side, your image of the scene moves back and forth behind the nearer object. If you focus your eyes on the background while moving your head from side to side, the image of the nearer object passes back and forth across the background. Head and body movements cause the images from the scene before us to change; the closer the object, the more it changes relative to the background. The information contained in this relative movement helps us to perceive distance.

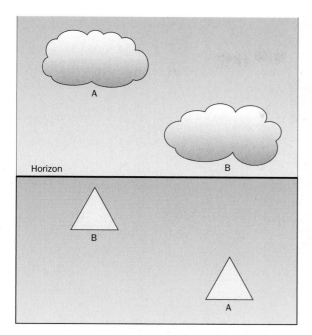

Figure 6.29 Depth cues supplied by elevation. The objects nearest the horizontal line appear furthest away from us.

Source: Adapted from Matlin, M.W. and Foley, H.J., *Sensation and Perception* (3rd edn). Boston: Allyn & Bacon, 1992.

Figure 6.30 illustrates the kinds of cue supplied when we move with respect to features in the environment. The top part of the figure shows three objects at different distances from the observer: a man, a house and a tree. The lower part shows the views that the observer will see from five different places (P_1–P_5). The changes in the relative locations of the objects provide cues concerning their distance from the observer. The phenomenon is known as **motion parallax** (*parallax* comes from a Greek word meaning 'change').

Constancies of visual perception

An important characteristic of the visual environment is that it is almost always changing as we move, as objects move, and as lighting conditions change. However, despite the changing nature of the image the visual environment casts on our retinas, our perceptions remain remarkably constant.

Visual perception across cultures

From birth onwards, we explore our environment with our eyes. The patterns of light and dark, colour and movement, produce changes in the visual system of the brain. There is evidence, however, that perception is not absolute, that it varies across cultures. Ecological variables such as those associated with geography, cultural codes and education influence perception.

The visual stimulation we receive, particularly during infancy, affects the development of our visual system. If the environment lacks certain features – certain visual patterns – then an organism might fail to recognise the significance of these features if it encounters them later in life (Blakemore and Mitchell, 1973). But this is not the only type of environment that can influence perception.

There may also be differences in the cultural codes found in pictorial representations (Russell *et al.*, 1997). Although artists have learned to represent all the monocular depth cues (except for those produced by movement) in their paintings, not all cues are represented in the traditional art of all cultures. For example, many cultures do not use linear perspective. Does the absence of particular cues in the art of a particular culture mean that people from this culture will not recognise them when they see them in paintings from another culture?

It is quite rare for a member of one culture to be totally unable to recognise a depiction as a depiction (Russell *et al.*, 1997). However, Deregowski *et al.* (1972) found that when the Me'en tribe of Ethiopia, a culture unfamiliar with pictures, were shown a series of pictures from a children's colouring book, they would smell them, listen to the pages while flexing them, examine their texture but would ignore the actual pictures. They did recognise depictions of indigenous animals, suggesting that the familiarity of a pictorial depiction is important for recognition within cultures. Familiar objects are sometimes depicted in an exaggerated way. Aboriginal depictions of the crocodile, for example, are distorted: the trunk is seen from above and the head and tail from the side (Dziurawiec and Deregowski, 1992), although this finding may be attributable to the fact that such animals are difficult to draw.

There are other geographical influences on perception. People who live in 'carpentered worlds', that is worlds in which buildings are built from long, straight pieces of material that normally join each other in right angles, are more likely to be subject to the Müller–Lyer illusion. This illusion is shown in Figure 6.31. Look at the two vertical lines and decide which is longer.

Actually, the lines are of equal length. Segall *et al.* (1966) presented the Müller–Lyer illusion (and several others) to groups of subjects from Western and non-Western cultures. Most investigators believe that the Müller–Lyer illusion is a result of our experience with the angles formed by the intersection of walls, ceilings and floors (Redding and Hawley, 1993). The angled lines can be seen as examples of linear perspective (see Figure 6.32). In fact, Segall and his colleagues did find that people from 'carpentered' cultures were more susceptible to this illusion: experience with straight lines forming right angles appeared to affect people's perception.

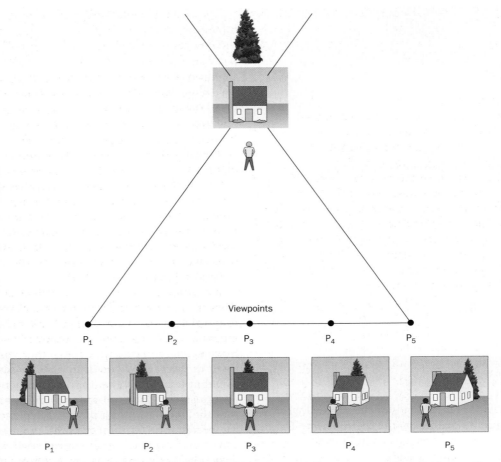

Figure 6.30 Motion parallax. As we move from P1 to P5, the relative locations of the man, tree and house change. These changes enable us to make inferences about the relative positions of these objects.

Source: From *HABER, Psychology of Visual Perception*, 1st ed. (c) 1973 Wadsworth, a part of Cengage Learning, Inc. reproduced by permission, www.cengage.com/permissions

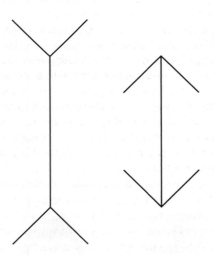

Figure 6.31 The Müller–Lyer illusion. The two vertical lines are actually equal in length, but the one on the left appears to be longer.

Figure 6.32 The impact of culture on the Müller–Lyer illusion. People from 'non-carpentered' cultures that lack rectangular corners are less likely to be susceptible to this illusion. Although the two vertical lines are actually the same height, the one on the right looks shorter.

Controversies in Psychological Science – How does language influence visual perception?

The issue

The effects on perception of another cultural code – language – have received much attention from psychologists for a good reason. Words for shades of light and colour seem to be more limited in some cultures than others. The Inuit, for example, have more than one name for various shades of snow, whereas Africans have different words for different shades of sand, presumably because these features form a crucial part of the culture's environment. There are also differences in the number of colour words that different cultures use. This has important implications for our understanding of the cross-cultural generalisability of colour perception which we discussed in Chapter 5. For example, do all cultures use all the primary and secondary colour terms? Does the word 'blue' mean the same across cultures? Do cultures have different words for various shades of blue? If so, why?

The evidence

In the mid-nineteenth century, the British statesman William Gladstone noted that the writings of the ancient Greeks did not contain words for brown or blue. Perhaps the ancient Greeks did not perceive these colours. Magnus (1880) investigated this hypothesis by gathering both linguistic and perceptual data. He sent questionnaires and colour chips to Western residents of European colonies and asked them to test the abilities of the native people to distinguish among the various colours. He assumed that language would reflect perceptual ability. If a language did not contain words to distinguish between certain colours, then the people who belonged to that culture would not be able to distinguish these colours perceptually.

Magnus was surprised to discover very few cultural differences in people's ability to perceive various colours. Linguistic differences did not appear to reflect perceptual differences. The issue emerged again in the mid-twentieth century with the principle of **linguistic relativity**. Briefly stated, this principle asserts that language used by the members of a particular culture is related to these people's thoughts and perceptions. The best-known proponent of this principle, Benjamin Whorf, stated that 'the background linguistic system. . . of each language is not merely a reproducing instrument for voicing ideas but rather is itself a shaper of ideas, the program and guide for the individual's mental activity, for his analysis of impressions, for his synthesis of his mental stock-of-trade' (Whorf, 1956, p. 212). This became known as the **Sapir–Whorf hypothesis** – the idea that language can determine thought (Kay and Kempton, 1984).

Proponents of linguistic relativity suggested that colour names were cultural conventions – that members of a given culture could divide the countless combinations of hue, satura-tion and brightness (defined in Chapter 5) that we call colours into any number of different categories (Kay et al., 1997). Each category was assigned a name, and when members of that culture looked out at the world, they perceived each of the colours they saw as belonging to one of these categories.

Two anthropologists, Berlin and Kay, examined this hypothesis in a linguistic study of a wide range of languages. They found the following eleven primary colour terms: black, white, red, yellow, green, blue, brown, purple, pink, orange and grey (Berlin and Kay, 1969; Kay, 1975; Kay et al., 1991). The authors referred to these as focal colours. Not all languages used all eleven (as English does). In fact, some languages used only two: black and white (Heider, 1972). Others, such as Russian, had two words for blue.

If a language contained words for three primary colours, these colours were black, white and red. If it contained words for six primary colours, these were black, white, red, yellow, green and blue. Berlin and Kay suggested that basic colour terms would be named more quickly than non-basic colour terms, that basic terms would be more salient, that is, they would be elicited first if you asked people to name colours spontaneously, and that basic terms would be more common in written communications such as texts. In fact, people do respond more quickly to basic than they do to non-basic colour terms across a range of languages; when asked to write down a list of as many colour words in five minutes as possible and draw a line under the last words written, every minute, basic terms invariably appear at the beginning of the list (Corbett and Davies, 1997). Similarly, Heider (1971) found that both children and adults found it easier to remember a colour chip of a focal colour (such as red or blue) than one of a non-focal colour (such as turquoise or peach).

In a famous cross-cultural study, Heider (1972) studied members of the Dani culture of New Guinea. The language of the Dani people has only two basic colour terms: *mili* ('black') and *mola* ('white'). Heider assembled two sets of colour chips, one containing focal colours and the other containing non-focal colours. She taught her participants arbitrary names that she made up for the colours. Even though the participants had no words in their language for any of the colours, the group learning names for focal colours learned the names faster and remembered them better.

Categorical perception of colour refers to our ability to discriminate between two colours that seem to fall along a continuum. However, speakers of Berinmo and Himba do not distinguish a boundary between green and blue, which suggests that categorical perception is not universal. Roberson et al. (2008) tested this hypothesis in a group of native Korean- and English-speaking adults. Koreans distinguish between

▶

Controversies in Psychological Science – *Continued*

yeondu and *chorok*. The boundary between the two was described as 'green' by English speakers. Korean speakers were faster at discriminating between colours marked as a boundary in Korean but not English, but not at distinguishing between colours that fell within a colour category. The faster participants showed categorical perception only when stimuli appeared in the right visual field; slower participants showed categorical perception in both visual fields, suggesting that categorical perception may be verbally mediated by the left hemisphere.

Conclusion

Colour is a difficult topic to study cross-culturally. The evidence suggests, however, that although there are cultural variations in the number of colour words used, there seems to be cross-cultural agreement on the colours considered as 'basic'.

Brightness constancy

People can judge the whiteness or greyness of an object very well, even if the level of illumination changes. If you look at a sheet of white paper either in bright sunlight or in shade, you will perceive it as being white, although the intensity of its image on your retina will vary. If you look at a sheet of grey paper in sunlight, it may in fact reflect more light to your eye than will a white paper located in the shade, but you will still see the white paper as white and the grey paper as grey. This phenomenon is known as **brightness constancy**.

Katz (1935) demonstrated brightness constancy by constructing a vertical barrier and positioning a light source so that a shadow was cast to the right of the barrier. In the shadow, he placed a grey square card on a white background. In the lighted area on the left of the barrier, he placed a number of shades of grey and asked participants to choose one that matched the grey square in the shadow (see Figure 6.33).

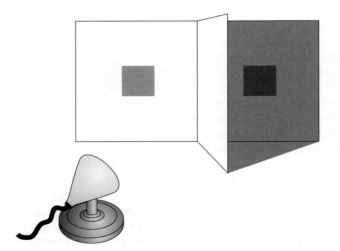

Figure 6.33 Brightness constancy as demonstrated by the experiment by Katz (1935).

His participants matched the greys not in terms of the light that the cards actually reflected but in terms of the light they would have reflected had both been viewed under the same level of illumination. In other words, the participants compensated for the dimness of the shadow. The match was not perfect, but it was much closer than it would have been if perception of brightness had been made solely on the basis of the amount of light that fell on the retina. The perception of white and grey, then, is not a matter of absolutes; rather, the colours are perceived relative to the surrounding environment.

Form constancy

When we approach an object or when it approaches us, we do not perceive it as getting larger. Even though the image of the object on the retina gets larger, we perceive this change as being due to a decrease in the distance between ourselves and the object. Our perception of the object's size remains relatively constant.

The unchanging perception of an object's size and shape when it moves relative to us is called **form constancy**. Psychologists also refer to size constancy, but size is simply one aspect of form. In the nineteenth century, Hermann von Helmholtz suggested that form constancy was achieved by **unconscious inference**, a mental computation of which we are unaware. We know the size and shape of a familiar object. Therefore, if the image it casts upon our retina is small, we perceive it as being far away; if the image is large, we perceive it as being close. In either case, we perceive the object itself as being the same size.

Form constancy also works for rotation. The drawing in Figure 6.34 (a) could be either a trapezoid or a rectangle rotated away from us. However, the extra cues clearly identify the drawing in Figure 6.34 (b) as a window, and experience tells us that windows are rectangular rather than trapezoidal; thus, we perceive it as rectangular. Obviously, this effect will not be seen in members of cultures that do not have buildings fitted with rectangular windows (or seen by people unfamiliar with the object).

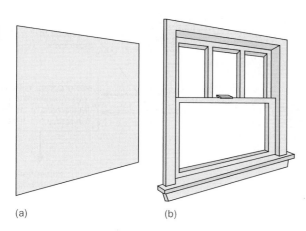

Figure 6.34 Form constancy. **(a)** This figure can be perceived as a trapezoid. **(b)** Because we recognise this figure as a window, we perceive its shape as rectangular.

Figure 6.35 Effect of perceived distance. Although both letterboxes are exactly the same size, the upper one looks larger because of the depth cues (perspective and texture) that surround it. If you turn the book upside-down and look at the picture, thus disrupting the depth cues, the letterboxes look the same size.

The process just described works for familiar objects. However, we often see unfamiliar objects whose size we do not already know. If we are to perceive the size and shape of unfamiliar objects accurately, we must know something about their distance from us. An object that produces a large retinal image is perceived as big if it is far away and small if it is close. Figure 6.35 illustrates this phenomenon. Although the two letterboxes are exactly the same size, the one that appears to be further away looks larger. If you turn the book upside-down and look at the figure again, the appearance of depth is greatly diminished, and the two letterboxes appear to be approximately the same size.

Perception of motion

Detection of movement is one of the most primitive aspects of visual perception (Milner and Goodale, 1995). This ability is seen even in animals whose visual systems do not obtain detailed images of the environment. Of course, our visual system can detect more than the mere presence of movement. We can see what is moving in our environment and can detect the direction in which it is moving.

Adaptation and long-term modification

One of the most important characteristics of all sensory systems is that they show adaptation and rebound effects. For example, when you stare at a spot of colour, the adaptation of neurons in your visual system will produce a negative after-image if you shift your gaze to a neutral background; and if you put your hand in some hot water, warm water will feel cool to that hand immediately afterwards.

Cutting edge – Content over style?

When we see a work of art, what do we perceive first – the content, the style, the colour? A new development in the study of art perception is microgenesis – the process whereby our perception of art can be broken down into sub-types of perception, each varying in complexity. For example, which perceptual features are necessary for us to identify an image presented for 1 ms or 50 ms?

Researchers from the University of Salzburg and Vienna used this technique to examine the point at which people were able to distinguish between two works of art that varied in style or content (Augustin *et al.*, 2008). The researchers pre-sented participants with two images on a computer monitor and asked them how similar they were. The images varied according to content (trees, flowers, houses, men/boys) and style (Cezanne, Chagall, Kirchner, Van Gogh). Presentation times were 10, 50, 202 and 3,000 ms. The time taken to make the judgement was recorded.

Participants were able to distinguish between content at all presentation times, but effects of style became apparent at 50 ms. That is, participants were able to distinguish between works of art of different styles even when presented for only 50 ms, despite having no prior education in art.

Motion, like other kinds of stimuli, can give rise to adaptation and after-effects. Tootell *et al.* (1995) presented participants with a display showing a series of concentric rings moving outwards, like the ripples in a pond. When the rings suddenly stopped moving, participants had the impression of the opposite movement – that the rings were moving inwards. During this time, the experimenters scanned the participants' brains to measure their metabolic activity. The scans showed increased activity in the motion-sensitive region of the visual association cortex, which lasted as long as the illusion did. Thus, the neural circuits that give rise to this illusion appear to be located in the same region that responds to actual moving stimuli.

Interpretation of a moving retinal image

As you read this book, your eyes are continuously moving. Naturally, the eye movements cause the image on your retina to move. You can also cause the retinal image to move by holding the book close to your face, looking straight ahead, and moving it back and forth. In the first case, when you were reading normally, you perceived the book as being still. In the second case, you perceived it as moving. Why does your brain interpret the movement differently in these two cases? Try another demonstration. Pick a letter on this page, stare at it, and then move the book around, following the letter with your eyes. This time you will perceive the book as moving, even though the image on your retina remains stable. Thus, perception of movement requires coordination between movements of the image on the retina and those of the eyes.

Obviously, the visual system must know about eye movements in order to compensate for them in interpreting the significance of moving images on the retina. Another simple demonstration suggests the source of this information. Close your left eye and look slightly down and to the left. Gently press your finger against the outer corner of the upper eyelid of your right eye and make your right eye move a bit. The scene before you appears to be moving, even though you know better. This sensation of movement occurs because your finger – not your eye muscles – moved your eye. When your eye moves normally, perceptual mechanisms in your brain compensate for this movement. Even though the image on the retina moves, you perceive the environment as being stationary. However, if the image moves because the object itself moves or because you push your eye with your finger, you perceive movement (see Figure 6.36).

In general, if two objects of different size are seen moving relative to each other, the smaller one is perceived as moving and the larger one as standing still. We perceive people at a distance moving against a stable background and flies moving against an unmoving wall. Thus, when an experimenter moves a frame that encloses

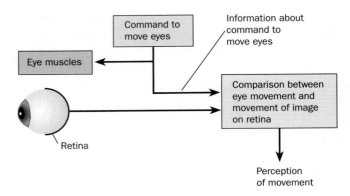

Figure 6.36 A schematic representation of the brain mechanisms responsible for the interpretation of a moving retinal image. This system must compensate for eye movements.

a stationary dot, we tend to see the dot move, not the frame. This phenomenon is also encountered when we perceive the moon racing behind the clouds, even though we know that the clouds, not the moon, are moving.

Perception of movement can even help us perceive three-dimensional forms. Johansson (1973) demonstrated just how much information we can derive from movement. He dressed actors in black and attached small lights to several points on their bodies, such as their wrists, elbows, shoulders, hips, knees and feet. He made films of the actors in a darkened room while they were performing various behaviours, such as walking, running, jumping, limping, doing push-ups, and dancing with a partner who was also equipped with lights. Even though observers who watched the films could only see a pattern of moving lights against a dark background, they could readily perceive the pattern as belonging to a moving human and could identify the behaviour the actor was performing. Subsequent studies (Kozlowski and Cutting, 1977; Barclay *et al.*, 1978) showed that people could even tell, with reasonable accuracy, the sex of the actor wearing the lights. The cues appeared to be supplied by the relative amounts of movement of the shoulders and hips as the person walked.

Combining information from successive fixations

As Chapter 5 showed, when examining a scene, our eyes do not roam slowly around; rather, they make rapid step-like movements called saccades. After each saccade, the eyes rest for a while, gathering information before moving again. These stops are called **fixations**. The visual system combines the information from each fixation and perceives objects too large or too detailed to see in a single glance. Obviously, in doing so, it must keep track of the locations of each of the fixations.

Figure 6.37 (a) illustrates an impossible object. At first glance, the lines represent a three-dimensional object. However, careful inspection shows that the object cannot

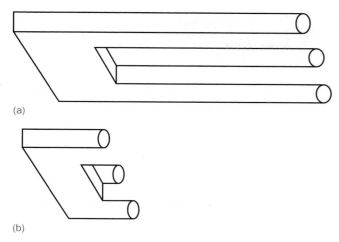

(a)

(b)

Figure 6.37 **(a)** An impossible figure. Only after carefully studying the figure do we see that it cannot be a drawing of a real three-dimensional object. **(b)** An unconvincing impossible figure. When the legs are short enough so that the entire figure can be perceived during a single fixation, the figure does not look paradoxical.

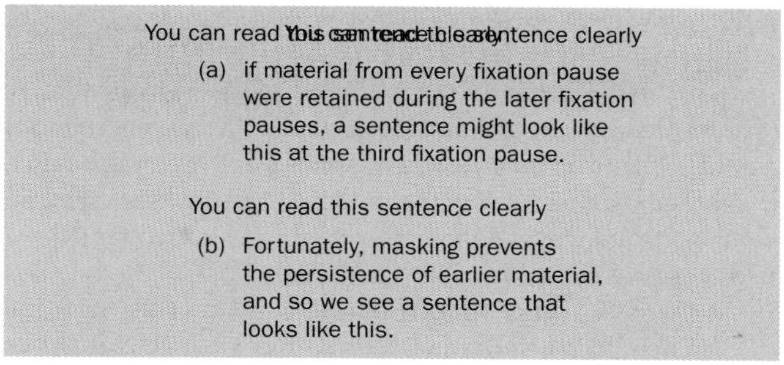

You can read **This can reade any**tence clearly

(a) if material from every fixation pause were retained during the later fixation pauses, a sentence might look like this at the third fixation pause.

You can read this sentence clearly

(b) Fortunately, masking prevents the persistence of earlier material, and so we see a sentence that looks like this.

Figure 6.38 The role of backward masking. If each saccade did not erase the remaining image from the previous fixation, we probably would not be able to read.

Source: From Margaret W. Matlin and Hugh H.J. Foley, *Sensation and Perception*, 3rd edn © 1992. Published by Allyn & Bacon, Boston, MA. Copyright © by Pearson Education. By permission of the publisher.

possibly exist. But the drawing in Figure 6.37 (b) creates a very different impression; it does not look at all like a unified three-dimensional object. The difference in the two impressions is that the details of the larger figure cannot be gathered in a single glance. Apparently, when we look from one end of the figure to the other, the information we gather from the first fixation is slightly modified to conform to the image of the second one. Of course, the two images do not exactly match, as a careful inspection shows.

Clearly, what we see during one fixation affects what we see in another. If two visual stimuli are presented, one after the other, the second stimulus could sometimes erase the image of the first. That is, under the appropriate conditions, the subject would fail to perceive the image that came first. This phenomenon is known as **backward masking** (Werner, 1935).

Normally, backward masking can be demonstrated only in the laboratory, where the shape and intensity of the stimuli and the time interval between them can be carefully controlled. Breitmeyer (1980) suggests that the explanation for this phenomenon lies in the nature of the saccadic movements made by the eyes when gathering information about the visual environment. For example, consider the saccadic movements that your eyes make as you read a line of text in this book. You do not stop and look at each letter or even at each word; instead, you make several fixations on each line. During each one, your visual system gathers information and begins decoding the letters and words. Your eyes move on, and you perceive more words. Breitmeyer suggests that each saccade erases the image remaining from the previous fixation, leaving only the information that has been analysed by the visual system. Figure 6.38 illustrates what might happen if this erasure did not occur.

Perception and the environment – An international perspective

A good science tries to create theories that apply generally to most contexts, events or people. In psychology's case, a good theory should apply to all people. However, there are instances where group differences test this assumption, such as when cultures are compared across some variable. For example, there is a small amount of evidence to suggest that differences in visual perception exist between Western people and those from East Asia – Westerners tend to perceive objects more analytically and in a more focused way; East Asians are more likely to attend to the context in which objects appear (i.e. they perceive a scene 'holistically') (Choi and Nisbett, 1998; Chua *et al.*, 2005a).

In one study where American and Japanese participants were asked to describe an underwater scene, Americans were more likely to describe objects in the water but the Japanese reported 60 per cent more information about the background environment (Masuda and Nisbett, 2001). In a different scenario, Americans were also able to identify an object (a tiger) more accurately than were the Japanese when it appeared against a different background from that in which it was originally seen. Why does this focal v. context effect occur? One reason might be the types of eye movement made by different cultures.

To test this hypothesis, Chua *et al.* (2005) asked American and Chinese participants to view scenes in which objects

Perception and the environment – *Continued*

appeared against complex backgrounds. The eye movement of participants as they viewed the object and scene were then tracked. Compared with the Chinese, Americans focused on specific objects and more quickly. The Chinese made more saccades – eye movements – to the background.

The researchers suggest that this effect could partly be explained by socialisation. East Asians grow up and live in complex social networks in which paying attention to context is important (perhaps more important than focusing on individual objects or people); Westerners, however, are educated to value individuality and independence (and eye movement is, therefore, directed accordingly). This extends even to cultural products. An analysis of advertising and popular texts in Western and Asian (Korea, Japan, China)/Mexican cultures found that the latter were more individualistic and less collectivistic (Morling and Lamoreaux, 2008).

Similar cultural effects can occur when rating facial expressions. Participants in one experiment were asked to rate the degree of emotion shown in cartoons depicting happy, sad, angry or neutral facial expressions. These faces were surrounded by other people expressing the same or different emotion (Masuda *et al.*, 2008). The surrounding stimuli influenced the ratings of Japanese participants significantly more than they did Westerners. This was evidenced by eye-tracking data. The Japanese spent more time looking at the surrounding stimuli than did the Westerners. The lack of self-absorption of Japanese participants was also seen in an experiment in which people completed a verbal fluidity task – where there was an opportunity to cheat – in front of a mirror (Heine *et al.*, 2008). North Americans were more self-critical and less likely to cheat in front of the mirror; the Japanese participants were unaffected by the presence of a mirror.

Perception of movement in the absence of motion

If you sit in a darkened room and watch two small lights that are alternately turned on and off, your perception will be that of a single light moving back and forth between two different locations. You will not see the light turn off at one position and then turn on at the second position. If the distance and timing are just right, the light will appear to stay on at all times, quickly moving between the positions. This response is known as the **phi phenomenon**. 'Moving' neon signs and some computer animations make use of it.

This characteristic of the visual system accounts for the fact that we perceive the images in cinema films, video tapes and television as continuous rather than separate. The images actually jump from place to place, but we see smooth movement.

see activity on mypsychlab

The psychology of art – An international perspective

Different nations and different cultures as well as groups within those nations and cultures produce art that can be as similar as it is different. Researchers, however, have found significant differences in the art and artistic depictions of people from the East and the West. In one study, Masuda *et al.* (2008) analysed the artistic styles in art sourced from the archives of various museums. A total of 365 Western and 218 Eastern landscapes were analysed and 286 and 151 portrait paintings from these cultures were compared.

Eastern landscape art was more likely to place the horizon higher than was Western art. This creates more space for field information. For portrait paintings, the size of the models was smaller in the Eastern sample – the Western sample was less likely to include more background.

In a second study, groups of American and Taiwanese, Korean, Japanese and Chinese students were asked to draw and photograph landscapes and portraits. The use of context was greater in both types of stimuli in the Eastern sample. It was more likely to draw the horizon in a high position and draw more objects. It was also more likely to use the zoom function to minimise the size of the model in portrait photographs and make the context larger.

Finally, American and East Asians students were asked to rate their preference for portrait photographs where the model and the background varied. Japanese participants were significantly less likely to prefer narrow backgrounds and larger models.

The findings are consistent with those of other studies. Miyamoto *et al.* (2006) took photographs of significant cultural institutions in the US and Japan. These included schools, post offices, hotels, etc. The institutions in Japan featured more objects and were visually more complex.

Why do these differences occur? Masuda *et al.* (2008) cite Cohen *et al*'s insider/outsider view of how we organise information about the world (Cohen and Gunz, 2002; Cohen *et al*, 2007). The insider is dominant in the West – this person dwells on his/her own private experiences and sees the world from his/her point of view. The outsider views the world from the point of view of an outsider looking at the self. It seems as if these roles can change. For example, people who have been exposed to Japanese scenes for a few minutes notice more context than those who are exposed to American scenes (Miyamoto *et al.*, 2006).

Brain mechanisms of visual perception

Although the eyes contain the photoreceptors that detect areas of different brightnesses and colours, perception takes place in the brain. As you saw in Chapters 4 and 5, the optic nerves send visual information to the thalamus, which relays the information to the primary visual cortex located in the occipital lobe at the back of the brain. In turn, neurons in the primary visual cortex send visual information to two successive levels of the visual association cortex. The first level, located in the occipital lobe, surrounds the primary visual cortex. The second level is divided into two parts, one in the middle of the parietal lobe and one in the lower part of the temporal lobe. Figure 6.39 illustrates the various regions involved in visual perception.

Visual perception by the brain is often described as a hierarchy of information processing. According to this scheme, circuits of neurons analyse particular aspects of visual information and send the results of their analysis on to another circuit, which performs further analysis. At each

step in the process, successively more complex features are analysed. Eventually, the process leads to the perception of the scene and of all the objects in it. The higher levels of the perceptual process interact with memories: the viewer recognises familiar objects and learns the appearance of new, unfamiliar ones. Deprivation of the visual system or damage to it during the early years of development can have significant consequences for visual function.

The primary visual cortex

Our knowledge about the characteristics of the earliest stages of visual analysis has come from investigations of the activity of individual neurons in the thalamus and primary visual cortex. For example, Hubel and Wiesel inserted microelectrodes – extremely fine wires having microscopically sharp points – into various regions of the visual system of cats and monkeys to detect the action potentials produced by individual neurons (Hubel and Wiesel, 1977, 1979). The signals detected by the microelectrodes are electronically amplified and sent to a recording device so that they can be studied later.

After positioning a microelectrode close to a neuron, Hubel and Wiesel presented various stimuli on a large screen in front of the anaesthetised animal. The anaesthesia makes the animal unconscious but does not prevent neurons in the visual system from responding. The researchers moved a stimulus around on the screen until they located the point where it had the largest effect on the electrical activity of the neuron. Next, they presented the animal with stimuli of various shapes in order to learn which ones produced the greatest response from the neuron.

From their experiments, Hubel and Wiesel (1977, 1979) concluded that the geography of the visual field is retained in the primary visual cortex. That is, the surface of the retina is 'mapped' on the surface of the primary visual cortex. However, this map on the brain is distorted, with the largest amount of area given to the centre of the visual field. The map is actually like a mosaic. Each piece of the mosaic (usually called a module) consists of a block of tissue, approximately 0.5 × 0.7 mm in size and containing approximately 150,000 neurons.

All of the neurons within a module receive information from the same small region of the retina. The primary visual cortex contains approximately 2,500 of these modules. Because each module in the visual cortex receives information from a small region of the retina, that means that it receives information from a small region of the visual field – the scene that the eye is viewing. If you looked at the scene before you through a straw, you would see the amount of information received by an individual module. Hubel and Wiesel found that neural circuits within each module analysed various characteristics of

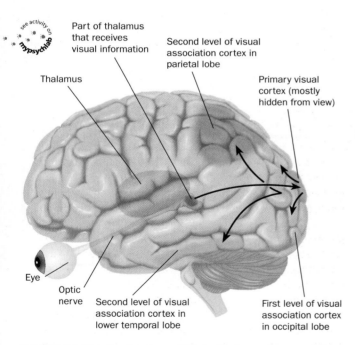

Figure 6.39 The visual system of the brain. Arrows represent the flow of visual information. Sensory information from the eye is transmitted through the optic nerve to the thalamus, and from there it is relayed to the primary visual cortex. The results of the analysis performed there are sent to the visual association cortex of the occipital lobe (first level) and then on to that of the temporal lobe and parietal lobe (second level). At each stage, additional analysis takes place.

their own particular part of the visual field, that is, of their **receptive field**. Some circuits detected the presence of lines passing through the region and signalled the orientation of these lines (that is, the angle they made with respect to the horizon). Other circuits detected the thickness of these lines. Others detected movement and its direction. Still others detected colours.

Figure 6.40 shows a recording of the responses of an orientation-sensitive neuron in the primary visual cortex. This neuron is located in a cluster of neurons that receive information from a small portion of the visual field. That is, the neuron has a small receptive field. The neuron responds when a line oriented at 50 degrees to the vertical is placed in this location – especially when the line is moving through the receptive field. This response is specific to that orientation; the neuron responds very little when a line having a 70-degree or 30-degree orientation is passed through the receptive field. Other neurons in this cluster share the same receptive field but respond to lines of different orientations. Thus, the orientation of lines that pass through this receptive field is signalled by an increased rate of firing of particular neurons in the cluster.

Because each module in the primary visual cortex receives information about only a restricted area of the visual field, the information must be combined somehow for perception to take place. This combination takes place in the visual association cortex.

How different are imagining and perceiving visual stimuli?

Does visual imagery use the same brain areas as those involved in visual perception? Does the imagining of different types of 'mental' content activate different brain areas and if so, are they areas that would be normally activated by the actual perception of such content? Would imagining faces, for example, activate the same area(s) as that or those activated by the viewing of actual faces?

In one study, functional Magnetic Resonance Imaging was used to determine whether the brain areas activated during the mental imagining of faces were similar to or different from those activated during the mental imagining of places (O'Craven and Kanwisher, 2000). A region at the back of the brain, the human fusiform face area (HFFA), was significantly more active during the mental imagining of faces than places. They also found that imagining places activated a region called the parahippocampal place area (PPA) to a much greater extent than did the faces (as for the HFFA, the PPA becomes active when people look at places). Both of these regions can be seen in Figures 6.41.

These results are similar to those obtained by Goebel *et al.* (1998), who found that the brain region activated during visual motion was also activated during the mental imagery of motion. Studies at the level of individual

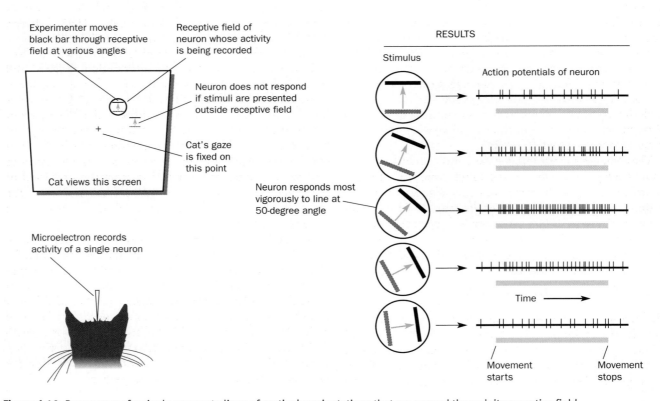

Figure 6.40 Responses of a single neuron to lines of particular orientations that are passed through its receptive field.

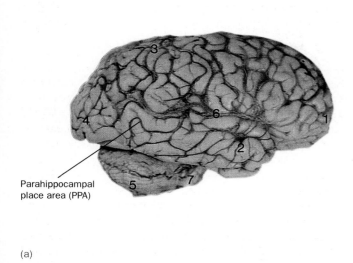

Parahippocampal
place area (PPA)

(a)

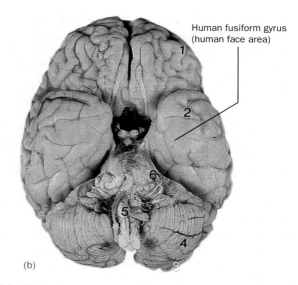

Human fusiform gyrus
(human face area)

(b)

Figure 6.41 The parahippocampal place area **(a)** and the fusiform face area **(b)** of the brain.

groups of cells also show overlap in activation during actual perception and imagination. Kreiman *et al.* (2000), for example, recorded electrical activity from 276 neurons from the lateral (side) regions of the brain (the medial temporal lobes) as participants imagined previously viewed faces, objects, spatial layouts and animals. The purpose of the experiment was to determine whether the same neurons would respond when viewing images as when imagining them. As predicted, the authors found that when neurons responded selectively to a stimulus (that is, responded to that stimulus but not to another, indicating that the response is stimulus-specific), the same neurons were active whether the person viewed or imagined the stimulus. There was a great deal of overlap between neural response during actual viewing and imagining what was viewed.

These studies suggest that the mechanisms responsible for visual perception of images and those responsible for the mental imagining of the same images are similar. The mechanisms may be shared – the results from O'Craven and Kanwisher's study (2000), for example, suggest that the difference in activation between the two types of condition (imagery v. viewing) was one of degree, rather than type.

The visual association cortex

The first level of the visual association cortex, which surrounds the primary visual cortex, contains several subdivisions, each of which contains a map of the visual scene. Each subdivision receives information from different types of neural circuit within the modules of the primary visual cortex. One subdivision receives information about the orientation and widths of lines and edges and is involved in perception of shapes. Another subdivision receives information about movement and keeps track of the relative movements of objects (and may help compensate for movements of the eyes as we scan the scene in front of us). Yet another subdivision receives information concerning colour (Zeki, 1993; Milner, 1998). You can see these subdivisions in Figure 6.42.

The two regions of the second level of the visual association cortex put together the information gathered and processed by the various subdivisions of the first level. Information about shape, movement and colour are combined in the visual association cortex in the lower part of the temporal lobe. Three-dimensional form perception takes place here. The visual association cortex in the parietal lobe is responsible for perception of the location of objects. It integrates information from the first level of the visual association cortex with information from the motor system and the body senses about movements of the eyes, head and body.

Researchers have studied the anatomy and functions of the visual association cortex in laboratory animals. Neuroimaging studies have also been used to locate comparable subregions in humans. For example, when a person looks at a display containing irregular patches of different colours, one region of the visual association cortex becomes active. When a person looks at a display of moving black-and-white squares, another region becomes active (see Figure 6.43). Presumably, these areas are involved in the analysis of colour and movement, respectively.

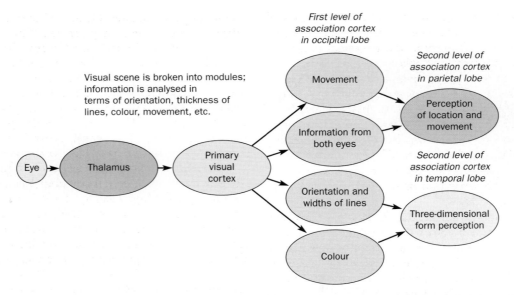

Figure 6.42 Schematic diagram of the types of analysis performed on visual information in the primary visual cortex and the various regions of the visual association cortex.

Brain damage and visual perception

see activity on mypsychlab

Research with laboratory animals and data from individuals with brain damage have shown that certain areas of the visual cortex, the lingual and fusiform gyri, are important for discriminating between colours (Damasio *et al.*, 1980; Davidoff, 1997). Damage

to this area causes **achromatopsia**, a form of colour blindness in which the world is seen in shades of grey, as Figure 6.44 shows.

Neuroimaging studies also suggest that these areas are active in healthy individuals during a simple task where participants perceive colours (McKeefry and Zeki, 1997). McKeefry and Zeki suggest that there is an area or areas outside the primary visual cortex – V4, in the ventral occipitotemporal cortex – which mediates colour perception.

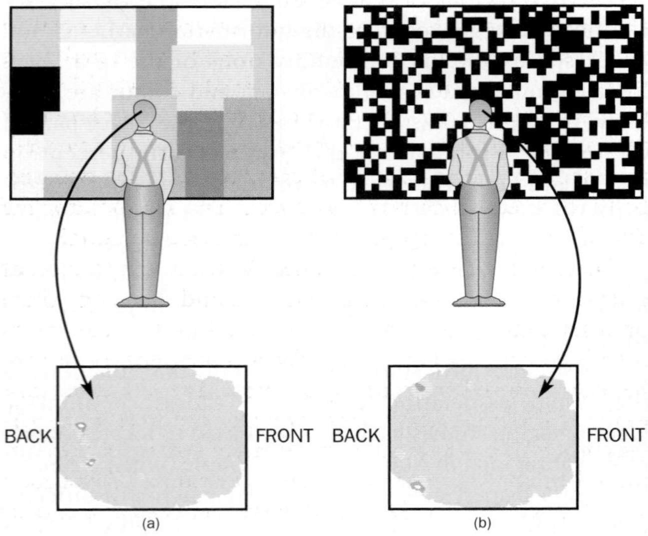

Figure 6.43 PET scans of the human brain showing regions of increased metabolic activity (indicating increased neural activity) when the subjects looked at multicoloured patterns **(a)** and moving black and white rectangles **(b)**.
Source: Adapted from Zeki, S., *La Recherche*, 1991, 21, 712–21.

Figure 6.44 A photograph illustrating the way the world would look to a person who had achromatopsia in the right visual field, caused by damage on the left side of the brain to the region of the visual association cortex.

The finding that damage to different parts of the visual system results in different types of impairment in visual perception suggests that some visual system pathways carry one type of information whereas others carry different types of information. Schneider (1969) had proposed that there were two major visual system pathways: a geniculostriate pathway which was responsible for identifying stimuli and discriminating between patterns, and a retinotectal pathway which was responsible for locating objects in space. Schneider's theory has since been modified, although the idea that different brain regions are responsible for the perception of an object's qualities and its location is valid.

Ungerleider and Mishkin (1982), for example, have suggested that different parts of the brain are involved in object identification and object location: the appreciation of an object's qualities is the role of the inferior temporal cortex; the ability to locate an object is the role of the posterior parietal cortex. Primates with posterior parietal cortex lesions make consistent errors in accurately reaching out for or grasping objects although their ability to discriminate between objects is intact. Similar damage in humans also results in difficulties performing visuospatial tasks such as estimating length and distance (Von Cramon and Kerkhoff, 1993; Jeannerod *et al.*, 1994). Recall from Chapter 4 that the parietal cortex plays an important role in visually guiding movement and in grasping or manipulating objects (Sakata, 1997). Importantly, Ungerleider and Mishkin distinguished between a ventral and dorsal pathway or stream which projected from the primary visual cortex (PVC) to these areas. Thus, although originating in the PVC, the two pathways were independent and projected to different areas of the brain (to the temporal and posterior parietal cortices, respectively).

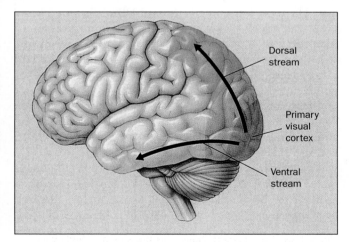

Figure 6.45 The two visual routes (ventral and dorsal) and their pathway from the visual cortex.

Source: From Pinel, John P.J., *Biopsychology*, 3rd edn © 1997. Published by Allyn & Bacon, Boston, MA. Copyright Pearson Education.

Goodale and Milner (1992; Milner and Goodale, 1995) developed the theory further. What is important, they argue, is not 'what' and 'where', but 'what' and 'how'. In Ungerleider and Mishkin's model, the ventral stream processes the 'what' component of visual perception (identification of an object) whereas the dorsal stream processes the 'where' component (the spatial location of an object). Goodale and Milner's research has focused on the 'what' and 'how' areas. The brain regions representing these streams can be seen in Figure 6.45.

Goodale and Milner have made an extensive study of DF, a woman with substantial bilateral damage to the occipital cortex (but sparing the PVC) resulting from carbon monoxide poisoning (Goodale and Milner, 1992; Milner and Goodale, 1995). DF is unable to discriminate between geometric shapes and is unable to recognise or identify objects, despite having no language or visual sensory impairment (Milner *et al.*, 1991). That is, she exhibits visual form agnosia (agnosia is described in more detail in the next section). DF is able to respond to objects. For example, she can place her hand into a slot of varying orientations or grasp blocks (Goodale *et al.*, 1991). However, when she is asked to estimate the orientation of the slot or the width of the box by verbally reporting or by gesturing, she is unable to do so. Why?

DF may be using the intact visuomotor processing system in the parietal cortex to perform the grasping and orientation tasks (Milner and Goodale, 1995; Milner, 1998). The guidance of motor behaviour relies on a primitive dorsal stream in the parietal cortex which is spared in DF. This is why the execution of her motor behaviour is accurate. When asked to indicate which of two boxes is a rectangle and which is a square, she can respond correctly when holding the boxes but less correctly when making a verbal response (Murphy *et al.*, 1996). DF would make partial movements towards one of the boxes before correcting herself. When these initial reaches were analysed, they showed the same level of accuracy as if she had verbally reported which box was which. Did DF monitor the size of her anticipatory grip before making a decision?

There is evidence that she does. When asked to look at a series of lines of varying orientation and then copy them on a separate piece of paper, DF would outline the line in the air before making a copy. When asked not to do this, her copies were still relatively accurate. She found the task easier if she imagined herself drawing the line: when she was asked to copy the line immediately – thereby preventing rehearsal from taking place – she failed (Dijkerman and Milner, 1997). DF must have generated a motor image of the lines to allow her to accomplish this task, a behaviour which would have been made possible by intact functioning of the frontal and parietal lobes.

On the basis of DF's behaviour, research from neuroimaging studies of motor movement and vision, and animal lesions to parietal and occipital areas, Milner and

Goodale (1995) propose that the dorsal stream sends information about object characteristics and orientation that is related to movement from the primary visual cortex to the parietal cortex. Damage to the ventral stream, which projects to the inferior temporal cortex, is what is responsible for DF's inability to access perceptual information.

Projections to the primary visual cortex

Two specific cellular pathways – the parvocellular (P) and magnocellular (M) pathways – run from the retina to the cortex and terminate in different layers of the primary visual cortex (V1). Other layers of V1 project to other dorsal and ventral stream areas. Layers 2 and 3 of V1, for example, provide input to the ventral stream areas whereas layer 4B sends input to dorsal stream areas. Layer 4B also receives input from the M and P pathways and projects to areas such as V5, a region known to be involved in motion perception. Many other circuits such as this are made within the visual system but comparatively little is known about how functionally relevant such connections are or how different types of cell contribute to the circuitry. One study has shown that different types of neurons in area V1 receive different signals from the M and P pathways and forward this information to other specific cortical areas (Yabuta *et al.*, 2001). The results of the study suggest that if two types of cell project to different layers, perhaps each type carries different types of information in the cortical visual system.

Perceptual disorders

When the brain is damaged and visual perception is impaired, the patient is said to exhibit a **perceptual disorder**. There are several perceptual disorders and each is associated with damage to different parts of the visual system. It is important to note that these disorders are strictly perceptual, that is, there is no underlying impairment in sensation (patients retain visual acuity and the ability to tell light from dark and so on). The basic visual sensory system itself is, therefore, unimpaired. Three of the most important perceptual disorders are blindsight, agnosia and spatial neglect. Each is important in its own way because they demonstrate how brain damage can affect different aspects of visual perception.

Blindsight

When the primary visual cortex is damaged, a person becomes blind in some portion of the visual field. Some individuals, however, can lose substantial areas of the PVC and yet show evidence of perceiving objects despite being 'cortically blind'. This phenomenon is called **blindsight** (Weiskrantz, 1986, 1997) because although patients are unable to see properties of objects they are aware of other aspects such as movement of objects. Moving objects are better detected than still ones, objects can be located if they are pointed at and they can detect movement and colour, despite being 'unable' to see the stimuli. (There are equivalent phenomena in the auditory and somatosensory systems called deaf hearing and blindtouch.)

The earliest case of blindsight was reported at the beginning of the last century (Riddoch, 1917). Riddoch was an army medical officer who had made a study of soldiers whose primary visual cortex had been damaged by gunshot wounds. Although none of the patients could directly describe objects placed in front of them (neither shape, form nor colour), they were conscious of the movement of the objects, despite the movement being 'vague and shadowy'. This suggested to Riddoch that some residual visual ability in the PVC remained which allowed the perception of object motion but no other aspect of visual perception. Some patients need to be prompted to 'guess' (Blindsight Type 1) whereas others will reports vague sensations (Blindsight Type 2) although both types claim that they cannot see anything. That the PVC is damaged led to the hypothesis that this area was responsible for conscious visual perception (Radoeva *et al.*, 2008).

Since Riddoch's study, several other cases of blindsight have been reported, notably Larry Weiskrantz's famous patient, DB (Weiskrantz, 1986). DB had undergone surgery for a brain tumour, which necessitated removal of the area of the visual cortex in the right occipital lobe. This surgery resulted in a scotoma – an area of complete blindness in the visual field. DB could indicate whether a stick was horizontal or vertical, could point to the location of an object when instructed, and could detect whether an object was present or absent. Other tasks presented greater difficulty: DB could not distinguish a triangle from a cross or a curved triangle from a normal one. The most intriguing feature of DB's behaviour, however, was a lack of awareness of the stimuli presented. According to DB, he 'couldn't see anything' when test stimuli were seen. Why could DB, and patients like DB, make perceptual decisions despite being unaware of visual stimuli?

One hypothesis suggests that perceptual tasks can be completed successfully because stray light emitted by stimuli makes its way from the intact field of vision because it reflects from surfaces outside the eye area – what is called extraocular scatter. Cowey (2004) has suggested that one way of controlling for this light scatter is to mask the blind field from view by placing a half-patch over the viewing eye, but this control is rarely employed. There can also be an intraocular source of light scatter – according to Cowey (2004), visual stimuli always 'smear' the retina. Because stimuli in blindsight studies have been presented very close to the eye, this has allowed the retina to be smeared with the image and to be stimulated, leading to crude visual perception.

The stray light hypothesis, however, appears to be an unlikely explanation because DB is able to make perceptual decisions in the presence of strong ambient light which reduces the amount of stray light emitted by stimuli. More to the point, this theory does not explain how DB can still make decisions based on the spatial dimensions of objects.

An alternative hypothesis suggests that the residual perceptual abilities of patients such as DB are attributable to the degrading of normal vision, possibly due to the presence of some residual striatal cortex ('islands' of PVC cortex that are undamaged) (Scharli *et al.*, 1999; Wessinger *et al.*, 1999). Implicit in this hypothesis is the notion that residual abilities are not attributable to the functioning of another visual system pathway. There are ten known pathways from the retina to the brain (Stoerig and Cowey, 1997). As you have seen, there appear to be two distinct pathways in the visual system which mediate different aspects of vision. The visual location of objects, for example, is thought to be a function of a system which includes the superior colliculus, the posterior thalamus and areas 20 and 21, whereas the analysis of visual form, pattern or colour is thought to be a function of the geniculostriate system which sends projections from the retina to the lateral geniculate nucleus, then to areas 17, 18 and 19, and then to areas 20 and 21. Blindsight could, therefore, conceivably be due to a disconnection between these two systems. Again, there are arguments against this hypothesis.

Curiously, DB, although unable to 'see' objects when presented to him – even 30 years after his deficit was first studied, appears to be aware of a visual 'after-image' after a stimulus on a monitor is switched off (Weiskrantz *et al.*, 2002). The colour and spatial structure of the stimulus can be described, a phenomenon that is correlated with increased prefrontal cortex activity (Weiskrantz *et al.*, 2003). It is unclear whether this ability is due to spared striate cortex, however, because DB has surgical clips which prevent him from undergoing an MRI scan which would demarcate the preserved cortex.

Another patient, GY, has no spared striate cortex, but still exhibits signs of blindsight (Azzopardi and Cowey, 2001). When the visual cortex of blindsight patients with spared striate cortex is imaged, there is no activation observed to visual stimuli that produce the blindsight phenomenon (Storeig *et al.*, 1998). Both lines of evidence suggest that the spared striate cortex explanation is weak (although not completely dismissible – perhaps the degree and type of spared cortex are the important factors).

What seems reasonable, but for which there is no hard evidence, is the hypothesis that blindsight relies on a primitive, early visual system that is not dependent on the striate cortex. A note of caution should be struck, however. Blythe *et al.* (1987), for example, found only 5 cases of blindsight in a sample of 25 patients; Marzi *et al.* (1986) found a similar ratio (4 patients out of 20) in their sample. The degree of variability in the appearance of blindsight following striatal removal, therefore, suggests some restraint in extrapolating from individual cases.

Visual agnosia

Patients with posterior lesions to the left or right hemisphere sometimes have considerable difficulty in recognising objects, despite having intact sensory systems. We saw an example of this in an earlier section when we discussed the perceptual impairments seen in patient DF. This disorder is called agnosia (literally 'without knowledge'), a term coined by Sigmund Freud. Agnosia can occur in any sense (tactile agnosia refers to the inability to recognise an object by touch, for example) but **visual agnosia** is the most common type (Farah, 1990; Farah and Ratcliff, 1994).

The existence of specific types of agnosia is a controversial topic in perception and neuropsychology. A distinction is usually made between two types of visual agnosia: associative and apperceptive. **Apperceptive agnosia** is the inability to recognise objects whereas **associative agnosia** is the inability to make meaningful associations to objects that are visually presented. Some neuropsychologists have argued that the boundaries between these two types are 'fuzzy' (DeRenzi and Lucchelli, 1993), and other sub-types of visual agnosia have been suggested (Humphreys and Riddoch, 1987a). Apperceptive agnosics have a severe impairment in the ability to copy drawings, as patient DF did. Associative agnosics, conversely, can copy accurately but are unable to identify their drawings. For example, Humphreys and Riddoch's patient, HJA, spent six hours completing an accurate drawing but was unable to identify it when he had finished. Figure 6.46 shows you an example of HJA's drawings.

Figure 6.46 The drawing of a building by HJA reflects great attention but he was unable to name it. The line drawings beneath are of very simple objects but HJA was unable to name them.
Source: Humphreys and Riddoch (1987). *To See or Not to See*. Andover: Psychology Press, reprinted by permission of Thomson Publishing Services.

There has been considerable debate concerning the specificity of visual object agnosia, that is, whether some patients are able to recognise some categories of object but not others (Newcombe *et al.*, 1994). The commonest dissociation is seen between living and non-living things. Generally, it has been found that recognition of living objects (such as animals) is less accurate in agnosic patients than is recognition of non-living objects (Warrington and Shallice, 1984; Silveri *et al.*, 1997). To determine whether different brain regions were responsible for this dissociation, Martin *et al.* (1996) conducted a PET study of healthy individuals' brain activity as the subjects named pictures of tools or animals. Both categories of words were associated with activation in the visual cortex and Broca's area (because the participants saw and spoke) but some areas were activated by the naming of animals (left occipital region) and others by the naming of tools (right premotor regions).

Some psychologists, however, have argued that these studies do not show differences between the categories of object but between the ways in which these two different types of stimulus are presented. Parkin and Stewart (1993), for example, have suggested that it is more difficult to recognise drawings of animate than inanimate objects. An inanimate object such as a cup, is a lot less detailed than an animate object, such as a fly. The dissociation seen in agnosic patients, therefore, may be due to the complexity and/or familiarity of the perceived stimulus. Stewart *et al.* (1992) have suggested that when these artefacts are controlled for, these dissociations disappear. However, the issue continues to be controversial. Sheridan and Humphreys (1993), for example, have shown that patients show such dissociations even under well-controlled conditions and a recent review suggests that specific brain regions may mediate the recognition of objects from different semantic categories (Gainotti, 2000).

Prosopagnosia

A more category-specific form of agnosia is **prosopagnosia**. Some individuals with damage to specific areas of the posterior right hemisphere (and sometimes left and right hemispheres) show an impairment in the ability to recognise familiar faces. This condition is known as prosopagnosia ('loss of knowledge for faces'). Some patients are unable to recognise famous faces (Warrington and James, 1967) or familiar people such as spouses (DeRenzi, 1986). This disorder, while rare, can have dramatic effects on a person's everyday life. For example, here are some comments from patients with prosopagnosia on how their condition affects them (all from Yardley *et al.*, 2008):

"I was getting off a bus and somebody got on it and grabbed me, and I pushed them out of the way and it was only when they opened their mouth that I realized it was my own mother."

"Sometimes if I see someone and I'm not sure if I know them I just try and keep out of their way and hope they don't see me, 'cause I don't know how to act."

"The condition makes me less interested in the social events, the partying, the getting to know lots of people, because that just gives me a whole set of things I'll get wrong."

"I'd try, spend three days chatting up some girl and then cut her dead in the street without knowing that I'd done it."

Barry Wainwright, who suffers from prosopagnosia: 'If I look at a photograph of myself, I don't know it's me. I don't recognise my wife or my seven children, either, even when I'm looking right at them.'

Source: From *The Guardian Weekend Magazine*, 22 November 2008, p. 12.

Much of the recent neuropsychological work on face recognition has exploited neuroimaging techniques in order to determine whether different regions of the human brain respond to faces selectively. One controversy in the area surrounds whether such selective activation is specific to faces or to some other perceptual aspect of faces, such as whether they appear in greyscale or in two-tone. Kanwisher *et al.* (1998), for example, found that the brain region which you encountered in the earlier section, the human fusiform face area (HFFA), was significantly activated when people viewed upright and inverted greyscale faces. Inverted two-tone faces, however, were associated with significantly reduced brain activation. The results suggest that the HFFA does not respond specifically to low-level features of faces (if it did, the inverted and upright two-tone faces would have produced similar activation) but does respond to face stimuli. The authors acknowledge, however, that this may not be the only brain region specialised for face processing.

Current neuroimaging data make HFFA a strong contender for the role of the brain's primary face processor. Its response is stronger when viewing faces, followed by whole humans and animal heads (Kanwisher *et al.*, 1999) and appears to be involved in remembering, as well as seeing, faces (Kuskowski and Pardo, 1999). Gorno-Tempini *et al.* (1998) compared the human brain's ability to process, implicitly or explicitly, famous and unknown face stimuli, proper names and object names and report that the perceptual analysis of faces was associated with selective activation of the HFFA in both hemispheres of the brain. Other regions were implicated in famous name processing (relative to common names). The same research group also reported a study in which activation to famous and non-famous faces and buildings was recorded (Gorno-Tempini and Price, 2001). In this experiment, they found that the HFFA and the PPA were selectively activated by faces and buildings, respectively, regardless of fame (although other regions were activated during exposure to the famous stimuli).

One view, however, suggests that the FFA, rather than being specialised for recognising faces, is responsible for distinguishing between members of a homogeneous class of objects (not just faces). A related argument suggests that the FFA is active when it distinguishes between members of object classes that we are expert in identifying. Because we are very familiar with faces, and expert at recognising them, the FFA is, therefore, active when we view faces. This argument also suggests, however, that expert identifiers should activate the FFA when they view objects they are expert in recognising (and not just faces).

To test these various hypotheses, Rhodes *et al.* (2004) set up two experiments in which people were either trained or were not trained to recognise Lepidoptera (moths and butterflies). Brain activation was monitored using fMRI while participants viewed faces and Lepidoptera. In the second experiment, experts in identifying moths and butterflies passively watched examples of the species while brain activity was recorded. If the FFA is active during expert discrimination, then it should be just as active during face perception and Lepidoptera perception in experts.

The authors found no support for this hypothesis. In the first experiment, the FFA was more significantly activated when people watched faces than Lepidoptera, regardless of whether people had been trained to recognise examples of the species. In the second experiment, activation was greater in the FFA when the butterfly experts watched faces than Lepidoptera. There was no overlap in the areas activated by faces and moths and butterflies.

The results suggest that the FFA contains neurons that allow 'individuation' of (i.e. discrimination between) faces.

Spatial neglect

Patients with lesions in the right parietotemporal cortex sometimes have difficulty in perceiving objects to their left (Vallar, 1998). In fact, in 80 per cent of patients with right hemisphere stroke, patients are unable to attend automatically to any stimuli in left space (Halligan and Marshall, 1994). This is called **spatial neglect** (or unilateral spatial hemineglect) and occurs on the side of the body that is contralateral to the side of the brain damage (the regions damaged can be seen in Figure 6.47). Neglect for the left side is more common than right neglect (which would be caused by damage to the left hemisphere).

Patients exhibiting spatial neglect behave as if half of the world does not exist. They may forget to attend to their clothing on the left-hand side, neglect food on the left side of the plate or ignore the left-hand side of their newspaper (Halligan and Cockburn, 1993; Halligan and Marshall, 1994).

Spatial neglect patients show a characteristic pattern of behaviour on visuospatial tests. For example, if they are required to bisect lines of varying length, they will err to the right. If they are presented with an array of stimuli (such as small lines) and asked to mark off as many as possible, they mark off those on the right-hand side but fail to mark off those on the left, as seen in Figure 6.48.

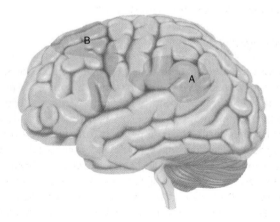

Figure 6.47 The areas of the brain damaged in spatial neglect patients. Most patients have damage to region A; some can have damage to region B.

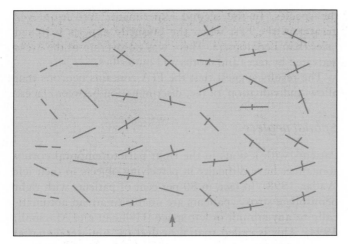

Figure 6.48 The line cancellation task. Spatial neglect patients consistently neglect one side of the display (in this example, the left side).

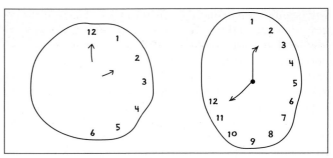

Figure 6.49 The famous clock-drawing task at which spatial neglect patients are impaired. Patients either neglect the numerals on the left side completely or bunch them up on the right.

Similarly, neglect patients, when asked to draw (or mentally imagine a scene) fail to draw or report details from the left side of the object or image (Halligan and Marshall, 1994; Guariglia *et al.*, 1993). Sometimes, patients will transfer details from the left to the right-hand side, as seen in Figure 6.49. This is called **allesthesia** or **allochiria** (Meador *et al.*, 1991).

The examples shown in Figure 6.51 illustrate the profound consequences that brain damage can have on perceptual behaviour, not just in terms of behavioural impairment but also in terms of disruption to a patient's life and work.

The reasons for spatial neglect are unclear (see Halligan and Marshall, 1994, and Mozer *et al.*, 1997, for a discussion).

Psychology in action – How does brain injury affect artists?

Losing the ability to speak, to recall information, or organise and plan everyday life efficiently are all unwelcome intruders in the world of the normally functioning. But what if the disrupted function is essential to the person's life and provides him or her with a livelihood? Beethoven composed symphonies, Evelyn Glennie plays exceptional xylophone, Stevie Wonder is an accomplished keyboardist; even James Joyce managed to produce *Ulysees* and *Finnegan's Wake* despite his chronic sight loss (although this is thought to explain some of Joyce's eccentric text). None of these, however, despite their sensory losses, sustained brain injury. Chatterjee (2004) has reviewed the type of effects brain injury has on an artist's performance and output.

The loss of the ability to perceive colour is clearly one of the most challenging problems for an artist who exploits his or her chromatic palette. Sacks (1995) describes an artist who developed an injury leaving him achromatopsic – the artist's world appeared 'dirty grey' and he reported being unable to imagine colours (or even being able to dream in colour). Before the accident leading to the injury, the patient painted colourful, abstract creations; after the accident, the paintings became figurative and abstract. Contrast, figure and form were good as was the patient's ability to understand and describe colour but his use of colour became haphazard.

Unilateral spatial neglect has more intriguing, if predictable, consequences. Jung (1974) described four early cases of painters who developed neglect following brain injury. One, the German artist Lovis Corinth, had suffered a right hemisphere stroke. His painting changed dramatically: the contours on the left of his work disappeared and details became misplaced. Blanke *et al.* (2003) reported the case of a 71-year-old artist who could colour the right side of her paintings normally and evenly but paid minimal attention to the left. Figure 6.50 gives an example of the patient's art following injury. Neglect for colour was greater than neglect for form in the majority of the patient's paintings. Painter IK showed right neglect where entire canvasses would be created in exuberant colour but the right side lacked detail and form (Marsh and Philwin, 1987).

Perhaps the most famous example of unilateral spatial neglect is the Italian film director, Federico Fellini, whose disorder was reported by Cantagallo and Della Sala (1998). At the age of 73, Fellini suffered a stroke in the middle cerebral artery of the right parietal lobe that caused left extrapersonal spatial

Psychology in action – *Continued*

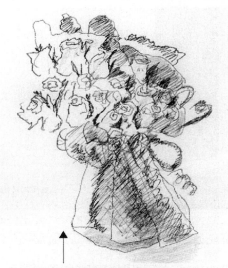

Drawing showing left colour neglect
Arrow indicates the middle of the page.

Figure 6.50 The colour neglect seen in a drawing by Blanke *et al.*'s patient.

Source: Plate 6.2 from *Human Neuropsychology*, 2nd edn, Pearson/Prentice Hall (Martin, G.N., 2006). Image kindly provided by Dr Olaf Blanke.

neglect that persisted for two months. As well as being a celebrated film director, Fellini was an accomplished cartoonist and his completion of neglect tests was peppered with his cartoonish embellishments. His original cartoons showed neglect of the left side. Figure 6.51 (a) and (b) illustrates some of Fellini's attempts.

Fellini's neglect did not appear to be representational (he could imagine both sides of his visual field) and he was completely aware of his deficits. Unlike patients in previous reports, his increased awareness did not lead to a decrease in his neglect (Guariglia *et al.*, 1993).

Halligan and Marshall (1997) reported the consequences of neglect for a 75-year-old artist and sculptor who had suffered a right hemisphere stroke. Six months after the stroke, his drawings were poorer and less elaborate than they were before the stroke. His family also noted that he seemed to concentrate on the right-hand side of the drawings. In fact, on all the standard tests of neglect, he showed impairment. Figure 6.52 (a)–(c) shows examples of the patient's sculptures before and 3 to 4 months after the stroke.

As Fellini did, some artists can recover their ability to attend to the left to some extent; sometimes they will use broader strokes than normal or may be more expressive, as the painters Loring Hughes and Lovis Corinth found.

(a)

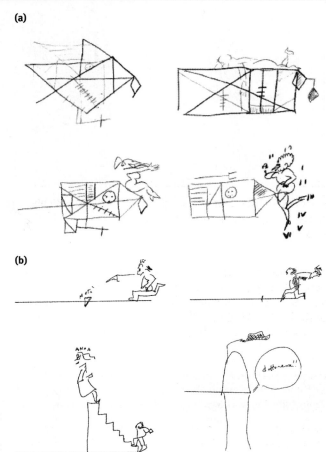

(b)

Figure 6.51 Italian film director Federico Fellini developed spatial neglect after suffering a stroke. As well as being a director, Fellini was also a talented cartoonist and he doodled comically on his psychological tests. **(a)** and **(b)** Examples of Fellini's spatial neglect test performance.

Source: Chatterjee, A. A madness to the methods of cognitive neuroscience? *Journal of Cognitive Neuroscience*, 2005, 17, 6, 847–9, © by the Massachusetts Institute of Technology.

At least neglect patients can recognise their creations. Some patients with visual agnosia are unable to do this. Wapner *et al.* (1978) report the case of a 73-year-old amateur artist who developed visual agnosia following a stroke. The artist would draw extremely laboriously but failed to recognise what he drew. He could identify the general shape of the object and describe its function, and even tried to identify it from its parts, but could not put a label to it. His agnosia was perceptual, rather than conceptual, because he would sometimes describe the functions of parts of the object he drew (e.g. what a telephone was for).

Psychology in action – *Continued*

(a)

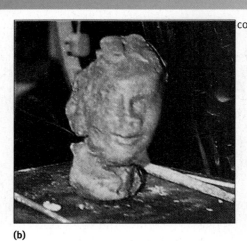
(b)

(c)

Figure 6.52 These show the effects of brain damage on the work of a sculptor. **(a)** A sculpture made before the injury. **(b)** Another sculpture made after the injury. **(c)** A drawing made by the same artist after injury.

Source: Halligan, P. and Marshall, J., *The art of visual neglect*, The Lancet, 1997, 350, July, pp. 139–140. © 1997 The Lancet Limited.

Agnosic patients can sometimes imagine the objects they would like to draw. Botez *et al.* (1985), however, report the case of a 38-year-old teacher and amateur charcoal drawer who was unable to imagine people, places or objects, following dilation of one of the brain's chambers. Copying objects presented little problem but when the object was removed from sight, her drawings became simple and schematic. When she was given the name of an object to draw, she could not do this competently.

Perception seems the most likely casualty in the artist's battle with brain damage but there are some cases of impairment to other functions which lead to some unusual artistic sequences. The Bulgarian artist Zlatio Boiyadjiev, exhibited a natural, pictorial style prior to the development of aphasia (Zaimov *et al.*, 1969). After the aphasia, his art became bold, rich and colourful, full of striking, energetic lines and replete with bizarre imagery. Another artist with aphasia, the Polish artist RL (an Assistant Professor in Lublin), was known for highly symbolic paintings. Following aphasia, he produced very well-executed charcoal drawings, self-portraits and landscapes (Kaczmarek, 1991). No matter how hard he tried, he never did recover the symbolism of his art that existed before the aphasia.

Chapter review

Perception of form

- Perception of form requires recognition of figure and ground. The Gestalt organisational laws of proximity, similarity, good continuation and common fate describe some of the ways in which we distinguish figure from ground even when the outlines of the figures are not explicitly bounded by lines.
- One hypothesis concerning the mechanism of pattern perception, or visual recognition of particular shapes suggests that our brain contains templates of all the shapes we can perceive. We compare a particular pattern of visual input with these templates until we find a fit. A second hypothesis suggests that our brain contains prototypes, which are more flexible than simple templates. Some psychologists believe that prototypes

are collections of distinctive features (such as the two parallel lines and the connecting diagonal of the letter N).

- Perception involves both bottom-up and top-down processing. Our perceptions are influenced not only by the details of the particular stimuli we see, but also by their relations to each other and our expectations. Thus, we may perceive a shape either as a loaf of bread in the kitchen or as a letterbox alongside a country road, for example.
- We can usually distinguish male and female faces on the basis of eyes, mouth and nose but rarely on the basis of single features alone.
- Lighting, form and contour significantly influence our ability to recognise faces correctly.

Perception of space and motion

- Because the size and shape of a retinal image vary with the location of an object relative to the eye, accurate form perception requires depth perception – perception of the locations of objects in space.
- Depth perception comes from binocular cues (from convergence and retinal disparity) and monocular cues (from interposition, size, linear perspective, texture, haze shading, elevation, and the effects of head and body movements).
- The Sapir–Whorf hypothesis suggests that language can strongly affect the way we perceive the world although there is not much research to support it. It is possible that experience with some environmental features, such as particular geographical features or buildings composed of straight lines and right angles, has some influence on the way people perceive the world.
- We perceive the brightness of an object relative to that of objects around it; thus, objects retain a constant brightness under a variety of conditions of illumination. In addition, our perception of the relative distance of objects helps us maintain form constancy.
- Because our bodies may well be moving while we are visually following some activity in the outside world, the visual system has to make further compensations. It keeps track of the commands to the eye muscles and compensates for the direction in which the eyes are pointing.
- Movement is perceived when objects move relative to one another. In particular, a smaller object is likely to be perceived as moving across a larger one. Movement is also perceived when our eyes follow a moving object, even though its image remains on the same part of the retina and supplies important cues about an object's three-dimensional shape.
- Because a complex scene, covering a large area, cannot be seen in a single glance, the visual system must combine information from successive fixations. The phenomenon of backward masking suggests that the image received from the previous fixation is erased immediately after a saccade so that blurring does not occur.
- The phi phenomenon describes our tendency to see an instantaneous disappearance of an object and its reappearance somewhere else as movement of that object. Because of the phi phenomenon, we perceive television shows and films as representations of reality, not as a series of disconnected images.

Brain mechanisms of visual perception

- Visual information proceeds from the retina to the thalamus, and then to the primary visual cortex (PVC). The PVC is organised into modules, each of which receives information from a small region of the retina.
- Neural circuits within each module analyse specific information from their part of the visual field, including the orientation and width of lines, colour and movement.
- The different types of information analysed by the neural circuits in the modules of the PVC are sent to separate maps of the visual field in the first level of the visual association cortex. The information from these maps is combined in the second level of the visual association cortex: form perception in the base of the temporal lobe and spatial perception in the parietal lobe.
- The brain seems to contain visual systems which process (1) features of objects and (2) the space indication of objects. The first, the ventral stream, projects from the PVC to the inferior temporal cortex; the second, the dorsal stream projects from the PVC to the posterior parietal cortex.
- Visual agnosia is the inability to perceive objects accurately (apperceptive agnosia) or assign meaning to visually presented objects (associative agnosia). Prosopagnosia is the inability to identify familiar faces and results from bilateral or unilateral posterior brain damage.
- The agnosic deficits seen in patient DF may be due to an intact dorsal stream but an impaired ventral stream.
- Blindsight refers to the ability to perform visual perceptual tasks despite a lack of awareness of the perceived stimuli; it is normally associated with damage outside the primary visual cortex.
- Spatial neglect is the inability to attend to stimuli in one half of space. Patients usually neglect the left-hand side as a result of right parietotemporal cortex damage (that is, the deficit is contralesional – occurs on the opposite side to the brain damage).

Suggestions for further reading

Perception – general

Coren, S., Ward, L.M. and Enns, J.T. (2003) *Sensation and perception* (6th edn). Chichester: Wiley.

Goldstein, E.B. (2004) *Blackwell Handbook of Sensation and Perception*. Oxford: Blackwell.

Levine, M.W. and Shefner, J.M. (2000) *Fundamentals of Sensation and Perception*. Oxford: Oxford University Press.

Ramachandran, V.S. and Rogers-Ramachandran, D. (2007) Paradoxical perceptions. *Scientific American Mind*, 18, 2, 18–20.

Schiffman, H.R. (2000) *Sensation and Perception: An integrated approach* (5th edn). Chichester: Wiley.

All of these books provide a good, solid description and evaluation of the topics covered in this (and the previous) chapter.

Visual perception: general aspects

Bruce, V., Green, P. and Georgeson, M. (2003) *Visual Perception* (4th edn). Hove: Psychology Press.

Snowden, R., Thompson, P. and Troscianko, T. (2006) *Basic Vision*. Oxford: Oxford University Press.

The Bruce et al. text gives a good introduction to the visual system, as does Snowden et al.

Visual recognition/awareness

Chatterjee, A. (2004) Neuropsychology of art. *Neuropsychologia*, 42, 1568–83.

Conway, B.R. and Livingstone, M.S. (2007) Perspectives on science and art. *Current Opinion in Neurobiology*, 17, 476–82.

Cowey, A. (2004) The 30th Sir Frederick Bartlett lecture: fact, artefact, and myth about blindsight. *The Quarterly Journal of Experimental Psychology*, 57A, 4, 577–609.

Goodale, M. and Milner, D. (2005) *Sight Unseen: An exploration of conscious and unconscious vision*. Oxford: Oxford University Press.

Gruter, T. (2006) Picture this – how does the brain create images in our minds? *Scientific American Mind*, 17, 1, 18–23.

This selection of very good readings covers various aspects of visual processing.

Visual agnosia and face perception

Bruce, V. and Young, A.W. (1998) *In the Eye of the Beholder: The science of face perception*. Oxford: Oxford University Press.

Farah, M.J. (2001) *The Cognitive Neuroscience of Vision*. Oxford: Oxford University Press.

Gruter, T. (2007) Forgetting faces. *Scientific American Mind*, 18, 3, 68–73.

Gruter, T., Gruter, M. and Carbon, C-C. (2008) Neural and genetic foundations of face recognition and prosopagnosia. *Journal of Neuropsychology*, 2, 79–97.

Johnston, V.S. (2006) Mate choice decisions: The role of facial beauty. *Trends in Cognitive Sciences*, 10, 1, 10–13.

Martin, G.N. (2006) *Human Neuropsychology* (2nd edn). Harlow: Prentice Hall Europe.

Taylor, M.J., Batty, M. and Itier, R.J. (2004) The faces of development: A review of early face processing over childhood. *Journal of Cognitive Neuroscience*, 16, 8, 1426–42.

Weiskrantz, L. (1997) *Consciousness Lost and Found: A neuropsychological exploration*. Oxford: Oxford University Press.

Some useful and interesting specific and general reading on agnosia and face perception.

Spatial neglect

Cantagallo, A. and Della Sala, S. (1998) Preserved insight in an artist with extrapersonal spatial neglect. *Cortex*, 34, 163–89.

A good description of the consequences of brain damage on spatial neglect.

Journals to consult

Brain

British Journal of Psychology

Cognitive Neuropsychology

Cortex

Journal of Experimental Psychology: Human perception and performance

Nature

Neuropsychologia

Neuropsychology

Neuroscience

Perception

Perception and Psychophysics

Perceptual and Motor Skills

Psychological Science

Quarterly Journal of Experimental Psychology

Trends in Cognitive Science

Trends in Neuroscience

Vision Research

Visual Neuroscience

Website addresses

http://coglab.wadsworth.com/
This is a site that will allow you access to various experiments and demonstrations in experimental psychology. The site requires you to register before viewing the material.

http://www.essex.ac.uk/psychology/interest.html
You'll find a collection of online experiments here on various aspects of visual perception.

http://www.exploratorium.edu
A collection of demonstrations of visual illusions from The Exploratorium.

http://cns-web.bu.edu/pub/laliden/WWW/Visionary/Visionary.html
An online dictionary of terms used in visual perception.

http://www.yorku.ca/eye
An online textbook called *The Joy of Visual Perception*, written by Peter Kaiser at York University.

http://www.faceresearch.org/exp
An excellent site featuring experiments on face perception run by the University of Aberdeen.

Learning and behaviour

CHAPTER 7

Luck can change your life

Ms V is a compulsive gambler. It wrecked her marriage and drained her wallet long ago. Her kids don't like her because she is always barely scraping by – and borrowing money from them – waiting for the next big win that she hopes will give her all the cash she needs to escape her current mess.

How did it all begin? The answer lies in the schedules of reinforcement. At college, one of her boyfriends liked to bet on the horses and V went along one day. She bet £10 on a filly named Flo and won £300. What a rush! Luck brought her a giant reinforcer without much effort – with no 'down side' in sight. Her boyfriend was excited, too. V saved the money and went back to the track several more times over the next several weeks – sometimes alone, sometimes with her boyfriend – making more £10 bets. Most lost. A few made small wins. But the betting was exciting, and there was lots of sensory stimulation when her horse took one of the front positions.

When V's £300 was about half gone, she bet on a long shot with big odds. No one expected Viceroy to win, but V put down £75 on a hunch. Viceroy. . . won by a nose. V walked away with £4,500 in her pocket. Early periods of generous reinforcement can have a big effect on our later behavioural decisions.

Source: adapted Baldwin and Baldwin (1998)

WHAT YOU SHOULD BE ABLE TO DO AFTER READING CHAPTER 7

- Describe the concept of habituation and the phenomena of classical conditioning and operant learning.
- Understand the principles underlying classical conditioning.
- Understand the principles underlying operant conditioning.
- Describe and explain conditioned aversions.
- Describe the nature of insight.
- Apply the principles of learning theory to behaviour.
- Describe some of the factors that influence academic learning.

QUESTIONS TO THINK ABOUT

- Do different aspects of learning have different underlying principles? Is learning to ride a bike governed by different principles from those used for learning to find your way around college or university or learning a foreign language?
- Does all learning have to be intentional? Can you learn something without knowing it or without wanting to learn it?
- Is learning a process that depends on innate ability, the ability to adopt successful learning strategies or both?
- What factors do you think enhance and promote the process of learning?
- What psychological factors can enhance (or impair) your academic learning?
- In what way is the brain like a computer (and vice versa)?

Explore the accompanying video, simulations, and animations on MyPsychLab. This chapter includes activities on: Acquisition of conditioned responses • Stimulus generalisation and stimulus discrimination • Classical conditioning of Little Albert • Schedules of reinforcement • Check your understanding and prepare for your exams using the multiple choice, short answer and essay practice tests also available

The purpose of learning

Behaviours that produce favourable consequences are repeated and become habits, but those that produce unfavourable consequences tend not to recur (Ouellette and Wood, 1998). In other words, we learn from experience. **Learning** is an adaptive process in which the tendency to perform a particular behaviour is changed by experience. As conditions change, we learn new behaviours and eliminate old ones.

This chapter considers three kinds of learning: habituation, classical conditioning and operant conditioning. All three involve cause-and-effect relations between behaviour and the environment. We learn which stimuli are trivial and which are important, and we learn to make adaptive responses and to avoid maladaptive ones. We learn to recognise those conditions under which a particular response is useful and those under which a different response is more appropriate. The types of learning described in this chapter serve as the building blocks for more complex behaviours, such as problem-solving and thinking, which we consider in later chapters.

Learning, however, cannot be truly observed in a direct sense; it can only be inferred from changes in behaviour. As you saw in Chapter 1, the influential field of behaviourism which dominated experimental psychology in the early twentieth century demanded that only observable behaviour could be valid subject matter for psychologists. However, even the founding father of behaviourism, John B. Watson, argued that there could be two categories of observable behaviour: explicit behaviour, which is directly observable to the eye, and implicit behaviour, which could be measured by special equipment (an example would be the measurement of bodily response using psychophysiological recording equipment).

But not all changes in behaviour are caused by learning. For example, your performance in an examination or the skill with which you operate a car can be affected by your physical or mental condition, such as fatigue, fearfulness or distraction. Moreover, learning may occur without noticeable changes in observable behaviour taking place. In some cases, learning is not apparent – at least, not right away – from our observable behaviour. In other cases, we may never have the opportunity to demonstrate what we have learned. For example, although you may have received training in how to conduct an orthogonally rotated factor analysis in your computer's statistics package, you may never need to demonstrate the results of your learning again. In still other cases, you may not be sufficiently motivated to demonstrate something you have learned. For example, a tutor might pose a question in a seminar but although you know the answer, you do not say anything because you get nervous when speaking in front of others.

Learning takes place within the nervous system. Experience alters the structure and chemistry of the brain, and these changes affect the individual's subsequent behaviour. Performance is the behavioural change (or new behaviour) produced by this internal change.

Habituation

Many events may cause us to react automatically. For example, a sudden, unexpected noise causes an **orienting response**: we become alert and turn our heads towards the source of the sound. However, if the noise occurs repeatedly, we gradually cease to respond to it; we eventually ignore it. **Habituation**, learning not to respond to an unimportant event that occurs repeatedly, is the simplest form of learning. As you will see in Chapter 12, even infants a few months old show evidence of habituation.

From an evolutionary perspective, habituation makes adaptive sense. If a once-novel stimulus occurs again and again without any important result, the stimulus has no significance to the organism. Obviously, responding to a stimulus of no importance wastes time and energy.

The simplest form of habituation is temporary, and is known as short-term habituation. Imagine entering a new room in an inhabited house. It is likely that you will perceive the distinctive odour of the room. Eventually, however, you begin not to notice the odour; you will have become habituated. If you return to the same house the next day, however, you will perceive that distinctive smell again but if you stay in the room for long enough, you will again become habituated.

Classical conditioning

Unlike habituation, **classical conditioning** involves learning about the conditions that predict that a significant event will occur. We acquire much of our behaviour through classical conditioning. For example, if you are hungry and smell a favourite food cooking, your mouth is likely to water. If you see someone with whom you have recently had a serious argument, you are likely to experience again some of the emotional reactions that occurred during the encounter. If you hear a song that you used to listen to with a loved one, you are likely to experience a feeling of nostalgia. If you listen to a piece of music that can be distinctly identified by nation, then people will buy more of that nation's wine. How does such classical conditioning take place?

...ne that you have an uninflated balloon directly ...u. Someone starts inflating the balloon with a ...e balloon gets larger and larger. What are you ...? You will probably grimace and squint your ...u realise that the balloon is about to burst in ...

...consider how a person learns to flinch defen-...t the sight of a tightly stretched balloon. Suppose ...e inflate a balloon in front of a young boy who has ...seen one before. The boy will turn his eyes towards ...larging balloon, but he will not flinch. When the ...n explodes, the noise and the blast of air will cause ...nsive startle reaction: he will squint, grimace, raise ...oulders and suddenly move his arms towards his ...A bursting balloon is an important stimulus, one ...auses an automatic, unlearned defensive reaction.

...e will probably not have to repeat the experience ...y times for the boy to learn to react the way we all ...- flinching defensively before the balloon actually ...sts. A previously neutral stimulus (the over-inflated ...loon), followed by an important stimulus (the explo-...n that occurs when the balloon bursts), can now ...gger the defensive flinching response by itself. The ...fensive flinching response has been classically condi-...oned to the sight of an over-inflated balloon. Two ...imuli have become associated with each other.

Pavlov's serendipitous discovery

In December 1904, the Russian physiologist Ivan Pavlov was awarded the Nobel Prize in physiology and medicine for his work on the digestive system. Invited to Stockholm to accept the award and to deliver an acceptance speech, the 55-year-old Pavlov did not speak of his pioneering work on digestion (Babkin, 1949). Instead, his address, entitled 'The first sure steps along the path of a new investigation', focused on his more recent work involving conditional reflexes or 'involuntary' responses. Pavlov's new line of research was to take him far from the research for which he was awarded the Nobel Prize, and today he is remembered more for his work in psychology than in physiology. But it was while studying the digestive system that Pavlov stumbled on the phenomenon that was to make a lasting impact on psychology (Windholz, 1997).

Pavlov's chief ambition as a physiologist was to discover the neural mechanisms controlling glandular secretions during digestion. He measured the secretions during the course of a meal by inserting a small tube in a duct in an animal's mouth and collecting drops of saliva as they were secreted by the salivary gland. During each of the test sessions, he placed dry food powder inside the dog's mouth and then collected the saliva. All went well until the dogs became experienced subjects. After several testing sessions, the dogs began salivating before being fed, usually as soon as they saw the laboratory assistant enter the room with the food powder. What Pavlov discovered was a form of learning in which one stimulus predicts the occurrence of another. In this case, the appearance of the laboratory assistant predicted the appearance of food.

Rather than ignoring this phenomenon or treating it as a confounding variable that needed to be controlled, Pavlov designed experiments to discover exactly why the dogs were salivating before being given the opportunity to eat. He suspected that salivation might be triggered by stimuli that were initially unrelated to eating. Somehow, these neutral stimuli came to control what is normally a natural reflexive behaviour. After all, dogs do not naturally salivate when they see laboratory assistants.

To do so, he placed an inexperienced dog in a harness and occasionally gave it small amounts of food powder. Before placing the food powder in the dog's mouth, Pavlov sounded a bell, a buzzer or some other auditory stimulus. At first, the dog showed only a startle response to the sound, perking its ears and turning its head towards the sound. The dog salivated only when the food powder was placed in its mouth. But after only a dozen or so pairings of the bell and food powder, the dog began to salivate when the bell rang. Placing the food powder in the dog's mouth was no longer necessary to elicit salivation; the sound by itself was sufficient. Pavlov showed that a neutral stimulus can elicit a response similar to the original reflex when the stimulus predicts the occurrence of a significant stimulus (in this case, food powder).

This type of learning is called classical or **Pavlovian conditioning**. Pavlov demonstrated that conditioning occurred only when the food powder followed the bell within a short time. If there was a long delay between the sound and the food powder or if the sound followed the food powder, the animal never learned to salivate when it heard the sound. Thus, the sequence and timing of events are important factors in classical conditioning. Classical conditioning provides us with a way to learn cause-and-effect relations between environmental events. We are able to learn about the stimuli that warn us that an important event is about to occur. Obviously, warning stimuli must occur prior to the event about which we are being warned.

Figure 7.1 shows the basic classical conditioning procedure – the special conditions that must exist for an organism to respond to a previously neutral stimulus.

A stimulus, such as food, that naturally elicits reflexive behaviour, such as salivation, is called an **unconditional stimulus (UCS)**. The reflexive behaviour itself is called the **unconditional response (UCR)**. If, for a certain dog, a bell signals food, then the bell may also come to elicit salivation through classical conditioning. Another dog may hear the sound of an electric can opener just before it is

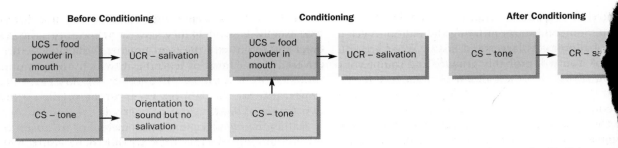

Figure 7.1 Basic components of the classical conditioning procedure. Prior to conditioning, the UCS but not the CS elicits a resp◌ (the UCR). During conditioning, the CS is presented in conjunction with the UCS. Once the conditioning is completed, the CS alon◌ elicits a response (the CR).

fed, in which case that sound will come to elicit salivation. A neutral stimulus paired with the unconditional stimulus that eventually elicits a response is called a **conditional stimulus (CS)**. The behaviour elicited by a conditional stimulus is called a **conditional response (CR)**. In the case of Pavlov's dogs, food powder was the UCS: it elicited the UCR, salivation.

At first, when Pavlov presented the sound of the bell or buzzer, the dogs did not salivate; the sound was merely a neutral stimulus, not a CS. However, with repeated pairings of the sound and the food powder, the sound became a CS, reliably eliciting the CR – salivation.

The biological significance of classical conditioning

Salivation is an innate behaviour and is adaptive because it facilitates digestion. Through natural selection, the neural circuitry that underlies salivation has become part of the genetic endowment of many species. Pavlov's experiments demonstrated that an innate reflexive behaviour, such as salivation, can be elicited by novel stimuli. Thus, a response that is naturally under the control of appropriate environmental stimuli, such as salivation caused by the presence of food in the mouth, can also come to be controlled by other kinds of stimulus.

Classical conditioning accomplishes two functions. First, the ability to learn to recognise stimuli that predict the occurrence of an important event allows the learner to make the appropriate response faster and perhaps more effectively. For example, hearing the buzz of a wasp near your head may make you duck and avoid being stung. Seeing a rival increases an animal's heart rate and the flow of blood to its muscles, makes it assume a threatening posture, and causes the release of hormones that prepare it for vigorous exercise.

The second function of classical conditioning is even more significant. Through classical conditioning, stimuli that were previously unimportant acquire some of the properties of the important stimuli with which the◌ been associated and thus become able to modify ◌ iour. A neutral stimulus becomes desirable when ◌ associated with a desirable stimulus or it becomes u◌ sirable when it is associated with an undesirable one. ◌ sense, the stimulus takes on symbolic value. For exam◌ we respond differently to the sight of a stack of mo◌ and to a stack of paper napkins. The reason for the s◌ cial reaction to money is that money has, in the pa◌ been associated with desirable commodities, such as foo◌ clothing, cars, electrical equipment and so on.

Basic principles of classical conditioning

Classical conditioning involves several learning principles, including acquisition, extinction, spontaneous recovery, stimulus generalisation and discrimination.

Acquisition

In laboratory experiments, a single pairing of the CS with the UCS is not usually sufficient for learning to take place. Only with repeated CS–UCS pairings does conditional responding gradually appear. The learning phase of classical conditioning, during which the CS gradually increases in frequency or strength, is called **acquisition**.

In one study (Trapold and Spence, 1960), a tone (CS) was paired with a puff of air into the eye (UCS). The puff of air caused the participants' eyes to blink automatically (UCR). Conditioning was measured as the percentage of trials in which conditional eyeblinks (CR) occurred. Note that at the beginning of the experiment, the tone elicited very few CRs. During the first 50 trials, the percentage of CRs increased rapidly but finally stabilised.

Two factors that influence the strength of the CR are the intensity of the UCS and the timing of the CS and UCS. The intensity of the UCS can determine how quickly the CR will be acquired: more intense UCSs usually produce more rapid learning. For example, rats will learn a conditioned fear response faster if they receive higher levels of a painful stimulus (Annau and Kamin, 1961). Classical conditioning of a salivary response in dogs occurs faster when the animals are given larger amounts of food (Wagner *et al.*, 1964). Generally speaking, the more intense the UCS, the stronger the CR.

The second factor affecting the acquisition of the CR is the timing of the CS and UCS. Classical conditioning occurs fastest when the CS occurs shortly before the UCS and both stimuli end at the same time. In his experiments on salivary conditioning, Pavlov found that one half-second was the optimal delay between the onset of the CS and the onset of the UCS. With shorter or longer delays between the CS and UCS, conditioning generally was slower and weaker (see Figure 7.2).

Extinction and spontaneous recovery

Once a classically conditioned response has been acquired, what happens to that response if the CS continues to be presented but is no longer followed by the UCS? This procedure, called **extinction**, eventually eliminates the CR. Returning to our classically conditioned eyeblink response, suppose that after we reduce the intensity of the UCS, we stop presenting the UCS (the puff of air). However, we do continue to present the CS (the tone).

It is important to realise that extinction occurs only when the CS occurs but the UCS does not. For example, the eyeblink response will extinguish only if the tone is presented without the puff of air. If neither stimulus is presented, extinction will not occur. In other words, the subject must learn that the CS no longer predicts the occurrence of the UCS– and that cannot happen if neither stimulus is presented.

Once a CR has been extinguished, it may not disappear from the organism's behaviour permanently. Pavlov demonstrated that after responding had been extinguished, the CR would often suddenly reappear the next time the dog was placed in the experimental apparatus. Pavlov referred to the CR's reappearance after a 'time out' period as **spontaneous recovery**. He also found that if he began presenting the CS and the UCS together again, the animals would acquire the conditional response very rapidly – much faster than they did in the first place.

Stimulus generalisation and discrimination

No two stimuli are exactly alike. Once a response has been conditioned to a CS, similar stimuli will also elicit that response. The more closely the other stimuli resemble the CS, the more likely they will elicit the CR. For example, Pavlov discovered that once a dog learned to salivate when it heard a bell, it would salivate when it heard a bell having a different tone or when it heard a buzzer. This phenomenon is called **generalisation**: a response produced by a particular CS will also occur when a similar CS is presented. Of course, there are limits to generalisation. A dog that learns to salivate when it hears a bell will probably not salivate when it hears a door close in the hallway.

In addition, an organism can be taught to distinguish between similar but different stimuli – a phenomenon called **discrimination**. Discrimination training is accomplished by using two different CSs during training. One CS is always followed by the UCS; the other CS is never followed by the UCS. For example, suppose that we regularly direct a puff of air at an animal's eye during each trial in which a low-pitched tone (CS+) is sounded, but on trials in which a high-pitched tone (CS–) is sounded, we present no air puff. At first, increased amounts of blinking will occur in response to both stimuli (generalisation). Gradually, however, fewer and fewer blinks will occur after the CS– but they will continue to be elicited by the CS+ (see Figure 7.3). Discrimination, then, involves learning the difference between two or more stimuli. An animal learns that differences among stimuli are important – it learns when to respond to one stimulus and when not to respond to a different stimulus.

Conditional emotional responses

Many stimuli are able to arouse emotional responses, such as feelings of disgust, contempt, fear, anger, sadness, tenderness, longing or sexual desire. Many of these stimuli, such as a place, a phrase, a song or someone's voice and face, originally had no special significance. But because these stimuli were paired with other stimuli that

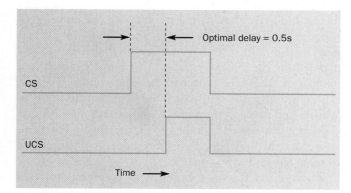

Figure 7.2 The timing of the CS and UCS in classical conditioning. The CS precedes the UCS by a brief interval of time, and both stimuli end simultaneously.

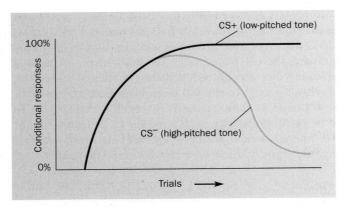

Figure 7.3 Behaviour produced through discrimination training. The CS+ is always followed by the UCS (a puff of air directed towards the eye); the CS− is always presented without the UCS.

elicited strong emotional reactions, they came, through classical conditioning, to take on emotional significance.

If you read or hear words such as 'enemy', 'ugly', 'bitter' or 'failure', you are likely to experience at least a weak negative emotional response. In contrast, the words 'gift', 'win', 'happy' and 'beauty' may elicit positive responses. These words had no effect on you before you learned what they meant. They took on their power through being paired with pleasant or unpleasant events or perhaps with descriptions of such events.

Staats and Staats (1957) found that if people read neutral nonsense words such as 'yof' or 'laj' while hearing positive or negative words, they later said that they liked those that had been associated with the positive words and disliked those that had been associated with the negative ones. The researchers found that this procedure could even affect people's ratings of the pleasantness of names such as Tom or Bill or nationalities such as Italian or Swedish (Staats and Staats, 1958). Berkowitz (1964) found that when people had received unpleasant electrical shocks while in the company of another person, they later acted in a hostile manner towards that person. Thus, classical conditioning may play a role in the development of ethnic prejudices and personal dislikes (and, of course, of positive reactions as well). We are often not aware of the reason for our emotional reactions, we simply feel them and conclude that there is something 'nice' or something 'nasty' about the stimulus (or the person).

Phobias

Many people are troubled by behaviours that they wish they could stop or by thoughts and fears that bother them. Phobias are unreasonable fears of specific objects or situations, such as spiders, cars or enclosed spaces, and we will look at phobias in more detail in Chapter 18.

Presumably, at some time early in life, the person having the phobia was exposed to the now-feared object in conjunction with a stimulus that elicited pain or fear. For example, being stuck in a hot, overcrowded lift with a group of frightened and sweating fellow passengers might be expected to lead to a fear of lifts or perhaps even to produce a fully-fledged phobia.

Classical conditioning can occur even without direct experience with the conditional and unconditional stimuli. For example, a child of a parent who has a snake phobia can develop the same fear simply by observing signs of fear in his or her parent. The child need not be attacked or menaced by a snake. In addition, people can develop phobias vicariously – by hearing about or reading stories that vividly describe unpleasant episodes. The imaginary episode that we picture as we hear or read a story (UCS) can provide imaginary stimuli (CSs) that lead to real conditional emotional responses (CRs).

The case of Little Albert

A famous example of an experimentally induced learned phobia is that of Little Albert. In Chapter 1 you came across the work and ideas of John B. Watson. To Watson, behaviour had to be observable in order to be measured. He was excited by Pavlov's finding that dogs could be conditioned to respond in a specific way to a previously neutral stimulus. He and Rosalie Rayner set up the first experiment in which fear was experimentally conditioned in a human being (Watson and Rayner, 1920).

At the age of nine months, a healthy infant called Albert B was shown to have no fear of live animals such as rats and rabbits (Albert is for ever known in textbooks as Little Albert). When a steel bar was unexpectedly struck by a claw hammer, however, he became distressed and frightened. Watson and Rayner attempted to condition fear of a previously unfeared object (a white rat) in Little Albert by pairing it with a feared stimulus (the noise of the hammer hitting the bar). They paired the rat with the noise seven times in two sessions, one week apart. When the rat was presented on its own, Albert became distressed and avoided the rat. Five days later, Albert was exposed to a number of other objects such as familiar wooden blocks, a rabbit, a dog, a sealskin coat, white cotton, the heads of Watson and two assistants and a Santa Claus mask. Albert showed a fear response to the rabbit, the dog and the sealskin coat. The initial conditioned response had generalised to some objects but not others.

Watson and Rayner's experiment is famous for two reasons. The first is the successful attempt at experimentally conditioning fear in a human being; the second is the number of inaccuracies reported in articles and textbooks describing the experiment (Harris, 1979). These include inaccurate information about Albert's age, the conditioned stimulus and the list of objects that Albert was believed to be frightened of after conditioning (the list includes fur pelt, a man's beard, a cat, a puppy, a glove, Albert's aunt and a teddy bear). These inaccuracies teach a valuable lesson, and that is the wisdom of consulting original sources of information. Because the study of Albert is part of psychology's history, details become distorted when information is passed down from textbook to textbook, a form of memory distortion described in more detail in the next chapter.

What is learned in classical conditioning?

Research shows that for classical conditioning to occur, the CS must be a reliable predictor of the UCS (Rescorla, 1991). Imagine yourself as the subject in a classical conditioning demonstration involving a tone as the CS, a puff of air into your left eye as the UCS and an eyeblink as the CR. Your psychology lecturer asks you to come to the front of the class and seats you in a comfortable chair.

Occasionally, a tone sounds for a second or two, and then a brief but strong puff of air hits your eye. The puff of air makes you blink. Soon you begin to blink during the tone, before the puff occurs. Now consider all the other stimuli in the seminar room – your tutor explaining the demonstration to the group, your colleagues' questions, squeaks from students moving in their chairs, and so on. Why don't any of these sounds become CSs? Why do you blink only during the tone? After all, some of these stimuli occur at the same time as the puff of air. The answer is that among the stimuli present during the demonstration, only the tone reliably predicts the puff of air. All the other stimuli are poor forecasters of the UCS. The neutral stimulus becomes a CS only when the following conditions are satisfied:

1 The CS must regularly occur prior to the presentation of the UCS.

2 The CS does not regularly occur when the UCS is absent.

Consider another example. The smell of food is more likely to elicit feelings of anticipation and excitement about supper if you are hungry than is the smell of your mother's cologne because the smell of the food is the best predictor of a meal about to be served. Similarly, the sound of footsteps behind you as you are walking is more apt to make you afraid than the sound of a car passing by or the wind blowing in the trees because the footsteps are better predictors of being mugged or threatened with danger.

It also appears that conditioned responses are more common to novel than familiar stimuli. Pavlov had observed that a novel CS was more successfully paired with a UCS than was a familiar one. This phenomenon is known as **latent inhibition** (Lubow, 1989), and because familiar stimuli are associated less successfully with conditioning than are novel ones, this effect is called the **CS pre-exposure effect** (because participants will have already been pre-exposed to the CS). Similarly, when an organism is presented with the UCS (which may be novel) before it is used as a UCS in the experiment proper, the link between CS and UCS is weaker. This is called the **UCS pre-exposure effect** (Randich and LoLordo, 1979).

Why does latent inhibition occur? No one quite knows for sure, but one explanation is related to the degree of exposure to the stimulus. A familiar CS is familiar to individuals by being in the environment; because the CS is part of the environment of context then the CS becomes merged into the context of the conditioning. To use a description from signal detection theory which you learned about in Chapter 5, the signal-to-noise ratio is weak – the CS sends a weak signal because it cannot be distinguished from the context very well.

Neurobiological correlates of Pavlovian conditioning

In an experiment to determine the brain regions involved in Pavlovian fear conditioning, participants were exposed to lights that signalled the appearance of a painful electric shock (conditioned stimulus, CS) or ones that did not (Knight *et al.*, 1999). Functional magnetic resonance imaging (fMRI) was used to monitor differences in brain activation. As training and learning progressed, the amount of neuronal activity seen during the warning CS increased in a part of the brain called the anterior cingulate, in the front of the brain. When the light and shock were not paired (i.e. they were not associated), this activation did not occur. Although the researchers suggest that this part of the brain may not be neccessary for learning fear, it does facilitate the learning of fear. Another crucial structure for fear conditioning is the amygdala, and you will discover more about its role in fear recognition and conditioning in Chapter 13.

After behaviourism

Pavlov's work greatly influenced his colleagues abroad, especially the pioneers of behaviourist thinking such as John B. Watson. Behaviourism was a robust and experimentally strict discipline whose principles were laid out by Watson in the first and second decades of the twentieth century. It viewed behaviour and learning in terms of stimulus and response and, as the next evolution of behaviourism described in the next section shows, reinforcement. The inner mind or introspective self-reports played no part in behaviourist thinking: these were unverifiable and held the same status as superstition to the behaviourist. Both stimulus and response could be observed and the effect of one on the other recorded. Behaviourism left a unique and historical legacy that is seen in almost all experimental work undertaken in psychology today; its effects were such that modern psychology has absorbed its principles and aims.

The torch-bearers of behaviourism, however, began to modify elements of its thinking in the mid-twentieth century and although the effects of these modifications made no significant or lasting impact on psychology by themselves, the attempts at modification did because other, more dominant approaches to studying behaviour arose from them. Two influential psychologists, whose specific work did not have a long-lasting effect on the way psychology is studied, but did bequeath a way of thinking about learning and behaviour, were Clark L. Hull (1884–1952) and Edward Chase Tolman (1886–1959).

Hull's computational approach to learning

Of all the learning theories reviewed in this chapter, Hull's is probably the most ambitious and complicated of them. In his two published books, *Principles of Behaviour* (1943) and *A Behaviour System* (1952), Hull made extremely detailed predictions about behaviour that could occur in specific situations. The books contained 153 theorems that ranged from considering how we learn to discriminate, to moving in space, to how we acquire our values, and Hull's aim was to develop a system whereby behaviour could be predicted from specified independent variables (IVs). You can quickly appreciate why the approach is seen as ambitious and complicated.

Hull organised his system by considering what Watson's behaviourism did not wish to: **intervening variables**, the variables that could modify the relationship between stimulus and response. In Hull's system, analysis of behaviour comprised four stages:

Stage 1 Analysis of the IVs from which behaviour was predicted.

Stage 2 Computing values for intervening variables.

Stage 3 Computing values at this stage, using values at stage 2.

Stage 4 Analysis of the dependent variables (DVs).

In summary, the stage process argued that knowing the values of an independent variable at stage 1 meant computing values of the intervening variables at stage 2, using these computed values to compute those at stage 3 and from this predict the outcome (or the dependent variable). Figure 7.4 summarises the main points of the system.

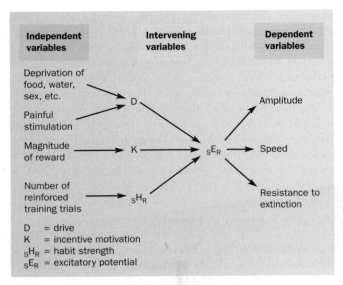

Figure 7.4 A simplified version of Hull's system.

Source: Adapted from Hill W.F., *Learning: A survey of psychological interpretation*, 7th edn. Published by Allyn & Bacon, Boston, MA. Copyright © 1997 by Pearson Education. By permission of the publisher.

The number of independent variables were limitless and could range from direct stimulation (the brightness of light or the loudness of noise) to events that preceded the moment of study (such as degree of exercise taken or the amount of food consumed) to experiential episodes (such as the number of times a person had responded to the stimulus before). To produce a response (the DV), the IV would interact with the intervening variables at stages 3 and 4.

These intervening variables were not directly observeable and were hypothetical states (you might see why Watson's behaviourism would have rejected Hull's approach). According to Hull, there were two types of intervening variable: habit strength and drive. You will find out more about these concepts and their validity in Chapter 13, but for now a simple definition of each would be: habit strength is the strength of the connections that had been learned between a stimulus and a response after reinforced practice had occurred; drive is a state of activation that propels an organism to seek stimulation (a reduction in the drive would serve as a reward). A drive represents a temporary state which is produced when the body has been deprived of something it needs, such as food, water, relief from pain, and so on. The greater the reward, therefore, the greater the reduction in drive: a slice of bread would not significantly reduce the drive for food, but a four course meal might. The greater the number of times a response was followed by reinforcement, the greater the formation of habit strength and the connections between a stimulus and its response. Hull also suggested another variable, incentive motivation, which would account for the organisms's response to rewards of increasing size.

As the above cursory description of the system suggests, Hull's theory was complex and followed detailed mathematical formulae. His second book contained 133 theorems which, for good measure, followed on from 17 postulates and 15 corollaries. The apparent beauty and strength of Hull's system was that one variable could be computed from another using these formulae. Where the system failed, however, was in using the values from a single experiment to predict later behaviour: this often did not work. Hull later stated that the values were meant to be regarded as illustrations rather than as fixed numbers and that, of course, values would vary across individuals. While Hull's work has not had the direct influence and impact on later theory of some other schools of learning and behaviour, it represented an ambitious and laudable attempt at pinning down behaviour to values that could be computed and used to predict later behaviour.

Tolman and the cognitive map

Like Hull, Tolman argued that there was more to the study of learning and behaviour than simply recording the stimulus and measuring the response. Tolman's view was that a theory of behaviour should consider the cognitive variables that intercede between stimulus and response: our thoughts, beliefs, attitudes, motivation to succeed and so on are all important determinants of our response to a stimulus.

Tolman's approach was called purposive behaviourism and although, like the behaviourism it followed, it concerned itself with objective and observable behaviour and the external influences that could change it, it was also concerned with the cognitive processes that guided or gave rise to that behaviour. Behaviour had a purpose; it was executed to achieve a goal, hence, purposive behaviourism.

According to Tolman, the behaviour that we engage in to achieve our goals is underpinned by our cognitions. Our cognitive processing can be measured by observing the way in which a person behaves or has experienced specific stimuli. For example, we might learn that chilli con carne tastes nicer with added ginger, cinnamon and three, rather than two, red chillies, so we make the chilli again adding these ingredients. None or any might make the chilli nicer but if none do, we experiment again either by adding or subtracting ingredients. Our experience – our cognitions – modifies our behaviour.

Tolman's most famous illustration of learning and the cognitions that lead to a response is that of reward loca-

tion. If an organism finds a way of locating a reward, it may eventually find a different, more efficient method, of locating it. If you imagine yourself in a strange town centre for the first time, your first successfully navigated route to a shop may be the longest, or least efficient one. With increasing knowledge of the environment, you will eventually find the shortest, quickest route to the shop you want.

In Tolman's experiment, rats were allowed to run on a table and through an enclosed alleyway which led to various elevated pathways at the end of one of which was some food (Tolman *et al.*, 1946). When the rat had learned the location of the food, the alleyway was removed and replaced with new routes which went in different directions. Figure 7.5 shows you the difference between the two conditions.

Tolman *et al.* found that, in the second condition, the rats did not take the route they had previously learned in order to obtain the food. Instead, they took a short-cut towards the direction of the food. According to Tolman, the rat had learned a 'cognitive map' of the routes and chose the shortest one. Although this seems eminently plausible, Tolman did not seem to consider that the rat may have taken the shortest route because the smell of the food led the rodent to it.

This objection aside, Tolman's influence was important because it rejected the stiff stimulus–response (S–R) approaches of behaviourism and encouraged an emphasis on the cognitive variables that shape behaviour. The essential principles of the approach can be seen in much

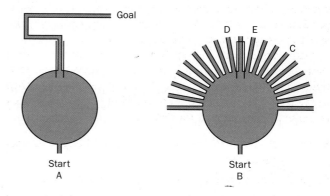

Figure 7.5 The two pathways used in Tolman's experiment. In the first, the rat takes the longer route in order to find the food. In the second, the original route is blocked and 18 new routes made available. The rats chose the tunnel marked C (that corresponding most closely to the location of the food), rather than D or E, the routes closest to that originally taken.

Source: Hill W.F., *Learning: A survey of psychological interpretation*, 7th edn. Published by Allyn & Bacon, Boston, MA. Copyright © 1997 by Pearson Education. By permission of the publisher.

Figure 7.6 A simulated view of a central corridor in a building used in Wilson *et al.*'s experiment.

Source: Wilson, P. N., Foreman N. and Stanton, D. Improving spatial awareness in physically disabled children using virtual environments. *Engineering Science and Education Journal*, 1999, 8(5), 196–200, reprinted by permission of the Institute of Electrical Engineers.

of modern-day experiments on transfer of learning: the principle whereby learning in one environment can be successfully transferred to a different one. Work in virtual reality technology, for example, has been able to present participants with 'virtual' versions of environments which participants can navigate and explore before encountering the actual environment, thereby assisting navigation in the real version (Wilson *et al.*, 1999). An example of one of these virtual images (part of an animated tour) can be seen in Figure 7.6. This image shows the ground floor central corridor of a simulated building (based on the psychology department at Leicester University, England).

Wilson *et al.* (1996a) found that severely disabled children who explored this computer simulation were able to point successfully to objects in the real building when they later encountered it. A group of undergraduates who guessed the location of the objects, without having had the benefit of exposure to the computer simulation, performed less accurately.

Tolman died just before the beginning of what is called in psychology, 'the cognitive revolution', which you read about in Chapter 1. However, his approach was a precursor to the cognitive revolution and prompted other disciplines, such as linguistics, to consider cognitive variables in their study. While Tolman's ideas were superseded to some extent by developments in cognitive psychology, his work could be seen as the bedrock on which cognitive psychology's general approach is based.

Operant conditioning

Habituation and classical conditioning teach us about stimuli in the environment: we learn to ignore unimportant stimuli, and we learn about those that predict the occurrence of important ones. These forms of learning deal with relations between one stimulus and another. In contrast, **operant conditioning** tells about the relations between environmental stimuli and our own behaviour; it is also called instrumental learning. The term 'operant' refers to the fact that an organism learns through responding – through operating on the environment. The principle behind operant conditioning is already familiar to you: when a particular action has good consequences, the action will tend to be repeated; when a particular action has bad consequences, the action will tend not to be repeated.

The law of effect

Operant conditioning was first discovered in the basement of a house in Cambridge, Massachusetts, by a 24-year-old man who would later become one of the twentieth century's most influential educational psychologists, Edward L. Thorndike. Thorndike placed a hungry cat inside a 'puzzle box'. The animal could escape and eat some food only after it operated a latch that opened the door. At first, the cat engaged in random behaviour: mewing, scratching, hissing, pacing and so on. Eventually, the cat would accidentally activate the latch and open the door. On successive trials, the animal's behaviour would become more and more efficient until it was operating the latch without hesitation. Thorndike called this process 'learning by trial and accidental success'.

Thorndike explained that the cat learned to make the correct response because only the correct response was followed by a favourable outcome: escape from the box and the opportunity to eat some food. The occurrence of the favourable outcome strengthens the response that produced it. Thorndike called this relation between a response and its consequences the **law of effect**.

The impact of Thorndike's discovery of the law of effect on the early development of scientific psychology would be difficult to overstate. It affected research in the study of learning in one very important way: it stimulated an enormous number of experimental studies aimed at understanding behaviour–environment interactions, a line of research that is known today as behaviour analysis. Nowhere was this effect more evident than in the work of B.F. Skinner.

see activity on mypsychlab

Skinner and operant behaviour

Although Thorndike discovered the law of effect, Harvard psychologist Burrhus Frederic Skinner championed the laboratory study of the law of effect and advocated the application of behaviour analysis and its methods for solving human problems (Skinner, 1953, 1971; Mazur, 1994). He devised objective methods for studying behaviour, invented apparatus and methods for observing it, and created his own philosophy for interpreting it (Bolles, 1979). Moreover, he wrote several books for the general public, including a novel, *Walden Two*, that showed how his discoveries might be used for improving society (Skinner, 1948).

One of Skinner's most important inventions was the **operant chamber** (or Skinner box), an apparatus in which an animal's behaviour can be easily observed, manipulated and automatically recorded (as seen in Figure 7.7).

For example, an operant chamber used for rats is constructed so that a particular behaviour, such as pressing on a lever, will occasionally cause a pellet of food to be delivered. An operant chamber used for pigeons is built so that a peck at a plastic disc on the front wall will occasionally open a drawer that contains some grain. Behaviour analysts who study human behaviour use special devices suitable to the unique characteristics of their human subjects (Baron *et al.*, 1991). In this case, instead of giving their participants some food, they give them points (as in a video game) or points exchangeable for money.

Behaviour analysts manipulate environmental events to determine their effects on response rate, the number of responses emitted during a given amount of time. Events that increase response rate are said to strengthen responding; events that decrease response rate weaken

responding. To measure response rate, Skinner devised the **cumulative recorder**, a device that records each response as it occurs in time.

The invention of the operant chamber and the cumulative recorder represent clear advances over Thorndike's research methods because subjects can (1) emit responses more freely over a greater time period, and (2) be studied for longer periods of time without interference produced by the experimenter handling or otherwise interacting with them between trials. Under highly controlled conditions such as these, behaviour analysts have been able to discover a wide range of important behavioural principles.

The three-term contingency

Behaviour does not occur in a vacuum. Sometimes a response will have certain consequences; sometimes it will not. Our daily behaviour is guided by many different kinds of discriminative stimuli – stimuli that indicate that behaviour will have certain consequences and thus sets the occasion for responding. For example, consider answering the telephone. The phone rings, you pick it up and say 'hello' into the receiver. Most of the time, someone on the other end of the line begins to speak. Have you ever picked up a telephone when it was not ringing and said, 'hello'? Doing so would be absurd, because there would be no one on the other end of the line with whom to speak. We answer the phone (make a response) only when the phone rings (the preceding event) because, in the past, someone with whom we enjoy talking has been at the other end of the line (the following event). Skinner referred formally to the relationship among these three items – the preceding event, the response and the following event – as the **three-term contingency** (see Figure 7.8).

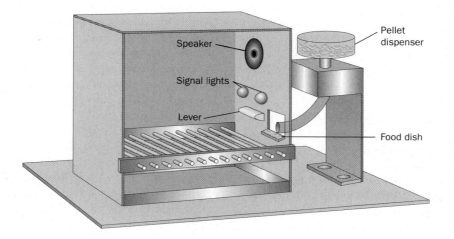

Figure 7.7 An operant chamber. (This operant chamber is used for lever pressing by rats.)

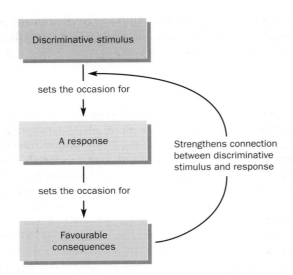

Figure 7.8 The three-term contingency.

The preceding event – the discriminative stimulus – sets the occasion for responding because, in the past, when that stimulus occurred, the response was followed by certain consequences. If the phone rings, we are likely to answer it because we have learned that doing so has particular (and generally favourable) consequences. The response we make – in this case, picking up the phone when the phone rings and saying 'hello' – is called an operant behaviour. The following event – the voice on the other end of the line – is the consequence of the operant behaviour.

Operant behaviour, therefore, occurs in the presence of discriminative stimuli and is followed by certain consequences. These consequences are contingent upon behaviour, that is, they are produced by that behaviour. In the presence of discriminative stimuli, a consequence will occur if and only if an operant behaviour occurs. In the absence of a discriminative stimulus, the operant behaviour will have no effect. Once an operant behaviour is established, it tends to persist whenever the discriminative stimulus occurs, even if other aspects of the environment change (Nevin, 1988; Mace *et al.*, 1990). Of course, motivational factors can affect a response. For example, you might not bother to answer the telephone if you are doing something you do not want to interrupt.

Reinforcement, punishment and extinction

Behaviour analysts study behaviour–environment interactions by manipulating the relations among components of the three-term contingency. Of the three elements, the consequence is the most frequently manipulated variable. In general, operant behaviours can be followed by five different kinds of consequence: positive reinforcement, negative reinforcement, punishment, response cost and extinction. These consequences are always defined in terms of their effect on responding.

Positive reinforcement

Positive reinforcement refers to an increase in the frequency of a response that is regularly and reliably followed by an appetitive stimulus. An appetitive stimulus is any stimulus that an organism seeks out. If an appetitive stimulus follows a response and increases the frequency of that response, we call it a positive reinforcer. For example, the opportunity to eat some food can reinforce a hungry pigeon's pecking of a plastic disc. Money or other rewards (including social rewards) can reinforce a person's behaviour. Suppose that you visit a new restaurant and really enjoy your meal. You are likely to visit the restaurant several more times because you like the food. This example illustrates positive reinforcement. Your enjoyment of the food (the appetitive stimulus) reinforces your going to the restaurant and ordering dinner (the response).

Negative reinforcement

Negative reinforcement refers to an increase in the frequency of a response that is regularly and reliably followed by the termination of an aversive stimulus. An aversive stimulus is unpleasant or painful. If an aversive stimulus is terminated (ends or is turned off) as soon as a response occurs and thus increases the frequency of that response, we call it a negative reinforcer. For example, after you have walked barefoot across a stretch of hot pavement, the termination of the painful burning sensation negatively reinforces your response of sticking your feet into a puddle of cool water.

It is important to remember that both positive and negative reinforcement increase the likelihood that a given response will occur again. However, positive reinforcement involves the occurrence of an appetitive stimulus, whereas negative reinforcement involves the termination of an aversive stimulus. Negative reinforcement is thus not the same as punishment.

Punishment

Punishment refers to a decrease in the frequency of a response that is regularly and reliably followed by an aversive stimulus. If an aversive stimulus follows a response and decreases the frequency of that response, we call it a punisher. For example, receiving a painful bite would punish the response of sticking your finger into a parrot's cage. People often attempt to punish the behaviour of their children or pets by scolding them.

Although punishment is effective in reducing or suppressing undesirable behaviour in the short term, it can also produce several negative side effects: unrestrained use of physical force (for example, child abuse) may cause serious bodily injury. Punishment often induces fear, hostility and other undesirable emotions in people receiving punishment. It may result in retaliation against the punisher. Through punishment, organisms learn only which response not to make. Punishment does not teach the organism desirable responses.

Reinforcement and punishment are most effective in maintaining or changing behaviour when a stimulus immediately follows the behaviour. It may occur to you that many organisms, particularly humans, can tolerate a long delay between their work and the reward that they receive for it. This ability appears to contradict the principle that reinforcement must occur immediately. However, the apparent contradiction can be explained by a phenomenon called conditioned reinforcement.

Why is immediacy of reinforcement or punishment essential for learning? The answer is found by examining the function of operant conditioning: learning about the consequences of our own behaviour. Normally, causes and effects are closely related in time; you do something, and something immediately happens, good or bad. The consequences of our action teach us whether to repeat that action. Events that follow a response by a long delay were probably not caused by that response.

It is important not to confuse punishment with negative reinforcement. Punishment causes a behaviour to decrease, whereas negative reinforcement causes a behaviour to increase.

Response cost

Response cost refers to a decrease in the frequency of a response that is regularly and reliably followed by the termination of an appetitive stimulus. Response cost is a form of punishment. For example, suppose that you are enjoying a conversation with an attractive person that you have just met. You make a disparaging remark about a political party. Your new friend's smile suddenly disappears. You quickly change the topic and never bring it up again. The behaviour (disparaging remark) is followed by the removal of an appetitive stimulus (your new friend's smile). The removal of the smile punishes the disparaging remark.

Response cost is often referred to as time-out from positive reinforcement (or simply time-out) when it is used to remove a person physically from an activity that is reinforcing to that person.

As we have just seen, there are four types of operant conditioning – two kinds of reinforcement and two kinds of punishment – caused by the occurrence or termination

of appetitive or aversive stimuli. Another way to change behaviour through operant conditioning is extinction, which involves no consequence at all. See Figure 7.9.

Extinction

Extinction is a decrease in the frequency of a previously reinforced response because it is no longer followed by a reinforcer. Behaviour that is no longer reinforced decreases in frequency: it is said to extinguish. For example, a rat whose lever pressing was reinforced previously with food will eventually stop pressing the lever when food is no longer delivered. People soon learn to stop dropping money into vending machines that don't work. A young boy will stop telling his favourite 'knock-knock' joke if no one laughs at it any more.

Extinction is not the same as forgetting. Forgetting takes place when a behaviour is not rehearsed (or a person does not think about a particular memory) for a long time. Extinction takes place when an organism makes a response that is no longer reinforced. If the organism does not have an opportunity to make that response, it will not extinguish. For example, if you go out of town for a few weeks, you will not forget how to operate the vending

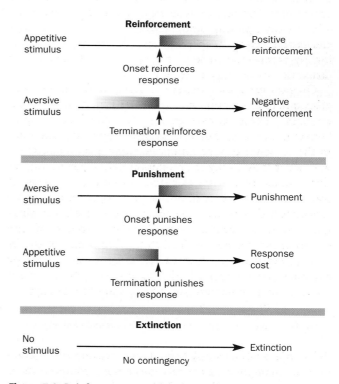

Figure 7.9 Reinforcement, punishment and extinction produced by the onset, termination or omission of appetitive or aversive stimuli. The upward-pointing arrows indicate the occurrence of a response.

machine where you often buy a bar of chocolate. However, if you put money in the machine and do not receive anything in return, your response will extinguish.

Other operant procedures and phenomena

The basic principles of reinforcement, punishment and extinction described above are used in other operant procedures to teach an organism a new response, to teach it when or when not to respond, or to teach it how to respond in a particular way.

Shaping

Most behaviour is acquired through an organism's interaction with reinforcing and punishing events in its environment. In fact, Skinner developed a technique, called **shaping**, to teach new behaviours to his subjects. Shaping involves reinforcing any behaviour that successively approximates the desired response. Imagine that we want to train a rat to press a lever when a red light is lit (the discriminative stimulus) in an operant chamber. Although the rat has used its paws to manipulate many things during its lifetime, it has never before pressed a lever in an operant chamber. And when it is first placed in the chamber, it is not likely to press the lever even once on its own.

The lever on the wall of the chamber is attached to an electrical switch that is wired to electronic control equipment or a computer. A mechanical dispenser can automatically drop pellets of food into a dish in the chamber. Thus, the delivery of a food pellet can be made dependent on the rat's pressing the lever.

Before we can shape lever pressing, we must make the rat hungry. We do so by letting the animal eat only once a day. When we know that it is hungry, we place the animal in the operant chamber and then train it to eat the food pellets as they are dispensed from the pellet dispenser. As each pellet is delivered, the dispenser makes a clicking sound. This sound is important. No matter where the rat is in the operant chamber, it can hear the sound, which indicates that the food pellet has been dispensed. Once the rat is hungry and has learned where to obtain food, we are ready to shape the desired response. We make the operation of the pellet dispenser contingent on the rat's behaviour. We start by giving the rat a food pellet for just facing in the direction of the lever. Next, we wait until the rat makes a move towards the lever. Finally, we give the rat a piece of food only if it touches the lever. Soon, our rat performs like Thorndike's cats: it makes the same response again and again.

Shaping is a formal training procedure, but something like it also occurs in the world outside the laboratory. A teacher praises poorly formed letters produced by a child who is just beginning to print. As time goes on, only more accurately drawn letters bring approval. The method of successive approximations can also be self-administered. Consider the acquisition of skills through trial and error. To begin with, you must be able to recognise the target behaviour – the behaviour displayed by a person having the appropriate skill. Your first attempts produce behaviours that vaguely resemble those of a skilled performer, and you are satisfied by the results of these attempts. In other words, the stimuli that are produced by your behaviour serve as reinforcers for that behaviour. As your skill develops, you become less satisfied with crude approximations to the final behaviour; you are satisfied only when your behaviour improves so that it more closely resembles the target behaviour. Your own criteria change as you become more skilled. Skills such as learning to draw a picture, catching a ball, or making a bed are all behaviours that are acquired through shaping. After all, when a child learns these skills, they first learn behaviours that only approximate the final level of skill that they will attain. This process is perfectly analogous to the use of changing criteria in training an animal to perform a complex behaviour.

Intermittent reinforcement

So far, we have considered situations in which a reinforcing stimulus is presented after each response (or, in the case of extinction, not at all). But usually not every response is reinforced. Sometimes a kind word is ignored; sometimes it is appreciated. Not every fishing trip is rewarded with a catch, but some are, and that is enough to keep a person trying.

The term **intermittent reinforcement** refers to situations in which not every occurrence of a response is reinforced. The relation between responding and reinforcement usually follows one of two patterns: each response has a certain probability of being reinforced, or responses are reinforced after particular intervals of time have elapsed. Probability-based patterns require a variable number of responses for each reinforcer. Consider the performance of an archer shooting arrows at a target. Suppose that the archer hits the bull's-eye one-fifth of the time. On average, he will have to make five responses for every reinforcement (hitting the bull's-eye); the ratio of responding to reinforcement is five to one. The number of reinforcers the archer receives is directly proportional to the number of responses he makes. If he shoots more arrows (that is, if his rate of responding increases), he will receive more reinforcers, assuming that he does not get tired or careless.

Behaviour analysts refer to this pattern of intermittent reinforcement as a ratio schedule of reinforcement. In the laboratory, the apparatus controlling the operant chamber may be programmed to deliver a reinforcer after every fifth response (a ratio of five to one), after every tenth, after every two hundredth, or after any desired number. If the ratio is constant – for example if a reinforcer is programmed to be delivered following every tenth response – the animal will respond rapidly, receive the reinforcer, pause a little while, and then begin responding again. This type of ratio schedule is called a **fixed-ratio schedule** (specifically, a fixed-ratio 10 schedule).

If the ratio is variable, averaging a particular number of responses but varying from trial to trial, the animal will respond at a steady, rapid pace. For example, we might programme a reinforcer to be delivered, on average, after every 50 responses. This type of ratio schedule is called a **variable-ratio schedule** (specifically, a variable-ratio 50 schedule). A slot machine is sometimes programmed to deliver money on a variable-ratio schedule of reinforcement. Variable in this instance means that the person cannot predict how many responses will be needed for the next pay-off.

The second type of pattern of reinforcement involves time. A response is reinforced, but only after a particular time interval has elapsed. Imagine that you wanted to know what the weather was going to be like because your friends are due to visit, but the weather where they are is quite snowy. In order to keep abreast of the weather, you listen to the half-hourly bulletin on your local radio station. This pattern of intermittent reinforcement is called an interval schedule of reinforcement. After various intervals of time, a response will be reinforced. If the time intervals are fixed, the animal will stop responding after each reinforcement. It learns that responses made immediately after reinforcement are never reinforced. Then it will begin responding a little while before the next reinforcer is available. This type of interval schedule is called a **fixed-interval schedule**.

If the time intervals are variable, an animal will respond at a slow, steady rate. That way, it will not waste energy on useless responses, but it will not miss any opportunities for reinforcement either. This type of interval schedule is called a **variable-interval schedule**. In a variable-interval 60-second schedule of reinforcement, a reinforcer would be delivered immediately following the first response after different time intervals had elapsed. The interval might be 30 seconds at one time, and 90 seconds at another, but, on the average, it will be 60 seconds. An animal whose behaviour is reinforced by this schedule would learn not to pause immediately after a reinforcer was delivered. Instead, it would steadily respond throughout the interval, regardless of the length of the interval.

Schedules of reinforcement are important because they show us that different reinforcement contingencies affect the pattern and rate of responding. Think about your own behaviour. How would you perform in subjects in which your grades were determined by a mid-term and a final exam, or by weekly quizzes, or by unannounced quizzes that occur at variable intervals? What kind of schedule of reinforcement is a salesperson on while waiting on potential customers?

Some people work at a slow, steady rate, but others work furiously after long periods of inactivity. Can it be that in the past their work habits were shaped by different schedules of reinforcement?

Resistance to extinction and intermittent reinforcement

A response that has been reinforced intermittently is more resistant to extinction. A response that has been continuously reinforced is much less likely to be so resistant. Baldwin and Baldwin (1998) illustrate this by citing the example of two girls who were prone to throwing temper tantrums. Connie (for it is she) received continuous reinforcement for her tantrums by her parents. Whenever she would throw a tantrum, her parents would pay her attention. Paula (for it is she), however, received only intermittent reinforcement – her parents had two other children and would only pay attention to her tantrums about once in every six episodes. This, as you now know, is a typical variable-ratio 6 method of reinforcement.

When they joined school, the teacher expressed unhappiness at the tantrums and suggested that the parents undertake a programme of extinction: they were asked to ignore all tantrums. What happened? On the first day of extinction, Connie actually experienced more tantrums (20 per cent more – Lerman and Iwata, 1995) but this dropped to zero in the next few days. Paula's behaviour, on the other hand, was less resistant to extinction. It took 2–3 weeks for the tantrums gradually to reduce. She continued to throw tantrums long after Connie had stopped.

Why? Well, Connie's behaviour changed because previously continuously reinforced behaviour was now not reinforced at all. Her behaviour received no reinforcement and because her tantrums did not attract the necessary attention, they stopped. They increased on the first day because Connie believed she had to produce more behaviour to receive her reinforcement. When she realised that this behaviour would not be reinforced, she stopped. Paula's behaviour, however, had previously been intermittently reinforced (every sixth tantrum) and so the new schedule had little effect on her tantrums because she had become accustomed to receiving no reinforcement for her behaviour. On the first day of the programme, therefore, she behaved as she normally would because it was pretty much like normal. Her extinction was gradual and longer than Connie's because it took a longer period to realise that reinforcement was completely absent rather than intermittent.

Generalisation and discrimination

In classical conditioning, generalisation means that stimuli resembling the CS also elicit the CR. In operant conditioning, generalisation means that stimuli resembling a discriminative stimulus also serve as discriminative stimuli for a particular response.

In operant conditioning, as in classical conditioning, generalisation can be reduced through discrimination training. In classical conditioning, discrimination means that CRs occur only in response to certain CSs and not to other, similar stimuli. In operant conditioning, discrimination means that responding occurs only when a particular discriminative stimulus is present – one that was present while responding was reinforced in the past. Responding does not occur when discriminative stimuli associated with extinction or punishment are present.

Obviously, recognising certain kinds of similarities between different categories of stimuli is a very important task in our everyday lives. When we encounter a problem to solve – for example, diagnosing a puzzling disease or improving a manufactured product – we attempt to discover elements of the situation that are similar to those we have seen in other situations and try to apply the strategies that have been successful in the past. That is, we try to generalise old solutions to new problems.

Discriminative stimuli can exert powerful control over responding because of their association with the consequences of such responding. In or out of the laboratory, we learn to behave appropriately to environmental conditions. For example, we usually talk about different things with different people. We learn that some friends do not care for sports, so we do not talk about this topic with them because we will receive few reinforcers (such as nods or smiles). Instead, we discuss topics that have interested them in the past.

Conditioned reinforcement and punishment

We have studied reinforcement mainly in terms of primary reinforcers and primary punishers. **Primary reinforcers** are biologically significant appetitive stimuli, such as food when one is hungry. **Primary punishers** are biologically significant aversive stimuli, such as those that produce pain. Behaviour can also be reinforced with a wide variety of other stimuli: money, a smile, kind words, a pat on the back, or prizes and awards. These stimuli, called **conditioned (or secondary) reinforcers**, acquire their reinforcing properties through association with primary reinforcers. Because it can be exchanged for so many different kinds of primary reinforcers in our society, money is the most common conditioned reinforcer among humans. That money is a conditioned reinforcer can be demonstrated by asking yourself whether you would continue to work if you could no longer exchange money for food, drink, shelter and other items.

Similarly, **conditioned punishers** acquire their punishing effects through association with aversive events. For example, the sight of a flashing light on top of a police car serves as a conditioned punisher to a person who is driving too fast because such a sight precedes an unpleasant set of stimuli: a lecture by a police officer and a ticket for speeding.

A stimulus becomes a conditioned reinforcer or punisher by means of classical conditioning. That is, if a neutral stimulus occurs regularly just before an appetitive or aversive stimulus, then the neutral stimulus itself becomes an appetitive or aversive stimulus. The primary reinforcer or punisher serves as the UCS because it produces the UCR – good or bad feelings. After classical conditioning takes place, these good or bad feelings are produced by the CS – the conditioned reinforcer or punisher. Once that happens, the stimulus can reinforce or punish behaviours by itself. Thus, operant conditioning often involves aspects of classical conditioning.

Conditioned reinforcement and punishment are very important. They permit an organism's behaviour to be affected by stimuli that are not biologically important in themselves but that are regularly associated with the onset or termination of biologically important stimuli. Indeed, stimuli can even become conditioned reinforcers or punishers by being associated with other conditioned reinforcers or punishers. The speeding ticket is just such an example. If an organism's behaviour could be controlled only by primary reinforcers and punishers, its behaviour would not be very flexible. The organism would never learn to perform behaviours that had only long-range benefits. Instead, its behaviour would be controlled on a moment-to-moment basis by a very limited set of stimuli. Conditioned reinforcers and punishers, such as money, grades, smiles and frowns, allow for behaviour to be altered by a wide variety of contingencies.

Conditioning of complex behaviours

The previous sections considered rather simple examples of reinforced behaviours. But people and many other animals are able to learn very complex behaviours. Consider the behaviour of a young girl learning to print letters. She sits at her school desk, producing long rows of letters. What kinds of reinforcing stimuli maintain her behaviour? Why is she devoting her time to a task that involves so much effort?

The answer is that her behaviour produces stimuli – printed letters – which serve as conditioned reinforcers. In previous class sessions, the teacher demonstrated how to print the letters and praised the girl for printing them herself. The act of printing was reinforced, and the printed letters that this act produces come to serve as conditioned reinforcers. The child prints a letter, sees that it looks close to the way it should, and her efforts are reinforced by the sight of the letter. Doing something correctly or making progress towards that goal can provide an effective reinforcer.

This fact is often overlooked by people who take a limited view of the process of reinforcement, thinking that it has to resemble the delivery of a small piece of food to an animal being taught a trick. Some people even say that because reinforcers are rarely delivered to humans immediately after they perform a behaviour, operant conditioning cannot play a major role in human learning. This assertion misses the point that, especially for humans, reinforcers can be very subtle events.

Aversive control of behaviour

Your own experience has probably taught you that punishment can be as effective as positive reinforcement in changing behaviour. Aversive control of behaviour is common in our society, from fines given to speeding motorists to the prison sentences given to criminals. Aversive control of behaviour is common for two main reasons. First, it can be highly effective in inducing behaviour change, producing nearly immediate results. A person given a fine for jumping a red light is likely, at least for a short while, to heed the sign's message. The very effectiveness of punishment as a means of behaviour change can serve as an immediate reinforcer for the person doing the punishing.

Secondly, society cannot always control the positive reinforcers that shape and maintain the behaviour of its members. However, it can and does control aversive stimuli that may be used to punish misconduct. For example, suppose that a young person's peers encourage antisocial behaviours such as theft. Society has no control over reinforcers provided by the peer group, but it can control stimuli to punish the antisocial behaviours, such as fines and imprisonment.

How punishing stimuli work

How does a punishing stimulus suppress behaviour? Punishment, like reinforcement, usually involves a discriminative stimulus. A child's shouting is usually punished in the classroom but not outdoors during a break. A dog chases a porcupine, gets stuck with quills, and never chases one again. However, it continues to chase the neighbour's cat.

Most aversive stimuli elicit some sort of protective or defensive response, such as cringing, freezing, hiding or running away. The response depends on the species of animal and, of course, on the situation. If you slap your dog for a misdeed, the dog will cower and slink away, looking clearly 'apologetic', because you are in a position of dominance. However, if the dog is struck by a stranger, it may very well react by attacking the person. Both types of behaviour are known as species-specific defence reactions (Bolles, 1970).

Escape and avoidance

Negative reinforcement teaches organisms to make responses that terminate aversive stimuli. These responses can make a stimulus cease or the organism can simply run away. In either case, psychologists call the behaviour an **escape response**: the organism endures the effects of the aversive stimulus until its behaviour terminates the stimulus. In some cases, the animal can do more than escape the aversive stimulus; it can learn to do something to prevent it occurring. This type of behaviour is known as an **avoidance response**.

Avoidance responses usually require some warning that the aversive stimulus is about to occur in order for the organism to be able to make the appropriate response soon enough. Imagine that you meet a man at a party who backs you against the wall and engages you in the most boring conversation you have ever had. In addition, his breath is so bad that you are afraid you will pass out. You finally manage to break away from him (an escape response). A few days later, you attend another party. You begin walking towards the buffet table and see the same man (discriminative stimulus) standing nearby. You decide that you will get some food later and turn away to talk with some friends at the other end of the room (an avoidance response).

As we saw earlier, phobias can be considered to be conditioned emotional responses – fears that are acquired through classical conditioning. But unlike most classically conditioned responses, phobias are especially resistant to extinction. If we classically condition an eyeblink response in a rabbit and then repeatedly present the CS alone, without the UCS (puff of air), the response will extinguish. However, if a person has a phobia for cockroaches, the phobia will not extinguish easily even if they encounter cockroaches and nothing bad happens. Why does the response persist?

Most psychologists believe that the answer lies in a subtle interaction between operant and classical conditioning. The sight of a cockroach makes a person with a cockroach phobia feel frightened, that is, they experience an unpleasant conditional emotional response. The person runs out of the room, leaving the cockroach behind and reducing the unpleasant feelings of fear. This reduction in an aversive stimulus reinforces the avoidance response and perpetuates the phobia.

Conditioning of flavour aversions

You have probably eaten foods that made you sick and now avoid them on the basis of their flavour alone. The association of a substance's flavour with illness, which is often caused by eating that substance, leads to **conditioned flavour-aversion learning**.

The study of flavour-aversion learning is important not only because it is a real-life experience, but also because it has taught psychologists about unique relations that may exist between certain CSs and certain UCSs. Just as punishment is a result of classical conditioning where a species-typical defensive response becomes classically conditioned to a discriminative stimulus, conditioned flavour aversions are acquired in the same way. The flavour is followed by an unconditional stimulus (sickness) that elicits the unpleasant responses of the autonomic nervous system, such as cramping and retching. Then, when the animal encounters the flavour again, the experience triggers unpleasant internal reactions that cause the animal to stop eating the food.

Many learning researchers once believed that nearly any CS could be paired with nearly any UCS to produce nearly any CR. However, in a now classic experiment, Garcia and Koelling (1966) showed that animals are more prepared to learn some types of relation among stimuli than others.

In the first phase of their experiment, Garcia and Koelling permitted rats to drink saccharine-flavoured water from a tube. Each lick from the tube produced three CSs: taste, noise and bright lights. This phase ensured that rats were equally familiar with each of the CSs. In the next phase, the rats were divided into four groups, each experiencing either 'bright-noisy' water or 'tasty' water. Each CS was paired with illness or electric shock.

After several trials, the experimenters measured the amount of saccharine-flavoured water the rats consumed. They found that the rats learned the association between flavour and illness but not between flavour and pain produced by electric shock. Likewise, the rats learned the association between the 'bright-noisy' water and shock-induced pain but not between the 'bright-noisy' water and illness. The results make sense; after all, the animal has to taste the flavour that makes it ill, not hear it, and in the world outside the laboratory, a particular flavour does not usually indicate that you are about to receive an electric shock.

This experiment draws two important conclusions: (1) rats can learn about associations between internal sensations (being sick) and novel tastes, and (2) the interval between the two stimuli can be very long. These facts suggest that the brain mechanisms responsible for a conditioned flavour aversion are different from the ones that mediate an aversion caused by stimuli applied to the outside of the body (such as a painful foot shock). It appears that conditioned flavour aversions serve to protect animals from poisonous foods by enabling them to learn to avoid eating them. Because few naturally occurring poisons cause sickness immediately, neural mechanisms that mediate conditioned flavour aversions must be capable of learning the association between events that are separated in time. Most other cause-and-effect relations involve events that occur close in time; hence the neural mechanisms that mediate an organism's ability to learn about them operate under different time constraints.

Some animals have eating habits quite different from those of rats; they eat foods that they cannot taste or smell. For example, some birds eat seeds that are encased in a tasteless husk. They do not have teeth, so they cannot break open the husk and taste the seed. Thus, they cannot use odour or taste as a cue to avoid a poison. However, Wilcoxon *et al.* (1971) found that quail (a species of seed-eating birds) can form a conditioned aversion to the sight of food that earlier made them sick. People can also acquire conditioned flavour aversions. A friend of mine often took trips on aeroplanes with her parents when she was a child. Unfortunately, she usually got airsick. Just before take-off, her mother would give her some spearmint-flavoured chewing gum to help relieve the pressure on her eardrums that would occur when the plane ascended. She developed a conditioned flavour aversion to spearmint gum. In fact, the odour of the gum still makes her feel nauseated.

Conditioned flavour aversions, like most learning situations, involve both classical and operant conditioning. From one point of view, we can say that the aversive stimuli produced by the poison punish the behaviour of eating a particular food. That is, the flavour serves as a discriminative stimulus for a punishment contingency (operant conditioning). However, it also serves as a conditioned stimulus for a classical conditioning situation: the flavour is followed by an unconditional stimulus (the poison) that elicits unpleasant responses of the autonomic nervous system, such as cramping and retching. Then, when the animal encounters the flavour at a later date, it experiences unpleasant reactions that cause it to leave the source of the stimulus and avoid the food.

Psychology in action – Flavour aversions

Because conditioned flavour aversions can occur when particular flavours are followed by feelings of nausea, even several hours later, this phenomenon has several implications for situations outside the laboratory. An unfortunate side effect of chemotherapy or radiation therapy for cancer is nausea. Besides killing the rapidly dividing cells of malignant tumours, both chemotherapy and radiation kill the rapidly dividing cells that line the digestive system and thus cause nausea and vomiting.

Knowing what we know about conditioned flavour aversions, we might predict that chemotherapy or radiation therapy would cause a conditioned aversion to the foods a patient ate during the previous meal. Bernstein (1978) showed that this prediction is correct. She gave ice cream to some cancer patients who were about to receive a session of chemotherapy and found that several months later, 75 per cent of these patients refused to eat ice cream of the same flavour. In contrast, control subjects who did not taste it before their chemotherapy said that they liked it very much. Only one trial was necessary to develop the conditioned flavour aversion. Even when patients have a clear understanding that the drugs are responsible for their aversion and that the food is really wholesome, they still cannot bring themselves to eat it (Bernstein, 1991). Thus, a conditioned food aversion is not a result of cognitive processes such as reasoning or expectation.

Questionnaires and interviews reveal that cancer patients develop aversions to the foods that they normally eat even if their treatment sessions occur several hours after the previous meal (Bernstein *et al.*, 1982; Mattes *et al.*, 1987). When patients receive many treatment sessions, they are likely to develop aversions to a wide variety of foods. Because a treatment that produces nausea may cause the development of a conditioned flavour aversion to the last thing a person has

eaten, Broberg and Bernstein (1987) attempted to attach the aversion to a flavour other than one that patients encounter in their normal diets. Cancer patients ate either a coconut or root beer Lifesaver (a sweet) after the last meal before a chemotherapy session. The experimenters hypothesised that the unique flavour would serve as a scapegoat, thus preventing a conditioned aversion to patients' normal foods. The procedure worked; the patients were much less likely to show an aversion to the food eaten during the last meal before the treatment.

Conditioned flavour aversions can also have useful applications. For example, psychologists have applied conditioned aversions to wildlife control. In regions where coyotes have been attacking sheep, they have left chunks of dog food laced with an emetic drug wrapped in pieces of fresh sheepskin. The coyotes eat the bait, become sick and develop a conditioned aversion to the smell and taste of sheep (Gustavson and Gustavson, 1985). These methods can help protect endangered species as well as livestock. Mongooses have been introduced into some islands in the Caribbean, where they menace the indigenous population of sea turtles. Nicolaus and Nellis (1987) found that a conditioned aversion to turtle eggs could be established in mongooses by feeding them eggs into which an emetic drug had been injected.

Evidence suggests that for some species, conditioned flavour aversions can become cultural traditions. Gustavson and Gustavson (1985) reported that after adult coyotes had developed a conditioned aversion to a particular food, their offspring, too, avoided that food. Apparently, the young coyotes learned from their mothers what food was fit to eat. However, Nicolaus *et al.* (1982) found that adult racoons having a conditioned aversion to chickens did not teach their offspring to avoid chickens. In fact, after seeing the young racoons kill and eat chickens, the adults overcame their aversion and began preying on chickens again.

Applications of operant conditioning to human behaviour

Instructional control

 Human behaviour is influenced not only by reinforcement but also by the interactions of reinforcement with rules, that is, verbal descriptions of the relation between behaviour and reinforcement. In fact, much of our everyday behaviour involves following rules of one sort or another. Cooking from a recipe, following directions to a friend's house, and obeying the speed limit are common examples. Because

rules have the potential to influence our behaviour in almost any situation, behaviour analysts are interested in learning more about how rules and reinforcement interact.

One way to investigate this interaction is to give subjects rules that are false, that is, rules that are inaccurate descriptions of the behaviour required for reinforcement (Galizio, 1979; Baron and Galizio, 1983). In such experiments, people may behave in accordance with either the rule or the reinforcement requirement. Other researchers have shown that people sometimes generate their own rules about the consequences of their behaviour (Lowe, 1979). Lowe argues that our ability to describe verbally the consequences of our behaviour explains why humans often respond differently from other animals when placed under similar reinforcement contingencies (Lowe *et al.*, 1983). When exposed to fixed interval schedules, animals do not respond immediately after each reinforcement. As time passes, though, responding gradually increases until the next reinforcer is delivered. Humans, on the other hand, tend to follow one of two strategies: responding very slowly or responding very rapidly. Those people who respond slowly often describe the schedule as interval-based and they respond accordingly. Those who respond rapidly usually describe the schedule as ratio-based – which it is not – and they respond accordingly. Thus, the language one uses may indeed exert some control over one's own behaviour. The extent to which language and other behaviours interact is the subject of ongoing experimental and theoretical work (Hayes, 1989; Cerruti, 1990).

Stimulus equivalence

Stimulus equivalence refers to the emergence of novel behaviour without direct reinforcement of that behaviour (Fields, 1993; Fields *et al.*, 1995). Imagine that you were asked to learn the relationship among a group of symbols: A, B and C. Suppose further that after training without reinforcement, you discovered that A = B and A = C. How then would you respond to the following question: does B = C? You would probably reason that if A = B and A = C, then B, too, is equal to C. But notice that you were never trained or received any direct reinforcement for learning that B = C. Rather, the equivalent relationship between B and C emerged from your previous learning; hence, the term 'stimulus equivalence'.

Stimulus equivalence is an important area of research because it represents one way we learn to use and understand symbols, such as language. For example, let A represent a picture of a dog, B represent the spoken word 'dog', and C represent the printed word 'dog'. Suppose that we teach a child to point to the picture of the dog (A) and say the word 'dog' (B). In this case, the child learns that A = B and B = A. Next, suppose that we teach the child to point to the picture of the dog (A) when he sees the printed word 'dog' (C). The child learns that A = C and that C = A. What we are really interested in, though, is whether the child will have learned that the spoken word 'dog' (B) is equivalent to, or means the same thing as, the printed word 'dog' (C).

This is precisely what children learn under these circumstances, even though the equivalent relationship, B = C, has not been directly trained (Sidman and Tailby, 1982). Rather, it emerged as a consequence of the child's learning history. Understanding how stimulus equivalence develops is likely to lead to a better understanding of language development.

Drug use and abuse

Soon after Skinner outlined the principles of operant behaviour, others were quick to apply them to the study of drug action and drug-taking (Thompson and Schuster, 1968). In fact, Skinner's three-term contingency is now partly the basis of an entirely separate discipline of pharmacology known as behavioural pharmacology, the study of how drugs influence behaviour. In this field, the terms 'discriminative stimuli', 'responding' and 'consequences' translate into drugs as discriminative stimuli, the direct effects of drugs on behaviour, and the reinforcing effects of drugs, respectively. Perhaps the most interesting discovery in behavioural pharmacology is the finding that most psychoactive drugs function as reinforcers in both humans and animals.

Controversies in Psychological Science – What is insight?

The issue

Many problems we have to solve in our daily lives require us to make responses that we have never made before and that we have never seen anyone else make either. We often think about a problem, looking at the elements and trying to imagine various solutions. We try various responses in our heads, but none seems to work. Suddenly, we think of a new approach: maybe this one will work. We try it, and it does. We say that we have solved the problem through insight (Sternberg and Davidson, 1996).

But what is insight? Some people see it as almost a magical process: a sudden flash of inspiration, a bolt from the blue. At the simplest level, it is a form of understanding that changes a person's perception of a problem and its solution (Dominowski and Dallob, 1996). Most people regard insight as a particularly human ability – or, at least, as an ability that belongs to our species and, perhaps, some of the higher primates. Some psychologists, however, regard the term as fairly meaningless.

The evidence

During the early part of the twentieth century, the German psychologist Wolfgang Köhler studied the problem-solving behaviours of chimpanzees. In one famous example (Köhler, 1927), he hung some bananas from the ceiling of an animal's

Controversies in Psychological Science – *Continued*

cage, just high enough to be out of reach. The cage also contained a large box. Sultan, one of the chimps, first tried to jump up to reach the bananas, then paced around the cage, stopped in front of the box, pushed it towards the bananas, climbed onto the box, retrieved and ate the fruit. Later, when the bananas were suspended even higher, he stacked up several boxes, and on one occasion when no boxes were present, he grabbed Köhler by the hand, led him over to the bananas and climbed on top of him. Figure 7.10 illustrates the attempts at solving the problem.

Köhler believed that the insightful problem-solving behaviour shown by the chimpanzees was different from the behaviour of Thorndike's cats as they learned to escape the puzzle boxes. The cats clearly showed trial-and-error behaviour, coming upon the solution by accident. The escape from the box served as a reinforcing stimulus, and eventually the animals learned to operate the latch efficiently. But the behaviour of the chimpanzees seemed very different. They suddenly came upon a solution, often after looking at the situation (and, presumably, thinking about it). Köhler saw no accidental trial-and-error behaviour. The problem used in Köhler's experiment is an example of an object-use problem. Another type of problem, a spatial insight problem (Dominowski and Dallob, 1996) is seen in Figure 7.11. This is the nine dot problem in which you have to connect all the dots using four straight lines and without lifting your pen from the page or retracing any of the lines.

Research suggests that insight may be less mysterious than it appears and may be based on combinations of behaviours initially learned through trial and error. In one study (Epstein *et*

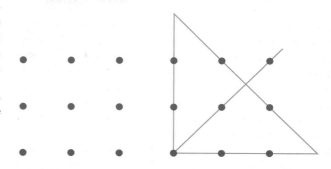

Figure 7.11 The nine dot problem. The challenge is to connect all nine dots using four straight lines without retracing any lines and without lifting your pen. The solution is seen in the figure on the right.

Source: Dominowski, R.L. and Dallob, P. Insight and problem solving. In Sternberg, R. and Davidson, J. (eds), *The Nature of Insight*. Cambridge, MA: MIT Press, 1996. Reproduced with permission from MIT Press.

al., 1984), the experimenters used operant procedures (with food as the reinforcer) to teach a pigeon two behaviours: (1) to push a box towards a target (a green spot placed at various locations on the floor), and (2) to climb onto a box and peck at a miniature model of a banana which was suspended overhead. Once these behaviours had been learned, the experimenters confronted the pigeon with a situation in which the box was in one part of the chamber and the banana was in another. The pigeon acted much the way that Sultan did:

> At first, the bird appeared to be confused: it stretched toward the banana, turned back and forth from the banana to the box, and so on. Then, rather suddenly, it began to push the box toward the banana, sighting the banana and readjusting the path of the box as it pushed. Finally, it stopped pushing when the box was near the banana, climbed onto the box, and pecked the banana.
>
> *Source*: Epstein, 1985, p. 132.

Pigeons will show insightful behaviour only after they have learned the individual behaviours that must go together to solve a problem. For example, only if pigeons have learned to push a box towards a goal will they move it under a model banana hanging from the top of the cage. It is not enough to have learned to push a box; they must have learned to push it towards a goal. Presumably, the chimpanzees' experience with moving boxes around and climbing on them was necessary for them to solve the hanging banana problem.

In Chapter 2, you read about the concept of nominal fallacy: we tend to think that we have explained a phenomenon simply by naming it. Simply labelling behaviour as insightful does not help us to understand it. If we do not know what

Figure 7.10 Insightful behaviour by a chimpanzee in an experiment similar to one performed by Köhler. The chimpanzee piles boxes on top of each other to reach the bananas hanging overhead.

Source: Powerstock/Superstock, reprinted by permission.

Controversies in Psychological Science – *Continued*

behaviours an animal has already learned, a novel and complex sequence of behaviours that solves a problem seems to come from nowhere. To understand the necessary conditions for insight to occur, we need to know more than what is happening during the current situation; we also need to know what kinds of learning experiences the animal has had.

Conclusion

The scientist's challenge is to dissect even the most complex behaviours and try to understand their causes. Perhaps

chimpanzees, like humans, are capable of solving problems by using some sort of mental imagery, testing possible solutions in their heads before trying them. But neither humans nor chimpanzees will be able to think about objects they have never seen or imagine themselves performing behaviours they have never performed or seen others perform. But the raw material for problem-solving – including the thinking that may accompany some forms of insightful behaviour – must come from experience. That is what this chapter has been all about.

When administered as a consequence of responding, these drugs will induce and maintain high rates of responding (Griffiths *et al.*, 1980). There is a very high correlation between drugs that will maintain animal responding in experimental settings and those that are abused by humans (Griffiths *et al.*, 1980). Cocaine, for example, maintains very high rates of responding and drug consumption, to the point that food and water consumption decreases to life-threatening levels. Unlimited access to cocaine in rhesus monkeys can lead, in some cases, to death. These findings have allowed psychologists to study the abuse potential of newly available drugs in order to predict their likelihood of becoming drugs of abuse. The realisation that drugs are reinforcers has, in turn, led behavioural pharmacologists to treat cocaine dependence in people successfully by scheduling reinforcement for non-drug-taking behaviour (Higgins *et al.*, 1994).

Just as the telephone ringing can serve as a discriminative stimulus for you answering it, the stimulus effects of drugs can also exert control over human behaviours that are reinforced by non-drug stimuli. People become more sociable under the influence of alcohol not only because the drug reduces their inhibitions, but also because people have some successful social interactions while under the drug's effects. These interactions reinforce their sociability. In fact, many laboratory studies have shown that certain drugs actually increase social responding and social reinforcement (Higgins *et al.*, 1989).

Observation and imitation

Normally, we learn about the consequences of our own behaviour or about stimuli that directly affect us. We can also learn by a less direct method: observing the behaviour of others. Evidence suggests that imitation does seem to be an innate tendency. Many species of birds must learn to sing the song of their species; if they are raised apart from other birds of their species,

they will never sing or they will sing a peculiar song that bears little resemblance to that of normally raised birds (Marler, 1961). However, if they hear the normal song played over a loudspeaker, they will sing it properly when they become adults. They have learned the song, but clearly there were no external reinforcement contingencies; nothing in the environment reinforced their singing of the song.

Classically conditioned behaviours, as well as operantly conditioned behaviours, can be acquired through observation. For example, suppose that a young girl sees her mother show signs of fear whenever she encounters a dog. The girl herself will likely develop a fear of dogs, even if she never sees another one. In fact, Bandura and Menlove (1968) reported that children who were afraid of animals – in this case, dogs – were likely to have a parent who feared dogs, but they usually could not remember having had unpleasant direct experiences with them. As you will see in Chapter 13, we tend to imitate, and feel, the emotional responses of people we observe.

Under normal circumstances, learning by observation may not require external reinforcement. In fact, there is strong evidence that imitating the behaviour of other organisms may be reinforcing in itself. However, in some cases in which the ability to imitate is absent, it can be learned through reinforcement. For example, Baer *et al.* (1967) studied three severely retarded children who had never been seen to imitate the behaviour of other people. When the experimenters first tried to induce the children to do what they themselves did, such as clap their hands, the children were unresponsive. Next, the experimenters tried to induce and reinforce imitative behaviour in the children. An experimenter would look at a child, say 'do this,' and perform a behaviour. If the child made a similar response, the child was immediately praised and given a piece of food. At first, the children were physically guided to make the response. If the behaviour to be imitated was clapping, the experimenter would clap their hands, hold the child's hands and clap them together, and then praise the child and give them some food.

The procedure worked. The children learned to imitate the experimenters' behaviours. More importantly, however, the children had not simply learned to mimic a specific set of responses. They had acquired the general tendency to imitate. When the researchers performed new behaviours and said 'do this', the children would imitate them.

Recent approaches to learning: computational modelling and neural networks

In his editorial of an issue of the journal *Perception*, Gregory (1998) asked, 'Is the brain a computer?' If a computer is anything that solves problems, then 'yes', says Gregory, 'the brain is a computer'. Similarly, if perception is problem-solving (such as being able to perceive an object from poor amounts of sensory data), then the visual brain is also a computer.

Although cognitive psychology has a history that dates back to the early part of the twentieth century, most of its philosophy and methodology has developed since the 1960s. During this time, the best-known physical device that performs functions similar to those of the human brain has been the general-purpose serial computer. Thus, it is the computer that provided (and still provides) much of the inspiration for the models of human brain function constructed by cognitive psychologists.

Modern general-purpose computers consist of four major parts:

- Input and output devices (or, collectively, I/O devices) permit us to communicate with the computer – to give it instructions or data and to learn the results of its computations.

- Memory permits information to be stored in the computer. This information can contain instructions or data we have given the computer or the intermediate steps and final results of its calculations.

- A central processor contains the electronic circuits necessary for the computer to perform its functions – to read the information received by the input devices and to store it in memory, to execute the steps specified by the instructions contained in its programs, and to display the results by means of:

- the output devices.

Modern general-purpose computers can be programmed to store any kind of information that can be coded in numbers or words, can solve any logical problem that can be explicitly described, and can compute any mathematical equations that can be written. Therefore, in principle, at least, they can be programmed to do the things we do: per-ceive, remember, make deductions, solve problems. The power and flexibility of computers seem to make them an excellent basis for constructing models of mental processes.

For example, psychologists, linguists and computer scientists have constructed computer-inspired models of visual pattern perception, speech comprehension, reading, control of movement, and memory (Rolls, 1997; 2008), as well as robots which can mimic aspects of behaviour. Some of these are more successful than others. The computer Deep Blue, for example, played a six-game chess match against the World Chess Champion Gary Kasparov in 1997, and won by two games to one (the players drew three times). The advantage that such a computer has is its speed of processing; its disadvantage is that its depth of understanding is limited and not as sophisticated as that of humans. It can be programmed with all the moves in chess that are known to date, but it may not understand why those moves may work. While speed is one of a computer's advantages – and at this they are far superior to humans: chips are faster than neurons – its disadvantage is seen clearly in exercises such as language translation, at which its performance is generally execrable. It can understand grammar and it may understand specific words, but it has no sense of the meaning of a sentence. Sentences such as 'He was killing time' are problematic for it. We understand this to mean occupying our time while we wait; a computer may understand this to mean murdering a clock.

Artificial intelligence

The construction of computer programs that simulate human mental functions is called **artificial intelligence**. The aim of such enterprises is to try to clarify the nature of mental functions. For instance, to construct a program and simulate perception and classification of certain types of pattern, the investigator must specify precisely what the task of pattern perception requires. If the program fails to recognise the patterns, then the investigator knows that something is wrong with the model or with the way it has been implemented in the program. The investigator revises the model/program, tries again, and keeps working until it finally works (or until they give up the task as being too ambitious). So far, no program is advanced enough to deal with more than a small fraction of the patterns a human can recognise.

Ideally, the task of discovering what steps are necessary in a computer program to simulate some human cognitive abilities tells the investigator the kinds of process the brain must perform. However, there is usually more than one way to accomplish a particular goal. Critics of artificial intelligence have pointed out that even if it is entirely possible to write a program that performs a task that the human brain performs – and comes up with exactly the

Scientists at the Massachusetts Institute of Technology have developed a number of 'intelligent' machines and instruments. The software worn by the pool player analyses the position of the balls on the table and then works out the easiest shot to attempt.

Source: Sam Ogden/Science Photo Library Ltd.

same results – the computer may perform the task in an entirely different way. In fact, some say, given the way that computers work and what we know about the structure of the human brain, the computer program is guaranteed to work differently.

Serial computers work one step at a time and each step takes time. A complicated program will contain more steps and will take more time to execute. But we do some things extremely quickly that computers take a very long time to do. One of the best examples is visual perception. We can recognise a complex figure about as quickly as we can a simple one. For us, it takes about the same amount of time to recognise a friend's face as it does to identify a simple triangle. The same is not true at all for a serial computer. A computer must 'examine' the scene through an input device something like a television camera. Information about the brightness of each point of the picture must be converted into a number and stored in a memory location. Then the program examines each memory location, one at a time, and does calculations that determine the locations of lines, edges, textures and shapes. Finally, it tries to determine what these shapes represent. Recognising a face takes much longer than recognising a triangle.

If the brain were a serial device, its maximum speed would probably be around ten steps per second, considering the rate at which neurons can fire (Rumelhart *et al.*, 1986). This rate is extremely slow compared with modern serial computers. Obviously, when we perceive visual images, our brain does not act like a serial device.

Parallel processing and neural networks

Instead, the brain appears to be a **parallel processor**, in which many different modules (collections of circuits of neurons) work simultaneously at different tasks. A complex task is broken down into many smaller ones, and separate modules work on each of them. Because the brain consists of many billions of neurons, it can afford to devote different clusters of neurons to different tasks, as we saw in Chapters 4 and 6. With so many things happening at the same time, the task gets done quickly.

Recently, psychologists have begun to devise models of mental functions that are based, very loosely, on the way the brain seems to be constructed. These models are called **neural networks**, and the general approach is called connectionism. One area of psychology where neural networks have been applied is language, and we turn to this in Chapter 10.

Computer simulation specialists have discovered that when they construct a network of simple elements interconnected in certain ways, the network does some surprising things. The elements have properties like those of neurons. They are connected to each other through junctions similar to synapses. Like synapses, these junctions can have either excitatory or inhibitory effects. When an element receives a critical amount of excitation, it sends a message to the elements with which it communicates, and so on. Some of the elements of a network have input lines that can receive signals from the 'outside', which could represent a sensory organ or the information received from another network. Other elements have output lines, which communicate with other networks or control muscles, producing behaviour. Thus, particular patterns of input can represent particular stimuli, and particular patterns of output can represent responses.

Investigators do not construct physical networks. Instead, they write computer programs that simulate them. The programs keep track of each element and the state of each of its inputs and outputs and calculate what would happen if a particular pattern of input is presented. Neural networks can be taught to 'recognise' particular stimuli. They are shown a particular stimulus, and their output is monitored. If the response on the output lines is incorrect, the network is given a signal indicating the correct response. This signal causes the strength of some of the junctions to be changed, just as learning is thought to alter the strength of synapses in the brain. After several trials, the network learns to make correct responses.

If the network uses a sufficiently large number of elements, it can be trained to recognise several different patterns, producing the correct response each time one of the patterns is shown to it. In addition, it will even recognise the patterns if they are altered slightly, or if only parts of the patterns are shown. Thus, neural networks can recognise not only particular patterns but also variations on that pattern. Thus, they act as if they had learned general prototypes, not specific templates. For example, they may learn that the letter A reproduced in Times Roman font is the same as an A reproduced in Palatino font.

So, does the brain work like a computer? The answer seems to be that it does, but not like the most familiar kind of computer, which cognitive psychologists first used as a basis for constructing models of brain function. The brain appears to be a parallel processor made up of collections of neural networks. Neural networks' attempts to simulate the functions of the brain have not met with considerable success (which is not surprising given the complexity of that organ). Most simulations have been of the very basic, perceptual kind. It is interesting to speculate that a strong artificial intelligence position on the nature of simulating brain function would effectively result in the creation of a conscious computer. How likely do you think this is?

Learning in practice: being a student

 So far, we have considered some of the important theories of learning that have made an impact on psychology and in applied contexts. Other elements of the learning process are covered in the next chapter on memory. The remainder of this chapter examines how various factors can affect academic learning and success. It explores how the use of different teaching methods can influence learning as might the type of material taught. It also considers how specific variables such as personality, learning style, group study and confidence can influence successful understanding of learned material.

Deep v. shallow learning

Perhaps the most consistently studied – and reliable – dichotomy in the psychology of learning is deep and shallow processing (or learning). In shallow learning, there is an emphasis on remembering facts, rather than on understanding them; in deep learning, there is an emphasis on knowing and understanding material, rather than on the straightforward process of remembering it.

For example, in the 1990s researchers suggested that learning could be conceptualised in five ways (Saljo, 1991; adapted from Hartley, 1998):

1 Learning is a means of acquiring knowledge.

2 Learning is a means of storing (remembering) information that could be used later.

3 Learning is the acquisition of facts, knowledge and methods.

4 Learning is the making sense of, or abstracting meaning from, material.

5 Learning is a process that assists the interpretation or understanding of reality.

Researchers found that those students who were classified as 'shallow' learners were most likely to adopt the first two of these learning strategies; 'deep' learners were more likely to adopt the last two. To examine whether 'depth' could be taught, Norton and Crowley (1995) studied the effect of incorporating workshops into a first-year psychology course on students' learning strategies. When the performance of those who attended all the workshops was compared with those who attended one or two or none, there was no increase in deep processing in the conscientious students. However, those who stayed with the workshops adopted a less shallow processing style as the course progressed. The results demonstrated that by encouraging students to think, to interpret and to discuss concepts and ideas – rather than asking them to learn their material by rote – this process could make them less shallow learners.

The idea was first proposed and demonstrated empirically in Sweden in the 1970s. Marton and Saljo (1976), for example, characterised deep learners as those who would agree with statements such as:

- I try to get the principal ideas.

- I try to find the main points of a chapter.

Whereas shallow learners were likely to agree with statements such as:

- I try to concentrate on remembering as much as possible.

That is, the deep learners tried to glean meaning from material whereas the shallow learners tried to remember the information. When a group of students was given a 1,400-word article on curriculum reform in Swedish universities and asked to summarise the author's main argument in one or two sentences, the results were – in light of what you now know – predictable. None of the students who were classified as shallow learners (based on their responses to a questionnaire) was able to do this; those classified as deep learners did this faultlessly.

In an article by Gibbs (1992) cited in Hartley (1998), the author lists factors which could encourage shallow processing and those which could foster deep learning. Here are some of those factors:

- Factors encouraging surface learning:
  - heavy workload;
  - excess course material;

- reduced opportunity to study a subject in depth;
- lack of choice in subject areas and methods of studying those subjects;
- assessment that is threatening and anxiety-provoking.

- Factors encouraging deep learning:
  - project work;
  - learning by doing;
  - problem-based learning;
  - work that does not rely solely on remembering;
  - work that allows reflection;
  - independent learning;
  - rewarding understanding and penalising memorisation;
  - involving students in the choice of assessment method.

So, the message that seems to be clear and consistent from research is: in the contexts studied, having a 'deep' approach to study is better than one driven by a need to remember.

Learning style

Psychologists have devised various ways of measuring students' learning styles and investigating whether students on different courses learn in different ways. One of these measures is the Student Process Questionnaire (SPQ) (Biggs, 1987), a 42-item measure of a deep approach to learning (evaluating material critically; reading widely; engaging in discussion), a surface approach to learning (e.g. rote learning) and an achieving approach to learning (where the student has a strong intention to succeed and obtain high grades). In a study of how chemistry students' learning style changes across their course (Zeegers, 2001), the deep approach to learning was the one most closely related to good grade outcome but the achieving approach was the one most likely to undergo fluctuations across the course. Students expressed less achievement-driven behaviour as the course progressed, suggesting that striving for high grades became less important as their education progressed. The surface approach increased in the first year of study but stabilised thereafter. Older students were significantly more likely to engage in deep learning and also show high achievement motivation. These students also received higher grades and completed more units on their courses.

In a similar study, researchers from the universities of Leiden and Amsterdam investigated whether factors such as personality and learning style correlated with academic performance in 409 Dutch first-year psychology undergraduates (Busato *et al.*, 2000).

Intellectual achievement and the motivation to do well were, as expected, positively related to academic performance. There was a relationship between an undirected learning style and performance. Students who adopted this approach did significantly worse than did students who adopted other styles. The personality variable most closely related to academic success was conscientiousness. Interestingly, performance in the first exam at university was the most important predictor of academic success.

Changes in students' views about their learning

The perception and understanding of material learned across a degree changes. A study at Princeton University found that the instructor's way of expressing him/herself, information about the course and an absence of criticism about the course from others was significantly related to

Cutting edge – Personality and academic success

An analysis of 109 studies examining the relationship between psychosocial and study skill factors, grade success and student retention (how likely students are to stay on their course) has shown that there is a moderately significant relationship between remaining in college and (i) keeping academic goals, (ii) a person's ability to assess the inability to succeed academically and (iii) good academic skills. The best predictors of grade success are motivation to achieve and the student's ability to assess accurately his/her ability to succeed (Robbins *et al.*, 2004). The results seem to tally with those from the workplace where highly motivated employees and those capable of self-evaluation are those who are most successful.

However, personality may be a better predictor of academic performance than grades or other factors. Openness to experience and agreeableness have been found to be significant predictors of academic success, but extraversion, neuroticism and conscientiousness have not (you will find a detailed description of these personality types in Chapter 14) (Farsides and Woodfield, 2003). Of all the variables studied, however, a non-personality factor – seminar attendance – was the strongest predictor of success. This said, a meta-analysis of studies exploring the relationship between personality and academic performance found that one personality variable in particular was important (Poropat, 2009). In a sample totaling over 70,000 participants from secondary and tertiary education the greatest correlation – it predicted performance better than did intelligence – was between performance and conscientiousness.

post-course evaluations in general (Babad *et al.*, 1999). The features that predicted evaluations at introductory level were not those that predicted evaluations at advanced 4. The only consistent feature was that workload and mark leniency were weak predictors of course selection.

For advanced courses, features which predicted evaluation were interesting readings, having an interesting course, and instructor's knowledge and expertise. None of the personality factors – such as the lecturer's sense of humour or approachability – predicted these students' evaluations of their course. Only for the introductory students was there a relationship between the instructor's humour and the post-course evaluation.

The study appears to show that as students progress through their degree, what they value in a course changes. They become more concerned with academic substance and less with 'lighter' features such as the instructor's sense of humour. At the beginning of their education, first year students are sampling the many different things that university or college has to offer. The instructor's sense of humour and expression was important to first year students, but advanced students valued the quality of their courses and teaching, such as the content of courses and how well they were taught and prepared. The authors argue that the respondents in their sample may not be representative (because Princeton undergraduates have different course structures to those of others) but suggest that the results could be generalised to similar institutions.

Chamorro-Premuzic *et al.* (2007) found that the personality characteristics of the lecturer interact with the students' own and these influence perceptions of teaching. Students tended to prefer lecturers with personalities similar to their own, unless they were neurotic. Particularly, they preferred lecturers who were emotionally stable and conscientious.

A study from the University of Missouri-Columbia found that by graduation, students placed less emphasis on extrinsic factors (such as earning money, gaining popularity and how they looked) and more on intrinsic factors (valuing community, intimacy and growth) (Sheldon, 2005). The greater the shift to intrinsic values, the greater the sense of psychological well-being students felt as they progressed through college. You might find that the findings of these studies mirror your own experience as a psychology student.

Confidence

One variable that might mediate the relationship between learning style and academic success is confidence. A small number of studies has shown that the relationship between a person's confidence in performing well and actual performance, however, may not be that great. Studies of students have shown that those who do best are those that do not express over-generous levels of confidence: the more modestly self-assessed students performed best. Conversely, those who rate their confidence in their ability highly tend not to do as well as their self-image would predict. In one study of students from university courses in Israel, the Netherlands, Palestine, Taiwan and the USA, confidence ratings were seen to be nation-dependent in some cases (Lundeberg *et al.*, 2000).

Palestinian students expressed greatest confidence in their ability (whether they were actually correct or incorrect in answering questions). Taiwan students were the least confident but were better able to discriminate between their performance when they knew they were right and when they knew they were wrong. That is, their confidence rating was higher when they got the answer right, and lower when they got the answer wrong. Other countries such as the USA, the Netherlands and Israel showed comparable performance and confidence scores. There was no significant difference between men or women in their confidence ratings and the relationship between this and performance.

There are aspects of learning that can be positively influenced by confidence, however. Participants who scored higher in conscientiousness and openness tend to be more confident about their reading and writing ability (Pulford and Sohal, 2006). Agreeableness and perfectionism predicted confidence in numeracy skills. People who expressed least confidence in speaking tended to be introvert, female, low on conscientiousness and were not especially motivated to be organised. Confidence in the ability to manage time was found in participants who were conscientious, extravert and motivated to be organised. All three personality traits predicted Grade Point Average in the first year (the greater the trait expressed, the higher the GPA).

The best way to understand a textbook

This textbook should provide you with enough basic information and further reading for you to understand important concepts, theories and findings in psychology research, to write your essays, sit your course exams or complete your course projects. But are there specific ways of reading this textbook that can maximise your learning?

According to research by Slotte and Lonka (1999), there is. They studied 226 high school students' methods of taking notes from a philosophical textbook, the content of which would be examined formally before students enrolled on a course. Half of the sample were asked to review their notes during note-taking; the other half were not given any explicit instructions. The quality and quantity of the notes was then analysed and were correlated with exam performance.

They found that reviewing notes during essay writing was associated with good performance on questions that required comprehension of the text and deep, detailed knowledge. However, reviewing these notes did not help with drawing original conclusions about the text. Importantly, they note that students summarising the text in their own words with their own subheadings and structure performed better than those students who took verbatim notes or took notes in the exact order in which the material appeared in the text. This finding suggests that deeper understanding (and better performance) comes from having read and understood material in a text. The key to this is being able to express the text's ideas in your own words. If you have not done this, you haven't understood the text.

Is learning by note-taking from this book different from note-taking from a lecture? A recent meta-analysis suggests that the relationship between note-taking and encoding of information in a text or during a lecture is significant but modest (Kobayashi, 2005). Inexperienced students benefited more from note-taking than did experienced ones, possibly because the latter could perform successfully without substantial note-taking. Taking notes from a visual presentation was less effective than taking notes from an audio source, presumably because paying attention to the lecture together with meeting the mechanical demands of note-taking interfered with the writing.

Can the internet be used to teach successfully?

The past decade has seen an expansion in the use of the World Wide Web to facilitate teaching and research. One innovation that has potentially important implications for tutors and students is the development of online courses (Kinney, 2001; Carr-Chellman and Duchastel, 2000; Martin *et al.*, 2005; Schweizer, 1999; Waschull, 2001). One benefit of these courses is that they allow you greater autonomy. If the teaching materials are clear, interactive and engaging, you do not need to be physically in the classroom with the tutor. This idea is not novel. The Open University in the UK has based its peda-

gogy extensively on this approach, via the use of video-based interactive learning. There are now online versions of courses in health psychology (Upton and Cooper, 2001), social work (Stocks and Freddolino, 1998), nursing (Cravener, 1999), introductory psychology (Martin *et al.*, 2005; Waschull, 2001), child development (Graham, 2001) and research methods (Wang and Newlin, 2000), among others.

One study comparing the effectiveness of teaching an introductory psychology course via the Web with teaching via traditional lectures found that those who followed an online course showed greater knowledge of the content of the syllabus than did those who followed a lecture-based course (Maki *et al.*, 2000). Examination performance was also better in this group. Web-based courses were praised for their convenience but when both types of course were evaluated by the students, the lecture-based format received the most positive ratings, suggesting that learning and satisfaction with the course can be independent of each other: a format which yields better academic performance may not necessarily be the one that is regarded most positively.

There is also evidence that the more the students use online material, the better they perform. Upton and Cooper (2001) found that the grades of undergraduates in psychology were higher when they undertook an online health psychology course than when they followed a conventional lecture-based course, but improvement was related to the increased time spent on the learning materials.

One criticism of online courses is that students may not spend very long on them. One study found that the time spent on an online cognitive psychology course varied from 6.69 hours to 11.96 hours (Taraban *et al.*, 2001). When asked how long they spent on it, however, students overestimated the time they spent on the modules by 100 per cent (the computer tracked students' actual usage so tutors could compare self-reported use with actual use). One way of ensuring that students do spend time on these courses is by providing a comprehensive series of exercises where the student is expected to provide some form of reflective feedback (as part of the course assessment) or where the answers might be forwarded to their tutor.

Studying psychology – An international perspective

You might think that most psychology students study similar topics over similar periods of time across the world. In a sense, this is right but some countries teach psychology in different ways; some have only recently developed psychology degrees; some teach psychology to achieve a particular end such as training in educational psychology. How does the teaching of psychology differ across the world?

In Australia, psychology departments exist in almost all universities (only three do not have one) (Wilson and Provost, 2006). Like those in the UK, departments in the older universities evolved from philosophy departments in the early twentieth century. Again, like the UK, the 1980s saw an expansion of Australian institutes calling themselves universities and thus offering university psychology degrees (the parallel in the UK is the transmogrification of the polytechnics into universities in the early 1990s). Like the UK, courses are accredited by a professional organisation (the Australian Psychological Society). Psychology students in Australia can study three types of psychology degrees: a three-year degree that does not prepare the student to practise psychology; a four-year degree, which does and involves the writing of a thesis and the study of ethics; and graduate degrees.

Courses are slightly different in Italy. Here, students can study for a three-year degree, which qualifies them to practise as a 'psychological assistant' in a restricted range of areas (Prandini and McCarthy, 2006), or a five-year degree which involves an additional two years of study which qualifies the student to practise. The student then pursues a graduate programme in a specific area to specialise further. All public school teachers in Italy have to complete a postgraduate course which involves training in psychology (Prandini and McCarthy, 2006).

Surprisingly for a country that is the birthplace of modern psychology, Germany only established its first professional curriculum in psychology in 1941 (Hodapp and Langfeldt, 2006). In the 1960s, there were 18 universities offering psychology to 2,000 students taught by 31 professors. In the 1980s, there were 30 universities teaching 18,000 students. Currently, there may be around 43 universities with 450 professors teaching 32,000 students (Hodapp and Langfeldt, 2006). Approximately 70 per cent of students are women, a figure that is echoed in the UK. German universities are chang-

ing and as of 2004, a Diplom qualification now entitles students to work in a profession related to psychology. As with all the degrees mentioned so far, the emphasis in German education is on teaching skills that will enable students to apply scientific principles to human behaviour.

The large number of departments in Germany, and other countries, isn't seen elsewhere. Greece, for example, has four psychology departments offering two types of 'undergraduate' degree: a Ptychion (Bachelor's) degree, lasting four years, and a Master's degree (Metaptychiako Diploma) in an area such as clinical, school/educational or organisational psychology – this can last up to three years and involves internship at a relevant institution (Georgas, 2006).

The compactness of provision in Greece contrasts with Russia: 100 psychology departments have been established in the past decade (Karandashev, 2006). Students at Russian universities can study for four (Bachelor's degree) or five years (Specialist degree), in programmes regulated by the Ministry of Education (Karandashev, 2006). The four-year course trains students in general psychology; the five-year course prepares them for professional work. While Russia has divested itself of its communist shackles (partly), China has not. Psychology became an independent university discipline in China in 1960 but, following the 'Cultural Revolution' of 1966–76 and the resultant closure of all universities, psychology was attacked as pseudoscience (Zhang and Xu, 2006). Since 1980, however, psychology has clawed its way back into the university curriculum and is now one of the most popular science subjects (Zhang and Xu, 2006).

Finally, and interestingly given the politically fractious times in which we live, what of Iran? Iran was no academic late-developer: it was running courses in psychology in the 1920s. Currently, 19 universities offer psychology courses, with the BS (Bachelor of Science) degree being awarded after four years of study (Alipour, 2006). Unlike some other countries, the psychological associations in Iran do not accredit courses. Around 34,000 psychology students study in Iran and specialise in four fields: general, clinical, exceptional children and industrial psychology (Alipour, 2006). Very interestingly, in 2003, the Islamic Iranian parliament passed a law that granted equal status to medical and psychological counselling services.

Chapter review

Habituation and classical conditioning

- Habituation screens out stimuli that experience has shown to be unimportant. This form of learning allows organisms to respond to more important stimuli, such as those related to survival and reproduction.
- Classical conditioning occurs when a neutral stimulus occurs just before an unconditional stimulus (UCS) – one that automatically elicits a behaviour. The response that an organism makes in response to the unconditional stimulus (the UCR) is already a natural part of its behaviour; what the organism learns to do is to make it in response to a new stimulus (the conditional stimulus, or CS). When the response is made to the CS, it is called the conditional response, or CR.
- The relationship between the conditional stimulus and unconditional stimulus determines the nature of the conditional response. Acquisition of the conditional response is influenced by the intensity of the unconditional stimulus and the delay between the conditional stimulus and unconditional stimulus.
- Extinction occurs when the conditional stimulus is still presented but is no longer followed by the unconditional stimulus; the conditional response may show spontaneous recovery later, even after a delay.
- Generalisation occurs when stimuli similar to the conditional stimulus used in training elicit the conditional response.
- Discrimination involves training the organism to make a conditional response only after a particular conditional stimulus occurs.
- Classical conditioning can also establish various classes of stimuli as objects of fear (phobia) or of sexual attraction (fetishes). For classical conditioning to occur, the conditional stimulus must not only occur immediately before the unconditional stimulus, but it must also reliably predict the occurrence of the unconditional stimulus.

After behaviourism

- Hull's theory of learning reduced behaviour to numerical values; using these values Hull's system sought to predict behaviour.
- Tolman's theory of learning argued that stimulus–response models were too simplistic and suggested the concept of intervening variables – variables which mediated the relationship between a stimulus and the response to it. Tolman's research led to the coining of the term cognitive map to describe our ability to manipulate three-dimensional environments in the mind.

Operant conditioning

- The law of effect specifies a relation between behaviour and its consequences. If a stimulus that follows a response makes that response become more likely, we say that the response was reinforced. If the stimulus makes the response become less likely, we say that it was punished. The reinforcing or punishing stimulus must follow the behaviour almost immediately if it is to be effective.
- The process of operant conditioning helps adapt an organism's behaviour to its environment.
- Skinner described the relation between behaviour and environmental events as a three-term contingency: in the presence of discriminative stimuli, a consequence will occur if and only if an operant response occurs.
- A reinforcer is an appetitive stimulus that follows an operant response and causes that response to occur more frequently in the future.
- A punisher is an aversive stimulus that follows an operant response and causes it to occur less frequently in the future.
- If an aversive stimulus is terminated after a response occurs, the response is reinforced through a process called negative reinforcement. The termination of an appetitive stimulus can punish a response through a process called response cost.
- Extinction occurs when operant responses are emitted but not reinforced, which makes sense because organisms must be able to adapt their behaviour to changing environments.
- Complex responses, which are unlikely to occur spontaneously, can be shaped by the method of successive approximations.
- Various types of schedule of reinforcement have different effects on the rate and pattern of responding. When a response is reinforced intermittently, it is more resistant to extinction, probably because an intermittent reinforcement schedule resembles extinction more than a continuous reinforcement schedule does.
- Discrimination involves the detection of essential differences between stimuli or situations so that responding occurs only when appropriate.
- Generalisation is another necessary component of all forms of learning because no two stimuli, and no two responses, are precisely the same. Thus, generalisation embodies the ability to apply what is learned from one experience to similar experiences.
- The major difference between classical conditioning and operant conditioning is in the nature of the contingencies: classical conditioning involves a contingency between stimuli (CS and UCS), whereas operant conditioning involves a contingency between the organism's behaviour and an appetitive or aversive stimulus. The two types of conditioning complement each other. The pairings of neutral stimuli with appetitive and aversive stimuli (classical conditioning) determine which stimuli become conditioned reinforcers and punishers.

Conditioning of complex behaviours

- Much behaviour is under the control of aversive contingencies, which specify particular behaviours that are instrumental in either escaping or avoiding aversive stimuli.

- In conditioned flavour aversions, there is a delay between tasting a poison and getting sick; the rule that a reinforcing or punishing stimulus must immediately follow the response cannot, therefore, apply.
- We are able to acquire both operantly and classically conditioned responses through observation and imitation; we can learn to modify and combine responses learned in other contexts to solve new problems. This is referred to as insight.
- Behaviour analysts argue that behaviour is governed by external causes, such as discriminative stimuli and environmentally based reinforcers and punishers; cognitive psychologists maintain that behaviour is controlled by internal causes, such as thoughts, images, feelings and perceptions.

Factors influencing learning in an academic context

- Research has shown that various factors can influence academic learning, including personality, learning style, group study, the type of learning materials and the style of teaching.

- Students normally begin courses by adopting superficial learning styles geared towards achieving grades and covering the basics; as they progress, learning becomes deeper and more thoughtful.
- While beginning students evaluate courses based on superficial factors, such as the lecturer's sense of humour, more advanced students value the lecturer's knowledge and the quality of the learning materials more.
- The key to understanding material in textbooks is to underline the parts that you consider relevant first and then to write these parts in your own words.
- Research on the use of the internet as a structured teaching tool suggests that it can bring academic benefits.
- Findings from studies that have compared students' performance on web-based courses and traditional classroom-based courses are mixed. Some show superior examination performance by the internet students but others report the opposite.

Suggestions for further reading

Learning – general reading

Baldwin, J.D. and Baldwin, J.I. (1998) *Behavior Principles in Everyday Life* (3rd edn). Hillsdale, NJ: Prentice Hall.

Malott, R.W. and Trojan, E.A. (2008) *Principles of Behaviour*. (6th edn). Boston: Prentice Hall.

Martin, G.L. and Pear, J. (2007) *Behaviour modification: What is it and how to do it*. Boston: Prentice Hall.

Olson, M. and Hergenhahn, B.R. (2009) *Introduction to the theories of learning*. Eighth edition. Boston: Prentice Hall.

Terry, S. (2009) *Learning and Memory*. (4th edn). Boston: Allyn & Bacon.

Good, comprehensive accounts of the psychology of learning.

Learning – specific reading

Bowden, E.W., Jung-Beeman, M., Fleck, J. and Kounios, J. (2005) New approaches to demystifying insight. *Trends in Cognitive Sciences*, 9, 7, 322–8.

Halpern, D.F. (2002) *Thought and Knowledge* (4th edn). London: Lawrence Erlbaum Associates.

Harris, B. (1979) Whatever happened to Little Albert? *American Psychologist*, 34(2), 151–60.

Hartley, J. (1998) *Learning and Studying*. London: Routledge.

Martin, G.N., Brunswick, N. and Jolic, N. (2005) Developing an on-line course in psychology. *Journal of Social, Environmental and Health Issues*, 6, 1, 11–26.

Staddon, J.E.R. and Cerutti, D.T. (2003) Operant conditioning. *Annual Review of Psychology*, 54, 115–44.

Watson, J.B. and Rayner, R. (1920) Conditioned emotional reactions. *Journal of Experimental Psychology*, 3, 1–14.

Watson and Rayner's original article on conditioned human fear is a classic of its kind – the first scientific study of conditioning of fear in a human being. Apart from its historical interest, it is also useful to read in order to avoid the mistakes highlighted in Harris's incisive review. Halpern's and Hartley's books give you good reviews of the psychology of learning in an academic context.

Journals to consult

Applied Cognitive Psychology

Behaviour Research and Therapy

British Journal of Psychology

Cognition

Ergonomics

Journal of Applied Behaviour Analysis

Journal of Applied Psychology

Journal of Experimental Psychology: Learning, memory and cognition

Learning and Individual Differences

Psychological Review

Psychological Science

Quarterly Journal of Experimental Psychology

Website addresses

http://psych.athabascau.ca/html/prtut/reinpair.htm
A site which allows you to explore the nature of positive reinforcement with an online demonstration.

http://www.biozentrum.uni-wuerzburg.de/genetics/behavior/learning/classical.html
A site which explores some of the ideas involved in classical conditioning.

http://www.biozentrum.uni-wuerzburg.de/genetics/behavior/learning/operant.html
A site from the same author of the classical conditioning link, this time on operant conditioning.

http://www.psychology.org/links/Paradigms_and_Theories/Behavior_Analysis/
An excellent collection of links to behaviour analysis/operant conditioning sites.

Memory

Clive had no idea that Tuesday 26 March 1985 would be his last day of conscious thought. We weren't ready... By morning, he could not answer a simple question or remember my name. The doctor said it was 'flu and lack of sleep caused the confusion.

'I'm never ill,' Clive used to say. And he never was. Then, all of a sudden, he was. But instead of a normal illness the doctors had some chance of recognizing, this one is rare, sneaky. Nobody knew what was wrong with him. . .

'A sudden virus had caused holes in Clive's brain; memories fell out. But nothing could touch what was in his heart. He couldn't remember a thing that had ever happened to him; but he remembered me and knew that he loved me.'

Source: Deborah Wearing (2005) *Forever Today* New York: Doubleday, pp. xi–xii.

Explore the accompanying videos, simulations, and animations on MyPsychLab. This chapter includes activities on: The phonological loop • Mnemonics • Experiencing the Stroop Effect • Interference – a theory of memory • Check your understanding and prepare for your exams using the multiple choice, short answer and essay practice tests also available.

WHAT YOU SHOULD BE ABLE TO DO AFTER READING CHAPTER 8

- Describe what is meant by 'memory' and describe the different types of memory process.
- Describe and understand theories of forgetting.
- Understand the term 'amnesia', be aware of different types of amnesia and understand the biological basis of the disorder.
- Distinguish between the processes of encoding and retrieval.
- Understand how memories are formed and can change over time (and how unreliable they can be).
- Be aware of the neural basis of learning and memory processes such as encoding and retrieval.
- Be aware of the practical applications of concepts from memory research and cognitive psychology.

QUESTIONS TO THINK ABOUT

- What do we mean when we refer to 'memory'?
- Are there different types of memory?
- Why do we forget?
- Can memories be manipulated, and if so, how?
- Would you expect the brain mechanisms that are responsible for memory acquisition also to be responsible for retrieval? Why?
- Is memory capacity finite?
- Without memory, do we have personality?
- Where, in the brain, are memories stored? Can they be stored?

Memory: an introduction

Memory is the process of encoding, storing and retrieving information. **Encoding** refers to the active process of putting stimulus information into a form that can be used by our memory system. The process of maintaining information in memory is called storage and the active processes of locating and using information stored in memory is called **retrieval**.

When psychologists refer to the structure of memory, they are referring to two approaches to understanding memory – a literal one and a metaphorical one. Literally, memory may reflect the physiological changes that occur in the brain when an organism learns. Metaphorically, memory is viewed as a store or a process made up of systems and subsystems. These divisions may not necessarily have neurological meaning but they are useful metaphorical shorthand for describing aspects of memory. They are a way of explaining aspects of memory.

Types of memory

Research suggests that we possess at least four forms of memory: sensory memory, short-term memory, working memory and long-term memory (Baddeley, 1996).

Sensory memory is memory in which representations of the physical features of a stimulus are stored for a very brief time, perhaps for a second or less. This form of memory is difficult to distinguish from the act of perception. The information contained in sensory memory represents the original stimulus fairly accurately and contains all or most of the information that has just been perceived. For example, sensory memory contains a brief image of a sight we have just seen or a fleeting echo of a sound we have just heard. Normally, we are not aware of sensory memory; no analysis seems to be performed on the information while it remains in this form. The function of sensory memory appears to be to hold information long enough for it to be transferred to the next form of memory, short-term memory.

Short-term memory (STM) refers to immediate memory for stimuli that have just been perceived. Its capacity is limited in terms of the number of items that it can store and of its duration. For example, most people who look at the set of numbers

1 4 9 2 3 0 7

close their eyes and recite them back, will have no trouble remembering them. If they are asked to do the same with the following set they might have a little more trouble:

7 2 5 2 3 9 1 6 5 8 4

Very few people can repeat 11 numbers. Even with practice, it is difficult to recite more than 7–9 independent pieces of information that you have seen only once. Short-term memory, therefore, has definite limits. However, there are ways to organise new information so that we can remember more than 7–9 items, but in such cases the items can no longer be considered independent.

Working memory is similar to short-term memory in that it involves short-term storage of information. But working memory is more than this in that it allows us to manipulate material in short-term memory. Remembering material while engaging in a different but related task, for example, illustrates working memory and you will find out more about this in a later section. If you had repeatedly recited the 11 numbers above until you had memorised them (rehearsal) you could have placed them in long-term memory. **Long-term memory (LTM)** refers to information that is represented on a permanent or near-permanent basis. Unlike short-term memory, long-term memory has no known limits and, as its name suggests, is relatively durable. If we stop thinking about something we have just perceived (that is, something contained in short-term memory), we may not remember the information later. However, information in long-term memory need not be continuously rehearsed. We can stop thinking about it until we need the information at a future time.

Some cognitive psychologists argue that no real distinction exists between short-term and long-term memory; instead, they see them as different phases of a continuous process. These psychologists object to the conception of memory as a series of separate units with information flowing from one to the next, as seen in Figure 8.1. Memory may be more complex than this model would have us believe, and the next sections explore the nature of sensory memory, STM, working memory, LTM and other types of memory process.

Sensory memory

Under most circumstances, we are not aware of sensory memory. Information we have just perceived remains in sensory memory just long enough to be transferred to short-term memory. In order for us to become aware of sensory memory, information must be presented very briefly so that we can perceive its after-effects. Although we probably have a sensory memory for each sense modality, research efforts so far have focused on the two most important forms: iconic (visual) and echoic (auditory) memory.

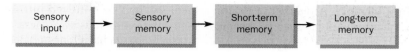

Figure 8.1 The information-processsing model of human memory.:

Iconic memory

Visual sensory memory, called **iconic memory** (icon means 'image'), is a form of sensory memory that briefly holds a visual representation of a scene that has just been perceived. To study this form of memory, Sperling (1960) presented visual stimuli to people by means of a tachistoscope, an apparatus for presenting visual stimuli for extremely brief durations. Sperling flashed a set of nine letters on the screen for 50 milliseconds (ms). He then asked people to recall as many letters as they could, a method known as the whole-report procedure. On average, they could remember only four or five letters, but they insisted that they could see more. However, the image of the letters faded too fast for people to identify them all.

To determine whether the capacity of iconic memory accounted for this limitation, Sperling used a partial-report procedure. He asked people to name the letters in only one of the three horizontal rows. Depending on whether a high, middle or low tone was sounded, they were to report the letters in the top, middle or bottom line (see Figure 8.2). When the participants were warned beforehand to which line they should attend, they had no difficulty naming all three letters correctly. But then Sperling sounded the tone after he flashed the letters on the screen. The participants had to select the line from the mental image they still had: they had to retrieve the information from iconic memory. With brief delays, they recalled the requested line of letters with perfect accuracy. For example, after seeing all nine letters flashed on the screen, they would hear the high tone, direct their attention to the top line of letters in their iconic memory, and 'read them off'. These results indicated that their iconic memory contained an image of all nine letters.

Sperling also varied the delay between flashing the nine letters on the screen and sounding the high, medium or low tone. If the delay was longer than 1 second, people could report only around 50 per cent of the letters. This result indicated that the image of the visual stimulus fades quickly from iconic memory. It also explained why participants who were asked to report all nine letters failed to report more than four or five. They had to scan their iconic memory, identify each letter and store each letter in short-term memory. This process took time, and during this time the image of the letters was fading. Although their iconic memory originally contained all nine letters, there was time to recognise and report only four or five before the mental image disappeared.

Echoic memory

Auditory sensory memory, called **echoic memory**, is a form of sensory memory for sounds that have just been perceived. It is necessary for comprehending many sounds, particularly those that constitute speech. When we hear a word pronounced, we hear individual sounds, one at a time. We cannot identify the word until we have heard all the sounds, so acoustical information must be stored temporarily until all the sounds have been received. For example, if someone says 'mallet', we may think of a kind of hammer; but if someone says 'malice', we will think of something entirely different. The first syllable we hear – 'mal' – has no meaning by itself in English, so we do not identify it as a word. However, once the last syllable is uttered, we can put the two syllables together and recognise the word. At this point, the word enters short-term memory. Echoic memory holds a representation of the initial sounds until the entire word has been heard; it seems to hold information for about four seconds (Darwin *et al.*, 1972).

Short-term memory

Short-term memory has a limited capacity, and most of the information that enters it is subsequently forgotten. Information in sensory memory enters short-term memory, where it may be rehearsed for a while. The rehearsal process keeps the information in short-term memory long enough for it to be

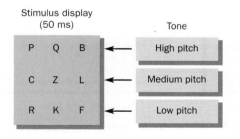

Stimulus display (50 ms)

Tone

Figure 8.2 The critical features of Sperling's iconic memory study.
Source: Adapted from Sperling, G., The information available in brief visual presentations, *Psychological Monographs*, 1960, 74, 1–29.

transferred into long-term memory. After that, a person can stop thinking about the information; it can be recalled later, when it is needed.

This simple story is actually inaccurate. First of all, information does not simply 'enter short-term memory'. For example, most people who read the letters

P X L M R

and put them in short-term memory, have a number of strategies for achieving this. Some would have repeated the letters to themselves or would have whispered or moved their lips. We can say the names of these letters because many years ago we learned them. But that knowledge is stored in long-term memory. Thus, when we see some letters, we retrieve information about their names from long-term memory, and then we hear ourselves rehearsing those names (out loud or silently). The five letters above contain only visual information, their names came from long-term memory, which means that the information put into short-term memory actually came from long-term memory.

To illustrate this, try the following experiment. Study the symbols below, then look away from the book, and try to keep them in short-term memory.

ζ ⵑ δ ɘ ⵗ

This task is extremely difficult because few people will have learned the names of these symbols. Because of this, there is no way of recording them in short-term memory. Figure 8.3 may, therefore, be a better description of the memory process than is Figure 8.1.

Information can enter short-term memory from two directions: from sensory memory or from long-term memory. When we are asked to multiply 7 by 19, information about the request enters our short-term memory from our sensory memory. Actually performing the task, though, requires that we retrieve some information from long-term memory. What does 'multiply' mean? What is a 7 and a 19? At the moment of the request, such information is not being furnished through our senses; it is available only from long-term memory. However, that information is not recalled directly from long-term

memory. It is first moved into short-term memory and then enters conscious awareness.

Psychologists have long debated the number of memory stores that we have – some view humans as having a short-term memory store and a long-term memory store (the dual-store model), whereas others argue that the distinction between these two stores is blurred and that we have one flexible memory store that deals with short-term and long-term memory retrieval (single-store model). Dual-store models were (and are) based on a simple paradigm: participants recall items from a list; if they recall from the end of this list, these items were retrieved from STM; words recalled from the beginning of the list were retrieved from LTM.

To determine whether this distinction was supportable, Talmi *et al.* (2005) set up an fMRI experiment in which participants were asked to remember and then recognise words from a list, as their brain activation was measured. Recognition of items appearing early in the list was associated with activity in regions of the brain associated with LTM (the hippocampus and related structures); recognition of items appearing later in the list was not associated with activation in these areas, providing some neuroimaging support for the distinction between dual memory stores.

Working memory

The fact that short-term memory contains both new information and information retrieved from long-term memory has led some psychologists to prefer the term 'working memory' (Baddeley and Hitch, 1974; Baddeley, 1986). Working memory acts on material we have just perceived and allows us to manipulate this in the short-term. It allows us to keep a new telephone number 'alive' in memory long enough to dial it or allows us to perform that multiplication task mentioned in the earlier paragraph. In short, it represents our ability to remember what we have just perceived and to think about it in terms of what we already know (Baddeley, 1986; Logie, 1996). We use it to remem-

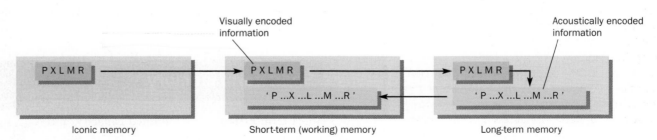

Figure 8.3 Relations between iconic memory, short-term memory and long-term memory. Letters are read, transformed into their acoustic equivalents and rehearsed as 'sounds' in the head. Information can enter short-term memory from both iconic memory and long-term memory. Visual information enters short-term memory from iconic memory, but what is already known about that information (such as names of letters) is moved from long-term memory to short-term memory.

ber whether any cars are coming up the street after looking left and then right, for example.

A widely used test of working memory is reading span (Daneman and Carpenter, 1980). One version involves asking people to read aloud and verify the truthfulness of sentences while, at the same time, trying to remember the last word of each sentence. This task, like many others of working memory, requires a person to maintain some information in memory (storage) while simultaneously manipulating other information (processing).

Another manipulation task in working memory might involve asking the participant to recite from memory a series of five letters forwards, backwards or in alphabetical order. After a delay, the participant is asked to match the number order of a given letter, according to the mental manipulation (e.g. forwards, backwards or alphabetical). So, if the letters B, M, T, E, I were presented and the participant was asked to alphabetise them, the number 4 (called a digit probe) should elicit the correct answer, M (because M is the fourth letter in the alphabetised string, B, E, I, M, T).

Although the terms 'short-term memory' (STM) and 'working memory' (WM) are sometimes used interchangeably, some psychologists make clear distinctions between them. Short-term memory has been referred to as information retained in long-term memory that is called on but not used in a sustained way. Working memory involves dual processing and actual manipulation of material in mental space, not simply the storage of material (Miyake, 2001). There is evidence that tests of working memory and STM measure different processes (Kail and Hall, 2001).

The components of working memory

Working memory was a model devised in the 1970s and later developed extensively by the British psychologists Alan Baddeley and Graham Hitch. They regarded this type of memory as having three components which allowed us to store temporarily verbal material and visuospatial material, and to coordinate the storage of this material. The component which stores verbal material was originally called the **articulatory loop** although this term has been superseded by the term **phonological loop** (Baddeley and Logie, 1992). The component that allows storage of visuospatial material is called the **visuospatial scratchpad** and the coordinating system is called the **central executive**. The working memory 'system' is illustrated in Figure 8.4 and is described next.

Phonological working memory

When we see a printed word, we say it, out loud or silently. If it is said to ourselves, circuits of neurons that control articulation are activated. Information concerning this activity is communicated within the brain to circuits of neurons in the auditory system, and the word is 'heard'. Information is then transmitted back to the articulatory system, where the word is silently repeated. The loop continues until the person's attention turns to something else or until it is replaced with new information.

This articulatory or phonological loop allows the retention of verbal phonetic information (so it acts as a phonological store) and operates like the loop of an audiotape (hence, the name). Lists of long words are remembered more poorly than lists of short words, for example, because there is less room on the loop for lists of long words (so the words 'encyclopaedia', 'constellation' and 'antediluvian' would be more difficult to recall than would the words 'clock', 'parrot' and 'daisy'). However, because the loop also allows the rehearsal of information by **subvocal articulation** (such as subvocally rehearsing a telephone number), the loss of information from the phonological store can be avoided. According to Baddeley *et al.* (1975), the capacity of the phonological loop is determined by how much material the participant can rehearse in two seconds. (Figure 8.5 illustrates how the phonological loop is represented in the brain.)

However, the operation of the loop can be defective under certain circumstances. For example, Salame and Baddeley (1982) found that irrelevant speech played in the background while participants learned visually presented

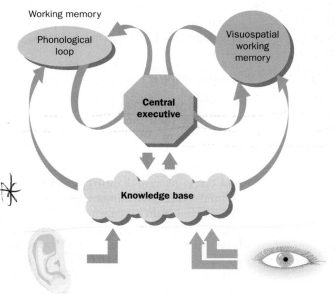

Figure 8.4 Logie's (1995) schematic drawing of the components of working memory.

Source: Adapted from Logie, R., *Visual Spatial Working Memory*, p. 127. © 1995. Reprinted by permission of Psychology Press Limited, Hove, UK.

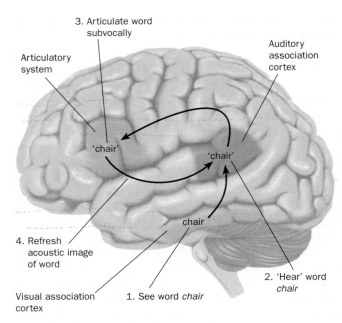

Figure 8.5 The articulatory loop. A hypothetical explanation of phonological working memory.

words interfered with the recall of these words, but the length of the words to be remembered had no significant effect on recall. However, the closer the irrelevant speech was to the words to be remembered, the greater the interference, suggesting that there was some interference in learning words while attending to the sound (or phonology) of similar ones. There is also evidence that non-speech-related material can have the same effect: even background noise can disrupt recall of verbal and arithmetical material (Banbury and Berry, 1998, and see Chapter 9).

Visuospatial working memory

Much of the information we process is non-verbal. We recognise objects, perceive their locations and find our way around our environment. We can look at objects, close our eyes and then sketch or describe them. We can do the same with things we saw in the past. The visuospatial scratchpad contains visual information either obtained from the immediate environment by means of the sense organs or retrieved from long-term memory.

An example of the ability to manipulate visual information in working memory comes from a famous experiment by Shepard and Metzler (1971). They presented people with pairs of drawings that could be perceived as three-dimensional constructions made of cubes. The participant's task was to see whether the shape on the right was identical to the one on the left; some were, and some were not. Even when the shapes were identical, the one on the right was sometimes drawn

as if it had been rotated. For example, in Figure 8.6(a) the shape on the right has been rotated clockwise 80 degrees, but in Figure 8.6(b) the two shapes are different.

Shepard and Metzler found that people were accurate in judging whether the pairs of shapes were the same or different but took longer to decide when the right-hand shape was rotated. Participants formed an image of one of the drawings in their heads and rotated it until it was aligned the same way as the other one. If their rotated image coincided with the drawing, they recognised them as having the same shape. If they did not, they recognised them as being different. The data supported what the participants said – the more the shape was rotated, the longer it took for people to rotate the image of one of the shapes in working memory and compare it with the other one.

The central executive

The above elements – the phonological loop and the visuospatial scratchpad – do not work independently but have to be regulated and supervised, via the central executive subsystem (Baddeley, 1986). This central executive not only allocates mental resources to working memory tasks but also supervises the updating of what is in working memory.

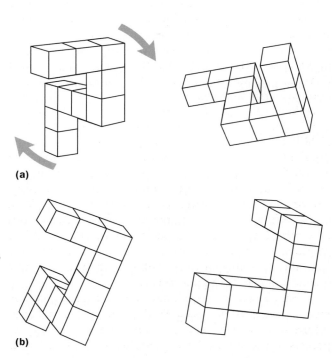

Figure 8.6 The mental rotation task. **(a)** The shape on the right is identical to the one on the left but rotated 80 degrees clockwise. **(b)** The two shapes are different.

Source: Adapted from Shepard, R.N. and Metzler, J., Mental rotation of three-dimensional objects, *Science*, 1971, 171, 701–3. © 1971 The American Association for the Advancement of Science.

How does working memory work?

Apart from allowing us to do the activities mentioned in the previous sections, working memory is also important for cognitive functions such as reading comprehension, academic ability and mathematics (Ashcraft and Kirk, 2001; Daneman and Hannon, 2001). Performance on a working memory span task involving numbers, for example, is a good predictor of spatial task performance (Kane *et al.*, 2001). WM performance is also a good predictor of reading comprehension or verbal ability if the working memory span tests involve verbal or numerical material (Daneman and Hannon, 2001; Hitch *et al.*, 2001; Shah and Miyake, 1996; see Chapter 10).

According to the 'resource sharing model' of Daneman and Carpenter (the name given to it by Hitch *et al.*, 2001), a reading span task measures how flexibly we can allocate mental resources to the processing and storage of material. In practical terms, if a person is a good reader, reading sentences for their truthfulness uses up very few cognitive resources and, therefore, frees up more 'cognitive space' for other activities (in this example, storage of the last word in the sentences). If readers are poor, on the other hand, the opposite pattern is seen and they, therefore, show poor working memory performance (Yuill and Oakhill, 1991). Working memory capacity is thought to be one factor which determines good reading comprehension ability, although this view has been challenged – some psychologists argue that working memory deficits occur with language impairment, rather than causing it (Nation and Snowling, 1998, 1999). They note that even poor readers can remember as many one-, two- or three-syllable words as good readers.

Daneman and Carpenter's view of working memory (1980) has attracted much support and has been the dominant, explanatory view of working memory. An alternative model of working memory, however, argues that it is our control of attention that leads to successful working memory performance (Engle *et al.*, 1999). What counts is how much information can be stored, and this is determined by attention capacity. Thus, you should be able to predict people's performance on attention tasks from their working memory reading span tasks and there is some evidence to support this link.

A final alternative explanation argues that working memory depends on a person's ability to ignore irrelevant information rather than on their limited capacity to process information (Hasher and Zacks, 1988). In order to achieve this goal, there must be good inhibition of irrelevant information and a focus on only relevant material. It is a persuasive argument. Performance on working memory tasks depends on, among other factors, the ability to inhibit the interference produced by items encountered in early experimental trials (Lustig *et al.*,

2001). It appears to be one of the keys to successful working memory performance.

Primacy and recency effects

When individuals are asked to listen to a long list of words spoken one at a time and then write down as many as they can remember (a free recall task), most participants will remember the words at the beginning and the end of the list and forget the words in between. The tendency to remember the words at the beginning of the list is called the **primacy effect**; the tendency to remember words at the end of the list is called the **recency effect**. Two factors may account for these effects.

The primacy effect appears to be due to the fact that words earlier in a list have the opportunity to be rehearsed more than do words in the other parts of a list. This makes good sense – the first words get rehearsed more because, at the experiment's outset, these are the only words available to rehearse. The rehearsal permits them to be stored in long-term memory. As more and more words on the list are presented, short-term memory becomes fuller so that words that appear later in the list have more competition for rehearsal time. Because the first words on the list are rehearsed the most, they are remembered better.

As Atkinson and Shiffrin (1968) point out, because the words at the end of the list were the last to be heard, they are still available in short-term memory. Thus, when you are asked to write the words on the list, the last few words are still available in short-term memory even though they did not undergo as much rehearsal as words at the beginning of the list.

A way of testing this would be to create a delay between the presentation of the last stimulus and its recall. Postman and Phillips (1965), for example, inserted a delay of 15 seconds between the last item and recall and had their participants engage in another task. The effect was to abolish the recency effect because STM was occupied and was not allowed to rehearse the last items in the list. When the delay involved no intervening activity, and so STM was unoccupied by another task, the recency effect remained intact (Baddeley and Hitch, 1977). However, the abolition of both recency and primacy effects seems to depend on the nature of the intervening task. If people are told to count backwards for 20 seconds after the presentation of a word list, primacy and recency effects are still shown (Tzeng, 1973). The instructions given to people are also important. If people are instructed to repeat the list in the order they heard the words, the recency effect is abolished (Tulving and Arbuckle, 1963). If they are allowed to recall the list spontaneously, the recency effect remains.

Recency (and primacy) effects extend beyond the recall of artificial word lists. They have been reported for the recall of parking positions (Pinto and Baddeley, 1991), operas attended over a quarter of a century (Sehulster, 1989) and names of American presidents (Roediger and Crowder, 1976; Healy *et al.*, 2000). Baddeley and Hitch (1977) found that when rugby players were asked to recall the teams they played, they named the most recently played teams first and with greater accuracy. Maylor (2002) asked 27 Methodist churchgoers and 27 non-churchgoers to place six verses of various hymns that were not carols and did not have a narrative, in the correct order. If serial positioning occurs in semantic memory, Maylor predicted, people would be better at identifying the first and last verses but would do less well in arranging the order of verses two to five. This is exactly what she found. Even practised participants showed the serial positioning effect. Serial positioning occurs when people remember more of the end or the begining of a list of items they are asked to remember. It suggests that items are better recalled from the beginnings and ends of lists because they are temporally distinctive: nearby items are more likely to be confused with each other than are items that are widely separated.

The primacy and recency effects are important because they demonstrate that memory is not a random process. Information is not just plucked from the environment and stored away randomly in the brain. Instead, the processing of information is much more orderly; it follows predictable patterns and is dependent on the contributions of rehearsal and short-term memory.

The limits of short-term and working memory

How long does information remain in short-term or working memory? The answer may lie in a classic study by Lloyd and Margaret Peterson (Peterson and Peterson, 1959). The experimenters presented participants with a stimulus composed of three consonants, such as JRG. With rehearsal, the participants easily recalled it 30 seconds later. The Petersons then made the task more challenging: they prevented participants from rehearsing. After they presented the participants with JRG, they asked them to count backwards by three from a three-digit number they gave them immediately after they had presented the set of consonants. For example, they might present participants with JRG, then say, '397'. The participants would count out loud, '397... 394... 391... 388... 385', and so on until the experimenters signalled them to recall the consonants. The accuracy of recall was determined by the length of the interval between presentation of the consonants and when recall was requested (see Figure 8.7). When rehearsal was disrupted by backward counting – which prevented individuals from rehearsing information in

short-term memory – the consonants remained accessible in memory for only a few seconds. After a 15–18-second delay between the presentation of the consonants and the recall signal, recall dropped to near zero.

What, then, is the capacity of short-term memory? Miller (1956), in a famous article entitled 'The magical number seven, plus or minus two', demonstrated that people could retain, on average, seven pieces of information in their short-term memory: seven numbers, seven letters, seven words or seven tones of a particular pitch. If we can remember and think about only seven pieces of information at a time, how can we manage to write novels, design buildings or even carry on simple conversations? The answer comes in a particular form of encoding of information that Miller called chunking, a process by which information is simplified by rules which make it easily remembered once the rules are learned.

A simple demonstration illustrates this phenomenon. Read the ten numbers printed below and see whether you have any trouble remembering them.

1 3 5 7 9 2 4 6 8 0

These numbers are easy to retain in short-term memory because we can remember a rule instead of ten independent numbers. In this case, the rule concerns odd and even numbers. The actual limit of short-term memory is seven chunks, not necessarily seven individual items. Thus, the total amount of information we can store in short-term memory depends on the particular rules we use to organise it.

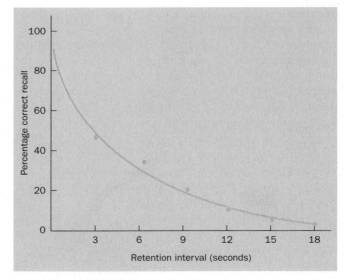

Figure 8.7 Limits of recall from working memory. Percentage correct recall of the stimulus as a function of the duration of the distractor task used in the study by Peterson and Peterson.

Source: Adapted from Peterson, L.M. and Peterson, J.M., Short-term retention of individual verbal items. *Journal of Experimental Psychology*, 1959, 58, 193–98.

In life outside the laboratory we are rarely required to remember a series of numbers. The rules that organise our short-term memories are much more complex than those that describe odd and even numbers. The principles of **chunking** can apply to more realistic learning situations. If we look at the following words:

> along got the was door crept locked slowly he until passage the he to which

and try to remember them, the task is difficult; there is too much information to store in short-term memory. If we repeat the process for the following group of words:

> He slowly crept along the passage until he got to the door, which was locked.

we would be much more successful. Once the same fifteen words are arranged in a sequence that makes sense, they are not difficult to store in short-term memory.

The capacity of short-term memory for verbal material is not measured by the number of letters, syllables or words it can retain but by how much meaning the information offers: this is working memory and long-term memory working together. The first set of words above merely contains fifteen different words. However, when the items are related, we can store many more of them. We do not have to string fifteen words together in a meaningless fashion but can let the image of a man creeping down a passage towards a locked door organise the new information.

Loss of information from short-term memory

The essence of short-term memory is its transience; hence, its name. Information enters from sensory memory and from long-term memory, is rehearsed, thought about, modified and then leaves. Some of the information controls ongoing behaviour and some of it causes changes in long-term memory, but ultimately, it is lost from short-term memory. What causes it to leave? The simplest possibility is that it decays, it fades away. Rehearsal allows us to refresh information indefinitely, thus preventing the decay from eliminating the information.

However, the most important cause appears to be displacement. Once short-term memory has reached its capacity, either additional information will have to be ignored or some information already in short-term memory will have to be displaced to make room for the new information.

One of the best examples of displacement of information in short-term memory comes from an experiment conducted by Waugh and Norman (1965). The people in this study heard lists of sixteen digits. The last digit, accompanied by a tone, was called the probe digit. When people heard it, they had to think back to the previous occurrence of the same digit and tell the experimenter the digit that followed that one.

Look at the sequence of numbers listed below. The last one, a 9, was accompanied by a tone, which told the person that it was the probe. If you examine the list, you will see that the earlier occurrence of a 9 was followed by a 4. Thus, the target, or correct, response was 4.

2 6 7 5 1 3 7 2 6 3 9 4 5 8 1 9

Notice that the 4 is separated from the second 9 by three numbers (5, 8 and 1). Waugh and Norman presented many different lists in which the location of the correct response varied. The distance between the target and the probe ranged from one to twelve items.

The study had two conditions. In one, the lists were presented rapidly, at four digits per second. In the other, they were presented slowly, at only one digit per second. The reason for this manipulation was to determine whether any effects they observed were caused by the mere passage of time rather than by displacement. They found that the more items that came between the target and the probe, the less likely it was that the target would be remembered. The critical variable seemed to be the number of items between the target and the probe, not the time that had elapsed (see Figure 8.8).

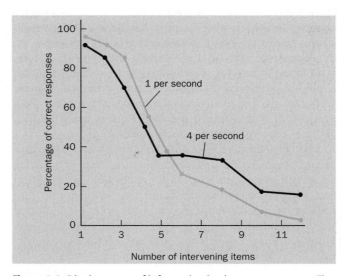

Figure 8.8 Displacement of information in short-term memory. The graph shows the percentage of correct responses as a function of intervening items presented at two different rates of time.
Source: Adapted from Waugh, N.C. and Norman, D.A., Primary memory. *Psychological Review*, 1965, 72, 89–104.

The results indicate that new information displaces old information in short-term memory. But at the longest delays (six or more intervening items), subjects performed more poorly when the items were presented slowly. Perhaps information in short-term memory does decay, but the effect is much less important than displacement.

Learning and encoding in long-term memory

What allows memory to move from short-term to long-term memory? Memory involves both active and passive processes. Sometimes, we use deliberate strategies to remember something (encode the information into long-term memory), for example, rehearsing the lines of a poem or memorising famous dates for a history exam. At other times, we simply observe and remember without any apparent effort, as when we tell a friend about an interesting experience we had. And memories can be formed even without our being aware of having learned something. What factors determine whether we can eventually remember an experience?

The consolidation hypothesis

The traditional view of memory is that it consists of a two-stage process (not counting sensory memory). Information enters short-term memory from the environment, where it is stored temporarily. If the material is rehearsed long enough, it is transferred into long-term memory. This transfer of information from short-term memory into long-term memory has been called consolidation (Hebb, 1949). Through rehearsal (for example, by means of the articulatory loop), the neural activity responding to sensory stimulation can be sustained; and if enough time passes, the activity causes structural changes in the brain. These structural changes are more or less permanent and solid (hence, the term 'consolidation'), and are responsible for long-term memory.

The **consolidation** hypothesis makes several assertions about the learning process. It asserts that short-term memory and long-term memory are physiologically different, and few investigators doubt that information that has just been perceived is stored in the brain in a different way from information that was perceived some time ago. However, some other features of the original consolidation hypothesis have been challenged. First, the hypothesis asserts that all information gets into long-term memory only after passing through short-term memory. Secondly, it asserts that the most important factor determining whether a particular piece of information reaches long-term memory is the amount of time it spends in short-term memory.

Levels of processing

Craik and Lockhart (1972) have pointed out that the act of rehearsal may effectively keep information in short-term memory but does not necessarily result in the establishment of long-term memories. They suggested that people engage in two different types of rehearsal: maintenance rehearsal and elaborative rehearsal. **Maintenance rehearsal** is the rote repetition of verbal information – simply repeating an item over and over. This behaviour serves to maintain the information in short-term memory but does not necessarily result in lasting changes. In contrast, when people engage in elaborative rehearsal, they think about the information and relate it to what they already know. **Elaborative rehearsal** involves more than new information. It involves deeper processing: forming associations, attending to the meaning of the information, thinking about that information, and so on. Thus, we elaborate on new information by recollecting related information already in long-term memory. We are more likely to remember information for an examination by processing it deeply or meaningfully; simply rehearsing the material to be tested will not be effective.

Craik and Tulving (1975) gave participants a set of cards, each containing a printed sentence including a missing word, denoted by a blank line, such as 'The _____ is torn'. After reading the sentence, the participants looked at a word flashed on a screen, then pressed a button as quickly as possible to signify whether the word fitted the sentence. In this example, 'dress' will fit, but 'table' will not. The sentences varied in complexity. Some were very simple:

She cooked the _____.
The _____ is torn.
Others were complex:
The great bird swooped down and carried off the struggling _____.
The old man hobbled across the room and picked up the valuable _____.

The sentences were written so that the same word could be used for either a simple or a complex sentence: 'She cooked the chicken' or 'The great bird swooped down and carried off the struggling chicken'. All participants saw a particular word once, in either a simple or a complex sentence.

The experimenters made no mention of a memory test, so there was no reason for the participants to try to remember the words. However, after responding to the sentences, they were presented with them again and were asked to recall the words they had used. The experimenters found that the participants were twice as likely to remember a word if it had previously fitted into a sentence of medium or high complexity than if it had fitted into a simple one. These results suggest that a memory is more effectively established if the item is presented in a rich context – one that is likely to make us think about the item and imagine an action taking place.

Craik and Lockhart (1972) suggested that memory is a by-product of perceptual analysis. A central processor, analogous to the central processing unit of a computer, can analyse sensory information on several different levels. They conceived of the levels as being hierarchically arranged, from shallow (superficial) to deep (complex). A person can control the level of analysis by paying attention to different features of the stimulus. If a person focuses on the superficial sensory characteristics of a stimulus, then these features will be stored in memory. If the person focuses on the meaning of a stimulus and the ways in which it relates to other things the person already knows, then these features will be stored in memory. For example, consider the word:

tree

This word is written in black type, the letters are lower case, the bottom of the stem of the letter 't' curves upwards to the right, and so on. Craik and Lockhart referred to these characteristics as surface features and to the analysis of these features as shallow processing. Maintenance rehearsal is an example of **shallow processing**. In contrast, consider the meaning of the word 'tree'. You can think about how trees differ from other plants, what varieties of trees you have seen, what kinds of foods and what kinds of wood they provide, and so on. These features refer to a word's meaning and are called semantic features. Their analysis is called **deep processing**. Elaborative rehearsal is an example of deep processing. According to Craik and Lockhart, deep processing generally leads to better retention than does surface processing (see Figure 8.9). As you saw in Chapter 7, a deep approach to learning also improves a student's performance.

Automatic versus effortful processing

Our retrieval of material from memory is enhanced by the extent to which we practise or rehearse information. Practising or rehearsing information, through either shallow or deep processing, is called **effortful processing**. As a student, you know that the more you concentrate on your studies, the more likely it becomes that you will do well in an exam. But your experience also tells you that you have stored information in memory that you had never rehearsed in the first place. Somehow, without any effort, information becomes encoded into your memory. This formation of memories of events and experiences with little or no attention or effort is called automatic processing.

Information that is automatically processed includes frequency (how many times have you read the word 'encode' today?), time (when did you experience your first kiss?), and place (where in the textbook is the figure of Sperling's data located?). Automatic processing helps us to

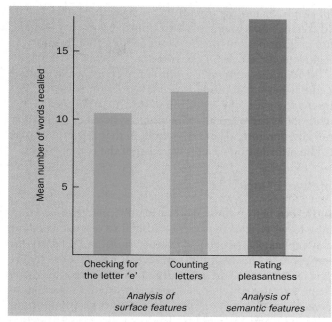

Figure 8.9 Shallow versus deep processing. Mean number of words recalled after performing tasks that required analysis of surface features or analysis of semantic features.

Source: Based on Craik, F.I.M. and Lockhart, R.S., Levels of processing: A framework for memory research. *Journal of Verbal Behavior*, 1972, 11, 671–84.

learn things with relative ease, which makes life a lot less taxing than having continually to process information effortfully. Unfortunately, perhaps because of its complexity, most textbook learning is effortful, not automatic.

Encoding specificity

Encoding specificity refers to the principle that the way in which we encode information determines our ability to retrieve it later. For example, suppose that someone reads you a list of words that you are to recall later. The list contains the word 'beet', along with a number of terms related to music, such as 'melody', 'tune' and 'jazz'. When asked if the list contained the names of any vegetables, you may report that it did not. Because of the musical context, you encoded 'beet' as 'beat' and never thought of the tuberous vegetable while you were rehearsing the list (Flexser and Tulving, 1978). Many experiments have made the point that meaningful elaboration during encoding is helpful and probably necessary for the formation of useful memories.

Mnemonics

When we can imagine information vividly and concretely, and when it fits into the context of what we already know, it is easy to remember later. **Mnemonic systems** (from the Greek *mnemon*, meaning 'mindful') – special techniques or strategies consciously used to improve memory – make use of information already stored in long-term memory to make memorisation an easier task.

Mnemonic systems do not simplify information but make it more elaborate. More information is stored, not less. However, the additional information makes the material easier to recall. Mnemonic systems organise new information into a cohesive whole so that retrieval of part of the information ensures retrieval of the rest of it.

Method of loci

In Greece before the sixth century BC, few people knew how to write, and those who did had to use cumbersome clay tablets. Consequently, oratory skills and memory for long epic poems (running for several hours) were highly prized, and some people earned their livings by using them. Because people could not carry around several hundred pounds of clay tablets, they had to keep important information in their heads. To do so, the Greeks devised the **method of loci**, a mnemonic system in which items to be remembered are mentally associated with specific physical locations (*locus* means 'place' in Latin).

To use the method of loci, would-be memory artists had to memorise the inside of a building. In Greece, they would wander through public buildings, stopping to study and memorise various locations and arranging them in order, usually starting with the door of the building. After memorising the locations, they could make the tour mentally, just as you could make a mental tour of your house to count the rooms. To learn a list of words, they would visualise each word in a particular location in the memorised building and picture the association as vividly as possible. For example, for the word 'love' they might imagine an embracing couple leaning against a particular column in a hall of the building. To recall the list, they would imagine each of the locations in sequence, 'see' each word, and say it. To store a speech, they would group the words into concepts and place a 'note' for each concept at a particular location in the sequence.

For example, if a person wanted to remember a short shopping list without writing it down and the list consists of five items: cheese, milk, eggs, soy sauce and lettuce, the person might first think of a familiar place, perhaps their house. Next, they would mentally walk through the house, visually placing different items from the list at locations – loci – in the house: a lump of cheese hanging from a coat rack, milk dripping from the kitchen tap, eggs lying in the hallway, a bottle of soy sauce on a dining chair, and a lettuce on the sofa (see Figure 8.10). Then, in the supermarket, the person mentally retraces his or her path through the house and notes what he or she has stored at the different loci.

Figure 8.10 The method of loci. Items to be remembered are visualised in specific, well-known places.

Figure 8.11 The peg-word method. Items to be remembered are associated with nouns that rhyme with numbers ('one' is a bun, etc.).

Peg-word method

A similar technique, the **peg-word method**, involves the association of items to be remembered with a set of mental pegs that are already stored in memory (Miller *et al.*, 1960). As with the method of loci, the goal involves visually associating the new with the familiar. One example is to take the numbers from one to ten and rhyme each number with a peg-word; for example, one is a bun, two is a shoe, three is a tree, four is a door, five is a hive, and so on. Returning to your grocery list, you might imagine the package of cheese in a hamburger bun, a shoe full of milk, eggs dangling from a tree, soy sauce on a door, and the lettuce on top of a bee hive (see Figure 8.11). In the supermarket, you review each peg word in order and recall the item associated with it. At first, this technique may seem silly, but there is ample research suggesting that it works (Marshark *et al.*, 1987).

Narrative stories

Another useful aid to memory is to place information into a **narrative**, in which items to be remembered are linked together by a story. Bower and Clark (1969) showed that even inexperienced people can use this method. The investigators asked people to try to learn twelve lists of ten concrete nouns each. They gave some of the people the following advice (p. 181):

> A good way to learn the list of items is to make up a story relating the items to one another. Specifically, start with the first item and put it in a setting which will allow other items to be added to it. Then, add the other items to the story in the same order as the items appear. Make each story meaningful to yourself. Then, when you are asked to recall the items, you can simply go through your story and pull out the proper items in their correct order.

Here is a typical narrative, described by one of the subjects (list words are italicised):

> A *lumberjack* darted out of the forest, *skated* around a *hedge* past a colony of *ducks*. He tripped on some *furniture*, tearing his *stocking* while hastening to the *pillow* where his *mistress* lay.

People in the control group were merely asked to learn the lists and were given the same amount of time as the people in the 'narrative' group to study them. Both groups could remember a particular list equally well immediately afterwards. However, when all the lists had been learned, recall of all 120 words was far superior in the group that had constructed narrative stories.

Cutting edge – Something to chew over

Of all the pressing issues psychologists could study, you wouldn't think that chewing gum was up there with mental illness, prejudice and the reduction of smoking. But some evidence suggests that chewing gum can improve memory, specifically, improvements in immediate and delayed word recall. Functional MRI evidence suggests increased blood flow when people chew gum and psychophysiologists report increased heart rate during the same.

But the picture is inconsistent. For each study showing positive effects of mastication, there is at least another showing no effect. Some researchers have even suggested that it is not the act of chewing that produces these supposed improvements, but the mint flavour released by the chum during mastication. The very immediate effect of chewing on cognitive performance – which may be due to an increase in

alertness/arousal – could be mediated by the perception of the peppermint/spearmint that is immediately released on chewing (and which dissipates the longer it is chewed).

To examine whether it is the flavour of the gum rather than the act of chewing which produces memory improvements, Johnson and Miles (2008) had participants either chew flavourless gum or taste mint-flavoured strips during the learning and recall of 15 nouns.

They found that chewing gum at encoding and retrieval or tasting mint strips during the same was no more likely to improve recall than conditions where no gum/strips were present at learning/recall or one was present at encoding/retrieval and the other was not.

Which suggests that this is another myth that is best spat out rather than digested.

Not all information can be easily converted to such a form, however. For example, if you were preparing to take an examination on the information in this chapter, figuring out how to encode it into lists would probably take you more time than studying and learning it by more traditional methods.

Long-term memory: episodic and semantic memory

Long-term memory contains more than exact records of sensory information that has been perceived. It also contains information that has been transformed – organised in terms of meaning. For example, the type of information that is personally meaningful to us (such as what we had for breakfast this morning or what we were doing last night) appears to be different from the type of information that is based on general knowledge (such as knowing the capitals of the world or the order in which Shakespeare wrote his plays). These two types of memory have been termed episodic and semantic memory, respectively, and the distinction was originally made by Tulving (1972). **Episodic memory** (or **autobiographical memory**) provides us with a record of our life experiences. Events stored there are autobiographical and there appears to be cross-cultural agreement on when such memories are acquired (even though cultures differ in terms of the type of memory encoded) (Conway *et al.*, 2005). **Semantic memory** consists of conceptual information such as general knowledge; it is a long-term store of data, facts and information. Our knowledge of what psychology is, the names of the authors of this book, the components of the human

sensory systems and how neuroimaging has helped localise the process of working memory should form part of your semantic memory. Semantic memories can, of course, interact with episodic ones.

The distinction between episodic and semantic memory reflects the fact that we make different uses of things we have learned: we describe things that happened to us, or talk about facts we have learned. Tulving (1983, 1984) revised his original views of the two systems, suggesting that episodic memory is a part of semantic memory, not a separate, independent system, so the debate is ongoing.

One way of determining a distinction between them would be to show that brain regions involved in one are not as involved in the other. Studies of brain injury have highlighted the involvement of the left prefrontal cortex in the retrieval of words in response to a cue (such as another word or a letter) and the temporal lobe in object naming and the retrieval of information about an object's characteristics (Martin and Chao, 2001). The processing of semantic information appears to involve a network of regions including the left prefrontal, parietal and posterior temporal cortex. When people are allowed to generate words to visually or auditorily presented cues, the posterior temporal cortex is activated regardless of whether the words are generated from the participants' native language or from their second language (Klein *et al.*, 1999; Tatsumi *et al.*, 1999).

Perhaps the most controversial data supporting the notion of semantic memory concerns stimulus specificity, the notion that one region of the brain is more involved than others in the perception or retrieval of certain categories of object. Well-known examples of this, as you saw in Chapter 6, are face recognition and the naming of inanimate and animate objects (Warrington, 1975; Warrington and Shallice, 1984; Warrington and

Autobiographical Memory – An international perspective

There seem to be real differences in the content of the autobiographical memories of people from different cultures. European Americans tend to recall their own roles in events and the feelings those events generated, whereas Asian Americans tend to recall details of social/group activities (Wang, 2004; Wang and Ross, 2005). One explanation for this is that American culture – at the most general level – is highly individualistic and emphasises and rewards autonomy and self-drive, whereas Asian cultures emphasise interdependence and the importance of social interaction/dependence.

To test this hypothesis, Wang (2008) asked Asian American to focus either on their American or their Asian background prior to recalling autobiographical memories. Those primed by the American condition recalled memories that were more self-focused and less social than were those whose Asianness had been primed. Participants who were not primed either way recalled the two types of content about equally.

McCarthy, 1987). Warrington's patients showed evidence of a dissociation between knowledge for living and non-living things. They were able to name non-living things but had considerable difficulty in naming living things, whether the stimuli to be named were verbal or non-verbal. In a later study, Warrington and Shallice (1984) interpreted their findings by suggesting that the two types of object-naming depended on different processing mechanisms. Living things would be processed primarily according to perceptual and visual features such as their size, colour, shape and so on, whereas non-living things would be processed according to their function.

Neuroimaging data have generally supported the proposition that certain brain regions are specifically activated by specific stimuli, but do not explain why. Pictures of tools have been found to generate more brain activity in the left posterior temporal cortex than do pictures of other objects and animals (Martin *et al.*, 1996; Chao *et al.*, 1999). An area of the brain called the fusiform gyrus, as you saw in Chapter 6, is activated during face recognition but is not as consistently or significantly activated by other types of stimuli. Other stimuli which selectively activate certain brain regions are buildings and houses (Epstein and Kanwisher, 1998).

Explicit and implicit memory

Another distinction is made between explicit and implicit memory. **Explicit memory** refers to memory for information we were aware of learning. A simple example would be our recollection of the 12 times table: this is a task that most of us were instructed to remember explicitly. Recognition and recall of material in explicit memory require active recollection of material that has been studied (McBride and Dosher, 1997). For example, we might ask participants to recall freely as many words as they can after being presented with a long list of them, or to indicate which stimuli from an array of visual stimuli were previously seen. Under these conditions, participants are explicitly instructed to recall or to recognise.

Implicit memory, however, does not appear to rely on conscious awareness. Instead, it is memory for information that is incidentally or unintentionally learned and which does not rely on the recognition or recall of any specific learning episode (Schacter, 1987; Cleermans, 1993). It is sometimes referred to as being synonymous with procedural memory, the memory for knowing how to do things (like riding a bike, operating a computer keyboard, or playing a musical instrument). There is some question, however, over whether implicit and procedural memory are truly synonymous. Procedural memory implies that some conscious effort has been made towards learning a skill such as riding a bike or playing a musical instrument; implicit memory would assume that skills were learned without such conscious effort, which seems highly unlikely. Also, there seems to be little procedural input to performing a stem-completion task (described below), which taps implicit memory. There continues to be debate about the number of memory systems, and whether these memory systems are separate or different forms of the same system.

The acquisition of specific behaviours and skills is probably the most important form of implicit memory. Driving a car, turning the pages of a book, playing a musical instrument, dancing, throwing and catching a ball, sliding a chair backwards as we get up from the dinner table – all these skills involve coordination of movements with sensory information received from the environment and from our own moving body parts. We do not need to be able to describe these activities in order to perform them. We may not be aware of all the movements involved while we are performing them. Implicit memory may have evolved earlier than explicit memory.

A good example of learning without awareness is provided by an experiment conducted by Graf and Mandler (1984). These investigators showed people a list of six-letter words and had some of them engage in a task that involved elaborative processing: they were to think about each word and to decide how much they liked it. Other people were given a task that involved processing superficial features: they were asked to look at the words and decide whether they contained particular letters. Later, their explicit and implicit memories for the words were assessed. In both cases the basic task was the same, but the instructions to the subjects were different. People were shown the first three letters of each word. For example, if one of the words had been 'define', they would have been shown a card on which was printed 'def' (this is called a word-stem completion task). Several different six-letter words besides define begin with the letters 'def', such as 'deface', 'defame', 'defeat', 'defect', 'defend', 'defied' and 'deform', so there are several possible responses. The experimenters assessed explicit memory by asking people to try to remember the words they had seen previously, using the first three letters as a hint. They assessed implicit memory by asking the people to say the first word that came to mind that started with the three letters on the card.

Deliberate processing (shallow or deep processing) had a striking effect on the explicit memory task but not on the implicit memory task. When people used the three letters as cues for deliberate retrieval, they were much more successful if they had thought about whether they liked the word than if they simply paid attention to the occurrence of particular letters. However, when people simply said the first word that came to mind, the way they had studied the words had little effect on the number of correct words that 'popped into their heads' (see Figure 8.12).

There is some evidence, however, that the distinction between implicit and explicit memory may not be gen-uinely dissociable. Buchner and Wippich (2000) suggest that these differences in test performance reflect nothing more than test demands. That is, that there are differences between measures of implicit and explicit memory (apart from the fact that they measure implicit and explicit memory) that produce these differences between groups. They note that whereas explicit measures are reliable, tests of implicit memory are relatively unreliable. The unreliability of implicit measures, therefore, may account for the lack of group differences that are reliably seen when explicit measures are used.

In one experiment, Buchner and Wippich required participants either (1) to recognise from a list of new and old words, words that had been previously seen, or (2) to complete word stems using words that had previously been seen. This last implicit task was used in a famous study of amnesics' memory and no differences were found between amnesics and controls. When the researchers analysed the reliability of these measures, the implicit measure was significantly less reliable than was the recognition measure. The study raises important questions about experiments which claim to show differences in memory performance based on implicit measures: it suggests that such differences may be due to methodological, rather than conceptual, reasons.

However, another study adopting a different method provides a different view. It puts forward the possibility that tests of explicit and implicit memory are dissociable because explicit tasks involve conceptual processing whereas implicit tasks involve perceptual processing. If both types of test are made conceptual, people may perform no differently on them (Brooks et al., 2001).

Remembering

Remembering is an automatic process. The word 'automatic' means 'acting by itself'. But this definition implies that no special effort is involved. What is automatic is the retrieval of information from memory in response to the appropriate stimulus. What sometimes requires effort is the attempt to come up with the thoughts (the internal stimuli) that cause the information to be retrieved. In psychology experiments, retrieval can be measured in two basic ways: participants either recall material they have learned unprompted (free recall) or they are asked to identify material they had previously seen; this material is presented amongst stimuli that had not been seen (this is called a recognition memory paradigm).

The retrieval of implicit memories is automatic: when the appropriate stimulus occurs, it automatically evokes the appropriate response. Explicit memories can be retrieved automatically. Whisper your name to yourself. How did you manage to remember what your name is? How did

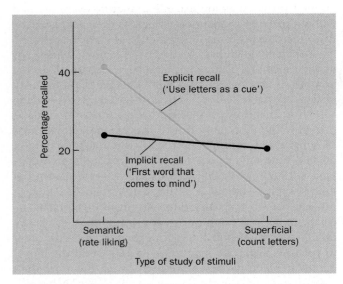

Figure 8.12 Explicit versus implicit memory. The graph shows the percentage of words recalled as a function of the type of study procedure. Deliberate processing improved performance of the explicit memory task but had little effect on the implicit memory task.

Source: Based on data from Graf, P. and Mandler, G., Activation makes words more accessible, but not necessarily more retrievable. *Journal of Verbal Learning and Verbal Behavior*, 1984, 23, 553–68.

you retrieve the information needed to move your lips in the proper sequence? Those questions cannot be answered by introspection. The information just leaps out at us when the proper question is asked (or, more generally, when the appropriate stimulus is encountered).

Reading provides a particularly compelling example of the automatic nature of memory retrieval. When an experienced reader looks at a familiar word, the name of the word occurs immediately, and so does the meaning. In fact, it is difficult to look at a word and not think of its name. Figure 8.13 contains a list of words that can be used to demonstrate a phenomenon known as the Stroop effect (Stroop, 1935; MacLeod, 1992). Look at the words in Figure 8.13 and, as quickly as you can, say the names of the colours in which the words are printed; do not read the words themselves.

Most people cannot completely ignore the words and simply name the colours; the tendency to think of the words and pronounce them is difficult to resist. The **Stroop effect** indicates that even when we try to suppress a well-practised memory, it tends to be retrieved automatically when the appropriate stimulus occurs.

But what about the fact that some memories seem to be difficult to recall? For most people, remembering information is effortless and smooth. It is something we do unconsciously and automatically – most of the time. Occasionally, though, our memory of a name or a place or something else fails. The experience is often frustrating because we know that the information is 'in there somewhere' but we just cannot seem to get it out. This is known as the **tip-of-the-tongue phenomenon** (you encountered the olfactory analogue, the tip-of-the-nose phenomenon, in Chapter 5). It was first studied carefully during the 1960s (Brown and McNeill, 1966), and since then we have learned a great deal about it (Jones, 1989; A.S. Brown, 1991). It is a common, if not universal, experience; it can occur about once a week and increases with age; it often involves proper names and knowing the first letter of the word; and is solved during the experience about 50 per cent of the time.

The active search for stimuli that will evoke the appropriate memory, as exemplified in the tip-of-the-tongue phenomenon, has been called **recollection** (Baddeley, 1982). Recollection may be aided by contextual variables, including

blue blue blue green
green yellow red
yellow yellow blue
red green yellow
yellow green yellow
yellow red yellow
green blue yellow
red blue green green
blue blue green red

Figure 8.13 The Stroop effect. Name the colour in which the words are printed as quickly as you can; you will find it difficult to ignore what the words say.

physical objects, suggestions, or other verbal stimuli. These contextual variables are called **retrieval cues**. The usefulness of these retrieval cues often depends on encoding specificity. Remember from the previous section that the encoding specificity principle states that information can only be retained if it has been stored and the way in which it is retrieved depends on how it was stored. One famous example is that of encoding and retrieving material above and under water. Godden and Baddeley (1975) asked skilled scuba divers to learn lists of words either under water or on land. The divers' ability to recall the lists was later tested in either the same or a different environment. The variable of interest was where subjects learned the list: in or out of the water. When lists were learned under water, they were recalled much better under water than on land, and lists learned on land were recalled better on land than in the water. The context in which information is learned or processed, therefore, influences our ability to recollect that information.

Psychology in action – Using odour to retrieve memories

One of the most celebrated examples of the use of odour as a memory prompt is that of Marcel Proust. In *À la recherche du temps perdu*, he recounts how the experience of dipping a cake into tea provoked a long autobiographical reverie because the memorable aroma percolating from the tea-soaked madeleine transported him back to his childhood. But, literary licence aside, is there sound evidence for the ability of odour to provoke genuine autobiographical memories?

Psychology in action – *Continued*

The evidence for the beneficial effects of odour on behaviour is mixed: some studies show strong positive effects, others show no effect of odour while still others show that exposure to pleasant scents can impair performance. Of the positive studies, exposure to a pleasant odour has been found to increase charitable behaviour (Baron, 1997), facilitate anagram formation (Baron and Thomley, 1994), create more favourable impressions of a casually dressed female job candidate but a less favourable one of a formally dressed candidate (Baron, 1983), enhance recall of verbal material when odour is presented at encoding and recall (Herz, 1997), generate more emotional memories than can words or sights (Herz and Cupchik, 1992), increase genital arousal in women exposed to male cologne during a specific stage of the menstrual cycle (Graham *et al.*, 2000), increase brain electrical activity associated with relaxation or lack of attention (Martin, 1998), and reduce anxiety in women waiting for dental surgery (Lehrner *et al.*, 2000). Exposure to a pleasant, relaxing odour can also impair vigilance (Gould and Martin, 2001) and mental arithmetic performance (Ludvigson and Rottman, 1989) and worsen pain perception (Martin, 2006) but can leave some tasks unaffected (Knasko, 1992).

In the field of memory, however, accurate recall of memories of events experienced years previously has been found when the odours present at those events are re-presented some time later (Aggleton and Waskett, 1999; Chu and Downes, 2000), illustrating a form of state-dependent learning. Cann and Ross (1989) reported that the presence of a pleasant perfume at the presentation of a series of photographic slides led to better recognition if it was also presented at recall. Schab (1990) found that participants who learned and recalled in the presence of an ambient chocolate odour recalled more antonyms than did a control group or a group presented with an odour at encoding but not retrieval. In a subsequent experiment, odour-related words were no better recalled than neutral words although there was benefit to having the same odour present at encoding and recall. But the recall of memories may depend on the emotional nature of the odour. People report more unhappy memories in the presence of an unpleasant odour, for example, than they do in a pleasant one, and happier memories in the presence of a pleasant odour (Ehrlichman and Halpern, 1988).

In a real-life study, Aggleton and Waskett (1999) asked participants to recall memories of their visit to the Viking Museum in York, England, during exposure to no odour or to odours that accompanied the exhibits at the museum. Participants who recalled memories in the presence of the odours they had previously been exposed to, remembered significantly more about the exhibits and about their visit than did those participants who received no such olfactory cues. This seems to confirm what Proust described at the beginning of the last century: odour may be an effective retrieval cue.

Reconstruction: remembering as a creative process

Much of what we recall from long-term memory may not be an accurate representation of what actually happened previously. One view of memory is that it is a plausible account of what might have happened or even of what we think should have happened. An early experiment by Bartlett (1932) drew attention to this possibility. This was Bartlett's view (p. 213):

> Remembering is not the reexcitation of innumerable fixed, lifeless and fragmentary traces. It is an imaginative reconstruction, or construction, built out of the relation of our attitude towards a whole active mass of organised past reactions or experience and to a little outstanding detail which commonly appears in image or in language form. It is thus hardly ever really exact, even in the most rudimentary cases of rote recapitulation, and it is not at all important that it should be so.

Bartlett had people read a story or essay or look at a picture. Then he asked them on several later occasions to retell the prose passage or to draw the picture. Each time, the people 'remembered' the original a little differently. If the original story had contained peculiar and unexpected sequences of events, people tended to retell it in a more coherent and sensible fashion, as if their memories had been revised to make the information accord more closely with their own conceptions of reality. Bartlett concluded that people remember only a few striking details of an experience and that during recall they reconstruct the missing portions in accordance with their own expectations.

Many studies have confirmed Bartlett's conclusions and have extended his findings to related phenomena. Spiro (1977, 1980) found that people will remember even a rather simple story in different ways, according to their own conceptions of reality. Two groups of people read a story about an engaged couple in which the man was opposed to having children. In one version, the woman was upset when she learned his opinion because she wanted to have children. In the other version, the woman also did not want to have children. After reading the story, people were asked to fill out some forms. While collecting the forms, the experimenter either said nothing more about the story or 'casually mentioned' that the story was actually a true one and added one of two different endings: the couple got married and have been happy ever since, or the couple broke up and never saw each other again.

Two days, three weeks or six weeks later, the participants were asked to recall the story they had read. If at least three weeks had elapsed, people who had heard an ending that contradicted the story tended to 'remember' information that resolved the conflict. For example, if they had read that the woman was upset to learn that the man did not want children but were later told that the couple was happily married, people were likely to 'recall' something that would have resolved the conflict, such as that the couple had decided to adopt a child rather than have one of their own. If people had read that the woman also did not want children but were later told that the couple broke up, then they were likely to 'remember' that there was a difficulty with one set of parents. In contrast, people who had heard an ending that was consistent with the story they had read did not remember any extra facts; they did not need them to make sense of the story. For example, if they had heard that the couple disagreed about having a child and later broke up, no new 'facts' had to be added.

People were most confident about details that had actually not occurred but had been added to make more sense of the story. Thus, a person's confidence in the accuracy of a particular memory is not necessarily a good indication of whether the event actually occurred.

However, some researchers have criticised Bartlett's findings and some have even argued that Bartlett himself drew conclusions that were not warranted (Ost and Costall, 2002). Edwards and Middleton (1987), for example, have argued that the studies reported by Bartlett, – these studies reported a form of memory called serial reproduction – did not assess the normal, everyday process of remembering. For example, participants in Bartlett's experiments wrote down alone what they could remember of a story read to them (rather than being retold to them, as you might expect in most everyday contexts). Others, such as Roediger *et al.* (2000), have argued that the material to be remembered was not particularly ecologically valid. One of the stories to be recalled, *The War of the Ghosts*, was quite exotic and unusual and not like everyday prose (Wynn and Logie, 1998; Roediger *et al.*, (2000), which made connections between parts of the story difficult to form. Bartlett did use more familiar material and found that participants made the typical reconstruction of the story. Bartlett's story is reproduced in Table 8.1, together with two recalled versions. Note the differences, and types of differences, between the actual story and the remembered one.

In an experiment in which the material to be remembered was relevant, Wynn and Logie (1998) quizzed undergraduates at two-month intervals about an incident at the beginning of the academic year and asked them to recall memories from that time. They found that memories were very resistant to change over time. However, although the study found that some distinctive memories could be accurately recalled, recent research suggests that memories can be very manipulable to the extent that false information introduced at recall can lead to this false information being incorporated into memory. The context in which memory and acquisition takes place can also influence our recall of events, as the next section shows.

Table 8.1 Three examples of *The War of the Ghosts* story. The first (a) is the original story; the second (b) is a version by a participant after 20 hours' delay; the third (c) is the same person's version of the story after eight days

(a) *The War of the Ghosts*

One night two young men from Egulac went down to the river to hunt seals, and while they were there it became foggy and calm. Then they heard war-cries, and they thought: 'Maybe this is a war-party.' They escaped to the shore, and hid behind a log. Now canoes came up, and they heard the noise of paddles, and saw one canoe coming up to them. There were five men in the canoe, and they said:

'What do you think? We wish to take you along. We are going up the river to make war on the people.'

One of the young men said: 'I have no arrows.'

'Arrows are in the canoe,' they said.

'I will not go along. I might be killed. My relatives do not know where I have gone. But you,' he said, turning to the other, 'may go with them.'

So one of the young men went, but the other returned home.

And the warriors went on up the river to a town on the other side of Kalama. The people came down to the water, and they began to fight, and many were killed. But presently the young man heard one of the warriors say: 'Quick, let us go home: that Indian has been hit.' Now he thought: 'Oh, they are ghosts.' He did not feel sick, but they said he had been shot.

So the canoes went back to Egulac, and the young man went ashore to his house, and made a fire. And he told everybody and said: 'Behold I accompanied the ghosts, and we went to fight. Many of our fellows were killed, and many of those who attacked us were killed. They said I was hit, and I did not feel sick.'

He told it all, and then he became quiet. When the sun rose he fell down. Something black came out of this mouth. His face became contorted. The people jumped up and cried.

He was dead.

Table 8.1 *Continued*

(b) *The War of the Ghosts*
Two men from Egulac went fishing. While thus occupied by the river they heard a noise in the distance.
'It sounds like a cry,' said one, and presently there appeared some men in canoes who invited them to join the party on their adventure. One of the young men refused to go, on the ground of family ties, but the other offered to go.
'But there are no arrows,' he said.
'The arrows are in the boat,' was the reply.
He thereupon took his place, while his friend returned home. The party paddled up the river to Kaloma, and began to land on the banks of the river. The enemy came rushing upon them, and some sharp fighting ensued. Presently someone was injured, and the cry was raised that the enemy were ghosts.
The party returned down the stream, and the young man arrived home feeling none the worse for his experience. The next morning at dawn he endeavoured to recount his adventures. While he was talking something black issued from his mouth. Suddenly he uttered a cry and fell down. His friends gathered round him.
But he was dead.

(c) *The War of the Ghosts*
Two young men from Egulac went fishing. While thus engaged they heard a noise in the distance. 'That sounds like a war-cry,' said one, 'there is going to be some fighting.' Presently there appeared some warriors who invited them to join an expedition up the river.
One of the young men excused himself on the ground of family ties. 'I cannot come,' he said, 'as I might get killed.' So he returned home. The other man, however, joined the party, and they proceeded on canoes up the river. While landing on the banks the enemy appeared and were running down to meet them. Soon someone was wounded, and the party discovered that they were fighting against ghosts. The young man and his companion returned to the boats, and went back to their homes.
The next morning at dawn he was describing his adventures to his friends, who had gathered round him. Suddenly something black issued from his mouth, and he fell down uttering a cry. His friends closed around him, but found that he was dead.

Source: Bartlett, F.C., *Remembering*. London: Cambridge University Press, 1932.

Psychology in action – How long does memory last?

In 1885, Hermann Ebbinghaus reported the results of the first experiment to determine the duration of memory. Using himself as a participant, Ebbinghaus memorised 13 nonsense syllables such as 'dax', 'wuj', 'lep' and 'pib'. He then studied how long it took him to relearn the original list after intervals varying from a few minutes up to 31 days. Figure 8.14 shows what he found. Much of what he learned was forgotten very quickly – usually within a day or two. But even after 31 days, he could still recall some of the original information.

Ebbinghaus's research dealt with remembering nonsense syllables and began a fruitful line of enquiry for psychologists interested in the length of time we can reasonably retain information before we begin to forget. For example, for how long might you remember the important experiences of your childhood? Or the information in this book? Or a well-known public event?

Schmolck *et al*. (2000) looked at the effect of **retention interval** – the period between encoding and retrieval – on memory for the O.J. Simpson trial verdict, announced on 3 October 1995. College students were asked about how they heard the news about the verdict three days after the result, 15 months later and 32 months later. There was a significant difference between recall at 15 and at 32 months. After 15 months, about 50 per cent of recollections were accurate and only 11 per cent

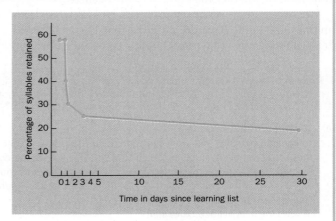

Figure 8.14 Ebbinghaus's (1885) forgetting curve.
Source: Adapted from Ebbinghaus, H., *Memory: A contribution to experimental psychology* (H.A. Ruger and C.E. Bussenius, trans.), 1885/1913. Teacher's College Press, Columbia University, New York.

contained major errors; at 32 months, only 29 per cent of the recollections were accurate and 40 per cent contained major distortions. Figure 8.15 shows you how memory became distorted in these participants over time. There may be some value

Psychology in action – *Continued*

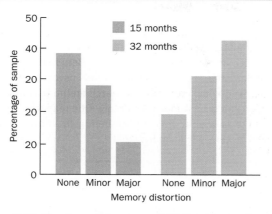

Figure 8.15 The degree of memory distortion (none, minor and major) for the O.J. Simpson trial verdict seen in Schmolck *et al.*'s study after 15 and 32 months.

Source: Schmolck, H., Buffalo, E.A. and Squire L.R., Memory distortions develop over time: Recollections of the O.J. Simpson trial verdict after 15 and 32 months. *Psychological Science*, 2000, 11(1), 39–45, reprinted by permission of Blackwell Publishers Ltd.

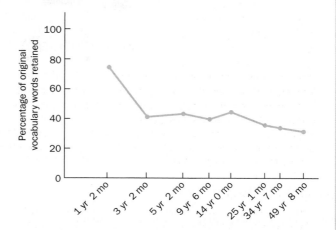

Figure 8.16 The forgetting curve for Spanish vocabulary.

Source: Adapted from Bahrick, H.P., Semantic memory content in permastore: Fifty years of Spanish learned in school. *Journal of Experimental Psychology: General*, 1984, 113, 1–29.

to this. There is neuroimaging evidence to suggest that the process of forgetting frees up regions of the brain: the forgetting of material that competes with more important information that we need to remember is associated with a decline in the activation of the prefrontal cortex, for example (Kuhl *et al.*, 2007).

In a well-known study, Bahrick *et al.* (1975) investigated how much information about their classmates (such as faces or names) graduates would remember 25 years after graduation. Bahrick found that the ability to recall classmates' names and to generate a name from a photo declined over time. The longer the retention interval (RI), the greater the decline. Recognition of faces and names and the matching of names to faces, however, was fairly robust. Ninety per cent of responses were correct over the first 15 years (although accuracy, again, declined when the RI became longer). Bahrick (1984) also reported that retention for Spanish learned at school declined in the first six years after graduating, stabilised for the next 35 years and then declined thereafter (see Figure 8.16).

Bahrick argued that the period of stability from 6 to 35 years represents a 'permastore'; this was a store of knowledge that was resistant to forgetting and which must have been learned deeply. An alternative interpretation, however, was suggested by Neisser (1984). He suggested that individuals have a schematic representation of a 'knowledge domain', that is, specific knowledge is not stored in a permanent way, but ways of representing that knowledge allow the retrieval of information. On the basis of this view, conceptual knowledge should be better retained (and retrieved) than would, say, straightforward facts.

Conway and co-workers (Conway *et al.*, 1991; Cohen *et al.*, 1992), measured students' retention of knowledge of cognitive psychology over twelve years (between 1978 and 1989) and found that memory declined in the first 36 months, then stabilised. However, the recall and recognition of proper names declined more rapidly than did memory for concepts. Why? If you accept Neisser's position, conceptual information should be better retained because memory is organised in such a way as to facilitate the retention of this type of information. Cohen (1990) further suggested that proper names lacked the semantic depth necessary for encoding concepts. Proper names did not need to be represented in abstract form and do not fall within a scheme of knowledge. In a follow-up study, Conway *et al.* (1992) found that coursework was a better predictor of retention than was exam performance because the learning for the former was distributed across the term whereas learning for the exam was, arguably, massed (being crammed).

In a separate study of how much first-year students thought they knew, guessed or remembered answers on a multiple choice examination on a range of psychology lecture courses, Conway *et al.* (1997) found the better students seemed to 'remember' more of the answers. For research methods courses, the same students 'knew' more, indicating that a **remember-to-know shift (R–K shift)** had occurred. Why, then, did better students not 'know' more after their lecture courses? One reason may be that the lecture courses contained more topics and that there was, therefore, greater variability in the types of knowledge domain to be learned

Psychology in action – *Continued*

(Conway *et al.*, 1997). Also, the research methods courses involved a large degree of repetition (as research methods courses do) and problem-solving is integral to the course: these factors might promote the R–K shift.

People's memory for their grades also declines with time (Bahrick *et al.*, 2008). One to 54 years after graduating, 276 participants were able to recall 3,025 of 3,967 grades. The better students made fewer errors. Of those who recalled their marks incorrectly, 81 per cent inflated the grade.

So, what can we conclude about long-term retention of knowledge? Non-schematic knowledge (such as the names of psychologists) declines more greatly than schematic knowledge (such as conceptual information). Better students also remember more of non-research methods psychology lecture courses and know more from research methods courses as well as recall grades more accurately. One reason for this is that there is a shift from remembering to knowing, from episodic to semantic memory.

The malleability of memory

An experiment takes place in which participants are asked to read short passages of text and then, one day later in a telephone conversation, are asked questions about the content of the text and the context in which the reading occurred. Six weeks later, they are asked the same questions and also whether they remembered answers given in their telephone conversation. This experiment by Loftus and her colleagues (see Joslyn *et al.*, 2001) found that while participants were remarkably good at remembering the correct answers they gave, they were significantly poor at remembering the questions they answered incorrectly. Perhaps the correct answers generated a positive mood or represented a more coherent memory.

This is one of several studies that indicate that our subjective beliefs about the context of content of memory can influence the recall of events. Research from social psychology and cognitive psychology shows how we can be misled into saying things or doing things we believe to be incorrect or which we are not sure about. The studies of Solomon Asch (described in Chapter 15) and Elizabeth Loftus (described below) show how malleable human behaviour can be, especially when we are faced with the pressure to conform.

Roediger *et al.* (2001) investigated whether conformity was simply a 'public' behaviour where a person wants to be seen to behave correctly and yet knows that their response is wrong, or a 'private' one, where the conversion in their belief is genuine. Studies of social psychology have shown that conformity is greater when participants make decisions in the company of others than when alone. Would the presence of another person who falsely claimed that an object had been in a room lead a participant also to claim that they remembered seeing an object in a room when no such object was present?

In one condition, a participant and a confederate watched slides of six household scenes featuring common household objects for either 15 or 60 seconds. In a collaborative recall task in which both individuals tried to recall as many objects in the scenes as they could, the confederate made occasional mistakes such as recalling items that were not in the slides. Some of these items were consistent with some of the items in the scene and other were not. After a short delay, the participant was asked to recall as many items from the scenes as they could. In a second condition, a similar experiment was carried out but no erroneous suggestions were made.

Participants in the company of those confederates who recalled objects that were not in the scenes recalled significantly more erroneous objects than did those in the control condition. This effect was magnified if people were exposed to the scenes for 15 seconds (presumably, reflecting the fact that such a short period leaves little time to monitor the scene and leads you to believe that there were objects presented that were not actually there). Participants who recalled these erroneous items were also more likely to report that they 'knew' the objects were in the scene rather than report they remembered seeing them.

Why were the participants influenced in this way? The authors interpret the results in terms of Johnson's source monitoring framework (Johnson *et al.*, 1993). This argues that because we receive information from many sources, we can recall this material but misattribute it to earlier events. The collaborative recall part of the experiment may be an example of an early event acting as a source of memory interference where more recent memories interfere with current retrieval. The more consistent the confederates' recall is with that of the event or scene, the stronger the social contagion will be; the more distinctive the recall, the less likely social contagion is to occur.

This susceptibility has significant consequences for important areas of life, especially those which can have serious repercussions, such as eyewitness testimony.

Eyewitness testimony

On 4 October 1992, an El Al plane lost its engine after take-off from Amsterdam Schiphol Airport. It returned to the airport but lost height and crashed into an 11-storey apartment building. Ten months later, Crombag *et al.* (1996) questioned 193 individuals about the crash. The event was widely reported in the news but was not actually filmed. When individuals were asked if they saw the plane hit the building, 55 per cent said that they had (they had not been present at the time of the accident); 59 per cent said that the fire started immediately on impact. In a follow-up study, 68 per cent said they had seen the crash and 67 per cent of participants said that they saw the plane hit the building horizontally (in fact, it hit the building vertically).

This experiment and those of Loftus and her colleagues (Loftus, 1997) suggest that our recollections of events may not be infallible. Loftus, for example, has reported that the kinds of questions used to elicit information after an event has been experienced can have a major effect on what people remember. Loftus's research shows that even subtle changes in a question can affect people's recollections. For example, Loftus and Palmer (1974) showed people films of car accidents and asked them to estimate vehicles' speeds when they 'contacted/ hit/bumped/collided/ smashed' each other. People's estimates of the vehicles' speeds were directly related to the force of the impact suggested by the verb, such as 'hit', that appeared in the question (see Figure 8.17). That is, the more expressive and dramatic the verb, the greater the estimated speed. In a similar experiment, people were asked a week after viewing the film whether they saw any broken glass at the scene (there was none). People in the 'smashed' group were most likely to say yes. Thus, a leading question that encouraged them to remember the vehicles going faster also encouraged them to remember that they saw non-existent broken glass. The question appears to have modified the memory itself.

Even very subtle leading questions can affect people's recollections. Loftus and Zanni (1975) showed people short films of an accident involving several vehicles. Some people were asked, 'Did you see a broken headlight?'; others were asked, 'Did you see the broken headlight?' The particular question biased the people's responses: although the film did not show a broken headlight, twice as many people who heard the article 'the' said that they remembered seeing one.

These are not the only examples of the ways in which memories can be altered. Individuals can be misled into thinking that a 'stop' sign was a 'give way' sign (Loftus *et al.*, 1978) and that a bare-handed thief wore gloves (Zaragoza and Mitchell, 1996). This misinformation effect is much stronger in older people (Jacoby *et al.*, 2005).

Experiments such as these have important implications for eyewitness testimony in courts of law. Wells and Seelau (1995) illustrate this point with the following examples:

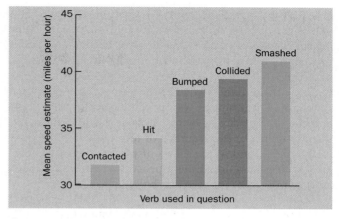

Figure 8.17 Leading questions and recall. Mean estimated speed of vehicles as recalled by people in the study of Loftus and Palmer (1974).

Source: Based on data from Loftus, E.F. and Palmer, J.C., Reconstruction of automobile destruction: An example of the interaction between language and memory. *Journal of Verbal Learning and Verbal Behavior*, 1974, 13, 585–89.

In 1984, Frederick Rene Dange was identified from a set of photographs and served 10 years in a Californian prison for rape, kidnapping, robbery and murder he did not commit. Dange was released in 1994 after a DNA test proved his innocence. In 1980, James Newsome was convicted of murder on the basis of eyewitness evidence. Fifteen years later, he was released after his fingerprints were submitted to new computer technology that implicated someone else as the murderer.

In a review of 205 cases of wrongful arrest, Rattner (1988) found that 52 per cent of these cases were associated with mistaken eyewitness testimony. In 1996, the National Institute of Justice found that 28 people had been wrongfully convicted based on eyewitness testimony (DNA evidence had exonerated the accused). Consequently, in 1998, the American Psychological Association issued a new series of rules and procedures designed to reduce errors made in considering eyewitness identification (Wells *et al.*, 1998).

Eyewitness identification

In a famous, historical case, *Frye* v. *The United States* (1923), the court ruled that scientific evidence was admissible only if it was generally accepted by the relevant scientific community. The judgment in a case called *Daubert* v. *Merrell Dow Pharmaceuticals, Inc.* 70 years later, however, ruled that judges would be the gatekeepers of scientific reliability in the US – they would judge the relevance, validity and reliability of scientific evidence. This makes the quality of evidence very important. Laypeople regard eyewitness reports, crime scene reports and police procedures as important contributions to their evaluation of testimony (Shaw *et al.*, 1999). They also regard the eye-witness's vision, knowledge of the suspect and emotional state during the crime as well as lighting at the crime scene and the time of day as being the factors which most frequently influence the accuracy of testimony. Do these lay views correspond to the views of professional psychologists who have studied these processes? And how much agreement is there between psychologists?

According to one study (Kassin *et al.*, 2001) experts in eyewitness identification agreed on the following:

- 98 per cent thought that testimony could be influenced by the way in which questions are worded
- 98 per cent thought that police line-up instructions could affect identification.
- 92 per cent agreed that the eyewitness's attitudes and expectations about the event could influence testimony.
- 87 per cent thought that eyewitnesses' confidence in their judgement is poorly correlated with the accuracy of the testimony.
- 83 per cent thought that memory loss is greatest immediately after witnessing the event.
- 81 per cent thought that the less time an eyewitness has to observe an event, the less well it will be remembered.
- 45 per cent thought that hypnosis improved testimony accuracy.
- 80 per cent thought that eyewitness confidence is malleable and influenced by factors unrelated to accuracy, that exposure to a mugshot increases the likelihood of the face in the mugshot being selected from a later line-up, that children are more susceptible than adults to leading questions, and that eyewitnesses are better at recognising perpetrators of their own race.

According to forensic psychologists Gary Wells and Amy Bradfield (1999), 'There is increasing evidence that mistaken eyewitness identifications from line-ups and photospreads are the most frequent cause of juries convicting innocent persons.' They examined how information given to a witness before and after making a line-up identification affected the witness's confidence in making the correct identification. Giving positive post-identification feedback (such as telling the witness they identified the right suspect when they had not) inflates confidence in their identification, but also makes them think that their view of the suspect was better, that they identified the suspect more quickly and that they paid more attention when they witnessed the suspect.

What do these famous lines have in common? 'Beam me up, Scotty', 'Me Tarzan, you Jane', 'You dirty rat', 'Play it again, Sam', 'Elementary, my dear Watson'? Their fame, yes. But none of these lines was actually said. This highlights how our memory can be very malleable.
Source: Paramount Television/The Kobal Collection.

In a twist to this type of experiment, Wells and Bradfield asked witnesses to think privately about how certain they were about their identification, how good their view was, how long they took to identify the suspect before being given false positive feedback. Another group of participants was given these instructions after receiving feedback and another was not instructed to think about its decision. In each case, the eyewitness had identified the wrong suspect.

The researchers found that when eyewitnesses were instructed to think about the decision prior to feedback, they were relatively unaffected by the false positive feedback. Those who were not instructed to think about their decision or were instructed to think after being given feedback, showed a significant inflation in their confidence which also extended to other aspects of their testimony.

'The solution to preventing feedback,' say Wells and Bradfield, 'is apparent from the argument that a properly conducted line-up is like a properly conducted experiment.' They suggest that the person with whom the witness communicates the decision about line-up identification should be unaware of who the suspect is and that confidence measures should be taken prior to the witness being told whether the suspect had been correctly identified. If not, false identification will be confounded by a false sense of inflated confidence.

Cutting edge – Unbelievable accents

Can your accent affect your plausibility as an eyewitness? We make assumptions about people based on little psychological information – from the way they look and dress to their voice and accent. A study from the US has found that eyewitnesses who used an accent (German, Mexican and Lebanese) were judged to be significantly less credible, accurate and prestigious and more deceptive than an American accent by US-born participants (Frumkin, 2007). The Lebanese accent was rated least favourably.

The study suggests that testimony delivered by a non-native speaker may be interpreted negatively by native speakers. The finding should make prosecutors and defence lawyers aware that seemingly trivial factors –such as a person's accent – can have serious effects on their plausibility.

The experiments reviewed in this section indicate that learning new information and recalling it later are active processes – information is not placed in a mental filing cabinet and picked up later. We organise and integrate information in terms of what we already know about life and have come to expect about particular experiences. Thus, when we recall the memory later, it may contain information that was not part of the original experience.

At first, this phenomenon may appear to be maladaptive because it means that eyewitness testimony cannot be regarded as infallible, even when a witness is trying to be truthful. However, it probably reflects the fact that information about an episode can be more efficiently stored by means of a few unique details. The portions of an episode that are common to other experiences, and hence resemble information already stored in long-term memory, need not be retained. If every detail of every experience had to be encoded uniquely in long-term memory, perhaps we would run out of storage space. Unfortunately, this process sometimes leads to instances of faulty remembering.

Interference

see activity on mypsychlab Although long-term memory is durable, it may also be susceptible to interference. The finding that some memories may interfere with the retrieval of others is well established. An early study by Jenkins and Dallenbach (1924) showed that people are less likely to remember information after an interval of wakefulness than after an interval of sleep, presumably because of new memories that are formed when one is awake (see Figure 8.18).

Subsequent research soon showed that there are two types of interference in retrieval. Sometimes we experience **retroactive interference**: when we try to retrieve information, other information, which we have learned more recently, interferes. You may have a hard time recalling your old telephone number because a new one has replaced it. When memories that interfere with retrieval are formed after the learning that is being tested, we experience retroactive interference.

At other times, retrieval is impaired by **proactive interference**, in which our ability to recall new information is reduced because of information we learned previously. Figure 8.19 illustrates the experimental procedure used to examine the effects of proactive interference.

In this procedure, the experimental group learns the words in both list A and list B. The control group learns only the words in list B. Both groups then experience a retention interval before they are asked to recall the words in list B. If the experimental group recalls fewer words in list B during the test than does the control group, proactive interference is said to have occurred.

As reasonable and intuitive as the principle of interference may be, it has not gone unchallenged. Researchers agree that interference can affect retrieval, but some argue that the kinds of recall task people are asked to perform in the laboratory are most likely to be affected by interference. In real life, such effects may not be so powerful. For

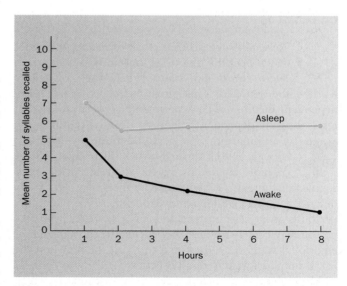

Figure 8.18 Interference in memory retrieval. The mean number of nonsense syllables recalled after sleeping or staying awake for varying intervals of time.

Source: Adapted from Jenkins, J.G. and Dallenbach, K.M., Oblivescence during sleep and waking. *American Journal of Psychology*, 1924, 35, 605–12.

Retroactive interference

Group	Initial learning	Retention interval	Retention test
Experimental	Learn A	Learn B	Recall A
Control	Learn A		Recall A

Proactive interference

	Initial learning		Retention interval	Retention test
Experimental	Learn A	Learn B		Recall B
Control		Learn B		Recall B

Figure 8.19 Retroactive and proactive interference illustrated.

example, meaningful prose, such as the kind found in novels, is resistant to interference. That said, however, a recent study demonstrated that when participants watched either a violent, sexually explicit or neutral television show featuring nine adverts, recall of the advertisements immediately after the exposure and 24 hours later was poorer in the violent and sexual television conditions (Bushman and Bonacci, 2002). The effect was robust whether the television programme was liked or disliked and whether the participant was male or female. It seems as if some stimuli are powerful or exciting enough to interfere with our memory, even outside the laboratory.

State-dependent memory: the effect of mood on recall

Research suggests that recall of memory is better when people's moods or emotional states match their emotional states when they originally learned the material. This phenomenon is called **state-dependent memory**. The experimental procedure used in tests of state-dependent memory usually requires the manipulation of a person's mood by hypnosis (Bower, 1981), through drugs (Eich *et al.*, 1975), or, more commonly, by the alteration of the environmental context, as exemplified by the scuba diver study described earlier (Godden and Baddeley, 1975). Next, the person is given a list of items to memorise. Later, when the person may or may not be experiencing the same mental or emotional state, they are asked to recall the items on the list. If the states match, recall is better.

Mood-dependent memory describes a context in which the person's mood at encoding and retrieval can affect the successful execution of these two processes (such as a well-liked song provoking memories of events experienced when the song was first heard). Although replications in which positive effects in mood-dependent memory are rare (Bower and Mayer, 1989), Eich (1995) suggests that when participants in these experiments experience strong/stable moods and are responsible for generating memory cues, mood-dependent memory is robust.

In one experiment, participants were asked to generate specific memories for events from autobiographical memory in response to common words (Eich *et al.*, 1994). Two to three days later, participants were allowed to free recall the memories generated in the experiment. Eich *et al.* found that more events were recalled when the mood matched the mood at testing. In another set of experiments, Eich (1995) found that the transfer of information from one environment to another is better if these environments feel similar. However, changes in the environment are not important if the moods at acquisition and reinstatement are the same. There is also evidence to suggest that individuals with mood disorders have a greater ability to discriminate between old and new stimuli if their moods at exposure and testing match (Eich *et al.*, 1997).

Does this evidence suggest that mood-dependent memory is genuinely robust? Smith (1995) and Eich himself (1995) suggest that mood-dependent memory effects may be explained by other factors. Smith, for example, suggests that active memories or pre-existing mood generated at the time of acquisition could have cued a representation of the initial context of the original event.

State-dependent memory may be related to **place-or context-dependent memory**, illustrated by the Godden and Baddeley experiment above. The demonstration of place-dependent memory (PDM) depends on the event to be remembered, the nature of encoding and retrieval, the ease by which people can mentally reinstate themselves, and the retention interval (Smith, 1979, 1988; McDaniel *et al.*, 1989; Wilhite, 1991). Reinstatement is important to PDM and refers to the process whereby the individual is placed in the same environment or is experiencing the same mood as when they originally encoded or generated information.

Because all of the factors listed above are important to PDM, the evidence for the phenomenon is mixed but generally supportive. In a meta-analysis of context-dependent memory studies in which retrieval and encoding were dependent on the explicit processing of aspects of the experimental environment, Smith and Vela (2001) found that context effects were very reliable. However, when people were encouraged to use non-contextual cues during encoding of material and its retrieval, the effects of environmental cues were reduced.

Flashbulb memories

For British sports fans, it was a blessing; for those bored with wall-to-wall sport and physical activity involving sticks and running around in circles, it was a prompt for a collective groan. On 6 July 2005, the United Kingdom was told that London's bid to hold the 2012 Olympic Games was successful. Scenes of celebration ensued in Singapore and in London. The morning after, one of the authors was listening to the BBC's News and Sports radio station where the regular phone-in turned to discussing the logistics of holding the games and whether the capital would be up to it. At 9.50 a.m., the presenter, Michael Bannister, was about to introduce a guest when he read out an announcement from London Transport indicating that Liverpool Street underground station in the financial district of London had been closed, due to a technical problem. Probably electrical, he said. This seemed unusual but, after 11 September 2001, nothing could be that unusual. The association with the 11 September attack was prescient. It later transpired that bombs had been detonated in two London underground stations. A bus travelling near Tavistock Square, the home of the British Medical Association, had its roof blown off by another bomb. A total of 53 people were murdered on 7 July 2005, including all of the British-born bombers.

The above recollection is an example of a **flashbulb memory** – the remembering of an event that is personally or socially important, novel, unexpected, vivid and has major long-term consequences. You will often hear people say that they knew exactly what they were doing when Kennedy was assassinated (Winograd and Killinger, 1983) in the same way that the author knew exactly where he was and what he was doing when news of the first of the 7 July London bombs exploding was heard.

The name 'flashbulb memories' was coined by Brown and Kulik (1977) to describe the vivid recollections from black and white respondents of the assassinations of Martin Luther King and President Kennedy. According to Brown and Kulik, the memory has a '"live" quality that is almost perceptual. . . like a photograph' (p. 74). Since Brown and Kulik's landmark paper was published, flash-

bulb memories have been reported for the death of the King of Belgium (Finkenauer *et al.*, 1998), the death of spectators at the Hillsborough football stadium, England (Wright, 1993; Wright *et al.*, 1998), the resignation of Margaret Thatcher as British prime minister (Conway *et al.*, 1994; Wright *et al.*, 1998), the Gulf War (Weaver, 1993), the assassination of Olaf Palme, the Swedish prime minister (Christianson, 1989), the 1986 American space shuttle disaster (Bohannon, 1988), the experience of being in an earthquake (Neisser *et al.*, 1996b), the fall of the Berlin Wall, by East and West Germans (Bohn and Bernsten, 2007), and the death of Diana, Princess of Wales (Hornstein *et al.*, 2003).

According to Christianson (1992), 'people remember. . . public negative emotional events better than ordinary events that occurred equally long ago', suggesting that these events are not only more salient than others but also more accurate. Recently, there has been some debate on whether flashbulb memories are genuinely different from other types of memory. According to Brown and Kulik, flashbulb memories are of surprising or consequential events which are stored in the brain 'unchanged'; they also operate via a mechanism that is different from that which allows the formation of other types of memory. Wright (1993; Wright *et al.*, 1998), however, has conducted an extensive study of memories of the Hillsborough disaster and the resignation of Margaret Thatcher and suggests that flashbulb memories do not require a special mechanism. Furthermore, memories for these events may not even be vivid.

Wright *et al.* (1998) considered three assumptions behind flashbulb memories: (1) that they are 'collective' in nature (i.e. most of us will experience them when encountering a surprising and important event); (2) that the subjective characteristics of memories are reliable (would changing the order of questions in the study alter recollective ability, for example, especially if certain orders cued memories better?); and (3) that flashbulb memories are actually vivid. The researchers looked at memories for the Hillsborough disaster – where 96 spectators were crushed to death at an English FA football semi-final – and the resignation of Margaret Thatcher on 22 November 1990. Memory for the resignation was more vivid than for Hillsborough but the Hillsborough event was considered more important. Twelve per cent of the sample had vivid recollections of the resignation whereas nine per cent had vivid recollections of Hillsborough. This contrasts markedly with the 86 per cent reported by Conway *et al.* (1994) for Thatcher's resignation. Perhaps age, or even a lack of interest in politics, could have accounted for the difference in the later study.

A problem with previous flashbulb memory research has been the absence of a 'control' group of memories: researchers have measured memories for flashbulb events over time but have not compared them with memories for

ipant has, for example, to determine which of two stimuli had been previously presented (where one stimulus is a distractor and not experienced before and the other is the stimulus previously seen/heard/etc.).

As you saw in Chapter 7, during instrumental learning the organism identifies a link between a stimulus and the response. It learns that by making a certain number of behavioural responses or making these responses at certain intervals it will be rewarded (or reinforced; the reward reinforces the behaviour and encourages it to be repeated to achieve the same outcome). In classical conditioning, the organism learns that if two previously unassociated stimuli are paired often enough, then the response normally elicited by the first will also be elicited by the other (although before they were paired it would not have done this).

Learning seems to involve a strengthening of connections between neurons. The theory was proposed by Hebb (1949) in his famous book, *The Organization of Behaviour*. Hebb proposed that each psychologically important event is conceived of as the flow of activity in a neuronal loop. This loop is made up of the interconnections between dendrite, cell body and the synapses on these structures. The synapses in a particular path become functionally connected to form what Hebb called a cell assembly. The assumption he made was that if two neurons are excited together, they become linked functionally. If the synapse between two neurons is repeatedly activated as the postsynpatic neuron fires, then the structure or chemistry of the synapse changes. This change strengthens the connection between neurons.

Hebb proposed that short-term memory resulted from reverberation of the closed loops of the cell assembly; long-term memory is the more structural, lasting change in synaptic connections. This long-term change in structure is thought to reflect **long-term potentiation (LTP)**, a term which desribes the strengthening of neuronal connections via repeated stimulation (Lomo, 1966). Lomo found that if the axonal pathway from the entorhinal cortex to the dendate gyrus was repeatedly, electrically stimulated, then there was a long-term increase in the size of potentials generated by the postsynaptic neurons. LTP, therefore, was produced by the activation of synapses and the depolarisation of postsynaptic neurons. Psychologists agree that long-term memory involves more or less permanent changes in the structure of the brain (Fuster, 1995; Horn, 1998). But where and how?

Where are long-term memories formed?

Long-term potentiation seems to predominate in the **hippocampus**. If the hippocampus is stimulated, long-term physical changes are observed (Bliss and Gardner-Medwin, 1973). The entorhinal cortex provides inputs to the hippocampus. The axons from the entorhinal cortex pass through a part of the subcortex called the perforant path and form synapses with cells in the dendate gyrus, a part of the hippocampal formation.

The hippocampal formation itself is composed of two distinct structures: Ammon's horn (often referred to as the hippocampus) and the dendate gyrus. Ammon's horn comprises the substructures CA1, CA2 and CA3. CA1 is sometimes referred to as 'Sommer's sector'. There is also significant hippocampal output to the mammillary body via a tract called the fornix. Damage to each of these structures is sometimes associated with memory loss although the evidence for the involvement of the fornix is mixed (Calabrese *et al.*, 1995).

Translating this process into the behaviour seen in classical conditioning, the unconditioned stimulus (the puff of air) makes strong synaptic connections with the neurons which produce the unconditioned response (the blink). Presenting the conditioned stimulus (the tone) alone, generates weak synapses. But pairing the tone with the unconditioned stimulus, leads to the conditioned stimulus forming very strong synaptic connections. The more often the pairing is made, the stronger the connection becomes. For this type of classical conditioning to occur, a functioning hippocampus appears to be necessary and the involvement of the structure would appear to be that of acquiring conscious knowledge of the relationship between the conditioned and unconditioned stimulus. The hippocampus is also involved in learning the relationship between the unconditioned and conditioned stimulus when there is a delay between the presentation of each, a process called trace conditioning (Clark and Squire, 1998).

The consolidation of memory seems to be time-dependent. For example, the initial period and the few hours after the learning of UCS and CS pairings appears to be the moment when memory is consolidated. Therefore, interruption of the process at these times will impede consolidation (Bourtchouladze *et al.*, 1998). The first period of consolidation may be dependent on a different neurotransmitter system to that involved in the second. These are the NMDA and dopaminergic systems, respectively.

Chemical modulation of long-term potentiation

The most important excitatory neurotransmitter in the nervous system is glutamic acid or glutamate. One subtype of glutamate, N-methyl-D-aspartate (NMDA) appears to be important for producing long-term potentiation (LTP) (Abel and Lattal, 2001). NMDA receptors are found in the CA1 sector of the hippocampus; blocking activity in NMDA receptors prevents long-term potentiation in CA1 and the dendate gyrus. Blocking activity does not prevent or reverse LTP that has already occurred. The key process is the entry of calcium ions through ion channels, a phenomenon mediated by NMDA receptors.

When calcium enters an ion channel, changes in the structure of the neuron are produced by an enzyme, called a calcium-dependent enzyme, CDE (Lynch *et al.*, 1988). One CDE is called calpain which breaks down proteins in the spines of dendrites. Without this entry of calcium, LTP does not occur. Weak synapses, resulting from weak activation, do not lead to depolarisation that allows calcium ions to enter ion channels. Strong synapses that are activated do lead to this depolarisation, suggesting that the NMDA receptor is vital for the process of learning acquisition (Steele and Morris, 1999).

However, LTP can occur in other parts of the brain, apart from the hippocampus, and not all forms of LTP involve the NMDA receptors. So, although the hippocampus and the NMDA receptors seem to be prime mechanisms for LTP, they may not be the only ones. There are structures such as the amygdala, for example, that are involved in the conditioning of fear. Temporarily inactivating part of the amygdala, for example, can impair an organism's ability to learn to fear whereas inactivating the same area after conditioning has taken place, still results in a fear response in the organism (Wilensky *et al.*, 1999). This finding suggests that this part of the amygdala may be involved in the acquisition, but not consolidation, of memory. The topic of fear conditioning is explored in more detail in Chapter 13.

One of the most important findings in the physiology of memory in recent decades has been that the hippocampal formation is essential for the formation or learning of new memories but it may not be involved in the long-term retention or retrieval of memory (Shors, 2004). What is unclear is why this dissociation should be.

Lee *et al.* (2004) have discovered that a type of gene, called *zif268*, is needed for the reconsolidation of context-dependent fear memory but another factor (called BDNF) is needed for initial consolidation. This shows how different physiological processes are involved in different aspects of memory formation: one type of factor is needed for immediate consolidation (but not reconsolidation) and another is involved in reconsolidation (but not immediate consolidation). The retrieval of fear memory also appears to recruit *zif268* but in another region of the brain – the anterior cingulate cortex (Frankland *et al.*, 2004). Frankland *et al.* found that remote memory for fear was associated with anterior cingulate involvement in mice. Both the studies report changes in the brain during fear conditioning.

Studies of memory in animals have now associated around 47 specific genes with good memory performance. In research with human participants, genetic clusters were examined in participants who learned a series of semantically-unrelated words for immediate free recall and then completed an unexpected delayed free-recall test 5 minutes later (de Quervain and Papassotiropoulos, 2006). The genes that encoded a certain protein (ADCY8), and five others, were related to better memory performance and with greater activation in those brain regions involved in autobiographical memory and delayed recall (areas described below).

Amnesia

Damage to particular parts of the brain can permanently impair the ability to form new long-term memories while leaving language and perception intact (Warrington and Weiskrantz, 1968). The inability to form new memories is called **anterograde amnesia**. The impairment in the ability to retrieve memories from before the brain injury is called **retrograde amnesia**. The brain damage can be caused by the effects of long-term alcoholism, severe malnutrition, stroke, head trauma or surgery (Parkin, 1996). In general, people with anterograde amnesia can still remember events that occurred prior to the damage. They can talk about things that happened before the onset of their amnesia, but they cannot remember what has happened since. They never learn the names of people they subsequently meet, even if they see them daily for years.

One of the most famous cases of anterograde amnesia was patient HM (Scoville and Milner, 1957; Milner, 1970; Corkin *et al.*, 1981). HM's case is interesting because his amnesia was both severe and relatively pure, being uncontaminated by other neuropsychological deficits. At the age of nine, HM suffered a head injury after a bicycle accident which left him epileptic. In 1953, when HM was 27 years old, a neurosurgeon removed part of the temporal lobe on both sides of his brain because the drugs used to treat his epilepsy were not effective. The surgery cured the epilepsy, but it caused anterograde amnesia (this type of operation is no longer performed). HM died in 2009.

HM could carry on conversations and talk about general topics not related to recent events. He could also talk about his life prior to the surgery. However, he could not talk about anything that had happened since 1953. He lived in an institution where he could be cared for and spent most of his time solving crossword puzzles and watching television. HM was aware that he had a memory problem. For example, here is his response to a researcher's question:

Every day is alone in itself, whatever enjoyment I've had, and whatever sorrow I've had ... Right now, I'm wondering. Have I done or said anything amiss? You see, at this moment everything looks clear to me, but what happened just before? That's what worries me. It's like waking from a dream; I just don't remember.

Source: Quoted in Milner, 1970, p. 37.

Clearly, HM's problem lay in his ability to store new information in long-term memory, not in his short-term memory. His verbal short-term memory was normal; he could repeat seven numbers forwards and five numbers backwards, which is about average for the general population. At first, investigators concluded that the problem was in memory consolidation and that the part of the brain that was destroyed during surgery was essential for carrying out this process. But subsequent evidence suggests that the brain damage disrupts explicit memory without seriously damaging implicit memory.

Recently, however, psychologists have questioned whether HM had a pure memory deficit, that is, one that prevents the acquisition or consolidation of new information for explicit recall but leaves other cognitive abilities (such as the ability to produce and comprehend language) intact (Mackay *et al.*, 1998). Mackay *et al.* cite studies in which participants described two meanings of ambiguous sentences presented visually (such as 'they talked about the problem with the mathematician') and compared these participants' performance with those of HM. HM's descriptions were 'less clear and concise and more repetitive than controls'. Independent judges also rated HM's descriptions as less grammatical and comprehensible.

Other investigators have found that people with anterograde amnesia can learn to solve puzzles, perform visual discriminations, and make skilled movements that require hand–eye coordination (Squire, 1987). Clearly, their brains are still capable of undergoing the kinds of change that constitute long-term memory, but the people fail to remember having performed the tasks previously. For example, they may learn the task on one occasion. When, the next day, the experimenter brings them to the experimental apparatus and asks if they have ever seen it before, they say no. They have no explicit, episodic memory for having spent some time learning the task. But then they go on to perform the task well, clearly demonstrating the existence of implicit long-term memory.

Graf and Mandler (1984) showed lists of six-letter words to amnesic and non-amnesic people and asked them to rate how much they liked them. They then administered two types of memory test. In the explicit memory condition, they asked people to recall the words they had seen. In the implicit memory condition, they presented cards containing the first three letters of the words and asked people to say the first word that started with those letters that came into their minds. The amnesic people explicitly remembered fewer words than the non-amnesic people in the control group, but both groups performed well on the implicit memory task (see Figure 8.20).

Amnesia is not an all-or-nothing phenomenon, however. Severe amnesia, for example, can leave facial familiarity recognition, the acquisition of school knowledge or knowledge of the meaning of words intact. The fact that amnesic patients can remember facts and describe experiences that occurred before the brain injury indicates that their ability to recall explicit memories acquired earlier is not severely disrupted. Of those parts of the brain necessary for establishing new explicit memories, the most important part seems to be the hippocampus, a structure located deep within the temporal lobe, and which forms part of the limbic system.

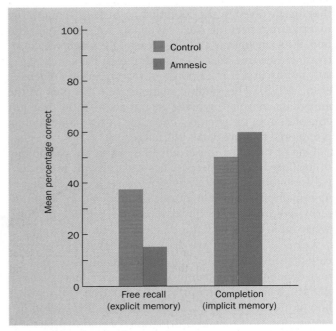

Figure 8.20 Explicit and implicit memory of amnesic patients and non-amnesic people. The performance of amnesic patients was impaired when they were instructed to try to recall the words they had previously seen but not when they were asked to say the first word that came into their minds.

Source: Adapted from Graf, P., Squire, L.R. and Mandler, G., The information that amnesic patients do not forget. *Journal of Experimental Psychology: Learning, memory and cognition*, 1984, 10, 164–78.

Psychology in action – Memory at the movies . . .

Common sense, as you saw in Chapter 1, may be common but does not make much sense in psychology. Sometimes people's misunderstandings of psychology, and science in general, can have serious consequences, such as distorting how mental illness and the mentally ill are viewed (see Chapter 18). In more light-hearted contexts, the misperception can seem comical. Films, television and novels exploit artistic licence to bend scientific facts sometimes to breaking point. An episode of the American sci-fi television programme, *The X Files*, had a protagonist confuse a technique used for measuring brain structure with one used for measuring brain activity. This protagonist was the medically qualified one. Even as this passage was being written, a journalist on a 24-hour television news channel is describing football supporters' reaction to a national football team manager as 'Pavlovian', thus misunderstanding Pavlov and, probably, football supporters.

Perhaps nowhere is artistic licence more vigorously exploited than in films. In an article in the *British Medical Journal*, Sallie Baxendale (2004), a clinical neurologist from the National Hospital for Neurology and Neurosurgery in London, has reviewed how films interpret and portray an important human phenomenon: memory loss. *The Bourne Supremacy, Total Recall, Memento, Men in Black, The Eternal Sunshine of the Spotless Mind*. . . several recent films have used amnesia as the hook with which to draw in cinema-goers and the hook is not new. At least ten silent movies released before 1926 featured amnesic characters.

Amnesia is an organic disorder with a neurological or psychiatric basis. Fugue states (where people experience lack of consciousness but appear conscious and wander around oblivious to their condition, ending up in, for example, a bus depot) or states where people believe they are someone else (dissociative disorders) are rare, as are changes in personality and identity. Amnesic patients have normal intelligence, normal attention span but show a severe inability to process new information. The most common causes of amnesia are neurosurgery, infection or stroke. Many films routinely flout these known facts in the cause of entertainment and Baxendale highlights a few of these.

In terms of causes of amnesia, she finds that many movies attribute memory loss to car crashes and assault. When Santa falls from a sleigh in the film *Santa Who?* he loses his identity and autobiographical memory. This cause and effect, as Baxendale suggests, is highly unlikely. Everyday memory difficulties are also rarely seen (although they should be one of the defining features of the disorder) and amnesic characters pursue new careers and social networks, unimpeded by their cinematic affliction. Trained assassins are especially prone to developing this trait, as seen in *The Bourne Identity* and *The Long Kiss Goodnight*. (Although in an unusual and knowing twist, *The Bourne Identity Crisis* features a protagonist who forgets he is gay and becomes a trained assassin.)

Two other films, best forgotten, are *Clean Slate* and *50 First Dates*. In the former, the hero is able to form new memories while awake but, after sleeping, forgets all he has learned. In the latter, Adam Sandler attempts to seduce Drew Barrymore who forgets each meeting they have had. As Baxendale pointedly notes, 'Some viewers might envy Ms Barrymore's ability to forget her romantic encounters with Mr Sandler, but her affliction seems to be the result of a head injury rather than the unconscious suppression of traumatic memories.' Cinematic forgetfulness reaches its zenith – humorously and deliberately – in *Groundhog Day* where Bill Murray's character exists in a world in which he perpetually relives the previous day.

In terms of recovery, Baxendale notes how television and movies are enamoured of the 'two are better than one' philosophy of head injury – a bang on the head can produce memory loss but a second bang can restore it. This happens in the Tom and Jerry cartoons and films such as *Tarzan the Tiger* and *Singing in the Dark*. In real life, a second blow does not make an effective rehabilitation strategy.

There are some honourable exceptions to this filmic hall of dishonour. Christopher Nolan's innovative film *Memento*, for example, features a character played by Guy Pierce who has severe anterograde amnesia and tries to recall the events leading to his wife's death. This is relayed in a narrative played backwards, as the character tries to piece together clues to his life. The character does not suffer retrograde amnesia, does not lose his identity and suffers severe everyday memory problems (like HM who, apparently, inspired the story). He writes every detail he thinks is important, and which may help him understand the past, in a clearly visible place such as his body (if he used a notebook, he would forget about it and forget what he wrote in it).

Ironically, the film that does portray amnesia in the most realistic form, according to Baxendale, does not feature humans at all. It is *Finding Nemo* and the fish, Dory, has severe difficulty in learning and remembering new information, recalling names and knowing where she is going and why. 'Although her condition is often played for laughs,' Baxendale writes, 'poignant aspects of her memory loss are also portrayed, when she is alone, lost, and profoundly confused.' This reflects real-life, human amnesia.

Does the accurate or inaccurate portrayal of amnesia in films matter? After all, we don't always go to the cinema to confront a mirror raised to real life. We go to suspend disbelief. We go to see fish, toys and ants talking, to see a man in an unlikely, figure-hugging suit swinging from buildings by

Psychology in action – *Continued*

(a) Leonard Shelby, played by Guy Pierce in the film *Memento*, is one of the few successful cinematic portrayals of amnesia. The most successful, however, appears to be Dory **(b)** , in *Finding Nemo*.
Source: (a) Summit Entertainment/The Kobal Collection Ltd.; (b) W. Disney/Everett/Rex Features.

sticky strings spurting from his wrists, to cheer for a group of hobbits, to boo an asthmatic, black-helmeted villain, or to see a boy in spectacles racing on a broom in a flying contest. Reality becomes important, however, if the reality is meant to be accurately portrayed. Dustin Hoffman's character in *Rain Man*, for example, although an extreme example, is an attempt at a serious portrayal of the social debilitation experienced by a person with Asperger's Syndrome. (The man who inspired the Hoffman character appears in Chapter 12.)

The general lesson, however, is this: don't go to the movies expecting to learn much about psychology. In fact, as this section demonstrates, you might as well forget it. . .

The role of the hippocampus in memory

The hippocampus, like many structures of the brain, is not fully mature at birth. In fact, it is not until a child is 2–3 years old that most of these structures are fully developed. As a result, many cognitive activities, such as the formation of semantic memories, are not particularly well developed until this age (Liston and Kagan, 2002). One reason that few people remember events that occurred during infancy may be the immaturity of the hippocampus.

The hippocampus receives information from all association areas of the brain and sends information back to them. In addition, the hippocampus has two-way connections with many regions in the interior of the cerebral hemispheres. Thus, the hippocampal formation is in a position to 'know' – and to influence – what is going on in the rest of the brain (Gluck and Myers, 1995). Presumably, it uses this information to influence the establishment of explicit long-term memories.

The structure appears to be very important for navigating or exploring our way around a spatial environment or in forming representations of the locations of objects (O'Keefe and Nadel, 1978). Morris *et al.* (1982), for example, placed rats in a pool of milky water that contained a platform just underneath the water.

In order to avoid swimming constantly, the rats had to find the platform hidden beneath the milky water.

Eventually, through trial and error, the rats would find the platform. Then, the researchers performed a series of experimental ablations. One group of rats received lesions to the hippocampus, another received lesions to the cerebral cortex and another received no lesion. When the rats were then allowed into the pool, the pattern of behaviour seen in Figure 8.21 was observed. Notice how those rats with the hippocampus lesion had extremely poor navigation compared with the cortex lesion and control group. Similarly, when rats had learned that there was a platform under water and were then allowed to explore the water with the platform removed, those with an intact hippocampus would spend longer in the part of the maze where the platform had been previously positioned. Those rats with hippocampal lesions, however, did not engage in this 'dwell time' in the quadrant where the platform once was (Gerlai, 2001). This suggests an important role for the hippocampus in spatial learning.

Both rodents and primates show deficits in what has been called spatial memory (Redish and Touretzsky, 1997). Spatial memory, the ability to encode and retrieve information about locations and routes is, like memory itself, not a unitary function. Kessels *et al.* (2001), for example, note that there is a difference between memory

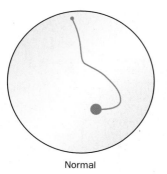
Normal

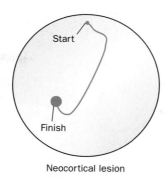
Start

Finish

Neocortical lesion

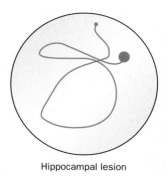
Hippocampal lesion

Figure 8.21 The effects of damaging a rat's hippocampus on its ability to find a platform in opaque water after having initially been trained to locate the platform successfully.

Source: Reprinted by permission from Macmillan Publishers Ltd: NATURE, Place navigation impaired in rats with hippocampal lesions, 182(297), pp. 681–683 (Morris, R.G.M. et al. 1982), Copyright 1982.

for routes and paths and the knowledge of spatial layouts which enables a person to find an object or a location. The role of the hippocampus in aspects of spatial memory have been well documented in animals, but O'Keefe and Nadel's view (1978) of hippocampal function has not gone unchallenged. Olton *et al.* (1979), for example, argued that the hippocampus was not exclusively responsible for spatial memory but was more involved in working memory. Tasks used in spatial memory tasks were, according to the theory, tests of short-term or working memory rather than spatial memory: all required the organism to keep information in mind while they engaged in another behaviour that used such information and this is the feature that was disrupted by damage.

In a meta-analysis of 27 studies that reviewed the consequences of hippocampal dysfunction, Kessels *et al.* (2001) found that whereas mild or moderate impairments were found on tasks requiring integration of information or navigation around a maze, there was little effect on spatial working memory. There was, however, a large impairment on tests of positional memory such as locating Xs in an array of letters. The lesions in patients showing mild to severe impairment were invariably to the right hippocampus, a finding that is consistent with O'Keefe and Nadel's hypothesis (1978) that the right hippocampus is specialised for mapping spatial information.

Neuroimaging and memory

Although much of our knowledge about the brain mechanisms that underlie memory has been derived from animal studies or from studies of individuals with brain injury, neuroimaging studies provide evidence from healthy individuals, and suggest that different regions of the brain are more involved than others in performing different types of memory task (Cabeza and Nyberg, 2000; Fletcher and Henson, 2001). As Horn

(1998) asked, 'If memory consists of a mark made in the brain by a particular experience, where is the mark and what is its nature?'

Spatial navigation

Maguire and her colleagues set up a novel and unusual experiment to see whether the hippocampus was active during spatial navigation (Maguire *et al.*, 1997). In their study, 11 London taxi drivers each with at least 14 years' experience of driving described the shortest legal route between two locations in London as a positron emission tomography (PET) scanner observed brain activity study. You can see a map of the route in Figure 8.22.

The taxi drivers were also asked to recall famous London landmarks (an examination of topographical memory). The activation during these tasks was compared with that during the recall of sequences from famous films. When the drivers described the route from one location to another, significant activation of the right hippocampus was found (but was not found with the landmark or film conditions), as Figure 8.23 illustrates.

This finding suggests that the right part of the hippocampus is important to retrieval of information that involves recall of movement in complex environments. In another PET experiment, participants were asked to navigate their way around a familiar but complex virtual town, using a pair of virtual reality goggles (Maguire *et al.*, 1998). Activation of the right hippocampus was again associated with knowing accurately where places were located and with navigating between them. The speed with which individuals navigated their environment was associated with right caudate nucleus activity. Also activated, however, were the right inferior parietal and bilateral medial cortices, which suggests, as many imaging studies do, that memory performance is not exclusively dependent on one region or structure.

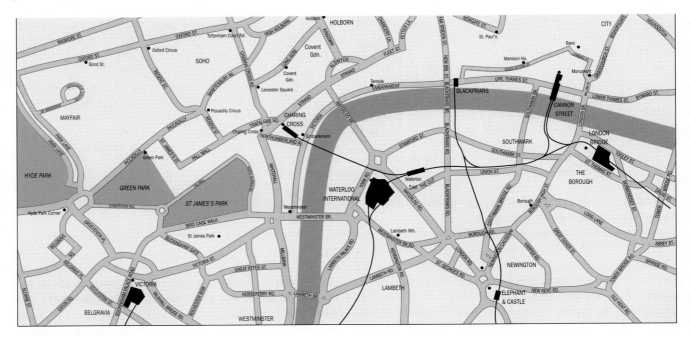

Figure 8.22 The route (in blue) that Maguire's taxi drivers had to describe.

Source: Maguire, E.A., Frackowiak, R.S.J. and Frith, C.D., Recalling routes around London: Activation of the right hippocampus in taxi drivers. *Journal of Neuroscience*, 1997, 17, 7103. © Society for Neuroscience.

Experienced taxi driving is one thing, but day-to-day navigation is another. A recent study, however, examined untrained people's ability to navigate (drive) their way around a virtual London, as fMRI measured brain activation to see which regions of the brain were recruited during this type of task (Spiers and Maguire, 2007). Starting, turning and stopping were associated with activation in the premotor, parietal and cerebellar regions of the brain. Swerving and avoiding collisions were associated with occipital and parietal, as well as premotor and insula activation. The right prefrontal lobe was especially active when observing road traffic rules, supporting other studies you read about in Chapter 4 (and will read about further in Chapter 13) that these regions play a role in moral reasoning.

The picture is not consistent, however. Rosenbaum *et al.* (2005) noted that Maguire *et al.*'s data showed that activation was actually seen in the parahippocampal gyrus, not the hippocampus. They also describe results from their own fMRI study which found that participants who were engaged in the recall of well-rehearsed knowledge about a city's topography showed greatest activation in the parahippocampal gyrus (there was slight activation in the hippocampus) (Rosenbaum *et al.*, 2004).

A case study, reported by Rosenbaum *et al.* (2005), provides another source of evidence against the involvement of the hippocampus in topographical memory. They studied SB, a patient with probable Alzheimer's disease who had been a taxi driver in Toronto, Canada, for 40 years. His remote memory for spatial locations in Toronto was compared with two other retired taxi drivers (with different illnesses) and a healthy control group. His ability to spatially navigate between various Toronto landmarks was comparable to the other participants. His most pronounced deficit was an inability to distinguish between Toronto landmarks and unknown buildings (an impairment that extended to world-famous landmarks). While the hippocampus may be necessary for the acquisition and retrieval of spatial information in the short-term, these results suggest that its role in long-term memory for old environments is much less certain.

This and the earlier study, together with those of amnesics who can recall the topography of the neighbourhood in which they grew up (e.g. Teng and Squire, 1999), provides a challenge to the view that the hippocampus is

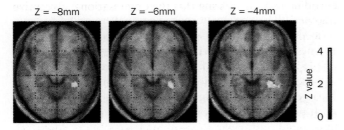

Figure 8.23 Areas of the brain activated by the recall of routes. Note the activation of the right hippocampus.

Source: Maguire, E.A., Frackowiak, R.S.J. and Frith, C.D., Recalling routes around London: Activation of the right hippocampus in taxi drivers. *Journal of Neuroscience*, 1997, 17, 7103. © Society for Neuroscience.

needed for the acquisition and retrieval of long-term topographical memories. However, Maguire *et al.* (2006) investigated the effects of brain injury on recall of routes in London in a taxi driver with damage to the hippocampus, the area which was active during route recall in the earlier imaging study. In the experiment, the driver and a matched control navigated their way through a virtual version of the city of London, along streets they had encoded 40 years ago.

They found that the injury did not affect the driver's ability to orientate himself around the city, his knowledge of landmarks and the spatial relationships between them or his ability to navigate the town. However, the driver did have difficulty when navigating routes that were not A-roads (major road arteries). It was as if complex routes were more problematic for him. It is possible, therefore, that coarse recall of topography is not affected by the hippocampus but recall of detailed, complex spatial relations might be.

Working memory

The ability to manipulate information in memory over a short space of time seems to be the primary responsibility of the frontal lobes (Fletcher and Henson, 2001), regions which, apparently contrarily, also become active during the retrieval of material that has been retained over long periods. Fletcher and Henson (2001) distinguish between two types of measures in working memory tasks: maintenance and manipulation. Working memory maintenance tasks involve measuring the process of keeping information in mind; working memory manipulation tasks involve measuring the reorganisation of material that is kept in mind.

A typical maintenance task involves presenting a participant with between three and nine stimuli and asking them to indicate whether a single stimulus presented subsequently formed part of the original array. The letter-based version of this task is usually associated with significant increases in activation in the left hemisphere, especially the ventrolateral frontal cortex, parietal lobe and premotor area (Awh *et al.*, 1996). When the task involves information about spatial relations or objects rather than words, activity is greater in the right hemisphere. Often, the same regions activated by letters or words in the left hemisphere are also activated in the right by spatial/object stimuli (Smith *et al.*, 1996).

Remember from earlier that one type of working memory manipulation task involves presenting the participant with a series of five letters and then asking them to recite the letters forwards, backwards or in alphabetical order, in mind. After a delay, the participant is asked to match the number order of a given letter, according to the mental manipulation (e.g. forwards, backwards or alphabetical). During the delay, there is usually activation seen in the ventrolateral and dorsolateral frontal cortex; during the reordering part of the task, activation is seen more in the dorsolateral part (D'Esposito *et al.*, 1999; Postle *et al.*, 1999).

In tasks that involve the generation of words, left dorsolateral activation is observed but not if words simply have to be repeated (Frith *et al.*, 1991). Word generation is a common 'frontal lobe' test: people with frontal lobe injury are poor at generating words from a given first-letter, for example.

Encoding and retrieval in episodic and semantic memory

Given that encoding and retrieval of information are two different cognitive tasks relating to the same function, you would expect these processes to have different underlying neural substrates. The left prefrontal cortex is activated when we learn and encode material whereas the right side is activated when we try to recall this material (Tulving *et al.*, 1994; Nyberg *et al.*, 1996; Fletcher *et al.*, 1998a, b).

The encoding of episodic memory is associated with activity in regions including the prefrontal and medial-temporal cortex and the cerebellum (Cabeza and Nyberg, 2000). Studies have usually found left-sided activation during episodic memory encoding, especially during the encoding of verbal material. The encoding of non-verbal material tends to be associated with bilateral activity in the frontal cortex. The role of the left prefrontal cortex in memory may be one of organising information: this part of the brain is responsible for our ability to group items on the basis of some characteristic or attribute.

Fletcher *et al.* (1998a) conducted a PET study in which participants listened to words that were either semantically organised, or disorganised but had to be put into categories. As expected, the condition in which the list was already organised produced the least amount of left prefrontal cortex activation whereas the task requiring the participant to generate an organisational structure resulted in greatest activation. A distractor task reduced activation during the organisation task but not during any other encoding task, suggesting that the organisational, executive role of the left prefrontal cortex can be disrupted.

Retrieval of episodic memory is consistently associated with prefrontal activation, sometimes in both cerebral hemispheres but usually in the right, although other regions are also activated depending on the type of material retrieved (Nyberg *et al.*, 1996; Fletcher *et al.*, 1996). Furthermore, there is evidence that the amygdala and the hippocampus contain neurons that encode our ability to recognise something and also when/where this something was originally seen. In one experiment, participants were asked to remember as many of 12 unique items, presented on a computer screen, as possible and also remember where on the screen they had seen them. The stronger the neurons' responses in these regions, the better the recall (Rutishauser *et al.*, 2008).

Remembering and long-term memory

Neuroimaging studies of long-term memory involve presenting the participants with several items that they are told to memorise (or given no memorisation instructions), and then asking them to recall the presented material some time later. Usually, the participant is asked to recognise the presented stimulus from a range of target and distractor stimuli. The process involves encoding and retrieval and neuroimaging research has highlighted the different brain regions involved in each type of process. If encoding is intentional or incidental, it is associated with left frontal cortex activation, as we have already seen. Simple retrieval of information is also associated with left frontal lobe activation (Fletcher and Henson, 2001).

If encoding and retrieval is successful, would greater brain activation be seen during encoding for those stimuli that were successfully encoded or for all stimuli regardless of how well they were retrieved? There is evidence from EEG studies that a specific type of electrical activity, called EEG theta, is greater during the encoding of successfully retrieved words than unsuccessfully retrieved ones (Klimesch *et al.*, 1997). In one neuroimaging study, Brewer *et al.* (1998) found that greater right frontal cortex activity was associated with successful encoding. Individuals were asked to view a series of indoor or outdoor scenes and decide whether each scene depicted outdoors or indoors. Thirty minutes later, they were given a recognition test and asked to indicate whether they remembered the scene, thought the scene was familiar but not well remembered or was forgotten. Memory for the scenes was predicted by frontal and parahippocampal activation with greater activation found for the remembered images.

Lateralisation of memory processes

A model called the HERA model has been proposed to account for the differences in brain activation seen during memory encoding and retrieval. HERA stands for Hemispheric Encoding-Retrieval Asymmetry, and the model argues that greater left than right frontal cortex activation is seen during episodic encoding whereas greater right than left frontal cortex activation is seen during episodic retrieval (Tulving *et al.*, 1994). The evidence reviewed above and more extensively in Fletcher and Henson (2001) and Cabeza and Nyberg (2000) suggests strong support for the model. In general, verbal encoding is associated with left frontal activation whereas right activation is more common during retrieval but, as

we have seen, such areas as well as others can be bilaterally active during encoding and retrieval. Why?

Fletcher and Henson (2001) put forward some interesting possibilities. Two are statistical and methodological and hinge on (1) the type of statistical parameters a study sets for statistical significance in neuroimaging research (different studies may set different parameters) and (2) the small number of samples used in neuroimaging research. A further reason may be the lack of clarity over the precise definition of cognitive processes in memory studies. Setting aside questions regarding what is verbal and what is non-verbal (and whether these two categories could be considered unitary), there are also questions regarding the nature of encoding and retrieval. Not all studies use the same measures of encoding or retrieval; perhaps the inconsistencies in findings can, therefore, be attributed to these different methodological approaches.

The nature of the model is challengeable, however. Dobbins and Wagner (2005) presented participants with various stimuli and then presented three images (two of which had been seen before) and asked them three different questions about each. The questions were 'Was this bigger before?' (the participant had to indicate whether an image previously seen had been bigger), 'Was it pleasant in the previous task?' (the participant was asked to indicate which of the stimuli was rated as pleasant or unpleasant in the previous task) and 'Is there a new item?' (participant was asked to identify the image that had not been seen before). Two areas of the left prefrontal cortex (specifically, the ventromedial/orbitofrontal cortex) were active in each of the retrieval conditions. There was greater activation in the anterior part of this region when participants retrieved conceptual information (pleasant condition) and in the posterior region during retrieval of conceptual and perceptual information (see Figure 8.24).

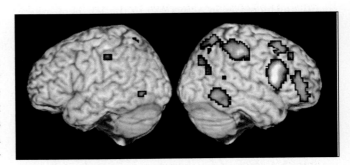

Figure 8.24 Domain-general and domain-sensitive prefrontal mechanisms.

Source: Dobbins, I.G. & Wagner, A.D. (2005) Domain-general and domain-sensitive prefrontal mechanisms for recollecting events and detecting novelty. *Cerebral Cortex*, 15, 1768–1178.

Memory-enhancing drugs

In recent years, pharmaceutical companies have become excited at the possibility that drugs may help improve memory or reduce the decline in memory performance seen with normal ageing or in people with probable Alzheimer's disease, the major cause of dementia (and a topic described on page 462 in Chapter 11). But do these drugs work? The Controversies in Psychological Science box sifts through some of the evidence.

Controversies in Psychological Science – Do 'smart drugs' work?

The issue

SHOULD WE JUST SAY NO TO SMART DRUGS?

All across India school children are popping little green and yellow pills – and claiming better grades as a result. Balding executives insist they are regaining lost hair as their memories improve. The country's Science Minister only half-jokingly prescribes the capsules for all members of Parliament. This new wonder drug, launched nationwide in January, is called Memory Plus, a compound derived from the brahmi plant found in India's marshlands. Memory Plus is just one of hundreds of so-called 'smart drugs' available around the world, either in the form of over-the-counter herbal mixtures or synthetic prescription formulas. Though these potions vary widely in composition, effectiveness and toxicity, they are all intended to enhance memory by stimulating neural activity.

This extract from *Time* magazine was not a one-off. 'Scientists boost memory power', proclaimed the BBC Health website; 'Smarten up your act', advised the *Sydney Morning Herald*; 'The making of a genius', declared the India Express News Service, hopefully.

What unites these stories is a fascination with a relatively new development in pharmacology: so-called smart drugs. Smart drugs are non-prescription pharmaceuticals that claim to improve memory, restore neural function or generally enhance intellectual function. The increase in the number of people getting older, together with the knowledge of the devastating consequences of Alzheimer's disease, suggests that there may be a large market for these drugs. But do they live up to their claims? Do they reverse memory decline and improve thinking?

The evidence

Drugs that claim to improve intellectual function have been called nootropics (from the Greek, *noos*, 'mind', and *tropein*, 'towards'). Although the word was used to describe a specific drug that increased neurotransmitter activity (Nicholson, 1990), it is now used to refer to any drug that claims to improve cognitive function or protect neurons from injury or insult. These drugs are not excitants, tranquillisers or antipsychotics and they have few side effects (Gabryel and Trzeciak, 1994).

Much of the excitement surrounding the use of memory-enhancing drugs in humans was based on findings from animal studies in which the animals' brains were found to respond positively to various drugs. Improvements in neural activity or memory performance in these animals led to trials with human participants. Many models of Alzheimer's disease, for example, are based on studies of neuronal degeneration in animals and so such research can be very useful. But could the animal findings be replicated in humans?

In a major review of every available peer-reviewed, systematic study of the effect of non-prescription compounds on memory enhancement, McDaniel *et al.* (2002) conclude that the evidence provides little scientific support for the drugs' claims. However, they concede that it is possible that such drugs may be effective in certain circumstances.

The six drugs which McDaniel *et al.*'s review investigated are listed in Table 8.2 together with the putative mechanisms for their action.

Phosphatidylserine (PS)

The drug phosphatidylserine (PS) has been found to reduce the neurobiological effects of ageing in animals and to restore memory function that has been lost. Its effects on humans, however, are less clear-cut. For example, McDaniel *et al.* found that the drug had no positive effect on the memory performance of people with probable Alzheimer's disease. However, people demonstrating cognitive decline associated with ageing showed some improvement in memory, especially in the ability to recall word lists. There were hardly any significant effects found on other memory tests.

Choline compounds

Drugs such as phosphatidylcholine (PC) and citicoline are called choline compounds because the chemical, choline, forms their basis. These drugs are thought to help with neurotransmitter activity associated with memory performance, although the few studies of PC on the memory performance of people with probable Alzheimer's disease have produced non-significant results. McDaniel *et al.* conclude that the efficacy of PC in improving memory in people without neuronal degeration is also open to question because there are no studies of this drug in normally ageing individuals. Although there are

Controversies in Psychological Science – *Continued*

Table 8.2 A list of the major drugs claimed to improve memory, and the proposed mechanisms for their effects

Drug	Mechanism
Phosphaidylserine (PS)	• Maintains neuron membrane • Increses number of neuronal receptors • Helps the branching of dendrites • Stimulates neurotransmitter release
Citicoline	• Maintains nueron membrane • Increases availability of neurotransmitter, acetylcholine • Promotes activity in the dopamine neurotransmitter system
Piracetam	• Facilities activity in the dopaminergic, cholinergic and noradrenergic systems • Protects neurons from toxins
Vinpocetine	• Increases blood flow to brain • Increases the uptake of glucose • Increases the availability of neurotransmitter, acetylcholine
Acetyl-L-carnitine	• Increases production of energy in neurons • Protects neurons from toxins • Maintains neurons' receptors • Increases the availabilty of acetylcholine
Antioxidants (e.g. Vitamins E, C)	• Protects neurons from toxins

Source: Adapted from McDaniel M.A., Maier, S.F. and Einstein, G.O., 'Brain-specific' nutrients: A memory cure? *Psychological Science in the Public Interest*, 2002, 3 (1), 12 –38.

hardly any studies investigating the effects of citicoline, the one double-blind study has found a significant increase in the accurate recall of stories in ageing individuals with no neuronal degeneration.

Piracetam

This drug is thought to improve the efficiency of neurons, increase the activity of neurotransmitters and combat the age-related decrease in the number of neuronal receptors. As with the other two drugs, McDaniel *et al.* found that piracetam did not produce memory improvement in patients with Alzheimer's disease or in old people whose memory was deteriorating.

Vinpocetine

Like many of the other drugs in this section, vinpocetine has been shown to have significant and positive effects on the neurobiology of animals. For example, studies have observed increases in blood flow and a reduction in the cell loss that results from blood flow loss in animals that were administered the drug. McDaniel *et al.* note that there is some evidence for the efficacy of the drug in humans. They cite three studies showing that administration of the drug to older adults with memory problems resulted in improvements in performance on tests measuring attention, concentration and memory when compared with a similar group that received a placebo drug. The effects of vinpocetine on episodic memory, however, were negligible.

Acetyl-L-carnitine

In animals, this drug has been found to reduce the number of receptor membranes that are lost through normal ageing; it is also thought to remove toxins from the brain. In humans, the drug has been found to increase performance on some memory tests performed by people with Alzheimer's disease but, according to McDaniel *et al.*, there are few significant differences between groups receiving the drug and groups receiving a placebo.

Antioxidants

As organisms age, the appearance of free radicals increases. Free radicals are not helpful to the organism; in fact, they are dangerous and they damage tissue wherever they exist. Antioxidants are drugs that combat the effects of free radicals and the thinking behind their use in studies of memory is that their administration will prevent the damage that these free radicals inflict on neurons. Antioxidants, such as vitamin E, however, have not been associated with any significant or consistent memory improvement in Alzheimer's disease or Parkinson's disease.

McDaniel *et al.* have found that although some studies appear to show positive benefits of drug administration on memory, closer observation of the data shows a more specific pattern of efficacy. A study of the drug Ginkgo-ginseng found an improvement in memory four weeks after drug administration to adults with normal memory (Wesnes *et al.*, 2000). This improvement was sustained for two weeks after the 12-week study. Scores on the memory tests, however, showed that the drug seemed to work only at a certain time of day. McDaniel *et al.* found that there was little difference in memory performance between the placebo and pill groups at 7.30 a.m. but there was a large and robust difference at 2.30 p.m. For almost all tests, performance in the pill group was better in the afternoon. Why?

McDaniel *et al.* suggest that two explanations could account for this improvement. It is well documented that the preference for the morning increases with increasing age. Older people's memory performance is worse in the afternoon than it is in the morning. It is possible, therefore, that in the

Controversies in Psychological Science – *Continued*

Wesnes *et al.* study, the drug helped halt the decline in memory seen in older people in the afternoon. It is also possible, however, that repeated testing resulted in proactive interference for tests completed later in the session. If this hypothesis were correct, you would expect the last test to show the poorest performance. In fact, this was the pattern found in both groups but the pill group outperformed the placebo group. This suggests that an alternative mechanism for the drug may be a reduction in the degree of proactive interference. Both of these explanations are plausible and future studies need to eliminate one or the other. This analysis of one study, however, shows that closer examination of data can reveal more specific patterns of behaviour than those originally presented.

Conclusion

The evidence reviewed by McDaniel *et al.* indicates that the results of studies examining the effects of smart drugs on memory performance in people with Alzheimer's disease, or older people with impaired memory performance, are patchy but suggestive. As each of the drugs examined claims to exert a specific effect on neuronal structure and function, perhaps it is unrealistic to administer just one of these drugs in the hope of achieving memory benefits; perhaps a combination would be more appropriate. One marketed drug, 'Memory 2000' manufactured by Natural Balance and mentioned in the *Time* magazine piece, already does this. McDaniel *et al.* (p. 35) conclude that the evidence, while not scientifically strong, lays open the possibility that drugs might be effective given in the right context in well-controlled environments. 'The current data', they say, 'do not allow strong scientifically based recommendations for any of these memory nutrients . . . [however,] the data do not allow us to conclude that these nutrients are ineffective in boosting memory.' Given the evidence you have read about the efficacy of 'smart drugs', would you recommend them? Why?

Chapter review

Sensory memory

- Memory is the process of encoding, storing and retrieving information. It exists in three forms: sensory, short-term/working and long-term. The characteristics of each differ, which suggests that they differ physiologically as well.
- Sensory memory provides temporary storage of information until the newly perceived information can be stored in short-term memory.
- Information in sensory memory lasts for only a short time. The partial-report procedure shows that when a visual stimulus is presented in a brief flash, all of the information is available for a short time (iconic memory). If the viewer's attention is directed to one line of information within a few hundred milliseconds of the flash, the information can be transferred into short-term memory. Echoic memory – sensory memory for sound – appears to operate similarly.

Short-term and working memory

- Short-term memory and working memory contain a representation of information that has just been perceived, such as a person's name or telephone number. Although the capacity of short-term memory is limited, we can rehearse the information as long as we choose, thus increasing the likelihood that we will remember it indefinitely.

- Information in short-term memory is encoded according to previously learned rules. Information in long-term memory determines the nature of the encoding.
- Working memory is different from short-term memory in that it allows the short-term storage and manipulation as opposed to simple storage of material in memory.
- Working memory comprises a phonological loop – a store of phonetic, verbal information – a visuospatial scratchpad – a store of spatial information and memories for movement – and a central executive responsible for supervising and updating the content of working memory.
- Short-term memory lasts for about 20 seconds and has a capacity of about seven items. We often simplify large amounts of information by organising it into 'chunks' of information, which can then be more easily rehearsed and remembered.
- When presented with a list of items, we tend to remember the items at the beginning of the list (the primacy effect) and at the end of the list (the recency effect) better than items in the middle of the list.
- The primacy effect occurs presumably because we have a greater opportunity to rehearse items early in the list and thus store them in long-term memory. The recency effect occurs because we can retrieve items at the end of the list from short-term memory.

- The existence of acoustical errors (rather than visual ones) in the task of remembering visually presented letters suggests that information is represented phonologically in short-term memory.
- Loss of information from short-term memory appears to be primarily a result of displacement; new information pushes out old information. However, a small amount of simple decay may also occur.

Learning and encoding in long-term memory

- Long-term memory refers to the very long-term retention of information and appears to consist of physical changes in the brain – probably within the sensory and motor association cortex.
- Consolidation of memories is likely caused by rehearsal of information, which sustains particular neural activities and leads to permanent structural changes in the brain.
- Short-term memories probably involve neural activity (which can be prolonged by rehearsal), whereas long-term memories probably involve permanent structural changes.
- Elaboration is important to learning. Maintenance rehearsal, or simple rote repetition, is usually less effective than elaborative rehearsal, which involves deeper, more meaningful processing.
- Encoding of information to be stored in long-term memory may take place automatically or with effort. Automatic processing of information is usually related to the frequency, timing and place (location) of events. Textbook learning entails effortful processing, most likely because of its complexity.
- Encoding specificity states that the way in which material is stored depends on how the material is retrieved. The most durable and useful memories are encoded in ways that are meaningful.
- Some psychologists have argued that shallow processing is a less effective way of encoding information than is deep processing (levels of processing, therefore, determine the success of retrieval). Critics, however, point out that shallow processing sometimes produces very durable memories, and the distinction between shallow and deep has proved to be impossible to define explicitly.
- Mnemonic systems are strategies used to enhance memory and usually employ information that is already contained in long-term memory and visual imagery. These are useful for remembering lists of items but are less useful for more complex material, such as textbook information.

The organisation of long-term memory

- Episodic memory refers to memories of events and people that are personally meaningful to us; it is synonymous with autobiographical memory.
- Semantic memory refers to memory for knowledge and facts.
- Most psychologists believe that episodic and semantic memories are parts of different systems although this is controversial.
- Explicit memory refers to recollection of information that was deliberately encoded and retrieved; implicit memory refers to memory for information that is unintentionally learned.

Remembering

- Remembering is an automatic process, although we may sometimes work hard at generating thoughts that will help this process along.
- Forgetting information occurs primarily in the first few years after it is learned and the rate of forgetting decreases slowly thereafter. Once we have learned something and retained it for a few years, the chances are that we will remember it for a long time afterwards.
- Recalling a memory of a complex event entails a process of reconstruction that uses old information.
- Our ability to recall information from episodic memory is influenced by retrieval cues, such as the questions people are asked in courts of law to establish how an event occurred. Sometimes, the reconstruction introduces new 'facts' that we perceive as memories of what we previously perceived.
- Remembering is strongly influenced by contextual variables involving mood and emotion. Some evidence suggests that remembering is easier when an individual's mood during the attempt to recall information is the same as it was when that information was originally learned; this is called state-dependent memory.
- We also tend to remember the circumstances that we were in when we first heard of a particularly emotional event such as the death of a famous person, a natural disaster, or an invasion of one country by another; these are called flashbulb memories.
- Sometimes recollecting one memory is made more difficult by the information contained in another memory, a phenomenon known as interference.
- In retroactive interference, recently learned information interferes with recollection of information learned earlier.
- In proactive interference, information learned a while ago interferes with recently learned information.
- Although interference has been demonstrated in the laboratory, interference may not operate so obviously in real life. Prose and other forms of everyday language appear to be more resistant to interference than are the nonsense syllables that people who participate in memory experiments are often required to learn.

Biological basis of memory

- Much of what we have learned about the biological basis of memory comes from studies involving humans with brain damage, from laboratory studies in which animals undergo surgical procedures that produce amnesia, and from neuroimaging studies of memory in healthy individuals.
- Learning seems to involve a strengthening of connections between neurons.
- Hebb proposed that short-term memory resulted from reverberation of the closed loops of the cell assembly; long-term memory is the more structural, lasting change in synaptic connections. This long-term change in structure is thought to reflect long-term potentiation (LTP), a term which describes the strengthening of neuronal connections via repeated stimulation.

- LTP is thought to originate in the hippocampus although it can occur elsewhere in the brain.
- A subtype of glutamate, N-methyl-D-aspartate (NMDA), appears to be important for producing long-term potentiation. NMDA receptors are found in the CA1 sector of the hippocampus; blocking activity in NMDA receptors prevents long-term potentiation in CA1 and the dendate gyrus.
- Anterograde amnesia refers to an inability to learn new memories after brain injury; these individuals can learn to perform many tasks that do not require verbal rules, such as recognising fragmentary pictures. Retrograde amnesia refers to the inability to retrieve remote memories.

- Patient HM showed an inability to store new information in long-term memory as a result of damage to the temproal lobes in general and the hippocampus in particular.
- The hippocampus is important for the learning of new material and for spatial navigation.
- The frontal cortex is involved in working memory and in the encoding and retrieval of material.
- Some recent studies have suggested that 'smart drugs' can improve memory function in people with poor memory. Evidence, however, is mixed with most studies showing no significant, positive effects on memory.

Suggestions for further reading

Memory – general

Baddley, A.D., Eysenck, M.W. and Anderson, M.C. (2009) *Memory*. Hove: Psychology Press.

Conway, M.A. (2009) Episodic Memories. *Neuropsychologia*, 47, 2305–2313.

Davachi, L. and Dobbins, I.G. (2008) Declarative memory. *Current Direction in Psychological Science*, 17, 2, 112–18.

Greenberg, D. (2005) Flashbulb memories. *Skeptic*, 11, 3, 74–80.

Schacter, D.L. (2003) *How the Mind Forgets and Remembers: The seven sins of memory*. Souvenir Press.

Some excellent introductions to memory and aspects of memory.

Cognitive psychology and applied cognitive psychology

Brasby, N. and Gellaty, A. (2004) *Cognitive Psychology*. Oxford: Oxford University Press.

Eysenck, M.W. and Keane, M.T. (2005) *Cognitive Psychology: A student's handbook*. (5th edn). Hove: Psychology Press.

Herrmann, D.J., Toder, C.Y., Gruneberg, M. and Payne, D.G. (2006) *Applied Cognitive Psychology: A textbook*. Hove: Psychology Press.

Good overviews of memory and other topics in cognitive psychology.

Working memory

Baddeley, A.D. (2002) *Working Memory, Thought and Action*. Oxford: Oxford University Press.

Conway, A.R.A., Kane, M.J., Bunting, M.F., Hambrick, D.Z., Eilhelm, O. and Engle, R.W. (2005) Working memory span tasks: A methodological review and user's guide. *Psychonomic Bulletin and Review*, 12, 5, 769–86.

Logie, R.H. (2003) Spatial and visual working memory: A mental workspace. *The Psychology of Learning and Motivation*, 42, 37–78.

Good, concise readable reviews of the current status of working memory research by leading psychologists in the field.

Biological basis of normal memory

Abel, T. and Lattal, K.M. (2001) Molecular mechanisms of memory acquisition, consolidation and retrieval. *Current Opinion in Neurobiology*, 11, 180–7.

Conway, M.A., Pleydell-Pearce, C.W., Whitecross, S. and Sharpe, H. (2002) Brain imaging autobiographical memory. *The Psychology of Learning and Motivation*, 41, 229–63.

Fletcher, P.C. and Henson, R.N.A. (2001) Frontal lobes and human memory. *Brain*, 124, 849–81.

Martin, G.N. (2006) *Human Neuropsychology* (2nd edn). Harlow: Prentice Hall, Chapter 9.

Piolino, P., Desgranges, B. and Eustache, F. (2009) Episodic auto-biographical memories over the course of time: cognitive, neuropsychological and neuroimaging findings. *Neuropsychologia*, 47, 2314–2329.

Rosler, F., Ranganath, C., Roder, B. and Kluwe, R. (2009). *Neuroimaging in Human Memory*. Oxford: Oxford University Press.

Squire, L.R. and Schacter, D.L. (2003) *Neuropsychology of Memory*. Hove: Psychology Press.

Squire, L.R., Stark, C.F.L. and Clark, R.E. (2004) The medial temporal lobe. *Annual Review of Neuroscience*, 27, 279–306.

Svoboda, E., McKinnon, M.C. and Levine, B. (2006) The functional neuroanatomy of autobiographical memory: A meta-analysis. *Neuropsychologia*, 44, 2189–208.

Wixted, J.T. (2004) The psychology and neuroscience of forgetting. *Annual Review of Psychology*, 55, 235–69.

A good selection of books and papers on the biology and neurology of memory.

Memory disorders

Baddeley, A.D., Kopelman, M. and Wilson, B.A. (2002) *Handbook of Memory Disorders*. Chichester: John Wiley.

Baxendale, S. (2004) Memories aren't made of this: Amnesia at the movies. *British Medical Journal*, 329, 1480–83.

Kopelman, M.D. (2002) Disorders of memory. *Brain*, 125, 2152–90.

Parkin, A.J. (1997) *Case Studies in the Neuropsychology of Memory*. Hove: Psychology Press.

Wearing, D. (2005) *Forever Today*. New York: Doubleday.

Memory disorders are frequently discussed in journals and there are many of these articles you can consult. A good start would be Kopelman's comprehensive article. Parkin's Case Studies provides a thoughtful and expansive collection of papers written about different kinds of memory disorder. Clive Wearing's memory disorder is described evocatively by his wife Deborah.

Manipulability of memory

Gardner, M. (2006) The memory wars, parts 2 and 3. *Skeptical Inquirer*, 30, 2, 46–50.

Haber, R.H. and Haber, L. (2000) Experiencing, remembering and reporting events. *Psychology, Public Policy and Law*, 6(4), 1057–1097.

Wells, G.L. and Olson, E.A. (2003) Eyewitness testimony. *Annual Review of Psychology*, 54, 277–95.

The malleability of memory is well described in these publications. Haber and Haber's article reviews and evaluates a wealth of research concerning the unreliability of memory and eyewitness testimony, in particular (although predominantly from a North American legal perspective). Gardner's paper critically examines the nature of recovered memories

Journals to consult

Applied Cognitive Psychology

Brain

British Journal of Psychology

Cognition

Cognition and Emotion

Cognitive Science

European Journal of Cognitive Psychology

Journal of Cognitive Neuroscience

Journal of Cognitive Psychology

Journal of Experimental Psychology

Journal of Memory and Language

Legal and Criminological Psychology

Memory

Memory and Cognition

Nature

Psychological Science

Psychonomic Bulletin and Review

Quarterly Journal of Experimental Psychology

Science

Website addresses

http://coglab.wadsworth.com/
This is a site that will allow you access to various experiments and demonstrations in experimental psychology. The site requires you to register before viewing the material.

http://www.psychology.org/links/Environment_Behavior_Relationships/Memory/
A collection of various links to memory-related sites.

http://www.psychologie.uni-bonn.de/online-documents/ lit_cog.htm
A site which gives you access to some full-text journal articles of relevance to memory.

http://spot.colorado.edu/~dubin/bookmarks/b/240.html
A collection of links to memory-related sites

Consciousness

CHAPTER 9

Court told of sleep deprivation clue in Selby train case

The man accused of causing the deaths of 10 people in the Selby rail crash had 'insufficient' sleep before setting off on his journey to work, a court heard today.

Professor James Horne, from Loughborough University, told a jury at Leeds Court he believed Gary Hart could not have maintained alert driving as he made his way along the M62 towards Great Heck, North Yorkshire. Mr Hart had only had a short nap in the previous 24 hours. [Prof. Horne] added: 'There is no doubt about it, it was insufficient.'

The prosecution claims that Mr Hart fell asleep at the wheel after chatting for five hours to Kristeen Panter, a woman he had met on the Internet.

Prof. Horne said that drivers were particularly prone to falling asleep at the wheel between 2am and 6am. They were most likely to fall asleep on dull and boring roads where there was little stimulation for the driver, such as the stretch of the M62 ahead of the crash site.

Source: from 'Court told of sleep deprivation clue in Selby train case', *The Guardian*, 30 November 2001, Copyright Guardian News & Media Ltd 2001.

WHAT YOU SHOULD BE ABLE TO DO AFTER READING CHAPTER 9

- Describe what psychologists and philosophers mean by consciousness.
- Understand the problems of studying consciousness.
- Be familiar with theories explaining consciousness.
- Understand the concept of selective and divided attention and give examples of it.
- Describe hypnosis and the reasons for hypnotically induced behaviour.
- Describe the behavioural and psychophysiological stages of sleep.
- Understand theories of sleep.
- Describe the symptoms of sleep disorders and their possible causes.

QUESTIONS TO THINK ABOUT

- What is consciousness?
- Can we measure it?
- Is consciousness unitary?
- How do we manage to attend to some stimuli in the environment while ignoring others?
- What is hypnosis and how does it work?
- How do we selectively attend to information in our environment?
- Why do we sleep?
- What are the effects of sleep deprivation on behaviour?

Explore the accompanying videos, simulations, and animations on MyPsychLab. This chapter includes activities on: Background noise • Split brain • Hypnosis • Sleep and circadian rhythms • Check your understanding and prepare for your exams using the multiple choice, short answer and essay practice tests also available.

Consciousness: an introduction

Consciousness poses the most baffling problems in the science of the mind. There is nothing that we know more intimately than conscious experience, but there is nothing that is harder to explain.   *Source:* Chalmers, 1995.

Why are we aware of ourselves, of our thoughts, our perceptions, our actions, our memories and our feelings? Is some purpose served by our ability to realise that we exist, that events occur, that we are doing things and that we have memories? According to James (1890), 'all people unhesitatingly believe that they feel themselves thinking. This belief is the most fundamental of all postulates of Psychology.'

Philosophers have puzzled over the questions raised above for centuries without finding a convincing answer (Block *et al.*, 1997). Psychologists, however, had generally neglected the problem of consciousness. Early behaviourists, as you saw in Chapter 1, denied that there was anything to explain and argued that the only subject matter for psychological investigation was behaviour, not consciousness. Several psychologists continue to believe that consciousness is a side effect of what we do – an epiphenomenon – that is not intrinsically interesting as a research question or a psychological topic. To illustrate psychology's lack of interest in this topic, consider the fate of one paper written by the influential neuro-psychologist, Jeffrey Gray. Over three decades ago, Gray (1971) published a paper outlining what he regarded as the hard problems of consciousness. Gray (1998) noted that in the ten years following the publication of the article, he received just two requests for a copy of the paper.

Recent years, however, have seen a revival in the scientific study of consciousness, with philosophers, neuroscientists, mathematicians and psychologists contributing ideas and theories to this area (Penrose, 1989; Dennett, 1991; Crick, 1994; Pinker, 1997; Gray, 1998; Blackmore, 2010).

Once the bane of behaviourists, consciousness is now provoking new research and concepts from psychologists, particularly those who seek the neural basis of consciousness. Popular accounts of theories of consciousness, such as Daniel Dennett's *Consciousness Explained* and Francis Crick's *The Astonishing Hypothesis*, reflect a renewed interest in the topic. This chapter reviews current thinking about consciousness and, more importantly, research findings in this complex area.

Philosophical approaches to consciousness

Historically, people have taken three philosophical positions about the nature of consciousness (Block *et al.*, 1997). The first and earliest position is that consciousness is not a natural phenomenon: it is not subject to the laws of nature that all scientists attempt to discover, laws involving matter and purely physical forces. This position states that consciousness is something supernatural and miraculous, not to be understood by the human mind.

The second position is that consciousness is a natural phenomenon but, for various reasons, we cannot understand it. Consciousness exists because of the nature of the human brain, but just how this occurs is not known. We can never understand consciousness because our brains are simply not capable of doing so; it would take a more complex brain than ours to understand the biology of subjective awareness. An alternative but related view is that everything can be explained, including all aspects of the human brain, but that consciousness is a vague, poorly operationally defined term (Wilkes, 1988; McGinn, 1989).

The third position is that people are indeed conscious, that this consciousness is produced by the activity of the human brain, and that there is every reason for us to be optimistic about our ability to understand this phenomenon (Crick, 1994).

The meaning of 'consciousness'

Although the word 'consciousness' is a noun, 'consciousness' itself does not exist. What exists are humans having the ability to do something that we describe as 'being conscious'. So, then, what does it mean to be conscious? Allport (1988) reported that, 'I find that I have no clear conception what people are talking about when they talk about consciousness or "phenomenal awareness", nor, for that matter, when they talk about its linguistic-conceptual Siamese twin, the conscious self.' Consciousness is a private experience, which cannot be shared directly. We experience our own consciousness but not that of others. We conclude that other people are conscious because they are like us and because they can tell us that they, too, are conscious. This, inevitably, has a subjective quality which makes consciousness difficult to study scientifically.

According to Chalmers (1995), consciousness investigators face easy problems and a hard problem. The easy problems include the ability to discriminate, categorise and react to stimuli, to integrate information by using a cognitive system, to report mental states and to access internal states, to control behaviour deliberately and to differentiate between wakefulness and sleep. All of these features are associated with consciousness but, according to Chalmers, they are the relatively easy topics of consciousness because they primarily involve the contents of consciousness; these features refer to functions or abilities. Understanding (or discovering) the neural correlates of consciousness is also an easy problem, according to Chalmers. A mental state is said to be conscious when this state can be verbally reportable or internally accessible; the organism is able to be conscious of some information, react to it and explain it. This is another easy problem. But this is only one side of the story. The hard problem lies in studying the experience of these mental events.

When we report these mental events we have an experience of reporting these mental events. Over and above this ability, we have the experience itself. There must be something 'that it is like' to be conscious (Nagel, 1974); there is a subjective quality about it and because of this, it poses a difficult problem. These conscious experiences are sometimes referred to as phenomenal consciousness or 'qualia'. In summary, the easy problems are understanding the functions and neurophysiology of consciousness; the hard problem is explaining why we have the experience of consciousness in the first place. The distinction between easy and hard problems is a controversial one and you yourself would probably challenge the notion that the understanding of the neural correlates of consciousness, for example, represents an easy problem. In the next section, we will consider some of the theories that have been proposed to account for the 'easy' and 'hard' aspects of consciousness.

Theories of consciousness

Neurobiological theories

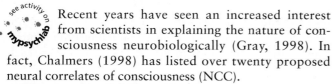

Recent years have seen an increased interest from scientists in explaining the nature of consciousness neurobiologically (Gray, 1998). In fact, Chalmers (1998) has listed over twenty proposed neural correlates of consciousness (NCC).

The essence of the neurobiological approach is that consciousness arises from the neural activity of the brain. Neurobiological approaches diverge, however, when they begin to specify which parts or elements of the brain give rise to the activity that is meant to represent consciousness. Neurobiological theories of consciousness derive their data from a number of sources, such as those described in Chapter 4 – neuroimaging and brain damage – and other branches of natural science, such as mathematics and quantum physics. Each type of study has yielded a different perspective on the NCC and some of the most important or influential of these theories are reviewed below.

Consciousness and brain damage

Brain damage can alter human consciousness. Patients with anterograde amnesia, for example, are unable to form new verbal memories but can learn some kinds of

tasks. However, they remain unaware that they have learned something, even when their behaviour indicates that they have. The brain damage does not prevent all kinds of learning, but it does prevent conscious awareness of what has been learned.

As you saw in Chapter 6, there are individuals who, if they have damaged the posterior parts of their brain, show a lack of awareness of stimuli presented to their visual field. Brain damage which impairs the perception of visual stimuli seems also to impair the ability. Blindsight patients have damage to the primary visual cortex and, although they are able to perform some visual perception tasks, they report being unaware of the task stimuli that had been presented in their visual field. Remember from Chapter 6 that individuals with certain types of agnosia are unable to recognise objects or may be unable to ascribe meaning to such objects. Another form of agnosia is characterised by the inability to identify familiar faces by using facial cues alone. All of these disorders involve some lack of awareness and may help us to understand the regional contribution of the brain to conscious awareness.

Blindsight patients have damage to an area called V1, the primary visual cortex. This is the region in the brain to which information from the retina travels. Does the activity of V1 reflect conscious awareness of visual stimuli? Crick and Koch (1995) have proposed the controversial idea that it does not. They argue that it is not involved in conscious visual perception because V1 does not directly project to the frontal cortex (which integrates information from other parts of the cortex); the areas surrounding V1, however – the extrastriate cortex – do, and it is the activity of these areas which may reflect conscious processing. Crick and Koch (1995) admit that this is a subtle and speculative proposal and have not undertaken an empirical test of this hypothesis. It remains an intriguing hypothesis.

Another form of brain damage, this time a surgical procedure designed to eliminate the symptoms of intractable epilepsy, gives rise to what has become known as the **split brain** or **callosal syndrome** (Bogen, 1993). Individuals who suffer epilepsy which cannot be controlled by drugs, experience violent storms of neural activity which begin in one hemisphere and shift to the other via the corpus callosum, the large bundle of axons that connect one cerebral hemisphere to another. This causes an epileptic seizure. These seizures can occur many times each day, preventing the patient from leading a normal life. Neurosurgeons discovered that by severing the corpus callosum, thereby 'splitting' the brain, they could reduce the frequency of these seizures (Sperry *et al.*, 1969). This is illustrated in Figure 9.1.

Roger Sperry and Michael Gazzaniga and their associates (Gazzaniga, 1970, 1998; Gazzaniga *et al.*, 1996;

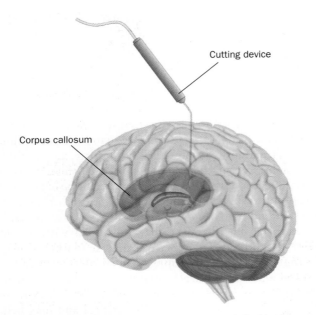

Corpus callosum

Cutting device

Figure 9.1 The split-brain operation. Holes are drilled in the top of the skull and a cutting device is introduced between the left and right cerebral hemispheres, severing the corpus callosum.

see activity on mypsychlab

Sperry, 1966) pioneered research into the psychological consequences of **split-brain surgery**. Sperry won the Nobel Prize in 1981 for his work on neurosurgery. Their work, initially with cats, demonstrated that the cerebral cortex of the left and right hemispheres normally exchange information via the corpus callosum. With one exception (described later), each hemisphere receives sensory information from the opposite side of the body and controls muscular movements on that side, as we saw in Chapters 4 and 6. The corpus callosum allows these activities to be coordinated, so that each hemisphere 'knows' what is going on in the other hemisphere (Hoptman and Davidson, 1994; Banich, 1995).

When the two hemispheres are disconnected after split-brain surgery, they appear to operate independently; their sensory mechanisms, memories and motor systems no longer appear to exchange information. The effects of these disconnections are not obvious to a casual observer, for the simple reason that only one hemisphere – in most people, as we will see in the next chapter, the left – controls speech. The right hemisphere of an epileptic person with a split brain allows the patient to understand speech reasonably well, but it is poor at reading and spelling. Because Broca's speech area is located in the left hemisphere, the right hemisphere is totally incapable of producing speech.

Given that only one side of the brain can 'talk about' what it is experiencing, a casual observer will not detect the independent operations of the right side of a split

brain. Even the patient's left brain has to learn about the independent existence of the right brain. One of the first things that these patients say they notice after the operation is that their left hand seems to have a mind of its own. This is called **alien hand** ('la main étrangère'). For example, patients may find themselves putting down a book held in the left hand, even if they are reading it with great interest. At other times, they surprise themselves by making obscene gestures with the left hand. Because the right hemisphere controls the movements of the left hand, these unexpected movements puzzle the left hemisphere, the side of the brain that controls speech. One hypothesis suggests that the inhibition of actions organised elsewhere, but originating in the frontal cortex, is lost in split-brain patients, hence the appearance of unusual, uninhibited behaviour in one hand. Another, different phenomenon is **intermanual conflict**. This refers to the apparently contradictory activity of the left and right hands; one might do up a set of buttons on a shirt, for example, while the other might undo them (Akelaitis, 1944/45).

If a patient with a split brain tries to use their right hand to arrange blocks to duplicate a geometrical design provided by the experimenter, the hand will hopelessly fumble around with the blocks. Often, the left hand (controlled by the right hemisphere) will brush the right hand aside and easily complete the task. It is as if the right hemisphere gets impatient with the clumsy ineptitude of the hand controlled by the left hemisphere.

The effects of cutting the corpus callosum suggest that consciousness depends on the ability of speech mechanisms in the left hemisphere to receive information from other regions of the brain. If such communication is interrupted, then some kinds of information can never reach consciousness.

There is still some controversy over whether split-brain patients are genuinely unable to perform the tasks that psychologists set them (see Martin, 2006, for a review). The degree to which split-brain patients can make decisions about stimuli presented to the left or right of their visual field may depend on the part of the corpus callosum damaged: normally, not all of the corpus callosum is cut, only parts of it (Sergent, 1987, 1990, 1991). In one study, two out of three patients when presented with circles in each hemifield could indicate which was bigger (Sergent, 1987). There are also other connections between the hemispheres, in addition to those made by the corpus callosum. Some neuropsychologists, such as Sergent, have argued that split-brain patients who do not show the typical split-brain profile are so because these channels of communication are intact – there is still some way in which the hemispheres can transfer information (Seymour *et al.*, 1994).

Crick's astonishing hypothesis

Other neurobiological models of consciousness specify more exact regions and neural elements which give rise to consciousness. Crick's theory (Crick, 1994), for example, suggests that consciousness is the result of the activity of collections of neurons called neural assemblies (this is the astonishing hypothesis). The behaviour of neurons is represented by 35–75 Hz oscillations in the cortex; these oscillations form the basis of consciousness and correlate with awareness in different sensory modalities. According to the theory, oscillation represents the way in which the information we process is bound. The concept of binding is important in consciousness; it refers to the process whereby separate pieces of information about a single entity are brought together and used for processing later (Chalmers, 1995).

Bringing together information about colour and shape to form an image of an object is one example of binding. When elements are bound together, Crick's theory argues, neural groups will oscillate in the same space and time. While Crick's theory has received much attention and credit for specifically tying consciousness to specific brain activity, it has been criticised for not being able to explain the importance of these oscillations. If these oscillations give rise to conscious experience, why? Again, this is exactly Chalmers's 'hard' problem, mentioned earlier.

Penrose's and Hameroff's quantum models

Another neurobiological approach to consciousness focuses on the importance of chaos or non-linear dynamics in explaining consciousness. Much of Penrose's work is rooted in some quite complex physics and mathematics and we need not dwell on the detail here. In essence, Penrose (1989, 1994) argues that consciousness is a form of non-algorithmic processing which is important to conscious mathematical insight (Penrose himself is a famous mathematician). That is, consciousness is not an all-or-nothing, straightforward, linear process; instead, it is an uneven, non-linear process.

Penrose's model relies on an understanding of quantum physics. Quantum physics suggests that although events are observable and seem to follow a logical order, these events themselves are altered by being observed (this is called the Heisenberg Uncertainty Principle). In a revision of the original model, Hameroff and Penrose (1996) and Hameroff (1998) have suggested that consciousness takes place in the skeletal structure of neurons (called **cytoskeleton**), specifically in parts of the neuron called **microtubules**, as seen in Figure 9.2.

Hameroff is an anaesthetist and his ideas have been based on the processes involved in anaesthesia which induce loss of consciousness. For example, under general anaes-

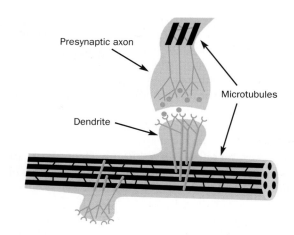

Figure 9.2 The black rods in the diagram represent microtubules. The green dots represent the neurotransmitter released by the presynaptic axon.

Source: From Hameroff, S.R., More neural than thou. In S.R. Hameroff, A.W. Kaszniak and A.C. Scott (eds) *Towards a Science of Consciousness II*. New York: Wiley, 1998.

thetic, individuals should not be able to move purposefully in response to a painful stimulus and should not be able to follow verbal commands (Franks and Lieb, 1998). The general process of anaesthesia is summarised in Table 9.1. There is some evidence that patients may be capable of remembering events/voices in the operating theatre during anaesthesia but this is quite controversial (Andrade, 1995).

Anaesthesia provides probably one of the most interesting challenges to researchers exploring the neural correlates of consciousness. One persuasive theory argues that anaesthesia is produced by blocking or disrupting sensory information that is processed via the thalamus. The activity of the thalamus, therefore, is a critical determinant of unconsciousness. Alkire *et al.* (2000) set up

Table 9.1 Stages of anaesthetic depth

Stage	Description
I	Analgesia. The patient is conscious but drowsy. The degree of analgesia (if any) depends on the anaesthetic
II	Excitement. The patient loses consciousness and does not respond to a non-painful stimulus. The patient may move, talk incoherently, be hypotensive or have other respiratory or cardiovascular irregularities
III	Surgical anaesthesia. Spontaneous movement ceases and ventilation becomes regular. As anaesthesia deepens, various reflexes are lost and the muscles relax
IV	Medullary depression. Respiration and vasomotor control cease, leading to death

Source: Rang, H.P., Dale, M.M. and Ritter, J.M., *Pharmacology*, New York: Churchill Livingstone. © 1995, with permission from Elsevier.

PET study in which 11 participants received two types of anaesthesia. Brain activity during anaesthesia/unconsciousness was monitored. The group found that during unconsciousness, there was a significant reduction in output from the thalamus to other parts of the cortex.

In Hameroff's specific model of consciousness, microtubules in the neuron are essential to consciousness. The function of microtubules is to transport material inside the neuron and define the shape of the processes that they inhabit; they, therefore, serve an important neural function. The model suggests that quantum events occur in or around these microtubules and that these events give rise to our conscious experience. It suggests this for a number of reasons, not least the reason that microtubules are important for the functioning of the neuron. However, this model could be criticised on the same grounds as Crick's in the way that it does not explain why such neural events should be associated with consciousness. In fact, Churchland (1998) has suggested that these microtubules might just as well be called pixie dust in the synapses – essence which magically gives rise to consciousness – although Hameroff (1998) has argued that the mechanism by which microtubules give rise to consciousness is detailed and not as vague as pixie dust. The model, because it is derived from data from anaesthesia, is a highly specific neural model of consciousness and, because of this, holds some promise.

Cognitive theories

Cognitive theories of consciousness, although recognising that consciousness arises from the activity of the brain, describe the way in which it occurs in more mentalistic, cognitive terms.

Baars's global workspace theory

The global workspace theory (Baars, 1988; Baars *et al.*, 1998) states that the contents of consciousness are contained in a central processor called a global workspace. This is used to mediate the activity of non-conscious processes. When such processes need to inform the rest of the system, they send information to the workspace, which is a little like a blackboard used by the rest of the system (Baars *et al.*, 1998). The model can thus explain how different types of conscious information are available to us but it does not explain why this information in the global workspace is experienced; in other words it does not solve the 'hard' problem (Chalmers, 1995).

Dennett's multiple drafts

The philosopher and cognitive scientist Daniel Dennett had proposed a complex theory of consciousness that relies on the idea that consciousness is not an all-or-nothing phenomenon that occurs in exactly the same way whenever it is evoked. Dennett (1991) begins the rationale for his theory by debunking the mind–body interactionism proposed by Descartes. The notion of the Cartesian theatre where mind and body are interacting protagonists is untenable according to Dennett. Instead, he argues that consciousness is not a theatre but the activation of revised collections of sensory information called 'drafts'. Because sensory information is received in various forms and at various times, conscious experience is an updating, constantly revising process a little like an author's manuscript which is in a constant state of redrafting and revision. Conscious experiences, therefore, result from multiple drafts of sensory information which are assembled at particular points in time. You can see why the theory is complex. One criticism of Dennett's theory is that, although it seems to abolish the notion of the Cartesian theatre, he is replacing it with a large number of theatres.

Shanon's theory

Shanon (1990, 1998) has argued, like Dennett and Baars, that consciousness is not unitary. Unlike Dennett and Baars, however, he invokes three components which he regards as making up consciousness: sensed being, mental awareness and reflection. Sensed being distinguishes between animate and living, and inanimate and dead; mental awareness refers to the idea that we are aware of thoughts that pass through our heads, that is, we are aware of the contents of consciousness; reflection refers to the idea that we are aware of our mental computations and that these 'mentations' can be the subject of future 'mentations'. According to Shanon, there are two types of reflection: meta-observation which reflects on the content of mental states, and monitoring or control which checks and evaluates thoughts; this control guides or governs our thinking process. According to Shanon, mental awareness is the core of consciousness whereas sensed being is a prerequisite and reflection is derived from it. How would one go about testing Shanon's theory, however? This would be difficult because the components are vaguely and generally described. It is also open to the criticism that it is too descriptive and actually explains very little.

Selective attention

We do not become conscious of all the stimuli detected by our sensory organs. For example, if you are writing an essay or laboratory practical report while the radio is on in the background and you have to meet an urgent deadline, you probably are unaware of what song is playing on the radio, or of the noises outside your room, of the hum of the refrigerator. Attention is completely devoted to your work. The process that controls our awareness of particular categories of events in the environment is called **selective attention**.

As you saw in Chapter 8, sensory memory receives more information than it can transfer into short-term (working) memory. Sperling (1960) found that although people could remember only about four or five of the nine letters he flashed onto the screen if they tried to remember them all, they could direct their attention to any of the three lines of letters contained in sensory memory and identify them with perfect accuracy.

The process of selective attention determines which events we become conscious of. Attention may be controlled automatically, as when an intense stimulus (such as a loud sound) captures our attention; it may be controlled by instructions ('Pay attention to that one over there'); or it may be controlled by the demands of the particular task we are performing. For example, when we are driving a car, we pay special attention to other road users, pedestrians, road signs and so on. Our attentional mechanisms serve to enhance our responsiveness to certain stimuli and to tune out irrelevant information.

Attention plays an important role in memory. By exerting control over the information that reaches short-term memory, it determines what information ultimately becomes stored in explicit long-term memory – the portion of long-term memory that we can talk about and can become conscious of, as you saw in Chapter 8. But the storage of information in implicit memory does not require conscious attention. Not all the information we do not pay attention to is lost.

Why does selective attention exist? Why do we not simply process all the information that is being gathered by our sensory receptors? We sometimes miss something important because our attention is occupied elsewhere. According to Broadbent (1958), the answer is that the brain mechanisms responsible for conscious processing of this information have a limited capacity. There is only so much information that these mechanisms can handle at one particular moment. Thus, we need some system to serve as a gatekeeper, controlling the flow of information to this system. The nature of this gatekeeper – selective attention – is the subject of ongoing research.

Dichotic listening

The first experiments to investigate the nature of attention scientifically took advantage of the fact that we have two ears. Cherry (1953) devised a test of selective attention called **dichotic listening**, a task that requires a person to listen to one of two messages presented simultaneously, one to each ear (dichotic means 'divided into two parts'). He placed headphones on his participants and presented recordings of different spoken messages to each ear, illustrated in Figure 9.3.

He asked the participants to shadow the message presented to one ear – to repeat back as quickly but as accurately as possible what that voice was saying. **Shadowing** ensured that they would pay attention only to that message.

The information that entered the unattended ear appeared to be lost. When questioned about what that ear had heard, participants responded that they had heard something, but they could not say what it was.

Figure 9.3 Dichotic listening and shadowing. A person listens to two different spoken messages simultaneously and continuously repeats back what one voice is saying.

Even if the voice presented to the unshadowed ear began to talk in a foreign language or read English backwards, participants do not notice the change (Wood and Cowan, 1995). Shadowing, however, is easier if the messages are physically different, that is, they are spoken by different sexes or one is louder than the other or one is speech and the other non-speech based. See Figure 9.4.

Other evidence shows that selective attention is not achieved by simply closing a sensory channel. Some information, by its very nature, can break through into consciousness. For example, if a person's name is presented to the unattended ear, they will very likely hear it and remember it later (Moray, 1959). Or if the message presented to the unattended ear contains sexually explicit words, people tend to notice them immediately (Nielsen and Sarason, 1981). The fact that some types of information presented to the unattended ear can grab our attention indicates that even unattended information undergoes some verbal analysis. If the unattended information is 'filtered out' at some level, this filtration must not occur until after the sounds are identified as words.

Several studies have shown that information presented to the unattended ear can affect our behaviour even if we do not become conscious of the information. To put it another way, the information can produce implicit memories, memories of which we are unaware (Cleermans, 1993). Von Wright *et al.* (1975) showed that words previously presented along with an unpleasant electrical shock would produce an emotional reaction when the words were presented to the unattended ear. Even when the participant was not consciously attending to the voice, the information produced a non-verbal response – a classically conditioned emotional reaction. Thus, the unattended information could trigger the recall of an implicit memory.

McKay (1973) showed that information presented to the unattended ear can influence verbal processing even when the listener is not conscious of this information. In the attended ear, participants heard sentences such as:

> They threw stones towards the bank yesterday.

While this sentence was being presented, the participants heard the word 'river' or 'money' in the unattended ear. Later, they were asked which of the following sentences they had heard:

> They threw stones towards the side of the river yesterday.
>
> They threw stones towards the savings and loan association yesterday.

Of course, the participants had heard neither of these sentences. McKay found that the participants' choices were determined by whether the word 'river' or 'money' was presented to the unattended ear. They did not specifically recall hearing the words presented to the unattended ear, but obviously these words had affected their perception of the meaning of the word 'bank'.

Treisman (1960) showed that people can follow a message that is being shadowed even if it switches from one ear to the other. Suppose a person is shadowing a message presented to the left ear, while the message to the right ear is unshadowed. In the example given in Figure 9.4, the person will probably say 'crept out of the swamp' and not 'crept out of flowers'. Apparently, the switch occurs when the message begins to make no sense. However, by the time the person realises that 'crept out of flowers' makes no sense, the rest of the message, 'the swamp', has already been presented to the right ear. Because the person is able to continue the message without missing any words, he or she must be able to retrieve some words from memory. Thus, even though an unshadowed message cannot be remembered later, it produces some trace that can be retrieved if attention is directed to it soon after the words are presented.

The cocktail-party phenomenon

Selective attention to auditory messages has practical significance outside the laboratory. For example, sometimes we have to sort out one message from several others without the benefit of such a distinct cue; we seldom hear one voice in one ear and another voice

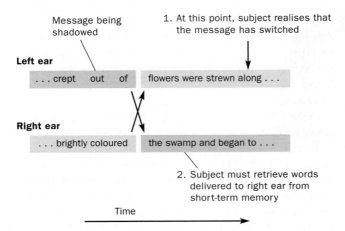

Figure 9.4 Shadowing a message that switches ears. When the message switches, the person must retrieve some words from memory that were heard by the unattended ear.

Controversies in Psychological Science – Does mobile phone use impair your driving?

The issue

The sale of mobile phones has been one of the marketing successes of the past few years: approximately 1 billion of them were in use worldwide in 2002 and it is estimated that 2.6 billion will be in use by the end of 2009. Mobile phones are portable, convenient and handy. So handy, that people often use them while doing other things. Surveys suggest that around 80 per cent of mobile phone users report having used the device while driving, despite the use of such devices being illegal in many countries (Goodman *et al.*, 1999). In 2003, for example, the UK passed an amendment to the Road Vehicles Act which made it an offence to drive a motor vehicle on a road while using a hand-held telephone (although not hands-free sets). The rationale for the ban is that factors such as holding the phone or dialling a number cause significant distraction and lack of control over the vehicle. Is there scientific evidence for this assumption?

The evidence

Strayer and Johnston (2001) have suggested that it is not the physical handling of mobile phones that leads to accidents but the conversations people have on them. They measured the errors made by drivers in a simulated driving task. These drivers either listened to a radio, listened to a book on tape, performed a word shadowing exercise on a mobile phone, held a conversation on a mobile phone or held a conversation using a hands-free set.

The authors cite previous studies that have shown a relationship between phone use and driving accidents. Redelmeier and Tibshirani's study (1997) of the phone records of those involved in driving accidents found that 24 per cent of people used their

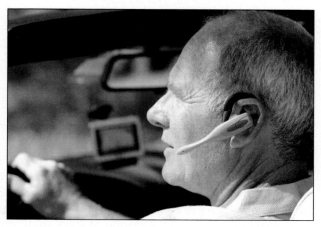

A hands-free set causes less distraction than a hand-held phone, when driving, but research suggests that it is the conversation you have that causes inattention'

Source: Corbis/Juice Images

phones within the 10 minutes before the accident. They argued that this rate suggested a danger that was as great as having excess alcohol in your bloodstream. Strayer and Johnston suggest that while the relationship appears causal, there may be other factors, such as the personality and disposition of the drivers, which caused the accident. Furthermore the study did not consider the conversational aspect of telephone use, although a study by Briem and Hedman (1995) suggested that holding a simple conversation did not significantly impair the ability to stay on the road.

Strayer and Johnston tested two hypotheses. The peripheral-interference hypothesis attributes driving accidents to non-conversational uses of the mobile phone such as holding and dialling. The attentional hypothesis attributes any driving impairment to the nature of the conversation taking place on the mobile phone.

In their simulated driving experiment, 48 undergraduates used a joystick to operate a cursor which they moved to follow a moving target on a computer screen. The target would move unpredictably, although not suddenly. Sporadically a green or red light would appear. If a green light appeared, the participant was asked to continue; if the red light appeared they were told to press a button which represented the brake on the joystick. The participants either conversed with a confederate on a mobile phone – they discussed President Bill Clinton's potential impeachment, and the Salt Lake City Olympic Committee bribery scandal – or conversed with a hands-free set or listened to a radio broadcast (which they could choose). The researchers found that the probability of missing a red light almost doubled when participants talked on the phone – whether hands-free or hand-held – compared with when they listened to the radio. There was no significant difference in the error rate between the two phone groups. Not only was the miss rate higher in these two groups, they were also slower to respond to the lights, as Figure 9.5 shows. People drove more poorly during the 'talking' portion of the conversation than the 'listening' portion.

To check that participants were listening to the material in the control condition – the authors did not assess this in their first experiment – and to ensure that the control condition was speech rather than music and speech-based, a second experiment required participants to complete the same simulated driving task but one group listened to a book on tape. This group did not perform significantly worse than the phone groups, suggesting that attending to verbal material is not enough to impair driving: active engagement in conversation is necessary for errors to be committed.

Controversies in Psychological Science – *Continued*

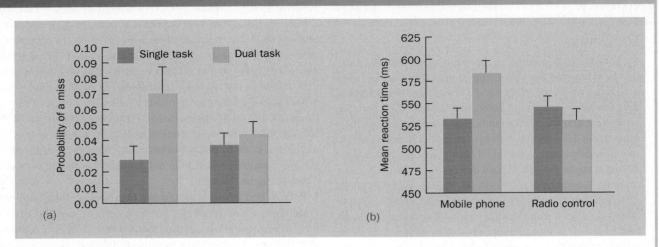

Figure 9.5 The probability of missing a red traffic light **(a)** and the reaction time to changing signals **(b)** when participants either performed the tracking task or performed the tracking task while having a conversation on a mobile phone or listening to the radio.

Source: Strayer, D.L. and Johnston W.A., Driven to distraction: Dual-task studies of simulated driving and conversing on a cellular telephone. *Psychological Science*, 2001, 12(6), 462–6, reprinted by permission of Blackwell Publishers Ltd.

In a final experiment, participants performed easy or difficult versions of the simulated driving task as they either repeated a word said to them by the experimenter over a mobile phone or as they generated a word beginning with a letter given to them by the experimenter over a mobile phone. While errors increased from the easy to the difficult conditions in the control (no phone) and dual-task (phone conditions), generating words was associated with significantly poorer performance than was the word repetition condition. This poor performance was especially pronounced in the difficult condition.

Conclusion

Strayer and Johnston provide persuasive evidence that holding a conversation on a mobile phone can impair driving. They suggest that the use of mobile phones while driving can impair attention when the context is an engaging one and not associated with the driving. Interestingly, they point to a study showing that as driving difficulty increases, conversation decreases (Parks, 1991). They also draw attention to the perhaps salient fact that, while eating a sandwich or holding a phone are activities under the sole control of the driver, a telephone conversation is not, and perhaps it is this lack of control which impairs driving performance.

This study is an intriguing one because it appears to contradict received and, indeed, legal wisdom: mobile phones do not cause accidents; conversations do.

in the other. We might be trying to converse with one person while we are in a room with several other people who are carrying on their own conversations. We can usually sort out one voice from another – an example of the **cocktail-party phenomenon.**

In this case, we are trying to listen to the person opposite us and to ignore the cross-conversation of the people to our left and right. Our ears receive a jumble of sounds, but we are able to pick out the ones we want, stringing them together into a meaningful message and ignoring the rest. This task takes some effort; following one person's conversation in such circumstances is more difficult when what they are saying is not very interesting. If we overhear a few words of another conversation that seems more interesting, it is hard to strain out the cross-conversation.

The original cocktail party effect study was reported in 1959 by Moray. The laboratory finding seemed to mirror that of hearing one's name mentioned in someone else's conversation at a party even though you were not attending to that conversation. However, in Moray's study, only 33 per cent of participants responded in this way. Is there some fundamental, psychological difference, therefore, between those who attend and those who do not, and would such a difference reflect different means of processing auditory or cognitive information?

According to a recent study, this difference could be working memory (Conway *et al.*, 2001). The researchers hypothesised that the least capable participants identified their names because they failed to demonstrate the working memory facility which would allow them to attend to the channel that they were meant to be attending to and ignore the channel they were not meant to.

Participants in the experiment were asked to complete a selective listening exercise similar to that of Moray. Participants listened to messages through headphones but were told only to attend to one channel; the participant's name would occur in the unattended channel. Participants also completed a working memory exercise that involved reading a simple mathematical equation followed by a word (e.g. 'Is (6 + 4)/2 = 5? DOG'), solving the equations and, at the end of all trials, writing down as many of the presented words as they could remember. The number of equation and word displays in each trial varied between two and six.

Those who excelled at this task were significantly better at ignoring their name than were those who performed less well.

> The critical factor seems to be the ability to block information from the irrelevant message. High-span subjects are more capable of this and were, therefore, less likely to hear their names, and they were also less susceptible to a consequential disruption of relevant task performance. Conway *et al.* 2005.

One of the behaviours we have become increasingly engaged in and which involves selective attention is mobile phone use. The use of these handsets has exploded over the past decade but their widespread availability and convenience has prompted some concern that they may be dangerous to use when, for example, driving. The assumption behind the concern is that holding a phone while driving reduces the controllability of the vehicle, impairs attention and, therefore, poses a threat to driver, pedestrians and other road users. But is there any scientific merit in this assumption? The Controversies in Psychological Science box above tackles this question and describes some recent, counter-intuitive findings.

Background noise

The opposite phenomenon to attention – where we try to exclude (become less conscious of) auditory information – has great practical

implications. Background noise, for example, is common in office environments and is a source of interference in open-plan offices (Klitzman and Stellman, 1989). Although there are very few controlled scientific experiments, existing studies report that background office noise is associated with stress, lack of concentration, low levels of performance and reduced employee efficiency (Loewen and Suedfeld, 1992; Sundstrom *et al.*, 1994).

Of course, we would not expect background noise to interfere with every type of behaviour. Music played in the background, for example, may even improve our performance. Are there specific auditory stimuli, therefore, that selectively impair the performance of specific tasks? Salame and Baddeley (1982), for example, have suggested that performance on a cognitive task can only be disrupted if the auditory stimulus doing the disruption is speech; others have suggested that stimuli other than speech can affect performance, giving rise to what has been termed the irrelevant speech effect (LeCompte *et al.*, 1997). The irrelevant speech effect suggests that any disruptive sound (delivered at conversational level) can impair memory for verbal material during serial (that is, when the material has to be recalled in a specific order) and free recall (Salame and Baddeley, 1990; Jones, 1995). An alternative to the speech effect is that the noise which disrupts performance has to show some variation (rather than being speech-like) before recall is disrupted. This is called the changing state hypothesis (Jones *et al.*, 1992). This theory would suggest that, in an office environment, performance would be disrupted by speech plus office noise.

To test this hypothesis, Banbury and Berry (1998) exposed undergraduates to office noise with speech, office noise without speech, speech alone or no noise while they (1) memorised a prose passage describing martial arts instructions for the correct and incorrect way of stretching muscles, and (2) solved a variety of arithmetical problems (division and subtraction). Memory for the prose passage was measured shortly afterwards. The experimenters found that office noise with speech and speech alone had a detrimental effect on memory for the prose passage; individuals in the office noise without speech condition, however, did not perform significantly differently from the control group, suggesting that the speech component of the noise was important (as Salame and Baddeley suggested). All three noise conditions, however, were associated with deficits in arithmetic performance. The experimenters noted that individuals were exposed to a greater duration of noise during the arithmetic task. Before the irrelevant speech effect explanation could be ruled out, therefore, the experimenters

Noise – An international perspective

The consequences of auditory distraction are discussed in Dylan Jones's review, 'The cognitive psychology of auditory distraction' (Jones, 1999).

> When a person's attention is directed elsewhere what degree of processing is undertaken on the material that the person is asked to ignore? Are all possible stimuli registered? Is their processing rudimentary, not going beyond, say, the representation of physical features, or is meaning also extracted? Jones, 1999.

A study of Dutch and Russian secretaries suggests that processing may be rudimentary. Zijlstra *et al.* (1999) looked at the work performance and psychological well-being of secretaries who were interrupted while undertaking a text-editing task. Contrary to expectations, interruptions made the participants work more quickly but no less efficiently, although these interruptions required more cognitive effort to deal with them. One strategy employed by participants was to ensure that their work had 'closure': that is, if they were interrupted mid-task, they would complete that task before dealing with the interruption. This would explain the increased speed in task performance.

These interruptions might be expected in a work environment and we may learn to adopt different strategies to avoid or ignore them. Noise over which we have little direct control may be more difficult to cope with. Aircraft noise or the noise of trains if you live under an airport flight path or near a railway track are examples of stimuli which can cause psychological impairment and annoyance. It has been estimated that 25 per cent of people in Europe have been exposed to noise level of 65dB or above (Berglund and Lindvall, 1995) and such people complain about the annoyance, the lack of sleep and the disruption to cognitive function that the noise causes (Smith and Jones, 1992).

Exposure to noise in children is correlated with deficits in reading, speech perception and long-term memory deficits (Evans and Lepore, 1993). Reading ability and long-term memory performance in children living next to a noisy, newly built airport in Munich was found to be severely impaired; those who had been exposed to airport noise and now lived near the old, closed airport, showed improvements in these tasks (Hygge *et al.*, 2002). Short-term memory also improved when the old airport closed.

suggested that length of exposure to noise needed to be extended in the prose recall condition. This they did by exposing individuals to office noise with speech, office noise without speech, meaningless speech or no noise during acquisition of the prose and during recall.

Extending the exposure period from five to nine minutes significantly and detrimentally affected memory performance when participants were exposed to office noise without speech and meaningless speech (duration did not affect performance in the office noise with speech condition). The greater impairment with greater exposure supported the results of other studies which showed that increasing the number of irrelevant background words presented during a primary task resulted in poorer memory performance (Bridges and Jones, 1996). This study, therefore, suggests that different categories of noise affect ongoing cognitive activity differently.

Models of selective attention

With all this evidence suggesting the robustness of selective attention, are we any closer to understanding how we selectively attend? In cognitive psychology, models of selective attention have been broadly divided into two: early selection models and late selection models. We consider the early selection models here.

Early selection models

The primary feature of early selection models (ESM) is that if items are not attended to they are not selected for perceptual analysis and so play no further part in information processing. Late selection models, on the other hand, argue that all information is attended to and is only selected later on in the information processing chain, that is, after perceptual analysis of the stimuli. Most of the influential ESM models were developed in the 1950s and 1960s when organisational psychology was making large inroads into workforce behaviour. Psychologists such as Donald Broadbent were interested in how psychological principles could be applied to understanding real-life problems, such as operating air traffic control systems or navigating a plane, both of which require extraordinary attention and selective attention.

Broadbent (1958) proposed a model of attention which was popular at the time because it was testable and falsifiable. However, evidence has shown that features of the model were incorrect. Broadbent proposed a filter theory of attention which suggested that processing information was a little like the operation of a filtering system: a channel of communication would process information and transmit this information to other cognitive systems for analysis. Specifically, Broadbent suggested that this filter initially processes information from a 'sensory store' and transfers it to other cognitive systems. This was an all-or-nothing model: only selected material would pass through the filter system. This selected material would then make its way to a limited capacity P(erceptual) system which would identify the material.

The all-or-nothing feature of the model can certainly explain why material presented to the unattended ear in dichotic listening experiments is not processed. A series of experiments by Moray (1959), however, suggested that the basic feature of the model was wrong. Moray found that when participants were instructed to switch attention from one ear to another during the experiment, they were able to do this when the instruction was along the lines of, 'Robyn, switch ears.' According to the model, this channel should have been blocked and should have remained unattended to: the participant should have been attending exclusively to another channel. Another set of experiments also demonstrated that listeners could follow messages that were switched from one ear to the other. For example, a narrative would begin in one ear and be switched to the previously unattended ear (Treisman, 1960, 1964). Participants, contrary to the filter model, would switch attention to the unattended ear to follow the narrative.

Treisman proposed her own model of selective attention which was 'weaker' than that of Broadbent. She argued that selective attention is certainly an early information processing activity but that not only would attended messages get through to the system, but unattended material would also get through but in weakened, attenuated form. This is called the attenuation model (Treisman, 1960).

Visual information

Sperling's studies of sensory memory, discussed in Chapter 8, demonstrated the role of attention in selectively transferring visual information into verbal short-term memory (or, for our purposes, into consciousness). Other psychologists have studied this phenomenon in more detail. For example, Posner *et al.* (1980) had participants watch a computer-controlled video display screen as a small mark in the centre of the screen served as a fixation point for the participants' gaze. They were shown a warning stimulus near the fixation point followed by a target stimulus – a letter displayed to the left or the right of the fixation point. The warning stimulus consisted of either an arrow pointing right or left or simply a plus sign. The arrows served as cues to the par-

ticipants to expect the letter to occur either to the right or to the left. The plus sign served as a neutral stimulus, containing no spatial information. The participants' task was to press a button as soon as they detected the letter.

Eighty per cent of the time, the arrow accurately pointed towards the location in which the letter would be presented. However, 20 per cent of the time, the arrow pointed away from the location in which it would occur. The advance warning clearly had an effect on the participants' response times: when they were correctly informed of the location of the letter, they responded faster. This is illustrated in the graph in Figure 9.6.

This study shows that selective attention can influence the detection of visual stimuli: if a stimulus occurs where we expect it, we perceive it more quickly; if it occurs where we do not expect it, we perceive it more slowly. Thus, people can follow instructions to direct their attention to particular locations in the visual field. Because gaze remained fixed on the centre of the screen in this study, this movement of attention was independent of eye movement. How does this focusing of attention work neurologically? The most likely explanation seems to be that neural circuits that detect a particular kind of stimulus are somehow sensitised, so that they can more easily detect that stimulus. In this case, the mechanism of selective attention sensitised the neural circuits that detect visual stimuli in a particular region.

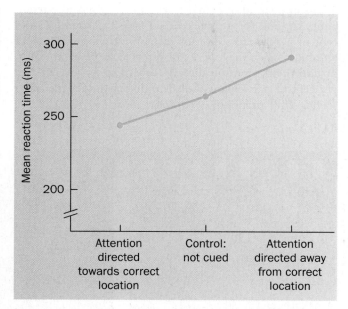

Figure 9.6 Location as a cue for selective attention. Mean reaction time in response to a letter displayed on a screen after subjects received a cue directing attention towards the location in which the letter appears was less than when no cue or an incorrect cue was received.

Inattentional blindness

Sometimes we don't see a visual stimulus because our attention has been drawn to something else, even if this something else is near the stimulus we can't see or is above or behind it. For example, if we are asked to fixate on a particular task or a spot on a screen, we can often ignore objects that ordinarily we would have no trouble in perceiving. This phenomenon is called **inattentional blindness** (Mack and Rock, 1998). It is similar to another seen in perception – change blindness – where participants do not notice (even very large) changes in the stimuli they are viewing if their attention is directed elsewhere. Examples include a failure to notice that the heads in two photographs have been switched – the switch would need to occur during an eye movement, otherwise it would be detectable (Grimes, 1996); and a failure to notice that a person giving directions has changed to another as a door was being carried between them (Simons and Levin, 1998).

In Mack and Rock's experiments, participants were asked to indicate which of the two arms of a visually presented cross was longer. At the fourth trial, an unexpected object was presented at the same time as the cross and participants were asked whether they were aware of this object appearing. The next trials followed, with participants being told that an unexpected object might appear, and a final trial explicitly asked participants to look for an unexpected object. Around 75 per cent of participants did not recognise the appearance of an object when they were not directed to be aware of it, or had their attention directly drawn to it. Twenty-five per cent of participants failed to do this under the other (divided/full attention) conditions.

The inattentional blindness effect can be seen in the most extraordinary contexts. A few years ago, a cinema advert (also available via youtube.com) was screened in which the viewers watched a basketball game between non-professional players. Cinema-goers were asked to pay attention to the number of passes made by the team in black or the team in white. After this, they were asked 'Did you see the gorilla?' This odd question was not as odd as the audience's reaction. Hardly any had seen the gorilla, even though a man in a gorilla suit walked along the screen during the game as the players participated.

The advert is based on an actual experiment designed and conducted by Daniel Simons and Christopher Chabris (Simons and Chabris, 1999). The audience behaved as the participants in their study behaved and the inattentional blindness was seen for a man who walked across the screen carrying an umbrella and even for the gorilla when it walked along the screen, stopped in the middle, turned to face the front, thumped its chest, turned and walked to the other side of the screen. This segment took nine seconds. The whole film lasted 62 seconds. You can see shots of the film in Figure 9.7.

Divided attention

Although all people seem to attend selectively to stimuli in the environment, they also sometimes have to undertake tasks that are made up of multiple components. Imagine cooking a meal, for example. Monitoring your boiling pasta while chopping up peppers and warming up your bolognese sauce requires you to attend to several stimuli. When attention is split in this way it is called **divided attention**.

Figure 9.7 Shots from Simon's gorilla and umbrella films

Source: Simons, D. J. and Chabris, C. F. Gorillas in our midst: sustained inattentional blindness for dynamic events. *Perception*, 1999, 28, 1059–74.

Various models have sought to explain divided attention and how we can (or, more often, cannot) undertake many tasks all at once. Single-capacity models, for example, suggest that there is one pool of resources available to deal with perceptual and cognitive challenges (Kahneman, 1973). You can probably gather from this that the more tasks an individual undertakes, the less capacity will be left to undertake these tasks effectively because each task is competing for the same pool of resources.

Resources are, then, normally allocated to the most important task. Single-capacity model theorists have found some support for this proposition in experiments where individuals have to undertake two tasks simultaneously (this is called **dual-task methodology**). When this occurs, performance on both tasks diminishes. Results like these suggest that when the resources necessary to complete tasks exceed the available single capacity, then performance will deteriorate. However, not all evidence supports this view. The anecdotal example of preparing a meal is one subjective example. Experiments in which typists were asked to transcribe text and complete a shadowing task at the same time found the participants were able to do this effectively (Shaffer, 1975). Sometimes, two tasks can be performed as well as one can.

An alternative to the single resource models are the multiple resource models. These argue that, in fact, we have several resource pools to deal with various cognitive and perceptual processes. It is because of these various pools that we can divide our attention between tasks successfully. These models suggest that when two tasks compete for the same resource, this will result in an impairment in task performance. When tasks compete for different resource pools, then they should be performed successfully. A problem with the resource model, however, is operationally defining a resource and the types of task that would use the different 'resources'. There is no general agreement on what the different types of resources are.

A final explanation for divided attention concerns the processes involved in various tasks. For example, Johnston and Heinz (1978) suggest that selective and divided attention clearly requires some form of selection. They divide the type of selection required into early (selecting perceptual/sensory information) and late (selecting meaning). Their process model does not agree that there is one structure or system which allows attention. It argues that early selection uses less capacity than late selection. To test this hypothesis, they asked participants to undertake a dichotic listening task where the stimuli differed in terms of their physical features (perceptual) or in terms of their meaning (semantic).

Concurrently, the participants undertook a reaction time task in which they had to press a button as soon as a light appeared. The experimenters found that although reaction time was slower when the participants listened to two messages, less capacity was required when the messages differed perceptually (such as the speaker's voice).

Brain mechanisms of selective attention

As we discussed earlier, one possible explanation for selective attention is that some components of the brain's sensory system are temporarily sensitised, which enhances their ability to detect particular categories of stimuli. For example, if a person were watching for changes in shapes, colours or movements (that is, if the person's attention were focused on one of these attributes), we might expect to see increased activity in the portions of the visual cortex devoted to the analysis of shapes, colours or movements.

This result is exactly what Corbetta *et al.* (1991) found. These investigators had participants look at a computerised display containing 30 coloured rectangles, which could change in shape, colour or speed of movement. The participants were asked to say whether they detected a change. On some trials, the participants were told to pay attention only to one attribute: shape, colour or speed of movement. The stimuli were counterbalanced so that the same set of displays was presented during each condition. Thus, the only difference between the conditions was the type of stimulus change that the participants were watching for.

In a PET study of brain activity during game watching, the experimenters found that paying attention to shape, colour or speed of movement caused activation of different regions of the visual association cortex. The locations corresponded almost precisely to the regions other studies have shown to be activated by shapes, colours or movements. Thus, selective attention towards different attributes of visual stimuli is accompanied by activation of the appropriate regions of the visual association cortex.

The left and right cerebral hemispheres seem to play different roles in attention. Focal attention (which involves attention to local cues) depends on the left hemisphere, whereas global attention (a holistic approach which takes in whole objects or scenes) is dependent on the right hemisphere (Fink *et al.*, 1996). This asymmetry of function may explain the symptoms seen in the perceptual disorder, spatial neglect, described in Chapter 6, in which brain-injured (usually right-hemisphere-damaged) patients are unable to report or respond to stimuli contralateral to the side of the brain injury.

Sustained attention has been associated with increased activation in the right prefrontal and parietal cortices, based on PET and fMRI findings, but generally there is a network of regions traversing the right fronto-parietal regions that are involved in sustained attention (Coull *et al.*, 1996), as Figure 9.8 shows.

Selective attention has been associated with increases in activation in posterior regions, but the region of activation depends on the type of attention that is selectively applied. If one sensory modality is attended to, regions associated with other modalities show suppressed activation (Haxby *et al.*, 1994; Ghatan *et al.*, 1998). Attending to a stimulus's movement has been associated with activation in the occipito-temporal region (Beauchamp *et al.*, 1997), with the prefrontal cortex and the cerebellum possibly modulating attention (Rees *et al.*, 1997a). Divided attention also recruits the prefrontal cortex, especially the left (Benedict *et al.*, 1998; Vandenberghe *et al.*, 1997). Posner and Petersen (1990) have characterised the ability to shift attention in three ways: the first component of attention allows the disengagement of attention from its current location (a function of the posterior parietal cortex); the second guides attention from the current location to the new location (a function of the superior colliculus, frontal eye fields and related structures); the third component allows the re-engagement of attention to the new location (a function of the thalamus).

Control of consciousness

Every culture appears to have methods of altering consciousness, from the ingestion of coffee, tea, alcohol or tobacco to taking marijuana or cocaine. Some of these you read about in Chapter 4. The urge to alter, expand, or even escape from one's consciousness does not require the use of drugs, however. There is some evidence that self-control may help to alter consciousness. The ancient Hebrews and early Christians often fasted for many days, undoubtedly because of the effects that their altered metabolism had on their consciousnesses. In earlier times, there was also much more emphasis on ritualised chants and movements, such as those of the early Jewish Hasidim and Cabbalists. In fact, the Christian Pentecostal sect and the Jewish Hasidic sects today practise dances and chanting that would not seem strange to thirteenth-century mystics, and these rituals encourage the 'taking over' of one's consciousness.

The one function that all methods of changing consciousness have in common is an alteration in attention. The various exercises can be divided into those that withdraw attention from the stimuli around us and those that increase attention to events that have become so commonplace that we no longer notice them, including our own behaviours that have become automatic and relatively non-conscious. We refer to exercises in both categories as meditation. Forms of meditation have developed in almost every culture. Zen Buddhism, Yoga, Sufism and Taoism are the best-known and most influential in Eastern societies, where they first developed, but there is also a tradition of meditation and contemplation in the Western world, still carried on in Christian monasteries. Even the ritualised recitation of the rosary and the clicking of the beads serve to focus a person's attention on the prayer they are chanting.

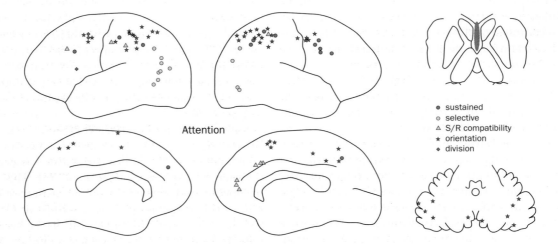

Figure 9.8 The areas of the brain involved in attention, according to recent neuroimaging data.

Source: Figure 4.6 from *Human Neuropsychology*, 2nd edn, Pearson/Prentice Hall (Martin, G.N., 2006).

Techniques for withdrawing attention

The goal of most meditation exercises is to remove attention from all sensory stimuli – to think of absolutely nothing. The various techniques require that the meditator directs their attention to a single object (such as a specially prepared symbol), to a spoken or imagined word or phrase (such as a prayer or mantra), to a monotonous sound (such as the rushing of a waterfall), or to a repetitive movement, such as breathing or touching the tips of each of the four fingers with the thumb (West, 1996).

By concentrating on an object, a sound or a repetitive movement we can learn to ignore other stimuli, a process called mental absorption. We achieve this kind of focus to some degree when we read a book intently or attempt to solve a problem. The difference is that the book or problem supplies a changing form of stimulation. Thoughts, words, images and ideas flow through our minds. In contrast, a person attempting to achieve a meditative trance selects an inherently static object of attention that leads to habituation. By concentrating on this unchanging source of information, continually bringing his or her attention back to it, the person achieves a state of utter concentration or nothing. Withdrawal of attention appears to have two primary goals: to reduce verbal control over non-verbal functions of the brain and to produce afterwards a 'rebound phenomenon' – a heightening of awareness and an increase in attention. The second goal is identical to that of consciousness-increasing exercises. Techniques similar to those found in attention withdrawal are used to achieve a hypnotic trance and these are reviewed in the next section on hypnosis.

Hypnosis

Hypnosis is a process whereby verbal suggestions made by one individual can be acted on by another who would not normally and voluntarily perform those acts. Under hypnosis, a person can be induced to bark like a dog, act like a baby or tolerate being pierced with needles. Although these examples are interesting and amusing, hypnosis is important to psychology because it provides information about the nature of consciousness and has applications in the fields of medicine and psychotherapy.

Hypnosis, or **mesmerism**, was discovered by Franz Anton Mesmer (1734–1815), an Austrian physician. He found that when he passed magnets back and forth over people's bodies (in an attempt to restore their 'magnetic fluxes' and cure them of disease), they would often have convulsions and enter a trance-like state during which almost miraculous cures

Psychology in action – Attention and pain

It was once thought that distraction was enough to help people take their mind off pain. Some studies, however, have shown that it is not necessarily distraction that is responsible for reducing pain but rather the emotional quality of the distractor. Positive stimuli, such as humour and laughter, are known to reduce pain perception (Cogan et al., 1987; Rotton and Shats, 1996) but increasing the attention required to complete cognitive tasks (distraction without emotion) does not (McCaul and Malott, 1984).

Minet de Wied and Marinus Verbaten from Utrecht University, the Netherlands, investigated whether high- and low-arousing neutral, negative or positive emotional stimuli affected people's experience of pain (de Wied and Verbaten, 2001). They presented pictures varying in emotional tone and arousal from the International Affective Picture System to 69 male students. The researchers hypothesised that if stimuli need to be emotionally distracting to reduce pain, then negative and positive pictures should reduce the experience of pain in a similar way. If stimuli prime the participant or help them appraise their state (so that a pleasant stimulus may put them in a positive mood but an unpleasant stimulus may put them in a negative mood), then pleasant and unpleasant stimuli will have different effects on the experience of pain. The pain induction task used was the cold-pressor task in which the participant keeps their arm in freezing water for as long as possible.

Exposure to pleasant pictures was associated with a greater tolerance of pain. In a second experiment, in which unpleasant pictures which contained either pain-related or pain-unrelated stimuli were presented, participants who viewed the pictures without pain cues tolerated the pain for longer than did those who viewed the pictures with pain cues. The results suggest that distraction by emotional cue may not be successful in reducing the experience of pain unless the distractor enhances positive mood (or does not produce a negative one, as experiment two showed).

could be achieved. As Mesmer discovered later, the patients were not affected directly by the magnetism of the iron rods; they were responding to his undoubtedly persuasive and compelling personality. We now know that convulsions and trance-like states do not necessarily accompany hypnosis, and we also know that hypnosis does not cure physical illnesses. Mesmer's patients apparently had psychologically produced symptoms that were alleviated by suggestions made while they were hypnotised.

The induction of hypnosis

A person undergoing hypnosis can be alert, relaxed, tense, lying quietly or exercising vigorously. There is no need to move an object in front of someone's face or to say 'you are getting sleepy'; an enormous variety of techniques can be used to induce hypnosis in a susceptible person. The only essential feature seems to be the participant's understanding that they are to be hypnotised. Moss (1965) reported having sometimes simply said to a well-practised subject, in a normal tone of voice, 'Please sit in that chair and go into hypnosis', and the subject complied within a few seconds. Sometimes, this approach even worked on volunteers who had never been hypnotised before.

The induction process normally involves suggestions for sleep or relaxation, followed by a set of suggestions aimed to produce arm lowering or lifting, hand clasping ('you cannot separate your hands'), hallucinations and amnesia.

Characteristics of hypnosis

Hypnotised people are very suggestible; their behaviour will conform with what the hypnotist says, even to the extent that they may appear to misperceive reality (Wagstaff, 1996). Under hypnosis, people can be instructed to do things that they would not be expected to do under normal conditions, such as acting out imaginary scenes or pretending to be an animal. Hypnotised people can be convinced that an arm cannot move or is insensitive to pain, and they then act as if that is the case. They can also be persuaded to have positive or negative hallucinations – to see things that are not there or not to see objects that are there.

One of the most dramatic phenomena of hypnosis is **posthypnotic suggestibility**, in which a person is given instructions under hypnosis and follows those instructions after returning to a non-hypnotised state. For example, a hypnotist might tell a man that he will become unbearably thirsty when he sees the hypnotist

Hypnos. The son of Nyx (night) and brother of Thanatos (death), the mythical Hypnos was thought to fan the weary to sleep.
Source: British Museum, London/The Bridgeman Art Library.

look at her watch. She might also admonish him not to remember anything upon leaving the hypnotic state, so that **posthypnotic amnesia** is also achieved. After leaving the hypnotic state, the man acts normally and professes ignorance of what he perceived and did during hypnosis, perhaps even apologising for not having succumbed to hypnosis. The hypnotist later looks at her watch, and the man suddenly leaves the room to get a drink of water.

Studies indicate that when changes in perception are induced in hypnotised people, the changes occur not in the people's actual perceptions but in their verbal reports about their perceptions. For example, Miller *et al.* (1973) used the Ponzo illusion to test the effects of hypnotically induced blindness. This effect is produced by the presence of the slanted lines to the left and right of two horizontal ones; if these lines are not present, the horizontal lines appear to be the same length. Through hypnotic suggestion, the experimenters made the slanted lines 'disappear'. But even though the participants reported that they could not see the slanted lines, they still perceived the upper line as being longer than the lower one. This result indicates that the visual system continues to process sensory information during hypnotically induced blindness; otherwise, the participants would have perceived the lines as being equal in length. The reported blindness appears to occur not because of altered activity in the visual system but because of altered activity in the verbal system (and in consciousness).

Theories of hypnosis

Most theories of hypnosis revolve around the question of whether hypnosis represents a different state of consciousness (Fellows, 1990; Lynn and Rhue, 1991). The state hypothesis of hypnosis suggests that this phenomenon is an example of an altered state of consciousness or a trance resulting from induction (Hilgard, 1986). Hilgard's neo-dissociation theory (Hilgard, 1978, 1991) suggests that we have multiple systems of control which are not all conscious at the same time. These systems are under the general, central control of an 'executive ego' which controls and motivates other systems. The theory suggests that when a person is under hypnosis, overall control is given up to the hypnotist who has access to various systems. Such a theory claims to find support from what is called the **'hidden observer'** phenomenon. This is where the experimenter places a hand on the shoulder of the hypnotised individual and appears to be able to talk to a hidden part of the person's body (Knox *et al.*, 1974).

The non-state hypothesis of hypnosis argues that the process does not reflect altered states of consciousness but more mundane psychological functions such as imagination, relaxation, role-enactment, compliance, conformity, attention, attitudes and expectations (Coe and Sarbin, 1991; Wagstaff, 1991, 1996). Wagstaff (1996), for example, has argued that hypnosis may well represent some altered state but the evidence suggests that hypnotic suggestion can be explained by what we already know about human behaviour and thought. Strategic role-enactment is common in psychological research, for example. The degree of role-taking depends on whether the participant is worried about giving up control or being manipulated. To experience a hand getting heavier, the individual can imagine a weight on their arm; to experience hypnotic 'amnesia', the individual can distract themselves. Of course, state theorists would argue that such compliance or acting out is part of hypnotic behaviour that occurs without subjective experience (Spanos, 1991, 1992).

Barber (1979) suggests that at least some aspects of hypnosis are related to events that can happen every day and argues that hypnosis should not be viewed as a special state of consciousness, in the way that sleep is a state of consciousness that differs from waking; rather, the hypnotised person should be seen as acting out a social role. The phenomena of hypnosis are social behaviours, not manifestations of a special state of consciousness. Hypnotised people willingly join with the hypnotist in enacting a role expected of them. Some of the rules governing this role are supplied by the direct instructions of the hypnotist, others are indirectly implied by what the hypnotist says and does, and still others consist of expectations that the people already have about what hypnotised people do.

For example, Spanos (1992) induced negative hallucinations in participants who reported being unable to see the number eight (although it was visible before them). When these participants were told that 'real' hypnotisable individuals, unlike 'fakers', do see the number briefly at the beginning, almost all subjects confirmed that they had seen it. In a more amusing experiment, Barber *et al.* (1974) asked a group of 'hypnotised' participants whether they could hear the experimenter, to which they replied 'no'!

People's expectations about hypnosis do indeed play an important role in their behaviour while under hypnosis. In lectures to two sections of an introductory psychology class, Orne (1959) told one section (falsely) that one of the most prominent features of hypnosis was rigidity of the preferred (that is, dominant) hand. Later, he arranged a demonstration of hypnosis during a meeting of students from both sections. Several of the students who had heard that the dominant hand became rigid showed this phenomenon when hypnotised, but none of the students who had not heard this myth developed a rigid hand. Similarly, if people become willing to follow a hypnotist's suggestions, perhaps they do so because they believe that this suggested behaviour is what is supposed to happen. Perhaps people willingly follow a hypnotist's suggestion to do something silly (such as bark like a dog) because they know that hypnotised people are not responsible for their behaviour.

Compliance, role-enactment and other psychological process can also explain examples of antisocial or strange behaviour that individuals can apparently be hypnotised into doing. Hypnotists have induced individuals to expose themselves indecently, pick up dangerous snakes, steal, verbally attack others, put their hands in nitric acid, throw acid at the experimenter, deal heroin, mutilate the Bible and make homosexual approaches (Orne and Evans, 1965; Wagstaff, 1993). However, Orne and Evans (1965) reported that non-hypnotised individuals could also be instructed to perform these acts. What produces this apparent unusual behaviour is the need to want to help the hypnotist or thinking that the antics were safe or that someone else would take responsibility for them (Udolf, 1983).

The hypnotist, entertainer and erstwhile disc jockey Paul McKenna, for example, invokes such psychological mechanisms to explain the odd behaviour he can induce in members of the public during his stage show. There is no real, special trance-like state, only the ability of individuals to become more-or-less compliant, to be more-or-less willing to please the hypnotist. For this reason, among others, McKenna was found not guilty in 1998 of being responsible for turning an audience volunteer into a violent and aggressive schizophrenic during his show.

Neurobiological correlates of hypnosis

You can see in the Controversies in Psychological Science section on hypnosis and pain that some researchers have suggested a role for the prefrontal cortex in hypnotic suggestion because this area mediates aspects of attention. There is good evidence for the link between attention and frontal cortex activity but there is evidence that two aspects of the hypnotic trance or state – relaxation and mental absorption – may also activate other areas. Hypnotic relaxation is induced when a participant listens to instructions to relax: these involve imagining feelings of warmth and heaviness, and drowsiness. Mental absorption is induced by having the participant listen carefully and continuously to the hypnotist's instructions and ignoring all other stimuli. A PET study of brain activity before and after hypnotic induction found that participants' self-ratings of relaxation and absorption was associated with activity in the anterior cingulate cortex, the thalamus and the brain stem, areas closely tied to states of consciousness (Rainville *et al.*, 2002). Mental absorption, in particular, was associated with activity in a network of cortical and subcortical regions, including the prefrontal cortex, as we would have predicted.

Controversies in Psychological Science – Can hypnosis reduce pain and stress?

The issue

Pain is the most unpleasant sensory experience humans can suffer. It can derive from many sources, although the commonest are illness and disease. Such pain is normally relieved by surgery or drugs (often the surgery itself causes pain and has to be relieved pharmacologically). There are instances, however, where surgical or pharmacological interventions in pain relief are not successful. Often, in such circumstances, patients turn to hypnotic analgesia as an alternative. **Hypnotic analgesia** refers to the ability to endure or eliminate surgical pain via hypnotic suggestion (Wagstaff, 1996). Does such analgesic intervention work?

The evidence

Hypnosis can play a useful role in medicine, dentistry and psychotherapy (Heap and Dryden, 1991). The analgesia – insensitivity to pain – produced by hypnosis has been reported to be more effective than that produced by morphine, tranquillisers such as Valium, or acupuncture (Stern *et al.*, 1977). Thus, it can be used to suppress the pain of childbirth or having one's teeth drilled or to prevent gagging when a dentist is working in a patient's mouth. It is also useful in reducing the nausea caused by the drugs used in chemotherapy for cancer. However, because not all people can be hypnotised, and because the induction of hypnosis takes some time, few physicians or dentists use hypnosis to reduce pain; drugs are easier to administer.

Barber (1996, 1998) has reviewed evidence which suggests that hypnotic treatment for acute pain resulting from medical procedures (chemotherapy, surgery) or recurring pain is effective. Of course, different types of condition produce different types of pain: some pains are constant, some intermittent. Osteoarthritis and trigeminal neuralgia, for example, produce almost constant pain whereas migraine and sickle cell disease and lower back pain caused by spinal nerve compression produce recurring pain.

To investigate whether hypnosis would help mediate the effects of a temporarily stressful event and whether any buffering effect would be accompanied by immune system changes, Kiecolt-Glaser *et al.* (2001) took blood samples from medical and dental students who were hypnotically suggestible. They did this during periods of low stress and then three days before their first exams. Exams have been found to provoke considerable distress in examinees. Wounds tend to heal significantly more slowly before an important examination, for example, than during an exam-free period (Marucha *et al.*, 1998). Half of the group were assigned to a hypnosis-generated relaxation-training condition in this interval; the other half received no relaxation training. The authors examined various immune system variables including lymphocyte number and interleukin-1 (which assists wound healing).

They found that students in the hypnosis condition showed a significantly greater proliferation of lymphocytes and an increase in interleukin-1 production during the examination period, compared with the control group. These students were also able to maintain baseline levels of these antibodies. The authors suggest that the effects are similar to those seen in surgical patients – hypnotic relaxation training in some patients is associated with shorter hospital stays, decreased

Controversies in Psychological Science – *Continued*

pain and more rapid recovery following surgery (Blankfield, 1991; Lang *et al.*, 2000). The findings highlight the role of hypnotic relaxation in reducing stress and in altering immune system functioning.

While evidence suggests that pain can be reduced following hypnotic suggestion, the cognitive or physiological mechanisms underlying this reduction are not known. There are 'non-hypnotic' factors which could be involved in pain reduction. For example, non-specific coping strategies, pain relief through feeling numb or cold, the use of relaxation and pre-operative preparation to alleviate anxiety are all successful in reducing the degree of reported surgical pain (Barber *et al.*, 1974; Chaves, 1989).

These results have been explained in terms of the ironic processes theory (Wegner, 1994). According to this theory, the control of mental events is made possible by two processes working together. The operating process retrieves material that puts the organism in a desirable state; the maintaining process searches consciousness for any content that is inconsistent with the desired state. When cognitive tasks reduce the resources available, the effectiveness of the monitoring process increases in comparison with the operating process (Eastwood *et al.*, 1998). Eastwood tested this hypothesis by requiring participants low and high in hypnotisability to report the degree of pain they were experiencing in a pain-induction task at regular intervals. The experimenters found that the frequency of pain reporting was associated with an increase in the level of experienced pain but that highly hypnotisable participants reported less pain.

The fact that only highly hypnotisable participants showed this effect explains why the published research has focused more on these individuals than on those who are not particularly susceptible to hypnotic suggestion (Crawford, 1994). Why are highly susceptible individuals more likely to report reductions in pain? Some psychologists have suggested that these individuals can partition their attentional resources more effectively (Hilgard and Hilgard, 1994). Crawford *et al.* (1993) have reported that highly susceptible individuals showed a bilateral increase in blood flow to the frontal cortex and somatosensory cortex during hypnotic analgesia and the experience of pain. According to Crawford *et al.* (1998), this evidence suggests that the frontal region deals with the active allocation of attention, whereas the posterior parts are concerned with the spatio-temporal aspects of pain perception (such as where and when the pain is experienced).

Conclusion

Wagstaff (1987) has suggested that many of the effects seen in hypnotic analgesia are the result of the same factors that result in other forms of hypnotism. These factors include social support, relaxation, covert modelling, placebo and social compliance. Belief in the efficacy of the hypnosis is also an important factor. Wagstaff and Royce (1994) found that although hypnotic suggestions for the alleviation of nail-biting was better than non-hypnotic suggestions, the best predictor of abstinence from nail-biting was belief in the efficacy of the procedure. There may, therefore, be a strong placebo effect seen in these studies.

What are the characteristics of a highly hypnotisable subject? How would you design an experiment to examine the effects of hypnotic analgesia on the pain induced by cancer and chemotherapy? How would you determine that any effect was attributable to hypnosis?

Sleep

Sleep is not a state of unconsciousness; it is a state of altered consciousness. During sleep, we have dreams that can be just as vivid as waking experiences, and yet we forget most of them as soon as they are over. Our amnesia leads us to think, incorrectly, that we were unconscious while we were asleep. In fact, there are two distinct kinds of sleep, and thus two states of altered consciousness. We spend approximately one-third of our lives sleeping, or trying to, although the reasons for why we sleep are not fully known.

The stages of sleep

Sleep is not uniform. We can sleep lightly or deeply; we can be restless or still; we can have vivid dreams, or our consciousness can be relatively blank. Researchers who have studied sleep have found that its stages usually follow an orderly, predictable sequence.

Most sleep research takes place in sleep laboratories. Because a person's sleep is affected by their surroundings, a sleep laboratory contains one or more small bedrooms, furnished and decorated to be as home-like and comfortable as possible. The most important apparatus of the sleep laboratory is the polygraph, a machine located in a

see activity on **mypsychlab**

separate room that records on paper the output of various devices that can be attached to the sleeper. For example, the polygraph can record the electrical activity of the brain through small metal discs pasted to the scalp, producing an **electroencephalogram** (**EEG**). It can record electrical signals from muscles, producing an **electromyogram** (**EMG**) or from the heart, producing an **electrocardiogram** (abbreviated as EKG or ECG). Or it can record eye movements through small metal discs attached to the skin around the eyes, producing an **electro-oculogram** (**EOG**). Other special transducers can detect respiration, sweating, skin or body temperature, and a variety of other physiological states (Andreassi, 2001).

The EEG record distinguishes between alert and relaxed wakefulness. When a person is alert, the tracing looks rather irregular, and the pens do not move very far up or down. The EEG shows high-frequency (15–30 Hz), low-amplitude electrical activity called **beta activity**. When a person is relaxed and perhaps somewhat drowsy, the record shows **alpha activity**, a medium-frequency (8–12 Hz), medium-amplitude rhythm.

When the individual relaxes and becomes drowsy, the EEG changes from beta activity to alpha activity. Figure 9.9 illustrates this and the subsequent stages of sleep.

The first stage of sleep (stage 1) is marked by the presence of some **theta activity**, EEG activity of 3.5–7.5 Hz. This stage is actually a transition between sleep and wakefulness; the EMG shows that muscles are still active, and the EOG indicates slow, gentle, rolling eye movements. The eyes slowly open and close from time to time. Soon, the person is fully asleep. As sleep progresses, it gets deeper and deeper, moving through stages 2, 3 and 4. The EEG gets progressively lower in frequency and higher in amplitude. Stage 4 consists mainly of **delta activity**, characterised by relatively high-amplitude waves occurring at less than 3.5 Hz. Our sleeper becomes less responsive to the environment, and it becomes more difficult to awaken him. Environmental stimuli that caused him to stir during stage 1 produce little or no reaction during stage 4. The sleep of stages 3 and 4 is called **slow-wave sleep**.

Stage 4 sleep is reached in less than an hour and continues for as much as a half hour. Then, suddenly, the EEG begins to indicate lighter levels of sleep, back through stages 3 and 2 to the activity characteristic of stage 1. The sleeper's heartbeat becomes irregular and his respiration alternates between shallow breaths and sudden gasps. The EOG shows that the person's eyes are darting rapidly back and forth, up and down. The EEG record looks like that of a person who is awake and active. Yet the sleeper is fast asleep. Although EMG is generally quiet, indicating muscular relaxation, the hands and feet twitch occasionally.

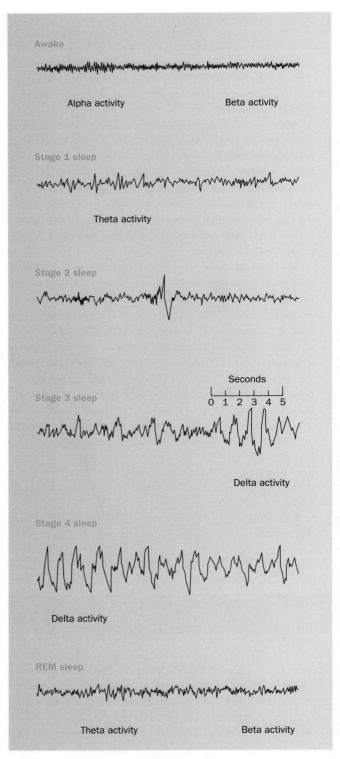

Figure 9.9 An EEG recording of the stages of sleep.

Source: Horne, J.A., *Why We Sleep: The functions of sleep in humans and other mammals*. Oxford: Oxford University Press, 1989. © 1988 Oxford University Press, reprinted by permission.

At this point, the subject is dreaming and has entered another stage of sleep, called **rapid eye movement (REM)** sleep. The first episode of REM sleep lasts 20–30 minutes and is followed by approximately one hour of slow-wave sleep. As the night goes on, the episodes of REM sleep get longer and the episodes of slow-wave sleep get shorter, but the total cycle remains at approximately 90 minutes. A typical night's sleep consists of four or five of these cycles. Figure 9.10 shows a record of a person's stages of sleep; the coloured shading indicates REM sleep. The double-exposure images in Figure 9.11 simulate the movement of the eyes during REM.

Regions of the brain also become more or less active during REM sleep, as Figure 9.12 shows. We will return to the significance of brain activity changes in sleep, consciousness and alertness at the end of the chapter.

Although a person in REM sleep exhibits rapid eye movements and brief twitches of the hands and feet, the EMG shows that the facial muscles are still. In fact, physiological studies have shown that, aside from occasional twitching, a person actually becomes paralysed during REM sleep. Males are observed to have partial or full erections. In addition, women's vaginal secretions increase at this time. These genital changes are usually not associated with sexual arousal or dreams of a sexual nature. Table 9.2 lists the principal characteristics of REM sleep and slow-wave sleep.

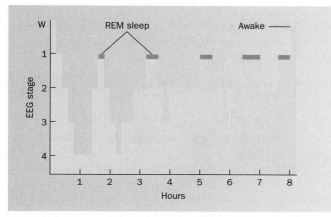

Figure 9.10 Typical progression of stages during a night's sleep. The dark blue shading indicates REM sleep.

Source: Hartmann, E., *The Biology of Dreaming*, 1967. Courtesy of Charles C. Thomas, Publisher, Ltd, Springfield, Illinois.

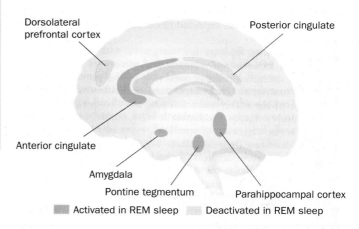

Figure 9.12 Areas of the brain activated and deactivated during REM sleep.

Source: From Hartmann, E., *The Biology of Dreaming*, 1967. Courtesy of Charles C. Thomas, Publisher, Ltd, Springfield, Illinois.

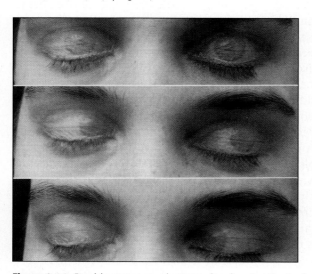

Figure 9.11 Double exposure photographs showing the typical movement of eyes during REM sleep.

Source: Hobson, J.A,. *Consciousness*. New York: W.H. Freeman, 1999.

Table 9.2 Principal characteristics of REM sleep and slow-wave sleep

REM sleep	Slow-wave sleep
Rapid EEG waves	Slow EEG waves
Muscular paralysis	Lack of muscular paralysis
Rapid eye movements	Slow or absent eye movements
Penile erection or vaginal secretion	Lack of genital activity
Dreams	

Cutting edge – Evening types are more creative, but also more maladaptive

Morning types or 'larks' are often viewed as conscientious, trustworthy and stable. Evening types or 'owls' are thought to be creative, unstable and have fractious social and family relationships (they also yawn more, Zilli *et al.*, 2007). Two studies have tried to determine whether there is empirical evidence for these characterisations.

In one study, evening and morning types completed a visual component of a well-known test of creativity, the Torrance Test of Creative Thinking (Giampietro and Cavallera, 2007). The test involved (i) drawing a picture using a shape provided by the experimenter and giving a name to it, and (ii) making complete shapes out of 10 incomplete straight and curved lines. Evening types out-scored morning types.

However, the increased creativity may be accompanied by maladaptive social behaviour. In a study which measured the IQ performance of adolescents classed as morning and evening types, in the morning and the evening, fluid intelligence was better if the time of testing matched the person's circadian preference. There were no circadian preference effects for crystallised intelligence (Goldstein *et al.*, 2007). Morning types, however, reported fewer attention problems, less aggression, were more competent socially in school and were engaged in more activities. One reason for this might be that evening types have difficulty in adjusting to the demands of early morning rises for school (Andershed, 2005).

Functions of sleep

Sleep is one of the few universal behaviours. All mammals, all birds and some cold-blooded vertebrates spend part of each day sleeping. Sleep is seen even in species that would seem to be better off without sleep. For example, the Indus dolphin (*Platanista indi*) which lives in the muddy waters of the Indus estuary in Pakistan (Pilleri, 1979). Over the ages, it has become blind, presumably because vision is not useful in the animal's environment (it has an excellent sonar system, which it uses to navigate and find prey). However, despite the dangers caused by sleeping, sleep has not disappeared. The Indus dolphin never stops swimming; doing so would result in injury, because of the dangerous currents and the vast quantities of debris carried by the river during the monsoon season. Pilleri captured two Indus dolphins and studied their habits. He found that they slept a total of seven hours a day, in very brief naps of 4 to 60 seconds each. If sleep did not perform an important function, we might expect that it, like vision, would have been eliminated in this species through the process of natural selection.

Sleep deprivation

The universal nature of sleep suggests that it performs some important functions (Hobson, 1988). One approach to discovering the functions of sleep is the deprivation study. Consider, for example, the function of eating. The effects of starvation are easy to detect: the person loses weight, becomes fatigued and will eventually die if they do not eat again. By analogy, it should be easy to discover why we sleep by seeing what happens to a person who goes without sleep.

Unfortunately, deprivation studies have not obtained persuasive evidence that sleep is needed to keep the body functioning normally. Horne (1978) reviewed over fifty experiments in which humans had been deprived of sleep. He reported that most of them found that sleep deprivation did not interfere with people's ability to perform physical exercise. In addition, they found no evidence of a physiological stress response to sleep deprivation. If people encounter stressful situations that cause illness or damage to various organ systems, changes can be seen in such physiological measures as blood levels of cortisol and epinephrine. Generally, these changes did not occur.

Although sleep deprivation does not seem to damage the body, and sleep does not seem to be necessary for athletic exercise, sleep may be required for normal brain functioning. Several studies suggest that sleep-deprived people are able to perform normally on most intellectual tasks, as long as the tasks are short. They perform more poorly on tasks that require a high level of cortical functioning after two days of sleep deprivation (Horne and Minard, 1985). In particular, they perform poorly on tasks that require them to be watchful, alert and vigilant. Female flight attendants working on international transmeridian flights, for example, perform attention tasks that require delayed responding more poorly than do their ground-bound colleagues (Cho *et al.*, 2000). People also show poor recency memory, but not recognition memory, after 36 hours' lack of sleep (Harrison and

Horne, 2000) and free recall of verbal material tends to be impaired after the loss of one night's sleep (Drummond *et al.*, 2000). The effects of sleep deprivation on working memory depend on the length of deprivation. There is little difference in performance between 24 and 35 hours of deprivation (Chee *et al.*, 2006b). The sleep deprivation was associated with a reduction in activation in two regions of the brain: the superior parietal cortex and the left thalamus. Participants allowed to sleep normally following sleep deprivation show greater activation in the frontal-parietal area and this correlates with improved working memory performance.

One study has reported that when sleep is restricted by 50 per cent, feelings of sociability and optimism decline by approximately 15 per cent (Haack and Mullington, 2005), and the ability to identify odours declines after 52 hours' sleep deprivation (McBride *et al.*, 2006). Wells and Cruess (2006) examined the effect of sleep loss on food consumption in a group of 50 undergraduates who were instructed to sleep for only 4 hours on the second day of the study (on the first they recorded their sleep quality and food intake). Respondents kept diaries of what they ate and so the study relied on self-reporting, with all the caveats that implies. After sleep loss, participants ingested fewer calories two days after sleep deprivation. They also chose foods for reasons other than health, naturalness and price. The study highlights the unexpected nutritional consequences of sleep loss.

The way in which we cope with stress may affect how well we sleep, regardless of the source of stress. Sadeh *et al.* (2004) measured the sleeping patterns and sleeping quality of 36 students during periods of low stress – a normal academic week, and high stress – when their eligibility for acceptance on an important clinical psychology course was being assessed. They were classed as problem-focused copers (PFC; they manage or alter the stress-causing problem); emotion-focused copers (EFC; they regulate emotional responses to the stressor); and disengagers (DE; they try to disengage from the thoughts and feelings generated by the threat). Individuals with a predominantly EFC style slept less whereas those who used EFC less slept more during the period of high stress. The low EFC participants also improved their sleep quality during the stressful period whereas high EFC participants' sleep worsened. A general effect was found for PFC – people scoring high in this style slept more, regardless of whether the period was stressful or stress-free.

One of the most dangerous consequences of sleep deprivation is poor driving. The Psychology in Action box below reviews the evidence for the effects of sleep loss on driving and how these effects may be combated with appropriate intervention.

During stage 4 sleep, the metabolic activity of the brain decreases to about 75 per cent of the waking level

(Sakai *et al.*, 1979). Thus, stage 4 sleep appears to give the brain a chance to rest. In fact, people are unreactive to all but intense stimuli during slow-wave sleep and, if awakened, act groggy and confused, as if their cerebral cortex has been shut down and has not yet resumed its functioning. These observations suggest that during stage 4 sleep the brain is, indeed, resting.

Sleep deprivation studies of humans suggest that although the brain may need slow-wave sleep in order to recover from the day's activities, the rest of the body does not. Another way to determine whether sleep is needed for restoration of physiological functioning is to look at the effects of daytime activity on night-time sleep. If the function of sleep is to repair the effects of activity during waking hours, then we should expect that sleep and exercise are related. That is, we should sleep more after a day of vigorous exercise than after a day spent quietly at an office desk. In fact, the relation between sleep and exercise is not very compelling.

Although bodily exercise has little effect on sleep, mental exercise seems to increase the demand for slow-wave sleep. In an ingenious study, Horne and Minard (1985) found a way to increase mental activity without affecting physical activity and without causing stress. The investigators told volunteers to show up for an experiment in which they were supposed to take some tests designed to test reading skills. In fact, when the people turned up, they were told that the plans had been changed. They were invited for a day out, at the expense of the experimenters. They spent the day visiting an art exhibition, a shopping centre, a museum, an amusement park, a zoo and stately home. After a scenic drive through the countryside they watched a film in a local cinema. They were driven from place to place and certainly did not become overheated by exercise. After the film, they returned to the sleep laboratory. They said they were tired, and they readily fell asleep. Their sleep duration was normal and they awoke feeling refreshed. However, their slow-wave sleep, particularly stage 4 sleep, was increased.

Sleep-dependent memory consolidation

One of the functions of sleep is to allow us to consolidate what we have learned while we were awake. This phenomenon is called sleep-dependent memory consolidation (Marshall and Born, 2007). For example, there is considerable evidence now to show that our procedural, declarative, sensory and motor memory are better after sleeping (Walker *et al.*, 2003; Cohen *et al.*, 2005; Born *et al.*, 2006) and each appears to be dependent on the appearance of certain sleep stages. Motor skills, for

Psychology in action – How sleep loss affects behaviour

At around 6 a.m. on 28 February 2001, Gary Hart, a 37-year-old builder from Lincolnshire, drove his Land Rover and trailer off the M62 near Great Heck in North Yorkshire, and plummeted down the embankment onto the east coast mainline. Within minutes, the vehicle was hit by a southbound express passenger train travelling at 117 mph. At 6.14 a.m. the passenger train collided with another train carrying 1,600 tons of coal. The collision killed 10 men and injured 76 people. Hart was convicted of death by dangerous driving. He admitted that he had not slept the night before but denied falling asleep at the wheel. He admitted having had only a short nap in the last 24 hours.

Most road traffic accidents occur between four and six o'clock in the morning, with a second, slightly smaller peak occurring in the middle of the afternoon (Horne and Reyner, 1999). Most researchers attribute this finding to sleeplessness and/or fatigue. A lack of sleep seems to exacerbate driving performance as does a feeling of fatigue and the ingestion of carbohydrates (London et al., 2004). Imagine the case of a person who has completed a night shift for the first time after having slept little in the past 24 hours, and who then drives the long, monotonous road journey home. All of these conditions present problems to the driver (Horne and Reyner, 1999), and driving performance is affected in those people who cut short their sleep to make an early morning journey. Even in the wakeful driver, prolonged driving induces subjective feelings of tiredness (Summala et al., 1999) and lane drifting (Brookhuis and DeWaard, 1993). Long-haul lorry drivers, in particular, experience increased fatigue and tension as the driving progresses, although it seems as if difficult driving conditions result in fewer driving mistakes than do monotonous ones, such as a straight road (Matthews and Desmond, 2002). Fatigue appears to have the same detrimental effect on driving as does alcohol (DeWaard and Brookhuis, 1991).

Combined with long work hours, sleep loss can be fatal. Researchers at the Harvard Work Hours, Health and Safety Group studied a group of 2,737 US medical residents in their first postgraduate year (interns) (Barger et al., 2005). The medical profession is notorious for having its physicians work long hours and shifts can frequently last longer than 24 hours. Forty per cent of the weeks in which interns worked involved them working for 80 hours; in 11 per cent, the physicians worked for over 100 hours. The researchers asked participants to note their work hours, extended work hours, documented motor vehicle crashes and near misses. Of the 320 crashes reported, 130 were severe enough to cause vehicle or person damage. The risk of a crash or near miss was significantly amplified if the physician was commuting after an extended rather than non-extended workshift. The majority of interns

reported spending as little as four hours asleep while working on extended shifts and they routinely worked 30 consecutive hours (see Table 9.3).

One way of preventing this erratic, lack-of-sleep-induced driving is to avoid it completely. But if this is not practical, one solution may be to ingest substances that are psychoactive and which might stimulate wakefulness. The most obvious example of such a substance is caffeine.

Reyner and Horne (2000) examined the effects of 200 mg of caffeine on the driving performance of individuals who had experienced significant sleep loss (no sleep during the night) or who had slept for only about five hours. The participants were collected at around 5.30 a.m. and were put in an immobile car which allowed them to make a simulated, computer-generated, dull, monotonous drive. The drivers were young and experienced and drove for two hours, from 6 to 8 a.m. Some participants received coffee with a 200 mg dose of caffeine, while others received no caffeine in their drink.

The caffeine significantly reduced the number of driving incidents (such as lane drifting) and subjective sleepiness in drivers who had experienced only five hours' sleep. For drivers deprived of all sleep, there were dramatic impairments on all measures and the experiment was abandoned after an hour. Even in these profoundly inattentive participants, caffeine reduced driving incidents in the first 30 minutes. The amount of caffeine they received was the equivalent of two to three cups (any more – five or more cups – would mean administering pharmacological amounts of caffeine). With most accidents occurring between 4 and 6 a.m. or mid-afternoon, a quick couple of coffees half an hour before setting off on a journey may help make drivers' behaviour safer. In separate experiments, Reyner and Horne (1998) found that two common interventions that drivers initiate when they feel sleepy – blowing cold air on the face or listening to the radio –

Table 9.3 The number of near misses and motor vehicle crashes in interns working extended (greater than 24 hours) and non-extended (less than 24 hours) shifts

	Extended work shift	Non-extended work shift
No. of crashes reported	58	73
No. of commutes	54,121	180,289
Rate (per 1,000 commutes)	1.07	0.40
Odds	2.3	1.0
No. of near misses reported	1,971	1,156
Rate (per 1,000 commutes)	36.42	6.41
Odds	5.9	1.0

Psychology in action – *Continued*

had only short-term effects on relieving sleepiness. However, combining caffeine intake with a nap improved driving performance and was associated with significantly less lane drifting (Horne and Reyner, 1996; Reyner and Horne, 1997).

A research group at the army and medical research centre in IMASSA in France found that healthy men who received 300 mg of slow-release caffeine at various points during 64 hours of uninterrupted wakefulness were more alert from the beginning of the experiment, compared with the placebo group. This vigilance was maintained to the end (Beaumont *et al.*, 2001). Alertness improved from the thirteenth hour, compared with the placebo group, and most tests of cognitive ability were better performed by the caffeine group in the early and middle stages of the experiment.

Gary Hart was convicted of death by dangerous driving after his car veered off a main road onto a railway line, and collided with a passenger train that subsequently collided with a coal train. The incident, which caused the deaths of 10 people, was found to be attributable to the fact that Hart had had only one brief nap in the previous 24 hours.
Source: © Corbis.

How long did these effects last and would they extend to the 'recovery' period after sleep deprivation? Would the person revert to normal fairly quickly regardless of whether they received caffeine or a placebo? The researchers measured EEG, sleepiness, sleep and cognitive function in the 42 hours of 'recovery' following the 64 hours of sleep deprivation in 16 healthy men who had received slow-release caffeine or a placebo (Beaumont *et al.*, 2005). In the two nights following deprivation, both groups showed a rebound of slow-wave sleep with the rebound of REM sleep seen during the second night. Cognitive function was similarly impaired in the placebo and caffeine groups on the first day of recovery and recovered – partially – to baseline levels on the second day.

Sleepiness does not 'just happen': it builds up and people try to fight it. People, however, may underestimate the point at which their sleepiness turns into actual sleep. Horne and Baulk (2004) examined the self-reported sleepiness, EEG and lane drifting of 38 sleep-restricted healthy adults who undertook a two-hour, monotonous simulated driving exercise in the afternoon. They found a strong, significant and positive correlation between subjective sleepiness and EEG changes indicative of sleepiness. Driving incidents followed reports/EEG indicators of sleepiness. When lane drifting occurred, the participants made a sharp corrective movement that momentarily increased arousal.

The results showed that the participants were aware of their sleepiness (and this correlated with predicted changes in EEG). Participants were asked to monitor their sleepiness, however, which may have drawn their attention more specifically to the way they felt. This suggests that drivers might be educated to reflect on the way they are feeling by prompting them to think about why they are opening windows, playing the radio loudly, etc.

The data reviewed here suggest that if a driver feels sleepy at the wheel, the first solution is to stop at a convenient place and take a nap. Coupling the nap with an intake of caffeine is an even better way of combating the potentially dangerous effects of sleepiness while driving. The practical consequences of this are clear: safer roads and, perhaps, a clearer head.

---

example, appear to be better consolidated after non-REM sleep or stage 2 sleep. Visual discrimination tasks are better remembered after slow-wave sleep and REM sleep (as evidenced by the findings that disrupting these sleep stages disrupts consolidation). The sleep after training appears to be resistant to the interference that you would expect to see during the delay between encoding and later retrieval. See Figures 9.13 and 9.14.

Slow-wave sleep (and lots of it) appears to be beneficial for remembering word pairs, remembering spatial locations and recognising words. REM sleep appears to be beneficial to non-declarative memory and emotional memory, i.e. those memory functions that rely less on encoding by the hippocampus. Studies of hippocampal function – navigation, for example – have found that after learning the navigation of a virtual town the hip-

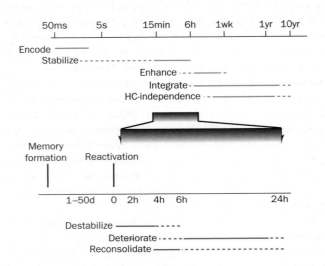

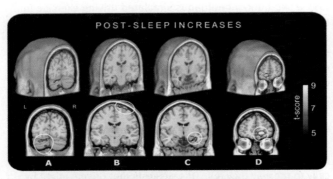

Figure 9.13 Time course of memory processes.

Source: Stickgold, R. and Walker, M. P. Sleep-dependent memory consolidation and reconsolidation. *Sleep Medicine* (2007), 8, 331–43, figure 2.

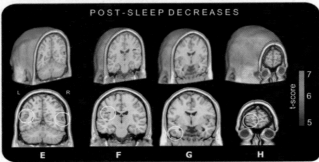

Figure 9.14 Sleep-dependent motor memory reorganisation in the human brain.

Source: Stickgold, R. and Walker, M. P. Sleep-dependent memory consolidation and reconsolidation. *Sleep Medicine* (2007), 8, 331–43, figure 2.

pocampus becomes active during slow-wave sleep. This activation correlates with memory performance the following day: the greater the activation, the greater the performance (Peigneux *et al.*, 2004). There is no evidence

that sleep helps you forget certain memories (Marshall and Born, 2007).

Dreaming

A person who is awakened during REM sleep and asked whether anything was happening will almost always report a dream. The typical REM sleep dream resembles a play or film – it has a narrative form. Conversely, reports of narrative, story-like dreams are rare among people awakened from slow-wave sleep. In general, mental activity during slow-wave sleep is more nearly static; it involves situations rather than stories and generally unpleasant ones. For example, a person awakened from slow-wave sleep might report a sensation of being crushed or suffocated. Unless the sleep is heavily drugged, almost everyone has four or five bouts of REM sleep each night, with accompanying dreams. Yet if the dreamer does not happen to awaken while the dream is in progress, it is lost for ever. Some people who claimed not to have had a dream for many years slept in a sleep laboratory and found that, in fact, they did dream. They were able to remember their dreams because the investigator awakened them during REM sleep.

The reports of people awakened from REM and slow-wave sleep clearly show that people are conscious during sleep, even though they may not remember any of their experiences then. Lack of memory for an event does not mean that it never happened; it only means that there is no permanent record accessible to conscious thought during wakefulness. Thus, we can say that slow-wave sleep and REM sleep reflect two different states of consciousness.

Functions of dreams

There are two major approaches to the study of dreaming: a psychological analysis of the contents of dreams, and psychobiological research on the nature and functions of REM sleep.

Symbolism in dreams

Since ancient times, people have regarded dreams as important, using them to prophesy the future, decide whether to go to war, or to determine the guilt or innocence of a person accused of a crime. In the last century, Sigmund Freud proposed a very influential theory about dreaming. He said that dreams arise out of inner conflicts between unconscious desires (primarily sexual ones) and prohibitions against acting out these desires, which we learn from society. According to Freud, although all dreams represent unfulfilled wishes, their contents are disguised and expressed symbolically. The latent content of the dream (from the Latin word for 'hidden') is transformed into the manifest content (the actual story-line or plot). Taken at face value, the manifest content is innocuous, but a knowledgeable psychoanalyst can supposedly recognise unconscious desires disguised as symbols in the dream. For example, climbing a set of stairs or shooting a gun might represent sexual intercourse. The problem with Freud's theory is that it is not disprovable; even if it is wrong, a psychoanalyst can always provide a plausible interpretation of a dream that reveals hidden conflicts disguised in obscure symbols.

Hall (1966), who agrees that symbols can be found in dreams, does not believe that they are usually hidden. For example, a person may plainly engage in sexual intercourse in one dream and have another dream that involves shooting a gun. Surely the 'real' meaning of shooting the gun need not be hidden from a dreamer who has undisguised dreams of sexual intercourse at other times or who has an uninhibited sex life during waking. Why should this person disguise sexual desires while dreaming? As Hall says, people use their own symbols, not those of anyone else. They represent what the dreamer thinks, and therefore, their meaning is usually not hidden from the dreamer.

Hobson (1988) proposed an explanation for dreaming that does not involve unconscious conflicts or desires. As we will see later, research using laboratory animals has shown that REM sleep occurs when a circuit of acetylcholine-secreting neurons in the pons becomes active, stimulating rapid eye movements, activation of the cerebral cortex and muscular paralysis. The activation of the visual system produces both eye movements and images. In fact, several

The song, 'Yesterday', apparently came to Paul McCartney in a dream. Waking up, he immediately beat out the melody on a piano. Originally titled 'Scrambled Eggs', it is now the most commercially successful song in history.

Source: Debra L. Rothenberg/Rex Features.

experiments have found that the particular eye movements that a person makes during a dream correspond reasonably well with the content of a dream; that is, the eye movements are those that one would expect a person to make if the imaginary events were really occurring (Dement, 1974). The images evoked by the cortical activation often incorporate memories of episodes that have occurred recently or of things that a person has been thinking about lately. Presumably, the circuits responsible for these memories are more excitable because they have recently been active. Hobson suggests that although the activation of these brain mechanisms produces fragmentary images, our brains try to tie these images together and make sense of them by creating a more-or-less plausible story.

We still do not know whether the particular topics we dream about are somehow related to the functions that dreams serve or whether the purposes of REM sleep are fulfilled by the physiological changes in the brain regardless of the plots of our dreams. Given that we do not know for sure why we dream, this uncertainty is not surprising.

Effects of REM sleep deprivation

As we saw, total sleep deprivation impairs people's ability to perform tasks that require them to be alert and vigilant, such as driving a car. What happens when only REM sleep is disrupted? People who are sleeping in a laboratory can be selectively deprived of REM sleep. An investigator awakens them whenever their polygraph records indicate that they have entered REM sleep. The investigator must also awaken control participants just as often at random intervals to eliminate any effects produced by being awakened several times.

When the person is no longer awakened during REM sleep, a rebound phenomenon is seen: the person engages in many more bouts of REM sleep than normal during the next night or two, as if catching up on something important that was missed.

Researchers have discovered that the effects of REM sleep deprivation are not very striking. In fact, medical journals contain reports of several patients who showed little or no REM sleep after sustaining damage to the brain stem (Lavie *et al.*, 1984; Gironell *et al.*, 1995). The lack of REM sleep did not appear to cause serious side effects. One of the patients, after receiving his injury, completed high school, attended law school and began practising law.

Several investigators have suggested that REM sleep may play a role in learning. For example, Greenberg and Pearlman (1974) suggest that REM sleep helps to integrate memories of events of the previous day – especially those dealing with emotionally related information – with existing memories. Crick and Mitchison (1983) suggest

Insomnia

Insomnia appears to affect around 10 per cent of the population, with the figure rising to 20 per cent in older adults (Ancoli-Israel, 2000). There is no single definition of insomnia that can apply to all people but a general definition is an inability to initiate or maintain sleep over at least three nights. The lack of sleep can create daytime distress and an impairment in social, work and physical functioning (Drake *et al.*, 2003; Irwin *et al.*, 2006). The amount of sleep that individuals require is quite variable, however. A short sleeper may feel fine with five hours of sleep; a long sleeper may still feel unrefreshed after ten hours. Insomnia, therefore, must be defined in relation to a person's particular sleep needs.

One study found that occupational stress, defined as the inability to stop worrying about work when not at work, was the most common predictor of poor sleep (Akerstedt *et al.*, 2002). Workers who anticipated having a bad next day showed less slow-wave sleep, an increase in the amount of stage 2 sleep, anxiety prior to sleeping and poorer quality of sleep than did those who did not anticipate having a challenging day (Kecklund and Akerstedt, 2006). Next-day apprehension was highly correlated with feelings of tension, nervousness, uneasiness and stress. The study leaves open the question of why the stress produces these changes. Is the group which is apprehensive about the next day habitually stressful or prone to feelings of anxiety, for example? Are they more vulnerable to stressors than are the non-apprehensive individuals?

Ironically, the most important cause of insomnia seems to be sleeping medication. Insomnia is not a disease that can be corrected with a medicine, in the way that diabetes can be treated with insulin. Insomnia is a symptom. If it is caused by pain or discomfort, the physical ailment that leads to the sleeplessness should be treated. If it is secondary to personal problems or psychological disorders, these problems should be dealt with directly. Patients who receive sleeping medications develop a tolerance to them and suffer rebound symptoms if they are withdrawn (Weitzman, 1981). That is, the drugs lose their effectiveness, so the patient requests larger doses from the physician. If a patient attempts to sleep without their accustomed medication or even takes a smaller dose one night, they are likely to experience a withdrawal effect: a severe disturbance of sleep. The patient becomes convinced that the insomnia is worse than before and turns to more medication for relief. This common syndrome is called drug dependency insomnia. Kales *et al.* (1979) found that withdrawal of some sleeping medications produced a rebound insomnia after the drugs were used for as few as three nights.

An alternative to pharmacology is psychology and a number of behavioural interventions – including cognitive behavioural therapy (CBT), described in more detail in Chapter 18 – have been found to be successful in improving sleep quality, lengthening the period of sleep and reducing the number of awakenings after sleep onset (Irwin *et al.*, 2006).

A common cause of insomnia, especially in older people, is **sleep apnoea** (apnoea means 'without breathing'): they cannot sleep and breathe at the same time. When they fall asleep, they stop breathing, the content of carbon dioxide in their blood builds up, and they awaken, gasping for air. After breathing deeply for a while, they go back to sleep and resume the cycle. Some people who suffer from sleep apnoea are blessed with a lack of memory for this periodic sleeping and awakening; others are aware of it and dread each night's sleep. Fortunately, some types of sleep apnoea in adults can be corrected by throat surgery.

Disorders associated with REM sleep

Two important characteristics of REM sleep are dreaming and paralysis. The paralysis results from a brain mechanism that prevents us from acting out our dreams. In fact, damage to specific regions of the pons of a cat's brain will produce just that result: the cat, obviously asleep, acts as if it were participating in a dream (Jouvet, 1972). It walks around stalking imaginary prey and responding defensively to imaginary predators.

This phenomenon can occur in humans, too. Several years ago, Schenck *et al.* (1986) reported the existence of an interesting syndrome: REM sleep behaviour disorder, the absence of the paralysis that normally occurs during REM sleep. Studies using laboratory animals have shown that the neural circuitry that controls the paralysis that accompanies REM sleep is located in the pons. In humans, **REM sleep behaviour disorder** seems to be produced by damage to this region (Culebras and Moore, 1989).

Dreams and muscular paralysis are fine when a person is lying in bed. But some people have periodic attacks of a sleep-related disorder called **cataplexy** (*kata-* 'down', *plessein* 'to strike'). They are struck down by paralysis while actively going about their business. They fall to the ground and lie there, paralysed but fully conscious. Attacks of cataplexy generally last less than a minute. The attacks are usually triggered by strong emotional states, such as anger, laughter or even lovemaking. People who have cataplectic attacks tend also to enter REM sleep as soon as they fall asleep, in contrast to the normal 90-minute interval.

Cataplexy is a biological disorder, probably involving inherited abnormalities in the brain. In fact, researchers have developed breeds of dogs that are subject to attacks of cataplexy so that they can study this disorder in the laboratory. As we saw, brain mechanisms responsible for

REM sleep are normally inhibited by serotonin-secreting neurons. Cataplexy can be treated by drugs that increase the activity of these neurons, thus increasing the inhibition.

Disorders associated with slow-wave sleep

Several phenomena occur during the deepest phase (stage 4) of slow-wave sleep. These events include sleepwalking, sleeptalking, night terrors and enuresis.

Sleepwalking can be as simple as getting out of bed and right back in again, or as complicated as walking out of a house and climbing into a car (sleepwalkers, apparently, do not try to drive). We know that sleepwalking is not the acting out of a dream because it occurs during stage 4 of slow-wave sleep, when the EEG shows high-amplitude slow waves and the person's mental state generally involves a static situation, not a narrative. Sleepwalkers are difficult to awaken; once awakened, they are often confused and disoriented. However, contrary to popular belief, it is perfectly safe to wake them up.

Sleepwalking seems to run in families; Dement (1974) reported a family whose grown members were reunited for a holiday celebration. In the middle of the night they awoke to find that they had all gathered in the living room – during their sleep.

Sleeptalking sometimes occurs as part of a REM sleep dream, but it more usually occurs during other stages of sleep. Often, one can carry on a conversation with the sleeptalker, indicating that the person is very near the boundary between sleep and waking. During this state, sleeptalkers are sometimes very suggestible. So-called truth serums are used in an attempt to duplicate this condition, so that the person being questioned is not on guard against giving away secrets and is not functioning well enough to tell elaborate lies. Unfortunately for the interrogators, there are no foolproof, reliable truth serums.

Night terrors, like sleepwalking, occur most often in children. In this disorder, the child awakes, screaming with terror. When questioned, the child does not report a dream and often seems confused. Usually, the child falls asleep quickly without showing any after-effects and seldom remembers the event the next day. Night terrors are not the same as nightmares, which are simply frightening dreams from which one happens to awaken. Apparently, night terrors are caused by sudden awakenings from the depths of stage 4 sleep. The sudden, dramatic change in consciousness is a frightening experience for the child. The treatment for night terrors, like that for sleepwalking, is no treatment at all.

The final disorder of slow-wave sleep, **enuresis**, or bed-wetting, is fairly common in young children. Most children outgrow it, just as they outgrow sleepwalking or night terrors. Emotional problems can trigger enuresis, but bed-wetting does not itself indicate that a child is psychologically unwell. The problem with enuresis is that, unlike the other stage 4 phenomena, there are after-effects that must be cleaned up. Parents dislike having their sleep disturbed and get tired of frequently changing and laundering sheets. The resulting tension in family relationships can make the child feel anxious and guilty and can thus unnecessarily prolong the disorder.

Fortunately, a simple training method often cures enuresis. A moisture-sensitive device is placed under the bed sheet; when it gets wet, it causes a bell to ring. Because a child releases only a few drops of urine before the bladder begins to empty in earnest, the bell wakes the child in time to run to the bathroom. In about a week, most children learn to prevent their bladders from emptying and manage to wait until morning. Perhaps what they really learn is not to enter such a deep level of stage 4 sleep in which the mechanism that keeps the bladder from emptying seems to break down.

Chapter review

The nature of consciousness

- Consciousness refers to our awareness of our own perceptions, thoughts and feelings and our experience of these.
- Some psychologists and philosophers regard consciousness as a by-product of cognitive processing and believe it is outside the scope of scientific study because of its subjective nature.
- Several theories seek to explain the nature of consciousness. These fall mainly into two camps: the neurobiological and the cognitive.
- The neurobiological explanations (such as those of Crick and Penrose) suggest that consciousness occurs when cell assemblies behave together or is generated by specific parts of a neuron.

- Perceptual disorders (such as blindsight and visual agnosia) and other deficits following brain injury (such as those seen after the split-brain operation) help demonstrate the importance of various brain regions to conscious awareness.

Attention

- The process of selective attention determines which stimuli will be noticed and which will be ignored. The factors that control our attention include novelty, verbal instructions and our own assessment of the significance of what we are perceiving.
- The cocktail-party phenomenon is an example of selective attention: we are able to detect relevant information in an environment that contains irrelevant and relevant information.

- Noise (such as office noise and speech) in the working environment can significantly impair memory for prose and arithmetic performance; the longer the duration of the noise, the greater the deficit.
- Dichotic listening experiments show that what is received by the unattended ear is lost within a few seconds unless something causes us to take heed of it; after those few seconds we cannot say what that ear heard. Even unattended information can produce implicit (as opposed to explicit) memories, however.
- Techniques of meditation have been used since the beginning of history and include methods for increasing or decreasing attention to the external world. In meditative techniques, a person pays strict attention to a simple stimulus such as a visual pattern, a word or a monotonous, repetitive movement.
- Studies of the effects of mobile phone use on attention have demonstrated that engagement in conversation impairs attention and driving performance, regardless of whether the phone is hand-held or hands-free. Listening to the radio does not produce these impairments.

Hypnosis

- Hypnosis is a form of verbal control over a person's consciousness in which the hypnotist's suggestions affect some of the person's perceptions and behaviours.
- State theorists argue that consciousness during hypnosis is a mysterious, trance-like state. Non-state theorists argue that it can be explained by psychological factors such as compliance, role-enactment, imagination and willingness to please. Evidence suggests invoking the concepts of trance or altered states of consciousness is unnecessary.
- Barber asserts that being hypnotised is similar to participating vicariously in a narrative, which is something we do whenever we become engrossed in a novel, a film, a drama or even the recounting of a friend's experience. When we are engrossed in this way, we experience genuine feelings of emotion, even though the situation is not 'real'.
- Although individuals under hypnosis appear to perform extraordinary, unusual or antisocial acts, non-hypnotic suggestion can result in the same behaviours being induced. People who would not normally perform antisocial or distasteful acts may do so because they (correctly) assume that the experimenter is responsible for what they do.
- Hypnosis has been shown to be useful in reducing pain, eliminating bad habits, reducing stress and helping people talk about painful thoughts and memories.
- The reasons for the efficacy of hypnotic analgesia have included highly hypnotisable participants' ability to partition attention and the role of the anterior brain regions in allocating attentional resources.

Sleep

- Sleep consists of several stages of slow-wave sleep, characterised by increasing amounts of delta activity in the EEG, and REM sleep. REM sleep is characterised by beta activity in the EEG, rapid eye movements, general paralysis (with twitching movements of the hands and feet), and dreaming.
- Sleep is a behaviour, not simply an altered state of consciousness.
- Although evidence suggests that sleep is not necessary for repairing the wear and tear caused by physical exercise, it may play an important role in providing an opportunity for the brain to rest.
- The consequences of sleep deprivation include fatigue, psychomotor and cognitive impairment and lack of vigilance.
- Although narrative dreams occur only during REM sleep, people often are conscious of static situations during slow-wave sleep. Freud suggested that dreams provided the opportunity for unconscious conflicts to express themselves through symbolism in dreams.
- Hobson suggested that dreams are the attempts of the brain to make sense of hallucinations produced by the activation of the cerebral cortex.
- The function of REM sleep in adults is uncertain, but it may be involved somehow in learning.
- Foetuses and infants engage in much more REM sleep than adults do, which suggests that REM sleep may play a role in brain development. Some experimental research supports this suggestion.
- The brain contains two biological clocks. One, located in the suprachiasmatic nucleus of the hypothalamus, controls circadian (daily) rhythms. This clock is reset when light strikes the retina in the morning. The second clock, located in the pons, controls the basic rest–activity cycle, which manifests itself in changes in activity during the day and alternating periods of slow-wave sleep and REM sleep during the night. A circuit of acetylcholine-secreting neurons in the pons, normally inhibited by serotonin-secreting neurons, turns on REM sleep. Slow-wave sleep is controlled by neurons in the preoptic area.
- Insomnia appears to be a symptom of a variety of physical and emotional disorders, not a disease. Although it is often treated by sleep medications, these drugs cause more sleep problems than they cure.
- Two neurological disorders involve mechanisms of REM sleep. REM sleep behaviour disorder occurs when brain damage prevents the paralysis that normally keeps us from acting out our dreams. Cataplectic attacks are just the opposite. They are caused by activation at inappropriate times of the mechanism that causes paralysis during REM sleep. Drugs that stimulate serotonin-secreting neurons are useful in treating cataplexy.
- The disorders of slow-wave sleep include sleepwalking, sleeptalking and night terrors.
- Sleepwalking and night terrors are primarily disorders of childhood. Sleeptalking is generally harmless so it probably should not even be considered a disorder.

Suggestions for further reading

Consciousness – general reading

Blackmore, S. (2003) *Consciousness: An introduction*. London: HodderArnold.

Blackmore, S. (2005) *Conversations on Consciousness: Interviews with twenty minds*. Oxford: Oxford University Press.

Hobson, J.A. (1999) *Consciousness*. New York: Scientific American Library.

Koch, C. (2005) The movie in your head. *Scientific American Mind*, 16, 3, 58–63.

Pickering, J. and Skinner, M. (1990) *From Sentience to Symbols: Readings on consciousness*. Hemel Hempstead: Harvester Wheatsheaf.

Rose, D. (2006) *Consciousness*. Oxford: Oxford University Press.

Consciousness is now well served by texts covering every aspect of its nature.

Attention

Engel, A.K., Debener, S. and Kranczioch, C. (2006) Coming to attention. *Scientific American Mind*, 17, 4, 46–53.

Logan, G.D. (2004) Cumulative progress in formal theories of attention. *Annual Review of Psychology*, 55, 207–34.

Marois, R. and Ivanoff, J. (2005) Capacity limits of information processing in the brain. *Trends in Cognitive Sciences*, 9, 6, 296–305.

Posner, M.I. and Rothbart, M.K. (2007) Research on attention networks as a model for the integration of psychological science. *Annual Review of Psychology*, 58, 1–23.

Styles, E.A. (2006) *The Psychology of Attention* (2nd edn). Hove: Psychology Press.

Several good items on attention and selective attention.

Biological basis of consciousness

Baars, B.J. (2001) How could brain imaging NOT tell us about consciousness? *Journal of Consciousness*, 8, 3, 24–29.

Revonsuo, A. (2001) Can functional brain imaging discover consciousness in the brain? *Journal of Consciousness*, 8, 3, 3–23.

Vaitl, D., Gruzelier, J., Jamieson, G.A., Lehmann, D., Ott, U., Sammer, G., Strehl, U., Birbaumber, N., Kotchoubey, B., Kubler, A., Miltner, W.H., Putz, P., Strauch, I., Wackermann, J. and Weiss, T. (2005) Psychobiology of altered states of consciousness. *Psychological Bulletin*, 131, 1, 98–127.

Special issue of Cortex, 2005, 41, 5.

A collection of good papers on the neural correlates of consciousness.

Hypnosis

Nash, M.R. and Benham, G. (2005) The truth and hype of hypnosis. *Scientific American Mind*, 16, 2, 46–53.

Wagstaff, G.F. (1996) Methodological issues in hypnosis. In J. Haworth (ed.) *Psychological Research*. London: Routledge.

There are few well-researched, scientific books, chapters or papers on the nature of hypnosis, perhaps reflecting scientists' general scepticism. Graham Wagstaff is a psychologist who has examined hypnosis from a scientific perspective and summarises what we know and do not know about the psychological processes involved in hypnosis in this very accessible chapter. The Scientific American Mind article does the same.

Sleep

Horne, J. (2007) *Sleepfaring*. Oxford: Oxford University Press.

Marshall, L. and Born, J. (2007). The contribution of sleep to hippocampus-dependent memory consolidation. *Trends in Cognitive Sciences*, 11, 10, 442–50.

Martin, P. (2003) *Counting Sheep: The science and pleasures of sleep and dreams*. London: Flamingo.

Stickgold, R. and Ellenbogen, J.M. (2008) Quiet! Sleeping brain at work. *Scientific American Mind*, August/September, 22–9.

These books and articles provide a good review of the activity which most of us spend one-third of our lives doing.

Journals to consult

Cognition and Consciousness

Imagination, Cognition and Personality

International Journal of Experimental and Clinical Hypnosis

Journal of Consciousness Studies

Journal of Experimental Psychology: Human perception

Philosophical Psychology

Psyche (**http://psyche.cs.monash.edu.au/**)

Sleep Medicine

Trends in Cognitive Sciences

Website addresses

http://www.psychology.org/links/Environment_Behavior_Relationships/Consciousness/
An excellent site featuring links to psychology of consciousness sites.

http://www.imprint.co.uk/jcs.html
This is a link to the Journal of Consciousness Studies. You can look at the journal's table of contents, abstracts of articles and the full text of some articles.

http://psyche.cs.monash.edu.au/index.html
This is a link to the online consciousness journal Psyche.

http://www.newscientist.com/nsplus/insight/big3/conscious/day1a.html
A link to a series of the magazine New Scientist's articles on consciousness.

http://www.perceptionweb.com/perc0999/simons.html
You can see shots of Simons's inattentional blindness experiment here

Language

CHAPTER 10

'Dyslex? You're making it up!'

A Labour MP has claimed dyslexia is a 'fictional malady' invented by the 'education establishment' to cover up bad teaching of reading and writing.

In an article for Manchester Confidential, Graham Stringer wrote: 'The education establishment, rather than admit that their eclectic and incomplete methods for instruction are at fault, have invented a brain disorder called dyslexia.'

The MP for Manchester Blackley said the dyslexia 'industry' should be 'killed off' through the 'magic bullet' of teaching children to read and write by using a phonetic system of sounding letters and words.

Mr Stringer said the disability had been eradicated in West Dunbartonshire where the council has eliminated illiteracy through a special programme.

'If dyslexia really existed then countries as diverse as Nicaragua and South Korea would not have been able to achieve literacy rates of nearly 100%. There can be no rational reason why this 'brain disorder' is of epidemic proportions in Britain but does not appear in South Korea or Nicaragua.'

But the British Dyslexia Association (BDA) says Mr Stringer 'misunderstands' the condition.

In a statement, they said: 'Mr Stringer assumes that literacy will solve the issue of dyslexia, however although many dyslexics have acquired the skills of reading, there is not doubt that they still remain dyslexic.

'It is concerning that an MP does not recognise dyslexia, which affects 10% of his constituents, even though his Government has taken steps to make sure dyslexic children and young people with dyslexia are recognised and supported.'

Source: http://video.news.sky.com/skynews/Home/Politics/Graham-Stringer-Labour-MP-Claims-Dyslexia-Is-A-Myth-Invented-To-Cover-Up-Bad-Teaching/Article/200901215203083, 14 January, 2009.

WHAT YOU SHOULD BE ABLE TO DO AFTER READING CHAPTER 10

- Define psycholinguistics and describe the nature of spoken language.

- Describe and explain various models of reading.

- Describe various language disorders including the aphasias, the acquired dyslexias and developmental dyslexia and indicate what these tell us about normal language processing.

- Identify the neural mechanisms which might underlie different aspects of language such as speech perception, reading and speech comprehension.

QUESTIONS TO THINK ABOUT

- What is language?

- Why have humans evolved language?

- Can other primates learn language? Would this language approximate our own?

- What is the role of sound in understanding written and spoken language?

- What stages does language development go through?

- How do people learn to read? What is the best way of doing this?

- How do people learn to recognise words?

- What causes dyslexia?

- What are the effects of brain injury on reading, writing and speaking?

- Do all humans have the same central mechanism for producing language regardless of which language they speak?

- How are we able to comprehend language?

Explore the accompanying videos, simulations, and animations on MyPsychLab. This chapter includes activities on: Morphemes • Dyslexia detector • The Wernicke-Geschwind model of language • Handedness • Check your understanding and prepare for your exams using the multiple choice, short answer and essay practice tests also available.

The use of language

Communication is probably one of the most important of all human behaviours. Our use of language can be private – we can think to ourselves in words or write diaries that are meant to be seen by no one but ourselves – but language evolved through social contacts among our early ancestors. Speaking and writing are clearly social behaviours: we learn these skills from other people and use them to communicate with them. An effective language system also abides by certain rules.

Although an exact definition is difficult to pin down (Harley, 2008), language can be characterised as a system of visual and/or vocal symbols which have meaning to the user and to the recipient. There are thought to be around 6,000 distinct languages in the world. The world's largest language is Chinese – it has more native speakers than any other – followed by English, Hindi/Urdu, Spanish and Arabic, as parts of Figure 10.1 and Table 10.1 show. The most popular foreign language is English (Montgomery, 2004) and Figure 10.2 shows the proportion of the population of selected European Union states which speak English (UK excluded).

We can use language to speak, write and read and we can also use it to remember and to think. Language also enables us to consider complex and abstract issues by encoding them in words and then manipulating the words according to specific rules. These rules are the subject of an area of study called linguistics.

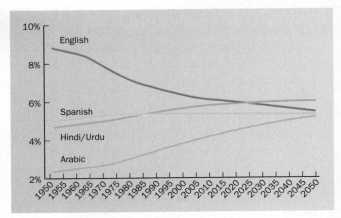

Figure 10.1 The projected survival and strength of the world's most successful languages.

Source: Reprinted with permission from 'The future of language' (Graddol, D.), *Science*, 303, 27 Feb., p. 1329. Copyright (2004) AAAS. Reprinted with permission from AAAS.

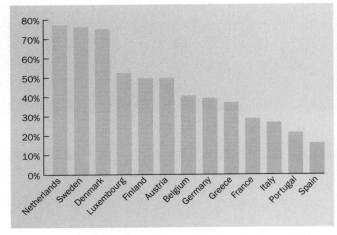

Figure 10.2 The percentage of the population of selected EU countries which speak English.

Source: Reprinted with permission from 'The future of language' (Graddol, D.), *Science*, 303, 27 Feb., p. 1330. Copyright (2004) AAAS. Reprinted with permission from AAAS.

Table 10.1 Estimates of native speakers of the most popular languages in the world (in 1995)

	Language	No. of speakers (millions)
1	Chinese	1113
2	English	372
3	Hindi/Urdu	316
4	Spanish	304
5	Arabic	201
6	Portugese	165
7	Russian	155
8	Bengali	125
9	Japanese	123
10	German	102

Psycholinguistics: the study of language acquisition and meaning

see activity on mypsychlab

The study of **linguistics** involves determining the 'rules' of language and the nature and meaning of written and spoken language. In contrast, **psycholinguistics**, a branch of psychology devoted to the study of verbal behaviour, examines the role of human cognition in language acquisition and comprehension: it is the integration of psychology and linguistics.

Psycholinguists are interested in how we acquire language – how verbal behaviour develops – and how we learn to speak from our interactions with others. In short, they are interested in the interaction between the structure and processing of language.

Psycholinguistics is a relatively recent, distinct branch of psychology although psychologists have studied language since the discipline's early experimental days. Wundt, for example, regarded as the father of psycholinguistics, argued that the sentence was the most basic element of speech production and comprehension. Speech production involved the transformation of thought process into sequences of speech segments; comprehension, on the other hand, was the reverse process. Wundt's view was not universally accepted. The linguist Hermann Paul, for example, argued that words, not sentences, were the building blocks of speech.

This essentially European debate became somewhat sterile during the 1920s and 1930s when the form of psychology championed by Wundt was usurped by behaviourism which, as you saw in Chapter 1, argued that psychology should concern itself only with observable behaviour. It was not until the 1950s that psychology began to take a renewed interest in the nature of language and, ironically, this interest was spurred by a linguist, Noam Chomsky. Chomsky's views of the nature of language are discussed later on in the chapter. This chapter reviews studies from psycholinguistics and cognitive psychology and introduces you to current understanding of the ways in which we produce and comprehend speech.

Perception of speech

Speech involves the production of a series of sounds in a continuous stream, punctuated by pauses and modulated by stress and changes in pitch. Sentences are written as sets of words, with spaces between them. Speech, however, is a more flexible means of communication than is writing. The sentences we utter are a string of sounds, some of which are emphasised (stressed), some are quickly glided over. We can raise the pitch of our voice when uttering some words and lower it when speaking others. We maintain a regular rhythmic pattern of stress. We pause at appropriate times, for example between phrases, but we do not pause after pronouncing each word. Thus, speech does not come to us as a series of individual words; we must extract the words from a stream of speech.

Recognition of speech sounds

The human auditory system is responsible for performing the complex task of enabling us to recognise speech sounds. The sound system of speech is called phonology.

These sounds vary according to the sounds that precede and follow them, the speaker's accent, and the stress placed on the syllables in which they occur. **Phonemes** are the elements of speech – the smallest units of sound that contribute to the meaning of a word. For example, the word 'pin' consists of three phonemes: /p/ + /i/ + /n/. It is important to note that phonemes are not the same as letters. The word 'ship', for example, has four letters but three phonemes: /sh/ + /i/ + /p/. Note that in linguistics phonemes are flanked by two forward-slanting lines to indicate that they are phonemes and not letters. The first step in recognising speech sounds, therefore, is the identification of phonemes.

Production of speech

The production of speech is the result of a coordinated set of muscles found in the face, mouth and throat. Those responsible for producing some common words are illustrated in Figure 10.3.

One detectable and distinctive phonetic feature is **voice onset time**, the delay between the initial sound of a voiced consonant and the onset of vibration of the vocal cords. Voicing refers to the vibration of the vocal cords. The distinction between voiced and unvoiced consonants allows us to distinguish between /p/ (unvoiced) and /b/ (voiced), between /k/ (unvoiced) and /g/ (voiced), and between /t/ (unvoiced) and /d/ (voiced).

For example, although the difference between uttering 'pa' and 'ba' are subtle, they are discernible. Uttering 'pa' involves building up pressure in the mouth. When the lips are opened, a puff of air comes out. The 'ah' sound does not occur immediately, because the air pressure in the mouth and throat keeps air from leaving the lungs for a brief time. The vocal cords do not vibrate until air from the lungs passes through them. Uttering 'ba', however, does not involve the initial build-up of pressure. The vocal cords begin vibrating as soon as the lips open. The delay in voicing that occurs when uttering 'pa' is slight, only 0.06 seconds.

An experiment by Lisker and Abramson (1970) illustrates this point. They presented participants with a series of computer-generated sounds consisting of a puff followed by an 'ah'. The sounds varied only in one way: the amount of time between the puff and the 'ah'. When we speak, we make a puff for 'pa' but not for 'ba'. However, even though the computer always produced a puff, participants reported that they heard 'ba' when the delay was short and 'pa' when it was long. Participants discriminated between the phonemes /p/ and /b/ strictly according to the delay in voicing. The experiment demonstrates that the auditory system is capable of detecting very subtle differences.

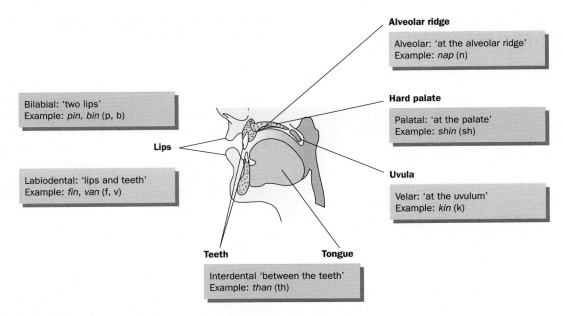

Figure 10.3 The areas in the vocal tract where production of consonants takes place.

Source: Payne, D.G. and Wenger, M.J, *Cognitive Psychology*. New York: Houghton Mifflin, 1998. Copyright © 1998 by Houghton Mifflin Company.

Although the fundamental unit of speech, logically and descriptively, is the phoneme, research suggests that psychologically the fundamental unit is larger. For example, the two syllables 'doo' and 'dee' each consist of two phonemes. When spoken, the same phoneme, /d/, is heard at the beginning. However, when Liberman *et al.* (1967) analysed the sounds of the syllables, they found that the beginning phonemes were not the same. In fact, they could not cut out a section of a tape recording of the two syllables that would sound like /d/.

These results suggest that the fundamental unit of speech consists of groups of phonemes, such as syllables. The perception of a phoneme is affected by the sounds that follow it (Ganong, 1980). Using a computer to synthesise a novel sound that fell between those of the phonemes /g/ and /k/, Ganong reported that when the sound was followed by 'ift', the participants heard the word 'gift', but when it was followed by 'iss', they heard 'kiss'. These results suggest that we recognise speech sounds in pieces larger than individual phonemes.

Errors in speech production

As you will see later in this chapter, some individuals with damage to a specific part of the brain have an inability to produce speech or will produce meaningless speech. Speech errors or slips of the tongue, however, are not confined to the brain-damaged (Fromkin, 1988; Dell *et al.*, 1997) and some of these will be very familiar to you. Table 10.2 lists some of the common speech production errors made by normal individuals.

One obvious error is where the beginnings of words are transposed. So, for example, instead of saying 'dear old queen', you might say 'queer old dean'. This is an example of a Spoonerism, named after the Oxford don William A. Spooner who was noted for making such mistakes as saying 'noble tons of soil' instead of 'noble sons of toil'.

Speech errors are interesting because although they are errors they still follow the rules of grammar. For example, one might confuse nouns in a sentence ('would you pass me that cupboard from the pepper') but you would not confuse a noun with a verb ('would you cupboard the pass from the pepper'). Errors thus reflect what we had intended to say rather than what we want to say (Levelt, 1989). Somehow, an error occurs between conception and execution.

When President Kennedy addressed his German audience with the inclusive pronouncement, *'Ich bin ein Berliner'*, what he actually said (to a Germanic ear) was – 'I am a cream pastry'. It is easy to see why we make such mistakes in languages which are unfamiliar, but why do you think that we make slips of the tongue in our native language?

Recognition of words: the importance of context

The perception of continuous speech involves different mechanisms from those used in the perception of isolated syllables. Because speech is full of hesitations, muffled sounds and sloppy pronunciations, many individual words can be hard to recognise out of context. For example, when Pollack and Pickett (1964) isolated individual words from a recording of normal con-

Table 10.2 Some common speech errors

1 Errors at phonemic segments
Consonant anticipation: a reading list/a leading list
Consonant deletion: speech error/peach error
Vowel exchange: fill the pool/fool the pill

2 Errors at phonetic features
Voicing reversal: big and fat/pig and vat
Nasality reversal: cedars of Lebanon/cedars of Lemadon

3 Errors at syllables
Syllable delection: unanimity of opinion/unamity of opinion
Syllable reversal: Stockwell and Schacter/Schachwell and Stockter

4 Errors of stress (with the stressed syllable given in capital leters)
apples of the Origin/apples of the oRigin
eCONomists: ecoNOMists, I mean, eCONomists

5 Errors of word selection
Word exchange: tend to turn out/turn to tend out
Word movement: I really musy go/I must really go

6 Errors at morphemes
Inflection morpheme error: cow tracks/tracks cows
Derivational morpheme error: easily enough/easy enough

7 Errors at phrases
A hummingbird was attracted by the red colour of the feeder/the red colour was attracted by a hummingbird of the feeder
My sister went to the Grand Canyon/the Grand Canyon went to my sister

8 Semantic and phonological word errors
Semantic substitution: too many irons in the fire/too many irons in the smoke
Phonological substitution: white Anglo-Saxon Protestant/white Anglo-Saxon Prostitute

9 Errors at morphologically complex words
Lexical selection error: it spread like wild fire/it spread like wild flower
Exchange error: ministers in our church/churches in our minister

Source: Adapted from Fromkin, V.A. Speech production, in J. Berko Gleason and N.B. Ratner (eds) *Psycholinguistics*. Fort Worth: Holt, Rinehart & Winston (Wadsworth 1997 edition).

versations and played them back to other people, those people correctly identified the words only 47 per cent of the time. When they presented the same words in the context of the original conversation, the participants identified and understood almost 100 per cent of them.

Understanding the meaning of speech

The meaning of a sentence (or of a group of connected sentences that are telling a story) is conveyed by the words that are chosen, the order in which they are combined, the affixes that are attached to the beginnings or ends of the words, the pattern of rhythm and emphasis of the speaker, and knowledge about the world shared by the speaker and the listener.

Syntax

The understanding of speech entails following the 'rules' of language. Words must be familiar and combined in specific ways. For example, the sentence, 'The two boys looked at the heavy box' is comprehensible; but the sentence, 'Boys the two looking heavily the box at' is not. Only the first sentence follows the rules of English grammar.

All languages have a **syntax**, or grammar, which is a set of rules governing the ways in which words are used to form sentences. They all follow certain principles, which linguists call syntactical rules, for combining words to form phrases, clauses, or sentences (syntax, like synthesis, comes from the Greek *syntassein*, 'to put together'). Our understanding of syntax is automatic although learned. We are no more conscious of this process, for example, than a child is conscious of the laws of physics when he or she learns to ride a bicycle.

The automatic nature of syntactical analysis can be illustrated by experiments performed with artificial grammars. For example, Reber and Allen (1978) devised a set of (complex) rules for combining the letters M, V, R, T and X. For example, MRTXV and VXTTV were 'grammatical', but MXVTR and VMRTX were 'ungrammatical'. They asked participants to look at 20 'grammatical' strings of letters, printed on index cards. The participants were told to 'pay the utmost attention to the letter strings' but were not instructed to do anything else. Later, the participants were presented with 50 different strings of letters, half of which were 'grammatical' and half of which were not. Some of the 'grammatical' strings were ones they had already seen, and some were new to them. The participants were asked to indicate whether the strings were 'grammatical'.

Although the participants did quite well – they correctly identified 81 per cent of the strings of letters – they could not express the rules verbally. The participants made statements like: 'The shapes of the items began to make sense.' 'Almost all my decisions are based on things looking either very right or very wrong. Sometimes for some reason things came out and glared at me saying, 'bad, bad, bad', other times the letters just flowed together and I knew it was an OK item.'

This finding and others like it suggests that syntactic rules are learned implicitly (or not at all). Knowlton *et al.* (1991) found that patients with anterograde amnesia were able to learn an artificial grammar even though they had lost the ability to form explicit memories. In contrast, as Gabrieli *et al.* (1988) observed, such patients are unable to learn the meanings of new words. Thus, learning syntax and word meaning appears to involve different types of memory and, consequently, different brain mechanisms.

Word order

Word order is important in English. In the sentences 'The boy hit the ball' and 'The ball hit the boy', word order tells us who does what to whom. In English, the first noun of the sentence is the subject, the second noun is the object and the part in between is usually the verb. This structure is referred to as S–V–O word order (for subject–verb–object) and around 75 per cent of the world's languages possess this sentence structure (Bernstein and Berko, 1993). Other languages, however, have different orders. Japanese, for example, uses the S–O–V order and both Welsh and Arabic use V–S–O. The assignation of words into meaningful categories (such as noun, verb, adjective and so on) is called parsing, and parsing involves being able to identify word classes.

Word class

Word class refers to the grammatical categories such as noun, pronoun, verb and adjective, and words can be classified as function words or content words. Function words include determiners, quantifiers, prepositions and words in similar categories: 'a', 'the', 'to', 'some', 'and', 'but', 'when', and so on. Content words include nouns, verbs and most adjectives and adverbs: 'apple', 'rug', 'went', 'caught', 'heavy', 'mysterious', 'thoroughly', 'sadly'. Content words express meaning; function words express the relations between content words and thus are very important syntactical cues.

Affixes

Affixes are sounds that we add to the beginning (prefixes) or end (suffixes) of words to alter their grammatical function. For example, we add the suffix '-ed' to the end of a regular verb to indicate the past tense (drop/dropped); we add '-ing' to a verb to indicate its use as a noun (sing/singing as in 'we heard the choir sing' and 'the choir's singing was delightful'); and we add '-ly' to an adjective to indicate its use as an adverb (bright/brightly). We are quick to recognise the syntactical function of words with affixes like these. For example, Epstein (1961) presented people with word strings such as the following:

> a vap koob desak the citar molent um glox nerf
>
> A vapy koob desaked the citar molently um glox nerfs

The people could more easily remember the second string than the first, even though letters had been added to some of the words. Apparently, the addition of the affixes 'y', '-ed' and '-ly' made the words seem more like a sentence and they thus became easier to categorise and recall.

Semantics

The meaning of a word – its **semantics** – provides important cues to the syntax of a sentence (semantics comes from the Greek *sema*, 'sign'). For example, consider the following set of words: 'Frank discovered a flea combing his beard'. The syntax of this sentence is ambiguous. It does not tell us whether Frank was combing Frank's beard, the flea was combing the flea's beard, or the flea was combing Frank's beard. But our knowledge of the world and of the usual meanings of words tells us that Frank was doing the combing, because people, not fleas, have beards and combs.

Function words and content words

Function words (such as 'the', 'and', 'some') help us determine the syntax of a sentence; **content words** help us determine its meaning. For example, even with its function words removed the following set of words still makes pretty good sense: 'man placed wooden ladder tree climbed picked apples'. You can probably fill in the function words yourself and get 'The man placed the wooden ladder against the tree, climbed it, and picked some apples.'

Prosody

Prosody is a syntactic cue which refers to the use of stress, rhythm and changes in pitch that accompany speech. Prosody can emphasise the syntax of a word or group of words or even serve as the primary source of syntactic information. For example, in several languages (including English), a declarative sentence can be turned into a question by means of prosody. Read the following sentences aloud to see how you would indicate to a listener which is a statement and which is a question.

> You said that.
>
> You said that?

We do this by intonation. In written communication, prosody is emphasised by punctuation marks. For example, a comma indicates a short pause, a full stop indicates a longer one along with a fall in the pitch of voice, and a question mark indicates an upturn in the pitch of voice near the end of the sentence. These devices serve as only partial substitutes for the real thing. Because writers cannot rely on the cues provided by prosody, they must be especially careful to see that the syntax of their sentences is conveyed by other cues: word order, word class, function words, affixes and word meaning.

The relationship between semantics and syntax

Sentences can be read or heard semantically in more than one way. Noam Chomsky (1957, 1965), the noted linguist, suggested that language can partly be explained by reference to sentence grammar. Although Chomsky's ideas underwent several revisions, the 1965 version of his theory suggests that there are three grammars. The first – generative grammar – represents the rules by which a speaker's ideas can be transformed into a final grammatical form. These transformed ideas or thoughts are called deep structures (the second grammar). The final output is the surface grammar or structure which is the end spoken product.

The deep structure represents the kernel of what the person intended to say. In order to utter a sentence, the brain must transform the deep structure into the appropriate surface structure: the particular form the sentence takes.

Most psychologists agree that the distinction between surface structure and deep structure is important (Tanenhaus, 1988; Bohannon, 1993; Hulit and Howard, 1993). Individuals with a language disorder known as conduction aphasia have difficulty repeating words and phrases, but they can understand them. The deep structure of other people's speech appears to be retained, but not its surface structure.

Knowledge of the world

Comprehension of speech also involves knowledge about the world and the particular situations encountered in it (Carpenter *et al.*, 1995). Schank and Abelson (1977) suggested that this knowledge is organised into scripts, which specify various kinds of events and interactions that people have witnessed or have learned about from others. Once a speaker has established which script is being referred to, the listener can fill in the details. For example, in order to understand what the speaker means in the following sentences:

> I learned a lot about the clubs in town yesterday. Do you have an aspirin?

we must be able to do more than simply understand the words and analyse the sentence structure (Hunt, 1985). We must know something about clubs; for example, that they serve alcohol and that 'learning about them' probably involves some drinking. We must also realise that imbibing these drinks can lead to a headache and that aspirin is a remedy for headaches. Hunt notes that when we describe an event to someone else, not all the details are spelled out. For example:

> Alison was hungry and so she went to a restaurant and ordered a pizza. When she had finished, she discovered that she had forgotten to take her purse with her. She was embarrassed.

In this story we need to understand that after eating in a restaurant, you are expected to pay.

What is meaning?

Words refer to objects, actions, or relations in the world. Thus, the meaning of a word (its semantics) is defined by particular memories associated with it. For example, knowing the meaning of the word 'tree' means being able to imagine the physical characteristics of trees: what they look like, what the wind sounds like blowing through their leaves, what the bark feels like, and so on. It also means knowing facts about trees: about their roots, buds, flowers, nuts, wood and the chlorophyll in their leaves. These memories are not stored in the primary speech areas but in other parts of the brain, especially regions of the association cortex. Different categories of memories may be stored in particular regions of the brain, but they are linked, so that hearing the word 'tree' activates all of them.

To hear a familiar word and understand its meaning involves first recognising the sequence of sounds that constitute the word. We must, therefore, have some form of memory store which contains the auditory representations of words. This store forms part of our auditory word recognition system. When we find the auditory entry for the word in our **mental lexicon** (lexicon means 'dictionary'), we must be able to access semantic information about this word. The region of the brain responsible for the auditory comprehension of words must somehow communicate with another region (or regions) which allows us to ascribe meaning to what we have just heard.

Is there a universal language?

Or, put less controversially, are there some features of language that are shared by most, if not all, languages? The answer seems to be yes. For example, all languages have nouns and words to represent states of action or states of being because we all need a way of referring to objects, people and events. Hockett (1960a, b) has suggested that all languages share similar features. These are listed in Table 10.3. Are there others that you think could be added to the list?

Table 10.3 The features that Hockett regards as common to all languages

Universal	Description
Arbitrariness	There is no inherent connection between symbols and the objects they refer to
Broadcast transmission	Messages are transmitted in all directions and can be received by any hearer
Cultural transmission	Language is acquired through exposure to culture
Discreteness	A distinct range of possible speech sounds exists in language
Duality of structure	A small set of phenomes can be combined and recombined into an infinitely large set of meanings
Interchangeability	Humans are both message perceivers and message producers
Productivity	Novel messages can be produced according to the rules of the language
Semanticity	Meaning is conveyed by the symbols of the language
Specialisation	Sounds of a language are specialised to convey meaning (as compared with non-language sounds)
Total feedback	The speaker of a language has auditory feedback that occurs at the same time as the listener receives the message
Transitoriness	Linguistic messages fade quickly
Vocal–auditory channel	Means of transmission of the language is vocal–auditory

Gesture and communication

When we communicate orally, we often gesture and gesture was probably the evolutionary forerunner of vocal language. Some have argued that our language is gestural in nature, rather than acoustic (Gentilucci and Corballis, 2006). Ploog (2002) has hypothesised that we have two neural systems which mediate vocal behaviour. The first is in the cingulate cortex (and is found in non-humans) and the second is neocortical (seen in humans), which controls contralateral voluntary motor movement. The function of gesture appears manifold: it is used to express feeling, tone and meaning. Many of the gestures we make are intended to communicate an idea or thought or request. We point in order to direct people where to go; we beckon with our hands if we want someone to come near us; we have a number of gestures signifying disapproval of others.

But can combining speech and gesture improve comprehension of another's intention? Kelly *et al.* (1999) set up a series of experiments in which they asked participants to watch video footage of a specially created scenario. For example, two characters, Adam and Bill, are going home when they meet each other in the street just outside their flat. Adam is on a bike and Bill is walking. Adam asks Bill if he had brought the burgers. Bill had not. Adam says to Bill that he had better get them. Bill protests that the burger bar is in another part of town. In one condition, Bill makes eye contact with Adam and gestures towards his friend's bike; in another, he maintains eye contact and just says the dialogue. In the experiment, participants are asked to indicate how they think the last person addressed in the scenario would react to what had been communicated. All scenarios featured indirect requests; in none was a target mentioned (in the example here, a bike) or an intended action explicitly suggested.

The authors found that those in the gesture and speech condition were almost twice as likely to understand the nature of the indirect request than were those in the speech-only condition. The authors found a similar result in another experiment in which participants had to remember information spoken by a woman who made or did not make meaningful gestures (e.g. shooting a basketball) when describing her brother, a basketball player.

To investigate whether speakers gesture to help listeners better understand what they are saying, Alibali *et al.* (2001) observed the gestures made by individuals who were asked to narrate to a colleague the contents of an animated cartoon. In one part of the experiment, the listener was face-to-face with the gesturer and could see the speaker's gestures; in the other, a screen blocked the view of the speaker. The gestures were filmed by a hidden camera and were classified into two categories: representational gestures, those used to gesture meaning in speech, and beat gestures, those which conveyed no semantic content and were simple and rhythmic.

The rate of beat gestures was comparable in the visible and the blocked condition but the rate of representational gesture varied according to condition. Specifically, speakers used more representational gestures when the listeners could see them than when they could not.

The researchers suggest that these results support the semantic information hypothesis of gesture. This states that a speaker's visibility to the listener influences the production of meaningful gestures. We seem to gesture to convey meaning when we speak, even when our listeners cannot see these gestures.

Gestures, like language, are very culture-specific bits of behaviour. A gesture in one language may mean something entirely different – or nothing at all – in another. To determine how well people could distinguish between real gestures and fake ones, Molinsky *et al.* (2005) asked native-born and non-native American students to view videotaped gestures which were genuinely used in America or ones which had been invented by the experimenter. Examples can be seen in Table 10.4.

Table 10.4 Examples of the types of fake and real gestures used in Molinsky *et al.*'s study (2005)

Real	Fake
Shoulder shrug	Twirl right finger in front of body from chest to above the head
Cup left hand around ear (so signify not being able to hear)	
Wave hand back and forth	Push front of nose inward with second finger
Slice throat with second finger of hand	Right hand in front of face, palm facing in; make downward motion like guillotine
Thumbs up	
Using first two fingers of hand to mine quotation marks	
Tap second finger of hand to head several times	Cup fist and twist towards the ground
Making circle with thumb and second finger (OK)	

There was a significant and positive relationship between accurate gesture recognition and length of stay in America – the longer participants had been there, the better the recognition. Specifically, however, the more competent they felt in communicating in their adopted culture, and the more motivated they were to learn about their new culture, the better they were at distinguishing fake from real gestures.

Reading

Speech first developed as a means of communication between two or more people facing each other, or at least within earshot of each other, and probably occurred around 200,000 to 300,000 years ago. Indo-European languages

see activity on mypsychlab

Psychology in action – Sex differences in communication

The prolific American linguist, Deborah Tannen, has reported some curious differences between men and women in the way they hold conversations and communicate with each other. Take the following example, from Tannen's book, *You Just Don't Understand* (1992):

> ' A married couple was in a car when the wife turned to her husband and asked, 'Would you like to stop for a coffee?'
>
> 'No, thanks,' he answered truthfully. So they didn't stop.
>
> The result? The wife, who had indeed wanted to stop, became annoyed because she felt her preference had not been considered. The husband, seeing his wife was angry, became frustrated. Why didn't she just say what she wanted?

This, according to Tannen's research, sums up one important difference between men's and women's language use: women often make a suggestion to start a negotiation. Men see it as a direct question to be answered directly. Another of Tannen's findings is that men's conversation can be a little like witnessing a verbal contest: it is a way of establishing dominance, not being pushed around, getting the upper hand. Women use conversation to encourage intimacy, closeness and support. Men are more independent, exemplified by a man's ability to make a unilateral decision which directly affects his partner without consulting her. Women try to win an argument by agreement – requests are formulated as proposals, not demands. Another difference is that men and women behave differently when dis-

pensing advice and understanding – when a woman expresses a problem or difficulty, a man will suggest a solution, when what is usually desired is understanding and reassurance.

A recent meta-analysis of men's and women's talkativeness and the type of speech they engage in has found some surprising differences (Leaper and Ayres, 2007). The researchers examined degrees of affiliative speech – that used to affirm or positively engage with another person – and assertive speech – that used to advance a point of view, be direct and give information.

Women, as predicted, engaged in more affiliative speech (but did not act unassertively during exchanges) but there was no general difference between the sexes in terms of assertive speech. The authors found the following specific results:

- Men were more talkative and used assertive speech more.
- Men used assertive speech less during interactions with strangers than close relations.
- Men were more likely to give suggestions in speech and approached conversations in a task-oriented way.
- Women made more critical statements.
- Female undergraduates used more affiliative and less assertive speech, but there was no difference in non-students.
- When mothers and fathers were with their child, the mother would talk more.
- Men were more talkative than women in mixed-sex interactions but there was no sex difference when interactions were with the same sex.
- Women were more likely to use affiliative speech in same-sex than mixed sex interactions.

Psychology in action – *Continued*

- Women disclosed more information than men but not in mixed-sex interactions.
- Women smiled more (and for longer in same-sex interactions).
- Men used assertive speech more in same-sex interactions (perhaps seeing the exchange as a form of competition).
- If a researcher was present, men used more assertive speech; when one was absent, the women did (although this finding was based on limited data).
- Greater affiliative speech in women and greater talkativeness in men was more likely when research was done in a university laboratory.
- Women were more likely to discuss socio-emotional-oriented topics; men discussed instrumental-oriented topics.

- Women were more assertive when interacting with children.
- Women used more affiliative speech when observed for brief periods (4–8 minutes), but not for 10–15 minutes or 20–300 minute periods.
- Talkativeness favouring men was greater in research published in top-tier journals.

The analysis suggests that sex differences in speech and the amount of speech can depend on a number of social and environmental factors, including the sex of the person the participant is interacting with, how long they interact, where they interact, how they interpret the situations they find themselves in, and whether they are students or non-students.

(144 tongues), for example, seem to have a common root, as Figure 10.4 shows.

The invention of writing, which made it possible for people to communicate across both space and time, was an important turning point in civilisation. The first system of writing appears to have been developed around 4000 BC in Sumeria (the location of present-day Iran and Iraq), apparently in response to the need to keep records of ownership and of business transactions. The earliest forms of writing were stylised drawings of real objects (pictographs), but most cultures soon developed symbols based on sounds. For example, Egyptian hieroglyphic writing used some symbols as pictographs but used others phonetically, to spell out people's names or words that denoted concepts not easily pictured (Ellis, 1992).

With the notable exception of Chinese (and other Asian writing systems based on Chinese), most modern languages use alphabetic writing systems in which a small number of symbols represent (more or less) the sounds used to pronounce words. For example, most European languages are represented by the Roman alphabet, originally developed to represent the sounds of Latin and subsequently adopted by tribes of people ruled or influenced by the Roman Empire. The Roman alphabet was adapted from the Greek alphabet, which in turn was adapted from the Phoenician alphabet. For example, the letter D has its origin in the Phoenician symbol 'daleth', which meant 'door'. At first, the symbol literally indicated a door, but it later came to represent the phoneme /d/. The Greeks adopted the symbol and its pronunciation but changed its name to delta. Finally, the Romans took it, altering its shape into the one we recognise in English today.

Scanning text

When we scan a scene, our eyes make rapid jumps called saccades. These same rapid movements occur during reading (a French ophthalmologist in the nineteenth century discovered saccadic eye movements while watching people read).

The study of eye movements is made possible by a device called an eye tracker. This device consists of an apparatus that holds a person's head in a fixed position and a special video camera that keeps track of the person's gaze by focusing on an eye and monitoring the position of the pupil. The person reads material presented by a computer on a video monitor.

Perception does not occur while the eyes are actually moving but during the brief **fixations** that occur between saccades. The average fixation has a duration of about 250 milliseconds, but their duration can vary considerably. Figure 10.5 shows the pattern of fixations made by both good and poor readers.

The ovals above the text indicate the location of the fixations (which occur just below the ovals, on the text itself), and the numbers indicate their duration (in milliseconds). The fixations of good readers were made in the forward direction; the poor readers looked back and examined previously read words several times (indicated by the arrows). In addition, the good reader took, on average, considerably less time to examine each word.

Familiar words tend to be skipped over more frequently than are visually similar non-words (Drieghe *et al.*, 2005). University students fixate on most words when they are asked to read text carefully enough to under-

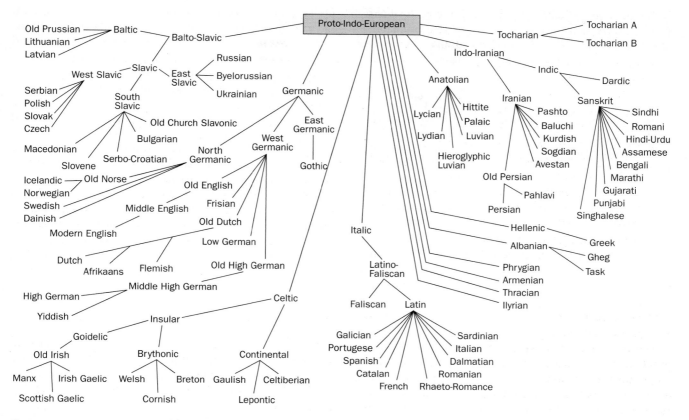

Figure 10.4 A language tree showing the suggested derivation of the most well-developed languages.
Source: 'Evolution of language', *Science*, 303, 27 February 2004, p. 1325, unnumbered figure.

stand its meaning. They fixate on 80 per cent of the content words but on only 40 per cent of the function words such as 'the' and 'and' (Just and Carpenter, 1980). Function words are generally shorter than content words, but the difference is not only a matter of size. Readers are more likely to skip over short function words such as 'and' or 'the' than over short content words such as 'ant' or 'run' (Carpenter and Just, 1983). For example, read the following sentence:

I love Paris in the
the springtime

You may not have noticed that second 'the' at the beginning of the second line and would have read the sentence as normal; we seem to be able to glide over function words such as 'the' without it detrimentally affecting the way in which we perceive and understand meaning.

As sentences are read, they are usually analysed word by word (Rayner and Pollatsek, 1989). Some words contribute more to our understanding than do others, and some sentences cannot make sense until we reach the end (compare and contrast: 'The capital of Kenya is Nairobi'; 'Nairobi is the capital of Kenya'). The more unusual a

word is, the longer a reader fixates on it. The word 'sable', for example, receives a longer fixation than the word 'table'. The word that follows an unusual word does not receive a longer-than-usual fixation, which indicates that the reader finishes processing the word before initiating the next saccade (Thibadeau *et al.*, 1982). Readers also spend more time fixating on longer words. In fact, if word familiarity is held constant, the amount of time a word receives is proportional to its length (Carpenter and Just, 1983). In addition, Just *et al.* (1983) found that the amount of time that Chinese readers spent fixating on a Chinese character was proportional to the number of brush strokes used to make it. Because all Chinese characters are of approximately the same size, the increased fixation time appears to reflect the complexity of a word rather than the amount of space it occupies.

Phonetic and whole-word recognition

Most psychologists who study the reading process believe that readers have two basic ways of recognising words: phonetic and whole-word recognition. **Phonetic reading** involves the decoding of the sounds that letters or groups of letters make (in a similar way to which the units of speech are called phonemes, the units of written language are called **graphemes**). For example, the ability to pronounce nonsense words depends on our knowledge of the relation between letters and sounds in the English language. Such knowledge is used to 'sound the word out'. When we do this we apply **grapheme–phoneme correspondence (GPC) rules**: the rules which govern the ways in which we are able to translate written letters into the appropriate sounds. This is called **whole-word reading**: reading by recognising a word as a whole. But do we have to 'sound out' familiar, reasonably short words such as 'table' or 'grass'? Probably not. Familiar words are perceived as whole words. However, consider this list of words: 'knave', 'shave', 'slave', 'have'. How did you pronounce the last word? You probably pronounced it to rhyme with 'slave'. This example illustrates that although whole-word reading would seem to be intuitively correct, our pronunciation of words can depend on the context in which words are used.

The process of reading

A relatively inexperienced reader will have to sound out most words and, consequently, will read rather slowly. Experienced, practised readers will quickly recognise most of them as individual units. In other words, during reading,

phonetic and whole-word reading are engaged in a race. If the word is familiar, the whole-word method will win. If the word is unfamiliar, the whole-word method will lose and the phonetic method will have enough time to compete.

When we read a word, we must have some store of knowledge which allows us to identify words as words. In the same way that the auditory store was considered part of the auditory word recognition system, the visual store can be considered part of the visual word recognition system. But is our recognition of written words purely visual? Or can we read by 'ear'?

To answer this question, Rubenstein *et al.* (1971) presented individuals with three types of non-word (strings of letters which make invalid English words): **pseudowords**, which conformed to the rules of English but had no meaning (for example GANK), non-words which were pronounceable but illegally spelled (for example MIRQ), and non-words which were unpronounceable and illegally spelled (for example HTTR). The participants had to decide whether these words, presented on a computer screen, were real English words or not (this is called a lexical decision task). The experimenters found that participants took longest to reject the pseudowords, followed by illegally spelled pronounceable words, followed by illegally spelled unpronounceable words. In a second experiment, Rubenstein *et al.*, included a set of words called **pseudohomophones**; these are words which are

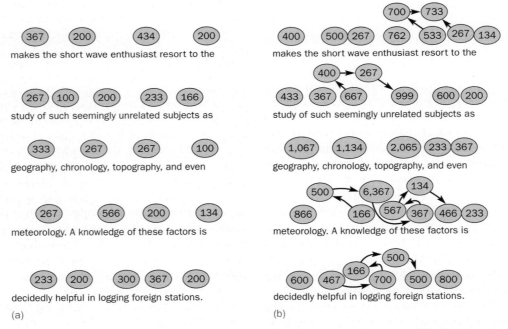

Figure 10.5 The pattern of fixations made by two readers. The ovals are placed above the locations of the fixations; the numbers within them indicate the durations of the fixations (in milliseconds). Arrows indicate backtracking to words already examined. **(a)** A good reader. **(b)** A poor reader.

Source: From Just, M.A. and Carpenter, P.A., *The Psychology of Reading and Language Comprehension* © 1987. Published by Allyn & Bacon, Boston, MA. Copyright © 1987 by Pearson Education. By permission of the publisher.

legally spelled, are pronounceable, sound like real words but have no meaning (for example PHICKS, which sounds like 'fix'). They would, therefore, pass an auditory word recognition system, but not the visual word recognition system. As predicted, pseudohomophones took longest to reject, followed by pseudowords.

Rubenstein *et al.* suggested that visual information is translated into a phonological code, a sound-based representation of the word, using grapheme to phoneme conversion. This representation is then checked by the auditory word recognition system which decides whether the word sounds like a real word or not. Pseudowords would fail this test – they do not sound like real words. Pseudohomophones, however, would pass because they do sound like real words. They, therefore, need to be checked by the visual word recognition system in order to determine whether the word is real. The visual word recognition system checks the orthography of a word (the way in which it is spelled). The recognition of words, therefore, involves phonic mediation: the conversion of written language into a sound-based representation.

Phonic mediation, however, appears to be necessary only for the recognition of unfamiliar words (Ellis, 1992). When we see a familiar word, we normally recognise it as a whole and say it aloud. If we see an unfamiliar word or a pronounceable non-word, we must try to read it phonetically. We recognise each letter and then sound it out, based on our knowledge of how letters are sounded out (phonetics).

Whole-word recognition is not only faster than phonetic decoding, but also essential in a language (such as English) in which spelling is not completely phonetic. In the following pairs of words:

cow/blow bone/one post/cost limb/climb

no single set of phonological rules can account for the pronunciation of both members of each pair (phonology refers to the relation between letters and the sounds they represent in a particular language). Yet all these words are familiar and easy to read. The ability to recognise words as wholes, therefore, may be necessary in order to read irregularly spelled words (although our 'have' example earlier on suggests how whole-word reading can fail).

Phonology, however, appears to be crucial for the development of language ability, as we will see later. Having good phonological skills appears to place children at an advantage linguistically. Gathercole and Baddeley (1990) found that 5-year-old children with good phonological skills were better at remembering nonsense words than were those with poor phonological skills. This ability to repeat nonsense words appears to be a good predictor of later, successful vocabulary acquisition (Gathercole *et al.*, 1992). The role of phonology (and other processes) in learning to read is the topic of the Psychology in Action section below. There is much debate over the best way to teach children how to learn to read, and psychologists have discovered much that teachers can use in their instruction.

The dual-route model of reading

The **dual-route model of reading** proposes that there are two routes that take the reader from spelling to sound (Coltheart, 1978; Morton and Patterson, 1980). The lexical route retrieves pronounced words from a lexicon, i.e. it 'looks up' words in an internal word pool which contains items learned through experience, a little like a personalised dictionary. This route is also known as the 'direct', 'lexical', 'lexico-semantic' or 'addressed' route: all refer to the same path. The sublexical route is the system which converts letters into sounds – a process called grapheme–phoneme correspondence. It 'translates' letters into sounds based on sound–letter associations that have been learned. Other terms for this route include indirect, assembled, sublexical and graphological. The lexical route would be able to identify all known words, regardless of whether they follow grapheme–phoneme correspondence rules; the sublexical route would be able to identify non-words using these rules (it would be able to recognise 'flound' as a non-word, for example, because the word follows normal grapheme–phoneme correspondence rules).

The model derived from studies of brain-injured patients who appear to rely more on one route than the other. People with a type of dyslexia called phonological dyslexia (see below), for example, appear to have access only to whole word forms (the direct, lexical route) and have difficulty in reading regularly spelled words (suggesting an impairment in the indirect, sublexical route). The reading of non-words is significantly worse than the reading of (familiar) words. An alternative to the dual-route model has argued that the same mechanisms underlie the reading aloud of words and non-words (such as 'nep' and 'cabe').

In a test of these competing models, Caccappoulo-van Vliet *et al.* (2004) described two patients with dementia who showed pure phonological dyslexia. These patients were unable to read non-words but they were able to read familiar, irregularly spelled words accurately. However, their phonological skills were intact, thus lending support to the dual-route model explanation of phonological dyslexia rather than the alternative (because phonological ability was generally unimpaired).

A meta-analysis of 35 neuroimaging studies of the dual-route model suggests that the two routes of reading can also be mapped in the healthy brain (Jobard *et al.*, 2003). Access to the visual representation of words was found to rely on two routes, but there was no consistent brain region devoted to storing the shapes of word forms. Instead, a general region located at the occipitotemporal junction

see activity on **mypsychlab**

appeared to be involved in the initial segmentation or classification of word-like stimuli. The phonological route was subserved by parts of the temporal lobe and also regions involved in working memory (because of the process involved in matching letters and sounds). The so-called direct route, according to this review, recruited a pathway linking the occipitotemporal cortex with those involved in semantic processing (these regions are found in or around the temporal cortex).

Connectionism and the dual-route model

Are both routes in the dual-route model activated simultaneously during reading? One view holds that both systems operate in parallel and are in some form of race, the winner being the system which produces the best pronunciation. A second view holds that the two processes are pooled until a match is made that would prompt articulation. No clear agreement on this process has been reached, although a great deal of excitement in cognitive psychology and psycholinguistics has been roused by the possibilities of connectionism, a form of computer modelling of human cognitive function, in solving this problem. This approach argues that there are no qualitatively different processes involved in recognising words and that there is no localised lexicon.

Connectionism takes as its starting point the view that the brain, or our information processing system, operates in a similar way to a computer and can, therefore, be modelled. Such a model should be capable of learning (as our brain is). This idea, of course, is not new. Rosenblatt (1962) had developed a parallel processing machine which was capable of simple learning. Modern, computer-based models of human computation, however, were pioneered by Seidenberg and McClelland (1989). Their **parallel distributed processing (PDP) model** did away with the notion of dual routes and instead posited one route only which

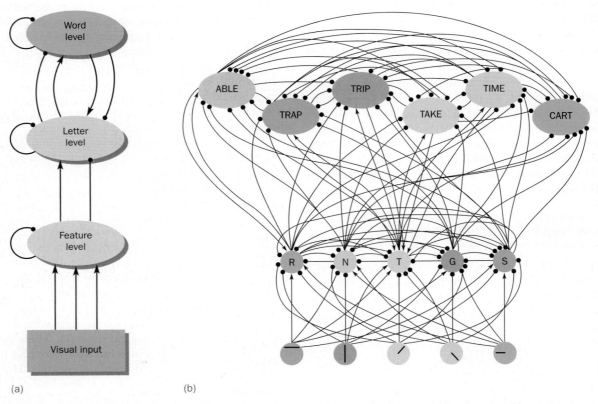

(a)   (b)

Figure 10.6 An example of the macrostructure **(a)** and microstructure **(b)** of McClelland and Rumelhart's activation model. The macrostructure illustrates the general organisation of the model. The microstructure shows how nodes within the model are connected. In these diagrams the arrows ending in points are excitatory connections, and the arrows ending in dots are inhibitory connections. The nodes at the bottom of **(b)** represent the physical features of words; the nodes at the next level represent the letters of words. Finally, the nodes at the top represent the actual words. You can see that there is an excitatory connection between the letter 'T' and the word 'TRIP' because the word contains this letter. However, there is an inhibitory connection between the letter 'N' and the word 'TRIP' because the word does not contain this letter.

Source: McClelland, J.L. and Rumelhart, D.E., An interactive activation model of context effects in letter perception. Part 1: An account of basic findings. *Psychological Review*, 1981, 88, 375–407. © 1981 The American Psychological Association, reprinted with permission.

was non-lexical. Their model is an example of a computational model of behaviour because it translates units of behavioural phenomena into computations. Seidenberg and McClelland's model was a three-layer neural network which sought to read regular, exception and non-words from spelling to sound. The three layers were: features, letters and words. Perception within each of these layers was argued to occur in parallel so that the system could analyse features while it identified letters and attempt to name the word a stimulus might represent (Zorzi *et al.*, 1998). An example of the type of network proposed by PDP can be seen in Figure 10.6.

However, the model has run into some difficulty. It cannot read non-words, for example, and it cannot simulate a form of dyslexia called surface dyslexia, which is described later in the chapter (Besner *et al.*, 1990; Coltheart *et al.*, 1993). The PDP model has been replaced by that of Plaut and colleagues (Plaut and McClelland, 1993; Plaut *et al.*, 1996) which seems to have met with some success in that it is at least capable of reading monosyllabic non-words but does not appear to account for the flexibility of human language (see Zorzi *et al.*, 1998, for a review). We will not say too much more about PDP and connectionism here. Although the PDP model and connectionism are difficult concepts to grasp it is important to take note of them because there is great debate in psychology over the relevance and validity of connectionism in trying to explain the process of visual word recognition.

Psychology in action – How children learn to read

Reading is an artificial activity and it must be taught to us (usually at an early age). A beginning reader has much of their work cut out because they have no vocabulary and no set of rules. Are there any cognitive skills (such as an awareness of rhyme or having an effective short-term memory) that can help develop the child's vocabulary and skills? Does reading develop naturally or in stages? And how can we best teach children to read?

To begin with, reading requires adequate sight, so a child would need to be visually competent. Of course, blind children can be taught Braille, but our concern here is with the development of visual word recognition and visual reading. The next important step is for the child to relate written letters or groups of letters to sounds. In some languages this is easier to do than it is in others. The rules needed to undertake this task are more complex in English, say, than in Finnish or Italian. Some of these rules will be simple – 'b' corresponds to /b/. Others are not – the 'c' in 'car' and 'mince' is sounded differently, for example. These general rules are called spelling-to-pronunciation correspondence rules or, more accurately, grapheme–phoneme correspondence rules. The essential feature of these rules is that the child must break up words into segments and put them back together again to form a pronounceable whole. This breaking and putting together again are called **segmentation** and **blending**, respectively, and are two tasks the beginning reader has great difficulty in undertaking.

According to Oakhill and Garnham (1988), the child's reading process is dependent on the development of a number of skills. Whether these skills give rise to reading, are associated with reading or develop from reading is an interesting psychological question that many developmental psychologists and psycholinguists have attempted to answer. However, this debate need not concern us here. What will concern us are the skills associated with reading development. Oakhill and Garnham's list includes the following features/skills: word con-

sciousness, awareness of lower-level features, orthographic awareness, phonemic awareness and use of analogy.

- *Word consciousness*. Word consciousness or **lexical awareness** refers to the ability to understand that speech and writing are composed of different, distinct elements called words. Of course, to us, as skilled readers, this is quite obvious. It is not, however, to a child who is learning to read and has not encountered such stimuli at any great length. Although it appears that young children have difficulties in indicating word boundaries (where one ends and another begins), children with strong lexical awareness tend to develop better reading ability (Ryan *et al.*, 1977).
- *Awareness of lower-level features*. A young child has a limited sight vocabulary and what it does have will have been learned through breaking down the elements of words into manageable, processable pieces. As suggested above, this is difficult for a young child to do. English, for example, although having an alphabet of 26 letters, has 45 phonemes. When Rozin *et al.* (1974) presented children with two words such as 'mow' and 'motorcycle' and asked them – auditorily – which one was 'mow', the maximum correct response varied from 50 per cent for suburban nursery children to 10 per cent for inner-city children.
- *Orthographic awareness*. The ability to recognise that writing systems have sets of rules that must be followed is called **orthographic awareness**. For example, in English, we know that some sequences of letters are acceptable (for example 'able') but know that others are not ('kqxg').
- *Phonological awareness*. Perhaps the most important skill a child needs in order to develop adequate reading ability is the capacity to appreciate sound and be able to identify letters with sounds (this is sometimes called **phonological awareness**). To explore the contribution of phonological processing to reading, Bradley and Bryant 1983; Bryant and

see activity on mypsychlab

Psychology in action – *Continued*

Bradley, 1985) have administered a series of phonological tasks to children at various stages of learning to read. Such tasks include finding the odd one out from the following two sets of spoken words: sun, sea, sock, rag; weed, need, peel, deed. (Notice how these two examples rely on the respondent noting both the beginning and ending sounds of words.) Good performance at tasks such as these is a good predictor of later reading ability.

- *Use of analogy*. Sometimes, children will not use grapheme–phoneme correspondence rules to read a word because it looks like another word. For example, Marsh *et al.* (1977) asked children and adults to pronounce nonsense words such as 'tepherd'. This word, if pronounced according to grapheme–phoneme correspondence (GPC) rules (with 'ph' pronounced as /f/) would be pronounced 'tefferd'. Children, however, pronounce it to rhyme with 'shepherd'. Adults do not. This is called children's use of analogy in reading.

The major ways in which children are taught to develop and use some or all of these skills are based on two systems: whole-word reading and phonics. Whole-word reading, as its name suggests, involves teaching the child to read whole words rather than analyse components of words and put them together to form whole words. This is sometimes called the look-and-say method because there is no room for segmentation of words. It is also called the meaning-based system because it encourages the child to think about the object the word represents. Words are usually displayed singly on cards and classrooms might have objects and pictures with word-labels attached to them. This means that the child begins to generate a pool of words which they will then be able to read in books after a sufficient number of words has been learned. Whole-word reading is easier for the child because it does not rely on segmentation. It also, as we have already mentioned, encourages the child to think about word meaning. One disadvantage of the system, however, is its inability to teach children how to decode new or unfamiliar words because no rule-based system is learned. If one considers that the average adult has a reading vocabulary of 50,000 words, the number of words a child would have to learn would be impracticable.

The alternative approach is called phonics. This rule-based system teaches the child correspondences between letters and sounds (that is, GPC rules, segmentation and blending). There are many forms of this teaching system and most teach the children letter-to-sound correspondences first before exposing them to actual words. Recently, a year-long comparison of phonics versus standard teaching methods in a group of English children found that phonics was associated with a reduction in reading difficulties (Shapiro and Solity, 2008). The disadvantages of the system are that it cannot cope well

with teaching the child irregular words and that 4–5-year-old children find the segmentation of phonemes difficult.

Many other teaching-of-reading systems exist. For example, one approach, the Initial Teaching Alphabet, reforms the orthography of irregular words by transforming them into regular words. Other approaches teach the child the letters of the alphabet first (success in which is a good predictor of reading ability). Another approach colour-codes letters in words. For example, a letter written in a certain colour can only be pronounced in one way. Yet another approach places marks underneath certain letters to indicate how they should be pronounced (the technical name for this is the 'diacritical marking system').

There is a close link between phonological skill and the ability to read. Some authors argue that is the key skill in the development of a child's reading ability. If this is so, one might hypothesise that if children are trained well in phonological awareness (an awareness of the sounds of words), they might develop better reading skills than those without the benefit of this training. Hatcher *et al.* (2004) tested this hypothesis by randomly assigning 410 British children of kindergarten age (4–5 years) to one of three teaching conditions or a control group. The conditions were Reading with Rhyme (a learning-to-read package with additional emphasis on rhyme), Reading with Phoneme (a learning-to-read package with additional emphasis on phoneme training such as syllable and word identification), and Reading with Rhyme and Phoneme (a combination of the first two). The control group was taught the standard reading programme. Measures of cognitive ability – including reading, arithmetic and literacy – were taken.

While children whose reading was progressing normally did not benefit significantly from the additional phonological training, children who had been identified as poor readers improved their reading skill and awareness of phonemes. The decline in reading ability was halted by the second school year in children who received phoneme training and by the third year in children who received the rhyme training.

Evidence suggests that children who learn transparent orthographies (where the letters are sounded out exactly as they are written) learn to read these languages more quickly than do those who learn to read opaque ones (where the relationship betweent what is written and how what is written is spoken is inconsistent). This is what Patel *et al.* (2004) found when they investigated the learning skills of 6–11-year-old Dutch and English children. Children learning to read Dutch (a transparent language) were more accurate and faster in reading words and non-words in their native language than the English (an opaque language) children were in theirs.

A study of 382 children from 21 primary schools in England found that phonological awareness was a significant predictor

Psychology in action – *Continued*

of later school success, including maths, reading and science performance, and teachers' positive assessments of the pupils (Savage *et al.*, 2007). 'Practically,' the authors conclude, 'screening of phonological awareness and basic reading skills by school staff in year 1 significantly enhances the capacity of schools to predict curricular outcomes in year 6' (p. 732).

Is there a 'best' approach amid these myriad of approaches? As you have seen, although some of the well-developed approaches have distinct advantages, all have certain disadvan-

tages. However, one consistent predictor of later reading ability is successful phonological awareness. Pronunciation is also better if the phonetic aspects of speech are emphasised during the early stages of teaching. This may explain why developmental dyslexics often have good cognitive ability but have poor phonological processing skills, a topic we discuss in the section on language disorders below. If you were teaching a child to read, how would you start? What aspect of reading would you consider the most important to teach at the initial stages?

Understanding the meanings of words and sentences

The meanings of words are learned through experience. The meanings of content words involve memories of objects, actions and their characteristics; thus, the meanings of content words involve visual, auditory, somatosensory, olfactory and gustatory memories. These memories of the meanings of words are distributed throughout the brain. Our understanding of the meaning of the word 'apple', for example, involves memories of the sight of an apple, the way it feels in our hands, the crunching sound we hear when we bite into it, and the taste and odour we experience when we chew it. The understanding of the meanings of adjectives, such as the word 'heavy', involves memories of objects that are difficult or impossible to lift.

A phenomenon known as semantic priming gives us some hints about the nature of activation of memories triggered by the perception of words and phrases. **Semantic priming** is a facilitating effect on the recognition of words having meanings related to a word encountered earlier. A particular word can be more easily read if the word preceding it is related in meaning. If an individual sees the word 'bread', they will be more likely to recognise a fuzzy image of the word 'butter' or an image that is presented very briefly by means of a tachistoscope (Johnston and Dark, 1986). Presumably, the brain contains circuits of neurons that serve as 'word detectors' involved in visual recognition of particular words (Morton, 1979; McClelland and Rumelhart, 1981). Reading the word 'bread' activates word detectors and other neural circuits involved in memories of the word's meaning. Apparently, this activation spreads to circuits denoting related concepts, such as butter. Thus, our memories must be linked according to our experience regarding the relations between specific concepts.

Context effects, an example of top-down processing, have been demonstrated through semantic priming. Zola (1984), for example, asked people to read sentences such as the following:

> 1 Cinemas must have adequate popcorn to serve their patrons.
>
> 2 Cinemas must have buttered popcorn to serve their patrons.

while he recorded their eye movements with an eye tracker.

Zola found that individuals fixated for a significantly shorter time on the word popcorn in the second sentence. Because the word 'adequate' is not normally associated with the word 'popcorn', individuals reading the first sentence were unprepared for this word. However, 'buttered' is commonly associated with popcorn, especially in the context of a cinema. The context of the sentence, therefore, activated the word detector for 'popcorn', making the recognition of the word easier.

Semantic priming studies have also shed some light on another aspect of the reading process, the development of a mental model. It has been suggested that when a person reads some text, he or she generates a mental model of what the text is describing (Johnson-Laird, 1983). If the text contains a narrative, for example, the reader will imagine the scenes and actions that are being recounted. These issues of semantic priming and semantic networks are taken up in Chapter 11.

On the relative importance of consonants and vowels

Do vowels provide more information to readers than consonants during visual word recognition, or vice versa? Or is there no difference between them? Some psychologists argue that consonants are the more useful of the two because they are of more help in decoding the sound of a word from its orthography – the way in which it is spelled – during the early stages of visual word recognition (Brown and Besner, 1987).

To examine which is the more important to word identification, Lee *et al.* (2001) designed a sophisticated eye tracking experiment which carefully noted the time participants spent fixated on words. On a computer monitor, participants read the following sentence:

> I went to the hardware store to buy a tgfx for the lamp in my bedroom.

An eye-tracking device followed the course of the participant's eye across the sentence. When it reached the word 'buy' the nonsense string 'tgfx' was replaced with either 'b-lb' or 'bu-b'. Participants were told to pay attention to the sentences as they would be asked questions about them later (in fact they were asked questions only about a quarter of the sentences). The change from nonsense string to word occurred while participants blinked. The amount of time the participant spent fixated on the actual word was measured. If vowels were processed more quickly than consonants then participants should fixate longer on the word with the missing vowel ('b-lb') than the one with the missing consonant ('bu-b'). The opposite would occur if consonants were processed more quickly.

The study found that gazes were longer when the consonant was missing and there was a 30 ms delay before the nonsense string was replaced by a word. However, this time difference disappeared when the delay was increased to 60 ms. The results suggest that in the early stages of visual word recognition, consonants are more important than vowels to readers when they try to identify words.

Language acquisition by children

Perception of speech sounds by infants

see activity on mypsychlab

Language development begins even before birth. Although the sounds that reach a foetus are somewhat muffled, speech sounds can still be heard. And some learning appears to take place prenatally (foetal learning is considered in more detail in Chapter 12). The voice that a foetus hears best and most often is obviously that of its mother. Consequently, a newborn infant prefers its mother's voice to that of others (DeCasper and Fifer, 1980). DeCasper and Spence (1986) even found that newborn infants preferred hearing their mothers reading a passage they had read aloud several times before their babies were born to hearing them read a passage they had never read before.

An infant's auditory system is well developed. Wertheimer (1961) found that newborns still in the delivery room can turn their heads towards the source of a sound. Babies 2 or 3 weeks of age can discriminate between the sound of a voice and other sounds. By the age of 2 months, babies can tell an angry voice from a pleasant one; an angry voice produces crying, whereas a pleasant one causes smiling and cooing.

One device used to determine what sounds a very young infant can perceive is the pacifier nipple, placed in the baby's mouth. The nipple is connected by a plastic tube to a pressure-sensitive switch that converts the infant's sucking movements into electrical signals. These signals can be used to turn on auditory stimuli. Each time the baby sucks, a particular sound is presented. If the auditory stimulus is novel, the baby usually begins to suck at a high rate. If the stimulus remains the same, its novelty wears off (habituation occurs) and the rate of sucking decreases. With another new stimulus, the rate of sucking again suddenly increases, unless the baby cannot discriminate the difference. If the stimuli sound the same to the infant, the rate of sucking remains low after the change.

Using this technique, Eimas *et al.* (1971) found that 1-month-old infants could tell the difference between the sounds of the consonants 'b' and 'p'. Like Lisker and Abramson (1970) in the study discussed earlier, they presented the sounds 'ba' and 'pa', synthesised by a computer. The infants, like the adult participants in the earlier study, discriminated between speech sounds having voice-onset times that differed by only 0.02 of a second. Even very early during post-natal development, the human auditory system is ready to make very fine discriminations. Table 10.5 lists some of the responses infants make to various types of speech sound.

Table 10.5 Examples of responses infants make to various speech sounds

Age of first occurrence	Response
Newborn	Is startled by a loud noise Turns head to look in the direction of sound Is calmed by the sound of a voice Prefers mother's voice to a stranger's Discriminates among many speech sounds
1–2 months	Smiles when spoken to
3–7 months	Responds differently to different intonations (e.g. friendly, angry)
8–12 months	Responds to name Responds to 'no' Recognises phrases from games (e.g. 'Peekaboo', 'How big is baby?') Recognises words from routines (e.g. waves to 'bye bye') Recognises some words

Source: From Berko Gleason, J., *The Development of Language*, 4th edn © 1997. Published by Allyn & Bacon, Boston, MA. Copyright © by Pearson Education. By permission of the publisher.

The pre-speech period and the first words – An international perspective

The first sound that a baby makes is crying, a useful noise for attracting the attention of its carers. At about 1 month of age, infants start making other sounds, including 'cooing' (because of the prevalence of the 'ooing' sound). Often during this period, babies also make a series of sounds that resemble a half-hearted attempt to mimic the sound of crying (Kaplan and Kaplan, 1970).

At around 6 months, a baby's sounds begin to resemble those that occur in speech. Even though their babbling does not contain words – and does not appear to involve attempts to communicate verbally – the sounds that infants make, and the rhythm in which they are articulated, reflect the adult speech that babies hear. Mehler *et al.* (1988) found that 4-day-old infants preferred to hear a voice speaking French, their parents' native language. This ability to discriminate the sounds and rhythms of the language spoken around them manifested itself in the infants' own vocalisations very early on. Boysson-Bardies *et al.* (1984) had adult French speakers listen to recordings of the babbling of children from various cultures. The adults could easily distinguish the babbling of 8–month-old French infants from that of babies with different linguistic backgrounds.

A study by Kuhl *et al.* (1992) provides further evidence of the effect of children's linguistic environment on their language development. Native speakers learn not to distinguish between slight variations of sounds present in their language. In fact, they do not even hear the differences between them. For example, Japanese contains a sound that comes midway between /l/ and /r/. Different native speakers pronounce the sound differently, but all pronunciations are recognised as examples of the same phoneme. When native speakers of Japanese learn English, they have great difficulty distinguishing the sounds /l/ and /r/; for example, 'right' and 'light' sound to them like the same word. Presumably, the speech sounds that a child hears alter the brain mechanisms responsible for analysing them so that minor variations are not even perceived. The question is, when does this alteration occur? Most researchers have supposed that it happens only after children begin to learn the meanings of words, which occurs at around 10–12 months of age.

Kuhl and her colleagues found, however, that this learning takes place much earlier. They studied 6-month-old infants in the USA and Sweden. The infants were seated in their mothers' laps, where they watched an experimenter sitting nearby, playing with a silent toy. Every two seconds, a loudspeaker on the infant's left presented the sound of a vowel. From time to time, the sound was altered. If the infant noticed the change and looked at the loudspeaker, the experimenter reinforced the response by activating a toy bear which pounded on a miniature drum.

The experimenters presented two different vowel sounds, one found in English but not in Swedish and the other found in Swedish but not in English. From time to time, they varied the sound slightly. The reactions of the Swedish infants and the American infants were strikingly different. Swedish infants noticed when the English vowel changed but not when the Swedish vowel changed; and American infants did the opposite. In other words, by the age of 6 months, the infants had learned not to pay attention to slight differences in speech sounds of their own language, but they were still able to distinguish slight differences in speech sounds they had never heard. Even though they were too young to understand the meaning of what they heard, the speech of people around them had affected the development of their perceptual mechanisms.

These results seem to support the **native language recognition hypothesis** – that infants have the ability to recognise words which belong to their native language (Moon *et al.*, 1993). Another hypothesis, the **general language discrimination hypothesis**, suggests that infants are capable of discriminating sentences from any two languages because they can extract sets of properties that these languages possess. The evidence above suggests that there is little support for this hypothesis. An alternative to these two hypotheses states that newborns are sensitive to prosody and can discriminate between languages on the basis of intonation and rhythm. This is called the rhythm-based language discrimination hypothesis (Nazzi *et al.*, 1998).

To test this hypothesis, Nazzi *et al.* compared the ability of 5-day-old infants to discriminate between rhythmic and non-rhythmic sentences in various languages. They found that infants were able to discriminate between English and Japanese but not English and Dutch, thereby supporting the rhythm hypothesis. This suggests that infants may be more attuned to the rhythmic as opposed to the phonetic quality of speech.

Interestingly, there is evidence to suggest that the ability to discriminate between phonetic sounds successfully may change with age. Stager and Werker (1997) have reported that 8–month-old infants are capable of discriminating phonetic detail in a task in which 14-month-old infants cannot. The researchers suggest that this represents a reorganisation in the infant's language processing capacity: it shifts from the processes needed to learn syllables to the process needed to learn words. This is advantageous to the infant as it grows and has to put names to objects, events and situations. Because these activities are computationally complex and involve a huge increase in input, the amount of detail that needs to be processed is, therefore, limited.

Infant communication

Even before infants learn to talk, they display clear intent to communicate. Most attempts at pre-verbal infant communication fall into three categories: rejection, request (for social interaction, for an object or for an action), and comment (Sachs, 1993). Rejection usually involves pushing the unwanted object away and using facial expression and characteristic vocalisations to indicate displeasure. A request for social interaction usually involves the use of gestures and vocalisations to attract the caregiver's attention. A request for an object usually involves reaching and pointing and particular vocalisations. A request for an action (such as the one described above) similarly involves particular sounds and movements. Finally, a comment usually involves pointing out an object or handing it to the carer, accompanied by some vocalisation.

Infants babble before they talk. They often engage in serious 'conversations' with their carers, taking turns 'talking' with them. Infants' voices are modulated, and the stream of sounds they make sound as though they are using a secret language (Menn and Stoel-Gammon, 1993). At about 1 year of age, a child begins to produce words. The first sounds children use to produce speech appear to be similar across all languages and cultures: the first vowel is usually the soft 'a' sound of 'father', and the first consonant is a stop consonant produced with the lips – 'p' or 'b'.

Thus, the first word is often 'papa' or 'baba'. The next feature to be added is nasality, which converts the consonants 'p' or 'b' into 'm'. Thus, the next word is 'mama'. Mothers and fathers all over the world recognise these sounds as their children's attempts to address them. The first sounds of a child's true speech contain the same phonemes that are found in the babbling sounds that the child is already making; thus, speech emerges from pre-speech sounds. During the course of learning words from their carers and from older children, infants often invent their own **protowords**, unique strings of phonemes that serve word-like functions. The infants use these protowords consistently in particular situations (Menn and Stoel-Gammon, 1993).

The development of speech sounds continues for many years. Some sequences are added very late. For example, the 'str' of string and the 'bl' of blink are difficult for young children to produce; they usually say 'tring' and 'link', omitting the first consonant. Most children recognise sounds in adult speech before they can produce them.

The two-word stage

At around 18–20 months of age, children start learning language by putting two words together, and their linguistic development takes a leap forward. It is at this stage that linguistic creativity begins.

As for first sounds, children's two-word utterances are remarkably consistent across all cultures. Children use words in the same way, regardless of the language their parents speak. Even deaf children who learn sign language from their parents put two words together in the same way as children who can hear (Bellugi and Klima, 1972). And deaf children whose parents do not know sign language invent their own signs and use them in orderly, 'rule-governed' ways (Goldin-Meadow and Feldman, 1977). Thus, the grammar of children's language at the two-word stage appears to be universal (Owens, 1992).

For many years, investigators described the speech of young children in terms of adult grammar, but researchers now recognise that children's speech simply follows different rules. Young children are incapable of forming complex sentences – partly because their vocabulary is small, partly because their short-term 'working' memory is limited (they cannot yet encode a long string of words), and partly because their cognitive development has not yet reached a stage at which they can learn complex rules of syntax (Locke, 1993).

How adults talk to children

When parents talk to children they use only short, simple, well-formed, repetitive sentences and phrases (Brown and Bellugi, 1964) called **child-directed speech** (Snow, 1986). Adults' speech to children is characterised by clear pronunciation, exaggerated intonations, careful distinctions between similar-sounding phonemes, relatively few abstract words and function words, and a tendency to isolate constituents that undoubtedly enables young children to recognise them as units of speech (deVilliers and deVilliers, 1978).

Another important characteristic of child-directed speech is that it tends to refer to tangible objects the child can see, to what the child is doing and to what is happening around the child (Snow *et al.*, 1976). Words are paired with objects the child is familiar with, which is the easiest way to learn them.

Adults, particularly carers who have a continuing relationship with a child, tend to act as tutors when talking to children. For example, Snow and Goldfield (1982) found that as a mother and child repeatedly read a book over a period of 13 months, the mother's speech became more and more complex, especially when they were discussing a picture that they looked at again and again.

Adults often expand children's speech by imitating it but putting it into more complex forms, which undoubtedly helps the child learn about syntactical structure (Brown and Bellugi, 1964):

Child: Baby highchair.

Adult: Baby is in the highchair.

Child: Eve lunch.

Adult: Eve is having lunch.

Child: Throw daddy.

Adult: Throw it to daddy.

People make allowances for the age of the child with whom they are talking. Mothers talk differently to 2-year-olds compared with 10-year-olds (Snow, 1972a). Even 4-year-old children talk differently to 2-year-olds compared with how they talk to adults or other 4-year-olds (Shatz and Gelman, 1973). It seems unlikely that these differentiated speech patterns are innately determined. Snow (1972a) compared the speech patterns of a mother talking to a child with her speech patterns when she only pretended to be talking to a child. The woman's speech when the child was absent was simpler than it would have been if addressed to an adult, but when the child was present, it was simpler still. Clearly, then, feedback from children is important.

The most important factor controlling adults' speech to children is the child's attentiveness. When a child looks interested, an adult continues with what they are doing. Signs of inattention in the child prompt an adult to advance or simplify the level of speech until the child's attention is regained. Stine and Bohannon (1983) found that when children give signs that they do not understand what an adult is saying the adult adjusts their speech by simplifying it.

Infants also exert control over what their carers talk about. The topic of conversation usually involves what the infant is playing with or is guided by what the infant is gazing at (Bohannon, 1993). This practice means that infants hear speech that concerns what they are already paying attention to, which undoubtedly facilitates learning. In fact, Tomasello and Farrar (1986) found that infants of mothers who talked mostly about the objects of their infants' gazes uttered their first words earlier than other infants and also developed larger vocabularies early in life.

One of the intriguing findings in the literature on the development of language is that twins tend to develop language later than do singletons. On average, the delay is about three months by the time infants have reached 3 years of age. Several reasons have been mooted for this discrepancy. Among these are obstetric complications, family background and the interaction between the mother and infant.

Rutter *et al*. (2005) measured the communication and language abilities of 96 pairs of twins and 98 pairs of singletons who were no more than 30 months apart in terms of chronological age. Measures were taken when the children were 20 months and 3 years old. The language ability of twins was 1.7 months below singletons when the infants were 20 months; this difference increased to 3.1 months at 3 years. There was no significant relationship between language development and obstetric/neonatal complications, birthweight or congenital abnormalities, thus ruling out these factors as probable causes of the language delay in twins.

In a second study, Thorpe *et al*. (2005) used the same sample but this time measured the degree of mother–infant communication. Having a mother who encouraged the child to speak, who elaborated the children's comments, who read with her child and who talked about the story she was reading was associated with significantly better language development. This interaction was significantly less apparent in the twin group. The mothers did not differ significantly in terms of their education or social background, which suggests that these factors had negligible effects on the results.

Acquisition of adult rules of grammar

The first words that children use tend to be content words: these words are emphasised in adult speech and refer to objects and actions that children can directly observe (Brown and Bellugi, 1964). As children develop past the two-word stage, they begin to learn and use more and more of the grammatical rules that adults use. The first form of sentence lengthening appears to be the expansion of object nouns into noun phrases (Bloom, 1970). For example, 'that ball' becomes 'that a big ball'. Next, verbs are used more frequently, articles are added, prepositional phrases are mastered and sentences become more complex. These results involve the use of **inflections** and function words. Table 10.6 shows the approximate order in which children acquire some of these inflections and function words.

It is more difficult for children to add an inflection or function word to their vocabulary than to add a new content word because the rules that govern the use of inflections or function words are more complex than those that govern the use of most content words. In addition, content words usually refer to concrete objects or activities. The rules that govern the use of inflections or function words are rarely made explicit. A parent seldom says, 'When you want to use the past tense, add '-ed' to the verb', nor would a young child understand such a pronouncement. Instead, children must listen to speech and figure out how to express such concepts as the past tense.

The most frequently used verbs in most languages are irregular. Forming the past tense of such verbs in English does not involve adding '-ed' (for example, go/went, throw/threw, buy/bought, see/saw). The past tense of such verbs must be learned individually. Because irregular verbs get more use than do regular ones, children learn

Table 10.6 The approximate order in which children acquire inflections and function words

Item		Example
1	Present progressive: *ing*	He is *sitting* down.
2	Preposition: *in*	The mouse is *in* the box.
3	Preposition: *on*	The book is *on* the table.
4	Plurals;– *s*	The *dogs* ran away.
5	Past irregular: e.g. *went*	The boy *went* home.
6	Possessive:– '*s*	The *girl's* dog is big.
7	Uncontractable copula *be*: e.g. *are*, *was*	*Are* they boys or girls? *Was* that a dog?
8	Articles: *the*, *a*, *an*	He has *a* book.
9	Past regular: *-ed*	He *jumped* the stream
10	Third person regulars:-s *s*	She *ran* fast.
11	Third person irregular: e.g. *has*, *does*	*Does* the dog bark?
12	Uncontractible auxiliary *be*: e.g. *is*, *were*	*Is* he running? *Were* they at home?
13	Contractible copula *be*: e.g. '*s*, *-re*	That's a spaniel. *They're* pretty.
14	Contractible auxiliary *be*: e.g. -'*s*, -'*re*	*He's* doing it. *They're* running slowly.

Source: Adapted from Clark, H.H. and Clark, E.V., *Psychology and Language: An introduction to psycholinguistics*, 1977. © 1977, reprinted with permission of H.H. Clark & E.V. Clark.

them first, producing the past tense easily in sentences such as 'I came', 'I fell down', and 'she hit me'. Shortly after this period, they discover the regular past tense inflection and expand their vocabulary, producing sentences such as 'he dropped the ball'. But they also begin to say 'I comed', 'I falled down', and 'she hitted me'. Having learned a rule, they apply it to all verbs, including the irregular ones that they were previously using correctly. It takes children several years to learn to use the irregular past tense correctly again.

Children's rudimentary understanding, or at least recognition, of language and parts of speech seems to begin in the first few months of life. Children learn to assign meaning to words – decide whether they are nouns, verbs and so on – and use these words to form semi-structured sentences. That is, the child begins to follow the rules of grammar. Grammatical words tend to be phonetically and structurally smaller than lexical words – nouns, verbs and so on – and the commonest of them ('in', 'a', 'and') are used more frequently in conversation than are the most common lexical words. Does the child, therefore, show a preference for spoken grammatical or lexical words?

One study exposed 6-month-old infants to spoken lexical and grammatical words and measured their preference for each type of stimulus (Shi and Werker, 2001). The researchers found that the infants showed a preference for

the lexical words. The authors suggest that although grammatical words are the most commonly used, lexical words may be more striking and acoustically interesting. Lexical words tend to be longer and have a more complex structure; mothers also tend to use lexical words in isolation (i.e. without the accompanying grammar). The preference for lexical words may help the child to give meaning to its world and act as a first essential step to developing more complex communication. It may be that children prefer and use lexical words first and then clamp them on to grammatical structures later.

Acquisition of meaning

The simplest explanation of why children use and understand language is that they hear a word spoken at the same time that they see (or hear, or touch) the object to which the word refers. After several such pairings, they add a word to their vocabulary. In fact, children first learn the names of things with which they interact, or things that change (and thus attract their attention). For example, they are quick to learn words like 'biscuit' or 'blanket', but are slow to learn words like 'wall' or 'window' (Ross *et al.*, 1986; Pease *et al.*, 1993).

Fast mapping

This quick learning of new, content words has been called **fast mapping** (Carey and Bartlett, 1978; Markman, 1989). There is some debate over whether fast mapping is specific to language or whether it is generated by other, cognitive processes. For example, if fast mapping is seen only for words then this would suggest that the process is language based; if fast mapping can extend to other domains, this suggests that the process is underpinned by general cognitive abilities (such as the ability to memorise).

In two experiments, Markson and Bloom (1997) taught 3–4-year-old children and a group of university undergraduates to learn a word referring to an object ('kobi') and a fact about this object. In one experiment, participants were told that this was an object given to the experimenter by her uncle. The participants' ability to remember and identify the object was tested immediately after learning, one week after or one month after. Although the adults were better at remembering the object and object name than were the children, all children performed comparably well when asked to retrieve the word, identify the object about which facts were presented, and to identify the object given to the experimenter by her uncle. The study suggests that fast mapping may not necessarily be specific to language processing but is made possible by learning and memory mechanisms that are not specific to the language domain.

Waxman and Booth (2000) replicated Markson and Bloom's original finding but suggested that there is a crucial difference between the principles underpinning noun learning and fact learning. They introduced pre-school children to an unfamiliar object, such as those seen in Figure 10.7, and required them to associate it with a noun ('This is a koba') or a fact ('My uncle gave this to me'). The researchers then investigated whether (1) the children were able to map the word or fact correctly by choosing the 'koba' or 'the object the uncle gave to the experimenter', from a series of 10 familiar objects and (2) the children were able to extend their knowledge of the object by identifying the object from unfamiliar ones. In the second condition, the children were asked, 'Is this one a koba?' (word condition), or 'Is this the one my uncle gave me?' (fact condition). The children were able to map successfully using the word or the fact. However, there was a difference between the two conditions when children had to extend their knowledge – the children extended the noun to other, similar objects but did not extend the fact.

In another study, 2–4-year-old children were taught a novel name for an object ('My cat stepped on this agnew') and given an arbitrary fact for a second, unfamiliar object (such as metal shelving brackets and Allen keys) (Behrend *et al.*, 2001). The children extended the novel name to more exemplars than they did facts, suggesting that some of the principles underpinning the learning of words and facts are different.

Overextension and underextension

Often a child may commit what are called errors of overextension or underextension. If a child has learned to identify a ball but says 'ball' when they see an apple or an orange, or even the moon, we must conclude that they do not know the meaning of 'ball'. This type of error is called **overextension** – the use of a word to denote a larger class of items than is appropriate. If the child uses the word to refer only to the small red plastic ball, the error is called

Table 10.7 Some overextensions that children make while learning new words

Word	Original referent	Application
mooi	Moon	Cakes, round marks on windows writing on windows and in books round shapes in books, round postmarks, letter *o*
buti	ball	Toy, radish, stone sphere at park entrance
ticktock	watch	All clocks and watches, gas meter, firehose wound on spool, bath scale round dial
baw	ball	Apples, grapes, eggs, squash, bell clapper, anything round
mem	horse	Cow, calf, pig, moose, all four-legged animals
fly	fly	Specks of dirt, dust, all small insects, child's own toes, crumbs of bread, a toad
wau-wau	dog	All animals, toy dog, soft house slippers, picture of an old man dressed in furs

Source: Adapted from Table 13.2 from *Psychology and Language: An introduction to psycholinguistics* by Herbert H. Clark and Eve V. Clark. © 1977, reprinted with permission of H.H. Clark & E.V. Clark.

an **underextension** – the use of a word to denote a smaller class of items than is appropriate. Table 10.7 lists some examples of children's overextensions while learning the meanings of new words.

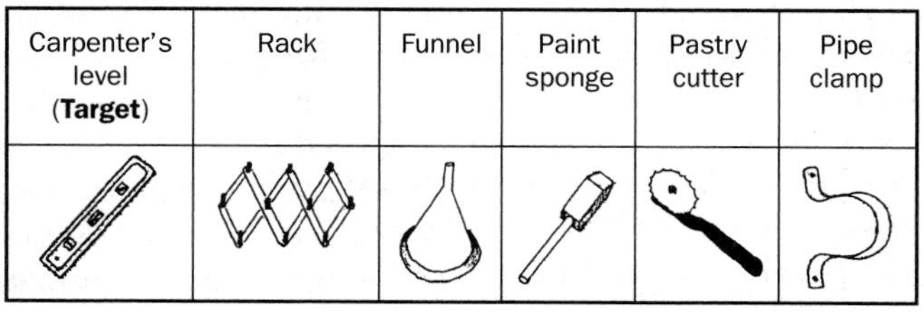

Both overextensions and underextensions are normal; a single pairing of a word with the object does not provide enough information for accurate generalisation.

Carers often correct children's overextensions. The most effective type of instruction occurs when an adult provides the correct label and points out the features that distinguish the object from the one with which the child has confused it (Chapman *et al.*, 1986). For example, if a child calls a yo-yo a ball, the carer might say, 'That's a yo-yo. See? It goes up and down' (Pease *et al.*, 1993).

Many words, including function words, do not have physical referents. For example, prepositions such as 'on', 'in' and 'towards' express relations or directions, and a child needs many examples to learn how to use them appropriately. Pronouns are also difficult; for example, it takes a child some time to grasp the notion that 'I' means the speaker: 'I' means me when I say it, but 'I' means you when you say it. In fact, parents usually avoid personal pronouns in speaking with their children. Instead, they use sentences such as 'Does [baby's name] want another one?'

Carpenter's level (**Target**)	Rack	Funnel	Paint sponge	Pastry cutter	Pipe clamp

Figure 10.7 Some of the unfamiliar objects referred to in Waxman and Booth's (2000) study.

Source: Waxman, S.R. and Booth, A.E., Principles that are invoked in the acquisition of words, but not facts. *Cognition*, 2000, 77, B33–B43. © 2000, with permission from Elsevier.

(meaning 'Do you want another one?'), and 'Daddy will help you' (meaning 'I will help you'). Abstract words such as 'apparently', 'necessity', 'thorough' and 'method' have no direct referents and must be defined in terms of other words. Therefore, children cannot learn their meanings until after they have learned many other words.

Bilingualism

The defining feature of bilingualism is the ability of the individual to meet the communication demands of the self or the individual's culture in two or more languages (Mohanty and Perregaux, 1997). **Bilingualism** is described as 'simultaneous' when two or more languages develop in childhood more or less simultaneously, spontaneously and naturally, and 'successive' when a second (and third) language is learned after the first, such as learning a second language during puberty (Romaine, 1989).

Until relatively recently, it was thought that bilingualism was detrimental to cognitive performance. The early studies, which compared Spanish–English bilinguals in America and English–Welsh bilinguals in Wales with monolinguals, showed that being able to speak two languages from childhood had negative consequences for intellectual development. It now appears that such conclusions are incorrect and that these early studies did not take into account socio-economic status, the degree of bilingualism or the skill in the second language (Lambert, 1977; Cummins, 1984). Rather than impairing cognitive ability, bilingualism seems beneficial to it (Perregaux, 1994). Mohanty (1982a, b, 1990) compared the cognitive performance of monolinguals with bilinguals in the Kond people of India; the bilinguals spoke Kui at home and Oriya outside the home environment. The bilinguals performed significantly better than the monolinguals on a series of cognitive and linguistic tasks. This superior performance in bilinguals was seen even in unschooled bilinguals (Mohanty and Das, 1987).

The learning of a second language can have two effects: additive and subtractive. A second language has an additive effect when it adds to cognitive ability allowed by the first language, that is, it enriches the use of the second language; a second language has a subtractive effect when it replaces the first language. For example, a second language might interfere with the production of words in the first language (you are speaking in one language but you can only remember some words in the other).

Is there a language acquisition device?

 According to Pinker (1984), 'In general, language acquisition is a stubbornly robust process; from what we can tell there is virtually no way to prevent it from happening, short of raising a child in a barrel.' The absence of barrels permitting, what shapes this linguistic learning process, and what motivates it?

There is vigorous controversy about why children learn to speak and, especially, why they learn to speak grammatically. Chomsky (1965) observed that the recorded speech of adults is not as correct as the dialogue we read in a novel or hear in a play; often it is ungrammatical, hesitating and full of unfinished sentences. In fact, he characterised everyday adult speech as 'defective' and 'degenerate'. If this speech is really what children hear when they learn to speak, it is amazing that they manage to acquire the rules of grammar.

The view that children learn regular rules from apparently haphazard samples of speech has led many linguists to conclude that the ability to learn language is innate. All a child has to do is to be in the company of speakers of a language. Linguists have proposed that a child's brain contains a **language acquisition device** which embodies rules of 'universal grammar'; because each language expresses these rules in slightly different ways, the child must learn the details, but the basics are already there in the brain (Chomsky, 1965; Lenneberg, 1967; McNeill, 1970).

The assertion that an innate language acquisition device guides children's acquisition of a language is part of a general theory about the cognitive structures responsible for language and its acquisitions (Pinker, 1990). The most important components are as follows:

- Children who are learning a language make hypotheses about the grammatical rules they need to follow. These hypotheses are confirmed or disconfirmed by the speech that they hear.

- An innate language acquisition device guides children's hypothesis formation. Because they have this device, there are certain types of hypothetical rule that they will never entertain and certain types of sentence that they will never utter.

- The language acquisition device makes reinforcement unnecessary; the device provides the motivation for the child to learn a language.

- There is a critical period for learning a language. The language acquisition device works best during childhood; after childhood, languages are difficult to learn and almost impossible to master.

Evaluation of the evidence for a language acquisition device

No investigator regards the first assertion – that children make and test hypotheses about grammatical rules – as tenable. Thus, we cannot simply ask children why they say what they do. Children's hypothesis-testing is a convenient metaphor for the fact that their speech sometimes follows one rule or another.

A more important – and testable – assertion is that the hypothesis testing is guided by the language acquisition device. The most important piece of evidence in favour of this assertion is the discovery of language universals: characteristics that can be found in all languages that linguists have studied. Some of the more important language universals include the existence of noun phrases ('the quick brown fox . . .'); verb phrases ('. . . ate the chicken'); grammatical categories of words such as nouns and adjectives; and syntactical rules that permit the expression of subject–verb–object relations ('John hit Andy'), plurality ('two birds'), and possession ('Rachel's pen').

However, the fact that all languages share certain characteristics does not mean that they are the products of innate brain mechanisms. For example, Hebb *et al.* (1973) observed that language universals may simply reflect realities of the world. When people deal with each other and with nature, their interactions often take the form of an agent acting on an object. Thus, the fact that all languages have ways of expressing these interactions is not surprising. Similarly, objects come in slightly different shapes, sizes and colours, so we can expect the need for ways (such as adjectives) to distinguish among them. It is not unreasonable to suppose that the same kinds of linguistic device have been independently invented at different times and in different places by different cultures. After all, archaeologists tell us that similar tools have been invented by different cultures all around the world. People need to cut, hammer, chisel, scrape and wedge things apart, and different cultures have invented similar devices to perform these tasks. We need not conclude that these inventions are products of a 'tool-making device' located in the brain. But even if some language universals are dictated by reality, others could indeed be the result of a language acquisition device. For example, consider the following sentences, adapted from Pinker (1990):

A1. Bill drove the car into the garage.

A2. Bill drove the car.

B1. Bill put the car into the garage.

B2. Bill put the car.

Someone (such as a child learning a language) who heard sentences A1 and A2 could reasonably infer that sentence B1 could be transformed into sentence B2. But the inference obviously is false; sentence B2 is ungrammatical. The linguistic rules that say that sentence A2 is acceptable but that sentence B2 is not very complex; and their complexity is taken as evidence that they must be innate, not learned. Pinker (1990, p. 206) concludes: 'The solution to the problem [that children do not utter sentence B2] must be that children's learning mechanisms ultimately do not allow them to make the generalisation.'

This conclusion rests on the assumption that children use rules similar to the ones that linguists use. How, the reasoning goes, could a child master such complicated rules at such an early stage of cognitive development unless the rules were already wired into the brain? But perhaps the children are not following such complex rules. Perhaps they learn that when you say 'put' (something) you must always go on to say where you put something. Linguists do not like rules that deal with particular words, such as put (something) (somewhere); they prefer abstract and general rules that deal with categories: clauses, prepositions, noun phrases and the like. But children learn particular words and their meanings – why should they not also learn that certain words must be followed (or must never be followed) by certain others? Doing so is certainly simpler than learning the complex and subtle rules that linguists have devised. It would seem that both complex and simple rules (or innate or learned ones) could explain the fact that children do not utter sentence B2.

The third assertion is that language acquisition occurs without the need of reinforcement, or even of correction. Brown and Hanlon (1970) recorded dialogue between children and parents and found that adults generally did not show disapproval when the children's utterances were ungrammatical and approval when they were grammatical. Instead, approval appeared to be contingent on the truth or accuracy of the children's statements. If there is no differential reinforcement, how can we explain the fact that children eventually learn to speak grammatically? It is undoubtedly true that adults rarely say, 'Good, you said that correctly', or, 'No, you said that wrongly'. However, adults do distinguish between grammatical and ungrammatical speech of children. A study by Bohannon and Stanowicz (1988) found that adults are likely to repeat children's grammatically correct sentences verbatim but to correct ungrammatical sentences. For example, if a child says, 'That be monkey', an adult would say, 'That is a monkey'. Adults were also more likely to ask for clarifications of ungrammatical sentences. Thus, adults do tend to provide the information children need to correct their faulty speech.

Chomsky's assertion about the defectiveness and degeneracy of adult speech is not strictly true, at least as far as it applies to what children hear. In fact, according to Newport *et al.* (1977), almost all the speech that a young child hears (at least, in industrialised English-speaking societies) is grammatically correct. If that is so, why should we hypothesise that a language acquisition device exists? Because, say some researchers, not all children are exposed to child-directed speech. 'In some societies people tacitly assume that children aren't worth speaking to and don't have anything to say that is worth listening to. Such children learn to speak by overhearing streams of adult-to-adult speech' (Pinker, 1990, p. 218).

Pinker's statement is very strong; it says that children in some cultures have no speech directed towards them until they have mastered the language. It implies that the children's mothers do not talk to them and ignores the fact that older children may not be quite so choosy about their conversational partners. To conclude that such an extreme statement is true would require extensive observation and documentation of child-rearing practices in other cultures. One of the strongest biological tendencies of our species is for a mother to cherish, play with and communicate with her offspring. If there really is a culture in which mothers do not do so, we need better documentation.

In fact, children do not learn a language that they simply overhear. Bonvillian *et al.* (1976) studied children of deaf parents whose only exposure to spoken language was through television or radio. This exposure was not enough; although the children could hear and did watch television and listen to the radio, they did not learn to speak English. It takes more than 'overhearing streams of adult-to-adult speech' to learn a language. The way that parents talk to their children is closely related to the children's language acquisition (Furrow *et al.*, 1979; Furrow and Nelson, 1986). Thus, the question is, just how much instruction (in the form of child-directed speech) do children need?

The fact that parents do not often reward their children's speech behaviours with praise or tangible reinforcers (such as sweets) does not prove that reinforcement plays no role in learning a language. We humans are social animals; our behaviour is strongly affected by the behaviour of others. It is readily apparent to anyone who has observed the behaviour of children that the attention of other people is extremely important to them. Children will perform a variety of behaviours that get other people to pay attention to them. They will make faces, play games and even misbehave in order to attract attention. And above all, they will talk.

The final assertion – that the language acquisition device works best during childhood – has received the most experimental support. For example, Newport and Supalla (1987) studied the ability of people who were deaf from birth to use sign language. They found that the earlier the training began, the better the person was able to communicate. Johnson and Newport (1989) also found that native Korean and Chinese speakers who moved to the USA learned English grammar better if they arrived during childhood. The advantage did not appear to be a result of differences in motivation to learn a second language. Such results are consistent with the hypothesis that something occurs within the brain after childhood that makes it more difficult to learn a language.

Conclusion

Observational studies such as these do not prove that a cause-and-effect relation exists between the variables in question. Johnson and Newport (1989) suggest that people's age (in particular, the age of their brain) affects their language-learning ability. But other variables are also correlated with age. For example, the Korean and Chinese speakers who moved to the USA as children spent several years in school; and perhaps the school environment is a particularly good place to learn a second language. In addition, adults are generally more willing to correct the grammatical errors made by children than those made by adolescents or other adults; thus, children may get more tutoring. It is certainly possible that the investigators are correct, but their results cannot be taken as proof that the brain contains an innate language acquisition device.

In one sense, a language acquisition device does exist. The human brain is a language acquisition device; without it, languages are not acquired. The real controversy is over the characteristics of this language acquisition device. Is it so specialised that it contains universal rules of grammar and provides innate motivation that makes reinforcement unnecessary?

The issue is made more interesting, if controversial, if we consider the ability of other higher primates to learn language. Other higher primates such as gorillas or chimpanzees do not naturally produce language although they have their own system of communication. Their vocal apparatus is different from that of humans so it would be unrealistic to assume that they would be able to articulate human language. However, these animals are the ones that are genetically closest to us; similar brain asymmetries, especially in those parts of the brain which are thought to mediate language, are seen in humans and apes. Would it be possible to teach primates human language? Do higher primates also possess an innate language acquisition device but need an environmental prompt for such a device to start working? These questions form the basis of the following Controversies in Psychological Science section.

Controversies in Psychological Science – Can other primates acquire language?

The issue

The members of most species can communicate with one another. Even insects communicate: a female moth that is ready to mate can release a chemical that will bring male moths from miles away; a dog can tell its owner that it wants to go for a walk by bringing its lead in its mouth and whining at the door. But, until recently, humans were the only species that had languages – flexible systems that use symbols to express many

Controversies in Psychological Science – *Continued*

meanings. But are other primates able to learn and use symbols in the same linguistic way that humans do?

The evidence

In the 1960s, Beatrice and Roger Gardner of the University of Nevada began Project Washoe (Gardner and Gardner, 1969, 1978), a remarkably successful attempt to teach sign language to a female chimpanzee named Washoe. Previous attempts to teach chimps to learn and use human language focused on speech (Hayes, 1952). These attempts failed because, as we noted above, chimps lack the control of tongue, lips, palate and vocal cords that humans have and thus cannot produce the variety of complex sounds that characterise human speech.

Gardner and Gardner realised this limitation and decided to attempt to teach Washoe a manual language – one that makes use of hand movements. Chimps' hand and finger dexterity is excellent, so the only limitations in their ability would be cognitive ones. The manual language the Gardners chose was based on ASL, the American sign language used by deaf people. This is a true language, containing function words and content words and having regular grammatical rules.

Washoe was 1 year old when she began learning sign language; by the time she was 4, she had a vocabulary of over 130 signs. Like children, she used single signs at first; then, she began to produce two-word sentences such as 'Washoe sorry', 'gimme flower', 'more fruit', and 'Roger tickle'. Sometimes, she strung three or more words together, using the concept of agent and object: 'You tickle me'. She asked and answered questions, apologised, made assertions – in short, did the kinds of things that children would do while learning to talk. She showed overextensions and underextensions, just as human children do. Occasionally, she even made correct generalisations by herself. After learning the sign for the verb 'open' (as in open box, open cupboard), she used it to say open faucet, when requesting a drink. She made signs to herself when she was alone and used them to 'talk' to cats and dogs, just as children will do. Although it is difficult to compare her progress with that of human children (the fairest comparison would be with that of deaf children learning to sign), humans clearly learn language much more readily than Washoe did.

Inspired by Project Washoe's success (Washoe died in 2007), several other investigators have taught primate species to use sign language. For example, Patterson began to teach a gorilla (Patterson and Linden, 1981), and Miles (1983) began to teach an orangutan. Washoe's training started relatively late in her life, and her trainers were not, at the beginning of the project, fluent in sign language. Other chimpanzees, raised from birth by humans who are native speakers of ASL, have begun to use signs when they are 3 months old (Gardner and Gardner, 1975).

Many psychologists and linguists have questioned whether the behaviour of these animals can really be classified as verbal behaviour. For example, Terrace *et al.* (1979) argue that the apes simply learned to imitate the gestures made by their trainers and that sequences of signs such as, 'please milk please me like drink apple bottle' (produced by a young gorilla) are nothing like the sequences that human children produce. Others have challenged these criticisms (Fouts, 1983; Miles, 1983; Stokoe, 1983), blaming much of the controversy on the method that Terrace and his colleagues used to train their chimpanzee.

Certainly, the verbal behaviour of apes cannot be the same as that of humans. If apes could learn to communicate linguistically as well as children can, then humans would not have been the only species to have developed language. The usefulness of these studies rests in what they can teach us about our own language and cognitive abilities. Through them, we may discover what abilities animals need to communicate as we do. They may also help us to understand the evolution of these capacities.

These studies have already provided some useful information. For example, Premack (1976) taught chimpanzees to 'read' and 'write' by arranging plastic tokens into 'sentences'. Each token represents an object, action or attribute such as colour or shape, in much the same way as words do. His first trainee, Sarah, whom he acquired when she was 1 year old, learned to understand complex sentences such as 'Sarah insert banana in pail, apple in dish'. When she saw the discs arranged in this order, she obeyed the instructions.

Chimpanzees can, apparently, use symbols to represent real objects and can manipulate these symbols logically. These abilities are two of the most powerful features of language. For Premack's chimpanzees, a blue plastic triangle means 'apple'. If the chimpanzees are given a blue plastic triangle and asked to choose the appropriate symbols denoting its colour and shape, they choose the ones that signify 'red' and 'round', not 'blue' and 'triangular'. Thus, the blue triangle is not simply a token the animals can use to obtain apples; it represents an apple for them, just as the word apple represents it for us.

Even though humans who the only primates who can pronounce words, several other species can recognise them. Savage-Rumbaugh (1990; Savage-Rumbaugh *et al.*, 1998) taught Kanzi, a pygmy chimpanzee, to communicate with humans by pressing buttons that contained symbols for words, as seen in Figure 10.8.

Kanzi's human companions talked with him, and he learned to understand them. Although the structure of his vocal apparatus prevented him from responding vocally, he often tried to do so. During a three-month period, Savage-Rumbaugh and her colleagues tested Kanzi with 310 sentences, such as 'Put a

Controversies in Psychological Science – *Continued*

toothbrush in the lemonade'. Three hundred and two of these had never been heard by the chimpanzee before. Only situations in which Kanzi could not have been guided by non-verbal cues from the human companions were counted; often, Kanzi's back was to the speaker. He responded correctly 298 times. Table 10.8 presents specific examples of these sentences and the actions that Kanzi took.

Conclusion

The most successful attempts at teaching a language to other primates are those in which the animal and the trainer have established a close relationship in which they can successfully communicate non-verbally by means of facial expressions, movements and gestures. Such interactions naturally lead to attempts at communication; and if signs (or spoken words) serve to make communication easier and more effective, they will most readily be learned.

Figure 10.8 Researcher Sue Savage-Rumbaugh taught her chimp, Kanzi, to communicate using a special keyboard.

Source: © 1999 Cable News Network, LP, LLP, All rights reserved.

Table 10.8 Semantic relations comprehended by Kanzi, a pygmy chimpanzee

Semantic relations	N	Examples (spoken)
Action–object	107	*'Would you please carry the straw?'* Kanzi looks over a number of objects on the table, select the straw, and takes it to the next room.
Object–action	13	*'Would you like to ball chase?'* Kanzi looks around for a ball, finds one in his swimming pool, takes it out, comes over to the keyboard, and answer 'Chase'
Object–location	8	*'Would you put out the grapes in the swimming pool?'* Kanzi selects some grapes from among several foods and tosses them into the swimming pool
Action–location	23	*'Let's chase to the A–frame,'* Kanzi is climbing in trees, has been ignoring things that are said to him. When he hears this he comes down rapidly and runs to the A-frame
Action–object–location	36	*'I hid the surprise by my foot,'* Kanzi has been told that a surprise is around somewhere, and he is looking for it. When he is given this clue, he immediately approaches the speaker and lifts up her foot
Object–action	9	*'Kanzi, the pine cone goes in your shirt,'* picks up a pine cone
Action–location–object	8	*'Go to the refridgerator and get out a tomato',* Kanzi is playing in the water in the sink. When he hears this he stops, goes to the refrigerator, and gets a tomato
Agent–action–object	7	*'Jeannine hid the pine needles in her shirt,'* Kanzi is busy making a nest of blankets, branches and pine needles. When he hears this, he immediately walks over to Jeannine, lifts up her shirt, takes out the pine needles, and puts them in his nest
Action–object–recipient	19	*'Kanzi, please carry the cooler to Penny,'* Kanzi grabs the cooler and carries it over to Penny
Other–object–action –recipient; action–recipient –location; etc.	69	

Source: Savage-Rumbaugh, E.S., Language acquisition in nonhuman species, *Development Psychobiology*, 1990, 23, 599–620. Copyright © 1990, this material is used by permission of John Wiley & Sons, Inc.

Brain development and language

In his book *The Biological Foundations of Language*, Lenneberg (1967) argued that the functional lateralisation of language – one cerebral hemisphere's superiority for processing language – begins at the same time as the child begins to acquire language and is complete at puberty. This conclusion was based on studies showing that in half a sample of children with lesions to the right or left sides of the brain, language was delayed if the lesion occurred in the first two years of life. The other half developed language normally (Basser, 1962). In adults and adolescents, language difficulties were associated with left-hemisphere lesions whereas mild language difficulties were associated with right-hemisphere lesions. Lenneberg thus argued that there was a sensitive period during which language should be acquired and lateralisation would develop.

Others (e.g. Krashen, 1973) argued that the hemispheres of the brain are equipotential at birth – each hemisphere is capable of undertaking the function for which the other becomes specialised. The critical period for lateralisation was complete by the age of 5 or 6 years. If lesions to the right hemisphere occurred before the age of 5 years, the child would show symptoms of aphasia, a disorder involving the inability to produce or comprehend speech. If damage occurred after the age of 5, no deficits in speech would arise suggesting that the normal left-for-language functional asymmetry had developed and was relatively complete. Krashen was involved in the study of an unusual case in which a young girl had been deprived of auditory stimulation and failed to develop normal language.

The case of Genie

Genie was a 13-year-old girl who had been chronically abused since infancy. The girl's father had harnessed her to a potty in a room in the back of the family house since she was at least 20 months old and deprived her of any linguistic stimulation. She slept in a crib covered with wire mesh. Her father was intolerant of noise and would beat her whenever she made any sound. Her mother fed her a diet of baby food, cereals and, occasionally, boiled eggs. When eventually spotted by social workers, the girl was 4 feet 6 inches tall and weighed 4 stone. She could not eat solid food and had nearly two complete sets of teeth. She was 13 years and 9 months old.

Her most remarkable psychological feature was her almost complete lack of language. She could not talk and had a vocabulary of about twenty words (she could understand concepts such as 'red' 'blue', 'green'). Her speech production was limited to 'nomore', 'stopit' and other negatives. Following her discovery, she was admitted to the Children's Hospital in Los Angeles for treatment. Researchers were interested in how handicapped Genie's language had become and what possible recovery could be made from such gross linguistic impairment (Fromkin *et al.*, 1972/73; Curtiss, 1977). There had been isolated instances of 'accidental' cases of language deprivation before, such as Victor, the 'wild boy of Aveyron', who had been found in 1800, lurking naked in front of a cottage in the Languedoc region of France. He had spent his 12 years from infancy living in the woods, surviving on a diet of acorns and potatoes. He had had his throat cut as a toddler and been left to die. Victor had no language, and while he never learned to speak, he achieved a rudimentary ability to spell.

A year after she was discovered, Genie's language ability underwent marked improvement. Her ability to structure according to rules was the equivalent of a 20-year-old's, and her spatial ability placed her in the adult ability category. She could tell the difference between singular and plural words and positive and negative sentences and could understand some prepositions. Her speech was limited to one or two word sentences, however, eventually becoming very descriptive and concrete ('big rectangular pillow', 'very, very, very dark-green box'). The 'explosion' of language, normally expected after such dramatic improvements, never materialised.

It became clear that Genie could develop new but basic language skills. She made a dramatic recovery from the time of her discovery to the time when the scientists had to abandon their studies. Yet, her language never fully recovered, remaining steadfastly descriptive, almost at the level one would expect primates to achieve with intensive language training. Her study showed, however, the remarkable, devastating effects of language and auditory deprivation on the development of language ability.

Plasticity and language development

In a series of famous experiments, Dennis and Whitaker (1976) and Woods (1980) found that the incidence of aphasia, an inability to produce or comprehend speech, following right-hemisphere damage was greater during infancy than if the lesions had occurred later in life. Other authors suggest that left-hemisphere lesions would produce the greatest deficits in language and speech if they occurred after the age of 5 or 6 years (Vargha-Khadem *et al.*, 1985). The evidence from the human literature was consistent with earlier experimental lesioning work in primates. This work found that if the brain of a monkey was lesioned during infancy, its recovery was significantly superior to that seen after the brain of an adult monkey was lesioned. This became known as the Kennard principle: the notion that recovery from brain damage during infancy is better than from damage during adulthood.

Another source of data suggesting a critical period for the development of asymmetry comes from studies of hemispherectomy, where one hemisphere is removed for medical reasons, usually because of the growth of a large tumour or because of intractable epilepsy. In adults, left hemispherectomies result in fairly severe aphasia, but left hemispherectomies in children are associated with almost complete recovery of language function (Searleman, 1977).

What these data suggest is that the brain has a degree of plasticity when it is developing. That is, specialised functions have not developed in any sophisticated way in one or other hemisphere during early growth. After a specific age, however, this specialisation has begun, but one or other hemisphere can undertake the functions of the other if the other is damaged.

For example, studies have shown that early brain lesions in children between 13 and 36 months old are associated with a delay in the development of expressive vocabulary, especially if damage is to the left side. However, there seems to be little effect on the next stage of language development, sentence production (Vicari *et al.*, 2000). If the damage occurs later, in adulthood, then it is hypothesised that the right hemisphere undertakes the language functions of the left (Hertz-Pannier *et al.*, 1999). One study has found that injury to the left temporal lobe is associated with subsequent increased activation of the right frontal lobe during verbal fluency (Voets *et al.*, 2006). MEG studies also suggest that lateralisation increases as a function of age (Ressel *et al.*, 2008).

Is half a brain enough?

In a novel experiment to explore the nature of plasticity, Hertz-Pannier *et al.* (2002) studied six children who underwent left hemispherectomy for intractable epilepsy (epilepsy that cannot be controlled by drugs) and monitored their brain activity during language tasks before and after the surgery. They hypothesised that if the brain shows evidence of plasticity, then we might expect the right hemisphere to take over the language function of the left. They used fMRI to study the children at age 6 years and 10 months and found the typical left lateralisation for language tasks such as word generation; there was little right hemisphere activity.

Following surgery, receptive language recovered quickly but expressive language and reading was slower to recover. When fMRI scanning was undertaken again at 10 years 6 months, there was a shift in activity to the right hemisphere during expressive and receptive language tasks. The regions that were activated – the inferior frontal temporal and parietal cortices – were analogous to those in the left hemisphere prior to the surgery.

This activation in the right hemisphere is also seen in adults recovering from aphasia. For example, Cappa *et al.* (1997) found that activation in the right temporoparietal region during the acute phase of recovery predicted improvement in auditory comprehension later on. More recently, a group of researchers has found that a period of intensive training in a group of patients who had suffered a stroke destroying parts of the left frontal cortex and who had difficulty in comprehending speech, led to increased activation in the bilateral network of regions associated with language. There were also increases in right hemisphere regions.

Another case study highlights how successful language development could be following such radical surgery (Battro, 2000). Nico is an Italian boy who was born with left hemiplegia. He managed to walk by age 18 months but developed intractable epilepsy at 22 months. Drugs and selective lesioning of the brain failed to halt the epilepsy and so, as a last resort and with the permission of Nico's parents, surgeons performed a right hemidecortication when the boy was 3 years and 7 months.

Nico recovered well and he did not lose his speech. His IQ was 107 and he learned to develop the basics of spelling and grammar at the same age as normal children through the use of a computer. He is still behind other children in his ability to draw and has difficulty forming letters of the alphabet and numbers with the right hand. The outcome of Nico's surgery suggests that the right hemisphere may be what Popper and Eccles (1977) described as a 'minor brain'. Without it, Nico has learned to develop the important function of language although his 'right hemisphere' functions, such as drawing, are impaired.

The neuropsychology of language and language disorders

You saw in Chapters 1 and 4 that neuropsychology aims to localise not only basic perceptual and sensory functions, such as touching, seeing, recognising objects and so on, but also quite sophisticated cognitive functions. The most extensively studied cognitive function is language, and our knowledge of the neuropsychology of language has come from three sources: studies of individuals with brain injury who show language impairment, individuals who do not develop language adequately, and neuroimaging studies in which activation of the brain in healthy individuals is monitored while they complete language tasks. These sources indicate that the mechanisms involved in perception, comprehension and production of speech are located in different areas of the cerebral cortex.

Language disorders

Brain damage can result from a large number of factors and can cause a wide variety of impairments in cognitive function. Some of the most pronounced impairments are those related to language. Some language impairments result directly from brain injury, others do not but are likely to be the result of disorganised or abnormal brain activity or structure. The most common language disorders are called the aphasias. The key feature of the aphasias is the loss of language function; the patient is unable to produce or comprehend speech. Other important disorders of language are reading impairment (dyslexia) and stuttering and all three of these disorders are considered in the next sections.

Aphasia

Aphasia literally means 'total loss of language function', although patients with the disorder do not lose all language: they are able to perform some language tasks, for example, depending on the site of the brain injury. Because of this, the term 'dysphasia' is sometimes used (dys- means 'partial loss of'). There are different types of aphasia, and the most common are summarised in Table 10.9. Two of the most common types are non-fluent (Broca's) aphasia and receptive (Wernicke's) aphasia. The areas of the brain which, when damaged, cause these aphasias can be seen in Figure 10.9.

Speech production: evidence from non-fluent (Broca's) aphasia

In order to produce meaningful communication, we need to convert perceptions, memories and thoughts into speech. The neural mechanisms that control speech production appear to be located in the frontal lobes. Damage to a region of the motor association cortex in the left frontal lobe (Broca's area) disrupts the ability to speak: it causes **non-fluent (Broca's) aphasia**, a language disorder characterised by slow, laborious, non-fluent speech (it is also called expressive, production or motor aphasia). When trying to talk with patients who have non-fluent aphasia, most people find it hard to resist supplying the words the patients are groping for. But although these patients often mispronounce words, the ones they manage to produce are meaningful. They have something to say, but the damage to the frontal lobe makes it difficult for them to express these thoughts.

Here is a sample of speech from a man with Broca's aphasia, who is telling the examiner why he has come to the hospital. His words are meaningful but what he says is not grammatical. The dots indicate long pauses.

Table 10.9 (a) Types of aphasia, their primary symptoms and the site of the associated brain lesion

Type of aphasia	Primary symptoms	Brain lesion to
Sensory (Wernicke's) aphasia	General comprehension deficits, neologisms, word retrieval deficits, semantic paraphasias	Post-perisylvian region: posterio-superior temporal opercular supramarginal angular and posterior insular gyri; planum temporale
Production (Broca's) aphasia	Speech production deficit, abnormal prosody; impaired syntaetic comprehension	Posterior part of the inferior frontal and precentral convolutions of the left hemisphere
Conduction aphasia	Naming deficits and impaired ability to repeat non-meaningful single words and word strings	Arcuate fasciculus, posterior parietal and temporal regions; left auditory complex, insula supramarginal gyrus
Deep dysphasia	Word repetition deficits; verbal (semantic) paraphasia	Temporal lobe, especially regions which mediate phonological processing
Transcortical sensory aphasia	Impaired comprehension, naming reading and writing, semantic irrelevancies in speech	Temporoparieto-occipital junction of the left hemisphere
Transcortical motor aphasia	Transient mutism and telegrammatic dysprosodic speech	Connection between Broca's area and the supplementary motor area; medial frontal lobe regions anterolateral to the left hemispheres frontal horn
Global aphasia	Generalised deficits in comprehension, repetiton, naming and speech production	Left perisylvian region, white matter, basal ganglia and thalamus

Source: G.N. Martin, *Human Neuropsychology* 2nd edn, Pearson/Prentice Hall

Table 10.9 (b) Symptomatology of aphasia

Type	Site of damage	Spontaneous speech	Comprehension	Paraphasia	Repetition	Naming
Broca's		Non-fluent	Good	Common	Poor	Poor
Wernicke's		Fluent	Poor	Uncommon	Poor	Poor
Conduction		Fluent	Good	Common	Poor	Poor
Global		Non-fluent	Poor	Variable	Poor	Poor

Source: G.N. Martin, *Human Neuropsychology* 2nd edn, Pearson/Prentice Hall (2006).

'Ah . . . Monday . . . ah Dad and Paul [patient's name] . . . and Dad . . . hospital. Two . . . ah doctors . . . , and ah . . . thirty minutes . . . and yes . . . ah . . . hospital. And, er Wednesday . . . nine o'clock. And er Thursday, ten o'clock . . . doctors. Two doctors . . . and ah . . . teeth. Yeah, . . . fine.'

Source: Goodglass, 1976, p. 278.

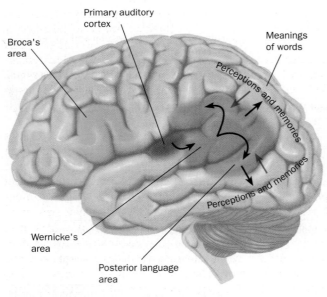

Figure 10.9 Words into thoughts and thoughts into words. The dictionary in the brain relates the sounds of words to their meanings and permits us to comprehend the meanings of words and translate our own thoughts into words. Black arrows represent comprehension of words; red arrows represent translation of thoughts or perceptions into words.

Lesions that produce non-fluent aphasia must be centred in the vicinity of Broca's area. However, damage restricted to the cortex of Broca's area does not appear to produce Broca's aphasia; the damage must extend to surrounding regions of the frontal lobe and to the underlying subcortical white matter (Damasio, 1989; Damasio *et al.*, 1996). Dronkers *et al.* (2007) used MRI to measure, in detail, the extent of the damage to the preserved brains of two of Broca's patients, including the famous Leborgne ('Tan').

They found that damage was much deeper than Broca reported (MRI was not available in his day) and other areas were also damaged including a large tract of fibre that connects the posterior and anterior language areas. Although damage to Broca's area can lead to transient impairment in speech production, it seems likely that damage to this fibre is necessary to produce severe speech difficulty.

Confusion about where – or what – Broca's area is exists even in the psychology literature today. A recent survey found that although 27 per cent of neuroimaging studies referred to Areas 44 and 45 as Broca's area, 52 per cent of the journal articles surveyed either did not define Broca's area or gave misleading or broad definitions of the region (Lindenberg *et al.*, 2007).

Wernicke (1874) suggested that Broca's area contains motor memories – in particular, memories of the sequences of muscular movements that are needed to articulate words. Talking involves rapid movements of the tongue, lips and jaw, and these movements must be coordinated with each other and with those of the vocal cords; thus, talking requires some very sophisticated motor control mechanisms. Because damage to the lower left frontal lobe (including Broca's area) disrupts the ability to articulate words, this region is the most likely candidate for the location of these 'programmes'. The fact that this region is located just in front of the part of the primary motor cortex that controls the muscles used for speech certainly supports this conclusion.

In addition to their role in the production of words, neural circuits located in the lower left frontal lobe appear to perform some more complex functions. Damage to Broca's area often produces **agrammatism**: loss of the ability to produce or comprehend speech that employs complex syntactical rules. For example, people with non-fluent aphasia rarely use function words. In addition, they rarely use grammatical markers such as '-ed' or auxiliaries such as 'have' (as in 'I have gone'). A study by Saffran *et al.* (1980) illustrates this difficulty. The following quotations are from agrammatic patients attempting to describe pictures:

> Picture of a boy being hit in the head by a baseball: 'The boy is catch . . . the boy is hitch . . . the boy is hit the ball.' (p. 229)
>
> Picture of a girl giving flowers to her teacher: 'Girl . . . wants to . . . flowers . . . flowers and wants to . . . The woman . . . wants to . . . The girl wants to . . . the flowers and the woman.' (p. 234)

In an ordinary conversation, non-fluent aphasics seem to understand everything that is said to them. They appear to be irritated and annoyed by their inability to express their thoughts well, and they often make gestures to supplement their scanty speech. The striking disparity between their speech and their comprehension often leads people to assume that their comprehension is normal. Their comprehension, however, is not normal. To test agrammatic people for speech comprehension, Schwartz *et al.* (1980) showed them a pair of drawings, read a sentence aloud and then asked them to point to the appropriate picture. The patients heard 48 sentences such as, 'The clown applauds the dancer' and 'The robber is shot by the cop'. For the first sample sentence, one picture showed a clown applauding a dancer, and the other showed a dancer applauding a clown. On average, the brain-damaged people responded correctly to only 62 per cent of the pictures (responses at chance levels would be 50 per cent). In contrast, the performance of normal people is around 100 per cent.

The agrammatism that accompanies non-fluent aphasia appears to disrupt patients' ability to use grammatical information, including word order, to decode the meaning of a sentence. Thus, their deficit in comprehension parallels their deficit in production. If they heard a sentence such as, 'The mosquito was swatted by the man', they would understand that it concerns a man and a mosquito and the action of swatting. Because of their knowledge of men and mosquitoes, they would have no trouble figuring out who is doing what to whom. But a sentence such as, 'The cow was kicked by the horse' does not provide any extra cues; if the grammar is not understood, neither is the meaning of the sentence.

Other experiments have shown that people with non-fluent aphasia have difficulty carrying out a sequence of commands, such as 'Pick up the red circle and touch the green square with it' (Boller and Dennis, 1979). This finding, along with the other symptoms described in this section, suggests that an important function of the left frontal lobe may be sequencing, both physically in terms of muscle movement (for example, the muscles of speech-producing words) and semantically in terms of sequencing actual words (for example, comprehending and producing grammatical speech). As you saw in the section on working memory in Chapter 8, the frontal cortex may be important for allowing us to sequence stimuli correctly. This sequencing role of the frontal cortex is returned to in the next chapter in relation to reasoning and in Chapter 13 in relation to organising social and emotional behaviour.

Speech comprehension: evidence from receptive (Wernicke's) aphasia

Comprehension of speech obviously begins in the auditory system, which is needed to analyse sequences of sounds and to recognise them as words. Recognition is the first step in comprehension. As we saw earlier in this chapter, recognising a spoken word is a complex perceptual task that relies on memories of sequences of sounds. This task appears to be accomplished by neural circuits in the upper part of the left temporal lobe – a region that is known as **Wernicke's area**.

Brain damage in the left hemisphere that invades Wernicke's area as well as the surrounding region of the temporal and parietal lobes produces a disorder known as **Wernicke's aphasia**. The symptoms of receptive aphasia are poor speech comprehension and production of meaningless speech (Wernicke's aphasia is also known as sensory or receptive aphasia). Unlike non-fluent aphasia, speech in receptive aphasia is fluent and unlaboured; the person does not strain to articulate words and does not appear to be searching for them. The patient maintains a melodic line, with the voice rising and falling normally. When you listen to the speech of a person with receptive aphasia, it appears to be grammatical. That is, the person uses function words such as 'the' and 'but' and employs complex verb tenses and subordinate clauses. However, the person uses few content words, and the words that he or she strings together just do not make sense. For example:

Well this is . . . . mother is away here working her work out o'here to get her better, but when she's looking, the two boys looking in other part. One their small tile into her time here. She's working another time because she's getting, too.

Source: Cookie Theft Picture Description from: Carroll, D. (1999) *Psychology of Language*, 3rd edn, Brooks/Cole Publishing Company.

Or this example of a conversation between a patient and a speech therapist:

Therapist: What did you have (to eat)?

PH: Today I haven't touched a/maiwa/d^/David. He had beastly tomorrow.

Therapist: Was the food good?

PH: Yes, it was fine.

Source: R.C. Martin (2003).

The failure of patients with Wernicke's aphasia to comprehend their own speech typically renders them unaware of their language processing problems and they will continue to participate in conversations, nodding in the appropriate places and taking turns to speak, blissfully unaware of their disorder.

A commonly used test of comprehension for receptive aphasia assesses the patient's ability to understand questions by asking them to point to objects on a table in front of them. For example, they are asked to 'point to the one with ink'. If they point to an object other than a pen, they have not understood the request. When tested this way, people with severe Wernicke's aphasia show poor comprehension.

Because Wernicke's area is a region of the auditory association cortex, and because a comprehension deficit is so prominent in receptive aphasia, this disorder has been characterised as a receptive aphasia. Wernicke suggested that the region that now bears his name is the location of memories of the sequences of sounds that constitute words. This hypothesis is reasonable; it suggests that the auditory association cortex of Wernicke's area recognises the sounds of words, just as the visual association cortex in the lower part of the temporal lobe recognises the sight of objects.

Wernicke's aphasia, like non-fluent aphasia, actually appears to consist of several deficits. The abilities that are disrupted include recognition of spoken words, comprehension of the meaning of words, and the ability to convert thoughts into words. Recognition is a perceptual task; comprehension involves retrieval of additional information from long-term memory. Damage to Wernicke's area produces a deficit in recognition; damage to the surrounding temporal and parietal cortex produces a deficit in production of meaningful speech and comprehension of the speech of others.

Brain damage that is restricted to Wernicke's area produces an interesting syndrome known as **pure word deafness** – a disorder of auditory word recognition, uncontaminated by other problems (Franklin *et al.*, 1994). Although people with pure word deafness are not deaf, they cannot understand speech. As one patient put it, 'I can hear you talking, I just can't understand what you're saying.' Another said, 'It's as if there were a bypass somewhere, and my ears were not connected to my voice' (Saffran *et al.*, 1976, p. 211). These patients can recognise non-speech sounds such as the barking of a dog, the sound of a doorbell, the chirping of a bird, and so on. Often, they can recognise the emotion expressed by the intonation of speech even though they cannot understand what is being said. More significantly, their own speech is excellent. They can often understand what other people are saying by reading their lips. They can also read and write, and, sometimes, they ask people to communicate with them in writing. Clearly, pure word deafness is not an inability to comprehend the meaning of words; if it were, people with this disorder would not be able to read people's lips or read words written on paper.

Wise *et al.* (2001) have suggested that the term 'Wernicke's area' has become meaningless because different research groups delineate the area in different ways and impute to it different functions. They re-analysed four brain imaging studies of Wernicke's area, defined generally as 'the left superior temporal cortex posterior to the primary auditory cortex'. The re-analysis identified two regions within 'Wernicke's area' which seemed to perform different functions. One part responded to speech and non-speech sounds, including the sound of the speaker's voice. The posterior part of this, near the parietal lobe, was active during speech production. The second part identified was more lateral and responded to external sources of speech; it was also active during the recall of word lists. This suggests that the functions of both parts are compatible with a hypothesis which states that the first region is involved in mimicking sounds and the second is involved in the transient representation of heard or internally generated phonetic sequences. Both processes, the authors argue, are important for the long-term memory of novel words.

If the region around Wernicke's area is damaged, but Wernicke's area itself is spared, the person will exhibit all of the symptoms of receptive aphasia except a deficit in auditory word recognition. Damage to the region surrounding Wernicke's area (the posterior language areas) produces a disorder known as **isolation aphasia**, an inability to comprehend speech or to produce meaningful speech accompanied by the ability to repeat speech and learn new sequences of words. The difference between isolation aphasia and Wernicke's aphasia is that patients with isolation aphasia can repeat what other people say to them; thus, they obviously can recognise words. However, they cannot comprehend the meaning of what they hear and repeat; nor can they produce meaningful speech of their own. Apparently, the sounds of words are recognised by neural circuits in Wernicke's area, and this information is transmitted to Broca's area so that the words can be repeated. However, because the posterior language area is destroyed, the meaning of the words cannot be comprehended.

Damage to other regions of the brain can disrupt particular categories of meaning in speech. For example, damage to part of the association cortex of the left parietal lobe can produce an inability to name the body parts. This disorder is called **autotopagnosia**, or 'poor knowledge of one's own topography' (a better name would have been autotopanomia, 'poor naming of one's own topography'). People who can otherwise converse normally cannot reliably point to their elbows, knees or cheeks when asked to do so, and they cannot name body parts when the examiner points to them. However, they have no difficulty understanding the meaning of other words.

Psychology in action – The man who lost his language: the phenomenology of aphasia

On Tuesday, 28 July we went to a party in London. I drive home because John had had too much to drink. At a red light I glanced at him, and saw on his face the expression of a man crazed by an apocalyptic vision. He laughed it off: 'Is that what you go around saying at parties, "Good evening, you have a crazed apocalyptic look on your face?" If I had known what that look meant, it is theoretically possible that I might have saved him . . .

Source: Sheila Hale (2002) *The Man Who Lost His Language*, p. 30.

On the morning of the 30 July 1992, just before nine o'clock, Sir John Hale, art historian and prolific author was found on his study floor, having the 'sweet witless smile of a baby' on his face and uttering only the words, 'the walls, the walls'. Hale had suffered a stroke. Sheila, his wife, had noted one of the signs just days before – a change in the musculature of his face. While most of the studies in this book emerge from academic journals, and are reported in the clinical way one would expect from such a source, Sheila Hale wrote a personal account of the disorder and its consequences, writing in careful and often touching detail about the day-to-day consequences of stroke and aphasia and how she coped with the virtual demolition of her husband's language.

Initially, John Hale was unable to speak or write or match written/spoken nouns to objects such as a razor, a chick, a pencil and some keys. He could surmise what people were saying from their gestures and tone of voice, laughing at jokes and following simple instructions. Reading for pleasure was difficult and he would turn over pages he could not follow. Curiously, he could understand academic journals and offprints which suggested a dissociation between reading for pleasure and reading for information. John was written off by his original consultant – at the time of the stroke, Hale was in his 60s and was felt to be unable to benefit from rehabilitation

– but an independent neurologist suggested that his intelligence alone might help his recovery. Sheila Hale discovered a series of language puzzle books designed for Roald Dahl's wife, Patricia Neal – who had become aphasic following a stroke – by Valerie Eton Griffiths, and recruited family and friends to use them with her husband. At this point, he began introducing new sounds into his conversation: *the*, *da* or *whoah*. He could copy shapes and words and perform mental arithmetic but was unable to write words independently.

At a new hospital, he was given a pad to write on. One of his earliest spontaneous examples of writing involved writing 'f' in the centre of the page and 'o', 'r' and 'k' diagonally to the right. He could sort Scrabble tiles into words – often punning with them. He could play Boggle and he could reconstruct sentences that had been cut up. Proof-reading his most recent book, he missed some errors but was able to direct his editor to the location of the references needed for the book.

His speech therapist originally thought that John could not benefit from therapy – ironically, because he was too exuberant and that anyone with his degree of expressiveness would not be sufficiently motivated to help themselves through the difficult process of rehabilitation. This view changed when, at a dinner party, she lifted up her arm and asked John what it was: 'John said *"da woahs"*. Elizabeth said, "No, John, listen to yourself. Now listen to me: *ahm*". John said *ahhhm*. "No, John, you're saying *ahhhm*. It's not quite right, is it? What is this? This is my . . . ?" John said *ahm*' (Hale, 2002, p. 191).

When Sheila asked the therapist how it could be that her husband could read German, English and French but not be able to write a sentence in any language, Elizabeth offered a series of illuminating metaphors: 'It is as though the road between Naples and Rome had been blown up. You can still travel between the two cities, but you have to make your way through the rubble to find an alternative route,' or 'The British Library has been shaken by an earthquake. The books have been

▶

Psychology in action – *Continued*

RICARDO WENT OUT SHOPPING TO BUY SOME FRUIT. HE BOUGHT A POUND OF _pears_ . AND A LARGE JUICY WATER _melan_ . HE ALSO WENT INTO THE OFF-LICENCE AND BOUGHT THREE BOTTLES OF _wine_ . HE WALKED HOME ALONG BY THE _river_ AND WATCHED THE MEN ROWING THE _boat_ . A VERY BEAUTIFUL _girl_ WAS SITTING ON A _bench_ SO HE SAT NEXT TO HER. SHE HAD LONG BLONDE _hair_ AND BIG BLUE _eyes_ . RICARDO SAID 'GOOD _morning_ IT'S A LOVELY _day_ ' SHE TURNED TO HIM AND _smiled_ SHOWING LOVELY WHITE _teeth_ . RICARDO OFFERED HER ONE OF HIS _pears_ . THEY TALKED HAPPILY FOR HALF AN HOUR AND THEN RICARDO ASKED HER OUT TO _dinner_ SHE AGREED AND THEY MET OUTSIDE THE _restaoran_ AT 7.30PM.

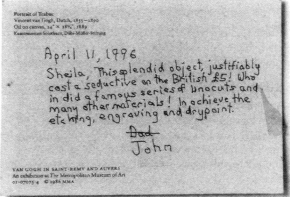

Some examples of John Hale's writing and attempts at written comprehension. The photograph shows Hale with his wife, Sheila.

Source: S. Hale (2002) *The Man Who Lost His Language*. London: Penguin.

Psychology in action – *Continued*

hurled off the shelves. They're all mixed up and the catalogues can't be found. The books are like your words: there they are, but you have no means of finding them' (Hale, 2002, p. 195).

John's understanding of words was excellent and he could recognise written and spoken reversed letter words, real words and non-words; he could match synonyms, and words to pictures. However, phonological segmentation was a problem: when presented with the words 'map' and 'gap' he was unable to indicate which sound had changed. He knew that both were different. He could identify the number of letters in a word and could fill in blanks in a story but sometimes made dysgraphic errors, writing 'borg' for 'dog'.

A curious deficit was his inability to recognise the subject of a sentence or picture. When presented with a picture of a boy on a bike and asked who was riding the bike, he would point to the word representing the verb ('riding' rather than the word 'boy'). He seemed to have lost understanding of 'who' words that stood for arguments. This lasted for two years. In 1995, his interest in reading for pleasure was rekindled, to such an extent that the house began to be over-run with biographies.

Three years after his stroke, John was able to speak the words: *haaloo, bye, I, fine, wine, bus, bow, bell, more, my, house* and *horse*. Sometimes, when trying to say one of these words, he would say 'arm' instead. Two years later, Sheila described a typical morning: 'Over lunch he tells me about his morning. *Mmmmmm* means walking along minding his own business. *Arrrr-up!* With his left hand describing an arc means that he has crossed a bridge. He meets a friend: broad smile, greeting gestures; they go into a pub; mime of conversation: *bahbahbahbahbah* – and drinking. Or John gets on a bus: sounds of changing gears, starting and stopping.'

Eventually, his non-language became less prosodic – he would introduce the words *um, oh, ah, aargh,* gah, *no* and *oh*

my God to stem the mellifluous aphasic flow. He took great pains to find the right word, a struggle observed in the brain-injured patient, Lt Zasetsky by Luria (1972) in his book, *The Man with a Shattered World.* 'It was so hard to write,' Zasetsky wrote, 'At last, I'd turned up a good idea. So I began to hunt for words to describe it and finally I thought up two. But by the time I got to the third word, I was stuck . . . Finally, I managed to write a sentence expressing an idea I had . . . sometimes I'll sit over a page for a week or two . . . But I don't want to give it up. I want to finish what I've begun. So I sit at my desk all day, sweating over each word.'

One October evening, Sheila Hale wrote, 'I was too weak to resist a quick, forbidden glance into the future. And what I saw was a succession of meals, sitting across a table from a husband who was no more, or less, companionable than an affectionate dog' (Hale, 2002, p. 61). John Hale hid his despair well until, one afternoon, his wife found him with his head bowed and his left hand covering his face: 'When I put my arms around him, I felt the tears on his face. He was crying for the first time since I had known him.'

Hale's book is testament to the support, love and care that can help an individual with aphasia deal with extreme communication difficulty. Despite the impairment in his speech, John continued to be charming, garrulous and intelligent company. David Chambers summed up the positive aspects of Hale when writing the historian's obituary in *The Times:* 'for those in his company, the infinitely modulated exclamations, chuckles and ironical groans which accompanied his enchanting smile seemed almost to amount to conversation. Gregarious as ever, he proved that, even in aphasia, life can be exhilarating.'

Specific language impairment

Some children have difficulties in producing or understanding spoken language, in the absence of known brain injury. The 3–4 per cent who exhibit this impairment are said to show **specific language impairment**. Grammar and phonology are the most affected aspects, but intelligence is within the normal range. When a 6-year-old with adequate hearing but specific language impairment is asked to repeat the sentence, 'Goldilocks ran away from the three bears because she thought they might chase her,' she says, 'Doedilot when away from berd. Them gonna chate her' (Bishop, 1997). A recent study suggests that one cause of these problems may be impaired auditory perception (B.A. Wright *et al.*, 1997). These researchers found that the children were impaired when perceiving tones that were brief, but not tones that were long.

Some language impairments, however, seem to occur in the absence of such auditory impairment. These impairments arise from a child's inability to acquire the rules of language early (Gopnik, 1997). One example of such a language impairment is the inability to produce the past tense. For example, in the following statement,

'Everyday he walks eight miles. Yesterday he . . .

some children would not be able to supply the past tense for 'walk' to complete the second sentence. These problems are seen in children who have normal auditory acuity and non-verbal and psychosocial skills, and, although they may have other difficulties such as dyslexia and depression, none of these factors has been reliably associated with these specific language impairments.

Table 10.10 The percentage of participants capable of marking novel words grammatically

Grammar	Language	Controls %	Impaired %
Past tense	English (in England)	95.4	38.0
	English (in Canada)	93.5	52.3
	Greek	87.1	20.0
	French	92.6	33.3
	Japanese	89.1	37.0
Plurals	English (in England)	95.7	57.0
	English (in Canada)	99.2	58.3
	Greek	79.8	42.1
Comparatives	English (in England)	74.0	21.0
Compounds	Japanese	80.5	20.2
	Greek	93.6	12.8
Diminutives	Greek	83.9	40.2

In each of these tests the subjects were given a context which required a grammatical rule to be applied to a novel word; for example, 'This pencil is weff' would require the participant to supply 'This pencil is even . . . [weffer]'.

In a review and theoretical analysis of these impairments, Gopnik (1997) has suggested there may be a strong genetic influence on their development because they tend to cluster in families and seem to occur in families cross-culturally.

Such impairments have also been found in languages such as English, Japanese, Greek and French. An example of the types of test used to determine specific language impairment is seen in Figure 10.10. Here, the participant is presented with a word they have never heard of (i.e. a non-word) and are given a grammatical rule to follow. The forms of impairment observed can be seen in Table 10.10.

Gopnik suggests that this specific impairment in the use of complex grammatical rules is universal, although critics have argued that auditory/articulation problems or general problems with cognition may be the source of the impair-

ment rather than a genetic, neural component. For example, children may leave off the /d/ sound when transforming an English word into the past tense. However, the problem does not seem to be specific to /d/ sounds. In languages where the past tense is transformed in a different way, the same specific language impairments have been observed. English, for example, has about four regular-form verbs; Greek has sixty. The number of mistakes in making past tenses seen in each language is proportional to the number of regular verbs they use. More to the point, as Gopnik notes, in French the final syllable is stressed so that it is not difficult to hear.

Speech and language disorders have been linked to chromosomes 3, 7, 13, 16 and 19. The genes underlying these are not fully identified, but one of these might be *FOXP2* located on chromosome band 7q31 (see Fisher, 2005 and Figure 10.11). Disruption of this gene leads to disruptions in articulation important for speech and seems to have evolved in the past 200,000 years. Striking evidence for this gene-linked disorder was found in a family where three generations were found to suffer from the impairment. Individuals with the genetic defect also have problems in expressing and understanding oral and written language. It is probably inaccurate to describe *FOXP2* as a 'language' gene, however, because it is also involved in other behaviour. To date, six chromosomes have been identified with links to specific learning impairment/dyslexia (Ramus, 2006).

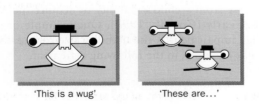

'This is a wug'   'These are...'

Figure 10.10 A task used to investigate a child's ability to understand grammar using novel words.

Source: Reprinted from Gopnik, M., Language deficits and genetic factors. *Trends in Cognitive Sciences*, 1997, 1(1) p. 7. © 1997, with permission from Elsevier Science.

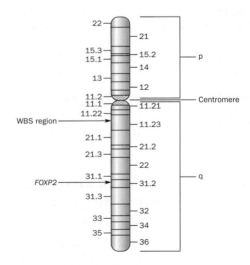

Figure 10.11 Recent research suggests that the *FOX P2* gene may be responsible for the development of speech and language disorders.

Source: Copyright © 2005 Massachusetts Medical Society. All rights reserved.

Dyslexia

The term **dyslexia** refers to a disorder involving impaired reading and it is one of the most common language disorders seen in children and adults. The incidence of the disorder lies between 5 and 17.5 per cent (Shaywitz, 1998). Although boys are thought to be affected more than girls, the evidence is unclear (Flynn and Rahbar, 1994). Many different types of dyslexia have been described but there are two broad categories: acquired dyslexia and developmental dyslexia. **Acquired dyslexia** describes a reading impairment resulting from brain injury in individuals with previously normal language. **Developmental dyslexia** refers to a difficulty in learning to read despite adequate intelligence and appropriate educational opportunity (Brunswick, 2009). The types of dyslexia and their symptoms are described in Table 10.11.

Acquired dyslexia

The most important forms of dyslexia which result from brain injury are visual word form dyslexia, phonological dyslexia, surface dyslexia and deep dyslexia. Visual word form dyslexia describes an inability to recognise words immediately but gradually with the naming of each letter (Warrington and Shallice, 1980). Sometimes a patient might commit a letter-naming mistake, pronouncing 'c, a, t . . . cat' when the word to be read is 'mat'. The disorder is thought to result from a disconnection between the region of the left hemisphere which mediates the recognition of word forms (Speedie et al., 1982) and the visual input system. Reading ability may rely on the perceptual and visual skills of the right hemisphere.

Phonological dyslexia refers to an inability to read pseudowords and non-words and is relatively rare (although phonological deficits are also seen in developmental dyslexia, described below). Phonological dyslexia provides evidence that whole-word reading and phonological reading involve different brain mechanisms and provides some support for the dual-route model of reading outlined earlier in the chapter (see Figure 10.12). Phonetic reading, which is the only way we can read non-words or words we have not yet learned, entails some sort of letter-to-sound decoding. It also requires more than decoding of the sounds produced by single letters, because, for example, some sounds are transcribed as two-letter sequences (such as 'th' or 'sh') and the addition of the letter 'e' to the end of a word lengthens an internal vowel ('can' becomes 'cane').

Surface dyslexia is the inability to recognise and read words based on their physical characteristics. Individuals are able to apply the grapheme–phoneme correspondence rules, however (described earlier in the chapter), but have difficulties with irregular words, using inefficient spelling-to-sound strategies (so, 'yacht' is pronounced as it reads and sounds).

Deep dyslexia refers to a severe inability to read; concrete words can sometimes be read but are commonly replaced by semantically related words. For example, a patient would read 'sleep' when the word is 'dream' (Coltheart et al., 1980). Abstract words are rarely pronounced accurately and neither are pronounceable non-words (indicating an inability to apply grapheme–phoneme correspondence rules).

Table 10.11 The dyslexias and the brain regions associated with them

Type of dyslexia	Primary symptoms	Brain regions implicated
Acquired dyslexia		
Visual word form dyslexia	Impaired sight reading; some decoding is possible	Disconnection between the angular gyrus of the dominant hemisphere and the visual input system
Phonological dyslexia	Deficits in reading pseudowords and non-words	Temporal lobe of the dominant hemisphere?
Surface dyslexia	Tendency to produce regularisation errors in the reading of irregular words	?
Deep dyslexia	Semantic substitutions, impaired reading of abstract words, inability to read non-words	Extensive damage to the dominant hemisphere
Developmental dyslexia	Impaired reading and spelling of words/non-words/pseudowords, poor phonological processing skills, sequencing and short-term memory, some visuo-perceptual defects	Temporo-parietal regions of the dominant hemisphere

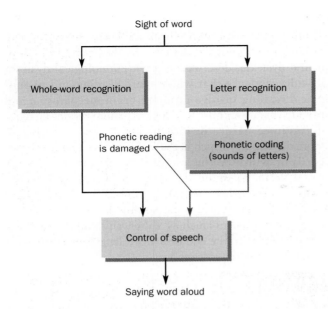

Sight of word

Whole-word recognition

Letter recognition

Phonetic reading is damaged

Phonetic coding (sounds of letters)

Control of speech

Saying word aloud

Figure 10.12 A hypothetical explanation of phonological dyslexia. Only whole-word reading remains.

Developmental dyslexia

The symptoms of developmental dyslexia resemble those of acquired dyslexias. Developmental dyslexia first manifests itself in childhood. It tends to occur in families, which suggests the presence of a genetic (and hence biological) component (Grigorenko *et al.*, 1997). Attempts have been made to categorise types of developmental dyslexia along the same lines as the acquired dyslexias. Such attempts usually distinguish between reading disorders which involve a deficit in 'sounding out' a word or in identifying words on the basis of visual form (Brunswick, 2009). Various names have been suggested for the two types such as dysphonetic v. dyseidetic (Fried *et al.*, 1981), phonological v. morphemic dyslexia (Temple and Marshall, 1983), and P (perceptual) and L (lingual) type (Bakker, 1992).

Although not all psychologists agree with such distinctions, a fairly constant factor in developmental dyslexia is poor awareness of the phonological features of sound, that is, poor phonological awareness (Stahl and Murray, 1994). The segmentation of words into sounds, being aware of alliteration, verbal repetition and verbal naming are all impaired in developmental dyslexia. For example, if children are asked to transpose the first sounds of the words 'mustard' and 'salad' (thereby producing 'sustard' and 'malad'), those with developmental dyslexia are unable to do this. Similarly, individuals with developmental dyslexia may be unable to perform phonological tasks such as indicating what is left when you take either the first or last sound away from a word such as 'mice'.

There also seems to be a deficit in the verbal or phonological memory of developmental dyslexics. For example, a number of studies have shown that these individuals have a poorer memory span than good readers for letter strings, words in a sentence and strings of digits. The stimuli do not have to be printed, the deficit is purely language-based; memory for unfamiliar faces or abstract patterns is intact (Lieberman *et al.*, 1982). Is this poor phonological memory the cause of the reading disorder?

Developmental dyslexia: possible neuropsychological causes

Visual pathway deficits

Some psychologists have argued that phonological impairments do not explain the persistent and severe nature of dyslexia (Hulme and Roodenrys, 1995). Reading is a complex task that requires phonology, memory and visual perception and there are various theories that attempt to explain developmental dyslexia in terms of dysfunctional neuronal systems in several areas of the brain (Habib, 2000). Stein and his colleagues (Stein, 1991; Stein and Walsh, 1997), for example, have suggested that developmental dyslexia is associated with poor visual direction sense, poor binocular convergence (described in Chapter 6), and visual fixation.

Stein's view argues that dyslexics are unable to process fast, incoming sensory information adequately. Most information from the retina to the cortex via the thalamus travels through one of three visual system pathways. One of these systems – the magnocellular (M) pathway – is thought to carry visual information about space, such as movement, depth, and the relationships between the positions of stimuli. Some researchers have implicated a malfunctioning M pathway in dyslexia but have had difficulty in explaining why the defective pathway makes reading difficult.

Studies have shown that poor visual fixation, poor tracking from left to right and poor binocular convergence appear to hinder the development of normal reading (Eden *et al.*, 1994). In an fMRI study of developmental dyslexia and the ability to process visual motion, Eden *et al.* (1996) found that moving stimuli (such as dots) failed to activate the cortical area that is projected to by the magnocellular pathway (area V5). In competent readers, this area was activated in both hemispheres during the task. Furthermore, the presentation of stationary patterns did not produce different patterns of brain activation in dyslexic individuals and controls, suggesting that the dyslexic sample had difficulties specifically with attending to moving stimuli.

One hypothesis suggests that the M pathway plays an important role in selective attention. It acts as an atten-

According to Agatha Christie, the world's most successful writer: 'I myself, was always recognised . . . as the 'slow' one in the family. It was quite true, and I knew it and accepted it. Writing and spelling were always terribly difficult for me. My letters were without originality. I was . . . an extraordinarily bad speller and have remained so until this day.'

Danny Glover **(a)**, Richard Branson **(b)**, Jay Leno **(c)** and Agatha Christie **(d)** . . . all very successful public figures. All are also dyslexic.
Source: (a) Frazer Harrison/Getty Images; (b) Chris Jackson/Getty Images; (c) Stephen Shugerman/Getty Images; and (d) Walter Bird/Getty Images.

tional spotlight which focuses on important stimuli and ignores all the clutter surrounding these stimuli. Vidyasagar and Pammer (1999) put this hypothesis to the test. They asked 21 reading-impaired children and age-matched normal readers to complete a standard visual search task in which they had to locate a stimulus that was characterised by a combination of colour and form (for example, looking for a grey triangle in a background of grey circles). The greater the number of distractors in this task, the greater the number of errors made by the reading-impaired group. When there were fewer than 36 distractors, the impaired readers did as well as their age-matched counterparts. When the number increased to 70, a significantly greater number of errors were committed by the impaired reading group, suggesting to the authors that in the dyslexic group visual search mechanisms are compromised when a visual scene is cluttered. Because reading places great demands on the attentional spotlight

– which detects the conjunction of features – an impairment in this process may be explained by deficits in the system that turns on and operates the spotlight.

A challenge was reported in a study which tested this explanation (Stuart *et al.*, 2006). People with developmental dyslexia have an impairment in one of the two visual pathways, the magnocellular pathway, which means that they are not sensitive to rapidly changing stimuli. A deficit in the auditory equivalent means that they have difficulty in segmenting speech, making accurate phonological representations of what they read and making grapheme–phoneme correspondences. Stuart *et al* measured auditory and visual contrast thresholds in adults with severe reading difficulties. This group showed normal ability to detect visual contrasts (and auditory contrasts). The data undermine the notion that the magnocellular pathway is defective in allowing a person to be sensitive to contrasts. Perhaps, the researchers suggest, the abnormality lies at the level of the interaction between this pathway and the other visual pathway, the parvocellular pathway.

Neural dysfunction

One of the consistent findings in neuroimaging studies of developmental dyslexia is that a decrease in blood flow is seen in temporal and inferior parietal areas, namely the areas involved in letter-to-sound conversion, the analysis of speech sounds and word form recognition (Brunswick *et al.*, 1999; Hoeft *et al.*, 2006, 2007; Aylward *et al.*, 2003; Horwitz and Braun, 2004). A study of 17 male dyslexics and a control group of 14 men, for example, found that blood flow to the superior part of the temporal lobe – a region called the angular gyrus – increased in normal readers with good reading performance: good reading skill was associated with greater blood flow to this area (Rumsey *et al.*, 1999). However, greater blood flow to this area was associated with poor reading skill in the dyslexic sample, suggesting that the good readers relied on this region to read and the region undertook the task adequately, but when the dyslexic readers also relied on the same region, it contributed to the task very poorly. Pugh *et al.* (2000) compared brain activation in impaired and normal readers who completed language tasks requiring minimal to considerable phonological processing. If tasks are print-related and involve no processing of the phonology of words, then there should be evidence of connectivity/activation between the angular gyrus and the superior temporal lobe in dyslexic participants. This is what Pugh *et al.* found.

Languages with fairly transparent reading systems, such as Italian, are less likely to present readers with difficulties. Paulesu *et al.* (2001) used PET to measure brain activation in French, English and Italian dyslexic participants and their respective control groups. Participants read either bisyllabic words or non-words aloud (an explicit reading

task) or as they made decisions about specific physical features of letters in words (an implicit reading task). Activity in the same region in the left hemisphere was reduced in all three dyslexic groups. The region included the left middle, inferior and superior temporal cortex.

A recent study has extended the study of dyslexia in other languages to Chinese. In logographic Chinese, graphic forms (characters) are mapped onto syllables whereas in English, units (letters) are mapped onto phonemes. For this reason, when Chinese people engage in working memory tasks, there is activation in the areas responsible for visuospatial manipulation and the left middle frontal gyrus. There is the reading of complex shapes and characters and orinunciation must be memorised by rote. Earlier studies had associated impaired reading in logographic Chinese with anomalous activation in the left middle frontal gyrus (Siok *et al.*, 2004). In a follow-up study, Siok *et al.* (2008) found reduced activation in the same area in people identified as dyslexic in Chinese. This finding is important because it suggests that the brain regions implicated in dyslexia depend on whether the language is alphabetic (e.g. English, Italian and so on) or non-alphabetic. See Figure 10.13.

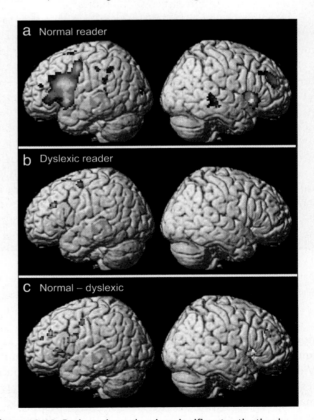

Figure 10.13 Brain regions showing significant activation in dyslexic and normal readers during a rhyme judgement task.

Source: Siok, W.T., Niu, Z., Jin, Z., Perfetti, C.A. and Tan, L.H. A structural–functional basis for dyslexia in the cortex of Chinese readers. *Proceedings of the National Academy of Sciences*, 2008, 105, 14, 5561–6.

Failure of lateralisation

One model of developmental dyslexia suggests that dyslexics have delayed or reduced left hemisphere function or have no lateralised preference (Bishop, 1990; Galaburda *et al.*, 1994). There is evidence that function and structure are more symmetrical in dyslexic samples. When good and poor readers respond to visual or auditory stimuli, brain electrical activity is symmetrical in dyslexic readers but typically left-based in controls (Cohen and Breslin, 1984; Brunswick and Rippon, 1994; Rippon and Brunswick, 1998). A group of North American researchers has found that the size and type of brain region correlates with degree of reading difficulty (Leonard *et al.*, 2006). In an MRI study of 11–16-year-old boys and girls with reading and language impairments, they found that smaller and more symmetrical brain structures were associated with considerable reading and language difficulties, and that larger, more asymmetric structures were associated with poor word reading (but not comprehension). The study also found, however, that 75 per cent of the children with developmental dyslexia showed asymmetry in a very important region for dyslexia: planum temporale (it was longer in the left, in contrast to some studies).

The planum temporale (PT) is a small region corresponding to the auditory association cortex in the temporal lobe. Because of the PT's prominence in the left hemisphere (where it is longer) and because it contains an area that is functionally the same as Wernicke's area, some researchers have suggested that this structure is important for language (see Beaton, 1997, for a thorough discussion). This idea, however, is speculative (Galaburda, 1995). For example, the leftward asymmetry of the planum temporale may simply be nothing more than a physical feature of the brain; it simply happens to be larger on the left than the right. However, there do seem to be more anomalies in asymmetry in dyslexics than in normal-reading samples. Control readers have a larger planum temporale in the left hemisphere than the right whereas dyslexic readers show a similarly sized structure in both hemispheres.

Best and Demb compared the degree of planum temporale asymmetry in a group of young dyslexic adults having a known M-pathway deficit with a control group (Best and Demb, 1999). Using three methods of brain imaging, the authors found little difference between the controls and the dyslexics: both showed the typical leftward PT asymmetry. However, some methods did point towards greater symmetry in the dyslexics. What this, and other independent evidence, suggests, the authors conclude, is that a sub-type of dyslexia may have the characteristic leftward asymmetry but not the M-pathway deficits.

Cerebellar dysfunction

The cerebellum is best understood as the region which contributes to motor function, posture and balance, although recent research implicates it in a variety of non-motor functions such as reading, speech perception and even emotional expression (Desmond, 2001; Justus and Ivry, 2001). Damage to the structure, for example, results in impairments in grammatical morphology (see Table 10.12).

It has also been implicated in developmental dyslexia. Nicolson *et al.* (1999) found that activation in the cerebellum was significantly lower in dyslexic than normal readers during the execution of familiar and novel motor tasks. The authors suggest that this cerebellar dysfunction affects the learning of new skills and the 'performance of automatic, overlearned skills'. Reading, they argue, is a complex behaviour composed of a number of interacting motor behaviours which need to be learned and improved over time. The dysfunctional cerebellum is not a cause of dyslexia but is a key structure in dyslexia.

Right-sided reduction in the front of the cerebellum has correctly predicted over 72 per cent of children with dyslexia: that is, the reduction in the region was correlated with poor reading (Eckert *et al.*, 2003). Other studies find that activation is more diffuse in the cerebellum in dyslexic children who generate appropriate verbs to a noun (Baillieux *et al.*, 2009). Rae *et al.* (2002) found that the side of the cerebellum that controlled the writing hand was

---

Table 10.12 Some grammatical errors made by patients with cerebellar damage

Italian patient (translation): I was watching [the] television. One moment after, immediately after, to feel one-half not to go. To have an attack, to be unable to speak. Upstairs there was my wife sleeping because it was midnight. I suddenly to stand up, suddenly to fall down. Not to do anything because there was the carpet . . .

Silveri *et al.* (1994)

Italian patient (translation): Razor hand. First there was razor and brush. A brush was used now instead spray. Foam on the hands then palm cream razor hand I do like this. I repeat operation against the growth. Same blade twice. Or electric razor. Face well dry. To use before pre-shave lotion. Batteries or current same thing. But electric razor skin used to must be.

Zettin *et al.* (1997)

Source: T. Justus, The cerebellum and English grammatical morphology: evidence from production, comprehension, and grammaticality judgements, *Journal of Cognitive Neuroscience*, 2004, 16 (7), 1115–30.

less well developed in dyslexic adults than controls. However, as Bishop (2002) argues, the development of the cerebellum depends on the degree of experience a person has with writing: a child with literacy problems is less likely to pick up a pen and use it frequently. Consequently, the cerebellum does not show the same strength of development seen in individuals who have a history of well-practised writing (Bishop, 2002).

Word recognition and production: neuroimaging studies

see activity on mypsychlab

Neuroimaging studies of normal readers generally conclude that the left hemisphere participates in language-related tasks more actively than does the right hemisphere and that specific regions of the left hemisphere are involved in the different components of language such as speech production, comprehension, processing of sound, meaning, and so on (Brunswick, 2004).

Petersen *et al.* (1988) were the first to conduct a PET investigation of language processing in healthy individuals. They found that the left posterior temporal cortex (including the primary auditory cortex and Wernicke's area) was significantly more active during passive listening of words than during a control condition. Repeating the nouns activated the primary motor cortex and Broca's area.

When people were asked to think of verbs that were appropriate to use with the nouns, even more intense activity was seen in Broca's area. Price *et al.* (1994) have also reported that greater activation in the left inferior and middle frontal cortices was found during performance of a lexical decision task whereas more temporal regions were activated during reading aloud and reading silently.

An important aspect of language analysis is, as you saw earlier in the chapter, phonological processing – the putting together of sounds to make meaningful words. Neuroimaging studies have found that when individuals discriminate between spoken words on the basis of phonetic structure, when they discriminate between consonants and when they make judgements about rhyme or engage in phonological memory tasks, activation in the left frontal cortex near Broca's area is found (Fiez *et al.*, 1995; Paulesu *et al.*, 1996; Zatorre *et al.*, 1996). Other studies report involvement of the temporal cortex and angular gyrus especially during tasks involving drawing analogies, repeating words and in reading words and pseudowords (Nobre *et al.*, 1994; Karbe *et al.*, 1998).

This evidence suggests that Broca's area and the frontal cortex are necessary for the phonetic manipulation of language but that the posterior temporal cortex is responsible for the perceptual analysis of speech (Zatorre *et al.*, 1996).

However, the picture may be a little more complex. Binder *et al.* (1997) compared the analysis involved in the phonetic and semantic perception of aurally presented words with the analysis of non-linguistic stimuli such as tones. A large network of left-hemisphere regions was activated during the semantic analysis, including areas in the frontal, temporal and parietal cortex. Activation, therefore, was not limited to one specific region.

Damasio *et al.* (1996), in a comprehensive study of its kind, evaluated the effects of language processing in individuals with brain lesions in both hemispheres, inside and outside the temporal regions. Damasio *et al.* hypothesised that there is no single mediating site for all words, but there are separate regions within a larger network that are activated by different kinds of word. There were three categories of words: persons, non-unique animals and non-unique tools, each of which should be processed by different parts of the frontal and temporal lobe. Although 97 individuals showed normal language, 30 did not; 29 of these had brain injury to the left hemisphere. While impaired retrieval of words was associated with temporal cortex damage, abnormal retrieval of animal words was found in patients with left interior temporal lobe damage and abnormal retrieval of tools was associated with posterolateral inferior temporal cortex damage.

Because we cannot infer normal function from brain damage, Damasio *et al.* conducted a second experiment in which healthy individuals performed the same language tasks while undergoing a PET scan. Although all words activated the left temporal cortex, specific categories were associated with activation of specific regions of the brain. Naming of tools activated the posterior, middle and inferior temporal gyri, for example, and animal naming activated other parts of the inferior temporal cortex. These results are similar to those of Martin *et al.* (1996), which showed that different categories of words appeared to activate different parts of the brain. A recent study has even suggested that silently naming the use of tools activates Broca's area and the left premotor and supplementary motor area (Grafton *et al.*, 1997). This suggests that even the naming of a tool's use can activate those parts of the brain that would be activated during the actual movement involved in using those tools.

There is significant overlap between neuroimaging and lesion studies in what they reveal about localisation of language processes. However, in neuroimaging experiments, it is unclear whether the activation in specific regions is necessary for the aspects of language processing studied. According to Price *et al.* (2003), one method of determining the necessity of these areas is to examine lesion data and investigate whether lesions to different areas are associated with different deficits.

Price *et al.* used fMRI to study two patients with acquired dyslexia. One patient had damage to all of the left temporal regions that are usually activated during normal reading. He was able to read some highly image-able words but was unable to read pseudowords and made meaning errors when reading others (saying 'wrong' when trying to read the word 'error'). The pattern is consistent with deficits seen in deep or phonological dyslexia and suggests that he relies on semantics when translating written words into sounds. The second patient also showed left temporal lobe damage but the lesion did not affect the superior temporal lobe (but did affect the inferior and anterior region). She could read regular words and most pseudowords but had greater difficulty in reading irregularly spelled words, a pattern typical of surface dyslexia. She had difficulty in reading words that required semantic processing, suggesting that the areas damaged might be important for semantic processing.

The first patient was asked to read highly imageable words during scanning; the second was asked to read one of a triad of regular three-letter words. For example, the word BUS would appear under two identical words. The first patient showed activation in all the language areas one would expect to be activated during normal reading, except for the area damaged. The second patient activated all the typical language areas but showed a reduction in areas associated with semantic processing. On the basis of these single-case studies, Price *et al.* suggest that translating written words to sounds is mediated by the left mid-fusiform gyrus in the temporal cortex. But, when semantic processing is impaired, the posterior part of this region and left frontal areas tries to undertake the function of translating the written word into phonology via semantics.

Is there a visual word form area?

People with visual word form dyslexia are unable to recognise the form of words presented visually. Studies with healthy individuals have localised the ability to identify visual letter strings as words – visual word form – in the left fusiform gyrus. Consequently, this area has been known as the visual word form area (Warrington and Shallice, 1980) because it responds to the visual, rather than auditory, forms of words (Giraud and Price, 2001).

Studies have suggested that damage to the ventral temporal lobe and fusiform gyrus are associated with an inability to recognise words while the ability to recognise individual letters is intact (Binder and Mohr, 1992); patients with fusiform gyrus damage engage in letter by letter reading (Beversdorf, *et al.*, 1997). Neuroimaging studies show that this region is active during the perception of word and word-like forms but it is less active during the perception of strings of letters that are unfamiliar such as consonant-string non-words (Buchel *et al.*, 1998). Polk and Farah (2002) found that the left ventral visual cortex was active during the recognition of pseudowords and words presented in normal case. Words and non-words which had alternating case letters activated the area just as strongly as did the pseudowords and words presented in regular form. The findings suggest that this region may respond to abstract letter identities rather than the font, size or case of the letters. The results were supported by the findings of another fMRI study which showed that activation in the left inferotemporal area was stronger during alphabetic letter strings than to chequerboards and was greater during word perception than during the perception of consonants (Cohen *et al.*, 2002).

Cutting edge – Irony–a look inside the brain

As neuroimaging methods and machinery become more complicated, so do the topics studied by psychologists who measure neural correlates of behaviour. Psychology has come a long way since the late 1980s when PET was used to measure brain activation during simple exercises such as reading or speaking single words. An example of the new complexity is a study in which researchers compared brain activation during the comprehension of literal, metaphoric or ironic sentences (Eviatar and Just, 2006). The aim was to discover whether different brain regions or systems were involved in these different types of comprehension.

Sixteen healthy adults read three-sentence stories that ended with a literal, metaphoric or ironic sentence. When utterances were metaphoric, activation was higher in the left inferior frontal gyrus and in both sides of the inferior temporal lobe than when utterances were ironic or literal. Irony was associated with more activation in the right superior and middle temporal gyri than were the literal statements (the metaphor condition fell in between the two).

The data suggest that different types of semantic information recruit different regions of the brain, especially the right temporal lobe. Irony is especially associated with right hemisphere activation, and this might reflect the 'processing of communicative intent or the construction of a coherent narrative.' (p. 2355). Metaphor processing has been associated with right hemisphere activity. The researchers suggest that when a task is more 'lexical', as theirs was, this would recruit the left hemisphere. If the participant had to make a judgement about the plausibility of a metaphor (a more 'holistic' task), this would recruit the right hemisphere.

Neuroimaging and language – An international perspective

Deep orthographies such as those found in English and French are a minefield of rules and linguistic irregularities. In English there are 1,120 ways of using graphemes (letters and strings of letters) to form 40 sounds (phonemes). Italian, on the other hand, has 33 graphemes representing 25 phonemes. When psychologists talk about the localisation of language, it is easy to forget that language is not a standard, unitary process but is heavily culture-bound. English, Russian and French, for example, all have different orthographical and phonological rules. Some authors have suggested that this explains the differences in word reading speed in English and Italian individuals (Italians are faster).

A recent meta-analysis of behavioural lateralisation studies (e.g. dichotic listening, visual field studies) of bilingualism has found differences between early and late bilinguals (Hull and Vaid, 2007). Early bilinguals (who acquired both languages before the age of 6), showed evidence of bilateral language representation; late bilinguals (who acquired language after the age of 6) showed greater left hemisphere dominance. In this second group, left hemisphere dominance was greater if participants were not proficient at the second language and if the second language was English.

Neuroimaging studies suggest more left hemisphere involvement in language by bilingual individuals and that similar cortical areas may be recruited during the processing of both languages. A study of French and English speakers, for example, found that performing language tasks in both languages was associated with activity in the left inferior frontal cortex (Klein *et al.*, 1995). Another study found that there was activation in different parts of Broca's area when people performed language tasks using a language learned in adulthood, but this activation was absent in those who had learned the language in childhood (Kim *et al.*, 1997). There was no difference in activation in Wernicke's area.

Some researchers have argued that such differences might reflect participants' proficiency in using language rather than the age at which the second language was acquired (Perani *et al.*, 1998). If there is an overlap in the language areas that mediate both tongues, this may be due to the similarity of the two languages spoken. Most studies, for example, have studied bilinguals who speak Indo-European languages (English, French, Italian and so on). Perani *et al.* (1996) compared brain activation in Italian–English speakers, where English was learned later in life, and Spanish–Catalan speakers, where Catalan was learned concomitantly with Spanish. Focal activity in the left hemisphere language regions was determined by expertise and not age of acquisition, a finding that has been replicated (Chee *et al.*, 1999; Dehaene *et al.*, 1997). Would the same overlap be seen if the two languages spoken were different in terms of syntax (meaning and grammar), morphol-

ogy (physical construction of the language) and phonology (the sound of the language)?

To test this hypothesis, Klein *et al.* (1999) measured cerebral blood flow in seven native speakers of Chinese (Mandarin) who had acquired English during adolescence. Mandarin uses pitch and tone to a greater extent than does English. The participants' task was to repeat words in Mandarin and English and to generate a verb in response to a noun in Mandarin and English. All words were presented auditorily and participants were asked to respond vocally. Klein *et al.* (1999) found that an area in the left frontal cortex was activated during speech production in Mandarin and English. A similar area was found to be active during French and English language processing in a previous study of Klein *et al.*'s (1995). Such findings can even extend to speakers of four or more languages.

Breillman *et al.* (2004), for example, used fMRI to measure the response of six quadrilingual participants who were asked to generate appropriate verbs to nouns; if the word 'fish' was presented, the participant might respond with 'swim'. Participants had knowledge of four to five common languages (English, German, Italian, French or Spanish) and completed the verbal task in each of their languages. As previous studies would predict, the task was associated with left-sided activation but, curiously, this activation was more pronounced in the languages in which participants were least proficient. This suggests that when people speak languages in which they are proficient the brain expends less energy – the process is more automatic and requires fewer cognitive resources for this reason. If people are not proficient in a language, there has to be a greater attempt at producing and understanding that language; this, in turn, recruits greater neural resources in order for the process to succeed.

In two PET studies, Paulesu *et al.* (2000) asked six English and six Italian university students either to read aloud words and non-words (experiment 1) or to perform a feature detection task (experiment 2) which involved paying attention to physical aspects of words presented visually rather than to the words themselves. They were not asked to read the words in experiment 2. The authors found that, across both experiments, the Italian speakers showed greater activation in those areas responsible for processing phonemes (left temporal regions) whereas the English speakers showed greater activation in other areas of the temporal cortex and frontal cortex (areas activated during word retrieval and naming). The areas activated can be seen in Figure 10.14.

This study was the first to show cultural effects on brain function related to language in healthy individuals and suggests that the neurophysiological difference may underpin the behavioural findings from word reading speed studies.

Neuroimaging and language – *Continued*

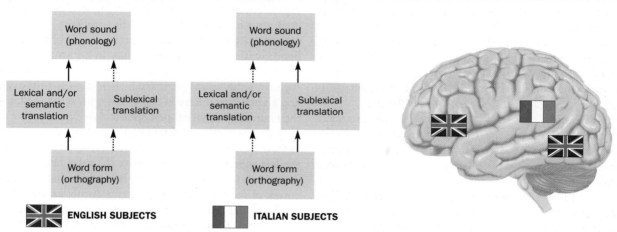

Figure 10.14 The different strategies used by English and Italian speakers are reflected in different types of brain activation.

Source: Fiez, J., Sound and meaning: How native language affects reading strategies. *Nature Neuroscience*, 2000, 3 (1), 3–5, reprinted by permission of the author and Nature Publishing Group.

The result is in keeping with studies of aphasia patients among different ethnic Chinese groups. Yu-Huan *et al.* (1990), for example, have reported that unilateral stroke leads to greater incidence of aphasia in dextrals with right-sided lesions (crossed aphasia) but only among the majority ethnic group called the Han. Crossed aphasia is rare among the minority ethnic group (the Uighur-Kazaks) and Wernicke's aphasia is generally rare in the Han. One explanation for this dissociation may lie in the way in which the languages of the groups differ: the Uighur-Kazak language is Indo-European-based and phonological in nature; the Han language,

conversely, is non-phonetic ('ideographical') where one sound can have multiple meanings.

A similar distinction is found in Japanese. Phonetic-based symbols (Kana) and logographic symbols (Kanji) are used routinely in written Japanese. Left-sided lesions are associated with impaired Kana reading in Japanese participants but preserved Kanji reading (Sasanuma, 1975). When healthy individuals are exposed to the different symbols in a typical visual field experiment, a left visual field advantage for Kanji is reported, suggesting right hemisphere involvement (Elman *et al.*, 1981).

Braille and Sign language

Gesturing preceded the sophisticated vocal communication of evolutionary modern times but, as you saw earlier, we still use gesture to communicate. More seriously, the congenitally deaf use American or British Sign Language. But to what extent does the brain have different systems for understanding the different types of communication – those that rely on our ability to hear and one that relies on our ability to decipher symbols or actions?

These questions assume an absolute definition of language. Goldberg has suggested that instead of referring to language per se, we should adopt the more general term 'descriptive systems' (Goldberg, 1989). Under this umbrella he includes various cognitive systems ('superstructures') which are normally employed to assemble the 'codes' received via the elementary 'feature detection' systems such as the visual and auditory cortices. Language,

as traditionally defined, is one such system. Others include mathematical or computational languages and musical notation. Early encounters with these systems are characteristically tentative, but gradual familiarity develops into automatic processing.

Schlesinger (1988) has observed a specific inability in some deaf children to manipulate the linguistic code, i.e. they experience difficulty in understanding questions, they are unable to formulate hypotheses, they have difficulty in conceptualising superordinate categories, and they appear to exist in a 'preconceptual, perceptual world'. In short, these people display precisely the syntactic and semantic deficits associated with isolated right hemisphere speech in those who have experienced left hemisphere damage in later life. Perhaps these deficits are caused by a shift from an initial stage of right hemisphere language to mature left hemisphere language. Neville *et al.* (1989), for example, have found that only deaf people with a perfect grasp of English grammar displayed 'normal' left hemisphere specialisation, concluding that both in the deaf and in those with normal hearing, grammatical competence is necessary and sufficient for left hemisphere specialisation if it occurs early. Early competence in spoken or signed language brings about this development of the left hemisphere and bestows an advantage on the right side of perceptual space, i.e. the right visual field and the right ear, via the dominant contralateral sensory pathways. Obviously, this perceptual advantage is grossly impaired following left hemisphere damage.

Unfortunately, this early exposure to signed language which brings about the shift of language functions to the left hemisphere is not always available to deaf children. Evidence has shown that hearing children of deaf parents and deaf children of deaf parents acquire sign language in infancy as a primary language and tend to show the shift to left hemisphere mediation of language (Grossi *et al.*, 1996). Many deaf children of hearing parents, however, have only restricted exposure to sign language during the critical period of development, a privation which may lead to a total arrest or delay, depending on the degree of deficiency of the linguistic experience, of cerebral maturation. In this situation, the child would continue to display signs of predominantly right hemisphere language as predicted in the absence of a shift to left hemisphere dominance.

Individuals who are deaf but have learned sign language appear to show activation in areas of the right hemisphere while signing. Using fMRI, Neville *et al.* (1998) measured brain activation in three groups of people: monolingual speakers of English who could hear; native deaf signers of American Sign Language (ASL); and bilingual users (of English and ASL) who could hear. Participants watched a videotape recording of a deaf signer producing sentences in ASL, and read English sentences presented on a computer monitor. The study found that although all groups activated the typical left hemisphere areas (Broca's and Wernicke's) when they processed English sentences, the native speakers of ASL also showed corresponding increases in the right hemisphere.

Could the results be due to the reorganisation of the cortex in the deaf participants? This is unlikely because both the hearing and deaf participants who were fluent ASL signers showed the same right hemisphere activation. Paulesu and Mehler (1998) have suggested that this pattern of activity may, instead, reflect the possibility that the right hemisphere holds the grammar for sign language because it requires representations of both sides of the body.

In the first brain imaging study of the perception of British Sign Language, nine hearing and nine congenitally deaf individuals had their brain activity measured by fMRI during the perception of sentences presented in BSL (MacSweeney *et al.*, 2002). An analogous auditory task in English was completed by hearing individuals. Regardless of the modality of communication, there was activation in Broca's area and in Wernicke's area – both bilaterally – during the language perception tasks. However, differences did emerge between tasks in temporal and occipital areas. The auditory task in hearing individuals was associated with increased activity in the auditory cortices. This activation was not found during BSL. BSL, on the other hand, was associated with activity in an area called V5 at the junction of the temporal and occipital cortex. V5 is the region of the visual cortex which responds to movement and so activation here is consistent with what we know of the neurology of visual perception.

When hearing and deaf people's responses to BSL were explored, however, deaf signers showed greater activation in the left superior temporal cortex than did hearing signers. This result is intriguing because it suggests that the auditory cortex of the temporal lobe is active during an auditory language task in hearing individuals but that it may respond to visual input in congenitally deaf individuals.

This part of the temporal lobe has been described as a multi-modal language area (Buchel *et al.*, 1998) because it can be activated by language processed in different modalities. The MacSweeney study indicated that this was so for sign language. Buchel *et al.* observed a similar phenomenon when studying blind participants reading Braille. When people engaged in tactile reading, the posterior left temporal area (Area 37) was active. Buchel *et al.* proposed that this area in blind, Braille-reading participants promotes activity in other parts of the brain that allows participants access to words. However, this area was active only during written word recognition, not spoken word recognition.

Neuropsychological models of language: a summary

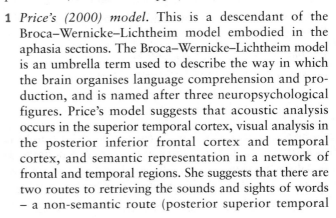

A recent review of neuropsychological models of language suggests that there are four competing and plausible frameworks for understanding the role of the brain in speech production and comprehension (Shalom and Poeppel, 2008).

1 *Price's (2000) model.* This is a descendant of the Broca–Wernicke–Lichtheim model embodied in the aphasia sections. The Broca–Wernicke–Lichtheim model is an umbrella term used to describe the way in which the brain organises language comprehension and production, and is named after three neuropsychological figures. Price's model suggests that acoustic analysis occurs in the superior temporal cortex, visual analysis in the posterior inferior frontal cortex and temporal cortex, and semantic representation in a network of frontal and temporal regions. She suggests that there are two routes to retrieving the sounds and sights of words – a non-semantic route (posterior superior temporal

cortex) and a semantic route (via posterior/inferior temporal cortex). Speech planning is governed by the anterior part of Broca's area and actual output is the responsibility of the motor cortex. The emphasis in Price's model is on semantic processing.

2 *Friederici's (2002) model.* This model makes two claims. The first is that the temporal lobe is responsible for semantic identification (such as the retrieval of memorised semantic information) and the frontal lobe constructs semantic relationships. The second is that the structure of syntax is built before semantic processing occurs and that these two interact later on in the processing stream.

3 *Hickok and Poeppel's (2004) model.* This utilises the distinction drawn in visual processing between the ventral and the dorsal streams (which you read about in Chapter 6 and also in the dyslexia section). They propose a visual and an auditory stream. The visual stream has two substreams, one (ventral) projecting to the temporal lobe and which is responsible for visual object recognition (the 'what') and a dorsal one projecting to the parietal and frontal lobes, which are involved in the visual representations of spatial attributes of language (the 'where'). The auditory stream is analagously conceptualised in the same way. The model, however, has little to say about the role of Broca's area.

4 *Indefrey and Levelt's (2004) model.* This proposes that Wernicke's area is involved in lexical analysis and in the representation of words but the posterior middle temporal lobe is involved in the phonological aspects of retrieval. It sees word production as involving five main types of representation (from appreciating the idea that a stimulus is lexical, to the breakdown of phonological output into syllables to production) each of which is processed at different times (from 175 ms after stimulus onset to 600 ms).

Although each says something slightly different about language processing and how it occurs in the brain, there are similarities between them. They suggest that:

- memorisation (learning and retrieval) occurs in the temporal lobe;

- analysis occurs in the parietal lobe;

- synthesising (creating combinations of representations) occurs in the frontal lobe;

and that:

- the inferior parietal lobe, inferior frontal lobe and the whole of the temporal lobe are involved in phonological processing;

- the middle areas are involved in syntactic processing;

- inferior areas are involved in semantic processing.

Caveats and complications

Sex differences

Early studies of language differences in men and women, utilising fairly basic methods, reported a greater right visual field (RVF) advantage when responding to words presented to the left and right visual fields in men. That is, information received by the left hemisphere (via the right visual field) is processed more quickly in men (Boles, 1984). Early neuroimaging studies showing greater left hemisphere activation in men when completing language tasks but a more symmetrical pattern of activation found in women (Pugh *et al.*, 1996), but the literature is mixed. Knaus *et al.* (2004), for example, found greater leftward asymmetry in the planum temporale in women whereas Sommer *et al.*'s (2004) meta-analysis of 14 functional imaging studies comprising 377 men and 442 women found no evidence for a sex difference in brain activity during language processing. The most recent review has found no differences in proficiency between the sexes: there is an early advantage for girls but this disappears into adulthood (Wallentin, 2009). There is no difference in brain activation or structure.

Language and the right hemisphere

The right side of the brain is not neglected in language. It takes on especial importance when the left hemisphere is damaged and may compensate for the language function lost after such damage. It is involved in the appreciation of metaphors (Bottini *et al.*, 1994) and in the processing of prosody and the affective tone of speech (Pell and Baum, 1997).

How good is the right hemisphere at processing language? And does it compensate well when the left hemisphere is damaged or removed during childhood? Evidence suggests that it does. Vanlancker-Sidtis (2004) examined the language and communication skills of an adult who had undergone a hemispherectomy at age 5. Consistent with what has previously been reported, the participant performed at normal levels on neuropsychological tests: he was able to pronounce, understand grammar, and understand word and sentence meaning at the levels we would expect of a control participant. However, slight impairments were found on three tests: the patient had difficulty in pronouncing phonemically complex words, comprehending linguistic contrasts in prosody (i.e. understanding the difference between the pronunciation of 'moving van' and 'moving van' when the stress is on 'moving' or 'van') and in deciding whether one of two line drawings matched a sentence spoken by the experimenter.

Interestingly, these impairments in prosody did not manifest themselves in the patient's everyday life. He could converse, use humour and take turns when in conversation at a level which belied his surgery. The research suggests, however, that although removal of the 'language' hemisphere does not impair most language functions, specific testing picks up on specific deficits. The author, however, could not rule out the possibility that the patient was naturally left-handed, and, therefore, had 'right-hemisphere' speech.

Handedness

Handedness refers to the degree to which individuals preferentially use one hand for certain activities (such as writing, unscrewing a jar, throwing a ball). It can also refer to the strength of hand skill. It is found in a variety of species and in most primates (from old/new world monkeys to great apes). Evidence of handedness or laterality goes back 2 million years; we seem to be the most lateralised of the primates. The right-left hand ratio in chimps is 2:1; in humans, it is 9:1 (Hopkins and Cantaloupo, 2008).

Handedness may be relevant to language because left- and right-handers may have speech localised in different hemispheres. According to a pioneering study by Rasmussen and Milner (1977), 96 per cent of right-handers and 70 per cent of left-handers in their study had left-hemisphere speech. Other, recent estimates place the figures at 95.3 per cent and 61.4 per cent, respectively (Segalowitz and Bryden, 1983). There are more men who are left-handers than women (Papadatou-Paston *et al*, 2008), possibly due to an X-linked allele.

The implication of these figures is that a proportion of left-handers do not have left-hemisphere speech but may have right-hemisphere or bilateral speech (this is why most neuroimaging studies of language indicate that their participants were all right-handed; this reduces the likelihood of variability in brain asymmetry). Right-handers are called dextrals and right-handedness is referred to as dextrality. Left-handers are called sinistrals and left-handedness is referred to as sinistrality. You can quickly see from these terms, that left-handers have not been treated

Ronald Reagan, George Bush Snr, Bill Clinton and, now, Barak Obama . . . the latest in a run of left-handed US Presidents'.
Source: Press Association Images/Molly Riley/AP

particularly fairly by language ('dextrous' means skilled; 'sinister' means menacing and evil; the French for left is *gauche*, which can also mean clumsy). There is even a theory that left-handers die sooner than right-handers (you can find more on this controversy in Martin, 2006).

A large neuroimaging study (*N*=188) of moderate and strong right-handers found that approximately 92 per cent of the sample showed left hemisphere language, with around 7 per cent showing right hemisphere activation during a language task (Knecht *et al.*, 2000a, b). There was no difference in lateralisation between men and women and there were no differences in task performance between the sexes.

The degree of activation in the right hemisphere during a word-generation task increases with the left-handedness of the participant (Knecht *et al.*, 2000a, b). Some psychologists have argued that human language evolved from gesture and that these gestures are 'behavioural fossils' which accompany speech. Corballis (1999), for example, argues that the proposition that language is gestural in origin might explain the relationship between handedness and cerebral asymmetry for language (of which, more later). Corballis cites evidence showing that right-handers primarily gesture with their right hand (which may not be surprising), but that left-handers (who have primarily left-hemisphere-based speech but show a more diverse pattern of localisation with some having speech in both hemispheres, or the right hemisphere), gesture with both hands. The logical consequence of the gestural hypothesis is that it was not language which distinguished *Homo sapiens* from other primates, but our ability to vocalise our communication instead of gesturing it.

The right shift theory

One theory of handedness suggests that the distribution of differences between the skills of both hands is determined by a single gene (Annett, 1985). Individuals who possess the rs+ allele have their hand distribution shifted to the right; their left hemisphere becomes dominant for speech. Individuals with the *rs++* gene show an even greater shift to the right hand (these individuals are called homozygotes) whereas those with the *rs+−* gene show a lesser degree of hand dominance (these individuals are called heterozygotes). Those without the rs+ allele (who express the rs− genotype) will show no overall bias in hand dominance.

This theory is called the **right shift theory** because it suggests that a single gene shifts dominance to one hand (this oversimplifies a complex theory but it is basically correct). Annett's theory is important because it suggests a relationship between hand skill and language (and even cognitive) ability. For example, Annett's theory predicts that heterozygotes (those with the rs+− allele) will be more advantaged on some skills than others, and that homozygotes (those with the rs++ or the rs− − allele) and those with the rs+ gene absent, will be disadvantaged.

Annett and her colleagues (Annett and Manning, 1989; Annett, 1992) have shown that extreme left- and right-hand dominance in hand skill is associated with poorer reading ability than is intermediate hand skill. Annett (1993) also reported that children with intermediate hand skill were more likely to be selected for elite schools in the UK. Individuals with the least bias to dextrality perform better in terms of arithmetical ability and spatial skill (Annett and Manning, 1990; Annett, 1992).

However, research from other laboratories has not found unequivocal evidence for Annett's theory. For example, McManus *et al.* (1993) assessed the handedness and intellectual ability of medical students and examined differences between three degrees of right-handedness, from weak to strong preference. He found no evidence of cognitive advantage or disadvantage between weak, intermediate and strong right-handers. Similarly, Resch *et al.* (1997) administered a series of cognitive ability tests to 545 students whose hand preference they also measured. They found that although those at the left end of the handedness continuum showed the poorest spelling, nonverbal IQ and educational success, there was no significant difference between this group and an intermediate and right-handed group, whereas Annett's theory might predict that strong right-handers would also exhibit poorer language ability. Palmer and Corballis (1996) have also found no relationship between hand preference and reading ability in 11–13-year-old children. Instead, reading ability was predicted by the overall level of hand skill rather than by the skill difference between hands.

Others have criticised Annett's model for other reasons. For example, Provins (1997) argues that handedness is a product of motor learning and environmental pressure. What is genetically determined, Provins argues, is not handedness but the motor capacity which could produce left- and-right hand preference, depending on the environment. Other critics such as Corballis (1997) have queried whether a single gene locus for handedness is reasonable: although the data would seem to fit a single-gene model, most genes have several loci, as we saw in Chapter 3 and will see again in Chapter 11 when we discuss the role of genetics in intelligence.

McManus (1985) has proposed that what is important is not hand skill, as Annett's model suggests, but hand preference. He proposes that a dextral allele (D) predisposes us towards right-hand preference while a chance allele (C) produces no directional bias. Individuals with the D allele (DD genotype) will develop a right-hand preference whereas those with the C allele (CC genotype) are equally likely to show left- or right-hand preference. Both models have attracted interest from researchers investigating the relationship between handedness and cognitive/language ability. Neither has fully explained this relationship but they provide an explanatory framework in which such relationships could operate.

Chapter review

Speech and comprehension

- Language can be defined as an orderly system of communication that involves the understanding or interpretation of vocal or written symbols.
- Phonemes are the basic elements of speech but research has also shown that the primary unit of analysis is not individual phonemes but groups of phonemes, perhaps syllables.
- Recognition of words in continuous speech is far superior to the ability to recognise them when they have been isolated. We use contextual information in recognising what we hear.
- Meaning is a joint function of syntax and semantics. All users of a particular language observe syntactical rules that establish the relations of the words in a sentence to one another. These rules are not learned explicitly. People can learn to apply rules of an artificial grammar without being able to say just what these rules are.
- The most important features that we use to understand syntax are word order, word class, function words, affixes, word meanings and prosody. Content words refer to objects, actions and the characteristics of objects and actions, and thus can express meaning even in some sentences having ambiguous syntax.
- Chomsky has suggested that speech production entails the transformation of deep structure (ideas, thoughts) into surface structure (actual sentence).
- Speech comprehension requires more than an understanding of syntax and semantics: it also requires knowledge of the world. We must share some common knowledge about the world with a speaker if we are to understand what the speaker is referring to.
- Speech errors, although incorrect, follow syntactical rules; the errors lie in the content of the speech.

Reading

- Recognition of written words (reading) is a complex perceptual task which involves scanning text, perceiving and understanding symbols and sounding out these visual symbols.
- The eye-tracking device allows researchers to study people's eye movements and fixations and to learn from these

behaviours some important facts about the nature of the reading process. For example, we analyse a sentence word by word as we read it, taking longer to move on from long words or unusual ones.

- Once a word has been perceived, recognition of its pronunciation and meaning takes place. Long or unfamiliar words are sounded out, that is, they are read phonologically by a process called phonic mediation.
- Short, familiar words are recognised as wholes. In fact, only whole-word reading will enable us to know how to pronounce words such as 'cow' and 'blow', or 'bone' and 'one', which have irregular spellings.
- The dual-route model of reading suggests that we have two routes for reading: one which does not rely on grapheme–phoneme correspondence rules and another which does.

Language acquisition

- Studies using the habituation of a baby's sucking response have shown that the human auditory system is capable of discriminating among speech sounds soon after birth.
- Human vocalisation begins with crying, then develops into cooing and babbling, and finally results in patterned speech. During the two-word stage, children begin to combine words creatively, saying things they have never heard.
- Child-directed speech is very different from that directed towards adults; it is simpler, clearer and generally refers to items and events in the present environment. As young children gain more experience with the world and with the speech of adults and older children, their vocabulary grows and they learn to use adult rules of grammar.
- Children seem to pay less attention to phonetic detail of language as they grow older, presumably because the process of acquiring vocabulary and understanding of objects and situations is computationally complex.
- Although the first verbs children learn tend to have irregular past tenses, once they learn the regular past tense rule (add '-ed'), they apply this rule even to irregular verbs they previously used correctly.
- A language acquisition device contains universal grammatical rules and motivates language acquisition. Although children's verbal performance can be described by complex rules, it is possible that simpler rules – which children could reasonably be expected to learn – can also be devised.
- Deliberate reinforcement is not necessary for language learning, but a controversy exists about just how important child-directed behaviour is.
- A critical period for language learning may exist which occurs between the ages of 5 and 14 years old; learning a new language after this is more difficult.
- Bilingualism refers to competence in two or more languages that are used to communicate with significant others. The languages activate similar brain areas, regardless of age of acquisition.

- Studies of other primates suggest that apes can be taught at least some of the rudiments of language.

Brain development and language

- Damage to either hemisphere is associated with better recovery of language when it occurs in childhood than adulthood.
- Some researchers have suggested that the lateralisation of language – left hemisphere dominance for language processing – is complete by around age 6; others argue that it continues until puberty.
- The ability of the brain to reorganise itself following injury in infancy and childhood, together with its ongoing development, is referred to as its plasticity.
- Children who have experienced surgical removal of an entire hemisphere, for medical reasons, do not experience significant impairments in function later in life.
- The ability of the child's brain to recover better than that of the adult's has been attributed to the ongoing development of lateralisation as well as the capacity of the right hemisphere to undertake the role of the language functions if disrupted.

Neuropsychology of language and language disorders

- The effects of brain damage suggest that memories of the sounds of words are located in Wernicke's area and that memories of the muscular movements needed to produce them are located in Broca's area.
- Wernicke's area is necessary for speech perception and Broca's area is necessary for its production.
- Wernicke's aphasia (caused by damage that extends beyond the boundaries of Wernicke's area) is characterised by fluent but meaningless speech that is lacking in content words but rich in function words.
- Broca's aphasia (caused by damage that extends beyond the boundaries of Broca's area) is characterised by non-fluent but meaningful speech that is lacking in function words but rich in content words.
- Damage restricted to Wernicke's area does not produce aphasia but produces pure word deafness, a deficit in speech comprehension unaccompanied by other language difficulties. Damage to the temporoparietal region surrounding Wernicke's area produces isolation aphasia – loss of the ability to produce meaningful speech or to comprehend the speech of others but retention of the ability to repeat speech.
- Dyslexia refers to an inability to read. There are two general types: acquired and developmental.
- Acquired dyslexia refers to reading disorder arising from brain injury and there are various types of dyslexia that result from brain injury such as deep dyslexia, phonological dyslexia and visual word form dyslexia. Although some regions of the brain are known to be involved in these disorders, their exact neural basis is unknown.

- Developmental dyslexia refers to a disorder of reading that occurs without brain injury and manifests itself in delayed reading development. Phonological processing (the ability to break down words into sounds and appreciate how they relate to each other) is severely impaired in developmental dyslexia.
- No one knows the exact causes of developmental dyslexia. Theories include delayed or disorganised left hemisphere development, an impairment in the function of the magnocellular pathway, a dysfunctional cerebellum, an inability to scan text efficiently and neuronal degeneration in the temporal cortex.

Neuroimaging and language

- Neuroimaging studies of language production and comprehension suggest that no one brain region is involved in language processing. Instead, there is a complex mosaic of regions which contributes to language and which interacts in a way which we only partially understand.
- Evidence suggests that Broca's area and the frontal cortex is necessary for the phonetic manipulation of speech but that the temporal cortex is necessary for the perceptual analysis of speech.
- The language areas of men and women are differently activated, with more bilateral activation in women, but the evidence is inconsistent.
- Handedness also interacts with degree of language proficiency, but in slightly irregular ways. Most right- and left-handers have left-hemisphere speech.

Suggestions for further reading

Language – general reading

Aitchison, J. (1998) *The Articulate Mammal* (4th edn). London: Routledge.

Burling, R. (2005) *The Talking Ape: How language evolved*. Oxford: Oxford University Press.

Diehl, R.L., Lotto, A.J. and Holt, L.L. (2004) Speech perception. *Annual Review of Psychology*, 55, 149–80.

Gentilucci, M. and Corballis, M.C. (2006) From manual gesture to speech: A gradual transition. *Neuroscience and Biobehavioral Reviews*, 30, 949–60.

Haesler, S. (2007) Programmed for speech. *Scientific American Mind*, 18, 3, 66–71.

Harley, T.A. (2008) *The Psychology of Language* (3rd edn). Hove: Psychology Press.

Lessmoellmann, A. (2006) Can we talk? *Scientific American Mind*, 17, 5, 44–9.

Pinker, S. (1994) *The Language Instinct*. London: Penguin.

Special issue of *Science* on 'Evolution of language', 2004, 303.

There are many books on language and specific aspects of language. These here are highly recommended. The special issue of Science has a number of articles on the development of language around the world.

Language development

Billingsley-Marshall, R.L., Simos, P.G. and Papanicolaou, A.C. (2004) Reliability and validity of neuroimaging techniques for identifying language-critical areas in children and adults. *Developmental Neuropsychology*, 26, 2, 541–63.

Friederici, A.D. (2005) Neurophysiological markers of early language acquisition: From syllables to sentences. *Trends in Cognitive Sciences*, 9, 10, 481–8.

Rayner, K., Foorman, B.R., Perfetti, C.A., Pesetsky, D. and Seidenberg, M.S. (2002) How should reading be taught? *Scientific American Mind*, March, 71–7.

Special issue of the *British Journal of Developmental Psychology* on 'The role of conversations in children's social, emotional and cognitive development', 2006, 24, 1.

Language is the most important intellectual function we develop and the way in which we develop it so quickly is astonishing but not well understood. These items give a comprehensive account of what we know about language acquisition and how it occurs. The article by Rayner et al. is a very accessible review of how children are taught to read.

Sex differences

Tannen, D. (1992) *You Just Don't Understand: Women and men in conversation*. London: Virago.

Tannen, D. (1996) *Gender and Discourse*. Oxford: Oxford University Press.

Tannen has written many best-selling books on how the sexes use language. These are two good examples.

Reading and reading disorders

Brunswick, N. (2009) *Dyslexia – A Beginner's Guide*. Oxford: Oneworld Publishers.

Brunswick, N. (2004) Developmental dyslexia: Evidence from brain research. In T. Nunes and P. Bryant (eds) *Handbook of Children's Literacy*. Dordrecht, The Netherlands: Kluwer Press.

Caccappoulo-van Vliet, E., Miozzo, M. and Stern, Y. (2004) Phonological dyslexia: A test case for reading models. *Psychological Science*, 15, 9, 583–90.

Demonet, J-F., Taylor, M.J. and Chaix, Y. (2004) Developmental dyslexia. *The Lancet*, 363, 1451–60.

Eckert, M. (2004) Neuroanatomical markers for dyslexia: A review of dyslexia structural imaging studies. *The Neuroscientist*, 10, 4, 362–71.

Excellent accounts of reading, reading development and dyslexia.

Neuropsychology and language

Brunswick, N. and Martin, G.N. (2006) The neuropsychology of language and language disorders. In G.N. Martin, *Human Neuropsychology* (2nd edn). Harlow: Prentice Hall.

Gernsbacher, M.A. and Kaschak, M.P. (2003) Neuroimaging studies of language production and comprehension. *Annual Review of Psychology*, 54, 91–114.

Hale, S. (2002) *The Man Who Lost His Language*. London: Penguin.

Hugdahl, K. and Westerhausen, R. (2009) What is left is right: How speech asymmetry shaped the brain. *European Psychologist*, 14, 1, 78–89.

Josse, G. and Tzourio-Mazoyer, N. (2004) Hemispheric specialization for language. *Brain Research Reviews*, 44, 1–12.

Linke, D.B. and Kersebaum, S. (2005) Left out. *Scientific American Mind*, 16, 4, 78–83.

Martin, R.C. (2003) Language processing: Functional organization and neuroanatomical basis. *Annual Review of Psychology*, 54, 55–90.

Turkeltaub, P.E., Gareau, L., Flowers, D.L., Zeffiro, T.A. and Eden, G.F. (2003) Development of neural mechanisms for reading. *Nature Neuroscience*, 6, 6, 767–73.

Special issue of *Cognition* on 'Towards a new functional anatomy of language', 2004, 92, 1–2.

Language disorders are some of the most common disorders studied by neuropsychologists, although not all of them are caused by brain injury. These items give good accounts of recent developments in the neuroimaging of language ability and language disorders. Hale's book is especially good, as she recounts the effects of stroke on her husband and her life.

Non-human language

Segerdahl, P. and Savage-Rumbaugh, S. (2005) *Kanzi's Primal Language*. London: Palgrave.

A nice book from one of the pioneering researchers in primate language.

Journals to consult

Brain and Language

British Journal of Developmental Psychology

British Journal of Psychology

Child Development

Cognition

Cognitive Neuropsychology

Developmental Psychology

Dyslexia

Journal of Child Language

Journal of Cognitive Neuroscience

Journal of Experimental Psychology: Learning, memory and cognition

Journal of Memory and Language

Language and Cognitive Processes

Laterality

Nature Neuroscience

Neuroimage

Psycholinguistics

Psychological Review

Psychological Science

Quarterly Journal of Experimental Psychology

Reading and Writing: An interdisciplinary journal

Science

Trends in Cognitive Sciences

Website addresses

http://www.psychology.org/links/Environment_Behavior_Relationships/Language/
A collection of links to language-related sites.

http://www.indiana.edu/~eric_rec/ieo/bibs/dyslexia.html
A collection of links to dyslexia-related sites.

www.psychologicalscience.org/newsresearch/publications/journals/pspi2_2.html
This gives the text to an article published in Psychological Science in the Public Interest reviewing the contribution of psychology to the teaching of reading.

Intelligence and thinking

Explore the accompanying videos, simulations, and animations on MyPsychLab. This chapter includes activities on: Standard intelligence measure • Gardner's theory of intelligence • An experiment in mental rotation • The mind's organisation of conceptual knowledge • Check your understanding and prepare for your exams using the multiple choice, short answer and essay practice tests also available.

CHAPTER 11

Lessons from a tragedy

St Anne's College, Oxford, 1962. I am on the sofa reading an essay to my English literature tutor. The door opens slowly and a woman with large blue-grey eyes and a helmet of rope-thick, not-so-clean hair appears with an old army blanket around her shoulders. She has a reputation for brilliance, eccentricity and lots of affairs of the heart. She is Iris Murdoch, distinguished philosopher, bestselling author, a noted teacher and student of human nature. As I expand on the character of Milton's Satan, I begin to quake under her gaze.

Cambridge University Department of Neurology, 2005. I am peering at a set of MRI scans of the grey matter belonging to the woman who once owned those fantastic blue-grey eyes . . . To a professional brain scientist's eye, the scans show that her neocortex is remarkably shrunken compared with a normal brain's. Slices of Iris Murdoch's brain, stored in a tissue bank in the same department, show protein deposits known as 'plaques' and 'tangles'.

It is probable that Iris Murdoch had Alzheimer's at 42 when, craving a cigarette, she walked into my tutor's room.

Source: John Cornwell, *The Sunday Times Magazine*.

WHAT YOU SHOULD BE ABLE TO DO AFTER READING CHAPTER 11

- Describe the ways in which intelligence has been defined.
- Understand the principles of intelligence testing.
- Describe the various models of reasoning.
- Evaluate the contribution of heredity and environment to intelligence.
- Be aware of and describe individual differences in intelligence.
- Describe and understand the effects of ageing on cognitive ability.
- Define and give examples of inductive and deductive reasoning.
- Appreciate the biases in human reasoning and why they occur.

QUESTIONS TO THINK ABOUT

- What is intelligence?
- How can intelligence be measured?
- Is it useful to invoke the concept of intelligence?
- Is there more than one 'intelligence'?
- Is there a difference between 'clever' and 'intelligent'?
- What factors contribute to the development of intelligent thought?
- Is intelligence inherited?
- What are the effects of ageing on functions such as language and remembering?
- What is dementia and are there different types of dementia with different symptoms?
- What causes dementia?
- How do we reason?
- Are there different ways of reasoning?
- In which ways can our reasoning be irrational?
- Why do we sometimes violate various logical rules?
- What is creativity? Can we measure and facilitate creativity experimentally?

What is intelligence?

In general, if people do well academically or succeed at tasks that involve their heads rather than their hands, we consider them to be intelligent. If a politician makes a useful policy decision, we call it an intelligent decision. If an author writes an erudite book on an arcane subject, we might describe him as having written an intelligent appraisal. But if asked to give a precise definition of intelligence, psychologists – in common with non-scientists – come slightly unstuck. Sternberg and Detterman (1986) asked a dozen theorists to provide definitions of intelligence and received a dozen different descriptions. Even according to one of psychology's historians, writing in the 1920s, intelligence has come to represent whatever intelligence tests measure (Boring, 1923).

In general, however, psychologists agree that the term **intelligence** describes a person's ability to learn and remember information, to recognise concepts and their relations, and to apply the information to their own behaviour in an adaptive way (Neisser *et al.*, 1996a). Where they diverge is in describing the nature of intelligence and how it works. For example, some psychologists argue that there is a general factor called intelligence but no different subtypes of intelligence; others argue intelligence is a series of abilities; yet others adopt a combinative approach arguing that there is general intelligence but there are also specific abilities. The number of these abilities depends on the theory one examines.

Theories of intelligence

Most theories of intelligence are based on the analysis of performance on tests which seek to measure specific abilities such as non-verbal and verbal intellectual competence. Much of the debate in the psychology of intelligence has focused on whether there is a single intelligence or there are multiple intelligences. Is our intellectual ability a unitary factor or is it made up of a number of different abilities? Are these abilities, if they do exist, completely separate from each other or are they related?

Intelligence tests yield a single number, usually called an IQ score, although this does not itself mean that intelligence is a single, general characteristic. Some investigators have suggested that certain intellectual abilities are completely independent of one another. For example, a person can be excellent at spatial reasoning but poor at solving verbal analogies. But psychologists disagree over whether specific abilities are totally independent or whether one general factor influences all abilities. The next sections consider some influential theories of intelligence.

Spearman's two-factor theory

Charles Spearman (1927) proposed that an individual's performance on a test of intellectual ability is determined by two factors: the *g* **factor**, which is a general factor, and the *s* **factor**, which is a factor specific to a particular test. Spearman did not call his *g* factor 'intelligence'; he considered the term too vague. He defined the *g* factor as comprising three 'qualitative principles of cognition': apprehension of experience, eduction of relations and eduction of correlates. A common task on tests of intellectual abilities – solving analogies – requires all three principles (Sternberg, 1985). For example, consider the following analogy:

LAWYER:CLIENT:DOCTOR: _____

This problem should be read as 'LAWYER is to CLIENT as DOCTOR is to _____'.

Apprehension of experience refers to people's ability to perceive and understand what they experience; thus, reading and understanding each of the words in the analogy requires apprehension of experience. Eduction (not 'education') is the process of drawing or bringing out, that is, making sense of, given facts. In this case, eduction of relations refers to the ability to perceive the relation between lawyer and client; namely, that the lawyer works for and is paid by the client. Eduction of correlates refers to the ability to apply a rule inferred from one case to a similar case. Thus, the person whom a doctor works for and is ultimately paid by is obviously a patient. Because analogy problems require all three of Spearman's principles of cognition, he advocated their use in intelligence testing.

Empirical evidence for Spearman's two-factor theory comes from correlations among various tests of particular intellectual abilities. The governing logic is as follows. If we administer ten different tests of intellectual abilities to a group of people and each test measures a separate, independent ability, the scores these people make on any one test will be unrelated to their scores on any other; the correlations among the tests will be approximately zero. However, if the tests measure abilities that are simply different manifestations of a single trait, the scores will be related; the intercorrelations will be close to 1.

In fact, the intercorrelations among a group of tests of intellectual abilities are neither zero nor 1. Instead, most of these tests are at least moderately correlated, so that a person who scores well on a vocabulary test also tends to score better than average on other tests, such as arithmetic or spatial reasoning. The correlations among various tests of intellectual ability usually range from 0.3 to 0.7, which means that they have between 9 per cent and 49 per cent of their variability in common (Ozer, 1985).

Spearman concluded that a general factor (*g*) accounted for the moderate correlations among different tests of ability. Thus, a person's score on a particular test depends on two things: the person's specific ability (*s*) on the particular test (such as spatial reasoning) and their level of the *g* factor, or general reasoning ability.

Evidence from factor analysis

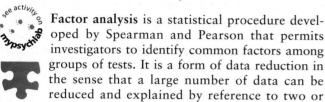 **Factor analysis** is a statistical procedure developed by Spearman and Pearson that permits investigators to identify common factors among groups of tests. It is a form of data reduction in the sense that a large number of data can be reduced and explained by reference to two or three factors (Kline, 1993). In the case of intelligence tests, these common factors would be particular abilities that affect people's performance on more than one test. If a group of people take several different tests of intellectual ability and each person's scores on several of these tests correlate well with one another, the tests may (at least partly) be measuring the same factor. A factor analysis determines which sets of tests form groups. For example, Birren and Morrison (1961) administered the Wechsler Adult Intelligence Scale (WAIS, an intelligence test described in the next section) to 933 people. This test consists of 11 different subtests. Birren and Morrison calculated the correlations between subtests and then subjected these correlations to a factor analysis. Table 11.1 shows the results of the analysis.

Table 11.1 Three factors derived by factor analysis of scores on WAIS subtests

| Subtest | Factors | | |
	A	B	C
Information	0.70	0.18	0.25
Comprehension	0.63	0.12	0.24
Arithmetic	0.38	0.35	0.28
Similarities	0.57	0.12	0.27
Digit span	0.16	0.84	0.13
Vocabulary	0.84	0.16	0.18
Digit symbol	0.24	0.22	0.29
Picture completion	0.41	0.15	0.53
Block design	0.20	0.14	0.73
Picture arrangement	0.35	0.18	0.41
Object assembly	0.16	0.06	0.59

Source: Adapted from Morrison, D.F. (1967) *Multivariate Statistical Methods*, New York: McGraw-Hill.

The factor analysis revealed three factors, labelled A, B and C. The numbers in the three columns in the table are called factor loadings; they are somewhat like correlation coefficients in that they express the degree to which a particular test is related to a particular factor. For the various subtests on factor A, the largest factor loading is for vocabulary, followed by information, comprehension and similarities. In the middle range are picture completion, arithmetic, picture arrangement and digit symbol. Digit span, object assembly and block design are the smallest. Verbal subtests make the most important contribution to factor A, so we might be tempted to call this factor verbal ability. But almost all tests make at least a moderate contribution, so perhaps this factor may reflect general intelligence. Digit span has a heavy loading on factor B (0.84), and arithmetic and digit symbol have moderate loadings. Factor B, therefore, is related to maintaining information in short-term memory and manipulating numbers. Factor C appears to be determined mainly by block design, object assembly, picture completion and picture arrangement, and might, therefore, represent the factor, spatial ability.

Although factor analysis can give hints about the nature of intelligence, it cannot provide definitive answers. The names given to factors are determined by the investigator and, although the names may appear to be quite appropriate, the process inevitably has a subjective element to it. There is also the danger of reification when conducting factor analysis. That is, the factors may wrongly be seen as concrete entities and not simply as labels used to describe a set of data as concisely and accurately as possible. Furthermore, factor analysis can never be more meaningful than the individual tests on which it is performed. To identify the relevant factors in human intelligence, one must include an extensive variety of tests in the factor analysis. The WAIS, for example, does not contain a test of musical ability. If it did, a factor analysis would undoubtedly yield an additional factor. Whether musical ability is a component of intelligence depends on how we decide to define intelligence; this question cannot be answered by a factor analysis.

Other psychologists employed factor analysis to determine the nature of intelligence. Louis Thurstone's study (1938) of students' performance on a battery of 56 tests extracted seven factors, which he labelled verbal comprehension, verbal fluency, number, spatial visualisation, memory, reasoning and perceptual speed. At first, Thurstone thought that his results contradicted Spearman's hypothesised *g* factor. However, Eysenck suggested a few years later that a second factor analysis could be performed on Thurstone's factors. If the analysis found one common factor, then Spearman's *g* factor would receive support. In other words, if Thurstone's seven factors themselves had a second-order factor in common, this factor might be conceived of as general intelligence.

Cattell performed a second-order factor analysis and found not one but two major factors. Horn and Cattell (1966) called these factors fluid intelligence (g_f) and crystallised intelligence (g_c). Fluid intelligence is reflected by performance on relatively culture-free tasks, such as those that measure the ability to see relations among objects or the ability to see patterns in a repeating series of items. Crystallised intelligence is defined by tasks that require people to have already acquired information, such as vocabulary and semantic information, and is therefore more culture-bound. Cattell regards fluid intelligence as closely related to a person's native capacity for intellectual performance; in other words, it represents a potential ability to learn and solve problems. In contrast, he regards crystallised intelligence as what a person has accomplished through the use of their fluid intelligence – what they have learned. Horn (1978) disagrees with Cattell by citing evidence suggesting that both factors are learned but are also based on heredity. He says that g_f is based on casual learning and g_c is based on cultural, school-type learning.

Figure 11.1 shows examples from five of the subtests that load heavily on fluid intelligence.

Tests that load heavily on the crystallised intelligence factor include word analogies and tests of vocabulary, general information and use of language. According to Cattell, g_c depends on g_f. Fluid intelligence supplies the native ability, whereas experience with language and exposure to books, school and other learning opportunities develop crystallised intelligence. If two people have the same experiences, the one with the greater fluid intelligence will develop the greater crystallised intelligence. However, a person with a high fluid intelligence exposed to an intellectually impoverished environment will develop a poor or mediocre crystallised intelligence. Table 11.2 presents a summary of tests that load on g_f and g_c.

No two investigators agree about the nature of intelligence. However, most believe that a small number of common factors account for at least part of a person's performance on intellectual tasks.

Sternberg's triarchic theory of intelligence

Sternberg (1985) has devised a theory of intelligence that derives from the information-processing approach used by many cognitive psychologists. Sternberg's theory has three parts; he calls it a **triarchic theory** (meaning 'ruled by three'). The three parts of the theory deal with three aspects of intelligence: componential intelligence, experiential intelligence and contextual intelligence. Taken together, these three components go beyond the abilities measured by most common tests of intelligence. They include practical aspects of behaviour that enable a person to adapt successfully to their environment. Table 11.3 provides a summary of the key concepts of Sternberg's triarchic theory.

Table 11.2 Summary of tests with large factor loadings on g_f or g_c

Test	Approximate factor loadings	
	g_f	g_c
Figural relations: Deduction of a relation when this is shown among common figures	0.57	0.01
Memory span: Reproduction of several numbers or letters presented briefly	0.50	0.00
Induction: Deduction of a correlate from relations shown in a series of letters, numbers, or figures, as in a letter series test	0.41	0.06
General reasoning: Solving problems of area, rate, finance, and the like, as in an arithmetic reasoning test	0.31	0.34
Semantic relations: Deduction of a relation when this is shown among words, as in an analogies test	0.37	0.43
Formal reasoning: Arriving at a conclusion in accordance with a formal reasoning process, as in a syllogistic reasoning test	0.31	0.41
Number facility: Quick and accurate use of arithmetical operations such as addition, subtraction and multiplication	0.21	0.29
Experimental evaluation: Solving problems involving protocol and requiring diplomacy, as in a social relations test	0.08	0.43
Verbal comprehension: Advanced understanding of language, as measured in a vocabulary reading test	0.08	0.68

Source: Adapted from Horn, J.L., Organization of abilities and the development of intelligence. *Psychological Review*, 1968, 75, 249. © 1968 by the American Psychological Association. Adapted by permission.

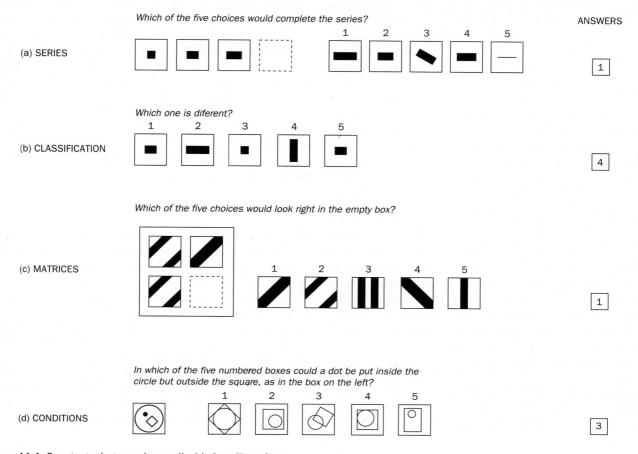

Figure 11.1 Four tests that correlate well with Cattell's g_f factor.

Table 11.3 An outline of Sternberg's triarchic theory of intelligence

Componential intelligence

Metacomponents (e.g. planning)
Performance components (e.g. lexical access)
Knowledge acquisition components (e.g. ability to acquire vocabulary words)

Experimental intelligence
Novel tasks
Automated tasks

Contextual intelligence
Adaptation (adapting to the environment)
Selection (finding a suitable environment)
Shaping (changing the environment)

Componential intelligence consists of the mental mechanisms people use to plan and execute tasks. The components revealed by the factor analyses of verbal ability and deductive reasoning are facets of componential intelligence. Sternberg suggests that the components of intelligence serve three functions. Metacomponents (transcending components) are the processes by which people decide the nature of an intellectual problem, select a strategy for solving it, and allocate their resources. For example, good readers vary the amount of time they spend on a passage according to how much information they need to extract from it (Wagner and Sternberg, 1985; cited in Sternberg, 1985). This decision is controlled by a metacomponent of intelligence. Performance components are the processes actually used to perform the task, for example word recognition and working memory. Knowledge acquisition components are those the person uses to gain new knowledge by sifting out relevant information and integrating it with what they already know.

The second part of Sternberg's theory deals with experiential intelligence. **Experiential intelligence** is the ability to deal effectively with novel situations and to solve automatically problems that have been previously encountered. According to Sternberg's theory, a person with good experiential intelligence is able to deal more effectively with novel situations than is a person with poor experiential intelligence. The person is better able to analyse the situation and to bring mental resources to bear on the problem, even if they have never encountered one like it before. After encountering a particular type of problem several times, the person with good experiential intelligence is also able to 'automate' the procedure so that similar problems can be solved without much thought, freeing mental resources for other work. A person who has to reason out the solution to a problem every time it occurs will be left behind by people who can give the answer quickly and automatically. Sternberg suggests that this distinction is closely related to the distinction between fluid and crystallised intelligence (Horn and Cattell, 1966). According to Sternberg, tasks that use fluid intelligence are those that demand novel approaches, whereas tasks that use crystallised intelligence are those that demand mental processes that have become automatic.

The third part of Sternberg's theory deals with **contextual intelligence** – intelligence reflecting the behaviours that were subject to natural selection in our evolutionary history. Contextual intelligence takes three forms: adaptation, selection and shaping. The first form, adaptation, consists of fitting oneself into one's environment by developing useful skills and behaviours. In different cultures, adaptation will take different forms. For example, knowing how to distinguish between poisonous and edible plants is an important skill for a member of a hunter–gatherer tribe. Knowing how to present oneself in a job interview is an important skill for a member of an industrialised society. The second form of contextual intelligence, selection, refers to the ability to find one's own niche in the environment. That is, individuals will decide on careers or activities which they both enjoy doing and do well.

The third form of contextual intelligence is shaping. Adapting to the environment or selecting a new one may not always be possible or profitable. In such cases, intelligent behaviour consists of shaping the environment itself. For example, a person whose talents are not appreciated by their employer may decide to start their own business.

Gardner's multiple intelligences theory

Gardner's theory of intelligence is based on a neuropsychological analysis of human abilities (Gardner, 1983). It argues that intelligence falls into seven categories: linguistic intelligence, musical intelligence, logical/mathematical intelligence, spatial intelligence, bodily/kinesthetic intelligence, and two types of personal intelligence. Bodily/kinesthetic intelligence includes the types of skill that athletes, typists, dancers or mime artists exhibit. Personal intelligence includes awareness of one's own feelings (intrapersonal intelligence) and the ability to notice individual differences in other people and to respond appropriately to them – in other words, to be socially aware (interpersonal intelligence).

Three of Gardner's types of intelligence – verbal intelligence, logical/mathematical intelligence and spatial intelligence – are not unusual, having been identified previously by many other researchers. The other four are rather unusual. According to Gardner, all seven abilities are well represented in the brain, in that specific brain damage can impair some of them but leave others relatively intact. For example, people with damage to the left parietal lobe can show apraxia, an inability to perform sequences of voluntary skilled movements. In contrast, people with damage to the right parietal lobe develop the spatial neglect described in Chapter 6. Individuals with frontal lobe damage, as you saw in Chapter 4 and will see later in this chapter and in Chapter 13, have difficulty evaluating the significance of social situations and making decisions about social matters (the frontal lobes used to be regarded as the region of the brain responsible for intelligence). These examples illustrate bodily/kinesthetic intelligence and both intrapersonal and interpersonal intelligence.

Gardner's theory has the advantage of being based on neuropsychological reality. It also accommodates the views of intelligence held by some non-Western cultures. For example, he would recognise the ability of a member of the Puluwat culture of the Caroline Islands to navigate across the sea by the stars as an example of intelligence.

Emotional intelligence

A different type of intelligence, one not based on any particular cognitive ability, was proposed by Goleman (1995, 1998). This type of intelligence refers to the social and emotional components of interactions with others: the more socially sensitive and emotionally sensitive you were to the needs and behaviours of others, the more successful your interaction would be. Goleman referred to this as **emotional intelligence** but there is some controversy over whether this is a separate, valid and reliable type of intelligence (Sjoberg, 2001).

There is certainly evidence that social skill is a key factor in understanding others' thoughts and feelings and this is one of the factors that Goleman cites as being important to success in business. A recent study suggests

Linguistic

James Joyce

Other well-known exemplars:
Marcel Proust
Martin Amis
Virginia Woolf
Dorothy Parker
Henrik Ibsen
P.G. Wodehouse
Jane Austen

Logical/mathematical

Isaac Newton

Other well-known exemplars:
Stephen Hawking
Richard Feynman
Albert Einstein
Jules-Henri Poincaré
Marie Curie
Trevor Bayliss
Tim Berners-Lee

Musical

Paul McCartney

Other well-known exemplars:
Wolfgang Amadeus Mozart
Vivaldi
Ivor Novello
Vince Clarke
Shania Twain
Madonna
Cole Porter

Spatial

Salvador Dali

Other well-known exemplars:
Leonardo Da Vinci
Henry Moore
Norman Foster
Christopher Wren
Marcel Duchamp
Stephen Spielberg
Paul Smith

Body/kinetic/kinesthetic

Darcey Bussell

Other well-known exemplars:
Margot Fonteyn
Rudolph Nureyev
Michael Jordan
David Beckham

Interpersonal

Oprah Winfrey

Other well-known exemplars:
Anthony Clare
Bill Clinton
Jerry Springer
Ricki Lake

Intrapersonal

Nelson Mandela

Other well-known exemplars:
Dalai Lama
Mahatma Gandhi
Mother Theresa

Well-known exemplars of the type of individuals who would show high levels of each of Gardner's multiple intelligences
Source: Press Association Images, Magnum Photos, Bettman/CORBIS.

that an interaction between intelligence and social skill may underlie some differences in job performance (Ferris *et al.*, 2001). Having low ability and social skill will do nothing for your career, but what if you had low ability and great social skill or great ability and low social skill?

The study asked 106 software engineers and programmers to complete a general ability scale which measured vocabulary, arithmetic, reasoning and spatial ability and also to rate their social skills, job performance and job dedication. These employees, their supervisors and their personnel managers were interviewed. A measure of personality was taken and salary level and sex were noted.

Neither high general mental ability nor high social skill was individually associated with high levels of performance or high salaries. Each factor seemed to influence the other. Social skill was highly correlated with performance and salary when workers were very mentally able; mental ability was highly correlated with job success when social skill was high. Having good social skills but low mental ability, however, resulted in lower salary levels. 'Perhaps individuals low in GMA [General Mental Ability]', the authors suggest, 'may attempt to overcompensate for their lack of intelligence by focusing a disproportionate amount of time and effort on social aspects of the job.'

They conclude that while the results suggest that social skill and intelligence interact and predict job performance and salary independently of personality, the next logical step would be to explore these relations by asking people – other than the employees themselves – to rate the employees' social skills.

It has been pointed out that Goleman's concept of emotional intelligence involves both social and emotional intelligence and that these may be separable. Measures of emotional intelligence seem to predict job success better than does interview performance (itself not a difficult achievement given the low correlation between interview performance and job performance), but empirical support for the concept is mixed (Mayer and Cobb, 2000).

Because the two factors involved in emotional intelligence may predict different behaviours, some researchers have developed specific scales to measure the emotional component only. Mayer *et al.* (1999), for example, have constructed such a scale and have defined emotional intelligence as 'the ability to perceive and express emotion, assimilate emotion in thought, understand and reason with emotion and regulate emotion in the self and others'. This scale seems to correlate well with questionnaires measuring empathy – a key feature of emotional intelligence – but its reliability and validity await more extensive testing. Some studies show that brief emotional intelligence measures predict commitment to a career but other authors have argued that the concept may not be as separate as some psychologists state. Sjoberg (2001), for example, argues that emotional intelligence may not be a measure of anything separate but is a factor that is 'secondary' to other concepts (which may be personality or cognitive ability).

Estimating intelligence – An international perspective

Although the proposition that men and women differ in intelligence is controversial, there is a great deal of evidence to suggest that males estimate their own IQ more highly than do females their own (Beloff, 1992; Byrd and Stacey, 1993). These beliefs seem to be unrelated to actual cognitive performance. The performance of males is significantly lower than their IQ estimate whereas that of females is also lower but not significantly so (Reilly and Mulhern, 1995).

A consistent finding is that participants of both sexes rate their fathers' IQ as being higher than their mothers' (Beloff, 1992; Furnham and Rawles, 1995). Not only are fathers rated as more intelligent than mothers, but boys are also rated as having a greater IQ than girls by their parents (Furnham and Gasson, 1998). These findings appear to generalise across the cultures studied to date.

To determine whether such sex differences in estimates are global (general IQ) or specific (related to specific abilities), Furnham *et al.* (1999a) asked 400 participants from the UK, Hawaii and Singapore to estimate their own parents' and siblings' IQ score for each of Gardner's multiple intelligences, using the test described in Figure 11.2. There were no sex differences in the estimated intelligence of siblings and parents but men estimated their own mathematical, spatial and bodily/kinetic intelligence as well as their overall intelligence to be higher than did women.

A similar study asked 140 Belgian, 227 British and 177 Slovakian students to estimate their multiple intelligence as well as that of their parents and siblings (Furnham *et al.*, 1999b). Men rated their own general intelligence, but not those of their parents or siblings, more highly than did women. When the researchers looked at specific types of intelligence, men rated their numerical (but not verbal or cultural) IQ higher than did women.

Few national differences were reported but those that were appeared to be attributable to the Slovakian women. They rated their own and their fathers' IQ more highly than did Slovakian men. They also rated their verbal intelligence more highly than numerical and cultural IQ (Slovakian men rated their cultural and numerical IQ to be similar but higher than their cultural IQ). This is the first study of its kind to find that women rate their own intelligence more highly.

A study comparing British and Turkish respondents found that men rated their father's intelligence as being higher than their mother's (based on Gardner and Sternberg's models) and men rated their overall, verbal, logical, spatial, creative and practical intelligence higher than did women (Furnham *et al*, 2009). Cultural differences were more pronounced than sex differences, however, with Turks rating their musical, body-kinesthetic, interpersonal, intrapersonal, naturalistic, creative, emotional and practical intelligence higher than did the Brits.

Estimating intelligence – *Continued*

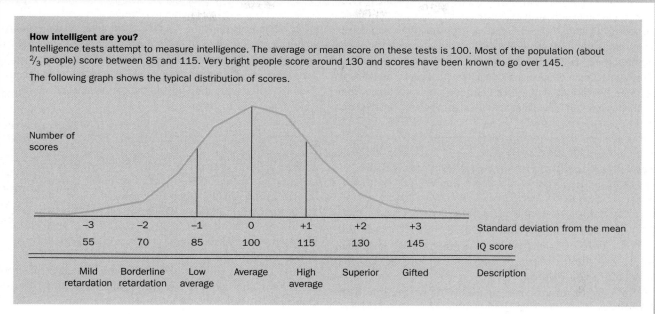

How intelligent are you?

Intelligence tests attempt to measure intelligence. The average or mean score on these tests is 100. Most of the population (about $^2/_3$ people) score between 85 and 115. Very bright people score around 130 and scores have been known to go over 145.

The following graph shows the typical distribution of scores.

Figure 11.2 Example of a test used to examine individuals' perception of their own and their relatives' intelligence.

Using the same intelligence measures, von Stumm *et al* (2009) compared estimates of men and women from 12 nations – Australia, Austria, Brazil, France, Iran, Israel, Malaysia, South Africa, Spain, Turkey, UK and USA. All nations overestimated their intelligence compared with actual scores obtained for each of the nations and men overestimated their own intelligence pretty universally (see Figure 11.3).

Finally, in an intriguing study, Furnham *et al.* (2002) asked British and American students to estimate their own overall intelligence and different types of intelligence, but also that of

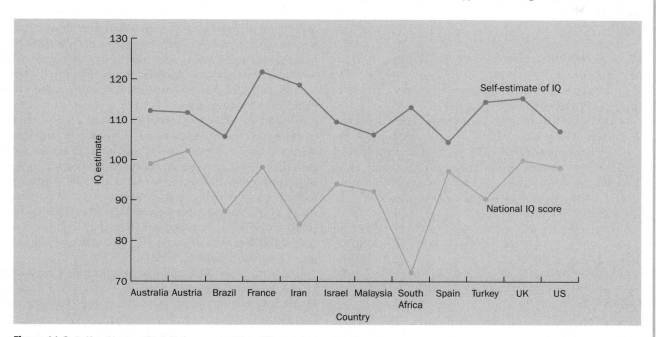

Figure 11.3 Self-estimates of intelligence and national IQ scores across nations

Source: von Stumm, S., Chamorro-Premuzic, T. & Furnham, A. (2009). Decomposing self-estimates of intelligence: Structure and sex differences across 12 nations. *British Journal of Psychology*, 100, 429–42.

Estimating intelligence – *Continued*

well-known figures such as Tony Blair, Bill Gates, Prince Charles and Bill Clinton. Men, as expected, estimated their verbal, logical and spatial IQ more highly than did women and women rated their male partners as having lower verbal IQ but higher spatial IQ than themselves. Of the famous figures, participants rated Bill Clinton and Prince Charles as less intelligent than themselves but Tony Blair and Bill Gates to be more intelligent.

These sex differences in the perception of relatives' intelligence perhaps underlie the sex differences seen in intellectual ability. There has been some controversy in psychology over whether men and women (and boys and girls) are better than each other on tests of cognitive ability. In fact, there do seem to be consistent sex differences in the performance of specific types of test (see below).

Are there consistent sex differences in cognitive ability?

see activity on mypsychlab

Take a look at Figure 11.4. At the moment, the glass is empty but imagine that it is half full. Using a pencil, draw a line across the glass where you think the top of the water should be. Do that now before you read on.

If you were a man, you probably drew the line horizontally across the glass; if you were a woman, you probably drew the line parallel to the direction in which the water glass is tipped. The correct line would be the horizontal one.

This phenomenon illustrates one of the most consistent sex differences in cognitive ability. The task is Piaget's Water Level Test, and men tend to be better at it than women (Halpern, 1992; Rilea, 2008). Other tests showing sex differences are summarised in Table 11.4.

Figure 11.4 The Water Level Test. The glass is meant to be half full of water. The participant's task is to indicate where the top of the water should be.

Source: Kalichman, S.C., The effects of sex and context on paper and pencil spatial task performance, *Journal of General Psychology*, 1989, 116, 133–9. Reprinted with permission of the Helen Dwight Reid Educational Foundation. Published by Heldref Publications, 1319 Eighteenth St., NW, Washington, DC, 20036–1802, www.heldref.org, copyright © 1989.

Why should males tend to be better at this task? One explanation for the Water Level Test result is that men and boys are intrinsically superior at tests of spatial ability than are women and girls (we will come on to reasons why this should be a little later). Spatial ability refers to 'skills in representing, transforming, generating and recalling symbolic, nonlinguistic information' (Linn and Petersen, 1985). The test of spatial ability which shows the most consistent and reliable sex difference is mental rotation (Masters and Sanders, 1993). In this task, individuals are presented with three sets of cubes and have to match the target set with one of the other two. The task is not straightforward because the cubes have to be mentally rotated before a match can be made, as you saw in Chapter 8 (Figure 8.6).

see activity on mypsychlab

The three-dimensional nature of the stimuli appears to be important. In one experiment the performance of 3- and 6-year-old boys and girls were compared on a two-dimensional task (a jigsaw puzzle) or a three-dimensional task (constructing Lego). It was found that although there was no difference between boys and girls on the two-dimensional task, boys performed better than girls at the three-dimensional task (McGuiness and Morley, 1991).

Is this sex difference consistent across all spatial ability tests? The answer is no. In other types of visuospatial test, women tend to outperform men. For example, women have been found to be consistently superior to men at tests involving visual recognition. It has been suggested that this may be so because of women's superior linguistic ability. Women, for example, are better than men at tests involving verbal fluency, such as naming as many objects as possible beginning with a specific letter (Halpern, 1997), and boys tend to be diagnosed with reading and speech disorders more commonly than are girls (Flynn and Rahbar, 1994).

The stimuli used can also be important. Rilea (2008) found that men were better at the Water Level Task but showed no advantage on mental rotation or paper folding. However, men were better at rotating polygons than stick figures (and they showed a right hemisphere advantage for the task; there was no right hemisphere advantage shown by women for either stimulus type).

Table 11.4 Cognitive tests and tasks that usually show sex differences

Type of test/task	Example
Tasks and tests on which women obtain higher average scores	
Tasks that require rapid access to and use of phonological, semantic and other information in long-term memory	Verbal fluency – phonological retrieval Synonym generation – meaning retrieval Associative memory Spellings and anagrams Mathematical calculations Memory for spatial locations
Knowledge areas	Foreign languages
Production and comprehension of complex prose	Reading comprehension Writing
Fine motor skills	Mirror tracing – novel, complex figures Pegboard tasks Matching and coding tasks
Perceptual speed	Multiple speeded tasks
Speech articulation	Tongue-twisters
Tasks and test on which men obtain higher average scores	
Tasks that require transformations in visual working memory	Mental rotation Piaget Water Level Test
Tasks that involve moving objects	Dynamic spatiotemporal tasks
Motor tasks that involve aiming	Accuracy in throwing balls or darts
Knowledge areas	General knowledge Maths and science knowledge
Test of fluid reasoning (especially in maths and science domain)	Promotional reasoning tasks Mechanical reasoning Verbal analogies Scientific reasoning

Source: Adapted with permission from Halpern, D.F., Sex difference in intelligence. *American Psychologist*, 1997, 52(10), 1091–102. © 1997 The American Psychological Association, reprinted with permission.

Contreras *et al.* (2007) suggest a stimulus-specific complicating factor: the tests of spatial ability used are static, not dynamic. Therefore, they set up a study in which men and women performed a dynamic test of spatial ability – guiding two dots towards a destination in the shortest time. They found that even when performance factors were taken into account, men outperformed women (i.e. differences in performance style did not explain the sex difference). On average, men took longer to decide on the first move of the dots, then guided the dots more quickly. These data suggest that 'spatial ability' is not an all-or-nothing concept but multidimensional. Different types of spatial ability test and different types of spatial stimuli produce sex differences; others do not.

Can sex differences be eliminated? There are some interesting answers. An experiment by McLoy and Koonce (1988, cited in Halpern, 1992) trained men and women on a standard simulated flight task and found that men were better at learning this task than were women. They also found that given sufficient training, women performed at about the same level as men; they simply needed more training to achieve this level of competence. Recently, a study manipulated participants' belief in performance and observed the consequences for behaviour. Men and women (in same sex groups) were asked to perform a mental rotation test but different groups were given different instructions (Moe, 2009). One group was told: 'Men are better than women at this task'; another: 'women are better than men'; and a third were given instructions with no reference to sex. Each group was also told that the test was either quite easy or very difficult. Women performed better when given the sex-positive instruction but task difficulty priming had no discernible effect. Men performed better when given sex-positive instructions, when told the test was easy and, if given control instructions, when the task was described as difficult. The sex-negative instructions had no effect on performance of either sex.

Sex differences in visuospatial ability might also be due to different processing styles. Pena *et al.* (2008) asked men and women to complete a visuospatial exercise in which they had to guide two differently coloured dots on a monitor to a colour-appropriate target area. Participants did this by using a cursor to alter the direction of an arrow button which guided the dots. Two interesting findings emerged. Men, as expected, performed better than women but the type of strategy employed during the task affected success on the task. They also found that when one type of strategy was adopted, sex differences were reduced; when the other was employed, sex differences remained strong.

The two strategy styles were described as 'segmentary' or 'planned and feedback-dependent holistic'. Segmentary strategy involved focusing on a particular portion of the task, to the exclusion of other aspects of the task or the screen (hence, 'segment'). Followers of this strategy would change the course of the dot frequently. Holistic strategists did not make as many course changes. Some of these planned their actions before the task ('planned') and some acted on feedback from the screen ('feedback-dependent'). Men used the holistic strategy more often than did women; women were more likely to adopt the segmentary strategy. When men used planned holistic and segmentary strategies, they performed better than women using the same strategies. However, when both sexes employed the planned strategy, this sex difference narrowed.

Why should men outperform women on spatial tasks? Theories of sex differences in cognitive ability fall into four general categories: evolutionary, psychosocial, biological and cognitive.

Evolutionary theories

The evolutionary point of view suggests that spatial superiority in men is a throwback to the evolution of men and women as hunters and gatherers (Eals and Silverman, 1994). This theory suggests that because men originally roamed and hunted (activities which rely on the manipulation of visuospatial features in the environment), and because women stayed 'at home' and gathered, it is not surprising that men are spatially superior. The greater visual recognition performance seen in women is meant to reflect women's evolutionary role as foragers (Tooby and DeVore, 1987).

According to evolutionary psychologists, one reason why men are better at spatial cognition than women is that men were the hunters who ranged far and wide for their prey and would, therefore, need to develop a well-tuned set of navigational skills. Women, the child-bearers and rearers, stayed at home and foraged. Some argue that women's ranging was limited to picking plants; men would hunt for game.

According to Ecuyer-Dab and Robert (2004), however, this dichotomy suggests that rather than showing a superior spatial advantage by men over women it shows how context can affect the way in which each sex expresses its specific spatial skills: spatial cognition in men would be used to navigate the environment for a mate and food whereas women's spatial cognition developed to deal with the immediate environment because they were more concerned with the survival of their offspring in the home. They, therefore, had no need to develop the navigational spatial skills that men did. In short, men developed and evolved large-scale navigation mechanisms and women evolved small-scale ones.

Ecuyer-Dab and Robert cite evidence from recent studies to support the hypothesis. Women, for example, were more likely than men to use landmarks when giving map directions. Men were more likely to provide more detail on direction and distance – although women are capable of doing this, they simply do not use these references as their primary source of information.

One objection to the theory that males are intrinsically superior to females on tests of mental rotation is that the results may be attributable to other causes. For example, because the task is timed, it has been argued that this is detrimental to women, who are more cautious when making decisions about rotation (Goldstein *et al.*, 1990). To test this hypothesis, Masters (1998) allowed male and female undergraduates either a short or unlimited time to perform a mental rotation task. She also used three different scoring procedures because previous studies had been criticised for basing their findings on using correct answers only (without looking at the number of incorrect responses too). Masters found that regardless of scoring procedure or time limit, men performed better than women. (Interestingly, however, some sex differences, such as female self-reported confusion over left and right, may be attributable to women rating themselves more critically than do men (Jordan *et al.*, 2006).)

However, as you saw in Chapter 3, evolutionary theories such as these are so broad as to be untestable. As Halpern (1997) also notes, you can explain almost any finding by indicating how it would be advantageous to hunters and gatherers.

Psychosocial theories

Psychosocial theories suggest that sex differences are learned through experience or imitation. Children, it is argued, fulfil sex-role stereotypes: boys are encouraged to play with toys which involve visuospatial manipulation; girls are not (we will come back to this in Chapter 12). It has also been suggested that boys and girls receive different models, rewards and punishment. One researcher has suggested that peer interaction is more likely to lead to stereotypical sex-role behaviour than is parent–child interaction, although this idea is controversial (Harris, 1995).

Another study, investigating the effect on spatial performance of the degree to which men and women internalise their sexual identity or behave in a stereotypically male or female way, on spatial test performance found a weak relationship between spatial ability and sex roles although the actual sex difference remained (Saucier et al., 2002).

Halpern (1992) cites fairly strong evidence against a psychosocial explanation for sex differences in cognitive ability. She noted that among individuals with high reasoning ability, right-handed men outperformed left-handed men on tests of spatial ability but were poorer than left-handed men at verbal tasks. Conversely, left-handed females were better at spatial tasks than were right-handers but the opposite pattern applied to verbal tasks. Any theory of psychosocial influence would have difficulty in explaining these findings: why should right- and left-handed boys and girls be socialised differently? It would also have difficulty in explaining why boys are more likely than girls to suffer from stuttering and reading disorders.

Biological theories

Biological theories suggest that sex differences in cognitive ability may be due to biological factors such as hormonal regulation and brain organisation. There is evidence that anatomical differences exist between the brains of boys and girls and between men and women (Martin, 2006). Witelson et al. (1995) reported that the number of neurons found in a structure thought to be important for language – the planum temporale (described in Chapter 10) – was 11 per cent greater in women than in men. A part of the tract of fibres that connects the two cerebral hemispheres (the corpus callosum) has also been found to be larger in women (Elster et al., 1990; Holloway et al., 1993). Some researchers have suggested that whereas men rely predominantly on one or other hemisphere to perform a specific function, women use both (Jancke and Steinmetz, 1994). The processing of phonemes – the constituent sounds of words – is associated with greater activation in both hemispheres in women than men (Shaywitz et al., 1995).

Apart from neuroanatomical differences, there may also be differences in the amount of, or sensitivity to, hormones (Collaer and Hines, 1995). Cognitive ability, for example, appears to fluctuate across the menstrual cycle (Hampson, 1990), and the amount of testosterone appears to correlate with spatial skill (Moffat and Hampson, 1996). In two interesting experiments, groups of individuals were given certain hormones for reasons other than enhancing cognitive ability. In one study, normal ageing men given testosterone to enhance their sex drive showed increased visuospatial performance (Janowsky et al., 1994). In another, transsexuals given testosterone as part of their preoperative sex change programme were found to show increased visuospatial ability and decreased verbal ability over a period of three months (Van Goozen et al., 1995).

Some studies have also found no relationship between hormone level and spatial ability (Liben et al., 2002). This may not mean that steroids are not involved. 'It may be', as the authors suggest, 'that such effects do occur but only under some as yet unidentified additional setting conditions (be they biological or experiential).'

An fMRI study has found that activation in the brain during mental rotation varies depending on a woman's point in her menstrual cycle and with hormone secretion in both sexes (Schoning et al., 2007). Twelve men and twelve women completed a three-dimensional mental rotation task and had their levels of testosterone and/or estradiol measured. Women were tested during the early follicular and midluteal phase of their cycle. Men and women showed activation in frontal and parietal regions. In men, greater testosterone was associated with greater left parietal lobe activation. In women, there was also a correlation between testosterone levels and activation in the follicular phase. Women's estradiol levels in both phases were associated with increased activation in frontal and parietal areas.

The study suggests that important factors, such as hormone level and point at the menstrual cycle, can significantly influence brain activation in neuroimaging studies of cognition.

Although appealing and persuasive in explaining the mechanism of some cognitive abilities, biological theories cannot account for some of the findings in sex differences research. If, for example, spatial ability is 'hard-wired' in the brain, how can improvements in spatial ability be brought about by training? Is the capacity there but the strategy for using this capacity absent?

Cognitive theories

Empathising and systemising are two ways of processing information, described by Simon Baron-Cohen (2003), in which people work at identifying someone's thoughts and feelings (perspective-taking, altruism, cooperativeness) or analysing relationships in non-social interactions (an interest in science, technology, the natural world, etc.). The approaches can be measured by two questionnaires, called the empathy quotient and the systemising quotient. Women are thought to be better at the former; men, the latter.

In a recent study, men were found to engage in higher levels of systemising than were women and non-heterosexual women higher than heterosexual women (Nettle, 2007). There were no differences between heterosexual and non-heterosexual men. Women did show a greater interest in the arts and culture, however, which may not be related to sociability/empathy.

Sex differences in general knowledge

When the most commonly used test of intelligence (the Wechsler Adult Intelligence Scale, described later) was validated, a curious finding emerged. The men scored more highly than did women. The same difference was found when the WAIS was revised 25 years later. The general knowledge section of the WAIS is quite short and so any sex difference in scores may not be entirely conclusive. The difference may be restricted to the narrow range of subjects in that subtest of the WAIS.

Whether sex differences exist in general intelligence is controversial. Investigating any differences between boys and girls is complicated by the fact that girls mature more quickly than boys, and that the growth spurt in boys is seen in late adolescence and this correlates with higher IQ. Researchers at the University of Western Ontario (Jackson and Rushton, 2006) examined the performance of 46,509 male and 56,007 female 17–18-year-olds on the 1991 Scholastic Assessment Test, a measure of academic success that correlates well with general intelligence.

They found that the boys/men scored, on average, 3.63 IQ points higher than the girls/women. This effect was found regardless of ethnic group and socio-economic status. The authors caution, however, that the results from this one test cannot be generalised to the general population.

To examine whether such sex differences in general knowledge could be replicated, Lynn and Irwing administered a much larger set of general knowledge questions to 1,047 science and arts undergaduates at the University of Ulster, Northern Ireland (Lynn and Irwing, 2003).

Tests were constructed which covered 19 areas of general knowledge and yielded six factors covering (1) Physical health and recreation, (2) Current affairs, (3) Family (this included, oddly, cookery and medicine), (4) Science, (5) Fashion, and (6) Arts. The experimenters also took measures of general intelligence and reasoning.

Some of the questions asked included, 'Who wrote *The Republic?*', 'What is the hardest substance?', 'What organ is impaired by glaucoma?', 'In what game is the best score 21?', 'Who is the leading black British model?' and 'What is the currency of Greece?'

Men scored, on average, better than women on questions covering literature, general science, games and finance. Women outscored men on questions involving medicine and fashion. In general, the men scored half a standard deviation (see Appendix) higher than women. When scores on the general intelligence measure were compared, there was no significant difference between men and women. Neither general intelligence, nor A level grades, appeared, therefore, to explain this difference.

The authors argue, on the basis of these results, that general knowledge ought to be considered an intelligence factor in its own right. They call it 'semantic memory'.

Intelligence testing

Assessment of intellectual ability, or intelligence testing, is a controversial topic because of its importance in modern society. Unless people have special skills that suit them for a career in sports or entertainment, their economic success may depend heavily on formal education. Many employers use specialised aptitude tests to help them select among job candidates. Test scores correlate with school and university grades, the number of years in education and adult occupational status (Neisser *et al.*, 1996a). There are hundreds of tests of specific abilities, such as manual dexterity, spatial reasoning, vocabulary, mathematical aptitude, musical ability, creativity and memory. All these tests vary widely in reliability, validity and ease of administration.

Early intelligence tests

Intelligence testing has a long and chequered history. As early as 2200 BC, Chinese administrators tested civil servants (mandarins) periodically to be sure that their abilities qualified them for their job. In Western cultures, differences in social class were far more important than individual differences in ability until the Renaissance, when the modern concept of individualism came into being.

The term 'intelligence' is an old one, deriving from the Latin *intellectus* (meaning 'perception' or 'comprehension'). However, its use in the English language dates only from the late nineteenth century, when it was revived by the philosopher Herbert Spencer (1820–1903) and by the biologist/statistician Sir Francis Galton (1822–1911). Galton was the most important early investigator of individual differences in ability. He was strongly influenced by his cousin Charles Darwin, who stressed the importance of inherited differences in physical and behavioural traits related to a species' survival. Galton observed that there were family differences in ability and concluded that intellectual abilities were heritable. Having noted that people with low ability were poor at making sensory discriminations, he decided that tests involving such discriminations would provide valid measures of intelligence.

In 1884, Francis Galton established the Anthropometric Laboratory (meaning 'human-measuring') at the International Health Exhibition in London. His exhibit was so popular that afterwards his laboratory became part of the South Kensington Museum. He tested over 9,000 people on 17 variables, including height and weight, muscular strength, and the ability to perform sensory discriminations. One task involved detecting small differences in the weights of objects of the same size and shape.

Galton made some important contributions to science and mathematics. His systematic evaluation of various large numbers of people and the methods of population statistics he developed served as models for the statistical tests now used in all branches of science. His observation that the distribution of most human traits closely resembles the normal curve (developed by the Belgian statistician Lambert Quételet, 1796–1874) is the foundation for many modern tests of statistical significance and can be seen in Figure 11.5.

Galton also outlined the logic of a measure he called correlation: the degree to which variability in one measure is related to variability in another. From this analysis, the British mathematician Karl Pearson (1857–1936) derived the correlation coefficient (r) used today to assess the degree of statistical relation between variables. In addition, Galton developed the logic of twin studies and adoptive parent studies to assess the heritability of a human trait.

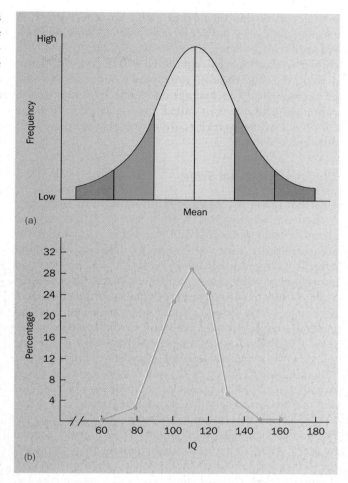

Figure 11.5 The normal curve and data from intelligence testing. **(a)** A mathematically derived normal curve. **(b)** A curve showing the distribution of IQ scores of 850 children two-and-a-half years of age.

Source: Terman, L.M. and Merrill, M.A., *Stanford–Binet Intelligence Scale*. Boston: Houghton-Mifflin, 1960. Copyright © 1960 by Houghton Mifflin Company.

Modern intelligence tests

The Binet–Simon Scale

Alfred Binet (1857–1911), a French psychologist, and a colleague (Binet and Henri, 1896) suggested that a group of simple sensory tests could not adequately determine a person's intelligence. They recommended measuring a variety of psychological abilities (such as imagery, attention, comprehension, imagination, judgements of visual space, and memory for various stimuli) that appeared to be more representative of the traits that distinguished people of high and low intelligence.

To identify children who were unable to profit from normal classroom instruction and needed special attention, Binet and Theodore Simon assembled a collection of tests, many of which had been developed by other investi-

gators, and published the **Binet–Simon Scale** in 1905. The tests were arranged in order of difficulty, and the researchers obtained norms for each test. **Norms** are data concerning comparison groups that permit the score of an individual to be assessed relative to his or her peers. In this case, the norms consisted of distributions of scores obtained from children of various ages. Binet and Simon also provided a detailed description of the testing procedure, which was essential for obtaining reliable scores. Without a standardised procedure for administering a test, different testers can obtain different scores from the same child.

Binet revised the 1905 test in order to assess the intellectual abilities of both normal children and those with learning problems. The revised versions provided a procedure for estimating a child's **mental age** – the level of intellectual development that could be expected for an average child of a particular age. For example, if an 8-year-old child scores as well as average 10-year-old children, their mental age is 10 years. Binet did not develop the concept of IQ (intelligence quotient). Nor did he believe that the mental age derived from the test scores expressed a simple trait called 'intelligence'. Instead, he conceived of the overall score as the average of several different abilities.

The Stanford–Binet Scale

Lewis Terman of Stanford University translated and revised the Binet–Simon Scale in the USA. The revised group of tests, published in 1916, became known as the Stanford–Binet Scale. Revisions by Terman and Maud Merrill were published in 1937 and 1960. In 1985, an entirely new version was published. The **Stanford–Binet Scale** consists of various tasks grouped according to mental age. Simple tests include identifying parts of the body and remembering which of three small cardboard boxes contains a marble. Intermediate tests include tracing a simple maze with a pencil and repeating five digits orally. Advanced tests include explaining the difference between two abstract words that are close in meaning (such as fame and notoriety) and completing complex sentences.

The 1916 Stanford–Binet Scale contained a formula for computing the intelligence quotient (IQ), a measure devised by Stern (1914). The **intelligence quotient (IQ)** represents the idea that if test scores indicate that a child's mental age is equal to their chronological age (that is, calendar age), the child's intelligence is average; if the child's mental age is above or below their chronological age, the child is more or less intelligent than average. This relation is expressed as the quotient of mental age (MA) and chronological age (CA). The result is called the **ratio IQ**. The quotient is multiplied by 100 to eliminate fractions. For example, if a

child's mental age is 10 and the child's chronological age is 8, then their IQ is (10 ÷ 8) × 100 = 125.

The 1960 version of the Stanford–Binet Scale replaced the ratio IQ with the deviation IQ. Instead of using the ratio of mental age to chronological age, the **deviation IQ** compares a child's score with those received by other children of the same chronological age (the deviation IQ was invented by David Wechsler, whose work is described in the next section). Suppose that a child's score is one standard deviation above the mean for their age. The standard deviation of the ratio IQ scores is 16 points, and the score assigned to the average IQ is 100 points. If a child's score is one standard deviation above the mean for their age, the child's deviation IQ score is 100 + 16 (the standard deviation) = 116. A child who scores one standard deviation below the mean receives a deviation IQ of 84 (100 – 16), as Figure 11.6 illustrates.

Wechsler Adult Intelligence Scale

see activity on mypsychlab

When David Wechsler was chief psychologist at New York City's Bellevue Psychiatric Hospital he developed several popular tests of intelligence. The Wechsler–Bellevue Scale, published in 1939, was revised in 1942 for use in the armed forces and was superseded in 1955 by the **Wechsler Adult Intelligence Scale (WAIS)**. This test was revised again in 1981 (the WAIS-R) and in 1997 (the WAIS-III). The **Wechsler Intelligence Scale for Children (WISC)**, first published in 1949 and revised in 1974 (the WISC-R), closely resembles the WAIS. Various versions of the WAIS-R have been devised for use with various populations (such as Irish, Scottish, Welsh and so on).

The current version, the WAIS-III, has widened age range for norms, is culturally up-to-date and includes more easy and difficult items. It is a large collection of individual tests (the test is called a 'battery') validated

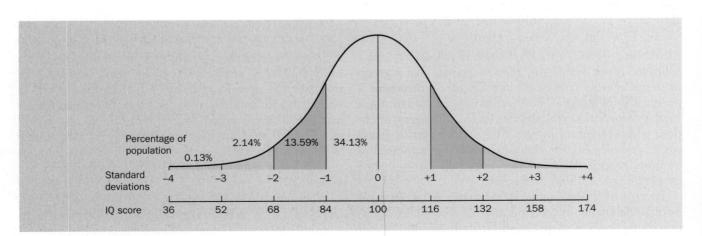

Figure 11.6 Calculating the deviation IQ score.

on 2,450 individuals from 13 age groups (from 16–17 years to 89). It was also administered to African American and Hispanic respondents, and rarely answered items were removed, thus giving the test a degree of culture-free face validity.

The WAIS-III comprises 14 subtests (11 are included from the WAIS-R) including vocabulary, arithmetic, block design, comprehension, object assembly and so on. Both the adult and children's versions comprise two major scales: verbal IQ (VIQ) and performance IQ (PIQ) which contribute to Full-Scale IQ (FS-IQ). Each major scale has various subscales (or subtests). For example, subtests of the verbal scale include tests of:

- information;
- comprehension (practical reasoning/interpretation of proverbs);
- similarities (abstraction and verbalisation of properties common to objects);
- arithmetic reasoning;
- digit span (repetition and reversal of numbers presented aurally);
- vocabulary (definitions).

Subtests of the performance scale include:

- digit symbols;
- picture completion (identification of missing features from line drawings);
- picture arrangement (arrangement of cartoon pictures in a meaningful order);
- block designs (block construction from a given design);
- object assembly (timed construction of puzzles).

The performance scale relies less on the retention of previously acquired information than does the verbal scale. As such, it is less dependent on formal education but is more vulnerable to ageing and conditions which impair perceptual and motor skills and speed (Rao, 1986). It is also susceptible to practice effects, as is the verbal scale but more so. An example of one of the performance scale tests can be seen in Figure 11.7. The norms obtained for the WAIS permit the tester to calculate a deviation IQ score.

The WAIS is the most widely administered adult intelligence test. An important advantage is that it tests verbal and performance abilities separately. Neuropsychologists often use it because people with brain damage tend to score very differently on the performance and verbal tests. In fact, it is so widely used that Lezak (1995) has called it the 'workhorse of neuropsychological assessment'. Comparisons of performance and verbal test scores suggest the presence of undiagnosed brain damage. Because people who have had few educational and cultural opportunities often do worse on the verbal tests

Figure 11.7 The block design subtest similar to that illustrated here is part of both of Wechsler's Scales, the WISC-R for children and the WAIS-R for adults.

Source: © Bob Daemmrich/The Image Works. Reproduced with permission.

than on the performance tests, the WAIS is useful in estimating what their score might have been had they been raised in a more favourable environment.

Reliability and validity of intelligence tests

The adequacy of a measure is represented by its reliability and validity (terms described in Chapter 2). In the case of intelligence testing, reliability is assessed by the correlation between the scores that people receive on the same measurement on two different occasions; perfect reliability is 1. High reliability is achieved by means of standardised test administration and objective scoring: all participants are exposed to the same situation during testing, and all score responses in the same way. The acceptable reliability of a modern test of intellectual ability should be at least 0.85. Validity is the correlation between test scores and the criterion – an independent measure of the variable that is being assessed.

However, most tests of intelligence correlate reasonably well with such measures as success in school (between 0.40 and 0.75). Thus, because intellectual ability plays at least some role in academic success, IQ appears to have some validity.

Are intelligence scores improving?

One of the most curious phenomena of intelligence measurement is that people appear to be getting significantly more intelligent or, more accurately, their IQ scores are increasing. This is called the Flynn effect after the psychologist James Flynn who noticed that the average level of intelligence has risen since the beginning of the twentieth century (Flynn, 1984, 1987). This is illustrated in Figure 11.8. It has been estimated that people living in the 1930s would have IQ scores that were one to two standard deviations below those living in 2000. The US population appears to have made a 20-point acceleration in IQ in 60 years. Scores on tests of fluid intelligence have doubled compared with scores on crystallised intelligence. In one Dutch study, an 18–20 point increase in IQ was observed within a generation (Flynn, 1999). There has also been an increase in sematic and episodic memory performance (Rönlund *et al*, 2008). Why?

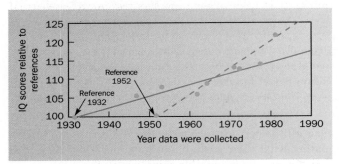

Figure 11.8 IQ increase over the twentieth century.

Source: Blair, C., Gamson, D., Thorne, S. and Baker, D., Rising mean IQ: Cognitive demand of mathematics education for young children, population exposure to formal schooling and the neurobiology of the prefrontal cortex, *Intelligence*, 2005, 33, 93–106, p. 94, figure 1.

The most obvious explanation would be improved schooling and education, especially in primary or elementary school where the focus has shifted towards teaching cognitive skills that reflect fluid intelligence (Blair *et al.*, 2005).

There is a significant association between national IQ and educational achievement. Lynn and Mikk (2007) correlated published national IQs scores in 2002 and 2006 with the educational attainment scores of children in 25 (10-year-olds) and 46 (14-year-olds) countries. Maths and science achievement correlated significantly with national IQ. IQ was also associated with per capita income: the greater the IQ, the greater the income.

The roles of heredity and environment

Abilities – intellectual, athletic, musical and artistic – appear to run in families. Why? Are the similarities owing to heredity, or are they solely the result of a common environment, which includes similar educational opportunities and exposure to people having similar kinds of interests?

According to Sternberg and Grigorenko (1997), we know three facts about the roles of heredity and environment in intelligence: (1) both contribute to intelligence, (2) they interact in various ways, and (3) poor and enriched environments influence the development of intellectual ability regardless of heredity.

What these facts illustrate is that the typical nature–nurture debate in intelligence is no longer valid. The nature–nurture argument suggests that, in its most stark form, behaviour or function is determined solely by the environment or solely by genetics/heredity. Psychologists have discovered that this argument is too simplistic. In fact, it is inaccurate. Almost all psychologists agree that

Cutting edge – Do you have to be smart to be rich?

This is the question Jay Zagorsky of Ohio State University asked when he examined IQ and income generation data from over 7,000 Americans born between 1957 and 1964 (Zagorsky, 2007). He found that although each point increase in IQ was associated with between $234 and $616 additional income per year, there was no statistically significant relationship between them. That is, while greater IQ was associated with greater income, the increase was not large enough to be statistically meaningful.

A slightly different finding was found in a study of IQ and career success (Strenze, 2007). This study found that intelligence measured before respondents had left formal schooling was significantly associated with later career/socio-economic success. However, parents' socio-economic status and school achievement was also associated with their offspring's success.

intelligence has a hereditary (as well as environmental) component. The debate now focuses on the degree to which each contributes to intelligence and the ways in which they interact to influence intellectual development.

The meaning of heritability

When we ask how much influence heredity has on a given trait, we are usually asking what the heritability of the trait is. **Heritability** is a statistical measure that expresses the proportion of the observed variability in a trait that is a direct result of genetic variability. The value of this measure can vary from 0 to 1. The heritability of many physical traits in most cultures is very high; for example, eye colour is affected almost entirely by hereditary factors and little, if at all, by the environment. Thus, the heritability of eye colour is close to 1.

Heritability is a concept that many people misunderstand. It does not describe the extent to which the inherited genes are responsible for producing a particular trait; it measures the relative contributions of differences in genes and differences in environmental factors to the overall observed variability of the trait in a particular population. An example may make this distinction clear. Consider the heritability of hair colour in the Eskimo culture. Almost all young Eskimos have black hair, whereas older Eskimos have grey or white hair. Because all members of this population possess the same versions of the genes that determine hair colour, the genetic variability with respect to those genes is in essence zero. All the observed variability in hair colour in this population is explained by an environmental factor – age. Therefore, the heritability of hair colour in the Eskimo culture is zero.

As with hair colour, we infer the heritability of a person's intelligence from their observed performance. Thus, looking at a person's IQ score is equivalent to looking at the colour of a person's hair. By measuring the correlation between IQ score and various genetic and environmental factors, we can arrive at an estimate of heritability. Clearly, even if hereditary factors do influence intelligence, the heritability of this trait must be considerably less than 1 because so many environmental factors also influence intelligence. The branch of psychology called behaviour genetics, which we came across in Chapters 1 and 3, predicts the degree of parental influence via genetic and environmental transmission on the development of the child's intellectual development. The proportion of the variance associated with genetic differences among individuals is called h; the remaining variation which is associated with environmental influences is referred to as $1-h$ (Neisser *et al.*, 1996a). The features which families share and have in common (such as choice of home) is sometimes referred to as c. Factor h

can be subdivided into two types: additive h, which refers to the amount of hereditary variance that is passed from parent to child, and non-additive h which refers to new, unique genetic expression in each generation. As children grow older, h increases and c decreases (McGue *et al.*, 1993). In childhood, the contribution of h and c to intelligence is similar; by adolescence h predicts about three-quarters of intellectual ability.

The heritability of a trait depends on the amount of variability of genetic factors in a given population. If there is little genetic variability, genetic factors will appear to be unimportant. Because the ancestors of people living in developed Western nations came from all over the world, genetic variability is likely to be much higher there than in an isolated tribe of people in a remote part of the world. Therefore, if a person's IQ score is at all affected by genetic factors, the measured heritability of IQ will be higher in, say, Western European culture than in an isolated tribe.

The relative importance of environmental factors in intelligence depends on the amount of environmental variability (EV) that occurs in the population. If environmental variability is low, then environmental factors will appear to be unimportant. In a society with a low variability in environmental factors relevant to intellectual development – one in which all children are raised in the same way by equally skilled and conscientious carers, all schools are equally good, all teachers have equally effective personalities and teaching skills, and no one is discriminated against – the effects of EV would be small and those of GV (genetic variability) would be large. In contrast, in a society in which only a few privileged people receive a good education, environmental factors would be responsible for much of the variability in intelligence: the effects of EV would be large relative to those of GV.

Although h and c give an indication of the degree of variance attributable to heredity and environment, they do not explain the mechanism by which intelligence is transmitted or developed (Neisser *et al.*, 1996a).

Sources of environmental and genetic effects during development

Biological and environmental factors can affect intellectual abilities prenatally and post-natally. Newborn infants cannot be said to possess any substantial intellectual abilities; rather, they are more or less capable of developing these abilities during their lives. Therefore, prenatal influences can be said to affect a child's potential intelligence by affecting the development of the brain. Factors that impair brain development will necessarily also impair the child's potential intelligence.

As the axons of developing neurons grow, they thread their way through a tangle of other growing cells, responding to physical and chemical signals along the way. During this stage of prenatal development, differentiating cells can be misguided by false signals. For example, if a woman contracts German measles during early pregnancy, toxic chemicals produced by the virus may adversely affect the development of the foetus. Sometimes, these chemicals can misdirect the interconnections of brain cells and produce mental retardation. Thus, although development of a human organism is programmed genetically, environmental factors can affect development even before a person is born.

Harmful prenatal environmental factors include physical trauma injury to the mother (for example, in a car accident) and toxic effects. A developing foetus can be exposed to toxins from diseases contracted by the mother during pregnancy (such as German measles) or from other sources. A pregnant woman's intake of various drugs can have detrimental effects on foetal development. Alcohol, opiates, cocaine and the chemicals present in cigarettes are harmful to foetuses. One of the most common drug-induced abnormalities, **foetal alcohol syndrome**, is seen in many offspring of women who are chronic alcoholics. Children with foetal alcohol syndrome are much smaller than average, have characteristic facial abnormalities, and, more significantly, are mentally retarded. Figure 11.9 shows the face of a child with foetal alcohol syndrome as well as the faces of a normal mouse foetus and of a mouse foetus whose mother received alcohol during early pregnancy.

Development can also be harmed by genetic abnormalities. Some of these abnormalities cause brain damage and consequently produce mental retardation. The best-known example of these abnormalities is Down syndrome, described in Chapter 3. Although Down syndrome is a genetic disorder, it is not hereditary; it results from imperfect division of the 23 pairs of chromosomes during the development of an ovum or (rarely) a sperm. Chapter 3 also described phenylketonuria (PKU), an inherited metabolic disorder that disrupts normal brain development. If left untreated, PKU can result in severe mental retardation.

From birth onwards, a child's brain continues to develop. Environmental factors can either promote or impede that development. Post-natal factors such as birth trauma, diseases that affect the brain, or toxic chemicals can prevent optimum development and thereby affect the child's potential intelligence. For example, encephalitis (inflammation of the brain), when contracted during childhood, can result in mental retardation, as can the ingestion of poisons such as mercury or lead.

Educational influences in the environment, including (but not limited to) schooling, enable a child to attain their potential intelligence. By contrast, a less than optimum environment prevents the fullest possible realisation of intelligence. Experience with mentally retarded people demonstrates this point. Known environmental causes account for only about 25 per cent of observed cases of mental retardation. In addition, people whose mental retardation has no obvious physical cause are likely to have close relatives who are also mentally retarded. These findings strongly suggest that many of the remaining 75 per cent of cases are hereditary. However, environmental causes (such as poor nutrition or the presence of environmental toxins) can produce brain damage in members of the same family; thus, not all cases of familial mental retardation are necessarily hereditary.

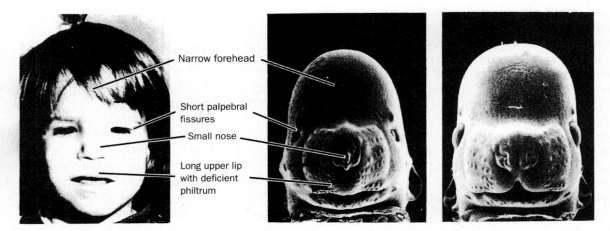

Figure 11.9 A child with foetal alcohol syndrome, along with magnified views of a mouse foetus whose mother received alcohol during pregnancy (left) and a normal mouse foetus (right).
Source: © Katherine K. Sulik.

Results of heritability studies

Estimates of the degree to which heredity influences a person's intellectual ability come from several sources. As you saw in Chapter 3, the two most powerful methods are comparisons between identical and fraternal twins and comparisons between adoptive and biological relatives.

Identical and fraternal twins

Scarr and Weinberg (1978) compared some specific intellectual abilities of parents and their adopted and biological children and of children and their biological and adopted siblings. They administered four of the subtests of the Wechsler Adult Intelligence Scale: arithmetic, vocabulary, block design and picture arrangement. The correlations between biological relatives were considerably higher than those between adoptive relatives, indicating that genetic factors played a more significant role than shared environmental factors. In fact, with the exception of vocabulary, adopted children showed little resemblance to other members of their family.

These results suggest that a person's vocabulary is more sensitive to their home environment than are other specific intellectual abilities. Presumably, such factors as the availability of books, parental interests in reading, and the complexity of vocabulary used by the parents have a significant effect on the verbal skills of all members of the household, whether or not they are biologically related.

A comprehensive survey of the differences between identical (monozygotic) and fraternal (dizygotic) twins on tests of spatial and verbal ability is illustrated in Figure 11.10 (reported in Plomin and DeFries, (1998)).

The figure illustrates the differences between the intelligence of groups across the lifespan from childhood to old age. What is remarkable about these data is that, across the lifespan, the similarity between identical twins is significantly greater than that between fraternal twins. Compare these results with those seen in Table 11.5. The table summarises data from a number of published studies of biological and adoptive families and adolescent and adult twins (Scarr, 1997). The table also shows that although identical twins reared in the same home show a higher concordance rate than identical twins reared apart, these concordance rates are still higher (significantly so) than those of fraternal twins reared together.

Recent studies have indicated that not only are monozygotic children closer in intellectual ability than their fraternal counterparts but that this difference extends to old age. Petrill *et al.* (1998) studied the degree of heritability of general intelligence in monozygotic and dizygotic twins longitudinally during infancy and early childhood. The researchers found that *h* increases from zero at 14 months to 0.64 at 36 months and begins to exert a significant effect by 24 and 36 months. The influence of shared environment began to attenuate at 36 months. One reason for the pronounced influence of

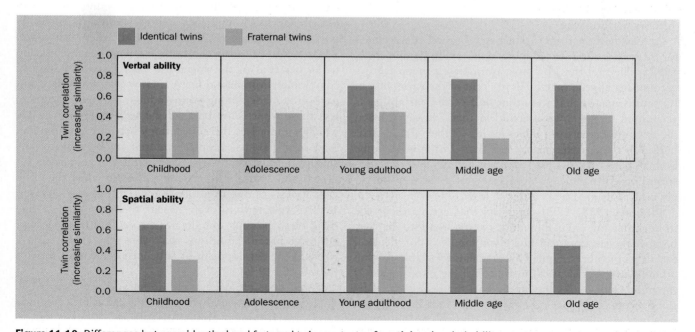

Figure 11.10 Differences between identical and fraternal twins on tests of spatial and verbal ability.

Source: Plomin, R. and DeFries, J.C., The genetics of cognitive abilities and disabilities. *Scientific American*, 1998, 287(5), pp. 40–47, reprinted by permission of Jennifer C. Christiansen.

Table 11.5 Intelligence test correlations of siblings from five behaviour-genetic studies of biological and adoptive families and twins (adolescents and adults).

Genetic r (correlation)	Relationship	Same home?	IQ correlation	Number of pairs
1.00	Same person tested twice	Yes	0.90	–
1.00	Identical twins	Yes	0.86	4672
1.00	Identical twins	No	0.76	158
0.50	Fraternal twins	Yes	0.55	8600
0.50	Fraternal twins	No	0.35	112
0.50	Biological siblings	Yes	0.47	26473
0.50	Biological siblings	No	0.24	203
0.00	Adoptive siblings	Yes	0.02	385

Source: Adapted with permission from Scarr, S. (1997). In *Intelligence, Heredity and Environments*, edited by R.J. Sternberg and E. Grigorenko. © 1997 Cambridge University Press, New York.

heredity at 36 months (and the attenuation of the influence of environment) may be the development of language, a function that is thought to be highly heritable.

The contribution of h to intelligence appears to increase from 0.3 in early childhood (Cherny *et al.*, 1994) to 0.8 in middle age (Finkel *et al.*, 1995). However, this influence may extend to very old age (over 80 years of age). In the first study of its kind, Petrill *et al.* (1998) examined the influence of h in monozygotic and dizygotic twins greater than 80 years of age taken from the OctoTwin sample of the Swedish Twin Registry which contains details of 90 per cent of the twins born in Sweden. The mean age of the participants was 82.7 years and all were free from dementia and motor handicap. Petrill *et al.* (1998) found that there was a significant influence of h on ability, especially on memory performance.

At least half the total variance in IQ scores is accounted for by genetic variance (Chipuer *et al.*, 1990; Plomin *et al.*, 1997). The fact that, by most estimates, genetic factors account for approximately 50 per cent of the variability in IQ scores means that the other half of the variability is accounted for by environmental factors. However, when the data are taken from tables such as Table 11.5, contribution of the environment is less than 25 per cent. Some estimates, based on comparisons of parents and their offspring raised together or apart, suggest a value of only 4 per cent. Why are these figures so low?

Plomin (1988, 1990) suggests that estimates of the importance of environmental factors tend to be low because the environment in a given family is not identical for all its members. Some environmental variables within a family are shared by all members of the family, such as the number of books the family has, the examples set by the parents, the places the family visits on holiday, the noisiness or quietness of the home, and so on. But not all of the environmental factors that affect a person's development and behaviour are shared in this way. For example, no two children are treated identically, even by family members; differences in their appearances and personalities affect the way other people treat them. Different members of a family will probably have different friends and acquaintances, attend different classes in school, and, in general, be exposed to different influences. And once people leave home, their environments become even more different.

Estimates of the contribution of environmental variability to intelligence based on measurements made during childhood tend to be higher than similar estimates based on measurements made during adulthood. The reason for this difference may be that, during childhood, family members share a more similar environment, whereas during adulthood their environments become less similar. As Plomin (1997) notes, studies of genetically unrelated children (of a mean age of under 10 years) adopted and raised in the same families, suggest that up to 30 per cent of the variability in IQ scores is due to common environmental factors. However, when the comparison is made among young adults, the figure drops to less than 3 per cent. This can be seen in Figure 11.11, which summarises the correlations between children and their birth parents, adopted children and their birth parents, and adopted children and their adoptive parents for verbal and spatial ability from the time when the child was 3 years of age to adolescence (Plomin and DeFries, 1998). Adopted children appear to become more like their birth parents but do not become more like their adoptive parents, findings that were also reported in a study of the development of antisocial behaviour in twins (Pike *et al.*, 1996).

Thus, once children leave home and are exposed to different environmental variables, the effect of a common family environment almost disappears. What is left, in the case of related individuals, is their common genetic heritage.

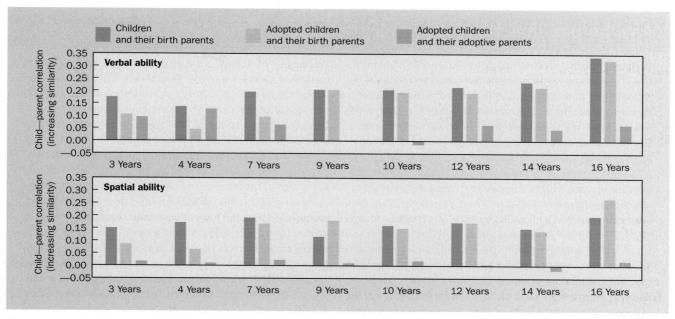

Figure 11.11 The Colorado Adoption Project monitored the spatial and verbal ability of (1) children and their birth parents; (2) adopted children and their birth parents; and (3) adopted children and their adoptive parents, from the child's third birthday to its sixteenth birthday. Notice how closely the adopted children's intelligence resembles that of their birth parents but that there is little resemblance between adopted children and their adopted parents.

Source: Plomin, R. and DeFries, J.C., The genetics of cognitive abilities and disabilities, *Scientific American*, 1998, 278, 5, 44, reprinted by permission of Jennifer C. Christiansen.

If intelligence is inherited, how does inheritance occur?

Given that our DNA is what makes us what we are, the first and most obvious locus of any genetic cause would be our chromosomes (Plomin, 1997). The DNA contains sequences of information which are divided into sections by enzymes (called restriction enzymes). Sometimes these sequences are repeated. These enzymes act as markers which can be used to locate chromosomes and defects on chromosomes. Some genetic disorders of behaviour are single-gene disorders, that is, only one chromosome is affected (such as that seen in PKU, as you saw in Chapter 3). More complex behaviours, however, are likely to have multiple genetic loci called quantitative trait loci. The question, therefore, is whether intelligence is inherited through one gene or multiple genes.

Plomin and his colleagues have pioneered research in this, one of the most difficult areas in behaviour genetics. Plomin *et al.* (1994a, b, 1995) have made an extensive study of DNA markers from Caucasian children of varying intelligence – from low IQ (less than 59) to high IQ (over 142) – and have found small genetic differences in intelligence between those with low and high IQ. Several of 100 identifiable DNA markers have been associated with intelligence, but no one marker has been consistently associated with it. A recent study has located a DNA marker for the gene on chromosome 6 which appears with greater frequency in a high IQ group (IQ over 136) than a control group (IQ = 103) (Chorney *et al.*, 1998). This is an exciting finding because it was replicated in a group with even higher IQ (over 160). The researchers caution, however, that the gene accounted for only a small portion of the genetic influence on intelligence and that many more genes may be implicated. Nonetheless, this new area of research may hold the key to identifying the genetic basis of intelligent behaviour.

Giftedness

Although having a high IQ may seem less of an intellectual impediment than having a low IQ, gifted children encounter equally serious but different problems at school (Winner, 1997). Gifted children are frequently described as bored in classes of children of the same age (Gross, 1993) and there is little provision in most schools for the teaching of the very bright and able (Westberg *et al.*, 1993).

Gifted children have been found to be able to induce the rules of algebra at 4–5 years (Winner, 1996), memorise musical scores (Feldman and Goldsmith, 1991), and identify prime numbers (Winner, 1996). Are there specific features of the gifted child, apart from high IQ, which

Psychology in action – Can low intelligence be improved?

Various projects, predominantly but not exclusively in the USA, have sought to discover whether early intervention in the schooling of poor children can lead to educational benefits beyond the period of intervention. In a recent review of the evidence for the long-term success of such programmes, Campbell *et al.* (2001) conclude that interventions are generally beneficial.

Some intervention programmes have shown that intervening early in a poor child's education can enhance their success at school (Johnson and Walker, 1991; Reynolds, 1994). Two such interventions include the Cognitive Acceleration Through Science Education programme (Adey and Shayer, 1994) and the Practical Intelligence for Schools Project (Sternberg and Wagner, 1986; Williams *et al.*, 1996). The former involves teaching children the pattern of thinking seen in science. In a two-year intervention study of 11–12-year-old children, there was a significant increase in science achievement test scores at the end of the intervention. The latter helps the child to build coping strategies based on knowing the strengths, weaknesses and demands of a task and applying the appropriate steps and strategies to complete these tasks. Again, intervention improved the intellectual skill of children when measured on practical and academic measures of writing, homework and test-taking. However, it is unclear whether these interventions make children think better or make them more intelligent.

Campbell *et al.* (2001) also draw attention to numerous other studies that have shown the positive benefit in middle childhood of early educational intervention. They also highlight the lack of studies beyond adolescence. They cite two studies in which children who received intervention were less likely to be placed in special needs classes while in school but (1) were not intellectually superior and (2) did not graduate any more quickly (Gray *et al.*, 1982). The second study, conversely, found that although intervention groups were less likely to be placed in special needs classes in school, they also performed better at school and, at 19 years old, performed better than the non-intervention group on tests of literacy (Weikart *et al.*, 1978).

The picture is clearly mixed, but if intervention programmes do show some evidence of success, why should this be? Campbell *et al.* suggest that intervention programmes directly affect a child's cognitive abilities by enabling it to 'meet the challenges of school'. The evidence, they argue, points towards a stronger role for these direct factors rather than indirect ones such as changes in motivation or the parents' perception of the child. The researchers explored some of these factors in a cohort of 104 largely African American children (98 per cent of total) from the Abecedarian project.

The Abecedarian project involved the study of the effects of educational intervention in children from low-income families. Fifty-seven of the infants were randomly assigned to the intervention group; the remainder to the control group. Intervention took the form of early education programmes in infancy for 8 hours a day, 5 days a week, 50 weeks a year. A special curriculum was designed to promote cognitive, perceptual and social development. The control group did not receive such consistent education and attended various day-care centres for different periods, with no experimental intervention. The researchers (Campbell *et al.*, 2001) conducted follow-up assessments when the participants were 21 years old and these assessments included tests of intelligence and evaluations of achievement.

The researchers found that cognitive test performance increased more steeply in the treated group during early childhood when compared with controls. From 3 to 21 years, however, there was a generally better performance in the treated group than in the controls. Reading and mathematics performance was better in the treated group but both groups' performance remained fairly stable from middle childhood onwards: performance showed little change over time and both groups' achievement developed in parallel. It was evident, however, that both groups showed a gradual decline in scores between 12 and 21 years, when compared with standardised scores for the general population. While the treated group performed better than the untreated group, both groups' performance compared unfavourably with the population average.

The results suggest that early intervention in a child's education can be beneficial for children from low-income families with poor maternal education compared with no intervention at all. The period from birth to 3 years or 5 years may be the key to explaining why other intervention programmes do not show such success (Gray *et al.*, 1982). These intervention programmes began when the children were 3 or 4 years old; they were also less time-intensive than the Abecedarian project.

distinguish them from a child of average intelligence? According to Davidson and Sternberg (1984), insight is a frequent characteristic of scholastic achievement; gifted children appear adept at selecting information and selectively encoding it. Similarly, gifted children may use the same memory strategies as other children but use them more effectively (Jackson and Butterfield, 1986). They also appear to think more independently and persistently than other children and require less structure in their work (Rogers, 1986).

What makes the brain of an intellectually gifted individual different from that of a less gifted one? Is there something about the way in which a gifted person's brain functions that distinguishes him or her?

A group of researchers from the USA and Australia used fMRI to compare brain activation in mathematically gifted adolescent males and control individuals while participants completed a three-dimensional mental rotation task (O'Boyle *et al.*, 2005). The same task is described in Chapter 8, Figure 8.6. In the gifted sample, activation was more bilateral during mental rotation while the control group showed more right-sided activation. Bilateral activation was especially prominent in the parietal lobes and was accompanied by bilateral activation in parts of the frontal lobe, such as the anterior cingulate. Activation in this region was almost completely absent in the control group.

The researchers suggest that this network might be activated or relied upon by the intellectually gifted or by individuals who are mathematically gifted. The prefrontal cortex, as you will see in this chapter, is more greatly activated during performance of tests of fluid intelligence.

Another MRI study has shown that the posterior parietal cortex is significantly more active in intellectually superior Korean adolescents than in Korean children of average intelligence (Lee *et al.*, 2006). The children completed two reasoning tasks, one which relied heavily on general intelligence (*g*), and another which relied on *g* less heavily. The study found that although both groups of adolescents recruited the prefrontal cortex and posterior parietal cortex during the task which relied heavily on *g*, activation was greater in the gifted children. The researchers suggest that superior intelligence is facilitated by activation in a fronto-parietal network which is itself facilitated by activation in the posterior parietal cortex.

IQ and nutrition

There is a clear, obvious and important link between intelligence and nutrition. Malnutrition can impair brain function (Brown and Pollitt, 1996) and IQ in the long term; iodine deficiency during pregnancy can lead to retardation and cretinism. In the late 1980s and early 1990s, a series of studies reported significant differences in non-verbal IQ between schoolchildren who received vitamin and mineral supplements (VMS) and those who received a placebo (Benton, 1992; Haller, 1995; Eysenck and Schoenthaler, 1997). Those who received the supplements scored significantly better.

Benton and Roberts (1988) administered either VMS or a placebo to 60 12-year-old Welsh schoolchildren and measured verbal and non-verbal IQ before and after the trial which lasted 9 months. They found that the non-verbal IQ of those children receiving VMS was significantly higher at the end of the trial compared with those receiving a placebo. In fact, non-verbal IQ was, on average, nine points higher. Schoenthaler *et al.* (1991a) also reported those receiving supplements had significantly higher non-verbal IQ (the placebo group's average IQ actually dropped a point). Two other studies confirmed the general findings from these reports (Benton and Buts, 1990; Benton and Cook, 1991). The largest study involved 615 Californian children (Schoenthaler *et al.*, 1991b). A placebo, VMS at the recommended daily allowance, VMS at half the RDA or VMS at twice the RDA was administered to the children each day for 12 weeks. As predicted, non-verbal IQ increased in all VMS groups.

Do these studies indicate that supplementation does have a genuine effect on cognitive performance? Do all studies agree? The answer, to the second question at least, is no. Some studies have failed to replicate the Benton

Cutting edge – The effect of intelligence on health

In recent years, psychologists have turned to an unusual factor as a predictor of long-term good health: intelligence. Studies have shown that people with lower IQ are more likely to die earlier than those with higher IQ, whatever socio-economic class they belong to (Batty *et al.*, 2007). A new study of 1,181 Scottish people born in 1936 and followed by researchers from 1963 to 2003 has confirmed this finding (Deary *et al.*, 2008).

People with higher intelligence and who were most dependable had a significantly lower rate of mortality. The 'hazard ratio' was 0.8 for intelligence and 0.77 for dependabil-

ity (i.e. very low). Children who were in the lower half of the dependability/intelligence dimension were twice as likely to die as those in the upper half. The hazard ratio was 2.82. Smoking, high cholesterol and high blood pressure in middle age is associated with a hazard ratio of 2.34 in women and 3.2 in men (Lowe *et al.*, 1998).

The researchers suggest that a number of explanations could account for this association. There is a relationship between genetics and intelligence and longevity, for example. This relationship may be mediated by socio-economic status and engaging in healthy behaviour.

and Schoenthaler findings. Nelson *et al.* (1990), for example, examined the effect of VMS and placebo on 227 7–12-year-old children over four weeks and found no evidence of significant improvement in non-verbal IQ. Benton (1992) and Eysenck and Schoenthaler (1997), in a review of these studies, suggest that a number of methodological differences could account for the contrary results. Differences in the length of trials, the types of test used, the method of administering tests, interpreting the results of tests, and the type of VMS may explain the results of those studies reporting no significant improvement in non-verbal IQ. More recently, researchers have found a significant relationship between iron and folate intake and total IQ and non-verbal IQ (Arija *et al.*, 2006). The greater the intake, the better the IQ. The results suggests that even in children who are well-nour-

ished and intelligent, some nutritional intervention might lead to better cognition.

If the effect seen in children is robust, why should VMS affect only non-verbal IQ? In all the published studies there has been no reported improvement in verbal IQ. Cast your mind back to the sections on types of intelligence earlier in this chapter. Verbal intelligence, as measured on the standard types of test, usually relies on information that has already been learned through experience. This type of intelligence is called 'crystallised' intelligence. Non-verbal intelligence, however, does not rely on previous knowledge and has been described as 'fluid'. If fluid intelligence reflects the potential to perform, it seems reasonable that administering VMS should affect this type of intelligence more than the type which is fixed and crystallised.

Controversies in Psychological Science – Is there a relationship between race and intelligence?

The issue

Of all the controversies in psychological science discussed in this book, perhaps the most controversial is that of the contribution of race to intelligence. *The Bell Curve*, a book written by a psychologist and a sociologist (Herrnstein and Murray, 1994), provoked a furore among psychologists and in the media across the world. The book asserted that psychologists agree that a general intelligence factor exists; that IQ tests measure what most people think of as intelligence; that IQ is almost impossible to modify through education and special training; that IQ is genetically determined; and that racial differences in IQ are the result of heredity. Whereas the chapter has so far discussed the first four assertions, this section addresses the last: whether race can influence IQ.

The evidence

Many studies have established the fact that there are racial differences in scores on various tests of intellectual abilities. For example, people who are identified as black generally score an average of 85 on IQ tests, whereas people who are identified as white score an average of 100 (Lynn, 1991; Jensen, 1985; Rushton, 1997). Although many blacks score better than many whites, on average whites do better on these tests. A statement endorsed by 52 professors indicated that, on average, whites' average IQ score is 100, African Americans' is 85, American-Hispanics' is somewhere between whites and African Americans', and Asians' is above 100 (*Mainstream Science*, 1994, cited in Suzuki and Valencia (1997)). Lynn's study (1996) of 2,260 children between 6 and

17 years of age found that Asian children scored an average of 107 IQ points, white children an average of 103 and black children an average of 89. Interestingly, black infants are more advanced than their white counterparts in the first 15 months of life (Lynn, 1998).

The controversy lies not in the facts themselves but in what these facts mean. Some authors have argued that the racial differences in scores on the tests are caused by heredity (Lynn, 1993; Rushton, 1995, 1997). *The Bell Curve* highlighted other racial aspects of intelligence such as the failure of intervention programmes to improve the IQs of black children.

The assertions made in *The Bell Curve* have not gone unchallenged. In response to the book and issues surrounding intelligence, the American Psychological Association set up a taskforce to report on the current state of knowledge regarding the nature and determinants of intelligence (Neisser *et al.*, 1996a). The evidence we have reviewed so far in the chapter has helped to clarify some of the issues raised in *The Bell Curve*.

Some investigators have attempted to use statistical methods to remove the effects of environmental variables, such as socio-economic status, that account for differences in performance between blacks and whites. However, these methods are controversial, and many statisticians question their validity. On the other hand, a study by Scarr and Weinberg (1976) provides unambiguous evidence that environmental factors can substantially increase the measured IQ of a black child. Scarr and Weinberg studied 99 black children who were adopted into white families of higher-than-average educational and socio-economic status. The expected average

Controversies in Psychological Science – *Continued*

IQ of black children in the same area who were raised in black families was approximately 90. The average IQ of the adopted group was observed to be 105.

Other authors have flatly stated that there are no racial differences in biologically determined intellectual capacity. But this claim, like the one asserting that blacks are inherently less intelligent than whites, has not been determined scientifically. It is an example of what Jensen (1980) has called the egalitarian fallacy – the 'gratuitous assumption that all human populations are essentially identical in whatever trait or ability the test purports to measure' (p. 370). Although we know that blacks and whites have different environments and that a black child raised in an environment similar to that of a white child will receive a similar IQ score, the question of whether any racial hereditary differences exist has not been answered. When we point to group differences in races we are referring to general, average differences in intellectual performance; there are considerable within-group differences which may even be larger than between-group differences (Suzuki and Valencia, 1997).

There is also a problem with what we mean by race. We can define race biologically by gene frequencies (Loehlin *et al.*, 1975) or we can define it as a social construct. For many people, race is whatever they believe it to mean; they themselves ascribe meaning to it (Omi and Winant, 1994). In this sense, the concept of race makes very little scientific sense.

Conclusion

Although the issue of race and intelligence as currently conceived does not appear to be meaningful, it would be scientifically interesting to study the effects of different environments on inherited intellectual capacity. The interesting and more valid questions concerning race are those addressed by social psychologists and anthropologists – questions concerning issues such as the prevalence of prejudice, ethnic identification and cohesiveness, fear of strangers (xenophobia), and the tendency to judge something (or someone) that is different as inferior.

Intelligence, thinking and ageing

Ageing and cognitive ability

As the body and the brain grow older, certain changes occur. The acuity of the senses may begin to decline, the ability to move quickly is reduced. On the cognitive level, there is also a decline in various functions such as the manipulation of information in working memory, retrieval of names, reaction time, declarative memory, information processing. Functions such as vocabulary, however, see some improvement with age (Woodruff-Pak, 1997). General IQ scores will peak at around 25 years of age and decline up to 65 years. After 65, the score drops rapidly (Woods, 1994). At the most severe end of cognitive decline, there is dementia – the gradual and relentless loss in intellectual function as the individual reaches the sixth decade of life and beyond. There may be great difficulty in separating the effects of normal ageing from the effects of dementia on cognitive ability (Alzheimer's disease, for example, can only be diagnosed with certainty post-mortem when the brain can be examined). Data from a Canadian sample suggest that the degree of cognitive impairment that is not related to dementia is around 16.8 per cent (the usual prevalence of dementia is 8 per cent) (Graham *et al.*, 1997).

Our categorisation of individuals into age groups is fairly arbitrary. In most developed countries, the age of retirement is set at 65 (an age originally set by Otto von Bismark, the German chancellor from 1871 to 1890), although this does not mean that those people who are 65 or older are incapable of holding down a job or lack the cognitive and physical capacity to hold down such a job. The distribution of the elderly population in the Western world in 1950 was pyramid-shaped, that is, there were fewer people reaching old and very old (over 80 years) age. It has been estimated that by 2030, this distribution will be pillar-shaped, with roughly equal numbers in the old and very old categories.

Improvements in health care, sanitation, crime prevention and nutrition are thought to be responsible for this increase in the number of years we are living. Psychologically, therefore, the more we learn about the effects of ageing – and in reversing its negative effects – the more important this information will become in countries where we are living longer.

What is ageing?

From a strict point of view, we age as soon as we emerge from the womb. We are born with all the neurons we will have in life and they begin dying as soon as we grow. There is a massive shedding of neurons and synapses during childhood; this continues to old age. Of course, this shedding does not leave us intellectually helpless. Although neurons are lost, new connections are formed between existing neurons (this is why, although neurons are lost, the brain increases in weight during childhood) and the existing neurons work more efficiently. It has been suggested that psychological ageing begins after maturity and that this is measured by behaviour that includes the ability to acquire, remember and retrieve words, people and events and the ability to process and manipulate information. This scientific study of the ageing process is called **gerontology**.

One problem with studying the ageing process, however, is the large variability between and within samples. For example, during a long period of study, older participants become susceptible to disease processes and illnesses which could directly affect the variables that gerontologists are interested in studying. This within-subject variation can also be seen in another capacity. If we take one age group, say the 50–60-year-old, and compare it with another on some cognitive measure, we are defining a group of individuals by an age category but all individuals within this group may not show the same degree of ageing. For example, although the ability to remember strings of digits declines with age, some individuals perform badly, some stay the same and some actually get better (Holland and Rabbitt, 1991). Group variation becomes more of a problem when we look at data from cross-sectional studies.

Cross-sectional studies, you will remember from Chapter 2, compare independent groups on some measure. In ageing research, a cross-sectional design would involve assigning individuals to age categories such as 18–25, 26–35, 36–45, 46–55 and so on. These groups would then complete a series of tests of cognitive ability, and differences between groups would be examined. If a difference in memory was found between the younger groups and the older groups, however, we could not attribute this finding to ageing and cite ageing as a cause. Can you see why? (This question was posed in Chapter 2.) The reason is that we are not really looking at the effects of ageing but at the effect of age groups. We are not following one individual across all age ranges, but have sampled from several different age ranges. Because of this, our groups may differ on variables that we had not anticipated, such as improvement in nutrition and healthcare. When one group influences the results in this way, the study is said to show a cohort effect. The conclusion we can draw is that age groups differ from each other.

A different type of design looks at age change and this is called a longitudinal design. Here, individuals are assessed across the lifespan and each individual acts as his/her own control (we could combine the two designs as well and compare individuals within one age group which vary on another characteristic, such as occupation or education level). A problem here is that with repeated testing, the individual will become increasingly familiar with the measures employed. When longitudinal and cross-

sectional measures are compared, the longitudinal assessments show least decline in ability (Schaie, 1990).

However, recent studies suggest that cross-sectional designs such as these can be meaningful and provide similar data to longitudinal studies. For example, Salthouse (2009) has summarised data showing the (fairly relentless decline) in cognitive ability as we get older, in a number of domains apart from vocabulary and general knowledge (which increase). You can see these data illustrated in Figure 11.12. The decline begins in adulthood and progresses thenceforth.

Memory decline

There is a gradual loss in performance for certain types of memory task with age. For example, older individuals have difficulty in retrieving names (Rabbitt *et al.*, 1995) and putting names to famous faces (Burke *et al.*, 1991). In Burke *et al.*'s experiment, participants were allowed one minute in which to name famous faces. The number of tip-of-the-tongue responses as people tried to put names to faces increased with age. When participants were allowed to try to remember the names on the tips of their tongues, however, 95 per cent of their responses were correct, which suggests that the information had been stored but that the participants had difficulty in retrieving it.

Older people also have difficulty in recalling where, when or how an event occurred, despite knowing that an event has occurred. This type of memory is called **source memory** because the emphasis is on the recall of the context in which an event occurred, rather than of the content/knowledge of the event (Johnson *et al.*, 1993). This type of memory seems more affected in the elderly than is memory for facts or items (Trott *et al.*, 1997), possibly because it relies on the integrity of the frontal lobe and the integrity of this brain region is challenged in elderly individuals, as you will see later.

Age-related impairments have been reported for declarative memory, efficiency of processing information and metamemory (Woodruff-Pak, 1997). **Metamemory** refers to 'knowing about knowing'; this knowledge of skills necessary to complete a task may be absent in the elderly. For example, elderly individuals may not spend sufficient amounts of time on a task that requires time to be spent on it (recall of digit names in serial order, for example). When they are instructed to spend a certain length of time on this task, however, they can recall accurately just as many series of digits as younger participants.

Prospective memory

Recent research on ageing and memory has focused on **prospective memory**, that is, remembering to perform an activity in the future (Maylor, 1996). This type of

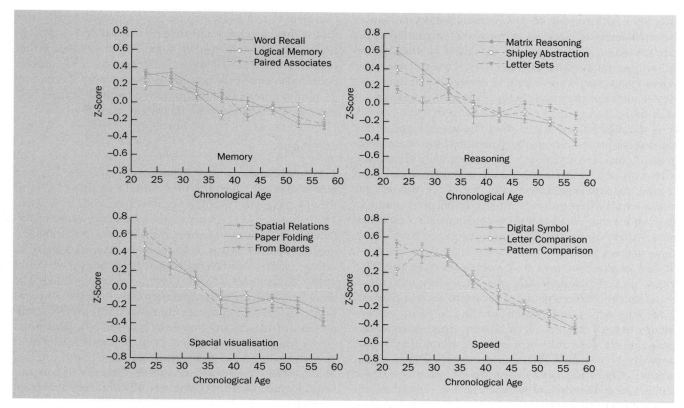

Figure 11.12 Mean scores and standard errors for 12 cognitive variables at 5-year age intervals.
Source: Salthouse, T.A. When does age-related cognitive decline begin? *Neurobiology of Aging*, 2009, 30, 507–14, figure 2.

memory may be especially important to the elderly given that such monitoring is essential for taking medicine at particular times, for example (Park and Kidder, 1996; Einstein *et al.*, 1998). In experiments where a handkerchief or comb is borrowed by the experimenter at the beginning of a test session and/or hidden in a drawer and the individual has to remember to ask for the return of the item, there is an age-related decline in memory.

Studies of prospective memory can be either 'time based' or 'event based'. In time-based experiments, the participant engages in a task and has to inform the experimenter when a certain time has elapsed (Einstein *et al.*, 1995). This may be analogous to remembering to telephone someone in an hour's time (Maylor, 1996). In one study, Maylor (1990) asked 52–95-year-olds to telephone her once a day for a week. Three-quarters of those who adopted a memory strategy or used external cues for remembering were more reliable at telephoning than were those who did not use such mnemonics. In event-based experiments, participants must make a response when a particular event occurs in a sequence of events.

Although age-related impairments have been observed for time-based tasks, event-based tasks show mixed results. Einstein *et al.* (1998), for example, gave a group of

young (mean age 19.8 years) and old (mean age 70.73 years) individuals 11 tasks to complete. The participants were told that during each task they should press a key on a keyboard once, thereby encouraging habitual prospective memory. In a divided attention condition, some participants were also told that they would hear a series of digits and were asked to press a hand-held counter when they heard two odd numbers. The young group performed the prospective memory task more effectively than did the old group and performance was worse in the divided attention condition, as expected. However, the impairment in the old group was made worse by divided attention. They omitted to make a response in 42 per cent of the first trials, and 12 per cent of the trials contained repetition errors. For trials occurring at the end of the experiment, 16 per cent contained omission errors whereas 42 per cent contained repetition errors.

During the experiment, participants were also presented with an external cue as a reminder that they should press the key. This cue resulted in the old group committing a greater number of omission errors, especially on later trials. One reason for this unexpected finding is that the old group came to rely on this (ineffective) external cue and not on an internal memory strategy.

The poor performance on prospective memory tasks may be attributable to reduced or impaired functioning of the frontal lobes (we will see later that there is some frontal lobe impairment with ageing). Given that prospective memory involves a considerable degree of planning, and that frontal lobe function declines with age, perhaps these two factors are related.

A study by Kliegel et al. (2000), however, suggests that the tests of prospective memory used in these experiments are not particularly realistic. These tests, they argue, usually require participants to make a single, isolated act within an experimental session. Everyday life, on the other hand, often involves more complicated planning than this. From cooking a three-course meal to air traffic control, the prospective memory required to perform these acts is complex.

The researchers asked 31 young (average age 26.5 years) and 31 older (average age 71.3 years) individuals to remind the experimenter to return to them a personal belonging (e.g. a wristwatch) at the end of the experiment. After having been given this instruction, participants were told that at some point they would complete a personal information questionnaire in the second part of the experiment after a short break and some tasks. This would be the cue for reminding the experimenter to return the belonging. Participants then completed various cognitive tasks that required them to follow a plan in order to perform these tasks successfully. They were then presented with the questionnaire.

While there was no difference between the two groups in their ability to remind the experimenter about the belonging, the older participants were significantly less likely to remember to initiate intended actions during the cognitive task phase of the experiment. The faithfulness with which participants executed their plans was no different between groups and both groups retained these plans equally well. The older participants, however, had difficulties in planning, initiating and executing the set of tasks.

The authors suggest that the findings may reflect superior working memory in the younger participants – the tasks required the maintenance and rehearsal of material in mind while undertaking other tasks, the critical feature of working memory and, as we have seen, a function of the frontal cortex.

A caveat

One note of caution, however, should be struck when interpreting these data. Some studies show that when memory instructions in some experiments are de-emphasised, age differences in performance disappear (Rahal et al., 2001). Age is also affected by the content of the test. So, for example, if people have to recall a narrative that is character-based, older people perform more poorly at it than if they recalled a narrative that was based on perceptual features – referring to a man or a woman, rather than to a character (Fung and Carstencens, 2003). Older people also appear to perform better between 8 a.m. and 11 a.m. whereas younger participants give of their best between 1 p.m. and 5 p.m. (Hasher et al., 1999).

Language

There are certain aspects of language processing that may not decline with age and may actually improve. One of the greatest gains is seen in vocabulary (Bayley and Oden, 1955; Jones, 1959). However, older individuals have difficulty in retrieving or accessing these words and exhibit a greater number of tip-of-the-tongue responses than do young individuals during retrieval (Bowles and Poon, 1985). According to LaRue (1992), the types of linguistic error made by elderly participants include: circumlocutions (giving inaccurate multi-word responses), nominalisations (describing functions not objects), perceptual errors (misidentifying stimuli) and semantic association errors (naming an object/feature associated with a target object). The elderly may also have difficulty in comprehending and initiating grammatically complex sentences (Kemper, 1992). Reasons for these, and other memory impairments, are discussed below.

Why does cognitive ability decline?

The evidence above indicates that cognitive ability, especially certain types of memory, declines with age. But is this the case? Ritchie (1997), for example, distinguishes between behaviour that is ageing-related and age-related. Ageing-related processes are the result of ageing; age-related processes occur only at a specific age. Huntington's disease, which was discussed in Chapter 3, is age – not ageing – related, for example. Is the decline seen in the elderly, therefore, not the result of ageing but of other age-related illnesses? Some European longitudinal data suggests that ageing may not be a factor (Ritchie et al., 1996; Leibovici et al., 1996). These researchers found that when controlling for physical illness, depression and signs of dementia, participants' cognitive performance improved over three years. They suggest that the decline that is commonly reported is due to pathology not ageing per se.

Processing speed and ageing

Several studies have shown a strong, positive association between our speed at processing information and intelligence. A new review of 172 studies, featuring over 53,000 participants, has now confirmed this association (Sheppard and Vernon, 2008). Intelligence measures were significantly associated with mental speed, an association which became stronger as the information processing task became more complex. Men and women also differed on some tests of information processing.

Over many years and several studies, Timothy Salthouse (1992, 1993; Craik and Salthouse, 2000) has argued that the elderly perform more poorly at cognitive tasks because they become slower at performing them. Older people have difficulty in activating, representing or maintaining information 'in mind', in attending to relevant stimuli in the environment and ignoring the irrelevant ones and in processing information speedily. If individual differences in speed are partialled out of these studies, then age-related differences disappear (Salthouse and Babcock, 1991). In fact, ageing could account for less than 1–2 per cent of the variance seen in such studies (Salthouse, 1993). This is a theory that has strong currency in gerontology. For example, several researchers have proposed that the cognitive decline seen in ageing may be attributable to reduced functioning of the frontal lobe (Parkin and Walter, 1992; West, 1996). The density of dopamine receptors declines in this area and dopamine is an important neurotransmitter in the performance of working memory tasks. The frontal cortex is also important for efficient information processing.

If there is significant frontal cortex decline with ageing, we might expect executive function, a key function of the frontal cortex, to be more significantly compromised in older participants. The support for this hypothesis, however, is mixed with some cross-sectional studies showing no differential decline and others showing decline on specific frontal lobe tests (one of these, a card sorting task, is described in the next major section on thinking) (Crawford et al., 2000).

The problem with suggesting that executive function may be specifically impaired, however, is that executive and non-executive task performance may be difficult to distinguish in elderly samples. The reason for this is the one cited by Salthouse (1996): all of these tasks may draw on a common resource such as speed of information processing.

The speed of processing explanation, however, may not account for the findings from prospective memory studies. Prospective memory tasks do not rely on speed but on retention of information for future use. It is possible that timed tasks impair the ability of the elderly. This was evident in experiments where participants could name famous faces if given enough time. Training also appears to be an important factor. In one study, older participants played video games for two hours a week for seven weeks or played no such games. Those who had played were faster at an experimental reaction time task

than those who had not, and were also faster on several difficulty levels (Clark et al., 1987).

Another factor which can help to protect against certain types of cognitive impairment is education. In one Australian study of elderly blue-collar workers and academics, degree of education was associated with stable crystallised intelligence but not other types of cognitive ability (Christensen et al., 1997). A Dutch study has also shown that education was associated with a slower rate of memory decline (Schmand et al., 1997). However, more recent studies (see, e.g. Andel et al., 2006) suggest that high levels of education and having a complex occupation accelerates cognitive decline, arguably because the person's 'cognitive reserve' has been expended.

The environment of the individual also contributes to the stability or decline of cognition. Individuals with cognitive impairment were three times as likely to be living in community healthcare institutions (Graham et al., 1997). Holland and Rabbitt (1991) found that when elderly participants were allowed ten minutes to recall autobiographical memories from each third of their lives, participants living in the community recalled significantly more memories from the recent than the remote period, in contrast to those in residential care who recalled more memories from the earliest period.

But why does such slowing occur in the first place? Why is memory performance one of the most consistently affected cognitive abilities? One suggestion is that cognitive decline is the result of changes in the central nervous system (Lowe and Rabbitt, 1997). In particular, researchers have focused on the hippocampus and the frontal cortex. There is a considerable loss in frontal lobe tissue over the course of the lifespan – around 17 per cent between the ages of 20 and 80 (Mittenberg et al., 1989; West, 1996). One PET study compared the encoding and retrieval of word pairs in young (mean age 26) and old (70 and over) adults (Cabeza et al., 1997). The young participants showed greater left prefrontal activation during encoding and right prefrontal activation during retrieval compared with the old sample. In fact, the old sample showed little frontal activation during encoding and more bilateral activation during retrieval. This pattern of activity suggested to the experimenters that the stimuli had been inefficiently processed or encoded. An fMRI study of recognition and encoding in young, middle-aged and older adults found that activation in brain areas involved in these memory processes declines across age groups but activation in areas that are irrelevant to the specific tasks increases (Grady et al., 2006). Other cognitive studies show that when material is learned thoroughly, then ageing has little effect on retrieval (Woodruff-Pak, 1997), although no neuroimaging study has explored this yet.

At the neural level, one might expect gross changes in the language areas. This would explain the deficits seen on some language tasks. However, little change occurs in the language areas of the elderly. This has led some researchers to suggest that this ageing-related impairment is not due to ineffective language processing but to deficiencies in attention, perception, speed, memory and executive function (Glosser and Deser, 1992).

An alternative (or complementary) view to the frontal lobe hypothesis suggests that ageing results in an impairment of cognitive differentiation – the degree to which behaviour is specialised for specific tasks. The decline, which is domain-independent, is reflected in neurons' inability to perform such differentiation. The cortical basis of visual differentiation may be the ventral visual cortex – this responds to faces, orthography and places – and shows less atrophy than other areas with age. In an fMRI study where 12-year-olds and 70-year-olds were asked to view faces, houses, pseudowords and chairs, less specialisation in activation in the ventral visual cortex was found in the elderly sample (Park *et al.*, 2004). Given that perceptual processing speed declines with age, perhaps such a slowness might be the result of a ventral visual cortex that shows less differentiation. Because there is less differentiation, older participants who are asked to make the same/different decisions about geometric pairs or digits (a standard perceptual processing speed task) are slower at doing so.

Dementia

Dementia refers to the gradual and relentless decline in cognitive ability and is characterised by impairment in short-term and long-term memory. There may also be confusion, change in personality and impaired abstract thinking and judgment. There are various types of dementia such as **dementia of the Alzheimer type** (DAT, the commonest type), vascular dementia (the second commonest, caused by stroke), Pick's disease dementia and Lewy body dementia (both are characterised by neural abnormality). There are many causes of dementia: the most common is **Alzheimer's disease**. It is important to differentiate between Alzheimer's disease and DAT: the former is the disease, the latter is the psychological consequence of this illness. It has been estimated that 24.3 million people worldwide suffer from dementia and that the number of people diagnosed with the illness is expected to double every 20 years until 2040 (Ferri *et al.*, 2005). In the EU, it is estimated that 1–2 million people over 65 years of age have dementia and 54 per cent of these cases are due to Alzheimer's disease (Lobo *et al.*, 2000).

Dementia of the Alzheimer type

According to **DSM-IV TR**, dementia of the Alzheimer type is characterised by:

- Cognitive decline exemplified by memory impairment (learning new information and recalling previously learned information) and one or more of: aphasia, apraxia, agnosia and executive function problems.

- Symptoms which cause significant decline from previous level of functioning.

- Gradual onset and continuing cognitive decline.

- Symptoms that are not due to other progressive CNS diseases or conditions causing dementia.

(DSM-IV TR is the manual used by the majority of the world's clinicians to diagnose mental illness and mental disorder (you'll find this described in more detail in Chapter 18).)

Although there are no completely accurate figures, it is estimated that between 5 per cent and 10 per cent of individuals over 65 years of age will develop Alzheimer's disease (Rocca *et al.*, 1986; Ritchie, 1997); it accounts for approximately 50 per cent of all cases of dementia (Fields, 1998). American studies show a 50 per cent incidence in people over 85 and 100 per cent incidence in one Dutch study of 19 centenarians – those over a hundred years old (Evans *et al.*, 1989; Hebert *et al.*, 1995; Blansjaar *et al.*, 2000). The percentage affected increases with age. Other studies suggest that some centenarians (around 30 per cent) are impervious to the disease (Andersen-Ranberg *et al.*, 2001; Silver *et al.*, 2001; Hagberg *et al.*, 2001). There is also evidence that patients over 65 years old who are later diagnosed with the disease show evidence of neuropsychological impairment at least three years before the diagnosis (Amieva *et al.*, 2005).

The disease was named after Alois Alzheimer at the beginning of the last century who reported the case of a 56-year-old female patient who exhibited cognitive impairment as a result of abnormal brain formations. These formations are the characteristics of Alzheimer's disease and include (1) neurofibrillary tangles, abnormal proteins which are found in various parts of the patient's brain, especially the temporal, parietal and frontal cortices (Foster *et al.*, 1997), and (2) senile plaques, abnormal nerve cell processes which surround the protein and are found in the cortex. These two features are illustrated in Figure 11.13. Animal models suggest that the specific protein which may contribute to the cognitive decline in Alzheimer's disease may be an assembly called AB*56 which is found outside cells (Lesne *et al.*, 2006). In the early, pre-clinical stage of the disease, plaques are seen in the parietal and medial prefrontal lobes (Mintun *et al.*, 2006).

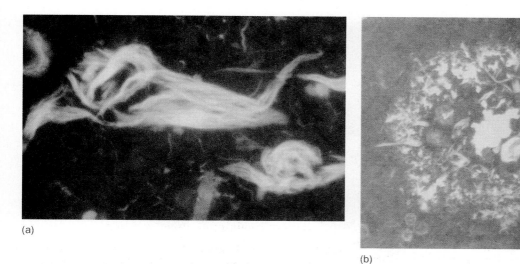

(a)

(b)

Figure 11.13 Images showing two of the characteristic neural features of Alzheimer's disease. **(a)** One of the neurofibrillary tangles that characterises brain cell abnormality in Alzheimer's disease. **(b)** The senile plaques seen in the nerve cell of a brain attacked by Alzheimer's disease.

Source: Beatty, J. (1995). *Principles of Behavioral Neuroscience*. New York: Brown and Benchmark/William C. Brown Communications Inc., 1995. Reprinted with permission.

There is significant neuron loss in Alzheimer's disease. The frontal and temporal gyri are thought to shrink by approximately 20 per cent and atrophy is found in the hippocampus, amygdala and other subcortical areas such as the raphe nuclei and nucleus basalis of Meynert. Figure 11.14 (a) and (b), and Figure 11.15 show how extensive this atrophy can be.

The disease can occur sporadically or in a genetic form called familial Alzheimer's disease. The familial form is thought to be autosomal-dominant with the gene carried on chromosome 21 and, possibly, chromosome 19. The gene expresses itself by producing the amyloid precursor protein from which the protein associated with the senile plaques is formed. Early-onset AD is associated

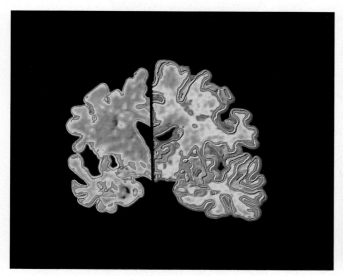

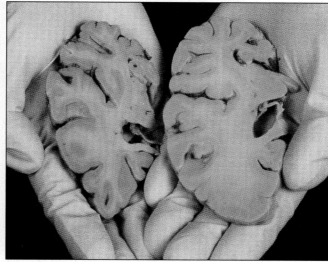

Figure 11.14 (a) Alzheimer's disease. A computer-enhanced photograph of a slice through the brain of a person who died of Alzheimer's disease (left) and a normal brain (right). Note that the grooves (sulci and fissures) are especially wide in the Alzheimer's brain, indicating degeneration of the brain. **(b)** Sections from a normal brain (right) and from a brain with Alzheimer's.

Source: (a) Alfred Pasieka/Science Photo Library (b) Plate 11.3 from *Human Neuropsychology*, 2nd edn, Pearson/Prentice Hall (Martin, G.N., 2006).

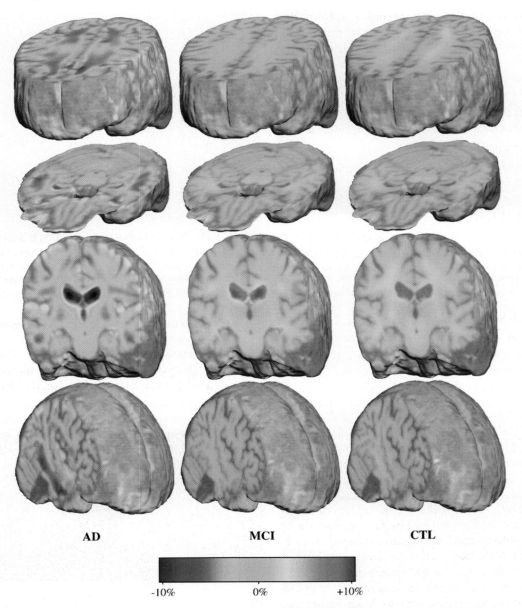

Figure 11.15 Comparison of brain volume atrophy in a patient with Alzheimer's disease (AD), an individual with mild cognitive impairment (MCI) and a healthy elderly control (CTL). The bluer the image, the greater the cell loss.

Source: Leow, A.D., Yanovsky, I., Parikshak, N. *et al.* Alzheimer's Disease Neuroimaging Initiative: A one-year follow-up study using tensor-based morphometry correlating degenerative rates, biomarkers and cognition. *NeuroImage*, 2009, 45, 645–55, figure 1.

with this marker and also with mutations on chromosomes 1 and 14 (Bird, 1999). Evidence from Scandinavian studies suggests that the heritability of Alzheimer's disease is between 0.6 and 0.75 (Bergem *et al.*, 1997; Gatz *et al.*, 1997). The E4 allele of the apolipoprotein gene also appears to be a risk factor in Alzheimer's disease and for cognitive impairment (Farrer *et al.*, 1997; Slooter *et al.*, 1997).

Clinical features of DAT

The major cognitive impairment in AD is loss of memory. This impairment is gradual and occurs in the presence of a normal level of consciousness but in the absence of any other CNS disease that might account for the symptoms. Some of the more marked deficits in memory include:

- An inability to recall autobiographical information from long-term memory (information about people, events and conversations, for example) is the major characteristic of the disease and appears early on in the disorder's development (Greene and Hodges, 1996a; Fleischman and Gabrieli, 1999).

- Impaired recall of previously learned information and, sometimes, memory for conceptual or factual information.

- Rapid forgetting.

- Explicit memory impairment (implicit memory is relatively preserved).

- Short- and long-term memory impairment (Fleischman and Gabrieli, 1998).

- Tendency to show a lack of a primacy effect but to show a recency effect – patients will more correctly recall items from the end of a list than the beginning (Bayley *et al.*, 2000).

- Interference by previously learned information when new material is learned.

- Attention and working memory impairment.

- Semantic memory impairment – inability to recall over-learned information.

- Circumlocution and paraphrasic errors.

- Delayed-memory impairment – this appears to be best at discriminating DAT patients from controls (Zakzanis *et al.*, 1999).

One difficulty in diagnosing Alzheimer's disease is that senile plaques are seen with normal ageing (tangles tend not to be) whereas tangles are seen in other types of dementia (Ritchie, 1997). Although the effects of ageing and dementia may be distinguished by the fact that abnormalities in the elderly affect the superficial cortex, they go much deeper in Alzheimer's disease. There are also biochemical abnormalities seen in Alzheimer's disease.

In particular, there is significant loss of certain neurotransmitter pathways linking various brain structures, such as the cerebral cortex and the hippocampus, in Alzheimer's disease.

Memory decline in Alzheimer's disease

The major cognitive impairment in Alzheimer's disease is memory loss and episodic memory retrieval is thought to be one of the most seriously affected. A person's inability to recall autobiographical information from long-term memory (information about people and events, for example) is a major characteristic of the disease and appears early on in the disorder's development (Fleischman and Gabrieli, 1999). Figure 11.16 plots the decline in memory function in a patient with Alzheimer's disease and a matched control, across the lifespan. Figure 11.17 (a) and

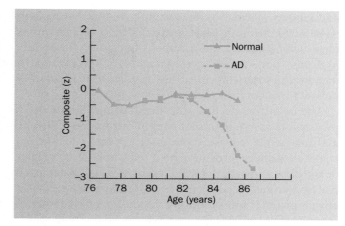

Figure 11.16 The decline in memory function in a patient with Alzheimer's disease and a matched control, across the lifespan.

Source: Galvin J.E., Powlishta, K.K., Wilkins, K., McKell, D.W. Jr., Xiong, C., Grant, E., Storandt, M., and Morris JC. (2005) Predictors of preclinical Alzheimer disease and dementia. *Archives of Neurology*, 65, 758–765.

(b) shows brain scans of patients with Alzheimer's disease who tried to retrieve episodic memory.

Explicit memory is more seriously affected than implicit memory and both short- and long-term memory are impaired (Fleischman and Gabrieli, 1998). Greene

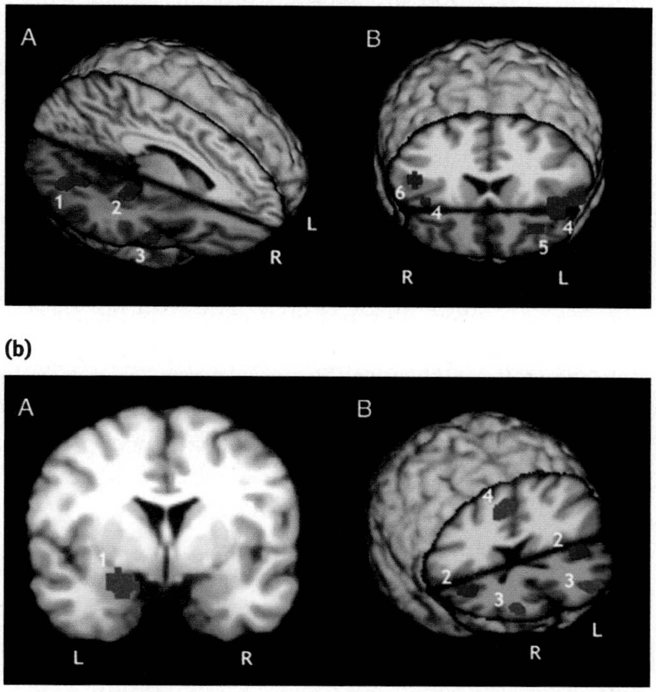

(a)

(b)

Figure 11.17 Comparison of brain activation between AD patients **(a)** across encoding studies, and **(b)** across retrieval studies.

Source: Schwindt, G.C. and Black, S.E. Functional imaging studies of episodic memory in Alzheimer's disease: a quantitative meta-analysis. *NeuroImage*, 2009, 45, 181–90, figures 2 and 3.

and Hodges (1996a, b), for example, found that patients with Alzheimer's disease performed poorly at naming, identifying and recognising famous faces from the present and past but also found that memory for personally meaningful events declined less rapidly than did public memory (memory for events in public life).

The cognitive decline seen in Alzheimer's patients is much more severe than that seen in disease-free individuals during the course of normal ageing, and various cognitive deficits correlate with a reduction in the volume of the hippocampus, the temporal cortex and thalamus. It can sometimes be difficult to distinguish between the effects of DAT and symptoms of mild cognitive impairment (MCI). MCI seems to occupy a halfway house between the cognitive decline seen with normal ageing and dementia. Sixty-one per cent of MCI patients begin with memory impairments (Storandt, 2006) and it, too, has some of the hallmarks of Alzheimer's disease, such as the amyloid-B deposits (Goedert and Spillantini, 2006). In a study of people who had not manifested the symptoms of dementia – the sample is the famous Framingham Study which follows a large cohort of people through life (Elias *et al.*, 2000) – two tests were associated with the later development of dementia – verbal memory and the similarities test of the WAIS. Poor performance on these predicted later development of dementia. Other tests are thought to be good predictors, especially those which involve planning and sequencing (Storandt *et al.*, 2006).

Attentional problems

Some psychologists have suggested that attention deficit may also be an early cognitive characteristic (Perry and Hodges, 1999) and may explain the deficit in episodic memory (Balota and Faust, 2001). What is unclear, however, is whether this deficit in attention is a global and unitary one – where all types of attention are impaired – or whether different types of attention are affected differently (Baddeley *et al.*, 2001).

Baddeley *et al.* administered three tests of attention deficit to three groups of participants: a group of 41 patients diagnosed with probable Alzheimer's disease, a group of 36 age-matched controls and a group of 36 young controls. In the first attention test, participants performed simple and choice reaction time exercises which involved pressing a key whenever a stimulus appeared on a monitor (this was called a test of focal attention). The second test investigated the participants' ability to ignore distractors in a visual search task (for example, ignoring other letters when looking for the letter Z in an array of letters). The third test involved the ability to divide attention between two simultaneously

performed exercises. In each of the tests, there were two levels of difficulty. So, for the visual search task, for example, participants looked for the letter Z in an array of similar or dissimilar (difficult condition) letters. The researchers hypothesised that participants with Alzheimer's disease would perform significantly more poorly than the control group at the difficult versions of the tasks.

The experimenters found that whereas both groups were impaired at the normal and difficult versions of the choice reaction time task, there was no significant difference between the two groups, indicating that this type of attention may be relatively immune to the effects of Alzheimer's disease. The ability to ignore distractors in a visual search exercise, however, was significantly impaired in Alzheimer's disease (although both demented and old performed worse than the young). The greatest effect of the disease was found in the dual-task exercise: performance on this task was significantly worse in the Alzheimer group than the control group.

The results suggest that attention is not globally affected by Alzheimer's disease – providing evidence against the unitary hypothesis – but that there is selective impairment in attention, specifically divided attention.

As well as selective impairments in attention, people with Alzheimer's disease also experience other subtle and more pronounced difficulties. Memory impairments – such as disorientation over finding their homes, forgetting people's names and faces, and not being able to follow the flow of a conversation – are key features. The inability to comprehend sentences, however, is more subtle and some psychologists have suggested that this deficit stems not from some linguistic problem or decline but from a work-

The author Terry Prachett, who has been diagnosed with dementia of the Alzheimer type.
Source: Getty Images/Peter Macdiarmid

ing memory impairment, similar to that seen when failing to follow conversation (Baddeley *et al.*, 1991). In 2003, the journalist and critic Adrian Gill wrote an article about his father, who suffers from Alzheimer's disease. Gill wrote:

> Conversations with Daddy are like talking to someone who can travel through walls. In the middle of a sentence, he can be somewhere else. I have to open empirical, rational doors to follow him. He glides through time and subjects in a way that logic and language prevent me. It's a sort of itinerant freedom.

Dementia and the novelist: the case of Iris Murdoch

Fellow novelist A.S. Byatt spared no sensitivity when she reviewed Iris Murdoch's last novel, *Jackson's Dilemma*. The book, Byatt averred, was 'an Indian rope trick . . . in which all the people have no selves and therefore there is no story and no novel'. Murdoch, however, was no novelistic novice. In 1978, she won the Booker Prize for *The Sea, The Sea* and was made Dame Commander of the British Empire in 1987 in recognition of her contribution to literature. Published criticism is an occupational hazard in the novelist's world but Byatt's criticism may have unwittingly reflected an organic, rather than creative, decline. Murdoch was diagnosed with Alzheimer's disease at the age of 76, just after she had finished writing *Jackson's Dilemma*; a post-mortem three years later confirmed the diagnosis.

Following the diagnosis of suspected AD, Garrard *et al.* (2005) monitored structural changes in Murdoch's brain, as part of her neurological assessment. In 1997, there was evidence of global atrophy, especially in the hippocampus (bilaterally), as seen in Figure 11.18 (a). You can see examples of her neuropsychological performance in Figure 11.18 (b).

When *Jackson's Dilemma* was published in 1995, the author had suffered severe writer's block and had become unexpectedly inarticulate at a question and answer session with the public a year later. The following summer, she was only able to describe her surroundings by reference to a city name and was unable to subtract or spell backwards. Her picture naming became circumlocutory: a bus was described as 'something carried along'; and her spelling became regularised. She would spell cruise as 'crewse', for example. Her retrograde memory was profoundly impaired and her narrative speech was grammatical but lacked real content. For example: 'the girl is just holding a plate and various pieces of . . . well . . . something useful . . . standing at a window . . .

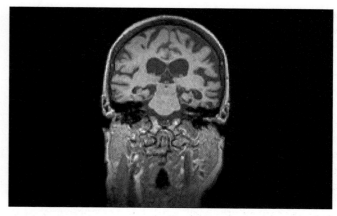

(a)

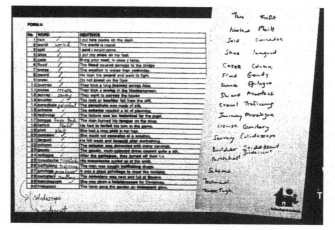

(b)

Figure 11.18 (a) A computer enhanced photograph of a slice through the brain of a patient with Alzheimer's disease; **(b)** Examples of Iris Murdoch's neuropsychological performance; **(c)** Iris Murdoch herself.

Source: (b) From Garrard, P., Maloney, L.M., Hodges, J.R. and Patterson, K. The effects of very early Alzheimer's disease on the characteristics of writing by a renowned author, in *Brain*, 2005, 128, pp. 250–60, by permission of Oxford University Press and Peter Garrard. (c) Bassouls Sophie/CORBIS Sygma.

whether the window is open is not quite clear to me. The thing where the water is running out. The girl doesn't bother. The window is open. Plate and two cups.'

Murdoch's disorder afforded Garrard *et al.* the opportunity to examine any relationship between the novelist's intellectual decline and the external manifestation of that decline – her final novel. The novelist regarded the work as being a true reflection of her output and requested no alterations be made to the text. Garrard *et al.* compared the vocabulary, syntax, grammatical class and lexical differences in this novel, in *Under the Net* (published in 1954) and in *The Sea, The Sea*.

The researchers found that her vocabulary was rich and innovative in the early work but was impoverished in the final novel. The number of words and class of words per sentence (ten sentences were taken from the first, middle and final chapters of each novel) was smallest in the last novel. There was no difference in word length between the novels but the final work contained more high frequency words, reflecting a decline in linguistic innovation. The use of high frequency words is, according to Garrard *et al.*, typical of temporal lobe pathology.

In a sense, of course, these data are correlational. The final novel exhibited the features described here and these features coincided with the development of the author's degenerative disease. Nonetheless, the data obtained from the analysis of the author's physical output reflects the behaviour observed by those closest to her.

Treatment for DAT

Is Alzheimer's disease reversible? The cost of caring for patients with DAT in the UK alone is estimated to be between £5 billion and £15 billion a year (Lowin *et al.*, 2001; McNamee *et al.*, 2001) but no treatment is able to halt the progress of the disease. Those treatments that have been attempted have focused on alleviating the memory impairments in DAT. The cholinergic hypothesis of Alzheimer's disease led to the development of drugs that specifically sought to redress the loss of cholinergic neurons and neurotransmitters (called cholinesterase inhibitors). Currently, five drugs have been approved for use by the US Drug and Food Administration (Robertson and Mucke, 2006). The mechanism of action for these drugs is the inhibition of the enzyme acetylcholinesterase, which divides the neurotransmitter at its receptors (Bullock, 2002). Three compounds currently used are donepezil, rivastigimine and galantamine.

Patients who have been given a course of either donepezil or rivastigimine have shown some improvement in memory performance (Cameron *et al.*, 2000; Evans *et al.*, 2000). Other drugs under review are anti-inflammatory drugs (because the incidence of Alzheimer's disease is low in sufferers of rheumatoid arthritis who take these drugs) and antioxidants such as vitamin E. Neither, however, has been shown to demonstrate consistent efficacy (Bullock, 2002). Perhaps the most innovative treatment under investigation involves vaccinating the individual, thereby giving them an antibody to remove the amyloid protein that causes cell degeneration. Trials in mice have been effective in relieving symptoms of the disease and in preventing the development of plaques (Schenk *et al.*, 1999) but there is no such vaccine for humans, as yet.

Thinking

One of the most important components of cognition is thinking: categorising, reasoning and solving problems. When we think, we perceive, classify, manipulate, and combine information. When we are finished, we know something we did not know before (although our 'knowledge' may be incorrect).

The purpose of thinking is, in general, to solve problems. These problems may be simple classifications (What is that, a bird or a bat?); they may involve decisions about courses of actions (Should I buy a new car or pay to fix the old one?); or they may require the construction, testing and evaluation of complex plans of action (How am I going to manage to earn money to continue my education so that I can get out of this dead-end job, and still be able to enjoy life?). Much, but not all, of our thinking involves language. We certainly think to ourselves in words, but we also think in shapes and images. And some of the mental processes that affect our decisions and plans take place without our being conscious of them. Thus, we will have to consider non-verbal processes as well as verbal ones (Reber, 1992; Holyoak and Spellman, 1993).

Classifying

When we think, each object or event is not considered as a completely independent entity. Instead, we classify things – categorise them according to their characteristics. Then, when we have to solve a problem involving a particular object or situation, we can use information that we have already learned about similar objects or situations. To take a very simple example, when we enter someone's house for the first time, we recognise chairs, tables, sofas, lamps and other pieces of furniture even though we may never have seen these particular items before. Because we recognise these categories of objects, we know where to sit, how to increase the level of illumination, and so on.

Concepts are categories of objects, actions or states of being that share some attributes: cat, comet, team, destroying, playing, forgetting, happiness, truth, justice. Most thinking deals with the relations and interactions among concepts. For example, 'the hawk caught the sparrow' describes an interaction between two birds; 'studying for an examination is fun' describes an attribute of a particular action; and 'youth is a carefree time of life' describes an attribute of a state of being.

Concepts exist because the characteristics of objects have consequences for us. For example, angry dogs may hurt us, whereas friendly dogs may give us pleasure. Dangerous dogs tend to growl, bare their teeth and bite, whereas friendly dogs tend to prance around, wag their tails and solicit our attention. Thus, when we see a dog that growls and bares its teeth, we avoid it because it may bite us; but if we see one prancing around and wagging its tail, we may try to pat it. We have learned to avoid or approach dogs who display different sorts of behaviour through direct experience with dogs or through the vicarious experience of watching other people interact with them. The point is, we can learn the concepts of dangerous and friendly dogs from the behaviour of one set of dogs while we are young and respond appropriately to other dogs later in life. Our experiences with particular dogs generalise to others.

Formal and natural concepts

Formal concepts are defined by listing their essential characteristics, as a dictionary definition does. For example, dogs have four legs, a tail, fur and wet noses; are carnivores; can bark, growl, whine and howl; pant when they are hot; bear live young; and so on. Thus, a formal concept is a sort of category that has rules about membership and non-membership.

Psychologists have studied the nature of formally defined concepts, such as species of animals. Collins and Quillian (1969) suggested that such concepts are organised hierarchically in semantic memory. Each concept has associated with it a set of characteristics. Consider the hierarchy of concepts relating to animals shown in Figure 11.19. At the top is the concept 'animal', with which are associated the characteristics common to all animals, such as 'has skin', 'can move around', 'eats', 'breathes' and so on. Linked to the concept 'animal' are groups of animals, such as birds, fish and mammals, along with their characteristics. These hierarchies are illustrated by Figure 11.19.

Collins and Quillian assumed that the characteristics common to all members of a group of related concepts (such as all birds) were attached to the general concept (in this case bird) rather than to all the members. Such an arrangement would produce an efficient and economical organisation of memory. For example, all birds have wings. Thus, we need not remember that a canary, a jay, a robin and an ostrich all have wings; we need only remember that each of these concepts belong to the category of bird and that birds have wings.

Collins and Quillian tested the validity of their model by asking people questions about the characteristics of

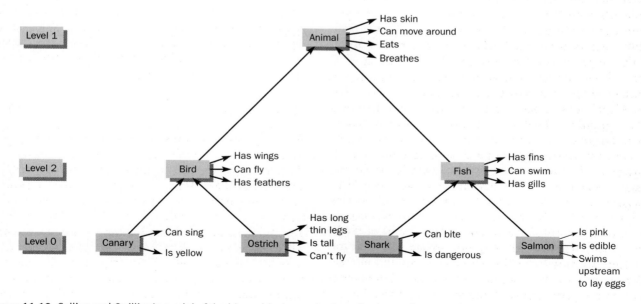

Figure 11.19 Collins and Quillian's model of the hierarchical organisation of concepts in semantic memory.

Source: From Robert L. Solso, *Cognitive Psychology*, 2nd edn. Published by Allyn & Bacon, Boston, MA. Copyright © 1988 by Pearson Education. By permission of the publisher.

various concepts. Consider the concept 'canary'. The investigators asked people to say true or false to statements such as, 'A canary eats'. When the question dealt with characteristics that were specific to the concept (such as 'can sing', or 'is yellow'), the subjects responded quickly. If the question dealt with a characteristic that was common to a more general concept (such as 'has skin' or 'breathes'), the subjects took a longer time in answering. Presumably, when asked a question about a characteristic that applied to all birds or to all animals, the participants had to 'travel up the tree' from the entry for canary until they found the level that provided the answer. The further they had to go, the longer the process took.

The model above is attractive but it does not reflect realistically the way in which we classify concepts and their characteristics. For example, although people may conceive of objects in terms of a hierarchy, a particular person's hierarchy of animals need not resemble that compiled by a zoologist. For example, Rips *et al.* (1973) found that people said yes to 'A collie is an animal' faster than they did to 'A collie is a mammal'. According to Collins and Quillian's model, animal comes above mammal in the hierarchy, so the results should have been just the opposite.

Although some organisation undoubtedly exists between categories and subcategories, it appears not to be perfectly logical and systematic. For example, Roth and Mervis (1983) found that people judged Chablis to be a better example of wine than of drink, but they judged champagne to be a better example of drink than of wine. This inconsistency clearly reflects people's experience with the concepts. Chablis is obviously a wine: it is sold in bottles that resemble those used for other wines, it looks and tastes similar to other white wines, the word 'wine' is found on the label, and so on. By these standards, champagne appears to stand apart. A wine expert would categorise champagne as a particular type of wine. But the average person, not being particularly well acquainted with the fact that champagne is made of fermented grape juice, encounters champagne in the context of something to drink on a special occasion, something to launch ships with, and so on. Thus, its characteristics are perceived as being rather different from those of Chablis.

Rosch (1975; Mervis and Rosch, 1981) suggested that people do not look up the meanings of concepts in their heads in the way that they seek definitions in dictionaries. The concepts we use in everyday life are natural concepts, not formal ones discovered by experts who have examined characteristics we are not aware of. **Natural concepts** are based on our own perceptions and interactions with things in the world. For example, some things have wings, beaks and feathers, and they fly, build nests, lay eggs and make high-pitched noises. Other things are furry, have four legs and a tail, and run around on the ground. Formal concepts consist of carefully defined sets of rules governing membership in a particular category; natural concepts are collections of memories of particular examples that share some similarities. Formal concepts are used primarily by experts (and by people studying to become experts), whereas natural concepts are used by ordinary people in their daily lives.

Rosch suggests that people's natural concepts consist of collections of memories of particular examples, called **exemplars**, that share some similarities. The boundaries between formal concepts are precise, whereas those between natural concepts are fuzzy – the distinction between a member and a non-member is not always clear. Thus, to a non-expert, not all members of a concept are equally good examples of that concept. A robin is a good example of bird; a penguin or ostrich is a poor one. We may acknowledge that a penguin is a bird because we have been taught that it is, but we often qualify the category of membership by making statements such as 'strictly speaking, a penguin is a bird'. Exemplars represent the important characteristics of a category – characteristics that we can easily perceive or that we encounter when we interact with its members.

According to Rosch *et al.* (1976), natural concepts vary in their level of precision and detail. They are arranged in a hierarchy from very detailed to very general. When we think about concepts and talk about them, we usually deal with **basic-level concepts** – those that make important distinctions between different categories – but do not waste time and effort with those that do not matter. For example, chair and apple are basic-level concepts. Concepts that refer to collections of basic-level concepts, such as furniture and fruit, are called **superordinate concepts**. Concepts that refer to types of items within a basic-level category, such as deckchair and Granny Smith's, are called **subordinate concepts**. These can be seen in Figure 11.20.

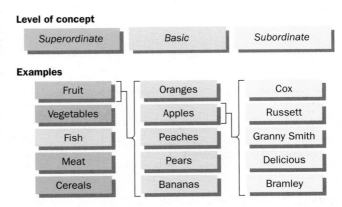

Figure 11.20 Examples of basic-level, subordinate and superordinate concepts.

The basic-level concept tends to be the one that people spontaneously name when they see a member of the category. That is, all types of chair tend to be called 'chair', unless there is a special reason to use a more precise label. People tend to use basic-level concepts for a very good reason: cognitive economy. The use of subordinate concepts wastes time and effort on meaningless distinctions, and the use of superordinate concepts loses important information. Rosch *et al.* (1976) presented people with various concepts and gave them 90 seconds to list as many attributes as they could for each of them. The subjects supplied few attributes for superordinate concepts but were able to think of many for basic-level concepts.

Subordinate concepts evoked no more responses than basic-level concepts did. Thus, because they deal with a large number of individual items and their characteristics, basic-level concepts represent the maximum information in the most efficient manner. When people think about basic-level concepts, they do not have to travel up or down a tree to find the attributes that belong to the concept. The attributes are directly attached to the exemplars that constitute each concept.

It is important to recognise that concepts can represent something more complex than simple exemplars or collections of attributes. Goldstone *et al.* (1991) showed participants groups of figures and asked them to indicate which were most similar to each other. When they showed the participants two triangles, two squares and two circles, the subjects said that the squares and triangles were most similar, presumably because both contained straight lines and angles. However, when they added a square to each of the pairs, the participants said that the two most similar groups were the triangles plus square and the circles plus square. The task is illustrated by Figure 11.21.

The concept this time was 'two things and a square'. If the participants were simply counting attributes, then the addition of a square to the pairs should not have changed their decision. As this study shows very clearly, concepts can include relations among elements that cannot be described by counting attributes.

Concepts are the raw material of thinking; they are what we think about. But thinking itself involves the manipulation and combination of concepts. Such thinking can take several forms, but the most common forms are deductive reasoning and inductive reasoning.

Deductive reasoning

Deductive reasoning consists of inferring specific instances from general principles or rules. For example, the following two series of sentences express deductive reasoning:

> John is taller than Phil
>
> Sue is shorter than Phil
>
> Therefore, John is taller than Sue
>
> All mammals have fur
>
> A bat is a mammal
>
> Therefore, a bat has fur

Deductions consist of two or more statements from which a conclusion is drawn. The first group of sentences presented above involves the application of a simple mathematical principle. The second group presents a syllogism. The syllogism, a form of deductive logic invented by Aristotle, is often found in tests of intelligence. A syllogism is a logical construction that consists of a major premise (for example, 'all mammals have fur'), a minor premise ('a bat is a mammal'), and a conclusion ('a bat has fur'). The major and minor premises are assumed to be true. The problem is to decide whether the conclusion is true or false.

People differ widely in their ability to solve syllogisms. For example, many people would agree with the conclusion of the following syllogism:

> All mammals have fur
>
> A zilgid has fur
>
> Therefore, a zilgid is a mammal

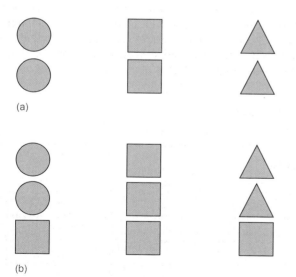

(a)

(b)

Figure 11.21 Concept formation. Participants were asked which of the groups of shapes were most similar. **(a)** Three pairs of geometrical shapes. **(b)** The same shapes with the addition of squares.

These people would be wrong; the conclusion is not warranted. The major premise says only that all mammals have fur. It leaves open the possibility that some animals that have fur are not mammals.

Mental models

Why are some people better than others at solving syllogisms? Johnson-Laird (1985) notes that syllogistic reasoning is much more highly correlated with spatial ability than with verbal ability. Spatial ability includes the ability to visualise shapes and to manipulate them mentally. Why should skill at logical reasoning be related to this ability? Johnson-Laird and his colleagues (Johnson-Laird and Byrne, 1991; Johnson-Laird *et al.*, 1992) suggest that people solve problems involving logical deduction by constructing **mental models**, mental constructions based on physical reality. When faced with a reasoning problem, people will generate a mental model of the puzzle and see what conclusions they can draw from parts of the mental model. They search for alternative models that might contradict the conclusion reached from the initial model; but if this falsification is not forthcoming, the conclusion is accepted. If the alternative model does falsify the conclusion reached by previous reasoning, the search goes on for an alternative model which may help us to reach the correct conclusion. For example, if you consider the following problem:

> A is less than C
>
> B is greater than C
>
> Is B greater than A?

in order to compare A with B, you must remember the order of the three elements. One kind of mental model is an imaginary line going from small to large in which you mentally place each item on the line as you encounter it.

Syllogistic reasoning – An international perspective

Several studies have suggested that illiterate, unschooled people in remote villages in various parts of the world are unable to solve syllogistic problems. Scribner (1977) visited two tribes of people in Liberia, West Africa – the Kpelle and the Vai – and found that tribespeople gave what Westerners would consider to be wrong answers. However, the people were not unable to reason logically but approached problems differently. For example, she presented the following problem to a Kpelle farmer. At first glance, the problem appears to be a reasonable one even for an illiterate, unschooled person because it refers to his own tribe and to an occupation he is familiar with.

> All Kpelle men are rice farmers
>
> Mr Smith is not a rice farmer
>
> Is he a Kpelle man?

The man replied:

Participant: I don't know the man in person. I have not laid eyes on the man himself.

Experimenter: Just think about the statement.

Participant: If I know him in person, I can answer that question, but since I do not know him in person, I cannot answer that question.

Experimenter: Try and answer from your Kpelle sense.

Participant: If you know a person, *if a question comes up* about him you are able to answer. But if you do not know the person, if a question comes up about him it's hard for you to answer.

Source: Scribner (1977), p. 490.

The farmer's response did not show that he was unable to solve a problem in deductive logic. Instead, it indicated that as far as he was concerned, the question was unreasonable. In fact, his response contained an example of logical reasoning: 'If you know a person . . . you are able to answer.'

Scribner found that illiterate people would sometimes reject the premises of her syllogism, replace them with what they knew to be true, and then solve the new problem, as they had defined it. For example, she presented the following problem to a Vai tribesperson.

> All women who live in Monrovia are married
>
> Kemu is not married
>
> Does she live in Monrovia?

The answer was yes. The respondent said, 'Monrovia is not for any one kind of people, so Kemu came to live there.' The suggestion that only married women live in Monrovia was absurd, because the tribesperson knew otherwise. Thus, if Kemu wanted to live there, she could – and did.

Clearly, the intellectual ability of people in other cultures cannot be measured against Western standards. In the world of traditional tribal people, problems are solved by application of logical reasoning to facts gained through direct experience. Their deductive-reasoning ability is not necessarily inferior, it is simply different, pragmatic.

Then, with all three elements in a row, you can answer the question. Figure 11.22 illustrates this.

In fact, when we solve problems concerning comparisons of a series of items, we tend to think about our own mental model that represents the information rather than about the particular facts given to us (Potts, 1972). For example, consider this passage:

After reading this passage, people can more easily answer

> Although the four craftsmen were brothers, they varied enormously in height. The electrician was the very tallest, and the plumber was shorter than him. The plumber was taller than the carpenter, who, in turn, was taller than the painter.
>
> *Source:* Just and Carpenter (1987), p. 202.

questions about pairs of brothers who largely differ in height. For example, they are faster to answer the question, 'Who is taller, the electrician or the painter?' than the question, 'Who is taller, the plumber or the carpenter?' This finding is particularly important because the passage explicitly states that the plumber was taller than the carpenter, but one must infer that the electrician was taller than the painter. Just and Carpenter's study shows that the result of an inference can be more readily available than information explicitly given. How can this be? The most plausible explanation is that when people read the passage, they construct a mental model that represents the four brothers arranged in order of height. The painter is clearly the shortest and the electrician is clearly the tallest. Thus, a comparison between the extremes can be made very quickly.

The type of syllogistic reasoning described in the previous section does not always lead to an alternative model being sought. Many reasoners rarely go beyond the initial model they construct (Evans *et al.*, 1999). Participants in Evans *et al.*'s experiment, for example, were more likely to accept conclusions that were consistent with their original model and reject conclusions that were inconsistent rather than construct a more accurate, reasonable model. This lack of ability to search for alternative models and accept conclusions that are inconsistent with the original mental models can have serious consequences for us, especially if people are making judgements about our character, demeanour and conduct. Nowhere is this more important than when judgements are made against a person accused of a crime in a court trial. In a later section, you will see how juries appear to make their decisions (and the factors that can affect the nature of this decision-making) and how biases in jurors' reasoning can affect their verdict.

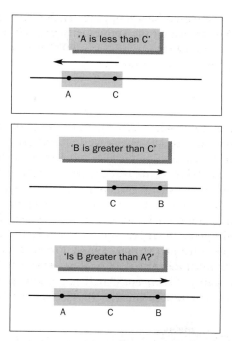

Figure 11.22 A mental model. Logical problems are often solved by imagining a physical representation of the facts.

Many creative scientists and engineers report that they use mental models to reason logically and solve practical and theoretical problems (Krueger, 1976). For example, the American physicist and Nobel laureate Richard Feynman said that he used rather bizarre mental models to keep track of characteristics of complex mathematical theorems to see whether they were logical and consistent. Here is how Feynman described his thought processes (1985, p. 70):

> When I'm trying to understand . . . I keep making up examples. For instance, the mathematicians would come in with a . . . theorem. As they're telling me the conditions of the theorem, I construct something that fits all the conditions. You know, you have a set [one ball] – disjoint [two balls]. Then the balls turn colours, grow hairs, or whatever, in my head as they [the mathematicians] put more conditions on. Finally, they state the theorem, which is some . . . thing about the ball which isn't true for my hairy green ball thing, so I say 'False!'

Such use of mental models by a talented and gifted scientist strengthens the conclusion that being able to convert abstract problems into tangible mental models is an important aspect of intelligent thinking.

There is some controversy in cognitive psychology at the moment regarding the spontaneity of people's search for alternative models.

Inductive reasoning

Deductive reasoning involves applying the rules of logic to infer specific instances from general principles or rules. This type of reasoning works well when general principles or rules have already been worked out. **Inductive reasoning** is the opposite of deductive reasoning; it consists of inferring general principles or rules from specific facts. In one well-known laboratory example of inductive reasoning, participants are shown cards that contain figures differing in several dimensions, such as shape, number and colour (Milner, 1964). On each trial, they are given two cards and asked to choose the one that represents a particular concept. After they choose a card, the experimenter indicates whether the decision is correct or not. The task is illustrated in Figure 11.23.

One trial is not enough to recognise the concept. If the first trial reveals that a card is correct, then the concept could be red, or four or triangle, or some combination of these, such as red triangle, four red shapes, or even four red triangles. Information gained from the second trial allows the subject to rule out some of these hypotheses – for example, shape does not matter, but colour and number do. The participant uses steps to solve the problem in much the same way as a scientist does: they form a hypothesis on the basis of the available evidence and test that hypothesis on subsequent trials. If it is proved false, it is abandoned, a new hypothesis consistent with what went before is constructed and this new hypothesis is tested.

Logical errors in inductive reasoning

Psychologists have identified several tendencies that interfere with people's ability to reason inductively. These include the failure to select the information they need to test a hypothesis, the failure to seek information that would be provided by a comparison group, and the disinclination to seek evidence that would indicate whether a hypothesis is false.

Failure to select relevant information

When reasoning inductively, people often fail to select the information they need to test a hypothesis. For example, consider the following task, from an experiment by Wason and Johnson-Laird (1972):

> Your job is to determine which of the hidden parts of these cards you need to see in order to answer the following question decisively:
>
> For these cards is it true that if there is a vowel on one side there is an even number on the other side?
>
> You have only one opportunity to make this decision; you must not assume that you can inspect the cards one at a time. Name those cards which it is absolutely essential to see.

The participants were shown four cards like those in Figure 11.24. Most people say that they would need to see card (a), and they are correct. If there was not an even number on the back of card (a), then the rule is not correct. However, many participants failed to realise that card (d) must also be inspected. True, there is no even number on this card, but what if there is a vowel on the other side? If there is, then the rule is (again) proved

Figure 11.23 A card sorting task. Participants are asked to sort cards according to a given criterion, such as colour or shape, that is unknown to them. After they have successfully determined this criterion, it is unexpectedly and unknowingly changed and the participant has to determine the new sorting criterion.

Source: From Pinel, P.J., *Biopsychology*, 3rd edn © 1997. Published by Allyn and Bacon, Boston, MA. Copyright © by Pearson Education. By permission of the publisher.

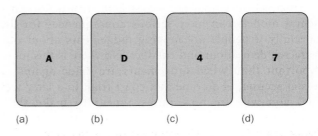

Figure 11.24 Cards used in a formal test of problem-solving.

wrong. Many participants also wanted to see card (c), but there is no need to do so. The hypothesis says nothing about whether an even number can be on one side of the card without there being a vowel on the other side.

People have to be taught the rules of logic; they do not automatically apply them when trying to solve a problem. But under certain circumstances, most people do reason logically. For example, Griggs and Cox (1982) presented a slightly different version of this test. They asked people to decide which cards should be checked to see whether the following statement was true: 'If a person is drinking beer, she must be over age 19.' The cards represented people; their age was on one side and their drink (beer or Coke) was on the other. Which card(s) would you check? (See Figure 11.25.)

Most participants correctly chose cards (a) and (d). They knew that if someone were drinking beer, she must be old enough. Similarly, if someone were 16 years old, we must check to see what she was drinking. The subjects readily recognised the fact that we do not need to know the age of someone drinking Coke, and someone 22 years old can drink whatever beverage she prefers. This study shows that experiments using puzzles designed to test people's reasoning ability do not always assess their ability to apply a logical rule to a practical situation.

In everyday life, people may commit biases in reasoning despite evidence showing that their reasoning is incorrect. The controversy in the UK concerning the possible role of the triple MMR (measles, mumps and rubella) vaccine in autism is an example of this. Some parents regard the multiple vaccination as potentially dangerous to their child and request single vaccines (one each for each of the infections). The reasoning is based on evidence from a study in which 12 children who received the MMR vaccine developed gut problems and symptoms of a developmental disorder called autism in which the child becomes withdrawn and does not engage in social and emotional communication. Other, larger, more sophisticated studies reporting no negative effect of the vaccine on child development did little to dispel the belief that MMR might cause autism.

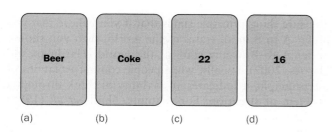

Figure 11.25 Cards used in a more realistic version of the problem-solving test.

This real-life example mirrors findings from the laboratory. In fact, laboratory studies try to investigate why some people commit these biases in reasoning and decision-making. In one study, participants were presented with hypothetical social reforms that would benefit the majority of people but would leave a small minority less well off (Baron and Jurney, 1993). Although participants agreed that such social policy decisions would be beneficial to all people, they voted against the proposals because some people might be worse off. This type of reasoning may explain why politicians behave in the way that they do.

Failure to utilise a comparison group

Another tendency that interferes with people's ability to reason inductively is their failure to consider a comparison group. Imagine that you learn that 79 per cent of the people with a particular disease get well within a month after taking a new, experimental drug (Stich, 1990). Is the drug effective? The correct answer to this question is: we cannot conclude anything – we need more information. What we need to know is what happens to people with the disease if they do not take the drug. If we find that only 22 per cent of these people recover within a month, then we would conclude that the drug is effective; 79 per cent is much greater than 22 per cent. On the other hand, if we find that 98 per cent recover without taking the drug, then we would conclude that the drug is worse than useless – it actually interferes with recovery. In other words, we need a control group. But most people are perfectly willing to conclude that, because 79 per cent seems like a high figure, the drug must work. Seeing the necessity for a control group does not come naturally; unless people are deliberately taught about control groups, they will not realise the need for them.

Failure to seek or use information that would be provided by a control group has been called ignoring base rate information. As several researchers have suggested, the problem here may be that we engage in two types of reasoning (Reber, 1992; Evans *et al.*, 1996; Stanovich, 1999). One type of reasoning is deliberate and conscious and involves explicit memories of roles that we can describe verbally. The other type of reasoning is unconscious and uses information we have learned implicitly. Because the explicit and implicit memory systems involve at least some different brain mechanisms, information from one system cannot easily interact with information from the other system. One of the most serious consequences of this reasoning error can be seen in so-called pseudo-diagnosticity tasks (Doherty *et al.*, 1979). This task involves making a medical diagnosis and is presented in the following way:

> A patient shows symptom A which is present in 95 per cent of patients suffering from disease B.
>
> Does this give grounds to suspect that the patient is suffering from disease B?

This decision can only be made by considering whether symptom A is also present in other illnesses; that is, the person must be aware of the base rate likelihood of disease B occurring relative to other diseases. If symptom A is present in other diseases, the data presented above do not give good grounds for an exclusive diagnosis of disease B. People who are untrained reasoners usually fail to consider this possibility: they are not sensitive to base rate information (Evans *et al.*, 2002).

If people are allowed to observe actual occurrences of certain events (that is, acquire the information about the base rate of occurrence automatically and implicitly), however, they can consider information about event frequency (Holyoak and Spellman, 1993). Furthermore, if people are given explicit instructions to consider alternative hypotheses, they will make decisions that take these alternative hypotheses into account (Klayman and Brown, 1993; Evans *et al.*, 2002).

Confirmation bias

see activity on mypsychlab Individuals may also show a disinclination to seek evidence that would indicate whether a hypothesis is false. Instead, people tend to seek evidence that might confirm their hypothesis; they exhibit the **confirmation bias**. For example, Wason (1968) presented people with the series of numbers '2, 4, 6' and asked them to try to figure out the rule to which they conformed. The participant was to test their hypothesis by making up series of numbers and saying them to the experimenter, who would reply yes or no. Then, whenever the participant decided that enough information had been gathered, they could say what the hypothesis was. If the answer was correct, the problem was solved. If it was not, the participant was to think of a new hypothesis and test that one.

Several rules could explain the series '2, 4, 6'. The rule could be 'even numbers', or 'each number is two more than the preceding one', or 'the middle number is the mean of the first and third number'. When people tested their hypotheses, they almost always did so by presenting several sets of numbers, all of which were consistent with their hypotheses. For example, if they thought that each number was two more than the preceding one, they might say '10, 12, 14' or '61, 63, 65'. Very few participants tried to test their hypotheses by choosing a set of numbers that did not conform to the rules, such as '12, 15, 22'. In fact,

the series '12, 15, 22' does conform to the rule. The rule was so simple that few participants figured it out: each number must be larger than the preceding one.

The confirmation bias is very strong. Unless people are taught to do so, they tend not to think of possible non-examples of their hypotheses and to see whether they might be true – the way that scientists do. But, in fact, evidence that disconfirms a hypothesis is conclusive, whereas evidence that confirms it is not.

The confirmation bias in inductive reasoning has a counterpart in deductive reasoning. For example, consider the following sentences (Johnson-Laird, 1985):

> All the pilots are artists
>
> All the skiers are artists
>
> True or false: All the pilots are skiers

Many people say 'true'. They test the truth of the conclusion by imagining a person who is a pilot and an artist and a skier – and that person complies with the rules. Therefore, they decide that the conclusion is true. But if they would try to disconfirm the conclusion – to look for an example that would fit the first two sentences but not the conclusion – they would easily find one. Could a person be a pilot but not a skier? Of course; the first two sentences say nothing to rule out that possibility. There are artist–pilots and there are artist–skiers, but nothing says that there must be artist–pilot–skiers.

The tendency to seek (and to pay more attention to) events that might confirm our beliefs is demonstrated by the way we have distorted the original meaning of the saying, 'the exception proves the rule'. Most people take this to mean that we can still consider a rule to be valid even if we encounter some exceptions. But that conclusion is illogical: if there is an exception, the rule is wrong. In fact, the original meaning of the phrase was, 'the exception tests the rule', which it does. The word 'prove' comes from the Latin *probare*, 'to test'.

Sure-thing principle

The sure thing principle states that if you believe that you prefer A to B in all states of the world, then you should prefer A to B in any state of the world (Hardman and Harries, 2002). Usually, when people commit violations of the principle, it indicates an inability to think through a problem or situation. For example, Shafir *et al.* (1993) asked students to imagine they were waiting for exam results and to plan for two outcomes: making a deposit for a holiday and deferring a decision on whether to go on holiday until after the exam results are published, or booking a cheap holiday immediately. Students who were told their

Cutting edge – Who believes in spoon bending?

'Would any one in the audience who believes in telepathy, please put my hand up', asked Emo Phillips in one of his stand-up routines. This chapter, as well as Chapter 15, shows that people can make very poor reasoners and can make ineffective use of evidence to make judgements or inform decisions. Our decisions are affected by our own biases, personal beliefs and convictions. A recent review has highlighted some of these elementary reasoning errors in people who are convinced of their belief in something a little strange: psychic ability (Wiseman and Watt, 2006).

The two commonest types of psychic ability are extra-sensory perception (ESP) and psychokinesis. ESP is the 'apparent ability to receive information via a channel of communication not presently recognised by mainstream science and includes alleged clairvoyance, telepathy and precognition (in which the information related to a future event)'. Psychokinesis is the 'apparent ability to influence physical objects and biological systems using unknown means, and encompasses a wide range of alleged phenomena, including causing objects to levitate, dice to roll at above chance levels and paranormal healing'. Is there something defective or unusual about the reasoning of the people who believe in such things?

Some psychologists have argued that believers in the paranormal have poor cognitive ability because they misattribute psychic causes to normal or natural phenomena – they cannot see a simple relationship between physical cause and effect (Alcock, 1981; Blackmore, 1992). There is some evidence of lower academic achievement in these individuals but the overall results are inconsistent.

People from the humanities are more likely to believe in psychic phenomena than are those with a science background but one study found that students of biology were greater believers than those from the humanities (Salter and Routledge, 1971). When asked to be critically evaluative of mock science papers, believers are less critical than nonbelievers (Gray and Mill, 1990). They are also poor at understanding probability. For example, if asked whether throwing 10 dice at the same time and getting 10 sixes is more or less likely than throwing one die 10 times and obtaining 10 sixes, believers underestimate the statistical likelihood (Musch and Ehrenberg, 2002). Believers are also more likely to see patterns in series of random dots (Blackmore and Moore, 1994) and to be prone to fantasy. 'The more the individual possesses the ability to find connections between their experiences and actual events,' writes Blackmore (1992), 'the more likely they are to view their experiences as psychic.'

---

result booked a holiday, whether the result was a pass or a fail. Students who were not told, however, elected to pay a small deposit and decide whether to go when the results were published. The evidence showed that even if those who deferred their holiday knew they had failed or passed, they would have booked the holiday. If they booked the holiday whatever their results were, why did they defer the holiday when they did not know the results?

Probability heuristic

The probability heuristic is similar to the confirmation bias in the sense that it shows how people can draw conclusions based on what they believe rather than on available evidence. The difference between them is that the probability heuristic shows how people can draw erroneous conclusions by not taking into account the probability of an outcome (Kahneman *et al.*, 1982; Tversky and Kahneman, 1983). The example in Table 11.6 illustrates the concept. Read through the example now and then come back to the text to see how you did.

In what position in life did you place Linda? If you responded like those participants in the original experiment, you would be significantly less likely to indicate that Linda was a bank teller than a bank teller and a feminist.

For some reason, people were not likely to consider bank tellers to be active feminists (or vice versa), thereby ignoring the principles of probability. This type of error, called a

---

Table 11.6 The Linda problem

Linda is 31 years old, single, outspoken and very bright. She majored in philosophy. As a student, she was deeply concerned with issues of discrimination and social justice, and also participated in anti-nuclear demonstrations.

Please rank the following by their probability, using I for the most probable and 8 for the least probable.

A Linda is a teacher in primary school
B Linda works in a bookstore and takes yoga classes
C Linda is an attractive feminist
D Linda is a psychiatric social worker
E Linda is a member of Woman Against Rape
F Linda is a bank teller
G Linda is an insurance salesperson
H Linda is a bank teller and is an active feminist

Source: Tversky, A. and Kahneman, D., Extensional versus intuitive reasoning: Conjunction fallacy in probability judgement. *Psychological Review*, 1983, 90, 293–315, © 1983 by the American Psychological Association, reprinted with permission.

conjunction error, is reduced when the initial description of the person is followed by text stating that 100 people fit the description they have read and the reader is asked how many of them are bank tellers and bank tellers and active feminists. When led in this way, people do not commit errors in reasoning that take little account of probability; without such guidance, these errors are committed.

An example of real-life decision-making is seen every time a juror reaches a verdict in a trial. Jurors' decisions carry great weight and in some cases can determine whether a person lives or dies. The Psychology in Action box describes some of the factors that can influence a juror's decision-making and tries to explain how jurors reach their decisions.

Cutting edge – How eBay works

Ever wondered why you missed out on that item you bid for on eBay? Why you were outbid, maybe at the last minute? Reasoning can often be tossed overboard in auctions because people's desire for an item, coupled with competition for that item, means that people will pay much more than the item is intrinsically worth. Researchers at the London Business School and Northwestern University in the USA sought to see what determines winning bids on internet auctions sites, like eBay, and whether the behaviour of bidders followed economic and logical rules (Ku *et al.*, 2006).

In a series of experiments, they used data collected from actual auctions (for shirts, rugs and cameras) run by sellers on eBay. They found that the greatest determinant of a high winning bid was a low starting price. So, for example, an item with a starting bid of $1 would attract more 'traffic' (i.e. bids) and a higher final price than would one with a starting price of $20. Despite the fact that bidders ought to reduce the maximum amount of their bid as the number of bids for an item increases, they failed to.

Of course, if you saw a holiday advertised at $1, this might ring alarm bells. Apart from the authenticity of the offer, you might question the value of the product or item. And this is what the researchers found. A low starting price affected the perception of the item's value, but because the amount of traffic attracted to the low price increased, the increase in bids means that the price was pushed up. This increase led to a re-evaluation of the item as valued.

Psychology in action – Jury decision-making

> Trial by jury itself, instead of being a security to persons who are accused, will be a delusion, a mockery and a snare.   Source: Lord Denman, Lord Chief Justice.

The outcomes of many famous trials by jury in Europe and the USA in recent years may give some credence to Denman's thoughts. The verdict in the O.J. Simpson case in the USA and the acquittal of the Maxwell brothers of fraud in the UK have led to calls for a review of the jury system (Doran and Jackson, 1997). The UK government is considering the abolition of juries for some offences. Jury systems exist in many countries. In England and Wales, for example, juries are considered part of the justice delivery system, but only 2 per cent of criminal cases go to trial by jury. In the UK, jurors are usually laypersons with no especial expertise in law or the subject of the trial; numbers vary between 12 (England and Wales) and 15 (Scotland). The lay nature of juries has made some question the verdicts of fraud trials, for example, where it is felt that the detailed evidence of fraud presented by the prosecution cannot be fully appreciated by a lay juror. In other countries, a jury may comprise a mixture of lay and expert jurors, called an 'escabinato jury'.

In Western societies, the jury symbolises all that is democratic, fair and just in a society. Jury decisions can call into question core values, and can have dramatic social consequences. For example, the 1992 Los Angeles riots, which left 50 dead and 2,300 injured, were sparked by the perception that an all-white jury had delivered an unjust verdict of 'not guilty' in the trial of white police officers accused of beating a black motorist. Several factors affect jury decision-making including the decision-making process itself, the number of people on a jury, jurors' prior beliefs, features specific to the case such as the sex, employment record and criminal history of the defendant, whether the crime involved the use of a weapon, and the availability of eyewitness testimony (Howitt, 2002).

Much of the research relies on experiments in which trials are simulated and mock juries hear (often genuine) court evidence, and draw their conclusions. The invented nature of

Psychology in action – *Continued*

much of these experiments obviously encourages us to be cautious when interpreting their results. However, many studies make their protocol as realistic as possible and encourage their participants to behave as if they were making real-life jury decisions.

Factors influencing juries' verdicts

The results make interesting reading. Allowing jurors to take notes or to ask questions leads to no significant change in the verdict reached or in the perception of the prosecution or defence (Penrod and Heuer, 1997), but makes the processing of complex evidence easier. The publicity given to a case (Otto *et al.*, 1994), the attractiveness of the victim (Kerr, 1978) and the order of evidence (Kassin *et al.*, 1990; Kerstholt and Jackson, 1998) have all been found to influence eventual verdicts. People who are anti-police are more likely to acquit than are those who do not hold anti-police views (Vidmar *et al.*, 1997), and people are more persuaded by an expert witness when the evidence is complex (Cooper *et al.*, 1996).

Jury size is important. In the case of *Willliams* v. *Florida*, the US Supreme Court ruled that six jurors were as effective as twelve. Juries usually require unanimity: in the UK this may be required at first but if this is not forthcoming a 10/12 majority is required. In Spain, on the other hand, there is what is called qualified majority voting. To reach a verdict of not guilty, a majority of 5/9 must be reached; for a verdict of guilty, 7/9 is required.

Large juries tend to result in hung verdicts (Zeisel, 1971; Saks and Marti, 1997) and spend longer deliberating on the verdict, engage in more irrelevant deliberations, make more assertions, regard trial evidence less meaningfully and are more intransigent than their unanimous-verdict counterparts (Arce *et al.*, 1998). Large juries are also likely to reach more guilty verdicts (Saks and Marti, 1997). Striking a note of caution, however, Saks and Marti found that although large mock juries reached more hung judgments, only 1 per cent of real juries were hung. When agreement between jurors is made compulsory, however, members do spend more time deliberating evidence in detail (Arce *et al.*, 1998).

In a study of 1,000 defendants on felony charges, Myers (1979) found that there were some specific features of the case that influenced verdicts. These included whether: a weapon was recovered, a large number of witnesses gave testimony or were prepared to, the defendant had previous convictions and was employed, whether the defendant was young or old; and the seriousness of the crime was also a factor. Factors not associated with the final verdict were the eyewitness testimony of the defendant, the testimony of experts and the defendant's relation to the victim.

How do jurors reach a verdict?

Psychologists have suggested two models which might account for this type of decision-making (Honess and Charman, 2002). The story model argues that jurors evaluate evidence/information in a step-by-step manner and construct a meaningful narrative using the evidence they hear. During the course of the trial, the juror begins to form a story and evaluates subsequent evidence in light of this (Pennington and Hastie, 1986, 1992). The second model is the dual-process model. This model argues that the juror engages in two types of processing during decision-making. The first type, systematic processing, involves paying close attention to case detail and engaging in close scrutiny of information. The second type, heuristic processing, involves paying less attention to detail but paying more attention to the social, emotional, subjective aspects of the case such as the persuasiveness of expert evidence, and the belief that there is 'no smoke without fire' (Eagly and Chaiken, 1993).

Current evidence suggests that the story model best accounts for jury decision-making (Carlson and Russo, 2001). The model also suggests that because all jurors have access to evidence, their construction of stories will depend on the juror's own beliefs, predispositions and personal experiences.

The personal and subjective nature of story construction was recently addressed by Carlson and Russo (2001). They argued that if a juror adopts a specific position at the beginning of the trial, then subsequent evidence will be interpreted in the context of this position. However, Carlson and Russo were not interested in the prior beliefs of the jurors but in the judgement they reached or beliefs they held about guilt or innocence in the early stages of a trial. Jurors interpret evidence according to the judgement predominating at the time (Russo *et al.*, 1996). Failure to ignore a judge's instructions or to dismiss evidence deemed inadmissible is thought to contribute to this bias in reasoning. Inadmissible evidence would still be evaluated, partially, according to the judgement the juror has already reached about the culpability of the defendant. Carlson and Russo call this 'predecisional distortion' because evidence is interpreted in a partial way before a verdict is reached.

'Predecisional distortion'/bias

Carlson and Russo found that predecisional bias was greater in prospective mock jurors than it was in a group of students. These jurors distorted evidence twice as much, held stronger prior beliefs and were more confident in their judgements than were the student juror group, possibly because the prospective jurors were older than the students or because the students were more analytical and reflective. This is a reasonable hypothesis given that the prospective group held strong prior beliefs that were not particularly susceptible to change.

▶

Psychology in action – *Continued*

If this bias is inherent in the system – because jurors are thinking individuals with differences in belief, thinking style and intellect – how can it be avoided? For a juror to reach a verdict before all the evidence is presented, and to interpret evidence in a way that is consistent with that verdict, is clearly problematic (Constantini and King, 1980). There is some evidence, however, that if people are given instructions not to develop biased thinking (either pro- or anti- an individual), then these biases can be removed. In mock jury settings, giving juries instructions before evidence is presented is more effective than instructing them after all the evidence has been heard (Bourgeois *et al.*, 1995).

There are some biases, however, that people would find very difficult to avoid. Pre-trial publicity is a good example of information presented prior to trial that could influence a juror's view of the evidence. Some judges in the UK consider such publicity could prejudice a defendant's case, as happened in 2001 when a judge ordered a retrial of two professional footballers accused of assaulting a man in Leeds city centre. A retrial was ordered after a national newspaper published an interview with the father of the assaulted man. The judge ruled that the defendants would not receive a fair trial. Although it seems intuitively reasonable, there is no systematic evidence to support the idea that pre-trial information could cause juror bias. More realistically, however, as Studebacker and Penrod (1997) note, there is no trial anywhere in the world where a juror would not be aware of some aspects of the crime.

Problem-solving

The ultimate function of thinking is to solve problems. We are faced with an enormous variety of them in our daily lives: fixing a television set, planning a picnic, choosing a spouse, navigating across the ocean, solving a maths problem, tracking some game, designing a bridge, finding a job. The ability to solve problems is related to academic success, vocational success, and overall success in life, so trying to understand how we do so is an important undertaking.

The spatial metaphor

According to Holyoak (1990), a problem is a state of affairs in which we have a goal but do not have a clear understanding of how it can be attained. As he notes, when we talk about problems, we often use spatial metaphors to describe them (Lakoff and Turner, 1989). We think of the solving of a problem as finding a path to the solution. We may have to get around roadblocks that we encounter or backtrack when we hit a dead end. If we get lost, we may try to approach the problem from a different angle. If we have experience with particular types of problem, we may know some short cuts.

In fact, Newell and Simon (1972) have used the spatial metaphor to characterise the problem-solving process. At the beginning of a person's attempt to solve a problem, the initial state is different from the goal state – if it were not, there would be no problem. The person solving the problem has a number of operators available. Operators are actions that can be taken to change the current state of the problem; metaphorically, operators move the current state from one position to another. Not all people will be aware of the operators that are available. Knowledge of operators depends on education and experience. In addition, there may be various costs associated with different operators; some may be more difficult, expensive or time-consuming than others. The problem space consists of all the possible states that can be achieved if all the possible operators are applied. A solution is a sequence of operators (a 'path') that moves from the initial state to the goal state.

Algorithms and heuristics

Some kinds of problem can be solved by following a sequence of operators known as an algorithm. **Algorithms** are procedures that consist of series of steps that, if followed in the correct sequence, will provide a solution. If you apply properly the steps of an algorithm (such as long division) to divide one number by another, you will obtain the correct answer. But many problems are not as straightforward as this. When there is no algorithm to follow, we must follow a heuristic to guide our search for a path to the solution. Heuristics (from the Greek *heuriskein*, 'to discover') are general rules that are useful in guiding our search for a path to the solution of a problem. Heuristics tell us what to pay attention to, what to ignore and what strategy to take.

Heuristic methods can be very specific, or they can be quite general, applying to large categories of problems. For example, management courses try to teach students problem-solving methods they can use in a wide variety of contexts. Newell and Simon (1972) suggest a general heuristic method that can be used to solve any problem: means–ends analysis. The principle behind **means–ends analysis** is that a person should look for differences between the current state and the goal state and seek ways to reduce these differences. The steps of this method are as follows (Holyoak, 1990, p. 121):

1 Compare the current state to the goal state and identify differences between the two. If there are none, the problem is solved; otherwise, proceed.

2 Select an operator that would reduce one of the differences.

3 If the operator can be applied, do so; if not, set a new subgoal of reaching a state at which the operator could be applied. Means–ends analysis is then applied to this new subgoal until the operator can be applied or the attempt to use it is abandoned.

4 Return to step 1.

At all times, the person's activity is oriented towards reducing the distance between the current state and the goal state. If problems are encountered along the way (that is, if operators cannot be applied), then subgoals are created and means–ends analysis is applied to solving that problem, and so on until the goal is reached.

Of course, there may be more than one solution to a particular problem, and some solutions may be better than others. A good solution is one that uses the smallest number of actions while minimising the associated costs. The relative importance of cost and speed determines which solution is best. Intelligent problem-solving involves more than trying out various actions (applying various operators) to see whether they bring you closer to the goal. It also involves planning. When we plan, we act vicariously, 'trying out' various actions in our heads. Obviously, planning requires that we know something about the consequences of the actions we are considering. Experts are better at planning than are novices. If we do not know the consequences of particular actions, we will be obliged to try each action (apply each operator) and see what happens. Planning is especially important when many possible operators are present, when they are costly or time-consuming, or when they are irreversible. If we take an irreversible action that brings us to a dead end, we have failed to solve the problem.

Where in the brain does decision-making occur?

For most of our complex, intelligent behaviour, a region in the front of the brain appears to be essential. Damage to the frontal lobes is associated with deficits in planning, putting stimuli in the correct order, behaving spontaneously and inhibiting incorrect responses (Adolphs *et al.*, 1996).

Damasio and colleagues' studies of patients with frontal lobe damage show that these individuals have great difficulty in making correct decisions (Damasio, 1995; Bechara *et al.*, 1996, 1997). Damasio suggests that the ability to make decisions leading to positive or potentially harmful consequences depends on the activation of somatic (that is, bodily) states. Damasio calls this the **somatic marker hypothesis** because such decisions involve automatic, endocrine and musculoskeletal routes. These routes mark events as important, but appear to be impaired in certain frontal lobe patients. When the decision can have a positive or negative outcome, the degree of physiological activity, such as heart rate and galvanic skin response (see Chapter 4) that is normally seen in healthy individuals is absent in these patients (Bechara *et al.*, 1997).

In a typical experiment, patients were taught to play a card game (the Iowa Gambling Task) where they were told to make as much money as possible (Bechara *et al.*, 1997). There are four decks of cards and some have a high probability of delivering a large immediate monetary reward or a large delayed monetary loss or a low immediate monetary reward or a low delayed monetary loss. No participant was told which deck contained the greatest probability of obtaining these outcomes and, therefore, had to learn from experience, turning over cards and remembering the outcomes. They had hunches. When a decision involved a high degree of risk, for example, a healthy individual would show a characteristic increase in physiological arousal; the frontal lobe patient, however, would not. Neuroimaging studies of the same task are associated with increases in blood flow to the ventromedial region of the frontal cortex (Elliott *et al.*, 1997; Grant *et al.*, 2000).

Bechara *et al.* found that the VM-damaged patients opted for the disadvantageous decks and failed to be sensitive to future consequences. Instead, they seemed to be guided by immediate reward. The researchers called this 'myopia for the future'. Even when the future consequences of behaving in a particular way were undesirable, these patients continued to behave in an inappropriate way. The group followed this up with a study showing that substance abusers performed within the same range as people with damage to the ventromedial cortex (Bechara *et al.*, 2001).

Manes *et al.* (2002) found that dorsolateral lesions were associated with working memory, set shifting and Iowa Gambling Task impairments; dorsomedial lesions were associated with planning and Iowa Gambling Task impairments, and orbitofrontal lesions were associated with performance at control level but showed prolonged deliberation on the Tower of London Task, a task that required forward planning (see Chapter 13 for an example of this task). However, the group with large frontal lesions showed great impairment and was the only group to show risky decision-making. According to Manes *et al.*'s criteria, patients in the Bechara studies would be classified as having large frontal lesions.

Reasoning and the brain

In healthy individuals, blood flow tends to increase in the frontal and parietal lobes during reasoning tasks (Goel *et al.*, 1997, 1998). According to theories of deduction, our ability to reason is either based on understanding the linguistic rules that underpin logic or based on whether visuospatial relations are involved in the reasoning (Goel, 2007). These two different interpretations probably explain why the results from neuroimaging have been inconsistent. Different types of reasoning tasks recruit different regions. For example, early studies, such as the PET studies of Goel – cited above – asked people to follow syllogisms such as:

> Some officers are generals
>
> No privates are generals
>
> Some officers are not privates

and found increased activation in the left frontal and temporal lobes.

Later studies, using fMRI, found increases in both sides of the prefrontal cortex, the left temporal lobe and both sides of the parietal lobe (Goel *et al.*, 2000; Goel, 2003).

Differences in activation are seen depending on whether the reasoning task involves conditional reasoning (participants have to follow if – then relations), complex conditional reasoning (such as the card sorting task described earlier), and transitive inferences (e.g. understanding that the relationship between A and B or B and C can be transferred to A and C). Left prefrontal activation is seen during the first, bilateral occipital, parietal and frontal activation during the second and frontal and parietal activation in the last. Goel and Dolan (2001), for example, using the third type, asked people to reason problems such as:

> Graham is taller than Mike
>
> Mike is taller than Lynn
>
> Graham is taller than Lynn

Knauff *et al.* (2003) extended this to action sentences:

> A dog is cleaner than a cat
>
> An ape is dirtier than a cat
>
> A dog is cleaner than an ape

and found similar activation.

According to Goel (2007), these studies suggest that the frontal-temporal pathway provides us with a heuristic system for reasoning – it helps us process conceptually coherent material – whereas the parietal lobe underpins a more formal system based on universal reasoning rules – it is involved in processing non-conceptual, incoherent material.

There is an exception to this model, however. Take a look at the following statements:

1 Mary is cleverer than John; John is cleverer than George; Mary is cleverer than George

2 Mary is cleverer than John; John is cleverer than George; George is cleverer than Mary

3 Mary is cleverer than John; Mary is cleverer than George; John is cleverer than George

Patients with damage to the left prefrontal cortex cannot process the first two types; patients with damage to the right are poor at processing the last, suggesting that there may be a degree of reasoning-related asymmetry in the brain.

In general, however, a small network of regions is involved in reasoning and, whatever the task, the prefrontal cortex is involved.

Brain activation in the very intelligent

Would more or less activation in the frontal lobes be apparent in very bright individuals? An early PET study indicated that individuals with high IQ had lower metabolic rates than those with low IQ during problem-solving (Haier *et al.*, 1988). When high and low IQ individuals were trained on a computer game, both groups' brain activity declined but the decline in the high IQ group was more rapid, suggesting that the highly intellectually able may need to use less of their neural machinery to think (Haier *et al.*, 1992).

A study by Chinese researchers, however, has found that intelligence is not simply related to activity in the frontal lobe but to connections between this region and other brain areas (Song *et al.*, 2008). They used fMRI to study 59 healthy adults and correlated intelligence scores with the strength of connections between the dorsolateral prefrontal cortex and other brain regions. They found that the greater the intelligence score, the greater the strength between the prefrontal cortex and the regions within it, and with the parietal, limbic and occipital cortices. The results suggest that intelligence can be correlated with increased brain activation, even when the brain is at rest.

Creative thinking

Creativity has almost as many definitions as intelligence. We recognise that the writing of

a novel, the design of a sculpture and the construction of a painting are creative products but what does it mean to be creative? Feldhusen and Goh (1995) define creativity as a 'complex mix of motivational conditions, personality factors, environmental conditions, chance factors and end products'. Vernon (1989) suggests that creativity is a person's capacity to produce ideas, inventions, artistic objects, insight and products evaluated highly by experts. Torrance (1975) defines creativity as a set of abilities, skills, motivations and states linked to dealing with problems. Others define the components of creative thinking as involving a realisation that a problem exists, formulation of questions to clarify the problem, determining the causes of the problem, clarifying the desired goal or solution and selecting a way to achieve this goal (Feldhusen, 1993). Still others have suggested that creativity involves producing a recognised, important end-product, not rubbish.

All of these definitions seem to have a common feature – that creativity involves some form of end-product. However, this end-product need not be material. Albert (1990), for example, has suggested that creativity is expressed through decisions not products. There do, however, seem to be different degrees of creativity. The production of a novel, painting or sculpture is undoubtedly creative, but solving inductive and deductive problems also involves a degree of creative thinking. However, artistic production seems to require creativity plus talent. These are high-level creative behaviours as opposed to the basic creative behaviour involved in solving deductive reasoning puzzles.

Given that psychologists cannot measure high-level creativity directly in the laboratory – they cannot ask individuals to come into the laboratory and write full-length novels, for example – they have devised other tests which tap the capacity to engage in creative thinking. The Torrance Tests of Creativity, for example, measure performance on a series of verbal and figural tasks such as naming as many objects as possible beginning with a specific letter or creating as many designs as possible using the same basic design (for example a circle). Torrance (1975) reports that performance on these tests predicts creative achievement, occupation and creative writing. Other tests include those by Wallach and Kogan (1965). These tests are verbal and measure verbal fluency – the ability to devise many uses for objects and the ability to detect similarities between stimuli. There is little evidence that performance on tests such as the Wallach and Kogan and the Torrance Tests – called tests of divergent thinking – predicts creativity (Brown, 1989).

Are there any features of the creative individual's personality that can predict creativity? Dacey (1989) has listed nine personality factors predictive of creativity and includes in this list flexibility, risk-taking and tolerance of ambiguity. Other factors suggested by other psychologists include: cognitive complexity, perceptual openness, field independence, autonomy and self-esteem (Woodman and Schoenfeldt, 1989), and fluency, flexibility, curiosity and humour (Treffinger *et al.*, 1990). Other personality factors that have recently attracted a great deal of interest are psychopathological or psychotic personality characteristics. Are creative people more prone to mental disorder? Does the mental disorder predispose the individual to creative thinking? These questions are discussed in the Controversies in Psychological Science box below.

In Greek mythology, Prometheus stole fire from the gods for mankind's use. Humans were thus able to use their own creativity and not rely on divine creation. The gods became displeased and released Pandora's Box on mankind – a casket of evil.

Source: Prometheus carrying fire (oil) Jan Crossiers (1600–71), Prado, Madrid, Spain. Index/Bridgeman Art Library Ltd.

Cutting edge – Creativity and romance

'In order to create,' said the great Russian violinist Igor Stravinsky, 'there must be a dynamic force – and what force is more potent than love?' Researchers at Arizona State University examined the relationship between romantic motives and creativity in a series of experiments (Griskevicius et al., 2006).

Men and women looked at photographs of attractive people of the opposite sex, or imagined being in a romantic scenario, and then completed subjective (writing a short story) and objective (the Remote Associates Test) creativity tests. The Remote Associates Test asks people to come up with one word that links three others in 15 seconds. For example, 'sun' would correctly bring together 'dress', dial' and 'flower'.

For men, thinking about an attractive woman as a potential romantic partner increased creativity. Women's creativity only increased when the man was perceived as trustworthy and committed. Men's increased creativity was therefore associated with attraction to a short-term mate, whereas women's was associated with attraction to a long-term mate. Women did not show increased creativity when thinking about a short-term or long-term mate who could not demonstrate good long-term viability as a partner. Although both sexes reported increased positive mood and arousal after appraising a person who might become a short-term partner, mood was unrelated to creativity.

The next step would be to examine not only the relationship between creativity and actual courtship, but also the relationship between the quality of the relationship and creativity.

Case studies in creativity

Mozart thought out symphonies, etc., entirely in his head . . . and then transcribed them, in completeness, onto paper. Beethoven wrote fragments of themes in notebooks, working on and developing them over years. The Mozartian type of genius is able to plumb the greatest depths of his own experience by the tremendous effort of a moment; the Beethovian must dig deeper and deeper into his consciousness, layer by layer . . .

Source: 'Making of a Poem', Stephen Spender, *Partisan Review* (1946).

According to the theory of creativity proposed by Sternberg and Lubart (1991), there are three features of creativity that highly creative individuals possess. These features are: (1) domain-relevant skills – abilities the individual has in their domain and their knowledge of the domain; (2) creativity-relevant processes – the personality, cognitive style or other individual differences which promote creativity; and (3) intrinsic task motivation – the internal drive which motivates the individual and which can be influenced by the individual's environment. Domains for creative individuals such as John Irving, Charles Darwin and Claude Monet, for example, would be fiction, science and art, respectively.

In a special issue of *American Psychologist* on creativity for the new millennium, introduced by Sternberg and Dess (2001), case studies of these and other creative individuals are presented and assessed for the features that make such individuals especially creative. Creative people are thought to produce products that are high in quality and novelty; intelligent, but not particularly creative, people can produce products of high quality but these may not be novel (Sternberg, 2001). The novel nature of creativity also suggests that its products 'defy the crowd'

(Sternberg and Lubart, 1995): creative individuals produce unusual (sometimes) counter-intuitive products (ideas, as well as physical items), and some individuals, like Darwin, attempt to persuade the crowd with their ideas. Creatives also analyse the many ideas they have or may redefine problems or make unexpected connections between two things.

Sternberg and Lubart (1991) also suggest that the creative individual is a little like a successful market trader: they buy low and sell high. That is, they identify a problem needing a solution or find/pose an important question, and are then the first to provide the solution, leaving others to elaborate on these solutions and refine them. Some creatives may not be well known because they try to pose too many questions or attempt solutions to too many problems. Martindale (2001) describes one such case: the British polymath, Thomas Young.

Young (1773–1829) was a physician and Fellow of the Royal Society (at the age of 21) whose legacy to science is phenomenal. He suggested an explanation for colourblindness, proposed the trichromatic theory of colour vision (described in Chapter 5), founded the modern wave theory of light in physics, explained Newton's rings (why colours are seen on thin films of soap bubbles), was the first to measure the diameter of the molecule, provided the first modern classification of disease, proposed a theory of tide movement that improved on Newton's and decoded the meaning of the Egyptian hieroglyphics on the Rosetta Stone. Despite all of this, he produced only 80 publications (which might suggest that the quality of the publications was more important than the quantity).

Martindale suggests that Young's behaviour supports Eysenck's (1995) theory of creativity. According to Eysenck, creative individuals possess characteristics designed to promote creativity. These features combine so that the absence of one can lead to a lack of creativity. Creative individuals think in analogical ways, are highly intelligent, love hard work and novelty, dislike the traditional, and have very high self-confidence. Young seems to possess all of these characteristics. Why, then, is he not as well known as other scientists? One reason, Martindale suggests, is that science became too specialised. Scientists in specific disciplines rarely step outside their own territory. Perhaps if he had focused on one discipline and worked within it, he may have made an even greater mark on science.

One of Young's most salient characteristics was his curiosity. This is a trait which, according to some psychologists, marks out the creative from the non-creative (Kashdan and Fincham, 2002). But is there a more fundamental characteristic of creativity which psychology's current questionnaires and measures do not tap? According to Sternberg (2002), there is. It is

the decision to be creative. People who create decide that they will forge their own path and follow it, for better or for worse. The path is a difficult one because people who defy convention often are not rewarded. Hence, at times, their self-esteem may be high, at other times, low. At times, they may work in groups, at other times individually. At times, they may feel curious, at other times, less so. But if psychologists are to understand and facilitate creativity, I suggest they must start, not with a kind of skill, not with a personality trait, not with a motivational set, and not with an emotional state, but rather, simply, with a decision . . . for creativity to occur, it must be preceded by a personal decision to think and act creatively, with all the risks attendant on doing so.

Controversies in Psychological Science – Are creativity and psychopathology related?

The issue

According to Dryden, 'Great wits are sure to madness near allied, and thin partitions do their bounds divide.' As if providing direct evidence for Dryden's poetic analysis, Lady Caroline Lamb once famously described Lord Byron as mad, bad and dangerous to know. Although the link between badness, danger and creativity has not been the source of much research in psychology, the link between creativity and madness (or psychopathology) has. (Chapter 18 provides more detail on the various types of mental illness that fall under the category of psychopathology.) Anecdotal evidence suggests that two types of mental illness, manic depression (alternating periods of elation and chronic sadness) and clinical depression exist preponderantly in novelists, poets, artists and performers. But what empirical evidence is there to link psychopathology and creativity? If there is a relationship, does creativity cause psychopathology or does psychopathology cause creativity? Is it possible to determine this?

The evidence

Kraepelin (1921) had originally described a disorder called manic-depressive insanity in which the manic aspect of the disorder would produce changes in thought that would increase creativity and thinking. A number of authors report that increases in creativity are common during the manic episodes of bipolar disorder (Jamison, 1989; Sutherland, 1987; Goodwin and Jamison, 1990). Jamison (1989), for

example, found that creative individuals, especially poets, reported states of mania during creation although she did not specify the direction of the change in behaviour (whether the poetry caused the mania or vice versa). There was also a high incidence of suicide in poets. Weisberg (1994), in studying the quantity and quality of the work of the composer Franz Schubert, who suffered what we would today call a bipolar disorder, found that although the quantity of the composer's work increased during manic episodes, the quality was not significantly improved.

In a famous study of the relationship between creativity and psychopathology, Ludwig (1994) compared 59 women writers from a Women Writers' Conference at the University of Kentucky and 59 women from a housewives' association, medical centre and university women's club. Ludwig found that the writers were more likely to suffer from mood disorders, drug abuse, panic attacks, general anxiety and eating disorders. The results of this study complement those of writers attending an Iowa writers' workshop, 90 per cent of whom were men (Andreasen, 1987). The study found a greater incidence of mood disorder in this group than in the general population (80 per cent v. 30 per cent) and a greater incidence of bipolar disorder. Shapiro and Weisberg (1999) sought to determine if the same relationship held for non-eminent samples. They gave a creativity and creativity personality questionnaire to 20 undergraduates (from a sample of 70) who met strict criteria for bipolar disorder. The presence of hypomanic or euphoric symptoms was found to be signifi-

Controversies in Psychological Science – *Continued*

Stephen Fry, Carrie Fisher, Richard Dreyfuss: creative individuals associated with manic-depression or clinical depression.

Source: Hugh Stewart/Corbis (t), Getty Images/WireImage (b).

cantly associated with creativity, although depressive symptoms were not. The authors speculated that the depressed effect may be a part of the creative individual's behaviour because the inability to be creative (because of pressures in other areas of life) makes the individual depressed.

In two studies of creativity, Post (1994, 1996) analysed extensively the biographies of 291 world-famous creative men (visual artists, composers, creative writers, scientists, scholars and statesmen). He found that 90 per cent of the writers in his sample exhibited some traits which would be classified as a personality disorder according to mental disorder diagnostic manuals; only one scientist showed this profile (Henry Babbage, inventor of the first computer). In addition, 73.4 per cent of scientists exhibited unremarkable sexual behaviour whereas only 39 per cent of writers did. Depressive episodes occurred in 72 per cent of the writers. These data suggested to Post that, although the study was retrospective, a 'causal nexus' existed between creativity and psychopathology. In a subsequent study of 100 American and British writers (Post, 1996), there was a high prevalence of mood disorder, as seen in Table 11.7. Poets showed the greatest degree of bipolar disorder, although the incidence of depression, marital/sexual problems and alcoholism in poets was low. Recently the degree of cognitive distortions found in the work of 36 eminent depressed and 36 non-depressed authors was analysed (Thomas and Duke, 2007). There were more distortions in the depressed writers, and poets exhibited more than did novelists.

A study of 40 innovative American jazz musicians from the 1940s, 1950s and 1960s found that about 50 per cent were addicted to heroin, and 27 per cent became dependent on alcohol (Wills, 2003). Only one of the sample (Bud Powell) was schizophrenic but 28 per cent had 'probable' depression. This study, according to the author, 'adds weight to the finding that outstanding workers in the arts can suffer from above-average levels of mental health problems but manage to produce exceptional work despite this'.

Table 11.7 Mood disorders found in a sample of 100 writers

	N	Bipolar psychoses	Unipolar psychoses	Severely disabling depressions	Milder depressions	Brief reactions only	Depressive traits only	Cyclothymic traits only	Totals
Poets	35	2	1	4	11	4	5	1	28
Poets/novelists	41	2	1	8	13	2	7	0	33
Playwrights	24	1	0	4	8	4	3	1	21
Totals	100	5	2	16	32	10	15	2	82

Source: Post, F., Verbal creativity, depression and alcoholism, *British Journal of Psychiatry*, 1996, 168, 545–55. Reproduced with permission of the Royal College of Psychiatrists.

Controversies in Psychological Science – *Continued*

If creativity and psychopathology are related, what creates this link? One personality trait which has been linked with creativity is psychoticism (Eysenck, 1995). **Psychoticism** refers to a cold, manipulative and indifferent personality style. A number of studies has shown that creative individuals score highly on tests of psychoticism (Fodor, 1994; Stavridou and Furnham, 1996). According to Kris (1952), creative people are able to shift between two modes of thinking called primary and secondary thinking. Primary thinking is artistic, free associative, analogical and relies on concrete rather than abstract concepts; secondary thinking is abstract and reality-oriented. There seems to be no link between psychoticism and primary thinking, however (Martindale and Dailey, 1996). Similarly, Aguilar-Alonso (1996) found no difference between high and low psychoticism on a measure of verbal and drawing creativity. Rawlings (1985) has suggested that individuals high in psychoticism show the same impulsive, non-conforming

processes that underlie creative thinking ability. Perhaps what underlies creativity and psychoticism is disinhibition, the ability not to inhibit behaviour and thought.

Conclusion

Retrospective evidence suggests that there is a strong link between mental disorder and creativity. The problem with retrospective studies, however, is that we cannot empirically examine the personalities of creative individuals who are dead: we have to rely on books, anecdotes, personal reminiscences of creative individuals' relatives, friends or lovers. The findings of some recent empirical studies have been inconsistent. Modern studies employ creativity tests thought to tap specific forms of thinking but these may be far removed from the creativity seen in a visual artist, a poet or a novelist. While we may still be able to describe creative individuals as bad or dangerous, their madness is still open to question.

Cutting edge – The key to creativity – shut up!

Evidence suggests that thinking aloud, surprisingly, impairs people's ability to be creative. A study from Tilburg and Amsterdam universities has shown that this is especially so when people are sensitive to what others think of them (de Vet and de Dreu, 2007).

In one experiment, they asked people to complete a standard test of creativity – specifically, to think of unusual uses for a tin can – while either thinking aloud as they did so or to keep quiet. Those in the quiet condition produced the same number of uses for the tin can but their efforts were judged to

be more original. When participants' sensitivity to what others thought of them was measured in a second experiment, the researchers found that the most sensitive produced less original ideas in the thinking-aloud condition.

The researchers argue that thinking aloud requires more in the way of cognitive resources than does keeping quiet, resources that could be used for thinking creatively and originally. Speech is also slower than thought and so it could be that speaking out loud prevents other, quicker, possibly more original and immediate thoughts from being generated.

Chapter review

Theories of intelligence

- Although intelligence is often represented by a single score – the IQ – modern investigators do acknowledge the existence of specific abilities. What is controversial is whether a general factor also exists.
- Factor analysis is a data reduction technique that attempts to explain a large amount of data with reference to one or two factors.

- Spearman argued that a general intelligence factor existed (which he called g) and demonstrated that people's scores on a variety of specific tests of ability were correlated. He also believed that specific factors (s factors) also existed.
- Thurstone performed a factor analysis on 56 individual tests that revealed the existence of seven factors, not a single g factor.
- Cattell's factor analysis on such data obtained two factors. The nature of the tests that loaded heavily on these two factors

suggested the names fluid intelligence (g_f) and crystallised intelligence (g_c), with the former representing a person's native ability and the latter representing what a person learns.

- Sternberg's triarchic theory of intelligence attempts to integrate laboratory research using the information processing approach and an analysis of intelligent behaviour in the natural environment.

- According to Sternberg, we use componential intelligence to plan and execute tasks. We use experiential intelligence to apply past strategies to new problems. Finally, we use contextual intelligence to adapt to, select, or shape our environment.

- Gardner's multiple intelligences theory is based primarily on the types of skill that can be selectively lost through brain damage. His definition of intelligence includes many abilities that are commonly regarded as skills or talents.

- Like Sternberg's theory, Gardner's theory emphasises the significance of behaviours to the culture in which they occur.

- The most consistent sex difference in cognition is for mental rotation – men are better at it than are females.

- Men overestimate their own IQ but both sexes rate their fathers and male children as having higher IQs than their mothers or female children.

Intelligence testing

- Although the earliest known instance of ability testing was carried out by the ancient Chinese, modern intelligence testing dates from the efforts of Galton to measure individual differences.

- Galton made an important contribution to the field of measurement, but his tests of simple perceptual abilities were abandoned in favour of tests that attempt to assess more complex abilities, such as memory, logical reasoning and vocabulary.

- Binet developed a test that was designed to assess students' intellectual abilities in order to identify children with special educational needs.

- Although the test that superseded his, the Stanford–Binet Scale, provided for calculation of IQ, Binet believed that 'intelligence' was actually a composite of several specific abilities. For him, the concept of mental age was a convenience, not a biological reality.

- Wechsler's two intelligence tests, the WAIS-III for adults (and its variants) and the WISC-R for children, are the most widely used tests of intelligence.

- The reliability of modern intelligence tests is excellent, but assessing their validity is still difficult. Because no single criterion measure of intelligence exists, intelligence tests are validated by comparing the scores with measures of achievement, such as scholastic success.

- Tests also need to be intelligible and quick to complete.

- Intelligence tests can have both good and bad effects on the people who take them. The principal benefit is derived by identifying children with special needs (or special talents) who will profit from special programmes.

The roles of heredity and environment

- Variability in all physical traits is determined by a certain amount of genetic variability, environmental variability, and an interaction between genetic and environmental factors.

- The degree to which genetic variability is responsible for the observed variability of a particular trait in a particular population is called heritability or h.

- Heritability is not an indication of the degree to which the trait is determined by biological factors; rather, it reflects the relative proportions of genetic and environmental variability found in a particular population.

- Intellectual development is affected by many factors, both prenatal and post-natal. Potential intelligence can be permanently reduced during prenatal or post-natal development by injury, toxic chemicals, poor nutrition or disease.

- Twin studies and studies comparing biological and adoptive relatives indicate that both genetic and environmental factors affect intellectual ability, which is probably not surprising. These studies also point out that not all of a person's environment is shared by other members of the family; each person is an individual and is exposed to different environmental variables.

- The evidence suggests that biological children who are adopted are intellectually more like their biological parents; this finding applies across all age ranges.

- Although there are differences between races in terms of IQ score, it is unclear whether this is due to heredity. There are also problems in defining race.

Thinking

- Formal concepts are defined as lists of essential characteristics of objects and events. In everyday life, we use natural concepts – collections of memories of particular examples, called exemplars.

- Concepts exist at the basic, subordinate and superordinate levels. We do most of our thinking about concepts at the basic level.

- Deductive reasoning consists of inferring specific instances from general principles.

- One of the most important skills in deductive reasoning is the ability to construct mental models that represent problems.

- Inductive reasoning involves inferring general principles from particular facts. This form of thinking involves generating and testing hypotheses.

- Without special training (such as learning the rules of the scientific method), people often ignore relevant information, ignore the necessity of control groups or show a confirmation bias – the tendency to look only for evidence that confirms one's hypothesis.

- Jury decision-making is one important real-life example of reasoning, and jurors can reach decisions that do not follow logic and that are influenced by factors other than trial evidence (such as jury size, pre-existing beliefs, aspects of the trial and so on).

- Current evidence suggests that jurors evaluate evidence in a step-by-step manner and construct a meaningful narrative using the evidence they hear.
- Problem-solving is best represented spatially: we follow a path in the problem space from the initial state to the goal state, using operators to get to each intermediate state. Sometimes a problem fits a particular mould and can be solved with an algorithm – a cut-and-dried set of operations.
- However, in most cases, a problem must be attacked by following a heuristic – a general rule that helps guide our search for a path to the solution of a problem. The most general heuristic is means–ends analysis, which involves taking steps

that reduce the distance from the current state to the goal. If obstacles are encountered, subgoals are created and attempts are made to reach them.

- The regions of the brain recruited most consistently during reasoning and decision-making are the prefrontal cortex and parietal lobe.
- Creativity has been defined in many ways but most psychologists agree that it describes a person's capacity to produce novel ideas, inventions, objects or products and to engage in successful problem-solving.
- Studies suggest a link between psychopathology (such as manic depression and depression) and creativity, but whether the link is causal is open to question.

Suggestions for further reading

Intelligence – general reading

Bartholomew, D.J. (2004) *Measuring Intelligence*. Cambridge: Cambridge University Press.
Flynn, J.R. (2007) Solving the IQ puzzle. *Scientific American Mind*, 18, 5, 24–31.
Flynn, J.R. (2009) *What is Intelligence?* Cambridge: Cambridge University Press.
Gardner, H. (2006) *Multiple Intelligences: New horizons in theory and practice*. New York: Basic Books.
Gray, J.R. and Thompson, P.M. (2004) Neurobiology of intelligence: Science and ethics. *Nature Reviews Neuroscience*, 5, 471–82.
Kliegel, M., McDaniel, M.A., and Einstein, G.O. (2007) *Prospective Memory: Cognitive, Neuroscience, Developmental, and Applied Perspectives*. London: Psychology Press.
Sternberg, R.J., Kaufman, J.C. and Grigorenko, E. (2008) *Applied Intelligence*. Cambridge: Cambridge University Press.
Some very good items on intelligence.

Genetics and the environment

Plomin, R. and Colledge, E. (2001) Genetics and psychology: Beyond heritability. *European Psychologist*, 6, 4, 229–40.
Special issue of *Psychology, Public Policy and Law* (2005) 11, 2, on race differences in cognitive ability.
Heredity is dealt with specifically in Plomin and Colledge's very good article. The special issue of PPPL is a lively collection of papers on a contentious topic.

Sex differences

Cahill, L. (2005) His brain, her brain. *Scientific American Mind*, May, 40–7.
Halpern, D.F., Benbow, C.P., Geary, D.C., Gur, R.C., Hyde, J.S. and Gernsbacher, M.A. (2007/2008) Sex, math and scientific achievement. *Scientific American Mind*, 18, 6, 44–51.

Halpern, D.F., Benbow, C.P., Geary, D.C., Gur, R.C., Hyde, J.S. and Gernsbacher, M.A. (2007) The science of sex differences in science and mathematics. *Psychological Science in the Public Interest*, 8, 1, 1–51.
Kimura, D. (2004) Human sex differences in cognition: fact not predicament. *Sexualities, Evolution and Gender*, 6, 1, 45–54.
For a good introduction to the complex area of sex differences in cognitive ability, these items are well recommended.

Ageing, dementia and intelligence

Cabeza, R., Nyberg, L. and Park, D. (2004) *Cognitive Neuroscience of Aging*. Oxford: Oxford University Press.
Craik, F.I.M. and Salthouse, T.A. (2000) *The Handbook of Aging and Cognition*. London: Lawrence Erlbaum Associates.
Hess, T.M. (2005) Memory and aging in context. *Psychological Bulletin*, 131, 3, 383–406.
Morris, R. and Becker, J. (2004) *Cognitive Neuropsychology of Alzheimer's Disease*. Oxford: Oxford University Press.
Naveh-Benjamin, M., Moscovitch, M. and Roediger, H.L. (2002) *Perspectives on Human Memory and Cognitive Aging*. Hove: Psychology Press.
Rabbitt, P. (2005) Cognitive gerontology: Cognitive change in old age. Special issue of *Quarterly Journal of Experimental Psychology Section A*. Hove: Psychology Press.
Neurobiology of Aging (2009), 30. This features a series of articles on age-related cognitive decline.
All these items are excellent introductions to the effect of ageing on intelligence and thinking.

Thinking and reasoning

Andre, D. and Fernand, G. (2008) Sherlock Holmes – an expert's view of expertise. *British Journal of Psychology*, 99, 109–25.
Gilhooly, K. (1996) *Thinking: Directed, undirected and creative*. Oxford: Academic Press.

Goel, V. (2007) Anatomy of deductive reasoning. *Trends in Cognitive Sciences*, 11, 10, 435–41.

Holyoak, K. and Morrison, R. (2005) *The Cambridge Handbook of Thinking and Reasoning*. Cambridge: Cambridge University Press.

Sutherland, S. (1992) *Irrationality*. London: Penguin.

Taleb, N.N. (2007) *The Black Swan*. London: Penguin.

Tavris, C. and Aronson, E. (2008) *Mistakes Were Made (but not by me)*. London: Pinter & Martin.

Good coverage of all the major aspects of thinking. Sutherland's book, in particular, is the best book on irrational thinking you can read.

Creativity

Dietrich, A. (2004) The cognitive neuroscience of creativity. *Psychonomic Bulletin and Review*, 11, 6, 1011–126.

Heilman, K.H. (2005) *Creativity and the Brain*. Hove: Psychology Press.

Runco, M.A. (2004) Creativity. *Annual Review of Psychology*, 55, 657–87.

Sawyer, R.K. (2006) *Explaining Creativity: The science of human innovation*. New York: Oxford University Press.

American Psychologist (2001), 56. Special issue on creativity.

A series of interesting items on creativity.

Journals to consult

Aging and Psychology

Applied Cognitive Psychology

British Journal of Psychology

Cognition

Cortex

Current Directions in Psychological Science

European Journal of Cognitive Psychology

European Psychologist

Intelligence

Journal of Experimental Psychology

Nature

Neuroscience

Personality and Individual Differences

Psychological Science

Psychology and Ageing

Quarterly Journal of Experimental Psychology

Science

Thinking and Reasoning

Website addresses

http://www.skeptic.com/03.3.fm-sternberg-interview.html
An interview with Professor Robert Sternberg in which he discusses the impact of The Bell Curve and the role of genetics/environment in intelligence.

http://www.uwsp.edu/acad/educ/lwilson/LEARNING/index.htm
A collection of links to creative thinking websites, as well as links to major theories in intelligence.

http://www.psychology.org/links/Environment_Behavior_Relationships/Intelligence/
http://www.personalityresearch.org/intelligence.html
Two collections of links to intelligence websites.

Developmental psychology

Explore the accompanying videos, simulations, and animations on MyPsychLab. This chapter includes activities on: Experiencing the visual cliff • Sexual identity development • Kohlberg's stage of moral reasoning • What makes a bully? • Check your understanding and prepare for your exams using the multiple choice, short answer and essay practice tests also available.

CHAPTER 12

Police refute Bridgend suicides link

Nico Hines

A total of 17 people aged between 15 and 27 and living in and around Bridgend have hanged themselves since January 2007. Local police, who have dismissed fears of a suicide cult, continue to deny any connection between the deaths.

At least ten of the victims seem to have been known to each other, however, with several having friendship links on Bebo, a social networking site. After their deaths, the profiles of many of the victims have quickly been transformed into virtual shrines with condolences.

Some commentators have suggested that the website allows the glorification of the deaths, promoting copycat suicides.

Source: *Times Online*, 19 February 2008.

WHAT YOU SHOULD BE ABLE TO DO AFTER READING CHAPTER 12

- Describe the major stages of psychological development from birth.
- Outline the nature of foetal development and learning.
- Describe how infant perception, memory and cognition develop.
- Describe the emotional and social development of the child from infancy to adolescence and attempt to explain how this occurs.
- Describe the psychological changes that occur during adolescence, adulthood and old age and attempt to explain why these changes occur.

QUESTIONS TO THINK ABOUT

- Can a foetus learn?
- How does a child learn to think and perceive?
- Does a child's cognitive development progress in discernible stages?
- Is an infant's ability to perceive certain stimuli, such as faces, innate?
- What is the relationship between brain development and cognitive development?
- What are a child's most important psychological functions?
- How valid are categories such as 'adolescence' and 'infancy'?
- How does the child interpret the perceptual world?
- When and how do children develop a sense of morality?
- What causes disorders of cognition and emotion in infants?
- How important is the nature of peer interaction to the social development of adolescents?
- Is adulthood marked by similar psychological milestones to those in infancy?
- How does social and cognitive behaviour change as people get older?
- Is cognitive decline in old age preventable?
- Are some cognitive abilities better preserved (or even improved) as we enter old age?

Developmental psychology

Apart from conception, development is probably the most astonishing thing we do. From birth to around late adolescence, we develop from a fairly unsophisticated bundle of reflexes and crude cognition to a fantastically efficient organism that can use language, perceive depth, colour, shape and motion, walk, run and jump, drive a car, or parachute from a plane, become a novelist, mathematician or physicist. There is an impressively rapid development of sensory, perceptual, social and cognitive ability during infancy and childhood and this, together with the further development of these abilities in adolescence and adulthood, is the subject matter of **developmental psychology**.

Developmental psychologists study both the similarities and the differences among people as they develop and change over the course of their life. Because of the longitudinal nature of this study, the area is sometimes described as lifespan developmental psychology, which acknowledges the fact that development does not end when adolescence ends.

The major developmental periods across the lifespan are the prenatal period, infancy and childhood, adolescence, adulthood, middle and late adulthood, and old age. This chapter considers the main developments that characterise each stage.

Prenatal development

The nine months between conception and birth is called the **prenatal period** and the length of a normal human pregnancy is 266 days, or 38 weeks. The prenatal period involves three developmental stages: the zygote, the embryo and the foetal stages.

Stages of prenatal development

Zygote stage

Conception, or the union of the ovum (egg) and sperm, is the starting point for prenatal development. During the **zygote stage**, which lasts about two weeks, the zygote, or the cell that is formed at conception, divides many times and the internal organs begin to form. By the end of the first week, the zygote consists of about 100 cells. Many of the cells are arranged in two layers, one for the skin, hair, nervous system and sensory organs, and the other for the digestive and respiratory systems and glands. Near

the end of this stage, a third layer of cells appears, those that will eventually develop into the circulatory and excretory systems and muscles.

Embryo stage

The second stage of prenatal development, the **embryo stage**, begins at about two weeks and ends about eight weeks after conception (see Figure 12.1).

During this stage, the zygote is transformed into an embryo and development occurs at a rapid pace. Within a month after conception, a heart has begun to beat, a tiny brain has started to function, and most of the major body structures are beginning to form. By the end of this stage, the major features that define the human body – the arms, hands, fingers, legs, toes, shoulders, head and eyes – are discernible. Behaviourally, the embryo can react reflexively to stimulation. For example, if the mouth is stimulated, the embryo moves its upper body and neck. This stage is also noteworthy because it is here that the embryo is most susceptible to chemicals that can cause birth defects. These chemicals include drugs such as alcohol or toxins produced by diseases such as German measles, and are called **teratogens** (from the Greek *teras*, meaning 'monster').

Sexual development begins during the embryo stage. The determining factor for sex is the Y chromosome, which is contributed by the male parent at conception. If it is present, the embryo will become a male (XY); if it is not, it will become a female (XX). Early in prenatal development, the embryo develops a pair of gonads that will become either ovaries or testes (the word 'gonad' comes from the Greek *gonos*, meaning 'procreation'). If a Y chromosome is present, a gene located on it causes the production of a chemical signal that makes the gonads develop into testes. Otherwise, the gonads become ovaries.

The development of the other sex organs is determined by the presence or absence of testes. If testes are present, they begin secreting a class of sex hormones known as **androgens** (*andros* in Greek means 'man'; *gennan* means 'to produce') which bring about the development of the male internal sex organs, the penis and the scrotum. Thus, these hormones are absolutely necessary for the development of a male. The most important androgen is testosterone and in Chapter 13 we will see how this hormone is involved in other behaviours such as dominance and aggression.

In contrast, the development of female sex organs (uterus, vagina and labia) occurs naturally, it does not need to be stimulated by a hormone. If the gonads completely fail to develop, the foetus becomes female, with normal female sex organs. Of course, lacking ovaries, such a person cannot produce ova. See Figure 12.2.

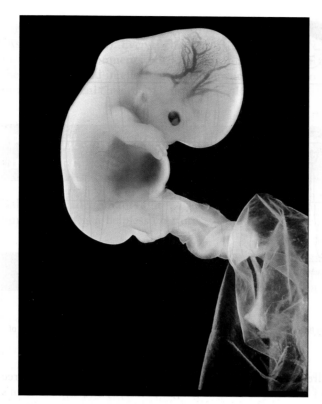

Figure 12.1 As this photograph of a six-week-old foetus illustrates, most of the major features that define the human body are present near the end of the embryonic stage of development (which starts at about two weeks and ends about eight weeks after conception).

Source: Neil Harding/Getty Images.

Foetal stage

The final stage of prenatal development is the **foetal stage**, which lasts about seven months. It officially begins with the appearance of bone cells and ends with birth. At the end of the second month of pregnancy, the foetus is about 3 cm long and weighs about 28 g. By the end of the third month, the development of major organs is completed and the bones and muscles are beginning to develop. The foetus is now 7–8 cm long and weighs about 90 g. The foetus may show some movement, especially kicking.

By the end of the fourth month, the foetus is about 18 cm long and weighs about 180 g. It is also now sleeping and waking regularly. Foetal movements also become strong enough to be felt by the mother, and the heartbeat is strong enough to be heard through a stethoscope. During the sixth month, the foetus grows to over 33 cm long and weighs almost 1 kg. The seventh month is a critical month because if the foetus is born prematurely at this point, it has a fair chance of surviving. However, foetuses mature at different rates, and some 7-month-old foetuses may be mature enough to survive whereas others may not.

During the last two months of prenatal development, the foetus gains weight at the rate of about 0.2 kg per week. On average, the foetus is about 50 cm long and weighs about 2.8 kg at the end of this period. The foetus is now ready to be born. Figure 12.3 shows how the body's shape changes from the embryo stage to adulthood.

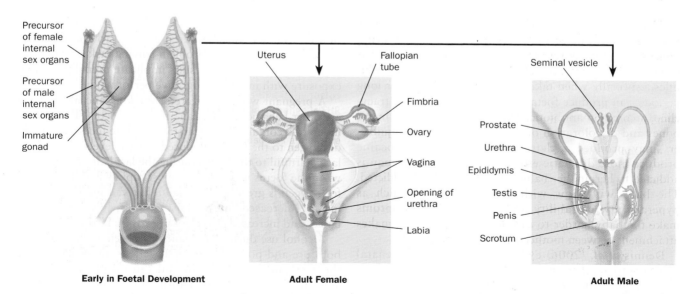

Figure 12.2 Differentiation and development of the sex organs.

Controversies in Psychological Science – *Continued*

and control stimulus. Greater sucking is meant to indicate greater interest or attention. Newborns show greater evidence of sucking when they hear their mother's voice or when they are presented with melodies or stories they were exposed to in the womb (DeCasper and Fifer, 1980; DeCasper *et al.*, 1994).

Another aspect of discriminatory learning that appears to occur prenatally is olfactory learning. Newborns are more attracted to the odour of amniotic fluid than other, unfamiliar odours (Schaal et al., 1995), and given a choice between a breast covered in amniotic fluid and one covered with an unfamiliar fluid, they choose to suckle on the nipple coated with amniotic fluid (Winberg and Porter, 1998). Even the mother's eating pattern can influence this 'learning'. Mothers who were garlic eaters gave birth to infants who 'recognised' the odour of garlic (Hepper, 1995). A group of French researchers exposed 3–4-day-old infants to a novel odour (camomile) placed on the mother's nipple and measured whether they preferred this odour to the odour of breast milk or a new odour when tested later (Delaunay-El Allam *et al.*, 2006). Preference was measured via head orientation in a paired odour choice paradigm in which the babies were presented with two odours. (Infants orient, or move, towards the stimuli they prefer.)

Those exposed to the novel odour preferred that odour to a new odour (those not exposed did not show this preference).

When the infants were presented with maternal milk and camomile odours, those exposed to camomile found both equally attractive; those not exposed to camomile preferred the breast milk. The results show that even 4–day-old infants can learn to express preferences for odours to which they have been previously exposed.

Conclusion

Does all of this evidence suggest that the foetus is capable of cognition? This depends on what we mean by cognition. If this means the ability to discriminate between stimuli, then neonates do demonstrate cognitive ability. They may be able to distinguish between the phonetic patterns in two stories, one of which was read to them when they were in the womb, but they clearly did not learn anything about the content or meaning of the story. Their learning was at a basic, perhaps even reflex, level. The auditory system may have sensed the phonetic nature of the story, but the neonate may not have been consciously aware of this sensation. The evidence suggests that the foetus is not simply an inactive, non-behaving organism, but a responsive and potentially discriminating human being.

Brain development

The brain allows the infant to process information around it, to assimilate this material and to act on it. As you saw in Chapter 10, during childhood the brain exhibits a degree of considerable 'plasticity'. A child can quite quickly recover from localised brain injury or damage, to a significantly greater extent than can adults. If damage occurs between infancy and 6 or 7 years old, the function undertaken by the damaged region can recover speedily as long as adequate rehabilitation and support from family and friends are present (as you saw in Chapters 4 and 10). The case of Nico, the child who had half of his brain removed to prevent epileptic fits, exemplified this relatively sophisticated recovery.

Another important feature of brain development is myelination – the process whereby nerve fibres (the axons) an covered in a milky sheath (myelin) which assists the propagation of nerve impulses sent down these fibres. The most dramatic, and the fastest, changes in myelination occur between birth and 6 months; there is slightly slower change between the age of 12 and 24 months and then a period of stable myelination that progresses until early adulthood (Hermoye *et al*, 2006; Miller *et al*, 2003).

Reflecting the functions that the infant relies on first, myelination is fastest in regions of the brain responsible for basic motor behaviour, the pons and cerebellum. Figure 12.4 shows myelination's milestones through childhood.

A number of factors influence the rate at which our brain grows and can impair this growth in the critical early stages when the cells of the brain are beginning to develop and make connections with other neurons. A lack of stimulation at a very early age can lead to a significant dysfunction in the nervous system. The failure to stimulate the visual system in animals, for example, leads to long-term disruption of this system's functioning (Blakemore and Mitchell, 1973). Malnutrition, discussed earlier, can have serious consequences for brain development and intellectual functioning.

Until recently, much of what we knew about the development of the brain and its function came from post-mortem studies, studies of acquired brain damage or rare case studies of children deprived of stimulation such as Genie or the Wild Boy of Aveyron, as you saw in Chapter 10. Even then, these rare studies did not tell us precisely what occurred during brain development. The techniques described in Chapter 4, however, such as functional magnetic resonance imaging (fMRI) and MRI have

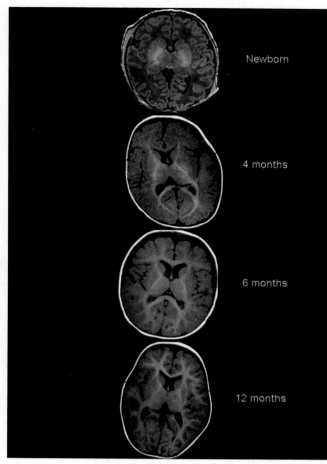

Figure 12.4 How myelination develops as the brain grows.
Source: Richmond, J. and Nelson, C.A. (2007). Accounting for change in declarative memory: A cognitive neuroscience perspective. *Development Review*, 27, 3, 349–73.

enabled researchers to compare stages of development across the lifespan both within a sample (that is, longitudinally) and between samples (cross-sectionally).

Giedd *et al.* (1999) compared the development of the brains of participants tested from age 4 to 20 years, at two-year intervals using MRI. They found that white matter increased steadily over time but the development of grey matter was slightly more irregular. Recall from Chapter 4 that grey matter is made up of blood vessels and neurons whereas white matter is made up of nerve fibres. The development of grey matter peaked just before adolescence and occurred in specific regions of the brain. Frontal and parietal lobe development peaked at 12 and 16 years, respectively, but occipital lobe development continued to 20 years. Although the initial sample was large (N=145), the number of individuals who underwent more than three scans was only 33, which suggests caution in interpreting the results. Nevertheless, the results suggest that development in some form continues past adolescence to adulthood.

Recently, an ambitious study mapped cortical development in 4–21-year-olds (Gogtay *et al.*, 2004). This study imaged grey matter changes every two years for 8–10 years and the findings can be seen in Figure 12.5. One of the principal observations is that higher order association cortices mature after lower order somatosensory and visual cortices. The regions of the brain considered to be the oldest were those which matured earliest (e.g. the entorhinal cortex, piriform cortex). Regions within the temporal lobe were the last to show grey matter maturity. An animated version of the development of these regions can be found at www.Pnas.org/cgi/content/full/0402680101/DC1.

Does the environment affect brain development?

see activity on mypsychlab

The nature–nurture controversy is one of the oldest in psychology. Normally, this controversy revolves around the origins of a particular behaviour, talent or personality trait. People ask, 'Is it caused by biological or social factors?', 'Is it innate or learned?', 'Is it a result of hereditary or cultural influences?', 'Should we look for an explanation in the brain or in the environment?' Almost always, biology, innateness, heredity and the brain are placed on the 'nature' side of the equation. Society, learning, culture and the environment are placed on the 'nurture' side. Rarely does anyone question whether these groups of items form a true dichotomy.

Studies using humans and laboratory animals show that interactions between hereditary and environmental factors – between nature and nurture – begin very early in life. Rosenzweig and his colleagues examined the effects of environmental stimulation on the development of the brain (see Rosenzweig, 1984, for a review) by dividing litters of rats and placing the animals into two kinds of environment: enriched and impoverished. The enriched environment contained items such as running wheels, ladders, slides and 'toys' that the animals could explore and manipulate. The experimenters changed these objects every day to maximise the animals' experiences and to ensure that they would learn as much as possible. The impoverished environments were plain cages in a dimly illuminated, quiet room.

The researchers found that the brains of rats raised in the enriched environment had a thicker cerebral cortex, a better blood supply, more protein content and more acetylcholine, a transmitter substance that appears to play an important role in learning.

What is the evidence from humans that environment is important for proper neuronal development? A group of researchers from Canada, Japan and Germany measured the electrical activity of the brains of twelve 4–6-year-olds as the participants listened to the tone of a violin or a

Figure 12.5 Scans showing the degree of brain development from 5 years old to 20 years old.

Source: from The Development of the brain, *Scientific American*, 241, pp. 106–17 (Cowan, W.M. 1979), with permission of Nelson H. Prentiss

burst of noise (Fujioka *et al.*, 2006). Over the course of a year, half of the children received music lessons; the other half did not. MEG was used to record brain activity at four points during the year.

The researchers found that a brain electrical potential recorded from the left hemisphere appearing 250 ms after the onset of the violin sound was larger, and appeared earlier, in those children who had received musical training. As you might expect, musical discrimination was better in the trained group, but so was non-musical working memory. The study suggests that musical training can influence the brain's ability to produce electrical potentials elicited by music, but not non-music, sounds.

In a natural experiment, Skeels (1966) had reported that children removed from orphanages and placed in mental institutions developed normal intelligence whereas those that stayed in orphanages did not. These marked effects of environment on cognitive development have been seen in a very real context. According to UNICEF, 1.5 million children in Central and Eastern Europe are in orphanages, as a result of war. An estimated 10–20 per 1,000 children between 0 and 18 years of age in Bulgaria, Russia and Romania and 5–10 per 1,000 in Poland, Hungary, Moldova, Lithuania, Latvia and Estonia are institutionalised (Brown *et al.*, 2004). In 2004, 23,000 international adoptions were made in the US, and most of

the children came from Eastern Europe, Russia and China (Nelson, 2007).

Many of the institutions may not encourage or nurture a child's intellectual ability. There is one caregiver per 15 children and there is little training for these caregivers. Sensory stimulation is basic – there is little patterned light, for example, and walls are usually painted white. Infants are left in cribs, rarely held, and strict dress codes are usually applied, as are eating times (Nelson, 2007). As the early Skeels study showed, institutionalisation's effects are not positive and these effects are seen in current institutions (Maclean, 2003). These negative effects include poor health, physical impairment, impaired brain development, delay in speech and language, inattention, hyperactivity, impaired cognition and behavioural problems (Johnson, 1997; 2000; Albers *et al.*, 1997; Rutter *et al.*, 1999).

Can the decline be reversed? Sir Michael Rutter and his colleagues from the Institute of Psychiatry, London, examined the extent of 'developmental catch-up' in a group of 111 Romanian orphans adopted into English families within 24 months of being born (Rutter and English and Romanian Adoptees Study Team, 1998). Compared with a control group of 52 English adopted children, the orphans showed poorer attainment of the typical developmental milestones. At 4 years of age, however, the orphans had 'caught up' with their English counterparts. The reason for such catching up is thought to be the brain's plasticity. According to Nelson (1999), neural plasticity 'can best be thought of as the subtle dance that occurs between the brain and the environment; specifically, it is the ability of the brain to be shaped by experience and, in turn, for this newly remolded brain to facilitate the embrace of new experiences'. It reflects the capacity of the brain to be flexibly organised and reorganised during the early years and seems to explain why brain injury in early childhood is more beneficial to cognitive development and speech than is injury sustained during adolescence or adulthood.

Two longitudinal studies of Romanian adoptees have found that lower IQ and higher degrees of behavioural and attachment problems are seen in children who spent eight months or more in an institution (Maclean, 2003). A comparison of Romanian adoptees and children adopted within the UK found that problems correlated with the length of institutionalisation (O'Connor and Rutter, 2000). The Bucharest Early Intervention Project has found similarly negative effects (Zeanah *et al.*, 2003). Children removed from institutions and fostered, however, appeared to show some improvement.

In terms of brain development, institutionalisation appears to be harmful. Eight-year-old Romanian children who had been institutionalised for an average of 38 months (and had been placed at the institution by the age of 18 months) showed reduced brain metabolism in the frontal lobes and were impulsive and had attention deficits, compared to a group of 10-year-old children with epilepsy (Chugani *et al.*, 2001). Institutionalised children also show reduced EEG activity (Marshall *et al.*, 2004).

Several factors can influence these outcomes – the time at which a child was placed in an institution, the length of stay and the quality of the institutional environment. But the problem with institutionalised children in Eastern Europe looks set to extend to elsewhere. Nelson (2007), for example, notes that Wasil Noor, Deputy Minister of Social Welfare in Afghanistan; has indicated than there are 1.6 million orphans in Afghanistan; 10,000 of these are living in institutions. If there ever was a case for using psychological research to improve the lot of a human being, it would be this.

Motor development

At birth, the infant's most important movements are reflexes – automatic movements in response to specific stimuli. The most important reflexes are the rooting, sucking and swallowing responses. If a baby's cheek is lightly touched, they will turn their head towards the direction of the touch (the rooting response). If the object makes contact with the baby's lips, the baby will open its mouth and begin sucking. When milk or any other liquid enters the mouth, the baby will automatically make swallowing movements. These reflexes are important for the baby's survival and for an infant's social development.

Normal motor development follows a distinct pattern, which appears to be dictated by maturation of the muscles and the nervous system. **Maturation** refers to any relatively stable change in thought, behaviour or physical growth that is due to the ageing process and not to experience. Although individual children progress at different rates, their development follows the same basic maturational pattern. Development of motor skills requires two ingredients: maturation of the child's nervous system and practice. Development of the nervous system is not complete at birth; considerable growth occurs during the first several months. In fact, some changes are still taking place in early adulthood.

Particular kinds of movement must await the development of the necessary neuromuscular systems. But motor development is not merely a matter of using these systems once they develop. Instead, physical development of the nervous system depends, to a large extent, on the baby's own movements while interacting with the environment. In turn, more complex movements depend on further development of the nervous system (Thelen, 1995). There is evidence that increased locomotion at 9 months is associated with more flexible memory. Crawlers, for example, are better able to imitate a set of actions when the original context in which these actions occurred is changed (Herbert *et al.*, 2007).

Perceptual development

If we want to study how older children or adults perceive the world, we can simply ask them about their experiences. We can determine how large an object must be for them to see it or how loud a sound must be for them to hear it. But we cannot talk to infants and expect to get any answers; we must use their non-verbal behaviour as an indicator of what they can perceive. Newborn infants indicate their taste preferences by facial expression and by choosing to swallow or not to swallow different liquids. When an infant is given a sweet liquid, the face relaxes in an expression rather like a smile; but when it is given a sour or bitter liquid, the face indicates displeasure. Newborn infants can even learn to recognise particular odours. Sullivan *et al.* (1991) presented 1-day-old infants with a citrus odour and then gently stroked them. The next day, these infants (but not control infants) turned towards a cotton swab containing the odour that had been paired with the stroking.

Most investigations of the perceptual abilities of newborn infants have taken advantage of the fact that babies have good control of movements of their head, eyes and mouth. We will look at the results of some of these studies next.

Perception of patterns

The visual perceptual abilities of infants can be studied by observing their eye movements as visual stimuli are shown to them. A harmless spot of infrared light, invisible to humans, is directed onto the baby's eyes. A special television camera, sensitive to infrared light, records the spot and superimposes it on an image of the display that the baby is looking at. The technique is precise enough to determine which parts of a stimulus the baby is scanning. For example, Salapatek (1975) reported that a 1-month-old infant tends not to look at the inside of a figure. Instead, the baby's gaze seems to be 'trapped' by the edges.

By the age of 2 months, the baby scans across the border to investigate the interior of a figure. Before the age of 2 months, infants seem to be more concerned with the contours of visual stimuli and rarely attend to internal features. This is called the **externality effect** (Bushnell, 1979). One reason for the externality effect could be that the infant's visual system is developing and does not possess the acuity or contrast sensitivity (the ability to discriminate between degrees of shade) necessary to perceive complex stimuli. Figure 12.6 shows how babies in the early weeks of life prefer to examine the periphery of a stimulus and stare at areas of high contrast (such as hairline or the chin of the face). At around 2 months, the child inspects the internal features of the stimulus, such as the features of the face (Bronson, 1991).

At around 3 weeks of age, newborns will prefer to look at chequerboards made up of large squares rather than smaller ones; at around 8 to 14 weeks, the preference shifts to the small squares (Brennan *et al.*, 1966). See Figure 12.7 for an example of the stimuli the newborns prefer at different ages.

One reason for this difference in preference may be due to the development of contrast sensitivity. A chequerboard with large squares, for example, will show great contrast because the white and the black blocks are big and, therefore, contrast with each other clearly. Small squares on a chequerboard allow little opportunity for contrast and the newborn may perceive these as a blur.

The work by Salapatek and his colleagues suggests that at the age of 1 or 2 months, babies are probably not perceiving complete shapes; their scanning strategy is limited to fixations on a few parts of the object at which they are looking. Their ability to focus on stimuli, and their visual acuity (the ability to discriminate elements within a stimulus) is relatively poor.

Infants can see objects at 6 metres that adults can at 200 (Courage and Adams, 1990). However, by 3 months, babies show clear signs of pattern recognition and the visual system develops quite rapidly. At 3 months, the babies' ability to focus is as good as adults'. Newborns show evidence of colour preference – they prefer to look at coloured stimuli rather than grey ones – but their ability to discriminate between individual colours is poor. The ability to discriminate between colours, however, is seen by 2 months (Brown, 1990) and this improves over the next three months.

Face perception at birth

Perhaps one of the most salient perceptual features of infant development is the gradual shift in preference from simple stimuli to patterned ones. For example, newborns prefer to look at stimuli that resemble the human face than at stimuli that do not (Rosser, 1994), and they prefer to look at scrambled faces than at a black and white oval stimulus (Fantz, 1961).

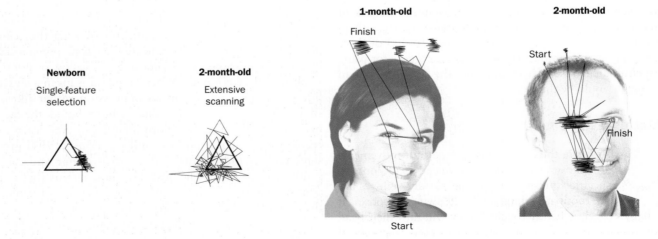

Figure 12.6 The ways in which an infant scans a face at 1 month and 2 months old.

Source: Adapted from Salapatek, P., Pattern perception in early infancy. In L.B. Cohen and P. Salapatek (eds) *Infant Perception: From sensation to cognition*. New York: Academic Press, 1975. Copyright 1975, with permission from Elsevier.

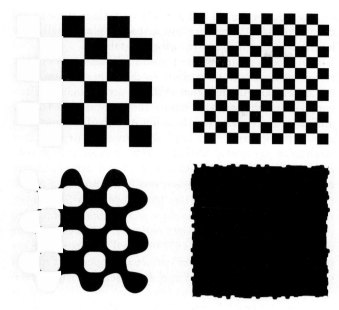

Figure 12.7 How the young infant perceives contrast. The two images at the bottom represent how the two images at the top, which differ in contrast, appear to young infants.

Source: Adapted from Banks, M.S. and Salapatek, P., Infant visual perception. In M.M. Haith and J.J. Campos (eds) *Handbook of Child Psychology. Vol. 2: Infancy and developmental psychobiology* (4th edn). New York: Wiley, 1983. Copyright © 1983, this material is used by permission of John Wiley & Sons, Inc.

As Chapter 6 showed, perceiving and recognising faces seems to rely on different perceptual mechanisms from those that allow us to recognise and perceive objects. At 2 years of age, infants show a preference for natural face arrangements rather than face arrangements that have disorganised features, which suggests that they show evidence of familiarity with the human face (Fantz, 1961). There are two hypotheses regarding the way in which young infants perceive faces and other visual stimuli. The first, the sensory hypothesis, suggests that visual perception occurs in two stages (Kleiner, 1993). The first involves the infant

Young infants' visual acuity is poor. The figure on the right is how the figure on the left would be perceived by a newborn.
Source: © DK Picture Library

comparing stimuli for contrast. If these stimuli are similar, then a second stage – the analysis of structure – takes place. This theory, therefore, suggests that if sensory characteristics are similar or identical, then preference for a stimulus will depend on the comparison of structure.

A competing hypothesis, the structural hypothesis, suggests that infants show a preference for face-like arrangements over non-face arrangements not because of the differences in the sensory properties of these stimuli but because infants have a specific device that contains information about the structural features of people's faces (Johnson and Morton, 1991). Johnson and Morton referred to this device which allows children to orient towards face-like stimuli as 'conspec'. Conspec is involved in perceiving the spatial relations between features of a face. For example, this device is responsible for perceiving that a cartoon face has elements in the right place to represent the mouth and eyes. Because conspec is a visual/perceptual device, it has a neural basis (in a subcortical structure called the superior colliculus, which guides the infant's attention to visual patterns). Another process allows the infant to learn about faces because they are guided towards paying attention to them – this is called 'conlearn'. Conlearn is thought to be a cortical function because it involves more sophisticated processing of information.

Current evidence is inconsistent regarding which hypothesis is correct, although the structural hypothesis has been successfully tested (Valenza *et al.*, 1996). Umilta and his colleagues, for example, presented healthy newborns with a variety of different face stimuli in a series of experiments. The aim of the experiments was to discover whether the sensory properties of faces accounted for babies' orienting response or whether the arrangement of features in faces was the most important determinant of orienting (Umilta *et al.*, 1996; Simion *et al.*, 1998). In one experiment, newborns were presented with two stimuli: one with facial features in correct arrangement, the other in a different order. The babies preferred to look at the correctly arranged stimulus (Umilta *et al.*, 1996). When face-like patterns were presented which differed only in their degree of sensory salience – the 'eyes' and 'nose' were either blobs or the outline of blobs – babies preferred to look at the outlined blobs.

In a further experiment, the researchers found that the babies also preferred stimuli whose sensory properties were pronounced. The researchers presented newborns with a face-like stimulus and a non-face-like stimulus that had optimal sensory properties but had features arranged in a different way. The structural hypothesis states that babies would prefer the correctly structured face to that which is incorrectly structured but visually more stimulating. In this experiment, newborns preferred to look at the face-like stimulus, thus providing evidence for the structural explanation of babies' preference for faces.

It was once thought that, up to the age of 10, children processed faces analytically – they looked at the individual features of a face when trying to recognise it. After this age, they began processing faces configurally – looking at the relations between features on a face in order to recognise it (Carey and Diamond, 1977). Research suggests that this is not the case and that both adults and children process faces configurally (Flin, 1985; Baenninger, 1994).

There is an improvement in face recognition with age, however (Itier and Taylor, 2004). The N170 **event-related potential (ERP)**, for example, appears to be associated with face recognition rather than general object recognition. It also appears to be larger, or delayed, when recognising inverted rather than upright faces (the former is difficult and is thought to be processed featurally rather than configurally). (The N170 is an evoked potential – described in Chapter 4 – that is seen approximately 170 milliseconds after the onset of a stimulus.)

Earlier ERP waves, such as the P100, which reflect sensory processing, were elicited in even very young children when viewing faces. However, the appearance of the N170 elicited by inverted faces started from mid-childhood (mid-teens), suggesting that the ERP data reflect maturational development in the neural systems that allows us to recognise faces.

The ability to see faces as wholes can be disrupted by visual deprivation during childhood (LeGrand et al., 2004). A group of 12 right-handed children who had been treated for bilateral congenital cataracts (they had been deprived of sight in early childhood but had recovered the sense) was asked to say whether the top halves of two faces were the same when the bottom halves were different. In a second condition, the top and bottom halves were misaligned so that the bottom half appeared to have been moved half way along the page. Normal individuals had difficulty in making this decision, but improved when the top and bottom halves were misaligned, suggesting that they processed the face holistically, as a whole. Children who had been deprived of sight, however, showed no evidence of holistic processing and performed better than controls when the top and bottom halves were aligned – they were 20 per cent more accurate and 175 ms faster. This suggests that holistic face processing can be disrupted by visual deprivation that can last for as little as three months.

Perception of space

The ability to perceive three-dimensional space and ability to judge the distance of objects from each other (depth perception) comes at an early age. Gibson and Walk (1960) placed 6-month-old babies on what they called a visual cliff – a platform containing a chequerboard pattern (see Figure 12.8). The platform adjoined a glass shelf mounted several feet over a floor that was also covered by the chequerboard pattern. Most babies who could crawl would not venture out onto the glass shelf. The infants acted as if they were afraid of falling.

You saw in Chapter 6 that several different types of cue in the environment contribute to depth perception. One cue arises from the fact that each eye gets a slightly different view of the world (Poggio and Poggio, 1984). The ability to perceive the world using information from both eyes – binocular depth cues – emerges at around 2–3 months of age and improves rapidly thereafter. Both eyes need to be properly aligned in order for depth perception to occur properly. If one eye is out of alignment, a condition called strabisimus arises (cross-eyedness). However, the infant usually never develops stereoscopic vision, even if the eye movements are later corrected by surgery on the eye muscles. Banks et al. (1975) studied infants whose eye movement deficits were later corrected surgically. If surgery occurred before 3 years of age, stereoscopic vision developed; if the surgery occurred later, it did not. This suggests that there is a critical period for the development of aspects of the visual system: if the aspect is developing, it can be modified; if it is complete, modification is not possible.

Other cues, such as kinetic depth cues and pictorial depth cues (such as those used by artists to draw in three dimensions and which allow us to view a receding railtrack as receding), also improve with age. For example, at the age of 3–4 weeks, babies will blink if an object looms towards them (Nanez, 1987).

The development of depth perception appears to be closely allied with motor development because the child's movement (especially of the head) helps the child to locate objects and helps them navigate their way around the environment. Babies who have considerable experience of crawling are more anxious about crossing the visual cliff than are those with little crawling experience (Bertenthal et al., 1984). These experienced crawlers are also better able to remember the location of objects and to find hidden objects (Bai and Bertenthal, 1992).

Figure 12.8 A visual cliff. The child does not cross the glass bridge.

Cognitive development in infancy and childhood

As children grow, their nervous systems mature and they undergo new experiences. Perceptual and motor skills become more complex and children become more competent at executing them. Children learn to recognise particular faces and voices, begin to talk and respond to the speech of others, and learn how to solve problems. Infants as young as 13 months are even able to form memories of specific events they experience (Bauer, 1997). In Chapter 10, you saw how psychologists and linguists have studied the development of language, written and spoken, from infancy onwards. This section considers our current understanding of the development of two other major aspects of cognitive development: memory and thinking.

Development of memory

Memory development in infancy

Memory is a difficult process to study in infants because they have yet to develop language and cannot give the sophisticated linguistic responses that older children can. It has been suggested that we have difficulty in retrieving memories from this period of our lives (before the age of 4 years) because our verbal ability and our memory structures are not yet sufficiently functional for us to be able to transfer material into long-term memory (Rubin, 1982; Eacott and Crawley, 1998). One-year-old infants, in particular, show rapid forgetting of material. The 'loss' of memory for events that occurs in infancy is called childhood or **infantile amnesia**.

Measures of memory in infancy

Because infants do not have sophisticated language, psychologists have had to devise other methods of studying the way in which their memory works.

Usually when presented with two stimuli, one of which is familiar and the other novel, infants who are older than 8–10 weeks will look longer at the novel stimulus. This suggests that the infant is capable of being distracted by stimuli which it perceives as new. The perception of a stimulus as new implies that there is a memory of the old stimulus which is used as a comparison.

A version of this task, the paired-comparison task, involves exposing the infant to a stimulus and then, after a short while, presenting it with the pre-exposed stimulus and a novel one. Memory is measured by monitoring the length of time the infant gazes at the stimuli (Fantz, 1958). For successful recognition, the length between the initial presentation and the subsequent recognition task depends on the infant's age. Nine-month-old infants can recognise a stimulus successfully after a delay of between 90 and 160 seconds, whereas 6-month-old infants require a much shorter interval.

Habituation paradigms involve the presentation of stimuli to infants repeatedly until they cease to make an orienting response to it, that is, they begin to ignore it because it does not seem to interest them. Attention tends to be paid to stimuli that are different from those that have been repeatedly presented. The longer the delay between the habituated stimulus and a novel stimulus, the more likely it is that the infant will produce a response to the habituated stimulus.

Operant conditioning makes use of the child's manipulation of mobiles. The child learns that if it moves its foot, which is attached to the mobile, the mobile moves and, therefore, catches its attention. The more vigorous the kicking, the greater the movement of the mobile (Rovee and Rovee, 1969). Technically, this paradigm is called the **mobile conjugate reinforcement paradigm**. A version of this paradigm involves a period of not being able to move the mobile, then a period of being able to move the mobile (via a ribbon attached to the child's foot) followed by a period of not being able to move the mobile again (Sullivan *et al.*, 1979). This indicates whether the child has learned the association between moving its foot and the resulting effect on the mobile (see Figure 12.9).

		First condition	Later condition
	Group A	Head turning causes mobile to move.	Head turning causes mobile to move.
		Babies learn to move head.	*Babies continue to move head.*
	Group B	Mobile remains stationary.	Head turning causes mobile to move.
			Babies do not learn to move head.
	Group C	Mobile intermittently moves on its own.	Head turning causes mobile to move.
			Babies do not learn to move head.

Figure 12.9 The importance of a responsive environment.
Source: Based on Watson, J.S. and Ramey, C.T., Reactions to responsive contingent stimulation in early infancy. *Merrill–Palmer Quarterly*, 1972, 18, 219–227.

Using this technique, researchers have found that young infants' recognition memory is relatively poor. Young infants of 2–3 months, although able to detect small changes in the mobile, are unable to recognise the mobile one day after training if the mobile has more than one element that has been changed, as measured by their reluctance to move the mobile (Rovee-Collier and Hayne, 1987). As the infant becomes older, however, the delay that can occur between presentations can become longer. For example, a 6-month-old infant can discriminate between a novel and a familiar stimulus after a delay of two weeks; an infant of 3 months can discriminate after a delay of only three days (Borovsky and Rovee-Collier, 1989).

The **deferred imitation paradigm** involves exposing the child to an adult who is performing some actions with a set of novel stimuli. After a delay, the 9–18-month-old infant is allowed to manipulate the objects used by the adult. Learning and memory is measured by the infant's ability to model its behaviour on the adult's (Meltzoff, 1988, 1995). If the toddler can understand instructions, it is given structured tasks, removed from the laboratory, returned again and asked to re-enact the activities it performed earlier. Memory performance for recently acquired actions (making a rattle) and familiar actions (putting a teddy to bed) is quite accurate (Bauer and Mandler, 1992; Mandler and McDonough, 1995).

Over the course of development from 1 to 2 years, the number of sequences of actions that the child can remember increases. At 20 months, for example, the child is able to remember three sequences (Bauer and Dow, 1994); at 24 months, the child can act out five (Bauer and Travis, 1993); at 30 months, the number of actions in the sequence can increase to eight. The finding that children can recall successively increasing series of steps with increasing age suggests that their memory capacity is increasing (or perhaps that their means of encoding is becoming more sophisticated and organised).

As age increases, so the delay between the initial learning period and recall sessions can also increase without any detriment to performance. By 14 months, for example, children have been found to be able to demonstrate the use of a series of observed props after a delay of one week (Meltzoff, 1988). The interesting question that arises from these findings is whether the child is engaging in imitation or in real reasoning. A recent study suggests that the child may be actually capable of reasoning, rather than imitating. Meltzoff's (1988) famous study of imitation learning in infants showed that when 14-month-old children watched an adult turn on a light box by touching the top of the box with the top of the head, two-thirds of the children attempted to switch on the light in this way a week later. None of the control group attempted to switch the light on in this way.

Gergely *et al.* (2002) repeated Meltzoff's study but instead of having the adult turn the light on with their head with hands free, they had adults either do the same as those in the Meltzoff study or had them occupy both hands. In the experiment, the hands-occupied condition was achieved by having adults wrap their arms and torso in a blanket. Twenty-seven infants viewed either the 'hands-free' or 'hands-occupied' adult switching on the light.

When the adult's hands were free, 69 per cent of infants used their heads to switch on the light; when the adult's hands were occupied, only 21 per cent of infants used their heads. The study suggests that infants may be capable of greater rationality than that implied in Meltzoff's seminal study. 'The early imitation of goal-directed actions', the authors conclude, 'is a selective, inferential process that involves evaluation of the rationality of the means in relation to the constraints of the situation.'

By around 3 months of age, the infant shows awareness of changes in its environment; by 6 months, it is able to remember temporal order of stimuli. At 8 months, it is able to recognise words spoken in a story that it heard a while before. For example, Jusczyk and Hohne (1997) exposed fifteen 8-month-old infants to three children's stories for ten days. After two weeks, infants heard words that either occurred frequently in the stories or did not occur frequently. The infants listened significantly longer to the words that had been part of the stories.

The findings of this study suggest that because a delay of two weeks had passed between exposure and recognition, the infant is already beginning to form long-term memories for words occurring in speech. This, of course, has implications for language development (as we saw in Chapter 10).

Memory in early childhood

Between the ages of 1 and 3 years, the child develops the rudimentary language that allows them to communicate and to express an awareness of memory (Bauer, 1997). This awareness of events experienced in the past is quite considerable. For example, a child of 3 years can recall a visit to McDonald's or report an event that occurred when they were 2 or younger (Nelson, 1986; Fivush *et al.*, 1987). When the child is prompted by an adult, the memory performance is even more impressive (Fivush, 1984; Bauer *et al.*, 1995). If the child is asked to act out the event, as opposed to providing a verbal report of it, they are able to recall twice as much information.

At this age, children's memory can be tested in more sophisticated ways than those used for very young infants. For example, two of the most commonly used measures of memory in young children involve object hiding and retrieval and the acting out of observed events. In the hidden object task, the child sees an object being hidden by an adult and after a delay is asked to retrieve it (DeLoache, 1984). In the observed actions task, the child is exposed to an adult performing a series of actions with props; either immediately after this, or after a delay (and, in both cases, without practice), the child is asked to act out this demonstration.

Children are able to perform such tasks, even at 1–2 years of age. Bauer and Dow (1994), for example, required 16- and 20-month-old infants to demonstrate a series of seen actions after a delay of one week. At the time of the initial exposure, the action was putting a child's toy character to bed; at the retrieval session (one week later), the props had changed to a small dog and a plastic crib. Although the props were changed, the performance of the demonstration after a week's delay was not significantly different.

Knowing where things are – spatial development at 2 years old

Toddlers are quite adept at demonstrating their knowledge of where an object is: very young children can use information about distance and geometry to determine the location of an object. However, this ability is tempered, especially in younger toddlers. This suggests that the neural mechanism that allows such location finding may be developing at this age. For example, when 16–36-month-old toddlers watch a toy being placed in a box and are then moved to the opposite side of the box and asked to find the toy, 22-month-old children are able to use landmarks in the room to guide their object location but younger children fail to do so (Newcombe et al., 1998). Two-year-old children forget more, after a delay between encoding and retrieval, than older infants, even when the effects of learning are kept constant (Bauer, 2006). This type of 'place learning' is thought to depend on the integrity of the hippocampus. When the context is changed or when a memory cue alters, infants remembering is impaired, perhaps because they interpret or perceive the cue and context as being a unitary representation, rather than considering both relatively and separately (Jones and Herbert, 2006). This ability to see relations between objects is thought to be attributable to the function of the hippocampus and this is not mature in infants.

Sluzenski et al. (2004) had 18–42-month-old infants complete tasks in which they had to remember multiple locations, learn the relations between objects and recall a learned location after a delay. For example, the two-location task involved the children observing two objects being hidden simultaneously in a box filled with sand. Whereas the performance of 18- and 24-month-old infants did not differ significantly when attempting to find the first toy, the 24-month-olds were better at finding

the second object. In another task, children were taught the spatial relation between two objects and were asked to search for one of these when another was revealed. Performance was poor in most of the children. In a retention task, children were asked to find an object after a delay between observing the object being hidden and retrieving it. The 18-month-olds performed more poorly than the other groups, especially the older ones.

The data suggest that specific changes in the ability to learn spatial relations occurs between 18 months and 24 months and beyond. While the authors were unable to measure hippocampal development and relate this to the changes they observe, they also note that the improvement they saw may be related to the development of structures surrounding the hippocampus.

Why does the child's memory improve dramatically from 1 to 4 years of age?

Three factors seem to account for the child's ability to recall information better with age: the formation of memory-related structures, the development of language and the development of metamemory, i.e. the realisation that using memory strategies will help the child to think and behave. The relative contribution of each is unclear but we know that the brain develops until the age of adolescence (and some parts become mature after this). Myelination, for example – the process whereby the axons of the brain become insulated and which allows them to transmit information to neurons more efficiently continues to adolescence – is correlated with speed of processing in children (Travis, 1998).

The development of language means that a child has the capability to encode material verbally instead of via some other representation such as visual representation. By the age of 3 years, for example, the child begins initiating conversation (Fivush et al., 1987). Interestingly, it has been suggested that it is not the verbal encoding of material per se that causes improvement in memory but the verbal expression of memory. That is, if a memory is verbally expressed, then this memory will be retained longer than if it had not been expressed (Nelson, 1993; Bauer and Wewerka, 1995).

It has also been suggested that the types of memory recalled from early and later infancy are dependent on whether the child is employing a narrative technique to give structure and meaning to events. Autobiographical memory develops later in infancy and this form of memory relies on the structuring and organisation of events to make them meaningful. Perhaps one reason why we can remember events as adults from the age of 4 years onwards but not before then is because we did not have a narrative structure in place before the age of 4 to give material meaning and depth (Nelson, 1993). This is quite a controversial idea.

The development of cognition: Jean Piaget

The most influential student of child development has been Jean Piaget (1896–1980), a Swiss psychologist, who viewed cognitive development as a maturational process. Piaget formulated the most comprehensive description of the process of cognitive development that we have. His conclusions were based on his observations of the behaviour of children – first, of his own children at home and, later, of other children at his Centre of Genetic Epistemology in Geneva. He noticed that children of similar age tend to engage in similar behaviours and to make the same kinds of mistakes in problem-solving. He concluded that these similarities are the result of a sequence of development that all normal children follow. Completion of each period, with its corresponding abilities, is the prerequisite for entering the next period.

According to Piaget, as children develop they acquire **cognitive structures** – mental representations or rules that are used for understanding and dealing with the world and for thinking about and solving problems. The two principal types of cognitive structure are schemata and concepts. **Schemata** ('schema' is the singular form) are mental representations or sets of rules that define a particular category of behaviour – how the behaviour is executed and under what conditions. A child is said to have a 'grasping schema' when they are able to grasp a rattle in their hand. Once they have learned how to grasp a rattle, they can then use the same schema to grasp other objects. A child has acquired a 'picking up schema' when they are able to lift the rattle from a surface.

Piaget suggested that as a child acquires knowledge of the environment, they develop mental structures called concepts – rules that describe properties of environmental events and their relations to other concepts. For example, concepts about the existence of various objects include what the objects do, how they relate to other objects, and what happens when they are touched or manipulated. Thus, an infant's cognitive structure includes concepts of such things as rattles, balls, crib slats, hands and other people.

Infants acquire schemata and concepts by interacting with their environment. According to Piaget, two processes help a child to adapt to its environment: assimilation and accommodation. **Assimilation** is the process by which new information is modified to fit existing schemata. For example, when a child moves a wooden block along a surface while making the rumbling sound of an engine, they have assimilated the wooden block into their schema of a car. **Accommodation** is the process by which old schemata are changed by new experiences. Accommodation produces either new schemata or changes in existing ones. For example, suppose that a young girl's concept of animal has three categories: doggies, kitties and teddies. If she sees a picture of a deer and calls it a kitty, she has assimilated the new information into an existing concept. However, if she decides that a deer is a new kind of animal, she will accommodate her animal concept to include the new category. Now this concept consists of doggies, kitties, teddies and deer.

Assimilation and accommodation are closely linked in that they both work together but there are periods in the child's life when it will assimilate more than it will accommodate (and vice versa). Piaget referred to this state as cognitive 'equilibrium'. When the child undergoes periods of quick and radical change, however, there is disequilibrium – new information does not match what the child knows and so the child has to accommodate the new information, rather than assimilate it. Once accommodation has taken place, the child returns to assimilation.

Piaget's four periods of cognitive development

Although development is a continuous process, the cognitive structures of children vary from age to age. We can make inferences about the rules that children of certain ages use to understand their environment and control their behaviour. Piaget divided cognitive development into four periods: sensorimotor, preoperational, concrete operational and formal operational. What a child learns in one period enables them to progress to the next period. This conception of stages was viewed as invariant – they always appeared in this order – and universal – they emerge in this way in all children. See Table 12.1 for a summary of Piaget's stages.

Table 12.1 The four periods of Piaget's theory of cognitive development

Period	Approximate age (years)	Major features
Sensorimotor	0–2	Object permanence; deferred imitation; rudimentary symbolic thinking
Preoperational	2–6 or 7	Increased ability to think symbolicaly and logically; egocentric; cannot yet master conservation problems
Concrete operational	6 or 7–11	Child can master conservation problems, can understand categorisation; cannot think abstractly
Formal operational	11 upwards	Child can think abstractly and hypothetically

The sensorimotor period

The **sensorimotor period**, which lasts for approximately the first two years of life, is the first stage in Piaget's theory of cognitive development. It is marked by an orderly progression of increasingly complex cognitive development ranging from reflexes to symbolic thinking. During this period, cognition is closely tied to external stimulation. An important feature of the sensorimotor period is the development of **object permanence**, the idea that objects do not disappear when they are out of sight. Until about 5 months of age, children appear to lose all interest in an object that disappears from sight – the saying 'out of sight, out of mind' seems particularly appropriate. In addition, cognition consists entirely in behaviour: thinking is doing.

At first, infants do not appear to have a concept for objects. They can look at visual stimuli and will turn their heads and eyes towards the source of a sound, but hiding an object elicits no particular response. At around 3 months, they become able to follow moving objects with their eyes. If an object disappears behind a barrier, infants will continue to stare at the place where the object has disappeared but will not search for it.

At around 5 months, infants can grasp and hold objects and gain experience with manipulating and observing them. They can also anticipate the future position of a moving object. If a moving object passes behind a screen, infants turn their eyes towards the far side of the screen, seeming to anticipate the reappearance of the object on the other side.

During the last half of their first year, infants develop much more complex concepts concerning the nature of physical objects. They grasp objects, turn them over and investigate their properties. By looking at an object from various angles, they learn that the object can change its visual shape and still be the same object. In addition, if an object is hidden, infants will actively search for it; their object concept now contains the rule of object permanence. For infants at this stage of development, a hidden object still exists. 'Out of sight' is no longer 'out of mind'.

By early in their second year, object permanence is well enough developed that infants will search for a hidden object in the last place they saw it hidden. However, at this stage infants can only keep track of changes in the hiding place that they can see. For example, if an adult picks up an object, puts it under a cloth, drops the object while their hand is hidden, closes the hand again and removes it from the cloth, infants will look for the object in the adult's hand. When they do not find the object there, they look puzzled or upset and do not search for the object under the cloth (see Figure 12.10).

Near the end of the sensorimotor period, two other interesting developments occur. First, children develop the ability to imitate actions that they have seen others per-

form, a behaviour that Piaget called **deferred imitation**. This behaviour is due to their increasing ability to form mental representations of actions that they have observed. These representations may then be recalled at a later time to direct particular imitative actions and symbolic play, such as pretending to feed a doll or taking a stuffed animal for a walk. Secondly, as having an imagination shows, 2-year-old children begin to think symbolically. They can use words to represent objects such as balls and animals. This is a critical developmental step because this skill is crucial to language development.

The preoperational period

Piaget's second period of cognitive development, the **preoperational period**, lasts from approximately age 2 to age 7 and involves the ability to think logically as well as symbolically. This period is characterised by rapid development of language ability and of the ability to represent

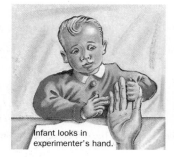

Object is in experimenter's hand.

Experimenter closes hand. . .

. . .puts hand under cloth. . .

. . .removes hand, leaving object under the cloth.

Infant looks in experimenter's hand.

Obviously upset, infant quits.

Figure 12.10 Object permanence. An infant will not realise that the object has been left under the cloth.

Source: Adapted from Bower, T.G.R., *Perception in Infancy* (2nd edn). San Francisco: W.H. Freeman, 1972.

things symbolically. The child arranges toys in new ways to represent other objects (for example, a row of blocks can represent a train), begins to classify and categorise objects, and starts learning to count and to manipulate numbers. By the age of $2^1/_2$ years, children have been shown to be able to treat objects such as kitchen utensils, bathroom items, animals, plants and so on as distinct categories of object (Bauer and Mandler, 1989).

Piaget asserted that development of symbolism actually begins during the sensorimotor period, when a child starts imitating events in his or her environment. For example, a child might represent a horse by making galloping movements with the feet or a bicycle by making steering movements with the hands. Symbolic representations like these are called signifiers: the motor act represents (signifies) the concept because it resembles either the movements that the object makes or the movements the child makes when interacting with the object.

Concepts can also be represented by words, which are symbols that have no physical resemblance to the concept; Piaget referred to such abstract symbols as signs. Signifiers are personal, derived from the child's own interactions with objects. Therefore, only the child and perhaps members of the immediate family will understand a child's signifiers. In contrast, signs are social conventions. They are understood by all members of a culture. A child who is able to use words to think about reality has made an important step in cognitive development.

Piaget's work demonstrated quite clearly that a child's representation of the world is different from that of an adult. For example, most adults realise that a volume of water remains constant when poured into a taller, narrower container, even though its level is now higher. However, early in the preoperational period, children will fail to recognise this fact; they will say that the taller container contains more water. The ability to realise that an object retains mass, number or volume when it undergoes various transformations is called **conservation**; the transformed object conserves its original properties.

Piaget concluded that the abilities to perceive the conservation of number, mass, weight and volume are attributes of increasing cognitive development. His studies showed number to be conserved by age 6, whereas conservation of volume did not occur until age 11. Presumably, conservation of number comes first because children can verify the stability of number once they learn to count, although conservation skill is seen in children who are not proficient counters (see Figure 12.11). This is an example of what Piaget called 'horizontal decalage' – the development of a skill within a period.

Another important characteristic of the preoperational period is **egocentrism**, or a child's belief that others see the world in precisely the way that they do. For example, a 3-year-old child may run to a corner, turn his back to you and cover his eyes in an attempt to hide during a game of hide and seek, not realising that he is still in full view. In a typical 'egocentric thinking' task, the child may be presented with models of three mountains which differ according to colour and features: some may have a cross on or snow or a house. A doll is placed at one end of the mountains and the child at the other. The child is then asked what they think the doll can see.

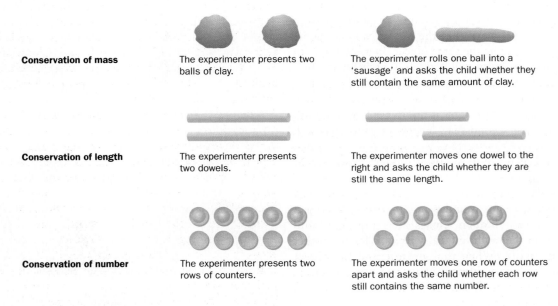

Conservation of mass	The experimenter presents two balls of clay.	The experimenter rolls one ball into a 'sausage' and asks the child whether they still contain the same amount of clay.
Conservation of length	The experimenter presents two dowels.	The experimenter moves one dowel to the right and asks the child whether they are still the same length.
Conservation of number	The experimenter presents two rows of counters.	The experimenter moves one row of counters apart and asks the child whether each row still contains the same number.

Figure 12.11 Various tests of conservation.

Source: Lefrancois, G.R., *Of Children: An introduction to child development*, Wadsworth (Lefrancois, G.R. 1983) with permission of Guy Lefrancois

Because giving a verbal response is difficult for the child, the child either selects the doll's view from ten images or is given models of the mountains and has to arrange them in such a way to represent the doll's viewpoint. Children aged 8–9 years perform poorly at this task, usually selecting the image that represents their, rather than the doll's, point of view. According to Piaget, the child was unable to 'decentre'. He concluded that the children 'really imagine that the doll's perspective is the same as their own' (p. 220; cited in Donaldson, 1978).

However, there have been challenges to Piaget's view of the child's cognitive development during this period. A significant series of studies, for example, has demonstrated that the child's egocentric thinking may not be as egocentric as Piaget suggested. If children are given familiar objects in the three mountains' task, for example, or are given alternative methods of giving a response – rather than choosing one of ten pictures which is difficult even for older children – even very young children show evidence that they can see viewpoints from another's perspective (Newcombe and Huttenlocher, 1992). If the difficulty and the unfamiliarity of a task are eliminated, therefore, children during this period do better than Piaget's conception would predict.

Young children also show evidence that they can engage in non-egocentric thinking: they change their language, depending on the context in which they find themselves. For example, 2-year-olds use shorter sentences when talking to their peers than when talking to adults suggesting that they are responsive to those interacting with them and possibly modify their own linguistic output accordingly (Gelman and Shatz, 1978).

Simplification of the tasks Piaget used has also shown that children in this period are capable of conservation. If the number of conserved items is reduced from six or seven to three, even 3-year-old children can perform the task correctly (Gelman, 1972). In one example of a conservation task, sugar is dissolved in water and the child is asked whether the sugar still exists. Although Piaget's studies suggested that children incorrectly responded that the sugar did not exist, recent research suggests that 3–5-year-olds are capable of responding that the sugar exists and can be tasted but that its particles are too small to be visible (Au *et al.*, 1993).

Children also seem to be more capable of understanding transformations than Piaget's theory suggests. For example, in an experiment where a dry cup becomes a wet cup or a wet cup becomes a dry one, 3-year-old children have difficulty in picking out the object that caused the cup to change its appearance (from water, cloth, feather), but 4-year-olds could perform the task correctly (McCabe and Peterson, 1988).

see activity on mypsychlab

The period of concrete operations

Piaget's third stage of cognitive development, the **period of concrete operations**, spans approximately ages 7 to 11 and involves children's developing understanding of the conservation principle and other concepts such as categorisation. Its end marks the transition from childhood to adolescence. This period is characterised by the emergence of the ability to perform logical analysis, by an increased ability to empathise with the feelings and attitudes of others, and by an understanding of more complex cause-and-effect relations. The child becomes much more skilled at the use of symbolic thought. For example, even before the period of concrete operations, children can arrange a series of objects in order of size and can compare any two objects and say which is larger. However, if they are shown that stick A is larger than stick B and that stick B is larger than stick C, they cannot infer that stick A is larger than stick C.

During the early part of this period, children become capable of making such inferences. However, although they can reason with respect to concrete objects, such as sticks that they have seen, they cannot do so with hypothetical objects. For example, they cannot solve the following problem: Judy is taller than Frank and Frank is taller than Carl. Who is taller, Judy or Carl? The ability to solve such problems awaits the next period of cognitive development.

The period of formal operations

During the **period of formal operations**, which begins at about age 11, children become capable of abstract reasoning. They can now think and reason about hypothetical objects and events. They also begin to understand that under different conditions their behaviour can have different consequences. Formal operational thinking is not 'culture free' – it is influenced by cultural variables, especially formal schooling (Piaget, 1972; Rogoff and Chavajay, 1995). Without exposure to the principles of scientific thinking, such as those taught at school, people do not develop formal operational thinking.

The period is also critical in another way. At around age 11 the child is beginning the journey into adolescence where physical, bodily changes are significant and where a type of formal operational egocentrism, the ability to imagine what others think about them and the belief that their views of others are shared by others, develops (Inhelder and Piaget, 1955). Teenagers seem to have two distinct views of themselves and others, believing that they are constantly on stage, performing to an imaginary audience and being the focus of attention (Elkind and Bowen, 1979), and believing that others are always talking or thinking about them. They feel they are special. These two views peak during this period and decline steadily throughout the adolescent years.

Although Piaget held that there are four periods of cognitive development, not all people reach the formal operational period, even as physically mature adults. In some tribal cultures, formal operations do not emerge at all, probably because there is a lack of opportunity to engage in hypothetico-deductive reasoning (Gellaty, 1987). In some cases, adults show formal operational thought only in their areas of expertise. Thus, a mechanic may be able to think abstractly while repairing an engine but not while solving maths or physics problems. A physicist may be able to reason abstractly when solving physics problems but not while reading poetry. However, once an individual reaches that level of thinking, they will always, except in the case of brain disease or injury, perform intellectually at that level.

However, a child does not necessarily reach this stage during the adolescent years. Some are capable of abstract reasoning at a much earlier age (6 years old) if the variables that are thought about are not many. The difficulty in the early years appears to revolve around understanding contradictory information. For example, Moshman and Franks (1986) found that if children younger than 10 years were presented with a reasoning problem that was unusual, for example:

> Dogs are bigger than elephants
>
> Elephants are bigger than mice
>
> Therefore, dogs are bigger than mice

they regarded the reasoning as illogical, probably because their knowledge of concrete objects (dogs, elephants, mice) interfered with general formal reasoning which required an understanding of the reasoning process rather than the objects referred to in the problem.

Play and its role in social and cognitive development

Play is often regarded as a social behaviour – children interact with each other or with objects in the environment in an enjoyable and positive way – but it is also a cognitive one in which children learn about these objects and the objects' relationship to the environment. Babies as young as 1 year begin to play with objects, although in an unsophisticated way. For example, objects may be picked up, sucked and thrown, but little more than this. However, as the infant grows older, it begins to play with objects in a more symbolic way. Through play, it appears to show evidence of developing cognition.

At 12–18 months, infants begin to play with objects symbolically – they pretend that the object is something else. For example, an object (a pencil) used for one purpose (writing), is used to carry out another behaviour (combing

the hair) (Belsky and Most, 1981). About half of the infants who reach 14 months can pretend that they are sleeping by putting their head on a pillow, but it takes a further six months before they are able to use a doll to signify sleeping by putting the doll to bed (Watson and Fischer, 1977). At the age of 4 years, children use play to find out more about their environment and the social values of the environment around them as well as its customs and traditions.

According to Piaget, play is the opposite of imitation. When children imitate, accommodation predominates over assimilation; when children play, the opposite occurs. According to Vygotsky (1976/1933), the meaning of an object in children's play completely usurps its actual physical meaning. In the comb and pencil example, the pencil had become the comb – it combed hair; it did not write messages on paper. This creativity in the child's use of objects increases in the presence of a parent but only if the parent joins in (Slade, 1987), which indicates that the parent's involvement in the child's developing imagination and exploration of objects is an important one.

Because of the complex nature of the activity, Piaget (1945/1951) saw play as a cognitive activity rather than a social one. He gave it the name **symbolic play** because infants used objects to symbolise other objects or used them to symbolise other activities (e.g. the pencil symbolised a comb). The transition from play to symbolic or pretend play occurred in two stages, according to Piaget.

The first stage occurs when the infant is between 0 and 4 years and, in typically Piagetian fashion, this stage is further subdivided into three substages. In substage 1, the child develops an idea of what an object is and preserves its unique characteristics; this enables it to project these characteristics onto other objects. The infants might observe a behaviour in those around them, develop a schema of those objects they observe and translate this schema into a different type of behaviour. For example, a child may observe an adult cleaning with one object but use another to carry out the same activity.

In substage 2, the child shows evidence of independence from the prop/object they use. That is, the knowledge of an object precedes the use of the object. A brush placed above the head is symbolically treated as an umbrella. The child not only has an awareness of what umbrellas do but is also able to use another object to signify the use of an umbrella. Another example is where the child plays hide and seek but plays the part of the person doing the hiding.

In substage 3, various actions are combined together to form an ensemble of meaning. This example comes from Piaget's study of one of his daughters: a shoe box is used as a bath, and a blade of grass is used as a thermometer. The child dips the blade into the shoe box and declares it too hot; a short while later, she repeats the action and declares that it is just right. This degree of imagination appears to occur at the same time as the creation of imaginary characters in the child's world. At this stage, this type of symbolic play becomes more organised.

How would you go about developing a test for determining which of Piaget's periods of cognitive development a child is in? What kinds of activity would you include in such a test and how would the child's behaviour with respect to those activities indicate the child's stage of development?

Evaluation of Piaget's contributions

Piaget's theory has had an enormous impact on research in developmental psychology (Beilin, 1990; Halford, 1990). However, not all of Piaget's conclusions have been accepted uncritically. One criticism levelled at Piaget is that he did not always define his terms operationally. Consequently, it is difficult for others to interpret the significance of his generalisations. Many of his studies lack the proper controls. Thus, much of his work is not experimental, which means that cause-and-effect relations among variables cannot be identified with certainty. Perhaps the greatest criticism of Piaget has been reserved for his periods of cognitive development. Attempts to verify the timetable of Piaget's periods of cognitive development have met with little success (Flavell, 1992). Children can be trained to perform Piaget's tasks correctly so that a child who should be operating at a level occurring in an early period might correctly attempt cognitive tasks that characterise a later developmental period (Beilin, 1978). This illustrates a problem with Piaget's theorising: there are not many abilities that are completely absent in one specific period and present in another. One view suggests that the child has the capacity for all of these abilities but they are present at different levels in different children, which would account for variations in children's cognitive performance.

Subsequent research has suggested that a child's ability to conserve various physical attributes occurs earlier than Piaget had supposed. Piaget also appears to have underestimated the ability of young children to understand another person's point of view, as you saw in the section on the pre-operational period. For example, Flavell *et al.* (1981) found that even a 3-year-old child realises that a person looking at the opposite side of a card to that which the child is examining will not see the same thing. Clearly, the child recognises the other person's point of view. Flavell and colleagues also showed that even very young children can tell the difference between appearance and reality. They presented a series of disguised items and asked children what the objects really were (Flavell *et al.*, 1989).

Piaget's prediction would be that children would identify the disguise, rather than the object underneath. However, Flavell *et al.* found that 3-year-old children were capable of correctly identifying the disguised object. They were also able to distinguish between the way an object felt and how it actually was. For example, although an ice cube held by a rubber glove was not perceived as cold, children were able to understand that the cube still maintained the property of coldness. Therefore, the children showed evidence of logical thinking before they reached the concrete operations period.

Piaget also largely discounted experience in his theory of development; periods would develop naturally and in order and did not depend on experience. However, culture does seem to have a significant effect on cognitive skills such as conservation. The children of the Hausa tribe in Nigeria, for example, do not go to school and do not understand conservation principles until they are around 11 years old (Fahrmeier, 1978), suggesting that some degree of daily activity involving conservation may be necessary before this concept is mastered.

Finally, it is interesting to discover that around 40–60 per cent of students fail Piaget's formal operations problems (Keating, 1979). Again, this may be because people are better able to reason abstractly with information that is familiar to them than with unfamiliar Piagetian information. Despite the fact that Piaget's method of observation led him to underestimate some important abilities, his meticulous and detailed observations of child behaviour have been extremely important in the field of child development and have had a great influence on educational practice. With Vygotsky (see below), Piaget has made probably the greatest contribution to our understanding of child development.

Vygotsky's sociocultural theory of cognitive development

Piaget's theory of cognitive development focuses on children's interactions with the physical world – children form internal representations of the world based on their experiences with physical objects. Another theorist, the Russian psychologist Lev Vygotsky, agreed that experience with physical objects is an important factor in cognitive development, but he disagreed that this is the whole story. Instead, he argued that the culture in which one lives also plays a significant role in cognitive development: the child's cognitive development was promoted by the interaction between the child and its social environment (Vygotsky, 1987). Although Vygotsky's work was conducted during the 1920s and early 1930s (he died of tuberculosis in 1934, aged 37), his writings have had a major impact on more recent conceptualisations of cognitive development during childhood (Smith *et al.*, 1997).

Vygotsky argued that children do not learn to think about the physical world in a vacuum. The cultural context – what they hear others say about the world and how they see others interact with physical aspects of the world – matters. Thus parents, teachers, friends and many others help children to acquire ideas about how the world works. We would expect, then, that the development of children raised in non-stimulating environments devoid of stimulating interactions with others, with books, and even television, would lag behind that of children raised in more stimulating environments. And this is exactly what has been found.

Vygotsky further believed that children's use of speech also influences their cognitive development. Piaget had argued that the private speech that children engage in was egocentric – children were unable to imagine others' points of view – and that this conversation would be rattled off as if in a stream of consciousness. As the child interacts with peers and as the child grows older and interacts with adults, this private speech is eliminated and the child engages in social speech – they listen to others talking and respond appropriately. Children up to about age 7 can often be observed talking to themselves. While drawing in a colouring book, a child may say, 'I'll colour her arms and face green and her trousers black.' Piaget would interpret such talk as being egocentric and non-social because it is directed at the self, because it may not make sense to a listener, and because its purpose is not to communicate information.

Vygotsky's (1934/1962) interpretation was different. He argued that the child's talk reflected the formulation of a plan that would serve as a guide to subsequent behaviour. According to Vygotsky, language is the basis for cognitive development, including the ability to remember, solve problems, make decisions and formulate plans. As children became better at tasks that involved attention, memorisation, planning and so on, then their private vocal speech would disappear and would be internalised instead. Studies have shown that children engage more in private speech if a task is challenging, if it makes them make mistakes or results in confusion about what to do next (Berk, 1992, 1994). The children who use such speech when faced with challenging tasks are more attentive and show better improvement in cognitive performance than are those who are less talkative (Behrend et al., 1992).

After about the age of 7 children stop vocalising their thoughts and instead carry on what Vygotsky labelled 'inner speech'. **Inner speech** represents the internalisation of words and the mental manipulation of them as symbols for objects in the environment. As children socially interact with their parents, teachers and peers, they learn new words to represent new objects. As the 'expertise' of the people they interact with increases, so does the children's cognitive skills. For example, Rogoff (1990) has shown that children become better problem solvers if they practise solving problems with their parents or with more experienced children than if they practise the problems alone or with children of similar cognitive ability. Vygotsky explained this process by referring to the **zone of proximal (or potential) development**. This describes a range of tasks or skills that a child is unable to master alone but can with the assistance of adults or their peers. The greater the interaction with adults, then the more adult the child's language becomes. But what aspect of the interaction is important for the change in development?

There are two possible candidates. One is a process whereby two people begin with a different understanding and by mutual discussion reach a common understanding. This has been called intersubjectivity (Newson and Newson, 1975) because one member of the dyad adjusts their point of view according to the behaviour of the other. The other possibility is that the interaction acts as a form of 'scaffolding' – peers and adults provide social support in the learning environment but this support can be adjusted (Bruner, 1983). Mothers who provide good social support while their child learns – and are, therefore, good scaffolders – produce children that generate more private speech and who are more successful than children with less social support when completing puzzles alone (Behrend et al., 1992).

Thus, while Piaget argued for a purely maturational view of children's cognitive development – skills developed within periods defined by cognitive characteristics as well as age – Vygotsky placed greater importance of sociocultural influences such as language and interactions with other people. As we have seen, research partially supports both theorists' ideas. However, Vygotsky's work has gone beyond Piaget's theory in explaining how cultural variables, especially language, influence cognitive development.

Developmental models of information processing in cognitive development

Both Piaget and Vygotsky saw cognitive development as a process of forming internal representations of the external world. Piaget focused on the development of schemata, the processes of assimilation and accommodation, and abstract reasoning. Vygotsky focused on the role of language in the development of problem-solving skills, decision-making, and formulating plans. An alternative approach is to view cognitive development in terms of information processing, which involves the storage, encoding and retrieval of information. Figure 12.12 shows you how cognitive performance, in terms of processing speed, improves from the age of 8 years onwards and then tails off in early adulthood. Two developmental models of information processing have emerged in recent years: Case's M-space model and Fischer's skill model.

Case's M-space model

According to Case (1985, 1992), cognitive development is a matter of a child becoming more efficient in using mental strategies. The heart of Case's model is **mental space (M-space)**, a hypothetical construct, similar to short-term or working memory, whose chief function is the processing of information from the external world. Expansion of M-space, or increases in a child's information processing capacity, is caused by a combination of three variables.

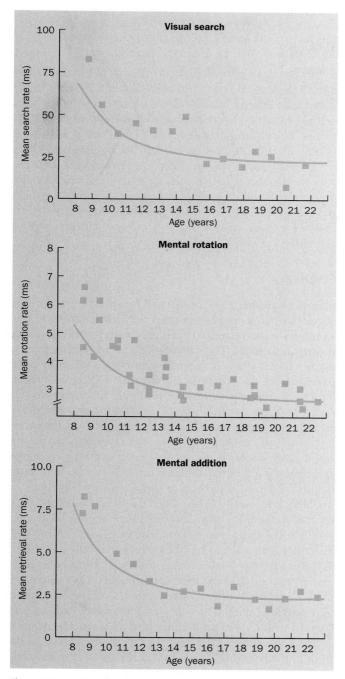

Figure 12.12 How the ability to engage in visual search, to rotate three-dimensional images mentally and to perform mental addition becomes faster from the age of 8 years onwards.

Source: Adapted from Krail, R., Developmental functions for speeds of cognitive processes. *Journal of Experimental Child Psychology*, 1988, 45, 361. Copyright 1988, with permission from Elsevier.

First, as the brain matures, so does its capacity to process greater amounts of information. Maturation of the brain, specifically the increasing number of networks of neural connections and increasing myelination of neurons, also enhances more efficient processing of information. Secondly, as children become more practised at using schemata, less demand is placed on cognitive resources, which can now be devoted to other, more complex cognitive tasks. For example, when children first learn to ride a bicycle, they must focus entirely on keeping their balance and steering the bike in a straight line. After they have acquired these skills, they no longer have to devote so much attention to steering the bike and not falling off. Now they can look around, talk to other bike riders and so on. Thirdly, schemata for different objects and events become integrated so that children now think in novel ways about these objects and events. The net result of such integration is the acquisition of central conceptual structures – networks of schemata that allow children to understand the relationships among the objects and events represented by schemata. As increasingly complex central conceptual structures are formed, children advance to higher levels of cognitive development, as represented in Piaget's stages. Each of the milestones in Piaget's theory, such as deferred imitation and conservation, requires increasing amounts of M-space.

Fischer's skill model

In Fischer's skill model, cognitive development involves the learning of skills, or the acquisition of competencies on particular tasks, such as those found in each of Piaget's developmental periods. Fischer emphasises the child's **optimal level of skill performance**, or the brain's maximal capacity for information processing. According to Fischer, as the brain matures, the child advances through stages of cognitive growth that parallel Piaget's periods of cognitive development (Fischer and Farrar, 1987; Fischer and Pipp, 1984). During each stage, the child's capacity to process information increases, as does the level of skill required for mastery of specific cognitive tasks, such as conservation tasks. As the child encounters different problems, new skills are acquired, practised and perfected. These skills become integrated, leading to increases in the child's ability to reason and think abstractly.

A child cannot progress from one Piagetian period to another until their brain has matured sufficiently to permit acquisition of the cognitive skills necessary to master tasks representative of the next period. For example, a preoperational child is not able to solve conservation tasks until their brain has matured sufficiently to permit acquisition of the necessary skills. Even if a parent explains the task, the child's brain will not be able to encode, store and later retrieve those instructions. When faced with the conservation problem later, the child will still be unable to solve it.

Both Case's M-space model and Fischer's skill model rely on brain maturation as the primary explanation for children's increasing ability to think logically and abstractly. And both models in essence rephrase Piaget's theory of cognitive development in information-processing terms. The purpose of these models has not been to discredit Piaget's theory. On the contrary, one important function of these models has been to reinterpret the theory in the language of modern cognitive psychology. Perhaps by conceptualising children's thought processes in terms of the interplay of Piaget's theory, brain maturation processes, and the acquisition of novel and more complex information processing abilities, further advances in understanding cognitive development will emerge.

Social and emotional development in infancy and childhood

Normally, the first adults with whom infants interact are their parents. In most cases, one parent serves as the primary carer. As many studies have shown, a close relationship called attachment is important for infants' social development. **Attachment** is a social and emotional bond between infant and carer that spans both time and space. It involves both the warm feelings that the parent and child have for each other and the comfort and support they provide for each other, which becomes especially important during times of fear or stress. This interaction must work both ways, with each participant fulfilling certain needs of the other.

Formation of a strong and durable bond depends on the behaviour of both people in the relationship. According to theorist John Bowlby (1969), attachment is a part of many organisms' native endowment. He and Mary Ainsworth have developed an approach that has succeeded in discovering some of the variables that influence attachment in humans (Ainsworth and Bowlby, 1991).

Infant attachment

see activity on mypsychlab Newborn infants rely completely on their parents (or other carers) to supply them with nourishment, keep them warm and clean, and protect them from harm. To most parents, the role of primary carer is much more than a duty; it is a source of joy and satisfaction. Nearly all parents anticipate the birth of their children with the expectation that they will love and cherish them. And when a child is born, most of them do exactly that. As time goes on, and as parent and child interact, they become strongly attached to each other.

What factors cause this attachment to occur? Evidence suggests that human infants are innately able to produce special behaviours that shape and control the behaviour of their carers. As Bowlby (1969) noted, the most important of these behaviours are sucking, cuddling, looking, smiling and crying.

Sucking

A baby must be able to suck in order to obtain milk. But not all sucking is related to nourishment. Piaget (1952) noted that infants often suck on objects even when they are not hungry. Non-nutritive sucking appears to be an innate behavioural tendency in infants that serves to inhibit a baby's distress. In modern society, most mothers cover their breasts between feedings or feed with a bottle, so a baby's non-nutritive sucking must involve inanimate objects or the baby's own thumb. But in Uganda, mothers were observed to give their babies access to a breast when they were fussy, just as mothers in other cultures would give them a dummy (Ainsworth, 1967).

Cuddling

Infants of all species of primates have special reflexes that encourage front-to-front contact with their mothers. For example, a baby monkey clings to its mother's chest shortly after birth. This clinging leaves the mother free to use her hands and feet. Human infants are carried by their parents and do not hold on by themselves. However, infants do adjust their posture to mould themselves to the contours of the parent's body. This cuddling response plays an important role in reinforcing the behaviour of the carer. Some infants, perhaps because of hereditary factors or slight brain damage, do not make the cuddling response and remain rigid in the adult's arms. Adults who hold such infants tend to refer to them as being not very lovable.

Harry Harlow (1974) conducted a series of experiments on infant monkeys and showed that clinging to a soft, cuddly form appears to be an innate response. Harlow and his colleagues isolated baby monkeys from their mothers immediately after birth and raised them alone in cages containing two mechanical surrogate mothers. One surrogate mother was made of bare wire mesh but contained a bottle that provided milk. The other surrogate was padded and covered with terry cloth but provided no nourishment.

The babies preferred to cling to the cuddly surrogate and went to the wire model only to eat. If they were frightened, they would rush to the cloth-covered model for comfort. These results suggest that close physical contact with a cuddly object is a biological need for a baby monkey, just as food and drink are. A baby monkey clings to and cuddles with its mother because the contact is innately reinforcing, not simply because she provides it with food.

Undoubtedly, physical contact with soft objects is also inherently reinforcing for human infants. The term 'security blanket' suggests that these objects are comforting during times of distress. Indeed, children are most likely to ask for their special blankets or stuffed animals before going to bed, when they are ill, or when they are in an unfamiliar situation.

Looking

For infants, looking serves as a signal to parents: even a very young infant seeks eye-to-eye contact with its parents. If a parent does not respond when eye contact is made, the baby usually shows signs of distress. Tronick *et al.* (1978) observed face-to-face interactions between mothers and their infants. When the mothers approached their babies, they typically smiled and began talking in a gentle, high-pitched voice. In return, infants smiled and stretched their arms and legs. The mothers poked and gently jiggled their babies, making faces at them. The babies responded with facial expressions, wiggles and noises of their own.

To determine whether the interaction was really two-sided, the experimenters had each mother approach her baby while keeping her face expressionless or mask-like. At first, the infant made the usual greetings, but when the mother did not respond, the infant turned away. From time to time, the infant looked at her again, giving a brief smile, but again turned away when the mother continued to stare without changing her expression. These interactions were recorded on videotape and were scored by raters who did not know the purpose of the experiment, so the results were not biased by the experimenters' expectations.

Each mother found it difficult to resist her baby's invitation to interact. In fact, some of the mothers broke down and smiled back. Most of the mothers who managed to hold out (for three minutes) later apologised to their babies, saying something like, 'I am real again. It's all right. You can trust me again. Come back to me' (Tronick *et al.*, 1978, p. 110). This study clearly shows that the looking behaviour of an infant is an invitation for the mother to respond.

Smiling

By the time an infant is 5 weeks old, visual stimuli begin to dominate as elicitors for smiling. A face (especially a moving one) is a more reliable elicitor of a smile than a voice is; even a moving mask will cause an infant to smile. At approximately 3 months of age, specific faces – those of people to whom the infant has become attached – will elicit smiles. In particular, the infant will engage in more generic smiling when gazing at its mother's face than when gazing elsewhere (Van Beek *et al.*, 1994). The infant also smiles when the mother smiles (Kaye and Fogel, 1980). Are these smiles indicative of genuine joy/positive emotion or are they reflective of some other process, such as imitation? When infants play, for example, they often smile with their mouths open. When 10–18-month-old children engage in social games, this is the facial response that dominates and one which makes the mother laugh (Jones *et al.*, 1990).

However, Fogel and colleagues have noted that infants engage in other forms of smiling such as that involving the raising of the cheeks. They found that while cheek-raising was characteristic of the early stages of tickling, open-mouth and cheek-raising smiling became more dominant as the tickling game progressed (Fogel *et al.*, 2000). When Fogel *et al.* examined the type of smiling elicited in a group of thirteen 1–6-month-old infants who interacted with their mother, they found that the infants generated distinct patterns of smiling depending on what the mother did. Cheek-raising smiles were associated with responding to the mother's positive affect; open-mouthed smiling was associated with visually engaging with the mother; and both of these facial movements were associated with a combination of visual engagement and response to the mother's positive affect (Messinger *et al.*, 2001).

Crying

For almost any adult, the sound of an infant's crying is intensely distressing or irritating. An infant usually cries only when it is hungry, cold or in pain (Wolff, 1969). In these situations, only the intervention of an adult can bring relief. The event that most effectively terminates crying is being picked up and cuddled, although unless the baby is fed and made more comfortable it will soon begin crying again. Because picking up the baby stops the crying, the parent learns through negative reinforcement to pick up the infant when it cries. Thus, crying serves as a useful means for a cold, hungry or wet child to obtain assistance.

Wolff (1969) suggested that babies have different patterns of crying. Konner (1972), who was studying a hunter-gatherer tribe in Africa, found that a pain cry caused all the people in earshot to turn towards the infant and induced several of them to run towards the child. However, only the child's carers responded to a hunger cry. More recent evidence suggests that babies' cries do not fall into need-specific categories – there is no 'hunger cry', no different cry for pain, and so on. Instead, cries simply vary in intensity, according to the level of the infant's distress. However, the onset of crying provides important information. If a baby suddenly begins crying intensely, mothers are more likely to assume that the baby is afraid or in pain. If the cry begins more gradually, mothers suspect hunger, sleepiness or a need for a nappy change (Gustafson and Harris, 1990).

The nature and quality of attachment

For an infant, the world can be a frightening place. The presence of a primary caregiver provides a baby with considerable reassurance when they first become able to explore the environment. Although the unfamiliar environment produces fear, the caregiver provides a secure base that the infant can leave from time to time to see what the world is like.

Stranger anxiety and separation anxiety

Babies are born prepared to become attached to their primary caregiver, who in most cases is their mother. Attachment appears to be a behaviour pattern that is necessary for normal development (Ainsworth, 1973; Bowlby, 1973). However, although attachment appears to be an inherited disposition, infants do not have a natural inclination to become attached to any one specific adult. Rather, the person to whom the baby becomes attached is determined through learning; the individual who serves as the infant's primary caregiver (or, in Bowlby's terms, 'attachment figure') is usually the object of the attachment.

Attachment partially reveals itself in two specific forms of infant behaviour: stranger anxiety and separation anxiety. **Stranger anxiety**, which usually appears in infants between the ages of 6 and 12 months, consists of wariness and sometimes fearful responses, such as crying and clinging to their carers, that infants exhibit in the presence of strangers. Male strangers generate the most anxiety in infants. Child strangers generate the least anxiety, while female strangers generate an intermediate amount of anxiety (Skarin, 1977). Stranger anxiety can be reduced and even eliminated under certain conditions. For example, if the infant is in familiar surroundings with its mother, and the mother acts in a friendly manner towards the stranger, the infant is likely to be less anxious in the presence of the stranger than it would if the surroundings were unfamiliar or if the mother was unfriendly towards the stranger (Rheingold and Eckerman, 1973).

Separation anxiety is a set of fearful responses, such as crying, arousal and clinging to the carer, that an infant exhibits when the carer attempts to leave the infant. Separation anxiety differs from stranger anxiety in two ways: time of emergence and the conditions under which the fear responses occur. It first appears in infants when they are about 6 months old and generally peaks at about 15 months – a finding consistent among many cultures (Kagan *et al.*, 1978). Like stranger anxiety, separation anxiety can occur under different conditions with different degrees of intensity. For example, if an infant is used to being left in a certain environment, say a daycare centre, it may show little or no separation anxiety (Maccoby, 1980). The same holds true for situations in which the infant is left with a sibling or other familiar person (Bowlby, 1969).

However, if the same infant is left in an unfamiliar setting, it will show signs of distress. Some infants show 'disorganised' attachment behaviour, that is, they show conflicting behaviour towards the carer. They may rush to the sound of an opening door when hearing the carer about to enter a room and then run away when the carer enters; they may also adopt a 'frozen' or still posture when the carer is in the room (Main and Solomon, 1990). A longitudinal study of disorganised attachment behaviour in 157 children (studied from 24 months to 19 years), found that disorganised behaviour was correlated with insensitive caring, living alone with the infant, neglect, physical and psychological neglect and an intrusive caring style (Carlson, 1998).

Ainsworth's Strange Situation

One measure of separation anxiety was devised by Ainsworth and her colleagues (Ainsworth *et al.*, 1978). They developed a test of attachment called the **Strange Situation** that consists of a series of eight episodes, during which the baby is exposed to various events that might cause some distress. The episodes involve the experimenter introducing the infant and the parent to a playroom and then leaving, the parent leaving and being reunited with the infant, or a stranger entering the playroom with and without the parent present. Each episode lasts for approximately three minutes. The Strange Situation test is based on the idea that if the attachment process has been successful, an infant should use its mother as a secure base from which to explore an unfamiliar environment. By noting the infant's reactions to the strange situation, researchers can evaluate the nature of the attachment. The characteristics of the different types of attachment are summarised in Table 12.2.

The use of the Strange Situation test led Ainsworth and her colleagues to identify three patterns of attachment. **Secure attachment** is the ideal pattern: infants show a distinct preference for their mothers over the stranger. Infants may cry when their carers leave, but they stop as soon as they return. Babies may also form two types of insecure attachment. Babies with **resistant attachment** show tension in their relations with their carers. Infants stay close to their mother before the mother leaves but show both approach and avoidance behaviours when the mother returns. Infants continue to cry for a while after their mother returns and may even push her away. Infants who display **avoidant attachment** generally do not cry when they are left alone. When their mother returns, the infants are likely to avoid or ignore them. These infants tend not to cling or cuddle when they are picked up.

Table 12.2 Episodes in the Strange Situation

Epsiode	Events	Attachment behaviour observed
1	Experimenter introduces parent and baby to playroom and then leaves	
2	Parent is seated while baby plays with toys	Parent as a secure base
3	Stranger enters, is seated, and talks to parent	Reaction to unfamiliar adult
4	Parent leaves room. Stranger responds to baby and offers comfort if baby is upset	Separation anxiety
5	Parent returns, greets baby, and offers comfort if necessary. Stranger leaves the room	Reaction to reunion
6	Parent leaves room	Separation anxiety
7	Stranger leaves room and offers comfort	Ability to be soothed by stranger
8	Stranger returns, greets baby, offers comfort if necessary, and tries to reinterest baby in toys	Reaction to reunion

Note: Episode 1 lasts about 30 seconds; each of the remaining episodes lasts about 3 minutes. Separation episodes are cut short if the baby becomes very upset. Reunion episodes are extended if the baby needs more time to calm down and return to play.

Source: from Berk, Laura E., *Child Development*, 4th edn © 1997. Published by Allyn and Bacon, Boston, MA. Copyright © Pearson Education. By permission of the publisher.

Although infants' personalities certainly affect the nature of their interactions with their carers and hence the nature of their attachment, mothers' behaviour appears to be the most important factor in establishing a secure or insecure attachment (Ainsworth *et al.*, 1978; Isabella and Belsky, 1991). Mothers of securely attached infants tend to be those who respond promptly to their crying and who are adept at handling them and responding to their needs. The babies apparently learn that their mothers can be trusted to react sensitively and appropriately. Mothers who do not modulate their responses according to their infants' own behaviour – who appear insensitive to their infants' changing needs – are most likely to foster avoidant attachment. Mothers who are impatient with their infants and who seem more interested in their own activities than in interacting with their offspring tend to foster resistant attachment.

The nature of the attachment between infants and carers appears to be related to children's later social behaviour. For example, Waters *et al.* (1979) found that children who were securely attached at 15 months were among the most popular and the most sociable children in their nursery schools at $3\frac{1}{2}$ years of age. In contrast, insecurely attached infants had difficulties with social adjustment later in childhood; they had poor social skills and tended to be hostile, impulsive and withdrawn (Erickson *et al.*, 1985).

While these attachment behaviours are seen cross-culturally, there are cultural differences. German babies, for example, appear to show more avoidant attachment than do American ones, possibly because German parents

encourage their children to be independent from an early age (Grossman *et al.*, 1985). Japanese babies are thought to exhibit more resistant attachment, possibly because Japanese mothers do not normally leave their charges in the care of others (Miyake *et al.*, 1985).

Predictors of secure attachment

Recall that Ainsworth and her colleagues found that the insecure attachment features just described were strongly related to attachment security. What is unclear from Ainsworth's study, however, is which aspects of the mother–child interaction, if any, are predictive of a secure attachment style. Are all the features listed above necessary for secure attachment or only one? Some researchers suggest that maternal sensitivity is the greatest predictor (Goldsmith and Alansky, 1987); others show different factors.

One problem with studies of attachment is the variation in methodology. Sometimes, conclusions are drawn from a single observation, others from multiple observations; the measures of attachment have ranged from asking parents about their attitudes to childcare to observing the frequency of physical contact (Frodi *et al.*, 1985; Benn, 1986; Kerns and Barth, 1995). As a result, the determinants of attachment are unclear because different studies adopt different research designs. In a meta-analysis of 66 attachment studies, De Wolff and van Ijzendoorn (1997) found that there was a moderately strong relationship between maternal sensitivity, defined as the ability to respond appropriately and promptly to the signals of the infant, and attachment.

Relationships with siblings

Along with parents and peers, siblings are the people with whom children share a close social and emotional relationship. Siblings may also cause resentment in older children because they attract most of the attention from parents and the older child may feel left out. Studies by Dunn and her colleagues, for example, have found that mothers are less warm towards their older children when their new baby is born (Dunn and Kendrick, 1982; Dunn, 1993). If the older child is over 2 years of age, they may also feel less secure and become more disruptive (Teti *et al.*, 1996). While this may draw attention to the child and maybe flag some underlying problem, the disruption can end up alienating the parent which itself may prolong the disruptive behaviour.

The elements of competition or jealousy between older and younger children is called sibling rivalry, but the degree of rivalry depends on a number of factors, including how secure the older child feels with its parents. Dunn and Kendrick (1982) found that if the first-born child already had a secure relationship with its parents, then its attitude towards the newborn was positive and the child adjusted reasonably well to the new arrival in the family. That said, there is often an element of tomfoolery in the siblings' relationships: one study found that disagreements and fights among siblings were as frequent as 56 an hour (Dunn, 1993). The disagreements, however, peter out by adolescence and the older sibling frequently takes the dominant role, initiating positive behaviours when engaging with the younger sibling. As siblings get older, there is a greater sense of equality between them and they eventually spend less time with each other and more time with their peers, as you will see in a later section on adolescence.

The relationship between parents is an important predictor of the security of sibling relationships. If parents get on, so do siblings. Similarly, if both parents are sensitive to the needs of all of their children, and are not selectively sensitive to one, there is less conflict between siblings (Brody, 1998). Parents' ability to stamp on skirmishes between siblings also predicts later conflict. The inability to do this is associated with increased conflict and aggressive, antisocial behaviour outside the home (Garcia *et al.*, 2000).

Of course, sibling relationships are not completely characterised by conflict. Siblings provide a source of emotional and social comfort to each other (Vandell, 2000). Older siblings often act as surrogate parents: one study found that in 57 per cent of 186 cultures studied, older siblings were the primary caregivers for younger siblings (Weisner and Gallimore, 1977). Older siblings are also often role models for their brothers and sisters and are often imitated by their younger siblings (Abramovitch *et al.*, 1980).

A recent study suggests that having a sibling can moderate the effects of stressful life events (Gass *et al.*, 2007). One hundred and thirty-two families participated – the average age of the youngest sibling at the first time of testing was 4.9 years (the average age difference between siblings was 5.6 years). The study found that having an affectionate older sibling was associated with less internalising behaviour following a stressful event.

Another study has found that intimacy between siblings is greatest in sisters during middle childhood and adolescence (Kim *et al.*, 2006). In a study of 200 white middle- and working-class families, intimacy in same-sex sibling relationships was found to be fairly stable across this period but mixed-sex sibling relationships showed a decline in intimacy across childhood and adolescence until mid-adolescence when intimacy increased. One reason for this is that middle adolescence heralds an interest in the opposite sex and having a sibling of the opposite sex might, therefore, be a useful sounding board for advice and strategy. First-borns experienced more conflict in early adolescence, second-borns experienced more conflict in middle childhood.

Finally, some children have no siblings because they are an only child. Do these children differ in some psychological way from children with brothers and sisters? Studies of only children have shown them to be high in self-esteem and in motivation to achieve; they are also more obedient and more intellectually able than children with siblings (Falbo and Polit, 1986; Falbo, 1992). Interestingly, one country has provided some useful data on the development of only children. In 1979, the People's Republic of China implemented a family planning policy stating that families should produce only one child. When these children were studied, their profile was comparable to their Western counterparts but they had higher scores on tests of intelligence and were more academically successful than their equivalents with siblings (Falbo and Poston, 1993).

Relationships with others

As well as forming relationships with parents and siblings, children also develop relationships with their peers, usually with children who are similar to them in terms of age and sex. The development of friendships marks an important trait in the child's life: the development of cooperation. Friends who play with each other are more likely to be cooperative than children who are not friends; friends also play in a more complex way than non-friends (Hinde *et al.*, 1985). On the other hand, such close relationships also lead to conflicts: these are more common among friends than among non-friends (Hartup and Laursen, 1992), clearly because they spend more time with each other. However, when conflicts do occur, friends make greater attempts at negotiation when solving disputes.

As relationships develop, children also show evidence of prosocial behaviour – they will automatically help another child. For example, if a child sees another crying, they will comfort that child, even before being taught to behave this

Social organisation – An international perspective

Do children from different cultures interact differently when in social groups? Children living in the US from Mexican families with mothers who had received limited schooling, US children whose mothers' had extensive schooling, and children of Mexican families with mothers who had extensive schooling were studied. Three children from each group were given a task – following instructions for origami – to complete together (Mejia-Arauz *et al.*, 2007).

The children from Mexican families with mothers who had received limited schooling were more likely to work together than were the other groups. The US children were more likely to work individually or in pairs – they were also more likely to chat more when interacting than interact non-verbally (which was the common form of interaction in the Mexican children).

The results seem to confirm studies showing that certain cultures – such as those in Mexico – are more likely to show evidence of collaboration on a shared task, even children from those cultures.

positively by a parent. The degree of prosocial behaviour that children show, however, can depend on the degree of encouragement they are given or on the prosocial disposition of the parents. Children who see others behaving in a generous and helpful way are more likely to be helpful and generous themselves (Eisenberg and Fabes, 1998). However, the father seems to be the more important role model for children: a positive correlation between the father's prosocial behaviour and the child's has been reported, but there was no such correlation found between the mother's and the child's (Eisenberg *et al.*, 1992).

Disorders of social cognition and emotion

You saw in Chapters 3 and 10 that some children are born with disorders associated with mental retardation (such as Down syndrome); or they can develop reading disorders that seem unrelated to the educational opportunities available to the child and to any underlying brain damage (such as developmental dyslexia). If there is no underlying intellectual retardation or physical cause, cognitive and emotional disorders are sometimes described as specific developmental disorders or disorders of psychological development (Rispens and van Yperen, 1997).

In earlier chapters, we discussed some disorders of childhood in some detail. This section describes disorders we have not come across yet: autism, conduct disorder and attention deficit hyperactivity disorder, and disorders of emotional regulation.

Autism

Characteristics of autism

Autism is a developmental disorder characterised by three features: social abnormality, language abnormality, and stereotypical and repetitive patterns of behaviour (Frith, 1989; Happé, 1994; Bailey *et al.*, 1996), all of which can extend to adulthood (Gillberg, 1991). Autism was originally reported in 1943 by Leo Kanner in an article in which he described 11 cases of 'autistic disturbance of affective contact and . . . desire for preservation of sameness'. The symptoms he described form the core of the classification of autism today.

The social abnormality includes the child's inability to reciprocate in social interactions, to form or develop loving relationships and to interact spontaneously with others. Autistic children and adults have an impairment in the appreciation of social cues.

One characteristic feature of autism is the inability to look for emotion in the behaviour or expression of others; this may give autistic children an aloof and cold demeanour because they may be judged emotionally unresponsive. In an experiment in which autistic and control children were asked to sort pictures of individuals according to a category, autistic children would sort by appearance (hat) rather than emotion (Weeks and Hobson, 1987). The impairment in interpersonal communication, however, appears to be limited to interpersonal understanding – not all social communication is impaired (Mundy *et al.*, 1986; Sigman, 1995).

Language development in autism is severely delayed and about half of autistics do not develop useful language. In addition to this delay, there is evidence of deviant communication in the form of the idiosyncratic use of language, the making up of new words (neologising) and little engagement in social chat. Rutter (1987) has argued that such poor communication skills arise from the autistic's impaired ability to use feedback. Other examples of deviant language use include a difficulty in maintaining a topic of conversation (Bailey *et al.*, 1996). There is also an impaired ability to play spontaneously with toys, possibly because autistic individuals do not know what the toys mean.

Stereotypical and repetitive behaviour includes an over-reliance on routines or rituals and an abnormal attachment to objects.

The development of autism

Autism develops in the first two years of a child's life and is four times as common in boys as it is in girls (Gillberg and Coleman, 1992; Rapin, 1997). The prevalence of the disorder is 1 in 1,000 across most of the countries in which autism has been studied (Bryson *et al.*, 1988; Gillberg and Coleman, 1992; Sugiyama *et al.*, 1992). Autism may recede when the child develops language and uses it to communicate socially.

Early signs of the disorder include a failure to maintain eye-to-eye contact, to reach out to familiar persons (Swettenham *et al.*, 1998), and to imitate (Klin *et al.*, 1992). Baron-Cohen's 'reading the mind in the eyes' test asks participants to judge the emotion emitted in a photograph that shows the eye region of a human face only. Baron-Cohen *et al.* (2001) administered the test to people with Asperger's syndrome and to high-functioning autistic individuals (people of normal intelligence who show autistic characteristics) and compared the performance of these groups with that of a control group. The performance of the experimental groups was significantly more impaired than that of the control group.

There are checklists available which enable parents to determine whether their child is exhibiting autistic tendencies and such checklists include Baron-Cohen *et al.*'s (1992) Checklist for Autism in Toddlers (CHAT) which aims to identify those at risk of developing the disorder. Mental retardation is common in cases of autism and is estimated to occur in 75 per cent of cases (Rutter, 1979; Rapin, 1997). Whereas performance on some cognitive tasks is low (such as comprehension), performance on others is high (such as block design) (Venter *et al.*, 1992). Some autistics also exhibit exceptional abilities in specific domains such as reading, spelling, maths and music. When these abilities become extreme and highly remarkable, autistic individuals are called 'idiot savants', although such exceptional abilities are not unique to autism (O'Connor and Hermelin, 1988).

Some researchers have also suggested that autism may be an inherited disorder because there is a high incidence of fragile X disorder in autistic children (Bailey *et al.*, 1996). Twin studies suggest a higher concordance rate in identical than fraternal twins (Steffenburg *et al.*, 1989; Bailey *et al.*, 1995). Currently, however, there is no evidence that autism is a simple inherited disorder and there is no clear-cut evidence for a genetic component (Rutter, 1994).

The outcome for autism is varied – some individuals develop little language whereas others are able to go on to full-time education, get married and start families (Rapin, 1997). The most important therapeutic interven-

Kim Peek, thought to be the inspiration for Dustin Hoffman's character, Ramond Babbitt, in *Rain Man* (although the character is not based on Peek) is an example of an autistic savant. He was able to read a Tom Clancy novel in under an hour and a half and name the Russian radio operator character from the book four months later (as well as give the page number of the passage describing the character). He memorised his first book at the age of 18 months and has learned 9000 to date, including Shakespeare and maps of all major US cities. He can read a page in 10 seconds. Not surprisingly, his friends have nicknamed him, 'Kim-puter'. Kim Peek's brain is unusual because his corpus callosum is absent.
Source: Adam Nadel/Polaris/Eyevinearchive.

tion appears to involve intensive education aimed at changing the behavioural and communication problems. As such, most interventions are designed for use by parents and teachers who have greatest contact with the children. Medical interventions have also been developed but these appear to be more effective in improving attention than in eliminating all the characteristics of the disorder (Cohen and Volkmar, 1997).

Autism and theory of mind

see activity on mypsychlab

In the late 1980s a theme emerged in autism research which suggested that autistic children had an impaired ability to make inferences about other people's mental states; that is, these children lacked, or had a defective, **theory of mind** (Leslie, 1987). According to this early model, a 2-year-old child can pretend play and understand others' mental states, desires and beliefs, but in autistic children the mechanism which allows this is impaired. As a result, the lack of pretend play would also be accompanied, later on, by an inability to interpret others' mental states.

Cutting edge – Loneliness and autistic tendency

A study from the US has associated autistic traits with loneliness (Jobe and White, 2007). Undergraduates who showed autistic characteristics such as rigidity, high attention to detail and preference for sameness, reported greater loneliness and fewer and shorter friendships than those who did not. These characteristics also correlated with the length of romantic relationships – the greater the autistic tendency, the longer the relationship (18.8 months, on average, compared to 11.3 months in people who showed less of a tendency to autism). This suggests that the preference for sameness may extend, in particular, to preference for romantic partner.

For example, Baron-Cohen *et al.* (1985) reported a study in which a child saw the unexpected transfer by a third person of an object from the location in which it was placed by the experimenter to a different location. The child's task was to predict where the experimenter would look for this object. Such tasks are now called 'theory of mind' tasks or tests of false belief. Four-year-old children could correctly indicate that the experimenter would look in the original location for the object; autistic children, however, could not, and predicted that the experimenter would look in the new location. The children seemed unaware that the experimenter would not know about the transfer of the object – they could not imagine the task from the other person's perspective. Baron-Cohen (1995) later used the term 'mindblindness' to refer to such inabilities to understand the thoughts of others. Deaf children perform significantly worse on false-belief tests than do hearing children, with older deaf children performing better than the younger deaf children, suggesting that there may be developmental delay in the ability to perform theory of mind tasks (Russell *et al.*, 1998). A study of deaf children from hearing families has found that their theory of mind ability develops significantly more slowly than those of deaf children from deaf families, whether they used spoken English or American Sign Language (Schick *et al.*, 2007). Curiously, when the language demands of a theory of mind task were reduced, deaf children from hearing families still performed less well.

A meta-analysis of studies examining the effect of age and language acquisition on understanding of theory of mind (measured via false-belief tasks) has found that theory of mind is associated with language ability, but not age (Milligan *et al.*, 2007). The more advanced the language understanding (general language, semantics, receptive vocabulary, syntax), the greater the false-belief understanding.

One view of theory of mind proposes that the child is a scientist, exploring the environment and constructing and testing hypotheses. This is Karmiloff-Smith's theory of representational redescription (Karmiloff-Smith, 1988, 1992). The child is seen as a theoretician who builds theories and explains events or stimuli that cannot be explained by sim-

plifying them. To become an expert 'scientist' the child passes through a series of stages that involve the child constructing representations of stimuli around them. In the beginning, behaviour is externally driven and the child makes many mistakes before getting better. This process involves reconstructing or redescribing representations (hence, theory of representational redescription) as development occurs. This perspective on theory of mind, however, has been challenged (Gellaty, 1997). Gellaty argues that this theory sees the child as an isolated individual, not as part of a community; he also suggests that the concept of 'scientific thinking' which the child is thought to develop, is too simplistic and assumes that all scientific thinking occurs in the same way.

Some researchers also suggest that theory of mind deficits are not common to all autistic individuals (Happé, 1993, 1994). The major deficit in autistic children, according to Frith and Happé (1994) is not impaired theory of mind but the inability to see situations and objects as wholes. Most of us see images and events as global images and events – we attend to the detail later. When you look at the television screen you do not attend to each individual detail of the image consciously (although your brain does do this), but you perceive a global image. The problem with autistic individuals, according to this view, is that they process information piecemeal and not in the context in which it appears.

There appears to be some evidence for this hypothesis. In experiments where participants have to find images within larger, more complex images, autistic children do very well (O'Riordan and Plaisted, 2001). An example of one of these exercises is shown in Figure 12.13.

Most normal participants have difficulty ignoring the large global image in which the 'hidden' image is embedded. Autistic children are also better than controls at discriminating among novel stimuli (but not familiar ones), indicating that they attend to specific features of stimuli (Plaisted *et al.*, 1998).

Frith and Happé (1994) suggest that two cognitive systems may be impaired in autism: one which normally allows theory of mind and another which determines the way in which information is processed. This model has

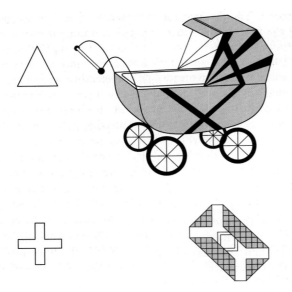

Figure 12.13 An example of the Embedded Figures Test. The task is to find the shape on the left which is embedded in the more meaningful, global image on the right. Autistic individuals are better at this task than non-autistic individuals.

Source: Happé, F., Autism: Cognitive deficit or cognitive style? *Trends in Cognitive Sciences*, 1999, 3(6), 216–222. Copyright 1999, with permission from Elsevier.

the benefit of accounting for the theory of mind deficits and the tendency of autistic individuals to segment information instead of perceiving it globally. However, the model does not explain why such impairments arise in the first place. One source of information suggests that this impairment may be neurological in nature, as the section below highlights.

Neuropsychology of autism and theory of mind

The idea that the frontal cortex is involved in theory of mind has received some support from studies in which patients with frontal lobe damage show evidence of poorer ability to draw inferences about other people's point of view than patients with damage to other brain areas (Stuss *et al.*, 2001). Rowe *et al.* (2001) found that patients with damage to the left and the right frontal lobes showed specific theory of mind deficits.

A review of neuroimaging data has concluded that a reduction in frontal lobe size and activation are some of the more consistent neuropsychological characteristics of autism (Deb and Thompson, 1998). Studies have reported reductions in the neurotransmitter dopamine in the prefrontal cortex only (Ernst *et al.*, 1997) and have found decreased volume in the frontal lobes of autistic individuals (Piven *et al.*, 1995). These features are more robust than most others and are consistent with a theory of autism that attributes impaired planning and organisation to frontal lobe dysfunction (Hughes *et al.*, 1994).

A single-case study, however, challenges this view. Bird *et al.* (2004) studied patient GT who had suffered brain damage as a result of stroke. There was extensive bilateral damage to the medial frontal lobes exclusively. GT showed the typical frontal lobe symptoms – impairments in planning and memory – but showed no evidence of impairment on 'theory of mind' tasks. This suggests that the medial frontal lobe may not be necessary for performing theory of mind tasks. Why, therefore, does neuroimaging evidence and some clinical neuropsychological evidence suggest otherwise? Bird *et al.* suggest that this could be because the medial frontal lobes are necessary for the acquisition of theory of mind but not for implementing theory of mind functions.

A similar idea was behind a neuroimaging study of high functioning autistic adults (Kennedy and Courchesne, 2007). The study referred to the idea that there are two different networks in the brain which perform different functions. One is thought to be impaired in autism; the other is intact. One network is responsible for doing cognitively demanding tasks and for engaging in externally directed behaviour. The second was activated when a person engaged in behaviour that involved a social or emotional component or which is introspective in nature (such as theory of mind). This is called the Task-Negative Network because there is a decrease in activation in specific brain areas during the performance of social or emotional tasks. This is the network that is affected in autism and this is what Kennedy and Courchesne (2007) found in their participants. The Task-Positive Network was unaffected.

Another region thought to be involved in autism is the amygdala. People with damage to the amygdala, as you will see in Chapter 13, have severe difficulties in recognising emotion, specifically fear. These patients also have difficulty in making complex social judgements such as assessing trustworthiness in someone's face. Autistic individuals are able to recognise basic emotions, unlike patients with bilateral amygdala damage, and discriminate between the intensity of emotions expressed through facial expression (Adolphs *et al.*, 2001). However, they are impaired at making social judgements about emotional facial expressions. For example, they rate faces as significantly more trustworthy than do control groups. The authors suggest that autistic individuals are capable of making perceptual judgements about faces and are capable of recognising basic emotions but are incapable of linking the perception of the face with the appropriate social judgement. Perhaps normal retrieval of social knowledge cued by faces is impaired or normal social knowledge has not been acquired. Critchley *et al.* (2000) found that although autistic individuals performed above chance levels when identifying emotional facial expressions, they performed more poorly than a control group. Autistic individuals did not activate the brain's 'face area' or the cerebellum when making judgements about emotional facial expression.

People with early damage to the amygdala are significantly impaired at theory of mind tests that require sophisticated understanding of communication (e.g. detecting tactless/ironic remarks and interpreting metaphors) (Shaw *et al.*, 2004). People with damage sustained during adulthood, however, performed no worse than the control groups. The findings suggest that the amygdala may be necessary for the development of theory of mind but may not be responsible for the ongoing reasoning involved in theory of mind tasks.

There may also be an association between autism and the levels of testosterone in the foetus. Auyeung *et al.* (2009) asked mothers to use two standard measures of autism to rate their children (aged between 6 and 10 years). These scores were then correlated with levels of testosterone measured from amniotic fluid during amniocentesis while the child was a foetus. The researchers found that levels of foetal testosterone were positively associated with the autism test measures: the higher the testosterone, the higher the score.

Finally, some researchers have hypothesised that autism may involve a dysfunction in the so-called mirror neuron system. Remember from Chapter 4 that these are neurons that fire when an organism reaches, for example, but also when the organism watches another reaching (hence,

'mirror'). The 'broken mirror' theory of autism suggests that the inability of autistic people to imitate is due to the dysfunction or impairment in these neurons (Williams *et al.*, 2004). However, imitation involves more than matching an action but visual analysis, selecting what is to be imitated and when to imitate it (Southgate and Hamilton, 2008). Different types of imitation are, therefore, possible. Researchers have also queried whether the imitation deficit in autism is robust and consistent. Some studies show that if an autistic child is instructed to imitate, he or she will (Hamilton *et al.*, 2007). They may fail to imitate meaningless action and facial expression, but they are able to imitate automatically (Bird *et al.*, 2007). It may be that normal children use cues from others to influence imitation – and when and what to imitate – but autistic children do not. That may be the failure in autism, not a failure to imitate itself (and, by extension, a failure of the mirror neuron system).

Asperger's syndrome

One disorder that is closely linked to autism is **Asperger's syndrome**. According to Asperger (1944), some individuals exhibit 'autistic psychopathy' that is reflected in poor social functioning and interpersonal communication; individuals usually have an obsessional and narrow range of interests. Because of these characteristics, some researchers

Theory of mind – An international perspective

In a typical false-belief task, person A places an object in a cupboard and leaves the room. Person B enters, puts the object in a different location and leaves the room. Person A re-enters, and the participant is asked where person A will look for the object.

Previous studies had shown that 5–6-year-olds can answer this question correctly – person A would look for the object in the cupboard. Younger children, however, make false-belief errors: they would answer that person A would look in the location to which the object had been moved. Recent studies, however, have shown that even 3-year-olds could perform such tasks successfully or improve on them.

In order to address these inconsistencies, Wellman *et al.* (2001) conducted a meta-analysis of 178 separate studies of theory of mind. A difficulty in comparing a few studies reporting inconsistent findings is that the studies may not be comparable – different methods, tests, measures, samples and so on are used. Meta-analyses take such inconsistencies into account by observing general patterns of results.

Their analysis showed that the results of the studies were consistent and robust. Children improved on false-belief tasks

from age 3 to 5. The understanding of belief and false belief was also found to be culture-free (at least, not specific to the cultures included in the analysis). Whether European, North American, East Asian, Australian or African, children acquired understanding of others' beliefs at around the same time. Some forms of task do improve performance when compared with others, however. There could be two reasons for this: either these forms are a more sensitive measure of theory of mind, or they are artefactually easy. The researchers, however, admit that the results of the meta-analysis cannot distinguish which explanation is correct. When studies across the developmental trajectory are analysed, there is a significant and discernible improvement with age, for easy and difficult tasks.

When the reliability of false-belief tasks was analysed, good reliability for judgements made within sessions was found, suggesting that a performance on one version of the task would be comparable to performance on another. The researchers conclude that one of the questions that the meta-analysis does not answer is how the developmental change in understanding of belief occurs.

have suggested that Asperger's is a milder form of autism (Schopler, 1996). There appears to be some support for this notion. When Asperger's original four cases were re-analysed, for example, they met current *DSM-IV TVR* criteria for autistic disorder, not Asperger's (Miller and Ozonoff, 1997). However, this finding could simply reflect the ways in which criteria for diagnosis have changed over the years. One way of determining the validity of a disorder would be to see if it was characterised by different features from those of related disorders.

Autistic individuals perform well on tasks that require them to assemble objects or to form a target abstract pattern from a set of blocks. If Asperger's syndrome is similar to autism, then we should see the same superior performance in both disorders. In a study comparing 120 Swedish individuals with Asperger's syndrome, autistic disorder or attention disorder on a range of tests from the WAIS-R, autistic individuals did better at the block design task and Asperger's individuals performed better at the verbal tasks and poorly at the object assembly task (Ehlers *et al.*, 1997). The result would suggest, therefore, that Asperger's can be distinguished from autism on the basis of spatial performance. However, whether this difference is meaningful is questionable. Abstract and portrait painters might be distinguished by some underlying characteristic, for example, but this does not negate the fact that they are both groups of artists using the same visuospatial and motor abilities. The fact that they differ on one dimension, does not make them totally different.

Conduct disorder/attention deficit hyperactivity disorder

Conduct disorder is a severe impairment in the ability of the child to inhibit its own behaviour and, specifically, to inhibit antisocial and deviant behaviour (Nicol, 1998). It is related to a specific disorder termed **attention deficit hyperactivity disorder (ADHD)** whose main features are poor sustained attention, impulsiveness and hyperactivity (Barkley, 1997). Recent conceptions of ADHD identify three types: Inattentive, Hyperactive/Impulsive and Co-morbid. The inattentive type is more likely to have problems performing executive or cognitive tasks than are the other two.

There is evidence that ADHD runs in families, especially behaviourally disordered families (Faraone *et al.*, 1997), and that conduct disorder is six times more common in children who have been sexually abused (Fergusson *et al.*, 1996; Herrenkohl *et al.*, 1997).

ADHD occurs in 3–7 per cent of the child population, with three times as many boys as girls exhibiting the disorder. Between 50 and 80 per cent of children with the disorder continue showing symptoms into adolescence;

30–50 per cent of affected adolescents show symptoms in adulthood. So, although the disorder recedes, it persists in a high percentage of cases. Because of the nature of the disorder, the problems associated with it can be cognitively damaging. ADHD has been associated with low academic achievement, school performance, suspension/expulsion from school, poor family and peer relationships, mental disorder and substance abuse (Barkley, 1997). Most of the 'treatment' approaches to the disorder involve some form of counselling, behaviour management and, sometimes, psychoactive medication (Toplak *et al.*, 2008). Some examples include managing behaviour in the classroom using praise, giving rewards to increase positive behaviour and ignoring inappropriate behaviour. This has met with some success (Chronis *et al.*, 2006). A treatment designed to normalise EEG frequencies that are dysfunctional in ADHD has also reported a decrease in the symptoms of inattention and hyperactivity (Heinrich *et al.*, 2004).

The causes of ADHD are unclear. Some biological evidence has associated the disorder with a problem in the connections between the frontal lobe, the cerebellum and a region called the striatum. Some studies have shown that brain volume – in the cortex and the cerebellum – is smaller in children with ADHD and that activation is more diffuse when participants complete a cognitive task (Durston, 2003). Cognitive theories attribute some role to disrupted cognitive or executive processes, which explains the involvement of the frontal lobe (Barkley, 2006).

Disorders of emotional regulation

Disorders of emotional regulation refer to problems that the child has in operating at an emotionally normal level. They represent behavioural problems which impair the ability to undertake day-to-day activities (Zeanah *et al.*, 1997). For example, the child may be abnormally distressed, depressed, show sleep disturbance or feeding problems or exhibit anxiety.

The degree of attachment that the child demonstrates towards its caregiver is often used as a good index of these behaviours. Because the child has no sophisticated language, it is difficult to diagnose an emotional disorder in the first three years of life. A depressed person can express their depression verbally (and even suggest causes); this language facility is not available to infants. As a result, emotional disorders tend to be reported by parents who see their child behaving in a way that is out of the ordinary.

Sometimes, however, the child's emotional problems may be associated with those of the carer, especially the mother. Given that the mother makes the greatest investment in caring for the child during its early years, perhaps this is not unexpected. Depressed mothers, for example, have been shown to express more negative emotion, show less positive engagement with, and less sensitivity to the child's behaviour during interactions with the child (Lyons-Ruth *et al.*, 1990). Mothers can be hostile, withdrawn and disengaged, and the child's interaction suffers accordingly. The child avoids the mother and shows great distress. If the mother is depressed for longer than three months after the birth of the child, the child can show developmental and growth delay (Field, 1992). Infants who interact with a nursery school teacher or non-depressed fathers have been found to show more positive and expressive behaviours than when interacting with their depressed mother (Pelaez-Nogueras *et al.*, 1994).

Murray *et al.* (1999) found fairly robust effects of the mother's depression on the long-term emotional adjustment of the child. The researchers looked at mother–child interaction and the ability of the child to adjust socially and behaviourally using reports from the mother, child and observation of the child playing freely. The children were studied at 18 months and 5 years after birth.

The mother's depression was associated with impaired relations between mother and child, behavioural disturbance at home and the child's impaired pattern of play. The quality of attachment at 18 months was the best predictor of the child's relationship with the mother. The findings suggest that early infant–mother relationships can have a significant impact on the child's behaviour later in childhood.

Emotion, attachment and hemispheric asymmetry

One model of emotional expression suggests that different sides of the frontal lobes regulate our experience of positive and negative emotions (you'll find more on this model in the next chapter). The left frontal region is thought to be responsive to positive emotion and the right frontal region is thought to be more responsive to negative emotion. Negative emotion may also be associated with reduced activity in the left frontal cortex (Davidson and Sutton, 1995).

Studies of distressed infants have highlighted similar asymmetries. For example, Davidson and Fox (1989) measured EEGs from infants they characterised as criers and non-criers (criers were those who became distressed when separated from their mother). The criers were distinguished from the non-criers by greater right-sided frontal EEG activation. Dawson *et al.* (1997) reported that the infants of depressed mothers (as well as the mothers themselves) showed reduced left frontal EEG activity. These asymmetries have also been found in studies comparing 4-year-old infants who are either happy and sociable or unhappy and unsociable. The sociable children showed greater left frontal activation (Fox *et al.*, 1995).

Behavioural inhibition in toddlers and infants refers to a temperamental pattern characterised by increased vigilance and decreased motor behaviour when children are confronted with a novel stimulus. These children are also more likely to avoid unfamiliar adults, show little spontaneous behaviour in the presence of unfamiliar peers and are regarded by their parents and peers as anxious and fearful. Children showing this pattern of behaviour also seem to show characteristic patterns of physiological and neural activity; some studies show that behavioural inhibition in children can be predicted by these physiological measures.

Depressed mothers who breastfed were more likely to raise infants who had a less negative temperament. These infants were also less likely to show increased right-sided EEG activation (characteristic of expressing negative emotion) than were infants of depressed mothers who breastfed less consistently. One reason for the interaction may be that the physical closeness of the mother and infant during breastfeeding offsets the negative temperament that might be provoked by a depressed mother who is less close to her child.

Four-month-old infants who display a consistent pattern of right frontal EEG activity are more likely to be behaviourally inhibited (Fox *et al.*, 2001). The EEG pattern was evident even at 9 months. Children who were initially assessed as inhibited but later became non-inhibited did not show this characteristic pattern of right-sided EEG activity. The researchers suggest that infants showing an increase in left-sided activity use approach (positive) behaviour to modulate negative affect; those infants who show right-sided activity are less likely to do this.

What seems unclear in these EEG studies, however, is the nature of cause and effect. Does the distress cause the EEG asymmetry or does the EEG asymmetry cause the distress? Does the asymmetry predispose the infant to distress? These are interesting and important questions. Because they have implications for theories of the nature of emotion and the neuropsychology of emotion, we discuss these in more detail in the next chapter.

The frontal lobes, as you saw in Chapters 4 and 11, also are involved in executive functions such as regulating behaviour (planning, changing strategies, responding emotionally). A study by Hughes *et al.* (1998) compared the performance of 3- or 4-year-old children, described as 'easy' or 'hard to manage', on a series of theory of mind, emotional understanding and executive function (frontal lobe) tasks. They found that the disruptive children showed poorer understanding of emotion and less successful performance on the theory of mind tasks.

If regional brain activity can discriminate sociable from non-sociable children, what do you think would be the implications of this for child welfare and education?

Development of sex roles in childhood

Physical development as a male or a female is only one aspect of sexual development. Social development is also important. A person's **sexual identity** is one's private sense of being a male or female and consists primarily of the recognition of membership in a particular group of people: males or females. Acceptance of this membership does not necessarily indicate acceptance of the sex roles or sex stereotypes that may accompany it. For example, a dedicated feminist may fight to change the role of women in her society but still clearly identify herself as a woman. **Sex roles** are cultural expectations about the ways in which men and women should think and behave.

Closely related to them are **sex stereotypes**, beliefs about differences in the behaviours, abilities and personality traits of males and females. Society's sex stereotypes have an important influence on the behaviour of its members. In fact, many people unconsciously develop their sex identity and sex roles based on sex stereotypes they learned as children.

Development of sexual identity

According to Kohlberg (1966), the ability of children to identify with their sex is determined in large part by their ability to classify objects as being boys' objects or girls' objects, that is, they begin to identify their own sex by observing how others class objects and people. In Kohlberg's model, the child undergoes three stages of sexual identity development: gender labelling, gender stability and gender consistency.

- *Stage 1 Gender labelling*. At the age of 2–3$\frac{1}{2}$ years, the child learns that they are of one sex. Labels that other people apply to them are learned and they attach these same labels to people of the same sex or objects associated with a sex.

- *Stage 2 Gender stability*. Between the ages of 3$\frac{1}{2}$ and 4$\frac{1}{2}$, children begin to realise that their sex is a constant and that this feature can often be seen in other's physical appearance. This time, therefore, is characterised by an increase in awareness of others' physical features.

- *Stage 3 Gender consistency*. At the age of 4$\frac{1}{2}$, children discover that people's sex does not change and that physical appearance does not affect their sexual identity. If a girl or boy dresses up as a member of the opposite sex, they are still regarded as a girl or boy despite their appearance.

By 2 years of age children begin to perceive themselves as being a boy or a girl. In the process of learning what it means to be boys or girls, children associate, in a stereotypical manner, certain toys, games, attitudes and behaviours, such as being aggressive or compliant, with one sex or the other (Huston, 1983; Jacklin and Maccoby, 1983; Picariello *et al.*, 1990). For example, consider an experiment conducted by Montemayor (1974), who invited children between the ages of 6 and 8 years to play a game that involved tossing marbles into a clown's body. Some of the children were told that they were playing a 'girl's game', some were told it was a 'boy's game', and others were told nothing. Boys and girls both said that the game was more fun when it had been described as appropriate to their sex, and they even attained better scores when it was.

Kohlberg's notion of identity development is echoed in recent work that tries to explain how this development occurs. **Gender schema theory**, for example, argues that children construct a 'schema' – a mental representation – of male and female and pay especial attention to features of their own sex (Bem, 1981; Martin and Halverson, 1981). Children's perception of sex is matched with information about others' sex that the child has already processed and understood (Ruble and Martin, 1998).

The ability to identify others' and the child's own sex emerges between the ages of 1 and 3 years. Usually, this is determined by asking children to look at photographs of boys and girls and to point to the person who is a boy or a girl or who is most like the child doing the looking (Etaugh *et al.*, 1989; Fagot and Leinbach, 1989). Children as young as 30 months can complete this task successfully and children as young as 36 months can sort photographs of boys and girls into two piles, without instructions to sort them according to sex.

By the age of 2, children are already beginning to spend more time preferentially playing with their own sex, with the time spent playing with the same-sex child multiplying eleven-fold by the time children reach 6 years (LaFreniere *et al.*, 1984).

Sexual identity and play

Sexual identity is also thought to emerge during play. Pre-schoolers, for example, will engage in role-play but in a sex-typical way: boys will play at being mechanics and bus drivers whereas girls will play at being teachers and cooks (Garvey, 1977). By the age of 1, children will play with sex-typical toys with their parents; by the age of 2, they may engage in this spontaneously without the interference of a parent (Fagot *et al.*, 1986; Roopnarine, 1986).

Some researchers, however, have noted that while children learn that the sexes differ on some dimensions, such as physical appearance, they do not differ on others

(Campbell *et al.*, 2002). Campbell *et al.* argue that sexual differentiation does not occur in all domains at certain age points. For example, they point to studies showing that children's ability to divide toys into 'girl' toys and 'boy' toys can be unrelated to the children's actual preference for those toys (Perry *et al.*, 1984). Furthermore, children who show sex-typed behaviour in one domain may not show it in another (Turner *et al.*, 1993).

To discover how well children could sex-type according to different behaviour domains, Campbell *et al.* studied 56 2-year-old children in various experimental conditions. In one condition, the child's mother would ask it to point to a male- and female-related stimulus that could be a toy or an activity. Male toys were described as cars, trains, water-pistols, blocks and balls whereas female toys were described as toasters, cookers, dolls, dustpans and brushes, and combs. Some of the female activities were described as drawing, whispering, playing with dolls or playing pat-a-cake; some of the male activities were described as chasing, jumping, climbing, wrestling and playing cowboys. In another condition, the child was presented with a photograph of itself and a photograph of a child of the opposite sex and was asked to point to the picture of the girl or boy. Finally, the children were observed in naturalistic settings. In one of these, a child was allowed to play with a selection of toys with the parent. In another, the child played with another child and their interaction was videotaped.

The researchers found that two-thirds of children could identify themselves as male or female, a finding supported by other studies of 3-year-old children (Fagot, 1985). About half of the group were able to point to the face of a boy or a girl accurately in photographs and around a quarter were able to differentiate toys according to whether they were boys' toys or girls' toys. Only one child in eight was able to identify activities according to their sex-type.

On the basis of these results, the researchers suggest that the child's awareness of its own sex and that of others is a 'developmental precursor' to the later sex-typing of toys and activities. The children in the study did prefer to play with sex-typed toys, however, whether they played alone or with another child. Lloyd and Duveen (1990) found that whereas $1\frac{1}{2}$ to $3\frac{1}{2}$ year-old boys played with boys' toys more than girls' toys, the girls played equally with boys' and girls' toys. When the children were paired with a same-sex partner, both sexes spent more time playing with their sex-typed toys.

According to Miller (1987), boys and girls are sensitive to the properties of toys that allow them to engage in specific behaviours. Thus, guns and swords offer the boy an opportunity for conflict whereas dolls and dolls' houses offer the girl an opportunity to nurture. Others, however, have noted that the attributes of objects may be related to sex but not to what the object actually does (the technical term for this is affordance). For example, when a typically female object such as a teapot was masculinised by painting it brown and covering it with spikes, boys were more inclined to play with it than were girls (Leinbach *et al.*, 1997). Furthermore, when a 6-month-old baby is dressed in either pink or blue (its actual sex is not apparent) and parents are asked to give it either a train (a boy's toy), doll (a girl's toy) or fish (a neutral toy), the baby in pink would be given the doll more often than would the baby in blue. The baby in pink was also smiled at more often (Will *et al.*, 1976).

Where do children learn sex stereotypes?

Parents play an especially important role in the development of sex stereotypes: they tend to encourage and reward their sons for playing with 'masculine' toys such as cars and trucks and objects such as baseballs and footballs (Fagot and Hagan, 1991) and encourage baby boys to generate gross motor activity, whereas they are more soothing and calming with baby girls (Smith and Lloyd, 1978). Parents also tend to encourage and reward their daughters for engaging in 'feminine' activities that promote dependence, warmth and sensitivity, such as playing house or hosting a make-believe tea party (Dunn *et al.*, 1987; Lytton and Romney, 1991). Parents who do not encourage or reward these kinds of stereotypical activity tend to have children whose attitudes and behaviour reflect fewer sex stereotypes (Weisner and Wilson-Mitchell, 1990).

In supposedly 'masculine' academic subjects, girls are perceived as performing less well than boys. Many reasons have been suggested for the discrepancy but one of the most frequently cited is socialisation: that is, parents and teachers are more likely to engage boys in science and scientific explanations than they are girls.

In an ingenious experiment to test this hypothesis, Crowley *et al.* (2001) sought the permission of parents visiting a Californian children's museum to film and record their interactions with their children as they made their way around the exhibitions. Data were collected from 298 interactions between mothers and fathers and their daughters and sons on 26 days over a 30-month period. Conversations were rated according to whether they involved explanations, descriptions of or directions for exhibitions.

The researchers found that parents were more likely to explain exhibits to their sons than to their daughters. If the behaviour of parents helps shape the behaviour of their children, the researchers suggest that this disparity could have a significant effect on the child's interest in and knowledge of science.

Moral development

The word 'morality' comes from a Latin word that means 'custom'. Moral behaviour is behaviour that conforms to a generally accepted set of rules, although whether these rules generally are accepted is quite controversial. With few exceptions, by the time a person reaches adulthood, they have accepted a set of rules about personal and social behaviour. These rules vary in different cultures and may take the form of laws, taboos and even sorcery (Chasdi, 1994). How does a child acquire morality?

Piaget's theory of moral development

According to Piaget, the development of morality occurs in three general stages: the premoral stage, the moral realism stage and the moral relativism stage. Table 12.3 outlines the features of each stage.

The first stage of moral development (ages 0–5 years) is **premoral**. During this period the child has little conception of rules or principles. The second stage, however, sees the beginning of rule adherence. This stage, **moral realism**, is characterised by egocentrism, or 'self-centredness', and blind adherence to rules.

Egocentric children can evaluate events only in terms of their personal consequences. Their behaviour is not guided by the effects it might have on someone else, because they are not capable of imagining themselves in the other person's place. Thus, young children do not consider whether an act is right or wrong but only whether it is likely to have good or bad consequences personally. Punishment is a bad consequence, and the fear of punishment is the only real moral force at this age. A young child also believes that rules come from parents (or other authority figures, such as older children or God), and that rules cannot be changed.

Older children and adults judge an act by the intentions of the actor as well as by the consequences of the act. A young child considers only an act's objective outcomes, not the subjective intent that lay behind the act. For example, Piaget told two stories, one about John, who accidentally broke fifteen cups, and Henry, who broke one cup while trying to do something that was forbidden to him. When a young child is asked which of the two children is the naughtiest, the child will say that John is, because he broke fifteen cups. They will not take into account the fact that the act was entirely accidental.

As children mature, they become less egocentric and more capable of empathy. Older children (older than age 7) can imagine how another person feels. This shift away from egocentrism means that children's behaviour may be guided not merely by the effects that acts have on themselves but also by the effects they have on others. At around 10 years of age, children enter Piaget's third stage of moral development, **moral relativism**, during which rules become more flexible as the child learns that many of them (such as those that govern games) are social conventions that may be altered by mutual consent.

Kohlberg's theory of moral development

Piaget's description of moral development was considerably elaborated on by Lawrence Kohlberg (1927–1987). Kohlberg (1971) had argued that, 'All individuals in all cultures go through the same order or sequence of gross stages of development, though they vary in rate and terminal point of development.' He studied boys of between 10 and 17 years of age, over the course of several years, by presenting them with stories involving moral dilemmas (Kohlberg, 1966; 1982). For example, one story described a man called Heinz whose wife was dying of a cancer that could only be treated by a medication discovered by a chemist living in the same town. This was the dilemma in full:

Table 12.3 Piaget's stages of moral development

Stage	Description
Premoral (0–5 years)	The child shows little understanding of rules or principles
Moral realism (5–10 years)	Rules are obeyed quite rigidly The child judges a person's action by its consequences The child develops a belief in punishment and justice
Moral relativism (10 years and over)	The child becomes more flexible in interpreting moral issues The child becomes aware that moral responses are relative, that rules can be broken and that people are not always punished

A woman is near death from cancer. One drug might save her, a form of radium discovered by a chemist living in the same town, who is selling the drug at ten times what it cost him to manufacture it. The sick woman's husband tried to borrow the money but could raise only half the price. He told the chemist that his wife was dying and asked him to sell the drug more cheaply or, at least, let him pay later, but the chemist refused. The desperate husband broke into the chemist's shop to steal the drug for his wife. Should he have done that?

For this dilemma and others, there is no correct answer. It is designed to discover more about how people engage in moral reasoning. On the basis of his research using such dilemmas, Kohlberg argued that moral development comprised three levels and seven stages (see Table 12.4). These stages are closely linked to children's cognitive development as outlined by Piaget.

The first two stages belong to the **preconventional level**, during which morality is externally defined. During stage 1, morality of punishment and obedience, children blindly obey authority and avoid punishment. When asked to decide what Heinz should do, children base their decisions on fears about being punished for letting one's wife die or for committing a crime. During stage 2, morality of naive instrumental hedonism, children's behaviour is guided egocentrically by the pleasantness or unpleasantness of its consequences to them. The moral choice is reduced to a weighing of the probable risks and benefits of stealing the drug.

The next two stages belong to the **conventional level**, which includes an understanding that the social system has an interest in people's behaviour. During stage 3, morality of maintaining good relations, children want to be regarded by people who know them as good, well-behaved children. Moral decisions are based on perceived social pressure. Either Heinz should steal the drug because people would otherwise regard him as heartless, or he should not steal it because they would regard him as a criminal. During stage 4, morality of maintaining social order, laws and moral rules are perceived as instruments used to maintain social order and, as such, must be obeyed. Thus, both protecting a life and respecting people's property are seen as rules that help maintain social order. This stage required people to expand their social perspectives, a requirement which was assisted by having attended university or working in a work setting that involved complex reasoning (Mason and Gibbs, 1993).

Kohlberg also described a final level of moral development – the **postconventional level**, during which people realise that moral rules have some underlying principles that apply to all situations and societies. During stage 5, morality of social contracts, people recognise that rules are social contracts, that not all authority figures are infallible, and that individual rights can sometimes take precedence over laws. During stage 6, morality of universal ethical principles, people perceive rules and laws as being justified by abstract ethical values, such as the value of human life and the value of dignity. In stage 7, the morality of cosmic orientation, people adopt values that transcend societal norms. This stage represents the zenith of moral development. Kohlberg believed that not all people reach the postconventional level of moral development.

Evaluation of Piaget's and Kohlberg's theories of moral development

Piaget's and Kohlberg's theories have greatly influenced research on moral development, but they have received some criticism. For example, Piaget's research indicated

Table 12.4 Levels and stages of Kohlberg's theory of moral development

Level and stage	Highlights
Preconventional level	
Stage 1: Morality of punishment and obedience	Avoidance of punishment
Stage 2: Morality of naive instrumental hedonism	Egocentric perspective; weighing of potential risks and benefits
Conventional level	
Stage 3: Morality of maintaining good relations	Morality based on approval from others
Stage 4: Morality of maintaining social order	Rules and laws define morality
Postconventional level	
Stage 5: Morality of social contracts	Obey societal rules for the common good, although individual rights sometimes outweigh laws
Stage 6: Morality of unversal ethical principles	Societal laws and rules based on ethical values
Stage 7: Morality of cosmic orientation	Adoption of values that transcend societal norms

that children in the second stage (moral realism) respond to the magnitude of a transgression rather than to the intent behind it. But even adults respond to the magnitude of a transgression. The theft of a few postage stamps by an office worker, for example, is not treated the same way as the embezzlement of thousands of pounds. In this sense, children's morality is quite adult-like.

While stages one to four of Kohlberg's model appear to be universal, the appearance of the later stages of moral reasoning seem to be culture-specific. Urban populations tend to express more mature moral judgements, i.e. reach the later stages of reasoning, than rural populations. For example, stages 5 and 6 are absent in semi-literate, peasant cultures (Kohlberg, 1969) and in folk villages (Snarey, 1985). One conclusion from this is that the stage model does not classify modes of reasoning that involve the types collective reasoning seen in less literate cultures (Snarey, 1985). For example, one 50-year-old Indian man justified Heinz's theft to save the life of a pet in terms of the 'unity of life' – all human life was sacred and needed to be preserved if possible. When Japanese and North American adults were given the Heinz dilemma, there was no difference in the moral stages of the two groups but the reasons for their decision were different (Isawa, 1992). Americans believed that the wife should live and that Heinz was right to steal the drug; the Japanese, however, were more concerned with the purity and cleanliness of life and decided that Heinz should not steal the drug.

Sobesky (1983) found that changes in the wording of Heinz's dilemma would drastically change people's responses. If the possibility of imprisonment was underscored, people tended to make more responses belonging to the preconventional level. Many researchers agree with Rest (1979), who concluded that Kohlberg's 'stages' are not coherent entities but do describe a progression in the ability of children to consider more and more complex reasons for moral rules.

A different type of criticism was levelled by Gilligan (1977, 1982), who suggested that Kohlberg's theory is sex-biased. According to her, Kohlberg's studies seem to suggest that men (in general) adhered to universal ethical principles, whereas women (in general) preferred to base their moral judgements on the effects these judgements would have on the people involved. Men's judgements were based more on abstract ideas of justice, whereas women's judgements were based more on concrete considerations of caring and concern for relationships. The criticism has some validity in the sense that the moral stages which Kohlberg suggested were based on data collected exclusively from boys: results show that when men and women study these dilemmas, their decisions place women at stage 3 and men at stage 5.

However, most researchers have not found that men's and women's moral judgements tend to be based on different types of values. For example, Donenberg and Hoffman (1988) found that boys and girls were equally likely to base their moral judgements on justice or caring and that the sex of the main character in the moral dilemma had no effect on their judgements. Adolescent girls reach the third stage of reasoning more quickly than do boys (Silberman and Snarey, 1993) and girls and women, across most cultures but not all, appear to express more care-related concerns when making moral judgements (Jaffe and Hyde, 2000; Leenders and Brugman, 2005; Raynauld et al., 1999). Johnson (1998), in a study of adults, also found that both sexes were capable of moral reasoning based on justice and caring. Walker (1989) tested 233 subjects ranging in ages from 5 to 63 years and found no reliable sex differences. However, while the available evidence does not appear to support Gilligan's conclusion that such concern is related to a person's sex, some studies do show sex differences in the type of real-life dilemmas. For example, women are more likely to report relationship-based dilemmas whereas men are more likely to report impersonal dilemmas when asked to describe actual moral dilemmas they have faced (Walker et al., 1987).

Alternative models of moral development

Although Kohlberg's model has been one of the most influential and widely studied models of moral reasoning, it is not the only one. Other models of moral development have focused on specific types of moral behaviour. For example, Damon (1977, 1980) has explored children's concept of sharing and distributing resources. In a typical scenario, a child is told that a class of children has received some money from the sale of paintings that the whole class had made. The child is given examples of how the money could be distributed – it could be distributed according to merit, need, equality or sex – and is asked which criterion is most appropriate. Based on responses to this scenario, Damon proposed that the child goes through four levels of moral reasoning, summarised in Table 12.5.

In Damon's model of distributive justice, the child begins the process of moral development by making decisions about sharing based on egocentric considerations. The child will make decisions based on their own desires and perspectives. This stage of reasoning occurs during the pre-schooler stage. Towards the end of this stage, children begin to introduce external factors into their reasoning and may distribute/share resources according to the size or ability of the recipient group. The second stage is observed in primary school children and is characterised by an increase in equality-based judgements, that is, the child believes that everybody should share in a reward regardless of their ability or merit. The third stage finds the child considering the merit and the achievement of others when deciding how to distribute resources. The

Table 12.5 Damon's model of distributive justice

Stage	Description
1	Pre-schoolers' decisions are based on their feelings and perspectives; decisions are egocentric At the end of the stage, external considerations influenced reasoning
2	Primary school children base their decisions on notions of equality
3	Equality gives way to considerations of merit and notions of reciprocity The distribution of resources is based on other's achievements
4	At age 10 to 11, the child exhibits evidence of fairness

fourth and final stage, which occurs at age 10 to 11 years, sees the child considering a large number of factors that could influence their judgements about distribution; at this stage, the children show evidence of the moral concept of fairness.

Damon's stages model finds considerable support in real-life decision-making by children. This type of thinking appears to follow a similar pattern, but the children exhibit greater levels of self-interest (Gerson and Damon, 1978). They will, for example, indicate that resources should be distributed according to merit if they themselves are seen as showing merit.

An alternative method of measuring moral reasoning and development is the socio-moral reflection method (SRM) of Gibbs *et al.* (1982). This is a dilemma-free measure which evaluates the importance of those issues, values and institutions that arise in Kohlberg's model and which are seen in every society and culture – contracts, truth, affiliation, life, property, law and legal justice (Gibbs *et al.*, 2007). For example, people's view of truth and contract might be prompted by the statement: 'Think about when you've made a promise to a friend'; affiliation would be explored by statements such as: 'Let's say a friend of yours needed help and may die and you're the only person who can save him or her.'

While this and other models have attempted to create chronologies of moral development, some researchers have questioned the catch-all nature of the term 'moral development'. For example, a distinction has been made between 'moral' and 'socio-conventional' reasoning (Turiel, 1998). Moral reasoning involves making decisions where the consequences of actions could lead to another person being physically or psychologically harmed. Socio-conventional reasoning concerns issues regarding conformity to social norms or conduct such as how to address others, how to behave at a dinner table. Both types of reasoning follow a rule system of some kind but the two are different in terms of their comparative moral importance. It is thought that children can make the distinction between these two types of reasoning by 6 or 7 years.

Adolescence

After childhood comes adolescence, the threshold to adulthood (in Latin, *adolescere* means 'to grow up'). The transition between childhood and adulthood is as much social as it is biological. In some societies, people are considered to be adults as soon as they are sexually mature, at which time they may assume adult rights and responsibilities, including marriage. In most industrialised societies, where formal education often continues into the late teens and early twenties, adulthood officially comes several years later. The end of adolescence is difficult to judge because the line between adolescence and young adulthood is fuzzy: there are no distinct physical changes that mark this transition. Erikson (1968) described adolescence as a 'psycho-social moratorium': a period in which the child begins to experiment with life and with living, testing social and emotional boundaries to see what is acceptable and what is not.

Physical development

Puberty (from the Latin *puber*, meaning 'adult'), the period during which a person's reproductive system matures, marks the beginning of the transition from childhood to adulthood. Many physical changes occur during this stage: people reach their ultimate height, develop increased muscle size and body hair, and become capable of reproduction. There is also a change in social roles. As a child, a person is dependent on parents, teachers and other adults. As an adolescent, they are expected to assume more responsibility. Relations with peers also suddenly change; members of one's own sex become potential rivals for the attention of members of the other sex.

Sexual maturation

The internal sex organs and external genitalia do not change much for several years after birth, but they begin to develop again at puberty. When boys and girls reach about

11–14 years of age, their testes or ovaries secrete hormones that begin the process of sexual maturation. This activity of the gonads is initiated by the hypothalamus, the part of the brain to which the pituitary gland is attached. The hypothalamus instructs the pituitary gland to secrete hormones that stimulate the gonads to secrete sex hormones. These sex hormones act on various organs of the body and initiate the changes that accompany sexual maturation.

The sex hormones secreted by the gonads cause growth and maturation of the external genitalia and of the gonads themselves. In addition, these hormones cause the maturation of ova and the production of sperm. All these developments are considered primary sex characteristics, because they are essential to the ability to reproduce. The sex hormones also stimulate the development of secondary sex characteristics, the physical changes that distinguish males from females. Before puberty, boys and girls look much the same, except, perhaps, for their hairstyles and clothing. At puberty, young men's testes begin to secrete testosterone; this hormone causes their muscles to develop, their facial hair to grow, and their voices to deepen. Young women's ovaries secrete oestradiol, the most important oestrogen, or female sex hormone. Oestradiol causes women's breasts to grow and their pelvis to widen, and it produces changes in the layer of fat beneath the skin and in the texture of the skin itself.

Development of the adult secondary sex characteristics takes several years, and not all characteristics develop at the same time. The process begins in girls at around age 11. The first visible change is the accumulation of fatty tissue around the nipples, followed shortly by the growth of pubic hair. The spurt of growth in height commences, and the uterus and vagina begin to enlarge. The first menstrual period begins at around age 13, just about the time the rate of growth in height begins to decline. In boys, sexual maturation begins slightly later. The first visible event is the growth of the testes and scrotum, followed by the appearance of pubic hair. A few months later, the penis begins to grow, and the spurt of growth in height starts. The larynx grows larger, which causes the voice to become lower. Sexual maturity – the ability to father a child – occurs at around age 15. The growth of facial hair usually occurs later; often a full beard does not grow until the late teens or early twenties.

In industrialised societies, the average age at the onset of puberty has been declining. For example, the average age at the onset of menstruation was between 14 and 15 years in 1900 but is between 12 and 13 years today. The most important reason for this decline is better childhood nutrition. It appears that this decline is levelling off in industrialised societies, but in many developing countries, the age of the onset of puberty is beginning to fall as these countries enjoy increasing prosperity.

Behavioural effects of puberty

The changes that accompany sexual maturation have a profound effect on young people's behaviour and self-concept. One pronounced change is sensitivity about their appearance. Many girls worry about their weight and the size of their breasts and hips (Kloep, 1999). Many boys worry about their height, the size of their genitals, their muscular development and the growth of their beards (Alsaker, 1996). At around the age of 13, girls have consistently more negative views of their body image than do boys (Kloep, 1999; Wichstrom, 1999). Findings such as these have been linked to the higher incidence of eating disorders such as anorexia nervosa and bulimia nervosa in girls (we return to the characteristics of anorexia and bulimia and their possible causes in much more detail in Chapter 13). In Europe, for example, between 1 and 3 per cent of girls are reported to show symptoms of one of these two disorders (Barnombudsmannen, 1997). A study of Scottish children found that although many of them considered themselves to be 'too fat', they were not significantly overweight for their age, showing an average body shape (Shucksmith and Hendry, 1998). The results indicate that puberty and the short period following it are characterised by a concern with body image, but a concern which does not appear grounded in reality.

An Australian study asked over five hundred 8–11-year-old boys and girls what they thought of their body image and whether they engaged in any thinking or behaviour that could lead to weight loss or muscle gain (McCabe and Ricciardelli, 2003). Body Mass Index was measured (see Chapter 13 to see how this is calculated), as was self-esteem.

As might be expected, children with high BMIs were those most concerned with losing weight and their self-esteem was associated with their body satisfaction. The poorer the self-esteem, the greater the dissatisfaction. Boys were more likely than girls to think about, and put strategies in place towards, increasing muscle. However, even girls were engaged in thinking about increasing their muscles. The study shows that even quite young children are concerned with their body image and already think about strategies for losing weight and/or increasing muscle.

In an American study of 165 girls and 139 boys with an average age of 15 years, Jones (2004) found that girls became increasingly dissatisfied with their bodies primarily through talking about their appearance with friends and comparing themselves with desirable others. As time progressed, the girls became highly preoccupied with their appearance and this preoccupation was related to the increase in dissatisfaction. Boys, however, seemed less concerned with making direct comparisons between themselves and their peers. Instead, those boys who reported being most dissatisfied with their bodies had an 'internalised' ideal of what a muscular body looked like: it was against this ideal that they compared themselves.

A more extensive study investigated how body image changed across almost two decades. The cross-sectional study of 3,127 college students from a North American university who completed body image questionnaires from 1983 to 2001 found that body image changed significantly across these years, especially in women (Cash *et al.*, 2004). White women, in particular, reported negative assessments of their body image and a preoccupation with being overweight in the 1980s and early 1990s. Their satisfaction with their upper and mid torso as well as their overall appearance declined over the period. Women who completed assessments more recently – mid-1990s onwards – reported more favourable body image and less concern with being overweight (despite being heavier than the 1980s, cohorts). Men were relatively unaffected over the years, with their body image remaining relatively stable.

In addition to concerns with bodily appearance, most adolescents display a particular form of egocentrism that develops early in the stage of formal operations: self-consciousness. Some developmental psychologists believe that self-consciousness results from the difficulty in distinguishing their own self-perceptions from the views other people have of them.

Because the onset of puberty occurs at different times in different individuals, young adolescents can find themselves to be more or less mature than some of their friends, and this difference can have important social consequences. Early-maturing boys feel more confident about themselves than do late-maturing boys and are also more satisfied with their looks and musculature (Cok, 1990). Early-maturing girls, however, seem to exhibit greater depression and unhappiness, although the evidence for this is mixed (Alsaker, 1992). Early-maturing girls do appear to have greater eating concerns (Brooks-Gunn, 1988) and show greater variability in self-esteem.

How do adolescents view puberty?

Adolescent boys and girls have different views of puberty. Whereas boys seem to look forward to the increasing strength, freedom and social status that the change brings, girls see limited benefits. Instead, they regard the onset of becoming a woman as being accompanied by the need to conform to society's view of women and this view is one that associates being a woman with lower social status (K.A. Martin, 1996). Girls perceive having less freedom than do boys because their parents insist on regulating aspects of their social lives, specifically, protecting them from predatory boys (K.A. Martin, 1996). Girls also seem unhappier at this time than are boys. Depression, for exam-

ple, appears to be more common in girls than in boys at puberty (Wichstrom, 1999). One possible reason may be their consistent concern over body image and the need to maintain a level of physical attractiveness – in short, the beginning of the development of sexual identity – two features that could meet with as much acceptance as rejection. As Figure 12.14 shows, girls become increasingly concerned with their weight and shape after the onset of puberty.

Changes in leisure activities reflect the move into young adulthood

One of the factors in an adolescent's life that marks the transition from childhood to adulthood is the type of leisure activity they engage in. The ways in which children engage in leisure activities before and after puberty seem to reflect an increased concern with becoming an adult and with divesting themselves of the clothes of childhood. In

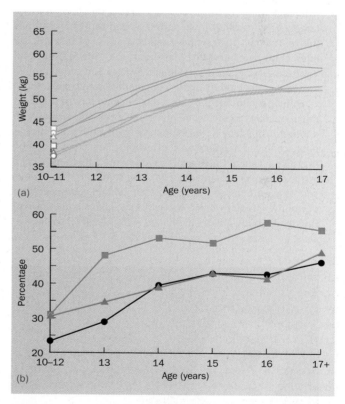

Figure 12.14 (a) Plots of three groups of girls' actual mean body weight (orange) against their preferred mean body weight (purple). Data came from a study of girls in London in 1972 (the line with the triangle), London in 1990 (the line with the circle) and Ottawa (Canada) in 1990 (the line with the square). **(b)** How the proportion of girls who wish to be thinner increases after puberty. Data came from the same samples as those used for part (a).

Source: Crisp, A., Sedgwick, P., Halek, C., Joughin, N. and Humphrey, H., Why may girls persist in smoking? *Journal of Adolescence*, 1999, 22, 657–672. Copyright 1999, with permission from Elsevier.

the early stages of adolescence, children might engage in social activities organised for them by adults, such as group- or club-based activities (the Brownies, Scouts, sports clubs, and so on). As the children progress through their teenage years, these activities are perceived as too controlling and as less exciting than they originally were. Instead, activities which children themselves control become more prominent; children will hang around street corners, shopping centres and parks, for example, or drink alcohol.

Studies of Swedish, Scottish and Norwegian children have all demonstrated that the two reasons that children consistently give for drinking alcohol are that either it makes them look more like an adult or it makes them more accepted as an adult (Kloep *et al.*, 2001). Eventually, after the initial experimentation with alcohol – which may lead to excessive and painful consumption – most learn to consume drink sensibly.

Psychology in action – Adolescents and the internet

Once there were pigeons, then the printing press, then Roland Hill's Penny Post, followed by television and telephony, and, in another technological upheaval, the internet. Humans create some enormously inventive ways of communicating with each other. In the 1980s and 1990s, the internet was a largely passive affair – we surfed to find things and to buy things. The past 10 years have seen the arrival of Web 2.0. The internet became interactive: Facebook, Flikr, Friends Reunited, YouTube, Skype, MSN messenger, Twitter and the like blossomed and the internet underwent another, small revolution.

Online communication has now become one of the most popular means whereby one human being communicates with another, especially if that human being is pubescent or pre-pubescent. Van den Eijnden *et al.* (2008) cite a study reporting that 84 per cent of Dutch adolescents were found to have used instant messaging or internet chat rooms. In 2007–08, serious concerns were raised about adolescents' and young people's use of the internet when a spate of 17 suicides in the town of Brigdend, South Wales were linked with the use of social networking sites. There was no evidence that these sites encouraged these suicides and it was more likely that the publicity generated on television and in newspapers provided more obvious encouragement.

This type of communication, however, is largely sterile and devoid of human contact. It may also be used by the lonely. Van den Eijnden *et al.*, therefore, sought to investigate whether online messaging was associated with any negative (or positive) effect on well-being.

They monitored instant messenger use and chat room visits by 663 12–15 year olds at two time points, separated by six months. Measures of loneliness and depression as well as compulsive internet use were administered at each session.

Using instant messaging and frequenting chat rooms – but not emailing – was positively related to compulsive internet use six months later: the greater the involvement in the former, the greater the compulsive internet use 6 months later. However, messenger use (but not chat room use or emailing) was also associated with increased depression six months later whereas loneliness was inversely related to instant messenger use. That is, those who reported being most lonely were less likely to use instant messaging, possibly because these lonely adolescents were adopting an 'avoidant' coping style (avoiding communication); research suggests that lonely people use the internet for entertainment, rather than contact (Seepersad, 2004).

Why was there an increase in reported depression? Perhaps depression arises because the person's social support is provided by online strangers. Such weak relations can not provide the social support that human contact can.

It seems, however, that adolescent boys can benefit more from this online communication than can girls – they feel that they are able to disclose more in an environment where there is no face-to-face or physical contact (Schouten *et al.,* 2007). The notion that the typical adolescent internet user is a generally lonely geek also appears to be a myth. Adolescents who are socially competent in 'real life' are more likely to use the internet –via messaging services, for example – to keep in touch with people (Bryant *et al.*, 2006).

Twenty years ago there was no internet as we know it. Now, this is an essential part of life, from childhood onwards.

Source: Getty Images

Social development, peer relations and delinquency

During adolescence a person's behaviour and social roles change dramatically. Adolescence is not simply a continuation of childhood; it marks a real transition from the dependence of childhood to the relative independence of adulthood. Adolescence is also a period during which many people seek out new experiences and engage in reckless behaviour – behaviour that involves psychological, physical and legal risks for them as well as for others (Arnett, 1995). Norm-breaking such as this is related to the adolescent's social network (Magnusson *et al.*, 1986). For example, early-maturing girls have been found to have older female friends who engage in more adult behaviour (such as drinking and smoking). Such girls are also likely to regard themselves as more accepted by older girls, to date more (Stattin and Magnusson, 1990), and be more sexually active. The picture in boys is unclear; there is no such consistent pattern in the nature of their peer network or their behaviour.

Early- and late-maturing 14-year-old boys report being involved in more crime and being more rebellious in school, such as being sent out of class, swearing at a teacher, expulsion from school and so on (Williams and Dunlop, 1999). Early and late maturers may engage in delinquent behaviour for different reasons – early maturers drink alcohol because this is what their peers do; late maturers drink in order to attract attention and gain popularity.

Of course, we cannot stop puberty, but we can try to stop delinquent behaviour. One way to do this is by trying to understand why such delinquent behaviour occurs. Delinquent behaviour can lead to further mental problems when the delinquent child becomes an adult. Researchers at the University of Rotterdam have reported that emotional and behavioural problems characteristic of delinquency in 706 Dutch 11–16-year-olds were significantly related to the development of psychopathology (according to psychiatric diagnostic criteria) when these children became adults (Ferdinand *et al.*, 1999). The children were followed up for almost nine years, making this longitudinal study of particular value. It does not suggest that the delinquency caused later psychopathology (because correlation does not mean causation), but those children characterised by behavioural or emotional disturbances later showed behaviour characteristic of mental disorder. The finding suggests that if the delinquency can be identified early enough, reducing the delinquent behaviour may lead to a healthier adult mental life.

Delinquency is associated with a range of intellectual problems. Children with conduct disorder, for example, may have low verbal IQ, impaired language ability and poor executive function, as you saw earlier. Although this pattern has been seen in young and adolescent children, a near identical pattern of intellectual impairment is seen in pre-school clinic-referred boys who met the standard criteria for conduct disorder (Speltz *et al.*, 1999). It would seem that the routine language testing of pre-school children exhibiting conduct disorder would be helpful in halting the decline in verbal IQ and language skill in these children.

Adolescence and mental health

Rates of depression increase in adolescence. Some studies have found that the prevalence increases from 1 per cent in children under 12 years of age to over 20 per cent by the end of adolescence (Kessler *et al.*, 2001). The biggest increase is seen between the ages of 15 and 18 (Hankin *et al.*, 1998), is twice as likely in girls (Glowinski *et al.*, 2003) and is even higher in pairs of female twins.

While some of the variance in mental health can be attributable to the momentous physical and social changes that the adolescent is going through, there are risk factors which can increase the likelihood of depression emerging. Sexual abuse, for example, (Putnam, 2003), is a serious risk factor for later depression which has also been associated with altered brain development (Teicher *et al.*, 2006). Studies have found that abuse experienced in childhood is associated with reduced hippocampus, corpus callosum, and frontal cortex grey matter (Andersen *et al.*, 2008). Depression, as you will see in the last chapter in the book, is associated with reduced hippocampal volume in adults. The pattern in depressed adolescents, however, is inconsistent. Some studies report a decrease in older adolescents who have major depression while others, fewer of them, show no reduction in adolescents with comparable problems (Andersen and Teicher, 2008).

Friendship

Friendship in childhood appears to have greater long-term consequences than might first be apparent (Newcomb and Bagwell, 1995). For example, pre-adolescent friendship and peer rejection are significant predictors of adult adjustment. Poor peer relations are associated with later maladjustment and mental health problems (J.G. Parker *et al.*, 1995). In an extensive longitudinal study, Bagwell *et al.* (1998) tracked 60 individuals from school age to 12 years after (when the mean age was 23 years 3 months). These researchers found that lower levels of pre-adolescent peer rejection predicted overall adjustment. Those with friends reported higher self-esteem as adults, whereas peer rejection and friendlessness was associated with mental disorder, especially depression. This evidence suggests that peer support and approval are important determinants of the adolescent's happiness and later adjustment. However, approval or rejection may not necessarily be causes of later adjustment or maladjustment. Perhaps these factors help to moderate maladjustment.

Psychology in action – Bullying

Bullying

Until relatively recently, the topic of bullying of schoolchildren by other schoolchildren featured briefly, if at all, in textbooks of social or developmental psychology. Aggression by children has always been a topic mined by psychology, but within the context of schooling it was largely ignored. In parts of Europe, however, there has been considerable research on bullying in the workplace: who bullies, why bullies do it, and how they get away with it. This research prompted others to explore the incidence, cause and prevention of bullying in school and an extensive research now exists in countries such as Australia, Canada, Norway, Sweden, the UK and the USA.

How common is bullying?

The incidence of bullying in secondary schools is high and is regarded by children themselves as a common problem (Smith *et al.*, 1999). According to Nicolaides *et al.* (2002, p. 106), bullying is 'a form of aggressive behaviour that causes injury or distress to the individual to whom it is directed'. This aggression can be physical (actual bodily violence), verbal, or psychological (such as social exclusion). The relationship between the bully and the victim is also unequal: perceived power tends to reside with the bully and bullies usually act repeatedly against their victims. The victim of a bully, therefore, is likely to be bullied on more than one occasion.

In a survey of bullying in English schools, Whitney and Smith (1993) reported the general incidence of bullying, who does the bullying and who becomes the victim. The study found that:

- 10–27 per cent of children reported being the victim of bullying at some time during school time.
- 6–12 per cent reported taking part in bullying at least once.
- Self-reports of bullying and being bullied declined as the children grew older (from 8 to 16 years).
- Boys were twice, and sometimes three, times as likely to be bullies as were girls.
- 35 per cent of bullies were spoken to by their teacher about their conduct.
- 30–35 per cent of victims spoke to teachers about their being bullied.
- 60 per cent of children reported disliking bullying.
- 20 per cent of children indicated that they would be willing to join in with bullying.

Since September 1999, it has been a legal requirement in England and Wales for schools to have an anti-bullying programme. Such programmes have been increasing across Europe, and Norway and Sweden have well-publicised anti-bullying campaigns. Such initiatives are considered important because studies have suggested that when schools are complacent about their bullying children or when the school's climate encourages bullying, then social relationships are harmed and the education that children in such schools receive is poor (Olweus, 1993; Rigby, 1997).

Boys are more likely to be physical bullies than are girls; girls are more likely to engage in 'psychological' bullying such as name-calling and excluding others. Teachers' perceptions of bullying and their awareness of the findings about bullying have generally been found to be accurate, but they usually under-report the incidence of bullying in their schools. One study found that teachers' estimate was 5–10 per cent, but the pupils' reports indicated that the incidence was over twice as high at 26 per cent (Pervin and Turner, 1994). The age and sex of the teacher also seems to be important: female teachers are more likely to have negative attitudes towards bullying and more positive attitudes towards the victim, but longer-serving teachers have a less positive attitude to the victim (Boulton, 1997).

Transitional life events, social dominance and bullying

Some psychologists have suggested that bullying becomes more prevalent during early adolescence and during transitional periods in the children's lives, for specific reasons. For example, aggression in early adolescence is viewed more positively by children's peers than it is later in adolescence (Bukowski *et al.*, 2000). According to Pellegrini and Long (2002), certain factors promote an increase in aggression at this time. They point to the obvious physical changes that occur, especially in boys. Hormonal changes lead to body size increase, the beginning of a sexual interest in the opposite sex and the visible expression of secondary sexual characteristics which mark the onset of young adulthood. The increase in body size, some researchers argue, leads to boys reviewing their position in their social environments and expressing a need for dominance within their social group (Hawley, 1999). One way of expressing this dominance is to use aggression, usually with the approval of peers (Maccoby, 1998).

Pellegrini and Long (2002) also note that, in addition to establishing social dominance, young adolescents also undergo a physical transition in their lives: moving school. This move appears to coincide with an increase in antisocial behaviour. In primary school, children are taught in well-established, close, friendly groups. The move to secondary school usually leads to the break-up of this close group and the child has to find new friends in a much bigger environment. Pellegrini and Long argue that if bullying is a way of establishing social dominance, the aggression should increase during this transition from primary to secondary school. Once social groups are established, the incidence of bullying should decrease.

Psychology in action – *Continued*

During the transition, bullying and aggression increase in the initial period but then decrease. Boys are more likely than girls to be bullies and are more likely to view bullying and aggression positively in the early stage of adolescence. After the transition to middle school, aggression decreased and dominance in social groups increased, providing some indirect evidence for the hypothesis that aggression is used to establish dominance but once dominance is established, continued aggression is unnecessary.

What makes a bully?

Are there personality characteristics that are specific to bullies? In an earlier study of teachers' views of bullies and victims, the personalities of victims were well described but the character of bullies less well-described (Siann *et al.*, 1993). One common view of the bully is of a person who is a lumpen, physically able individual who is socially inept (Nicolaides *et al.*, 2002). Research suggests, however, that this stereotype is inaccurate. The school bully is likely to be cold, manipulative and very socially adept. This is one reason why they are able to convince others to condone, endorse or join in with the bullying.

To test whether bullies are sensitive to emotional and social events, Sutton *et al.* (1999) first administered a questionnaire to 193 English schoolchildren aged between 7 and 11 years to determine who were bullies, followers, defenders of the victim, victims, and who did not get involved in bullying. The children then participated in an experiment in which they were read 11 short stories and asked questions about these stories which relied on an awareness of social cognition and manipulation. For example, in one of the studies, 'Mike' has a stomach ache but knows that if his mother sees him in pain, he will not be allowed out to play. He asks his mother if he can. The participants were shown four pictures of Mike's face and asked: (1) which facial expression represents how he really feels (the control question) and (2) which facial expression he shows to his mother when he asks her if he can go out (the experimental question).

The researchers found that bullies who initiated aggression were more accurate in answering social manipulation questions than were bullies who helped or supported the ringleader bullies, the victims, or the defenders. This finding suggests that the bully is not a socially inept individual but one who is aware of the power of manipulation.

A study of American children by Schwartz *et al.* (2000) found that those who were exposed to a harsh, hostile home environment early in life were more likely to be victimised by peers three years later. However, this occurred only in children who had few friends. Those children with hostile family backgrounds but who had numerous friendships experienced little peer victimisation. Friendship may be a moderating factor in peer victimisation, the authors argue.

Relations with parents

Philip Larkin, in his poem *This Be the Verse*, famously remarked, 'They fuck you up your mum and dad/They may not mean to but they do./They fill you with the faults they had/And add some extra just for you.' The relationship between adolescents and their parents can be fractious. As adolescents begin to define their new roles and to assert them, they almost inevitably come into conflict with their parents. Adolescents and their parents tend to have similar values and attitudes towards important issues (Youniss and Smollar, 1985). Family conflicts tend to be provoked by minor issues, such as messy rooms, loud music, clothes, curfews and household chores. These problems tend to begin around the time of puberty; if puberty occurs particularly early or late, so does the conflict (Paikoff and Brooks-Gunn, 1991).

Adolescence is said to be a time of turmoil, characterised by unhappiness, stress and confusion. When McGue *et al.* (2005) asked 1,330 11-year-old twins to rate the warmth and degree of conflict experienced in their relationship with parents and then asked them to do the same three years later (1,176 children did), the children's perception of their relationship declined significantly in three years – conflicts increased significantly and reported warmth decreased. Girls experienced these changes more significantly than did boys.

Whereas a few adolescents are unhappy most of the time (and most are unhappy some of the time), studies have found that the vast majority of teenagers generally feel happy and self-confident (Offer and Sabshin, 1984; Peterson and Ebata, 1987). But mood states do seem to be more variable during the teenage years than during other times of life. Csikszentmihalyi and Larson (1984) randomly sampled the mood states of a group of teenage students. They gave them electronic beepers that sounded at random intervals that were, on average, two hours apart. Each time the beepers sounded, the students stopped what they were doing and filled out a questionnaire that asked what they were doing, how they felt, what they were thinking about, and so on. The investigators found that the students' moods could swing from high to low and back again in the course of a few hours. The questionnaires also revealed conflicts between the participants and other family members. Although the subjects of the conflicts were usually trivial, they nevertheless concerned the teenagers deeply.

The degree of parental conflict the child is exposed to can have devastating consequences later in life, especially in terms of the child's adjustment (Fincham, 1998). Although divorce may seem an obvious cause of problems for the child, evidence suggests that the negative effects of divorce are evident before separation occurs (Doherty and Needle, 1991). Parental conflict has been associated with poor academic performance, depression (Meyer *et al.*, 1993) and antisocial behaviour (Loeber and Dishion, 1983). Longitudinal studies suggest that high degrees of parental conflict at the age of 3 are associated with later adjustment problems in adulthood (Neighbors *et al.*, 1997). Although not all children will be affected detrimentally by parental conflict, this behaviour has consistently clear and negative effects on the child's immediate and future behaviour.

Adulthood: beyond adolescence

It is much easier to outline child or adolescent development than adult development; children and adolescents change faster, and the changes are closely related to age. Adult development is much more variable because physical changes in adults are more gradual. Mental and emotional changes during adulthood are more closely related to individual experience than to age. Some people achieve success and satisfaction with their careers, while some hate their jobs. Some marry and have happy family lives; others are happy to live without children, and others never adjust to the roles of spouse and parent. No single description of adult development will fit everyone. Because of this variability, there is no single 'normative' change that occurs from adolescence onwards: puberty is the last single period during a person's development where significant and consistent changes in physical and cognitive behaviour occur.

Muscular strength peaks during the late twenties or early thirties and then declines slowly thereafter as muscle tissue gradually deteriorates. By age 70, strength has declined by approximately 30 per cent in both men and women (Young *et al.*, 1984). However, age has much less effect on endurance than on strength. Both laboratory tests and athletic records reveal that older people who remain physically fit show remarkably little decline in the ability to exercise for extended periods of time (Spirduso and MacRae, 1990).

Although it is easy to measure a decline in the sensory systems (such as vision, hearing and olfaction), older people often show very little functional change in these systems. Most of them learn to make adjustments for their sensory losses, using additional cues to help them decode sensory information. For example, people with a hearing loss can learn to attend more carefully to other people's gestures and lip movements; they can also profitably use their experience to infer what is said.

Functional changes with age are also minimal in highly developed skills. For example, Salthouse (1984, 1988) found that experienced older typists continued to perform as well as younger ones, despite the fact that they performed less well on standard laboratory tests of sensory and motor skills, including the types of skill that one would expect to be important in typing. The continuous practice they received enabled them to develop strategies to compensate for their physical decline. For example, they tended to read farther ahead in the text they were typing, which enabled them to plan in advance the patterns of finger movements they would have to make. However, as you saw in Chapter 11, the neurological diseases that accompany ageing can have devastating intellectual and personal consequences.

Middle adulthood: a period of contentment?

By the time people reach middle adulthood, they have achieved or have chosen to achieve, almost all of the major life decisions available to them. Marriage or cohabitation, having children, setting up a home, beginning a career – decisions on all of these major life changes will have been made by the time that people reach their late thirties/mid-forties.

Because the major life decisions have been made, people during this period in life generally feel comfortable and contented, and a conventional way of life becomes the norm. People become quite satisfied with their lives at this time; they feel at their most confident, most in control and most productive (Lachman *et al*, 1994; Chiriboga, 1997; Tikoo, 1996; Shek, 1996). Depression, for example, although present in the middle-aged, declines during this period in life (Pearlin and Mullan, 1992). Middle-aged women regard themselves as having a better ability to cope with life's difficulties (Stewart and Ostrove, 1998). Women's interest in sex appears to decline from the mid-40s (Helson and Soto, 2005), as Figure 12.15 shows.

Erikson (1968) argued that the adult years consist of three psychosocial stages – intimacy versus isolation, generativity versus stagnation, and integrity versus despair – during which life is reviewed either with a sense of satisfaction or with despair. During intimacy versus isolation, people succeed or fail in loving others; during generativity versus stagnation, people either withdraw inwardly and focus on their problems or reach out to help others; during integrity versus despair, life is reviewed with either a sense of satisfaction or with despair.

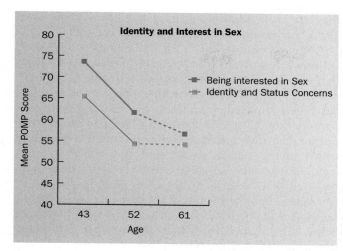

Figure 12.15 How interest in sex, as well as occupation with status, varies between the age of 40 and 60.

Source: Helson, R. and Soto, C.J. (2005). Up and down in middle age: monotonic and nonmonotonic changes in roles, status and personality. *Journal of Personality and Social Psychology*, 89, 2, 194–204.

Another attempt to understand stages of adult development is suggested by Levinson *et al.* (1978). They interviewed 40 men – business executives, blue collar workers, novelists and biologists – and analysed the biographies of famous men and examined stories of men's lives as portrayed in literature. They claimed to have discovered a pattern common to most men's lives. Instead of proceeding smoothly, their lives were characterised by several years of stability punctuated by crises. The crises were periods during which the men began to question their life structures: their occupations, their relations with their families, their religious beliefs and practices, their ethnic identities, and the ways they spent their leisure time. During times of transition – which caused considerable anxiety and turmoil – the men re-evaluated the choices they had made and eventually settled on new patterns that guided them through another period of stability. Periods of transition lasted four or five years, whereas the intervening periods of stability lasted six or seven years.

For Levinson *et al.*, the most important crises occur early in adulthood, when choices must be made about career and marriage, and at mid-life (during the early to mid-forties), when realities about one's life structure must finally be faced. Although Levinson and colleagues did not invent the notion of the mid-life crisis, they certainly helped bring it to the attention of the general public and helped make the term a part of everyone's vocabulary. They concluded that the mid-life crisis happened to all men. Men whose life structures do not yet meet their prior goals and expectations realise that the future will probably not bring the success that up until then has eluded them. Men who have succeeded begin to question whether the goals they had set for themselves were meaningful and worthwhile. All men, successful or not, also begin to confront the fact that they are getting older. They are starting to detect some signs of physical decline, and they are witnesses to the death of their parents or their parents' friends.

Several investigators have defined objective criteria for the presence of a mid-life crisis and have looked for its presence in representative samples of participants. For example, Costa and McCrae (1980) administered a Midlife Crisis Scale to 548 men aged 35–79 years. The scale contained items asking whether the participants were experiencing any of the symptoms of a mid-life crisis, such as dissatisfaction with job and family, a sense of meaninglessness, or a feeling of turmoil. They found no evidence for a mid-life crisis. Some people did report some of the symptoms, but they were no more likely to occur during the early to mid-forties than at any other age. A study of 60 women (Reinke *et al.*, 1985) also found no evidence of a mid-life crisis.

These findings do not mean that middle-aged people do not periodically contemplate or question the important issues in their lives. But there appears to be no crisis – in the dramatic sense – inherent to these reflective periods.

Adult development occurs against the backdrop of what many developmental psychologists consider to be the two most important aspects of life: love and work. For most of us, falling in love is more than just a compelling feeling of wanting to be with someone. It often brings with it major responsibilities, such as marriage and children. Work, too, is more than just a way to pass time. It involves setting and achieving goals related to income, status among peers and accomplishments outside the family.

Parenthood

One of the most significant events in a couple's life is the birth of a child. It brings about an upheaval in the social, emotional and intellectual lives of parents who find that demands on their time become more pressing and who are exposed to the additional stress of having responsibility for the care of another human being.

Generally speaking, mothers assume more responsibilities than do fathers for the day-to-day care of children (Biernat and Wortman, 1991). As a result, they spend more time doing housework and less time talking to their husbands (Peskin, 1982), which can place strain on their marital happiness. However, if husband and wife can find time together in the evenings, and if the husband is able to share in the parenting and household chores, the stress of adapting to family life is lessened considerably (Daniels and Weingarten, 1982). Even men who take parental leave report that they do so to look after their children, not to do housework (Brandt and Kvande, 1998). There seem to be exceptions to this pattern, however. A Danish study found that if both parents had successful careers, then the housework and childcare were distributed more equitably (Hestbaek, 1998).

The general pattern of greater involvement in the day-to-day running of the household by women may be why they perceive the personal costs of having a child to be greater than those perceived by men (Beckman, 1987). Men's priorities, it seems, remain the same after the birth of the child as they were before: they still want the attention of their wives or partners, they still want to engage in an active social life and they still want the freedom to pursue other interests outside the family (Watson *et al.*, 1995). With the inconvenience of childbirth, it is perhaps not surprising that men regard their marriages as being less satisfactory after the birth of a child (Chalmers and Meyer, 1996). The introduction of another human being into the dyad can also bring clear stresses. Parents may find that the time they have to spend with each other is reduced, especially if their child has additional medical or behavioural problems (Schuchts and Witkin, 1989).

Parenting adolescents

As children grow older and become more self-sufficient in caring for themselves, the day-to-day burdens of raising a family taper off and husbands and wives are able to spend more time with each other. However, adolescents pose new problems for their parents: they may question parental authority, and their burgeoning social agenda may put a wrinkle in their parents' personal and social calendars. For many parents, rearing adolescents, particularly during the time just prior to their leaving home, represents the low point of marital happiness (Cavanaugh, 1990). Most of the tensions revolve around issues of responsibility and mutual respect. The adolescent is slowly groping towards adulthood and wishes to be regarded as an individual who is responsible enough to lead their life without parental interference. Parents, however, still feel that their child requires guidance and has not earned the right to be regarded as fully independent.

Generally speaking, once a family's youngest child has left home, marital happiness increases and continues to do so through the remainder of the couple's life together. The average age of a child when they leave the parental home appears to be getting older, at least in the UK. According to Coleman and Hendry (1999), this age increased from 17 to 23 years in the previous decade. It was once thought that the 'empty nest' posed problems for the middle-aged couple, particularly for the mother, who was thought to define her role solely around her children. Chiriboga (1991) found that mothers undergo a fairly turbulent series of emotions once the child has flown the nest. Initial depression and a feeling of loss lead to further unhappiness but then to a sense of pride when

they see their adult child making a life of their own. These changes do not appear to be seen in fathers.

Although parents may miss daily contact with their children, they also feel happy (not to mention relieved) that a major responsibility of life – raising self-reliant children who become responsible members of society – has been completed successfully. Just as importantly, the parents now have time for each other and freedom to pursue their own interests. It may be true that an empty nest is a happy nest. Research tends to support this statement. In one study, only 6 per cent of empty-nest couples reported that life prior to their last child leaving home was better than their empty-nest experience. Over 50 per cent of the couples interviewed said that their lives were better now than before their children had left home (Deutscher, 1968; Neugarten, 1974).

Parenting during adolescence

Not all parenting is done by adults. There has been an increasing trend for parenthood to occur earlier in life, during the teenage years rather than young or middle adulthood. Childbirth during adolescence has been associated with a multitude of problems – social, educational and practical and, mostly, these are problems for the mother rather than the father. Adolescent mothers may face increased financial hardship and a reliance on state benefits, decreased employment prospects, a disruption in their education and the opprobium of others who disapprove of their behaviour (Dennison and Coleman, 1998). They also have to cope with the normal disruptions and changes that accompany adolescence itself.

However, the picture is not as gloomy as it first appears. When mothers themselves are asked about how they are coping with the responsibility of raising a child, they report problems but also indicate that the experience can be a positive one (Dennison and Coleman, 1998). Many report coping well, and receive support from their own mothers and family during the pregnancy and after the birth of the child (Phoenix, 1991).

Work

The task of raising a family is balanced with one or both parents having a career. In fact, events that occur in the workplace often affect the quality of home life. A promotion and a pay rise can mean that the family can now do things that they could not before. Working long hours to get that pay rise, however, can decrease the amount of time that a couple can spend together with their children. According to Chiriboga (1997), work is the major source of stress for most men but for only around one-fifth of women.

With the dramatic increase in the number of women entering the workforce since the 1970s many psychogists have focused their research efforts on understanding dual-earner marriages – those in which both parents work full- or part-time. Compared with single-earner marriages, dual-earner families generally have a better standard of living in terms of material possessions and savings for their children's education and for retirement. Another important benefit accrues, especially to the wife: she is able to achieve recognition and independence outside the home (Crosby, 1991). Most husbands in dual-earner marriages support their wives' working. In addition, they find their wives to be more interesting, essential and helpful (Schaie and Willis, 1992).

Coping with unemployment

When adults find themselves unemployed, however, there may be serious consequences for the person who is made unemployed and their relationships with others. Arguments with a partner can increase, there is less satisfaction with the partnership or marriage and there is a strong likelihood of divorce if the dissatisfaction and arguments continue (Liem and Liem, 1990). Unemployment, however, seems to exaggerate already existing problems. The risk of divorce, for example, occurs primarily in partnerships that have already experienced problems prior to unemployment.

If the unemployed person identifies very closely with their work – in a sense, 'living and breathing' their work – then the consequences of removing the opportunity to do that much-valued work will be psychologically damaging. This is especially true if the person is in middle adulthood rather than young adulthood. A study of middle-aged unemployed Israeli women, for example, found that they were least likely to reject job offers and experienced declining health following unemployment (Kulik, 2000). What may make this life change so difficult to cope with at middle adulthood is the reduced likelihood of re-entry into the workplace. If people over 40 years of age who have been made redundant by their company actively seek work but do not secure employment after a year of searching, they experience feelings of uselessness and resignation (Henkens *et al.*, 1996). These feelings might also lead to increased mental distress, the increase being greater than that observed in younger or older people who have been made unemployed (Theodossiou, 1998).

Men and women seem to respond to unemployment differently, however. Men appear to engage in activities that give structure to their lives, such as claiming state benefit, attending benefit interviews or job hunting, whereas women will engage in more domestic chores. Women will also use this time to engage in self-improvement activities such as seeking out alternative careers or retraining; men, on the other hand, may spend this time watching television or developing hobbies (Walsh and Jackson, 1995). The effects of unemployment on health are considered again in Chapter 17.

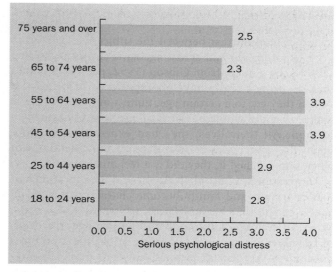

Figure 12.16 Percentage of age group reporting symptoms of severe psychological distress.
Source: National Center on Health Statistics (2006) Health, United States, 2006.

Late adulthood and the menopause

One of the inevitable features of ageing is that the process is visible. The outer shell of age is easy to see: a young person may not be served alcohol based on their appearance, and similar judgements – often, more harmful – are made about people as they pass from middle into late adulthood. Although middle-aged and older individuals may feel full of vitality, youth and vigour, this is not the impression their physical appearance indicates to others (Featherstone and Hepworth, 1993). Despite the subjective feeling of vitality, some physical changes are inevitable.

There is also an increase in reported mental health symptoms in the 45–64 year old group, as well as in older samples who are retired or out of work, as Figure 12.16 shows.

At late adulthood the body undergoes a shift, especially in women. Alteration in the endocrine system leads to the pituitary gland and the hypothalamus releasing hormones that prevent the ovaries from controlling menstruation. This physical change is called the menopause and is sometimes accompanied by 'hot flushes', sweating during sleep, fatigue and irritability (Dan and Bernhard, 1989). In one Scottish study, over half of the sample had reported experiencing one of 15 menopause-related symptoms, but only 22 per cent of respondents felt the symptoms to be a problem (Porter *et al.*, 1996). In fact, many women experience and value the sense of freedom that the menopause brings (Robinson, 1996). They feel that this time of life brings enhanced social status and psychological well-being. There are also cross-cultural differences in people's responses to the menopause. Japanese women, for example, report fewer menopausal symptoms than do American or Canadian women (Lock, 1998).

Old age

see activity on mypsychlab

The contrast between the subjective experience of ageing and actual ageing is clearly illustrated by a quote from Gibson (1992, p. 59) who notes that we do not really have an experience of being old: 'When they get to a certain age, quite a number of people realise that the whole business of age status is rather an illusion. All their lives, they had expected to be 'old' when they reached a certain date on the calendar, but when they reached it, they did not feel different.'

Despite the way people feel, physical deterioration and loss of friends and family become characteristics of old age, a period that begins almost arbitrarily at 65 years. Whereas in young adulthood and middle age, the death of friends is a non-normative event, in old age it becomes normative. Very few milestones, however, mark the transition to old age. There are socially constructed events, such as compulsory retirement from work, which indicate that old age has arrived, but few other events as certain as this mark out the last and longest period in a person's life (Hendry and Kloep, 2002).

There is a tendency in some people to disguise the effects of old age – they may dress in a way they think young people do or may engage in activities they associate with youth, or attempt to conceal the physical effects of ageing by applying cosmetics. These individuals feel that they still need to compete, to be sexy and to be seen as attractive to younger people rather than accept the ageing process. This is unusual because when people are asked which age they would like to be, the ideal age is quite close to their actual age (Uotinen, 1998). General optimism appears to increase with age, but optimism related to health and thinking declines (Isaacowitz, 2005). Interestingly, when 3,793 adults aged between 34 and 74 years of age were asked to rate how satisfied they were with their life in the past, the present or future, there was little difference between the young and old samples in terms of actual satisfaction but the older participants anticipated their satisfaction would get worse and the younger sample expected it would get better (Lachman *et al.*, 2008). The under 65s found the present more satisfying than the past; the over 65s found the past and present equally satisfying.

What constitutes successful ageing? Researchers and older people alike agree on the principal factors which contribute to successful ageing but laypeople tend to consider more 'psychological' factors as additionally important, as Table 12.6 and Figure 12.17 show. Biomedical theorists, for example, emphasise longevity as a measure of successful ageing and focus on the absence of illness/risk factors for illness, as well as the maintenance of cognitive and physical function as important constituents (Bowling and Dieppe, 2005). One study of 601 Australian men in their

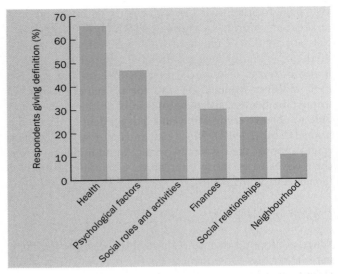

Figure 12.17 Most common definitions of successful ageing given by 854 people aged ⩾ 50 in Britain

Source: From Thoughts for Today, *British Medical Journal*, 2005, Vol. 331, p. 1550, unnumbered figure (24–31 December 2005) with permission from the BMJ Publishing Group.

80s, found that three-quarters of them aged well, mentally, and that education and the degree of physical activity they were involved in were good predictors of successful mental health (Almeida *et al.*, 2006). Psychosocial theorists emphasise older people's satisfaction with life, personal growth and social participation as important constituents. Laypeople, when asked, highlight social, psychological and physical factors as important to growing old successfully. One study of 854 people aged 50 and over found that 75 per cent of the sample regarded themselves as ageing very well; they cited good health and functioning as a definition of successful ageing (Bowling and Dieppe, 2005).

There is evidence that ageing may not be an entirely negative experience. A study of young people found that not only did they want to be older but also that they were less positive about their own age and worried about their personal inadequacies (Montepare, 1991). Older people who accepted the process of ageing, on the other hand, felt good about themselves, feared ageing less and were more satisfied with life (Montepare and Lachman, 1989). Data from the Amsterdam Longitudinal Aging Study suggest that having a partner, a good family, social support and high self-esteem can lead to better coping with chronic illness in old age (Penninx *et al.*, 1998), which indicates that there are factors which can mitigate the effects of old age.

There is an element of loss of power in old age, however. Compulsory retirement from work – a milestone introduced by the German chancellor, Bismarck, in the nineteenth century – is the first step to removing a sense of power from old people. There is no relationship between a person's ability to function as an employee and their age

Table 12.6 View of what constitutes successful ageing

Theoretical views

Life expectancy
Life satisfaction and well-being
Mental and psychological health, cognitive function
Personal growth, learning new things
Physical health and functioning
Percieved control, autonomy, coping, self-esteem, goals
  sense of self
Social community, leisure activities, intergration and participation
Social networks, support, participation

Additional lay definitions

Accomplishments
Enjoyment of diet
Financial security
Nieighbourhood
Physical appearance
Productivity/contribution to life
Sense of humour
Sense of purpose
Spirituality

Source: adapted from What is successful ageing and who should define it?, *British Medical Journal*, 331, pp. 1548–51 (Bowling, A. and Dieppe, P. 2005), reproduced with permission from the BMJ Publishing Group.

(Salthouse and Maurer, 1997), but almost all professions have a compulsory retirement age. In fact, politicians are one of the few professions not to have such a compulsory milestone, an irony given that the original compulsory retirement age was determined by a politician. If there is no relationship between an employee's work performance and their age, how can a retirement age be justified?

At retirement, old people may become eligible for state benefits and other monetary or social benefits that the state sees fit to bestow on them. Because of this dependence, old age is sometimes characterised as a 'second childhood' (Hockey and James, 1995). As Jacques says in his seven ages of man speech in *As You Like It*, (II, VII, 163–6):

> Last scene of all,
>
> That ends this strange eventful history,
>
> Is second childishness and mere oblivion;
>
> Sans teeth, sans eyes, sans taste, sans everything.

Old people fear becoming a burden to others and fear the loss of autonomy that old age can bring (Dittman-Kohli, 1990). The prejudice that they may face can also be problematic and can become a self-fulfilling prophecy. If old people are presented with subliminal messages that are derogatory about old people's abilities, for example,

they perform less well on a subsequent task of cognitive ability than would those old people not exposed to such messages (Levy, 1996).

How language use changes as we get older

While research suggests that we respond to negative emotion less readily as we get older, research into the psychology of expressive writing also suggests that we become less egocentric. Pennebaker and Stone (2003) compared the language used in written or spoken expression by people who had taken part in 32 experiments in which they expressed how they feel and think about a recently experienced trauma. This technique, and what it is used for, is discussed in more detail in Chapter 18.

These experiments require participants to write about personal and traumatic experiences. There were 1,925 participants in the 15–24-year-old group, 494 in the 25–39 group, 132 in the 40–54 group and 62 in the 55–69 group. In a follow-up experiment, the researchers also followed the linguistic development of ten established, professional writers including Shakespeare, Austen, Dickens, George Eliot and Wordsworth.

One of the most pronounced differences in young and older authors' and speakers' language development was the use of the first person singular: I. There was a significantly lower tendency to use 'I' in communication in the older groups, suggesting that as people get older, they become more topic-focused and less self-referential. The same reduction in the use of 'I' seen in the experimental samples is also seen in the samples of fiction studied, particularly in Austen's and Wordsworth's work.

In the older samples, there was also significantly less evidence of referring to other people. In the younger samples there was a significantly greater reference to other people. Perhaps this change reflects the possibility that as we grow up, we are much closer to and dependent on other people and refer to ourselves in terms of others' behaviour or expectations (such as those of parents or older siblings).

Older participants in both studies made more use of the future-tense than did the younger ones while using fewer past-tenses. Conversely, the youngest sample made the greatest use of the past-tense and least use of the future-tense. Time references (such as day, minute and clock) were more common in the younger samples whereas the use of words of six letters or more was more common in the older samples (but there were no differences between groups for fiction, perhaps reflecting the probability that professional authors' vocabulary is already fairly well-developed at the beginning of their writing career).

Although the largest portion of the study was cross-sectional, it suggests that older people's use of language differs in significant and interesting ways from that of younger samples. The most important of these differences is a reduction in the egocentric use of 'I' in older people.

Death and bereavement

'I'm not afraid of death,' said Woody Allen. 'I just don't want to be there when it happens.' Death is the final event of life. It is a biological and social event – family and friends are emotionally affected by the death of a loved one. Although a death may claim a life at any time, most people die when they are old. One question that developmental psychologists have asked about death and dying among the elderly is, how do old people view the inevitability of their own death?

As you might expect, elderly people contemplate their death more often than do younger people but, generally speaking, they fear death less than do their younger counterparts (Kalish, 1976) and tend to cope better with loss (McCrae and Costa, 1993). Although depression can occur immediately someone close dies, this decreases over the next one to two years (Thompson *et al.*, 1998). No one knows why this is so, but a tentative explanation may be that older people have had more time to review the past and to plan for the future knowing that bereavement is close at hand. Thus, they are able to prepare themselves psychologically (and financially) for death. The sense of loss, however, can continue until the bereaved die (Wortman *et al.*, 1993).

Contemplating and preparing for death, though, is not like knowing that you are actually dying. The changes in attitude that terminally ill people experience, have been studied by Kübler-Ross (1969, 1981). After interviewing hundreds of dying people, she concluded that people undergo five distinct phases of psychologically coping with death. The first stage is denial. When terminally ill people learn of their condition, they generally try to deny it. Anger comes next – now they resent the certainty of death. In the third stage, bargaining, people attempt to negotiate their fate with God or others, pleading that their lives might be spared. While bargaining, they actually realise that they are, in fact, going to die. This leads to depression, the fourth stage, which is characterised by a sense of hopelessness and loss. According to Kübler-Ross, 'When the terminally ill patient can no longer deny his illness, when he is forced to undergo more surgery or hospitalization, when he begins to have more symptoms or becomes weaker or thinner, he cannot smile it off anymore.' The fifth and final stage, acceptance, is marked by a more peaceful resignation to the facts or 'positive submission'. 'It is as if the pain had gone,' according to Kübler-Ross, 'the struggle is over.'

Kübler-Ross's work highlights the psychological factors involved in dying and has provided an initial theory about how the dying come to grips with their fate. Her work, though, has not been accepted uncritically. Her research was not scientific – her method for interviewing people was not systematic, and her results are largely

Elizabeth Kübler-Ross (1926–2004), psychiatrist.
Source: Press Association Images.

anecdotal. Moreover, of the five stages, denial is the only one that appears to be universal. Apparently, not all terminally ill people have the same psychological response to the fact that they are dying.

However, despite its flaws, Kübler-Ross's work is important because it has prompted an awareness, both scientific and public, of the plight of the terminally ill. The scientific response, as you might guess, has been to do more medical research in the hope of prolonging the life of people with cancer or other terminal illness. The public response has involved the attempt to provide support for the dying and their families through hospice services (Aiken, 1994). In the past, hospices were places where strangers and pilgrims could find rest and shelter. Today, hospices are special places that provide medical and psychological support for the dying and their families. In cases in which the dying person wishes to die at home, hospice volunteers work in that setting. The primary functions of hospice services are two fold: to provide relief from pain and to allow the person to die with dignity. No attempt is made to prolong life through technology if doing so would diminish the self-respect of the dying person and their family. To die with dignity is perhaps the best death possible – for, together, the dying and their loved ones are able to experience, for the last time together, reverence for the experience of life.

Chapter review

Prenatal development

- The three stages of prenatal development span the time between conception and birth. In just nine months, the zygote grows from a single cell, void of human resemblance, into a fully developed foetus, complete with physical features that look much like yours and mine, except in miniature.
- Sex is determined by the sex chromosomes. Male sex organs are produced by the action of a gene on the Y chromosome that causes the gonads to develop into testes.
- The testes secrete androgens, a class of hormones that stimulates the development of male sex organs. If testes are not present, the foetus develops as a female.
- The most important factor in normal foetal development is the mother's nutrition; malnutrition leads to abnormal development and impaired cognition.
- Normal foetal development can be disrupted by the presence of teratogens, chemicals which can cause mental retardation and physical deformities; one teratogen is alcohol – when consumed by a pregnant woman, this may lead to foetal alcohol syndrome.
- There is evidence that the human foetus is capable of discriminating between sensory stimuli while in the womb, suggesting that it is capable of a rudimentary form of cognition.

Physical and perceptual development in infancy and childhood

- A newborn infant's first movements are reflexes that are crucial to its survival. For example, the rooting, sucking and swallowing reflexes are important in finding and consuming food.
- Sophisticated movements, such as crawling and standing, develop and are refined through natural maturation and practice.
- A newborn's senses appear to be at least partially functional at birth. However, normal development of the senses, like that of motor abilities, depends on experience.
- The brain appears to develop throughout infancy and adolescence, with myelination being the key characteristic of maturation.
- Because the infant lacks language, most studies of motor and perceptual development examine the child's non-verbal response to stimulation. These responses include movements involving the head, mouth and eyes.
- If an infant is deprived of the opportunity to practise them during a critical period, these skills may fail to develop, which will affect the child's performance as an adult.
- Before the age of 2 years, infants seem to be more concerned with the contours of visual stimuli – a phenomenon called the externality effect.

Cognitive development in infancy and childhood

- The first step in a child's cognitive development is learning that many events are contingent on its own behaviour. This understanding occurs gradually and is controlled by the development of the nervous system and by increasingly complex interactions with the environment.
- By around 3 months, the infant shows awareness of changes in its environment; by 6 months, it is able to remember temporal order of stimuli. At 8 months, it is able to recognise words spoken in a story that it heard a while before.
- Over the course of development from 1 to 2 years the number of sequences of actions that the child can remember increases.
- Three factors seem to account for the child's ability to recall information better with age: the formation of memory-related structures, the development of language, and the development of metamemory – the realisation that using memory strategies will help the child to think and behave.
- According to Piaget, as children develop they acquire cognitive structures – mental representations or rules that are used for understanding and dealing with the world and for thinking about and solving problems. The two principal types of cognitive structure are schemata (mental representations or sets of rules that define a particular category of behaviour) and concepts (rules that describe properties of environmental events and their relations to other concepts).
- According to Piaget, two processes help a child to adapt to its environment: assimilation, the process by which new information is modified to fit existing schemata, and accommodation, the process by which old schemata are changed by new experiences.
- Piaget divided a child's cognitive development into four periods – a system that is widely, if not universally, accepted. These periods are determined by the child's experiences and the maturation of its nervous system.
- An infant's earliest cognitive abilities are closely tied to the external stimuli in the immediate environment; objects exist for the infant only when they are present (the sensorimotor period).
- Gradually, infants learn that objects exist even when hidden. The development of object permanence leads to the ability to represent things symbolically, which is a prerequisite for the use of language (the preoperational period).
- Next, the ability to perform logical analysis and to understand more complex cause-and-effect relations develops (the period of concrete operations).
- Around the age of 11 years, a child develops more adult-like cognitive abilities – abilities that may allow the child to solve difficult problems by means of abstract reasoning (the period of formal operations).

- Piaget's critics point out that, in some cases, his tests of cognitive development underestimate children's abilities. For example, if tested appropriately, it is evident that they conserve various properties earlier than he thought, and that their egocentrism is less pronounced than his tests indicated.
- Vygotsky's writings and the research they have stimulated have showed that the sociocultural context in which children are raised has a significant impact on their cognitive development.
- In particular, language appears to influence how children learn to think, solve problems, formulate plans, make decisions and contemplate ideas.
- Two information processing accounts of cognitive development have been developed recently. Case's M-space model argues that cognitive development proceeds according to expansion of mental space, or the brain's information processing capacity. M-space expands due to three causes: brain maturation, practice using schemata, and the integration of schemata for different objects and events.
- Fischer's skill model focuses on the relation between brain maturation and a child's ability to learn new cognitive skills specific to particular tasks, such as conservation. Maturation of the brain permits the child to acquire new cognitive skills necessary to solve increasingly complex tasks. Both of these models in essence reinterpret Piaget's theory in the language of information processing.

Social development in infancy and childhood

- Because babies are totally dependent on their parents, the development of attachment between parent and infant is crucial to the infant's survival.
- Some of the behaviours that babies possess innately are sucking, cuddling, looking, smiling and crying. These behaviours promote parental responses and are instrumental in satisfying physiological needs.
- Play is a social and cognitive behaviour – children interact with each other or with objects in the environment in an enjoyable and positive way and learn about these objects and the objects' relationship to the environment. At around 12–18 months, infants begin to play with objects symbolically – they pretend that the object is something else. At the age of 4 years, children use play to find out more about their environment and its social values as well as its customs and traditions.
- Ainsworth's Strange Situation theory allows a researcher to determine the nature of the attachment between infant and caregiver. By using this test, several investigators have identified some of the variables – some involving infants and some involving mothers – that influence attachment.
- Maternal sensitivity (as measured by the mother's ability to respond positively to the baby's signals) appears to be the best predictor of secure attachment.
- Interaction with peers is probably the most important factor in social development among children and adolescents. However, a caregiver's style of parenting can also have strong effects on the social development of children and adolescents.

- Children rate people who speak their own 'national' language and in their own accent more positively than they do ethnically different groups.
- Autism is a childhood disorder in which the child shows abnormal patterns of social interaction (indifference and unwillingness to make eye or physical contact), delayed and/or idiosyncratic language, and stereotypical and repetitive behaviour.
- An influential theory of autism suggests that autistic children lack a theory of mind: they are unable to imagine the thoughts, actions or feelings of others.
- Others theories suggest that autistic children have an impairment of executive function or that they are unable to see wholes (instead of features); these theories are based on the finding that not all autistic children experience theory of mind difficulties.
- There seems to be a reduction in dopamine in the frontal regions of autistic children which may suggest an impairment in executive function and some studies have suggested that theory of mind tasks are mediated by the frontal lobe.
- Asperger's syndrome describes impaired interpersonal communication and social functioning but seems to differ from autism in also being characterised by individuals having a narrow and obsessional range of interests.
- Attention deficit hyperactivity disorder (ADHD) describes a failure of the child to inhibit its own antisocial and deviant behaviour; these children are impulsive, hyperactive and have a poor attention span.
- Evidence suggests that maternal depression is associated with poor social interaction with the child and poor sensitivity to the infant's behaviour; infants of depressed mothers are more expressive with caregivers than with the mother.
- Emotional distress may be predicted by decreased left frontal EEG activation and increased right frontal activation.

Development of sex roles in childhood

- A person's sexual identity refers to one's private sense of being a male or female and consists primarily of the recognition of membership in a particular group of people: males or females.
- According to Kohlberg, the ability of children to identify with their sex is determined in large part by their ability to classify objects as being boys' objects or girls' objects.
- Gender schema theory argues that children construct a 'schema' – a mental representation – of male and female and pay special attention to features of their own sex. Children's perception of sex is matched with information about others' sex that the child has already processed and understood.
- The ability to identify others' and the child's own sex emerges between the ages of 1 and 3 years.
- Research has shown that both parents and peers tend to encourage children to behave in sex-appropriate ways, especially with regard to play activities and toys.

Moral development

- Piaget suggested that moral development consists of three principal stages: the premoral stage, characterised by little understanding of rules or principles; the moral realism stage, characterised by egocentrism and blind adherence to rules; and the moral relativism stage, characterised by empathy and a realisation that behaviour is judged by the effects it has on others.

- Kohlberg suggested that moral development consists of three levels, with seven stages.
- During the preconventional level, morality is based on the personal consequences of an act.
- During the conventional level, morality is based on the need to be well regarded and on sharing a common interest in social order. During the postconventional level, which is achieved by only a few people, morality becomes an abstract, philosophical virtue.
- Critics of Piaget and Kohlberg point out that the stages of moral development are, to a certain degree, products of the measuring instruments. Although it does not appear, as Gilligan originally suggested, that females follow different moral rules from males, her work has sensitised researchers to the importance of including both sexes in studies of human development. Subtle changes in the way that moral dilemmas are posed can produce very different answers.
- Damon's model of redistributive justice argues that the child begins the process of moral development by making decisions about sharing based on egocentric consideration.
- Eventually, the child makes moral decisions based on concepts of fairness and merit.

Adolescence

- Adolescence is the transitional stage between childhood and adulthood. Puberty is initiated by the hypothalamus, which causes the pituitary gland to secrete hormones that stimulate maturation of the reproductive system.
- Puberty marks a significant transition, both physically and socially. Early maturity appears to be socially beneficial to boys, because early maturers are more likely to be perceived as leaders. The effects of early maturity in girls is mixed; although their advanced physical development may help them acquire some prestige, early-maturing girls are more likely to engage in norm-breaking behaviour.
- Whereas boys seem to look forward to the increasing strength, freedom and social status that puberty brings, girls regard the period as one in which they need to conform to society's view of women and as one that restricts freedom.
- The nature of friendship changes during adolescence. Girls seek out confidantes rather than playmates, and boys join groups that provide mutual support in their quests to assert their independence. Insecure friendships at this time can lead to increased psychopathology later in life.
- Bullying can be physical (actual bodily violence), verbal or psychological (such as social exclusion) and increases during the transition from primary to secondary school; contrary to received wisdom, the bully is not socially inept but very aware of the power of manipulation.

- Although adolescence brings conflicts between parents and children, these conflicts tend to be centred on relatively minor issues. Most adolescents hold the same values and attitudes concerning important issues as their parents do. Mood swings during adolescence can be dramatic but, on the whole, teenagers report that they are generally happy and self-confident.

Adulthood: beyond adolescence

- Up to the time of young adulthood, human development can reasonably be described as a series of stages: a regular sequence of changes that occurs in most members of our species. But development in adulthood is much more variable and few generalisations apply.
- Older people are more likely to exhibit gradual changes, especially in abilities that require flexibility and in learning new behaviours.
- Intellectual abilities that depend heavily on crystallised intelligence – an accumulated body of knowledge – are much less likely to decline than are those based on fluid intelligence – the capacity for abstract reasoning.
- Erikson and Levinson have both proposed that people encounter a series of crises that serve as turning points in development. Erikson's stages span the entire life cycle, from infancy to old age, whereas Levinson's stages concentrate on mid-life development.
- By the time people reach middle adulthood, they have achieved or have chosen to achieve, almost all of the major life decisions available to them such as marriage or cohabitation, having children, setting up a home or establishing a career. People during this period in life generally feel comfortable and contented, and a conventional way of life becomes the norm. People feel at their most confident, most in control and most productive. Depression declines during this period in life.
- There appears to be no scientific evidence to support the idea that people experience a mid-life crisis.
- Marriages seem to be happiest just after the birth of children and after the children have left home. It appears to be unhappiest just before the children leave home – possibly owing to the emotional and time demands that adolescents place on their parents.
- Men and women seem to respond to unemployment differently. Men appear to engage in activities that give structure to their lives such as claiming state benefits, attending benefit interviews or job hunting, whereas women will engage in more domestic chores.
- At late adulthood, the body undergoes a shift, especially in women. Alternation in the endocrine system leads to the pituitary gland and the hypothalamus releasing hormones that prevent the ovaries from controlling menstruation. This physical change is called the menopause and is sometimes accompanied by 'hot flushes', sweating during sleep, fatigue and irritability.
- Having a partner, good family and social support and high self-esteem can lead to better coping with chronic illness in old age.

- With old age and retirement, people feel less independent and more of a burden than they did when working. The dependence on others and on state benefits has led to this period in life being described as a second childhood.

- Kübler-Ross's interviews with terminally ill people have revealed that many of them seem to experience a five-stage process in facing the reality that they are going to die.

Suggestions for further reading

General development

Bee, H. and Boyd, D. (2010) *The Developing Child*. (12th edn). Boston: Allyn & Bacon.

Bergen, D. (2008) *Human Development: Trends and contemporary theories*. Boston: Prentice Hall.

Berk, L.E. (2009) *Child Development* (8th edn). Boston: Allyn & Bacon.

Boyd, D. and Bee, H. (2009) *Lifespan Development*. (5th edn). Boston: Allyn & Bacon.

Dixon, W.E. (2003) *20 Studies That Revolutionised Child Psychology*. Boston: Allyn & Bacon.

Feldman, R.S. (2008) *Development Across the Lifespan*. (5th edn). Boston: Allyn & Bacon.

Foos, P.W. and Clark, M.C. (2008) *Human Aging*. (2nd edn). Boston: Allyn & Bacon.

Gottesman, I.I. and Hanson, D.R. (2005) Human development: Biological and genetic processes. *Annual Review of Psychology*, 56, 263–86.

Hackman, D.A. and Farah, M.J. (2009) Socioeconomic status and the developing brain. *Trends in Cognitive Sciences*, 13, 2, 65–73.

Liben, L.S. (2009). *Current Directions in Developmental Psychology*. Boston: Allyn & Bacon.

Schaffer, H.R. (2003) *Introducing Child Development*. Oxford: Blackwell.

Schaffer, H.R. (2006) *Key Concepts in Developmental Psychology*. London: Sage.

There are dozens of books available on all aspects of development which makes choosing the best text to recommend a little troublesome. The titles above are recommended as good introductory texts to general development.

Infancy

Berk, L.E. (2008) *Infants and Children: Prenatal through middle childhood*. (6th edn). Boston: Prentice Hall.

Muir, D. and Slater, I. (2000) *Infant Development: The essential readings*. Oxford: Blackwell.

Slater, A. and Lewis, M. (2002) *Introduction to Infant Development*. Oxford: Oxford University Press.

Special section on 'face processing' in *Journal of Child Psychology and Psychiatry*, 2004, 45, 7.

These books provide well-researched introductions to infant development, with the issue of JCCP providing some recent research on the development of face processing.

Cognitive development

Oates, J. and Grayson, A. (2004) *Cognitive and Language Development in Children*. Oxford: Blackwell.

This excellent book provides an in-depth and fairly up-to-date account of what we know about the development of thinking and remembering in childhood.

Social cognition

Kraft, U. (2006) Detecting autism early. *Scientific American Mind*, 17, 5, 68–73.

Treffert, D.A. and Christensen, D.D. (2005) Inside the mind of a savant. *Scientific American*, December, 108–13.

Special issue of *Clinical Neuroscience Research on advances in autism research*, 2006, 6, 3–4, 111–24.

Interesting items giving a good background to theory of mind (and autism).

Moral reasoning

Gibbs, J.C. (2010) *Moral Development and Reality: Beyond the theories of Kohlberg and Hoffman*. (2nd edn). Boston: Allyn & Bacon.

Langford, P.E. (1995) *Approaches to the Development of Moral Reasoning*. Hove: Psychology Press.

These texts will give you more detailed information about the child's moral reasoning ability.

Piaget and Vygotsky

Smith, L. (1996) *Critical Readings on Piaget*. London: Routledge.

Smith, L., Dockrell, J. and Tomlinson, P. (1997) *Piaget, Vygotsky and Beyond*. London: Routledge.

Piaget and Vygotsky are very much alive in developmental thinking and these two books critically assess the contributions of these thinkers to developmental psychology.

Social development

Brody, G.H. (2004) Siblings' direct and indirect contributions to child development. *Current Directions in Psychological Science*, 13, 1, 124–6.

Schafer, M. (2005) Stopping the bullies. *Scientific American Mind*, 16, 2, 76–81.

Smith, P.K. (2004) *Bullying in Schools*. Cambridge: Cambridge University Press.

The child's relationships with others are examined in these books and papers.

Adolescence and adulthood

Adams, G. and Berzonsky, M. (2005) *The Blackwell Handbook of Adolescence*. Oxford: Blackwell.

Bee, H.L. and Boyd, D. (2005) *Lifespan Development* (4th edn). New York: Addison Wesley Longman.

Berk, L.E. (2003) *Development Through the Lifespan* (3rd edn). Boston: Allyn & Bacon.

Blakemore, S-J. and Choudhury, S. (2006) Development of the adolescent brain: Implications for executive function and social cognition. *Journal of Child Psychology and Psychiatry*, 47, 3/4, 296–312.

Burke, D.M. and Shafto, M.A. (2004) Aging and language production. *Current Directions in Psychological Science*, 13, 1, 21–4.

Lachman, M.E. (2004) Development in midlife. *Annual Review of Psychology*, 55, 305–32.

Papalia, D.E., Sterns, H., Feldman, R.D. and Camp, C. (2006) *Adult Development and Aging*. Maidenhead: McGraw-Hill.

Reyna, V.F. and Farley, F. (2007) Is the teen brain too rational? *Scientific American Mind*, 17, 6, 58–65.

Willis, S.L. and Martin, M. (2005) *Middle Adulthood*. London: Sage.

Very readable accounts of the main phases of development after childhood.

Ageing

Burke, D.M. and Shafto, M.A. (2004) Aging and language production. *Current Directions in Psychological Science*, 13, 1, 21–4.

Charles, S.T. (2009) *Current Directions in Adulthood and Ageing*. Boston: Allyn & Bacon.

Craik, F.I.M. and Salthouse, T.A. (2000) *The Handbook of Aging and Cognition*. London: Lawrence Erlbaum Associates.

Morris, R.G. (2004) Neuropsychology of older adults. In L.H. Goldstein and J.E. McNeil (eds) *Clinical Neuropsychology: A practical guide to assessment and management for clinicians*. Chichester: John Wiley & Sons.

Naveh-Benjamin, M., Moscovitch, M. and Roediger, H.L. (2002) *Perspectives on Human Memory and Cognitive Aging*. Hove: Psychology Press.

Rabbitt, P. (2005) Cognitive gerontology: Cognitive change in old age. *Special issue of Quarterly Journal of Experimental Psychology Section A*. Hove: Psychology Press.

Sachdev, P.S. (2003) *The Ageing Brain*. Hove: Psychology Press.

Special issue of *The American Journal of Geriatric Psychiatry* on 'Successful ageing', 2006, 14, 1.

A good selection of books, chapters and articles on ageing

Journals to consult

Ageing and Psychology

Autism

British Journal of Developmental Psychology

British Journal of Educational Psychology

Child Development

Developmental Neuropsychology

Developmental Psychology

Developmental Psychopathology

Developmental Review

Developmental Science

International Journal of Aging and Human Development

Journal of Adolescence

Journal of Child Psychology and Psychiatry

Journal of Educational Psychology

Journal of Experimental Child Psychology

Journal of Gerontology, Psychological and Social Sciences

Journal of Reproductive and Infant Psychology

Psychological Science

Website addresses

http://www.psychology.org/links/Environment_Behavior_Relationships/Child/

A collection of links to psychology of children material.

http://www.psychology.org/links/Environment_Behavior_Relationships/Infant/

A short collection of links to information about infant development.

http://www.psychology.org/links/Environment_Behavior_Relationships/Adolescent/

A collection of general and science-based links about adolescent development.

http://www.psych.ox.ac.uk/babylab/

A link to The University of Oxford's Babylab – features links to published papers and to other relevant sites.

http://www.psychology.org/links/Environment_Behavior_Relationships/Geriatric/

A collection of links on the psychology of ageing.

http://www.psychology.org/links/Environment_Behavior_Relationships/Death_and_Dying/

Links to the psychology of death and dying.

Motivation and emotion

CHAPTER 13

How happiness can be catching

Sarah Boseley, Health editor

Happiness is catching, new research has confirmed, and depends on how cheerful about life your friends feel.

Happiness is spread through social networks and exists in clusters of close friends and neighbours, according to a study published in the *British Medical Journal. Being* around happy people at work does not help, the research found – happiness is most contagious in your street. Living next door to somebody who becomes happy can increase your own chances of happiness by 34%.

Source: from 'How happiness can be catching', *The Guardian*, 5 December 2008 (Boseley, S.), Copyright Guardian News & Media Ltd. 2008.

Explore the accompanying videos, simulations and animations on MyPsychLab. This chapter includes activities on: Effects of the hypothalmus on eating behaviour • Recognising facial expressions of emotion • The classic case of Phineas Gage • The James-Lange theory of emotion • Check your understanding and prepare for your exams using the multiple choice, short answer and essay practice tests also available

WHAT YOU SHOULD BE ABLE TO DO AFTER READING CHAPTER 13

- Define motivation.
- Describe and understand the processes involved in starting and stopping a meal.
- Outline the basic psychology and physiology of thirst.
- Describe the major eating disorders, anorexia nervosa, bulimia nervosa and obesity, and outline their possible causes.
- Describe and understand the process of sexual development and orientation.

- Evaluate the theories explaining aggression and describe the factors which lead to aggressive behaviour.
- Describe the ways in which psychologists have defined and studied emotion.
- Evaluate the 'fundamental emotion' debate.
- Outline the major theories of emotion.
- Describe current understanding of the biological basis of emotion.

QUESTIONS TO THINK ABOUT

- What motivates us to eat, drink, be aggressive and have sex?
- What influences sexual preference and orientation?
- What causes eating disorders?
- What strategies can an overweight person adopt to lose weight and, more importantly, maintain this loss?

- How does aggressive behaviour manifest itself and what theories could account for it?
- How would you define emotion?
- Are there basic emotions? If so, how many and what distinguishes one from the other?
- What role do physiology and the brain play in the expression and recognition of emotions of different types?

Motivation

Why do people behave differently? Why do some individuals eat particular foods whereas others eat different foods? Why do we eat in the first place? What makes us attracted to different sexual partners, or any sexual partner? Why do we become aggressive?

Most of these questions can probably be answered by motivation. When commonly used, **motivation** refers to a driving force that moves us to a particular action. More formally, motivation is a general term for a group of phenomena that affect the nature of an individual's behaviour, the strength of the behaviour and the persistence of the behaviour.

Motivation includes two types of phenomenon. First, stimuli that were previously associated with pleasant or unpleasant events motivate approach or avoidance behaviours. For example, if something reminds you of an interesting person you met recently, you may try to meet that person again by consulting your mobile and sending a message. Secondly, being deprived of a particular reinforcer increases an organism's preference for a particular behaviour. Besides obvious reinforcers such as food or water, this category includes more subtle ones. For example, after spending a lot of time performing routine tasks, we become motivated to go for a walk or meet with friends.

Motivation affects all categories of behaviour. This chapter considers three important categories of motivated behaviour: eating, sexual behaviour and aggression. Other types of motivation such as intention and being influenced by real or imaginary others will be discussed in Chapters 15 and 16.

Biological needs

Biological needs can be potent motivators. To survive, we need air, food, water, various vitamins and minerals, and protection from extremes in temperature. Complex organisms possess physiological mechanisms that detect deficits or imbalances associated with these needs and **regulatory behaviours** that bring physiological conditions back to normal. Examples of regulatory behaviours include eating, drinking, hunting, shivering, building a fire and putting on a warm coat. This process of detection and correction, which maintains physiological systems at their optimum value, is called **homeostasis** ('stable state'). Deficits or imbalances motivate us because they cause us to perform the appropriate regulatory behaviours.

A regulatory system has four essential features: the **system variable** (the characteristic to be regulated), a **set point** (the optimum value of the system variable), a **detector** that monitors the value of the system variable,

and a **correctional mechanism** that restores the system variable to the set point. A simple example of such a regulatory system is a room where temperature is regulated by a thermostatically controlled heater. The system variable is the air temperature of the room, and the detector for this variable is a thermostat. The thermostat can be adjusted so that contacts of a switch will close when the temperature falls below a pre-set value (the set point). Closure of the contacts turns on the correctional mechanism – the coils of the heater. You can see this process illustrated in Figure 13.1.

If the room cools below the set point, the thermostat turns the heater on, which warms the room. The rise in room temperature causes the thermostat to turn the heater off. Because the activity of the correctional mechanism (heat production) feeds back to the thermostat and causes it to turn the heater off, this process is called **negative feedback**. Negative feedback is an essential characteristic of all regulatory systems.

The **drive reduction hypothesis** was the earliest attempt to explain the nature of motivation and reinforcement. This theory stated that biological needs, caused by deprivation of the necessities of life, are unpleasant. The physiological changes associated with, say, going without food for several hours produce an unpleasant state called hunger. Hunger serves as a drive, energising an organism's behaviour. The organism then engages in behaviours that in the past have obtained food. The act of eating reduces hunger, and this drive reduction is reinforcing, as seen in Figure 13.2.

Not all drives are based on homeostasis, on biological needs like the ones for food and water. The most obvious example is the drive associated with sexual behaviour. An individual can survive without sexual behaviour; but the sex drive is certainly motivating, and sexual contact is certainly reinforcing. Similarly, most organisms placed in a featureless environment will soon become motivated to seek something new; they will work at a task that gives them a view of the world outside.

The drive reduction hypothesis of reinforcement has fallen out of favour for two primary reasons. The first is that drive is almost always impossible to measure. For example, suppose you obtain pleasure from watching a set of colour slides taken by a friend while on holiday. According to the drive reduction hypothesis, your 'exploratory drive' or 'curiosity drive' is high, and looking at holiday slides reduces it, providing reinforcement. Or consider a woman who enjoys listening to music. What drive induces her to turn on her iPOD? What drive is reduced by this activity? There is no way to measure 'drive' in either of these examples and confirm that it actually exists; thus, the hypothesis cannot be tested experimentally.

The second problem is that if we examine our own behaviour we find that most events we experience as rein-

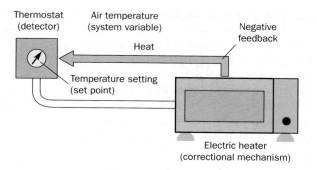

Figure 13.1 An example of a regulatory system.

see activity on mypsychlab

forcing are also exciting, or drive-increasing. The reason a roller-coaster ride is fun is certainly not because it reduces drive. The same is true for skiing, surfing or viewing a horror film. Likewise, an interesting, reinforcing conversation is one that is exciting, not one that puts you to sleep. And people who engage in prolonged foreplay and sexual intercourse do not view these activities as unpleasant because they are accompanied by such a high level of drive. In general, the experiences we really want to repeat (that is, the ones we find reinforcing) are those that increase, rather than decrease, our level of arousal.

Physiology of reinforcement

To understand the nature of reinforcement we must understand something about its physiological basis. Olds and Milner (1954) discovered quite by accident that electrical stimulation of parts of the brain can reinforce an animal's behaviour. For example, rats will repeatedly press a lever when the brain is electrically stimulated.

The neural circuits stimulated by this electricity are also responsible for the motivating effects of natural reinforcers such as food, water or sexual contact, and of

drugs such as heroin, alcohol and cocaine. Almost all investigators believe that the electrical stimulation of the brain is reinforcing because it activates the same system that is activated by natural reinforcers and by drugs that people commonly abuse. The normal function of this system is to strengthen the connections between the neurons that detect the discriminative stimulus (such as the sight of a lever) and the neurons that produce the operant response (such as a lever press). The electrical brain stimulation activates this system directly.

Researchers have discovered that an essential component of the reinforcement system consists of neurons that release dopamine as their transmitter substance. Thus, all reinforcing stimuli appear to trigger the release of dopamine in the brain.

Optimum-level theory

Although events that increase our level of arousal are often reinforcing, there are times when a person wants nothing more than some peace and quiet. In this case, avoidance of exciting stimuli motivates our behaviour. As you saw in Chapter 7, the removal (or avoidance) of an aversive stimulus produces negative reinforcement. In an attempt to find a common explanation for both positive and negative reinforcement, some psychologists have proposed the **optimum-level hypothesis** of reinforcement and punishment: when an individual's arousal level is too high, less stimulation is reinforcing; when it is too low, more stimulation is desired (Hebb, 1955; Berlyne, 1966). Berlyne hypothesised two forms of exploration: diversive exploration is a response to understimulation (boredom) that increases the diversity of the stimuli the organism tries to come in contact with; specific exploration is a response to overstimulation (usually because of a specific need, such as lack of food or water) that leads to the needed item, thereby decreasing the organism's drive level.

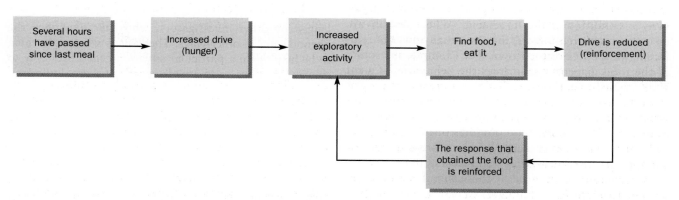

Figure 13.2 The drive reduction hypothesis of motivation and reinforcement.

The hypothesis that organisms seek an optimum level of arousal is certainly plausible. Any kind of activity, even the most interesting and exciting one, eventually produces satiety; something that was once reinforcing becomes bothersome. Presumably, participation in an exciting behaviour gradually raises an organism's arousal above its optimum level. However, the logical problem that plagues the drive reduction hypothesis also applies to the optimum-level hypothesis. Because we cannot measure an organism's drive or arousal, we cannot say what its optimum level should be. Thus, the optimum-level hypothesis remains without much empirical support.

Effects of intermittent reinforcement

You saw in Chapter 7 that when an organism's behaviour is no longer reinforced, the behaviour eventually ceases, or extinguishes. If the behaviour was previously reinforced every time it occurred, extinction is very rapid. However, if it was previously reinforced only intermittently, the behaviour persists for a long time. Intermittent reinforcement leads to **perseverance**, even when the behaviour is no longer reinforced.

Many human behaviours are reinforced on intermittent schedules that require the performance of long sequences of behaviours over long intervals of time. A person's previous experience with various schedules of reinforcement probably affects how long and how hard the person will work between occasions of reinforcement. If all attempts at a particular endeavour are reinforced (or if none are), the person is unlikely to pursue a long and difficult project that includes the endeavour. If we knew more about a person's history with various schedules of reinforcement, we would probably know more about their ability to persevere when the going gets difficult (that is, when reinforcements become variable).

The role of conditioned reinforcement

Another phenomenon that affects the tendency to persevere is conditioned reinforcement. When stimuli are associated with reinforcers, they eventually acquire reinforcing properties of their own. For example, the sound of the food dispenser reinforces the behaviour of a rat being trained to press a lever.

Motivation is not merely a matter of wanting to do well and to work hard. It also involves the ability to be reinforced by the immediate products of the work being done. If a person has regularly been exposed to particular stimuli in association with reinforcers, that person's behaviour can be reinforced by those stimuli. In addition, if the person has learned how to recognise self-produced stimuli as conditioned reinforcers, the performance of the behaviours that produce them will be 'self-reinforcing'.

Failure to persist: learned helplessness

A large body of evidence suggests that organisms can learn that they are powerless to affect their own destinies. Two social psychologists, Maier and Seligman (1976), reported a series of experiments demonstrating that animals can learn that their own behaviour has no effect on an environmental event. This result is exactly the opposite of what has been assumed to be the basis of learning. All the examples of learning and conditioning cited so far have been instances in which one event predicts the occurrence of another. **Learned helplessness** involves learning that an aversive event cannot be avoided or escaped.

Overmeier and Seligman (1967) conducted the basic experiment. They placed a dog in an apparatus in which it received electrical shocks that could not be avoided; nothing the animal did would prevent the shocks. Next, they placed the dog in another apparatus in which the animal received a series of trials in which a warning stimulus was followed by an electrical shock. In this case the animal could avoid the shocks simply by stepping over a small barrier to the other side of the apparatus. Dogs in the control group learned to step over the barrier and avoid the shock, but dogs that had previously received inescapable shocks in the other apparatus failed to learn. They just squatted in the corner and took the shock as if they had learned that it made no difference what they did. They had learned to be helpless.

Seligman (1975) has suggested that the phenomenon of learned helplessness has important implications for behaviour. When people have experiences that lead to learned helplessness, they become depressed and their motivational level decreases. The change in motivation occurs because the helplessness training lowers their expectation that trying to perform a task will bring success. Seligman also suggested that learned helplessness has the characteristics of a personality trait; that is, people who have had major experiences with insoluble tasks will not try hard to succeed in other types of task, including ones they could otherwise have solved.

Seligman's theory of learned helplessness has been challenged by other investigators, who have explained the phenomenon in other ways. The issue is whether learning to be helpless in a particular situation generalises only to similar situations or to a wide variety of them. For example, McReynolds (1980) observed that when people experience a situation in which reinforcements are not contingent on their responding, their responding extinguishes. If the situation then changes to one in which responding will be reinforced, the people will continue not to respond unless they perceive that the schedule of reinforcement has changed. The more similar the second situation is to the first, the more likely it is that the person will act helpless. This explanation describes the phenomenon of learned helplessness as a failure to discriminate between the condition under which responding is reinforced and the condition under which it is not. Further research will have to determine whether learned helplessness is, as Seligman asserts, a stable personality trait or whether it can be explained by the principles of instrumental conditioning. We will return to learned helplessness in the depression section of Chapter 18 (see p. 821).

Ingestion: drinking and eating

Much of what an animal learns to do is motivated by the constant struggle to obtain food and drink. The need to eat certainly shaped the evolutionary development of our own species. Simply put, motivation to eat is aroused when there is a deficit in the body's supply of stored nutrients, and it is satisfied by a meal that replenishes this supply. A person who exercises vigorously uses up the stored nutrients more rapidly, and loses water, and consequently must eat more food and ingest more fluid. Thus, the amount of food and drink a person normally ingests is regulated by physiological need. But what, exactly, causes a person to start eating and drinking, and what stops these behaviours? These are simple questions, yet the answers are complex. There is no single physiological measure that can tell us reliably whether a person should be hungry or thirsty; hunger and thirst are determined by a variety of conditions. So, instead of asking 'What is the cause of hunger or thirst?' we should ask, 'What are the causes?'

Thirst

A popular theory at the turn of the twentieth century argued that thirst was caused by a dry mouth and that it was this dryness that regulated how much water we ingested. When the salivary glands reduced the amount of fluid they secreted, this made the mouth dry and was the cue for drinking. While plausible, the theory was not supported by evidence because even if water was made available to the mouth but was prevented from reaching the stomach, drinking would continue: the mouth was being kept wet, not dry, and yet drinking continued because the fluid did not reach the stomach. Why?

Osmometric thirst

A later theory suggested that thirst was caused by dehydration within cells (Gilman, 1937). The fluid in cells is called intracellular fluid and contains a little sodium but large amounts of potassium and other metabolites. The other source of fluid in the body is extracellular fluid and this is found in two places. Interstitial fluid surrounds the cell body and is salty; blood plasma is found in the capillaries, arteries and veins and allows living cells and blood to be suspended within it. Extracellular fluid comprises about 20 per cent of the body's weight; intracellular fluid comprises about 40 per cent of body weight. Gilman administered solutions of sodium chloride to animals. The membranes surrounding cells are not very permeable to sodium and so water is drawn from the intracellular fluid to the extracellular fluid by a process called osmosis, whereby water moves through a semi-permeable membrane from a region where there is a low concentration of solutes to one where there is a high concentration. This reduces the concentration of sodium available across the membrane and the movement of water by osmosis dehydrates and shrinks the body's cells. This is what Gilman found and the type of thirst is called **osmometric thirst**. Because the organism needs to be aware of this thirst, there must be cells in the body which serve to inform the central nervous system that dehydration is occurring. These cells are called osmoreceptors and are located in the brain. When salt solutions are injected into the brain, drinking increases, but if sodium chloride is injected into the general blood supply, no such increase is observed (Wood *et al.*, 1977).

The precise locus of the osmoreceptors seems to be a part of the brain called the lateral preoptic area. If even small lesions are made to this region, the typical increase in drinking seen in response to dehydration is reduced (Mason, 1980). When neurons are exposed to urea, salt and sucrose – neurons are impermeable to salt and sucrose but not to urea – those neurons stimulated by salt and sucrose and which caused increased drinking were located in the lateral preoptic area (Peck and Novin, 1971).

Volumetric thirst

Osmometric thirst is caused by dehydration within cells. There is another type of thirst that results from dehydration outside cells, that is, a reduction in the level of blood plasma. This is called **volumetric thirst** because the thirst is provoked by a reduction in the volume of blood plasma. One obvious way in which volumetric thirst can occur is through bleeding – a loss of blood leads to a great loss of extracellular fluid with all the substances that the fluid contains. People who suffer from haemophilia experience thirst during a bleeding episode and this is alleviated by an infusion of blood.

Volumetric thirst can also result from low levels of salt in the diet. The loss of extracellular fluid produces the movement of water from the extracellular fluid and into cell bodies, by the process of osmosis described earlier. This process leads to drinking.

Given that blood plasma is lost as a result of extracellular/volumetric thirst, you might hypothesise that receptors detecting this loss are located in the vascular or circulatory system. One important structure in this system is the kidney. If blood flow to the kidney is inhibited, the total volume of blood in the body does not change, but there is

of nutrients are absorbed from the intestines into the bloodstream. Therefore, the body's supply of fuel is not replenished until quite some time after the meal begins. If you were to continue to eat until the nutrients actually entered the bloodstream, your stomach would burst. Therefore, some other detectors must be responsible for stopping the meal.

Although evidence suggests that the primary cause of hunger is not an empty stomach, the primary cause of satiety (that is, the cessation of hunger caused by eating) seems to be a full stomach. Many studies have shown that satiety is caused by entry of a sufficient quantity of nourishing food into the stomach. Therefore, the stomach must contain detectors that sense the presence of food. We have known for a long time that hunger can be abolished by injecting food into an animal's stomach by means of a flexible tube. Even though the animal does not get to taste and smell the food, it will not subsequently eat. Davis and Campbell (1973) showed how precisely the stomach can measure its contents. The investigators allowed hungry rats to eat their fill and then removed some food from their stomachs. When they let the rats eat again, they ate almost exactly as much as had been taken out.

The stomach appears to contain detectors that inform the brain about the chemical nature of its contents as well as the quantity. The ability to detect the chemical nature of food that has entered the stomach is important, because eating should stop relatively soon if the food is very nutritious but should continue for a longer time if it is not. Deutsch et al. (1978) injected either milk or a dilute salt solution into hungry rats' stomachs and 30 minutes later allowed them to eat. The rats that had received injections of milk ate less than the ones that had received the salt solution. Because the rats could not taste what was put in their stomachs, the effect had to come from detectors there. The nature of these detectors is not known, but they must respond to some chemicals present in food. You can try an experiment of your own: drink two glasses of water when you are very hungry and see whether they satisfy your appetite.

Detectors that measure the amount and nutritive value of food in the stomach contribute only to short-term control of eating – the termination of a single meal. Long-term factors also control food intake. For example, when people eat especially nutritious food, they soon learn to eat less. When they begin to exercise more, and hence burn up their store of nutrients faster, they soon start eating more.

There may also be characteristics of food that may make us eat more or less of it. Some psychologists have argued that the variety and sensory properties of food can reduce or increase our intake; these reductions are associated with a reduction in ratings of the food's pleasantness. The section below reviews some of this evidence.

Sensory-specific satiety

Have you ever experienced the feeling when, after eating a big savoury meal, you could still manage to eat dessert? Or that you have had enough of eating peanuts but could quite happily contemplate eating a packet of crisps?

These experiences reflect **sensory-specific satiety (SSS)** – the decrease in the pleasantness and consumption of specific food after eating it to satiety. The satiety is sensory-specific because individuals may become sated eating foods of specific tastes, shapes, sizes and textures but not foods of different taste, shape, size and texture (Rolls et al., 1986). This phenomenon explains why, if we eat a meal composed of a variety of foods, we eat more because there is greater sensory stimulation available from a varied meal (we would consume a greater quantity of a meal consisting of a bowl of soup, sausages, egg and bacon, and chocolate mousse than we would a meal comprising solely of sausages). SSS also has survival value because if we become bored with eating one food but not another, this increases the likelihood of a variety of foods being eaten.

If a food is eaten to satiety, a second course of the same food will result in a reduction in intake of around 50 per cent (Rolls et al., 1981). In Rolls's early experiment, all foods, with the exception of roast beef, produced sensory-specific satiety. In one study, participants ate either a four-course meal of sausages, bread and butter, chocolate dessert and bananas or ate only one of these foods to satiety. The researchers found that consumption was 60 per cent higher when foods were presented together than when presented separately (Rolls et al., 1986). At a post-satiety tasting session, those foods presented alone were also rated as less pleasant than those eaten as part of a four-course meal (Rolls et al., 1984). Even colour and shape influence the amount of food eaten. When a variety of pasta shapes is presented for consumption, more is eaten than when only one pasta shape is presented; people also eat more food if it is made up of different colours than one colour (Rolls et al., 1982). The effect of varying the shape and variety of food can be seen in Figures 13.4(a), (b).

SSS is also seen in the sense of smell. In an experiment where participants were asked to rate the pleasantness of the odours of banana, satsuma, fish paste, chicken and rose water before and after consuming bananas and chicken to satiety, the pleasantness of chicken and banana odours (but not other foods) significantly declined after satiety (Rolls and Rolls, 1997).

Why should this be? SSS allows us to enjoy and consume a greater variety of food and, therefore, represents a mechanism that enables us to consume a variety of nutrients. There is also evidence that certain regions of the brain may be responsible for our feeling of satiety. The hypothalamus, as you have seen, is important to feeding.

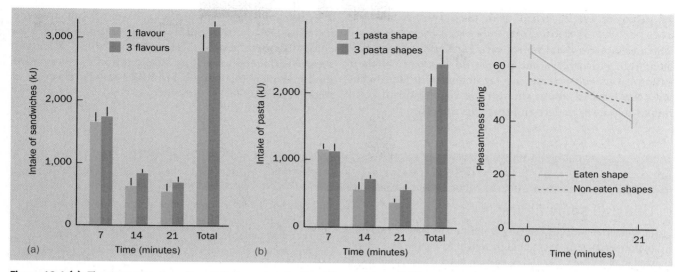

Figure 13.4 (a) The amount eaten of a one-flavoured and a three-flavoured meal. **(b)** The effect of varying the type of pasta shape on food intake and pleasantness ratings of the taste of the shapes. In both these examples, the sensory properties of the food influence intake and ratings of pleasantness.

Source: Reprinted from Rolls, B.J., Rolls E.T. and Rowe E.A., How sensory properties of foods affect human feeding behaviour, *Psychology and Behaviour*, 1982, 29, 409–417. © 1982, with permission from Elsevier Science; and Rolls and Rolls (1997).

Neurons in this region in monkeys stop responding to the sight and taste of food when the food has been eaten to satiety (Rolls *et al.*, 1986). Small *et al.* (2001b) and others, however, suggest that a key region involved in satiety is the orbitofrontal cortex (OFC).

An fMRI study in which the odour of banana was presented before and after people had eaten bananas to satiety found that activation in the OFC decreased when people sniffed the odour of banana after satiety (O'Doherty *et al.*, 2000). No such decrease was observed when people sniffed the odour of vanilla, suggesting that the OFC response was a specific response to a specific property of the food eaten to satiety. One role for the prefrontal cortex in this process may be that of responding to reward. When we have eaten to satiety, the OFC will not respond because the brain does not feel rewarded. Rolls *et al.* have reported that OFC taste cells in monkeys reduce their firing to food stimuli when these monkeys have eaten to satiety.

In another study, volunteers ate chocolate to satiety as a PET scanner measured brain activation (Small *et al.*, 2001a). Participants first ate a chunk of chocolate, rated it for pleasantness and were then asked if they would like another. If they did, they were given another piece and asked to rate its pleasantness again. This continued until the participants felt that they had consumed enough chocolate.

The researchers found that when participants ate chocolate they found pleasant, there was increased blood flow in a collection of regions including areas beneath the corpus callosum, a part of the OFC called the caudomedial OFC, the insula, striatum and midbrain. When participants were sated, blood flow increased in the parahippocampal gyrus and a different part of the OFC (the caudolateral OFC) than was activated during initial eating. What could this activation represent?

Small *et al.* suggest that the activity with chocolate reflects two different systems which mediate two aspects of behaviour: approach and withdrawal. That is, when the brain responds to reward, it activates the insula and part of the OFC. This reflects an 'approach' behaviour because we tend to approach things we like and this generates a positive emotion. When the brain responds to non-reward or stimuli that do not provide an opportunity for reward (such as food we no longer want to eat) brain regions involved in 'withdrawal' are recruited. These are involved in withdrawal because we tend to withdraw from stimuli we do not like and we find such stimuli unpleasant (or at the very least, do not find them pleasant).

This is an interesting hypothesis because it is in keeping with a model of emotion which argues that the frontal cortex is the region that becomes active during the experience of positive and negative emotion. We will describe and evaluate this model in the emotion section of the chapter (see p. 589).

The region is also activated while looking at food-related stimuli after fasting (Porubska *et al.*, 2006). Twelve lean participants were asked look at food- and non-food-related stimuli after five hours of fasting. Functional MRI measured brain activation as they did this. The left side of the OFC was significantly more active when participants viewed the food slides (the insula on both sides of the brain was also more active). As self-reported appetite increased, so did activation in the insula bilaterally, the left operculum and the right putamen. The data suggest that all of these regions are involved in the motivation to eat.

Obesity

The mechanisms that control eating generally do an efficient job. However, some people do not control their eating habits and become too fat or too thin. Does what we have learned about the normal regulation of food intake help us to understand these disorders?

Obesity is extremely difficult to treat, but attempts have been made to design intervention programmes for clinically obese people. The evidence for the success of these treatments, as well as a description of obesity and its consequences, can be found in the Psychology in Action section.

Psychology in action – The problem of obesity and its treatment

Obesity: some figures

In Western countries, obesity is defined as having body fat that exceeds 25 per cent of body weight in women and 18 per cent in men (Bray, 1998). The amount of fat is estimated using a measure called body mass index (BMI). This takes a person's weight in kilograms and divides it by their height in metres squared. This figure is expressed as X kg/m2. To be diagnosed as clinically obese, a person must have a BMI that is equal to or greater than 30 kg/m2 (World Health Organization, 1998). Figure 13.5 shows you how to calculate BMI.

The prevalence of being overweight in 6–11-year-old children had increased from 6 per cent in 1980 to 10.65 per cent in 1994 (Troiano and Flegal, 1998). Only a minority of adults have the desired BMI of 18.5 to 24.9 kg/m2 and this shift towards being overweight is thought to carry severe health risks. The risk of mortality increases by around 30 per cent in people with a BMI of 30 kg/m^2; this percentage continues upward to 40 per cent when BMI exceeds 40 kg/m^2 (Manson et al., 1995). A study of 14,403 Norwegian men aged between 40 and 49 and initially free of coronary heart disease (CHD) has shown that body mass index was a risk factor for the subsequent development of the disease later in life (Haheim et al., 2007). The causes of death in obese people include stroke, diabetes and cancer (these correlate with obesity). Obese people also suffer social and physical complications (Wadden et al., 2002). Obese girls complete fewer years in school, despite having just as good grades as those who remain, are less likely to marry, and earn less than their non-obese counterparts. Obese people also elicit negative aesthetic judgements from others (as you saw in Chapter 3): people tend to prefer partners with a specific shape and size (and it is not obese).

Consequences of obesity and rationale for intervention

Interventions are recommended when a person has a serious BMI statistic and a risk of developing ill health. For people with a BMI of below 27 kg/m2, clinicians recommend an increase in physical activity and a decrease in fat and sugar intake, coupled with self-directed efforts to maintain weight loss and the taking of a doctor's advice (Wadden et al., 2002). For people with higher BMIs, the same intervention may be implemented but if this does not work more drastic measures may be adopted such as drugs or, for those with a BMI in excess of 40 kg/m2, surgery (this is called **bariatric surgery**). The side effects of surgery are considerable, but weight loss is produced more efficiently (Yanovski and Yanovski, 2002). It is expensive, costing around £17,000 per operation (Bauchowitz et al., 2005).

Initial success at weight loss depends on the goals of the person losing the weight. First, people need to be motivated to lose weight. Secondly, they need to realise that weight reduction programmes are designed for health rather than aesthetic reasons. For example, until recently interventions were guided towards helping people achieve their ideal weight (rather than a weight which would reduce the risk of ill health). Current emphasis, however, is on reducing health complications and so a loss of 5–15 per cent can be effective in producing this reduction, even though the patient/client may not be happy with having lost so little weight and expect a weight loss of 20–35 per cent (Blackburn, 1995; O'Neil et al., 2000). Wadden et al. cite one study which reported that weight reduction of 7 kg/m2 combined with 150 minutes of exercise a week reduced the likelihood of developing diabetes by 58 per cent (Diabetes Prevention Program Research Group, 2002, cited in Wadden et al., 2002). A meta-analysis of obesity prevention programmes for children has found that only 21 per cent of 64 programmes showed evidence of weight gain prevention in children (Stice et al., 2006). The effect was greater for children and adolescents (rather than pre-adolescents) and for girls.

Psychological interventions

Difficulty in restricting food intake is increased during holiday periods which the overweight regard as high-risk periods because of family celebrations or national holiday celebrations. One way in which this difficulty could be reduced is by self-monitoring, the act of closely observing what is eaten and when and in which contexts. Boutelle et al. (1999) examined the effect of self-monitoring during this high-risk holiday period in a group of overweight individuals on a weight-loss programme. Forty-nine obese people who had been on the programme for at least a month, were known to self-monitor rarely and who were willing to be contacted in a two-week holiday period (Christmas–New Year), took part in the study.

Psychology in action – *Continued*

Height (Feet)	100	105	110	115	120	125	130	135	140	145	150	155	160	165	170	175	180	185	190	195	200	205	210	215	220	225	230	235	240	245	250
5'0"	20	21	21	22	23	24	25	26	27	28	29	30	31	32	33	34	35	36	37	38	39	40	41	42	43	44	45	46	47	48	49
5'1"	19	20	21	22	23	24	25	26	26	27	28	29	30	31	32	33	34	35	36	37	38	39	40	41	42	43	43	44	45	46	47
5'2"	18	19	20	21	22	23	24	25	26	27	27	28	29	30	31	32	33	34	35	36	37	37	38	39	40	41	42	43	44	45	46
5'3"	18	19	19	20	21	22	23	24	25	26	27	27	28	29	30	31	32	33	34	35	35	36	37	38	39	40	41	42	43	43	44
5'4"	17	18	19	20	21	21	22	23	24	25	26	27	27	28	29	30	31	32	33	33	34	35	36	37	38	39	39	40	41	42	43
5'5"	17	17	18	19	20	21	22	22	23	24	25	26	27	27	28	29	30	31	32	32	33	34	35	36	37	37	38	39	40	41	42
5'6"	16	17	18	19	19	20	21	22	23	23	24	25	26	27	27	28	29	30	31	31	32	33	34	35	36	36	37	38	39	40	40
5'7"	16	16	17	18	19	20	20	21	22	23	23	24	25	26	27	27	28	29	30	31	31	32	33	34	34	35	36	37	38	38	39
5'8"	15	16	17	17	18	19	20	21	21	22	23	24	24	25	26	27	27	28	29	30	30	31	32	33	33	34	35	36	36	37	38
5'9"	15	16	16	17	18	18	19	20	21	21	22	23	24	24	25	26	27	27	28	29	30	30	31	32	32	33	34	35	35	36	37
5'10"	14	15	16	17	17	18	19	19	20	21	22	22	23	24	24	25	26	27	27	28	29	29	30	31	32	32	33	34	34	35	36
5'11"	14	15	15	16	17	17	18	19	20	20	21	22	22	23	24	24	25	26	26	27	28	29	29	30	31	31	32	33	33	34	35
6'0"	14	14	15	16	16	17	18	18	19	20	20	21	22	22	23	24	24	25	26	26	27	28	28	29	30	31	31	32	33	33	34
6'1"	13	14	15	15	16	16	17	18	18	19	20	20	21	22	22	23	24	24	25	26	26	27	28	28	29	30	30	31	32	32	33
6'2"	13	13	14	15	15	16	17	17	18	19	19	20	21	21	22	22	23	24	24	25	26	26	27	28	28	29	30	30	31	31	32
6'3"	12	13	14	14	15	16	16	17	17	18	19	19	20	21	21	22	22	23	24	24	25	26	26	27	27	28	29	29	30	31	31
6'4"	12	13	13	14	15	15	16	16	17	18	18	19	19	20	21	21	22	23	23	24	24	25	26	26	27	27	28	29	29	30	30

Height (Feet)	255	260	265	270	275	280	285	290	295	300	305	310	315	320	325	330	335	340	345	350	355	360	365	370	375	380	385	390	395	400
5'0"	50	51	52	53	54	55	56	57	58	59	60	61	62	62	63	64	65	66	67	68	69	70	71	72	73	74	75	76	77	78
5'1"	48	49	50	51	52	53	54	55	56	57	58	59	60	60	61	62	63	64	65	66	67	68	69	70	71	72	73	74	75	76
5'2"	47	48	48	49	50	51	52	53	54	55	56	57	58	59	59	60	61	62	63	64	65	66	67	68	69	70	70	71	72	73
5'3"	45	46	47	48	49	50	50	51	52	53	54	55	56	57	58	58	59	60	61	62	63	64	65	66	66	67	68	69	70	71
5'4"	44	45	45	46	47	48	49	50	51	51	52	53	54	55	56	57	58	58	59	60	61	62	63	64	64	65	66	67	68	69
5'5"	42	43	44	45	46	47	47	48	49	50	51	52	52	53	54	55	56	57	57	58	59	60	61	62	62	63	64	65	66	67
5'6"	41	42	43	44	44	45	46	47	48	48	49	50	51	52	52	53	54	55	56	56	57	58	59	60	61	61	62	63	64	65
5'7"	40	41	42	42	43	44	45	45	46	47	48	49	49	50	51	52	52	53	54	55	56	56	57	58	59	60	60	61	62	63
5'8"	39	40	40	41	42	43	44	44	45	46	46	47	48	49	49	50	51	52	52	53	54	55	55	56	57	58	59	59	60	61
5'9"	38	38	39	40	41	41	42	43	44	44	45	46	47	47	48	49	49	50	51	52	52	53	54	55	55	56	57	58	58	59
5'10"	37	37	38	39	39	40	41	42	42	43	44	44	45	46	47	47	48	49	50	50	51	52	52	53	54	55	55	56	57	57
5'11"	36	36	37	38	38	39	40	40	41	42	43	43	44	45	45	46	47	47	48	49	50	50	51	52	52	53	54	54	55	56
6'0"	35	35	36	37	37	38	39	39	40	41	41	42	43	43	44	45	45	46	47	47	48	49	50	50	51	52	52	53	54	54
6'1"	34	34	35	36	36	37	38	38	39	40	40	41	42	42	43	44	44	45	46	46	47	47	48	49	49	50	51	51	52	53
6'2"	33	33	34	35	35	36	37	37	38	39	39	40	40	41	42	42	43	44	44	45	46	46	47	48	48	49	49	50	51	51
6'3"	32	32	33	34	34	35	36	36	37	37	38	39	39	40	41	41	42	42	43	44	44	45	46	46	47	47	48	49	49	50
6'4"	31	32	32	33	34	35	35	36	37	37	38	38	39	40	40	41	41	42	43	43	44	44	45	46	46	47	47	48	49	

Figure 13.5 How to determine BMI in adults.

Here is a shortcut method for calculating BMI (if you are too short or too tall for the table: Step 1, multiply weight (in pounds) by 703; Step 2, multiply height (in inches) by height (in inches); Step 3, divide the answer in Step 1 by the answer in Step 2 to get your BMI. Example: for a person who is 5 feet 5 inches tall weighing 149 lbs. Step 1, 149 x 703 = 104747; Step 2, 65 x 65 = 4225; Step 3; 104747 divided by 4225 = 24.8.

Source: Shape Up America! www.shapeup.org.

Self-monitoring took the form of examining food intake and taking weight measurements daily. Two groups – an intervention group and a non-intervention group – were observed and both groups were encouraged to do this basic level of self-monitoring. However, the intervention group also received daily mailings (comics and literature about self-monitoring and weight loss) from the researchers as well as one or two phone calls in each week in the two-week period reminding them to self-monitor.

Those in the intervention group self-monitored more frequently but also managed their weight more effectively than did those in the non-intervention group. Both groups had difficulty in managing their weight, however (the comparison group putting on a pound, on average). Those in the self-monitoring

Psychology in action – *Continued*

In 2008, chef Jamie Oliver launched a campaign called 'Pass It On' to get the people of Rotherham in the North of England eating well and heathily. One resident, Julie Critchlow (pictured here), was so unimpressed she took take-away orders from disgruntled schoolchildren outside the school railings. She was eventually won over.

Source: Corbis: Peter Dench (l), Ross Parry Agency: (r);

group lost more weight and there was a strong association between self-monitoring and weight loss.

The difficulty in maintaining weight loss is one of the most serious problems obese people face. Studies of 20-week intervention programmes, such as the one described, have found that people can lose up to 9 kg (around 9 per cent of body weight) but when the intervention programme stops, people can regain as much as one-third of their weight in the following 12 months (Foreyt and Goodrick, 1993; Wing, 2002). Clinicians, therefore, have focused their attention on how to achieve the maintenance of weight loss.

This can be done by creating detailed behavioural plans for the client to follow, as well as by controlling the portions of food the client eats. Replacing normal meals and snacks with portion-controlled meals, for example, can lead to an 8 per cent reduction in weight over a sustained period of dietary regime control. The longer the intervention, the greater the weight loss, but most of the loss is seen in the first six months (Perri *et al.*, 1989; Flechtner-Mors *et al.*, 2000). The greatest predictor of whether people maintain their loss is their ability to engage in physical activity. Those who do, tend to maintain their weight-loss programmes, as Figure 13.6 shows. Those who exercise at home are more successful at maintenance than are those who attend gyms or leisure centres (Perri *et al.*, 1997).

Surgical interventions

If psychological interventions do not succeed in producing weight loss, more aggressive interventions such as surgery are sometimes implemented if the person is morbidly obese, i.e. the person has a BMI of over 40 kg/m². There are two methods of surgically effecting weight loss in the obese. The first, called an intestinal bypass, worked by bypassing a part of the digestive system called the jejenum (Mason and Ito, 1969). The effect of this was to produce dramatic weight loss – in the order of 45 kg – but also very serious side effects such as liver failure. The second, and the one that is most commonly adopted, is also a form of gastric bypass. A 50 ml pouch is attached to the gullet which restricts food intake. The pouch is connected to the jejenum, bypassing the stomach and part of the intestine called

Every overweight person's dream: a pill that reduces fat. Pharmaceutical companies are working on such products constantly but no pill is currently totally effective.

Source: Copyright © News Group Newspapers Ltd

the duodenum. The effect of this is to reduce weight by around 30 per cent in the first-year-and-a-half after surgery (Albrecht and Pories, 1999) and a sustained loss over a decade later.

Pharmacological interventions

Surgery is not the only physical intervention for obesity. Another possibility might be drugs and, in recent years, several companies have sought to deliver the perfect anti-obesity drug or 'fat-buster'. Historically, such drugs have been used for other purposes – for depression (fenfluramine, sibutramine) or to combat smoking (rimonabant). Customised drugs have focused on the substances in the body which regulate hunger and satiety, such as the hormone, cholecystokinin (CCK), amylin, insulin and glucagons. All of these are released when we eat and help limit meal size (Woods *et al*, 2006; Naslund and Hellstrom, 2007). One, ghrelin, is released in the stomach and affects the vagus nerve and hypothalamus and increases food intake. Drugs which mimic the effects of these hormones produce an increase in the feeling of satiety. Drugs that antagonise ghrelin receptors decrease the feelings of hunger (Moran, 2006). There are also chemicals, melanocortins, which are released by

Psychology in action – *Continued*

leptin's action on a group of neurons in the arcuate nucleus. When melanocortin receptors are activated, there is a decrease in feeding and an increase in energy expenditure. Drugs are being developed which act as agonists for melanocortin receptors (Nargund *et al.*, 2006). Other drugs being developed include histamine 3 antagonists which may help to reduce weight gain (Ebenshade *et al.*, 2006). None of these drugs have met with long-term success, as yet, but the quest to develop the perfect weight-loss drug continues.

Policy for the future

Wadden *et al.* (2002) suggest five ways in which the obesity problem might be tackled. These are:

- Regulating the food advertising aimed at children, especially the advertising of sugary and fatty food.
- Prohibiting fast foods and drinks from schools.
- Subsidising the sale of healthy foods.
- Taxing unhealthy foods.
- Providing resources for physical activity.

Some of these steps may probably never happen, because they are quite stark and potentially expensive, especially for the manufacturer who will see its goods taxed and the advertising of these goods reduced. The authors do acknowledge that these steps may not even achieve the aims they set out to achieve. Of course, there is also the important issue of choice and freedom of choice: people can decide not to consume

sugary or fatty food and some people enjoy eating such foods in moderation. For those who consume sensibly to reduce or impede access to such foods, by reducing their advertising or taxing them heavily, would it be psychologically (perhaps morally) beneficial?

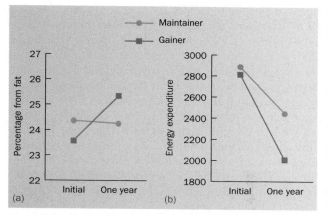

Figure 13.6 The number of calories obtained from fat **(a)** and the weekly kcal expenditure **(b)** in a group of people who gained weight or maintained weight loss after undergoing a weight loss programme.

Source: McGuire, T., Wing, R.R., Klem, W., Lang, M.L. and Hill, J.O., What predicts weight regain in a group of successful weight losers? *Journal of Consulting and Clinical Psychology*, 1999, 67(2), 177–185. Copyright © 1999 by the American Psychological Association, reprinted with permission.

What causes obesity?

Various psychological variables may be a cause of obesity, including lack of impulse control, poor ability to delay gratification, and maladaptive eating styles (primarily eating too fast). However, in a review of the literature, Rodin *et al.* (1989) found that none of these suggestions has received empirical support. Rodin and her colleagues also found that unhappiness and depression seem to be the effects of obesity, not its causes, and that dieting behaviour seems to make the problem worse.

There is no single, all-inclusive explanation for obesity, but there are many partial ones. Habit plays an important role in the control of food intake. Early in life, when we are most active, we form our ideas about how much food constitutes a meal. Later in life, we become less active, but we do not always reduce our food intake accordingly. We fill our plates according to what we think is a proper-sized meal (or perhaps the plate is filled for us), and we eat everything, ignoring the satiety signals that might tell us to stop before the plate is empty.

One reason why many people have so much difficulty losing weight is that metabolic factors appear to play an

important role in obesity. In fact, a good case can be made that obesity is most often not an eating disorder but rather a metabolic disorder. Metabolism refers to the physiological processes, including the production of energy from nutrients, that take place within an organism. Just as cars differ in their fuel efficiency, so do people. Rose and Williams (1961) studied pairs of people who were matched for weight, height, age and activity. Some of these matched pairs differed by a factor of two in the number of calories they ate each day. People with an efficient metabolism have calories left over to deposit in the long-term nutrient reservoir; thus, they have difficulty keeping this reservoir from growing. In contrast, people with an inefficient metabolism can eat large meals without getting fat. Thus, whereas a fuel-efficient automobile is desirable, a fuel-efficient body runs the risk of becoming obese.

Genetic influences

Are people who suffer from excessive weight gain genetically different from those with normal weight or is it true that, as Bray (1998) suggests, 'genes load the gun, the environment pulls the trigger'? Differences in metabolism appear to have a hereditary basis. Griffiths and Payne (1976) found that the children of obese parents weighed more than other children even though they ate less. Stunkard *et al.* (1986) found that the body weight of a sample of people who had been adopted as infants was highly correlated with their biological parents but not with their adoptive parents. Thus, a person's weight (presumably closely related to their metabolic efficiency) is influenced by genetic factors.

Why are there genetic differences in metabolic efficiency? James and Trayhurn (1981) suggest that under some environmental conditions metabolic efficiency is advantageous. That is, in places where food is only intermittently available in sufficient quantities, being able to stay alive on small amounts of food and to store up extra nutrients in the form of fat when food becomes available for a while is a highly adaptive trait. Therefore, the variability in people's metabolisms may reflect the nature of the environment experienced by their ancestors. For example, physically active lactating women in Gambia manage to maintain their weight on only 1,500 calories per day (Whitehead *et al.*, 1978). This high level of efficiency, which allows people to survive in environments in which food is scarce, can be a disadvantage when food is readily available because it promotes obesity.

Another factor – this one non-hereditary – can influence people's metabolism. Many obese people diet and then relapse, thus undergoing large changes in body weight. Some investigators have suggested that starvation causes the body's metabolism to become more efficient. For example, Brownell *et al.* (1986) fed rats a diet that made them become obese and then restricted their food intake until their body weights returned to normal. Then they made the rats fat again and reduced their food intake again. The second time, the rats became fat much faster and lost their weight much more slowly. Clearly, the experience of gaining and losing large amounts of body weight altered the animals' metabolic efficiency.

Steen *et al.* (1988) obtained evidence that the same phenomenon (called the yo-yo effect) takes place in humans. They measured the resting metabolic rate in two groups of adolescent wrestlers: those who fasted just before a competition and binged afterwards and those who did not. The investigators found that wrestlers who fasted and binged developed more efficient metabolisms. Possibly, these people will have difficulty maintaining a normal body weight as they get older.

The role of leptin

For a long time, investigators believed that fat tissue provided some chemical signal that could be detected by the brain. When too much fat began accumulating, more of this chemical was secreted, and the person began eating less. If the amount of body fat began to decrease, the level of the chemical fell and the person began eating more.

After many years of searching for such a chemical signal, researchers have finally succeeded in finding one. The discovery came after years of study with a strain of genetically obese mice. The ob mouse (as this strain is called) has a low metabolism, overeats and gets monstrously fat. It also develops diabetes in adulthood, just as many obese people do. Recently, researchers in several laboratories have discovered the cause of the obesity (Campfield *et al.*, 1995; Halaas *et al.*, 1995; Pelleymounter *et al.*, 1995). A particular gene, called *OB*, normally produces a protein known as **leptin** (from the Greek word *leptos*, 'thin'). Leptin is normally secreted by fat cells that have absorbed a large amount of triglyceride. Because of a genetic mutation, the fat cells of ob mice are unable to secrete leptin.

Leptin has profound effects on metabolism and eating, acting as an anti-obesity hormone. If ob mice are given daily injections of leptin, their metabolic rate increases, their body temperature rises, they become more active and they eat less. As a result, their weight returns to normal. The treatment works even when the leptin is injected directly into the brain, indicating that the chemical acts directly on the neural circuits that control eating and metabolism. Figure 13.7 shows a photograph of an untreated ob mouse and an ob mouse that has received injections of leptin.

Maffei *et al.* (1995) discovered that leptin is found in humans and that the level of leptin in the blood is correlated with obesity; thus, this chemical signal appears to be present in our species as well as in mice. But if leptin is produced by human fat cells, why do some people nevertheless overeat and become obese?

As you saw in Chapter 4, hormones act on their target cells by stimulating receptor molecules located on these cells. Using the techniques of molecular genetics, Tartaglia *et al.* (1995) discovered the leptin receptor. In order for leptin to reduce weight, the brain must contain function-

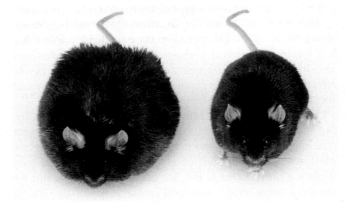

Figure 13.7 The effects of leptin on obesity in mice of the ob (obese) strain. The ob mouse on the left is untreated; the one on the right received daily injections of leptin.

Source: Photo courtesy of Dr J. Sholtis, The Rockefeller University. © 1995 Amgen, Inc.

Controversies in Psychological Science – Can the bitter gene cause obesity?

The issue

If the media are to be believed, we in the well-resourced West are turning into lumpen couch potatoes, gorging on criminally inedible food and staring gormlessly at *Big Brother* while mentally eyeing up the next kebab. This pattern of unhealthy eating seems to be particularly prominent in adults and children from poorer backgrounds. For example, the Head Start programme in the US, a pre-school programme for children from low-income families, found that obesity was greater in these children than in the general population – 15 per cent were obese compared to 10 per cent for the general population (Feese *et al.*, 2003). Various reasons have been suggested for this, but one possible factor may be surprising: obesity may be caused by the gene that allows us to perceive bitter tastes.

The evidence

Around 30 per cent of Europeans are thought to be unable to taste the bitter substances, 6-n-propylthiouracil (PROP) and pehylthiocarbamide, an ability thought to be mediated by a specific gene called *TAS2R38*. People who are able to taste PROP have been found to have a lower BMI than do non-tasters (Tepper and Ullrich, 2002) but evidence is mixed. One study found no difference and another reported that the effect was found for boys but that girl tasters had higher BMIs than girl non-tasters (Keller *et al.*, 2002; Keller and Tepper, 2004).

Being able to taste or not taste bitter substances has evolutionary advantages. As you saw in Chapter 5, most poisons are bitter and so it is to our advantage to have a gene that codes for this taste because it can prevent harm and assist survival. Those who cannot taste bitterness, however, can ensure that they ingest a wider range of (non-poisonous) foods, thereby ensuring a healthy diet and a healthy life. The ability to taste PROP is associated with several quirky behavioural features: PROP-tasters have more food aversions, dislike (and eat fewer) vegetables, think that vegetables taste bitter (especially broc-

coli, orange/grapefruit juice and spinach), and prefer sweeter foods (Keller *et al.*, 2002; Dinehart *et al.*, 2006). When child PROP-tasters are allowed to eat what they like, they eat fewer bitter-tasting vegetables and fewer vegetables in general than do non-tasters (Bell and Tepper, 2006). This selective diet may be related to the obesity seen in PROP-tasting children.

To test this explicitly, a recent study asked 81 children attending a Head Start pre-school to taste a solution of PROP and indicate whether it tasted of water or 'like something else' (Lumeng *et al.*, 2008). Because the children were around $3–3^{1}/_{2}$ years-old, facial expression was used as a measure of bitterness perception (children would exhibit the 'yuck' response if they tasted bitter). The children's BMI was measured, along with their diet, their neophobia (whether they were afraid or spurned new or unfamiliar foods) and the mother's race, BMI, weight, height, etc.

There were 18 non-tasters and 63 tasters in the sample. The tasters had a significantly higher BMI than did the non-tasters and were more overweight. The mother's BMI and tasting status were the two strongest predictors of the child's obesity.

Conclusion

The researchers note that the study has limitations –such as using facial expression to index response and that children from high-income homes were not included. The research raises an important question, however: why do children from low-income families and who are tasters have a higher BMI? The researchers point to studies showing that feeding is less restrictive in low-income families and meal times are less structured. Their consumption of fruit and vegetables is lower, they eat more fatty and sugary foods, and consume more fast food. Given that PROP tasters find vegetables less palatable and prefer sweet foods, this characteristic, combined with the vegetable-light/fat and sugar-heavy diet of low-income family children, could lead to the increased BMI in this group.

---

ing leptin receptors. Perhaps, researchers speculate, some people have leptin receptors that do not respond normally to the presence of leptin in the blood. The overgrown fat cells of these people secrete high levels of leptin, but the effect the hormone produces in the brain is less intense than normal. Hence, people overeat.

How emotion affects food intake

One reason for why they do so given by people who eat excessively is that it makes them feel better. Some researchers have linked this increased positive mood to the

dopamine release caused by carbohydrate and fat (which the foods people crave tend to be full of – crisps, sweets, biscuits and so on). A new study of healthy men, however, suggests that the relationship can be quite complex: if a man is exposed to a stimulus that creates happiness, his appetite for chocolate increases; if he is exposed to one that causes sadness it decreases (Macht *et al.*, 2002).

Macht *et al.* asked men to abstain from eating for either two or eight hours before watching film clips designed to elicit anger, fear, sadness and happiness (e.g. a sequence from the film *Cry Freedom* was used to generate anger). After this, participants were given up to four pieces (5 g) of their preferred chocolate to eat and were asked to rate their appetite for chocolate and how much they liked what they ate.

Men in the happiness condition ate more chocolate and rated it as more pleasant than did men in the sadness condition. The findings suggest that emotion can affect eating in two ways: one involves people eating nice food when in a good mood and rating the food in a way that is congruent with their mood. The other involves people regulating their emotion through eating: people may, like binge eaters, eat tasty food to feel better.

Some research, however, suggests that when it comes to mood, ingesting chocolate does not necessarily improve positive mood but instead reduces negative mood. Macht and Mueller (2007) asked 48 men and women of normal weight to eat a 5 g piece of chocolate or drink some water after watching film clips designed to elicit positive, negative or neutral mood states. Mood was measured after seeing the clips and before and after ingesting the chocolate.

The chocolate eaters reported less negative mood compared to the water drinkers but the food had no effect on the other mood states. The authors suggest that this reduction in bad mood was attributable to the chocolate's palatability. In a second study, therefore, participants ate either palatable or unpalatable chocolate – one that was not rated as particularly pleasant – just after watching mood-inducing films. The palatable chocolate reduced negative mood, but the unpalatable chocolate did not. The benefit disappeared after three minutes.

The results suggest that emotional eating may arise from palatable food's ability to reduce negative mood, such as that experienced during periods of stress.

A study by researchers from Wales and Germany has found that the taste of sweet but not bitter foods can be affected by the taster's mood. Greimel *et al.* (2006) induced joy or sadness in participants by presenting them with video clips designed to elicit these emotions. Participants then rated the pleasantness and sweetness of a sweet chocolate drink, a bitter quinine solution and a bitter-sweet drink. Emotion significantly influenced pleasantness and sweetness ratings of the sweet drink: those who had been made sad rated the drink as less pleasant and sweet; those who had been made happy, rated it as more pleasant and sweeter. There was no effect of emotion on the ratings of the bitter and bitter-sweet drinks. 'The results fit the motivational and cognitive properties of the two emotions', the authors conclude. 'Whereas joy is associated with an increased readiness to savour the world, sadness is associated with a focus on inner experiences' (p. 267).

Anorexia nervosa

Anorexia nervosa is an eating disorder characterised by a severe restriction of eating. The literal meaning of the word 'anorexia' suggests a loss of appetite, but people with this disorder generally do not lose their appetite (DSM-IV TR, 2001). Their limited intake of food – especially fats and carbohydrates – occurs despite intense preoccupation with food, its preparation

---

Cutting edge – Mood food

Go into any restaurant or café and you'll invariably hear the sound of music coming through the PA system. It is designed to create an ambiance, a feeling of relaxation (or excitement) befitting the establishment. A study from the US has also shown that this music can affect not only how long you eat for, but also how much (Stroebele and de Castro, 2006).

In a diary study, 78 college students made a note of what they ate and for how long for seven consecutive days. They also noted where and when they ate, whether there was music present, how loud and fast/slow this music was, and how many people were present.

The researchers found that listening to music was significantly associated with higher food intake and meals of longer duration, regardless of whether the food was a proper meal or a snack. The speed and volume of music was not significantly associated with either of these variables. People ate more and longer when more people were present but the effect of music

on meal duration was eliminated when the number of people present was taken into account. This number, rather than the music, was the better predictor of meal length.

On a related note, research shows that we eat less in the presence of a stranger of the opposite sex than one of the same sex. We often adjust our eating depending on what the other person is doing. To explore this further, researchers from the US and Canada paired participants either with friends, partners or strangers and then asked them to eat as many biscuits and crackers as they wanted (Salvy *et al.*, 2007).

Men and women ate more in the presence of those they knew than when with strangers. But certain men and women were likely to eat more. Women in couples ate more than any of the other female samples; and men who ate with friends ate more than men in any other pairing. Eating is facilitated by social interaction, especially, it seems, in men.

and with their own disorder (Hermans *et al.*, 1998). Their average intake is around 100 calories a day; for healthy adult women, the recommended calorie intake is between 1,500 and 2,000. They may enjoy preparing meals for others to consume, collect recipes, and even hoard food that they do not eat. They have an intense fear of becoming obese, and this fear continues even if they become dangerously thin. There is a significant disturbance in the perception of body shape and size, with anorexics consistently overestimating body size and shape (Smeets *et al.*, 1997). Many exercise excessively by cycling, running, or almost constant walking and pacing. The prevalence of the disorder is between 0.5 and 1 per cent.

Bulimia nervosa

A different eating disorder, **bulimia nervosa**, is characterised by a loss of control of food intake. The term bulimia comes from the Greek *bous*, 'ox', and *limos*, 'hunger'. People with bulimia nervosa periodically gorge themselves with food, especially dessert or snack food, and especially in the afternoon or evening. These behaviours must occur at least twice a week for three months for a diagnosis of bulimia nervosa to be made (DSM-IV TVR, 2001). These binges are usually followed by self-induced vomiting or the use of laxatives, along with feelings of depression and guilt (Mawson, 1974; Halmi, 1978). This behaviour is called purging, although not all bulimics use this behaviour as a means of compensating for the binge eating. With this combination of bingeing and purging, the net nutrient intake (and consequently, the body weight) of bulimics can vary; Weltzin *et al.* (1991) report that 44 per cent of bulimics undereat, 37 per cent eat a normal amount, and 44 per cent overeat. Episodes of bulimia are seen in some patients with anorexia nervosa. Bulimics seem to be less concerned with food but are excessively preoccupied with body shape (Lovell *et al.*, 1997). The prevalence rate is a little higher than that for anorexia and ranges between 1 and 3 per cent. Despite a reported increase in the prevalence of the disorder over many decades, some recent research suggests that it is declining, with data from the UK, the USA and The Netherlands showing reduced prevalence of bulimia (Keel *et al.*, 2005; Currin *et al.*, 2005; Hoek and van Hoeken, 2003).

Aetiology of anorexia and bulimia nervosa

Because anorexia is characterised by constraint, reduced affect and emotion, and an ascetic way of life, and bulimia is characterised by impulsivity and sensation-seeking, the causes of each might be different. Some researchers have suggested that bulimia might be attribut-

able to some neurophysiological problem, such as an imbalance of serotonin (a neurotransmitter involved in mood, eating and impulsive behaviour). Serotonin disturbances are seen in the disorder during and after the illness (Kaye, 2008) and one mechanism for the process might be that gonadal steroids affect the regulation of 5HT during puberty. Bulimics, like anorexics, might discover that reducing intake also affects serotonin and mood because the lack of food reduces blood levels of a chemical called tryptophan. In the short term, they might experience an improvement in mood but with continued calorie restriction, the effect on serotonin is to make their mood worse (Kaye, 2008).

The fact that anorexia nervosa is seen primarily in young women has prompted a number of biological, cognitive and sociocultural explanations. There is good evidence, primarily from twin studies, that hereditary factors play a role in the development of anorexia (Russell and Treasure, 1989). The existence of hereditary factors suggests that abnormalities in physiological mechanisms may be involved. However, most psychologists believe that the emphasis our society places on slimness, especially in women, is largely responsible for this disorder. Others suggest that the excessive need to control eating (which is, in turn, caused by Western societies' preoccupation with shape and weight) is the characteristic feature (Fairburn *et al.*, 1999).

Body dissatisfaction in healthy and eating- disordered women

see activity on **mypsychlab**

Around 50 per cent of girls and undergraduate women report being dissatisfied with their bodies (Bearman *et al.*, 1986), and this can occur as early as 7 years of age and across cultures (Dohnt and Tiggemann, 2006). This dissatisfaction with one's body is seen as a significant risk factor for the development of eating disorders (Grabe *et al.*, 2007). A number of studies has shown that such body dissatisfaction is significantly higher in young women than it is in middle-aged women. One theory that could account for this dissatisfaction is Frederickson and Roberts's self-objectification theory (1997). This argues that most Western cultures regard the female body as something to be viewed and evaluated. In such cultures, there is a tendency in women to monitor their appearance, judging it as others (mostly, men) would view it. Noting that the body does not meet the ideal – or the perceived notion of an ideal – the woman becomes dissatisfied about her appearance. One consequence of such monitoring is increased anxiety and shame about the body. Ultimately, it could be argued, such monitoring leads to eating disorder, anxiety and sexual dysfunction.

Strahan *et al.* (2006) found that women rated their appearance more negatively than did men and also compared their bodies with very attractive women, especially unrealistic ones such as models, more often than they did less attractive ones. This bias was eliminated by removing the salience of 'cultural norms', i.e. the emphasis on what people find attractive in women and what magazines and television portray as being the ideal of womanly pulchritude and physical perfection. When cultural norms are minimised, women compare themselves with their (more realistic and relevant) peers. However, when cultural norms are made salient, women are more likely to compare themselves with models (and consequently feel worse about themselves when they make such comparisons).

The widespread portrayal of such norms, and women's susceptibility to their psychologically pernicious effects, might explain their insecurity with their bodies. A recent television advertisement for a well-known UK pharmacist showed a woman nervously standing amongst a beach of sunbathers, as the voice-over conveyed her inner thoughts about whether she was slim enough to expose herself in the summer sun. 'The most dreaded moment of the year', the voice-over intoned. A newspaper commentator takes up the story: 'Her fellow baskers turn en masse to judge her. She nervously reveals smooth, caramel limbs, thus enabling the meerkats to return to their sunbathing, safe in the knowledge that they won't have to look at her bingo wings and stubble for the rest of the day' (Raeside, 2007).

This manipulation has some basis in fact. Frederick et al. (2006) found that more women than men felt too heavy, unattractive and avoided wearing a swimsuit in public (16 per cent of men versus 31 per cent of women). Men felt better about their bodies than did women but underweight women were most happy with their bodies, alarmingly. Slender women were more satisfied than those with higher BMIs. Various studies have shown that women, particularly young women, are overly concerned with their appearance and with how others view them; self-objectification seems to occur when the women have the maximum potential for reproduction.

To investigate the relationship between weight, age and self-objectification, Tiggemann and Lynch (2001) asked 322 Australian women aged between 20 and 84 to rate how they viewed their physical appearance. The researchers found that although body dissatisfaction was consistent across all ages, self-objectification, habitual body monitoring, appearance anxiety and symptoms of eating disorders was greatest in the younger sample and decreased with age. Previous studies – and the self-objectification theory – would predict this change over time. Although women become dissatisfied with their bodies, they attach less importance to physical appearance as they get older. Such responses may be affected by culture and class. For example, young Australian female undergraduates express greater body dissatisfaction and lower body esteem than

their Pakistani equivalents. However, when the Pakistani group is divided into Urdu-medium (middle social class) or English-medium (upper social class) groups, the latter group express more concern with body shape than the former (Mahmud and Crittenden, 2007). Although the BMI of the Australians was higher, the findings remained even when physical weight was taken into consideration. The researchers suggest that 'Pakistani women, by virtue of belonging to a collectivist society, where identities are based more on one's group membership rather than on one's personal attributes, may be less likely to face pressures and shape-related criticism' (p. 194).

One source of women's body dissatisfaction is the media. Thin women are portrayed as paragons of their kind: they are healthy, better-looking, attract the most desirable men and so on. Films, magazines and television programmes emphasise the thinness of women (Fouts and Burggraf, 1999), there are fewer fat people portrayed on television and portrayals now are thinner than on television in the past and thinner than is normal in the population (Greenberg et al., 2003; Silverstein et al., 1986; Fouts and Burggraf, 1999). Women who watch thin media images of other women express a significantly greater negative body image than when watching average-sized women, especially if the viewers are under 19 years old and are concerned with their body weight (Groesz et al., 2002; Grabe et al., 2007). Culturation theory argues that increased exposure to material makes this material the norm over time and people come to accept it as real (Gerbner et al., 2002): if this is what women are like, women might think, this is how I need to be, too. If women with a negative body image watch a seven-minute analysis of how the media portrays women, they engage less in social comparison – comparing themselves to an imagined ideal – and are affected less by seeing images of thin, beautiful women (Posavac et al., 1998).

The effects of watching television and fashion magazine images appear to be different: seeing thin women in fashion magazines is associated with a greater activation of what psychologists call 'internalisation of thin ideals', the ability to evoke a stereotype of the most desirable (thin) woman (Tiggemann, 2003). Interestingly, women with eating disorders report less anxiety about their body when watching magazine advertisements featuring average-sized models (Halliwell et al., 2005). The advertisements featuring very thin and average-sized women were rated as just as effective as each other, suggesting that advertisements need not recruit the thinnest of stick-thin women so sell their wares.

About one anorexic patient in 30 dies of the disorder. Many anorexics suffer from osteoporosis, and bone fractures are common. When the weight loss becomes severe

In 2004, the company Dove launched its campaign for Real Beauty (top) using models which contrasted with those normally seen in adverts for similar products (bottom). Of course, both types are designed to sell us thing we do not really need.

Source: The Advertising Archives.

enough, anorexic women cease menstruating (this is called amenorrhoea). Another possible cause is that changes in a young woman's endocrine status alter her metabolism or the neural mechanisms involved in feeding, but because prolonged fasting and the use of laxatives have many effects, interpreting these differences is difficult (Halmi, 1978). Recent neuroimaging research, however, has shed some light on the neurobiological mechanisms of the disorder. Uher *et al.* (2003) reported that women with anorexia who had been successfully tested showed differences in activation in the anterior cingulate and prefrontal cortex when looking at pictures of food. Wagner *et al.* (2008) went a step further and used fMRI to measure brain activation in 16 women who had recovered from anorexia and 16 controls who tasted sucrose or water. They found reduced activation in the insula, anterior cingulate and striatum in the recovered anorexic group. The pleasantness ratings of the tasters were correlated with brain activation, as Figure 13.8 shows.

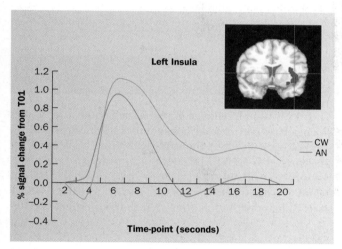

Figure 13.8 Changes in the brain's insula region while recovering anorexic women and healthy women tasted sucrose. Activation was reduced in the recovering group suggesting that this brain region plays a role in the eating disorder.

Source: Reprinted, with permission from Elsevier, from *Physiology and Behaviour*, vol. 94, issue 1, Walter Kaye, 'Neurobiology of anorexia and bulimia nervosa', pages 121–35, copyright 2008.

Cutting edge – Body size, television size and other people's attractive parts

Curiously, women's response to watching other women's bodies on television, as well as their intake of crisps and chocolates, can be affected by the size of the television screen they watch. One study had female students of normal weight eat snacks while watching a 30-minute film of beautiful girls in a frame size that was either in 4:3 ratio (normal) or 16:9 (where the image is stretched) (Anschutz *et al.*, 2008). Restrained eaters felt worse and ate less in the thinner condition.

Furthermore, if women are asked to look at photographs of themselves and other women and identify a part of their own and others' bodies they find unattractive, women with higher BMI judged their bodies to be less attractive (Roefs *et al.*, 2008). Eye-tracking technology showed that they would spend more time looking at their unattractive body parts and more time looking at other women's attractive parts.

Eating disorders – An international perspective

It is almost a cliché to say that eating disorders have increased significantly in the past few decades and that this increase is most obvious in young women raised in 'the West'. Like most clichés, however, it is underpinned by a strong element of truth and evidence. Eating disorders are still more common in Western cultures and more common in girls and women than boys and men. According to Prince (1985), the most well-known eating disorder (after obesity) is anorexia nervosa and there is evidence that this disorder may be culture-bound, that is, one limited to culture 'primarily by reason of certain of their psychosocial features'.

In a review of the extent to which anorexia and bulimia nervosa are culture-bound, Keel and Klump (2003) showed that anorexia has been reported in every non-Western region of the world but that bulimia nervosa appears most frequently in Western cultures. Although suggesting that the former may be culture-bound, the authors caution that anorexia is a more widely studied and accepted disorder than is bulimia and the lack of extensive evidence on the prevalence of bulimia may explain its greater appearance in studies of Western participants.

If we humour the study's conclusion, however, and try to explain why the discrepancy should arise, one factor that might be important is the availability of high-sugar, fatty, palatable foods. Binge eating involves eating these foods to excess; there must, therefore, be a ready source of them. The great prevalence of bulimia in the West may, therefore, reflect the fact that more of this food is available. It does not explain, however, why the bingeing occurs in the first place. The authors suggest a possible genetic predisposition to bulimia, citing evidence that the disorder may share genetic transmission with other 'neuroses' such as phobia. This idea may be too general to be valid, however. Why should genetic predisposition to bingeing be transmitted along with genetic predisposition to being afraid of a spider?

Sexual behaviour

The motivation to engage in sexual behaviour can be very strong. However, sexual behaviour is not motivated by a physiological need, in the way that eating is. Because we must perform certain behaviours in order to reproduce, the process of natural selection has ensured that our brains are constructed in such a way as to cause enough of us to mate with each other that the species will survive.

Effects of sex hormones on behaviour

Sex hormones – hormones secreted by the testes and ovaries – have effects on cells throughout the body. In general, these effects promote reproduction. For example, they cause the production of sperms, build up the lining of the uterus, trigger ovulation, and stimulate the production of milk. Sex hormones also affect nerve cells in the brain, thereby affecting behaviour, but they do not cause behaviours. Behaviours are responses to particular situations and are affected by people's experiences in the past. Sex hormones affect people's motivation to perform particular classes of reproductive behaviours. We therefore start our exploration of sexual behaviour with the motivational effects of sex hormones.

Effects of androgens

see activity on mypsychlab

As you saw in Chapter 12, androgens such as testosterone are necessary for male sexual development.

During prenatal development, the testes of male foetuses secrete testosterone, which causes the male sex organs to develop. This hormone also affects the development of the brain. The prenatal effects of sex hormones are called **organisational effects** because they alter the organisation of the sex organs and the brain. Studies using laboratory animals have shown that if the organisational effects of androgens on brain development are prevented, the animal later fails to exhibit male sexual behaviour. In addition, males cannot have an erection and engage in sexual intercourse unless testosterone is present in adulthood. These effects are called **activational effects** because the hormone activates sex organs and brain circuits that have already developed.

J.M. Davidson *et al.* (1979) performed a carefully controlled double-blind study of the activational effects of testosterone on the sexual behaviour of men whose testes failed to secrete normal amounts of androgens. The men were given monthly injections of a placebo or one of two different dosages of a long-lasting form of testosterone. When the men receiving testosterone were compared with the men in the control group, the effect of testosterone on total number of erections and attempts at intercourse during the month following the injection was found to be large and statistically significant, and the larger dosage produced more of an effect than did the smaller dosage. Thus, we may conclude that testosterone definitely affects male sexual performance.

If a man is castrated (has his testes removed, usually because of injury or disease), his sex drive will inevitably decline. Usually, he first loses the ability to ejaculate, and then he loses the ability to achieve an erection (Bermant and Davidson, 1974). But studies have shown that some men lose these abilities soon after castration, whereas others retain at least some level of sexual potency for many months. Injections or pills of testosterone quickly restore potency. Possibly, the amount of sexual experience prior to castration affects performance afterwards. Rosenblatt and Aronson (1958) found that male cats who had copulated frequently before castration were able to perform sexually for much longer periods of time after the surgery. Perhaps the same is true for men.

Testosterone affects sex drive, but it does not determine the object of sexual desire. A homosexual man who receives injections of testosterone will not suddenly become interested in women. If testosterone has any effect, it will be to increase his interest in sexual contact with other men.

Although evidence shows clearly that testosterone affects men's sexual performance, humans are uniquely emancipated from the biological effects of hormones in a special way. Not all human sexual activity requires an erect penis. A man does not need testosterone to be able to kiss and caress his partner or to engage in other non-coital activities. Men who have had to be castrated and who cannot receive injections of testosterone for medical reasons report continued sexual activity with their partners. For humans, sexual activity is not limited to coitus.

Androgens appear to activate sex drive in women as well as in men. Persky *et al.* (1978) studied the sexual activity of 11 married couples ranging in age from 21 to 31. The subjects kept daily records of their sexual feelings and behaviour, and the experimenters measured their blood levels of testosterone twice a week. Couples were more likely to engage in intercourse when the woman's testosterone level was at a peak. In addition, the women reported finding intercourse more gratifying during these times.

Effects of progesterone and oestrogen

In most species of mammals, the hormones oestradiol and progesterone have strong effects on female sexual behaviour. The levels of these two sex hormones fluctuate during the menstrual cycle of primates and the **oestrus cycle** of other female mammals. The difference between these two cycles is primarily that the lining of the primate uterus – but not that of other mammals – builds up during the first part of the cycle and sloughs off at the end. A female mammal of a non-primate species – for example, a laboratory rat – will receive the advances of a male only when the levels of oestradiol and progesterone in her blood are high. This condition occurs around the time of ovulation, when copulation is likely to make her become pregnant. During this time, the female will stand still while the male approaches her. If he attempts to mount her, she will arch her back and move her tail to the side, giving him access to her genitalia. In fact, an oestrus

female rat often does not wait for the male to take the initiative; she engages in seductive behaviours such as hopping around and wiggling her ears. These behaviours usually induce sexual activity by the male (McClintock and Adler, 1978).

A female rat whose ovaries have been removed is normally non-receptive, even hostile, to the advances of an eager male. However, if she is given injections of oestradiol and progesterone to duplicate the hormonal condition of the receptive part of her oestrus cycle, she will receive the male or even pursue him. In contrast, women and other female primates are unique among mammals in their sexual activity: they are potentially willing to engage in sexual behaviour at any time during their reproductive cycles. Some investigators have suggested that this phenomenon made monogamous relationships possible: because the male can look forward to his mate's receptivity at any time during her menstrual cycle, he is less likely to look for other partners.

In higher primates (including our own species), the ability to mate is not controlled by oestradiol and progesterone. Most studies have reported that changes in the level of oestradiol and progesterone have only a minor effect on women's sexual interest (Adams *et al.*, 1978; Morris *et al.*, 1987). However, as Wallen (1990) points out, these studies have almost all involved married women who live with their husbands. In stable, monogamous relationships in which the partners are together on a daily basis, sexual activity can be instigated by either of them. Normally, a husband does not force his wife to have intercourse with him, but even if the woman is not physically interested in engaging in sexual activity at a particular moment, she may find that she wants to do so because of her affection for him. This fact poses an interesting question. If all of a woman's sexual encounters were initiated by her, without regard to her partner's desires, would we find that variations in oestradiol and progesterone across the menstrual cycle affect her behaviour? Studies using monkeys suggest that this may be the case (Wallen *et al.*, 1986). And as Alexander *et al.* (1990) showed, women taking oral contraceptives (which prevent the normal cycles in secretion of ovarian hormones) were less likely to show fluctuations in sexual interest during the menstrual cycle.

Sexual orientation

When people reach puberty, the effects of sex hormones on their maturing bodies and on their brains increase their interest in sexual activity. As sexual interest increases, most people develop a special interest in members of the opposite sex – they develop a heterosexual orientation. Why does opposite-sex attraction occur? And why does same-sex attraction sometimes occur? Research has not yet provided definite answers to these questions, but it has provided some hints.

Homosexual behaviour (engaging in sexual activity with members of the same sex; from the Greek *homos*, meaning 'the same') is seen in male and female animals of many species. The widespread occurrence of homosexual behaviour means that we should not refer to it as unnatural. However, humans are apparently the only species in which some members regularly exhibit exclusive homosexuality. Other animals, if they are not exclusively heterosexual, are likely to be bisexual, engaging in sexual activity with members of both sexes. In contrast, the number of men and women who describe themselves as exclusively homosexual exceeds the number who describe themselves as bisexual.

Traditional theories of sexual orientation have stressed the importance of a person's early environment. In the early twentieth century, most mental health professionals regarded homosexuality as a disorder, caused by a faulty home environment, for example as the result of having been raised by an overprotective mother and an indifferent father. More recent research has refuted these conclusions. First, there is no evidence that homosexuality is a disorder. The adjustment problems that some homosexuals have occur because others may treat them differently. Therefore, even if we observe more neuroses in homosexuals than in heterosexuals, we cannot conclude that their maladjustment is directly related to their sexual orientation. In a society that was absolutely indifferent to a person's sexual orientation, homosexuals might be as well adjusted as heterosexuals. In fact, a large number of homosexuals are well adjusted and happy with themselves (Bell and Weinberg, 1978), suggesting that homosexuality is not necessarily associated with emotional difficulties.

Sexual orientation appears to be determined prior to adolescence and prior to homosexual or heterosexual activity and most homosexual men and women have engaged in some heterosexual experiences during childhood and adolescence (Bell *et al.*, 1981). But unlike heterosexuals, they found these experiences unrewarding. The most important single predictor of adult homosexuality was a self-report of homosexual feelings, which usually occurred three years before first genital homosexual activity. This finding suggests that homosexuality is a deep-seated tendency. It also tends to rule out the suggestion that seduction by an older person of the same sex plays an important role in the development of homosexuality.

As the researchers admit, the results of the study are consistent with the hypothesis that homosexuality is at least partly determined by biological factors. That is, biological variables may predispose a child to behaviour that is more typical of the other sex and eventually to sexual arousal by members of their own sex.

What might be the biological causes of homosexuality? We can immediately rule out the suggestion that male homosexuals have insufficient levels of testosterone in their blood; well-adjusted male homosexuals have normal levels of testosterone (Tourney, 1980).

A more likely cause of male homosexuality is the pattern of exposure of the developing brain to sex hormones. Some experiments suggest that if a female rat is subjected to stress during pregnancy, the pattern of secretion of sex hormones is altered, and the sexual development of the male offspring is affected (Ward, 1972; Anderson *et al.*, 1986). Various laboratories have studied the brains of deceased heterosexual and homosexual men and have found differences in the size of two different subregions of the hypothalamus and in a bundle of axons that connects the right and left temporal lobes (Swaab and Hofman, 1990; LeVay, 1991; Allen and Gorski, 1992). We cannot necessarily conclude that any of these regions is directly involved in people's sexual orientation, but the results do suggest that the brains may have been exposed to different patterns of hormones prenatally.

When the organisational effects of androgens are blocked in male laboratory animals, the animals fail to develop normal male sex behaviour. Nature has performed the equivalent experiment in humans (Money and Ehrhardt, 1972; Ris-Stalpers *et al.*, 1990). Some people are insensitive to androgens. They have **androgen insensitivity syndrome**, caused by a genetic mutation that prevents the formation of androgen receptors. Because the cells of the body cannot respond to the androgens, a genetic male with this syndrome develops female external genitalia instead of a penis and scrotum. The person does not develop ovaries or a uterus.

If an individual with this syndrome is raised as a girl, all is well. Normally, the testes (which remain in the abdomen) are removed because they often become cancerous. At the appropriate time, the person is given oestrogen pills to induce puberty. Subsequently, the individual will function sexually as a woman. Women with this syndrome report average sex drives, including normal frequency of orgasm in intercourse. Most marry and lead normal sex lives. Of course, lacking a uterus and ovaries, they cannot have children.

Although little research has been done on the origins of female homosexuality, Money *et al.* (1984) found that the incidence of homosexuality was several times higher than the national average in women who had been exposed to high levels of androgens prenatally. The cause of the exposure was an abnormality of the adrenal glands, which usually secrete very low levels of these hormones. Thus, sexual orientation in females may indeed be affected by biological factors.

There is also some evidence that genetics may play a role in sexual orientation. Twin studies take advantage of the fact that identical twins have identical genes, whereas the genetic similarity between fraternal twins is, on average, 50 per cent. Bailey and Pillard (1991) studied pairs of male twins in which at least one member identified himself as homosexual. If both twins are homosexual, they are said to be concordant for this trait. If only one is homosexual, the twins are said to be discordant. Thus, if homosexuality has a genetic basis, the percentage of identical twins concordant for homosexuality should be higher than that for fraternal twins. And this is exactly what Bailey and Pillard found; the concordance rate was 52 per cent for identical twins and 22 per cent for fraternal twins. In a subsequent study, Bailey *et al.* (1993) found evidence that heredity plays a role in female homosexuality, too. The concordance rates for female identical and fraternal twins were 48 per cent and 16 per cent, respectively.

A study by Canadian and American academics has found a significant relationship between handedness, homosexuality and the number of older brothers (Blanchard *et al.*, 2006). A previous meta-analysis had found a significant positive association between the number of older brothers (but not sisters) and homosexuality in men (Blanchard, 2004). Blanchard *et al.* (2006) combined five samples of participants to give 1,774 right-handed heterosexuals, 287 non-right-handed heterosexuals, 928 right-handed homosexuals and 157 non-right-handed homosexuals. They found that homosexuality was greater in those who had older brothers, but only if participants were right-handed. In participants who had no older brothers, homosexuals were more likely to be non-right-handed than were heterosexuals.

The data suggest that fraternal birth order and handedness interact to influence sexual orientation. The authors speculate that some factor (such as higher levels of foetal testosterone) associated with non-right-handedness 'increases the odds of homosexuality in first male births'. Of course, these data are correlational and do not suggest that one factor causes the other.

Neurobiological correlates of sexual behaviour

Arnow *et al.* (2002) have used fMRI to determine which regions of the brain were recruited when heterosexual young men watched 'explicitly erotic' video material, or relaxing or sports-related material. During viewing, penile turgidity was measured using a custom-built device. Figure 13.9 identifies regions of activation during arousal.

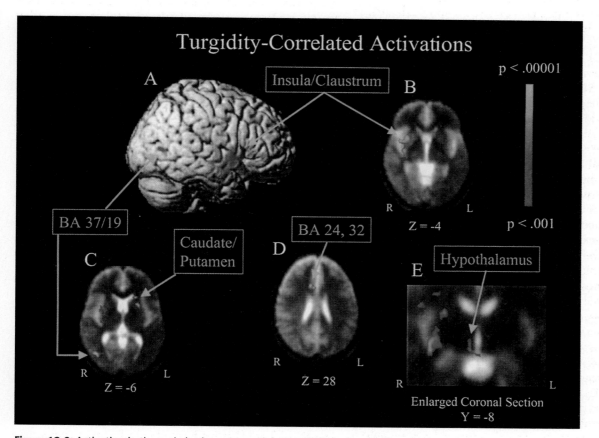

Figure 13.9 Activation in the male brain, measured during fMRI, during penile erection.

Source: From Arnow, B.A. et al., Brain activation and sexual arousal in healthy, heterosexual males, *Brain*, 2002, Vol. 125, 1014–23. Reprinted by permission of Oxford University Press and Bruce Arnow.

The right hemisphere showed the most consistent activation during arousal. Various regions, including the premotor region, subcortical parts of the motor system and the occipital and temporal cortex, were activated during tumescence (much more so than during non-tumescence). The authors suggest that the results are consistent with other, differently designed studies. However, they cite a study showing that there is little overlap between the areas activated in men and those in women. 'Further studies will be needed', the authors say, 'to determine if such discrepancies reflect gender or paradigm differences in sexual arousal related brain activation.'

Aggressive behaviour

Aggression is a serious problem for humans: every day, we hear or read about incidents involving violence and cruelty and, undoubtedly, thousands more go unreported. Many factors probably influence a person's tendency to commit acts of aggression, including childhood experiences, peer group pressures, hormones and drugs, and malfunctions of the brain. Various aspects of aggressive behaviour have been studied by zoologists, physiological psychologists, sociologists, social psychologists, political scientists and psychologists who specialise in the learning process.

Ethological studies of aggression

The utility of species-typical behaviours such as sexual activity, parental behaviour, food gathering and nest construction is obvious; we can easily understand their value to survival. But violence and aggression are also seen in many species, including our own. If aggression is harmful, one would not expect it to be so prevalent in nature. Ethologists – zoologists who study the behaviour of animals in their natural environments – have analysed the causes of aggression and have shown that it, too, often has value for the survival of a species.

Intraspecific aggression

Intraspecific aggression involves an attack by one animal upon another member of its species. Ethologists have shown that intraspecific aggression has several biological advantages. First, it tends to disperse a population of animals, forcing some into new territories, where necessary environmental adaptations may increase the flexibility of the species. Secondly, when accompanied by rivalry among males for mating opportunities, intraspecific aggression tends to perpetuate the genes of the healthier, more vigorous animals.

Human cultures, however, are very different even from those of other species of primates. Perhaps intraspecific aggression has outlived its usefulness for humans and we would benefit by its elimination. Whatever the case may be, we must understand the causes of human aggression in order to eliminate it or direct it to more useful purposes.

Threat and appeasement

Ethologists have discovered a related set of behaviours in many species: ritualised **threat gestures** and **appeasement gestures**. Threat gestures enable an animal to communicate aggressive intent to another before engaging in actual violence. For example, if one dog intrudes on another's territory, the defender will growl and bare its teeth, raise the fur on its back (making it look larger to its opponent), and stare at the intruder. Almost always, the dog defending its territory will drive the intruder away. Threat gestures are particularly important in species whose members are able to kill each other (Lorenz, 1966; Eibl-Eibesfeldt, 1989). For example, wolves often threaten each other with growls and bared teeth but rarely bite each other. Because an all-out battle between two wolves would probably end in the death of one and the serious wounding of the other, the tendency to perform ritualised displays rather than engage in overt aggression has an obvious advantage to the survival of the species.

Aggression shows distinct sex differences. During play, young boys often display more aggression than do young girls (Fabes and Eisenberg, 1992). In an American longitudinal study of elementary and high school students, males were shown to be more aggressive than were females and patterns of aggression were found to be less stable for males than for females (Woodall and Matthews, 1993).

However, sex differences in aggression may vary in different cultures. In some cultures and subcultures, girls may join gangs that are involved in aggressive activities. For example, in Chihuahua, Mexico, a girl being initiated into a gang must fist-fight a gang member. Girl gangs often join their 'brother' gangs in defending their turf against other male gangs. Girl gangs also fight other girl gangs, and such fights may involve knife-fighting and rock-throwing as well as fist-fighting.

Hormones and aggression

In birds and most mammals, androgens appear to exert a strong effect on aggressiveness. Do hormones also influence aggressive behaviour in humans? Men are generally more aggressive than women (Knight *et al.*, 1996) although such differences are attenuated when factors such as provocation are considered (Bettencourt and Miller, 1996). The fact that a man's sexual behaviour depends on the presence of testosterone suggests that this hormone may also influence aggressive behaviour. Some cases of aggressiveness – especially sexual assault – have been treated with drugs that block androgen receptors and thus prevent androgens from exerting their normal effects (Heim and Hursch, 1979; Brain, 1984, 1994). The rationale is based on animal research that indicates that androgens promote both sexual behaviour and aggression in males. However, the efficacy of treatment with anti-androgens has yet to be established conclusively (Mazur and Booth, 1998).

Another way to determine whether androgens affect aggressiveness in humans is to examine the testosterone levels of people who exhibit varying levels of aggressive behaviour in the laboratory and outside the laboratory. Testosterone is secreted into the bloodstream sporadically and so changes in levels can be measured easily. Levels are greatest in the morning and lower in the afternoon (Dabbs, 1990). Clearly, in the laboratory it is unethical (and probably undesirable) to encourage aggression. Psychologists, therefore, have used measures that increase feelings of hostility rather than generate hostility itself and have reported a significant correlation between these measures and testosterone levels: increased testosterone levels were associated with increased feelings of hostility. Most studies, however, report negative results, that is, no relationship between testosterone level and hostility (Mazur and Booth, 1998).

Outside the laboratory, the findings are slightly different. Dabbs *et al.* (1987), for example, measured the testosterone levels of 89 male prison inmates and found a significant correlation between these levels and (1) the violence of the crime, and (2) their fellow prisoners' ratings of their toughness. These effects were also found in female prison inmates. Dabbs *et al.* (1988) found that women prisoners who showed unprovoked violence and had several prior convictions also showed higher levels of testosterone. It is reported that 17–18-year-old criminals with high testosterone levels were more likely to have committed violent crimes and to have violated prison rules (Dabbs *et al.*, 1991). The picture is not entirely uniform, however. One study found no significant difference between the testosterone levels of those individuals charged with violent offences and those charged with property crime (Bain *et al.*, 1987).

In an experimentally controlled study, researchers have noted that losing a tennis match or a wrestling competition causes a fall in blood levels of testosterone (Mazur and Lamb, 1980; Elias, 1981). In a very elaborate study, Jeffcoate *et al.* (1986) found that the blood levels of a group of five men confined on a boat for 14 days changed as they established a dominance-aggression ranking among themselves: the higher the rank, the higher the testosterone level was. Increases have also been reported in individuals about to play a chess match, with

greater increases found in winners than losers after the match (Mazur *et al.*, 1992), and in Brazilian supporters who saw their team on television win the 1994 World Cup Final against Italy; the (losing) Italian viewers showed relatively lower levels (Fielden *et al.*, 1994, cited in Mazur and Booth, 1998).

Testosterone seems to have masculinising (androgenic) and anabolic (building protein tissue) effects. Some athletes take anabolic steroids in order to increase their muscle mass and strength and, supposedly, to increase their competitiveness. Anabolic steroids include natural androgens and synthetic hormones having androgenic effects. Several studies have found that anabolic steroids increase aggression. For example, Yates *et al.* (1992) found that male weightlifters who were taking anabolic steroids were more aggressive and hostile than those who were not. But, as the authors note, we cannot be certain that the steroid is responsible for the increased aggressiveness; it could simply be that the men who were already more competitive and aggressive were the ones who chose to take the steroids.

Testosterone and dominance

What could account for the relationship between testosterone and aggression? Mazur and Booth (1998) have recently proposed that a reciprocal relationship exists between these two factors. Specifically, high levels of testosterone encourage dominant behaviour which maintains high status. The model is reciprocal because testosterone and dominance are seen as reinforcing each other in contrast to the basal model which suggests that the individual has a static, basal level of testosterone which routinely predicts his behaviour. These authors suggest that reciprocal relationships can obviously only be observed across time and at different testing points. They point to a study in which testosterone levels in American Air Force veterans were low during marriage but increased during divorce as evidence for their model (Mazur and Michalek, 1998). The authors interpreted this finding in terms of competition. Divorce is a stressful, but competitive, process. Marriage, on the other hand, is a positive experience, free of competition and – if successful – stress.

The way in which women view themselves is directly related to the degree of testosterone they secrete (Grant and France, 2001). Women with the higher levels of testosterone used more 'dominant' adjectives to describe themselves than did those with lower levels, providing additional evidence for a link between testosterone and dominance. There is also an unusual link between testosterone and communication. Men high in testosterone are less likely to get married, more likely to get divorced and report a lower quality of interaction in marriages they stay in (or leave). Testosterone, it has been argued, promotes simple thinking and not abstract, subtle or complex thought. This, of course, is highly controversial and is based on indirect evidence. Pennebaker *et al.* (2004) correlated testosterone level with natural written language in two people who were undergoing testosterone therapy for the development of upper body strength (male) or as part of a transgender procedure (female). The longer the time since the last testosterone injection, the fewer words describing social relations were used in the participants' text.

Testosterone: status, relationships and empathy

People showing comparatively high and low levels of testosterone tend to react differently in simple social settings, suggesting that the hormone plays some part in assertiveness (Dabbs *et al.*, 2001). Dabbs *et al.* found that participants with low testosterone looked around a room more when entering (to the left and the exit) and focused less frequently on a camera present than did high-testosterone participants.

There is evidence that when high testosterone-level persons feel that their status is threatened, they try to regain this quickly – usually through physical challenge. Researchers have also begun to examine the mismatch effect – where people normally low in testosterone are placed in positions of great status.

In one experiment, researchers placed high and low testosterone students in high and low status positions – making sure they completed a short or long version of a spatial intelligence test accurately (Josephs *et al.*, 2006). Those who completed the task first would put their hand up and say 'done' thus signalling status: they were intellectually superior.

Low testosterone individuals were more emotionally aroused, focused more on their status and performed worse on the test if they were in the high status position. The same pattern was seen in the high testosterone individuals only when they were in the low status position, thus demonstrating the mismatch effect. The same effect for emotional arousal and poor cognition was replicated in a separate experiment with a different type of cognitive test (mathematics) and when heart rate was measured. In a final experiment, the researchers found that levels of testosterone were better predictors of dominance than were self-report measures such as questionnaires.

What are the implications of these findings? 'It is possible that after an increase in status', say Josephs *et al*, 'a person's physiology will gradually change in concert to the new position. . . When testosterone increases, this informs the individual that the environment is safe for further attempts at maintaining or enhancing status. When testosterone decreases, the individual is being flashed a sell signal and should flee the situation to avoid further loss of status' (p. 1011).

Does being with a partner increase or decrease a person's testosterone level? A study by Canadian researchers measured testosterone in men and women who were single, in long-distance relationships or in relationships with people living in the same city. Testosterone was higher in single men than those in relationships (whether long-distance or same-city). Testosterone was lower in women with same-city partners than single women or those with long-distance relationships. The results suggest that hormone levels can increase or decrease depending on a person's relationship status. A cross-sectional and longitudinal study of heterosexual and 'non-heterosexual' men and women has reported that testosterone was lower in heterosexual men and non-heterosexual women (but not non-heterosexual men and heterosexual women) (van Anders and Watson, 2006). The longitudinal study found that having a partner was associated with low testosterone: those with low testosterone were more likely to be partnered at follow-up.

Having a high level of testosterone has also been associated with lack of empathy, although whether it causes this lack of empathy or whether it is only correlated with it is open to question. To test this hypothesis, Hermans *et al.* (2006) administered testosterone to 20 healthy women whose facial muscles were recorded while they observed happy and angry faces. Empathy was measured by participants' mimicry of others' facial expression of emotions. Testosterone was found to be associated with a decrease in facial mimicry, suggesting that the hormone has a role in empathy.

Imitation and aggression

A large percentage of non-violent people may have been hit or punished at least once when they were children, with no obvious harm. But when parents habitually resort to aggression, their children are likely to do the same. In the extreme case of child abuse, parents who beat their children usually turn out to have been victims of child abuse themselves; this unfortunate trait seems to be passed along like an unwanted family heirloom (Parke and Collmer, 1975).

Another factor which is thought to influence aggression in children is exposure to violence on television, in films, video games and in comics. Does the continued observation of violence in the mass media lead children to choose aggressive means to solve their problems? Or are the television companies' representatives correct when they argue that children have no trouble separating fact from fantasy and that the mass media only give us what we want anyway?

Field studies suggest that long-term viewing of violence on television is associated with an increase in children's violent behaviour. For example, Lefkowitz *et al.* (1977) observed a correlation of 0.31 between boys' viewing of

Psychology in action – Aggression at work

Sometimes, work isn't as pleasant as it should be. You turn up to work in a bad mood: it's raining, you overslept, you had too many bill reminders in the post, your train was half an hour late (for which you are told off), the ticket assistant was rude to you, your boss appears to be irritated with you and all morning you've had the most annoying customers in the world on the phone or at your cash desk. These slings and arrows may make you wonder why you're doing the job you're doing. These quotidian irritations pale into insignificance, however, compared to real workplace troubles – assault and murder.

Aggression in the workplace has been studied for some years, and was pioneered in Europe by research in Scandinavia, but we still know too little about how to prevent it. Or, perhaps more pertinently, employers still do too little to put what we know about it into practice.

Workplace aggression refers to psychological acts (such as shouting) and physical assault that can harm another or cause offence in the workplace (Dupre and Barling, 2003). One researcher has specifically characterised workplace aggression as involving either expressions of hostility (which can be verbal or non-verbal, such as giving someone the 'silent treatment'); acts of obstruction (deliberately hampering a person's ability to do their job); and overt physical aggression (Baron *et al.*, 1999).

The chances of your being verbally or physically assaulted by a work colleague, however, are comparatively rare. In fact, most aggression in the workplace is committed by members of the public (customers) or people outside the company. In 1997, 866 Americans were murdered at work; 85 per cent of these murders were committed by outsiders (US Bureau of Labor Statistics, 1998). A study of eight Californian cities found that 90 per cent of non-fatal assaults were caused by non-workmates (Peek-Asa *et al.*, 2001).

In a review, LeBlanc and Barling (2004) highlighted some of the causes of workplace aggression (and, therefore, how aggression could be reduced)

LeBlanc and Barling have identfied four types of aggression. Type I aggression involves an assailant that is not remotely related to the victim (those most at risk are people who handle money with members of the public). Type II aggression involves an assailant who has a legitimate relationship with the organisation (e.g. a customer). Type III aggression involves an offence where the aggressor is a current or former employee of the company or organisation. The fourth type involves aggression by a current employee against another.

Psychologically, the last two types may be the more interesting and important to explore because whereas you might expect a degree of irritation and anger from customers (as you might have felt when listening to your rude ticket assistant), you can take physical steps to protect yourself against them. It is more difficult to protect yourself physically from work colleagues – largely because there should be no need to because you are working together.

So, what predicts workplace aggression? Several factors appear to be involved. Being under surveillance, for example, increases aggression towards an employee's supervisor but not colleagues (Greenberg and Barling, 1999).

The two most important predictors, however, are alcohol consumption and perceived organisational injustice. Organisational injustice refers to perceived wrongdoing or unfairness by the company and/or supervisors. These two factors have been found to predict aggression against colleagues and subordinates. Excessive drinking can also interact with job insecurity to produce aggression towards colleagues: those who don't feel secure in their job and drink excessively are more likely to be aggressive than heavy drinking people who are more secure in their job. These feelings of insecurity and aggression increase if people feel they are being mistreated (Jockin *et al.*, 2001).

A sense of justice is important to every employee. We expect to be treated with politeness, dignity and respect. Supervisors who are perceived as abusive were likely to see their employees quit. But those who remain, and still felt that they were being abused, were likely to be less satisfied with life and would experience more psychological distress and conflicts between work and family (Tepper, 2000). These are the people likely to show less job commitment and satisfaction. Those who felt they could find other jobs felt better.

The conclusion from the studies reviewed by LeBlanc and Barling (2004) seems clear. A happy workforce is one where supervisors are not over-controlling, where decision-making is transparent, where employees, views are respected and addressed (not simply acknowledged and disregarded), where people are not prevented from doing their job properly and where individuals are appropriately rewarded for their efforts. It all seems quite simple, doesn't it?

---

violence and their later behaviour. They reported that the greater the boys' preference for violent television at age 8, the greater their aggressiveness was both at that age and ten years later, at age 18. Girls were found to be much less aggressive, and no relation was observed between television viewing and violence.

Feshbach and Singer (1971) carried out a bold and interesting field study in an attempt to manipulate directly the amount of violence seen by boys on television, and thus to determine whether the viewing would affect their later aggressiveness. With the cooperation of directors of various private boarding schools and homes for neglected children, half the teenage boys were permitted to watch only violent television programmes, the other half only non-violent ones. Six months later, no effect was seen on the behaviour of the boys in the private schools. The boys in the homes for neglected children who had watched violent programmes tended to be slightly less aggressive than subjects who had watched the non-violent ones.

Two factors prevent us from concluding from this study that violent television programmes promote pacifism or at least have no effect. First, by the time people reach their teens, they may be too old to be affected by six months of television viewing; the critical period may come earlier. Secondly, some of the boys resented not being allowed to watch their favourite (in this case, violent) television programmes, and this resentment may have made them more aggressive. As with many other complex social issues, we lack definitive evidence that television violence makes people more aggressive.

Emotion

Most psychologists who have studied emotion have focused on one or more of the following questions: What kinds of situations produce emotions? What kinds of feelings do people say they experience? What kinds of behaviours do people engage in? What physiological changes do people undergo in situations that produce strong emotions? What exactly is an emotion?

The word 'emotion' comes from Latin and means 'to move' or 'to stir up'. In general terms, **emotion** is used by psychologists to refer to a display of feelings that are evoked when important things happen to us. Emotions are relatively brief and occur in response to events having motivational relevance (or to their mental re-creation, as when we remember something embarrassing that we did in the past and experience the feelings of embarrassment again). Emotions are the consequence of events that motivate us. When we encounter reinforcing or punishing stimuli, stimuli that motivate us to act, we express and experience positive or negative emotions. The nature of the emotions depends on the nature of the stimuli and on our prior experience with them.

There are problems, however, associated with defining emotions. We have a multitude of ways of expressing what we think are emotional behaviours. Davitz (1970), for example, found 556 words and phrases that were emotion-related.

Some psychologists view emotion as being produced by reinforcing stimuli or by a set of interacting brain regions or by our awareness of bodily feelings. Given the disparate nature of these definitions, LeDoux (1995b) was right when he concluded that emotion had 'proved to be a slippery concept for both psychologists and neuroscientists'.

If the definition is unclear, then perhaps we can agree on examples of emotions and can describe a core set of basic, fundamental emotions. Yet, even here, the evidence is ambiguous. There are psychologists who have argued that a set of basic emotions exists (Ekman, 1973; Izard, 1977, 1992; Plutchik, 1980). The number of basic emotions has ranged from six or seven (Ekman, 1984, 1992) to eight (Plutchik, 1980), to ten (Izard, 1992). To Ekman, the basic emotions are sadness, joy (happiness), surprise, fear, anger, disgust and contempt (or fear), and these can be universally seen in facial expression (see Figure 13.10).

To Plutchik, the basic emotions are fear/terror, anger/rage, joy/ecstasy, sadness/grief, acceptance/trust, disgust/loathing, expectancy/anticipation and surprise/astonishment. There are other psychologists who have argued that because we have no satisfactory criteria on which to base any concept of 'basic-ness' then we cannot conclude that any emotions we care to list are basic ones (Ortony and Turner, 1990). Yet others argue that the methods used to determine basic emotions are flawed and that the findings are not wholly conclusive (Russell, 1994; cf. Ekman, 1994). What, therefore, is the evidence for basic emotions?

Basic emotions

Charles Darwin (1872) suggested that human expressions of emotion have evolved from similar expressions in other animals. He said that emotional expressions are innate, unlearned responses consisting of a complex set of movements, principally of the facial muscles. Thus, a man's sneer and a wolf's snarl are biologically determined response patterns, both controlled by innate brain mechanisms, just as coughing and sneezing are. Some of these movements resemble the behaviours themselves and may have evolved from them. For example, a snarl shows one's teeth and can be seen as an anticipation of biting.

Darwin performed what was probably the first cross-cultural study of behaviour. He obtained evidence for his conclusion that emotional expressions were innate by observing his own children and by corresponding with people living in various isolated cultures around the world. He reasoned that if people all over the world, no matter how isolated, show the same facial expressions of emotion, these expressions must be inherited instead of learned. The logical argument goes like this. When groups of people are isolated for many years, they develop different languages. Thus, we can say that the words that people use are arbitrary; there is no biological basis for using particular words to represent particular concepts. However, if facial

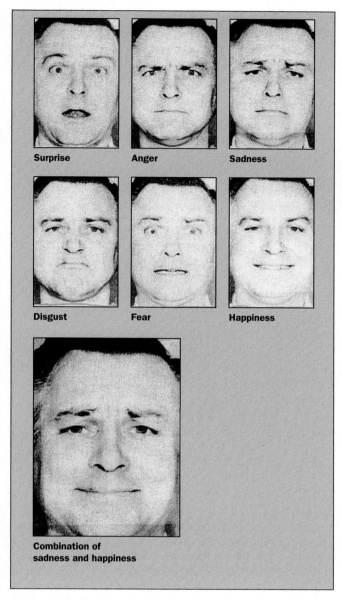

Figure 13.10 The six basic emotions shown in facial expression, and a combination of two, as suggested by Ekman.

Source: From Pinel, John P.J., *Biospychology*, 3rd edn © 1997. Published by Allyn and Bacon, Boston, MA. Copyright © by Pearson Education. By permission of the publisher.

expressions are inherited, they should take approximately the same form in people from all cultures, despite their isolation from one another. And Darwin did, indeed, find that people in different cultures used the same patterns of movement of facial muscles to express a particular emotional state. Of the basic emotions that we experience most often, it has been argued that sadness and happiness are the two most common. Recent research, however, suggests that we may experience happiness more often than was

originally thought. Studies also suggest that the degree of positive mood that we exhibit in our facial expression may correlate with other expressions of positive behaviours in our lives. The Controversies in Psychological Science section below reviews this research.

The biology of emotion

Perhaps one way of determining whether an emotion is basic or not is by observing the neural machinery activated by these so-called basic emotions. If these emotions are distinct then it follows that different brain regions or pathways might mediate them. In animal research, much of the work on understanding the neural correlates of emotion has focused on fear because this emotion is easy to condition in the laboratory. Evidence from animal work and from studies of brain-damaged humans suggests that the amygdala is an important structure for the recognition and expression of fear. Other neuropsychological evidence suggests that other brain regions may also be involved in different types of emotion.

All emotional responses contain three components: behavioural, autonomic and hormonal. The behavioural component consists of muscular movements that are appropriate to the situation that elicits them. For example, a dog defending its territory against an intruder first adopts an aggressive posture, growls and shows its teeth. If the intruder does not leave, the defender runs towards it and attacks. Autonomic responses – that is, changes in the activity of the autonomic nervous system – facilitate these behaviours and provide quick mobilisation of energy for vigorous movement. As a consequence, the dog's heart rate increases, and changes in the size of blood vessels shunt the circulation of blood away from the digestive organs towards the muscles. Hormonal responses reinforce the autonomic responses. The hormones secreted by the adrenal glands further increase heart rate and blood flow to the muscles and also make more glucose available to them.

One of the more important neurotransmitters for emotion is dopamine. When we experience even a slight lift in our mood – or positive affect – the increase is accompanied by an increase in dopamine in two of the major pathways that send dopamine projections to the brain. This does not mean to say that no dopamine was being carried along these pathways in the first place – there are levels of dopamine in the brain, even at rest – but it does mean that a change in behaviour resulted in an increase in these levels.

Emotional responses, like all other responses, can be modified by experience. For example, we can learn that a particular situation is dangerous or threatening. Once the learning has taken place, we will become frightened when we encounter that situation. This type of response, acquired through the process of classical conditioning, is called a conditioned emotional response. A **conditioned emotional response** is produced by a neutral stimulus that has been paired with an emotion-producing stimulus. If an organism learns to make a specific response that avoids contact with the aversive stimulus (or at least minimises its painful effect), most of the non-specific 'emotional' responses will eventually disappear. That is, if the organism learns a successful coping response – a response that terminates, avoids or minimises an aversive stimulus – the emotional responses will no longer occur.

Controversies in Psychological Science – What is the key to enduring happiness?

The issue

Freud, in one of his more perspicacious moments, once remarked that our common mental state is unhappiness. This we punctuate with attempts, of varying success, at relieving it. The American Declaration of Independence accords the right to all American citizens the 'pursuit of happiness'. The intuitive psychology behind this right seems to be the belief that we all deserve happiness and should pursue it without hindrance. This, however, is easier said than done. Research shows that lottery winners have a short-term boost in well-being but no significant long-term increase in happiness. That said, the famous North American Nun study (a longitudinal study of ageing and Alzheimer's disease in nuns from the School Sisters of Notre Dame) found an association between positive thoughts expressed in handwritten diaries and longer living (Danner *et al.*, 2001).

The evidence

A recent study by Zelenski and Larsen (2000) reported that, contrary to the view that we make sporadic attempts at happiness injections, positive emotions are the ones we experience most frequently during the day. For three times a day over the course of a month, their 82 undergraduates reported the degree of various emotions that they experienced. The researchers found that positive emotions dominated the participants' self-reports, as Table 13.1 shows.

The intensity and frequency of positive emotions far outnumbered negative emotions. The researchers also found that some emotions were frequently experienced together. Examples included fear and sadness, sadness and anger, and anger and disgust. Jealousy was the most commonly experienced secondary emotion.

Would people who outwardly express positive emotions also show high degrees of positive affect in their 'inner' life? To try to answer this question, Harker and Keltner (2001) took the unusual step of taking photographs of women printed in their college yearbook and relating the degree of affect expressed in their faces to personality later in life. Ratings of the women's disposition was also obtained from independent observers.

Table 13.1 The frequency of types of emotion experienced in everyday life by 5,642 respondents. 0 = experienced not at all; 7 = experienced very much

Emotion	Mean frequency
Excited	1.73
Interested	1.80
Enthusiastic	1.84
Happy	2.92
Relaxed	2.63
Quiet	1.84
Bored	0.98
Sad	0.60
Guilty	0.42
Lonely	0.64
Frustrated	1.13
Anxious	1.21
Disgusted	0.35
Angry	0.47
Afraid	0.30

Source: Adapted from Zelenski, J.M. and Larsen, R.J., The distribution of basic emotions in everyday life: A state and trait perspective from experience sampling data. *Journal of Research in Personality*, 2000, 34, 178–197.

High degrees of positive affect expressed in the photographs correlated with self-reported traits of affiliation, competence and low negative affect. Positive facial expression was also positively correlated with having a good marriage and enhanced well-being, up to 30 years after the photograph was taken. When observers rated the personalities of the women based only on information provided by the yearbook photographs, women showing positive affect were judged more positively. These were the women with whom observers expected to have more rewarding exchanges.

The researchers admit that the measure of positive emotional expression was very limited. They say that 'it is hard to think of a thinner slice of behaviour'. They also concede that the study focused on women exclusively.

Controversies in Psychological Science – *Continued*

The results of the study, however, are consistent with another showing that very happy people are likely to have stronger social and romantic relations than their less happy counterparts. Diener and Seligman (2002) screened 222 undergraduates for self-reported happiness and compared the 10 per cent who scored most highly on happiness and well-being measures (*N*=22) with a sample of those who scored in the average range (*N*=60) or below-average (*N*=24). Comparison measures included personality, social relations, romantic relations, exercise and psychopathology.

Very happy people were found to have a rich social life and to spend less time alone than did the moderately happy people. They had stronger romantic and social relationships than did the less happy groups and were more extraverted, agreeable and less neurotic. Unhappy people's social relations were worse than moderately happy people's. The very happy people did not experience a greater number of objectively defined good events in their lives than did the other groups but no one factor was sufficient for happiness, that is, there was no one factor which was common to all very happy people. Even the very happy people were not consistently happy – they occasionally experienced negative moods.

Sheldon and Houser-Marko (2001) sought to see whether people who pursued and attained happiness, actually sustained this sense of happiness. The authors referred to the 'self-concordance model' to underpin their research. This model suggests that the intrinsically motivated personal goals we set ourselves will lead to greater happiness and a sense of fulfilment than will goals that seem to be determined by context or environment.

North American undergraduates were contacted at the beginning of their university course and asked to rate their adjustment to college life and to generate eight personal goals. Parents were also contacted at this point and asked how well they thought their children would adjust to college life. Halfway through the semester, the students were contacted again and asked how well they had pursued their goals. The adjustment measure was taken later in the semester. In the January following this exercise, participants generated goals again for the second semester (they were allowed to keep the goals set in semester 1). Two months later, the students were asked to rate how well they had achieved their goals. They were also asked to give their peers questionnaires which evaluated the students' ability to adjust and students' success in achieving adjustment.

Students who were self-concordant, that is, set goals that were personally meaningful, were more likely to achieve their goals. Greater attainment in semester 1 predicted increased feelings of self-concordance in semester 2. Those most likely to achieve their goals in semester 2 showed best adjustment and sense of growth at the end of the study. They were also likely to have a higher average mark across all courses, even though the goals may not have been specifically class-related.

The experimenters suggest that the new level of well-being brought about by goal attainment may extend to further semesters, and studies are needed to answer this question and to see whether older students show the same pattern of achievement as their younger counterparts.

More recently, the Framingham study (which is the study described in the vignette in the chapter opening) has found that people who surround themselves with happy people who are central to their social network are more likely to be happy in future (Fowler and Christakis, 2009). In the study, 4,739 individuals were studied from 1983 to 2003.

Conclusion

The secret to generating happiness, however, remains elusive. As Diener and Seligman conclude: 'There appears to be no single key to high happiness that automatically produces this state . . . High happiness seems to be like beautiful symphonic music – necessitating many instruments, without any one being sufficient for the beautiful quality.'

Emotion – An international perspective

In the late 1960s, Ekman and Friesen undertook a series of cross-cultural observations that validated those of Darwin (Ekman *et al.*, 1972). They visited an isolated tribe in a remote area of New Guinea – the South Fore tribe, a group of 319 adults and children who had never been exposed to Western culture. If they were able to identify accurately the emotional expressions of Westerners as well as they could identify those of members of their own tribe, and if their own facial expressions were the same as those of Westerners, then the researchers could conclude that these expressions were not culturally determined.

Because translations of single words from one language to another are not always accurate, Ekman and Friesen told little stories to describe an emotion instead of presenting a single word. They told the story to a subject, presented three photographs of Westerners depicting three different emotions, and asked the subject to choose the appropriate one. This they

Emotion – *Continued*

Table 13.2 Cross-cultural accuracy [%] in recognising of emotion

Expression	US	Chile	Brazil	Argentina	Japan
Happiness	97	90	92	94	87
Fear	88	78	77	68	71
Disgust	84	85	86	79	82
Anger	68	76	82	72	63
Surprise	91	88	81	93	87
Sadness	87	91	82	88	80
Average	86	85	83	82	78

Adapted from: Elfenbein, H.A. and Ambady, N. (2003) Universals in cultural differences in recognising emotions. *Current Directions in Psychological Science*, 12, 5, 159–164.

were able to do. In a second study, Ekman and Friesen asked Fore tribespeople to imagine how they would feel in situations that would produce various emotions, and the researchers videotaped their facial expressions. They showed photographs of the videotapes to American college students, who had no trouble identifying the emotions. Four of them are shown in Figure 13.11. The caption describes the story that was used to elicit each expression. Table 13.2 shows the degree of accuracy of various cultures at recognising facial expressions of emotion.

However, not all psychologists have agreed with Ekman's conclusions. While the finding that facial expressions can be identified cross-culturally is robust, there is little agreement on what these findings mean. Zajonc (1985), for example, has suggested that facial expressions are epiphenomena – not important of themselves and, in fact, serving another purpose, such as conveying social information. Critics such as Fridlund (1992, 1994) have argued that all facial expressions are commu-

nicative and that to single out a group of emotional facial expressions ignores the fundamental social nature of facial expression. Expressions may not be emotional signals but social tools used for communications: we can communicate happiness or approval via a smile but this smile may not be generated by genuine emotion but by social cues or needs. This objection is difficult, in part, to counter because expressions may sometimes be used for non-emotional purposes. Smiling may indeed be an expression of joy, but it can also be an expression of sarcasm or even, in sinister contexts, threat. What critics suggest is that facial expressions do not reflect the emotion but the social signalling of the emotion; the two are different.

Other critics, such as Russell (1991, 1994), have even questioned whether the cross-cultural findings are robust. Russell has argued in some detail that the faults in the methodology in these experiments, particularly the method of presenting each emotion sequentially and asking respondents to choose from a list of alternative descriptions the expression they have seen, make the conclusions of these studies uninterpretable.

Two large-scale explorations of emotion recognition and experience across cultures, suggest that there is great consistency between cultures but there are also specific differences between them. Members of individual cultures, for example, may be more accurate in judging emotions in the faces of people from their own culture (or 'in-group').

European American, Asian American, Japanese, Indian and Hispanic students were asked to report their emotional experiences over a one-week period and indicate how many pleasant and unpleasant emotions they generally experienced (Scollon *et al.*, 2004). Individuals from Asian cultures reported less life satisfaction and fewer pleasant emotions than did North Americans, a finding also evident within a nation – Asian Americans showed this pattern more than did European Americans, for example (Diener *et al.*, 1995; Okazaki, 2000).

  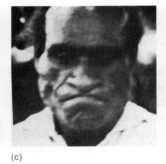 

(a)   (b)   (c)   (d)

Figure 13.11 Portraying emotions. Ekman and Friesen asked South Fore tribesmen to make faces (shown in the photographs) when they were told stories. (a) Your friend has come and you are happy. (b) Your child has died. (c) You are angry and about to fight. (d) You see a dead pig that has been lying there a long time.
Source: © Paul Ekman.

Emotion – *Continued*

The group also found other significant diferences between cultures. Hispanic Americans reported greatest levels of pride, whereas the three Asian samples reported the least, with the Indian sample reporting the least within these (suggesting that pride is not greatly valued in these cultures and may be a negative emotion rather than a positive one). No cultural differences emerged for sadness but did for guilt. Japanese and Asian Americans reported greater levels of guilt than did the European Americans and Hispanics. The Indian sample reported the least guilt. The three Asian cultures reported significantly fewer pleasant emotions (and more negative emotions) than did the other cultures.

The notion that there is an in-group advantage for recognising emotions has been challenged (Beaupre and Hess, 2005). These Canadian researchers measured emotional recognition in a sample of French-Canadian, sub-Saharan Africans and Chinese participants living in Canada. All samples performed similarly when asked to recognise expressions of emotion in the in-group and out-group faces but some groups were better at this task in general (regardless of the nationality of the face). The French-Canadians recognised sadness more accurately than did the other two cultures and recognised shame more accurately than did the Chinese. The authors argue that because the stimuli used in the experiment derive from North American investigations, this benefited the French-Canadians and might explain their accuracy.

A study of native Japanese and American Japanese people's facial expression suggests that aspects of facial expression can be a clue to cultural background and can be used a bit like phonetic accents: subtle communication cues that reveal a person's background (Marsh *et al.*, 2003). Around 80 American and Canadian undergraduates, largely native white participants, were asked to determine the cultural background of American Japanese and native Japanese people based on facial expressions of emotion. If culture/background produced differences in facial expression, these might be seen as non-verbal 'accents'.

While participants could distinguish between cultures when the faces expressed an emotion, they were poor at doing so when the facial expressions were neutral. This, the authors suggest, indicates that people can judge the cultural background of people based on their facial expression of emotion just as they would do so based on a person's accent. It would be interesting to examine how important such a cue can be – would it predict our ability to distinguish between English-speaking Scots, Welsh, Irish or English people, for example?

The amygdala

The amygdala, located in the temporal lobe, just in front of the hippocampus, plays an important role in the expression of conditioned emotional responses. According to Aggleton and Mishkin (1986), it represents 'the sensory gateway to the emotions'. It serves as a focal point between sensory systems and the systems responsible for behavioural, autonomic and hormonal components of conditioned emotional responses (Kapp *et al.*, 1982; LeDoux, 1995a). (The location of the amygdala can be seen in Chapter 4, Figure 4.36.)

Many studies have found that damage to the amygdala disrupts the behavioural, autonomic and hormonal components of conditioned emotional responses. After this region has been destroyed, animals no longer show signs of fear when confronted with stimuli that have been paired with aversive events (LeDoux, 1995a, 1996). Le Doux and his group have identified two routes by which conditioning to fear can occur. The first is a direct – fast and dirty – route linking the thalamus to the amygdala and a second, slower route which links the two via the visual or auditory cortex (depending on the type of stimulus). The first carries the emotional content of the conditioning; the second carries the sensory content. Take a look at Figure 13.12 to see how this system would operate when a person sees a snake.

When the amygdala is stimulated by means of electricity or by an injection of an excitatory drug, animals show physiological and behavioural signs of fear and agitation. Long-term stimulation of the amygdala produces gastric ulcers (Henke, 1982). These observations suggest that the autonomic and hormonal components of emotional responses controlled by the amygdala are among those responsible for the harmful effects of long-term stress.

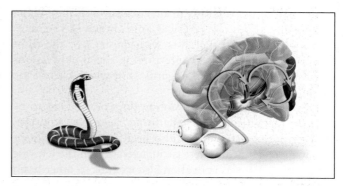

Figure 13.12 What happens in the brain when we fear a snake. Le Doux's model suggests that there are two pathways in the brain which mediate this response. Both are highlighted here.
Source: Science Photo Library Ltd./Claus Lunan/Bonnier Publications

The role of the amygdala in human emotion

The effects seen in animals are mirrored in humans. Individuals with damage to the amygdala are unable to recognise fear in facial expressions, are unable to draw a fearful expression (although they can draw other emotional expressions) and are impaired at recognising fear by sound (Adolphs *et al.*, 1994, 1995, 1999; Calder *et al.*, 1996; Scott *et al.*, 1997; Brooks *et al.*, 1998).

Neuroimaging data suggest that the amygdala is relatively more involved than other brain regions in the perception of fear-related material. Morris *et al.* (1996) reported that not only did activation increase in the left side of the amygdala when individuals were watching fearful facial expressions but they also found that this activation was greater when the facial expression was more intense. Other fMRI and PET studies have confirmed this activation in the amygdala during the perception of fear in facial expression (Morris *et al.*, 1998), and in the perception of sad expressions, but not angry ones (Blair *et al.*, 1999). Adolphs *et al.* (1999) reported a case study of a 31-year-old woman who sustained damage to both sides of her amygdala. They asked her to rate facial expressions, words and sentences along two dimensions: how arousing they were and how pleasant they were. While she was able to distinguish pleasant from unpleasant emotions, she was unable to recognise emotional arousal in those expressions conveying negative emotions, specifically fear and anger. The authors argue that these results support a role for the amygdala in responding to highly negative, threat-related stimuli that require quick responses, although there are results showing that if we keep negative thoughts in mind, this maintenance, and the subsequent bad feeling it generates, is associated with increases in amygdala activity (Schaefer *et al.*, 2002).

Patients with amygdala damage are significantly poor at identifying social (hostility, friendliness) or cognitive (pensiveness) expressions in faces, although they make judgements about the physical appearance of the faces (Shaw *et al.*, 2005). Patients with damage to the right frontal lobe were poor at interpreting social expressions that were negatively hued, regardless of which part of the frontal lobe was damaged.

The amygdala's role in emotion does not appear to be tied to recognising or generating negative emotion. Viewing positive stimuli has also been found to be associated with a significant increase in activation in the left side of the amygdala; this activation also extends to other brain areas known to be involved in drug addiction and reward (Hamann *et al.*, 2002). Watching diseased and mutilated bodies stimulated both sides of the amygdala (but little beyond it). The notion that the amygdala is active when encoding and retrieving positive memories suggests that its role here may be due to its role in remembering positive events. That said, the amygdala has many parts (and parts that PET may not have been sensitive enough to measure), and Hamann *et al.* suggest that different regions within the structure may play different roles.

The amygdala is not the only region to be involved in mediating human emotional response. Perceiving the meaning of social situations is obviously more complex than perceiving individual stimuli, such as the expression of fear on people's faces; it involves experiences and memories, inferences and judgements. These skills are not localised in any one part of the cerebral cortex, although research does suggest that one region of the brain – the orbitofrontal cortex – appears to play a special role.

The orbitofrontal cortex and emotion

The **orbitofrontal cortex (OFC)** is located at the tip of the frontal lobes (see Figure 13.13). It covers the part of the brain just above the orbits – the bones that form the eye sockets – hence the term 'orbitofrontal'. The orbitofrontal cortex receives information from the sensory system and from the regions of the frontal lobes that control behaviour. Thus, it knows what is going on in the environment and what plans are being made to respond to these events. It also communicates extensively with the limbic system, which is known to play an important role in emotional reactions. In particular, its connections with the amygdala permit it to affect the activity of the amygdala, which, as we saw, plays a critical role in certain emotional responses.

Neuroimaging studies implicate the orbitofrontal cortex in emotion. One experiment compared those brain regions that were activated during pleasant or neutral touch, smell and taste (Francis *et al.*, 1999). Participants had their hands stroked by either a velvet glove or a piece of wood as their brain activity was monitored. The pleasant touch (velvet) was associated with significantly greater activation in the orbitofrontal cortex than was the neutral touch (wood). The more intense touch (the neutral wood) was associated with activation in the part of the brain that represents touch. When participants tasted the pleasant sensation of glucose and the pleasant aroma of vanillin, similar but different parts of the orbitofrontal cortex were activated, as were other parts of the brain.

The strongest evidence for the involvement of the orbitofrontal cortex in emotion, however, comes from individuals who have suffered injury to the area. The first – and most famous – case was reported in the mid-nineteenth century and you read about him in Chapter 1. Phineas Gage, the railroad worker, was using a steel rod to ram a charge of dynamite into a hole drilled in solid rock. The

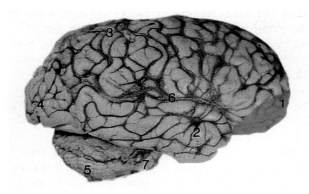

Figure 13.13 The orbitofrontal cortex.
Source: Science Photo Library.

charge exploded and shot the rod into his cheek, through his brain and out of the top of his head. He survived, but he was a different man. Before his injury, he was serious, industrious and energetic. Afterwards, he became childish, irresponsible, boorish and thoughtless of others (Harlow, 1848, 1868). He was unable to make or carry out plans, and his actions appeared to be capricious and whimsical. His accident largely destroyed the orbitofrontal cortex (Harlow, 1848;

Table 13.3 Some of the personality changes that can follow frontal lobe injury

Exaltation/depression
Decreased concern with social propriety
Apathy and indifference
Lack of judgement
Diminished reliability
Facetiousness
Childish behaviour
Anxiety
Social withdrawal
Irritability
Inertia
Lack of ambition
Indifference to opinions of others
Lack of restraint
Restlessness
Purposelessness
Slowness in thinking
Decreased self-concern
Impulsive
Distractibility
Egocentricity

Source: Adapted with permission from Stuss, D.T., Gow, C.A. and Hetherington, C.R., 'No longer Gage': Frontal lobe dysfunction and emotional changes. *Journal of Consulting and Clinical Psychology*, 1992, 60(3), 349–359. Copyright © 1992 by the American Psychological Association, adapted with permission.

Damasio *et al.*, 1994). Figure 13.14 shows the plotted trajectory of the iron rod through Gage's head.

Over the succeeding years, physicians reported several cases similar to that of Phineas Gage. In general, damage to the orbitofrontal cortex reduced people's inhibitions and self-concern; they became indifferent to the consequences of their actions. A list of the behaviours associated with orbitofrontal cortex damage appears in Table 13.3.

Given the large list of impairments in Table 13.3, what exactly is the role of the orbitofrontal cortex in emotion? Eslinger and Damasio (1985) found that their patient, EVR, who sustained bilateral damage of the orbitofrontal cortex displayed excellent abstract social judgement. When he was given hypothetical situations that required him to make decisions about what the people involved should do – situations involving moral, ethical or practical dilemmas – he always gave sensible answers and justified them with carefully reasoned logic. However, his personal life was a disaster.

EVR frittered away his life savings on investments that his family and friends pointed out were bound to fail. He lost one job after another because of his irresponsibility. He became unable to distinguish between trivial decisions and important ones, spending hours trying to decide where to have dinner but failing to use good judgement in situations that concerned his occupation and family life. As the authors noted, 'He had learned and used normal patterns of social behaviour before his brain lesion, and although he could recall such patterns when he was questioned about their applicability, real-life situations failed to evoke them' (p. 1737). Recall from the section on reasoning and the brain in Chapter 11, that Damasio proposed a somatic marker hypothesis of orbitofrontal cortex function. This suggests that our ability to make social and emotional decisions depends on our being able to make sense of somatic information that the body generates in response to specific events. If we are making a risky decision, this risk will be associated with a physiological response which will reflect our uncertainty about the decision we have made. In frontal lobe patients, Damasio argues, these connections between somatic states and an appreciation of them, are missing.

The type of behaviour seen in EVR is also seen in many patients with orbitofrontal cortex damage. Hornak *et al.* (1996) found that their group of patients with frontal lobe damage were impaired at identifying facial and vocal emotional expression. Some of the comments made by orbitofrontal lobe patients on their disorder might help to illuminate the phenomenology of the social impairment – it shows us in very personal terms how the brain damage has affected that person's behaviour. Some of the comments made by Hornak *et al.*'s patients appear in Table 13.4.

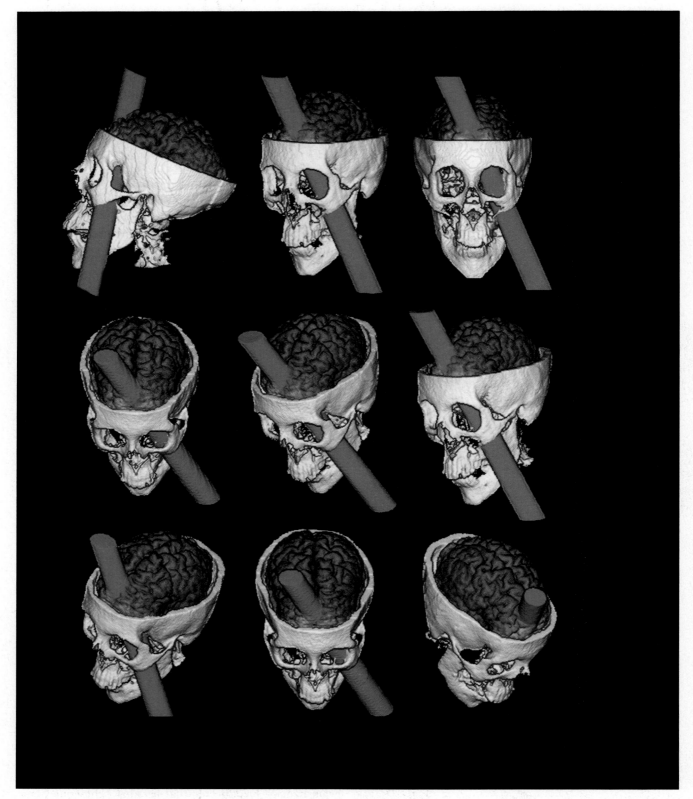

Figure 13.14 The trajectory of the iron bar through Phineas Gage's head.

Source: From H. Damasio, T. Grabowski, R. Frank, A.M. Galaburda and A.R. Damasio, The return of Phineas Gage: Clues about the brain from a famous patient. *Science*, 1994, 246: 1102–1105. Department of Neurology and Image Analysis Facility, University of Iowa.

Table 13.4 Some responses of frontal lobe patients after their injury

Case 2
'If I have something to say, I can't wait and have to say it straight away.'

Case 4
'Emotion, tears, that's all gone out of the window. If I saw someone cry I'd just laugh – people look really silly getting upset.'
'I'm much more aggressive and I feel less fear. I go fighting for no reason.'
'Since I've taken up body building, I tend to show off a bit.'

Case 5
'Anger and irritability had increased; anxiety had decreased.'

Case 7
'I ain't scared of nobody. I'm not frightened of opening my mouth and speaking my mind. If I think someone's in the wrong, I'll tell them and not give a monkey's what they think of me.'

Case 8
'I'm not the woman he married; much more outspoken.'

Source: Adapted from Hornak, J., Rolls, E.T. and Wade, D., Face and voice expression identification in patients with emotional and behavioural changes following ventral frontal lobe damage. *Neuropsychologia*, 1996, 34(4), 247–61.

Emotional processing deficits and social conduct problems seen in frontal lobe patients most often accompany damage to the right (ventromedial) prefrontal cortex, rather than the left (Tranel *et al.*, 2002). Patients with damage to the left side show normal skin conductance response when faced with the risky gambling task described in Chapter 11 and show little antisocial behaviour. Those with damage to the right side, however, show reduced skin conductance to the gambling task and meet the criteria for antisocial personality disorder, suggesting that the right prefrontal cortex plays a more involved role than the left in emotional regulation. The idea that the prefrontal cortex responds asymmetrically during the experience of emotion is reviewed, in a slightly different context, below.

Some patients with frontal lobe damage are unable to inhibit making incorrect responses on some cognitive tasks (although others can). Do you think that this lack of inhibition may be related to the emotional changes seen after damage to the orbitofrontal cortex?

Left–right frontal asymmetry and emotion

Other evidence implicates the anterior cortex in emotion but in a different way. It has generally been thought that the right hemisphere was the dominant hemisphere for processing emotion. We now know, however, that this is far too crude a characterisation of a complex behaviour and function. While the right hemisphere is superior to the left at recognising and perceiving emotional stimuli – such as distinguishing neutral from emotional faces and distinguishing sentences that vary according to their emotional tone – the left hemisphere plays a more important role in the experience of emotion. This hypothesis has been suggested and tested

most prolifically by Richard Davidson and his colleagues at the University of Wisconsin (Tomarken *et al.*, 1990; Wheeler *et al.*, 1993; Davidson and Sutton, 1995). In Davidson's experiments, participants were exposed to film clips designed to elicit specific emotions – positive and negative – as EEG activity was recorded. Participants indicated when they were experiencing these positive and negative emotions during viewing.

Using such a paradigm – but employing only women participants – Davidson has found that left frontal activation in a specific EEG waveband (alpha) is associated with the experience of positive emotion, whereas increased relative right frontal activation and left frontal reduction in activation is associated with the experience of negative emotion (R.J. Davidson *et al.*, 1979; Wheeler *et al.*, 1993). One study measured resting EEG in men and women at two sessions separated by six weeks (Sutton and Davidson, 2000). At the second session, participants were given a word-pair judgement task. Participants were required to indicate which of two word pairs went together the best. The words were manipulated for emotional tone so that some word pairs were pleasant and some were unpleasant (although the associative strength between words in all pairs was the same).

Participants with greater left-sided activation were more likely to select the pleasant word pairs as being the two that went best together. The results, the authors suggest, show an attentional bias towards positive stimuli in healthy individuals who show frontal left-sided baseline EEG. In a variation of these experiments, Ekman *et al.* (1990) investigated whether the type of EEG activity associated with a genuine smile (the so-called **Duchenne smile**) would differ from that generated by false smiles. The Duchenne smile is known as the genuine smile because it spontaneously activates the

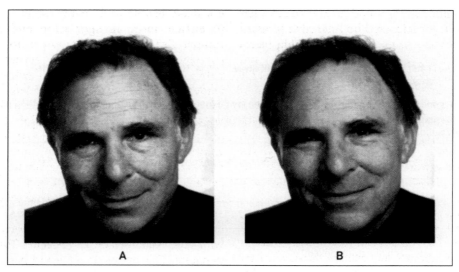

Figure 13.15 The Duchenne smile. The face is that of Paul Ekman
Source: The Orion Publishing Group Ltd.

zygomatic muscles around the corners of the mouth and the orbicularis occuli muscles around the corners of the eyes, as you can see from Figure 13.15. It is also associated with better long-term adjustment, that is, people who express Duchenne smiles seem to be those who are better adjusted in the long-term (Papa and Bonanno, 2008).

Ekman *et al.* (1990) found that the Duchenne smiles were associated with greater left-sided activation in temporal and parietal regions. On the basis of these and other studies, Davidson suggested that the frontal asymmetry reflects motivational tendencies to withdraw or approach. That is, pleasant stimuli should be approachable and, therefore, activate the left frontal region whereas unpleasant stimuli would be avoided or withdrawn from and would activate the right frontal region (and decrease activity in the left frontal region). Coupled with this motivational model is the idea that asymmetry predisposes individuals to react in a specific emotional way. Greater baseline right frontal activation, for example, may predict the intensity of response to negative stimuli but this activation is a necessary but not sufficient condition for this response to occur (this is called the **diathesis model**).

A recent study has extended this research to feelings during the menstrual cycle (Hwang *et al.*, 2008). The researchers used MEG to measure changes in frontal brain asymmetry across the menstrual cycle in 16 healthy women. They found that women in their ovulatory period showed higher right frontal activity whereas higher left was found during the menstrual period. The researchers suggest that this change reflects the effects of hormonal changes which themselves modify brain activity.

Two studies highlight the role of the left and right frontal cortex in depression and anxiety. In one longitudinal study, people who showed relatively greater right frontal EEG activation at the beginning of the study were more likely to report greater trait anxiety one year later (Blackhart *et al.*, 2006). A study of EEG activation to various film clips has also implicated the right hemisphere (Hagemann *et al.*, 2005a). Resting EEG and self-reported emotions after watching film clips on four occasions were analysed. Participants with greater right-sided EEG activation (and smaller left-sided activation) reacted more intensely to the film clips, regardless of the emotion they were designed to elicit. The researchers suggest that this highlights a role for the right hemisphere in automatically generating emotional responses; the left hemisphere they argue, is more involved in the control or modulation of emotion.

Exercise, music and EEG asymmetry

Similar studies have shown that variables such as the type of music you listen to or the degree of exercise you undertake or even the types of words you read, correlate with changes in mood and frontal EEG activity. For example, Petruzzello *et al.* (2001) measured EEG activity from very fit or low to moderately fit adults before and during a 30-minute session on the treadmill. Measures of mood were taken after the exercise.

Their findings were similar to those found in Sutton and Davidson's (2000) experiment: relative left-sided activity at baseline predicted the degree of positive affect experienced after exercise. The greater the left-sided activation, the better the mood of participants post-exercise. However, this prediction held only for the highly fit individuals. This suggests that resting baseline EEG and predisposition to positive affect may be mediated by other variables (such as fitness). Those with greater left-sided activity also expended the greatest energy.

Schmidt and Trainor (2001) found greater relative left frontal EEG activity in participants who listened to pleasant musical excerpts (pleasant–calm: *Spring* by Vivaldi; pleasant–intense: *Brandenburg Concerto No. 5* by Bach) and greater relative right frontal EEG activity in participants who listened to unpleasant excerpts (unpleasant–calm: *Adagio* by Barber; unpleasant–intense: *Peter and the Wolf* by Prokofiev). No asymmetrical pattern of activation was found when the intense and calm excerpts were compared. However, overall frontal cortex activity declined as the pieces became more intense. Activity declined from the unpleasant–intense, pleasant–intense, pleasant–calm and unpleasant–calm.

The results are consistent with the emotional asymmetry model outlined above. While some studies have supported the frontal asymmetry model, however, some recent evidence has suggested that the type of asymmetry seen depends on the methods of analysis and the EEG recording procedures one uses (Hagemann *et al.*, 1998). Hagemann *et al.* (2005b), for example, have found that EEG asymmetry to emotional stimuli can change from one testing session to the next. In one study, they even found that right-sided activation most consistently predicted the strength of people's emotional responses to emotional stimuli (Hagemann *et al.*, 2005a). In a recent study, it was found that right frontal activation was more common in the morning and during the autumn, suggesting that the EEG can be influenced not only by time of day but also season (Petersen and Harmon-Jones, 2009).

What are the limitations of the approach–withdrawal model of emotion? Can you think of a stimulus that is both approachable and repelling? Would this compromise the model?

Emotional experience: anger and disgust

One study examining the response of the cortex during the recognition of anger in facial expressions found that as the intensity of the angry expression increased so did activity in the right oribitofrontal cortex and the anterior cingulate gyrus (ACC) (Blair *et al.*, 1999). Previous studies have linked activation in the ACC with watching intense emotional facial expression. There was no significant increase in amygdala activity when the men saw angry expressions. The authors propose that the results signify a clear model: there is no unitary system that responds to negative stimuli, but two systems. One system mediates responses to negative stimuli involved in social aversive conditioning (sadness, fear); the other mediates responses to negative stimuli (anger and related stimuli) that curtails behaviour (the emotion is thought to suppress behaviour).

Anger is conceivably an approach tendency because there is motivation to engage in competitiveness or physical harm (Carver and Harmon-Jones, 2009). Anger does not make people walk away, rather it makes them want to engage more in aggression and readies them for combat. But anger, by definition, is not necessarily a positive emotion. This presents the asymmetry model above with a paradox of sorts. If it is genuinely an approach tendency, we should see increased left frontal brain activity when people experience it. If this increase is found, does not then give the left frontal lobe an exclusive role in positive affect – it can also be activated by a negative emotion. Harmon-Jones (2004), however, suggests that there may be an alternative explanation: that people who get angry actually like being angry and, therefore, anger can be seen, via this logic, as a positive emotion.

To test this hypothesis, he took baseline EEG measurements from men and women and correlated this activity with their responses on an Attitudes Towards Anger questionnaire. This questionnaire asked participants to agree or disagree with a series of statements about anger (e.g. 'I like the feeling of power I get from expressing anger'). Measures of aggression were also taken and were used to divide the participants into those who expressed high levels of trait anger. The results showed that the most angry and aggressive of the group showed greater left frontal brain activity than did their milder counterparts. There was no significant relationship between attitudes towards anger and brain asymmetry: those who found anger to be a positive emotion were no more likely than those who did not view it so to produce left frontal EEG. The study is important because it suggests that the role of the frontal cortex in emotion might be more usefully seen as one involving motivational tendencies rather than emotional valence.

Research from Texas A&M University has found that individuals high in trait anger show greater EEG activation in the left frontal area of the brain when they view pictures designed to make them angry (Harmon-Jones, 2007). The same research group examined whether manipulating frontal asymmetry could affect aggressive response. Peterson *et al.* (2008) asked participants to contract their hand to increase activation in the contralateral hemisphere (contracting the right hand leads to left hemisphere activation and contracting the left, the right hemisphere). After being insulted and then being given the opportunity to show to aggression against their tormentor in a game, participants who contracted their right hand showed more aggression than did left-hand contractors. Left-frontal EEG was also associated with greater aggression. This EEG work has been extended to neuroimaging. In an fMRI experiment, participants were insulted and then asked to think about the incident (Denson *et al.*, 2008). The researchers found that feelings of anger induced by the insult were associated with activation in the anterior cingulate cortex. Activation in the hippocampus, insula and cingulate cortex were associated with thinking about the insult.

Another emotion regarded as negative is disgust and there appears to be a curious link between the recognition of this emotion and the degenerative motor disorder, Huntington's disease (HD) described in Chapter 3. Sprengelmeyer *et al.* (1996, 1997b) found that patients who showed symptoms of HD were poor at recognising facial expressions of disgust (but not other emotions), a finding replicated by Gray *et al.* (1997) who tested carriers of the gene for the disease but who had not yet developed the disease's symptoms. Patients with Gilles de LaTourette and obsessive-compulsive disorder also show this selective deficit in recognition (Sprengelmeyer *et al.*, 1997a). People who have just been diagnosed with the illness are also impaired in recognising disgust in facial expressions, although the ability to detect disgust in people's voices and the ability to experience disgust appear unaffected (Sprengelmeyer *et al.*, 2006). However, in an extensive study of 475 individuals with Huntington's disease, Johnson *et al.* (2007) have found that patients are not likely to show an impairment in recognising disgust specifically, as some studies have suggested. Instead, such patients are impaired at recognising negative emotions in general – anger, disgust, fear, sadness, as well as surprise but not happiness. The greater the patients' motor deficit, the greater their emotion recognition impairment.

The region of the brain that is dysfunctional in HD and these disorders is the fronto-striatal area, especially the basal ganglia. Early fMRI research that explored the neuroanatomical basis of disgust recognition in healthy individuals found increased activation in the putamen – a part of the basal ganglia (Phillips *et al.*, 1997; Sprengelmeyer *et al.*, 1998). This region is also implicated in Parkinson's disease (PD) and this finding prompted Sprengelmeyer *et al.* (2003) to hypothesise that recognition of disgust might also be impaired in patients with PD. They reported that medicated and unmedicated PD patients were poorer at recognising disgust than was a control group; the unmedicated group gave the poorest performance.

Neuroimaging data from healthy participants implicate more cortical regions in tasks where individuals recognise emotions. Using fMRI, Schienle *et al.* (2005) asked 63 women to rate how disgusting they considered 40 generally disgusting scenes and 40 neutral scenes to be. They found that activation was greater in the left orbitofrontal cortex, left medial OFC, the occipitotemporal lobe and left and right amygdala when the women viewed the disgusting stimuli. A broadly similar result was reported in a group of men and women who viewed disgust- and fear-inducing pictures (Schienle *et al.*, 2005). This study found increased activation in the left medial and dorsolateral prefrontal PFC cortex in both sexes.

Schienle *et al.* interpret their results in terms of Rolls's theory of emotion. Briefly, Rolls (1999) has proposed that visual affective stimuli are initially processed by the occipital lobe. The ventral visual system then projects to the amygdala and PFC via the inferior temporal area. The PFC 'decides' on the reward value of the stimuli – do they afford reward or punishment? This 'decision' then leads to a behavioural outcome and the individual either withdraws or approaches.

Using display rules

We all realise that other people can recognise our expressions of emotions. Consequently, we sometimes try to hide our true feelings, attempting to appear impassive or even to display an emotion different from what we feel. At other times, we may exaggerate our emotional response to make sure that others see how we feel. For example, if a friend tells us about a devastating experience, we make sure that our facial expression conveys sadness and sympathy. Researchers have studied all these phenomena.

Attempting to hide an emotion is called **masking**. An attempt to exaggerate or minimise the expression of an emotion is called **modulation**. And an attempt to express an emotion we do not actually feel is called **simulation**. According to Ekman and Friesen (1974), the expression of emotions often follows culturally determined **display rules** – rules that prescribe under what situations we should or should not display signs of particular emotions. Although the patterns of muscular movements that accompany particular feelings are biologically determined, these movements can, to a certain extent, be controlled by display rules. See Figure 13.16.

Each culture has a particular set of display rules. For example, in Western culture, it is impolite for a winner to show too much pleasure and for a loser to show too much disappointment. The expression of these emotions is supposed to be modulated downwards. Also, in many cultures, it is unmanly to cry or to show fear and unfeminine to show anger.

Context is important in encouraging genuine facial expression of emotion. Participants were asked to listen to stories which varied in funniness and were told by a friend or a stranger (Jakobs *et al.*, 1999). The stories were either told on tape recorder, face-to-face or on the telephone. The researchers found that participants who listened to a stranger smiled less than when listening to a friend, as previous research would predict. Motivation to express an emotion was enhanced by face-to-face encounters, but only when listening to a friend. Simply listening to a friend did not affect this motivation, but the interaction between storyteller and channel of communication did. The study shows that the facial expression of emotion in response to listening to a story of varying emotional content can depend not just on the storyteller but the medium through which that storyteller tells the story. The interpersonal distance between a person and a target who smiles is shorter than the distance between them and a target with a neutral smile or a non-enjoyment smile (Miles, 2009).

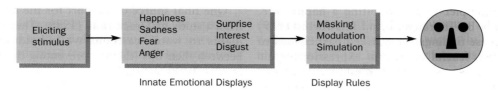

Figure 13.16 Controlled facial displays. Innate emotional displays can be modified by display rules.
Source: Adapted from Ekman, P. and Friesen, W., *Semiotica*, 1969, 49–98.

Recent neuroimaging research suggests that we remember smiling faces better than ones with neutral expressions (Tsukiura and Cabeza, 2008). In an fMRI study, people were presented with either smiling or non-smiling faces and were asked to associate the face with a name that was also presented with each face. Participants were then presented with the names and asked to retrieve the facial expression associated with that name. People remembered smiling faces better and faster than neutral ones. The OFC and hippocampus were particularly involved in successful encoding, especially when stimuli were smiling faces. The connections between these two regions were also stronger during the retrieval of smiling than neutral faces.

The results suggest that a smiling face can enhance retrieval. Furthermore, the rewarding nature of the smile is reflected in activation in the OFC. This activation, the researchers suggest, strengthens the hippocampal activation (itself a reflection of strengthened encoding).

Ekman and his colleagues (Ekman *et al.*, 1972; Friesen, 1972) attempted to assess a different kind of culturally determined display rule. They showed a distressing film to Japanese and American college students, singly and in the presence of a visitor, who was described to the subjects as a scientist. Because the Japanese culture discourages public display of emotion, the researchers expected that the Japanese students would show fewer facial expressions of emotion when in public than when alone.

The researchers recorded the facial expressions of their participants with hidden cameras while the participants viewed a film showing a gruesome and bloody coming-of-age rite in a pre-literate tribe. The results were as predicted. When the participants were alone, American and Japanese subjects showed the same facial expressions. When they were with another person, the Japanese participants were less likely to express negative emotions and more likely to mask these expressions with polite smiles. Thus, people from both cultures used the same facial expressions of emotion but were subject to different social display rules.

When people attempt to mask the expression of a strongly felt emotion, they are usually unable to do so completely, that is, there is some **leakage**, or subtle sign of the emotion (Ekman and Friesen, 1969). Ekman and Friesen (1974) investigated this phenomenon. They showed an unpleasant film of burns and amputations to female nursing students. After watching the film, the participants were interviewed by an experimenter, who asked them about the film. Some of the participants were asked to pretend to the interviewer that they had seen a pleasant film. The experimenters videotaped the participants during the interviews and showed these tapes to a separate group of raters, asking them to try to determine whether the people they were watching were being honest or deceptive. The raters were shown videotapes of the participants' faces or bodies. The results indicated that the raters could detect the deception better when they saw the subjects' bodies than when they saw their faces. Apparently, people are better at masking signs of emotion shown by their facial muscles than those shown by muscles in other parts of their body. Presumably, people recognise the attention paid to the face and learn to control their facial expressions better than they do the movements of the rest of the body.

Facial feedback hypothesis

The use of display rules suggests that we are capable of manipulating our facial expression to influence others. It has also been suggested that our own facial expressions can influence our own feelings. That our awareness of facial expression influences the way in which we feel is at the heart of the **facial feedback hypothesis** (Tourangeau and Ellsworth, 1979; Lanzetta *et al.*, 1976). If this is so, then manipulating a person's facial expression should result in the feeling of the expression-appropriate emotion. You cannot be angry with a smile on your face, for example. This idea has its origin in a remark by Darwin (1872), who had argued that 'the free expression by outward signs of an emotion intensifies it . . . the repression, as far as this is possible, of all outward signs softens our emotions'.

A test of the facial feedback hypothesis was undertaken by Laird (1974), who asked participants to view photographs while electrical activity from the face muscles was ostensibly recorded. The individuals were told that they would feel emotion-related muscle changes and, to counteract these changes, their muscles would be contracted or relaxed. In fact, the facial manipulation resulted in the participants expressing either a happy or angry face. As predicted, participants who then responded to specific photographs were angrier when exhibiting an angry

defended says that this order of sequence is incorrect . . . The more rational statement is that we feel sorry because we cry, angry because we strike, afraid because we tremble, and not that we cry, strike, or tremble because we are sorry, angry or fearful, as the case may be.

James suggested that our own emotional feelings are based on what we find ourselves doing and on the sensory feedback we receive from the activity of our muscles and internal organs. Where feelings of emotions are concerned, we are self-observers. Thus, patterns of emotional responses and expressions of emotions give rise to feelings of emotion. By this reasoning, feelings of emotions are simply by-products of emotional responses. The James–Lange model is illustrated in Figure 13.18.

James's and Lange's theory was not entirely correct, however. As Cannon (1927, 1931) pointed out:

1 Separating the viscera from the central nervous system did not result in changes in emotional behaviour.

2 Emotional and non-emotional states can be associated with the same physiological changes.

3 Visceral changes are too slow to be able to reflect emotional changes.

4 Inducing visceral change that should result in emotional change usually does not produce these changes.

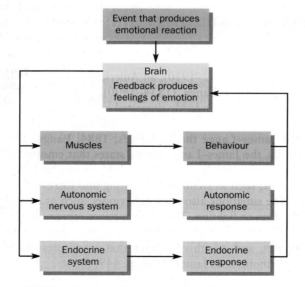

Figure 13.18 A diagrammatic representation of the James–Lange theory of emotion. An event in the environment triggers behavioural, autonomic and endocrine responses. Feedback from these responses produces feelings of emotion.

Schachter and Singer's model

Schachter (1964) proposed that feelings of emotions are determined jointly by perception of physiological responses and by cognitive assessment of a specific situation. Thus, to Schachter, emotion is cognition plus perception of physiological arousal. Both are necessary. Schachter and Singer (1962) tested this hypothesis by inducing physiological arousal in groups of participants placed in various situations. All participants were told that they were part of an investigation on the effects of a vitamin called 'suproxin' on visual perception (no such vitamin exists). The investigators gave some participants injections of adrenalin, a hormone that stimulates a variety of autonomic nervous system effects associated with arousal, such as increased heart rate and blood pressure, irregular breathing, warming of the face and mild trembling. Other participants received a control injection of a salt solution, which has no physiological effects.

Next, the researchers placed some participants in an anger-provoking situation in which they were treated rudely and subjected to obnoxious test questions such as, 'How many men, besides your father, has your mother slept with? (a) one, (b) two, (c) three, (d) four or more.' Others were treated politely and saw the antics of another 'participant' (a confederate who was hired by the experimenters) who acted silly and euphoric. The experimenters hoped that these two situations, together with the physiological reactions produced by the injections of adrenalin, would promote either negative or positive emotional states.

Finally, some participants were correctly informed that the injections they received would produce side effects such as trembling and a pounding heart. Others were told to expect irrelevant side effects or none at all. Schachter and Singer predicted that the participants who knew what side effects to expect would correctly attribute their physiological reactions to the drug and would not experience a change in emotion. Those who were misinformed would note their physiological arousal and conclude that they were feeling especially angry or happy, as the circumstance dictated. All participants reported their emotional states in a questionnaire.

The results were not as clear-cut as the experimenters had hoped. The adrenalin did not increase the intensity of the participants' emotional states. However, participants who expected to experience physiological arousal as a result of the injection reported much less of a change in their emotional states than did those who did not expect it, regardless of whether they had received the adrenalin or the placebo. These results suggest that we interpret the significance of our physiological reactions rather than simply experience them as emotions.

Nisbett and Schachter (1966) provided further evidence that participants could be fooled into attributing their own naturally occurring physiological responses to a drug and thus into feeling less 'emotional'. First, they gave all participants a placebo pill (one having no physiological effects). Half the participants were told that the pill would make their hearts pound, their breathing increase and their hands tremble; the other half (the control subjects) were told nothing about possible side effects. Then, the researchers strapped on electrodes and gave the participants electrical shocks. All participants presumably experienced pain and fear, and, consequently, their heart rates and breathing increased, they trembled, and so on. Yet the participants who perceived their reactions as drug-induced were able to tolerate stronger shocks than were the control subjects, and they reported less pain and fear. Thus, cognition can affect people's judgements about their own emotional states and even their tolerance of pain.

The precise nature of the interaction between cognition and physiological arousal has not been determined. For example, in the Nisbett and Schachter experiment, although the verbal instruction about effects of the placebo affected the participants' reactions to pain, it did not seem to do so through a logical, reasoned process. In fact, Nisbett and Wilson (1977) later reported that participants did not consciously attribute their increased tolerance of pain to the effects of the pill. When participants were asked whether they had thought about the pill while receiving the shocks or whether it had occurred to them that the pill was causing some physical effects, participants typically gave answers such as, 'No, I was too worried about the shock' (Nisbett and Wilson, 1977, p. 237).

Evolutionary theories

Evolutionary theories of emotion view emotions as adaptive traits – they help the organism to adapt to the demands of the environment and thereby survive (Izard, 1977; Plutchik, 1984).

Plutchik's structural, psychoevolutionary theory of emotion

In common with other evolutionary theories of emotion, Plutchik's (1984) psychoevolutionary theory regards emotions as being important to adaptation and survival. However, he argues that in order to understand the nature of emotions, they must be organised in a certain way. He argues, therefore, that emotions can be distinguished on the basis of intensity (anger is less intense than rage, for example), similarity (surprise may engage the same feelings as happiness), polarity (that is, opposites: grief is the opposite of joy), and whether they are primary or secondary (the secondary emotions derive from the primary ones).

Plutchik lists eight behavioural patterns, such as destruction, rejection and reproduction, which can be seen in all organisms; each of his primary emotions (described in an earlier section) is associated with these behavioural patterns.

Shaver's prototype theory

Shaver *et al.*'s (1992) model of emotion also uses the notion that we react to the environment using a limited behavioural repertoire and argues that, like emotional facial expression, these repertoires should be universal. Furthermore, the assumption that emotions are universal suggests that they have a biological basis. Emotions are viewed as 'action tendencies' that arise from an appraisal of the environment. Because the similarities in environmental events are more common than dissimilarities, the theory argues, appraisals will be similar across cultures. Shaver and his colleagues suggest that such a view is supported by evidence from three countries – the USA, Italy and China – in which there was substantial overlap in the words that individuals listed as basic emotions.

Frijda's 'action tendencies'

Shaver adopted the concept of 'action tendencies' from Frijda's (1988) model which also views emotions as adaptive. There is a small number of these tendencies which represents the individual's readiness to respond to the environment in emotional ways. These tendencies mediate the individual's relationship with the environment and Frijda proposed ten of them. Like Plutchik's model, Frijda's argues that emotions are adaptive in that they are used by individuals to solve problems posed by the environment. Unlike Plutchik's, it disagrees that the model can apply to any organism – it is specifically related to human behaviour. However, Frijda also argues that there is little difference between the action tendency and the emotion associated with it, emotion perhaps being the state of awareness of these action tendencies. He also suggests that these emotions (and tendencies) follow on from an individual's appraisal of the environment. That is, the individual first monitors the environment and appraises the threat or problem posed by this environment. Frijda *et al.* (1989) have found that action tendencies and emotions can be predicted from individuals' appraisals of the environment.

This notion of appraisal is important to a number of models and theories of emotion. In general, such theories argue that emotion is dependent on the individual's appraisal of environmental events and situations. Schachter and Singer's model, although described as a physiological model, involved a strong appraisal component. Other models, however, include appraisal as a more explicit feature.

Cognitive theories

Lazarus's model

Lazarus's original model of emotion suggested that emotion arose from the individual's appraisal of the environment (Lazarus, 1966). **Primary appraisal** involved the initial evaluation of the environment – is it positive, negative or neutral; secondary appraisal involved the individual's evaluation of how best to cope with this environment and what options were available to facilitate this coping. **Secondary appraisal** was composed of two types: emotion-focused coping and problem-focused coping. Emotion-focused coping refers to the defence mechanisms that the individual might adopt, such as fleeing the situation or denying negative thoughts and feelings. Problem-centred coping is directed more at finding solutions to the problems posed by the environment when there are changes in the environment.

This original model, however, was devised to explain how people respond to stressors – factors which cause stress (this is discussed in more detail in later chapters). The later reformulation of the model (Lazarus, 1991) was designed to be a general theory of emotion which Lazarus called the 'cognitive–motivational–relational' theory of emotion. Primary appraisal now comprises the components: goal-relevance (Is the environment related to the goal that the individual wants to pursue?), goal congruency/incongruency (Is the goal possible or will it be prevented?) and ego-involvement (Does the environment have consequences for the individual's self-esteem?). Secondary appraisal assesses the environment in terms of how the individual might cope with it and how such coping might affect future relations. Lazarus proposed that the appraisal of situations which might involve harm to the individual were innate; however, secondary appraisal could override the decisions derived from primary appraisal.

Weiner's model

Weiner's model also utilises the concept of appraisal but is based on the notion that individuals make attributions to the environment and behaviour (Weiner, 1985). The environment provides the individual with a range of positive and negative stimuli which produce initial emotional reactions of pleasure and displeasure. These reactions are triggered automatically and are not emotional responses that rely on the individual's attributions, such as experiencing depression because failure is attributed to poor ability and general worthlessness. These emotions are fairly primitive and reflect conditioned emotional reactions.

The individual's account of how events in the environment were caused determines which positive and negative emotions are elicited. This attribution-dependent model suggests that these explanations depend on three factors: (1) whether the cause of the emotion is internal to the individual or external and caused by the environment; (2) whether the cause is stable or will change over time; and (3) whether the cause of the emotion is controllable or uncontrollable. Abramson *et al.* (1978) later added a fourth dimension: whether the environment affected the individual's whole life (global change) or a specific part of it (specific change). According to this model, the attributions for success or failure will determine whether positive or negative emotions are experienced.

The hedonic treadmill theory

In 1971, Brickman and Campbell published a theory of emotion and well-being in which they suggested that we adapt to emotional events in our lives, in the same way that we adapt to a new smell when we enter an unfamiliar house. Studies published in the late 1970s appeared to support this theory. Lottery winners, for example, were no more happy than lottery losers and non-winners and people with paraplegia were similarly not less happy than those who could walk. The theory suggests that experiences inducing happy emotions are transitory; they are transitory because of adaptation.

Recently, however, new research has forced a revision of the theory and Diener *et al.* (2006) describe some of these new developments. For example, the treadmill view suggests that after we experience a highly emotional event, we return to a neutral state soon after. Once you've got your fantastic exam result, for example, or received that promotion, there is a period in which you are elated. The elation then subsides. Research has shown, however, that (exceptional events aside – such as getting that promotion) people are generally happy most of the time, according to self-reports. The European Values Study Group and World Values Survey Association (2005) data indicate that 80 per cent of respondents reported being quite or very happy, suggesting that the baseline is 'happy' rather than 'neutral'. Of course, there is variability in these 'set points'; different people have different set points. You also saw earlier in the book how positive affect declines with age but that negative affect also decreases.

The theory also states that people cannot do very much to change the long-term degree of happiness they experience – because of the return to a neutral state. However, studies of widows and widowers, as well as of people who have been laid off from work, show initially very low levels of happiness but this happiness is restored (but usually, only after a very long period – years, for example). The early data from people with severe disability has also been challenged, with Diener *et al.* (2006) citing evidence from patients with disabilities showing that they experienced a drop in life satisfaction after the disability, a drop that did not recover significantly.

Other models

Other models of emotion assume that thoughts and feelings represent nodes in a network. Thus a node for a specific emotion triggers off activation of other related nodes. Joy, for example, might trigger nodes that recall past achievement or motivate the individual to achieve even greater success by generating creative plans for the future. Failure might trigger nodes related to failure (such as negative feelings of self-worth and thoughts that previous successes may not have been deserved). This outline describes one model devised by Bower (1981; Bower and Cohen, 1982) which explained how mood-dependent memory occurred, that is, why we are more likely to recall happy events if we were happy at encoding and unhappy events if we were unhappy at encoding.

However, as you saw in Chapter 8, mood-dependent memory is not a particularly robust phenomenon and appears to be influenced by factors other than the encoding and retrieval conditions. Another problem is that in mood-dependent memory experiments it is unclear whether positive conditions increase accessibility to positive thoughts and feelings or reduce accessibility to negative ones. Bower (1987) later took account of this by arguing that the individual must realise that the material they learn is usefully related to the mood they are in. How this fits in with the network model, however, is unclear.

Other models such as those of Lang (1979, 1984) suggest that emotions may not be unitary phenomena but comprise three systems: verbal report, behaviour and physiology. This theory suggests that we can express emotion in one of these systems without experiencing it in another. For example, a depressed individual may show a positive disposition to those close around them (by verbal report) but their behaviour (withdrawal, quietness) and physiology suggest another emotion.

Two other models are also worthy of note. Leventhal and Scherer's model (1987) suggests that the emotion system is made up of three components. At the sensory motor level, individuals may respond to situations and events automatically. This automatic reaction is present from birth onwards. The schematic level is also an automatic level of processing but the automatic behaviour derives from learned associations. Finally, the conceptual level represents reactions that are not automatic but depend on the individual's memories about emotion, expectations, goals, plans and so on. The conceptual level places the event that causes the emotion in a long-term context, that is, how would it affect the individual's future behaviour? In addition to these levels, the model proposes that the stimuli giving rise to emotional reactions are evaluated along various dimensions including novelty, pleasantness, their relevance to goals and plans, the potential to cope with them and their compatibility with social norms and the individual's self-concept.

Finally, Oatley and Johnson-Laird's model (1987; Oatley, 1992) argues that because we often encounter environments in which multiple goals are possible one of these goals must receive priority over the others. Emotion, according to the model, provides the means by which goals are prioritised. This is achieved by two mechanisms: one is primitive and has no symbolic significance (it is almost hormonal); the other is prepositional and symbolic (it has an internal structure and is more 'conscious' than the other mechanism). The model proposes five basic emotions: happiness, sadness, fear, anger and disgust, with other emotions derived from these.

Complex emotions, the theory argues, are likely to involve only one of these emotions although others have suggested that one or two may be necessary (Jones and Martin, 1992). All five of these emotions are related to the achievement of goals so that one type of emotion leads to the achievement of a goal whereas others are related to failure to achieve goals. However, it is difficult to reconcile these goals with certain emotions. Disgust, for example, as Power and Dalgleish (1997) have pointed out, is unlikely to violate only a 'gustatory goal' because disgust can be elicited by smells, sights and even sounds. In addition, why should the emotional reaction to a malodour be part of a goal – what would be the purpose?

Cutting edge – Keeping your emotional distance

Your understanding of psychology so far should tell you that a small change in the environment can have a large effect on behaviour. The section on EMG and emotion is a good example. The beauty of the best psychology is that it reveals something about our behaviour that is astonishing and unexpected. That even placing dots wide apart on a sheet of paper makes you emotionally distant, for example. This is what Williams and Bargh (2008) found.

They reviewed a theory suggesting that when we think about distant events we think about them in the abstract, but when we think about recent events we think and talk about them in more concrete terms (Trope and Lieberman, 2003). This even extends to social and physical distance (we think more concretely about people and places near us (Fujita *et al.*, 2006). Think about where you live now and describe it to yourself. You probably used concrete

▶

Cutting edge – *Continued*

language – it's a first floor flat, it's in a certain part of town, it has two bedrooms and so on.

Williams and Bargh (2008) reasoned that this relationship could be inverted. That is, priming the thought of distance could make people think more distantly. They asked participants to plot a pre-assigned series of points on a graph paper – see Figure 13.19. Some participants had to plot the points far apart from each other; other participants had to plot them near to each other. They were then asked to rate and judge various objects, scenarios and film clips.

Those who had been primed by plotting distal points derived greater enjoyment in film clips depicting embarrassing events, showed less emotional distress when watching violent material, gave lower estimates for the calorie content in unhealthy food and reported weaker ties to family members and the place where they grew up.

And all this from two points placed in graph paper.

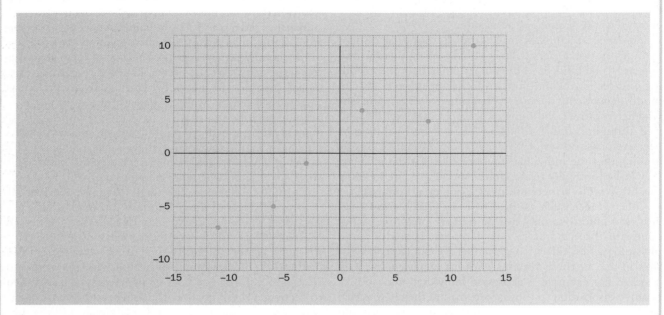

Figure 13.19 The graph paper on which Williams and Bargh's participants placed pre-determined dots

Is a good mood good for cognition?

Brewer's model of emotion is based in part on evidence which showed that individuals in a negative or a positive mood would recall material better if the material matched their mood. For example, individuals exposed to a malodour would recall more negative memories than they would if exposed to a pleasant odour. Similarly, they would recall more pleasant memories in the pleasant condition (Ehrlichman and Bastone, 1992). You saw in Chapter 8 that individuals who encode information in a pleasant environment will recall better if retrieval also occurs in the pleasant environment. What effects, therefore, does a person's emotional state have on that person's ability to perform cognitive operations?

In a famous series of experiments, Isen and colleagues have demonstrated that being in a positive mood can have positive and negative consequences for behaviour. For example, in a laboratory-based study, Isen and Patrick (1983) reported that while positive mood led to undergraduates betting larger amounts in a gambling game than did controls, these bets were only large when the probability of winning was high. Isen *et al.* (1988) reasoned that either the positive mood predisposed people to believe that losing was likely or that thinking about negative events made them think that their positive mood might be lost. Isen and Geva (1987) found that those in a positive mood did indeed think about loss more than the controls did.

Positive mood has also been found to affect decisions made in more real-life risk situations (although these were still laboratory-based). Individuals in a positive mood are more likely to choose a risky treatment for back pain than are those in a control group (Deldin and Levin, 1986).

In an investigation of the effect of induced positive mood on creative and executive thinking, Oaksford *et al.* (1996) tested two hypotheses. The facilitation hypothesis suggests that positive mood benefits creative thinking by facilitating it; the suppression hypothesis suggests that positive and negative moods take up resources that would normally be available for performing the cognitive task that the individual is presented with. Ellis *et al.* (1997), for example, found that negative mood was associated with impaired performance on a test in which participants looked for contradictions in a passage of text. The authors suggested that impairment occurred because intrusive and irrelevant thoughts impaired comprehension. Positive and negative mood should, therefore, also impair performance on reasoning and planning tasks, if a change in mood results in a reallocation of resources.

In an earlier experiment, Isen *et al.* (1987) had reported a beneficial effect of positive mood on a creative problem-solving task. The task was to support a lighted candle on a door using tacks, some matches in a matchbox and the candle (the solution, just in case you are not in a positive mood, is to tack the box to the door and place the candle lit with the matches, on top of the box). Those individuals who had watched some comedy were better at solving this problem than those exposed to a neutral or negative film or those exposed to no film.

Oaksford extended this study by having participants complete creative and reasoning tasks after watching either a comedy programme, a neutral, wildlife programme or a negative documentary about stress. The researchers found that although positive and negative mood impaired performance on a deductive reasoning task, the positive mood only was associated with poor performance on the Tower of London Task which involves forward planning and reasoning. Some examples from the task can be seen in Figure 13.20.

The results of Oaksford's study provide some support for the suppression hypothesis in that a test requiring executive function (forward planning and sequencing of events) was disrupted by a positive mood. It also suggests that a positive mood may not always be beneficial to the performance of some cognitive tasks. The results of this and other research suggest that being in a good mood may not necessarily lead to better cognitive performance.

A study from the University of New South Wales in Australia has found that people in a *negative* mood were much more successful than those in a *positive* mood at convincing others to agree with statements such as 'Student fees should be increased/decreased' or 'Aboriginal land rights should be preserved/restricted in Australia' (Forgas, 2007). People in a negative mood were more likely to persuade others to believe an unpopular view than were people in a positive mood. Why did this effect occur? When the researcher examined the content of the arguments adopted, people in a negative mood were more likely to use concrete messages in their persuasion. This, in turn, led to more effective persuasion. Mood had influenced participants' processing style.

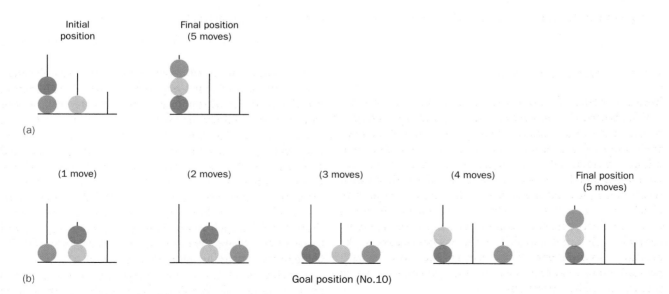

Figure 13.20 The Tower of London task. In (a) the participant is required to move the balls from the initial position to the target position in five moves; (b) shows how this is done.

Controversies in Psychological Science – Dark clouds gathering, sunny spells later . . .

The issue

Is there a relationship between the weather and a person's mood? Many people long for summer months when they can jet off to sunny climes, soak in the sun and lounge on the beach while creatively avoiding skin cancer. People in countries where natural sunlight is restricted appear to have a higher incidence of unhappiness or depression. We know that the mood of the general population appears to decline in the winter months (Harmatz *et al.*, 2000) and that one treatment for **seasonal affective disorder** – the appearance of depression in the dark, winter months (see Chapter 18) – is exposure to artificial light. This seems to improve mood in depressed and non-depressed people (Leppamaki *et al.*, 2002; 2003). Serotonin increases or decreases as naturally occurring sunlight increases or decreases, respectively (Lambert *et al.*, 2002). But, treatment for SAD aside, is there any evidence from healthy people that climate and temperature significantly influences mood? And if one does influence the other, why?

The evidence

In a study published in *Psychological Science*, Keller *et al.* (2005) review a variety of studies investigating the relationship between climate and mood and cognition. Task performance in one study peaked at 22°C and dropped at cooler or warmer temperatures than 22°C (Allen and Fischer, 1998). More heuristic and less systematic processing has been found in people during sunny and warm days than on cloudy or cool days (Sinclair *et al.*, 1994). Studies such as this have led to the suggestion that low humidity and high levels of sunlight (and high barometric pressure and temperature) are associated with positive mood whereas high temperatures alone led to a negative mood or no change in mood. Evidence, however, is not entirely consistent.

For example, daily mood reports collected from almost five hundred undergraduates in Dallas during the autumn or spring found no relationship between season and mood (Watson, 2000). A study of shoppers recruited on sunny or cloudy, rainy days found that people recalled more of the ten unusual objects placed at a checkout when the weather was rainy (Forgas *et al.*, 2009). Others report that behaviour such as violence increases during high temperatures (Anderson, 2001) and that stock market returns are higher in the summer (Saunders, 1993), perhaps reflecting the possibility that temperature inures traders to risk or makes them less risk-averse. Seasonal studies are also problematic in that sunny and warm days can be experienced in 'cooler' seasons (e.g. autumn). And there is a possibility that sunny days in spring and autumn can produce different effects (they are less novel

in the spring, for example?). Do people need to be directly exposed to this weather for mood to change, i.e. do they need to be outdoors? One study found that 93 per cent of the people in the individual countries studied spent their time indoors during good weather (Woodcock and Custovic, 1998).

To test these hypotheses, Keller *et al.* (2005) set up three experiments. In the first, they examined whether temperature or the length of time spent outdoors in warm weather affected mood. Data were collected from 97 people from April to June. They found no direct relationship between barometric pressure and temperature, and mood. But they did find a positive relationship between mood and time spent outside. A similar relationship was found for creativity, cognitive flexibility, openness to experience and digit span performance. People who spent more than 30 minutes outdoors on clear days had higher digit spans and showed a more flexible thinking style.

In a second experiment, the researchers manipulated the time spent outdoors. The first session took part indoors; participants then either danced or walked around a track or walked outdoors or on a treadmill. Again, temperature did not appear to affect mood but the outdoor condition did. When people were outdoors on days that were warm, clear and characterised by high pressure, their mood was significantly more positive than those indoors during the same meteorological conditions. (The mood of those indoors decreased.)

In both studies, participants were from a northern climate. In a third study, the researchers recruited 387 participants from the internet who indicated they were from either North America/Canada, southern US or Europe. They found that the more time that participants spent outdoors in the spring, the greater the association between temperature and mood. As temperatures increased in the summer, there was a negative relationship between time spent outdoors and mood: those who were outside in high temperatures showed reduced mood. The best temperature for mood improvement was 19.7°C. This mood declined after 45 minutes outdoors.

Conclusions

Keller *et al.* have shed some light on the relationship between mood and weather. It seems as if the important factor is the time people spend outdoors in warm weather on clear days. This improvement is not just seen in mood but also on some measures of cognitive ability. The length of time people spend outdoors appears to be important and the effects may be season-dependent. The positive effects found in spring may be because 'people have been deprived of such weather during the winter' (p. 724).

Emotion without cognition?

Related to research on mood and cognition is a broader issue in emotion research. This is whether emotion can occur without cognition. Some psychologists, such as Lazarus (1984), believe that emotions are produced only by cognitive processes – by anticipating, experiencing, or imagining the outcomes of important interactions with the environment. Others, such as Zajonc (1984), insist that cognitive appraisal is not necessary and that emotions are automatic, species-typical responses heavily influenced by classical conditioning.

Although the two sides of the debate appear to have been drawn sharply, it seems clear that both automatic processes and conscious deliberation play a role in the expression and feelings of emotion. Some examples of emotions clearly involve cognitive processes. For instance, a person can become angry after realising that someone's 'kind words' actually contained a subtle insult. This anger is a result of cognition. But sometimes, emotional reactions

and their associated feelings seem to occur automatically. As we saw, through the process of classical conditioning, stimuli can evoke emotional reactions before we have time to realise what is happening. In some cases, we may be acting in a hostile and angry manner without realising what we are doing. If cognitive processes are responsible for our anger, they are certainly not conscious, deliberate ones.

One of the problems with this debate (as with many other debates) is that the opponents sometimes define the same terms in different ways. For example, not everyone agrees which operations of the brain should be regarded as cognitive and which should not. According to Lazarus, (1984) many cognitive processes are unconscious and relatively automatic. But if cognitive processes need not be conscious, how can we tell whether a given process is cognitive? And if we cannot tell, how can we hope to decide whether cognition is necessary for all emotions? If our definition of cognition is too general, we would have to conclude that all responses require cognition.

Chapter review

Motivation

- Motivation is a general term for a group of phenomena that affects the nature, strength and persistence of an individual's behaviour. It includes a tendency to perform behaviours that bring an individual into contact with an appetitive stimulus or that move it away from an aversive one.
- Regulatory systems include four features: a system variable (the variable that is regulated), a set point (the optimum value of the system variable), a detector to measure the system variable and a correctional mechanism to change it.
- Psychologists believed that aversive drives were produced by deprivation and that reinforcement was a result of drive reduction. However, the fact that we cannot directly measure an individual's drive level makes it impossible to test this hypothesis. Many reinforcers increase drive rather than reduce it. Thus, most psychologists doubt the validity of the drive reduction hypothesis of reinforcement.
- The discovery that electrical stimulation of parts of the brain could reinforce behaviour led to the study of the role of brain mechanisms involved in reinforcement. Apparently, all reinforcing stimuli (including addictive drugs) cause the release of dopamine in the brain.
- Because high levels of drive or arousal can be aversive, several investigators proposed the optimum-level theory of motivation and reinforcement. This theory suggests that organisms strive to attain optimum levels of arousal; thus, reinforcement and punishment are seen as two sides of the same coin.

- Because drive cannot be directly measured, we cannot determine whether an individual's drive is above or below its optimum level.
- Perseverance is the tendency to continue performing a behaviour that is no longer being externally reinforced and is determined by the organism's previous history with intermittent reinforcement and its opportunity to develop behaviours that produce conditioned reinforcers.
- Learned helplessness involves learning that an aversive event cannot be avoided or escaped.

Eating and drinking

- The fluid in cells is called intracellular fluid and contains a little sodium but large amounts of potassium and other metabolites. The other source of fluid in the body is extracellular fluid and this is found in two places. Interstitial fluid surrounds the cell body and is salty; blood plasma is found in the capillaries, arteries and veins and allows living cells and blood to be suspended within it.
- The reduction in the concentration of sodium available across the membrane and the movement of water by osmosis dehydrating and shrinking the body's cells is called osmometric thirst.
- Another type of thirst (volumetric thirst) results from dehydration outside cells, i.e. a reduction in the level of blood plasma.
- Hunger is the feeling that precedes and accompanies an important regulatory behaviour: eating.

- Eating begins for both social and physiological reasons. Physiologically, the most important event appears to be the detection of a lowered supply of nutrients available in the blood.
- Detectors in the liver measure glucose level, and detectors elsewhere in the body measure the level of fatty acids. Both sets of detectors inform the brain of the need for food and arouse hunger.
- Detectors responsible for satiety, which appear to be located in the walls of the stomach, monitor both the quality and the quantity of the food that has just been eaten.
- Long-term control of eating appears to be regulated by the chemical leptin, which is released by overnourished fat tissue and detected by cells in the brain. It decreases meal size and increases metabolic rate, thus helping the body to burn up its supply of triglycerides.
- Genetic and environmental factors may interact to cause the person's weight to deviate from the norm.
- To be diagnosed as clinically obese a person must have a body mass index that is equal to or greater than 30 kg/m².
- Intervention programmes for obese people are successful if individuals self-monitor and continue to adopt the strategies they have been taught after the intervention period is over.
- In extreme cases, surgery of the intestine is an effective means of helping a person lose weight (bariatric surgery).
- People differ genetically in the efficiency of their metabolisms and this efficiency can easily lead to obesity. Particular eating habits, especially those learned during infancy, can override the physiological signals that would otherwise produce satiety.
- Experiences such as repeated fasting and refeeding (the yo-yo effect) are often accompanied by overeating.
- Sensory-specific satiety refers to a reduction in the pleasantness of a food eaten to satiety whereas the pleasantness of others is relatively unaffected.
- People eat more of a four-course than of a one-course meal and more of a meal containing a variety of pasta shapes and colours than one containing one shape and one colour.
- The hedonic response to food after satiety is thought to be mediated by the secondary taste cortex; the primary taste cortex helps to identify the food.
- Anorexia nervosa is an eating disorder in which the individual is obsessed with food and weight but deliberately reduces their intake of food and avoids it; the prevalence of the disorder is between 0.5 and 1 per cent worldwide, and most anorexics are young women.
- Studies have found metabolic differences in anorexic patients, but we cannot determine whether these differences are the causes or the effects of the disorder.
- Bulimia nervosa is an eating disorder which involves a loss of control of food intake; bulimic individuals will often binge and then use laxatives or vomiting to get rid of the consumed food.

Sexual behaviour

- Testosterone has two major effects on male sexual behaviour: organisational and activational.

- In the foetus, testosterone organises the development of male sex organs and of some neural circuits in the brain; in the adult, testosterone activates these structures and permits erection and ejaculation to occur.
- The sexual behaviour of female mammals with oestrus cycles depends on oestradiol and progesterone, but these hormones have only a minor effect on women's sexual behaviour.
- Women's sexual desire, like that of men, is much more dependent on androgens.
- The development of sexual orientation appears to have biological roots. A large-scale study of homosexuals failed to find evidence that child-rearing practices fostered homosexuality.
- Studies have identified three regions of the brain that are of different sizes as between in homosexual and heterosexual males. These results suggest that the brains of these two groups may have been exposed to different patterns of hormones early in life. In addition, twin studies indicate that homosexuality has a genetic component as well.

Aggressive behaviour

- Ethological studies of other species suggest that aggression is a means of averting violence: threat gestures warn of an impending attack, and appeasement gestures propitiate the potential aggressor.
- In males of most animal species, androgens have both organisational and activational effects on aggressive behaviour.
- Testosterone appears to increase in a variety of situations and contexts. Increases have been found before chess players play matches and in winners after matches; increased levels have been reported in prisoners convicted of violent crime and described by fellow inmates as being tough. These data are, however, correlational.
- Field studies on the effects of televised violence are not conclusive. Observational studies have revealed a modest relation between preference for violent television shows and boys' aggressiveness, but we cannot be sure that watching the violence causes the aggressiveness.
- An attempt to manipulate aggression by forcing children to watch violent or non-violent television programmes was inconclusive because many children resented their loss of choice.

Emotion

- Emotion refers to behaviours, physiological responses and feelings evoked by appetitive or aversive stimuli, although psychologists have defined emotion in various ways.
- Darwin believed that expression of emotion by facial gestures was innate and that muscular movements were inherited behavioural patterns.
- Ekman and his colleagues showed that members of the South Fore tribe recognised facial expressions of Westerners and made facial gestures that were clear to Westerners, suggesting that emotional expressions are innate behaviour patterns and universally found.

- There is controversy, however, over whether facial expressions reflect true emotions or whether they reflect the social communication of an emotion.
- A number of theorists have suggested that there is a group of basic emotions, although the exact number is controversial, as is the notion that there are basic emotions. The most widely accepted number of basic emotions is six or seven.
- Research has shown that those who are outwardly happy are most likely to have high self-esteem and are happy in other aspects of their lives.
- Expressions of emotion are not always frank and honest indications of a person's emotional state. They can be masked, modulated or simulated according to culturally determined display rules.
- When a person attempts to mask their expression of emotion, some leakage occurs, particularly in movements of the body. Presumably, we learn to control our facial expressions better because we are aware of the attention that other people pay to these expressions.
- Destruction to parts of the amygdala prevents the recognition of fear in facial expressions and activation in the amygdala is seen in healthy individuals exposed to facial expressions of fear. In healthy individuals, the left side of the amygdala is active during the experience of positive emotion.
- The orbitofrontal cortex is also important to emotion and may be involved in the regulation of socially appropriate behaviour that involves complex decision-making.
- People with damage to the orbitofrontal region are able to explain the implications of complex social situations but are unable to respond appropriately when put in these situations. Thus, this region appears to be necessary for translating judgements about the personal significance of events into appropriate actions and emotional responses.
- The affective asymmetry of emotion model suggests that EEG activation of the left frontal region may be involved in the experience of positive emotion whereas activation of the right frontal region is involved in the experience of negative emotion.
- James and Lange suggested that the physiological and behavioural reactions to emotion-producing situations were perceived by people as states of emotion and that emotional states were not the causes of these reactions.
- Although emotional states are sometimes produced by automatic, classically conditioned responses, some psychologists have suggested that the perception of our own emotional state is not determined solely by feedback from our behaviour and the organs controlled by the autonomic nervous system. It is also determined by cognitive assessment of the situation in which we find ourselves.
- Schachter and his colleagues found that information about the expected physiological effects of drugs (or placebos) influenced subjects' reports about their emotional state. In one study, subjects even tolerated more intense electrical shocks, apparently discounting their own fear.
- Appraisal theories suggest that emotion is experienced after the environment has been evaluated for threat, fear, joy or any other influential factor.
- Evolutionary theories argue that emotions are a means of adapting to change in the environment; these changes produce a restricted set of responses which are universal (hence, the emotions associated with them should also be universal).
- The debate over whether cognition is necessary for emotion continues. Ultimately, the argument rests on how cognition is defined.

Suggestions for further reading

Motivation – general reading

Deckers, C. (2010) *Motivation: Biology, Psychology and Environment*. (3rd edn). Boston: Allyn & Bacon.
Sheldon, K. (2010) *Current Directions in Motivation and Emotion*. Boston: Allyn & Bacon.
Two very good introductions to the topic of motivation.

Ingestion

Bulik, C.M., Reba, L., Siega-Riz, A-M., Reichborn-Kjennerud, T. (2005) Anorexia nervosa: Definition, epidemiology and cycle of risk. *International Journal of Eating Disorders*, 37, S2–S9.
Eggers, C. and Libers, V. (2007) Through a glass, darkly. *Scientific American Mind*, 18, 2, 30–5.
Grimm, O. (2007) Addicted to food? *Scientific American Mind*, 18, 2, 36–9.
Kaye, W. (2008) Neurobiology of anorexia and bulimia nervosa. *Physiology and Behavior*, 94, 121–35.
Macht, M. (2007) Feeding the psyche. *Scientific American Mind*, 18, 5, 64–9.
Steingarten, J. (1997) *The Man Who Ate Everything*. London: Hodder.
Steingarten, J. (2002) *It Must Have Been Something I Ate*. London: Hodder.
Wadden, T.A., Brownell, K.D. and Foster, G.D. (2002) Obesity: Responding to the growing epidemic. *Journal of Consulting and Clinical Psychology*, 70(3), 510–25.
A variety of easy-to-read books and papers on ingestion and eating disorders. In particular, Grimm reviews what mechanisms contribute to overeating, and Macht, one of the leading researchers in the area, reviews some evidence of how mood affects food intake.

Sexuality

Hock, R.R. (2010) *Human Sexuality* (2nd edn). Boston: Allyn & Bacon.
An up-to-date general account of the topic.

Aggression and testosterone

Adams, D.B. (2006) Brain mechanisms of aggressive behavior: An updated review. *Neuroscience and Biobehavioral Reviews*, 30, 304–18.
Archer, J. (2006) Testosterone and human aggression: An evaluation of the challenge hypothesis. *Neuroscience and Biobehavioral Reviews,*30, 319–45.
Baumeister, R.E. (2006) Violent pride. *Scientific American Mind*, 17, 4, 54–9.
Booth, A., Granger, D.A., Mazur, A. and Kivlighan, K.T. (2006) Testosterone and social behavior. *Social Forces*, 85, 1, 165–91.
Janowsky, J.S. (2006) Thinking with your gonads: Testosterone and cognition. *Trends in Cognitive Sciences*, 10, 2, 77–82.
LeBlanc, M.M. and Barling, J. (2004) Workplace aggression. *Current Directions in Psychological Science*, 13, 1, 9–12.
Strueber, D., Lueck, M. and Roth, G. (2007) The violent brain. *Scientific American Mind*, 17, 6, 20–29.

Emotion – general reading

Adolphs, R. (2006). Perception and emotion. *Current Directions in Psychological Science*, 15, 5, 222–6.
Barrett, L.F. and Wager, T.D. (2006). The structure of emotion. *Current Directions in Psychological Science*, 15, 2, 79–83.
Barrett, L.F., Mesquita, B., Ochsner, K.N. and Gross, J.J. (2007). The experience of emotion. *Annual Review of Psychology*, 58, 373–403.
Damasio, A. (2000) *The Feeling of What Happens*. London: Vintage.
Ekman, P. (2007). *Emotions Revealed.* (2nd edn). Austin, Texas: Holt, Rinehart & Winston.
Elfenbein, H.A. and Ambady, N. (2003) Universals in cultural differences in recognizing emotions. *Current Directions in Psychological Science*, 12, 5, 159–64.

Fox, E. (2008). *Emotion Science*. London: Palgrave.
Jenkins, J.M., Oatley, K. and Stein, N. (1998) *Human Emotions*: A reader. Oxford: Blackwell.
Keltner, D., Jenkins, J.M., and Oatley, K. (2006) *Understanding Emotions* (2nd edn). Oxford: Blackwell.
Manstead, A.S.R., Frijda, N. and Fischer, A. (2004) *Feelings and Emotions*. Cambridge: Cambridge University Press.
Naqvi, N., Shiv, B. and Bechera, A. (2006). The role of emotion in decision making. *Current Directions in Psychological Science*, 15, 5, 260–4.
Russell, J.A., Bachorowski, J-A., Fernandez-Dols, J-M. (2003) Facial and vocal expressions of emotion. *Annual Review of Psychology*, 54, 329–49.
Schubert, S. (2006). A look tells all. *Scientific American Mind*, 17, 5, 26–31.
Some excellent books and papers on general emotion topics.

Biological perspectives on emotion

Bartz, J.A. and Hollander, E. (2006). The neuroscience of affiliation: Forging links between basic and clinical research on neuropeptides and social behavior. *Hormones and Behavior*, 50, 518–28.
Canli, T. and Amin, Z. (2002) Neuroimaging of emotion and personality: Scientific and ethical considerations. *Brain and Cognition*, 50, 414–431.
DeVignemont, F. and Singer, T. (2006). The empathic brain: How, when and why? Trends in *Cognitive Science*, 10, 10, 435–41.
McGaugh, J.L. (2004) The amygdala modulates the consolidation of memories of emotionally arousing experiences. *Annual Review of Neuroscience*, 27, 1–28.
Murray, E.A. (2007). The amygdala, reward and emotion. *Trends in Cognitive Sciences*, 11, 11, 489–97.
Wager, T.D., Phan, K.L., Liberzon, I. and Taylor, S.F. (2003) Valence, gender, and lateralization of functional brain anatomy in emotion: A meta-analysis of findings from neuroimaging. *NeuroImage*, 19, 513–31.
An excellent selection of books and review papers on various aspects of the biology of emotion.

Journals to consult

Appetite
Cognition and Emotion
Emotion
Health Psychology
Hormones and Behavior
International Journal of Eating Disorders
Journal of Abnormal Psychology
Journal of Consulting and Clinical Psychology
Journal of Personality and Social Psychology
Motivation and Emotion
Nature
Personality and Individual Differences
Physiology and Behaviour
Psychological Bulletin
Psychological Science
Social Neuroscience

Website addresses

http://www.psychology.org/links/Environment_Behavior_
Relationships/Emotion/
A collection of links to emotion sites.

http://www.psychology.org/links/Environment_Behavior_
Relationships/Motivation/
A collection of links to motivation sites.

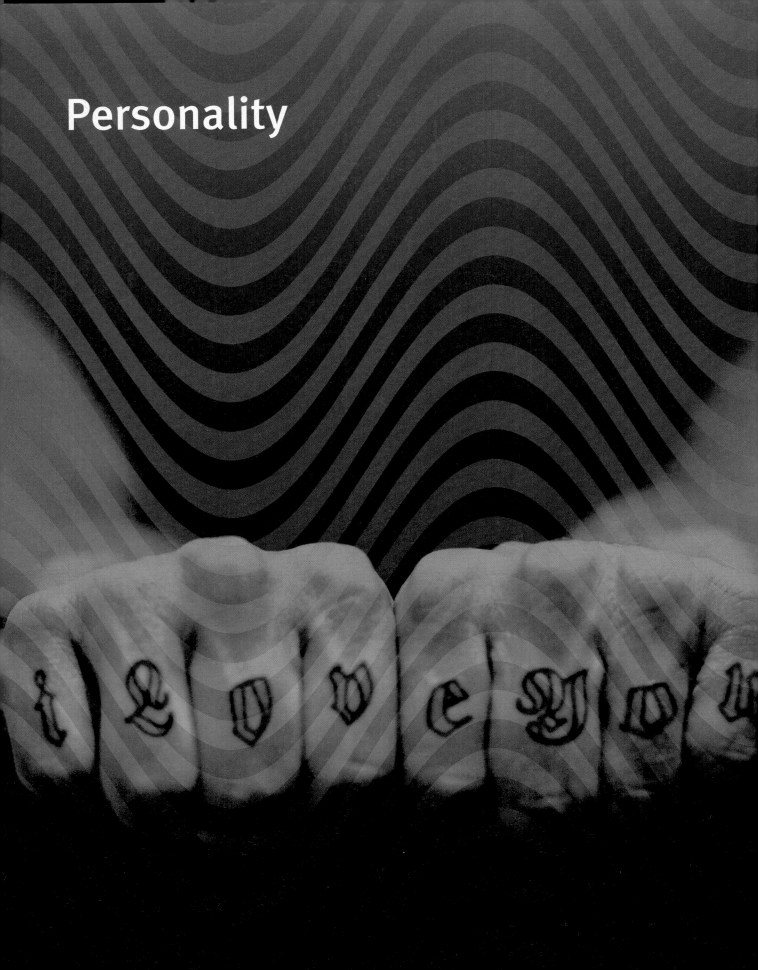

Personality

CHAPTER 14

Mapped out: Britain's personality clusters

Jonathan Leake and Helen Brooks

You are where you live. The growing mobility of modern Britain is creating, or reinforcing, particular personality types in different regions.

Londoners appear to be changing fastest, displaying sharply elevated levels of creativity, intellect, open-mindedness and extroversion when compared with people living in Wales, Scotland, Northern Ireland and the rest of Ireland.

People living in Wales, by contrast, emerge from the Cambridge University study as less extrovert, less conscientious and more anxious than the English, Scots or Northern Irish.

Similar differences appear in the English regions, with people from Devon, Cornwall, Northumberland and Tyneside being the least outgoing and the most neurotic.

Source: *The Sunday Times*, 14 April 2009.

WHAT YOU SHOULD BE ABLE TO DO AFTER READING CHAPTER 14

- Describe what psychologists mean by 'personality'.
- Describe and understand the methods used by psychologists to study personality.
- Describe and explain what is meant by trait theory and situationism.
- Describe and evaluate psychodynamic personality theory and humanistic approaches to personality.
- Describe and evaluate the trait theories of Cattell, Eysenck and Costa and McCrae.
- Evaluate the validity and reliability of personality tests.

QUESTIONS TO THINK ABOUT

- What is personality?
- Can we measure personality scientifically? If so, how?
- If individuals possess personality characteristics, how do we explain people's behaviour when they act out of character?
- Does personality mean the same thing in every culture? Is personality a linguistic rather than behavioural phenomenon?
- Does personality have a biological basis?
- Does personality change over time?
- Are there national differences in personality?

Explore the accompanying videos, simulations and animations on MyPsychLab. This chapter includes activities on: Locus of control • The psychodynamic approach • Maslow's hierarchy of needs • Self-actualisation • Check your understanding and prepare for your exams using the multiple choice, short answer and essay practice tests also available.

Towards a definition of personality

People have different styles of thinking, of relating to others, and of working, all of which reflect differences in personality – differences crucial to defining us as individuals. Common experience tells us that there is no one else just like us. There may even be significant differences in the personal characteristics of identical twins.

Such everyday observations provide a starting point for psychology's study of personality. But unlike such informal observations, psychology's approach to studying personality is considerably more calculated. For example, to many people, personality is nothing more than 'what makes people different from one another'. To psychologists, however, the concept is generally defined much more narrowly. **Personality** is a particular pattern of behaviour and thinking that prevails across time and situations and differentiates one person from another.

Psychologists do not draw inferences about personality from casual observations of people's behaviour. Rather, their assessment of personality is derived from results of special tests designed to identify particular personality characteristics. The goal of psychologists who study personality is to discover the causes of individual differences in behaviour.

This goal has led to two specific developments in the field of personality psychology: the development of theories that attempt to explain such individual differences and the development of methods by which individual patterns of behaviour can be studied and classified. Merely identifying and describing a personality characteristic is not the same as explaining it. However, identification is the first step on the way to explanation. What types of research effort are necessary to study personality? Some psychologists devote their efforts to the development of tests that can reliably measure differences in personality. Others try to determine the events – biological and environmental – that cause people to behave as they do. Thus, research on human personality requires two kinds of effort: identifying personality characteristics and determining the variables that produce and control them.

Trait theories of personality

As you will see in this chapter, the word 'personality' means different things to different people. The way in which personality is used by trait theorists is similar to the way in which we often think of personality in everyday life: a set of personal characteristics that determines the different ways we act and react in a variety of situations.

Personality types and traits

It has long been apparent that people differ in personality. The earliest known explanation for these individual differences is the humoral theory, proposed by the Greek physician Galen in the second century AD and based on then-common medical beliefs that had originated with the ancient Greeks. The body was thought to contain four humours, or fluids: yellow bile, black bile, phlegm and blood. People were classified according to the disposition supposedly produced by the predominance of one of these humours in their systems. Choleric people, who had an excess of yellow bile, were bad tempered and irritable. Melancholic people, who had an excess of black bile, had gloomy and pessimistic temperaments. Phlegmatic people, whose bodies contained an excessive amount of phlegm, were sluggish, calm and unexcitable. Sanguine people had a preponderance of blood (*sanguis*), which made them cheerful and passionate.

Although later biological investigations discredited the humoral theory, the notion that people could be divided into different **personality types** – different categories into which personality characteristics can be assigned based on factors such as developmental experiences – persisted long afterwards. For example, Freud's theory, which maintains that people go through several stages of psychosexual development, predicts the existence of different types of people, each type having problems associated with one of these stages. We discuss some of these problems later in this chapter.

Personality types are useful in formulating hypotheses because, when a theorist is thinking about personality variables, extreme cases are easily brought to mind. But after identifying and defining personality types, one must determine whether these types actually exist and whether knowing a person's personality type can lead to valid predictions about their behaviour in different situations.

Most modern investigators view individual differences in personality as being in degree, not kind. Tooby and Cosmides (1990) have, for example, argued that the nature of human reproduction makes the evolution of specific personality types unlikely – fertilisation produces a reshuffling of the genes in each generation, making it highly unlikely that a single, unified set of genes related to personality type would be passed from one generation to the next.

Rather than classify people by categories, or types, many investigators prefer to measure the degree to which an individual expresses a particular personality trait. A **personality trait** is an enduring personal characteristic that reveals itself in a particular pattern of behaviour in different situations. A simple example illustrates the difference between types and traits. We could classify people into two different types: tall people and short people. Indeed, we use these terms in everyday language. But we all recognise that height is best conceived of as a trait – a dimension on which people differ along a wide range of values. If we measure the height of a large sample of people, we will find instances all along the distribution, from very short to very tall, as Figure 14.1 illustrates. It is not that people are only either tall or short (analogous to a personality type) but that people vary in the extent to which they are one or the other (analogous to a personality trait).

We assume that people tend to behave in particular ways: some are friendly, some are aggressive, some are lazy, some are timid, some are reckless. Trait theories of personality fit this common-sense view. However, personality traits are not simply patterns of behaviour: they are factors that underlie these patterns and are responsible for them.

Identification of personality traits

Trait theories of personality do not pretend to be all-encompassing explanations of behaviour. Instead, they are still at the stage of discovering, describing and naming the regular patterns of behaviour that people exhibit (Goldberg, 1993). In all science, categorisation must come before explanation; we must know what we are dealing with before we can go about providing explanations. The ultimate goal of the personality psychologist is to explain what determines people's behaviour – which is the ultimate goal of all branches of psychology.

Allport's search for traits

Gordon Allport (1897–1967) was one of the first psychologists to search systematically for a basic core of personality traits. He began by identify-

ing all the words in an unabridged dictionary of the English language that described aspects of personality (Allport and Odbert, 1936). He found around 18,000 words, which he then further analysed for those that described only stable personality characteristics. He eliminated words that represented temporary states, such as 'flustered', or evaluations, such as 'admirable'. This still left him with over 4,000 words. Allport was interested in learning how many traits are needed to describe personality and exactly what these traits may be. For example, many of those 4,000 words, such as 'shy' and 'bashful', are synonyms. Although each synonym presumably makes some sort of distinction about a trait, a group of synonyms together might be used to describe the same underlying trait. Many trait theorists believe that the most basic set of personality traits ranges from 3 to 16 traits.

Allport's research stimulated other psychologists to think about personality in terms of traits or dispositions. In fact, most modern trait theories can be traced to Allport's earlier theoretical work. Like Allport, modern trait theorists maintain that only when we know how to describe an individual's personality will we be able to explain it.

Cattell: sixteen personality factors

In Chapter 11 you read about the importance of using factor analysis in defining intelligence. Factor analysis identifies variables that tend to be correlated. To use factor analysis to study personality, researchers must observe the behaviour of a large number of people. Usually, the observations are limited to responses to questions on paper-and-pencil tests, but occasionally, investigators observe people's behaviour in semi-natural situations. Statistical procedures then permit investigators to determine which items a given person tends to answer in the same way; they can then infer the existence of common factors. For example, a shy person would tend to say no to statements such as 'I attend parties as frequently as I can' or 'When I enter a room full of people, I like to be noticed.' In contrast, outgoing people would tend to say 'yes' to these statements.

To the degree that people possess orderly personality traits, they tend to answer certain clusters of questions in particular ways. Raymond Cattell (b. 1905) began his search for a relatively small number of basic personality traits with Allport and Odbert's (1936) list of adjectives. In addition, he collected data on people's personality characteristics from interviews, records describing their life histories, and from observing how people behave in particular situations. From this list, Cattell began to construct preliminary versions of a questionnaire called the 16PF. Then, using factor analysis, he analysed responses from thousands of people to whom the inventory had

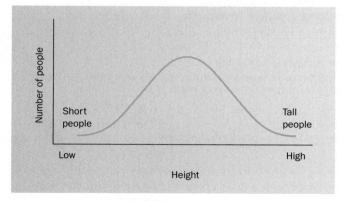

Figure 14.1 The distribution of height. We can measure people's height, a trait, on a continuous scale. We can also look at the extremes and divide people into the categories 'short' and 'tall' types.

been administered. Eventually, he identified 16 personality factors.

Cattell referred to these 16 traits as source traits because, in his view, they are the cornerstones upon which personality is built: they are the primary factors underlying observable behaviour. He called groups of similar types of observable behaviour surface traits; he included such traits as kindness, honesty and friendliness because they are visible to others. They represent the surface of personality and spring forth from source traits, which lie deeper within the personality. Figure 14.2 illustrates a personality profile of a hypothetical individual rated on Cattell's 16 factors. The factors are listed in order of importance, from top to bottom. Look at the ratings to see whether you think they would help you to predict the person's behaviour.

Eysenck: three factors

 Hans Eysenck (1916–1997) also used factor analysis to devise his theory of personality (Eysenck,

1970; Eysenck and Eysenck, 1985). His research identified three important factors: extraversion, neuroticism and psychoticism. These factors are bipolar dimensions. Extraversion is the opposite of introversion, neuroticism is the opposite of emotional stability, and psychoticism is the opposite of self-control. **Extraversion** refers to an outgoing nature and a high level of activity; **introversion** refers to a nature that shuns crowds and prefers solitary activities.

Neuroticism refers to a nature full of anxiety, worries and guilt; **emotional stability** refers to a nature that is relaxed and at peace with itself. **Psychoticism** refers to an aggressive, egocentric and antisocial nature; **self-control** refers to a kind and considerate nature, obedient of rules and laws. Eysenck's use of the term 'psychoticism' is different from its use by most clinical psychologists; his term refers to antisocial tendencies and not to a mental illness. A person at the extreme end of the distribution of psychoticism would receive the diagnosis of antisocial personality disorder.

Table 14.1 lists some questions that have high correlations or factor loadings on Eysenck's three factors. The

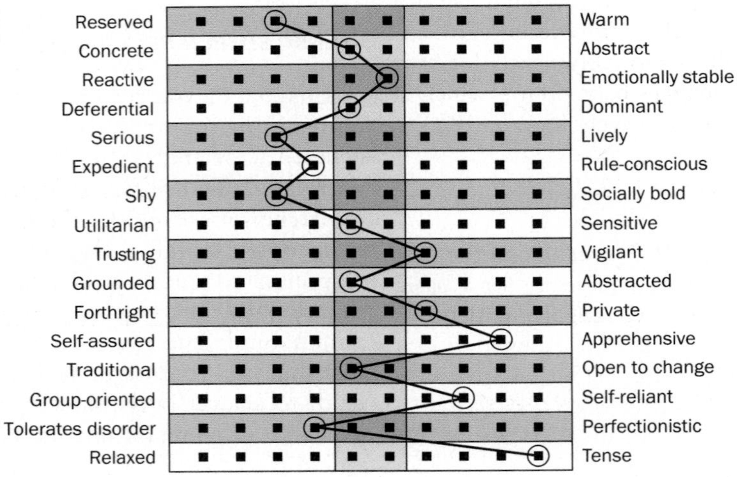

Reserved								Warm
Concrete								Abstract
Reactive								Emotionally stable
Deferential								Dominant
Serious								Lively
Expedient								Rule-conscious
Shy								Socially bold
Utilitarian								Sensitive
Trusting								Vigilant
Grounded								Abstracted
Forthright								Private
Self-assured								Apprehensive
Traditional								Open to change
Group-oriented								Self-reliant
Tolerates disorder								Perfectionistic
Relaxed								Tense

Figure 14.2 A hypothetical personality profile using Cattell's sixteen personality factors.

Source: from *16PF® Fifth Edition Administrator's Manual.* Copyright © 1993 by the Institute for Personality and Ability Testing, Inc., Champaign, Illinois, USA. All rights reserved. Reproduced with permission. '16PF' is a registered trademark of IPAT Inc. IPAT is a wholly owned subsidiary of OPP Ltd.

Cutting edge – Personality and music preferences

Can personality traits predict how you use the music you listen to? A study from the UK has found that British and American undergraduates who were open and intellectually engaged (enjoyed the arts, problem-solving, engaging in debate) and who had high IQ were more likely to use music in a cognitive or rational way (paying attention to it and appreciating the composition/musicianship) (Chamorro-Premuzic and Furnham, 2007). Neurotic, introverted and non-conscientious participants, on the other hand, were more likely to use music in an emotionally manipulative way – to cheer them up after a bad day, for example.

best way to understand the meaning of these traits is to read the questions and to imagine the kinds of people who would answer yes or no to each group. If a factor loading is preceded by a minus sign, it means that people who say 'no' receive high scores on the trait; otherwise, high scores are obtained by those who answer 'yes'.

According to Eysenck, the most important aspects of a person's temperament are determined by the combination of the three dimensions of extraversion, neuroticism and psychoticism – just as colours are produced by the combinations of the three dimensions of hue, saturation and brightness. Figure 14.3 illustrates the effects of various combinations of the first two of these dimensions – extraversion and neuroticism – and relates them to the four temperaments described by Galen.

More than most other trait theorists, Eysenck emphasises the biological nature of personality (Eysenck, 1991). For example, consider the introversion–extraversion dimension, which is biologically based, according to Eysenck, on an optimum arousal level of the brain.

Eysenck believes that the functioning of a neural system located in the brain stem produces different levels of arousal of the cerebral cortex. Introverts have relatively high levels of cortical excitation, whereas extraverts have relatively low levels. Thus, in order to maintain the optimum arousal level, the extravert requires more external stimulation than does the introvert. The extravert seeks stimulation from external sources by interacting with others or by pursuing novel and highly stimulating experiences. The introvert avoids external stimulation in order to maintain their lower arousal level at an optimum state. Different states of arousal are hypothesised to lead to different values of the extraversion trait for different people. This hypothesis is reviewed in the section on the biological basis of personality.

Most trait theorists accept the existence of Eysenck's three factors because they have emerged in factor analyses performed by many different researchers; these appear, in fact, to have the highest validity of all proposed personality factors (Kline, 1993).

Table 14.1 Some items from Eysenck's tests of extraversion, neuroticism and psychoticism

Factor	Loading
Extraversion	
Do you like mixing with people?	0.70
Do you like plenty of bustle and excitment around you?	0.65
Are you rather lively?	0.63
Neuroticism	
Do you often feel fed up?	0.67
Do you often feel lonely?	0.60
Does your mood often go up and down?	0.59
Psychoticism	
Do good manners and cleanliness matter much to you?	−0.55
Does it worry you if you know there are mistakes in your work?	−0.53
Do you like taking risks for fun?	0.51

Source: Adapted from Eysenck, H.J. and Eysenck, M.W., *Personality and Individual Differences: A natural science approach*. New York: Plenum Press, 1985.

Cutting edge – How extraverted is 'honey.bunny77@hotmail.de?'

Have you ever wondered if people's email addresses – the ones they themselves chose – reflect their personality or mask it? And is your impression of someone who emails you coloured by the email moniker they use? A group of German researchers examined 599 email addresses from young adults, measured the users' personality and then asked others to rate these emailers' personality based solely on the email address (Back *et al.*, 2008). The researchers found a remarkable correspondence between the nature of the email address and personality type, with independent observers showing high levels of agreement with the users' own assessment of their personality. This was true for neuroticism, openness, agreeableness, conscientiousness and narcissism but not extraversion.

The five-factor model and the Big Five

Languages reflect the observations of a culture; that is, people invent words to describe distinctions they notice. An analysis of such distinctions by Tupes and Christal (1961), replicated by Norman (1963), led to the most widely accepted mode of personality traits: the **five-factor model** (FFM; McCrae and Costa, 1985, 1987, 1990). The FFM proposes that personality is composed of the following five primary dimensions:

1 Neuroticism

2 Extraversion

3 Openness

4 Agreeableness

5 Conscientiousness

These factors can be measured by the Neuroticism, Extraversion, and Openness Personality Inventory, or NEO-PI, which consists of 181 items that potentially describe the person being evaluated (McCrae and Costa, 1990). Studies have shown that people's assessment of their own personality agrees well with ratings by spouses and those who know them. The test items are brief sentences, such as 'I really like most people I meet' or (for ratings by someone else) 'She has a very active imagination'. The person taking the test rates the accuracy of each item on a scale of 1 to 5, from strong disagreement to strong agreement. The scores on each of the five factors consist of the sums of the answers to different sets of items.

McCrae *et al.* (1986) validated the FFM through the factor analysis of a list of adjectives contained in a test called the California Q-Set. This test consists of 100 brief descriptions (such as 'irritable', 'cheerful', 'arouses liking' and 'productive'). The items were provided by many psychologists and psychiatrists who found the words useful in describing people's personality characteristics. Thus, the words are not restricted to a particular theoretical orientation. McCrae and his colleagues found that factor analysis yielded the same five factors as the analysis based on everyday language: neuroticism, extraversion, openness, agreeableness and conscientiousness.

The FFM is regarded by most personality psychologists as a fairly robust model of personality (Magai and McFadden, 1995). A study of the personalities of 163 men over 45 years found that neuroticism, extraversion and openness were positively correlated throughout the 45 years and that the traits remained relatively stable (Soldz and

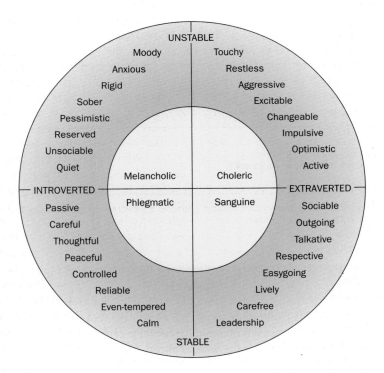

Figure 14.3 Eysenck's original theory illustrated for two factors. According to Eysenck, the two dimensions of neuroticism (stable versus unstable) and introversion–extraversion combine to form a variety of personality characteristics. The four personality types based on the Greek theory of humours are shown in the centre. Eysenck later added 'psychoticism' as the third trait.

Source: Eysenck, H.J., *The Inequality of Man*. London: Temple Smith, 1973. Reprinted with permission.

Vaillant, 1999). The Big Five Personality Inventory has been used to investigate various relationships between personality and other psychological variables, as you will see in this chapter and throughout he book – when a study has investigated conscientiousness or openness to experience, it is using the FFM model. For example, Zhao and Seibert (2006) investigated the differences between the personalities of managers and entrepreneurs. In a meta-analysis, they found that entrepreneurs scored more highly on the dimension of conscientiousness and openness to experience but scored lower on neuroticism and agreeableness. There was no difference between the two groups for extraversion.

Another group explored whether those who are always late for appointments differed in personality traits from those who turned up on time or early. Participants completed a personality questionnaire (the Big Five) and were invited to participate in an experiment a few days later (Back *et al.*, 2006). The researchers then examined whether any of the personality variables were related to the degree of punctuality. They examined three dependent measures – time of arrival, earliness and lateness. As you might predict, conscientiousness was significantly associated with punctuality – the more conscientious the participant, the less likely he or she was to turn up late and the more likely he or she was to turn up early. Agreeableness was associated with turning up on time and neuroticism was associated with turning up early. The researchers speculate that more specific components of these general traits – such as dependability – might better predict punctuality.

Personality – An international perspective

Any truly grand theory of personality must be able to encompass all cultures, countries and languages. If personality comprises three or five factors, which we all exhibit to a lesser or greater extent, then these factors should be exhibited or reported cross-culturally. If not, then the theory is culture-specific and describes only personality within a limited number of cultures.

One immediate problem in testing the universality of trait theories is that the way in which they are measured depends on language, and different cultures have slightly different words that they use to describe things. They also have words to represent events and objects that other cultures do not. Inuit, for example, have tens of words to describe the quality of snow. Individuals in less Arctic climes would obviously have no need for such a large vocabulary because snow appears only irregularly and does not impinge on their life in such a regular and intrusive way.

In personality, problems in demonstrating universality lie in taxonomy. Do the same words mean the same thing across cultures? For example, various cultures have attributed different meanings to the conscientiousness factor of the Big Five model (Caprara and Perugini, 1994). This factor means something different to the Dutch, Hungarians and Italians, and to the Americans, Germans, Czechs and Poles. Some reviewers have suggested that the best one can do is to find acceptable counterparts of the Big Five in all cultures; the first three factors of the model can be found in most cultures but the cross-cultural validity of others may be questionable (De Raad, 1998). However, there are more consistencies than inconsistencies across cultures.

McCrae *et al.* (2005) asked college students from 50 cultures, including Arabic and Black African cultures, to identify a man or woman they knew well and rate them using the third person version of the Revised NEO Personality Inventory. The Big Five structure was replicated in almost all cultures (Morocco and Nigeria were two of the half dozen or so not to show this pattern). Women were more positive than men in rating others, especially when rating other women.

In a separate study of the geography of personality traits, Allik and McCrae (2004) examined whether respondents from 36 cultures differed according to the Big Five personality dimension. Cultures that were geographically close shared similar personality traits: the greatest geographical distinction was between European and American cultures, and Asian and African cultures. Americans and Europeans were significantly more extravert and open to experience but less agreeable than peoples from other cultures. Why?

The authors suggest that the results may be due to shared gene pools (China and Korea, for example, share genetic ancestry) or to features of those cultures. Studying the process of acculturation – the assimilation of a person's behaviour with that person's culture – might help identify which is correct. For example, a study of Chinese peoples who emigrated to Canada found that differences between these people and European Canadians attenuated the longer the Chinese lived in Canada (McCrae *et al.*, 1998). Openness and agreeableness, in particular, increased in the immigrant group but introversion remained stable and did not match levels seen in European Canadians. These data suggest that some personality traits might be adopted or enhanced by acculturation, but others may not.

Can cultures also differ according to the implicit or lay trait or context theories they hold? Implicit theories describe what people think about the stability (trait) or variability (context) of

▶

Personality – *Continued*

personality traits, how consistent they believe such traits are across situations, how they predict behaviour from a person's personality traits, how they form an idea of a person's traits from little behavioural information and so on. Church *et al.* (2005) investigated cross-cultural implicit beliefs about personality in what they called two individualistic cultures – America and Australia – and two collectivistic cultures – Mexico and the Philippines. They hypothesised that the more individualistic the culture, the greater or stronger the culture's beliefs in traits, rather than situations, as determinants of behaviour. Implicit trait beliefs were stronger in Americans than in Mexicans or Filipinos, but implicit contextual beliefs were weaker.

We often hold stereotypes of our own and other nations that may not necessarily be true. The Brits have stiff-upper lips, Americans let it all hang out, Australians don't stand on ceremony and the French are supercilious. None might be accurate; some might.

To investigate whether our perceptions of our own and the culture of others are supported by empirical data, a team of international researchers asked respondents from 49 cultures across six continents to complete a National Character Survey which asked them to describe a typical member from a culture. These responses were compared with personality data collected via the NEO-PI-R (Terracciano *et al.*, 2005).

These was a significant relationship between cultural traits described by others and objectively assessed personality for only four cultures – New Zealand, Australia, Poland and Lebanon. The only significant relationships between self-reported cultural characteristics and personality scores were found in Poland and Japan. Poland, therefore, was the only culture where the people's views of the nation's characteristics were supported by objective data.

The study highlights the power of national stereotypes in our views of others and members of our own culture: such stereotypes are contradicted by empirical data.

Stability of personality traits across the lifespan

Longitudinal studies of personality show remarkable stability in personality factors (especially, extraversion). Cross-sectional studies, however, show less stability – not surprisingly, perhaps, because cross-sectional studies include people who differ in age (and, therefore, share different cultural influences).

A meta-analysis of American studies of undergraduates' personalities in the years between 1966 and 1993 (Twenge, 2001) found that correlations between year of study and extraversion were positive and strong: extraversion seemed to increase as the years went by. The increase in extraversion was large and explained between 14 and 19 per cent of the variance in personality over this time. Does this mean that extraversion increased across the years? The author cautions that this may not necessarily be true. It is possible, for example, that people had become more willing to describe themselves as extravert.

A review of the stability of personality in 152 longitudinal studies (allowing for 3,217 examples of test–retest reliability) found that the consistency of personality increased from childhood to young adulthood, increased still further from adulthood to 30 years, and stabilised between the ages of 50 and 70 years (Roberts and DelVecchio, 2000). These data suggest that personality traits are fairly stable across the lifespan, certainly until the age of 50. Even then, stabilisation is not so great as to indicate a marked change in personality.

The results were confirmed by Caspi *et al.* (2000) who monitored the personalities of children born between April 1972 and March 1973 in Dunedin, New Zealand, the country's fourth largest city. The children were studied from 3 years of age to 21. At the age of 3, children were classified by temperament and, in adulthood, they were asked to rate their own temperament. They also had their temperament rated by others (official records were also used to form an assessment of their temperament).

Children regarded as uncontrollable at the age of 3 grew up to be impulsive, unreliable and antisocial. Children who were regarded as inhibited were more likely to grow up to be more depressed, unassertive and have fewer sources of social support. The authors suggest that behaviour early in life may be strong predictors of behaviour later in life and argue that the earliest that one could use such measures to predict personality would be 2 years because this is when the child begins to develop adequate memory and strategies for remembering. At this point, children also become aware of being embarrassed and of being ashamed.

A Dutch study of 2,494 adults ranging in age from 16 to 91 years of age has found age differences in personality type (Allemand *et al.*, 2008). Although personality was fairly stable across all age groups, there were some differences. Specifically, older adults were more agreeable and more conscientious than were middle-aged or younger adults. The researchers suggest that this reflects 'an increase in personality maturity, in the sense of becoming emotionally more predictable and more attuned to social demands' (p. 767).

Cutting edge – Sex and profession differences in personality

A study of Israeli professionals has found significant personality differences between men and women and between members of different professions (Rubinstein and Strul, 2007). Women were found to be significantly more neurotic and extravert than were men, and artists were found to be more neurotic than were doctors, lawyers and clinical psychologists; artists were also more open to experience than were doctors.

More general sex differences were reported in a 55-culture study by Schmitt et al. (2008). In a sample of just over 17,500 participants, they found that women reported higher levels of neuroticism, extraversion, agreeableness and conscientiousness than did men and that these differences were much more pronounced in cultures that are healthy, prosperous and more egalitarian.

One study has suggested that some personality traits are more fluid than others. McCrae and Costa and their international team of researchers looked at changes in the Big Five personality traits from the age of 14 years to 30 years in a sample of Germans, British, Spaniards, Czechs and Turks (N=5085) (McCrae et al., 2000). They found that neuroticism, extraversion and openness to experience decreased from 14 to 30 years but that agreeableness and conscientiousness increased. Similar trends were found after 30 years, but the changes were not as pronounced.

A similar pattern – some decline, some stability, but largely some change – has also been noted in a meta-analysis of longitudinal studies. Roberts et al. (2006) found that social dominance (a feature of extraversion), conscientiousness and emotional stability increase between the ages of 20 and 40, whereas social vitality and openness increase during adolescence, then decline to old age. Results from meta-analyses such as these suggests that personality traits are not fixed and immutable but are subject to change and evolution (although, generally, this change is not pronounced – a 35-year-old introvert is unlikely to become an uncontrollable 55-year-old extravert).

How we view ourselves in the past and the present

see activity on mypsychlab

Anecdotal evidence suggests that we view our present selves more positively than we do our younger selves: we feel happier, more successful, able to get on better with others and so on. You saw in Chapter 12 that middle age is associated with general contentment (depression is less common in this period of life). Research, however, can be patchy. Some studies show that young and middle-aged people rate their present selves more positively than their younger selves, whereas older individuals (mean age, 73 years) feel more positively about the present for some attributes, more negatively about others and neutral about still others (Ryff, 1991). Other studies show that people rate themselves to be happier in the present than the past.

In a systematic study of people's appraisals of their past and present selves, Wilson and Ross (2001) asked university undergraduates to provide descriptions of their present selves and how they remember themselves at 16 years of age. People were more positive about their present than past selves. In a second study, participants

Cutting edge – Do you get better looking each day?

The country and western singer, Mac Davis, probably tongue-in-cheek, once sang 'Oh Lord, it's hard to be humble/When I'm perfect in every way/And I can't wait to look in the mirror/Because I get better looking each day.' A study from the University of Cardiff, however, lends support to Davis's cod-vanity.

Geoffrey Haddock (2006) asked women students to rate their present (now) and past selves (beginning of the academic year) for physical attractiveness. They were also asked how important physical attractiveness was to their sense of self. Participants rated their present selves as physically more attractive, but only if physical attraction was a feature they thought was important to their sense of self. In a second experiment, participants judged their current physical attrac-

tiveness and estimated how physically attractive they would be in five years' time. Participants rated their future selves to be more attractive than their current selves. However, this result was found only in participants who tended to make social comparisons with others.

While the results may reflect the fact that students actually do believe that they get more attractive with time, they could also suggest that our appraisals of ourselves are affected by time and that these are relative: we are more positive about the present than the past and are more positive about the future than the present. Whether Mac was right or not, Haddock's participants could have been singing the same tune.

evaluated themselves using a list of desirable attributes (broad-minded, common sense, self-confident, good coping skills, good social skills) and undesirable attributes (dishonest, rude, dull/boring). The same pattern emerged: past selves were viewed less favourably. Even a period of two months was sufficient to produce a less favourable view of the past self compared with the present self. In two more studies, the researchers found that people judged themselves to have improved more significantly than acquaintances. When people compared their past self to a peer at that age, they regarded themselves more favourably than they did their peer.

There are various explanations for why people regard their current self more positively than they do their past self. Perhaps people revise the past because they wish to see their present selves in a favourable light. Revising the past downward may be easier than inflating the past upward. By criticising their past selves, they can feel better about themselves without inflating their current view of themselves. The authors suggest that one way in which this research can be developed is by asking those who have views about the variability of attributes to rate themselves. For example, people who hold that attributes are fixed and relatively stable may regard their past and present selves differently from those who believe that attributes can change over time.

Heritability of personality traits

Several trait theorists, including Cattell and Eysenck, have asserted that a person's genetic history has a strong influence on their personality. Many studies have shown that some personality traits are strongly heritable (Emde *et al.*, 1992; McGue *et al.*, 1993; Jang *et al.*, 1998). As you saw in Chapter 3, the heritability of a trait can be assessed by comparing identical (monozygotic, MZ) with fraternal (dizygotic, DZ) twins, comparing twins raised together with twins raised apart, and comparing biological with adoptive relatives. Many studies have found that identical twins are more similar to each other than are fraternal twins on a variety of personality measures, which indicates that these characteristics are heritable (Loehlin, 1992).

Using various tests of Eysenck's factors of extraversion, neuroticism and psychoticism, Zuckerman (1991) found that identical twins were more similar than fraternal twins on every measure. Similar data have been reported for the Big Five (e.g., Loehlin *et al.*, 1998; Yamagata *et al.*, 2006) with correlations between MZ twins being consistently higher than those for the DZ twins.

The results of Big Five and ENP studies suggest that heredity accounts for between 40 and 70 per cent of the variability in these three personality traits. Concordance rates for extraversion in MZ twins range between 0.45 and 0.60, and for DZ twins, between 0.15 and 0.3 (Zuckerman, 2005). When people rate the personalities of MZ and DZ twins they see on video, the CR rating for the MZ twins is 0.59 and for the DZ twins 0.23 (so viewers think the MZ twins behave more similarly than the DZ twins, even though they are not aware of their twin status). A similar pattern is seen for peer ratings. The concordance rates for MZ twins reared apart is between 0.3 and 0.6; for DZ twins, it is 0.

Slightly lower correlations are found for neuroticism, but the direction is the same; the CRs are higher for the MZ than DZ twins (Zuckerman, 2005). Thus, it would appear that the remaining 30–60 per cent of the variability is caused by differences in environment. In other words, some family environments should tend to produce extraverts, others should tend to produce introverts, and so on. But research indicates that the matter is not so simple.

Zuckerman (1995) reviewed several studies that measured the correlation in personality traits of pairs of identical twins raised together and raised apart. If family environment has a significant effect on personality characteristics, then the twins raised together should be more similar than those raised apart. But they were not. Taken as a group, these studies found no differences, indicating that differences in family environment account for none of the variability of personality traits in the twins who were tested. Another approach, comparing the personality traits of parents with those of their adopted children, suggests that family environment may account for approximately 7 per cent of the variability (Scarr *et al.*, 1981). If approximately 40–70 per cent of the variability in personality traits is caused by heredity and 0–7 per cent is caused by family environment, what is responsible for the remaining 23–50 per cent of the variability? The answer is that heredity and environment interact.

The major source of the interaction seems to be the effect that people's heredity has on their family environment (Plomin and Bergeman, 1991). That is, people's genetic endowment plays an important role in determining how family members interact with them. Identical twins agreed on their ratings of cohesion, expressiveness, conflict, achievement, culture, activity, organisation and control much more than the fraternal twins did; that is, identical twins were much more likely to have experienced similar family environments.

There are two possible explanations for these results: the family environments could have been more similar for identical twins than for fraternal twins, or the family environments could really have been the same in all cases but were simply perceived as different by the fraternal twins. Evidence suggests that the first possibility is correct, that is, the family environments really were more similar for identical twins (Loehlin, 1992). How can this be? One might think that each family has a certain environment and that everyone in the household comes under its influence.

Although there are aspects of a family that are shared by the entire household, the factors that play the largest role in shaping personality development appear to come from social interactions between an individual and other family members. These social interactions are different for different people. Because of hereditary differences, one child may be more sociable; this child will be the recipient of more social interaction. Another child may be abrasive and disagreeable; this child will be treated more coldly. In the case of identical twins, who have no hereditary differences, the amount of social interaction with each twin is likely to be similar.

Even physical attributes (which are largely hereditary) will affect a child's environment. A physically attractive child will receive more favourable attention than will an unattractive child. In fact, studies that examined videotaped interactions between mothers and their children confirm that heredity does have an important influence on the nature of these interactions (Plomin and Bergeman, 1991). Thus, although a child's environment plays an important part in their personality development, hereditary factors play a large role in determining the nature of this environment.

One caution about this interpretation is in order. Although the studies cited have been replicated in several cultures, none has investigated the effects of the full range of cultural differences in family lives. That is, when comparisons have been made between twins raised together and those raised apart, almost all have involved family environments within the same culture. It is possible that cultural differences in family environments could be even more important than the differences produced by a person's heredity; only cross-cultural studies will be able to test this possibility.

Are all personality traits a product, direct or indirect, of a person's heredity? The answer is no. Some personality characteristics show a strong effect of shared environment but almost no effect of genetics. For example, twin studies have found a strong influence of family environment, but not of heredity, on belief in God, involvement in religion, masculinity/femininity, attitudes towards racial integration, and intellectual interests (Loehlin and Nichols, 1976; Rose, 1988). Thus, people tend to learn some important social attitudes from their family environments.

Neurobiological basis of personality

Patients with damage to the front of the brain, the orbitofrontal cortex, as you saw in the last chapter and Chapter 4, behave differently from those with damage to other areas of brain; they are more impulsive, engage in more inappropriate behaviour and report more anger and less happiness (Berlin *et al.*, 2004). Traumatic brain injury to the frontal lobe in children as young as 5 or as old as 14 is associated with personality changes 6 and 12 months following injury (Max *et al.*, 2006). Curiously, given the marked changes in 'personality' normally observed in frontal lobe patients, Berlin *et al.* (2004) found no significant differences between the groups on a standard measure of personality (the Big Five). Where, therefore, if anywhere, do the neural correlates of personality reside?

Several psychologists have attempted to relate extraversion, neuroticism and psychoticism to underlying physiological mechanisms (Eysenck and Eysenck, 1985; Gray, 1987; Zuckerman, 1995; Canli, 2006). Zuckerman (1995), for example, suggested that the personality dimensions of extraversion, neuroticism and psychoticism are determined by the neural systems responsible for reinforcement, punishment and arousal. People who score high on extraversion are particularly sensitive to reinforcement – perhaps their neural reinforcement systems are especially active. Table 14.2 summarises Zuckerman's hypothetical explanations for the three major personality dimensions.

Cutting edge – Personality and birth order

Do you have a brother or sister? Do you think that he or she is similar to or different from you? If you have many siblings, and you are the youngest or the oldest, have you noticed that you might behave slightly differently from brother or sister?

A study from the US of families with large numbers of siblings (equal to or greater than six) has found differences in personality between brothers/sisters which is dependent on birth order (Dixon *et al.*, 2008). The youngest sibling, as well as the three youngest siblings, was significantly more extravert than the oldest, and oldest three siblings, when compared with their own family members and those from the other families. A review published in the 1980s concluded that younger siblings were more sociable.

One explanation for the finding may be that the younger sibling has to try harder for parental attention because of competition from other siblings: increased extraversion is reflected in increased assertiveness.

Table 14.2 Zuckerman's hypothetical biological characteristics that correspond to personality dimensions

Personality trait	Biological characteristics
Extraversion	High sensitivity to reinforcement
Neuroticism	High sensitivity to punishment
Psychoticism	Low sensitivy to punishment; high optimal level of arousal

Infants who later become extraverts show higher activity levels, whereas adult extraverts show more reinforcement-seeking behaviour. Adult extraverts participate in more social activities, tend to shift from one type of activity to another, are optimistic and expect that their pursuits will result in reinforcing outcomes. However, unlike people who score high on psychoticism, they are sensitive to the effects of punishment and can learn to act prudently. People who score high on neuroticism are anxious and fearful. If they also score high on psychoticism, they are hostile as well. These people are particularly sensitive to the punishing effects of aversive stimuli. Zuckerman therefore suggests that the personality dimension of neuroticism is controlled by the sensitivity of the neural system responsible for punishment, which appears to involve the amygdala.

People who score high on psychoticism have difficulty learning when not to do something. Zuckerman suggests they have a low sensitivity to punishment and also have a high tolerance for arousal and excitation; in other words, we could say that their optimum level of arousal is abnormally high. As you saw in Chapter 13, some theorists hypothesise that people seek situations that provide an optimum level of arousal: too much or too little arousal is aversive. Therefore, a person with a high optimum level of arousal (a high tolerance for excitement) seeks out exciting situations and performs well in them. A neurotic would find these situations aversive, and their behaviour would become disorganised and inefficient. A person with a high tolerance for excitement makes a good warrior but does not fit in well in civilised society. This is a reformulation of Eysenck's original theory. He argued that extraverts were less reactive to cortical excitation and, therefore, sought out stimulation. Extraverts do need more stimulation to feel good. Introverts, conversely, are cortically over-aroused which leads to them seeking out or avoiding situations that are stimulating. Eysenck's theory was constructed at a time when EEG and ERP were the only useful methods of measuring excitation. Neuroimaging data show a complicated pattern. Introverts show more activation in some brain regions than do extraverts; conversely, extraverts show more activation in some brain regions than do introverts (Haier *et al.*, 1987).

Canli *et al.* (2001) predicted that extraversion would be correlated with greater brain activation when people watch pleasant images whereas neuroticism would be correlated with greater brain activation when participants watch unpleasant images. Their hypothesis was based on the assumption that extraverts would be more positively disposed and would respond enthusiastically to pleasant stimuli whereas neurotic participants would react intensely to negative stimuli. This is the pattern they found in an fMRI study of 14 women.

Canli *et al.* (2002) also found, however, that extraversion was associated with amygdala activation when participants watched happy faces. The more extravert the individual, the greater the activation in this structure. No other interaction between emotion and personality was found. Canli *et al.*'s findings are illustrated in Figure 14.4.

In a more explicit examination of personality and brain activation, Sigura *et al.* (2000) used Cloninger's (1986) idea that we have three heritable personality types and correlated these types with regional blood flow using a form of PET. According to Cloninger, the three types are 'novelty-seeking' – a tendency towards seeking out novel stimuli and events; 'harm avoidance' – a tendency to avoid punishment and harm because individuals respond intensely to such stimuli; and 'reward dependence' – a tendency to seek reward and respond intensely to reward. Significant associations between novelty-seeking and brain activation were found in the left insula and the anterior cingulate cortex; a negative correlation was found between harm avoidance and activation in the left parahippocampal gyrus and regions of the frontal, temporal and parietal lobes.

The picture, therefore, is complex – perhaps not surprisingly given the febrile nature of personality and debate over whether it is a genuinely fixed series of traits. Perhaps the biological basis of personality may be found at a more genetic level. There have been associations reported, for example, between the presence of a serotonin gene (5HTT or SERT) and neuroticism scores (Lesch *et al.*, 1996). There are two variants of this gene – a long one and a short one. The short-allele version has been associated with high harm avoidance and neuroticism scores, and lower agreeableness scores (Lesch *et al.*, 1996; Hamer *et al.*, 1999; Greenberg *et al.*, 2000), and with depression and hostility (Mossner *et al.*, 2001; Sen *et al.*, 2004). Novelty-seeking and sensation-seeking have been associated with the presence of a specific dopamine receptor (D4DR) (Ebstein *et al.*, 1996). Its allele has two forms and the longer one has been linked to high-novelty seeking (Baijan *et al.*, 1996), although in reviews of all relevant studies, around half show this pattern (Prolo and Lincino, 2002). In one study of 4-year-old children, mothers of those children with the long form of the D4DR allele described them as having more problems with aggression (Schmidt *et al.*, 2004).

Of course, if this allele is important to more 'negative' personality types, perhaps those with the allele might respond in a specific way when they view negative images, such as fearful faces. Predicting that viewing such faces would lead to greater amygdala activation in these allele carriers, Hairi *et al.* (2002) found this activation in an fMRI study of 28 individuals.

Perhaps, in terms of understanding the possible genetic causes of personality expression, Wilson (1998, p. 247) best sums up our current status:

> Reductionism across all levels is not a realistic goal for science. . . One could conceivably find all the particular genes that contribute to the genetic variance in a personality trait but not be able to account for the complex interactive influences with environment that shaped the trait. Genes and environment interact throughout development and although environment cannot change genes, it can affect this expression through releasor genes. Genes do not make personality traits or behavioural traits, they simply make proteins that in turn make nerves, biochemicals, and these affect physiology and ultimately, behaviour.

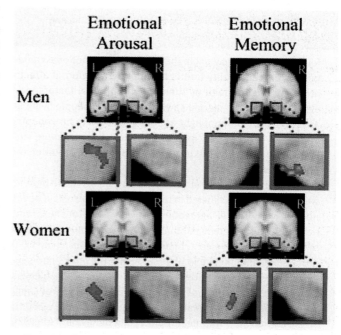

Figure 14.4 Areas of activation in the amygdalae of men and women as they recalled arousing, emotional pictures.
Source: Plate 10.1 from *Human Neuropsychology*, 2nd edn, Pearson/Prentice Hall (Martin, G.N., 2006).

Controversies in Psychological Science – The state you're in: a psycho-geography of personality

The issue

Can country or a state be said to have a 'personality'? In what was perhaps the earliest study to explore this in a systematic way, the Catell 16PF was administered to six regions of the US (Krug and Kulhavy, 1973). It found that people from north-eastern, mid-west and west coast states had higher 'creative productivity' scores than those in south-eastern, south-western and mountain regions. Another report from the 1970s found that subscriptions to cultured and sophisticated magazines were more common in the north-east and west central parts of the US than the South (Zelinsky, 1974). A more recent study of self-perception in nine US regions found that respondents in the mid and south Atlantic regions rated themselves as 'nervous' or 'worrying' whereas those in New England, the mid Atlantic and Pacific regions scored more highly on broad-mindedness, curiosity and sophistication (Plaut *et al.*, 2002). The development of well-validated personality measures, such as the Five Factor Model which is biologically rooted and predicts stability in traits across time, has sparked a plethora of cross-cultural and transnational studies.

The evidence

Why should these different states show these different patterns of personality? In a recent review, Rentfrow *et al.* (2008) suggest at least three reasons: (1) people migrated to places that met their psychological and physical needs; (2) a social founder effect, where the intellectual history, customs and culture of a place established social norms for that environment which influenced behaviour and personality, and (3) socialisation, where personality traits are acquired that are consistent with the behaviour seen in the environment people were in, i.e. people behaved in a way that was consistent with the behavioural norm for that region.

In terms of social migration, Rentfrow *et al.* argue that a person high in extraversion, for example, might escape a suffocating small town to one where there is greater stimulation and creativity, and there is evidence from social psychology demonstrating that people seek out social situations that are consistent with their own beliefs and attitudes (Buss, 1987). Extraverts seek out stimulating environments; neurotic people do not (Furnham, 1981). The social influence of the social

Controversies in Psychological Science – *Continued*

founder effect might work in the same way as emotional contagion – if a personality trait is common in a region, it affects others and is imbibed by them. Environmental factors may also be important – as you saw in Chapter 11, people living in areas with little natural light are more inclined to be unhappy and those living in hot climates tend to experience more violence than those in cold ones (Magnusson, 2000; Anderson and Anderson, 1996).

In their ambitious study, Rentfrow *et al.* investigated whether US regions differed in terms of their extraversion, openness to experience, agreeableness, conscientiousness and neuroticism. They predicted that extraversion would be related to community involvement, preference for enterprising or social professions and interest in physical health (as others had suggested before: Ozer and Benet-Martinez, 2006); agreeableness would be related to religiosity, longevity and low levels of criminality (Ozer and Benet-Martinez, 2006; Roberts *et al.*, 2007); conscientiousness with health-protecting behaviour, longevity and low levels of crime; neuroticism with criminal behaviour and poor coping; and openness to experience with unconventional belief and preference for creative professions.

Rentfrow *et al.* used the internet to recruit 619,397 participants from 50 US states and Washington DC. Information about ethnicity, socio-economic status, education, etc. was requested, as was information about personality. Fifty-five per cent were women.

Conclusion

Rentfrow *et al.*'s findings were as follows (see also Figure 14.5 (a) – (e)):

- Levels of *extraversion* were associated with social involvement (such as club meetings, time spent in bars), involvement in business in healthcare professions (e.g. sales/nursing), high rates of robbery and murder, high religiosity and a higher proportion of people in artistic/investigative professions; but lower levels of jogging/exercising.

- Levels of *agreeableness* were associated with low crime and activities that were social (but not bar/club-related), religiosity and involvement in artistic/entertainment professions.

- Levels of *conscientiousness* were positively associated with murder and robbery (strangely – although when demographic variables were taken into account, this effect disappeared), religiosity and less time spent in bars.

- Levels of *neuroticism* were associated with incidents of robbery and murder and in less exercise taken at home.

- Levels of *openness to experience* were associated with liberal values, preference for artistic/investigative professions, and more tolerant views on marijuana, abortion and gay marriage.

(a)

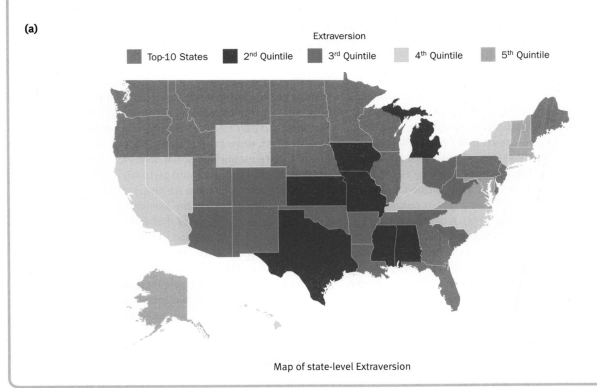

Map of state-level Extraversion

Controversies in Psychological Science – *Continued*

(b)

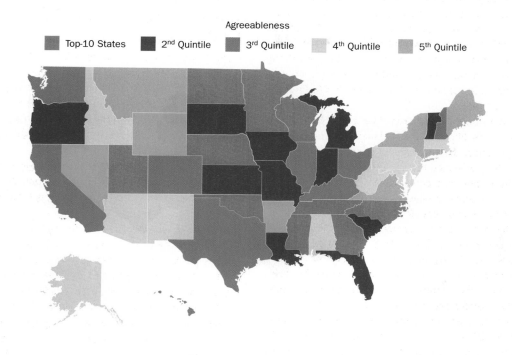

Map of state-level Agreeableness

(c)

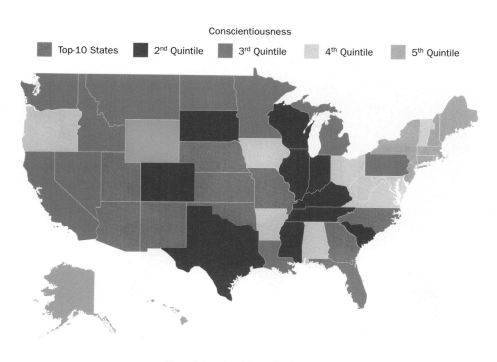

Map of state-level Conscientiousness

Controversies in Psychological Science – *Continued*

(d)

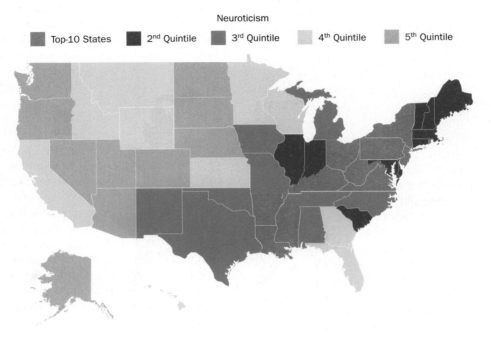

Map of state-level Neuroticism

(e)

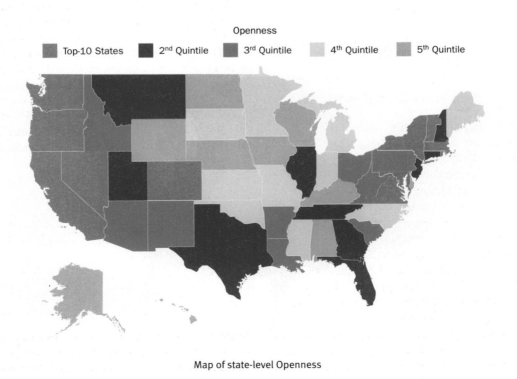

Map of state-level Openness

The social learning approach

Some psychologists, such as Cattell and Eysenck, are interested in the ways in which people differ with respect to their personality traits. Other psychologists are more interested in the ways in which a person's personality is affected by environmental and cognitive variables. These psychologists view personality and its development as a process in which behavioural, cognitive and environmental variables interact to produce a person's personality. **Social learning theory** embodies the idea that both the consequences of behaviour and an individual's beliefs about those consequences determine personality.

Social learning theory stems partially from Skinner's experimental analysis of behaviour. Although Skinner's work has influenced contemporary personality theory, he should not be mistaken for a personality theorist. He was definitely not one. For Skinner, behaviour is explained entirely in terms of its consequences. Behaviour is consistent from one situation to the next because it is maintained by similar kinds of consequences across those situations. Behaviour changes only when the consequences for behaving change. Skinner's ideas have attracted the attention of some personality researchers because they are experimentally based and provide testable hypotheses for predicting an individual's behaviour within and across situations. Social learning theorists have modified and applied Skinner's ideas to their own work. One such researcher is Albert Bandura (b. 1925), who blended Skinner's ideas with his own ideas about how cognitive factors may influence behaviour.

Expectancies and observational learning

Cognitive processing, including the individual's interpretation of the situation, is central to social learning theory (Bandura, 1973, 1986). An important aspect of cognition for Bandura and other social learning theorists is **expectancy**, the individual's belief that a specific consequence will follow a specific action. Expectancy refers to how someone perceives the contingencies of reinforcement for their own behaviour. If a person does something, it may be because they expect to be rewarded or punished. In different situations, expectancies may vary. For example, a child may learn that he can get what he wants from his younger sister by hitting her. However, on one occasion, his parents may catch him hitting his sister and punish him. His expectancy may now change: he may still get what he wants by behaving aggressively, but if he is caught, he'll be punished. This new expectancy may influence how he behaves towards his sister in the future (especially around his parents).

Expectancies also permit people to learn actions vicariously, that is, without those actions being directly reinforced. The vicarious nature of some learning experiences is obvious in children as they imitate the actions of others. A 3-year-old who applies deodorant to herself does so not because this behaviour has been reinforced in the past, but rather because after watching her mother do it, she expects it would be 'fun' for her to do so too.

Vicarious learning is better known as observational learning, which is learning through observing the kinds of consequence that others (called models) experience as a result of their behaviour. **Observational learning** is a form of learning in which an expectancy about reinforcement is formed merely by observing another's behaviour and the consequences it produces. Your own experience is no doubt filled with examples of observational learning – learning to dance, to make a paper aeroplane, to write italic, and to engage in many other activities. The more complex the behaviour, the more times we must observe it being executed and practise what we have observed before we can learn it well. Learning to tie a shoelace requires more attention to detail than learning to roll a ball across the floor.

Reciprocal determinism and self-efficacy

Unlike many personality researchers, Bandura does not believe that either personal characteristics (traits) or the environment alone determine personality (Bandura, 1978). Rather, he argues for **reciprocal determinism**, the idea that behaviour, environmental variables and person variables, such as perception, interact to determine personality, as illustrated in Figure 14.6. We know that our actions can affect the environment. We also know that the environment can affect our behaviour. Likewise, our thoughts may affect the ways in which we behave to

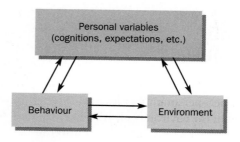

Figure 14.6 Patterns of interaction in reciprocal determinism. According to Bandura, behaviour, environment and personal variables, such as cognitions and expectations, interact to determine personality.

change the environment and, in turn, those changes can influence our thoughts. When our acts of kindness are met with kindness in return, we perceive the environment as friendly and are apt to show kindness under other, similar circumstances. Likewise, when we are treated rudely, we perceive the environment as unfriendly (perhaps hostile) and will be likely to attempt to avoid or change similar environments in the future.

According to Bandura (1982), **self-efficacy**, or one's expectations of success in a given situation, is an important determinant of whether one will attempt to make changes in one's environment. Each day, we make many decisions based on our perceptions of the extent to which our actions will produce reinforcement. Our actions are based on our evaluation of our competency. Moreover, self-efficacy not only determines whether we will engage in a particular behaviour, it also determines the extent to which we will maintain that behaviour in the face of adversity. For example, if you believe that you are unqualified for a job even though you really desire it, you are apt not to apply for an interview for that job. However, if you are confident of your qualifications for the job, you will surely attempt the interview. Even if you are turned down for that job, you may interview for a similar position because you are sure of your abilities. Low self-efficacy can hamper both the frequency and the quality of behaviour–environment interactions, and high self-efficacy can facilitate both.

Related to self-efficacy is the extent to which an individual feels optimistic or pessimistic about their life's circumstances. Seligman and Schulman (1986) have found that people (in the case of their study, life insurance agents) who can find something positive in less than desirable circumstances are generally more successful than are people who view those circumstances negatively. It seems that otherwise cheerless circumstances stimulate optimists to seek creative means of 'putting the circumstances right'. Pessimists are more likely to throw up their arms in despair and to give up. Thus, if there is a solution to be found for a problem, the optimist has the better chance of finding it.

Person variables

Like Bandura, Walter Mischel (b. 1930) believes that much of one's personality is learned through interaction with the environment. Also like Bandura, Mischel emphasises the role of cognition in determining how one learns the relationship between one's behaviour and its consequences. In addition, though, Mischel argues that individual differences in cognition, or **person variables** as he calls them, account for differences in personality. Mischel (1984) proposed five person variables that figure significantly in social learning:

1 *Competences.* We each have different skills, abilities and capacities. What we know and the kinds of behaviour that have been reinforced in the past influence the kinds of action in which we will probably engage in the future.

2 *Encoding strategies and personal constructs.* We also differ in our ability to process information. The way we process information determines how we perceive different situations. One person may perceive going on a date as fun, and so look forward to it; another person may perceive going on a date as potentially boring, and so dread it.

3 *Expectancies.* On the basis of our past behaviour and our knowledge of current situations, we form expectancies about the effects of our behaviour on the environment. Expecting our behaviour to affect the environment positively leads to one course of action; expecting our behaviour to affect it negatively leads to another.

4 *Subjective values.* The degree to which we value certain reinforcers over others influences our behaviour. We seek those outcomes that we value most.

5 *Self-regulatory systems and plans.* We monitor our progress towards achieving goals and subject ourselves to either self-punishment or self-reinforcement, depending on our progress. We also modify and formulate plans regarding how we feel a goal can best be achieved.

Mischel's view is a dynamic one – people's thoughts and behaviours are undergoing constant change as they interact with the environment. New plans are made and old ones reformulated; people adjust their actions in accordance with their competences, subjective values and expectancies of behaviour–environment interactions. This is taken up in the Controversies in Psychological Science section.

Locus of control

Other social learning theorists, such as Julian Rotter (b. 1916), have argued that the extent to which one perceives oneself to be in control of particular situations is also an important element of personality. **Locus of control** refers to whether one believes that the consequences of one's actions are controlled by internal, person variables or by external, environmental variables (Rotter, 1954, 1966). A person who expects to control their own fate – or, more technically, who perceives that rewards are dependent upon their own behaviour – has an internal locus of control. A person who sees their life as

Controversies in Psychological Science – Do traits or situations best predict behaviour?

The evidence

Social learning theorists stress the importance of the environment to behaviour and place less emphasis on the role of personality traits. They argue that the situation often plays a strong role in determining behaviour. In contrast, trait theorists argue that personality traits are stable characteristics of individuals and that knowing something about these traits permits us to predict an individual's behaviour. Which of these views is correct? Is there a correct view?

see activity on mypsychlab

The issue

Mischel (1968, 1976) has suggested that stable personality traits do not exist – or if they do, they are of little importance. Situations, not traits, best predict behaviour. He asks us to consider two situations: a party to celebrate someone's winning a large sum of money and a funeral. People will be much more talkative, cheerful and outgoing at the party than at the funeral. How much will knowing a person's score on a test of intraversion–extraversion enable you to predict whether he or she will be talkative and outgoing? In this case, knowing the situation has much more predictive value than knowing the test score.

Mischel cites several studies in support of his position. One of the first of these studies was performed over 70 years ago. Hartshorne and May (1928) designed a set of behavioural tests to measure the traits of honesty and self-control and administered them to over 10,000 students in elementary school and high school. The tests gave the children the opportunity to be dishonest – for example, to cheat on a test, lie about the amount of homework they had done, or keep money with which they had been entrusted. In all cases, the experimenters had access to what the children actually did, so they could determine whether the child acted honestly or dishonestly. They found that a child who acted honestly (or dishonestly) in one situation did not necessarily act the same way in a different situation. The average correlation of a child's honesty from situation to situation – the cross-situational consistency – was below 0.3. The authors concluded that 'honesty or dishonesty is not a unified character trait in children of the ages studied, but a series of specific responses to specific situations' (p. 243).

Mischel (1968) reviewed evidence from research performed after the Hartshorne and May study and found that most personal characteristics showed the same low cross-situational consistency of 0.3 or lower. He concluded that the concept of personality trait was not useful. People's behaviour was determined by the situations in which they found themselves, not by any intrinsic personality traits. In a study of personality change following 11 September 2001 (Petersen and Seligman, 2003), researchers made use of the internet to run an online experiment on positive emotion. Visitors to the website were asked to rate themselves on various positive psychological traits, such as bravery, gratitude, kindness, spirituality, hope, industry and so on. There were 24 traits in all. The questionnaire was uploaded in the spring of 2001 and the researchers were able to compare the responses of those who responded before 11 September with those who completed the survey after that date. Over 900 people had completed the survey before 11 September, while over 3,000 responded after that date. The majority of respondents were American.

When responses immediately before and after the event were compared, seven of the traits showed evidence of a significant increase. People responding after 11 September regarded themselves as more grateful, hopeful, kind, loving and spiritual than did pre-11 September respondents. They also declared a greater sense of leadership and emphasised the importance of teamwork more.

Other psychologists disagree with Mischel. For example, Epstein (1979) noted that personality traits are more stable than some of these measures had suggested. He noted that assessments of cross-situational consistency usually test a group of people on two occasions and correlate their behaviour in one situation with their behaviour in the other. He showed that repeated measurements across several days yielded much higher correlations. In a study of his own, a group of 28 undergraduates kept daily records of their most pleasant and most unpleasant experiences for a month. For each experience, they recorded the emotions they felt, their impulses to action and their actual behaviour. The correlation between a person's emotions, impulses, or behaviour on any two days was rather low – of the order of 0.3. However, when he grouped measurements (that is, correlated the ratings obtained on odd-numbered days with those obtained on even-numbered days), the correlation rose dramatically – up to around 0.8.

Although Mischel is sceptical about the value of the concept of personality trait, he has acknowledged that particular personality traits may be important as predictors of behaviour (Mischel, 1977, 1979). He also points out that some situations by their very nature severely constrain a person's behaviour, whereas others permit a wide variety of responses. For example, red lights cause almost all motorists to stop their cars. In this case, knowing the particular situation (the colour of the traffic light) predicts behaviour better than knowing something about the personality characteristics of the drivers. Conversely, some situations are weak and have little control over people's behaviour. As Zuckerman (1991) points out, an

Controversies in Psychological Science – *Continued*

amber light is such a situation; when drivers see an amber traffic light, some will stop if they possibly can and others will accelerate and rush through the junction. The difference between the two behaviours is likely determined by individual personality traits.

Personality and situations are usually conceived of as independent variables, but they are not always independent. In laboratory settings, experimenters assign people to various situations. Here, situation and personality are truly independent. However, as Bem and Allen (1974) pointed out, people in life outside the laboratory are able to exert some choice over the situations they enter. For instance, a party is a moderately powerful situation and tends to produce extraverted behaviours. Introverted people may stay away from parties to avoid situations that encourage behaviours with which they are not comfortable. Similarly, extraverts may avoid situations in which they are alone. The fact that people choose their own situations means that personality traits interact with situations. Emmons *et al.* (1986) found that people do, indeed, show consistent patterns in the types of situations they

choose; and when circumstances force them to be in situations they do not normally choose, they feel uncomfortable.

Conclusion

Acknowledging the stability of personality over many situations and the interaction between personality and situations, most psychologists agree that the original question, 'Which is more important in determining a person's behaviour, the situation or personality traits?' has proved too simplistic. Some types of personality trait will prevail in most situations; some situations will dictate the behaviour of most people. But some interactions between situation and personality require the analysis of both variables. Figure 14.7 illustrates some of the important variables that control an individual's personality development.

Fred enjoys most sports and he enjoys most social activities such as drinking and partying. Sometimes, however, he prefers to spend some time by himself. Are we justified in arguing that Fred has a 'sociability' trait? Or does the situation determine his behaviour?

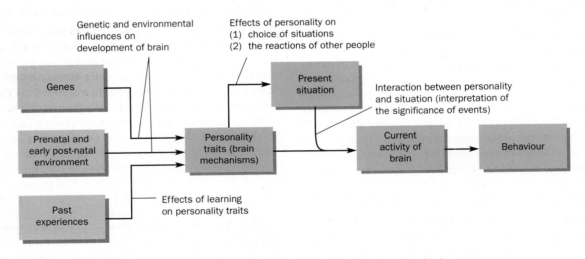

Figure 14.7 Personality traits and the interactions between traits and situations that determine behaviour.

being controlled by external forces unaffected by their own behaviour has an external locus of control, as you can see from Figure 14.8.

Rotter developed the I–E Scale, which assesses the degree to which people perceive the consequences of their behaviour to be under the control of internal or external variables. The I–E Scale contains 29 pairs of statements to which a person indicates their degree of agreement. A typical item would be:

The grades that I achieve depend on my abilities and how hard I work to get them.

The grades that I achieve depend mostly on my teacher and his or her tests.

The scale is scored by counting the number of choices consistent with either the internal or the external locus of

Figure 14.8 Internal and external loci of control. People having internal loci of control perceive themselves as being able to determine the outcomes of the events in their lives. People having external loci of control perceive the events in their lives to be determined by environmental variables.

control orientation. Scores may range from 0 to 23, with lower scores indicative of greater internal locus of control. Of all the populations Rotter has assessed with the I–E Scale, the highest level of internal locus of control was obtained from a group of Peace Corps volunteers (Rotter, 1966).

Rotter's scale has been used in hundreds of studies of social behaviour in a wide variety of situations. Consider some of the findings obtained from research using the I–E Scale:

- People having internal locus of control orientations will work harder to obtain a goal if they believe that they can control the outcome in a specific situation. Even when told that a goal could be obtained with their own skill and effort, those having external orientations tended not to try as hard as those having internal orientations (Davis and Phares, 1967).

- People having internal orientations are also more likely to be aware of and to use good health practices. They are more apt to take preventive medicines, to exercise regularly and to stop smoking than are people having external orientations (Strickland, 1979). They are, however, more likely to blame themselves when they fail, even when failure is not their fault (Phares, 1984).

Psychology in action – Personality and romance

Since the pioneering study of Terman (1938) psychologists have sought to determine which factors contribute to a successful romantic relationship. One view suggests that the more similar two people are, the more successful their relationship. An alternative view, however, suggests that a successful relationship arises from the compatibility of a partner with a person's idea of an ideal mate.

To test this hypothesis, Zentner (2005) studied non-married students for nine months and examined the relationship between their satisfaction with their partner and the partner's qualities (whether similarities or proximities to the ideal partner). The study found that the closeness between a partner and a person's ideal of a romantic partner were better predictors of a satisfied relationship than was the similarity between partners. This gives rise to all manner of questions. For exam-

ple, if we say that we are attracted to people who share our personality characteristics, why does the similarity between the personality of ourselves and a partner play little role in successful romantic attraction?

Another factor that might predict romantic success (its longevity) is family history. The quality of parenting, for example, might influence the ways in which offspring form and develop their own relationships because of the ways in which children are brought up. Recent research examining the effect of parenting style and individual differences on competence in romantic relationships in young mid-western Americans has found that parenting styles that are nurturing are associated with more successful romantic relationships in offspring, even when the offspring's personality characteristics were taken into account (Donnellan *et al.*, 2005).

The psychodynamic approach

The work of Sigmund Freud had a profound and lasting effect on twentieth-century society but little long-term effect on modern psychology. Terms such as ego, libido, repression, rationalisation and fixation are as familiar to many Western laypeople as to clinicians. Before Freud formulated his theory, people believed that most behaviour was determined by rational, conscious processes. Freud was the first to claim that what we do is often irrational and that the reasons for our behaviour are seldom conscious. The mind, to Freud, was a battleground for the warring factions of instinct, reason and conscience; the term **psychodynamic** refers to this struggle.

The development of Freud's theory

Sigmund Freud (1856–1939) was a Viennese physician who acquired his early training in neurology in the laboratory of Ernst Wilhelm von Brücke, an eminent physiologist and neuro-anatomist. Freud's work in the laboratory consisted mostly of careful anatomical observation rather than experimentation. Careful observation also characterised his later work with human behaviour; he made detailed observations of individual patients and attempted to draw inferences about the structure of the human psyche from these cases.

Freud left Vienna briefly and studied in Paris with Jean Martin Charcot, who was investigating the usefulness of hypnosis as a treatment for hysteria. Patients with hysteria often experience paralysis of some part of the body or loss of one of the senses, and no physiological cause can be detected. The fact that hypnosis could be used either to produce or to alleviate these symptoms suggested that they were of psychological origin. Charcot proposed that hysterical symptoms were caused by some kind of psychological trauma. Freud was greatly impressed by Charcot's work and became even more interested in problems of the mind.

Freud returned home to Vienna, opened his medical practice and began an association with Josef Breuer, a prominent physician. Freud and Breuer together published a book called *Studies on Hysteria*, and one of the cases cited in it, that of Anna O., provided the evidence that led to some of the most important tenets of Freud's theory. Breuer had treated Anna O. 12 years before he and Freud published their book. She suffered from a great number of hysterical symptoms, including loss of speech, disturbances in vision, headaches, and paralysis and loss of feeling in her right arm. Under hypnosis, Anna was asked to think about the time when her symptoms had started.

Each of her symptoms appeared to have begun just when she was unable to express a strongly felt emotion. While under hypnosis, she experienced these emotions again, and the experience gave her relief from her hysterical symptoms. It was as if the emotions had been bottled up, and reliving the original experiences uncorked them. This release of energy (which Breuer and Freud called catharsis) presumably eliminated the hysterical symptoms.

The case of Anna O. is one of the most frequently reported cases in the annals of psychotherapy. However, Breuer's original description appears to be inaccurate in some of its most important respects (Ellenberger, 1972). Apparently, the woman was not cured at all by Breuer's hypnosis and psychotherapy. Ellenberger discovered hospital records indicating that Anna O. continued to take morphine for the distress caused by the disorders Breuer had allegedly cured. Freud appears to have learned later that the cure was a fabrication, but this fact did not become generally known until recently. However, Breuer's failure to help Anna O. with her problems does not mean that we must reject psychoanalysis. Although Breuer's apparent success inspired Freud to examine the unconscious, Freud's theory of personality must stand or fall on its own merits when evaluated by modern evidence.

The case of Anna O., along with evidence obtained from his own clinical practice, led Freud to reason that human behaviour is motivated by instinctual drives, which, when activated, supply 'psychic energy'. This energy is aversive, because the nervous system seeks a state of quiet equilibrium. According to Freud, if something prevents the psychic energy caused by activation of a drive from being discharged, psychological disturbances will result.

Freud believed that instinctual drives were triggered by traumatic events in a person's life. During such an event, the individual is forced to hide strong emotion. Because it cannot be expressed normally, the emotion is expressed neurotically, that is, with excessive anxiety. The individual cannot recall the emotions or the events that produced them because they are embedded in the **unconscious**, the inaccessible part of the mind. Unconscious memories and emotions exert control over conscious thoughts and actions, causing the neurotic symptoms to linger and the emotions of the original traumatic event to stay secret.

Freud also believed that the mind actively prevents unconscious traumatic events from reaching conscious awareness. That is, the mind represses the memories of traumatic events, most of which are potentially anxiety-provoking, preventing their being consciously discovered. He used the idea of an iceberg as a metaphor to describe the mind. Only the tip is visible above water; the much larger and more important part of it is submerged. Likewise, the conscious mind hides a larger and more important part of the mind – the unconscious. To understand a person's personality, we must tap his or her unconscious.

Freud, then, argued that our personalities are determined by both conscious and unconscious powers, with the unconscious exerting considerable influence on the conscious. To understand how the unconscious exerts its control over conscious thought and action, we need to explore Freud's view of the structure of personality.

Structures of the mind: id, ego and superego

Freud was struck by the fact that psychological disturbances could stem from events that a person apparently could no longer consciously recall, although they could be revealed during hypnosis. This phenomenon led him to conclude that the mind consists of unconscious, preconscious and conscious elements. The unconscious includes mental events of which we are not aware, the conscious entails mental events of which we are aware, and the preconscious involves mental events that may become conscious through effort.

Freud divided the mind into three structures: the id, the ego and the superego. The operations of the **id** are completely unconscious. The id contains the **libido**, which is the primary source of instinctual motivation for all psychic forces; this force is insistent and is unresponsive to the demands of reality. The id obeys only one rule: to obtain immediate gratification in whatever form it may take – this is called the **pleasure principle**. If you are hungry, the id compels you to eat; if you are angry, the id prompts you to strike out or to seek revenge or to destroy something. Freud (1933, p. 65) conceived of the id as

> the dark, inaccessible part of our personality . . . We approach the id with analogies: we call it a chaos, a cauldron full of seething excitations . . . It is filled with energy reaching it from the instincts, but it has no organisation, produces no collective will, but only a striving to bring about the satisfaction of the instinctual needs subject to the observance of the pleasure principle.

The **ego** is the self; it controls and integrates behaviour. It acts as a mediator, negotiating a compromise among the pressures of the id, the counterpressures of the superego and the demands of reality. The ego's functions of perception, cognition and memory perform this mediation. The ego is driven by the **reality principle**, the tendency to satisfy the id's demands realistically, which almost always involves compromising the demands of the id and superego. It involves the ability to delay gratification of a drive until an appropriate goal is located. To ward off the demands of the id when these demands cannot be gratified, the ego

uses defence mechanisms (described later). Some of the functions of the ego are unconscious.

The **superego** is subdivided into the conscience and the ego-ideal. The **conscience** is the internalisation of the rules and restrictions of society. It determines which behaviours are permissible and punishes wrongdoing with feelings of guilt. The **ego-ideal** is the internalisation of what a person would like to be – their goals.

Freud believed the mind to be full of conflicts. A conflict might begin when one of the two primary drives, the sexual instinctual drive or the aggressive instinctual drive, is aroused. The id demands gratification of these drives but is often held in check by the superego's internalised prohibitions against the behaviours the drives tend to produce. Internalised prohibitions are rules of behaviour learned in childhood that protect the person from the guilt that they would feel if the instinctual drives were allowed to express themselves.

The result of the conflict is compromise formation, in which a compromise is reached between the demands of the id and the suppressive effects of the superego. According to Freud, phenomena such as dreams, artistic creations and slips of the tongue (we now call them Freudian slips) are examples of compromise formation.

In what many consider to be his greatest work, *The Interpretation of Dreams*, Freud wrote, 'The interpretation of dreams is the royal road to a knowledge of the unconscious activities of the mind' (1900, p. 647). To Freud, dreams were motivated by repressed wishes and urges. By analysing dreams, Freud thought repressed wishes and memories could be rediscovered. For example, Freud believed that the **manifest content** of a dream – its actual storyline – is only a disguised version of its **latent content** – its hidden message, which is produced by the unconscious. The latent content might be an unexpressed wish related to the aggressive instinctual drive.

For example, a person may desire to hurt or injure another person, perhaps a co-worker with whom they are competing for a promotion. However, if the person acted out this scenario in a dream, they would experience guilt and anxiety. Therefore, the aggressive wishes of the unconscious are transformed into a more palatable form – the manifest content of the dream might be that the co-worker accepts a job offer from a different company, removing any competition for the promotion. The manifest content of this dream manages to express, at least partly, the latent content supplied by the unconscious.

In addition to analysing his patient's dreams, Freud also developed the technique of free association to probe the unconscious mind for clues of intrapsychic conflict. **Free association** is a method of analysis in which an individual is asked to relax, clear his or her mind of current thoughts and then report all thoughts, images, perceptions and feelings that come to mind. During free association, Freud looked for particular patterns in his patient's report that might reveal wishes, fears and worries that the patient's mind might be keeping hidden. For example, free association might reveal, among other things, the thought of beating someone up, an image of a knife, and perhaps a feeling of relief. Recognising a pattern in his patient's report, he may draw conclusions about the client's hidden desire to harm someone and about the reasons motivating both that desire and the relief experienced once the aggressive urge is satisfied.

Defence mechanisms

According to Freud, the ego contains **defence mechanisms** – mental systems that become active whenever unconscious instinctual drives of the id come into conflict with internalised prohibitions of the superego. The signal for the ego to utilise one of its defences is the state of anxiety produced by an intrapsychic conflict. This unpleasant condition motivates the ego to apply a defence mechanism and thus reduce the anxiety. The six important defence mechanisms are summarised in Table 14.3.

Repression

Repression is responsible for actively keeping threatening or anxiety-provoking memories from our conscious awareness. For example, a person may have witnessed a brutal murder but cannot recall it later because of the uncomfortable emotions it would arouse. Freud believed that repression was perhaps the most powerful of the defence mechanisms.

Reaction formation

Reaction formation involves replacing an anxiety-provoking idea with its opposite. An often-cited example of a reaction formation is that of a person who is aroused and fascinated by pornographic material but whose superego will not permit this enjoyment. They become a militant crusader against pornography. Reaction formation can be a very useful defence mechanism in this situation, permitting acceptable interaction with the forbidden sexual object. The crusader against pornography often studies the salacious material to see just how vile it is so that they can better educate others about its harmful nature. Thus, enjoyment becomes possible without feelings of guilt.

Projection

Projection involves denial of one's own unacceptable desires and the discovery of evidence of these desires in the behaviour of other people. For example, a man who is experiencing a great deal of repressed hostility may per-

Table 14.3 Freudian defence mechanisms

Defence mechanism	Description	Example
Repression	The mind's active attempt to prevent memories of traumatic experiences from reaching conscious awareness	Failure to remember the death of a loved one or other highly upsetting events that occurred earlier in your life
Reaction formation	Replacing an anxiety-provoking idea with its opposite	Having intense feelings of dislike for a person but acting in a friendly manner towards them
Projection	Denial of one's unacceptable feelings and desire and finding them in others	Denying that you have negative feelings towards someone, but asserting that person to have negative feelings towards you
Sublimation	Channelling psychic energy from an unacceptable drive into a more acceptable one	Diverting energy from the sex drive to produce a work of art
Rationalisation	Creating an acceptable reason for a behaviour that is actually performed for a less acceptable reason	Asserting that you donate money to charities because you truly are a generous person when really you want the tax relief for the donation
Conversion	The manifestation of a psychic conflict in terms of physical symptoms	A psychic conflict, perhaps aroused by a particular person, causes you to develop symptoms of deafness or blindness to avoid contact with them

ceive the world as being full of people who are hostile to him. In this way, he can blame someone else for any conflicts in which he engages.

Sublimation

Sublimation is the diversion of psychic energy from an unacceptable drive to an acceptable one. For example, a person may feel strong sexual desire but find its outlet unacceptable because of internalised prohibitions. Despite repression of the drive, its energy remains and finds another outlet, such as artistic or other creative activities. Freud considered sublimation to be an important factor in artistic and intellectual creativity. He believed that people have a fixed amount of drive available for motivating all activities, therefore surplus sexual instinctual drive that is not expended in its normal way can be used to increase a person's potential for creative achievement.

Rationalisation

Rationalisation is the process of inventing an acceptable reason for a behaviour that is really being performed for another, less acceptable reason. For example, a man who feels guilty about his real reasons for purchasing a pornographic magazine may say, 'I don't buy the magazine for the pictures. I buy it to read the interesting and enlightening articles it contains.'

Conversion

Conversion is the provision of an outlet for intrapsychic conflict in the form of a physical symptom. The conflict is transformed into blindness, deafness, paralysis or numbness. (This phenomenon has also been called hysteria, which should not be confused with the common use of the term to mean 'running around and shouting and generally acting out of control'.) For example, a person might develop blindness so that they will no longer be able to see a situation that arouses a strong, painful intrapsychic conflict. Anna O.'s problem would be described as a conversion reaction.

Freud's psychosexual theory of personality development

see activity on mypsychlab Freud believed that personality development involves passing through several psychosexual stages of development – stages that involve seeking pleasure from specific parts of the body called erogenous zones. As we will see, each stage of personality development involves deriving physical pleasure from a different erogenous zone. Freud used the term 'sexual' to refer to physical pleasures and the many ways an individual might seek to gratify an urge for such pleasure. He did not generally use the term to refer to orgasmic pleasure.

Freud's theory of personality development has been extremely influential because of its ability to explain personality disorders in terms of whole or partial fixation – arrested development owing to failure to pass through an earlier stage of development. Freud believed that a person becomes fixated at a particular stage of development when they become strongly attached to the erogenous zone involved in that stage. Although normal personality development involves passing successfully through all the psychosexual stages, Freud maintained that most people become more or less fixated at some point in their development.

Because newborn babies can do little more than suck and swallow, their sexual instinctual drive finds an outlet in these activities. Even as babies become able to engage in more complex behaviours, they continue to receive most of their sexual gratification orally. The early period of the **oral stage** of personality development is characterised by sucking and is passive. Later, as babies become more aggressive, they derive their pleasure from biting and chewing.

Fixation at the oral stage may result from early (or delayed) weaning from breast to bottle to cup. Someone whose personality is fixated at the early oral stage might be excessively passive. 'Biting' sarcasm or compulsive talking can represent fixation at the later, more aggressive phase of the oral stage. Other oral stage fixation activities include habits such as smoking and excessive eating.

The **anal stage** of personality development begins during the second year of life; now babies begin to enjoy emptying their bowels. During the early part of this stage, called the expressive period, babies enjoy expelling their faeces. Later, in the retentive period, they derive pleasure from retaining them. Improper toilet training can result in fixation at the anal stage. People fixated at the anal expressive period are characterised as destructive and cruel; anal retentives are seen as stingy and miserly.

At around age 3, a child discovers that it is pleasurable to play with his penis or her clitoris, and enters the **phallic stage** (phallus means 'penis', but Freud used the term bisexually in this context). Children also begin to discover the sex roles of their parents, and they unconsciously attach themselves to the parent of the opposite sex. A boy's attachment to his mother is called the **Oedipus complex**, after the mythical Greek king who unknowingly married his mother after killing his father. For a time, Freud believed that a girl formed a similar attachment with her father, called the **Electra complex**, but he later rejected this concept. In Greek mythology, Electra, aided by her brother, killed her mother and her mother's lover to avenge her father's death.

In boys, the Oedipus complex normally becomes repressed by age 5, although the conflicts that occur during the phallic stage continue to affect their personalities throughout life. A boy's unconscious wish to take his father's place is suppressed by his fear that his father will castrate him as punishment. In fact, Freud believed that young boys regarded females as castrated males. The conflict is finally resolved when the boy begins to model his behaviour on that of his father so that he achieves identification with the father. Failure to resolve this conflict causes the boy to become fixated at this stage. The boy then becomes preoccupied with demonstrations of his manhood, continually acting 'macho'.

Girls supposedly experience fewer conflicts than boys do during the phallic stage. According to Freud, the chief reason for their transfer of love from their mothers (who provided primary gratification during early life) to their fathers is penis envy. A girl discovers that she and her mother lack this organ, so she becomes attached to her father, who has one. This attachment persists longer than the Oedipus complex, because the girl does not have to fear castration as revenge for usurping her mother's role. Freud believed that penis envy eventually becomes transformed into a need to bear children. The missing penis is replaced by a baby. A girl who becomes fixated during the phallic stage develops strong feelings of being inferior to men, which are expressed in seductive or otherwise flirtatious behaviour. For example, she may become attracted to older men ('father figures') and attempt to seduce them to demonstrate her power over them and thereby relieve her feelings of inferiority.

After the phallic stage comes a **latency period** of several years, during which the child's sexual instinctual drive is mostly submerged. Following this period, the onset of puberty, the child, now an adolescent, begins to form adult sexual attachments to age-mates of the other sex. Because the sexual instinctual drive now finds its outlet in heterosexual genital contact, this stage is known as the **genital stage**.

Further development of Freud's theory: the neo-Freudians

Freud's theory created controversy in the Victorian era in which it was unveiled. Its emphasis on childhood sexuality and seething internal conflicts seemed preposterous and offensive. Yet the theory's proposal that our thoughts and behaviour as adults stem from unconscious forces as well as from our early childhood experiences was revolutionary and these were recognised by many scholars as genuinely original ideas. Freud attracted a number of followers who studied his work closely but who did not accept it completely. Each of these people agreed with Freud's view on the dynamic forces operating within the psyche. Each of them disagreed with Freud, though, on how much importance to place on the role of unconscious sexual and aggressive instincts in shaping personality. Four psychodynamic theorists, Carl Jung, Alfred Adler, Karen Horney and Erik Erikson, have been particularly influential in elaborating psychodynamic theory.

Carl Jung: analytical psychology

Early in the twentieth century, several students of psychoanalysis met with Freud to further the development of psychoanalysis. One of these people was Carl Jung (1875–1961). Freud called Jung 'his adopted eldest son, his crown prince and successor' (Hall and Nordby, 1973, p. 23). However, Jung developed his own version of psychodynamic theory that de-emphasised the importance of sexuality. He also disagreed with his mentor on the structure of the unconscious. Unfortunately, Freud had little tolerance of others' opinions. After 1913, he and Jung never saw each other again. Jung continued to develop his theory after the split by drawing ideas from mythology, anthropology, history and religion, as well as from an active clinical practice in which he saw people with psychological disorders.

To Jung, libido was a positive creative force that propels people towards personal growth. He also believed that forces other than the id, ego and superego, such as the collective unconscious, form the core of personality. To Jung, the ego was totally conscious and contained the ideas, perceptions, emotions, thoughts and memories of which we are aware. One of Jung's more important contributions to psychodynamic theory was his idea of the **collective unconscious**, which contains memories and ideas inherited from our ancestors. Stored in the collective unconscious are **archetypes**, inherited and universal thought forms and patterns that allow us to notice particular aspects of our world (Carver and Scheier, 1992). From the dawn of our species, all humans have had roughly similar experiences with things such as mothers, evil, masculinity and femininity. Each one of these is represented by an archetype. For example, the shadow is the archetype containing basic instincts that allow us to recognise aspects of the world such as evil, sin and carnality. Archetypes are not stored images or ideas – we are not born with a picture of evil stored somewhere in our brain – but we are born with an inherited disposition to behave, perceive and think in certain ways.

Alfred Adler: striving for superiority

Like Jung, Alfred Adler (1870–1937) studied with Freud. Also like Jung, Adler felt that Freud overemphasised the role of sexuality in personality development. Adler argued that feelings of inferiority play the key role. Upon birth, we are dependent on others for survival. As we mature, we encounter people who are more gifted than we are in almost every aspect of life. The inferiority we feel may be social, intellectual, physical or athletic. These feelings create tension that motivates us to compensate for the deficiency. Emerging from this need to compensate is a striving for superiority, which Adler believed to be the major motivational force in life.

According to Adler (1939), **striving for superiority** is affected by another force, social interest, which is an innate desire to contribute to society. Social interest is not wholly instinctual though, because it can be influenced by experience. Although individuals have a need to seek personal superiority, they have a greater desire to sacrifice for causes that benefit society as a whole. Thus, while Freud believed that people act in their own self-interest, motivated by the id, Adler believed that people desire to help others, directed by social interest.

Karen Horney: The Flight of the Vagina

Karen Horney (pronounced 'horn-eye'; 1885–1952), like other Freudian dissenters, did not believe that sex and aggression are the primary themes of personality. She did agree with Freud, though, that anxiety is a basic problem that people must address and overcome.

According to Horney, individuals suffer from basic anxiety caused by insecurities in relationships. People often feel alone, helpless or uncomfortable in their interactions with others. For example, a person who begins a new job is often unsure of how to perform their duties, whom to ask for help, and how to approach their new colleagues. Horney theorised that to deal with basic anxiety, the individual has three options (Horney, 1950):

1 *Moving towards others.* Accept the situation and become dependent on others. This strategy may entail an exaggerated desire for approval or affection.

2 *Moving against others.* Resist the situation and become aggressive. This strategy may involve an exaggerated need for power, exploitation of others, recognition or achievement.

3 *Moving away from others.* Withdraw from others and become isolated. This strategy may involve an exaggerated need for self-sufficiency, privacy or independence.

Horney believed that these three strategies corresponded to three basic orientations with which people approach their life. These **basic orientations** reflect different personality characteristics. The self-effacing solution corresponds to the moving towards others strategy and involves the desire to be loved. The self-expansive solution corresponds to the moving against others strategy and involves the desire to master oneself. The resignation solution corresponds to the moving away strategy and involves striving to be independent of others.

Horney maintained that personality is a mixture of the three strategies and basic orientations. As the source of anxiety varies from one situation to the next, so may the strategy and basic orientation that is used to cope with it. Like Adler, Horney thought environmental variables influenced personality development. In her view, outlined in her book, *The Flight of the Vagina*, in order to understand personality one must consider not only psychodynamic forces within the mind, but also the environmental conditions to which those forces are reacting.

Erik Erikson: identity crisis

Erik Erikson (1902–94) studied with Anna Freud, Sigmund Freud's daughter. He emphasised social aspects of personality development rather than biological factors. He also differed from Freud about the timing of personality development. For Freud, the most important development occurs during early childhood. Erikson emphasised the ongoing process of development throughout the lifespan. Erikson proposed that people's personality traits develop as a result of a series of crises they encounter in their social relations with other people. Because these crises continue throughout life, psychosocial development does not end when people become adults.

Erikson's theory of lifelong development has been very influential, and his term 'identity crisis' has become a familiar one. However, because his theory does not make many empirically testable predictions, it has received little empirical support.

Evaluation of psychodynamic theory and research

Freud's psychodynamic theory has had a profound effect on psychological theory, psychotherapy and literature. His writing, although nowadays regarded as sexist, is lively and stimulating, and his ideas have provided many people with food for thought. However, his theory has received little empirical support, mainly because he used concepts that are poorly defined and that cannot be observed directly. How is one to study the ego, the superego or the id? How can one prove (or disprove) that an artist's creativity is the result of a displaced aggressive or sexual instinctual drive? The writings of the neo-Freudians have had even less influence on modern research. Although the theories of Jung, Adler, Horney and Erikson have their followers, scientific research on personality has largely ignored them.

The emphasis by Freud and his followers on the potentially harmful effects of particular types of childhood environment has led some psychotherapists to conclude that their patients' maladjustments and mental disorders are, by and large, caused by their parents. Many parents have blamed themselves for their children's disorders and have suffered feelings of severe guilt. But many forms of mental disorders – particularly the most serious ones – are largely a result of heredity and are not affected much by family environment. Hence, the teachings of Freud and his followers have compounded the tragedy of mental illness by causing parents to be accused unjustly of poor parenting practices.

The one Freudian phenomenon that has undergone experimental testing is repression. This phenomenon is very important to Freud's theory because it is one of the primary ego defences and because it operates by pushing memories (or newly perceived stimuli) into the unconscious. Thus, experimental verification of repression would lend some support to Freud's notions of intrapsychic conflict and the existence of the unconscious.

The results of research on repression have not been conclusive. Typically, the researchers in repression experiments ask participants to learn some material associated with an unpleasant, ego-threatening situation, and they then compare their memory for the information with that of participants who learned the material under non-threatening conditions. If repression occurs, the threatened participants should remember less of the material than the non-threatened participants will. Some studies have reported positive results, but later experiments have shown that other, non-Freudian phenomena could explain them more easily (D'Zurilla, 1965). Perhaps the most important point here is that none of the experiments can really be said to have threatened the participants' egos, producing the level of anxiety that would lead to the activation of a defence mechanism. Any experimental procedure that did so would probably be unethical. Thus, it is difficult to test even the most specific prediction of Freud's theory. It is very hard, perhaps impossible, to prove that a person's behaviour and personality are products of unconscious conflicts. If a person admits to their sexual urges, psychoanalytic thinking would accept this as fitting the theory; if they deny them, they are repressing these urges and denying their existence. Can you see a problem here in scientifically accepting psychoanalytic explanations of personality?

The humanistic approach

The **humanistic approach** to the study of personality seeks to emphasise the positive, fulfilling elements of life. Humanistic psychologists are interested in nurturing personal growth, life satisfaction and positive human values. They believe that people are innately good and have an internal drive for **self-actualisation** – the realisation of one's true intellectual and emotional potential. The two most influential humanistic theorists have been Abraham Maslow and Carl Rogers.

Maslow and self-actualisation

For both Freud and Abraham Maslow (1908–70), motivation is one of the central aspects of personality. However, where Freud saw strong instinctual urges generating tensions that could not be completely resolved, Maslow saw positive impulses that could be easily overwhelmed by the negative forces within one's culture. According to Maslow (1970), human motivation is based on a hierarchy of needs. Our motivation for different activities passes through several levels, with entrance to subsequent levels dependent on first satisfying needs in previous levels, as illustrated by Figure 14.9. If an individual's needs are not met, they cannot scale the hierarchy and so will fail to attain their true potential.

In Maslow's view, understanding personality requires understanding this hierarchy. Our most basic needs are physiological needs, including the need for food, water, oxygen, rest and so on. Until these needs are met, we cannot be motivated by needs found in the next level (or any other level). If our physiological needs are met, we find ourselves motivated by safety needs, including the need for security and comfort, as well as for peace and freedom from fear. Once the basic survival and safety needs are met, we can become motivated by attachment needs, the need to love and to be loved, to have friends and to be a friend. Next, we seek to satisfy esteem needs – to be competent and recognised as such. You are probably beginning to get the picture: we are motivated to achieve needs higher in the hierarchy only after first satisfying lower needs. If we are able to lead a life in which we have been able to provide ourselves with food and shelter and to surround ourselves with love, we are free to pursue self-actualisation.

Maslow based his theory partially on his own assumptions about human potential and partially on his case studies of historical figures whom he believed to be self-actualised, including Albert Einstein, Eleanor Roosevelt, Henry David Thoreau and Abraham Lincoln. Maslow examined the lives of each of these people in order to assess the common qualities that led each to become self-actualised. In general, he found that these individuals were very self-accepting of themselves and of their lives' circumstances, were focused on finding solutions to pressing cultural problems rather than to personal problems, were open to others' opinions and ideas, were spontaneous in their emotional reactions to events in their lives, had strong senses of privacy, autonomy, human values and appreciation of life, and had a few intimate friendships rather than many superficial ones.

Maslow (1964) believed that the innate drive for self-actualisation is not specific to any particular culture. He

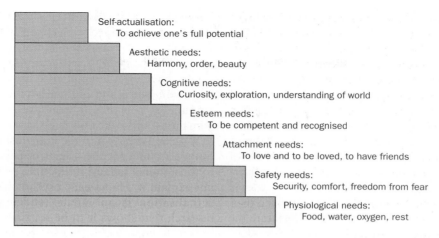

Figure 14.9 Maslow's hierarchy of needs. According to Maslow, every person's goal is to become self-actualised. In order to achieve this goal, individuals must first satisfy several basic needs.

viewed it as being a fundamental part of human nature. In his words, 'Man has a higher and transcendent nature, and this is part of his essence . . . his biological nature of a species which has evolved' (p. xvi).

Rogers and conditions of worth

Carl Rogers (1902–87) also believed that people are motivated to grow psychologically, aspiring to higher levels of fulfilment as they progress towards self-actualisation (Rogers, 1961). Like Maslow, Rogers believed that people are inherently good and have an innate desire for becoming better. Rogers, though, did not view personality development in terms of satisfying a hierarchy of needs. Instead, he believed that personality development centres on one's self-concept, or one's opinion of oneself, and on the way one is treated by others.

Rogers argued that all people have a need for positive regard, or approval, warmth, love, respect and affection flowing from others. Young children, in particular, show this need when they seek approval for their actions from parents and siblings. In Rogers's view, children often want others to like them to the extent that gaining positive regard is a major focus of their lives. The key to developing a psychologically healthy personality, though, is to develop a positive self-concept or image of oneself. How does one do this? Rogers's answer is that we are happy if we feel that others are happy with us. Likewise, we are also unhappy with ourselves when others are disappointed in or unsatisfied with us.

Thus, our feelings towards ourselves depend to a large extent on what others think of us. As children, we learn that there exist certain conditions or criteria that must be met before others give us positive regard. Rogers called these criteria **conditions of worth**.

Positive regard is often conditional. For example, parents may act approvingly towards their young child when he helps in the kitchen or in the garden but not when he pinches his younger sister or tells a lie. The boy learns that what others think of him depends on his actions. Soon, too, he may come to view himself as others view him and his behaviour: 'People like me when I do something good and they don't like me when I do something bad.'

Although conditions of worth are a necessary part of the socialisation process, they can have negative effects on personality development if satisfying them becomes the individual's major ambition. As long as the individual focuses chiefly on seeking positive regard from others, they may ignore other aspects of life, especially those that lead to positive personality growth. In Rogers's view, then, conditions of worth may stand in the way of self-actualisation. An individual may devote her life to satisfying the expectations and demands of others in lieu of working towards realising her potential. In this sense, the need for positive regard may smother an individual's progress towards self-actualisation.

According to Rogers, the solution to this problem is **unconditional positive regard,** or love and acceptance that has no strings attached. In a family setting, this means that parents may establish rules and expect their children to obey them, unless doing so would compromise the children's feelings of worth and self-respect. For example, if a child misbehaves, the parents should focus on the child's behaviour and not the child. In this way, the child learns that her behaviour is wrong but that her parents still love her. Unconditional positive regard allows people to work towards realising their potential unfettered by what others think of them.

In developing his theory, Rogers used unstructured interviews in which the client, not the therapist, directed the course of the conversation. He believed that if the therapist provided an atmosphere of unconditional positive regard, a client would eventually reveal their true self, the kind of person they now are, as well as their ideal self, the kind of person that they would like to become. Rogers also gave the Q sort test to many of his clients. This test consists of a variety of cards, each of which contains a statement such as 'I am generally an optimistic person' or 'I am generally an intolerant person'. The client's task is to sort the cards into several piles that vary in degree from 'least like me' to 'most like me'. The client sorts the cards twice, first on the basis of their real self and next in terms of their ideal self. The difference between the arrangement of the cards in the piles is taken as an index of how close the client is to reaching their ideal self. Rogers's goal as a therapist was to facilitate the client's becoming their ideal self. Rogers's approach to therapy is discussed in more detail in Chapter 18.

Evaluation of the humanistic approach

The humanistic approach is impressive because of its emphasis on people seeking a healthy well-being. Indeed, the approach has wide appeal to those who seek an alternative to the more mechanistic and strictly biologically or environmentally determined views of human nature. However, critics point up two closely related problems with this approach.

First, many of the concepts used by humanistic psychologists are defined subjectively and so are difficult to test empirically. For example, how might we empirically examine the nature of self-actualisation? Few published studies have even attempted to answer this question. By now, you know the hallmark of a good theory – the amount of research it generates. On this count, the humanistic approach comes up short.

A second criticism of the humanistic approach is that it cannot account for the origins of personality. It is subject to the **nominal fallacy**; it describes personality, but it does not explain it. Humanistic psychologists believe that self-actualisation is an innate tendency, but there is no research that shows it to be so. Conditions of worth are said to hamper a child's quest for self-actualisation and thus to alter the course of personality development away from positive psychological growth. However, the humanistic approach provides no objective explanation of this process. Although the humanistic approach may offer a positive view of human nature and give apparent purpose to life, this view is largely unsubstantiated. Before moving on to the next section, take time to look at Table 14.4 which summarises the major theories of personality we have discussed so far.

Table 14.4 A summary of the major personality theories

Theory	Primary figures	Primary emphases	Primary strengths	Primary limitations
Trait	Allport, Cattell, Eysenck	An individual's traits determine personality	Focuses on stability of behaviour over long periods; attemps to measure traits objectively	Largely descriptive; ignores situational variables that may affect behaviour
Psychobiological	Eysenck, Zuckerman	The role of genetics and the brain and nervous system in personality development	Emphasis on the interaction of biology and environment in determining personality; rigorous empirical approach	Reliance on correlation methods in determining the role of genetics in personality
Social learning	Bandura, Mischel, Rotter	Personality is determined by both the consequences of behaviour and our perception of them	Focuses on direct study of behaviour and stresses rigorous experimentation	Ignores biological influences on personality development; often more descriptive than explanatory
Psychodynamic	Freud, Jung, Adler, Horney, Erikson	Unconsious psychic conflicts; repression of anxiety-provoking ideas and desires	The idea that behaviour may be influenced by forces outside conscious awareness	Basic concepts are not empiracally testable
Humanistic	Maslow, Rogers	Stresses the positive aspects of human nature and how to become a better person	Useful in therapeutic settings	Contains vague and untestable concepts; primarily descriptive

Assessment of personality

Think for a moment of your best friend. What is he or she like? Outgoing? Impulsive? Thoughtful? Moody? You can easily respond yes or no to these alternatives because you have spent enough time with your friend to know him or her quite well. After all, one of the best ways to get to know people – what they are like and how they react in certain situations – is to spend time with them. Obviously, psychologists do not have the luxury of spending large amounts of time with people in order to learn about their personalities. Generally, they have only a short period to accomplish this goal. From this necessity, personality tests were first developed. The underlying assumption of any personality test is that personality characteristics can be measured. This final section of the chapter describes the two main types of personality test: objective tests and projective tests.

Objective tests of personality

see activity on mypsychlab

Objective personality tests are similar in structure to classroom tests. Most contain multiple-choice and true/false items, although some allow the person taking the test to indicate the extent to which they agree or disagree with an item. The responses that subjects can make on objective tests are constrained by the test design. The questions asked are unambiguous, and explicit rules for scoring the subjects' responses can be specified in advance. Examples include the Eysenck Personality Inventory and the NEO-PI, described earlier.

One of the oldest and most widely used objective tests of personality is the **Minnesota Multiphasic Personality Inventory (MMPI)**, devised by Hathaway and McKinley in 1939. The original purpose for developing the test was to produce an objective, reliable method for identifying various personality traits that were related to a person's mental health. Improvement in people's scores over the course of treatment would indicate that the treatment was successful.

In devising this test, Hathaway and McKinley wrote 504 true/false items and administered the test to several groups of people in mental institutions in Minnesota who had been diagnosed as having certain psychological disorders. These diagnoses had been arrived at through psychiatric interviews with the patients. Such interviews are expensive, so a simple paper-and-pencil test that accomplished the same result would be valuable. The control group consisted of relatives and friends of the patients, who were tested when they came to visit them. (Whether these people constituted the best possible group

of normal participants is questionable.) The responses were analysed empirically, and the questions that correlated with various diagnostic labels were included in various scales. For example, if people who had been diagnosed as paranoid tended to say true to 'I believe I am being plotted against', this statement would become part of the paranoia scale.

The current revised version of the MMPI, the MMPI-2, has norms based on a sample of people that is much more representative ethnically and geographically than the original sample (Graham, 1990). It includes 550 questions, grouped into ten clinical scales and four validity scales. A particular item can be used on more than one scale. For example, both people who are depressed and those who are hypochondriacal tend to agree that they have gastrointestinal problems. The clinical scales include a number of diagnostic terms traditionally used to label psychiatric patients, such as hypochondriasis, depression or paranoia.

The four validity scales were devised to provide the tester with some assurance that subjects are answering questions reliably and accurately and that they can read the questions and pay attention to them. The '?' scale ('cannot say') is simply the number of questions not answered. A high score on this scale indicates either that the person finds some questions irrelevant or that the person is evading issues that they find painful.

The L scale (lie) contains items such as 'I do not read every editorial in the newspaper every day' and 'My table manners are not quite as good at home as when I am out in company'. A person who disagrees with questions like these is almost certainly not telling the truth. A high score on the L scale suggests the need for caution in interpreting other scales and also reveals something about the participant's personality. In particular, people who score high on this scale tend to be rather naive; more sophisticated people realise that no one is perfect and do not try to make themselves appear to be so.

The F scale (frequency) consists of items that are answered one way by at least 90 per cent of the normal population. The usual responses are 'false' to items such as 'I can easily make other people afraid of me, and sometimes do it for the fun of it', and 'true' to items such as 'I am liked by most people who know me'. A high score on this scale indicates carelessness, poor reading ability or very unusual personality traits.

The K scale (defensiveness) was devised to identify people who are trying to hide their feelings to guard against internal conflicts that might cause them emotional distress. A person receives a high value on the K scale by answering 'false' to statements such as 'Criticism or scolding hurts me terribly' and 'At periods, my mind seems to work more slowly than usual'. People who score very low on this scale tend to be in need of help or to be unusually immune to criticism and social influences.

Some psychologists argue that validity scales are useless or even harmful in most testing situations. For example, consider the following item: 'Before voting, I thoroughly investigate the qualifications of all candidates'. According to Crowne and Marlowe (1964), anyone who answers 'yes' to such a question has to be lying. But as McCrae and Costa (1990) note, people taking tests do not necessarily respond passively to each item, taking it at face value. Instead, their response is based on their interpretation of what they think the question means. They suggest (p. 40) that most people will say to themselves:

> Surely these psychologists didn't mean to ask if I actually study the voting records of every single political candidate, from President to dogcatcher. No one does, so that would be a stupid question to ask. What they must have meant to ask was whether I am a concerned citizen who takes voting seriously. Since I am and I do, I guess I should answer yes.

There is evidence to support McCrae and Costa's suggestion. When psychologists calculate a person's score on the MMPI, they usually apply a correction factor derived from the validity scales. Several studies have shown that the application of the correction factors to the scores of normal subjects actually reduces the validity of these scores. McCrae and Costa suggest that when the MMPI is administered to normal subjects for research purposes, such corrections should not be made. However, validity scales may be useful in situations in which subjects may be motivated to lie (for example, when a personality test is used to screen job applicants) or in cases in which the test is being used clinically to evaluate the possibility of mental illness or personality disorder.

As well as being used in clinical assessment, the MMPI has been employed extensively in personality research, and a number of other tests, including the California Psychological Inventory and the Taylor Manifest Anxiety Scale, are based on it. However, the MMPI has its critics. As we saw earlier, the five-factor model of personality has received considerable support. Some of its advocates have noted that the MMPI misses some of the dimensions measured by the NEO-PI, which includes tests of neuroticism, extraversion, openness, agreeableness and conscientiousness (Johnson *et al.*, 1984). Thus, these factors will be missed by a clinician or researcher who relies only on the MMPI. For this reason, many researchers, especially those interested in the psychobiology of personality, no longer use the MMPI.

Projective tests of personality

Projective tests of personality are different in form from objective ones and are derived from psychodynamic theories of personality. Psychoanalytically oriented psychologists believe that behaviour is determined by unconscious processes more than by conscious ones. Thus, they believe that a test that asks straightforward questions is unlikely to tap the real roots of an individual's personality characteristics.

Projective tests are designed to be ambiguous so that the person's answers will be more revealing than simple agreement or disagreement with statements provided by objective tests. The assumption of projective tests is that an individual will 'project' his or her personality into the ambiguous situation and thus make responses that give clues to this personality. In addition, the ambiguity of the test makes it unlikely that subjects will have preconceived notions about which answers are socially desirable. Thus, it will be difficult for a subject to give biased answers in an attempt to look better (or worse) than he or she actually is.

The Rorschach Inkblot Test

One of the oldest projective tests of personality is the **Rorschach Inkblot Test**, published in 1921 by Hermann Rorschach, a Swiss psychiatrist. The Rorschach Inkblot Test consists of ten pictures of inkblots, originally made by spilling ink on a piece of paper that was subsequently folded in half, producing an image that is symmetrical in relation to the line of the fold. Five of the inkblots are black and white, and five are colour. The participant is shown each card and asked to describe what it looks like. Then the cards are shown again, and the participant is asked to point out the features they used to determine what was seen. The

A client completing a Rorschach Inkblot test.
Source: Science Photo Library Ltd.

responses and the nature of the features the participant uses to make them are scored on several dimensions.

In the following example described by Pervin (1975), a person's response to a particular inkblot might be 'Two bears with their paws touching one another playing a game or could be they are fighting and the red is the blood from the fighting'. The classification of this response, also described by Pervin (p. 37), would be: large detail of the blot was used, good form was used, movement was noted, colour was used in the response about blood, an animal was seen, and a popular response (two bears) was made. A possible interpretation of the response might be:

> Subject starts off with popular response and animals expressing playful, 'childish' behaviour. Response is then given in terms of hostile act with accompanying inquiry. Pure colour response and blood content suggest he may have difficulty controlling his response to the environment. Is a playful, childlike exterior used by him to disguise hostile, destructive feelings that threaten to break out in his dealings with the environment?

Although the interpretation of people's responses to the Rorschach Inkblot Test was originally based on psycho-analytical theory, many investigators have used it in an empirical fashion. That is, a variety of different scoring methods have been devised, and the scores obtained by these methods have been correlated with clinical diagnoses, as investigators have done with people's scores on the MMPI. However, the validity of these scoring techniques and the validity of the test in general is questionable (Groth-Marnat, 1997).

The Thematic Apperception Test

Another popular projective test, the **Thematic Apperception Test (TAT)**, was developed in 1938 by the American psychologists Henry Murray and C.D. Morgan to measure various psychological needs. People are shown a picture of a very ambiguous situation and are asked to tell a story about what is happening in the picture, explaining the situation, what led up to it, what the characters are thinking and saying, and what the final outcome will be. Presumably, the participants will 'project' themselves into the scene, and their stories will reflect their own needs. As you might imagine, scoring is difficult and requires a great deal of practice and skill. The tester attempts to infer the psychological needs expressed in the stories. Consider the responses of one woman to several TAT cards, along with a clinician's interpretation of these responses (Phares, 1979, p. 273). The questions asked by the examiner are in parentheses.

> *Card 3BM.* Looks like a little boy crying for something he can't have. (Why is he crying?) Probably because he can't go somewhere. (How will it turn out?) Probably sit there and sob hisself to sleep. *Card 3GF.* Looks like her boyfriend might have let her down. She hurt his feelings. He's closed the door on her. (What did he say?) I don't know. *Card 10.* Looks like there's sorrow here. Grieving about something. (About what?) Looks like maybe one of the children's passed away.
>
> *Interpretation.* The TAT produced responses that were uniformly indicative of unhappiness, threat, misfortune, a lack of control over environmental forces. None of the test responses were indicative of satisfaction, happy endings, etc. . . . In summary, the test results point to an individual who is anxious and, at the same time, depressed.

The pattern of responses in this case is quite consistent; few people would disagree with the conclusion that the woman is sad and depressed. However, not all people provide such clear-cut responses. As you might expect, interpreting differences in the stories of people who are relatively well adjusted is much more difficult. As a result, distinguishing among people with different but normal personality traits is hard.

One major problem with the TAT is in quantifying responses, such as the ones above. Often, responses are analysed qualitatively which makes assessing the reliability of the test difficult. Others have argued that subjecting the test to quantitative rigorous examination defeats the object of using the test which is to help guide a clinician's assessment of a patient's personality. However, even here, there are problems in that there is little agreement between clinicians regarding the assessment of the individual's responses on the TAT (Groth-Marnat, 1997).

Controversies in Psychological Science – Are projective tests reliable and valid?

The issue

Most empirical studies find that projective tests, such as the Rorschach Inkblot Test and the TAT, have poor reliability and little validity. For example, Eron (1950) found no differences between the scores of people admitted to mental hospitals and a group of college students. In a review of over 300 studies, Lundy (1985) found that the validity of the TAT appears to be lower when it is administered by an authority figure, in a classroom setting or when it is represented as a test. Lundy (1988) suggests that in such situations, the participants are likely to realise that they are talking about themselves when they tell a story about the cards and may be careful about what they say. Why are projective tests so unsuccessful?

The evidence

Projective tests have met with little success for a number of reasons: (1) there are few standardised procedures because different clinicians can present tests and present different parts of them in different ways; (2) norms are rarely available so that comparisons between how an individual performs and how he or she performs compared to the population cannot be reliably made; (3) the tests have low reliability – people can respond differently on a test depending on the examiner; and (4) the tests have low validity – they do not measure what they purport to measure.

Scott Lilienfeld and his colleagues at Texas, Emory and Pittsburgh Universities have conducted a comprehensive and critical review of the scientific status of projective tests. (Lilienfeld *et al.*, 2000). The review raises some important questions about the ways in which the tests are administered, used and interpreted. These concerns take on added significance when you consider that over 30 per cent of clinical psychologists who were members of the American Psychological Association reported using projective techniques either always or frequently, according to one survey (Watkins *et al.*, 1995), and over 80 per cent used the tests at least once or occasionally.

The most popular of the projective techniques used by respondents in the Watkins *et al.* (1995) study was the Rorschach Inkblot Test. The test was criticised in the 1950s and 1960s for poor standardisation. These criticisms were taken on board and when the test was corrected in the 1970s, detailed instructions for the administration and interpretation of the test, as well as the provision of some norms, were included (Exner, 1974). The correction became known as the Comprehensive System. Despite the improvement in standardisation, Lilienfeld *et al.* (2000) found that reliability continued to be low: clinicians agreed on only half of the characteristics

that the test purports to reveal about the individual (the test involves the clinician rating the individual's responses on over 100 characteristics).

The test also showed poor validity; although clinicians claimed that the test could identify mental disorder, researchers found that it was poor at detecting depression, anxiety and psychopathy. Some studies claimed to show that tests did reveal these disorders; others not: the picture was clearly inconsistent. This highlights the danger in using the test unthinkingly: it could identify people as mentally ill when they are not. Lilienfeld *et al.* (2001) cite a study of 123 volunteers at a blood donation centre who were asked to complete the test: one in six was identified as showing signs of schizophrenia.

The scores they receive on one day are often very different from those they receive on another day. But a test of personality is supposed to measure enduring traits that persist over time and in a variety of situations. The TAT has also been criticised for potential sex bias, mostly because of what are considered male-dominated themes, such as power, ambition and status, used to score the test (Worchel *et al.*, 1990).

According to Lilienfeld *et al.* (2000), the TAT suffers from the same early problems as the Rorschach: there are no standardised procedures (so clinicians can administer as many or as few of the scenes and in any order, as they wish) and no way of scoring the test in a standardised way (clinicians interpret the responses to the scenes intuitively). In fact, the number of psychologists using a standardised scoring system for TAT has been reported to be as low as 3 per cent. The TAT also suffers from the unavailability of population norms and from poor test–retest reliability. Attempts have been made to provide standardised scoring systems for the TAT (Westen *et al.*, 1990) which seem to show that it is good at describing people's perceptions of others, but these attempts may not be sufficiently rigorous to be clinically applicable.

Conclusion

Lilienfeld *et al.* (2000) suggest that we can draw six conclusions from a review of studies of the scientific status of projective tests:

1 the use of projective tests continues to be very controversial and psychiatrists need to be aware of this;

2 people can 'fake' responses on these tests;

3 the techniques are used for purposes for which they were not intended;

4 scoring can be unreliable and poor;

Controversies in Psychological Science – *Continued*

5 norms are either absent or poorly described;

6 the techniques may show a cultural bias favouring North Americans.

If projective tests such as the Rorschach and the TAT have been found to be of low reliability and validity, why do many clinical psychologists and psychiatrists continue to use them?

The primary reason seems to be tradition. The use of these tests has a long history and the rationale for the tests is consistent with psychodynamic explanations of personality. Many psychodynamic and clinical psychologists still argue that the tests are valuable for discovering and evaluating inner determinants of personality, whatever the evidence to the contrary.

Chapter review

Trait theories of personality

- We can conceive of personality characteristics as types or traits. The earliest theory of personality classified people into types according to their predominant humour, or body fluid. Today, most psychologists conceive of personality differences as being represented by degree, not kind.
- Personality traits are the factors that underlie patterns of behaviour. Presumably, these factors are biological in nature, although they may be the products of learning as well as heredity.
- The search for core personality traits began with Allport, who studied how everyday words are used to describe personality characteristics. Although he never isolated a core set of traits, his work inspired others to continue the search for such traits.
- Several researchers developed their theories of personality through factor analysis, a statistical method of reducing a large amount of data to two or three themes or ideas (called factors).
- Cattell's analyses indicated the existence of 16 personality factors; Eysenck's research suggested that personality is determined by three dimensions: extraversion (versus introversion), neuroticism (versus emotional stability) and psychoticism (versus self-control).
- McCrae and Costa's five-factor model, based on an analysis of words used to describe people's behavioural traits, includes extraversion, neuroticism, agreeableness, openness and conscientiousness. There is strong cross-cultural agreement on the first three factors but not on the fifth.

Psychobiological approaches

- Studies of twins and adopted children indicate that personality factors, especially extraversion, neuroticism and psychoticism, are affected strongly by genetic factors. However, there is little evidence for an effect of common family environment, largely because an individual's environment is strongly affected by heredity factors, such as personality and physical attributes.

- Zuckerman argues that extraversion is caused by a sensitive reinforcement system, neuroticism is caused by a sensitive punishment system (which includes the amygdala), and psychoticism is caused by the combination of a deficient punishment system and an abnormally high optimum level of arousal.
- Extraversion is associated with increased amygdala activation when viewing happy faces.

The social learning approach

- Social learning theory blends Skinner's notion of reinforcement with cognitive concepts such as expectancy to explain social interaction and personality.
- According to Bandura, people learn the relation between their behaviour and its consequences by observing how others' behaviour is rewarded and punished. In this way, people learn to expect that certain consequences will follow certain behaviours.
- Bandura has also argued that personality is the result of reciprocal determinism – the interaction of behaviour, environment and person variables such as perception.
- The extent to which a person is likely to attempt to change his or her environment is related to self-efficacy, the expectation that he or she will be successful in producing the change. People with low self-efficacy tend not to try to alter their environments; the opposite is true for people with high self-efficacy.
- Mischel has argued that personality differences are due largely to person variables – individual differences in cognition. These variables include competences, encoding strategies and personal constructs, expectancies, subjective values, and self-regulatory systems and plans.
- Rotter's research has shown that locus of control – the extent to which people believe that their behaviour is controlled by person variables or by environmental variables – is also an important determinant of personality.

- Traits and situations interact: some people are affected more than others by a particular situation, and people tend to choose the types of situation in which they find themselves. People's personality traits directly affect situational variables.

The psychodynamic approach

- Freud believed that the mind is full of conflicts between the primitive urges of the id and the internalised prohibitions of the superego.
- According to Freud, these conflicts tend to be resolved through compromise formation and through ego defences such as repression, sublimation and reaction formation. His theory of psychosexual development, a progression through the oral, anal, phallic and genital stages, provided the basis for a theory of personality and personality disorders.
- Freud's followers, most notably Jung, Adler, Horney and Erikson, embraced different aspects of Freud's theory, disagreed with other aspects, and embellished still other aspects.
- Jung disagreed with Freud about the structure of the unconscious and the role of sexuality in personality development, and saw libido as a positive life force.
- Adler also disagreed with Freud on the importance of sexuality. Instead, Adler emphasised the need to compensate for our inferiority and our innate desire to help others as the major forces in personality development.
- Horney argued that personality is the result of the strategies and behaviours people use to cope with anxiety, which she believed is the fundamental problem that all people must overcome in the course of normal personality development.
- Erikson maintained that personality development is more a matter of psychosocial processes than of psychosexual processes. He viewed personality development as involving eight stages, each of which involves coping with a major conflict or crises. Resolution of the conflict allows the person to pass to the next stage; failure to resolve it inhibits normal personality development.
- Although Freud was a brilliant and insightful thinker, his theory has not been experimentally verified, primarily because most of his concepts are unobservable and, therefore, untestable.

The humanistic approach

- The humanistic approach attempts to understand personality and its development by focusing on the positive side of human nature and people's attempts to reach their full potential: self-actualisation.

- Maslow argued that self-actualisation is achieved only after the satisfaction of several other important but lesser needs, for example, physiological, safety and attachment needs.
- Maslow's case study analysis of people whom he believed to be self-actualised revealed several common personality characteristics including self-acceptance, a focus on addressing cultural problems and not personal ones, spontaneity, preservation of privacy, an appreciation of life, and possession of a few very close friends.
- According to Rogers, the key to becoming self-actualised is developing a healthy self-concept. The primary roadblocks in this quest are conditions of worth – criteria that we must meet to win the positive regard of others. Rogers maintained that too often people value themselves only to the extent that they believe other people do. As a result, they spend their lives seeking the acceptance of others instead of striving to become self-actualised. Rogers proposed that only by treating others with unconditional positive regard could we help people to realise their true potential.
- Although the humanistic approach emphasises the positive dimensions of human experience and the potential that each of us has for personal growth, it has been criticised for being unscientific.
- Critics argue that its concepts are vague and untestable and that it is more descriptive than explanatory.

Assessment of personality

- Objective tests contain items that can be answered and scored objectively, such as true/false or multiple-choice questions.
- One of the most important objective personality tests is the Minnesota Multiphasic Personality Inventory (MMPI), which was empirically devised to discriminate among people who had been assigned various psychiatric diagnoses. It has since been used widely in research on personality.
- The MMPI's validity scales have been challenged by researchers who suggest that most people's responses can be taken at face value. More recently, researchers interested in personality have turned to tests not based on people with mental disorders, such as the NEO-PI.
- Projective tests, such as the Rorschach Inkblot Test and the Thematic Apperception Test, contain ambiguous items that elicit answers that presumably reveal aspects of participants' personalities; because answers can vary widely, test administrators must receive special training to interpret them. Unfortunately, evidence suggests that the reliability and validity of such tests is poor.

Suggestions for further reading

Personality – general reading

Allen, B. (2006) *Personality Theories: Development, growth and diversity* (5th edn). Harlow: Pearson Education.

Carver, C.S. and Scheier, M.F. (2008) *Perspectives on Personality* (6th edn). Boston: Allyn & Bacon.

Cloninger, S.C. (2008) *Theories of Personality* (5th edn). Boston: Prentice Hall.

Costa, P.T. and McCrae, R.R. (2005) *Personality in Adulthood*. New York: Guilford Press.

Gregory, R.J. (2007) *Psychological Testing* (5th edn). Boston: Allyn & Bacon.

Lombardo, G.P. and Foschi, R. (2002) The European origins of 'personality psychology'. *European Psychologist*, 7(2), 143–5.

Mischel, W. (2004) Toward an integrative science of the person. *Annual Review of Psychology*, 55, 1–22.

Monte, C.F. and Sollod, R.N. (2002) *Beneath the Mask* (7th edn). Chichester: Wiley.

Pervin, L.A. (2002) *The Science of Personality*. Oxford: Oxford University Press.

Each of the titles in these two sections is a very good introduction to personality.

Issues and controversies in personality research

Canli, T. (2006) *Biology of Personality and Individual Differences*. Hove: Psychology Press.

Eysenck, H. (1985) *Decline and Fall of the Freudian Empire*. London: Pelican.

Matthews, G., Deary, I.J. and Whiteman, M.C. (2003) *Personality Traits* (2nd edn). Cambridge: Cambridge University Press.

McCrae, R.R. (2004) Human nature and culture: A trait perspective. *Journal of Research in Personality*, 38, 3–14.

Pervin, L. (2002) *Current Controversies and Issues in Personality* (3rd edn). Chichester: Wiley.

Zimmer, C. (2005) The neurobiology of the self. *Scientific American Mind*, 93–101.

Zuckerman, M. (2005) *Psychobiology of Personality* (2nd edn). Cambridge: Cambridge University Press.

Special issue of *The Psychologist* on 'Freud's Influence', 2006, 19, 9.

Journals to consult

British Journal of Psychiatry

British Journal of Psychology

European Journal of Personality

European Psychologist

International Journal of Psychology

Journal of Personality

Journal of Personality and Social Psychology

Journal of Research in Personality

Perceptual and Motor Skills

Personality and Individual Differences

Personality and Social Psychology Bulletin

Psychological Reports

Psychological Science

Website addresses

http://pmc.psych.nwu.edu/personality
The Personality Project at Northwestern University website. This excellent site has links to further reading, personality descriptions, related websites and much more.

http://www.personalityresearch.org/
The Great Ideas in Personality website provides an account of exactly that.

http://www.psychology.org/links/Environment_Behavior_Relationships/Measurement/
A collection of links to psychological testing and test sites.

http://www.psychology.org/links/Environment_Behavior_Relationships/Disposition-Personality/
A collection of links to personality sites.

Social cognition and attitudes

Michael A. Hogg, Dominic Abrams and G. Neil Martin

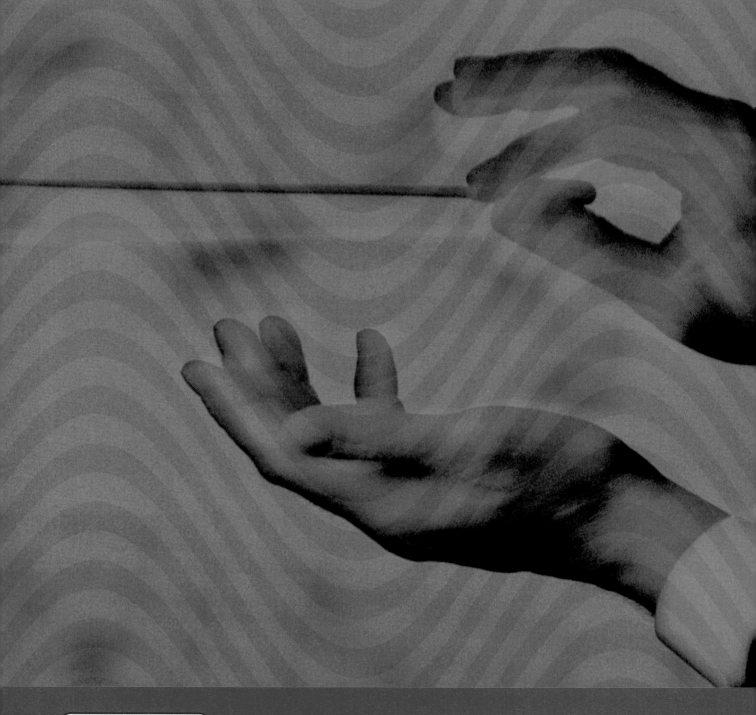

Explore the accompanying videos, simulations and animations on MyPsychLab. This chapter includes activities on: Impression formation • The actor-observer effect • Unconscious stereotyping • Cognitive dissonance • Check your understanding and prepare for your exams using the multiple choice, short answer and essay practice test also available.

CHAPTER 15

'MI5' fantasy conman faces life sentence for deception

Simon Freeman

A conman who wove an elaborate web of deceit – likened to the plot of a James Bond film – was facing a life sentence today after a decade preying sexually and financially on his credulous victims. In reality, Robert Hendy-Freegard, 34, was a barman at the Swan pub near the Harper Adams Agricultural College in Newport, Shropshire.

In the fabulous fantasy world that he constructed around him, he was an MI5 spy on an undercover investigation into an IRA cell.

Using sophisticated mental manipulation techniques and violence he convinced a number of students of his credentials and, under the guise of recruiting them to assist in his pretend missions, took over their lives.

Six were women, all were seduced – he was in sexual relationships with five at the same time – and most became engaged to him. Among the victims was a solicitor, who rated his bedroom techniques '11 out of 10', a psychologist and a pregnant company director.

Source: Times Online, 23 June 2005.

WHAT YOU SHOULD BE ABLE TO DO AFTER READING CHAPTER 8

- Define social psychology and understand what social psychologists do.

- Understand how we process, store and use information about ourselves and other people.

- Understand the motives that influence how we form a conception of who we are.

- Understand how self-concept influences our perceptions and treatment of other people.

- Understand how we make inferences, especially causal inferences, about others' behaviour, and also about our own behaviour.

- Understand how attitudes are formed and changed

QUESTIONS TO THINK ABOUT

- Are the problems facing social psychology different from those in other branches of psychology?

- What makes social psychology similar to sociology, and what makes it similar to neuroscience?

- Does it matter where and when social psychology research is conducted?

- How quickly can you form a mental image of another person? What does the image contain? Is it purely visual, or does it capture something about their personality, group membership, or other 'social' information? How are such impressions formed?

- What determines whom you like and dislike? Why do you sometimes change your mind about a person?

- Why do you use stereotypes and is it possible to avoid them?

- Who are you? Would you answer this question differently if different people asked it? Why?

- Who would you trust to make an accurate judgement about your future prospects: a teacher, parent or yourself? What might influence the judgement made by each of these people?

- Try to persuade someone using a line of argument with which you personally disagree. Is persuasion simply a matter of using the right technique or are there other reasons why this is a difficult task? What tactics do you use, and why?

Social psychology

Most human activity is social. We spend most of our waking hours interacting with, thinking about, or being directly or indirectly influenced by other people. Our behaviour affects the way others think, feel and act and, in turn, their behaviour affects our thoughts, feelings and actions. Not for nothing is the great American social psychologist Elliot Aronson's best-selling book on social psychology called *The Social Animal* (latest edition published in 2007). Human interaction also structures the norms, conventions and institutions that make up the societies we live in.

The field of psychology that studies social behaviour is called **social psychology**. According to Gordon Allport (1968, p. 3), social psychology is study of 'how the thoughts, feelings, and behaviour of individuals are influenced by the actual, imagined, or implied presence of others'. In the next two chapters we explore the way in which people, as individuals or in groups, affect one another. We examine the complex interplay of basic cognitive processes and cognitive structures that we use to process and store information, and the nature of human relations and interactions that occur in everyday life. In this chapter we focus on social cognition and attitudes – how people process and store social information, and how social information affects social behaviour. In the following chapter we focus on social interaction between individuals, between groups, and among people within groups.

Doing social psychology

To a large extent we are all social psychologists but rather than being empirical scientists, we are more like intuitive social psychologists (Heider, 1958). To get by in life we need to have a well-developed understanding of why people behave as they do, what causes particular behaviours, and what effect our behaviour has on others. These common-sense understandings are often quite accurate, but sometimes they are not. For example, we 'know' that 'birds of a feather flock together' (similarity leads to attraction), but we also 'know' that 'opposites attract'. So, which is correct? Many of us may also think that friendship between people from different racial groups should reduce prejudice – but does it? How can we be sure? Under what circumstances is someone most likely to help someone in distress? To get someone to do you a favour, should you first make a modest request that they will agree to and then scale it up to the real request, or should you first make an outrageously large request that nobody in their right mind would agree to and then scale it down?

To answer these questions, social psychologists use a wide range of scientific methods including laboratory experiments, field experiments, surveys, observation of naturally occurring behaviour, and the analysis of what people say and write. Controlled laboratory experiments predominate because they are so well suited to establishing the causes of behaviour. However, some research questions are difficult to address in the laboratory. For example, it would be difficult to study a riot or an established street gang in the laboratory. Can you think of any other experiment which you would think would be impossible to set up (you'll be surprised at some of the experiments psychologists have conducted. . .)? Social psychologists can be quite tenacious and inventive. One early researcher tried to instigate a riot in the laboratory by wafting smoke under the locked door of the laboratory – some groups of participants kicked the door open and disengaged the smoke generator, and other groups calmly discussed the possibility that they were being observed (French, 1944).

Social psychologists develop formal theories about human behaviour that, unlike common-sense theories, are carefully grounded in data from systematic and well-controlled research. These theories sometimes confirm common-sense knowledge, but sometimes they do not, and many theories are concerned with how people develop and use this common-sense social psychological knowledge in the first place.

Social cognition and social knowledge

At the heart of social behaviour is a our ability to make sense of a social situation in order to know what to expect and what to do. We often have ready-made explanations and interpretations of people and situations – explanations that are readily accessible in the society in which we live. In this way, people's social interpretations can vary from culture to culture, group to group, and across time. For example, Moscovici (1976) explored how Freudian concepts, such as unconscious motives, Oedipus complex, displacement and so forth, have become widely accepted and used in contemporary mass culture to account for people's behaviour. These **social representations** of the way people's minds work provide a framework for making sense of the world. This framework develops through many means, such as mass communication, informal conversation, and adherence to prescriptions of scientific and religious movements, and other group ideologies (Moscovici, 1983; also see Lorenzi-Cioldi and Clémence, 2001).

Social representations have far-reaching consequences for how we deal with one another. For example, whether insanity is considered to have a moral, biological, religious, physical or social cause will determine how it is responded to by policy-makers and the public (Jodelet, 1991). When Peter Sutcliffe, the British 'Yorkshire Ripper', was convicted in 1981 in the UK of over 20 rapes and murders he was deemed to be 'criminal' rather than 'insane', and was therefore imprisoned rather than hospitalised. Such distinctions are dependent more on society's current social representations of good and evil, sanity and insanity than they are on objectively measurable criteria. However, as you will see in Chapter 18, criteria for diagnosing mental illness have progressed dramatically since then.

Against the background of particular social representations, values and norms, cognitive-inferential processes affect the way we understand, use and respond to our social environment (Augoustinos and Walker, 1995). For example, Echebarria-Echabe *et al.* (1994) examined how smokers and non-smokers account for the causes of smoking. Two representations appeared to be common: one which emphasised the psychological weakness of people who fall prey to the attractions of tobacco and another (defensive representation) which associated smoking with facilitative social factors and favourable stereotypes of smokers. When the potential conflict between non-smokers and smokers was made more salient, smokers became significantly more likely to adhere to the defensive representation.

Our ability to interpret social situations involves a range of basic cognitive-inferential processes, including memory for people, places, and events; concept formation skills; and sensory and perceptual abilities. Social cognition rests on an array of basic cognitive-inferential processes and on the way in which social information is stored, structured and retrieved from memory. Fiske and Taylor (1991, p. 13) have characterised the individual as a **motivated tactician,**

> a fully engaged thinker who has multiple cognitive strategies available and chooses among them based on goals, motives, and needs. Sometimes the motivated tactician chooses wisely, in the interests of adaptability and accuracy, and sometimes. . . defensively, in the interests of speed or self-esteem.

A central and dominant theme in social psychology has been the development of our understanding of social cognition – how people attend to, perceive, interpret, store and respond to social information.

Forming impressions of people

All of us form impressions of others: friends, neighbours, lecturers, foreigners – virtually everyone we meet. We assign all sorts of characteristics to them. We may, for example, think of someone as friendly or hostile, helpful or selfish. Note that these are terms that not only describe the type of person someone is, but which also critically evaluates them. One of the major tasks of social psychology is to understand how we form these impressions. In Solomon Asch's words, 'How do the perceptions, thoughts, and motives of one person become known to other persons?' (Asch, 1952, p. 143).To answer questions like this, psychologists study **impression formation**, the way in which we form impressions, often first impressions, of others and attribute specific characteristics to them.

Cognitive algebra

One perspective on impression formation argues that our evaluation of other poeple is critically important as it underpins fundamental judgements of danger and safety and thus approach-avoidance decisions. Impressions of people are largely evaluative. This process has been referred to as **cognitive algebra** (Anderson, 1978). This perspective argues that people intuitively represent traits in terms of their desirability: they effectively assign values to traits, e.g. +1, 0, –1, –2), and they integrate the value of traits they assign to a person in order to arrive at an overall evaluation of that person. This information can be integrated in three different ways:

- *summation* – the larger the number of positive traits the more positive the overall impression;
- *averaging* – a limited number of highly positive traits yields a more positive impression than lots of positive traits with many of them only marginally positive (marginal traits bring down the average);
- *weighted averaging* – not only are traits averaged, but some traits are considered more important than others in a particular context and are thus weighted more heavily. Research suggests that the weighted averaging model best characterises impression formation.

Several factors influence weighting. For example, the same information may be weighted differently if you are forming an impression of a potential friend rather than a potential colleague. Weightings of particular attributes may also be influenced by what other person attributes are present. The meanings of specific attributes, and overall meaning of a combination of attributes, may influence the meaning and the valence of a particular attribute.

Generally, although attribute valence is important, so is the meaning of an attribute – when we evaluate someone as 'cruel' we not only evaluate that person negatively, but also know something about their behaviour. These and other considerations suggest people may not form impressions in such a piecemeal manner, but in a more holistic or gestalt manner that places a greater importance on the meaning of attributes. This idea underpins Asch's **configural model** of impression formation.

Asch's configural model

Over half a century ago, Asch (1946) noted that our impressions of others are formed by more complex rules than just a simple sum of the characteristics that we use to describe people. Asch was able to show that when we form impressions of other people, some perceptual features seem to have more influence than others in our final impression. For example, your impression of someone may be swayed by whether people are intelligent or not, and a friend's may be swayed by whether people are approachable or not. Kelly (1955) refers to these idiosyncratic views of what is most important in characterising people as **personal constructs**. In one context, intelligence may be a more relevant dimension than approachability (e.g. evaluating someone as a member of a research team), whereas in another context the opposite may be true (e.g., evaluating someone as a charity fund-raiser). Asch called characteristics that are disproportionately influential in impression formation **central traits**. Central traits are very useful for organising and summarising large amounts of diverse information about a person you encounter.

To demonstrate this, Asch (1946) provided participants with a list of traits describing a hypothetical person. Some received a list that included the trait 'warm', whereas others received an identical list, except that the trait 'warm' was replaced by 'cold'. Participants given the list including 'warm' were more likely to see the person as generous, happy and altruistic. But not all traits seemed to be so important. When the words 'polite' and 'blunt' were substituted for 'warm' and 'cold', no differences were observed in participants' impressions. Kelley (1950) replicated Asch's study in a more naturalistic setting where the target person was not hypothetical, but was a real person who really gave a guest lecture to a class. Kelley found the same results. Students who had had the lecturer described as 'cold' rated him to be more unsociable, self-centred, unpopular, formal, irritable, humourless and ruthless, than did those who had had him described as 'warm'. Our perception of others seems to be based partially on central traits – which can vary from context to context, or from person to person.

Biases in impression formation

What determines whether a trait is central or not? One factor is the order in which information is available or is processed. Research suggests that the first information we process is the most important – there is a marked **primacy effect**. Getting to know someone takes time and usually requires many interactions. Perhaps the first time you saw someone was at a party when she was loud and boisterous, having a good time with her friends. But later, you learn that she is a mathematics student with excellent grades who is generally quite reserved. What is your overall impression of this person: loud and boisterous, or bright and shy? To determine whether first impressions might overpower later impressions, Asch (1946) presented one of the following lists of words to each of two groups of participants:

> Intelligent, industrious, impulsive, critical, stubborn, envious
>
> Envious, stubborn, critical, impulsive, industrious, intelligent

Notice that these lists contain the same words but in reverse order. After they saw the list, Asch asked the participants to describe the personality of the person having these characteristics. People who heard the first list evaluated the person much more favourably than people who heard the second list – a clear primacy effect.

Although sometimes more recent information can be influential (for example, when there is a lot of information and we are distracted), the general rule is that first impressions are most impactful and most enduring (Jones and Goethals, 1972).

The impressions we form of people are also disproportionately influenced by negative information. We tend to pay more attention to negative information, and although we like to think the best of people, bad impressions, once formed, are very difficult to change. By contrast, good impressions can easily change. One reason for this negativity bias is that people are probably especially sensitive to negative information because it can signify potential harm or danger (Skowronski and Carlston, 1989).

It will not surprise you to learn that sometimes there are social conventions and norms (sometimes legislation) that actually discourage us from forming impressions at all. For example, most of us would resist forming impressions based on race, gender or disability, particularly if we were serving on a selection panel for job applicants. People make an assessment of **social judgeability**, a perception of whether there is a legitimate and adequate basis for judging a specific person before forming an impression. Sometimes, merely believing you are in a position to make a judgement (but in reality you lack good evidence) results in your making unwarranted evaluations of other people (Leyens *et al.*, 1992).

Impressions are also influenced by physical appearance. Immediate first impressions, which as we have just seen can be quite enduring, are often based on what we see, because other information about people's 'character' is not yet available. According to Zebrowitz and Collins (1997), appearance-based first impressions can actually be surprisingly accurate. However, there are obvious pitfalls. For example, the tendency to form more favourable first impressions of physically attractive people may cause one to hire people who are delightfully decorative but not much good at getting the job done (Heilman and Stopeck, 1985).

Schemas and categories

A central theme for social cognition is the concept of **schema** – although 'schemata' is the correct plural, social cognition theorists, perhaps embarrassingly, refer to 'schemas' (Fiske and Taylor, 1991). A schema is a mental framework or body of knowledge that organises and synthesises information about something. Schemas contain information about attributes and the relationship between attributes. We have schemas for specific people (for example, one's best friend), groups of people (for example, traffic wardens), ourselves, events (for example, how to order food at a restaurant), roles (for example, how the pilot of an aeroplane should behave in the cockpit), places and objects.

Schemas aid us in interpreting the world. The first time you visited your psychology professor in their office, for example, there were probably few surprises. Your 'professor' schema guided your expectations. However, you would probably be surprised if you saw that your professor's office was filled with skateboarding trophies, autographed photos of heavy metal bands, or dead animals mounted on the walls as hunting trophies. Such possessions are probably inconsistent with your impression of professors.

As an example of how schemas guide our interpretations, try to make sense of the following passage:

> The procedure is actually quite simple. First you arrange things into different groups. Of course, one pile may be sufficient depending on how much there is to do . . . It is important not to overdo things. That is, it is better to do too few things at once than too many. In the short run this may not seem important, but complications can easily arise. A mistake can be expensive as well. At first the whole procedure will seem complicated. Soon, however, it will become just another facet of life.
>
> *Source*: Bransford and Johnson (1972), p. 722.

Does this passage make sense to you? What if I tell you that the title of the passage is 'Washing Clothes'? Now you can interpret the passage easily. The sentences make perfect sense within the context of your schema for washing clothes. Not surprisingly, research has demonstrated that understanding is improved when people know the title of the passage before it is read (Bransford and Johnson, 1972). Imagine a time when you turned on the radio and a discussion or phone-in left you clueless as to the topic being talked about because the exchanges were so vague and generic that you could only make sense of them when the interviewer gave a reminder of the topic that was under discussion.

Categories, prototypes and exemplars

Once you categorise a person (as an individual or as a member of a particular group), the schema of that person or group is activated. Research suggests that schemas can be organised as **prototypes** (Cantor and Mischel, 1979) or as **exemplars** (Smith and Zárate, 1992). A prototype is an abstract fuzzy set of attributes that define the category, where no instance may actually embody the attributes. An exemplar is a specific instance of the category. For example, if your schema of French people is the actor Gerard Depardieu then you have an exemplar representation, whereas if what comes to mind is a general notion of baguettes, cafés, berets, striped jumpers, and so forth then you have a prototype representation. Note that both types of schema are equally accurate or inaccurate as a 'true' description of the category as a whole.

Social categories simplify the social world by reducing an infinite diversity of people to a more limited number of categories of people, each described by a schema – men, women, Catholics, Danes, doctors, and so forth. Categories only form and persist to the extent that they make sense of the world and one's place within it. Of course, any specific person can fit into many categories (e.g. someone can be a female, an Italian, and an engineer), but the key point is that once a person is categorised the appropriate schema comes into play to influence perceptions, expectations and interaction.

Categories vary in inclusiveness. Highly inclusive categories have many members (for example, a nation) and thus tend to gloss over potentially important differences between people. More exclusive categories have fewer members (for example, a family). Although they capture differences more precisely, an exclusive category structure would produce too many categories – it is a too fine-grained segmentation of the world. In general, the most cognitively accessible social categories are **basic level categories** which are neither too inclusive nor too exclusive. Basic level categories are default categories that we first use to generate context-specific schemas of people – these are often based on visible cues such as skin colour, physiognomy, sex and dress (Zebrowitz, 1996). However, many factors, including the social interactive context, our interaction goals, and our own personal history, can influence basic level categories and what categorisation and associated schema comes into play in a particular context.

Schema acquisition and development

We tend to acquire and develop our schemas through exposure to instances of the category – face-to-face encounters, media presentations, second-hand accounts, and so forth. As one encounters more instances of a category one's schema is likely to become less exemplar-based and more prototype-based. Research suggests that such prototype-based schemas can become tightly organised into a single mental construct that is very rapidly activated in an all-or-nothing fashion by category cues (Schul, 1983). Such schemas are highly resistant to change (Fiske and Neuberg, 1990), which can be particularly problematic in the case of schemas of groups.

see activity on **mypsychlab**

Group schemas and stereotypes

Schemas of social groups are particularly significant since they characterise large numbers of people in terms of a small number of properties that submerges the variety of differences that exist between people. Schemas of social groups are almost always shared among people in one group. For example British people often believe that Americans are 'brash', the French think the British are 'cold', and so forth. Shared schemas of social groups are best described as **stereotypes**, and because they are closely associated with prejudice, discrimination and intergroup relations we will return to them in the next chapter (Leyens *et al.*, 1994).

According to Tajfel (1981), such stereotypes are learned early in childhood through normal socialisation rather than direct experience. Research suggests that children's use of stereotypes and expression of negative attitudes towards out-groups peak at around the age of 7 and then decline by 8 or 9 years of age. This may reflect cognitive developmental changes that affect the way children understand the meaning of categories and attributes, and changes in role-taking skills (Aboud, 1988; Durkin, 1995). Prejudice, a topic discussed in much greater depth in the next chapter, usually refers to a person's expression of negative views of and behaviours

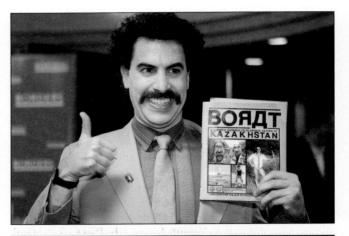

Some of the best comedy comes from caricature – the exaggeration of stereotypes or stereotypical features. Two recent colourful examples are Sasha Baron-Cohen's creations, Borat and Bruno

towards members of an ethnic group that differs from their own (Brown, 1995). A key component of prejudice is the belief that the ethnic or 'out-group' is highly dissimilar to the 'in-group' (the person's own social or racial group).

Language is one important factor that can enhance or magnify perceived dissimilarities between groups and this is no more evident than when comparing different nationalities or cultures (Giles and Johnson, 1987; Giles and Coupland, 1991). Language is a communicative glue, bonding otherwise highly dissimilar individuals. Not only can it allow communication between the in-group members, it can also prevent or inhibit communication with out-group members.

Durkin and Judge (2001) explored whether people's speaking a language that was unfamiliar would affect children's view of them. They reviewed evidence showing that children as young as 4 can show prejudicial attitudes towards ethnic groups (Aboud and Skerry, 1984; Aboud, 1988). While the prejudice 'increases' up to age 6 or 7, there is evidence of a tailing off in the behaviour from middle childhood onwards (Doyle and Aboud, 1995). Children rate people who speak their own 'national' language and in their own accent more positively than they do ethnically different groups (Doyle *et al.*, 1988). Some have suggested that children hold these views about out-groups because they interpret different external signs as threatening and as alien to them. As children get older, they are able to realise – because their capacity for thinking is enhanced – that external attributes can be overlooked and that internal attributes can be appreciated.

Durkin and Judge (2001) found that when children viewed videotapes of foreign families or English-speaking families that behaved badly or not, 6-year-olds judged the foreign-language family least favourably. When the family behaved badly, this placed it at even greater social distance from the children. At age 8, social distance from the anti-social foreign-language family was still significantly great but liking and attributions did not differ between the different family types. These 8-year-olds also placed social distance between themselves and the prosocial foreign-language family, a greater distance than that between them and the prosocial English-speaking family. Language-based differences were all but eliminated in the 10-year-old group, a finding that is compatible with other studies showing that 'prejudice' is less evident in this group.

While the younger children's negative views of the foreign-language family may be due to distrust or to the perception of this family as the out-group, an alternative explanation could be that the foreign-language family was difficult to understand: it was perceived as less likeable and viewed less positively because they could not be understood, not because they were foreign. Alternatively, the children may be motivated to view their own in-group more positively than they did out-groups, because they had a more favourable view of that group, a notion proposed in social identity theory (Tajfel and Turner, 1986). A consequence of this view is that the positive gloss that people place on their own group extends to individuals within that group; the esteem in which the group is held enhances the esteem of the individual. The theory would

predict, for example, that identifying with your nation would be closely associated with an in-group preference for that nation. But research suggests that this relationship is not always evident (Rubin and Hewstone, 1998; Verkuyten, 2001).

Verkuyten (2001) hypothesised that children who have a strong sense of national identification would report greater feelings of self-esteem after positively evaluating their in-group; evaluating the out-group will not raise self-esteem significantly. For those children who do not have a great sense of national identity, it was hypothesised that positively evaluating the in-group and the out-group leads to a momentary feeling of self-esteem. These hypotheses were tested in 21 classrooms in 12 Dutch primary schools. There were 484 children, aged between 10 and 12, all of Dutch nationality and having parents who were born in the Netherlands.

The children were asked what they thought about having friends from different nationalities (Dutch, American, German and Turkish) and, immediately after assessing their feelings about each nation, were asked to indicate how they felt at that moment (on a seven-point scale from 'very good' to 'very bad'). National identification was also assessed (the children were asked how important it was for them to be Dutch, whether they considered themselves to be really Dutch, and so on). Finally, the children were asked how socially distant they felt from other nationalities. The story given was that a child in the class was being frequently excluded socially because they came from another country. The children were asked whether their teacher would do something about it, whether other children in the classroom would disapprove and whether children would report this to their teacher.

Those children who regarded themselves as having a strong sense of national identity reported less social distance between themselves and other Dutch children and greater distance between themselves and children from other countries than did children who showed a low sense of national identity. Changes in the level of esteem, however, seemed unrelated to national identity. Reporting less social distance between them and the in-group and out-group temporarily improved mood. National identity did affect the magnitude of these increases, however. For example, Dutch children with a great sense of national identity and who reported little social distance between themselves and their in-group, reported more positive feelings after rating the in-group. There was little increase after rating the out-group. The children who had a low sense of national identity and who showed little social distance between the in- and out-groups, reported similar positive feelings after rating each group.

The study indicates that the association between these children's views of other nationalities and their perception of their own nation depends on (1) how greatly they identify with their own nation and (2) the social distance they perceive between themselves and children from the same or different countries.

Automaticity of stereotypes

Images of another group (the out-group) are generally less favourable than images of one's own group (the in-group) and provide a relatively positive evaluation of oneself. For example, a stereotype that characterises an out-group as lazy and unmotivated is an excellent justification for an intergroup relationship where your own group has control over that group.

Once someone is categorised as a member of a particular group, the schema of that group (stereotype) influences the impression of that person. For example, if students believe that professors are pompous, boring and opinionated, then once you, as a student, categorise someone as a professor you will automatically tend to assume that they are pompous, boring and opinionated, and that impression will influence the entire interaction. The expectation may even, over a period of time, change the professor's behaviour to conform to your schema (Snyder, 1984).

Like other schemas, stereotypes are relatively automatically and unconsciously activated in particular contexts (Bargh, 1989) – they have the property of **automaticity**. Particular cues (for example, a Welsh accent) can automatically activate a categorisation (Welsh), which in turn automatically engages the appropriate stereotype. For example, in a classic study, Devine (1989) presented people with (negative) African-American primes (words like 'lazy', 'slavery', 'Negroes') far too quickly for people to be aware of them. She found that participants interpreted a subsequent neutral act, by someone merely called Donald, in ways that were consistent with negative stereotypes of African-Americans. Whether someone scored high or low on a racial prejudice scale did not affect susceptibility to preconscious priming – an effect that was replicated by Fazio *et al.* (1995). Other research has, however, shown that the effect is more marked for people who score high on unobtrusive measures of possessing racist attitudes (Lepore and Brown, 1997).

The property of automaticity has been exploited by the **implicit association test** (IAT; Greenwald *et al.*, 2002) which is able quite reliably to elicit our hidden prejudices. The test has been placed on the Web (see address at end of this chapter) – so you can discover if you are prejudiced, or rather, just how prejudiced you are.

Implicit biases or prejudice can be expressed towards various types of people, the obese for example (Teachman *et al.*, 2003). Beachgoers in Connecticut were given a newspaper article which stated that obesity was caused either by genetics, or by overeating and lack of exercise. The IAT was then administered in which participants

decided whether words paired with the adjective 'good' or 'bad' were appropriately paired. So, the pairing of 'thin people' with 'good' and 'fat people' with 'bad' would be expected to be responded to more quickly as an appropriate pairing than would 'fat people' and 'good'. Participants also completed a questionnaire measuring their attitudes towards obesity and obese people.

Although the participants claimed to hold no explicit biases towards fat people, their implicit responses suggested otherwise. People associated 'fat people' with more negative attributes (lazy, bad) than positive ones (motivated, smart). In line with Crandall's (1994) reasoning, this bias was greater when people had been previously primed to think that obesity was caused by controllable factors such as overeating and lack of exercise than by uncontrollable genetic factors.

In a follow-up study, the implicit test was prefaced by stories which evoked sympathy towards fat people, or evoked sympathy towards people who use wheelchairs (what the researchers called a comparable 'stigmatised' group) or were neutral. Ninety women participated at Yale University. Reading empathic stories about fat people did not reduce implicit fat bias, compared with reading neutral stories. When overweight participants were added to this sample, there was evidence of in-group bias. Fat people were more likely to show less implicit bias after reading the empathetic material.

The results suggest that while people may claim that they do not hold negative (stereotypical) views of fat people, their implicit cognitions and behaviour suggest otherwise.

If stereotyping is largely an automatic process over which we have only limited conscious control, what can be done to combat it? One solution might be to make the category–stereotype link more conscious by thinking hard about it and suppressing the stereotype immediately it comes to mind. Over time, stereotype suppression might inhibit stereotype activation. An alternative view, which makes equal sense, is that the more you try to suppress the stereotype the firmer the cognitive or associative link between the category and the stereotype, and thus the more entrenched the automatic activation effect. Macrae *et al.* (1994) call this effect 'stereotype rebound'.

When good intentions backfire: stereotypes, influence and behaviour

A female assistant is working alongside her male boss on a complex decision task. Will he treat her any differently from a male assistant? Research by Vescio *et al.* (2005) examined the idea that powerful men use stereotypes to judge women when the stereotype seems contextually relevant and when they are focusing on the weakness of women in that context, that is, if the task is in an area in which women are stereotyped as weak.

Male and female students believed they were participating in an academic competition involving teams. Half the participants were led to believe that good leaders focused on eliminating weaknesses in their teams; the other half that good leaders focused on maximising strengths. Their task was to select from among four male and four female members those who should represent the team, and assign them roles of team captain, player and non-player. They were also asked to email an explanation for their decision to each member. The results showed that weakness-focused men, not women, used their stereotypes of subordinate women more strongly by assigning fewer valued positions in the group to those women. At the same time, these men praised the subordinate women more highly, as shown in Table 15.1. So these powerful men effectively acted in a patronising way towards subordinate women, denying them an opportunity for advancement but delivering positive messages to them.

Next Vescio and colleagues investigated how male leaders who patronised and focused on weakness might affect the behaviour of male and female subordinates. Being patronised makes people angry but because women tend to avoid overtly aggressive responses Vescio and colleagues predicted that low-power women may respond more passively to being patronised. In contrast, low-power men seemed likely to respond competitively, by endeavouring to perform better. A male leader assigned male or female participants a low-power role as a team member, and then either praised the member or did not, and assigned the member to a valued or devalued position in the group. Both male and female team members reported feeling angrier when they were patronised than when they were not but, as shown in Table 15.2, on a 23-item test males performed better after being patronised whereas females did not. As Vescio and colleagues conclude, leadership styles often focus on eliminating weaknesses, but people are likely to be more motivated and perform better, and

Table 15.2 Performance as a function of position assignment, praise, and participant's gender

	Valued position		Devalued position	
	Praised	Not praised	Praised	Not praised
Female participants	10.48	9.69	9.02	9.99
Male participants	10.00	10.19	11.86	10.5

less likely to be the unwitting victims of patronising stereotypes, when leaders focus on ways in which subordinate group members can promote the goals of the group.

Facing racial stereotypes

Physical appearance is a powerful cue to category membership. For example, we rely heavily on sex or skin colour to assign people to gender or racial/ethnic categories, and then generate stereotypical assumptions about their attributes and behaviours. We can even be quite discriminating in our perception of and reaction to physical appearance cues. For example, research in the United States has shown that African-American prisoners who have more Afro-centric facial features receive more severe sentences than African-American prisoners with less Afro-centric features.

Blair *et al.* (2004) analysed the facial features of a random sample of black and white prison inmates who had been given equivalent sentences. They hypothesised that strongly Afro-centric facial features might unwittingly (or wittingly) influence sentencing decisions. They defined Afro-centric features as being typical of those seen in African-Americans – e.g. 'dark skin, wide nose, full lips'.

The sample comprised 216 black and white inmates at the Florida Department of Corrections and their facial photographs were presented to two groups of undergraduates who rated the degree to which facial features were typical of African-Americans. While there was little difference in the severity of the sentence given to the black and white prisoners, there were significant differences in the harshness of the sentence within the black sample. Those with stereotypically Afro-centric features were significantly more likely to have received harsher sentences than were those with less Afro-centric physical characteristics.

The results indicate that although bias and stereotyping were not evident in sentencing – black and white criminals with equivalent criminal histories were given comparable sentences – more subtle forms of stereotyping were significantly influencing sentencing decisions.

Table 15.1 Position assignment and praise of female subordinates as a function of leader's gender and social influence focus

	Male leaders		Female leaders	
	Weakness focused	Strength focused	Weakness focused	Strength focused
Position assignment	3.79	4.47	4.76	4.58
Praise	4.42	3.84	3.69	3.62

Cutting edge – Sexist humour: does it make you sexist?

People who express sexist attitudes – an antagonism towards women (perhaps, itself, a sexist definition) – tend to suppress them for external reasons rather than internal ones. That is, these views would violate some social norm and are, therefore, not expressed. Sexist jokes tend to re-enforce sexist beliefs. Highly sexist men are far more likely to accept a sexist norm after exposure to sexist jokes: when asked to pretend to be managers who had made sexist remarks to a woman employee, highly sexist men felt less guilty about it after reading sexist jokes than neutral ones (Ford *et al.*, 2001). But can exposure to sexist humour create sexist beliefs?

A group of US researchers asked participants to read a series of scenarios and pretend to empathise with people in them (Ford *et al.*, 2008). In the scenario, participants were told that a discussion has taken place about workmates' favourite jokes. Some of these jokes were sexist (e.g. 'How can you tell if a blonde's been using the computer? There's Tippex on the screen'). The next scenario involved a discussion of views in which sexist beliefs were defended seriously. Finally, a vignette was presented in which the National Council of Women's aims were stated and its request for donations made clear. Participants were asked how much they would give to the organisation.

Highly sexist people exposed to sexist humour were less likely to give to the organisation. In a second experiment, the amount of money participants would cut from the organisation was measured. Sexist individuals exposed to sexist humour recommended greater budget cuts than those exposed to neutral comedy.

Conceptual and historical issues in social psychology

So far, you have seen how social psychologists have studied basic social behaviours such as impression formation and stereotypes. That social psychologists study these topics and in an experimental way owes a lot to the branch's history and development. The empirical study of social behaviour emerged in the second half of the nineteenth century (with a group in Germany calling themselves students of *Völkerpsychologie* – folk psychology – who focused on the collective mind, in contrast to Wundt).

In the early 1900s, America superseded Germany as the powerhouse of social psychology – a process which was accelerated in the 1930s by an enormous influx of leading German social psychologists fleeing Nazism. The ensuing global conflict, the Second World War, then posed urgent applied social psychological questions that created an explosion of research activity that focused on, for example, small group processes (Lewin, 1951), attitudes and attitude change (Hovland *et al.*, 1953), and prejudice (Adorno *et al.*, 1950).

From the late 1940s, social psychology grew prodigiously, in terms of programmes, publications, and profile within psychology. During the 1950s and early 1960s small group research flourished (for example, the study of group cohesion, leadership, communication networks, group influence – Shaw, 1976), as did the study of interpersonal relationships as social exchanges (Thibaut and Kelley, 1959), and the study of attitude change as the resolution of cognitive dissonance (Festinger, 1957). The mid-1960s through the 1970s was characterised by attri-

bution theories that focused on how people, as intuitive scientists, develop causal explanations of their social world as a basis for behaviour (Kelley, 1973).

Generally speaking, there are two camps in social psychology: those who believe that group behaviour is not qualitatively different from individual or interpersonal behaviour (we can call them 'individualists') and those who believe it is ('collectivists'). The debate mostly bubbles along in the background, but from time to time it seems to become a major preoccupation. The 1960s was one such occasion, when social psychology seemed to be deep in crisis (Elms, 1975). Critics felt that the discipline was asking the wrong questions, providing inadequate explanations of trivial behaviours and using primitive methodologies. The resolution of the crisis had two contrasting prongs. Social psychologists in the United States developed social cognition (discussed extensively in this chapter) in a drive for better methodology and better theory (Fiske and Taylor, 1991), and social psychologists in Europe developed what they called a more social social psychology (Tajfel, 1984) in a drive for socially relevant research (for example, the study of prejudice and intergroup conflict) and theories that linked cognitive and social processes

The late 1960s and early 1970s, therefore, saw the emergence of a crisis of confidence in social psychology. Social psychologists were concerned that social psychology was theoretically immature, methodologically unsophisticated, inappropriately dependent on scientific method, and focused too much on individuals and interpersonal interaction and too little on language and collective phenomena. Out of this angst arose a diversity of 'resolutions'. The two most successful are social cognition with sophisticated methodologies and theories that continue to dominate social psychology (Nisbett and

Ross, 1980; Fiske and Taylor, 1991; Devine *et al.*, 1994; Moskowitz, 2005), and social perspectives that focus on culture (Smith *et al.*, 2006), collective representations (Moscovici, 1976), and intergroup relations and social identity (Tajfel, 1984; Hogg and Abrams, 1988).

There is another set of responses that rejects traditional social psychological methods, theories and research foci altogether, and instead focuses on subjectivity, language and qualitative methods (Potter and Wetherell, 1987; Edwards, 1997). Two recent trends in social psychology are evolutionary social psychology (Buss and Kenrick, 1998) and social neuroscience (Ochsner and Lieberman, 2001). The former focuses on the evolutionary and adaptive origins of social behaviours and social-cognitive processes. The latter maps social behaviours and social-cognitive processes onto functions, structures and processes within the brain.

Self and identity

Some of the most significant and influential schemas are those we have about ourselves. Not surprisingly, the self is an important focus for social psychological research – a review published in 1997 found that there had been 31,000 social psychological publications on the self over the preceding 20 years (Ashmore and Jussim, 1997), and journal exists dedicated to the topic (*Self and Identity*).

Self-knowledge

Knowledge about ourselves is very much like knowledge about other people. If you were asked who you were, how would you respond? You might say your name, that you are a student and perhaps that you are also an athlete or have a part-time job. Alternatively, you could talk about your family, your nationality, ethnicity or religion. There are many ways you could potentially describe yourself, all of which would reflect your **self-concept** – your knowledge, feelings and ideas about yourself. In its totality, the self is a person's distinct individuality. At the core of the self-concept is the **self-schema** – a mental framework that represents and synthesises information about who you are. The self-schema is a cognitive structure that organises the knowledge, feelings and ideas that constitute the self-concept.

Social psychologists believe that we have many different selves that can be more or less discrete and come into play in different contexts – the subjective experience of self is highly context dependent. Selves not only describe how we are, but also how we would like to be, called possible selves (Markus and Nurius, 1986). Higgins (1987) takes this idea further in his **self-discrepancy th**[...] guishes between the actual self (how on[...] ideal self (how one would like to be), and [...] (how one thinks one ought to be). The latte[...] guides' which mobilise different types o[...] self-related behaviours. The ideal self engages 'promotional' goals – we strive towards achieving the ideal, whereas the 'ought' self engages 'prevention' goals – we strive to avoid doing what we ought not to do (Higgins, 1998).

How do we learn who we are – how do we form self-schemas? Introspection is one way, but the overwhelmingly social nature of human existence means that we learn much more about ourselves from how others treat us, and from how we think others view us. Research on **self-fulfilling prophecies** shows that others' expectation about us can change the way we behave. For example, Snyder (1984) reports a series of studies in which experimental participants behaved in a more extravert manner simply because others were primed with the false expectation that they, the participants, were extraverts. Expectations constrained participants to behave in a more extravert manner, and biased interpretations of neutral behaviour so it appeared more extravert. In this way participants gradually really did behave in a more extravert manner. Another example comes from research by Steele and Aronson (1995) into **stereotype threat**, which shows that because African-American students are aware of social expectations concerning academic underperformance, they can actually reduce effort and thus underperform.

Social impact on behaviour can affect self-conception because, according to self-perception theory (Bem, 1972), we often learn most about ourselves by simply observing how we behave. If there is no obvious coercion to behave as we do, then we assume that the behaviour reflects the type of person we are (see attribution theory, below). If you notice that you often drink coffee of your own free will you would be forgiven for deducing that you are the kind of person who likes coffee.

In addition to introspection and self-perception, another powerful source of self-knowledge is social comparison. According to **social comparison theory** (Festinger, 1954) people need to feel confident about the validity of their perceptions, attitudes, feelings and behaviours. This sense of validity often comes from the fact that other people who are similar to us agree with us. In this way, attitudes about ourselves may be grounded in belonging to groups of people who have similar views about who we are – views that reinforce and confirm our own self-attitudes.

Orientations of self-knowledge

We are all aware of two contrasting orientations to life – one in which we are adventurous, optimistic and approach-oriented (the glass is half full), and one in which we are more cautious, avoidant and defensively-oriented (the glass is half empty). This general distinction has recently been reconceptualised by **regulatory focus theory** (Higgins, 1997, 1998). Regulatory focus theory proposes that people have two separate self-regulatory systems, termed promotion and prevention, which are concerned with the pursuit of different types of goals.

The *promotion system* is concerned with the attainment of one's hopes and aspirations, termed *ideals*. It generates sensitivity to the presence or absence of positive events. People in a promotion focus adopt *approach-strategic means* to attain their goals. For example, promotion-focused students are likely to seek ways to improve their grades, to find new challenges and to treat problems as interesting obstacles to overcome. Promotion-focused individuals are also especially likely to recall information relating to the pursuit of success by others (Higgins and Tykocinski, 1992) and are most inspired by positive role models, who emphasise strategies for achieving success (Lockwood *et al.*, 2002). In addition, they tend to show especially high motivation and persistence on tasks that are framed in terms of gains and non-gains (Shah *et al.*, 1998).

The *prevention system* is concerned with the fulfilment of one's duties and obligations, termed *oughts*. It generates sensitivity to the presence or absence of negative events. People in a prevention focus use *avoidance strategic means* to attain their goals. For example, prevention-focused students might be more concerned with avoiding new situations or new people, to concentrate more on avoiding failure rather than achieving the highest possible grade. Prevention-focused individuals are especially likely to recall information relating to the avoidance of failure by others (Higgins and Tykocinski, 1992) and are most inspired by negative role models, who highlight strategies for avoiding failure (Lockwood *et al.*, 2002). In addition, they tend to show high motivation and persistence on tasks that are framed in terms of losses and non-losses (Shah *et al.*, 1998).

The two self-regulatory systems can be activated either chronically or temporarily. Differences in chronic promotion and prevention focus can arise from differences in the quality of a child's relationship with a caregiver (Higgins and Silberman, 1998). Caregivers can initiate a chronic promotion focus by, for example, hugging and kissing a child for behaving in a desired manner (a positive event) and withdrawing love as discipline (absence of a positive event). Conversely, a chronic prevention focus will likely result if caregivers encourage a child to be especially alert to potential dangers (absence of a negative event) and punish and shout at a child when they behave undesirably (a negative event).

In addition to these chronic individual differences, regulatory focus can also change more quickly from situation to situation. Situational variability can be induced experimentally through, for example, task feedback or task instructions. In one study (Higgins *et al.*, 1994), students were asked to report on either how their hopes and aspirations had changed over time (activating a promotion focus) or how their sense of duty and obligation had changed over time (activating a prevention focus). The participants read about several episodes that occurred over the course of a few days in the life of another student. In each of these episodes the student was pursuing a desired goal by employing either approach strategic means ('Because I wanted to be at school for the beginning of my 8.30 psychology class which is usually excellent, I woke up early this morning'), or avoidance strategic means ('I wanted to take a class in photography at the community centre, so I didn't register for a class in Spanish that was scheduled at the same time'). Higgins *et al.* predicted that participants would recall better the episodes which described strategic means that were consistent with their induced self-regulatory focus. Consistent with this prediction, participants in a promotion focus recalled better the episodes in which the student used approach strategic means whereas participants in a prevention focus recalled better the episodes in which the student used avoidance strategic means.

One interesting line of research has applied the principles of regulatory focus theory to intergroup discrimination (Sassenberg *et al.*, 2003). Participants with either a chronic or temporarily induced promotion or prevention focus were asked to distribute positive resources (money) or negative resources (withdrawal of money) between anonymous members of their own laboratory group (in-group) and anonymous members of another laboratory group (out-group).

Given that promotion-focused individuals have been shown to be especially sensitive to the presence or absence of positive outcomes whereas prevention-focused individuals are especially sensitive to the presence or absence of negative outcomes, Sassenberg *et al.* predicted that intergroup discrimination would be shown only when the available means for favouring the in-group were consistent with participants' chronic (or temporary) regulatory focus. Consistent with this prediction, participants discriminated under a promotion focus when positive but not negative resources had to be distributed and under a prevention focus when negative but not positive resources had to be distributed. In other words, under a promotion focus, group members focused on approaching positive in-group events and under a prevention focus group members focused on avoiding negative events.

Self-awareness

The above may give the impression that people spend all their time thinking about themselves, but this is not the case. People are not consciously aware of themselves all the time – if people were, then probably very little would ever get done. **Self-awareness** comes and goes for different reasons and with different consequences. Often we just get on with life without being particularly aware of ourselves, whereas at other times we can be obsessively self-absorbed or absolutely mortified over how others view us.

Duval and Wicklund (1972) believe that self-awareness is a state in which one is aware of oneself as an object, much as one might be aware of a tree or another person. Not surprisingly, standing in front of a mirror is a very effective way to become self-aware. Carver and Scheier (1981) argue that self-awareness can have at least two foci: the private self (one's private thoughts, feelings and attitudes), and the public self (how others see one, one's public image). Hence, self-awareness can also be raised simply by being in the presence of other people – for example, giving a public talk or performance. Private self-awareness directs behaviour at matching one's internal standards, whereas public self-awareness directs behaviour at promoting a good impression in the eyes of others. In contrast to heightened self-awareness, reduced self-awareness can produce a sense of **de-individuation** (Zimbardo, 1970; Diener, 1980) that may be associated with disinhibited, impulsive and anti-normative behaviour.

Being self-aware causes one to exert effort to try to address any discrepancy between one's actual self and how one feels one would like to be or ought to be. According to self-discrepancy theory (Higgins, 1987), described above, failure to resolve a discrepancy between the actual and the ideal self produces dejection-related emotions (disappointment, dissatisfaction, sadness), whereas failure to resolve an actual, 'ought' discrepancy produces agitation-related emotions (anxiety, fear).

Types of self and identity

Actual and possible selves can take many different forms. The enormous variety of human existence offers us a dazzling kaleidoscope of different ways in which we can define and conceptualise our selves. However, since selves are largely grounded in human interaction, various forms of human interaction may produce a more limited number of types of self. In particular, researchers distinguish between selves and identities that are grounded in individuality, interpersonal relationships, and group and category memberships.

Social identity theorists such as Hogg and Abrams (1988) and Tajfel and Turner (1986) distinguish between the personal self (personal identity: self defined in terms of idiosyncratic attributes or personal relationships) and the collective self (social identity: the self defined in terms of group attributes). Brewer and Gardner (1996) distinguish among individual self (defined by personal traits that differentiate one from all other people), relational self (defined by dyadic relationships), and collective self (defined by group memberships). From a more cultural perspective (see below), Markus and Kitayama (1991) distinguish between the independent self (self defined as autonomous and separate from other people) and the interdependent self (self defined in terms of specific relationships people have with others). These distinctions are certainly not the same as one another, but there is a general notion that people can define themselves perhaps as I, you and I, or we.

Social identity

Social identity theory distinguishes between personal self/personal identity, and collective self/social identity (Tajfel and Turner, 1986; Hogg and Abrams, 1988). Social identity theorists believe that one's self-concept comprises a large array of different identities that fall into two broad types: personal identities that derive from our close interpersonal relationships (for example, friendships and romantic relationships) and our idiosyncratic characteristics (for example, being humorous), and social identities that derive from the social groups to which we belong (ethnicity, gender, profession, age group). Features of the immediate social context – situation, people, goals, activities and so forth – influence what aspect of the self-concept we experience and use to process information and plan action in that particular context.

Social identities are uniquely associated with group behaviours – for example, the stereotypes we spoke of above, but also other group behaviours such as conformity and discrimination that we discuss in the next chapter. Social identities are attached to group memberships and derive their descriptive and evaluative properties from perceptions of the nature of the evaluative relations (for example, status) that exist between groups. In this way, intergroup relations influence self-conception. Social identity is associated with group and intergroup behaviours because the process of categorising ourselves and others as group members causes us to view ourselves and others only in terms of the defining attributes of membership of the relevant group, called the group prototype (Turner *et al.*, 1987). This causes us to perceive and treat others stereotypically, and causes us and fellow group members to enact the defining features (perceptions, attitudes, feelings, behaviours) of our group.

Self-motives

What motivates the different ways that we may want to conceptualise ourselves? Research suggests that there are three general classes of motivations. One motive is self-assessment – a desire to find out the truth about ourselves however disappointing or unfavourable the truth may be (Trope, 1986). Another motive is self-verification – a desire to confirm what we already know about ourselves, by looking for self-consistent information (Swann, 1987). The third motive is self-enhancement – a desire to find out favourable things about ourselves (Kunda, 1990). Sedikides (1993) conducted a series of six experiments to compare the relative strength of these three motives, and concluded that self-enhancement is by far the strongest, with self-verification a distant second, and self-assessment an even more distant third.

Because self-enhancement is so important, people have a formidable repertoire of strategies and techniques to construct or maintain a favourable self-concept (Baumeister, 1998). For example, they take credit for suc-cess but deny blame for failure; they forget failure feedback more readily than success feedback; they accept praise uncritically but receive criticism sceptically and dismiss it as being based on prejudice; and they self-interestedly interpret ambiguous self-attributes and perform a biased search of self-knowledge.

Self-esteem

The reason why people pursue self-enhancement is because it elevates **self-esteem**. Research overwhelmingly shows that it is adaptive for people to have a relatively positive sense of themselves, there is a positivity bias, and that a negative self-image can be quite dysfunctional (Taylor and Brown, 1988). People vary in their general level of self-esteem. People with higher self-esteem tend to pursue self-enhancement, whereas people with lower self-esteem tend to avoid self-derogation. Using the language of Higgins's (1998) regulatory focus theory, the former have a promotion orientation and the latter a prevention orientation. Although low self-esteem can be dysfunctional, research tends to discredit the popular

---

Cultural differences in self and identity – An international perspective

The same person can experience self in an array of different personal or collective ways depending on context. There is, however, another tradition of research that focuses on enduring differences in self-conception that are grounded in cultural differences (Markus and Kitayama, 1991; Oyserman et al., 2002; Triandis, 1989).

The key cultural difference is between individualistic and collectivist societies (Hofstede, 1980). Western societies such as Britain and the United States tend to be individualistic – they emphasise the unique individual and separateness from others, and encourage individual choice and loose ties among people. Eastern societies such as Japan and India tend to be collectivist – they emphasise group loyalty, relations among people, and the collective good. According to Triandis et al. (1985), collectivist societies are associated with allocentrism (people who value cooperation, social support, equality and honesty), and individualistic societies with idiocentrism (people who strive for achievement, pleasure, social recognition and a comfortable life, and who experience anomie and a degree of social alienation).

More recently, Markus and Kitayama (1991) have identified the key cultural difference in self-conception to be between independent and interdependent self-construal. The independent construal emphasises the uniqueness of the self, its autonomy from others, and self-reliance. Although other people have an influence on a person's behaviour, a person's self-concept is largely defined independently. The interde-pendent construal emphasises the interconnectedness of people and the role that others play in developing an individual's self-concept. In the interdependent construal, what others think of the individual, or do to the individual, matter – the person is extremely sensitive to others and strives to form strong social bonds with them.

Students from India (a collectivist Eastern culture) judge the self to be more similar to others, whereas American students (members of an individualist culture) judge the self to be more dissimilar to others (Markus and Kitayama, 1991). Markus and Kitayama have also shown that Japanese students tend to associate positive feelings with interpersonal behaviours and tend not to associate such feelings with personal achievements. In contrast, American students tend to feel satisfaction in their accomplishments. In a similar vein, comparing workers' intentions to leave their organisations, Abrams et al. (1998) found that Japanese workers were influenced by the evaluations they expected from their friends, family and co-workers, whereas British workers were not.

Vignoles et al. (2000) note that despite cultural differences in self-conception, the need to have a distinctive and integrated sense of self is universal; however, self-distinctiveness means something different in individualist and in collectivist cultures. In the former it is the isolated and bounded self that gains meaning from separateness, whereas in the latter it is the relational self that gains meaning from its relations with others.

belief that low self-esteem is associated with social problems such as violence (Baumeister *et al.*, 1996). On the contrary, violence is more closely associated with narcissism – high self-esteem in conjunction with a feeling of being superior and special.

People may not pursue self-esteem for its own sake. Leary *et al.* (1995) suggest that self-esteem is an internal indicator of social acceptance and belonging – it is a 'sociometer'. The idea here is that the most basic human motive is to belong and to be properly socially connected. Feeling good about one's self – self-esteem – is an extremely powerful indicator that one has succeeded in this pursuit.

Social inference

Causal attribution

As mentioned right at the start of this chapter, we are all intuitive social psychologists (Jones, 1990), using naive or common-sense psychological theories (Heider, 1958) to make sense of our social world. In order to interact with people and get on in life we need to have a basic understanding of how people work – we need to know why people do what they do. This knowledge is essential if we are to be able to navigate our way through life in such a way that we can make good things happen for us and avoid bad things that might happen to us. The most powerful knowledge we can have about people is causal knowledge – if we know what causes people to behave in certain ways then we are able to predict and influence what people will do. For example, most of us know that if we are nice to people they are likely to agree to do small favours for us, and that people who feel threatened or cornered can often lash out aggressively. The explanation of how people develop a common-sense causal understanding of human behaviour is called **attribution theory** (Hewstone, 1989). Strictly speaking, there are a number of variants of attribution theory that emphasise different aspects. Kelley's (1967) covariation model is probably the best established, and so we will focus on that.

Disposition versus situation

In deciding the causes of behaviour, the most important thing we need to know is whether the behaviour is a reflection of the person's disposition to behave in that way or a reflection of situational constraints that made them behave in that way. We need to assess the relative importance of situational and dispositional factors (Heider, 1958). **Situational factors** are stimuli in the environment. **Dispositional factors** are individual personality character-

istics. One of the tasks of socialisation is to learn what behaviours are expected in various situations. Once we learn that in certain situations most people act in a specific way, we develop schemas for how we expect people to act in those situations. For example, when people are introduced, they are expected to look at each other, smile, say something like 'How do you do?' or 'It's nice to meet you', and perhaps offer to shake the other person's hand. If people act in conventional ways in given situations, we are not surprised. Their behaviour appears to be dictated by social custom – by the characteristics of the situation.

As we get to know other people, we also learn what to expect from them as individuals. We learn about their dispositions – the kinds of behaviours in which they tend to engage across all sorts of situations. We learn to characterise people as friendly, generous, suspicious, pessimistic or greedy by observing their behaviour in a variety of situations. Sometimes, we even make inferences from a single observation (Krull and Erickson, 1995). If someone's behaviour is very different from the way most people would act in a particular situation, we attribute their behaviour to internal or dispositional causes. For example, if we see a person refuse to hold a door open for someone in a wheelchair, we assign that person some negative dispositional characteristics.

Kelley's covariation theory of attribution

Kelley (1967) has suggested that we attribute the behaviour of other people to external (situational) or internal (dispositional) causes on the basis of consideration of three aspects of the behaviour: its consensus, its consistency and its distinctiveness (Kelley, 1967; Kelley and Michela, 1980).

Consensual behaviour – a behaviour shared by many people – is usually attributed to external causes. The behaviour is assumed to be constrained or demanded by the situation. For example, if someone asks an acquaintance for the loan of a coin to make a telephone call, we do not conclude that the person is especially generous if they comply. The request is reasonable and costs little; lending the money is a consensual behaviour – most people would do it. However, if a person has some change but refuses to lend it, we readily attribute the behaviour to dispositional factors such as being a stingy or mean person.

We also base our attributions on **consistency** – on whether a person's behaviour occurs reliably in the same situation. For example, if you meet someone for the first time and notice that she speaks slowly and without much expression, stands in a slouching posture, and sighs occasionally, you will probably conclude that she has a sad disposition. Now, suppose that after she has left, you mention to a friend that the young woman seems very passive. Your friend says, 'No, I know her well, and she's usually very cheerful.' With this new evidence about her behaviour you may reassess and wonder what happened to make her act so sad – was it something in the situation? If a person's pattern of behaviour is consistent, we attribute the behaviour to internal causes. Inconsistent behaviours lead us to seek external causes.

Finally, we base our attributions on **distinctiveness** – the extent to which a person performs a particular behaviour only in a particular situation. Behaviours that are distinctively associated with a particular situation are attributed to situational factors; those that occur in a variety of situations are attributed to dispositional factors. For example, suppose that your partner is always very attentive towards you and other people but seems very dismissive to you whenever a particular group of his friends are around. You are unlikely to conclude that he is a dismissive type of person; you are more likely to conclude that this particular group of friends has a bad influence on him. Because his dismissive behaviour occurs only under a distinctive circumstance (the presence of the group of friends), you attribute it to external causes. Table 15.3 summarises Kelley's ideas about the factors that determine internal or external attributions.

Implications and extensions of attribution theory

Attribution theory has a number of interesting implications and extensions. Earlier in this chapter we described how people can learn about themselves by investigating the causes of their behaviour. According to **self-perception theory** (Bem, 1972), if people can internally attribute their behaviour then they have gained knowledge about themselves.

Another intriguing idea, suggested by Schachter (1964), is that the emotions we experience have two distinct components: an undifferentiated state of generalised physiological arousal and a cognitive label attached on the basis of an attributional analysis of what caused the arousal. So, arousal in the presence of a snarling lion is experienced as fear whereas arousal in the presence of an attractive member of the opposite sex may be experienced as sexual desire or passion. If Schachter is right, then there are interesting therapeutic implications – for example, if someone who is anxious can be persuaded to reattribute their arousal to something amusing then anxiety could be transformed into happiness (Valins and Nisbett, 1972).

Schachter and Singer (1962) conducted an experiment that did indeed show that different emotions could be produced by different labels. Participants were injected with a drug that produces arousal and were told that the cause of the arousal was the drug, or they were not told anything. All participants then waited in a room with a euphoric or an angry confederate. Participants who had not been informed of the cause of the arousal attributed their arousal to the behaviour of the confederate and actually reported feeling euphoric or angry. This was a controlled laboratory experiment. Subsequent research has shown that the nature of physiological arousal associated with different emotions, particularly strong emotions, is often different and so the emotions are intrinsically different – emotions may be based less on cognitive labelling than Schachter first suggested (Reisenzein, 1983; Forsterling, 1988). However, anyone who has observed small children will know how easily tears can be changed to laughter by simply doing something funny to entertain the child.

Attributional biases

Although causal attribution is an important way in which people make sense of their world, it is quite clear that we do not rely on causal attributions all the time. If we did then we would be completely immobilised by cogitation. Attribution and other inferential processes help us to con-

---

Table 15.3 Kelley's theory of attribution

Principle	Attribution of external causality	Attribution of internal causality
Consensus	*High.* Person lends coin for telephone call, performing a socially acceptable behaviour	*Low.* Person refuses to lend coin and seems mean
Consistency	*Low.* Usually cheerful person acts sad and dejected; we wonder what event has caused the sadness	*High.* We meet a person who speaks slowly and slouches, and conclude that we have met a person who is sad by nature
Distinctiveness	*High.* A child is rude only when playing with a certain friend; we conclude that the friend is a bad influence	*Low.* A child acts impudently and says mean and nasty things to everyone they meet. We conclude that the child is rude

struct representations and theories of the world, and in many cases simple cues rapidly engage these fully-fledged interpretations. In other words, we often rely on fully-fledged schemas, such as stereotypes, as described in detail earlier in this chapter.

When we do perform causal attributions we are actually doing something quite complex. Formal science is all about understanding the causes of things, and we all know how difficult formal science is. Not surprisingly, lay attributions fall well short of the rigour of formal science. Although day-to-day attributions are adequate for our everyday social interactional needs, attributional accuracy is compromised by the nature of human information processing and social cognition – it is marked by an array of biases and errors (Nisbett and Ross, 1980).

Actor–observer effects and the fundamental attribution error

When attributing someone's behaviour to possible causes, an observer tends to overestimate the significance of dispositional factors and underestimate the significance of situational factors. This kind of bias is called the **fundamental attribution error** (Ross, 1977) or the correspondence bias (Gilbert and Malone, 1995). It also reflects essentialism (Haslam *et al.*, 1998) – a tendency to consider behaviour to reflect underlying and immutable, often innate, properties (essences) of people or the groups they belong to.

For example, if we see a driver make a mistake, we are more likely to conclude that the driver is careless than to consider that external factors (perhaps a crying baby in the back seat) may have temporarily distracted him.

The fundamental attribution error is remarkably potent (but see below). Even when evidence indicates otherwise, people seem to prefer dispositional explanations to situational ones. For example, consider a well-known study by Jones and Harris (1967). Students read essays that other students had either freely chosen or been instructed to write in support of or in opposition to Fidel Castro. The students had to infer the writers' true attitude towards Castro. Where the writers had been free to choose, the students reasoned that those who wrote a pro-Castro essay were in favour of him, and those who wrote an anti-Castro essay were against him. Surprisingly, even when it was made quite clear that the writers had been instructed what essay to write, the students still believed that those who wrote a pro-Castro essay were in favour of him, and those who wrote an anti-Castro essay were against him. The students disregarded situational factors and made a dispositional attribution, thus committing the fundamental attribution error.

In contrast, when trying to explain our own behaviour, we are much more likely to attribute it to characteristics of the situation than to our own disposition. In other words, we tend to see our own behaviour as relatively variable and strongly influenced by the situation, whereas we see the behaviour of others as more stable and due to personal dispositions. When we try to explain our own behaviour, we are not likely to make the fundamental attribution error (Sande *et al.*, 1988). The fact that we tend to make different kinds of attributions for our own and others' behaviour is called the **actor–observer effect**.

A study of college-age male–female couples demonstrates the actor–observer effect (Orvis *et al.*, 1976). Each partner was asked separately to describe disagreements in the relationship, such as arguments and criticism. Each partner was also asked to explain his or her attribution of the underlying causes of the disagreements. When describing their own behaviour, each person tended to refer to environmental circumstances, such as financial problems or not getting enough sleep. However, when describing their partner's behaviour, participants often referred to specific negative personality characteristics, such as selfishness or low commitment to the relationship.

Why do we tend to commit the fundamental attribution error when we observe the behaviour of others but not when we explain the causes of our own behaviour? Jones and Nisbett (1971) suggested two possible reasons. First, we have a different focus of attention when we view ourselves. When we are doing something, we see the world around us more clearly than we see our own behaviour. However, when we observe someone else doing something, we focus our attention on what is most salient and relevant: that person's behaviour, not the situation in which they are placed.

A second possible reason for these differences in attribution is that different types of information are available to us about our own behaviour and that of other people. We have more information about our own behaviour and we are thus more likely to realise that our own behaviour is often inconsistent. We also have a better notion of which stimuli we are attending to in a given situation. This difference in information leads us to conclude that the behaviour of other people is consistent and thus is a product of their personalities, whereas ours is affected by the situation in which we find ourselves.

Even though we may be aware of the difference in attributions that we make as actors or observers, this does not seem to prevent the actor–observer effect. For example, Krueger *et al.* (1996) asked pairs of participants (one actor and one observer) to describe the actor on a series of trait adjectives and to rate the consistency of relevant behaviour. Participants then predicted one another's ratings. The actor–observer effect was obtained. Moreover, actors, but not observers, were aware that observers rated actors' behaviour as more consistent than actors themselves did.

The fundamental attribution error is also less 'fundamental' than was once thought – it is influenced by culture. As you might expect from our earlier comparison of individualist and collectivist cultures, it is more prevalent in the former than the latter types of society (Morris and Peng, 1994). People in individualist societies are more inclined to explain behaviour in terms of individual dispositions and free will, whereas people in collectivist societies are more inclined to explain behaviour in terms of social obligations and situational constraints.

The fundamental attribution error is also influenced by more immediate social contexts and individual goals. For example, Schmid and Fiedler (1998) examined closing speeches made by trainee lawyers and university students acting as prosecutors or defending lawyers. Prosecutors tended to attribute internal causality to the defendants, whereas defence lawyers tried to support negative intentional attributions to the victim. When an audience of laypeople was asked to judge the speeches, and recommend sentencing, its decisions reflected the attributions made in the speeches.

False consensus

Another attribution error is the tendency for people to believe that their own behaviour is widely shared and that their own views are consensual – an error called **false consensus**. For example, Sherman *et al.* (1984) found that male school students who smoked believed that a majority of their peers did so too, whereas non-smokers believed that a majority did not smoke. Obviously, both groups cannot be correct.

One explanation for false consensus is that people tend to surround themselves with similar others and thus actually encounter a disproportionate number of people who behave like they do (Ross, 1977). Thus, when people conclude that other people are more similar to themselves than they actually are, the error may be a result of a bias in selecting people to be with. Another possible explanation is that we dwell so much on our own behaviour that it effectively inhibits proper comparisons that might lead us to realise that others do not necessarily think or act as we do. A third possibility is that in order to have a stable perception of reality we need to believe that our perceptions, attitudes and behaviours are correct, and so we exaggerate the degree of consensual support we have. If you believe the world is flat, then it helps you believe this is true if you can believe that lots of other people agree with you (Marks and Miller, 1987). However, recent research suggests that this social projection of one's own beliefs involves the inclusion of others in the same social category as oneself (Spears and Manstead, 1990; Krueger and Clément, 1997), and it is increased when we are more self-attentive or self-conscious (Fenigstein and Abrams, 1993).

Self-serving biases

Some biases seem to be designed to protect or enhance our self-esteem or self-image (Hoorens, 1993) – these are called **self-serving biases**. These may take a number of forms, and sometimes we may not even be aware of them. For example, people seem to feel more positive about letters of the alphabet that are contained within their own names as compared with letters that do not appear in their name (the 'name letter effect'). Hoorens and Nuttin (1993) examined the name letter effect among children and university students. Participants tended to think these letters appeared more frequently in other words relative to non-name letters. Moreover, because of their association with oneself, 'mere ownership' of the name letters was sufficient to make them more attractive.

Self-serving biases of this type also find expression in the attributions we make. For example, when we attempt to attribute causes to our own behaviour – to explain the reasons for our actions – we tend to attribute our accomplishments and successes to internal causes and our failures and mistakes to external causes. Suppose that you receive an outstanding score on a test. If you are like most people, you will feel the high score is well deserved. After all, you are an intelligent individual who studied hard for the test. Your attributions reflect internal causes for the test score: you are bright and a hard worker. Now suppose that you fail the test – what sorts of attribution do you tend to make? Again, if you are like most people, you may blame your low score on the fact that it was a difficult, even unfair, test, or on the lecturer for being so picky about the answers they counted as wrong. Your attributions in this case blame external causes for the low score – the test's difficulty and the pickiness of your lecturer in marking it. One possible explanation for the self-serving bias is that people are motivated to protect and enhance their self-esteem (Sedikides and Gregg, 2003). Simply put, we protect our self-esteem when we blame failure on the environment and we enhance it when we give ourselves credit for our successes.

However, people differ in their **attributional style** – the extent to which they attribute their outcomes to stable and global causes (Metalsky *et al.*, 1987). In general, people with a 'depressogenic' style are more likely to attribute their failures to these stable and global causes (for example, lack of ability that will affect performance in many ways), resulting in a sense of hopelessness and depression. On the other hand, there is some evidence that depressogenic attributional style is associated with very high levels of achievement among students, perhaps because such students actively test the limits of their capability, and set very high standards for themselves (Houston, 1994).

This sort of bias can also occur at the group level, where it is called the **ultimate attribution error**. People tend to attribute in-group failures and out-group successes to external factors such as luck, and in-group successes and out-group failures internally to properties of the groups and their members (Pettigrew, 1979). This clearly makes the group that you belong to, the in-group, appear much more positive than the group you do not belong to, the outgroup, and thus is a self-serving bias.

Another self-serving attributional phenomenon is the **belief in a just world** – the belief that people get what they deserve in life (Lerner, 1977; Furnham, 2003). According to this idea, when misfortune or tragedy strikes, people tend to blame the victim instead of attributing the source of the problem to situational factors outside the victim's control. As a result, an innocent victim may be blamed for circumstances over which they had no control, and any suffering is seen as being deserved. Common examples of this include the tendency to blame unemployed people, destitute people, rape victims, and even victims of genocide for their plight. People may also be complacent about HIV infection because they overly attribute it to risky behaviour by homosexuals (the belief that 'gays deserve AIDS') and thus not relevant to themselves (Ambrosio and Sheehan, 1991).

Although there is a sense in which the belief in a just world may reflect the fundamental attribution error, social psychologists believe it is also, and perhaps more importantly, a self-serving bias. By seeing people as bringing bad things on themselves by being bad people, we can reason that we are good, sensible people and thus these things will not happen to us. In this way the world appears more within our control and less fickle and unpredictable. An interesting twist, which is consistent with this idea, is self-blame. People may sometimes blame themselves for their plight in order to avoid the frightening conclusion that the world is a completely unpredictable place where anything may happen irrespective of what you do (Miller and Porter, 1983). Belief in a just world also varies across cultures. In a study of people from 12 countries, Furnham (1983) discovered that the susceptibility to the belief in a just world attribution error was positively correlated with wealth and social status. That is, across many countries (which included countries from both Eastern and Western cultures), a person was more likely to commit this kind of attributional error if they were wealthy and had high social status.

Psychology in action – Attributional processes in relationships

People do not always engage in attributions in order to understand their world. However, people do tend to spend a great deal of time communicating their attributions, or negotiating with one another over their attributions. This is particularly the case in close interpersonal relationships (friendship and marriage), where attributions are communicated to fulfil a variety of functions – to explain, justify or excuse behaviour, or to attribute blame and instil guilt (Hilton, 1990).

Interpersonal relationships seem to go through three basic phases: formation, maintenance and dissolution. At each stage attributional communications can take a different form and serve different functions. During the formation stage, attributions reduce ambiguity and facilitate communication and an understanding of the relationship – they bring people together by providing a shared attributional framework. In the maintenance phase, the need to make attributions decreases because stable personalities and relationships have been constructed. The dissolution phase is characterised by an increase in attributions in order to regain an understanding of the relationship, or to deal with divergent attributions.

A notable feature of many interpersonal relationships is precisely this attributional conflict, where partners proffer divergent causal interpretations of behaviours, and disagree over what attributions to adopt. Often partners cannot even agree on a cause–effect sequence, one exclaiming, 'I withdraw because you nag', the other, 'I nag because you withdraw'.

Correlational studies show that happily married (or non-distressed) spouses tend to credit their partners for positive behaviours by citing internal, stable, global and controllable factors to explain them. Negative behaviours are explained away by ascribing them to causes viewed as external, unstable, specific and uncontrollable. Distressed couples behave in exactly the opposite way. In addition, it appears that while women engage in attributional thought about the relationship, men do so only when the relationship becomes dysfunctional. In this respect, and contrary to popular opinion, men may be the more diagnostic barometers of marital dysfunction.

Do attributional dynamics produce dysfunctional marital relationships, or do dysfunctional relationships distort the attributional dynamic? This important causal question has been looked at by Fincham and Bradbury (1987), who obtained responsibility attributions, causal attributions and marital satisfaction measures from 39 married couples on two occasions 10–12 months apart. Attributions made on the first occasion were found reliably to predict marital satisfaction 10–12 months later, but only for wives. Another longitudinal study (though only over a two-month period) confirmed that attributions do have a causal impact on subsequent relationship satisfaction. Subsequent, more extensive and

Psychology in action – *Continued*

better-controlled longitudinal studies have replicated these findings for both husbands and wives.

Srivastava *et al.* (2006) asked over 100 couples to indicate their satisfaction with their romantic relationship and investigated whether optimists were more satisfied (and whether partners of optimists were more satisfied). Both results were found: those who were most optimistic, and those partnered with very optimistic people, were significantly more likely to be satisfied with their relationship. A feature of this satisfaction that was important was perceived support – when they argued, partners who sought quick conflict resolution through conversation, for example, were more satisfied with the way in which the argument was resolved after a week had passed.

How long-term is this effect of optimism? When the researchers followed up couples after a year, it was men's overall optimism that predicted relationship success. Male optimists' relationships lasted longer than did non-optimists'.

Why is optimism so important? Srivastava *et al.* (2006) suggest that optimists may attribute a partner's negative outbursts or behaviour as temporary, reflecting a state-specific reaction rather than a global personality disposition. They may also focus more on a partner's positive characteristics, thus ignoring or playing down a partner's negative mood. They act as a more 'secure base' for their partners and thus provide much needed social support that is always there, unconditionally.

Heuristic judgements

Social cognition refers to ways in which we make inferences about people, social inferences, and the world we live in, and then store these inferences as schemas that guide our perception and judgement. An important basis for social inference is, as we have seen, to find causes for people's behaviour through attribution processes. However, as we have also seen, these processes are often not very accurate or reliable. Often we do not use attribution processes at all to make inferences about people, but instead use cognitive short-cuts or inferential rules called **heuristics**. Two of the most important heuristics that people use are representativeness and availability (Tversky and Kahneman, 1974).

The representativeness heuristic

When we meet someone for the first time, we notice their clothes, hairstyle, posture, manner of speaking, hand gestures and many other characteristics. Based on our previous experience, we use this information to make tentative conclusions about other characteristics that we cannot immediately discover. In doing so, we attempt to match the characteristics we can observe with schemas or stereotypes we have of different types or groups of people. If the person seems representative of one of these schemas, we conclude that they fit that particular category (Lupfer *et al.*, 1990). In making this conclusion, we use the **representativeness heuristic** – we classify an object into the category to which it appears to be the most similar.

The representativeness heuristic is based on our ability to categorise information. We observe that some charac-

teristics tend to go together (or we are taught that they do). When we observe some of these characteristics, we conclude that the others are also present. Most of the time this strategy works; we are able to predict people's behaviour fairly accurately. Tversky and Kahneman (1974) describe someone called Steve: he is 'very shy and withdrawn, invariably helpful, but with little interest in people or in the world of reality. A meek and tidy soul, he has a need for order and structure, and a passion for detail'. Chances are you will infer that Steve is a librarian rather than a farmer, surgeon or trapeze artist – and you are probably quite likely to be correct. What we know about Steve seems to be quite representative of what we 'know' about librarians.

In relying on the representativeness heuristic we often subscribe to the **base-rate fallacy** – we overlook statistical information about the relative size of categories and therefore the probability that the person will belong to the category. If you described a person as being athletic and interested in surfing you are probably better off simply inferring she is Chinese than Australian (for every Australian there are 60 Chinese).

Learning to play the odds, so to speak, and so to avoid being misled by distinctive characteristics, is particularly important in certain intellectual endeavours. For example, doctors who are experienced in making diagnoses of diseases teach their students to learn and make use of the probabilities of particular diseases and not to be fooled by especially distinctive symptoms. In fact, Zukier and Pepitone (1984) posed a problem to first-year medical students and to residents who had completed their clinical training. The inexperienced students were tricked by the base rate fallacy but the residents played the odds, as they had been taught to do.

The availability heuristic

When people attempt to assess the importance or the frequency of an event, they tend to be guided by the ease with which examples of that event come to mind – by how available these examples are to the imagination. This mental short-cut is called the **availability heuristic**. In general, the things we are able to think of most easily are more important and occur more frequently than things that are difficult to imagine. Thus, the availability heuristic works well – most of the time.

Some events are so vivid that we can easily picture them happening. We can easily picture getting mugged while walking through the heart of a large city at night or being involved in an aeroplane crash, probably because such events are often reported in the news and because they are so frightening. Thus, people tend to overestimate the likelihood of such misfortunes happening to them. Tversky and Kahneman (1982) demonstrated the effect of availability by asking people to estimate whether English words starting with 'k' were more or less common than words with 'k' in the third position (for example, 'kiss' versus 'lake'). Most people said that there were more words starting with 'k'. In fact, there are more than twice as many words having 'k' in the third position as those having 'k' in the first position. But because thinking of words that start with a particular letter is easier than thinking of words that contain the letter in another position, people are misled in their judgement.

Many variables can affect the availability of an event or a concept and thus increase its effect on our decision-making. For example, having recently seen a particular type of event makes it easier for us to think of other examples of that event. This phenomenon is called priming. Many first-year psychology students demonstrate this phenomenon when, after first learning the symptoms of various clinical disorders, they start 'discovering' these very symptoms in themselves.

Higgins *et al.* (1977) demonstrated the effects of priming on judging the personality characteristics of strangers. They had participants work on a task that introduced various descriptive adjectives. Next, the experimenters described an imaginary person, saying that he had performed such feats as climbing mountains and crossing the Atlantic in a yacht. Finally, they asked the participants to give their impressions of this person. Those participants who had previously been exposed to words such as 'adventurous' reported favourable impressions, whereas those who had been exposed to words such as 'reckless' reported unfavourable ones. The priming effect of the descriptive adjectives had biased their interpretation of the facts.

The availability heuristic also explains why personal encounters tend to have an especially strong effect on our decision-making. For example, suppose that you have decided to buy a new car. You have narrowed your choice down to two makes, both available for about the same price. You read an article in a consumer magazine that summarises the experiences of thousands of people who have purchased these cars, and their testimony shows clearly that one of them has a much better repair record. You decide to purchase that make, and mention the fact to a friend later that day. She says, 'Oh, no! Don't buy one of those. I bought one last year, and it has been nothing but trouble. I'd had it for only two weeks when it first broke down. I got it towed to a garage, and they had to order a part from the manufacturer. Since then, I've had trouble with the air conditioner and the transmission.' Would this experience affect your decision to buy that make of car?

Most people would take this personal encounter very seriously. Even though it consists of the experience of only one person, whereas the survey in the consumer magazine represents the experience of thousands of people, a vivid personal encounter is much more available and memorable than a set of statistics, and tends to have a disproportionate effect on our own behaviour (Borgida and Nisbett, 1977).

The cognitive accessibility of social information can also have dramatic effects on our behaviour and performance. Bargh *et al.* (1996) found that when participants had been primed with the stereotype of elderly people, they walked away from the experiment more slowly than unprimed participants. Dijksterhuis *et al.* (1998) extended this intriguing research to explore the effects of making specific individuals salient. Participants were first asked to unscramble some sentences that contained within them words that describe the traits associated with the elderly stereotype. This primed the elderly stereotype by making the attributes of elderly people more accessible in participants' minds. Next, half the participants were asked to make judgements about a specific elderly person, Princess Julianna, the 89-year-old Dutch Queen Mother. This made a specific 'exemplar' accessible. Participants were then directed to the lifts at the end of the corridor where another experimenter was waiting. The time taken for them to reach this second experimenter was recorded. In contrast to Bargh *et al.*'s (1996) results, when Princess Julianna was primed, participants walked significantly faster than when the general stereotype of elderly people had been primed.

These two studies illustrate that when general stereotypes are activated we may automatically adopt some of the stereotypical characteristics ourselves, but when images of specific extreme individuals are activated we automatically make a contrast between ourselves and the exemplar, making us react in opposition to the characteristics of the individual. We assimilate ourselves to stereotypes but contrast ourselves from individuals. For example, Dijksterhuis *et al.* (1998) also found that participants performed better on a test when the stereotype of professor had been primed than when the stereotype of a supermodel had been primed. However, they performed worse on the test when the specific example of Albert Einstein had been primed than when the specific example of Claudia Schiffer had been primed.

Attitudes and attitude change

The study of **attitudes** – relatively enduring sets of beliefs, feelings and intentions towards an object, person, event or symbol – is one of the most important fields of study in social psychology (Pratkanis *et al.*, 1989; Eagly and Chaiken, 1993). Some early definitions of social psychology actually defined social psychology as the study of attitudes.

The nature of attitudes

Many social psychologists believe that attitudes have three different components: affect, behavioural intention and cognition. The affective component consists of the kinds of feeling that an attitude object (person, activity, physical object) arouses. The behavioural intentional component consists of an intention to act in a particular way with respect to a particular object. The cognitive component consists of a set of beliefs about an object. Social psychologists have studied all three aspects of attitudes.

Affective components of attitudes

Affective components of attitudes can be very strong and pervasive. The bigot feels disgust in the presence of people from a certain religious, racial or ethnic group; the nature lover feels exhilaration from a pleasant walk through the woods. Like other emotional reactions, these feelings are strongly influenced by direct or vicarious classical conditioning (Rajecki, 1989).

Direct classical conditioning is straightforward. Suppose that you meet someone who seems to take delight in embarrassing you. She makes clever, sarcastic remarks that disparage your intelligence, looks and personality. Unfortunately, her remarks are so clever that your attempts to defend yourself make you appear even more foolish. After a few encounters with this person, the sight of her or the sound of her voice is likely to elicit feelings of dislike and fear. Your attitude towards her will be negative.

Vicarious classical conditioning undoubtedly plays a major role in transmitting parents' attitudes to their children. People are skilled at detecting even subtle signs of fear, hatred and other negative emotional states in people, especially when they know them well. Thus, children often vicariously experience their parents' prejudices and fears even if these feelings are unspoken. Children who see their parents recoil in disgust at the sight of members of some ethnic group are likely to feel the same emotion and thus, over time, develop the same attitude.

Simply being exposed repeatedly to an otherwise neutral object or issue over time may influence our attitude towards it – generally in a favourable direction. This attraction for the familiar is called the **mere exposure effect**. One of the first studies to demonstrate this effect used several neutral stimuli – towards which there were no positive or negative feelings – such as nonsense words, photographs of the faces of unknown people, and Chinese characters (Zajonc, 1968). The more the participants saw the stimuli, the more they liked the stimuli later. Stimuli that were seen only once were liked more than ones never seen before. Even when the stimuli were flashed so briefly that they could not be recognised, participants usually preferred a stimulus that had been previously presented to a novel one that they could not recognise (Kunst-Wilson and Zajonc, 1980). The mere exposure effect probably reflects our tendency to feel positive about things that do not pose a threat to us. Our feelings towards a person, event or object will naturally improve if, on repeated exposure, we discover that no threat is posed.

Cognitive components of attitudes

We acquire most beliefs about a particular attitude object quite directly: we hear or read a fact or opinion, or other people validate our expressed beliefs. However, we can often develop fairly nebulous likes and dislikes (affect) and then develop our beliefs subsequently, to justify our feelings. For example, you may feel you dislike Honda cars, but really not have many beliefs about them. This affective orientation will guide the sorts of belief you subsequently hold about Hondas – you are more likely then to believe unfavourable than favourable things about Hondas. This illustrates an important point: although we can separate out different components of attitudes in order to describe them in a textbook, in reality they are inextricably linked.

We form and change our attitudes throughout our lives; however, children have an enormous task ahead of them: they come into the world with no attitudes, and so have very rapidly to learn attitudes in order to orient themselves to people, events and objects in their world. One way they do this is by simply imitating the behaviour of people who play an important role in their lives.

Children usually repeat opinions expressed by their parents. In Northern Ireland, many children label themselves as Catholics or Protestants long before they know the values for which these religious organisations stand. Often they ask their parents, 'Are we Catholics or Protestants?' without considering whether they might have any choice in the matter. The tendency to identify with the family unit (and, later with peer groups) provides a strong incentive to adopt the group's attitudes.

Attitudes and behaviour

Attitudes have a behavioural intention component – a motivation or expressed intention to behave in some way or other that is consistent with the affective and cognitive components of an attitude. For example, many people have negative attitudes towards smoking and express the intention not to smoke. However, we all know that the expressed intention to behave according to an attitude certainly does not guarantee that we actually behave in that way – people who intend not to smoke often smoke. Intentions and behaviour are not the same thing.

People do not always behave as their expressed attitudes and beliefs would lead us to expect. In a classic example, LaPiere (1934) drove across the western United States with a Chinese couple. They stopped at over 250 restaurants and lodging places and were refused service only once. Several months after their trip, LaPiere wrote to the owners of the places they had visited and asked whether they would serve Chinese people. The response was overwhelmingly negative; 92 per cent of those who responded said that they would not. Clearly, their behaviour gave less evidence of racial bias than their expressed attitudes did. This study has been cited as evidence that attitudes do not always influence behaviour – indeed hundreds of studies of the relationship between attitudes and behaviour suggest, that on average, attitudes predict only 2–3 per cent of behaviour (Wicker, 1969). One way to think of this is that only 2 or 3 times out of 100 do people actually do what they say – perhaps we should not be quite so harsh on our politicians.

However, all is not lost. If it were, then commercial advertising would be a waste of time, as advertising largely tries to change behaviour by changing people's attitudes towards products. There are ways in which we can be much more accurate at predicting behaviour from attitudes. Attitude specificity is one important influence on attitude–behaviour congruence. If you measure a person's general attitude towards a topic, you will be unlikely to be able to predict their behaviour. Behaviours, unlike attitudes, are specific events. However, as the attitude being measured becomes more specific, the person's behaviour becomes more predictable.

For example, Weigel *et al.* (1974) measured people's attitudes towards a series of topics that increased in specificity from 'a pure environment' to 'the Sierra Club' (an American organisation that supports environmental causes). They used the participants' attitudes to predict whether they would volunteer for various activities to benefit the Sierra Club. A person's attitude towards environmentalism was a poor predictor of whether they would volunteer; their attitude towards the Sierra Club itself was a much better predictor (see Table 15.4). For example, a person might favour a pure environment but also dislike organised clubs or have little time to spare for meetings. This person would express a positive attitude towards a pure environment but would not join the club or volunteer for any activities to support it.

In another study, Davidson and Jacard (1979) monitored women's attitudes towards birth control as a predictor of use of the contraceptive pill over the next two years. They found that pill use over the next two years was most strongly predicted by a very specific measure of 'Attitude towards using birth control pills during the next two years' (a correlation of 0.57), and least strongly in contrast to the most general measure of 'Attitude towards birth control' (correlation of 0.08).

Reasoned action and planned behaviour

Probably the most systematic account of how attitudes and behaviour are related has been developed by Fishbein and Ajzen (see Ajzen, 1989) in their **theories of reasoned action** and of **planned behaviour**. Someone's intention to behave in a certain way is strengthened if (1) they have a positive attitude towards the behaviour, (2) they believe many people that matter also have a favourable attitude towards the behaviour, (3) they believe they have the resources and opportunity to engage in the behaviour, and (4) the intention is very specific to one particular behaviour. For example, consider someone who loves going to Wagnerian operas, all of whose friends also love

Table 15.4 Correlation between willingness to join or work for the Sierra Club and various measures of related attitudes

Attitude scale	Correlation
Importance of a pure environment	0.06
Pollution	0.32
Conservation	0.24
Attitude towards the Sierra Club	0.68

Source: Based on Weigel, R., Vernon, D.T.A. and Tognacci, L.N., Specificity of the attitude as a determinant of attitude–behavior congruence, *Journal of Personality and Social Psychology*, 1974, 30, 724–8.

going to Wagnerian operas, and who has a ticket to go to *The Ring*, which is on in his city tonight and who has nothing else to do tonight. If he expressed the strong intention of going to *The Ring* tonight which he is likely to do, then you can probably pretty accurately predict that this is what he will do. In contrast, consider someone who loves going to Wagnerian operas, but all of whose friends do not, and who has no ticket to the opera. He is unlikely to express a strong intention of going to *The Ring* tonight, and you are much less likely to know exactly what he will be doing.

D. Parker *et al.* (1995) surveyed almost 600 drivers in Britain, and found that they could quite accurately predict whether those drivers would engage in specific reckless driving behaviours, for example cutting in and reckless weaving, by measuring their attitudes towards the behaviour, the amount of support they perceived for this behaviour from their friends, and whether they had the resources and opportunity to behave in this way (for example, they had a car, they could get away with it, they had done it in the past and so knew what to do).

Attitude accessibility and attitude strength

Attitudes are cognitively represented in memory. Thus, like any other cognitive representations they are likely to have a greater influence on behaviour if they are readily accessible – easily and readily recalled. Indeed, research does show that attitudes affect behavioural intentions, and thus behaviour, more strongly if the attitudes are more accessible in memory (Doll and Ajzen, 1992). Our attitudes can also vary in strength. A strong attitude is one that has a strong associative link with the attitude object and thus, once activated, the attitude has a more automatic link with behavioural intentions and ultimately behaviour (Fazio *et al.*, 1986). So, for example, if you absolutely love chocolate and think about eating chocolate all the time then your attitude towards chocolate is strong and accessible and is probably a very good predictor of your intention to eat chocolate – an intention which probably maps tightly onto your behaviour. If, on the other hand, you quite like lobster and occasionally think about eating lobster then your attitude towards lobster is less strong and accessible, and is a poor predictor of your intentions and behaviour.

Social identity and norms

Another factor that influences the attitude–behaviour relationship is the extent to which an attitude is an important aspect of the kind of person we are. Self-defining attitudes, ones that define our identity, particularly our social identity as a group member, are more likely to be expressed as behaviour. More specifically, attitudes are more likely to express themselves as behaviour if the attitudes (and associated behaviour) are normative properties of a social group with which people identify (Terry and Hogg, 1996). To test this idea, Terry and Hogg (1996) measured attitudes and intentions relating to taking regular exercise and adopting sun-protective behaviours. They found a much tighter attitude–intention link among student participants who identified strongly with a student peer group for whom they felt regular exercise and adopting sun-protective behaviour was a strong group-defining norm.

Attitude change and persuasion

People often attempt to persuade us to change our attitudes. Social psychological research on persuasion has taken its form from an early and highly influential programme of research by Hovland *et al.* (1953). Hovland and colleagues famously asked, 'Who says what to whom and with what effect?' – a question which identifies the three key aspects of persuasive communication: the source of the communication, the content of the message and the audience or target of the communication.

The source

Credibility and attractiveness are two aspects of the source of a message that have a major affect on persuasiveness. A message tends to be more persuasive if its source is credible. Source credibility is high when the source is perceived as knowledgeable and is trusted to communicate this knowledge accurately. For example, in one study, people developed a more favourable attitude towards different types of medicine when the information appeared in the prestigious medical journal *New England Journal of Medicine* than when it appeared in a mass-circulation tabloid (Hovland and Weiss, 1951). Research by Bochner and Insko (1966) showed that credible sources are not only more persuasive but they can also induce the greatest amount of attitude change. Bochner and Insko took advantage of the fact that their student participants believed that 8 hours of sleep a night was required to maintain good health. They then exposed them to one of two sources of opinion, a high credibility Nobel Prize-winning sleep physiologist or a less credible YMCA instructor, who said that less sleep was optimal. Both sources shifted the students' attitudes when the sources advocated between 7 and 3 hours' sleep, but when they advocated 1 or 2 hours the credible source was significantly more effective than the less credible source at changing attitudes.

Messages also have more impact when the source is physically attractive. For example, physically attractive people are more likely than physically unattractive people to persuade others to sign a petition (Chaiken, 1979).

Individuals who are asked to endorse products for advertisers are almost always physically attractive or appealing in other ways. Since people tend to like people who are similar to them more than people who are not, similarity should have the same effect. However, this does not seem to be the case. People are more persuaded by similar others when the issue is a matter of taste (for example, musical preference), but more persuaded by dissimilar others when the issue is a matter of fact (for example, who won the Tour de France in a particular year) (Petty and Cacioppo, 1981).

The message

As you would expect, aspects of the message itself are important in determining its persuasive appeal. For example, is an argument that provides only one side of an issue more effective than one that presents both sides? The answer depends on the audience. If the audience either knows very little about the issue or already holds a strong position with respect to it, one-sided arguments tend to be more effective. If the audience is well informed about the issue, however, a two-sided argument tends to be more persuasive (McAlister *et al.*, 1980).

How effective are scare tactics embedded in the message in changing someone's attitude? Some research suggests that frightening messages are very effective. Leventhal *et al.* (1967) found that people were more likely to stop smoking when the message was accompanied by a graphic video of surgery on a patient affected by lung cancer. Other research finds the opposite. Janis and Feshbach (1953) found much more improvement in dental hygiene practices among participants who had been exposed to a low-fear message (facts about tooth decay and gum disease) than those exposed to a high-fear message (graphic visual images of disease). Yet other research has shown that scare tactics may be effective in bringing about change, but only when combined with instructive information about how to change one's behaviour (Cialdini *et al.*, 1981). According to Janis (1967), a little bit of fear is good for motivation to attend to the message and to change one's attitudes and behaviours, but too much fear can distract us from the message so that we are unable to conceive of ways to put the message into action (Keller and Block, 1995).

The audience

Research on the audience or target of the communication identifies a number of factors that influence how easily persuaded people may be. One finding is that people who have very low or very high self-esteem are less easily persuaded than people with average self-esteem, because the former are either too anxious to pay attention or too self-

assured to be influenced (Rhodes and Wood, 1992). There are no straightforward sex differences in persuadability, but complex interactions (Carli, 1990). For example, Covell *et al.* (1994) studied the effect of tobacco and alcohol advertisements on Canadian adult and adolescent males and females and discovered a sex difference among the adolescents only – female adolescents were more influenced than male adolescents by advertisements that were strongly image-oriented. As with sex, there is no clear relationship between age and persuadability – some research finds no age effect whereas other studies find that younger and older people are more easily persuaded than people in their middle years (Visser and Krosnick, 1998).

The process of attitude change through persuasion

Petty and Cacioppo (1986) have proposed the **elaboration likelihood model** to account for attitude change through persuasion (Figure 15.1). According to this model, persuasion can take either a central or a peripheral route. The central route requires a person to think critically about the argument being presented, to weigh its strengths and weaknesses, and to elaborate on the relevant themes. At issue is the substance of the argument, not its emotional or superficial appeal. The peripheral route, on the other hand, refers to attempts at persuasion in which the change is associated with positive stimuli – a professional athlete, a millionaire, or an attractive model – which actually may have nothing to do with the sub-

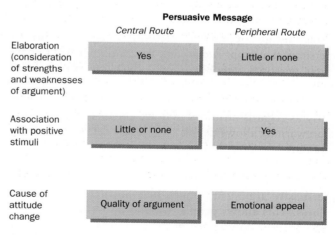

Figure 15.1 The elaboration likelihood model of attitude change. Persuasive messages may centre either on a substantive argument that requires an individual to think about the argument's strengths and weaknesses (the central route) or on a superficial argument that is associated with positive stimuli (the peripheral route).

stance of the argument. Selling products by associating them with attractive people or by implying that buying the product will result in emotional, social or financial benefits are examples of the use of peripheral attitude change techniques.

Very closely related to Petty and Cacioppo's distinction between central and peripheral route processing, is Chaiken's distinction between systematic and heuristic processing (Bohner *et al.*, 1995). People can systematically consider all aspects of a message, or they can very superficially rely on simple heuristics such as thinking that longer arguments or arguments with more statistical facts and figures must be more true, or that all messages from politicians are lies. People are more likely to resort to heuristic processing if they have limited time to process the message or if they are in a good mood. So, to change attitudes towards consumer products it is quite effective to bombard hurried people with advertisements that put them in a good mood and present statistical/scientific information from people dressed as scientists. This encourages heuristic processing and encourages the heuristic that messages backed by science must be true. One difference between the elaboration likelihood model and the heuristic–systematic model is that whereas a message is processed either centrally or peripherally at any one time, it can be processed systematically and heuristically at the same time.

Resistance to persuasion

Far more attempts at persuasion fail than succeed. Researchers have identified three major factors: reactance, forewarning and inoculation. Reactance refers to a tendency to resist persuasion, or even move one's attitudes in an opposite direction, when a deliberate persuasion attempt is detected. People do not like to have their personal freedom limited by being pressured to change their attitudes. When people are forewarned of an influence attempt they are less easily influenced, particularly as regards attitudes that are considered important. Forewarning allows people to generate defensive counter-arguments to protect their attitudes.

Related to forewarning, is inoculation. Inoculation is a process where people are exposed to a weak version of a persuasive argument – much like inoculation against an illness. This allows people to build up resistance, in this case specific counterarguments, against the full-blown persuasive attempt. Research on inoculation was prompted by the way that American prisoners of war in the Korean War of the 1950s were easily brainwashed to denounce the American way of life and endorse Communism. It was thought that this had happened because the soldiers had never heard any attacks on the

American way of life, and so were completely unprepared to protect their attitudes (McGuire, 1964). McGuire and Papageorgis (1961) conducted a study where student participants who strongly endorsed truisms such as 'It's a good idea to brush your teeth after every meal', were exposed to a strong attack on these truisms and then had their attitudes remeasured. Some participants were prepared for the attack by being provided with supporting arguments defending their position, some were inoculated by being exposed to a mild form of the attack, and some were not prepared at all. Supportive defence and inoculation reduced attitude change relative to no defence, but inoculation was significantly more effective.

What kinds of argument do you think would be effective in persuading you to change your attitude towards a prominent political figure? How would you describe these arguments in psychological terms? Based on social psychological knowledge about the relationship between attitudes and behaviour, what advice would you give an organisation that wanted to combat waste (for example, excessive paper use, excessive energy use)? Would you recommend changing employees' attitudes in order to change their behaviour?

Cognitive dissonance

Although we usually regard our attitudes as causes of our behaviour, our behaviour also affects our attitudes. Two major theories attempt to explain the effects of behaviour on attitude formation: cognitive dissonance and self-perception.

The oldest theory is cognitive dissonance theory, developed by Leon Festinger (1957). According to **cognitive dissonance theory**, when we perceive a discrepancy between our attitudes and behaviour, between our behaviour and self-image, or between one attitude and another, an unpleasant state of anxiety, or dissonance, results. For example, a person may successfully overcome a childhood racial prejudice but may experience unpleasant emotional arousal at the sight of a racially mixed couple. The person experiences a conflict between the belief in their own lack of prejudice and the evidence of prejudice from their behaviour. This conflict produces dissonance, which is an aversive state that people are motivated to reduce. A person can reduce dissonance by (1) reducing the importance of one of the dissonant elements, (2) adding consonant elements, or (3) changing one of the dissonant elements.

Suppose that a student believes that he is very intelligent but he invariably receives poor grades in his courses. Because the obvious prediction is that intelligent people get good grades, the discrepancy causes the student to experience dissonance. To reduce this dissonance, he may decide that grades are not important and that intelligence is not very closely related to grades. He is using strategy 1, reducing the importance of one of the dissonant elements – the fact that he received poor grades in his courses. Or he can dwell on the belief that his lecturers were unfair or that his job leaves him little time to study. In this case, he is using strategy 2, reducing dissonance by adding consonant elements – those factors that can account for his poor grades and hence explain the discrepancy between his perceived intelligence and grades. Finally, he can use strategy 3 to change one of the dissonant elements. He can either improve his grades or revise his opinion of his own intelligence.

Induced compliance

Most of us believe that although we can induce someone to do something, getting someone to change an attitude is much harder. However, Festinger's theory of cognitive dissonance and supporting experimental evidence indicate otherwise. Under the right conditions, when people are coerced into doing something or are paid to do something, the act of **compliance** – simply engaging in a particular behaviour at someone else's request – may cause a change in their underlying attitudes.

Cognitive dissonance theory predicts that dissonance occurs when a person's behaviour has undesirable outcomes for self-esteem; there is a conflict between the person's belief in their own worth and the fact that they have done something that damages this belief. The person will then seek to justify the behaviour. For example, a poorly paid vacuum cleaner sales representative is likely to convince himself that the shoddy merchandise he sells is actually good. Otherwise, he must question why he works for a company that pays him poorly and requires him to lie to prospective customers about the quality of the product in order to make a sale. Conversely, an executive of one of the celebrity gossip magazines may know that the magazines she produces are sleazy, mindless drivel, but she is so well paid that she does not feel bad about producing them. Her high salary justifies her job and probably also provides her with enough self-esteem that she has decided that the public gets what it deserves anyway.

Festinger and Carlsmith (1959) verified this observation by having participants perform very boring tasks, such as putting spools on a tray, dumping them out, putting them on the tray again, dumping them out again, and so on. After the participants had spent an hour on exercises like this, the experimenter asked each participant whether they would help out in the study by trying to convince the next person that the task was interesting and enjoyable. Some participants received $1 for helping out; others received $20. Control participants were paid nothing. The experimenters predicted that participants who were paid only $1

would perceive the task as being relatively interesting. They had been induced to lie to a 'fellow student' (actually, a confederate of the experimenters) for a paltry sum. Like the vacuum cleaner sales representative, they should convince themselves of the worth of the experiment to maintain their self-esteem. Poorly paid participants did in fact rate the task better than did those who were well paid (Figure 15.2). Clearly, our actions have an effect on our attitudes. When faced with inconsistency between our behaviour and our attitudes, we often change our attitudes to suit our behaviour.

Arousal and attitude change

Festinger's theory hypothesises that dissonance reduction is motivated by an aversive drive. A study by Croyle and Cooper (1983) obtained physiological evidence to support this hypothesis. The experimenters chose as their participants Princeton University students who disagreed with the assertion 'Alcohol use should be totally banned from the Princeton campus and eating clubs'. Each participant was induced to write an essay containing strong and forceful arguments in favour of the assertion or in opposition to it. While the participants were writing the essay, the experimenters measured the electrical conductance of their skin, which is known to be a good indicator of the physiological arousal that accompanies stress. Some participants were simply told to write the essay. Other participants were told that their participation was completely voluntary and that they were free to leave at any time; they even signed a form

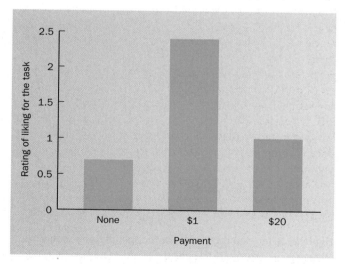

Figure 15.2 Effects of induced compliance. People who received $1 to lie about a boring task later indicated that they liked the task more than did people who received $20.

Source: Based on data from Festinger, L. and Carlsmith, J.M., Cognitive consequences of forced compliance. *Journal of Abnormal and Social Psychology*, 1959, 58, 203–210.

emphasising the voluntary nature of the task. Of course, all participants felt social pressure to continue the study, and all of them did. Those who were simply told to write the essay should have felt less personal responsibility for what they wrote and would therefore be expected to experience less cognitive dissonance than those who believed that they had exercised free choice in deciding to participate.

Participants in the 'free choice' condition who had written essays contradicting their original opinions showed both a change in opinion and evidence of physiological arousal. Those participants who were simply told to write the essay or who wrote arguments that they had originally agreed with showed little sign of arousal or attitude change (Figure 15.3).

Attitudes and expenditures

Festinger's theory of cognitive dissonance accounts for another relation between behaviour and attitudes: our tendency to value an item more if it costs us something. For example, some people buy extremely expensive brands of cosmetics even though the same ingredients are used in much cheaper brands. Presumably, they believe that if an item costs more, it must work better. Following the same rationale, most animal shelters sell their stray animals to prospective pet owners, not only because the money helps defray their operating costs, but also because they assume that a purchased pet will be treated better than a free pet.

Aronson and Mills (1959) verified this phenomenon. The experimenters subjected female college students to varying degrees of embarrassment as a prerequisite for joining what was promised to be an interesting discussion about sexual behaviour. To produce slight embarrassment, they had the participants read aloud five sex-related words (such as prostitute, virgin and petting – remember that this research was conducted in the 1950s) to the experimenter, who was male. To produce more severe embarrassment, they had the women read aloud 12 obscene four-letter words and two sexually explicit passages of prose. The control group read nothing at all. The 'interesting group discussion' turned out to be a tape recording of a very dull conversation.

Festinger's theory predicts that the women who had to go through an embarrassing ordeal in order to join the group would experience some cognitive dissonance. They had suffered an ordeal in order to take part in an interesting discussion that turned out actually to be very dull. These negative and positive experiences are inconsistent and dissonance arousing, and should make them view the 'discussion' more favourably so that their effort would not be perceived as having been completely without value. The results were as predicted: the participants who had been embarrassed the most rated the discussion more favourably than did the control participants or those who had experienced only slight embarrassment. We value things at least partly by how much they cost us. One controversial implication is that people might value social goods like education and national parks more highly if they personally paid (more) for them.

Self-perception

Bem (1972) proposed an alternative to the theory of cognitive dissonance. Drawing on attribution theory, which we discussed earlier in this chapter, he defined **self-perception theory** in the following way:

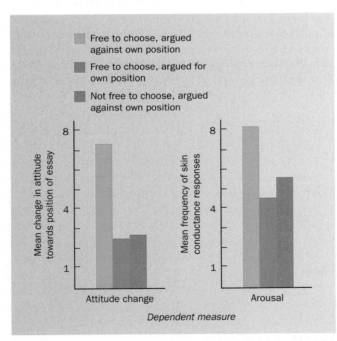

Figure 15.3 Physiological evidence for cognitive dissonance. Mean change in attitude towards the position advocated by the essay and mean frequency of skin conductance responses (a physiological index of arousal) in participants who argued for or against their own positions.
Source: Based on data from Croyle, R.T. and Cooper, J., Dissonance arousal: Physical evidence. *Journal of Personality and Social Psychology*, 1983, 45, 782–91.

> Individuals come to 'know' their own attitudes, emotions, and other internal states partially by inferring them from observations of their own overt behaviour and/or the circumstances in which this behaviour occurs. Thus, to the extent that internal cues are weak, ambiguous, or uninterpretable, the individual is functionally in the same position as an outside observer, an observer who must necessarily rely on those same external cues to infer the individual's inner states.

Bem noted that an observer who attempts to make judgements about someone's attitudes, emotions or other internal states must examine the person's behaviour for clues. For example, if you cannot ask someone why they are doing something, you must analyse the situation in which the behaviour occurs to try to determine the motivation. Bem suggested that people analyse their own internal states in a similar way, making attributions about the causes of their own behaviour.

You will recall the experiment by Festinger and Carlsmith (1959) in which students who were paid only $1 later rated a boring task as more interesting than did those who were paid $20. How does self-perception theory explain these results? Suppose that an observer watches a participant who has been paid $1 to deliver a convincing speech to another student about how interesting a task was. Because being paid such a small sum is not a sufficient reason for calling a dull task interesting, the observer will probably conclude that the student actually enjoyed the task. Lacking good evidence for external causes, the observer will attribute the behaviour to a dispositional factor: interest in the task. Bem argued that the participant makes the same inference about themself. Because the participant was not paid enough to tell a lie, they must have enjoyed the task. The principal advantage of self-perception theory is that it makes fewer assumptions than does dissonance theory; it does not postulate a motivating aversive-drive state.

But as Croyle and Cooper's (1983) experiment on essay writing showed, some conflict situations do produce arousal. Perhaps self-perception and cognitive dissonance occur under different conditions, producing attitude changes for different reasons. One factor that may determine whether dissonance or self-perception processes come into play involves the idea that attitudes have ranges of acceptable behaviour. For example, a pacifist might agree with using force to protect a helpless child from attack but would not agree with using force to react to a personal insult. According to Fazio *et al.* (1977), a pacifist who used force to protect a child might change his attitudes through self-perception (the behaviour falls within the latitude of acceptable behaviours), whereas a pacifist who struck out in retaliation for an insult would experience dissonance (the behaviour falls outside the latitude of acceptable behaviours). Using a slightly different logic, Cooper and Fazio (1984) suggest that when counter-attitudinal behaviour has undesirable consequences, we go through an attributional/self-perception process where we decide whether the behaviour was voluntary. If it was, then we experience dissonance.

Chapter review

Social psychology

- Social psychology is the study of how the thoughts, feelings and behaviour of people are influenced by the actual, imagined or implied presence of other people.
- Social psychologists employ the scientific method – they formulate theories of human behaviour and test them using a wide range of empirical methods.
- Social psychology has its roots in late-nineteenth-century German folk psychology. By the 1920s, America had taken the lead and social psychology was a branch of general psychology. The Second World War gave impetus to a focus on groups and attitudes. This was gradually replaced from the mid-1960s by a focus on individual cognition and inference in its social context. Contemporary social psychology is very diverse, embracing a wide range of emphases on social cognition, groups, intergroup relations, close relationships and attitudes.

Social cognition and social knowledge

- Social cognition refers to the way we process and represent the social world and our place in it. Social cognition is governed by cognitive parsimony, but it is also motivated by our own goals.

- Impressions of people are strongly influenced by central traits, negative information and information that one encounters first (primacy effect).
- Our thoughts, feelings, perceptions and beliefs about the world are organised in mental frameworks, or schemas, which help us manage and synthesise information about our social world.
- Schemas can be tied closely to specific instances of a category (called exemplars) or they can be fuzzy abstractions of defining features (called prototypes).
- Schemas that are widely shared within a group, and are held about another group, are stereotypes.
- Schemas tend to be activated automatically once we have categorised a person, object or event.

Self and identity

- Our self-concept is based on schemas that organise and synthesise personal knowledge and feelings we have about ourselves.
- We often try to bring our behaviour, and thus our own self-conception, in line with how we would like to be, or we feel we ought to be.

- There are cultural and situational differences in the extent to which self-schemas are based on being an individual, a member of a group, or in a relationship with specific other people.
- The way we conceptualise ourselves is most strongly motivated by a desire for an evaluatively positive self-concept that contributes to a sense of positive self-esteem.

Social inference

- In making attributions about the causes of another person's behaviour, we consider the relative contributions of dispositional and situational factors.
- In some circumstances we may gain an understanding of what sort of person we are and how we feel, by trying to discover what the causes of our behaviour might be.
- In making attributions about others' behaviour we tend to overestimate the role of dispositional factors and underestimate the role of situational factors (the fundamental attribution error); however, we do the opposite for our own behaviour.
- Attributions also tend to be self-serving. We attribute our own and our groups' good behaviours internally and bad behaviours externally. We also tend to think bad things happen to bad people and good things to good people.
- In making inferences about people we tend to rely on cognitive short-cuts or heuristics, such as how available something is to memory, and how superficially representative something is of a category.

Attitudes and attitude change

- Attitudes have affective, cognitive and behavioural intention components and may be learned through mere exposure to the object of the attitude, classical conditioning processes and imitation.
- Attitudes are poor predictors of behaviour unless very specific attitudes and very specific behaviours are measured. Prediction is even better if attitudes towards behaviours are measured, and if normative support is strong and opportunity and resources to perform the behaviour are available.
- To understand explicit attempts to change a person's attitude, we must consider both the source of the intended persuasive message and the message itself.
- A message tends to be persuasive if its source is credible or attractive and if it is pitched correctly at its intended audience.
- There are at least two routes to persuasion. The central route involves careful consideration of the message, whereas the peripheral route involves superficial reliance on heuristics such as the attractiveness of the message source.
- Cognitive dissonance is an aversive state that occurs when our attitudes and behaviour are inconsistent. Resolution of dissonance often involves changing attitudes in line with behaviour.
- Our own observations of our behaviour and situation also influence attitude development.

Suggestions for further reading

Social psychology in general

Aronson, E. (2007) *The Social Animal* (7th edn). NY: Freeman
Carr, S.C. (2003) *Social Psychology*. Australia: Wiley.
Hogg, M.A. and Cooper, J. (eds) (2003) *Sage Handbook of Social Psychology*. London: Sage.
Hogg, M.A. and Vaughan, G.M. (2005) *Social Psychology* (4th edn). London: Pearson Education.
Aronson's classic is a brilliant introduction to social psychology. The last three items are comprehensive texts which integrate European and North American research (Hogg et al.) and these territories and Australasia (Carr's is a lively book).

Self

Baumeister, R.F. (ed.) (1999) *The Self in Social Psychology*. Philadelphia: Psychology Press.
A set of key readings, presenting contemporary and classic published work.

Culture and social psychology

Smith, P.B., Bond, M.H. and Kagitcibasi, C. (2006) *Understanding Social Psychology Across Cultures*. London: Sage.
This is a completely up-to-date text on social psychological similarities and differences between cultures.

Social cognition and attitudes

Fiske, S.T. and Taylor, S.E. (2008) *Social Cognition: From brain to culture*. New York: McGraw-Hill.
Moskowitz, G.B. (2005) *Social Cognition: Understanding self and others*. New York: Guilford.
Tesser, A. and Schwartz, N. (eds) (2001) *Blackwell Handbook of Social Psychology: Intraindividual processes*. Oxford: Blackwell.
Some very good texts on social cognition. Fiske and Taylor's is a revision of an outstanding classic.

Journals to consult

Basic and Applied Social Psychology

British Journal of Social Psychology

European Journal of Social Psychology

European Review of Social Psychology

Journal of Applied Social Psychology

Journal of Community and Applied Social Psychology

Journal of Experimental Social Psychology

Journal of Personality and Social Psychology

Personality and Social Psychology Bulletin

Personality and Social Psychology Review

Self and Identity

Social Cognition

Website addresses

http://www.socialpsychology.org/
Social Psychology Network, maintained by Scott Plous. This site has excellent links to most areas of psychology and has a search facility. Well worth a visit.

http://www.psych.neu.edu/ISSI/
The International Society for Self and Identity (ISSI) is a scholarly association dedicated to promoting the scientific study of the human self.

http://www.indiana.edu/~soccog/scarch.html
Social cognition – social psychology paper archive

http://www.psych.purdue.edu/~esmith/scarch.html
Social Cognition Paper Archive and Information Center website, maintained by Eliot R. Smith at Purdue University, USA. Links to journals, papers, researchers and interactive demonstrations specific to social cognition (for example, implicit association test).

http://www.philosophy.ucf.edu/pi.html
An online bibliography organised under the following categories: self, person, personal identity, self-consciousness, pathologies of the self, personalism, consciousness, self-knowledge (and others).

http://implicit.harvard.edu/implicit
Go to this site to test how prejudiced you are according to Greenwald and Banaji's (e.g. Greenwald et al., 2002) Implicit Association Test. This site has already been visited by hundreds of thousands of people.

The sites mentioned in Chapter 16 may also be relevant.

Interpersonal and group processes

Michael A. Hogg and Dominic Abrams and G. Neil Martin

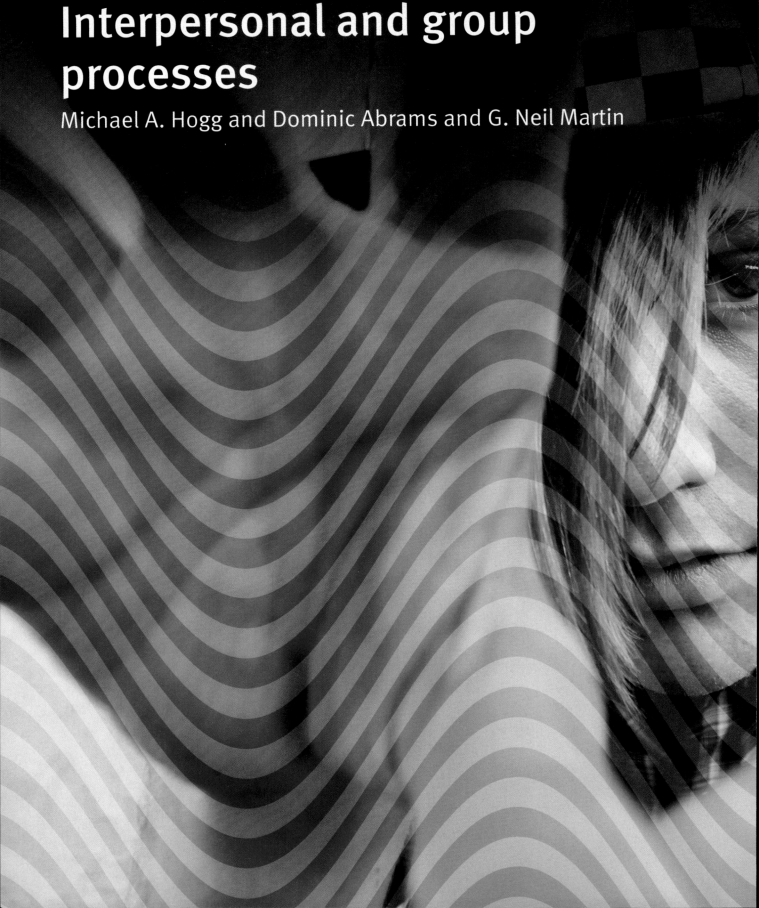

McKeown, 37, of no fixed address, launched a tirade of abuse after spotting Mohammed Mahmood, who was wearing traditional Muslim dress, as he walked along Victoria Road, Cambridge, on July 7. McKeown shouted: 'Look what you've done to London you terrorist, go back to your own country', before following him along the road hurling further abuse and threatening him with violence. Police said the incident was an unprovoked attack on a 'very calm, quiet man', and welcomed McKeown's 130-day prison sentence.

Source: *Cambridge Evening News*, 16 December 2005.

Explore the accompanying videos, simulations animations on MyPsychLab. This chapter includes activities on: Obedience • The Milgram experiment • Deindividuation • The rewards and costs of helping • Check your understanding and prepare for your exams using the multiple choice, short answer and essay practice tests also available.

WHAT YOU SHOULD BE ABLE TO DO AFTER READING CHAPTER 16

- Understand how people are influenced by individuals, authority, group norms and minorities.
- Know what affects people's performance of tasks in groups, and how groups make decisions and are influenced by leaders.
- Know why intergroup conflicts and prejudices are so difficult to change, and what underlies crowd behaviour and social movements.
- Understand some of the causes of human aggression, and what influences people's inclination to help others.
- Understand why we like who we do, and the path taken by love and close relationships.
- Appreciate the role of language, speech and non-verbal communication in social life, and what factors influence how we communicate.

QUESTIONS TO THINK ABOUT

- If someone ordered you to do something that caused serious harm to another person, would you do it?
- How does the presence of an audience affect the way you perform?
- Is there such a thing as team spirit? If so, which psychological processes are involved?
- What makes a great leader? What would ten such leaders have in common?
- If you try hard to suppress your prejudices, do you think they will gradually disappear?
- Can contact between racial groups reduce racial prejudice?
- Are men more aggressive than women?
- What sort of person are you attracted to, and why?
- Does attraction lead to love or vice versa?
- 'It's not what you do; it's the way that you do it.' Is this true when considering communication between people?

Social influence

At the end of Chapter 15 we discussed attitude change. The social process responsible for attitude change is social influence. However, social influence is in fact a much wider topic because it also addresses changes in people's behaviour that are not associated with changed attitudes. Sometimes people simply do what people tell or ask them to do, without necessarily changing their underlying attitudes. A key distinction in the social influence literature is between **compliance** (a surface change in behaviour which is not associated with true underlying cognitive changes) and **conformity** (a deep-seated cognitive change, usually in response to the existence of self-defining group norms).

Compliance

 Research on compliance focuses on the conditions under which people will go along with a request or do someone a favour. For example, how can you get someone to lend you some money, fix your car, pop down to the shops for you, fill out a questionnaire, and so forth? You simply want people to do what you request – you are not looking for deep-seated changes in their attitudes and values.

Ingratiation

One very effective method is **ingratiation**, which involves getting people to like you – flattery may not get you everywhere, but it is surprisingly effective. People are much more likely to agree to a request from someone they like or find attractive. One reason for this is that an attractive person, by association, makes the request appear more attractive. Advertisers regularly pay tribute to the effectiveness of association when they use attractive models and celebrities to endorse their products. For example, Smith and Engel (1968) showed two versions of an advertisement for a new car. One version included an attractive young woman and the other did not. When the participants subsequently rated the car, those who saw the advertisement with the attractive young woman rated the car as faster, more appealing, more expensive-looking and better designed.

Besides making products or opinions more attractive by being associated with them, attractive people are better able to get others to comply with their requests because people want to be liked by attractive people. People believe that being liked by attractive people makes them more desirable, too. Thus, people tend to emphasise their associations with attractive and important people. We have all encountered name-droppers who want us to think that they are part of a privileged circle of friends. This phenomenon is even demonstrated by fans of sports teams. Cialdini *et al.* (1976) found that students were more likely to wear sweatshirts featuring their university name on the day after the university football team had won a game than after the team had lost. Also, Wann and Dolan (1994) have shown that spectators identify with, and are biased in favour of, fellow spectators who support the same team.

Although attractive people may influence our behaviour, it is possible that they may only influence our underlying attitudes when we do not consider the underlying message carefully. You will recall from the section on attitude change in Chapter 15 that, according to Petty and Cacioppo's (1986, 1996) **elaboration likelihood model**, people can process information either via a central or a peripheral route. Attractive people may influence us via the peripheral route, and can thus be less influential if we adopt central route processing.

Reciprocity

Another effective method for ensuring others will comply with your requests is first to do them a favour. This takes advantage of a powerful human expectation of **reciprocity** – the tendency to return favours others have done for us. When someone does something for us, we feel uncomfortable until we have discharged the debt. For example, if people invite us to their house for dinner, we feel obliged to return the favour in the near future. Owing a social debt to someone we do not like is especially distasteful. Often people will suffer in silence rather than ask for help from someone they dislike. Reciprocity is pervasive – every culture is known to have some form of the 'golden rule' (Cialdini, 1993). It establishes a basic guideline for behaviour in a wide range of situations, and its emergence in evolutionary history is considered to be crucial to the development of social life.

Reciprocity does not require that the 'favour' be initially requested or even wanted. The debt of obligation can be so strong that reciprocity can be exploited by people who want us to comply with their requests when we would otherwise not do so. For example, people trying to sell something often try to capitalise on the reciprocity rule by giving the potential customer a free sample. Once the person has accepted the 'gift', the sales representative tries to get them to return the favour by making a purchase. Many of us avoid accepting free samples because we dislike being manipulated into buying something we do not want.

Experiments conducted by social psychologists have confirmed the strength of reciprocity in human interactions. For example, Regan (1971) enlisted the participation of university students in an experiment that supposedly involved art appreciation. During a break in the experimental session, some participants were treated to a soft drink by another 'participant' (a confederate) or by the experimenter; others received nothing. After the experiment, the confederate asked each participant to purchase some raffle tickets he was selling. Compliance with the request was measured by the number of tickets each participant bought. The participants treated to a soft drink by the confederate purchased the most raffle tickets.

Multiple requests

A third technique for gaining compliance involves the use of multiple requests. The focal request is either preceded by a smaller request that everyone will agree to (called foot-in-the-door), or preceded by a much larger request that everyone will refuse (door-in-the-face), or accompanied by all sorts of sweeteners (low-balling).

To investigate the **foot-in-the-door tactic**, Freedman and Fraser (1966) sent a person posing as a volunteer worker to call on homeowners in a residential California neighbourhood. The volunteer asked the homeowners to perform a small task: to accept a 3-inch-square sign saying 'Keep California Beautiful' or 'Be a Safe Driver' or to sign a petition supporting legislation favouring one of these goals. Almost everyone agreed. Two weeks later, the experimenters sent another person to ask these people whether they would be willing to have public service billboards erected in front of their houses. To give them an idea of precisely what was being requested, the 'volunteer worker' showed the homeowners a photograph of a house almost completely hidden by a huge, ugly, poorly lettered sign saying 'Drive Carefully'. Over 55 per cent of the people agreed to this obnoxious request. In contrast, only 17 per cent of householders who had not been contacted previously (and asked to accept the smaller sign) agreed to have such a billboard placed on their property.

The foot-in-the-door tactic works even better when the focal request is preceded by a graded series of smaller requests leading up to the focal request (Dolinski, 2000). So, if you wanted to persuade someone to go out with you, it might be useful to get them first to agree to study with you in the library, and once they say yes, say, 'How about going for coffee?', and then once they agree, pose the focal request of asking them to go out with you.

The foot-in-the-door tactic probably works because once people have committed themselves to a course of action they are loath then to change their mind. Commitment probably increases compliance for several reasons. First, the act of complying with a request in a particular category may change a person's self-image. Through the process of self-attribution, people who accept a small sign to support safe driving may come to regard themselves as public-spirited – what sensible person is not in favour of safe driving? Thus, when they hear the billboard request, they find it difficult to refuse. After all, they are public-spirited, so how can they say no? Saying no would imply that they did not have the courage of their convictions. Thus, this reason has at its root self-esteem. To maintain positive self-esteem, the person must say yes to the larger request.

Commitment may also increase compliance because the initial, smaller request changes people's perception of compliance in general. Evidence supporting this suggestion was provided by Rittle (1981). While sitting in a waiting room before taking part in an experiment, some adult participants were approached by an 8-year-old child who was having trouble operating a vending machine. Later, while answering a series of questions designed to disguise the true nature of the experiment, they were asked to rate their perceptions of how unpleasant it might be to provide help to other people. After the participants had answered all the questions and the study was apparently over, the interviewer asked them whether they would volunteer between 30 minutes and 4 hours of their time to participate in a research project. Participants who had helped the child rated helping as less unpleasant and were more willing to participate in the research project than were people who had not helped the child (see Figure 16.1).

The second multiple request tactic, the **door-in-the-face**, is the opposite of the foot-in-the-door. Here, the focal request is preceded by a much larger request that no one is likely to comply with. Cialdini *et al.* (1975) tested this tactic by approaching students with a huge request: 'Would you serve as a voluntary counsellor at a youth offenders' centre two hours a week for the next two years?' Virtually no one agreed. However, when the researchers then asked for a considerably smaller request, 'Would you chaperone a group of these offenders on a two-hour trip to the zoo?', 50 per cent agreed. When the second request was presented alone, less than 17 per cent

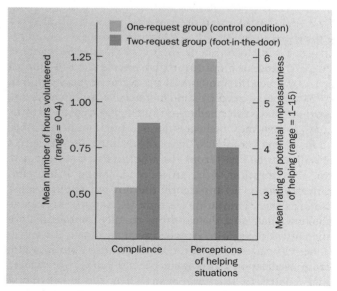

Figure 16.1 The effect of commitment on compliance and perceptions of the potential unpleasantness of helping situations. Mean number of hours volunteered (compliance) and mean rating of potential unpleasantness of volunteering, for control participants and participants who first helped a child.

Source: Based on data from Rittle, R.H., Changes in helping behaviour: Self versus situational perceptions as mediators of the foot-in-the-door technique. *Personality and Social Psychology Bulletin*, 1981, 7, 431–37.

complied. For the tactic to be effective, the final request should come from the same person who made the initial request. According to Cialdini and associates, participants perceive the scaled-down request as a concession by the influencer, and consequently they feel pressure to reciprocate. If some other person were to make the second request, reciprocation would not be necessary.

The final multiple request tactic is called **low-balling**. The effectiveness of low-balling depends on people's disinclination to change their mind once they have already made a commitment. For example, some of you may have had dealings with car sales agents. You are shown a beautiful car that you fall in love with and the agent commits you to purchasing the car which includes CD-player, GPS, air-conditioning, sunroof, electric windows and so forth, as well as all the various dealer costs. The agent now goes to get the paperwork ratified by their boss and comes back with the disappointing news that many of the 'extras' are not included. A rational choice would now be to decline to buy the car. However, because you are committed to your decision you are actually very likely still to purchase the car.

The effectiveness of low-balling was experimentally demonstrated by Cialdini *et al.* (1978). They asked half their participants to be in an experiment that began at 7 a.m. The other half were asked first to commit themselves to participating in an experiment, and then were informed that it would start at 7 a.m. The latter group, in the low-balling situation, complied more often (56 per cent) than the control group (31 per cent), and also tended to keep their appointments.

Obedience

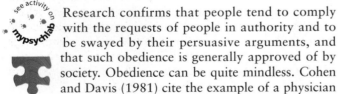

Research confirms that people tend to comply with the requests of people in authority and to be swayed by their persuasive arguments, and that such obedience is generally approved of by society. Obedience can be quite mindless. Cohen and Davis (1981) cite the example of a physician who prescribed ear-drops for a hospitalised patient with an ear infection. His order read 'place in R ear'. Unfortunately, he apparently did not put enough space between the abbreviation for right (R) and the word ear – the nurse delivered the ear drops rectally. Neither she nor the patient thought to question such treatment for an ear ache. Other research in the United States confirms that many medication errors occur because nurses overwhelmingly defer to doctors, even when the nurses have concerns about the wisdom or correctness of the doctors' directions (Lesar *et al.*, 1997).

The classic study of blind obedience is a series of experiments performed by Stanley Milgram (1963), who advertised for participants in local newspapers in order to obtain as representative a sample as possible. The participants served as 'teachers' in what they were told was a learning experiment. A confederate (a middle-aged account-ant) serving as the 'learner' was strapped into a chair 'to prevent excessive movements when he was shocked', and electrodes were attached to his wrist. The participants were told that 'although the shocks can be extremely painful, they cause no permanent tissue damage'.

The participant was then brought to a separate room housing an apparatus having dials, buttons and a series of switches that supposedly delivered shocks ranging from 15 to 450 volts. The participant was instructed to use this apparatus to deliver shocks, in increments of 15 volts for each 'mistake', to the learner in the other room. Beneath the switches were descriptive labels ranging from 'Slight shock' to 'Danger: severe shock'.

The learner gave his answers by pressing the appropriate lever on the table in front of him. Each time he made an incorrect response, the experimenter told the participant to throw another switch and give a larger shock. At the 300-volt level, the learner pounded on the wall and then stopped responding to questions. The experimenter told the participant to consider a 'no answer' as an incorrect answer. At the 315-volt level, the learner pounded on the wall again. If the participant hesitated in delivering a shock, the experimenter said, 'Please go on'. If this admonition was not enough, the experimenter said, 'The experiment requires that you continue', then, 'It is absolutely essential that you continue', and finally, 'You have no other choice; you must go on'. The factor of interest was how long the participants would continue to administer shocks to the hapless victim. A majority of participants gave the learner what they believed to be the 450-volt shock, despite the fact that the learner pounded on the wall twice and then stopped responding altogether (see Figure 16.2).

In a later experiment, when the confederate was placed in the same room as the participant and his struggling and apparent pain could be observed, 37.5 per cent of the participants – over one-third – obeyed the order to administer further shocks (Milgram, 1974). Thirty per cent were even willing to hold his hand against a metal plate to force him to receive the shock.

Even the once most powerful man in the world feels the need to obey authority: G. W. Bush's handwritten note at the UN on 14 September 2005, asking if he can go to the lavatory.
Source: REUTERS/Rick Wilking.

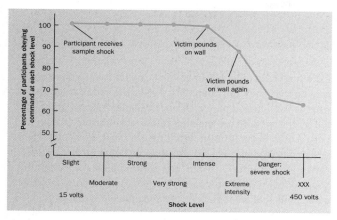

Figure 16.2 Data from one of Milgram's studies of obedience.

Source: From Baron, R.A. and Byrne, D., *Social Psychology: Understanding human interaction*, 8th edn © 1997. Published by Allyn & Bacon, Boston, MA. Copyright © by Pearson Education. By permission of the publisher.

Milgram's experiments indicate that a significant percentage of people will blindly follow the orders of authority figures, no matter what the effects are on other people. Most people find this surprising. They cannot believe that for such a large proportion of people the social pressure to conform to the experimenter's orders is stronger than the participant's own desire not to hurt someone else. As Ross (1977) points out, this misperception is an example of the **fundamental attribution error**. People tend to underestimate the effectiveness of situational factors and to overestimate the effectiveness of dispositional ones. Clearly, the tendency to obey an authority figure is amazingly strong. However, one factor that can dramatically reduce obedience is social support for non-compliance. In one of his studies, Milgram had two confederates work with the participant. When the confederates were obedient, so was the participant – obedience increased to 92.5 per cent. However, when the confederates were disobedient so was the participant – obedience dropped dramatically to 10 per cent.

Understandably, much of the attention given to Milgram's research focused on its considerable ethical implications (Elms, 1995). Many people, psychologists and non-psychologists alike, have attacked his research on the grounds that it involved deception and too much emotional strain on the participants. Indeed, Milgram's research helped prompt psychologists to strengthen ethical guidelines for conducting research with humans.

In his defence, however, it should be stressed that Milgram conducted an extensive debriefing at the end of each experimental session in which the true purpose of the experiment was explained to the participants. The participants were told that their behaviour was quite typical of the way most people responded to the situation posed by the experiment. In addition, the participants were later sent a detailed written report of the experimental procedure and a follow-up questionnaire asking them about their feelings regarding their participation. Eighty-four per cent of the participants said that they were glad to have participated in the experiment, and only 1.3 per cent indicated that they wished they had not participated.

An additional objection to Milgram's research is that people may have had to confront a disturbing aspect of their own behaviour – the self-realisation that they were capable of actions that they find reprehensible. Milgram replied that at least some of his participants considered their enhanced insight into their own behaviour to have been enough to justify their participation. Of course, Milgram could not guarantee that somebody, somewhere, who had participated in his research might not be deeply troubled by his participation. And therein lies another moral dilemma: to what extent is knowledge about behaviour, in general, and insight about one's own behaviour, in particular, to be avoided in case some people think that others might find this knowledge disturbing? That is not an easy question to answer and one that psychologists must grapple with each time they perform research such as that conducted by Milgram.

Cutting edge – Milgram and obedience to authority, 2007

Most psychologists thought it would never happen but, in 2007, a psychologist from Santa Clara did it. On 3 January 2007, the American current affairs programme, *Primetime*, featured a replication of Milgram's study, conducted by Jerry Burger. The programme was timely. Milgram's findings have been thought to explain aberrations ranging from the Holocaust of the Second World War, to the Mai Lai massacre, to the torture and humiliation that was allowed to fester at Abu Ghraib. For decades, psychologists and others have debated whether Milgram's findings were of their time or whether, in this multimedia age, they could transcend temporal boundaries. But no psychologist has replicated Milgram's study for over 30 years (Blass, 2000) because professional societies' guidelines on the ethical treatment of participants would prevent such experiments from being conducted (Elms, 1995).

However, Burger (2009) alighted on a solution. Most of controversy surrounding Milgram's studies focuses on his fifth experiment. This is where participants were asked to administer shocks from between 15 and 450 volts to an unseen person. At 150 volts, the participants heard the cries of protest from the victim and the victim's expressions of pain. At up to 300 volts, the victim yelled that he was in pain. After 330 volts,

Cutting edge – *Continued*

he fell silent. 65 per cent of people administered the shocks, at the experimenter's instigation, at the maximum voltage. The point at which participants began to become reluctant to give the shock was 150 volts. When psychiatrists, students and members of the public are asked at what point they would stop, 150 volts is their threshold (Milgram, 1974). This is an important figure because of those who reached this level, 79 per cent were prepared to continue to 450 volts, the maximum.

Burger used this fact to inform his replication. The assumption would be that if participants were willing to deliver a shock at this level, it is highly likely that they would have administered a higher shock (regardless of whether they said they would not). Burger carefully screened his participants, making sure that they had seen a clinical psychologist beforehand and that there was no indication of vulnerability. Participants were also informed, three times, that they could withdraw at any point and still keep the money they were promised for participating. They were told that the learner had also been offered the opportunity to leave at any point. Participants were told immediately after the experiment that the learner had received no shock (a long time elapsed in Milgram's study). In addition, the experimenter in Burger's study was a clinical psychologist who was instructed to stop immediately if any unacceptable signs of distress were observed. Twenty-nine men and forty-one women participated. The experiment was run using an almost identical protocol to that in Milgram's studies. In one condition, participants saw another confederate refuse the experimenter's instructions.

Seventy per cent of participants were willing to go beyond the 150-volt limit and had to be prevented from doing so. Even when they saw a confederate refuse instructions they continued to deliver the shock, indicating that seeing others disobey did not inhibit the giving of punishment. There was no significant difference between men and women (Milgram's studies recruited, largely, men). And while those who reported being highly empathetic expressed a reluctance to continue earlier than did those who were less empathetic, this empathy did not prevent them from physically continuing with the experiment and delivering the shocks.

It seems as if, almost 30 years after Milgram's original experiment, people will behave in almost exactly the same way now as they did then. Of course, the jaded might ask whether we needed an experiment, Milgram's experiment, to tell us that people are inclined to obey authority. 'Of course not', writes Blass (2009). 'What he did teach us is just how strong this tendency is – so strong, in fact, that it can make us act in ways contrary to our moral principles . . . Milgram showed that it does not take evil or aberrant persons to carry out actions that are reprehensible and cruel' (p. 40).

A copy of the participant recruitment advert that Milgram used.
Source: TopFoto: The Granger Collection, New York.

The social psychology of attribution – An international perspective

People frequently talk of differences between the East and the West. Almost any psychological quirk in people from these two terrains can be attributed to one group having a 'Western' style of thinking or behaving and the other an 'Eastern' one. But is there any psychological evidence to support the cliché?

Interestingly, social psychology has provided some. Research on people's perception of the causes of behaviour has found a striking result: people from the West, largely the US, tend to explain others' behaviour in terms of people's characteristics, that is, they commit the fundamental attribution error. People from the East, on the other hand, such as East Asians, attribute people's behaviour to situational factors (Lee *et al.*, 1996; Morris and Peng, 1994). In Morris and Peng's study, for example, the researchers analysed American and Chinese newspaper reports of mass murder and compared how often each nation attributed the murderers' actions

The social psychology of attribution – *Continued*

to personal or situational characteristics. The US journalists tended to focus on negative personality characteristics of the murderers; the Chinese journalists focused more on situational/contextual factors.

Research also shows that the West, at least those living in the North American part of it, tends to hold single individuals responsible for actions whereas East Asians hold groups or communities responsible (Chiu *et al.*, 2000; Menon *et al.*, 1999). Chui *et al.* asked people to determine who was responsible when a pharmacist dispensed the incorrect medicine. Americans believed it was the specific pharmacist; Chinese participants believed it was the pharmacy as a unit. Americans also believe there are fewer reasons for the causes of people's behaviour than do other Asian nations, such as Korea (Choi *et al.*, 2003).

In a recent study, European Americans and Asian Americans were asked to list their perceptions of consequences of various actions, including a shot in billiards and turning an area into a national park (Maddux and Yuki, 2006). When considering the consequences of taking a shot at bil-liards, the Asian Americans thought that a single shot would have a much greater impact on subsequent shots than did the European Americans. Japanese participants also listed more indirect consequences of creating a national park.

When the groups had to consider the consequences of a social act such as firing someone or causing an accident, the Japanese thought that these events would affect more people than did the Americans. They also felt more responsible, felt worse and were more likely to apologise to those affected.

The authors make an interesting extrapolation from their findings. The crime rate in Japan may be lower because the Japanese perceive their acts as affecting more people. The Japanese are also the only people to suffer from the culture-dependent psychological disorder, *taijin kyofusho* – an extreme fear of hurting or offending others and of being harshly judged by others. 'For East Asians,' the authors suggest, 'a sense of interdependence with others may extend farther outward in a temporal and physical manner, leading to a heightened sense of responsibility' (p. 680).

Conformity

Compliance and obedience produce changes in people's behaviour, but in general such changes do not correspond to a change in people's attitudes or other internal cognitive structures. These deeper changes are more likely to be wrought by group influence where we conform to what we perceive to be group norms (Turner, 1991).

Norms

People, particularly in individualistic Western societies, often think that they are not very influenced by norms and conventions. Indeed, conforming is often viewed as undesirable, as an indication of a weak personality, a lack of individual autonomy, and so forth. In reality, almost everything we think and do is, to varying degrees, grounded in social norms and conventions. Language itself is a normative way of communicating and representing the world to ourselves and others. If people did not agree on how to construct sentences or on what sounds to use to refer to what objects, then communication would be impossible. What we eat, when we eat, what side of the road we drive on, how we behave in restaurants – these are all normative behaviours.

Norms (in statistics) can take the form of explicit rules that are enforced by legislation and sanctions (for example, societal norms to do with private property, pollution and aggression), or they can be the implicit, unobserved, taken-for-granted background to everyday life (Garfinkel, 1967).

Garfinkel believed that these latter, implicit, norms and social regularities are hidden because they are so commonplace and integral to everyday life. They account for much behaviour that is often labelled native, instinctive and innate. Garfinkel coined the term **ethno-methodology** to describe the way that ordinary people (hence 'ethno') make sense of and maintain the normative regularities of the social order. Garfinkel believed that because these ethnomethods are usually tacit they are most easily noticed or brought to attention when they are violated. To demonstrate this point, Garfinkel had students act at home for 15 minutes as if they were boarders – that is, be polite, speak formally, and only speak when spoken to. Their families reacted with astonishment, bewilderment, shock, embarrassment and anger, backed up with charges of selfishness, nastiness, rudeness and lack of consideration. An implicit norm for familial interaction was revealed, and its violation provoked a strong reaction. The existence of an implicit norm is often revealed only when it is violated.

One of the earliest and most influential studies of how group norms emerge and then influence us was conducted by Sherif (1936). Sherif was able to show empirically how norms can arise out of social interaction, and then how these norms exert influence on behaviour. Sherif's study was based on a perceptual illusion, originally discovered by astronomers, called the **autokinetic effect**: a small stationary pin-point of light, when projected in an otherwise completely darkened room, appears to move. The illusion is so strong that even if someone is aware of the effect, the apparent movement often persists.

Sherif first placed participants in the room individually and asked each of them how far the light was moving at different times. The answers were quite variable; one person might see the light move 6 cm on average, whereas another might see it move an average of 300 cm. Next, Sherif had groups of three people observe the light together and call out their judgements of movement one after the other. Finally, the participants would again observe the light individually. The most interesting result of the study was that when people made their judgements together they very rapidly converged on a narrow range of judgements that was pretty close to the average of their individual judgements, and their subsequent individual judgements also fell within this narrow range. The group had established what Sherif referred to as a collective frame of reference – a group norm. Even when tested by themselves on a subsequent day, the group members still conformed to this frame of reference.

MacNeil and Sherif (1976) were able to show that even an arbitrary norm can have the same effect. They had a group with only one true participant and three confederates – the confederates made very extreme judgements that produced an extreme norm. MacNeil and Sherif gradually replaced all the confederates with real participants whose individual autokinetic judgements were nowhere near as extreme as the group norm – and yet, they still conformed tightly to the norm.

Sherif's autokinetic findings are not too surprising if we consider that the participants found themselves in an uncertain situation. It makes sense to use others' opinions or judgements as a frame of reference when you are not sure what is going on. But just how strongly do group norms influence individual behaviour when the situation is unambiguous – when we are certain that we perceive things as they really are? The answer to this question was provided in a series of elegant studies conducted by Asch (1951, 1952, 1955).

Majority influence

Asch's studies were less to do with the emergence of norms and more to do with how a numerical majority can influence a single person. Asch asked several groups of seven to nine students to estimate the lengths of lines presented on a screen. A sample line was shown at the left, and the participants were to choose which of the three lines to the right matched it (Figure 16.3). The participants gave their answers orally. In fact, there was only one true subject in each group; all the other participants were confederates of the experimenter. The seating was arranged so that the true subject answered last. On 12 of the 18 trials the confederates made unanimously incorrect responses. When this happened, about 25 per cent of true subjects remained unaffected, but the rest conformed to the erroneous majority on at least one trial. Five per cent conformed to all the incorrect judgements. Overall conformity occurred 33 per

Some people, like this protesting Greek student, believe so passionately in a point of view that they are prepared to go to great lengths to disobey (this is a work of art; the blood is paint).

cent of the time when it could have occurred. Under control conditions, when the confederates responded accurately, fewer than 1 per cent of the true subjects' estimations were errors – the task was quite unambiguous.

Group pressure did not affect the participants' perceptions; it affected their behaviour. That is, the participants went along with the group decision even though the choice still looked wrong to them – and even though the other people were complete strangers. When they were questioned later, they said that they had started doubting their own eyesight or had thought that perhaps they had misunderstood the instructions. The participants who did not conform felt uncomfortable about disagreeing with the other members of the group. The Asch effect shows how strong the tendency to conform can be. Faced with a simple, unambiguous task while in a group of strangers who showed no signs of disapproval when the participant disagreed with them, the vast majority of participants nev-

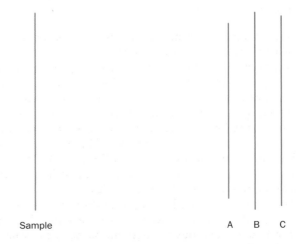

Sample   A   B   C

Figure 16.3 An example of the stimuli used by Asch (1951).

ertheless ignored their own judgements and agreed with the obviously incorrect choice made by the other people.

Presumably, people conformed because they thought that the other members of the group might ridicule them, or at least secretly think badly of them, if they did not. If this is true then conformity should entirely disappear if participants could give their responses privately, without the other members of the group knowing what they had done. To investigate this, Deutsch and Gerard (1955) conducted an Asch-type study where participants gave their responses privately in cubicles. Conformity dropped but certainly did not disappear – it occurred at a rate of 23 per cent.

Subsequent conformity research sought to discover factors that would reduce conformity. Probably the most important influence on conformity was found to be the unanimity of the erroneous majority. Asch's original experiment employed a unanimous erroneous majority to obtain a conformity rate of 33 per cent. However, Asch also found that a correct supporter (i.e. a member of the majority who always gave the correct answer – and thus agreed with and supported the true participant) reduced conformity from 33 per cent to 5.5 per cent. Other experiments have confirmed that conformity is greatly reduced if the majority is not unanimous (Allen, 1975).

However, support itself may not be the crucial factor in reducing conformity. Any sort of lack of unanimity among the majority seems to be effective. For example, Asch found that a dissenter who was even more incorrect than the majority was equally effective. Allen and Levine (1971) conducted an experiment in which participants who were asked to make visual judgements were provided with a supporter who had normal vision, or a supporter who wore such thick glasses as to raise serious doubts about his ability to see anything at all, let alone accurately judge lines. In the absence of any support, participants conformed 97 per cent of the time. The 'competent' supporter reduced conformity to 36 per cent, but most surprising was that the 'incompetent' supporter reduced conformity as well, to 64 per cent.

The process of conformity

Why do people conform? Or rather, what is the process by which people conform? There are at least three reasons why people conform (Turner, 1991). The first is that people like to think their perceptions and attitudes are accurate and valid. So, if people are uncertain or find that others disagree with them, they may think they are wrong and feel a need to change their perceptions and attitudes in line with those of other people. This form of social influence is called **informational influence** (Deutsch and Gerard, 1955). It would have been present in the autokinetic studies, but not the Asch studies.

The second reason why people conform is that people like to be liked and approved of by others and therefore do not like to stand out as different, particularly when in the physical presence of other people. This form of social influence is called **normative influence** (Deutsch and Gerard, 1955). It would have been present in both the autokinetic studies and the Asch studies, but not in the Deutsch and Gerard study.

The third reason why people conform is that they feel a sense of belonging with the group defined by the norm – this is a process of **referent informational influence** (Turner, 1991), which is associated with social identity processes (Turner et al., 1987; Hogg and Abrams, 1988). Group norms map out the defining attributes of a group. Thus, when people identify with the group they use the norms of the group to define themselves as group members. The process is fairly automatic – the group's norms are cognitively represented as a prototype (a fuzzy set of features that define the in-group and distinguish it from out-groups). When people categorise themselves as group members, they assimilate self to the relevant prototype and thus their behaviour is transformed so that it conforms to the prototype/norms. In the Sherif and Asch situations, other people's behaviour becomes a self-defining norm that is internalised to regulate one's own behaviour as a group member. Abrams et al. (1990) found that conformity in both the Sherif and the Asch paradigms was reduced when the source of influence was categorised as an out-group rather than an in-group.

The Stanford Prison experiment

see activity on mypsychlab

On a par with the ethical vortex that is Milgram's obedience experiments is Phillip Zimbardo's Stanford Prison experiment, another of social psychology's ground-breaking studies (Zimbardo, 1982). Zimbardo's involvement was motivated by several reported examples of guard brutality in US prisons. He sought to discover whether bad prison guards were inherently bad or were shaped by the situation in which they found themselves. In the original study, Zimbardo had the Palo Alto police arrest students, for various misdemeanours, assign them prisoner numbers and lock them up in a mocked-up real-life prison cell in a basement at Stanford University. Every attempt was made to ensure the authenticity of the prison environment (you can find our more details here: www.prisonexp.org). The students were randomly assigned to playing prisoners or guards. They knew the situation was not real but, as Zimbardo himself has noted, 'No one expected what happened'. The experiment was meant to run for 14 days; it was stopped after less than a week. The researchers expected the prisoners to sit around, behind bars, reading books and playing guitars. But the prisoners began to rebel. On the second morning, they began protesting vocally and physically. It was at this point that the atmosphere changed. The guards became increasingly brutal, as if they were determined to demonstrate who had the real power in this context (remember that both groups were students). As the prisoners became increasingly humiliated, the guards' behaviour worsened. Faced with this authoritarian onslaught, the prisoners became increasingly compliant. This simply made the guards more sadistic. You can see how the guards' behaviour changed, and changed dramatically, in these quotes from one of the students who played a guard.

Diary entry, before the experiment

As I am a pacifist and non-aggressive individual, I cannot forsee a time when I might maltreat other living things.

Day 3 of the study

This was my first chance to exercise the kind of manipulative power that I really like.

Day 5 of the study

I harass Sarge, who continues to stubbornly over-respond to commands. I have singled him out for special abuse both because he begs for it and because I simply don't like him.

Now, imagine if these were real prisoners and real guards, and maltreatment of prisoners was either condoned or not seen. What do you think would be likely to happen? The BBC 're-created' the experiments in 2003, not entirely to Zimbardo's satisfaction (see his interview in Cohen, 2004). But a real-life illustration emerged a few years ago with the revelation of the treatment of prisoners at the Iraqi prison, Abu Ghraib.

Minority influence

Conformity research tends to focus on the way that a numerical majority influences the attitudes and behaviour

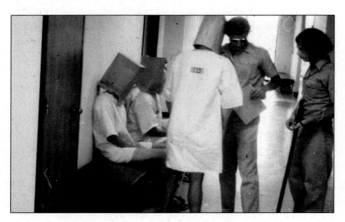

A still from the original Stanford Prison Experience.
Source: Philip G. Zimbardo, Phd.

of a minority. A valid question arises then as to whether a minority can influence the majority – what facilitates **minority influence**. After all, everyday experience tells us that people do not always conform to majorities. Sometimes a minority can be persuasive. Indeed social change – from new trends and fashions to social movements and political revolutions – would not be possible if active minorities could not have influence over the masses (Moscovici, 1976). Asch (1952) looked at this in one of his studies. He had 16 naive participants facing one confederate who gave incorrect answers. The participants found the confederate's behaviour ludicrous, and openly ridiculed him and laughed at him. Even the experimenter found the situation so bizarre that he could not contain his mirth and ended up laughing at the poor confederate. Clearly, in this context a minority was pretty ineffectual.

But in the Asch paradigm, who really is the majority and who the minority? Moscovici and Faucheux (1972) make the point that in a standard Asch experiment the hapless lone participant is faced by a small group of people who actually behave extremely bizarrely – in the real world, no one would make the judgements that the confederates make in the experiment. In reality, the majority is a minority, and the studies actually show how a minority viewpoint can be persuasive. This clever insight raises the question of how minorities are influential.

Because minorities have to combat a pervasive consensus that often has the support of a powerful elite, they need to adopt particular behavioural styles in order to be effective (Mugny, 1982). Minorities need to challenge the dominant consensus by providing an alternative viewpoint that is strongly consensual among minority members and has marked consistency across time. A consistent minority (1) disrupts the majority norm and thus produces uncertainty and doubt; (2) draws attention to itself as an entity; (3) conveys the existence of an alternative coherent point of view; (4) demonstrates certainty in, and unshakeable commitment to, its point of view; and (5) shows that the only solution to the conflict that has arisen is espousal of the minority viewpoint.

Minorities are also more effective if they are seen to have made significant personal or material sacrifices for their cause, to be acting out of principle rather than from ulterior motives, and to have some flexibility around their core message. There is also some evidence that minorities may be more effective if they are viewed by the majority as being a relevant in-group. This is usually difficult to bring about because, by definition, the majority protects itself by emphasising the out-group status of the minority. It can work, however, if the minority is able to establish its legitimate in-group credentials before it espouses a minority viewpoint (Crano and Alvaro, 1998) – in effect behaving like a wolf in sheep's clothing.

A consistent, but not rigid or inflexible, minority has what is called 'latent influence' that produces a conversion effect. Majority members cogitate about the minority position, but still conform to the majority position, until at a later point they suddenly appear to be converted to the minority's position and switch their allegiance and change their behaviour. This distinction, between the majority having relatively surface influence and the minority having a deeper latent influence leading to conversion, resembles to some extent the distinction made by social cognition and attitude researchers between peripheral and central route processing (Petty and Cacioppo, 1986) that we discussed in Chapter 15.

Moscovici and Personnaz (1980) conducted an intriguing experiment to test the conversion and latent influence ideas. Participants called out the colour of a series of blue slides, which varied only in intensity, after they had heard a confederate who was described as either a member of the majority (82 per cent of people) or a member of a minority (18 per cent of people) describe the slide as green. Moscovici and Personnaz also had participants describe the chromatic after-image they saw when the slide had been removed – participants did not realise that the after-image of blue is yellow, and of green is purple. Participants exposed to majority influence (the confederate who was a member of the majority) showed a tendency to call the blue slides green, but their after-image was unaffected – it remained yellow, indicating that although they may have complied with the majority they certainly had not changed what they actually saw. Participants exposed to minority influence, however, continued to call the slides blue, but remarkably their after-image had shifted towards purple, and the effect had become a little stronger when they were tested individually at a later stage. Although they had not changed their surface behaviour, there was a deeper latent change in their perception as a consequence of minority influence.

People in groups

see activity on mypsychlab

Human beings are unmistakably social creatures: a great deal of our lives is spent in the company of others. By itself, this is not an especially profound observation, but it leads to some interesting implications, particularly for social psychologists. We do not merely occupy physical space with other people. We affiliate psychologically and form groups with each other. A **group** is a collection of individuals who have a shared definition of who they are and what they should think, feel and do – people in the same group generally have common interests and goals. Groups are very diverse in size, form and longevity – they include ethnic groups, nations, organisations, departments, teams, clubs and even

families. However, by the definition above, not all aggregations of people are groups in a psychological sense – a crowd of people shopping or some people standing at a bus stop are unlikely to be a group.

People aggregate, affiliate, or form groups for all sorts of reasons. One set of reasons is very instrumental. Being in a group provides protection and allows people to do things that they cannot do alone. For example, it is probably better to walk down dangerous back streets in a crowd rather than alone, and a community can put up a barn more quickly than a lone individual. There are, however, some more basic psychological reasons for joining groups. A group of people with similar attitudes and behaviours to your own provides a wonderfully comforting sense of self-validation. Groups can reduce anxiety (Schachter, 1959), provide confirmation of the validity of one's perceptions (Festinger, 1954), and reduce uncertainty about one's self and one's place in the world (Hogg, 2000).

Baumeister and Leary (1995) believe that the need to belong is one of the most fundamental of all human motives. They may well be right. Williams (2001) has shown in a series of vivid experiments that simply being ignored or excluded from social interaction can have quite profound effects. Indeed, many societies use ostracism or shunning as a potent punishment. In Williams's studies, a naive participant ostensibly waiting with two other people (actually experimental confederates) for an experiment to begin is excluded by the confederates from a spontaneous game of passing a ball that they have found in the room. The participant showed signs of genuine distress – fidgeting, disengagement, displacement activities and so forth.

In 2007, the UK saw its first 'run' on a bank. Within hours of rumours of the extent of the bank's debt, Northern Rock's customers began queuing to withdraw their money. Some claimed that such images fuelled greater panic and exacerbated the bank's problems.
Source: Getty Images: Peter Macdiarmid

The treatment of marginal group members and deviants

Many of the groups we are in, our in-groups, provide the psychological environment for the self and are therefore fundamental, or even primary, to our sense of who we are (Allport, 1954; Yzerbyt *et al.*, 2000). They matter psychologically so much to us that we can be inordinately concerned and upset if we feel marginalised or rejected by the group, and we can go to great lengths to protect the integrity of the group by treating deviant members harshly. For example, people are much more willing to derogate a deviant member of the in-group than a similarly deviant member of an out-group – a phenomenon known as the 'black sheep effect' (Marques *et al.*, 1988). Moreover, this effect is particularly strong when people identify strongly with their group (Branscombe *et al.*, 1993).

Marques *et al.* (2001) proposed that this effect reflects the operation of 'subjective group dynamics', whereby people try, psychologically, to sustain the sense of validity of their in-group's norms. In one experiment, Abrams *et al.* (2000) asked psychology students to evaluate normative or deviant group members who were either psychology students (in-group) or customs officers (out-group) who made statements about the UK's policy on asylum seekers. The norm for psychology students was to leave the existing policy unchanged, whereas the norm for customs officers was to advocate tighter restrictions. Two types of deviant were presented in each group. The anti-norm psychologist and anti-norm customs officer actually both expressed an identical (slightly restrictive) attitude which tended towards the views of the opposing group. Evaluations of these anti-norm members showed the classic black sheep effect. The out-group deviant was preferred over the in-group deviant. However, when the deviants expressed extreme positions that exaggerated the norm of their own group (i.e. a very restrictive customs officer and a very lenient psychologist) they were evaluated much more negatively, and positively, respectively. This pattern of results is shown in Figure 16.4.

The opposing reactions to the anti-norm and pro-norm deviants shows that people may be more concerned to ensure that they maintain the difference between in-group and out-group norms than to ensure that all members of their group conform. Equally important is that people do not necessarily reject out-group members more than in-group members. They may favour out-group members who lend apparent support to the validity of in-group norms. Other research (Yzerbyt *et al.*, 1999; Hutchison and Abrams, 2003) shows that group members who identify more highly are likely to reject an anti-norm deviant from the stereotypical image of the group. All of this suggests that people are strongly motivated to sustain the idea that their in-group is a coherent entity.

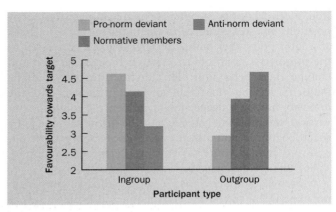

Figure 16.4 Favourability towards anti-norm and pro-norm deviants relative to normative members of the in-group and out-group.

Source: Based on Abrams, D., Marques, J.M., Brown, N.J. and Henson, M., Pro-norm and anti-norm deviance within and between groups. *Journal of Personality and Social Psychology*, 2000, 78, 911.

Which is more important – the individual or the group?

There is evidence that people may store information about the individual and collective self in separate cognitive 'baskets' (Trafimow *et al.*, 1991), that is, when people think of their personal qualities they are unlikely also to think about their group memberships, and vice versa. This means it is possible to test whether the individual or collective self has primacy in terms of people's motivation. Despite evidence that people will defend their collective in-group norms, some researchers argue that the individual self-concept provides the most powerful motivational force for behaviour. Gaertner *et al.* (2002) proposed that the individual self has primacy both because the individual self is the unit of natural selection and because attributes of the self seem to remain stable over time, and changes occur only slowly over the lifespan, presumably because people defend their individual self against threatening feedback, and they selectively accept or pursue information that confirms their self-image as an individual.

A further possibility is that either the individual or collective self may have primacy, depending on the context. For example, Markus and Wurf (1987) assume that the self is defined by a 'working self-concept', which draws on the relevant attributes in relation to the current situation. More radically, Turner *et al.*'s (1987) self-categorisation theory holds that the context and situation have a very strong effect on how the self is defined. In particular, self is defined in terms of a social category to which one belongs relative to a category to which one does not belong within a situation. For example, at a football match people define themselves primarily in terms of which team they support (Cialdini *et al.*, 1976), whereas when taking part in an election they define themselves in terms of which party they support.

Gaertner and Insko (2000) showed that participants would allocate more money to the in-group than an out-group only if they believed their personal earnings could be influenced by other in-group members. In another set of studies Gaertner *et al.* (1999) showed that people whose individual self was threatened considered the threat to be more severe, felt more negative and angry and derogated the source of the threat more than did those who experienced a threat to the collective self. For example, in their experiment participants anticipated playing a game with an individual partner (dyad condition) or joined two others to play against another three-person group. Participants rated their initial feelings of anger, and then after completing an initial comprehension task, participants received positive or insulting feedback from the opposing person/team that they 'did well/seems to know what is going on', or 'did not do well, must be a little slow'. Participants then rated their feelings of anger again. Figure 16.5 shows that participants felt angrier when their individual self was insulted than when their collective self was insulted.

To compare evidence for these different views, Gaertner *et al.* (2002) conducted a meta-analysis (statistical summary across a series of different studies) to examine how people respond to threats to the individual and collective self, and how they respond to opportunities to enhance the self. In these experiments threats and enhancements were manipulated either by directing negative or positive feedback or linking positive or negative information to the individual or collective self. Across 37 different items of research evidence, Gaertner *et al.* found that people responded more strongly to both threats and enhancements of the individual self than to comparable threats to the collective self or the contextual self.

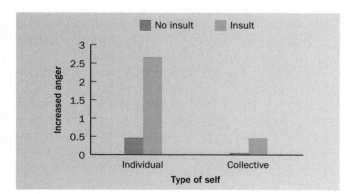

Figure 16.5 Increases in anger as a result of an insult to the individual or collective self.

Source: Based on Gaertner, L., Sedikides, C. and Graetz, K., In search of self-definition: Motivational primacy of the individual self, motivational primacy of the collective self, or collective primacy? *Journal of Personality and Social Psychology*, 1999, 76, 13.

Social facilitation

You saw in the above discussion of social influence that the behaviour of other people has a powerful effect on our behaviour. Studies have shown that the mere presence of other people can affect a person's behaviour. Triplett (1897) published the first experimental study of **social facilitation** – the enhancement of a person's performance by the presence of other people. He had people perform simple tasks, such as turning the crank of a fishing reel. He found that his participants turned the crank faster and for longer if other people were present. Although many other studies found the same effect, some investigators reported just the opposite effect. If the task was difficult and complex, the presence of an audience impaired the participants' performance. We're all probably familiar with the sound of audience laughter accompanying a sitcom on television. More often than not, this laughter is real not canned and we know that – despite what people might say – people laugh more and find the comedy funnier if they watch or listen to the material with audience laughter present (Martin and Gray, 1996).

Zajonc (1965) has suggested an explanation for social facilitation. He claims that the presence of people who are watching a performer (or of people whom the performer perceives as watching) raises that person's arousal level and produces 'drive'. The increase in arousal has the effect of increasing the probability of performing dominant responses: responses that are best learned and most likely to occur in a particular situation. When the task is simple, the dominant response is generally the correct one (by definition an easy task is one which you get right all the time), so an audience improves performance. When the task is difficult the dominant response is generally not the correct one (by definition a difficult task is one which you get wrong all the time), so an audience impairs performance.

Subsequent experiments have supported Zajonc's explanation. For example, Martens (1969) tested the prediction that the presence of a group increases a person's level of arousal or drive. While participants performed a complex motor task alone or in the presence of ten people, the experimenter determined physiological arousal by measuring the amount of sweat present on the participants' palms. The presence of an audience produced a clear-cut effect: the participants who performed in front of other people had sweatier palms.

Markus (1978) tested the effects of an audience on task performance. She had student participants get undressed and then dress up in either their own clothes (an easy task where the dominant response is to get it right) or in unfamiliar clothing involving a special lab coat and special shoes (a difficult task where the dominant response is to make mistakes). Some participants did this alone whereas others did this while being watched.

Relative to those who did the task alone, those who were being watched were faster on the easy task and slower on the difficult task – clear support for social facilitation.

Zajonc (1965) believed that the mere presence of other people produces arousal and drive. Baron (1986) proposed an alternative view. He argued that people are distracting and that trying to concentrate on a task while being distracted causes arousal and drive. There is some support for this idea. Any form of distraction, for example loud noise, produces social facilitation effects – improved performance of easy tasks and degraded performance of difficult tasks. Baron has also suggested that perhaps the notion of arousal or drive is unnecessary. People have a limited capacity for attention. In order to perform a task successfully you need to attend to a range of cues and procedures. The presence of other people is an additional tax on attention, which people combat by narrowing their attention onto the task cues and procedures. Difficult tasks require more attention than easy tasks, and thus narrowing of attention causes you to fail to attend to some important cues – task performance deteriorates. Easy tasks require less attention, so narrowing of attention actually causes you to attend more to the task than you ordinarily would – task performance improves.

A final perspective on how being in the presence of other people affects task performance builds on the idea that people make you self-aware (Carver and Scheier, 1981; Higgins, 1987; see also the section on 'Self awareness' in Chapter 15). Being self-aware motivates people to try to bring their actual self (their actual task performance) into line with their ideal self (how they would like or feel they ought to perform the task). Where the discrepancy is small, the additional motivation improves performance, but where the discrepancy is large and insurmountable, people tend to give up trying and task performance deteriorates.

Social loafing

Working together on a task, rather than merely being watched by others or simply being in the presence of others, can have additional effects: the presence of a group sometimes results in a decrease in effort, or **social loafing**. Thus, a group is often less than the sum of its individual members. Many years ago, Ringelmann (1913) measured the effort that people made when pulling a rope in a mock tug-of-war contest against a device that measured the exerted force. Presumably, the force exerted by eight people pulling together in a simple task would be at least the sum of their individual efforts or even somewhat greater than the sum because of social facilitation. However, Ringelmann found that the total force exerted was only about half what would be predicted by the simple combination of individual efforts. The participants exerted less force when they worked in a group.

The reduced performance could be due to at least two reasons. The people pulling on the rope could have distracted each other or interfered in other ways, or the people pulling the rope could simply have tried less hard – this is a distinction between **coordination losses** and **motivation losses** (Steiner, 1972). To tease these two possibilities apart, Ingham et al. (1974) replicated Ringelmann's study, but with two experimental conditions: one in which real groups of varying size pulled on a rope, and the other involving pseudo-groups with only one true participant and a number of confederates. The confederates were instructed only to pretend to pull on the rope while making realistic grunts to indicate exertion. The true participant was in the first position and so did not know that the confederates, who were behind, were not actually pulling. Participants in pseudo-groups pulled less strongly than participants pulling on their own. Because there was no coordination, there can be no loss due to poor coordination; the decrement can be attributed only to a loss of motivation. In real groups, there was an additional decrement in individual performance that can be attributed to coordination loss.

Scores of more recent studies have confirmed these results and have extended them to other behaviours, such as clapping, shouting, cheering and brainstorming (Williams et al., 2003). Formally defined, loafing is 'a reduction in individual effort when working on a collective task (in which one's outputs are pooled with those of other group members) compared to when working either alone or coactively' (Williams et al., 1993, p. 131).

Several variables have been found to influence the tendency to loaf. One of the most important of them is identifiability. Williams et al. (1981) asked participants to shout as loud as they could individually or in groups. Participants who were told that the equipment could measure only the total group effort shouted less loudly than those who were told that the equipment could measure individual efforts. The latter did not loaf – they shouted just as loudly in groups as they did alone. These results suggest that a person's efforts in a group activity are affected by whether other people can observe their individual efforts.

Another variable that determines whether social facilitation or social loafing occurs is individual responsibility. If a person's efforts are duplicated by those of another person (and if their individual efforts are not identifiable), the person is likely to exert sub-maximum effort. Harkins and Petty (1982) had participants work in groups of four on a task that required them to report whenever a dot appeared in a particular quadrant of a video screen. In one condition, each participant watched an individual quadrant and was solely responsible for detecting dots that appeared there. In the other condition, all four participants watched the same quadrant; thus, the responsibility for detecting dots was shared. Participants did not loaf when they were responsible for their own quadrants.

In a review of the social loafing literature, Karau and Williams (1993) noted that two variables – sex and culture – appear to moderate people's tendency to loaf. Although all people in different cultures are susceptible to social loafing, the effect is smaller for women than for men and for people living in Eastern cultures than for those living in Western cultures. Karau and Williams offer a reasonable explanation for this finding: both women and people living in Eastern cultures tend to be more group- or collectively-oriented in their thinking and behaviour than are men and people living in Western cultures. That is, women and people living in Eastern cultures tend to place greater importance on participating in group activities, which partially buffers them from social loafing effects.

Although research tends to show that loafing is the rule in groups, there are some studies which show that groups sometimes motivate people to work harder than they do alone. For example, Zaccaro (1984) had male and female participants construct 'moon tents' out of sheets of paper in two- or four-person co-active groups. The usual loafing effect emerged. However, other participants who believed they were competing against an out-group, and for whom the attractiveness and social relevance of the task was accentuated, behaved quite differently. The loafing effect was reversed: individuals performed at a higher rate in the larger group. This effect may represent **social compensation**, in which people work harder collectively than co-actively in order to compensate for anticipated loafing by others on important tasks or in important groups.

Why do people loaf? There are many reasons. For example, people are often anxious about having their performance evaluated, and so when their individual performance cannot be identified, they can avoid the possibility of evaluation by simply doing less. When their performance can be evaluated they are motivated to work harder in order to avoid an unfavourable evaluation. Another reason why people loaf may be because they feel that in a group they are dispensable – their effort is not really necessary to the group's overall performance because so many others are making a contribution.

Karau and Williams (1993; Williams *et al.*, 2003) have proposed an integrative model they call the **collective effort model**. It states that people will work hard on a collective task only to the degree that they expect their efforts to be instrumental in leading to outcomes that they value personally. Thus loafing will occur if people view the outcomes of the group performance or collective task as trivial or inconsistent with their own desires. Valued outcomes can be objective, say pay and rewards, or subjective such as personal satisfaction and feelings of growth, belonging or enjoyment. Even if people do value the outcomes, they will still loaf if they do not believe that their own efforts can help achieve those outcomes.

The collective effort model identifies a number of factors that moderate loafing. Because people work harder on collective tasks when they expect their effort to be instrumental in obtaining valued outcomes, loafing will be reduced when people: (1) believe their collective inputs can be evaluated; (2) work in smaller rather than larger groups; (3) view their contributions to the collective task as unique or important rather than redundant or trivial; (4) work on tasks that are meaningful, high in personal involvement, important to respected others, or intrinsically interesting; (5) work in cohesive groups or in situations that activate a salient group identity; (6) expect their co-workers to perform poorly; and (7) have a dispositional tendency to value collective outcomes.

Suppose that you have been asked by your psychology lecturer to organise a small group of class members to prepare a presentation. As the leader of the group, what steps might you take to prevent the individual members of your group from becoming social loafers?

Group decision-making

One of the most significant tasks that people perform in groups is decision-making. Group decision-making usually involves discussion that transforms a diversity of opinions into a single group decision.

Because it can be useful to predict what decision a group will come to from an initial distribution of diverse views (for example, juries, parliament, summits and other committees), research has identified a small number of explicit or implicit decision-making rules that groups can adopt, called **social decision schemes** (Davis, 1973). These are:

1 unanimity (discussion pressurises deviants to conform);

2 majority wins (discussion confirms the majority position, which is then adopted as the group position);

3 truth wins (discussion reveals the position that is demonstrably correct);

4 two-thirds majority (unless there is a two-thirds majority, the group is unable to reach a decision); and

5 first shift (the group ultimately adopts a decision consistent with the direction of the first shift in opinion shown by any member of the group).

If you know the decision rule that is being adopted, and you know the initial distribution of positions, then you can predict the group decision with a respectable degree of accuracy (Stasser and Dietz-Uhler, 2001).

Group decision-making involves social interaction, and so is subject to a range of effects that do not impact on individual decision-making, e.g. social facilitation and social loafing may affect the decision-making process. Here we will discuss four group decision-making phenomena that have been the subject of research: brainstorming, group remembering, group polarisation and groupthink.

Cutting edge – Creativity and brainstorming

One model of group interaction and creative thinking suggests that creativity is improved if you add new individuals, with differing views, to the group. Nemeth and Ormiston (2007) tested this by having three people (psychology undergraduates) brainstorm on a given issue then move on to a completely new group or remain in the original brainstorming group. The participants discussed issues such as 'How to decrease traffic congestion in the San Fransisco Bay area' and 'How to increase tourism in the San Fransisco Bay area'. The ideas generated were coded and judged for creativity.

When people remained in the original brainstorming group, participants felt more comfortable and perceived the group to be creative, but were actually no more creative. When membership changed, participants felt less comfortable but the number of creative ideas generated increased.

Brainstorming

Brainstorming is a group decision-making process that involves generating as many ideas as possible as quickly as possible (Osborn, 1957). Group members are told not to be inhibited or concerned about quality (simply to say whatever comes to mind), to be non-critical, and to build on others' ideas when possible. This process is intended to facilitate creative thinking and thus make the group more creative. Popular opinion is so convinced that brainstorming works that the activity is widely used in business organisations and advertising agencies. However, scientific research on brainstorming paints a rather different picture. According to a review by Stroebe and Diehl (1994), individual creativity and productivity are actually reduced, primarily due to interference effects from contending with others generating ideas at the same time as one is trying to generate one's own ideas. This is what Steiner (1972) would classify as a coordination loss. Brainstorming is effective, however, if it is engaged in electronically rather than face-to-face, and if the brainstorming group is very heterogeneous in its membership.

Group remembering

For groups to make decisions they need to marshal a substantial amount of material that is stored in memory. Do groups facilitate or impede memory? Research shows that groups are better than individuals at recalling simple information – such as names of performers or capital cities (Clark and Stephenson, 1995). This is because the group can pool unshared information and can recognise what is true and what is false. However, in more complex memory tasks, like recalling a police interrogation, the group's memory tends to be a creative reconstruction rather than regurgitation of facts. Group remembering is often a constructive process, characterised by negotiation of an agreed joint account of some part of experience. Some individuals' memories will contribute to the developing consensus while others' will not. In this way the group shapes a version of the truth that gains its subjective veracity from the degree of consensus. The group in effect constructs a version of the truth that guides individuals about what to store as a true memory and what to discard as an incorrect memory.

Another way to look at group remembering is to focus not on what a group recalls, but on how a group stores information. Groups tend to have **transactive memory** structures (Moreland *et al.*, 1996). Within the group, different people specialise in remembering different things, but through interaction (transactions) all members of the group remember who is the memory specialist in different domains. Transactive memory has clear advantages in dealing with remembering large amounts of information. However, there are pitfalls. In the context of organisations, if someone leaves then their memory domain disappears and it can take a while for someone else to occupy that domain. The other side of the coin is that new members of organisations may take some time to learn the transactive memory structure of the organisation. In both cases, group processes are disrupted. Disruption can be minimised by making sure that people occupying important memory domains have 'understudies', and that new members are formally taught the transactive memory structure of the organisation.

Group polarisation

We often think of committees and other small decision-making groups as being cautious and conservative in making decisions. Indeed this is often the case – such groups arrive at group decisions that smooth out and average individual variability, which is precisely what one would expect from Sherif's (1936) research on group norms, described above. So, the social psychology community was most interested in Stoner's research (1961) – Stoner found that a group would actually make a more risky decision than the average of the positions held by the group members if the members themselves already leaned towards such a decision. Group discussion produced a risky shift.

Subsequent research has shown this phenomenon to be part of a more general tendency for a group decision to be more extreme than the mean of its members' positions, in the direction favoured by the mean – a phenomenon called

group polarisation (Moscovici and Zavalloni, 1969). If the group leans towards taking a risk, group discussion will produce a more risky decision, if it leans towards caution then the group decision will be more cautious; if it leans towards joining the single European currency the decision will strongly favour joining; if it leans against joining it will be even more opposed; and so forth.

One important consequence of group polarisation is attitude change. For example, suppose that you join a local environmental group because you have a desire to protect the environment. After attending several meetings and discussing environmental issues with other group members, you may find that your pro-environment attitude has become even stronger: you are more of an environmentalist than you thought you were. The fact that group discussion can effect attitude change so powerfully has been documented in many psychology experiments. For example, Myers and Bishop (1970) found that the initial level of racial prejudice voiced by groups was altered through group discussion. Discussion caused the group with an initially low level of prejudice to become even less prejudiced and discussion caused the group with an initially high level of prejudice to become even more prejudiced.

What causes group discussion to lead to polarisation? Although several explanations have been offered, three seem the most plausible: those concerning informational and normative influence (Isenberg, 1986), and social identity processes (Turner *et al.*, 1989). Informational influence involves learning new information germane to the decision to be made. When you are in a group that is already slanted towards one decision, group discussion will bring to light new information that supports your position but that you have not heard before. This supportive novel information will strengthen commitment to your position, and across the members of the group this will encourage the group to endorse a more extreme decision.

Normative influence involves comparison of one's individual views with that of the group. Just as we discussed in the earlier section on conformity, people strive for social approval and do not like to stand out from the crowd. Discussion reveals what appears to be the socially desirable position, and thus members of the group strive to be seen by the other members of the group to be adhering to the 'popular' position. In this way the group becomes more extreme and is able to endorse a more extreme decision.

Social identity processes involve people in the group constructing a group norm to define their membership in the decision-making group and then conforming to that norm. If the group's mean initial position is relatively extreme, this implies that people who are not in the group (or who are in a specific out-group) are less extreme. In order to distinguish the group from 'other people', the in-group norm is perceptually polarised away from 'most other people'. The process of self-categorisa-tion and depersonalisation associated with group identification (Turner *et al.*, 1987) causes people to conform to the polarised norm and thus endorse a polarised group decision. Research has supported this analysis by showing that group polarisation occurs only if people perceive the extreme mean to be a group norm rather than merely an aggregate of positions, and if they identify with the group defined by the norm (Mackie, 1986; Turner *et al.*, 1989; Abrams *et al.*, 1990).

Groupthink

Irving Janis has studied a related phenomenon that sometimes occurs in group decision-making – **groupthink**, the tendency to avoid dissent in the attempt to achieve group consensus (Janis, 1972, 1982). He developed the notion of groupthink after studying the poor decision-making that led President John F. Kennedy to order the ill-fated attempt to overthrow the Castro regime in Cuba in 1961. The decision to embark on the Bay of Pigs invasion was made by Kennedy and a small group of advisers. After studying the conditions that led to this decision and other important group decisions that altered the course of twenti-eth-century history (such as the 1941 Japanese attack on Pearl Harbor), Janis proposed his theory of groupthink.

The theory specifies the conditions necessary for group-think as well as its symptoms and consequences (see Figure 16.6). The conditions that foster groupthink include a stressful situation in which the stakes are very high, a cohesive group of people who already tend to think alike and who are isolated from others who could offer criticism of the decision, and a strong group leader who makes their position well known to the group. In the Bay of Pigs example, the overthrow of one of America's arch-enemies was at stake, Kennedy's group of advisers were like-minded regarding the invasion and met in secret, and Kennedy was a forceful and charismatic leader who made his intentions to invade Cuba known to the group.

Janis also notes five symptoms of groupthink, all of which were present during the decision to invade Cuba: (1) group members share the illusion that their decision is sound, moral and right – in a word, invulnerable; (2) dissent from the leader's views are discouraged, further supporting the illusion that the group's decision is the right one; (3) instead of assessing the strengths and weaknesses of the decision, group members rationalise their decision, looking only for reasons that support it; (4) group members are closed-minded – they are not willing to listen to alternative suggestions and ideas; and (5) self-appointed 'mindguards' exist within the group who actively discourage dissent from the group norm.

Combined, these symptoms lead to flawed decision-making. They contribute to the tendency to conduct only incomplete or no research on the issue about which a decision is being made, to fail to examine alternative

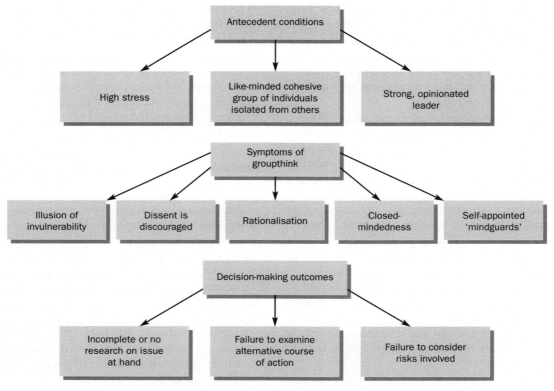

Figure 16.6 A summary of Janis's conception of groupthink.

courses of action specified by the decision, and finally, to fail to consider potential risks inherent in the decision.

Janis argues that groupthink may be avoided by taking several precautions: (1) criticism by group members should be encouraged; (2) relevant input should be sought from appropriate people who are not members of the group; (3) the group should be broken down into sub-groups in which different ideas and opinions are generated and developed; and (4) the group leader should not overstate their position

on the matter and should be on guard for rationalisation, closed-mindedness and illusions of invulnerability. An unlikely last word on this topic goes to former US President Ronald Reagan. He perceptively understood the dangers of groupthink: 'You risk becoming isolated. People tell you about what you want to hear and are reluctant to tell you about somebody who might not be pulling his weight or doing something hurtful to your administration. Not many people close to you are willing to say: "You're wrong".'

Psychology in action – The social psychology of drunkenness

How does alcohol affect your behaviour? Is it any different when you are alone or in a group? Are groups more risky or dangerous when they are drinking? Research into the effects of alcohol shows that individuals take more risks when they have been drinking. They are likely to be sexually irresponsible, aggressive, emotional, and to drive dangerously. Why?

According to Steele and Joseph's (1990) 'alcohol myopia' model, alcohol makes social behaviour more extreme because it blocks response conflicts by reducing cognitive constraints on affective preferences. Fromme *et al.* (1997) argued that drinkers maintain relatively automatic expectation of positive outcomes but they do not engage in systematic processing that is needed to evaluate potential negative outcomes. As a

result, people become riskier in their choices. Research on groups suggests that people also change the way they view risks and social relationships when they make decisions in groups (Janis, 1972).

Curiously, almost all of the research into these effects of alcohol examines only the behaviour of individuals. This is surprising given that such a large proportion of alcohol consumption happens in social settings, often in groups of three or more people.

Abrams *et al.* (2006) investigated whether moderate alcohol intake affected students' attraction to risk. Half of the students consumed enough alcohol to bring them to the legal limit for driving in the UK and USA (roughly 2 pints of beer or 4 glasses

Psychology in action – *Continued*

of wine). The other students consumed a placebo that tasted like alcohol but contained almost none. In one condition students were asked to complete tasks alone. In another condition students completed the same tasks together in groups of four. Members were asked to rate how attractive a series of 16 bets was to them and were told that they would be expected to spend some of their participation payment on these bets.

If *group polarisation* occurred, the group consensus should be more extreme than the average initial tendency of their individual members (Moscovici and Zavalloni, 1969). Given that alcohol myopia should make individuals risky, group polarisation should make them riskier still, so that the effect of alcohol is larger for groups than individuals. The group might also exhibit *deindividuation*, where group members become less self-conscious and less inhibited than individuals (Diener, 1980). Being in a group and drinking could add together to increase riskiness. A third possibility, *group monitoring*, argues that by sharing information, groups are often able to solve problems more reliably than their individual members (Laughlin and Ellis, 1986). The group monitoring hypothesis states that even when moderately intoxicated, group members will be able to attend to one another sufficiently to be reminded that perspectives other than their own should be considered during decision-making. This mutual monitoring within the group may compensate for the effects of alcohol on individuals' riskiness. Alcohol would make individuals but not groups riskier if group monitoring occurs.

Abrams and colleagues found the results supported the group monitoring hypothesis. Individuals found the bets significantly more attractive if they had consumed alcohol than if they were sober. However, when students were in groups, alcohol made no difference to the attractiveness of the bets. Adding further support to the group monitoring explanation is that whereas individuals completed the tasks more quickly after drinking alcohol (suggesting they were paying less attention), groups were significantly slower if they had been drinking alcohol. This fits with the idea that the groups were devoting time to monitoring and discussing their decisions.

Most people's drinking is likely to be moderate and relaxed social drinking, perhaps in the context of an informal meeting, or a drink after work. Under these circumstances it seems that groups might be able to compensate for the negative effects of alcohol on individuals' attentional capacities and loss of inhibition.

Leadership

Our discussion of groupthink has identified the important role of leaders in group decision-making. Indeed, it is very difficult to envisage groups without leaders. Almost all groups are structured into one or more people who have greater influence and take the lead, and others who are more influenced and act as followers. Leadership is endemic to group processes.

One approach to leadership focuses on the way that particular leadership styles are suited to different leadership situations – these are called **contingency theories** because they argue that the effectiveness of a particular style is contingent on situational factors. The best known of these is Fiedler's (1965) contingency theory. Fiedler believed that people differ in their leadership styles – some people are task-oriented and others relationship-oriented. Task-oriented leaders are authoritarian, value group success, and derive self-esteem from task accomplishment rather than being liked by the group; relationship-oriented leaders are relaxed, friendly, non-directive and sociable, and gain self-esteem from happy and harmonious group relations. Fiedler also believed that leadership situations could be classified in terms of what he called situational control. At one extreme were situations in which leaders had legitimate authority, good leader–member relations and the task was well structured; at the other extreme, legitimacy was low, leader–member relations poor and the task poorly structured. Fiedler predicted that relationship-oriented leaders were more effective than task-oriented leaders except if situational control was either very high or very low, when task-oriented leaders would be more effective. There is general support for this analysis, except that critics have suggested that it is too static a view of leadership, and that it underplays the fact that leadership is very much a group process that involves the relationship between leaders and followers.

Leader–follower relations are a more central focus of **transactional theories of leadership**. For example, Hollander (1958) argues that for leaders to be effective they need to develop a relationship with the rest of the group that allows them to be innovative and to exert influence over the group. Hollander suggests that leaders need to accumulate what he calls idiosyncrasy credits. This can be done by (1) initially conforming closely to established group norms, (2) ensuring that the group feels it has democratically elected you as the leader, (3) making sure that you are seen to have the competence to fulfil the group's objectives, and (4) being seen to identify with the group, its ideals and its aspirations.

Another transactional model of leadership is **leader–member exchange theory** (Graen and Uhl-Bien, 1995). To be effective, leaders need to establish very different individualised exchange relationships with different members of the group. However, in doing this, leaders need to be careful to treat all members with respect as valued group members, and not to create destructive internal divisions by showing too much preference for some members over others.

A development of transactional models of leadership focuses on **transformational leadership** (Bass, 1998). Transformational leaders' transactions with followers are characterised by charisma, inspirational motivation, intellectual stimulation and individualised consideration, which motivate followers to work for group goals that transcend immediate self-interest. Transformational leaders are those who respond positively to change and who actively induce change. Great leaders often do seem to behave in this way but critics worry that too much emphasis is now being placed on charisma as a personality attribute.

A different approach to the explanation of leadership has been proposed by social identity theorists (Hogg, 2001; Hogg and van Knippenberg, 2003). In groups, people tend to rest their evaluation and endorsement of leaders on the extent to which leaders match schemas they have of good leadership. However, where people identify strongly with a group that is important to self-definition, people's evaluations of their leaders are increasingly influenced by how prototypical of the group the leader is perceived to be.

There are many implications of this idea. For example, in very cohesive and salient groups with which people identify strongly, poor leaders (those who do not match effective leadership schemas) may prevail simply because they are highly prototypical of the group. Leaders are also presumably aware that they can increase their leadership effectiveness of such groups by being seen to be prototypical. They will engage in a rhetoric of prototypicality in which they talk up their own prototypicality (Reicher and Hopkins, 1996). Leaders of cohesive groups may behave differently as a function of how prototypical they are (van Knippenberg and van Knippenberg, 2003). Leaders who are highly prototypical are often aware that their prototypicality is not in question – they are thus able to be innovative and non-conformist. The prototypicality of less prototypical leaders still needs to be established – these leaders need to be much more conformist and thus less able to be innovative.

Negotiation, teamwork and leadership – An international perspective

From selling detergent to securing peace in Northern Ireland or the Middle East, the ability to negotiate with others is an important social skill. The outcome of a transaction or interaction can turn on not only how well you negotiate, but on how you work as a team and the leadership you show. A recent review by Gelfand et al. (2007) summarises how these three characteristics vary across nations and how this variation affects decisions.

Research on negotiation has shown that, in the US, people are more likely to show self-serving biases and make internal attributions about other negotiators' behaviour (Gelfand and Christakopoulou, 1999). North Americans are more likely to see conflicts as being about winning or violating an individual's rights (Gelfand et al. 2001), to share information directly with their colleagues during negotiation, and achieve high goals that both parties want to attain (Adair et al., 2001). They are more likely to make concessions at the end of the negotiation than at the beginning (Hendon et al., 2003), and are most satisfied with a negotiation when their economic gains have been maximised (Ma et al., 2002).

Japanese negotiators, in contrast, see conflicts as a violation of duty but also as an opportunity to compromise (Gelfand et al., 2001). The Chinese are more susceptible to the influence of fellow negotiators than are Americans (Liv et al., 2005), and the Japanese, Russians and participants from Hong Kong are more likely to seek out information during a negotiation through a pattern of offers (Adair et al., 2001).

Unlike US negotiators, Asian negotiators are more likely to make generous concessions early on in an exchange and gradually reduce these concessions as the negotiation goes on (Hendon et al., 2003). Unlike Americans, Estonians see a successful negotiation ending when both parties are the recipients of equivalent outcomes (Ma et al, 2002).

The ways in which teams operate and are perceived also differ across cultures. For example, Americans view their team less favourably if they – as individuals – do well but the team performs poorly. You don't see such an interpretation in Chinese participants (Chen et al., 1998). Taiwanese participants view their teams more negatively if membership changes often (compared with Australian participants, who don't) (Harrison et al., 2000). Individuals from collectivistic cultures are more likely to view teams as 'entities' and as 'acting as one' (Chiu et al., 2000). In Japan, indirect personal ties between group members is important for engendering trust amongst the team; in the US, this trust is fostered by team participants belonging to some shared membership category, such as the school they went to (Yuki et al., 2005). Teams of people from collectivistic cultures cooperate better and are more successful (Eby and Dobbins, 1997).

What if the team is made up of people from different cultures? The research suggests that these teams show considerable evidence of ethnocentrism and strong in-group biases (Cramton and Hinds, 2005; Von Glinow, 2004). When

Negotiation, teamwork and leadership – *Continued*

the team leaders prevent communication breakdown, however, multicultural teams perform as well as monocultural teams (Ayoko *et al.*, 2002). A person's culture/nation becomes important in team negotiations when either very few or very many members share the same background (Randel, 2003). Here, performance is worse than in more homogeneous groups (Thomas, 1999). Over time, however, Harrison *et al.* (2002) have found that this performance improves, presumably because team members have begun to familiarise themselves with each other and have learned about each other's behaviour. Also, the more heterogenous the team, the better the performance (compared with moderately varied teams) (Earley and Mosakowski, 2000).

Finally, we all know of leaders who seem capable of persuading others and of turning the minds of people who appear to hold entrenched, immutable opinions – Bill Clinton intervening to negotiate with the violently opposed political factions in Northern Ireland; Tony Blair persuading Bill Clinton to release ground troops in Kosovo which, ultimately, put an end to Milosevic's ethnic cleansing; Bob Geldof persuading a few popstars to sing a tune and then subsequently persuading millions to help feed the millions of starving in Africa and, more recently, persuade the eight richest nations in the world to tackle poverty in developing countries. (Of course, there are those whose persuasion is not as honourable or which leads to outcomes that are not as positive – such as those who can persuade young men that crashing a plane into a building or detonating a bomb on a tube train is a good idea or, more historically, Jim Jones, leader of the People's Temple – a Californian cult – who in 1978 ordered almost 800 people to commit suicide.)

Is there any trait that leaders such as this share? In individualistic cultures there is a tendency for leaders to use coercive power to achieve aims whereas in collectivistic cultures, the tendency is to use expert power. According to the Global Leadership and Organizational Behaviour Effectiveness Project (cleverly acronymed as GLOBE) which looked at 17,000 middle managers in 62 cultures, two traits stand out in good leaders: being charismatic and being a team-player (House *et al.*, 2004). The best senior managers were described as innovative, visionary and courageous; those at a lower level were described as being attentive to subordinates and were good at team building.

Gelfand *et al.* (2007) note that charisma varies across nations. They cite the example given by Den Hartog and Verburg (1997). They found that a strong, ululating voice was described as enthusiastic in Latin American cultures, and therefore a vehicle for charisma, whereas a monotonous tone was described as worthy of respect and self-control in Asian cultures, a uniformity that was considered charismatic.

Crowds and social movements

Crowds are clearly group events; however, they seem to be somewhat different from other group phenomena we have discussed. We have all seen media coverage of football riots, and of crowd aggression in, for example, the Middle East and Northern Ireland, and many of us may have been involved in protests or demonstrationss that have turned ugly. We are also familiar with vivid literary accounts of the great riots and demonstrations associated with the French and Russian revolutions. Crowds tend to be volatile, unruly and often violent. They are, of course, not always like this – the crowds attending the funeral of Queen Elizabeth, the Queen Mother, in London in 2002 or those outside the Vatican hearing the Papal address, were certainly not. However, research on crowds has traditionally focused on the antisocial and violent portrayal of crowds. The assumption is that, sometimes, just being part of a crowd can be sufficient to transform our otherwise civil behaviour into unruly, violent acts.

Many social psychologists explain these acts in terms of **deindividuation**, in which one loses one's sense of individuality and personal responsibility. In collective settings, people 'blend' into the crowd, achieving a sense of anonymity that causes them to assume less responsibility for their actions (Diener, 1980). Consider a study of empathy towards strangers conducted by Zimbardo (1970). In one condition, young women were easily identifiable: they wore name tags and were called by their names. In another condition, a different group of young women were not so easily identifiable: they wore large coats and hoods without name tags and were never referred to by their names. The two groups of women were given chances to administer electric shocks to a stranger, who was actually a confederate of Zimbardo's. The young women who were unidentifiable gave nearly twice as many electric shocks to the stranger as did the young women whose identities were known. Thus, the amount of aggression Zimbardo observed in his participants was strongly correlated with the extent to which their identities were known, reinforcing the idea that antisocial behaviour observed in some groups is due to the loss of personal identity of its individual members.

People in crowds are not always antisocial, and crowds themselves are not always aggressive. Deindividuation may not be an automatic consequence of crowds, or it may be a process that is less mechanically tied to antisocial behaviour. Taylor *et al.* (1994) characterise deindividuation as a process wherein one's personal identity – one's sense of self – is replaced by identification with the group's values and goals (see also Reicher *et al.*, 1995).

This idea has been more fully explored in terms of social identity theory, which we discussed earlier in this chapter. Reicher (1987, 2001) suggests that crowds are events where people from the same group, and thus with a common social identity, come together to achieve goals (which may or may not involve violence). The strong sense of common social identity ensures that people are highly attuned to the appropriate group norm, and thus conform tightly to it. There is no loss of identity or responsibility, no deindividuation, rather a change of identity. For Reicher, crowds are not fickle or irrational. They are group events in which there are clear limits to acceptable behaviour – limits set by the identity of the crowd. Local conditions and goals will influence how the crowd's social identity expresses itself within these limits. For example, Stott and colleagues have analysed the role of police behaviour in situations when football fans become violent, such as the 1998 World Cup Final, and conclude that the more heavy-handed the police are in their approach to policing the more violent and antagonistic the fans will be (e.g. Stott and Adang, 2004; Stott *et al.*, 2001).

This rational model of crowds links crowd action to various forms of social protest that may be part of a social movement. The key question in the study of social protest is what causes individual discontents or grievances to be transformed into collective action: how and why do sympathisers become mobilised as activists or participants? Klandermans (1997) argues that this involves the relationship between individual attitudes and behaviour (see Chapter 15). Sympathisers hold, by definition, sympathetic attitudes towards an issue yet these attitudes do not translate into behaviour. Participation also resembles a social dilemma (see below). Protest is generally for a social good (such as equality) or against a social ill (for example, pollution), and as success benefits everyone irrespective of participation but failure harms participants more, it is tempting to 'free ride' – to remain a sympathiser rather than become a participant.

When crowds go wrong: football hooliganism

Since the early 1970s European, but particularly English, football has become strongly associated with hooliganism. Football 'hooliganism' involves groups of people behaving in the same way. It is also a set of behaviours which is often associated in the popular mind with crowd behaviour, the popular image of a riot or other violent and antisocial collective event. Popular hysteria tends to characterise football hooliganism in terms of the familiar stereotypical image of football fans on the rampage (Murphy *et al.*, 1990).

Deindividuation theories offer a group-oriented analysis of this phenomenon. A football match is a crowd context where people feel anonymous and unidentifiable; they lose their sense of individual identity and thus no longer feel that it is necessary to act in socially acceptable ways. This perspective assumes that people are fundamentally antisocial and aggressive, and that the only reason people do not ordinarily act in this way is that they are usually identifiable in a society whose norms strongly proscribe such behaviour. Hooliganism is primitive unsocialised behaviour which lies deep in all our psyches, and which is released in crowd settings like a football match. Although recognising the group context of hooliganism, this analysis is also rather individualistic. The crowd releases individual aggressive instincts – and in fact any (non-group) context that makes one feel deindividuated may have the same effect (for example, darkness, or clothing which conceals who we are). One problem with this analysis is that it cannot easily explain why most people at football matches do not indulge in hooliganism. Perhaps they are not deindividuated – but why? Perhaps they are deindividuated, but deindividuation does not inevitably produce hooliganism, in which case alternative or additional processes must operate to produce hooliganism.

A different, more genuinely group-oriented analysis of football hooliganism is provided by Marsh *et al.* (1978). According to their analysis, violence by football fans is actually orchestrated far away from the stadium and long before a given match. What might appear to be a motley crowd of supporters on match day can actually consist of several distinct groups of fans with different status. By participating in ritualised aggression over a period of time, a faithful follower can be 'promoted' into a higher group and can continue to pursue a 'career structure'. Rival fans who follow their group's rules quite carefully can avoid real physical harm to themselves or others. For example, chasing the opposition after a match ('seeing them off') need not necessarily end in violence since part of the agreed code is not actually to catch anyone. Seen in this light, football hooliganism is a kind of staged production and is not the example of an uncontrollable mob sometimes depicted by the media. When real violence does take place it tends to be both unusual and attributable to particular individuals.

Football hooliganism can also be understood in more broadly societal terms. For example, Murphy *et al.* (1990) described how football arose in Britain as an essentially working-class sport, and that by the 1950s working-class values to do with masculine aggression had already become associated with the game. Attempts by the government (seen as middle class) to control this aspect of the sport can backfire because these attempts merely enhance class solidarity and encourage increased violence that generalises beyond matches. This sort of explanation points towards an analysis in terms of intergroup relations and subcultural norms that prescribe and legitimate aggression. Fans derive a sense of who they are – a sense of identity – from being part of a group of supporters. Some people, particularly those with few other valued sources of identity, identify more strongly than others. The attitudinal, dress and behavioural norms of the group are strongly adhered to, particularly in situations where the group is very salient, for example, at or around a match when supporters of opposing teams are present in the stadium, in the streets and on public transport. The actual norms of the groups reflect the historical origins of the sport and the intrinsically competitive and masculine nature of the game. Football hooliganism is largely a display of controlled aggression and machismo that reflects strong identification with group norms (this sort of group-oriented analysis owes much to social identity theory).

Protestors marching after the riots in Paris of October/ November 2005, which led to debates on integration and discrimination in France, and to what extent French of North African descent could have a French national identity.
Source: Christophe Ena/Press Association Images.

Intergroup relations and prejudice

Our discussion of social protest leads neatly into this next topic. Social protest involves one group of people protesting against another group – often a minority group protesting against the government. It is a manifestation of intergroup relations. Sherif (1962, p. 5) has provided a classic definition of **intergroup relations**:

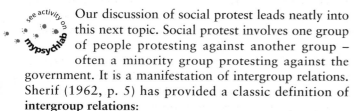

Intergroup relations refer to relations between two or more groups and their respective members. Whenever individuals belonging to one group interact, collectively or individually, with another group or its members in terms of their group identifications we have an instance of intergroup behaviour.

Relations between groups vary enormously from being relatively harmonious to being massively destructive, but almost always they tend to be characterised by some degree of competitive orientation that seeks to maintain the groups as distinctive entities. Because the extreme and harmful aspect of intergroup behaviour is so damaging (it includes war and genocide), research has tended to focus on that aspect and in particular on intergroup conflict and on the attitudinal aspect of hostile intergroup relations – prejudice.

Intergroup behaviour

Intergroup behaviour tends to be competitive and ethnocentric, that is, people tend to view all attributes of their group as being better than all attributes of any out-group they compare themselves with.

Realistic conflict and interdependence

One explanation of why and how this happens was developed on the basis of a series of three famous field experiments conducted by Sherif and his colleagues in 1949, 1953 and 1954 at summer camps for young boys in the United States (see Sherif, 1966). The participants, 11-year-old boys, were randomly assigned to one of two cabins that were isolated from each other. Friends were split up to be in different cabins. During the first week, the boys in each cabin spent their time together as a group, fishing, hiking, swimming, and otherwise enjoying themselves. The boys formed two cohesive groups, which they named the Rattlers and the Eagles. They became attached to their groups and strongly identified with them.

Next, the experimenters arranged a series of formal competitive events between the two groups. The best team was to win a trophy for the group and individual prizes for its members. As the competition progressed, the boys began taunting and insulting each other. Then the Eagles burned the Rattlers' flag, and in retaliation, the Rattlers broke into the Eagles' cabin and scattered or stole their rivals' belongings. Although further physical conflict was prevented by the experimenters, the two groups continued to abuse each other verbally and seemed to have developed a genuine hatred for each other – stereotypes and prejudices developed and were expressed verbally and physically.

Finally, in one of the studies the experimenters arranged for the boys to work together in order to accomplish shared goals that both groups valued but neither group could accomplish alone. The experimenters sabotaged the water supply for the camp and had the boys fix it; they had the boys repair a truck that had broken down; and they induced the boys to pool their money to rent a movie. After the boys worked on cooperative ventures, rather than competitive ones, the level of intergroup conflict diminished markedly.

To explain the results of these studies, Sherif developed **realistic conflict theory**. Sherif argued that the way people behave towards one another is strongly influenced by people's goals and their perception of the goal relations between people. When people have a common goal that requires interdependent action for its achievement, then people cooperate to help one another to achieve the goal, and this produces a sense of solidarity and oneness that underpins group formation. This is what happened in the first stage of the studies. When two groups have mutually exclusive goals, in other words when only one group can achieve the goal at the expense of the other group, then the groups compete and hinder each other from achieving their goal. This spawns mutual dislike, conflict and hostility. This is what happened in the second stage of the studies. When two groups have a common goal that cannot be achieved by one group alone (called a superordinate goal), then the two groups cooperate to help one another to achieve the goal. This reduces hostility and generates more positive intergroup attitudes. This is what happened in the final stage of the studies.

Frustrated goals and relative deprivation

A key feature of realistic conflict theory is the argument that intergroup conflict rests on competitive goals that cause each group to impede or frustrate each other's attempts to achieve their goals. Collective goal frustration may contribute to hostile intergroup relations. This idea has its roots in Dollard *et al.*'s (1939) **frustration–aggression hypothesis**. When people's goals are frustrated they can feel a sense of anger (technically called an 'instigation to aggress') that can be dissipated only by aggression, often not directed at the cause of the frustration but at a scapegoat that is weak and vulnerable. According to Berkowitz (1962), frustration is most likely to translate into collective aggression against an out-group when the instigation to aggress is associated with other generally aversive conditions, there are aggressive cues in the environment, and people are in the presence of others who are acting aggressively.

Generally, conflict between groups arises when a group has an acute feeling of being deprived. **Relative deprivation** can be most acute when a period of rising expectations (how things ought to be) and rising achievements (how things are) comes to an abrupt end because achievements suddenly drop off. This J-curve hypothesis (Davies, 1969) has been used to explain large-scale intergroup conflicts, for example, the French and Russian revolutions, and the rise of anti-Semitism in Europe after the economic crash of 1929.

Although relative deprivation can be based on diachronic (over time) comparisons between one's circumstances now and how they used to be, Runciman (1966) suggests that synchronic (here and now) self–other comparisons are much more immediate and powerful. These comparisons can be between one's self and individual others (interpersonal comparisons) or between one's own group and another group (intergroup comparisons). The former generates a sense of **egoistic relative deprivation** that is associated with stress, depression and demotivation. It is the latter that generates a sense of **fraternalistic relative deprivation** that is associated with collective protest, intergroup conflict, prejudice and so forth (Vanneman and Pettigrew, 1972).

There are at least three conditions that seem to amplify the impact of fraternalistic deprivation on competitive intergroup behaviour: (1) people need to identify strongly with their group (Abrams, 1990); (2) people need to feel that their deprived state relative to another group rests not only on an unjust distribution of resources (distributive injustice), but also on unjust procedures (procedural injustice) (Tyler and Smith, 1998); and (3) there is a perception of real intergroup conflict over scarce resources (see our discussion of realistic conflict theory, above).

Social identity

Although competitive goals and a sense of relative deprivation certainly do encourage conflict and hostile intergroup attitudes and behaviour, there is also substantial evidence that the mere existence of social categories or groups can be sufficient to provide the framework for this behaviour. Tajfel *et al.* (1971) conducted an experiment in which school students were randomly assigned to groups (ostensibly on the basis of preferences for paintings by the artists Klee and Kandinsky, who were unknown to the students). The participants did not interact and did not know who was in their group or who was in the other group. Nevertheless they subsequently discriminated against the out-group by repeatedly allocating less money to the out-group than their own group (even though they personally did not benefit financially from this allocation). This paradigm, the **minimal group paradigm**, and variants of it, have been used many hundreds of times over the last 35 years or so to replicate this effect – people who are categorised on a minimal, trivial, and often random basis tend to show a competitive and discriminatory orientation towards an out-group.

It should be noted that minimal social categorisation can sometimes not produce discrimination. Experimental participants need to feel they belong to the minimal group, and this sense of belonging or identification is enhanced where people feel uncertain about themselves and their place in the social context (Hogg, 2000). Also, discrimination can disappear when participants, rather than allocating rewards, are asked to allocate punishments or withhold rewards – called the positive–negative asymmetry effect (Mummendey and Otten, 1998).

The initial minimal group finding was an important catalyst for the development, originally by Tajfel and then by Turner and his associates, of **social identity theory** (Tajfel and Turner, 1986; Turner *et al.*, 1987; Hogg and Abrams, 1988; Hogg, 2006 – see also the section in Chapter 15 on self and identity). According to social identity theory, group and intergroup behaviour is associated with social identity (self-definition in terms of the defining attributes of an in-group), not personal identity (self-definition in terms of idiosyncratic traits or close interpersonal relationships). People cognitively represent social groups in terms of a fuzzy set of attributes (called a prototype) that simultaneously captures in-group similarities and intergroup differences. Prototypes are catered to specific contexts in order to maximise entitativity – the property of a group that makes it a distinct entity with sharp boundaries and clear consensual defining attributes. Self-inclusive social categories with high entitativity and clear prescriptive prototypes are very effective at reducing self-conceptual, attitudinal and behavioural uncertainty (Hogg, 2000).

When a particular intergroup categorisation seems best to account for what is going on in a particular situation it then becomes psychologically salient, that is, people categorise themselves and others in terms of the categorisation. Social categorisation causes people to view others and themselves not as unique individuals, but in terms of the relevant in-group or out-group prototype – a process called **depersonalisation** because perception is based on group membership and group attributes not individuality and personal attributes. Depersonalisation explains why, in intergroup contexts, we tend to see out-group members stereotypically, why we conform to in-group norms relating to perceptions, feelings, attitudes and behaviours, and why we tend to accentuate intergroup differences and intragroup similarities on all available and relevant dimensions of comparison. This cognitive aspect of social identity theory is called **self-categorisation theory** (Turner *et al.*, 1987).

Because groups define and evaluate who we are, it is important that the groups we belong to have attributes that we consider to be evaluatively positive. Intergroup behaviour is a struggle for positive distinctiveness for our own group relative to relevant out-groups. This furnishes a favourable social identity, and this in turn contributes to an underlying sense of self-esteem. The struggle for positive social identity can be framed in terms of a struggle for status, with dominant groups protecting their high-status position of advantage and privilege, and subordinate groups striving to rectify their lower-status position and associated disadvantage. According to social identity theory, the form that this struggle takes depends upon people's perceptions of the nature of status relations between groups (Ellemers, 1993; Tajfel and Turner,

1986). The focus is largely on how lower-status groups respond to their social position.

Where status relations are considered legitimate but the boundaries between groups are believed to be permeable, members of lower-status groups pursue social mobility – they disidentify from their group and try to gain admittance for themselves and their immediate family to the higher-status group. This is almost always unsuccessful. It leaves people with a marginal social identity – rejected by their in-group and not accepted by the out-group. Where status relations are considered to be relatively legitimate and highly stable and boundaries are impermeable, lower-status group members pursue a strategy of social creativity. They try to improve their social identity by seeking a redefinition of in-group properties – different, more positive attributes and a re-evaluation of existing properties. They also focus on comparisons with groups who are even lower in status than their own. Finally, where people recognise the illegitimacy of their lower-status position, feel that status relations are unstable, and can envisage ways to achieve a change in status relations, they engage in direct social competition. They go head-to-head with the higher-status groups – this can take the form of democratic political action, social protest, or revolution and war.

The social identity analysis of intergroup behaviour has gathered substantial support as an account of the dynamics of intergroup behaviour. For example, regarding the role of **self-esteem**, Hunter *et al.* (1996) studied the intergroup relationship between Catholic and Protestant 16-year-olds in Northern Ireland. Participants first completed some measures of self-esteem and then evaluated the two groups. Self-esteem was then measured again. Among those who expressed in-group bias when they evaluated the groups (favouring their own group over the other), self-esteem was raised on dimensions such as honesty, academic ability and physical appearance.

Regarding the motivational role of uncertainty reduction, a series of experiments has shown that discrimination in the minimal group paradigm occurs only if people are categorised under conditions of subjective uncertainty that causes them to identify with the minimal group (Hogg, 2000). Regarding intergroup conflict, there is an entire literature in the area of language and social psychology which shows that ethnolinguistic groups (ethnic groups for whom language is a defining feature) thrive or perish depending on perceptions of the stability, legitimacy and permeability of status relations, exactly as predicted by social identity theory (Giles and Johnson, 1987). Finally, there is evidence that in-group prototypes do enhance entitativity and that people conform to such norms when they identify with their group (Abrams *et al.*, 1990), and that this is associated with out-group stereotyping (Oakes *et al.*, 1993; Leyens *et al.*, 1994).

Ostracism

Research by Zadro *et al.* (2005) shows that people can feel worse when they are the target of ostracism (being excluded and ignored in the presence of others) than the target of a verbal dispute. Furthermore, those who are the source of the behaviour actually feel better when they ostracise you than when they target you with verbal dispute.

To demonstrate this, Zadro and colleagues conducted three role-playing experiments in which they constructed a mock train ride in the laboratory – three rows, one right behind the other, of three chairs. To further cue the 'train ride' aspect there were some of the usual signs found in trains, such as 'no smoking' and 'do not place your feet on the seats'. Student participants were randomly assigned the role of target or source – targets sat in the middle of rows and sources sat at the ends.

The scenario was described as one in which they were travelling home by train and the sources were cross with the target because he or she had not invited them to a party. In the ostracism condition the sources were told to express their anger by talking to one another across the target but ignoring the target. In the dispute condition they were told to express their anger by directly arguing with the target. The role-play lasted about five minutes, after which participants completed a questionnaire indicating how they felt – more specifically, to what extent they felt the four basic needs of belonging, control, self-esteem and meaningful existence were being met.

The results of the first study, with 35 students, showed that targets of ostracism felt all four needs were less satisfied than did targets of dispute – they felt less belonging, less control, lower self-esteem, and less meaningful existence. Sources who used ostracism felt greater control than did sources who used dispute. The second study, with 57 participants, was virtually identical with some minor changes to increase the realism of the role-play. Once again targets of ostracism felt all four needs were less satisfied than did targets of dispute. The final study,

with 138 participants, used a slightly different scenario – the target had refused to provide notes for the sources to catch up on a class they had missed – but was the same in other respects. Yet again, targets of ostracism felt all four needs were less satisfied than did targets of dispute – but here the difference was significant only on belonging and meaningful existence. In addition, sources of ostracism felt greater belonging and more superiority than did sources of dispute. This last study also had a control condition in which the target was explicitly included by the sources – as one would expect, inclusion caused both targets and sources to feel their needs were being better satisfied than did ostracism or dispute.

These studies by Zadro *et al.* (2005) are part of an extensive programme of research by Williams and his associates on the psychological effects of ostracism (Williams, 2001). These studies have used some very vivid paradigms – for example, in one paradigm a participant ostensibly waiting with two others for an experiment is initially included in a ball-tossing game and then excluded (e.g. Williams and Sommer, 1997). The ball-tossing paradigm has been adapted for a web-based experiment on cyber-ostracism (Williams *et al.*, 2000).

Prejudice

Intergroup attitudes are a core component of intergroup behaviour. Attitudes toward the out-group tend to be shared among the in-group members, and tend to devalue the out-group relative to the in-group – they are stereotypes and are a defining feature of prejudice. Indeed, **prejudice** can be defined as a shared attitude, generally negative, towards a social out-group, and thus towards members of that group purely on the basis of their membership in that group (see Chapter 11 for some discussion of the development of prejudice). Some of the most pernicious prejudices are those based on people's race, ethnicity, religion, age, sex, sexual orientation, and mental and physical health. But people have a remarkable ability

Cutting edge – Being left out in the cold

Research on ostracism shows that having one's existence ignored or denied by others is one of the most averse situations that people can face – underscoring the fundamentally social nature of human existence and the way that our sense of self and of reality is grounded in social recognition. We feel isolated. What is astonishing is that this isolation can also make us feel, literally, cold. Zhong and Leonardelli (2008) found that when people were asked to recall an experience in which they felt socially isolated, they estimated the tempera-

ture of the room to be lower than did those who recalled an experience in which they were socially included. In a follow-up study, they manipulated exclusion directly. Participants played an online game of pass the ball with three other players. What the participants did not know is that some of them would not have the ball passed to them. They would be excluded. Those who were excluded found the room colder and expressed a greater desire for warm food and drink than did those who were included.

to be prejudiced against almost any group you care to mention – powerfully illustrated by the 2006 Oscar-winning film *Crash*. Like other attitudes, prejudices have a cognitive component. In this case the cognitive component is, as discussed in the social cognition section of Chapter 15, a stereotype or schema – a set of interrelated (and shared) beliefs about members of the group that influences perception once we categorise someone as being a member of the group. Again, like other attitudes, there is no guarantee that prejudice will be expressed as behaviour, but when it is, that behaviour is called **discrimination**.

Theories of prejudice

Because prejudice is repugnant and can have such appalling effects, such as genocide, prejudice is often traced to individual differences and personality attributes. One of the most widely promulgated theories of prejudice is the **authoritarian personality** (Adorno *et al.*, 1950). Children who are brought up in families where their parents use harsh disciplinarian methods to secure love and dependence develop a love–hate relationship with their parents, which is unendurably stressful. The stress is resolved by idealising their parents and all authority figures and redirecting their hatred onto weaker others. This resolution becomes a deep-seated and immutable personality syndrome, authoritarianism, which frames relations for the rest of the person's life. It predisposes people to be prejudiced. Another personality explanation has been proposed by Rokeach (1948), who argues that some people, for whatever reason, have a general cognitive style that is rigid and dogmatic. These people are predisposed to be prejudiced because they strive for a rigidly stratified social world, are resistant to belief change in the light of contradictory evidence, and are inclined to ground their beliefs in authority and orthodox belief systems.

An individual differences explanation of prejudice, called **social dominance theory**, has been proposed by Pratto *et al.* (1994). They describe a relatively sophisticated, but nonetheless 'individual differences', analysis of exploitative power-based intergroup relations. People who desire their own group to be dominant and superior to out-groups have a high social dominance orientation that encourages them to reject egalitarian ideologies, and to accept myths that legitimise hierarchy and discrimination. These kinds of people are more inclined to be prejudiced than are people who have a low social dominance orientation.

Critics of personality and individual differences explanations of prejudice (Pettigrew, 1958; Billig, 1976) note that prejudice is not a sporadic individual matter, but rather it is a collective behaviour engaged in by large numbers of people in a relatively coordinated and highly targeted manner. They also provide evidence that personality is actually a poor predictor of prejudice, and that the nature of intergroup relations is a better predictor. In general, most social psychologists now believe that prejudice is a part of intergroup behaviour and therefore needs to be understood as part of a theory of intergroup behaviour. Although prejudice, stereotypes and discrimination are expressed by individuals, they are genuinely intergroup phenomena: individuals are prejudiced because they belong to groups that have developed certain relations with one another that are characterised by unequal status and advantage, and by conflict and hatred (Brown, 1995).

Cognitive processes in prejudice

We have already see one way in which cognitive processes are involved in prejudice – the categorisation of people into in-group and out-group seems to lay the groundwork for intergroup behaviour and possible prejudice. It may do this because it affects self-conception: it encourages people to view themselves as group members and think of themselves in terms of social identity, which can be considered a type of self-schema. Social categorisation causes people to view out-group members in terms of stereotypes, and to behave in ways that favour the in-group and maintain the distinctiveness of in-group identity.

Another cognitive process that is involved in stereotyping and prejudice is illusory correlation. Recall from Chapter 15 that the availability heuristic involves people assuming that distinctive, easily imagined items occur more frequently. This phenomenon probably explains why people overestimate the rate of violent crime (because an act of violence is a frightening, distinctive event) and overestimate the relative numbers of violent crimes committed by members of minority groups (because members of minority groups tend to be more conspicuous). This tendency is an example of an **illusory correlation** – the perception of an apparent relation between two distinctive elements that does not actually exist or is enormously exaggerated (Hamilton and Gifford, 1976).

Another fallacy that promotes stereotyping is the **illusion of out-group homogeneity**. People tend to assume that members of other groups are much more similar than are members of their own group (Linville, 1982). This tendency is even seen between the sexes: women tend to perceive men as being more alike than women are, and men do the opposite (Park and Rothbart, 1982). The same is true for young people and old people (Linville *et al.*, 1989). However, this effect can sometimes be reversed so that people think their own group is more homogeneous than the out-group. Simon and Brown (1987) suggest that one situation in which this can happen is when the in-group is a minority group in terms of status. The reason for this is that solidarity and thus homogeneity may have a special value for minorities.

Under-representation of women in academia – An international perspective

Although women make up approximately half of the student population, and in the UK and the Netherlands constitute the clear majority of psychology students, women are less well represented further up the academic ladder: faculty staff. According to one study, the proportion of women academic staff in universities around the world never exceeds 25 per cent (Lie *et al.*, 1994).

The further up the ladder we progress, the fewer women there are – even in liberal Western democracies. For example, Osborn (1998) found that the percentage of full-time women professors, across all disciplines, in 13 out of 16 European countries was 10 per cent or less; in North America, the figure was 13 per cent and in Australia, 14 per cent. Why? One reason might be that women are less committed to work because of competing commitments associated with child-rearing. Another reason is that employers have a gender stereotypical view of women employees that makes women appear less committed and therefore more of an employment risk.

Ellemers *et al.* (2004) tested these hypotheses in a study of students undertaking Ph.D. research at universities in the Netherlands and in Italy. In the Dutch study, the researchers found no differences between men and women Ph.D. students in terms of measured work commitment or work satisfaction, although the women themselves reported spending more time on household tasks than work. However, when staff from the same university were asked to judge these students, women doctoral students were perceived as being less committed than men students, even by women staff.

These findings were replicated in the Italian sample (although the women students reported greater team-oriented commitment). However, the biased judgement of women staff was even greater than in the Dutch sample, suggesting that the most stereotypical views of women are actually held by women.

Stigma and disadvantage

One of the principal problems with prejudice is that it stigmatises and disadvantages entire groups of people: 'Stigmatised individuals possess (or are believed to possess) some attribute, or characteristic, that conveys a social identity that is devalued in a particular social context' (Crocker *et al.*, 1998, p. 505). The targets of prejudice and discrimination are members of stigmatised groups, and thus they are stigmatised individuals. Stigma persists for a number of reasons.

An fMRI study of stigma suggests that our unstated prejudices might be revealed by our brain activation. Krendl *et al.* (2006) asked 22 men to make explicit (do you like this person?) or implicit (is this a man or a woman?) judgements about people with well-established stigma (obesity, unattractiveness, transexuality, etc). Areas of the brain normally activated by negative emotional stimuli, as well as regions involved in control and inhibition, were activated. However, when the most negatively perceived faces were judged in the implicit condition, activation was much greater in the amygdala and prefrontal cortex. Perhaps as one increased (in the amygdala), the other area responded to inhibit its activation.

A relatively positive sense of self can be gained by comparing others unfavourably with oneself. Stigma can legitimise inequalities of status and resource distribution that favour a dominant group – such groups are certainly going to ensure that the stigma remains in place, because it serves a system justification function (Jost and Hunyadi, 2002). Finally, people may need to stigmatise groups that have different world views from their own, because if one did not degrade and discredit out-groups in this way then the frail sense of certainty in, and controllability of, life that one gains from one's own world view would be shattered (Solomon *et al.*, 1991).

Members of stigmatised groups can experience **attributional ambiguity**. They can continually read prejudice and discrimination into innocuous behaviours and even into behaviours favouring them: Was I served first at the bar because I am black and the bartender was trying to conceal her hidden prejudice? Members of stigmatised groups can also suffer depressed self-esteem, self-worth and efficacy that can reduce motivation. For example, because stigmatised groups know exactly the negative stereotypes that others have of them, they experience what Steele *et al.* (2002) have called **stereotype threat**. Stigmatised individuals are aware that others may judge and treat them stereotypically, and thus, on tasks that really matter to them, they worry that through their behaviour they may even confirm the stereotypes. These concerns not only increase anxiety, but can also impair task performance. For example, an academically ambitious West Indian Briton, aware of

Cutting edge – Shoot me, I'm black

The social psychology literature is bursting with studies demonstrating prejudice against black people, as well as other similarly stigmatised groups. Researchers at the universities of Colorado and Chicago have now found that making stereotypes about people accessible influences a person's decision to shoot those individuals during a videogame (Correll *et al.*, 2007).

In the experiment, participants had to press a key indicating 'shoot' if they saw a person with a gun in the game they were playing. If the person was not carrying a gun, they were to press a key indicating 'don't shoot'. Half of the characters in the game were white, half were black. Before playing the game, people were asked to read newspaper articles in which armed robberies committed by either black or white felons were reported.

People who read about the black criminals were significantly more likely to shoot black targets in the videogame – regardless of whether these targets were armed or unarmed – than white (even armed) targets. So, by making stereotypical information accessible (the link between black people and violence), the researchers found that people's tendency to engage in stereotype-driven behaviour increased.

stereotypes of intellectual inferiority, may be extremely anxious when answering a question in class – she would be worried that the slightest mistake would be interpreted stereotypically. This anxiety may actually impact adversely on behaviour.

In general, however, although some stigmatised individuals are vulnerable to low self-esteem, diminished life satisfaction and, in some cases, depression, most members of stigmatised groups are able to weather the assaults and maintain a positive self-image (Crocker and Major, 1989). There are many ways in which people can do this. One way is to deny personal disadvantage. For instance, Crosby (1982) has identified the 'paradox of the contented female worker'. Women workers compare their salaries and working conditions with those of other women, which narrows the potential for recognising much larger sex-based inequalities in pay and conditions (Major, 1994).

Stereotype threat

Why do some groups in society underperform in particular areas – for example, academic underachievement of African-Americans, and mathematical and scientific underachievement of women? Coining the term 'stereotype threat', Steele and his colleagues argue that underachievement is a psychological response to stereotypes that characterise one's in-group (e.g. women) as inferior to a relevant outgroup (men) on a specific task (maths) in a specific domain (school) (Steele *et al.*, 2002). The negative stereotype is a cognitive and emotional burden that impedes performance and paradoxically actually produces an effect consistent with the negative expectation. Stereotype threat has two repercussions: anxiety about confirming the stereotype and thus being judged as possessing the negative attribute, and disen-

gagement with the task and the domain. These two effects lead to underachievement (Steele, 1997; Aronson *et al.*, 1999).

Much of the original research had been conducted with African-American students in the American schooling system. For example, African-American students have been found to perform less well than their white counterparts in testing situations where negative stereotypes about African-Americans are relevant (Steele and Aronson, 1995). This may be due to the potential recognition that failure could confirm a negative stereotype of their in-group (and, by extension, the self). The stereotype threat effect has been investigated with different stigmatised groups and in several domains including white men's maths ability when compared to Asian-American men (traditionally associated with higher maths ability; Aronson *et al.*, 1999) and children from low socio-economic backgrounds in academic testing situations (Croizet and Claire, 1998).

A principal aim of social psychological research into stereotype threat has been to discover what psychological variables (at both the social and individual levels) affect individuals' vulnerability to this effect. Some basic processes and issues have been identified, for example:

1 *Domain identification.* Stereotype threat only occurs in individuals for whom performing well in a given domain is important (Steele, 1997). Aronson *et al.* (1999) measured white male students' identification with maths and then asked them to complete a maths test either in the context of the stereotype that Asians are superior at maths (stereotype threat condition) or not (control condition). Performance on the maths test was significantly worse in the stereotype threat condition, but only for participants who identified highly with the maths domain (even when controlling for previous standardised aptitude test (SAT) scores).

Interestingly, this study not only provides evidence for domain-specific identification but also demonstrates that stereotype threat can affect traditionally non-stigmatised groups (American white male students).

2 *Cognitive load.* It is possible that the stereotype threat effect is more pronounced when people are under high cognitive load as there is an extra pressure to disconfirm negative stereotypes. Spencer *et al.* (1999) examined this possibility in two experimental studies of high-achieving male and female American university students. Women are believed to experience stereotype threat in maths-related domains. Participants in the first study did a maths test that was either easy or difficult. There was no difference in the performance of male and female students on the easy test, but females performed significantly worse on the difficult test. The increased cognitive load of stereotype threat impeded performance on a task that also demanded greater cognitive capacity. In a second study, Spencer *et al.* showed that this gender difference in performance on the difficult test was accentuated when the test was explicitly introduced in terms of gender differences in maths ability. This finding lends further credibility to the idea that performance differences do indeed result from stereotype threat rather than from real differences between males' and females' maths ability.

3 *Self-categorisation with the stereotyped group.* Research suggests that priming the social identity of the stigmatised group will automatically prime the negative stereotype and in turn affect performance in a stereotype consistent manner. One study clearly demonstrates this effect in the maths performance of Asian-American women (Shih *et al.*, 1999). In contrast to the negative connotations of being female in the maths domain, Shih *et al.* reasoned that Asian-American identity is associated with a positive stereotype of maths ability. Indeed, female Asian-Americans who were primed with their Asian-American identity significantly outperformed participants who were primed instead with their gender identity ('women').

4 *Individual level of identification with the stereotyped group.* Schmader (2002) demonstrated that the degree to which a person identifies with a relevant category also affects how strongly the stereotype influences their performance. White American students completed a maths test in either a gender-relevant domain or a gender-irrelevant domain. In the gender-irrelevant domain there was no difference between men's and women's performances on the test. However, in the gender-relevant domain, only the female participants who identified

highly with their gender underperformed compared with males. Thus, vulnerability to stereotype threat seems to depend on whether people see themselves as representative of the stereotyped category.

Given the deleterious consequences of stereotype threat, is it possible to train people to combat or overcome stereotype threat? Aronson *et al.* (2002) conducted an intervention study to trial a method of helping students resist their responses to stereotype threat. African-American and Caucasian male and female undergraduates participated in a laboratory study ostensibly concerning a penpal mentoring system for younger students. They were randomly divided into three groups. A battery of attitude change techniques were used to teach them and help them internalise the idea that intelligence is malleable (intervention-specific group) or that people have different intelligence orientations (intervention-only group – in case intervention alone boosts performance). The third group was a no-intervention control. The results showed that several weeks after the lab session the students in the intervention-specific group (where the negative stereotype was challenged) reported greater academic identification and enjoyment and higher grades compared with the other intervention style and the control group. This was particularly the case for African-American students whose academic performance and identification were depressed as a reaction to stereotype threat in the other conditions. It is interesting to note that there were no differences between groups on stereotype threat scores per se, suggesting that the specific intervention changed the participants' responses to stereotype threat and not their perceptions of it.

Modern forms of prejudice

Prejudice can express itself in many different ways. We are all familiar with what has been called old-fashioned prejudice – name-calling, abuse, persecution, assault and discrimination. This kind of expression of prejudice is now illegal and socially censured in all Western democratic societies, and so it is rarely encountered. Not surprisingly, research on racism in the United States shows a dramatic reduction in expressed anti-black attitudes since the 1930s (Devine and Elliot, 1995).

However, it may not be so much that prejudice is vanishing but that it is changing its form. This new form of prejudice (the research focuses mainly on racism), has a number of different names – aversive racism, modern racism, symbolic racism, regressive racism or ambivalent racism (Gaertner and Dovidio, 1986; Hilton and von Hippel, 1996). However, the general idea is that people now experience a conflict between deep-seated emotional antipathy towards racial out-groups, and modern egalitarian values that exert pressure to behave in a non-prejudiced manner. The resolution of this conflict, which produces **modern racism** or subtle forms of racism, is achieved by avoidance and denial of racism – separate lives, avoidance of the topic of race, denial of being prejudiced, denial of racial disadvantage, and thus opposition to affirmative action or other measures to address racial disadvantage. Although this analysis is mainly focused on racism in the USA, it can also apply to sexism (Swim *et al.*, 1995), and to racial attitudes in Europe (Pettigrew and Meertens, 1995).

Modern forms of prejudice can, by definition, be very difficult to detect, because people try to conceal their prejudices. To detect prejudice, researchers need to be ingenious in designing unobtrusive and indirect measures. Many different methods have been devised (Crosby *et al.*, 1980). For example, social cognition research shows that stereotypes can be automatically generated by categorisation, and categorisation can automatically arise from category primes (an accent, a face, a costume) (Bargh, 1989).

Another powerful unobtrusive measure of prejudice is to analyse the subtext of what people say. Racism can very subtly and quite unintentionally be embedded in the words we use, the way we express ourselves, and the way we communicate with and about racial out-groups (Potter and Wetherell, 1987, Edwards, 1997). For example, van Dijk (1987) found evidence of prejudice from a detailed analysis of spontaneous everyday talk among whites in the Netherlands and in southern California about other races (blacks, East Indians, North Africans, Hispanics, Asians). One hundred and eighty free-format interviews conducted between 1980 and 1985 were qualitatively analysed to show how racism is embedded in and reproduced by everyday discourse. People can use particular forms of language to communicate their prejudiced attitudes in ways that disarm the charge of being a racist. A common example is the disclaimer 'I'm not racist, but . . .' that can precede a clearly racist comment.

A more cognitive index of language and prejudice is the **linguistic intergroup bias** effect (Maass, 1999). Maass discovered that people tend to use concrete language that simply describes events when talking about positive out-group (and negative in-group) characteristics, but use much more general and abstract terms that relate to enduring traits when talking about negative out-group (and positive in-group) characteristics. In this way we can detect negative out-group attitudes: people start to become abstract and general when talking about their prejudices.

Can we reduce prejudice?

How can prejudice and intergroup conflict be reduced? Research suggests that propaganda, public service advertising and formal education have a limited effect – these methods are effective in conveying official societal expectations, but then, of course, they fail if they are conducted against a background of powerful and entrenched day-to-day informal endorsement of prejudice. So, are there any techniques that work and, if so, how?

On a larger scale, a popular view about how to reduce prejudice is the **contact hypothesis**: if people from different races could just get to know one another through coming together to interact then prejudice would disappear (Allport, 1954). Although this idea has immediate appeal, and indeed it was part of the scientific justification for the racial desegregation of the American schooling system in the 1950s, it is fraught with problems. For intergroup contact to work, people have to come together for prolonged equal-status, meaningful interaction that is pleasant and capable of changing stereotypes of entire groups not just attitudes towards the individuals with whom one interacts. Contact can often produce interracial friendships, but it rarely changes racial stereotypes. More often than not, contact can confirm and accentuate intergroup perceptions and further entrench stereotypes. There is often so much anxiety associated with intergroup encounters that groups avoid contact or find contact unpleasant and attribute this to the out-group (Stephan and Stephan, 2000).

Nevertheless, contact between members of different groups may promote positive attitudes. Indeed, a recent statistical survey of 515 studies of the effects of contact concluded that, all things being equal, contact does promote more positive intergroup relationships (Pettigrew and Tropp, 2006).

Contact may foster good interpersonal relationships ('decategorisation' of group members; Brewer and Miller, 1984), or it may foster a sense of common membership in a superordinate ingroup ('recategorisation'; Gaertner *et al.*, 1993), or it may allow the recognition of positive features of other groups while preserving a sense of in-group distinctiveness (mutual positive differentiation; Hewstone, 1996). Dovidio *et al.* (1997) asked sets of six participants to work first as two three-person groups. These groups then interacted and participants judged one another. Half of the participants were then encouraged to think of themselves as one larger (six-person) category. These recategorised participants were less likely to show evaluative preferences for their own sub-group, or to show a preference for self-disclosing to and helping members of their own sub-group.

Other research by S. C. Wright *et al.* (1997) has shown that that intergroup attitudes can improve if people witness or have knowledge of rewarding intergroup friendships between others – if my friend John has close out-group friends then maybe the out-group isn't quite as bad as I thought. Pettigrew (1998) concluded that friendship across group boundaries is an important way that contact allows people to learn about out-groups and to feel less anxious about future interaction with other members of these groups. This makes it more likely that people will generalise their positive feelings about an out-group friend to the out-group as a whole. Similar conclusions were reached by Brown and Hewstone (2005), who also emphasise the way that contact can influence emotions and feelings, and trust between groups, which in turn can promote more positive intergroup relationships.

Prejudices are intergroup psychological mechanisms for protecting and enhancing our self-image and our material well-being. Not surprisingly, threats to racial or cultural identity are unlikely to reduce prejudice. Thus, nations that try to assimilate ethnic minorities threaten those minorities and cause them to react to protect themselves, which in turn threatens the dominant majority and fuels prejudice. One strategy that does seem to help is pluralism or multi-culturalism – a social policy that recognises cultural diversity within the confines of a common superordinate national identity (Hornsey and Hogg, 2000).

Many people are unaware of their stereotypes and preconceptions about members of other groups because, as noted in the social cognition section of Chapter 15, stereotypes are automatically linked to categories (Bargh, 1989). Although making people aware of their stereotypes can persuade people that their beliefs are unjustified, this can backfire if people then try too hard to suppress their stereotypes. In one study, participants were shown a picture of a skinhead and then wrote a passage about a day in the life of that person (Macrae *et al.*, 1994). Half of the participants were instructed not to rely on stereotypes. Consistent with the instructions, participants in the no-stereotype condition used less stereotypical descriptions.

Next, participants were shown a picture of a second skinhead and were asked to write about a day in his life, but without suppression instructions. In this second stage, those who had been given the suppression instructions previously now showed a substantially increased use of stereotypical descriptions (see Table 16.1).

In a further experiment, compared with those in a control condition, participants who had first been in a suppress condition subsequently chose to sit further away from a chair they thought would be occupied by a skinhead. Macrae *et al.* reasoned that the effort involved in suppressing the stereotype actually makes the content of the stereotype more accessible. Thus, once a person is no longer actively suppressing the stereotype this content

Table 16.1 Ratings of passage stereotypically as a function of task instruction in Macrae *et al.*, Experiment 1

	Instruction	
Passage	Suppress stereotype	Control
1	5.54	6.95
2	7.83	7.08

Source: Macrae, C.N., Bodenhausen, G.V., Milne, A.B. and Jetten, J., Out of mind but back in sight: stereotypes on the rebound. *Journal of Personality and Social Psychology*, 1994, 67, 808–17. Copyright © 1994 by the American Psychological Association, reprinted with permission.

becomes 'hyperaccessible' (Wegner and Erber, 1992), resulting in a stereotype rebound effect (see also Plant and Devine, 2001).

The knack would seem to be to get people to have insight into their stereotypes – to understand them and see through them rather than merely to suppress them. The best solution may be to teach people to become less cognitively lazy and to take the time to reflect about their biases. For example, Langer *et al.* (1985) gave a group of children specific training in thinking about the problems of people with disabilities. They thought about such problems as the ways that a person with disabilities might drive a car and the reasons why a blind person might make a good newscaster. After this training, they were found to be more willing to go on a picnic with a person with disabilities than were children who did not receive the training. They were also more likely to see the specific consequences of particular disabilities rather than to view people with disabilities as 'less fit'. For example, they were likely to choose a blind child as a partner in a game of pin the tail on the donkey because they realised that the child would be likely to perform even better than a sighted child. Thus, at the individual level, people can learn to recognise their biases and to overcome their prejudices.

Devine (1989) proposed that even when a person has knowledge of a stereotype that is automatically linked to a category membership, the explicit application of a stereotype is a controllable process. It seems that people who are high and people who are low in prejudice towards a particular group may both share the same knowledge of the stereotype but low-prejudiced people may suppress or control the stereotype. However, the connection between categorising a person and applying a stereotype turns out to be complex. Lepore and Brown (1997) found that white British people's stereotypes of West Indians were similar regardless of whether participants were high or low scorers on a measure of prejudice.

The important message from this research is that even though people may share knowledge of a stereotype, they apply the stereotype differently when a categorisation is activated. That is, high-prejudiced people seem more likely to apply the negative aspects of the stereotype automatically, whereas low-prejudiced people are more likely to apply the positive aspects of the stereotype automatically.

What happens when a stereotype is activated directly at the same time as the category? For example, images conveyed by the music press often involve extreme representations of aggressive blacks (for example, rappers), or highly feminised and sexual images of women. It seems likely that such stereotypical images might override people's initial levels of prejudice. In line with this idea, Lepore and Brown (1997) found that when they primed participants with negative stereotype content (rather than just category labels) people who scored higher or lower on the prejudice scale were affected by the prime in the same way. Both sets of participants rated the target more negatively following the prime than when no prime was used. Thus, when the stereotype is activated directly, low- and high-prejudiced people apply negative stereotypical traits more readily.

With practice, stereotypes can be overcome: that is, when people either choose to, or are requested to, resist stereotypes over a period of time, the automatic associations they make with a particular category can be altered. A study by Kawakami et al. (2000) showed how people might be trained to avoid stereotyping. Participants were presented with a set of pictures and words. Half the participants were asked to say 'yes' if the word and picture were congruent (for example, a picture of a black person and a word that fits the stereotype of black people), and 'no' if they were incongruent (black person with a white stereotype word). The other half of the participants were in a stereotype negation condition. They were asked to say 'no' when the word and picture were congruent, and 'yes' when they were incongruent. This manipulation weakened the automatic linkage between the categorisation of the picture as black or white and the stereotype content associated with it. In the 'yes' condition but not the 'no' condition, participants categorised black and white faces faster when they were preceded by stereotype-consistent words.

The question is: how do low-prejudiced people sustain their low levels of prejudice in the face of pervasive social stereotypes? Monteith et al. (2002) argue that low-prejudiced people are especially sensitive to 'cues for control'. In essence, when automatic stereotype activation results in a reaction that is inconsistent with the way we think we should respond, this results in a negative sense of self – a sense of guilt or unease. This activates a behavioural inhibition system which ensures that behaviour matches the standards one sets for oneself. Over time, people learn that certain situational or other cues give advance warning that an undesired response is likely (for example, if race is mentioned in a conversation you might be alerted to the possibility that you could say something prejudicial).

Monteith et al. argued that when low-prejudiced individuals see images of black people linked with stereotypical content (for example, the statement 'this person spends a lot of time on the streets') this evokes guilt about the stereotypical association, and this in turn acts as a well-established cue for control.

In Monteith et al.'s research, participants who had completed measures of prejudice earlier in the year were asked to engage simultaneously in what they believed were two separate tasks. The first task was to decide whether pictures (of black and white people) had been presented before in the original format or as a mirror image. The second task was to decide what categories would best fit people described by a series of sentences (for example, the description 'this person has to do a lot of reading' fits the category 'college student'). Monteith et al. reasoned that if a picture of a black person happened to be presented in conjunction with a black stereotype description then this would constitute a cue for control among low-prejudiced people. Indeed, when these participants were presented with this combination of stimuli their decision times slowed down, relative to trials when the same sentences were paired with white faces. In contrast, participants who were high in prejudice were not expected to try to control their reactions, and in fact they responded with equal speed regardless of whether the black stereotypical sentences were paired with white or black faces. See Figure 16.7.

Various methods are available by which we could reduce prejudice but many of them rely on the consistent and motivated involvement of the prejudiced. With this involvement, the techniques might work. But this section provokes many questions. For example, how is it that we sometimes make important errors when we make judge-

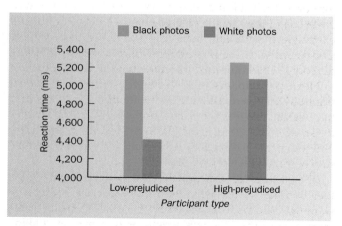

Figure 16.7 Reaction times as a function of race of photo and participant type.

Source: Based on Monteith, M.J., Ashburn-Nardo, L., Voils, C.I. and Czopp, A.M., Putting the brakes on prejudice: On the development and operation of cues for control. *Journal of Personality and Social Psychology*, 2002, 83, 1029–50.

ments about other people? Why do we have immediate, 'gut' reactions to people and events, and what are the advantages and pitfalls?

Think about the amount of contact you have with people who are ethnically different from yourself. Maybe you live in a diverse neighbourhood or have gone on holiday to countries which are ethnically quite different from your own. In what ways do you think this may have changed (or not changed) your images of other ethnic groups as a whole? When have these encounters resulted in more positive attitudes to that group and when have your attitudes become more negative?

Finally, if you were hired by an organisation to design and implement a strategy to reduce harmful ethnic prejudice among employees within the organisation, what would your strategy comprise?

Aggression and helping behaviour

Aggression

Human **aggression** is often considered to be an innate component of our biological inheritance, a behaviour which is a necessary part of the evolutionary process that ensures survival of the fittest (Lorenz, 1966). Chapter 13 described some of the basic functions of aggression. The ability to hurt others may well have these roots; however, social psychologists tend to be more interested in discovering situational factors that encourage or inhibit aggression and explain the huge diversity of human aggression (Baron and Richardson, 1994).

Many factors can cause aggression. When important goals are frustrated, people can feel angry and express this as aggression, particularly when there is an available target for aggression without fear of retaliation, and when the person who is frustrated has few other coping mechanisms available. According to social learning theory (Bandura, 1977), aggression can be learned by simply observing other people being reinforced for behaving aggressively. Aggression can also become more likely in a given situation if a person who has a tendency to respond aggressively is aroused, even if the arousal has nothing to do with anger (it could be arousal from a gym workout, a film, a sexual encounter).

People with a type A personality or elevated testosterone levels are also more likely to be aggressive. Testosterone is the male hormone, so, not surprisingly males tend to be more physically aggressive than females, but the hormonal cause can be very difficult to dissociate from the fact that men are typically socialised to be more aggressive than are females. There is little difference in verbal aggression between males and females (Harris,

1992). There is also evidence that disinhibition, caused perhaps by deindividuation, which we described earlier in this chapter, can increase the probability of aggression. Aggression, in the form of assaults in Minneapolis, has even been shown to increase with increasing temperature, peaking at around 25° C and then dropping off as it gets even hotter (Cohn and Rotton, 1997).

There are many paths to aggression – not surprisingly, aggression is an enduring problem for society. Consider the following scenario. A male with a type A personality and elevated testosterone is driving home in a hurry from the gym in traffic where people are successfully cutting in. He is in a large car with dark windows and the CD on full blast. What do you think might happen if you were driving rather slowly in front of him, or took rather a long time to pull away from the traffic lights?

Alcohol and aggression

Alcohol consumption is often associated with aggression. Research suggests that alcohol makes people more prone to social influence while at the same time less able to think through the consequences of their actions for themselves or others. Together this facilitates aggression when people drink in groups in societies that glorify aggression (Bushman and Cooper, 1990). Causal links are complex. For example, perhaps aggressive people like to go drinking in groups, and they would be aggressive even if they had not been drinking? However, controlled studies have shown that people who had consumed alcohol were more likely to act aggressively when encouraged by a confederate than were those who had consumed a placebo.

Media violence and aggression

Many people believe that the mass media, particularly films and television, have much to do with aggression. There is no denying that these media portray a great deal of aggression and in the majority of cases the aggression brings rewards to the aggressor – violence seems to pay. **Social learning theory** makes the clear prediction that much of the aggression in our society is caused or amplified by excessive violence on television and in films. However, research is inconclusive about the causal links (Phillips, 1986): perhaps aggressive people watch or pay more attention to media aggression, whereas non-aggressive people either do not watch media aggression or simply do not pay much attention to it. Similar arguments hold for the evidence that violent pornography is associated with more aggressive attitudes and behaviours towards women: perhaps misogynistic attitudes encourage men to view violent pornography rather than vice versa.

Prosocial and helping behaviour

Aggression is generally regarded as antisocial and undesirable. The flip side of this kind of behaviour is **prosocial behaviour** and behaviour oriented towards helping others. Just as aggression may have an evolutionary dimension, so does prosocial behaviour – cooperative helping behaviour among people is the foundation of human endeavour, and so it would be expected that over millions of years predispositions to behave in this way would have a selective advantage (Wilson, 1978). But again, as with the study of aggression, social psychologists are more concerned to identify situational factors that encourage people to behave prosocially and to help other people.

Cooperation and social dilemmas

Despite the possibility of an evolutionary advantage to cooperative prosocial behaviour, people are remarkably uncooperative. One popular research paradigm involves the **prisoner's dilemma** (Rapoport, 1976), which you read about in Chapter 3. In one variant, two obviously guilty suspects are questioned separately by detectives who have only enough evidence to convict them of a lesser offence. The suspects are separately offered a chance to confess, knowing that if one confesses but the other does not, the confessor will be granted immunity and the confession will be used to convict the other of the more serious offence. If both confess, each will receive a moderate sentence. If neither confesses, each will receive a very light sentence. The prisoners are faced by a dilemma as to whether to trust one another in order to obtain the best joint pay-off. Although mutual non-confession produces the best joint outcome, mutual suspicion and lack of trust almost always encourage both to confess. This finding has been replicated in hundreds of prisoner's dilemma experiments, using a variety of experimental conditions and pay-off matrices (Dawes, 1991).

Many other **social dilemmas** involve a number of individuals or groups exploiting a limited resource (Kerr and Park, 2001) under conditions where, if everyone cooperates, an optimal solution for all is reached, but if everyone competes then everyone loses. These are called **commons dilemmas** because they are modelled on the 'tragedy of the commons'. English towns used to have common pasture on which people were free to graze their cattle. If all used it in moderation it would replenish itself and continually benefit them all. Imagine, however, 100 farmers surrounding a common that could support only 100 cows. If each grazed one cow, the common would be maximally utilised and minimally taxed. One farmer, however, might reason that if they grazed an additional cow, output would be doubled, minus a very small cost due to overgrazing – a cost borne equally by all 100 farmers. So this farmer adds

a second cow. If all 100 farmers reasoned in this way they would rapidly destroy the common, thus producing the tragedy of the commons. The commons dilemma is an example of a replenishable resource dilemma. The commons is a renewable resource that will continually support many people provided that all people show restraint in 'harvesting' the resource. Many of the world's most pressing environmental and conservation problems are replenishable resource dilemmas – for example, rainforests and the world's population of ocean fish are renewable resources if harvested appropriately.

Another type of social dilemma is called a public goods dilemma. Public goods, such as public health, national parks, clean air, and road networks are provided for everyone. Because public goods are available to all, people are tempted to use them without contributing to their maintenance.

Experimental research on social dilemmas finds that when self-interest is pitted against the collective good, the usual outcome is competition and resource destruction even when appeals are made to cooperative and altruistic norms (Kerr, 1992). People can, however, act more cooperatively when they identify with the common good (Brewer and Kramer, 1986). In other words, when people derive their social identity from the entire group that has access to the resource, self-interest becomes subordinate to the common good (de Cremer and van Vugt, 1999). However, the same research indicates that when different groups, rather than individuals, have access to a public good, then the ensuing intergroup competition ensures ethnocentric actions which are far more destructive than mere self-interest. International competition over limited resources such as rainforests, whales and wetlands tragically accelerates their disappearance.

Another way in which social dilemmas can be resolved is by putting in place various structural solutions. These include a range of measures such as limiting the number of people accessing the resource (via permits), limiting the amount of the resource that people can take (via quotas), handing over management of the resource to an individual (a leader) or a single group, facilitating free communication among those accessing the resource, and shifting the pay-off to favour cooperation over competition. The problem with structural solutions is that they require an enlightened and powerful authority to implement measures, manage the bureaucracy and police violations. This can be hard to bring about (Rutte and Wilke, 1984).

Bystander intervention

People sometimes find themselves in a situation where they witness an emergency where someone needs their help. When are people most likely to help and why?

In 1964 in New York City, a woman named Kitty Genovese was chased and repeatedly stabbed by an assailant, who took 35 minutes to kill her. The woman's screams apparently went unheeded by at least 38 people who watched from their windows. No one, it seemed, tried to stop the attacker; no one even made a quick, anonymous telephone call to the police. When the bystanders were questioned later, they could not explain their inaction. 'I just don't know,' they said.

As you can imagine, people were shocked by the bystanders' response to the Genovese murder. Commentators said that the apparent indifference of the bystanders demonstrated that American society, especially in urban areas, had become cold and apathetic. Experiments performed by social psychologists suggest that this explanation is wrong – people in cities are not generally indifferent to the needs of other people. The fact that Kitty Genovese's attack went unreported is not remarkable because 38 people were present; it is precisely because so many people were present that the attack was not reported. Recent research, however, including a detailed review of the case suggests that this picture is not as clear-cut as it has usually been portrayed in textbooks. The Controversies in Psychological Science section reveals some remarkable facts about the case and undermines some persistent myths.

Controversies in Psychological Science – What did Kitty Genovese's witnesses really witness?

The issue

Kitty Genovese is one of the most well-known women not only in social psychology, but in psychology in general. The horrific ordeal she went through gave rise to a theory of social behaviour and intervention and sparked a series of now-famous experiments on the bystander effect, described in the text. It was identified as a 'signal crime' – one that issued a warning about the breakdown in society's collective moral fabric (Innes, 2004). But was this research based on an enormous series of false premises? According to a review of the evidence by Manning *et al.* (2007), it was.

The evidence

These are the facts of Kitty Genovese's murder and the response to it:

In the early morning of 13 March 1964, Kitty Genovese was sexually assaulted and then murdered in the Kew Gardens district of Queens in New York. According to almost all textbooks you will read which report the case, 38 people witnessed the assault and murder at some point from a nearby building but did nothing to intervene or alert the police. Curiously, although the case was reported in the local paper the next day, reference to the 38 witnesses only appeared in a newspaper, *The New York Times*, two weeks later, on 27 March – '38 who saw murder didn't call the police,' the story boldly surmised and went on: 'Apathy at stabbing of Queens woman shocks inspector.'

However, research by a local historian and lawyer, Joseph de May Jnr, began to cast doubt on this interpretation. He found that:

- not all of the 38 alleged witnesses were eyewitnesses – some only heard noise from the assault;

- the police were called immediately;
- despite reports that witnesses had seen Kitty Genovese for 30 minutes, this was impossible because, given the geography and chronology of the assault, she could only have been visible for a few seconds;
- Kitty Genovese was still alive when the police arrived – she was not seen being murdered.

The story then becomes even more intriguing because no list of the 38 witnesses has ever been made available and the three witnesses in court said that their first glimpse of what transpired could not lead them to believe that what they were witnessing was a murder (Manning *et al.*, 2007). According to the District Attorney, only half a dozen people were found who saw something of relevance. None actually saw the stabbing and one reported shouting at the assailant. This scared him off. After this first attack, Kitty Genovese made her way around the corner of the building and tried to make her way to the entrance of her flat. She would have been out of sight of most witnesses. At the site of the second attack, the stairwell of 92–96 Austin Street, only one person could have seen what happened.

Despite reports to the contrary, some residents did try to contact the police. An affidavit sworn by a 15-year-old boy stated that his father called the police. At the appeal of the murderer in 1995, several of the residents stated that they had tried to call the police but were unsuccessful. There was no '911' service at that time and calls to the local police station were not always welcome. There were regular reports of trouble at a nearby bar and police found the constant aggravation troublesome. This bar had closed earlier than usual on the night of Genovese's murder. One resident was even reported to have telephoned another resident, called the police and went to Genovese's side.

Controversies in Psychological Science – *Continued*

Conclusion

What does this curious collection of facts demonstrate? First, it clearly demonstrates that you should never believe what you read in the papers. The hoo-ha over the YK2 Millennium Bug and other spurious fears, many of which are detailed in Nick Davies's *Flat Earth News* (2008), and the Controversies in Psychological Science section in Chapter 2, provides further evidence in support of the recommendation. Misreporting, however, is alive and well. Recall the supposition, guesswork, accusations and rumour that surrounded Portugal resident Robert Murat and the media's assumption of his involvement of the kidnapping of Madeleine McCann in 2007. Second, far from sounding the death knell of the responsible citizen and the intervening bystander, it appears to show that citizen intervention was in reasonably good health.

The case of Kitty Genovese may, in Manning *et al.*'s words, be 'a stubborn and intractable urban myth'. It illustrates explicitly the value of evaluating everything you read, including this CiPS section.

Darley and Latané have extensively studied the phenomenon of **bystander intervention** – the actions of people witnessing a situation in which someone appears to require assistance. Their experiments have shown that in such situations the presence of other people who are doing nothing inhibits others from giving aid. For example, Darley and Latané (1968) staged an 'emergency' during a psychology experiment. Each participant participated in a discussion about personal problems associated with college life with one, two or five other people by means of an intercom. The experimenter explained that the participants would sit in individual rooms so that they would be anonymous and hence would be more likely to speak frankly. The experimenter would not listen in but would get their reactions later in a questionnaire. Actually, only one participant was present; the other voices were simply tape recordings. During the discussion, one of the people, who had previously said that he sometimes had seizures, apparently had one. His speech became incoherent and he stammered out a request for help.

Almost all participants left the room to help the victim when they were the only witness to the seizure. However, when there appeared to be other witnesses, the participants were much less likely to try to help. In addition, those who did try to help reacted more slowly if other people were thought to be present (see Figure 16.8).

Darley and Latané reported that the participants who did not respond were not indifferent to the plight of their fellow student. Indeed, when the experimenter entered the room, they usually appeared nervous and emotionally aroused, and they asked whether someone was helping the victim. The experimenters did not receive the impression that the participants had decided not to act; rather, they were still in conflict, trying to decide whether they should do something.

Thus, it seems that whether bystanders will intervene in a particular circumstance depends in part on how they perceive the situation. Latané and Darley (1970) have proposed a model describing a sequence of steps bystanders face when confronted with a potential emergency:

1 The event must come to their attention or be noticed.
2 They must assume some responsibility for helping the victim.
3 The possible courses of action must be considered and compared.
4 Finally, they must actually implement the chosen course of action.

Of course, this sequence takes place rapidly and without much awareness on the bystander's part, as is true of many situations to which we respond daily.

Unfortunately, at least from the perspective of the victim, obstacles may arise at any stage in this decision-making process, which make it unlikely that a bystander

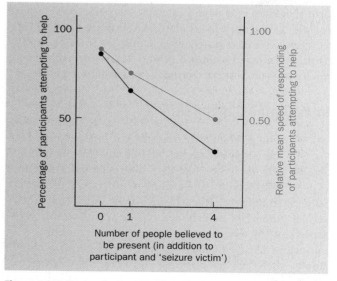

Figure 16.8 Bystander intervention. Percentage of participants attempting to help as a function of the number of other people the participants believed to be present.

Source: Based on data from Darley, J.M. and Latané, B., Bystander intervention in emergencies: Diffusion of responsibility. *Journal of Personality and Social Psychology*, 1968, 8, 377–83.

will intervene. In many cases, the bystander who is aware that others are available to help may not feel any personal responsibility to do so, a phenomenon called **diffusion of responsibility**. This factor is considered to be responsible for the finding that help is less likely to be offered when there are several bystanders present. In addition, the bystander may not feel competent to intervene or may be fearful of doing so; consequently, no action is taken. Shotland and Heinold (1985) staged an accident in which a person seemed to be bleeding. Bystanders who had received training in first-aid treatment were much more likely to come to the victim's aid, and they did so whether or not bystanders were present. Because they knew how to recognise an emergency and knew what to do, they were less likely to fear doing the wrong thing.

In life-saving and first-aid classes, people are taught to take control in emergency situations. For example, in a situation in which a person appears to be drowning, they assign onlookers specific responsibilities, such as calling emergency services, fetching rescue equipment, and so on. To what extent does taking control in this manner enhance bystander intervention? What effect might it have on the onlookers' tendency towards diffusion of responsibility?

Attraction and relationships

One of the most pervasive and immediate aspects of social life is our interpersonal relationships. It is, therefore, no accident that soap operas and celebrity magazines have a huge following, and they focus almost exclusively on close relationships – friendships, enmities, family life, romance and so forth. For most of us, much of our day-to-day happiness or misery rests on how our personal relationships are faring.

Interpersonal attraction

 One of the key features of our interpersonal relationships is whether we like someone or not, and whether they like us – **interpersonal attraction**. Many factors determine interpersonal attraction. Some factors are characteristics of the individuals themselves; others are determined by the socially reinforcing aspects of the environment. Interpersonal attraction is an important aspect of more enduring and closer relationships, such as friendships; however, the bases of attraction can change as one moves through different stages of a relationship (Duck, 1992). Physical appearance and attitudinal similarity can be very important in the initial stages of a relationship, whereas deeper personality similarities and complementarities of needs may become more important later on.

Physical appearance

Despite such maxims as 'Beauty is in the eye of the beholder', 'Never judge a book by its cover', and 'Beauty is only skin-deep', research confirms that we tend to like physically attractive people more than physically less attractive people (Langlois *et al.*, 2000). Social reinforcement provides a likely explanation for this phenomenon. Someone who is seen in the company of an attractive person and is obviously favoured by this person is likely to be well regarded by other people.

Walster *et al.* (1966) studied the effects of physical appearance at a dance at which university students were paired by a computer. Midway through the evening, the experimenters asked the participants to rate the attraction they felt towards their partners and to say whether they thought they would like to see them in the future. For both sexes, the only characteristic that correlated with attraction was physical appearance. Intelligence, grades and personality variables had no significant effect.

When people first meet someone who is good-looking, they rate the person as probably holding attitudes similar to their own and tend to assume that they have a good personality, a successful marriage and high occupational status (Dion *et al.*, 1972). In fact, physically attractive people usually do possess many of these characteristics, probably because they receive favourable treatment from society (Hatfield and Sprecher, 1986).

However, among same-sex heterosexual individuals, physical appearance may have its drawbacks, especially if members of the other sex are involved. For example, consider a study in which females were shown photos of the same woman dressed either casually or provocatively and either talking or not talking to a man in the presence of his female companion (Baenninger *et al.*, 1993). The female participants rated the 'other woman' in the photos more negatively when she was provocatively dressed than when she was casually dressed. Thus, we seem to take into account the particular circumstances under which we meet another person – their sex and the other people who may be present – when making judgements about that person and their attractiveness.

Proximity

Not surprisingly, the mere physical proximity of one person to another is a potent facilitator of attraction (Sprecher, 1998). Festinger *et al.* (1950) found that the likelihood of friendships between people who lived in an apartment house was related to the distance between the apartments in which they lived: the closer the apartments, the more likely the friendship was. People were also unlikely to have friends who lived on a different floor unless their apartments were next to a stairway, where they would meet people going up or down the stairs.

Proximity enhances familiarity, and familiarity has been shown to increase liking. We tend to grow to like things that become familiar to us over repeated exposure. Repetition generally increases our preference for a stimulus. This phenomenon applies to people as well. Even in the brief time it takes to participate in an experiment, familiarity affects interpersonal attraction. Saegert *et al.* (1973) had female university students participate in an experiment supposedly involving the sense of taste. Groups of two students (all were participants; no confederates this time) entered booths, where they tasted and rated various liquids. The movements of the participants from booth to booth were choreographed so that pairs of women were together from zero to ten times. Afterwards, the participants rated their attraction to each of the other people in the experiment. The amount of attraction the participants felt towards a given person was directly related to the number of interactions they had had – the more interactions, the more attracted they were to those persons (see Figure 16.9). And as you saw in Chapter 13, those who smile more are liked more.

Reciprocity

Liking follows the reciprocity principle – we tend to like those who like us. Dittes and Kelley (1956) led students in small discussion groups to believe, by way of anonymous written evaluations (actually written by the experimenters), that other group members either liked or disliked them. Results showed that students who believed they were liked were more attracted to the group than were those who believed they were disliked. More recently, Sprecher (1998) found reciprocal liking to be one of the major determinants of interpersonal attraction.

However, people with low or high self-esteem respond differently. People with high self-esteem base their liking for others less strongly than do people with low self-esteem on whether other people like them. In addition, we tend to like others who grow to like us, and dislike those who initially like us and then cool off on us – this is called the **gain–loss hypothesis** (Aronson and Linder, 1965). There are two possible explanations for this effect. When rejection changes to acceptance, the anxiety over rejection is reduced so that we experience the pleasure of being liked. Alternatively, it is possible that we regard those who like us from the beginning as undiscriminating, and this reduces the value of their praise. Those who dislike us to begin with but then re-evaluate as they get to know us better are discerning people, so their praise is worth more.

Similarity and need complementarity

Another factor that influences interpersonal attraction is similarity – similarity in looks, interests and attitudes. Couples tend to be similar in attractiveness. In fact, couples

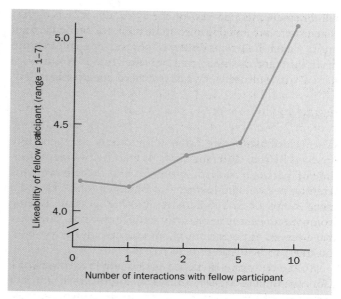

Figure 16.9 Familiarity, exposure and attraction. The rated likeability of a fellow participant as a function of number of interactions.

Source: Based on data from Saegert, S.C., Swap, W. and Zajonc, R.B., Exposure, context, and interpersonal attraction. *Journal of Personality and Social Psychology*, 1973, 25, 234–42.

who are mismatched in this respect are the most likely to break up (White, 1980). Although we might think that people would seek the most attractive partners that they could find, people tend to fear rejection and ridicule. Men especially tend to be afraid of approaching attractive women for this reason (Bernstein *et al.*, 1983).

Couples (and groups of friends) also tend to hold similar opinions. Presumably, a person who shares our opinions is likely to approve of us when we express them. Also, having friends who have similar opinions guarantees that our opinions are likely to find a consensus; we will not often find ourselves in the unpleasant position of saying something that invites disapproval from other people. Byrne (1971) confirmed, in a series of laboratory experiments, the important role of attitude similarity in relationships. The results were so reliable and consistent that Byrne formulated a 'law of attraction': attraction towards a person bears a linear relationship to the proportion of attitudes associated with the person. The more that other people agree with you, the more reinforcing they are and the greater your attraction to them. For example, if you suddenly discover that someone you are going out with likes the same obscure rock group as you, your liking for that person will suddenly increase.

Similarity of attitudes is not the only factor determining the strength of interpersonal attraction. Other kinds of similarity are also important, such as age, occupational status and ethnic background. Friends tend to have similar backgrounds as well as similar attitudes. In addition, liking can sometimes rest on dissimilarity. Winch (1958) suggested that under some circumstances, particularly in more developed relationships, people seek others who have different qualities from ourselves and who can thus best satisfy our needs – we pursue **need complementarity**.

Loving

The relationships we have with others are generally marked by two different kinds of emotion: **liking**, a feeling of personal regard, intimacy and esteem towards another person, and **loving**, a combination of liking and a deep sense of attachment to another person. Loving someone does not necessarily entail romance. You may have several close friends whom you love dearly yet have no desire to be involved with romantically.

Romantic love, also called **passionate love**, is an emotionally intense desire for sexual union with another person (Hatfield, 1988). Feeling romantic love generally involves experiencing five closely intertwined elements: a desire for intimacy with another, feeling passion for that person, being preoccupied with thoughts of that person, developing feelings of emotional dependence on that person, and feeling wonderful if that person feels romantic love towards you and dejected if not.

'Falling in love' and 'being in love' are common expressions that people use to describe their passionate desires for one another. Passionate love may occur at almost any time during the life cycle, although people involved in long-term cohabitation or marriages seem to experience a qualitatively different kind of love. The partners may still make passionate love to one another, but passion is no longer the defining characteristic of the relationship. This kind of love is called **companionate love** and is characterised by a deep, enduring affection and caring for another. Companionate love is also marked by a mutual sense of commitment, or a strong desire to maintain the relationship. How passionate love develops into companionate love is an unanswered question, although it is likely that the sort of intimacy that punctuates romantic love is still a major force in the relationship. An important feature of intimacy is self-disclosure, or the ability to share deeply private feelings and thoughts with another. Indeed, part of loving another is feeling comfortable sharing deeply personal aspects of yourself with that person.

Sternberg (1988b) has developed a theory of how intimacy, passion and commitment may combine to produce liking and several different forms of love (see Table 16.2). According to this theory, liking involves only intimacy, infatuation involves only passion, and empty love involves only commitment. Combining any two of these elements produces still other kinds of love. Romantic love entails both intimacy and passion but no commitment. Companionate love

see activity on mypsychlab

Table 16.2 Sternberg's theory of love

According to Sternberg, love is based on different combinations of intimacy, passion and commitment. These elements may combine to form eight different kinds of relationship

	Intimacy	Passion	Commitment
Non-love			
Liking	*****		
Infatuated love		*****	
Empty love		*****	
Romantic love	*****	*****	
Companionate love	*****		*****
Fatuous love		*****	*****
Consummate love	*****	*****	*****

***** indicates that the element is present in the relationship; a blank space indicates that the element is absent or is present only in low quantities
Source: After Sternberg, R.J., *The Triangle of Love*. New York: Basic Books, 1988.

entails both intimacy and commitment but no passion. Fatuous love (a kind of love marked by complacency in the relationship) entails both passion and commitment but no intimacy. The highest form of love, consummate love, contains all three elements.

Sternberg's theory is descriptive. It characterises different kinds of love but it does not explain the origins of love. What function has love served in the evolution of our species? The answer can be summed up very succinctly: procreation and child-rearing. Although love of any kind for another person is not a necessary requirement for sexual intercourse, a man and a woman who love each other passionately are more likely to have sex than are a man and a woman who do not. And if their union produces a child, then love serves another function – it increases the likelihood that both parents will share in the responsibilities of child-rearing. Our capacity for loving, then, contributes in very practical ways to the continued existence of our species.

Is Sternberg's theory of love an accurate account of your own experience with different kinds of love? Are there kinds of love that you have experienced that are not included in his theory?

Maintaining and ending relationships

Research on the maintenance of relationships has mainly dealt with heterosexual marriages in Western societies. Marital satisfaction seems to rest on companionate love and role complementarity, coupled with a sense of security and a shared search for new excitements and stimulation.

Commitment, the desire or intention to continue in the relationship, is crucial. Highly committed partners have a greater chance of staying together (Adams and Jones,

1997), and the very idea of subjectively committing oneself to a relationship can be more important than the conditions that led to commitment (Berscheid and Reis, 1998). Commitment has also been linked to the level of marital satisfaction, pro-relationship behaviour and trust. Two longitudinal studies by Wieselquist *et al.* (1999) revealed that commitment-inspired acts, such as accommodation and willingness to sacrifice, are good indicators of someone's pro-relationship motives. This is a cyclical model: such acts in turn elicit the partner's trust and reciprocal commitment and subsequent dependence on the relationship.

Adams and Jones (1997) pinpointed three factors that contribute to an ongoing relationship: (1) personal dedication (positive attraction to a particular partner and relationship); (2) moral commitment (a sense of obligation, religious duty or social responsibility, as controlled by a person's values and moral principles); and (3) constraint commitment (factors that make it costly to leave a relationship, such as lack of attractive alternatives, and various social, financial or legal investments in the relationship). More informally, relationship maintenance depends on people's feelings that: (1) they want to continue the relationship; (2) they ought to continue it; (3) they must continue it.

The end of a relationship is heralded by four factors (Levinger, 1980): (1) a new life seems to be the only solution; (2) alternative partners are available; (3) there is an expectation that the relationship will fail; and (4) there is a lack of commitment to a continuing relationship. Rusbult and Zembrodt (1983) believe that once deterioration is identified, it can be responded to in any of four ways. A partner can take a passive stance and show loyalty by waiting for an improvement to occur, or neglect, by allowing the deterioration to continue. Alternatively, a partner can take an active stance and show 'voice' behaviour, by working at improving the relationship, or exit behaviour, by choosing to end the relationship.

Duck (1992) describes a **relationship dissolution model** of four phases that partners pass through when a break-up occurs. There is an intrapsychic phase that involves brooding and some needling of the partner. The next phase is the dyadic phase. The pair will discuss the relationship, identify problems and make attributions of blame. The third phase is the social phase. In saying that the relationship is near an end, the partners may negotiate with friends, both as a means of social support for an uncertain future and for reassurance of being right. The social network will probably take sides, pronounce on guilt and blame and, like a court, sanction the dissolution. The final grave-dressing phase involves elaborating an acceptable account of the relationship that preserves one's reputation for reliability in future relationships. This 'grave-dressing' activity seeks a socially acceptable version of the life and death of the relationship.

Attraction is usually seen as a positive thing, but to what extent is it likely to be an advantage or a problem if people within a workplace (classroom, office, military unit) are attracted to one another? How likely is this to happen, and why?

Communicating and language

In many ways, communication is the essence of human social life, and the use of language to communicate is almost exclusively a human quality. People communicate both using language and non-verbally, and in recent years computer-mediated communication has become an entire new dimension of communication.

Speech and language

Spoken language communicates information in many different ways. First of all, what we actually say communicates information – if a person says, 'It's very hot in this room', then that tells you something about temperature. Sometimes, however, what we mean may not be evident in what we say. There is often a hidden subtext to language and the meaning of what we say can only be found by a detailed analysis of the entire discourse or text – what we say, to whom, and in what immediate and broader social context. You saw in Chapter 10 how context is important when revealing sex differences in communication.

Computer-mediated communication

In the past, people communicated with one another by speaking face-to-face, and if that was not possible by writing letters. Text communication has been with us for thousands of years, but its form and function has dramatically and very suddenly altered with the advent of computer-mediated communication (CMC). In the developed world we now conduct our business and personal relationships overwhelmingly by email, instant messaging, texting, in chat rooms, and so forth. Things have changed so quickly that research on CMC is in its infancy – as yet relatively fragmented, unprogrammatic, and a-theoretical (Hollingshead, 2001). The study of CMC recruits what we know about non-verbal communication and group processes. From research so far there are at least four general findings:

1 CMC restricts non-verbal communication channels and other accompaniments to spoken language (stress, pitch, speed, tone pauses), called paralanguage. This has relatively little effect on communication between

strangers, but it has a detrimental effect on interaction between people who have a closer relationship. Some non-verbal and paralanguage cues can, however, be introduced into CMC by emphasis, for example 'YES!!!', or by means of emoticons such as the sideways 'smiley' :-).

2 CMC can suppress the amount of information that is exchanged, which in turn can lead to poorer communicative outcomes. Generally, procedural aspects of group discussion that improve information exchange and group decisions in face-to-face settings may not have the same effect in computer-mediated settings.

3 CMC has a 'participation equalisation effect' that evens out many of the status effects that occur in face-to-face communicative contexts. People may feel less inhibited because they are less identifiable and may be deindividuated (Postmes et al., 1998). However, the effect does depend on how completely identity and status markers are concealed by the electronic medium (Postmes et al., 2001; Sassenberg and Boos, 2003). For example, emails often have a signature that clearly indicates the identity and status of the communicator.

4 Although, on balance, CMC initially hinders interaction and group performance, over time people adapt quite successfully to their mode of communication (Walther, 1996). Indeed, in many ways people gradually respond to CMC as if it was not computer-mediated. For example, Williams et al. (2000) found that when people are ignored in email interactions or chat rooms, they can interpret it as ostracism (called cyberostracism) and can react much as they would in face-to-face settings.

One interesting line of research on CMC focuses on sex differences. Do men and women use the medium differently? After all, men and women do differ in how they communicate non-verbally when interacting with each other. Thompson and Murachver (2001) investigated students' email messages, and found clear sex differences even when the sex of the target person was unknown to the sender. The differences were small, but when used in combination allowed quite accurate classification of a male or a female sender. Here are some differences. Female students used more intensive adverbs (for example 'it was *really* good'), hedges ('it was *sort of* interesting'), emotive references ('I was *upset*') and provided more personal information (for example, where they worked). On the other hand, male students were more insulting (for example, 'you were stupid to take that course') and offered more opinions ('the protest was worthwhile'). Perhaps with your own knowledge of sex-stereotypical behaviour these findings do not surprise you.

Non-verbal communication

see activity on mypsychlab

Verbal communication is accompanied by a smorgasbord of non-verbal cues that are richly communicative (DePaulo and Friedman, 1998). **Non-verbal communication** provides information about feelings and intentions (for example, non-verbal cues are often reliable indicators of whether someone likes you). It also can be used to regulate interactions (non-verbal cues can signal the approaching end of an utterance, or that someone else wishes to speak), to express intimacy (touching and mutual eye contact), to establish dominance or control (non-verbal threats), and to facilitate goal attainment (for example, pointing).

Cutting edge – What's in a name?

The British sitcom character, Hyacinth Bucket in *Keeping Up Appearances*, was so snobbishly offended by her surname, she adopted the phonological moniker, 'Bouquet'. Hilarity ensued as people would read her name as Bucket only for the character to disdainfully and brusquely upbraid them for their mispronunciation. People with the surname Pratt must have a difficult life. Some names appear guaranteed to produce a stereotypical response.

But is there any good evidence that your name influences people's reactions to you? Researchers in management at the Universities of California and Yale suggest that there is. They have found that, astonishingly, students whose names begin with the letters A or B achieved a higher grade point average (GPA, the American system of combining and averaging scores for end-of-school performance) than did those whose names

began with C or D (Nelson and Simmons, 2007). If the students liked their initials, the effects were even more pronounced, i.e. if they liked the letters A and B, they were even more likely to have a high GPA. The inference is that those letters were associated with better and poorer grades, respectively. Those students with C/D names moved onto graduate schools of poorer quality and reputation than did those with A/B names.

These data are correlational. But when the researchers set up a study to see whether name actually influenced task performance, they found that participants solved fewer anagrams when a consolation prize shared their first initial than when it didn't.

So, if your name is Adam Boulton, you're blessed. But where this leaves Celine Dion is anyone's guess.

People tend to have less control over non-verbal than verbal communication, and people are often unaware that they are sending or receiving non-verbal cues. Non-verbal sensitivity improves with age, is more advanced among successful people, and is compromised among people with various psychopathologies. Women are generally more adept than men at detecting and sending non-verbal communications; however, they differ less in conscious awareness of precisely what information has been communicated by which non-verbal channel, and they are worse than men at recognising covert messages such as discrepant or deceptive communications (Hall, 1984). These differences are probably due to child-rearing strategies that encourage girls more than boys to be emotionally expressive and attentive.

Because the eyes are often considered to be the windows of the soul, eye contact, now technically called **gaze**, communicates an enormous amount of information (Kleinke, 1986). For example, people gaze more at people they like, and lower-status people gaze more at higher-status people than vice versa except when a higher-status person wants to exert control over a lower-status person. Because white adults tend to gaze more when listening than when speaking, a speaker who increases gaze signals that they are about to stop speaking, and a listener who reduces gaze indicates that they are about to start speaking.

More general facial expressions are a rich indicator of people's feelings. Research shows that facial expressions are universal indicators of six basic emotions: happiness, surprise, sadness, fear, disgust and anger (Ekman, 1982). There are, however, strong cultural differences in the expression of emotion – for example, the expression of emotion is encouraged in Mediterranean cultures but discouraged in Asian cultures (Gallois, 1993).

The body itself is a means of communication, via postures and gestures. For example, postures can communicate liking – people who like one another tend to lean forward, maintain a relaxed posture and face one another. It can also communicate status – higher-status individuals adopt a relaxed, open posture, with arms and legs asymmetrically positioned and a backward lean to the body, whereas lower-status individuals adopt a more rigid, closed and upright posture, with arms close to the body and feet together (Mehrabian, 1972). Gestures are more straightforward – pointing at one's chest refers to self, beckoning with an upturned finger invites someone to approach, and so forth.

Touching means different things depending on the type of touch, the context within which the touch occurs, who touches whom, and what the relationship is between the interactants (Jones and Yarbrough, 1985). For example, touching can communicate liking, control, playfulness, and so forth. The prevalence and acceptability of touching varies markedly between cultures – northern Europeans hardly touch at all, whereas Latin Americans touch a great deal. Jourard (1966) observed people in cafés, and noted, in a one-hour period, no touching at all in London and 180 touches in Puerto Rico.

Finally, how close people position themselves relative to other people, **interpersonal distance**, communicates intimacy and liking. Hall (1966) has identified four interpersonal distance zones: intimate (up to 0.50 m), personal (0.5–1.25 m), social (1.25–4 m) and public (4–8 m). Clearly, if you want to become intimate with someone you will stand close, and if that person would rather not be that intimate they will move away.

Speech style

Language also communicates information by the way we say things – the language, accent, or **speech style** we use. For example, just saying 'Hello' conveys entirely different information if it is said in French or English, with an American or South African accent, in a lively, cheerful manner or a flat, depressed manner. Language contains **social markers** that convey information about the context, the person who is speaking, and the person who is being spoken to (Scherer and Giles, 1979). Social markers tell us, for example, about someone's mood or health, the formality of the situation, and the social category membership of the interactants – their age, sex, socio-economic status, ethnicity, and so forth.

The study of social category markers, particularly ethnicity markers, shows that language use and speech style in particular contexts are influenced to a significant extent by the relative social standing of identities that are cued by language and speech style, and that even second language proficiency is influenced in this way.

Because language is often an integral aspect of ethnic identity, indeed many groups effectively define themselves through their language (called **ethnolinguistic groups**), intergroup dynamics that affect whether a group thrives or not can also impact language. Languages can thrive, revive or die. The key variable here is **subjective ethnolinguistic vitality**, which refers to people's overall perception of the status of their language, how much support it has from society and social institutions, how many people speak the language and whether numbers are increasing or decreasing (Harwood *et al.*, 1994). High vitality encourages continued use of the language and thus ensures its survival and the survival of the ethnolinguistic group itself as a distinct entity in society. Low vitality is associated with declining use of the ethnic language, its gradual disappearance, and often the disappearance of the ethnolinguistic group as a distinct entity: that is, there is language death or language suicide. This analysis has been used to help understand the French language revival in Quebec over the past 30 years (Bourhis, 1984), and the loss of Japanese culture and language by third-generation Japanese in Brazil (Kanazawa and Loveday, 1988).

Because language is so tied up with identity, identity dynamics may impact one's motivation to become proficient in a second language. Many societies are multilingual with a dominant language – for example, in Britain English is the dominant language, but there are large numbers of people for whom Urdu or Hindi are their native tongue. What influences whether these people acquire native-like rather than classroom proficiency in English? According to Giles and Byrne (1982), it is all a matter of motivation, which hinges on the perception of whether or not native-like proficiency adds something of value to one's identity or subtracts from one's identity (Sachdev and Wright, 1996).

Low ethnic identification, low subjective vitality and a belief that one can 'pass' linguistically into the dominant group, coupled with a large number of other potential identities of which many are high status, are conditions that motivate the individual to acquire native-like mastery in the second language. Proficiency in the second language is considered economically and culturally useful; it is additive to one's identity. Realisation of this motivation will be facilitated or inhibited by the extent to which one is made to feel confident or anxious about using the second language in specific contexts. The converse set of sociopsychological conditions motivates people to acquire only classroom proficiency. Through fear of assimilation, the second language is considered subtractive in that it may attract in-group hostility and accusations of ethnic betrayal. Intelligence and aptitude will also affect proficiency.

How one speaks says much about one's status in society, and so it is not surprising to discover that we can change our speech style in different contexts to address issues of status – we can do this deliberately, but to a great extent this is an automatic process. **Speech accommodation theory** (Giles, 1984) describes the type of accommodation that occurs as a function of the social orientation that two speakers have towards one another. Where an interpersonal orientation exists, such as that between two friends, bilateral speech convergence occurs. Higher-status speakers shift their accent or speech style 'downwards' towards that of lower-status speakers, who in turn shift 'upwards'. Convergence increases interpersonal speech style similarity and thus enhances interpersonal approval and liking, particularly if the convergence behaviour is clearly intentional.

Where an intergroup orientation exists between the speakers, accommodation depends on the perceived nature of the relations between the two groups. If the lower-status group has low subjective vitality coupled with a belief in social mobility (i.e. that one can pass, linguistically, into the higher-status group), there is unilateral upward convergence on the part of the lower-status speaker and unilateral speech divergence on the part of the higher-status speaker. In intergroup contexts, divergence achieves psycholinguistic distinctiveness: it differentiates the speaker's in-group on linguistic grounds from the out-group. Where an intergroup orientation exists and the lower-status group has high subjective vitality coupled with a belief in social change (i.e. that one cannot pass into the higher-status group), bilateral divergence occurs: both speakers pursue psycholinguistic distinctiveness.

The social psychology of gossip

According to the Machiavellian intelligence or social brain hypothesis of how our minds evolved, the intelligence of primates evolved in order to solve social, rather than non-social, technological problems (such as finding food). The hypothesis is partly supported by research showing that when people are allowed to converse freely, two-thirds of their conversation comprises social topics – gossip (rather than work, leisure, arts, politics). Researchers from the

Cutting edge – I don't mean to be rude, but . . .

People often think that if they preface saying something socially difficult or unpleasant with a self-effacing disclaimer, the difficult or unpleasant thing will be more positively received. A recent study has tested whether such disclaimers work (El-Alayli et al., 2008). In the first study, participants rated the arrogance of people who began what they were saying with 'I don't mean to sound arrogant, but . . .' These people were only rated as arrogant when the disclaimer was actually followed by an arrogant statement. Similar findings were found when the disclaimer involved selfishness or laziness.

The researchers found that a tendency to believe that a person is what they claim to be (selfish, arrogant, lazy etc.) is enhanced not because we categorise them using the information we have available but because we make assumptions about their personality, based on the same information. Making the arrogance salient, then following it up with an arrogant statement means that the disclaimer has backfired because the initial information has already shaped our view of the speaker.

Of course, there are different sorts of disclaimers, as the researchers point out: 'I'm not prejudiced but . . .', 'I could be wrong, but . . .' and 'This may sound mad, but . . .' Would these also undermine the meaning of what a person is trying to convey?

universities of St Andrews and Liverpool investigated the type of social information that was better transmitted from person to person (Mesoudi *et al.*, 2006).

In one study, they found that when participants read about social interactions, their recall of these interactions was no different for gossip or non-gossip content. The interactions they read about involved very 'social' topics such as infidelity, deception and pregnancy. However, transmission was more accurate when there were a number of third party people interacting, i.e. the more people there were to gossip with, the more accurate the recall of that gossip. The authors suggest that this supports the Machiavellian hypothesis although perhaps the type of material described as gossip might have some other feature that might explain why it was more salient. If the protagonist had violated a social norm, for example, this would be more salient than if somebody had given a man, who was not her boyfriend, a lift into work early that morning.

Chapter review

Social influence

- Compliance with a request can be strengthened by ingratiation, reciprocity, or making multiple requests to prepare the target for the focal request – foot-in-the-door, door-in-the-face, low-balling.
- People have a tendency to blindly obey orders from people in authority, even when the consequence of obedience is terrible suffering for others. Obedience drops dramatically when there is social support for disobedience.
- Social interaction, particularly when people are uncertain or are in need of social approval, produces group norms that subsequently regulate behaviour.
- People conform because they are unsure, in need of approval, or define themselves – their identity – in terms of a group that is defined by the norms.
- Although people usually conform to majorities, minorities can change attitudes and behaviour through a conversion process. To do this, minorities need to be internally consensual in repeatedly, but not dogmatically, promulgating the same message.

People in groups

- The presence of other people enhances the performance of a well-learned behaviour but interferes with the performance of complex or poorly learned behaviour.
- When a group of people must collectively perform a task, the effort of any one individual is usually less than we would predict had the individual attempted the task alone – a behaviour known as social loafing.
- Loafing is reduced among people who value their group and feel they must compensate for others' performances. It is also reduced when people feel more identifiable and when they feel the task is important.
- Groups often exist to make decisions. Effective group decision-making can be hampered by elements of the discussion leading to the decision. This can cause groups to make very extreme decisions (polarisation) or very bad decisions (groupthink).
- Groups often need to remember a great deal of information. One way to do this effectively is to have a transactive memory structure in which different individuals or different sub-groups are responsible for remembering different information, but all members of the group know who is responsible for what.
- Groups usually have leaders. Leadership effectiveness ultimately rests on whether the group perceives the leader as being legitimate, as having the requisite skills, as being a loyal and focal group member, and as having the appropriate relationships with followers.
- People in crowds can sometimes behave antisocially because they feel anonymous and not responsible for the consequences of their actions – they are deindividuated.
- Collective events can also change people's identities so that they identify with the identity of the crowd and conform strongly to group norms.

Intergroup relations and prejudice

- Intergroup relations exist whenever people belonging to one group interact collectively or individually with another group or its members in terms of their group identifications.
- Where groups have the same goal, but only one group can achieve the goal at the expense of the others, then intergroup relations become highly conflictual. Where groups have the same goal, but the goal can only be achieved by the groups working cooperatively together, intergroup relations are more harmonious.
- Where groups feel their goals are being frustrated by another group, or that they are deprived relative to another group, conflict and negative attitudes arise – the target is often a weaker scapegoat group.
- The framework of intergroup competition or hostility is also contained in the mere fact of the existence of different categories – in-groups and out-groups.
- People derive a sense of who they are – a social identity – from the groups they belong to, and thus they are prepared to protect these groups against other groups. Because groups define and evaluate one's identity, and thus self-concept, people strive to evaluate their groups more positively than other groups.
- Prejudice is an attitude, usually negative, towards a particular group. Its cognitive component is stereotypes, and its behavioural manifestation is discrimination.

- Stereotypes and prejudices may be strengthened because people inflate the co-occurrence of negative behaviours and distinctive groups, and also exaggerate the perceived homogeneity of out-groups.
- Some people may be more prejudiced than others, but generally we can all be prejudiced if the social conditions favour prejudice. Prejudice stigmatises and disadvantages other people, but prejudice can be difficult to detect where social norms and legislation outlaw blatant prejudice.
- Teaching people to think about members of other groups as individuals and to consider them in terms of their personal situations and characteristics can reduce prejudices and tendencies towards stereotyping.
- Although initially appealing, simply bringing different groups into contact with one another, so that they become familiar with one another, is not reliably effective in reducing prejudice.

Aggression and helping behaviour

- Arousal, frustration, disinhibition and elevated testosterone levels are all factors that can lead to human aggression.
- People can also learn to be aggressive by witnessing other people being reinforced for aggressive behaviour.
- Alcohol and media violence may also contribute to aggression.
- People often find it difficult to sacrifice their own personal short-term gains for long-term collective gains. This is the social dilemma that underpins many of the world's greatest environmental problems. Social dilemmas can be reduced when people feel themselves part of a community or group that accesses a resource. Leadership, resource management and limited access to a resource, can also help.
- People often fail to help in an emergency (called bystander apathy) if there are many other potential helpers available or if they feel they do not have the resources to help. Misperception of norms can sometimes inhibit people from offering assistance in an emergency.

- Bystander intervention is facilitated if there are only few bystanders present and if they feel they have the resources (time, ability and so forth) to help.

Attraction and relationships

- We tend to be attracted to others who think positively of us, who are similar to us, who are physically attractive, and who live, work or play near us.
- Sternberg's theory of love describes how the elements of intimacy, passion and commitment are involved in the different kinds of love.
- The course of a relationship is strongly influenced by the degree of commitment the partners have to the relationship.

Communication and language

- Speech conveys information not only through the words we use but also through how we say things. The speech style we adopt (language, accent) is a reliable cue to group membership (age, sex, ethnicity and so on).
- Language and accent are often defining features of groups, particularly ethnic groups. Whether an ethnic languages thrives or perishes is influenced by the vitality of the language and the group it defines – a high-vitality language is one that has substantial material and social support in society, and contributes positively to one's sense of self.
- Because speech style cues group membership, people can consciously or unconsciously accentuate or de-emphasise their speech style to conceal or to publicise their group membership.
- Speech is accompanied by non-verbal cues that are particularly important for communicating feelings and relationships, and for regulating conversation. Some of the most important non-verbal channels are gaze, facial expression, postures, gestures, touch and interpersonal distance.

Suggestions for further reading

Group and intergroup processes

Brown, R.J. (2000) *Group Processes* (2nd edn) Oxford: Blackwell.
Brown, R.J. and Gaertner, S.L. (eds) (2001) *Blackwell Handbook of Social Psychology: Intergroup processes*. Oxford: Blackwell.
Hogg, M.A. and Tindale, R.S. (eds) (2001) *Blackwell Handbook of Social Psychology: Group processes*. Oxford: Blackwell.
Stangor, C. (2004) *Social Groups in Action and Interaction*. New York: Psychology Press.
Zimbardo, P. (2007) *The Lucifer Effect*. London: Ebury.
The first four books are accessible and readable introductions to a wide range of topics in the areas of group processes and intergroup relations. The last is an excellent review of why apparently good people do bad things.

Cooperation and leadership

Kozlowski, S.W. J. and Ilgen, D.R. (2007) The science of team success. *Scientific American Mind*, 18, 3, 54–61.
Reicher, S.D., Haslam, S.A. and Platow, M.J. (2007) The new psychology of leadership. *Scientific American Mind*, 18, 3, 22–9.
Sebanz, N. (2007). It takes two to . . . *Scientific American Mind*, 17, 6, 52–7.
The first item reviews the advantages of groupwork in decision-making; the second reviews some of the recent research on the social psychology of leadership; the third is a good article on the social psychology of cooperation.

Social influence

Cialdini, R.B.(2007) *Influence: The psychology of persuasion*. New York: HarperCollins.

Special issue of *American Psychologist* on Milgram's obedience studies (2009) 64, 1.

Interpersonal processes and relationships

Fletcher, G.J.O. and Clark, M.S. (eds) (2001) *Blackwell Handbook of Social Psychology: Interpersonal processes*. Oxford: Blackwell.
This is a single-volume handbook (one of the four separate volumes of the Blackwell Handbook of Social Psychology) that focuses on interpersonal processes, and covers attraction and close relationships.

Journals to consult

Basic and Applied Social Psychology

British Journal of Social Psychology

European Journal of Social Psychology

European Review of Social Psychology

Group Processes and Intergroup Relations

Journal of Experimental Social Psychology

Journal of Language and Social Psychology

Journal of Personality and Social Psychology

Journal of Social Issues

Journal of Social and Personal Relationships

Organizational Behavior and Human Decision Processes

Personality and Social Psychology Bulletin

Personality and Social Psychology Review

Psychological Science

Social Neuroscience

Website addresses

www.understandingprejudice.org
A site with information and links to researchers of prejudice. Also includes demonstrations and exercises (for example, the Ambivalent Sexism Inventory). This is a supplementary site to the book *Understanding Prejudice and Discrimination* (McGraw-Hill).

http://www.spssi.org
Society for the Psychological Study of Social Issues website. Contains many useful links, including areas of current activity where social psychologists are seeking to influence policy.

http://www.social-inclusion.org.uk
Website for a series of seminars on issues such as intergroup contact, prejudice reduction, processes underlying inclusion and exclusion of individuals within and between groups.

http://www.as.wvu.edu/~sbb/comm221/primer.htm
'Steve's Primer of Practical Persuasion and Influence'. Steve Booth-Butterfield's (West Virginia University) site that takes you through different persuasion techniques in an upbeat and amusing style.

Health psychology

CHAPTER 17

Which? Calls for 'fat tax' on unhealthy food

Rebecca Smithers

The government is being urged to consider a 'fat tax' on foods high in fat, salt and sugar, in a report which says existing policies aimed at ending the obesity crisis through healthier eating are confusing. In the report, called *Hungry for Change*, the consumer group *Which?* calls on the government to explore a range of radical financial incentives to encourage families to eat more healthily, including imposing an extra tax on foods deemed unhealthy.

Source: from 'Which? Calls for 'fat tax' on unhealthy food', *The Guardian*, 11 March 2009 (Smithers, R.), Copyright Guardian News & Media Ltd 2008.

Explore the accompanying videos, simulations and animations on MyPsychLab. This chapter includes activities on: Factors that contribute to health • Selye's general adaptation syndrome • Why do you drink? • What personality type are you? • Check your understanding and prepare for your exams using multiple choice, short answer and essay practice tests also available.

WHAT YOU SHOULD BE ABLE TO DO AFTER READING CHAPTER 17

- Define health psychology.
- Describe some of the factors that can lead to (or prevent) overeating, cigarette smoking, sexually transmitted disease, alcohol use and physical inactivity.
- Evaluate the psychological strategies that have been employed to reduce ill health.
- Describe and understand the process of stress and its effects on the immune system.
- Define psychoneuroimmunology and understand its significance to health.
- Evaluate the role of personality and specific styles of behaving in the maintenance of health and ill health.

QUESTIONS TO THINK ABOUT

- What is health psychology and how does it differ from abnormal psychology?
- What illnesses can psychology help to prevent? How can it do this?
- How can people stop eating fatty food, smoking or be encouraged to take up physical exercise?
- What is the role of personality in the development or prevention of illness?
- What effect do stressors have on health and the immune system?
- Can public health education campaigns change behaviour? How would you design an effective one?

Health psychology: a definition

The particular behaviours that make up an individual's way of life have important consequences for that individual's quality of life. Whether a person smokes, drinks alcohol, eats specific foods, exercises, has regular health checks and is susceptible to stress can all have an impact on a person's health and beliefs about their health. Such beliefs and behaviour are at the core of what health psychology seeks to understand. **Health psychology** is the branch of psychology that applies psychological principles to the understanding of health and illness. Factors influencing health can be external (in the form of stressors, health promotion, advertising of health-impairing products) or internal (in the form of thoughts, beliefs, decision-making and coping responses).

According to Matarazzo (1982), the aims of health psychology are to promote and maintain health, to prevent and treat illness, to identify the causes and symptoms of illness and the causes of health, and to analyse and improve healthcare systems/policy. It is a relatively new branch of psychology and, as its subject matter suggests, has a slight overlap with clinical psychology. Both health psychology and clinical psychology study stress and how people cope with it, but health psychology tends to concern itself with bodily illness whereas clinical psychology is primarily concerned with mental illness. (Clinical psychology is the subject of the next chapter.) Many of the theories and explanations for health-related behaviour and experience derive from work in cognitive and social psychology. Because of this fusion of psychologies and because of the subject matter of health psychology, the sub-area was not regarded as a distinct branch of the discipline until relatively recently.

Health and ill health

The starting point for all health psychologists is the definition of health and the determinants of health. Health has been defined as 'a positive state of physical, mental and social well-being – not simply the absence of injury or disease – that varies over time along a continuum. At the wellness end of the continuum, health is the dominant state. At the other end of the continuum, the dominant state is illness or injury' (Sarafino, 2002). A healthy lifestyle is one that can enhance an individual's physical and mental well-being; an unhealthy lifestyle is one that diminishes physical and psychological well-being. According to Whitehead (1995), the determinants of good health can be conceived of in the way suggested in Figure 17.1.

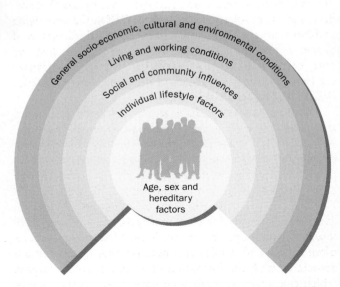

Figure 17.1 The types of factor which Whitehead suggests are contributors to health.
Source: Whitehead, M., Tackling health inequalities: An agenda for action. In M. Benzenal, K. Judge and M. Whitehead (eds) *Tackling Inequalities in Health: An agenda for action*, p. 23. London: King's Fund, 1995. © 1995 King's Fund. Reprinted by permission

In this model, the individual is at the centre and possesses immutable characteristics which can influence health (such as age, sex, race, genetic make-up). Surrounding the individual are four interacting layers which represent external determinants of health. These include the individual's lifestyle, their social and community influences, living and working conditions, and the general cultural and environmental conditions in which the individual lives.

Some specific examples of factors within each of these layers include nutrition, alcohol consumption, smoking, sexual behaviour and exercise. Health psychologists attempt to understand the factors which influence health and, if these factors are detrimental to health, apply psychological techniques in order to promote good health and discourage unhealthy behaviour. They are also involved in psychological aspects of healthcare and in determining the effects of government health policy on behaviour. The following sections evaluate the role of specific behaviours – eating, exercising, smoking, drinking alcohol and having unprotected sex – in health and illness.

Nutrition

Over the past 150 years or so, our diet has changed considerably: it is higher in fat and lower in fibre, largely because processed foods, fast food and sweets are high in fat and low in fibre. Diets too high in saturated fats (those fats found in animal products and a few vegetable oils) and too low in fibre have been associated with specific health disorders, such as **coronary heart disease (CHD)**, the narrowing of blood vessels that supply nutrients to the heart, and cancer, a malignant and intrusive tumour that destroys body organs and tissue (Cohen, 1987). CHD and cancer are two of the leading causes of death in Western nations (World Health Organization, 2007).

The chief culprit in CHD is **serum cholesterol**, a chemical that occurs naturally in the bloodstream where it serves as a detoxifier. Cholesterol is also the source of lipid membranes of cells and steroid hormones. It is a vital substance and we would die without it. Cholesterol has two important forms: HDL (high-density lipoprotein) and LDL (low-density lipoprotein). HDL is sometimes called 'good' cholesterol because high levels of it are inversely associated with CHD; it seems to play a protective role in the bloodstream. LDL is often called 'bad' cholesterol because high levels of it are associated with the formation of atherosclerotic plaques, which clog arteries. Fibre is an important dietary component because it helps to reduce LDL cholesterol levels (and aids digestion). People with pre-existing heart complaints are prescribed the cholesterol-reducing drugs, statins.

Cohen (1987) has shown that cultures having the highest death rates due to breast cancer are those in which large amounts of fats are consumed. People in countries such as the UK, the Netherlands, Canada and the USA have a relatively high fat intake and relatively high death rates due to breast cancer. In contrast, people in countries such as Japan and Thailand have both relatively low fat intake and relatively low death rates due to breast cancer. There is

evidence that specific lifestyles within these cultures can help to reduce the risk of cancer and other illnesses, and this is discussed below.

Of course, bad nutrition is different from malnutrition and the latter is more serious. According to the World Health Organization's (2007) estimates, 55 million children under 5 years of age show signs of wasting/malnutrition, and the global pattern of stunting in children can be seen in Figure 17.2. The highest number of these children live in south central Asia.

Heart disease and eating – explaining the French paradox

A paradox familiar to health researchers and gourmands alike is this: the French diet is laden with highly palatable saturated fat, and the nation's blood cholesterol level is high yet the incidence of death caused by heart disease is lower in France than it is in the United States. Of course, a highly fatty diet may not necessarily lead to heart disease and there could be other explanations for the French paradox including genetic differences, metabolism, a less stressful life, differences in attitudes towards illness, different eating patterns, greater exercise and so on (Rozin, 1999).

The body mass index of French people tends to be significantly lower than that of Americans: they are leaner. One reason for the leanness, despite the content of the diet, may be that they actually eat less. Although the diet may appear superficially frightening in terms of its nutritional content, it is a diet of moderation, rather than excess.

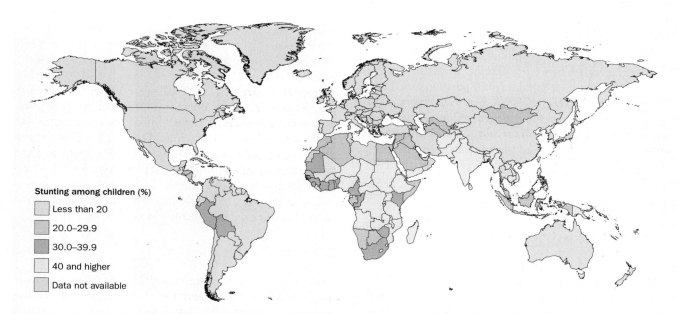

Figure 17.2 Geographical pattern of stunting in children under 5 years of age.
Source: World Health Statistics, 2007.

To examine whether this could explain the French paradox, Paul Rozin and a group of researchers at the University of Pennsylvania, USA, and CNRS in Paris, examined portion sizes in French and American fast-food restaurants (e.g. Pizza Hut, McDonald's, Hard Rock Café, Quick, Burger King, etc.), more upmarket restaurants (e.g. bistros) and supermarkets (Rozin *et al.*, 2003). The study took place in Pennsylvania and Paris. The portion sizes described in the cities' respective *Zagat* guide (a restaurant guide) were also compared.

When supermarket and restaurant foods were analysed, the French portions were indeed smaller. Of course, even small portions can be calorifically intense but the eating of many small, highly-calorific portions does not appear to occur in the French diet. The French also spent more time eating than did the Americans suggesting that the eating experience for the French amounts to more than the ingestion of food: it is a social, cultural – possibly, emotional – experience.

Physical fitness

People in developed countries lead increasingly sedentary lives; our work has changed (it is less physical) as have our leisure opportunities (we can watch more television, surf the internet and play computer games). Like high-fat, low-fibre diets, lack of exercise is correlated with increased risk of CHD (Peters *et al.*, 1983; Powell *et al.*, 1987). People who exercise regularly appear to accumulate less body fat and to be less vulnerable to the negative effects of stress than are people who do not exercise regularly (J.D. Brown, 1991).

There is some evidence that regular exercisers are likely to live longer (Paffenbarger *et al.*, 1986). This evidence comes from a longitudinal study of the lifestyles of 17,000 Harvard University alumni. Between 1962 and 1978, 1,413 of the original 17,000 participants died, 45 per cent from CHD and 32 per cent from cancer. Significantly more of these deaths occurred in participants who had led sedentary lives. Those alumni who reported that they exercised the equivalent of 30–35 miles of running or walking per week faced half the risk of dying prematurely compared with those who reported exercising the equivalent of five or fewer miles per week. On average, those who exercised moderately (an equivalent of 20 miles running or walking per week) lived about two years longer than those who exercised less than the equivalent of five miles.

These results have been replicated in a sample of elderly individuals. The relationship between the time that elderly (61–81 years old) non-smoking participants spent walking and the death rate was monitored over a period of 12 years (Hakim *et al.*, 1998). Men who walked more than two miles a day lived significantly longer than those who exercised less. Only 21.5 per cent of the two-mile walkers had died after 12 years, whereas 43 per cent had died in the group that undertook less exercise. Cancer and CHD was also lower in the walkers: this effect occurred even when other factors (such as blood pressure, alcohol consumption, medical condition, cholesterol level) had been taken into account. However, diet was not considered and there is the possibility that healthy eating may have been responsible for the reduced death rate. If a factor (such as walking or diet) can benefit health or make an individual less susceptible to illness or ill health, this factor is called a protective factor. In other words, this factor protects the individual from ill health. (Of course, it cannot prevent an illness, only protect a person from developing it.)

Although a brisk walk is often recommended to those who are not as agile as they once were, many elderly individuals continue to lead a sedentary lifestyle. Our immune system, the part of the body that fights infection (as you'll see later on), deteriorates with age, and this may expose the elderly to an increased risk for illnesses, such as upper respiratory tract infection.

To see if regular exercise could protect against infection, a group of researchers at the University of Tokyo measured immune system response on three occasions over 12 months in a group of normally sedentary elderly individuals who engaged in two bouts of 60-minute exercise a week for the duration of the study (Akimoto *et al.*, 2003). Participants, who were aged 65 years and older, engaged in resistance training (back, chest and inner thigh exercises) and endurance training (aerobic exercise such as 'step' and ball games).

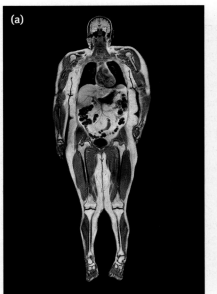 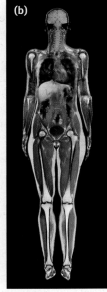

MRI scans of a clinically obese and a healthy individual.
Source: Marty Chobot/National Geographic Image Collection.

The secretion and concentration of an important antibody (a chemical produced by the body to fight infection) increased significantly over the period of study – before training, 4 months in and 12 months in – suggesting the benefits of this simple exercise regime to immune system functioning. Although the study did not use a control group, or examine the possible different effects of resistance and endurance training, the findings suggest a relatively easy way of protecting immune system functioning in a group that is susceptible to immune system decline.

Types of exercise

According to Cooper (1985), aerobic exercises such as running, walking, cycling and swimming are superior to other forms of exercise for improving cardiovascular health. **Aerobic exercises** are those which expend consid-erable energy, increase blood flow and respiration and thereby stimulate and strengthen the heart and lungs and increase the body's efficiency in using oxygen. Running at least two miles in less than 20 minutes four times a week (or any equivalent aerobic exercise), significantly increases cardiovascular health (Cooper, 1985). One study showed that aerobic exercise had an additional benefit: reduced heart response to mental stress (Kubitz and Landers, 1993). Two groups of students who had not exercised for at least three months prior to the study were divided into two groups. One group rode an exercise bike three times a week for 40 minutes for eight weeks; the other group did not perform any aerobic exercises. At the end of the eight-week period, both groups were given timed colour perception and maths tests. Participants in the aerobic exercise programme showed lower absolute heart rates in response to the tests than did the participants who did not exercise.

Controversies in Psychological Science – Can exercise improve mood?

The issue

Exercisers frequently report that they feel better after a bout of vigorous exercise (the so-called feel-good effect). They feel an increase in positive mood and self-confidence that can sometimes translate into better work performance or cognitive ability. But is there scientific evidence demonstrating the positive effects of exercise on mood?

The evidence

Although exercise can have significant immediate effects on mood, these effects are dependent on the types of exercise taken (Biddle, 1995; Scully et al., 1998). Petruzello et al. (1997), for example, found that exercise reduced state anxiety (the anxiety felt at the time) only after aerobic exercise. When trait anxiety was examined (the anxiety that individuals consistently feel, independently of their environment), a training programme lasting ten weeks reduced anxiety.

An analysis of a large number of studies investigating the effect of exercise on depression has found a moderate effect of acute and chronic exercise on depression, with those requiring clinical treatment showing the greatest reduction in depression (North et al., 1990). In fact, exercise seems to be better than psychotherapy in alleviating negative mood, and exercise and psychotherapy seem to be better than exercise alone (Martinsen, 1995).

Other studies suggest similar effects of exercise on mood but in more specific contexts. Mondin et al. (1996), for example, examined the effects of exercise deprivation on the mood of ten volunteers who regularly exercised for 45 minutes a day, 6–7 days a week. The participants exercised for a day, took three days off and resumed exercise on the fifth day. Depriving participants of exercise was associated with an increase in self-reported mood disturbance, state anxiety, tension, depression, confusion and a decrease in vigour. These changes were reversed when exercise resumed. Of course, one could attribute these results to factors other than exercise. Perhaps the disturbance in these individuals' routine affected their performance.

In a comparison of participants' mood before and after aerobic dance exercise, soccer, tennis or bowling, Rudolph and Kim (1996) found that mood improved only after the aerobic exercise and soccer. Biddle's review (Biddle, 1995) suggests that intensity of exercise may be a factor in enhanced mood, and perhaps this explains the result of this study. Running at intense levels over short durations increased stress but running over long distances increased arousal (Kerr and van den Wollenberg, 1997).

If exercise does improve mood, how much is needed and at what intensity? Hansen et al. (2001) measured mood before and after resting (sitting quietly) and before and after three bouts of exercise, lasting 10, 20 and 30 minutes, respectively, in a group of 20–25-year-olds. During the exercise conditions, participants worked on a bicycle ergometer (in essence, an exercise bike) which allowed participants to exercise with moderate intensity. After 10 minutes of cool-down – the post-exercise period – mood was measured again.

▶

Cigarette smoking – *Continued*

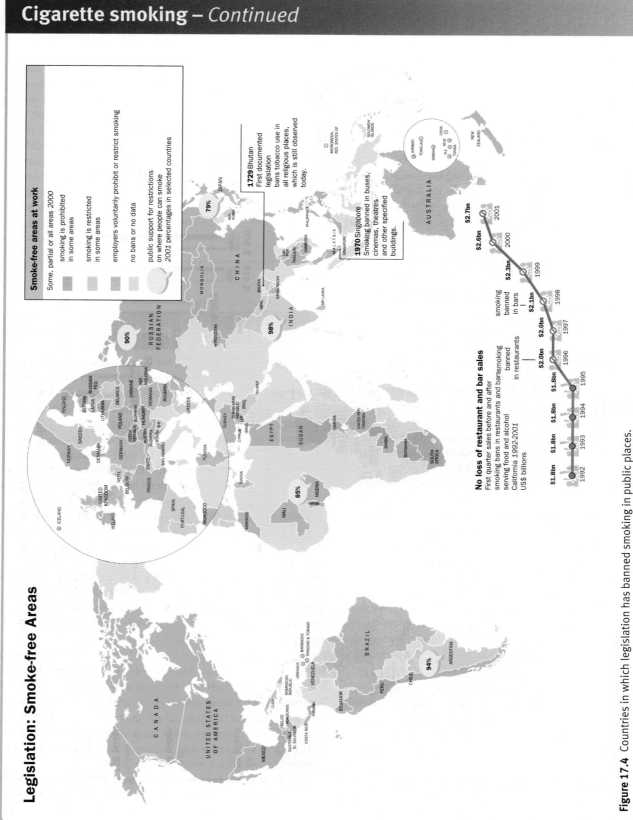

Figure 17.4 Countries in which legislation has banned smoking in public places.

Source: www.who.int/tobacco/statistics/tobacco_atlas/en/; by permission of the World Health Organization.

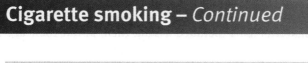

Cigarette smoking – *Continued*

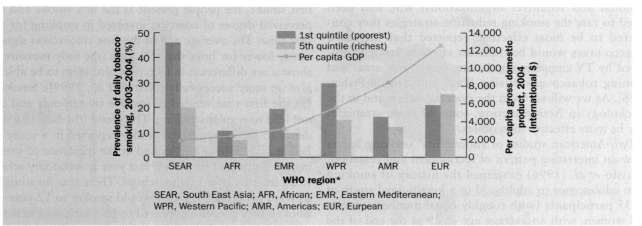

Figure 17.5 Daily tobacco smoking among adults aged 18 years and older, by income quintile and WHO region.

Source: World Health Statistics, 2007.

A 'stigmatised habit'

People hold justifiably negative views of smoking and because of this it has been labelled a 'stigmatised habit' (Furnham *et al.*, 2002). Their research showed that when people are asked to prioritise who should receive healthcare, for example, smokers are normally given the lowest priority. A study at University College London confirmed this view. The researchers asked 100 adults to rank 16 hypothetical patients in terms of priority for treatment for three medical conditions: heart transplantation, *in vitro* fertilisation (IVF) and cosmetic surgery. Participants were told that these patients would be treated by a UK National Health Service hospital, that is, a hospital directly funded by public taxation and which offers treatment free at the point of delivery. Information about patients varied according to age, annual income, smoking behaviour and whether the patient had children. The researchers found that young people, non-smokers and those on a low annual income were given highest priority and smokers the lowest priority. The existence of children only influenced decisions about IVF and heart transplant.

The results are consistent with other studies of people's attitudes to smokers, with young people preferentially prioritised for kidney dialysis treatment (Furnham and Briggs, 1993) and smokers given lower priority (Furnham *et al.*, 2000). As dialysis is unrelated to smoking, this result coupled with the findings from Furnham *et al.*'s study indicates little sympathy towards those who smoke. Smoking appears to be a 'stigmatised habit' which can

cloud perceptions of smokers and their treatment for illnesses unrelated to their habit. Of course, these studies asked for the general public's attitudes, and not doctors'.

Factors which promote the initiation and maintenance of smoking

What causes people, especially adolescents, to begin smoking? Psychologists know that both imitation and peer pressure contribute to the acquisition of the smoking habit (Lynskey *et al.*, 1998). Adolescents who have favourable impressions of a smoker are likely to imitate that person's actions. Cigarette manufacturers use this knowledge to advertise their products: they often portray smoking as a glamorous, mature, independent, and sometimes rebellious behaviour. In a longitudinal study of 643 14–17-year-olds and their smoking behaviour, the best predictor of smoking was peers' smoking six months earlier; parental smoking also predicted smoking (Biglan *et al.*, 1995).

The news and entertainment media are powerful shapers of our opinions, beliefs and behaviours. Magazine advertisements generally portray cigarette smokers as young, healthy, attractive and exciting individuals, despite the reality. A survey of European women's magazines reported that only four of the highest selling weekly and monthly magazines refused tobacco advertising (Amos *et al.*, 1998).

Some of the strategies which may prevent the recruitment of smokers include price increases, limiting access to young people, developing non-smoking policies for

Psychology in action – *Continued*

patient counselling visit and counselling by telephone. The group which received the intensive counselling maintained significantly higher quit rates over five years. Factors, apart from the intervention programme, which were associated with successful quitting included having 12 years of education, having the intention to quit and having high self-belief.

Between 2000 and 2001, the American Cancer Society trialled a telephone counselling programme for smokers who wanted to quit (Rabius *et al.*, 2004). Over 3,000 callers notified the Society of their intent to quit; of these, 420 were aged between 18 and 25 years. When intention to give up smoking was measured, quit rates were significantly higher among older and younger smokers who received telephone coun-

selling (compared with those who received a self-help booklet). Although cessation was reported by the participant – and there was no attempt to verify this – the results suggest that telephone counselling may be a useful way of helping smoking cessation.

The psychological evidence suggests that a number of specific factors can trigger smoking: these include visual, social and physiological cues. Evidence from studies in which an attempt is made to stop smoking by engaging smokers in an intervention programme shows that the studies' success rate is variable but that specially designed intervention programmes are more effective than doing nothing at all to stop smoking.

The physiology of smoking

Cigarette smoking, like other forms of drug use, is addictive: the nervous system may develop a tolerance to the drug or become physically dependent on the drug. Tolerance simply means that the neurons in the central nervous system (CNS) respond progressively less to the presence of the drug; larger doses of the drug are required to produce the same CNS effects that smaller doses produced earlier. Physical dependence means that CNS neurons now require the presence of the drug to function normally. Without the drug in the CNS, the individual will experience withdrawal symptoms, or uncomfortable physical conditions, such as sweating, tremors and anxiety. In addition to tolerance and physical dependence, many drugs, including the nicotine in cigarette smoke, produce psychological dependence, a craving to use the drug for its pleasurable effects. Consequently, obtaining and using the drug become focal points of an individual's life. An objective way of describing psychological dependence is to say that it involves behaviour that is acquired and maintained through positive reinforcement. A reinforcing drug is one that strengthens or maintains the behaviour that constitutes seeking, acquiring and using the drug.

The nicotine contained in cigarette smoke exerts powerful effects on the CNS and heart by stimulating postsynaptic receptors sensitive to the neurotransmitter acetylcholine (these are called nicotinic acetylcholine receptors). This stimulation produces temporary increases in heart rate and blood pressure, decreases in body temperature, changes in hormones released by the pituitary gland, and the release of adrenalin from the adrenal glands, as well as changes in motor and cognitive behaviour.

In common with all reinforcers, natural and artificial, it also causes secretion of dopamine in the brain; the release of dopamine in the brain is reinforcing, so this effect contributes to the maintenance of cigarette smoking. An

injection of nicotine increases firing in dopamine neurons in one part of the brain (ventral tegmental area) and enhances its release in another (Besson *et al.*, 2007). When the ventral tegmental area is injected with nicotine, this increases self-administration of nicotine (David *et al.*, 2006). Cigarette smoking may also be maintained by negative reinforcement. People who try to quit smoking usually suffer withdrawal symptoms, including headaches, insomnia, anxiety and irritability, and at a neurophysiological level, the acetylcholine receptors might be desensitised. These symptoms are relieved by smoking another cigarette. Such negative reinforcement appears to be extremely powerful. Over 60 per cent of all smokers have tried to quit smoking at least once, but have started again in order to escape the unpleasant withdrawal symptoms.

Nicotine alone cannot be blamed for the health risks posed by cigarette smoking. These risks are caused by the combination of nicotine with other toxic substances, such as the carbon monoxide and tars found in cigarette smoke. For example, while nicotine causes an increase in heart rate, the carbon monoxide in smoke deprives the heart of the oxygen needed to perform its work properly. The smoker's heart undergoes stress because it is working harder with fewer nutrients than normal. Over a period of years, this continued stress weakens the heart, making it more susceptible to disease than is the heart of a non-smoker.

Alcohol use

Alcohol is probably the most widely used and abused substance that requires the consumer to be of a given age before it is sold or used. When psychologists refer to substance abuse, they mean that the substance is used in a way that poses a threat to the safety and well-being of the user, to another, or to both. Most people who use alcohol do not abuse it, and not all people who abuse alcohol are alcoholics. People who drive under the influence of alcohol pose a serious threat to both themselves and others, but they may not be alcoholics.

Data suggest that people in the age range typically representing students (18–24 years) drink more alcohol than their non-student counterparts (O'Malley and Johnston, 2002); over 40 per cent of students say that they are heavy or binge drinkers (Wechsler *et al.*, 2002). According to a study of 300 first-year students at the University of South Florida, however, this heavy drinking may be dependent on the year in which the students are studying; it may not, for example,

appear in the first year (Del Boca *et al.*, 2004). Students were asked to self-report their monthly alcohol consumption during their first year at university. About a fifth of the students were abstinent during the 32-week period of the study. Binge drinking varied from week to week but did not exceed 30 per cent. Drinking was heaviest during the holiday period.

Figures 17.8 (a) and (b) show the pattern of drinking consumption in the EU, recorded in 2002. Figures 17.9 (a) and (b) show the pattern of mortality from alcohol-related illness in men and women (such as cirrhosis and head/neck cancers) in the EU.

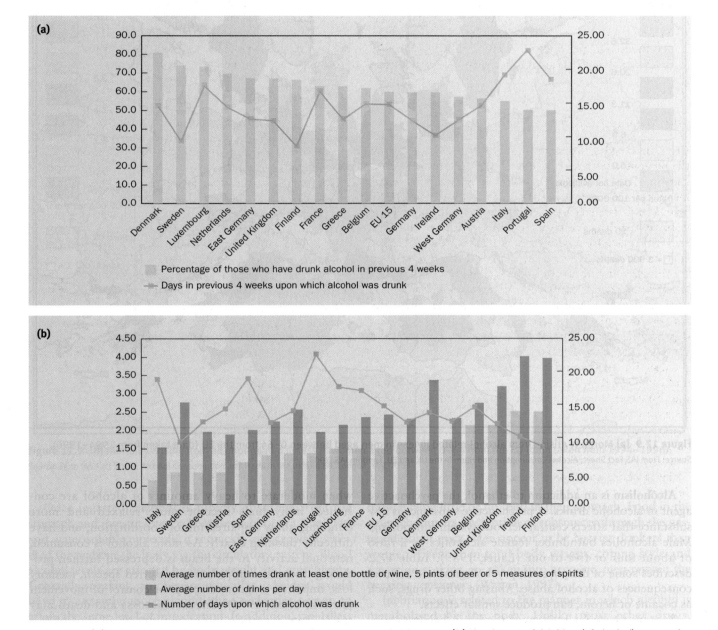

Figure 17.8 (a) The incidence of alcohol consumption in the European Union in 2002. **(b)** The degree of drinking (of alcohol) reported by European Union members in 2002.

Source: From IAS Fact Sheet: Alcohol Consumption and Harm in the UK and EU; London: IAS, 2003.

(for example, using a condom) if they have a positive view of condoms and think that others would approve (Abraham *et al.*, 1998).

Critics of the social cognitive models argue that the models do little to explain AIDS-related behaviour change and that intention to act does not explain behaviour change (Joffe, 1996, 1997; Fife-Shaw, 1997). Others, however, suggest that there is considerable evidence for the efficacy of the models (Abraham *et al.*, 1998). Sheeran *et al.* (1997) (cited in Abraham *et al.*, 1998), for example, reported a positive correlation between behavioural intention and condom use. Abraham *et al.* (1998) also note that interventions based on theory are more effective than those based on information-giving (Kalichman *et al.*, 1996).

The most successful interventions are those which combine information-giving and the teaching of behavioural skills (Fisher and Fisher, 1992). A school curriculum intervention programme based on social cognitive models was significantly more effective in changing feelings and cognitions about HIV and safe sex than was standard Dutch sex education (Schaalma *et al.*, 1996). At the beginning, 45 per cent reported inconsistent condom use; this had been reduced to 36 per cent by the end of the intervention.

Although prevention programmes have been partially successful in reducing high-risk sexual behaviours, they are least successful in situations in which a person's personal or cultural values prevent them from engaging in safe sex practices (Herdt and Lindenbaum, 1992). These values generally involve misperceptions of what practising safe sex means. Some men refuse to wear condoms because doing so would detract from their conception of what it means to be a man. Many people, especially young people, have the mistaken belief that they are invulnerable to any type of misfortune, including contracting an STD or AIDS.

Attitudes towards HIV and AIDS

Despite widespread media coverage of the AIDS epidemic throughout the world and instructional programmes designed to educate the general public about AIDS, the disease remains the most feared, stigmatised and publicly misunderstood contagious disease of our time (Rushing, 1995). When negative behaviour of this sort occurs, especially on a collective, widespread social basis, it is referred to as fear of contagion. Historical analyses of previous epidemics, such as the Black Death (bubonic plague) that struck Europe during the fourteenth century and the outbreak of cholera in Europe and the USA in the seventeenth century, have shown that fear of contagion is likely to occur only when four conditions are met: the disease must

be deadly, it must appear suddenly, it must have no apparent explanation, and people must believe that many people are at risk of contracting it (Rushing, 1995).

The AIDS epidemic meets these four conditions. It is deadly and it appeared suddenly: the first cases of AIDS were reported in 1981, a year in which 295 diagnoses of AIDS were made worldwide and 126 people died from it. Only ten years later, in 1991, 41,871 new cases were reported and 31,381 people had died from AIDS. According to the World Health Organization (2007), an estimated 40 million had been infected by AIDS by 2006.

It is relatively easy to explain fear of contagion during the periods of the bubonic plague and cholera. At that time, medical science was unsophisticated and lacked the technology needed to understand basic physiology. Fear of contagion in the time of AIDS is not so easily explained.

Bishop (1994) offers three possible explanations. First, some people may reason that just because no evidence currently exists that AIDS is spread through casual contact, it does not mean that such evidence may not be discovered. Medical experts tend to describe the transmission of AIDS through casual contact as being 'near impossible' or 'very unlikely', which leaves room for doubt in many people's minds.

Secondly, some people may mistake AIDS as having the same general characteristics of more typical contagious diseases such as chicken pox or influenza. People often use prototypes to represent concepts. Recall that a prototype represents the typical member of a class of things and that people organise information about other members in that class around the prototype. For example, if you think of influenza as a prototypical contagious disease, you may then apply the characteristics of this disease to other members of the same category, such as AIDS. Thus, because you know that influenza is a contagious disease spread by casual contact, you extend this same characteristic to AIDS and believe that it, too, is spread by casual contact.

Finally, the availability heuristic may also play a role in people's thinking about the transmission of AIDS. Recall from the discussion of the availability heuristic in Chapter 15 that when people attempt to assess the importance or the frequency of an event, they tend to be guided by the ease with which examples of that event come to mind. In the case of contagious diseases, AIDS has captured the world's attention.

Managing HIV and AIDS

Although psychologists and other health professionals have helped to develop programmes for the prevention of AIDS by devising interventions based on safe sex practices, these programmes are clearly too late for those with the HIV virus who may later develop AIDS. Psychology's contribution to the management of the virus has focused on the degree of support given to carriers, the reduction of risky sex following a positive diagnosis, and in helping to maintain a regular drug regime for those infected.

For example, the standard drugs for treating the HIV virus are currently nucleoside analogue reverse transcriptase inhibitors (NARTIs), which interfere with the ability of the virus to produce DNA needed for cell replication (Perelson *et al.*, 1996; Kelly *et al.*, 1998). However, this drug is currently taken in combination with other drugs called protease inhibitors. Protease inhibitors reduce the viral load in patients, that is, they reduce the viral quantity in blood. The NARTIs attack the virus in its early stages, the protease inhibitors attempt to halt the maturation of cells that have already developed. The difficulty with such combination therapy, however, is that these drugs are taken at various dosages at various times of the day; some need refrigeration, some cannot be taken on a full stomach (whereas others must be).

Even brief lapses in the drug regime can cause an increase in viral load and replication of the HIV virus (it is also an expensive lapse). Some of the factors which can influence a successful adherence to the drug regime include a belief that the drugs are effective and beneficial (Geletko *et al.*, 1995) – this is sometimes difficult when the effects of the drugs are not seen for a considerable time – and personal involvement in decision-making (Becker and Maiman, 1980), that is, the patient believes that the regime is constructed for their condition and that they have responsibility for this regime. The absence of negative affect and the availability of social support also enhance successful adherence (Freeman *et al.*, 1996).

Another problem associated with HIV infection is continued risky sexual and drug-use behaviour (Kelly and Kalichman, 1998). Between 30 and 35 per cent of HIV-infected individuals engage in unprotected sex and in unsafe needle-sharing drug practices, and a recent longitudinal study of women who were tested for HIV and given HIV counselling, showed no disengagement from high-risk sexual behaviour (Ickovics *et al.*, 1998). A more recent study, however, showed that if the support given is HIV-specific and not general, risky HIV behaviour is reduced (Darbes and Lewis, 2005).

Two models have been formulated for the prediction of HIV-relevant risk behaviour. The information–motivation–behaviour model (Fisher and Fisher, 1992) argues that the factors which influence risk reduction are knowledge about AIDS risk reduction, a change in motivation and the presence of behavioural skills that can reduce risky practice. An alternative model, the Aids risk reduction model (Catania *et al.*, 1990), suggests that a change in risky behaviour depends on the perception of the problem, a change in commitment and taking action. These factors can significantly influence the decision to use condoms (Kelly *et al.*, 1990).

With the seriousness of the illness being the most obvious and most pressing source of concern for carriers of the disease, the psychological effects of the disease have not been widely studied. There is insidious, cognitive impairment as the disease progresses (it is called a dementia) and this is well documented (Grant *et al.*, 1999). The social, personal consequences of the disease and its effects on mental health are less well understood. Studies reviewed by Emmelkamp (1996) suggest that individuals who have not accepted their homosexuality, who have received little or no social support and who have denied the effects of illness to themselves, are those most likely to develop severe psychological disturbances. In general, however, the degree of psychological distress is comparable to those of psychiatric outpatients or seronegative (those low in antibodies) homosexuals: that is, after the initial shock of discovering their positive status, patients are not more depressed or anxious than are those who were diagnosed negative.

Stress and health

Stress is a term that causes psychologists headaches. There is a great deal of controversy over what the term means and whether the term reflects a genuine psychological variable. This controversy is not helped by the suggestion that the man who popularised it probably meant another word that was similar, as you will see later. In general terms, stress is a pattern of physiological, behavioural, emotional and cognitive responses to real or imagined stimuli that are perceived as preventing a goal or endangering or otherwise threatening well-being. These stimuli are generally aversive and are called stressors. Stress is not a direct product of cultural evolution but is a product of natural selection. It is a behavioural adaptation that helped our ancestors to fight or flee from wild animals and enemies. Stress often helps us to confront or escape threatening situations (Linsky *et al.*, 1995).

Stressors come in many forms. They may be catastrophic, such as floods and rape, or they may be relatively trivial, such as being stuck in traffic when you are late for an appointment. Stressors are not always bad. Some stressors, such as athletic competition, having to perform in front of an audience or sitting an exam, can affect behaviour in positive ways. However, when stress is extended over long periods, it can have negative effects on both a person's psychological health and a person's physical health (Selye, 1991).

from assault by viruses, microbes, fungi and other types of parasite. Study of the interactions between the immune system and behaviour is called **psychoneuroimmunology**. Before discussing the effect of stressors on immune system functioning, it is useful to have an understanding of how the immune system works.

The immune system

The function of the **immune system** is to protect the body from infection. It is a network of organs and cells that protects the body from invading bacteria, viruses and other foreign substances, and is one of the most complex systems of the body. Because infectious organisms have developed devious tricks through the process of evolution, our immune system has evolved devious tricks of its own.

The immune system derives from white blood cells that develop in the bone marrow and in the thymus gland. Some of the cells roam through the blood or lymph glands and sinuses; others reside permanently in one place. The immune reaction occurs when the body is invaded by foreign organisms.

There are two types of specific immune reaction: chemically mediated and cell mediated. Chemically-mediated immune reactions involve antibodies. All bacteria have unique proteins on their surfaces, called **antigens**.

These proteins serve as the invaders' calling cards, identifying them to the immune system. Through exposure to the bacteria, the immune system learns to recognise these proteins. The result of this learning is the development of special lines of cells that produce specific **antibodies** – proteins that recognise antigens and help to kill the invading micro-organism. One type of antibody is released into the circulation by **B lymphocytes**, which receive their name from the fact that they develop in bone marrow. These antibodies, called **immunoglobulins**, are chains of protein. Each of five different types of immunoglobulin is identical except for one end, which contains a unique receptor. A particular receptor binds with a particular antigen, just as a molecule of a hormone or a transmitter substance binds with its receptor. When the appropriate line of B lymphocytes detects the presence of an invading bacterium, the cells release their antibodies, which bind with the bacterial antigens. The antibodies either kill the invaders directly or attract other white blood cells which then destroy the invaders. This process is illustrated by Figure 17.13.

One class of antibody, **secretory immunoglobulin A (sIgA)** is secreted by and covers the mucosal surfaces such as those found in the respiratory and gastrointestinal tracts. Its role appears to be to provide protection against infection by creating a barrier to invading organisms (Kraehenbuhl and Neutra, 1992). Because this antibody

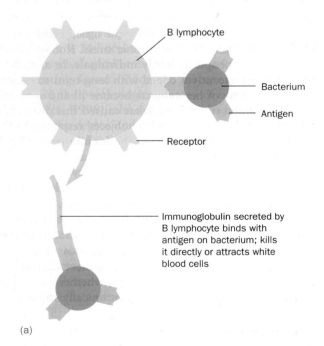

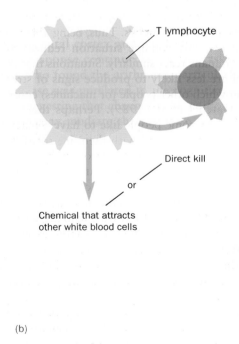

(a)

(b)

Figure 17.13 Immune reactions. **(a)** Chemically mediated reaction. The B lymphocyte detects an antigen on a bacterium and releases a specific immunoglobulin. **(b)** Cell-mediated reaction. The T lymphocyte detects an antigen on a bacterium and kills it directly or releases a chemical that attracts other white blood cells.

can be measured from saliva, it has been one of the most widely researched of the antibodies (Evans *et al.*, 1997).

The other type of defence mounted by the immune system, cell-mediated immune reactions, is produced by **T lymphocytes**, which develop in the thymus gland. An example of T lymphocyte appears in Figure 17.14.

T lymphocytes also produce antibodies, but the antibodies remain attached to the outside of the cell's membrane. T lymphocytes primarily defend the body against fungi, viruses and multicellular parasites. When antigens bind with their surface antibodies, the cells either kill the invaders directly or signal other white blood cells to come and kill them.

In addition to the immune reactions produced by lymphocytes, natural killer cells continuously prowl through tissue. When they encounter a cell that has been infected by a virus or that has become transformed into a cancer cell, they engulf and destroy it. Thus, natural killer cells constitute an important defence against viral infections and the development of malignant tumours. Although the immune system normally protects us, it can cause us harm, too. Allergic reactions occur when an antigen causes cells of the immune system to overreact, releasing a particular immunoglobulin that produces a localised inflammatory response. The chemicals released during this reaction can enter the general circulation and cause life-threatening complications. Allergic responses are harmful, and why they occur is unknown.

The immune system can do something else that harms the body – it can attack its own cells. Autoimmune diseases occur when the immune system becomes sensitised to a protein present in the body and attacks the tissue that contains this protein. Exactly what causes the protein to be targeted is not known. What is known is that autoimmune diseases often follow viral or bacterial infections. Presumably, in learning to recognise antigens that belong to the infectious agent, the immune system develops a line of cells that treat one of the body's own proteins as for-

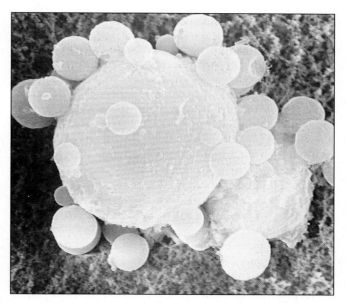

Figure 17.14 A T lymphocyte at work destroying tumour cells.
Source: Andrejs Liepins/Science Photo Library/Photo Researchers Inc.

eign. Some common autoimmune diseases include rheumatoid arthritis, diabetes, lupus and multiple sclerosis.

Neural control of the immune system

Stress can suppress the immune system, resulting in a greater likelihood of infectious diseases, and it can also aggravate autoimmune diseases. It may even affect the growth of cancers. What is the physiological explanation for these effects? One answer, and probably the most important one, is that stress increases the secretion of glucocorticoids, and these hormones directly suppress the activity of the immune system. All types of white blood cell have glucocorticoid receptors, and suppression of the immune system is presumably mediated by these receptors (Solomon, 1987).

Cutting edge – Telomeres – what are they and can they predict stress?

Telomeres are sequences of DNA that cap the tops of chromosomes and help maintain the stability of cells (Epel, 2009). However, there are enzymes that cannot replicate chromosomes fully or completely at the tips which means that, in essence, they are missing. As cells replicate, these telomeres become shorter. The relevance of this to health psychologists is that shorter telomeres in white blood cells are associated with the development of chronic disease such as stroke (Fuster and Andres, 2006). There is also some evidence to suggest that stressors are associated with shorter telomeres. For example, parents who cared for a child with a chronic illness had lower levels of the enzyme that prevents shortening and had shorter telomeres (Epel *et al.*, 2004). Similar telomere shortening is seen in people who care for people with dementia, in the depressed (Damjanovic *et al.*, 2007; Simon *et al*, 2006), and in women with low occupational status (Cherkas *et al.*, 2006). Current evidence points to a role for these genetic anomalies in stress-reactions, but research is at an early stage.

Stress and the immune system

The immune system does not appear to react to different types of stressor in the same way. Chronic stressors such as bereavement of a close friend or relative, caring for a relative with Alzheimer's disease and marital disharmony, tend to result in reduced immune system functioning (Kiecolt-Glaser *et al.*, 1993; Zisook *et al.*, 1994). Kiecolt-Glaser *et al.* (1995), for example, reported that wounds took nine days longer to heal in carers for individuals with Alzheimer's disease than in age- and income-matched 'stress-free' controls. Figures 17.15 (a) and (b) show the relationship between caregiving and wound healing and wound size over the recovery period. Acute stress, however, does not appear to have the same effect. Acute stress appears actually to increase the number of natural killer cells (Delahanty *et al.*, 1996) and the levels of sIgA (Zeier *et al.*, 1996). Caregivers in these studies tend to be 'informal' caregivers – they are not paid to look after ill people but are relatives or friends who willingly look after a seriously ill family member or friend. A meta-analysis of 23 published studies examining the health of caregivers and non-caregivers and its relationship to caregiving found that caregivers' levels of stress hormones were 23 per cent higher and their antibody responses 15 per cent lower than those of non-caregivers (Vitaliano *et al.*, 2003). While the authors stress that it is impossible to tell from these studies whether the stress of caregiving causes changes in physical condition, they point out that caregiving is a potentially risky behaviour.

Evans *et al.* (1993) have reported that lower quality of life (such as experiencing more undesirable or fewer desirable experiences) is associated with lower levels of sIgA. However, undergraduates asked to present a piece of work orally in front of their colleagues, showed an increase in the levels of this antibody (Evans *et al.*, 1994). Levels of sIgA tend to decrease during examination periods (Jemmott and Magloire, 1988) which suggests that short- and long-term stressors have different effects on the immune system. Exam stress seems to cause more than just nerves, panic and sleepless nights. It also seems to affect brain activation. Lewis *et al.* (2007) measured EEG during periods of low exam stress and high stress in 49 students. While cortisol levels did not change between testing periods, surprisingly, frontal EEG did: leftward asymmetry in the frontal area during low exam stress shifted to rightward asymmetry during high exam stress. This increase in the right frontal area also correlated with self-reports of poorer health. The results are consistent with the model of EEG frontal asymmetry which you read about in Chapter 13.

The immune system has recently been studied in experiments designed to examine the effects of laughter and humour on stress and coping with stress. The evidence

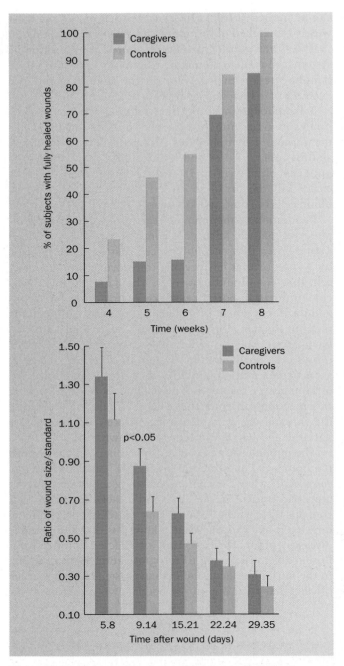

Figure 17.15 The progress of wound healing in Alzheimer's disease. **(a)** Percentage of caregivers and controls whose wounds had healed in time. **(b)** Average wound size during first five weeks of study.

Source: Kiecolt-Glaser, J.K., Marucha, P. T., Malarkey, W.B., Mercado, A.M. and Glaser, R., Slowing of wound-healing by psychological stress. *The Lancet*, 346, 1194–96. © 1995 The Lancet Limited.

for the role of humour and laughter in mediating the effects of the immune system is discussed in the Controversies in Psychological Science section.

Controversies in Psychological Science – Can humour reduce stress?

The issue

In 1979, Norman Cousins published a rather unusual book called *The Anatomy of Illness*. In it, he described the way in which he used laughter to help him recover from a degenerative spinal condition. Since 1979, a number of popular and scientific accounts have suggested that using humour can help to combat stress and ill health. One contributor to the field has suggested that 'happy breathing, simulated smiles and transcendental breathing' can uplift spirits (Holden, 1993). 'Don your Super-Humour-Person cape,' he exhorts, 'and save the world from the arch-villain over-seriousness.' While we can dismiss accounts like this as minor eccentricities of little psychological importance, more thoughtful researchers have examined whether humour does help us to cope with ill health and stress and provide immunity from these problems. These researchers have focused upon the effects of humour from several perspectives. Perhaps the most important of these are: producing humour, appreciating humour and using humour as a coping mechanism.

The evidence

Laughter is an intriguing behaviour: it can induce laughter in a passive listener, can enhance the enjoyment of comedy, despite people's claimed dislike of audience laughter (Martin and Gray, 1996), and provides vigorous muscle exercise. According to Hans Selye, laughter is a form of eustress: a positive, life-enhancing type of stress or pressure. In one experiment, 20 men and women endured pressure-induced discomfort after either having listened to a 20-minute laughter tape, a relaxation tape or a dull narrative (Cogan *et al.*, 1987). For both the laughter and relaxation conditions, discomfort thresholds were higher, that is, participants could endure greater stress.

Does this suggest that comedy is good for you? The picture is not altogether clear-cut. In a well-controlled experiment where the effect of the appreciation of humour on stress reduction was examined, the experimenters found no relationship between appreciation and stress reduction (Martin and Lefcourt, 1983). They did, however, find a slight moderation of the stress when humour was produced by participants. Another study found that this moderating effect was significant for depression but not anxiety symptoms (Nezu *et al.*, 1988). This finding suggests that it may not necessarily be the blanket appreciation (watching, listening) of humour that is important but the way in which humour is used.

Martin and Lefcourt and their colleagues have conducted a number of experiments in which they examined the relationship between a person's sense of humour, their use of humour as a coping mechanism and their response to stress.

In a small number of detailed studies, the experimenters took measures of individuals' physical stress by sampling their salivary immunoglobin A concentrations (sIgA). In one study, 40 participants provided saliva samples, completed a Daily Hassles Scale (a measure of the degree of stress experienced daily), and a sense of humour questionnaire. The experimenters found a negative correlation between low scores on the sense of humour questionnaire and sIgA levels. A different experiment measured sIgA concentrations before and after the presentation of humorous stimuli and examined whether the presentation would interact with the participants' sense of humour (Lefcourt *et al.*, 1990). The researchers found that not only did saliva concentrations increase after presentation of humour but also those participants with the greatest sense of humour had larger concentrations of sIgA after exposure to an audio comedy tape.

More recently, Lefcourt *et al.* (1997) examined the relationship between pain endurance, coping and blood pressure in men and women. There is evidence to suggest that men and women do use humour in different ways. Men are reported to make more frequent attempts at humour, for example, and use it for more negative reasons than do women (Myers *et al.*, 1997). In Lefcourt *et al.*'s experiment, women who used coping humour a great deal exhibited lower systolic blood pressure than did low-scoring women. Men, on the other hand, showed the reverse pattern. On the basis of the participants' responses to the stressful tasks, the experimenters concluded that humour may moderate the effect of uncontrollable and passively experienced stress but that stressful problem-solving tasks involving active participation are less susceptible to these moderating effects.

In a recent review of studies examining the relationship between humour and good health, Rod Martin (R.A. Martin, 2001) concludes that evidence is mixed at best. Some studies show beneficial effects of exposure to humour on health, others no effect. Furthermore, stimuli that are perceived as generally pleasant stimulate similar responses to those elicited by humour. Conversely, a stimulus need not be pleasant to reduce a painful experience. Studies have shown that both positive and negative emotional stimuli can reduce the perception of pain, for example. Martin suggests that experiments need to distinguish more clearly between effects that are specific to humour and effects that are general to positive emotional stimuli.

Conclusion

From what you have read so far, are you convinced that humour can help reduce the effect of stress? What influences your decision? Can you think of better ways of measuring the

Controversies in Psychological Science – *Continued*

effects of sense of humour, or perceiving humour or generating humour, on stress reduction? Would you expect the effects of sense of humour on stress reduction to be long term? If so, why? If not, why not?

Finally, in an ingenious test of the hypothesis that laughter and humour help us combat the effects of stressful events,

Rotton (1992) examined the death rates of comedians, literary humorists and non-humorous individuals by examining published biographical details. He found no significant difference between the lifespan of humorous entertainers and that of others.

Infectious diseases

A wide variety of stress-producing events in a person's life can increase the susceptibility to infectious diseases. For example, Glaser *et al.* (1987) found that medical students were more likely to contract acute infections – and to show evidence of suppression of the immune system – during final examinations than before. In addition, autoimmune diseases often get worse when a person is subjected to stress, as Feigenbaum *et al.* (1979) found for rheumatoid arthritis.

Stone *et al.* (1987) attempted to see whether stressful events in people's daily lives might predispose them to upper respiratory infection. If a person is exposed to a micro-organism that might cause such a disease, the symptoms do not occur for several days, that is, there is an incubation period between exposure and signs of the actual illness. The authors therefore reasoned that if stressful events suppressed the immune system, one might expect to see a higher likelihood of respiratory infections several days after such stress. To test their hypothesis, they asked volunteers to keep a daily record of desirable and undesirable events in their lives over a 12-week period. The volunteers also kept a daily record of any discomfort or symptoms of illness.

The results were as predicted: in the 3–5 days just before showing symptoms of an upper respiratory infection, people experienced an increased number of undesirable events and a decreased number of desirable events in their lives. Stone *et al.* (1987) suggest that the effect is caused by decreased production of a particular immunoglobulin (IgA) that is present in the secretions of mucous membranes, including those in the nose, mouth, throat and lungs. This immunoglobulin serves as the first defence against infectious micro-organisms that enter the nose or mouth. When a person is unhappy or depressed, IgA levels are lower than normal. The results suggest that the stress caused by undesirable events may, by suppressing the production of IgA, lead to a rise in the likelihood of upper respiratory infections.

However, this study did not manipulate exposure to the illness directly. In an extraordinary and well-controlled experiment, Cohen *et al.* (1998) exposed individuals to one of two common cold viruses, measured various personality and behavioural variables (such as sex, alcohol consumption, sleep pattern), and monitored which individuals developed a respiratory infection that led to the cold. Eighty-four per cent became infected but only 40 per cent developed a cold. Those who did were reported to have endured chronic life stressors for at least a month; those who had endured little stress or experienced the effect of stressors for less than a month did not, on average, develop the cold. Other factors which were positively related to developing a cold were smoking, fewer than three exercise sessions a week, poor sleep, drinking fewer than two alcoholic drinks a day, ingesting less than 85 mg of vitamin C and being introverted.

Bereavement

Bereavement, another source of stress, also suppresses the immune system. Cancer and other illnesses have been observed to occur at higher than average rates among people who are widowed. To investigate the possibility that bereavement suppresses the immune system, Schleifer *et al.* (1983) drew blood samples from 15 men whose wives were dying of terminal breast cancer. Two blood samples were drawn, the first before the spouse's death and the second within two months afterwards. Each time, an agent that normally stimulates blood lymphocyte activity was mixed with the lymphocytes, and the resultant level of activity was measured. On average, the activity level of blood lymphocytes after the spouse's death was less than before her death, which meant that the bereaved spouses were more susceptible to illness. Taken together, the results of these studies (and many other similar studies) suggest a strong link between stress and weakening of the immune system.

Loneliness

Loneliness, the feeling or perception of being alone, is stressful and is associated with poor health. Loneliness does not depend on having a small social network: even people with lots of friends and acquaintances can feel lonely. A factor that can facilitate good relations with others, and therefore predict good/ill health, is sociability, defined as 'the quality of seeking others and being agreeable' (Cohen *et al.*, 2003). Two of the dimensions of the Big Five personality scale you read about in Chapter 14 seem to measure this behaviour: extraversion and agreeableness. Cohen *et al.* used these measures and another which measures how well people develop good relations with others (and how often they interact with others) to examine whether high scorers were less prone to illness.

The researchers took baseline measures of sociability in over 300 adults aged between 18 and 54, then exposed participants to one of two rhinoviruses which caused the common cold. Five days after exposure, physical symptoms were noted and any infection development measured. Four weeks later, blood samples were taken to verify whether an illness had developed.

Sociability predicted susceptibility to the common cold: the greater the degree of sociability, the less likely the person was to develop a cold. The highly sociable individuals had more social relationships and relationships of greater quality than less sociable ones but the link between sociability and the development of illness remained even when these factors were taken into account. This suggests that it is not simply being sociable which could be a protective factor against illness but that it is the trait of sociability which acts as the protector. Interestingly, high extraversion scores, high agreeableness scores and positive relations individually predicted the decreased likelihood of a cold developing. However, when the measures were combined, the effect was greater.

In a direct examination of whether loneliness (and the size of a person's social network) influenced health, a group of North American researchers investigated the antibody response to influenza immunisation in first-year students whose social networks and degrees of loneliness throughout their first semester were assessed (Pressman *et al.*, 2005). These measures were then used to predict the degree of health or ill health experienced by the students.

Students experiencing either the greatest degree of loneliness or the smallest social networks showed poorer antibody response to one viral component of the vaccine (there were four in total). Those who were most lonely and who also had the smallest social networks showed the lowest antibody response of all. People who were lonely also had more circulating cortisol, slept less well, experienced greater stress and experienced more negative (and less positive) emotion. These outcomes were not significantly affected by social network size. The antibody responses at 1 and 4 months can be seen in Figures 17.16 (a) and (b).

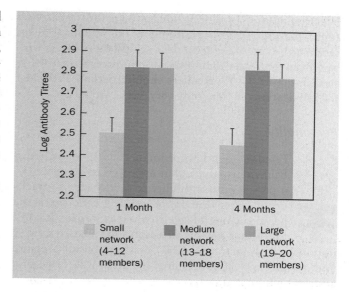

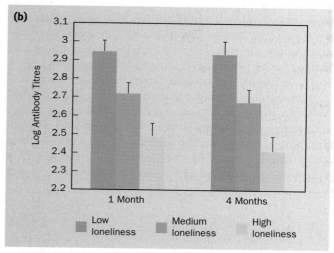

Figure 17.16 (a) Antibody levels at 1 month and 4 months, according to size of social network. **(b)** Antibody level at 1 month and 4 months, according to degree of loneliness.

Procrastination

Procrastination refers to the tendency to put off tasks and chores that could be done immediately. You might think that in the short term, this produces less stress because the individual is under less pressure to perform. In a study of procrastination among health psychology students, Tice and Baumeister (1997) noted the date on which students submitted coursework and took measures of procrastination from each. Not surprisingly, procrastinators submitted their coursework significantly later. They also received lower grades. However, and oddly, they also seemed to experience less stress than did non-procrastinators. In a term-long study, the researchers found that this was true, but only at the beginning of the term; at the end of the term their symptoms of stress were significantly greater than those of non-procrastinators, as seen in Figure 17.17. Readers should, perhaps, consider the implications of this study very, very carefully.

Personality

see activity on mypsychlab

Friedman and Rosenman (1959) identified a behaviour pattern that appeared to be related to a person's susceptibility to CHD. Heart attacks occur when the blood vessels that serve the heart become blocked, whereas strokes involve the blood vessels in the brain. The two most important risk factors in CHD are high blood pressure and a high level of cholesterol in the blood. Friedman and Rosenman characterised the disease-prone **type A pattern** as one of excessive competitive drive, an intense disposition, impatience, hostility, fast movements and rapid speech. People with the **type B pattern** were less competitive, less hostile, more patient, easy-going and tolerant, and they moved and talked more slowly; they were also less likely to suffer from CHD. Friedman and Rosenman developed a questionnaire that distinguished between these two types of people. The test is rather interesting, because the person who administers it is not a passive participant. The interviewer asks questions in an abrupt, impatient manner, interrupting the subject if they take too much time to answer a question. The point

of such behaviour is to try to elicit type A behaviour from the subject.

Researchers have devoted much attention to the relation between the type A personality and CHD. The Western Collaborative Group study (Rosenman *et al.*, 1975), which studied 3,154 healthy men for eight years, found that the type A behaviour pattern was associated with twice the rate of CHD relative to non-type-A behaviour patterns.

Research since has not been so conclusive, however. For example, one large study found that although people classified as type A were more likely to have heart attacks, the long-term survival rate after having a heart attack was higher for type A patients than for type B patients (Ragland and Brand, 1988). In this case, it would seem better to be type A, at least after having a non-fatal heart attack. Other studies have failed to find a difference in the likelihood of CHD in people with type A and type B personalities (Dimsdale, 1988).

The personality characteristic of submissiveness has been associated with lower rates of CHD in a group of Scottish individuals (Whiteman *et al.*, 1997). Submissiveness refers to a preference for staying in the background, letting others lead/dominate, and lacking self-assurance and self-confidence. Submissiveness, however, is not type B behaviour because submissive people do not have the type B personality's sense of security.

Other characteristics which seem to be part of the type A personality are a greater need for control (Furnham, 1990), placing less value on avoiding problems and responsibilities (Smith and Brehm, 1981), and greater alertness and focus (Matthews and Brunson, 1979). Williams *et al.* (1980) suggested that one aspect of the type A personality – hostility – is of particular importance in CHD. Several studies carried out in the early to mid 1980s confirmed that hostility was an important risk factor for CHD, but more recent studies have not.

Personality type may also be hazardous in another way. While a study of 108 drivers found that type A behaviour was associated with faster driving but not increased accidents (West *et al.*, 1993), a study of bus drivers in India and the USA (Evans *et al.*, 1987), however, found that type A behaviour was associated with high traffic accident rates per month, a finding that was replicated in Italian traffic policemen (Magnavita *et al.*, 1997).

There also seems to be a relationship between the competitive aspect of type A personalities and blood pressure and heart rate. In one study, blood pressure and cardiovascular activity was measured in 36 male and female undergraduates who took part in a motorised racing game experiment (Harrison *et al.*, 2001) where they played alone, or in competition with the experimenter, or in collaboration with the experimenter.

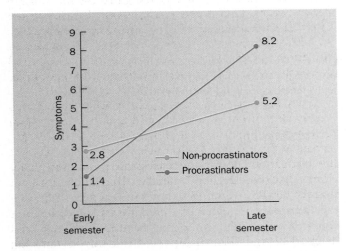

Figure 17.17 The number of symptoms reported by student procrastinators and non-procrastinators across a term on a health psychology course.

Source: Tice, D.M. and Baumeister, R.F., Longitudinal study of procrastination, performance, stress and health: The costs and benefits of dawdling. *Psychological Science*, 1997, 8(6), 454–8. Reprinted by permission of Blackwell Publishers Ltd.

The competitive condition was associated with significant increases in blood pressure and heart rate whereas the cooperative condition produced barely discernible changes in activity, a finding that echoes reports in the literature of reduced or stable cardiovascular activity in response to stress in the presence of a supportive person. As expected, the competitive condition was rated the most competitive condition and the cooperative condition was rated the most cooperative while the solo condition was rated the least difficult and engaging of the three.

Competitiveness and need to win were associated with increased blood pressure and heart rate, suggesting that the heart rate increases seen in the type A personality may be due to competitiveness. It is possible, however, that more physical activity may be exerted in tasks requiring competition. Perhaps it is the excess effort which produces the changes.

Occupational stress

Occupational stress refers to the degree of stress experienced by members of different professions. This area of research is a popular one in organisational psychology and the Whitehall study of CHD in British civil servants is a good example of the type of work carried out in this area. This study has shown that the lower the grade of employment in the civil service, the higher the mortality rate from CHD. The Whitehall II Study followed a different cohort and investigated whether two factors might be associated with CHD-related mortality: high psychosocial pressure and low control over their environment (Marmot *et al.*, 1997).

Swedish studies suggest that sickness-related absenteeism from work is more common in blue-collar than white-collar workers (Steers and Rhodes, 1984). Several factors can influence the rate of sickness, including the physical work environment, psychosocial factors, risk of unemployment, education level and absentee culture (Drago and Wooden, 1992). In an extensive study of absenteeism in 84,319 individuals in two counties in Sweden, Knutsson and Goine (1998) found that the professions showing highest degrees of absenteeism for men were shop assistants, repairmen and welders, whereas loggers and mechanics were absent for the fewest days. The professions with the highest absenteeism rates for women were shop assistants, assistant nurses and secretaries (the lowest rates were for primary school teachers). Of course, these findings do not necessarily suggest that these professions are marked by acute stress (and, therefore, by high rates of absenteeism) although they might, but they suggest that some professions may be more susceptible to stressors.

As the books of the chefs Anthony Bourdain and Marco Pierre White, and television shows such as Gordon Ramsay's *Hell's Kitchen* and *Kitchen Nightmares* illustrate, working in a professional kitchen is a hard, time-consuming and stressful occupation.
Source: OnEdition/Rex Features.

Much of the applied work in occupational or organisational psychology has been directed towards helping people to cope with the stress generated by heavy workloads or excessive working hours (Warr, 1990; Buunk *et al.*, 1998). This work can lead to 'burn-out'. Burn-out has been defined as 'a unique affective response to stress [and] a multidimensional construct consisting of emotional exhaustion, physical fatigue, and cognitive weariness' (Melamed *et al.*, 2006). In the workplace, it can result from constant and persistent exposure to stressors. Melamed *et al.* (2006) investigated the relationship between burn-out and risk of cardiovascular disease and reported an association with ill health, sleep disturbance and impaired immune system functioning. 'The evidence', the authors suggest, indicates that 'burn-out and vital exhaustion pose an increased risk of incident myocardial infarction, stroke and sudden cardiac death' (p. 339).

There appears to be a significant relationship between the number of hours worked and the degree of physical and mental illness an employee experiences, but the extent of this relationship is unclear: most conclude that the two are related but the relationship is not particularly strong (Sparks *et al.*, 1997). Studies from Japan, however, suggest that individuals who work in excess of 11 hours a day are more at risk of myocardial infarction than are those who work a moderate number (Sokejima and Kagamimori, 1998). In Japan, it is thought that long working hours can cause sudden fatal heart attacks, called 'karoshi' (Uehata, 1991, cited in Kageyama *et al.*, 1997). Kageyama *et al.*'s study of working commuters suggests that those with the longest commuting times and who work the most overtime show greater variability in heart rate than do those who commute and work less.

The ferocious work ethic of the Japanese is famed: they work longer hours than the British, Germans or North Americans. This devotion has been blamed for the estimated drop in birth rate from 1.28 to 1.26 per couple in 2006: people are too busy working to procreate and bring up a family.

A study of 968 Canadian employees has found that those in higher-status occupations suffer greater conflicts between home and work than do those in lower-status occupations (Schieman *et al.*, 2006). This conflict was most pronounced in the self-employed, those with greater job authority and those who worked longer hours.

Psychology in action – The health benefits of saintliness – when it is better to give (and forgive) . . .

Psychologists know that forgiving is better for mental health than is harbouring a grudge. Hostility, anger and blame – the behavioural litany of the aggrieved – have been associated with increased risk of coronary heart disease and even premature death, although no study has directly examined the relationship between forgiveness and physical health.

Research on the effects of hostility on people's respiratory function has found that increased hostility is associated with reduced lung function such as lung capacity and the ability to expire air (Jackson *et al.*, 2007). The group collected data from over 5,000 18–30-year-old US dwellers from metropolitan cities. Our pulmonary (lung) function peaks in young adulthood and plateaus thereafter: the poorer this function, the more likely we are to develop illness; it is also a risk factor for increased mortality. Researchers have found that some illnesses, such as myocardial infarction, increase in middle- to old-aged men who are hostile (remember that some personality characteristics, such as Type A behaviour, are associated with increased risk of cardiovascular disease). Jackson *et al.* sought to discover whether high levels of hostility predicted pulmonary function.

This is what they found, regardless of the participant's sex, age, height, socio-economic status, smoking, asthma or ethnicity. However, the group cautions against drawing cause-and-effect conclusions. They argue that low pulmonary function might cause high hostility, rather than vice versa, although this is unlikely.

One study has found that unforgiving thoughts produce greater aversive emotion and higher heart rate, blood pressure and brow muscle activity than do forgiving thoughts (Witvliet *et al.*, 2001). Over 70 men and women were asked either to rehearse hurtful memories and to bear grudges against real-life offenders, or to respond in a more forgiving way (such as imagining granting forgiveness). Participants felt more negative, aroused, angry, sad and less in control when they imagined being unforgiving. These cognitive and emotional responses were partnered by increased muscle tension at the brow, an index of anxiety.

The researchers suggest that although people cannot undo the wrong done to them in the past, they can change their response to the wrongdoing in such a way as to protect their physical and mental health.

A Finnish study has reported that women who gave, rather than received, support in intimate relationships took fewer days off sick from work (Vaananen *et al.*, 2005). A different pattern, however, was seen in men. They took fewer days off if they received more support from their partner than they gave.

Researchers at the University of Michigan looked at the relationship between mortality and the giving and receiving of social and emotional support in a group of 423 elderly married couples (Brown *et al.*, 2003). In the late 1980s, participants were interviewed about how much social support they gave to relatives, neighbours and spouses, such as running errands, shopping, helping with housework, providing transport or childcare, and so on. They were also asked whether they made their spouse feel loved and whether they were willing to listen to their spouse in times of need. In addition, respondents were asked how often they were the recipients of such support. Five years after the interviews took place, the mortality rate in the sample was assessed and correlated with the survey responses.

Surprisingly, those who reported giving support to others showed least risk for mortality, whether the support was social or emotional. This relationship held even when demographic, personality and health variables were controlled for.

Conscientiousness – the ability to delay gratification, to plan appropriately, to follow rules and norms and so on – may be another saintly trait that protects against ill health. Studies since the 1990s have suggested that this trait correlated with longevity (Friedman *et al.*, 1993). In a meta-analysis of 194 studies in which conscientiousness-related traits were associated with risk factors for mortality such as smoking, drinking alcohol, using drugs, being sexually promiscuous and so on, Bogg and Roberts (2004) found that the relationship between conscientiousness and risky health-related behaviours was weak but the relationship between this trait and beneficial health-related behaviours was significant. The more conscientious the participants were, the fewer symptoms of ill health they reported.

Unemployment

Almost all of us have to earn a living: money allows us to do many of the things we want to do and employment gives structure and meaning to our lives. Unemployment, however, has been associated with an increase in ill health and psychological disturbance – see Figure 17.18.

One consequence of unemployment is increased isolation and loss of social context (Donovan and Oddy, 1982). A Danish study of employed and unemployed single mothers found that isolation can lead to depression (Beck-Jorgensen, 1991) and that lower self-esteem is characteristic of people who become unemployed (Winefield and Tiggemann, 1994). A longitudinal study of 1,060 young people who were monitored over five years since their last term at school in northern Sweden found that unemployment was correlated significantly with increases in depressive symptoms, even when their initial health status was accounted for (Hammarstrom and Janlert, 1997).

However, it is possible that being in a job that you loathe may be just as detrimental to your physical and psychological well-being. Broom *et al.* (2006) investigated this possibility in a group of 2,500 40–44-year-old Australians. They found, as perhaps expected, that unemployed people reported generally worse health than those who were employed. However, people who had job insecurity, low marketability and experienced great strain at work expressed poorer health than did those who were in jobs with few or no stressors. If all three negative outcomes were reported, those people reporting them indicated that it was no better than being unemployed.

'These findings challenge the assumption that any job is better for health than is no job at all,' say the authors, 'suggesting that the quality of work tempers the health benefits of employment' (p. 583).

Optimism

Optimism refers to a disposition to believe in positive outcomes. Evidence suggests that dispositional optimists (those who are characteristically optimistic) are more successful at coping with ill health (Stanton and Snider, 1993), are not as emotionally perturbed by stressors (Aspinwall and Taylor, 1992), can cope better with breast cancer surgery (Stanton and Snider, 1993), report better physical health (Scheier and Carver, 1992), have a better quality of life (Fitzgerald *et al.*, 1993), and show an increase in helper T cells and natural killer cells (Segerstrom *et al.*, 1998). Optimism is also associated with better adjustment in university (Segerstrom *et al.*, 1998) and to the stress generated by missile attack (Zeidner and Hammer, 1992). A study of 163 early-stage breast cancer patients found that 5–13 years after surgery the degree of initial optimism expressed before treatment was positively related to people's feelings of well-being later on (medical variables predicted very little of reported well-being at follow-up) (Carver *et al.*, 2005). Similar findings are found in gerontology. A study of 128 men and women aged between 65 and 80 years found that optimism was associated with not smoking, moderate alcohol consumption, vigorous physical exercise and brisk walking (Steptoe *et al.*, 2006).

A study of middle-aged men and women supports the hoary idea that looking on the bright side leads to a healthier life (Steptoe *et al.*, 2005). The 216 participants came from the longitudinal British Whitehall II study in which 10,308 London-based civil servants have been followed since 1985–8 to monitor correlates of risk for heart disease. Those who showed more positive affect – as measured by noting the moments of happiness the participants experienced over the course of the working day – were more likely to show reduced neuroendocrine, inflammatory and cardiovascular activity. This effect was found regardless of sex, age, socio-economic position, body mass and smoking status and was also found on leisure days. Happiness was also associated with lower heart rate across the day.

Social support

Although all of us experience stress, the experience is a subjective and private matter. Nobody else can truly know what we feel. However, being confronted by a stressor and coping with stress are often social matters.

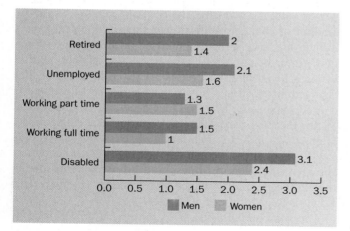

Figure 17.18 Average depression score for adults ages 63–73, by workstatus.

Source: from The impact of work on the psychological health and well-being of older Americans, *Annual Review of Gerontology and Geriatrics*, 26, pp. 153–174 (James, J.B. and Spiro, A. 2007) (c) Springer Publishing Company, Reproduced with the permission of the Springer Publishing Company, LLC, New York, NY 10036

We learn as children to seek others – parents, siblings and friends – when we need help. This is a pattern of coping that continues over the lifespan. Social support – the help that we receive from others in times of stress – is an important coping strategy for many people for two reasons. First, we can benefit from the experience of others in dealing with the same or similar stressors. Other people can show us how to cope, perhaps by teaching us how to reappraise the situation. Secondly, other people can provide encouragement and incentives to overcome the stressor when we may otherwise fail to cope with the stressful situation.

Eighty-nine first-year undergraduates completed a battery of depression, stress, social support and friendship measures at the beginning and end of their first term (Brissette *et al.*, 2002). When greater optimism was expressed at the beginning of the term, smaller increases in stress and depression and greater perception of social support were reported later in the term. The number of friends in the social network, however, did not seem to affect response to stress. Social support was found to contribute significantly to the better adjustment experienced by the optimistic, suggesting that this could be a mediating factor.

Coping with everyday stress

see activity on mypsychlab

The degree to which we experience stress and the degree to which stress impairs our health depends to a large extent on our perception of the threat posed by the stressor. The number of potential stressors is very large. Depending on the individual, almost any aspect of the environment can be perceived as a stressor.

Sources of stress

Stress can be induced by changes that threaten or otherwise complicate life. The death of a spouse, being promoted at work, changes in social activities, getting married, and sustaining a personal injury or illness are significant life changes that cause stress and disrupt everyday life (Holmes and Rahe, 1967). Some evidence has accumulated that suggests that if an individual experiences enough changes in lifestyle over a short time period, they are likely to develop a physical illness within the next two years (Rahe and Arthur, 1978). Other research suggests that not all people who encounter a series of significant stressors over a short period are at risk of illness (DePue and Monroe, 1986). Why? Once again, the answer lies in the way that people perceive stressors. Recall Lazarus's idea of cognitive appraisal: the amount of stress induced by a stimulus perceived to be a stressor is determined by how significant we believe its threat to be and whether we feel competent to cope with that threat.

Stressors do not have to be catastrophic or cause significant changes in lifestyle to induce stress. Often, the everyday hassles we experience are enough to leave us feeling stressed out. Locking our keys in the car, being late for an appointment, or having a disagreement with a friend are examples of stressful everyday events.

A common source of daily stress comes simply from making routine choices about what to do, how to do it or when to do it. Consider, for example, a choice between studying tonight for a test you have tomorrow or going to a party with some friends. You want to do both, but you can only do one (you are back into the classic self-control situation again – the choice between a small, short-term reward and a larger, long-term reward). Psychologists refer to this as an approach–approach conflict because the choice involves two desirable outcomes. Other choices involve approach–avoidance conflicts – one outcome is desirable and the other is not. For example, you live in Kent, want to visit Oslo and decide to travel by sea because you are afraid of flying. Still other choices involve avoidance–avoidance conflicts in which both outcomes are undesirable. For instance, choosing between having a root canal procedure or having a tooth extracted creates stress because you do not want to have either one of them, yet one needs to be done.

Several different tests have been developed to measure the severity of various stressors on people. Among the first measures to be developed was Holmes and Rahe's (1967) Social Readjustment Rating Scale (SRRS), which was devised on the assumption that any change in a person's life is a stressor. The test asks people to rate the amount of change or adjustment caused by recent events in their life, such as getting married or divorced, getting a new job or being sacked, moving to a new location, and losing a loved one. Responses are given in terms of life-change units (LCUs) – how much change or adjustment is caused by specific events. Once a person completes the SRRS, the LCUs are summed, resulting in a single score. High scores indicate high levels of stress and low scores low levels of stress. People who get high scores have been shown to have more illness and adjustment problems than have people who get lower scores (Holmes and Rahe, 1967; Monroe *et al.*, 1992).

Another commonly used scale, the Daily Hassles and Uplifts Scale, measures daily events that are either troublesome (hassles) or pleasant (uplifts) (DeLongis *et al.*, 1988). This scale requires people to rate, at the end of each day, the extent to which an event, such as the weather, deadlines, family, or physical appearance, served as a hassle or uplift for them on that day. This scale may be completed daily over extended periods to provide a picture of how the routine events of everyday life create stress for people. Daily hassles yield a more accurate prediction of physical illness and adjustment problems than do daily uplifts (DeLongis *et al.*, 1988) and major life events (Garrett *et al.*, 1991).

Coping styles and strategies

So far, we have considered the negative effects of stress: its damaging effects on the body and mind. However, each of us can learn to control stress. We may not always be able to predict when and where we will encounter stressors or to control their intensity, but we can mitigate their damaging effects by adopting coping strategies that are consistent with our lifestyles. A **coping strategy** is simply a plan of action that we follow, either in anticipation of encountering a stressor or as a direct response to stress as it occurs, which is effective in reducing the level of stress we experience.

According to Lazarus and Folkman (1984; Folkman and Lazarus, 1991), there are two types of coping response: problem-focused and emotion-focused. **Problem-focused coping** is directed towards the source of the stress. For example, if the stress is job related, a person might try to change conditions at work or take courses to acquire skills that will enable them to obtain a different job. **Emotion-focused coping** is directed towards a person's own personal reaction to the stressor. For example, a person might try to relax and forget about the problem or find solace in the company of friends. Obviously, if the source of a stress-producing problem has a potential solution, problem-focused coping is the best strategy. If it does not, then emotion-focused coping is the only option.

We each have our own idiosyncratic ways of dealing with stress that can be categorised as being emotion-focused. In fact, health psychologists have shown several of these methods to be effective in controlling stress, including aerobic exercise, cognitive reappraisal, progressive relaxation training and social support. Some people engage in other activities such as smoking, although evidence suggests that smoking results in no significant self-reported decrease in anxiety.

Resilience

You have already seen how various personality factors can act as protective agents against stress and ill health. Optimism is one – an optimistic disposition is associated with significantly fewer symptoms of ill health and stress.

Another factor is resilience. People are sometimes said to have 'bounced back' from some misfortune or some adversity, suggesting that they are resilient. Some psychologists have likened resilience to the property of metals: cast iron is hard and brittle (not resilient) whereas wrought iron is soft and malleable (resilient). Resilient individuals, in a psychological rather than metallurgical sense, are said to be able to bounce back from negative experiences and adapt to changing, adverse environmental conditions: they are optimistic, energetic, curious and express high degrees of positive emotion. Some psychological research has explored whether these positive emotions are a by-product of resilience or whether they are essential to resilient people's ability to cope.

Tugade and Fredrickson (2004) induced stress by asking participants to prepare a speech and deliver it to a video camera. The participants were told that their performance would be evaluated by their peers. In fact, this was an experimental ruse and there was no evaluating group. Cardiovascular and psychological responses were measured during and after the delivery of the speech.

Individuals who characteristically expressed positive emotion were more likely to show cardiovascular recovery after the stressful task (giving a speech). They were also more likely to find positive meaning in negative events. Given that increased cardiovascular reactivity produced by negative events predicts ill health, this degree of resilience suggests that the factor may protect against such ill health by reducing one of its predictors.

The study based their characterisation of resilience on participants' self-report. It would be useful to see whether a group of individuals rated by peers as resilient would show a similar pattern of behaviour. Furthermore, it would be useful to see whether this resilience is constant or whether it fluctuates and is affected by different types of negative experiences.

Some people use retrieval of positive memories to offset the unpleasant emotion created by negative experiences. Joormann and Siemer (2004) examined whether undergraduates' ability to cope with negative mood involved evoking positive memories. People who were slightly depressed were unlikely to evoke positive memories to cope with the unhappy memories; those who did not experience depression but were unhappy did use positive emotion. Even when the depressed participants were asked to recall only pleasant memories, they still reported being unhappy.

Cognitive reappraisal

Aerobic exercise is not the coping strategy of choice for everyone. Some people find that simply altering their perception of the threat posed by stressors reduces stress. This coping strategy is called **cognitive reappraisal** (or cognitive restructuring) and is an extension of Lazarus and Folkman's idea of cognitive appraisal. The rationale underlying this strategy is easy to grasp: if our cognitive appraisal of a stressor is a determining factor in producing stress, then by reappraising that stressor as being less threatening, stress should be reduced. Sometimes, simply learning to substitute an incompatible response, such as replacing a negative statement with a positive one, is sufficient to reduce stress (Lazarus, 1971; Meichenbaum, 1977). For example, students who suffer from test anxiety perceive tests as extremely threatening. They may say to themselves, 'I am going to fail the exam tomorrow', or, 'That test is going to be far too hard'. To reappraise the stressor in this case would involve replacing these statements with ones such as 'I'm going to pass that test tomorrow' or 'Yes, the test will be difficult, but I'm ready for it'.

Cognitive reappraisal is an effective coping strategy because it is often a more realistic approach to interpreting the threat posed by stressors than is the original appraisal. We have good reason to appraise a charging bear as a real threat, but not a university examination. After all, we may not be able to deal with the bear, but we can always learn how to take tests and improve our study habits. An additional benefit of cognitive reappraisal is that it teaches the individual that they can take control of stressful situations.

Relaxation training

Another coping strategy is simply learning to relax when confronted with a stressor. Relaxing is based on the same principle as cognitive reappraisal: substitute an incompatible response for the stress reaction. One procedure for producing relaxation is the **progressive relaxation technique**. It involves three steps: (1) recognising your body's signals informing you that you are experiencing stress; (2) using those signals as a cue to begin relaxing; and (3) relaxing by focusing your attention on different groups of muscles, beginning with those in the head and neck and then those in the arms and legs. Imagine that when confronted by a stressor, for example an exam, you respond by tensing certain muscles: those in your hand and fingers that you use to hold your pen or pencil and those around your mouth that you use to clench your teeth. Once you become aware of these responses, you can use them as cues to relax the muscle groups involved.

Some have also suggested that the use of aromas can alleviate stress and anxiety; this is sometimes called aromatherapy. Aromatherapy is, in fact, a misnomer because there is usually more to aromatherapy than just the presentation of odour; clients normally receive massage as well. The evidence for a long-term, or even short-term, effect of odour on mental health is sparse; few studies have investigated this relationship scientifically and those

that have done so have serious methodological or statistical flaws (see G.N. Martin, 1996, for a review).

Stress inoculation training

According to psychologist Donald Meichenbaum, the best way to cope with stress is to take the offensive – to have a plan in mind for dealing with stressors before you are actually confronted by them. In other words, people should not wait until they are faced with a stressor to cope with it; instead, they should anticipate the kinds of stressor most likely to affect them and develop the most effective coping plan for dealing with specific stressors. Meichenbaum (1985), in fact, has devised a problem-focused coping method, called **stress inoculation training**, which focuses on helping people to develop coping skills that will decrease their susceptibility to the negative effects of stress. Stress inoculation training has been found to be effective in reducing stress levels among people working in a variety of settings, including nurses, teachers, police trainees (Bishop, 1994) and professional athletes (Cox, 1991).

In Meichenbaum's words (1985, p. 21), stress inoculation training

> is analogous to the concept of medical inoculation against biological diseases . . . Analogous to medical inoculation, [stress inoculation training] is designed to build 'psychological antibodies', or coping skills, and to enhance resistance through exposure to stimuli that are strong enough to arouse defenses without being so powerful as to overcome them.

Stress inoculation training usually occurs in a clinical setting involving a therapist and a client and takes place over three phases aimed at achieving seven goals, summarised in Table 17.5.

The first phase is called the conceptualisation phase and involves two basic goals. Goal 1 involves learning about the transactional nature of stress and coping. Stress and coping are strongly influenced by the interaction of cognitive and environmental variables. A person experiences stress to the extent that they appraise the stressor – an environmental variable – as taxing or overwhelming their ability to cope with it – a cognitive variable. In Meichenbaum's view, coping is any behavioural/cognitive attempt to overcome, eliminate or otherwise control the negative effects caused by the stressor (see also Lazarus and Folkman, 1984).

Goal 2 involves becoming better at realistically appraising stressful situations by taking stock of, or self-

Table 17.5 Summary of the phases and goals of Meichenbaum's stress inoculation training programme

Conceptualisation phase

Goal 1:   Learning the transactional nature of stress and coping

Goal 2:   Learning to become better at realistically appraising stressful situations by learning self-monitoring skills with respect to negative or maladaptive thoughts, emotions and behaviours

Skills acquisition and rehearsal phase

Goal 3:   Learning problem-solving skills specific to the stressor

Goal 4:   Learning and rehearsing emotion-regulation and self-control skills

Goal 5:   Learning how to use maladaptive responses as cues to implement the new coping strategy

Application and follow-through phase

Goal 6:   Learning to practise imagery rehearsal using progressively more difficult or stressful situations

Goal 7:   Learning to apply new coping skills to other, perhaps unexpected, stressors

Source: Adapted from Meichenbaum, D., *Stress Inoculation Training.* New York: Pergamon Press, 1985.

monitoring, patterns in maladaptive thinking, feeling and behaving. A person may keep a diary, or a 'stress log', to record stressful events, the conditions under which these events occur, and their reactions to these events.

The second phase is called the skills acquisition and rehearsal phase and involves goals 3–5. Goal 3 involves learning specific problem-solving skills aimed at reducing stress. For example, a person may learn to identify and define a specific stressor and outline a plan for dealing with it in behavioural terms. The plan should include developing alternative ideas for dealing with the stressor and considering the possible consequences that correspond to each alternative. At this point, a person may find relaxation training and self-instructional training, in which they learn to make positive self-statements when confronted by a stressor, helpful.

Goal 4 involves learning and rehearsing emotion-regulation and self-control skills. These skills help people to remain calm and rational when confronted with a stressor. Goal 5 involves learning how to use maladaptive responses as a cue to invoke the new coping strategy. For example, when faced with a stressor, you may feel yourself getting tense. This feeling of tension is your cue to implement specific aspects of your inoculation training, which presumably would reduce your level of stress.

The third and final phase of Meichenbaum's programme is called the application and follow-through phase and comprises goals 6 and 7. Goal 6 involves imagery rehearsal, in which a person practises coping with the stressor by imagining being confronted by that stressor in progressively more difficult situations. The purpose of rehearsing the coping skills is to build confidence in one's ability to use the new coping strategy. Goal 7 involves learning to apply new coping abilities to both expected and unexpected stressors. This might be accom-

plished by imagining several situations in which you feel anxious, imagining implementing the coping strategy in response to the anxiety, and, finally, imagining feeling relieved as a result of coping with the stressor.

Stress is an inevitable consequence of environmental change. Both large changes, such as a natural disaster or changing jobs, and small changes, such as remembering that we have an exam tomorrow, contribute to the overall level of stress that we experience at any one time. Whether stress impairs our health depends on three variables: the extent to which we appraise the stressor as threatening, whether we engage in good health practices, and the extent to which we use coping strategies effectively. The combined effects of these variables on the relationship between stress and health are summarised in Figure 17.19.

Do psychological interventions reduce stress?

Psychologists know that psychological stress is linked to immune system responses: one causes disruption of the other. If psychological factors can affect the immune system, it seems reasonable to hypothesise that psychological factors that play a large part in intervention treatment can also affect immune system response. Over 85 intervention studies of the effect of psychological variables on stress have now appeared in journals, most of them appearing since the 1980s (Miller and Cohen, 2001).

Miller and Cohen's review suggests that the success of interventions are modest. The authors reviewed studies which examined the effects of different types of intervention on immune system functioning. These included (1) stress management interventions which are normally undertaken with patients with medical illness; these interventions involve educating the person about the illness, and providing coping skills training and psychological sup-

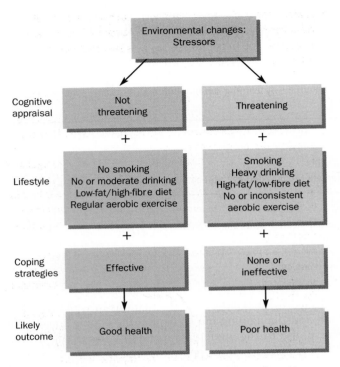

Figure 17.19 The effects of stress on health are mediated by cognitive appraisal, lifestyle and coping abilities.

port; (2) relaxation interventions which involve muscle relaxation; (3) disclosure interventions which usually ask participants to write about their stressful experiences; (4) hypnosis; and (5) conditioning interventions in which a neutral stimulus is paired with an immune system facilitator so that the presentation of the neutral stimulus alone will produce the immune system response.

The researchers found that stress management interventions altered immune responses very little; relaxation interventions also showed little evidence of producing immune response changes; disclosure interventions were modestly successful in enhancing immune system response; hypnosis showed that participants could use hypnotic suggestion to alter immune responses; and conditioning interventions were also modestly successful in changing immune system response.

Although two of these interventions met with some success, none of the interventions were found to be beneficial to people suffering stress caused by illness. Perhaps such interventions are inappropriate for counteracting the stress experienced by medically ill individuals (those suffering from cancer, for example). The authors suggest that people most likely to benefit from stress management and relaxation are those suffering ongoing, chronic stress such as the bereaved and those who have been involved in natural disasters.

Chapter review

Health psychology and unhealthy behaviour

- Health psychology applies psychological principles to the study of health and illness. It examines the effects of various psychological and physical factors on health and can also evaluate the effect of health policy and health education on behaviour.
- Behaviours which have implications for health psychology include smoking, eating, sexual behaviour, exercise and alcohol use.
- Protective factors are those which make the individual less susceptible to ill health.
- Evidence suggests that people who have high-fat, low-fibre diets tend to be more susceptible to coronary heart disease (CHD) and cancer than are people who have low-fat, high-fibre diets.
- Weight gain and increased low-density lipoprotein (LDL) cholesterol levels are both risk factors for CHD and cancer.
- The decision to begin smoking is influenced by peer pressure, low income and poor education; smoking normally begins in adolescence and is rarely initiated in adulthood.

- Smoking cessation programmes have met with limited success; a combination of nicotine replacement and psychological treatments appears to show the best outcome.
- Exercise appears to be effective in increasing positive mood and alleviating mild depression.
- The best precautionary measure against contracting any sexually transmitted disease (STD) is the practice of safe sex.
- Acquired immune deficiency syndrome (AIDS) refers to a disease resulting from infection by virus (HIV). There are 21 million people living in the world with AIDS; HIV can be contracted through unprotected homosexual and heterosexual sex, intravenous injection and transfusion of contaminated blood.
- Programmes aimed at preventing the spread of STDs and AIDS focus on teaching people the relationship between their behaviour and the likelihood of contracting one or more of these diseases and how to use safe sex strategies.

Stress and health

- Stress is defined in terms of our physiological and psychological response to stimuli that either prevent us from obtaining a goal or endanger our well-being.
- Selye's model describes how prolonged exposure to stress leads to illness and sometimes death.
- The stress response, which Cannon called the fight or flight response, is useful as a short-term response to threatening stimuli but is harmful in the long term. This response includes increased activity of the sympathetic branch of the autonomic nervous system and increased secretion of epinephrine, norepinephrine and glucocorticoids by the adrenal gland.
- Although increased levels of epinephrine and norepinephrine can raise blood pressure, most of the stressor-related harm to health comes from glucocorticoids.
- Prolonged exposure to high levels of these hormones can increase blood pressure, damage muscle tissue, lead to infertility, inhibit growth, inhibit the inflammatory response and suppress the immune system.
- The most important predictor of ill health produced by stressors is the nature of a person's coping response.
- Personality characteristics which may serve as protective factors against stress include submissiveness and optimism.
- Type A behaviour pattern refers to behaviour that is competitive, hostile, rapid and intense; some of these variables, especially hostility, may predict the likelihood of CHD, but the research findings are mixed.
- Psychoneuroimmunology is the study of the effects of psychological stressors on the immune system.
- The immune system consists of several types of white blood cell that produce chemically-mediated and cell-mediated responses. The immune system can cause harm when it triggers an allergic reaction or when it attacks the body's own tissues in autoimmune diseases.
- The most important mechanism by which stress impairs immune function is by increasing blood levels of glucocorticoids. Neural input to the bone marrow, lymph nodes and thymus gland may also play a role; naturally occurring opioids appear to suppress the activity of internal killer cells.

- A wide variety of stressful situations, such as the death of a spouse or caring for a relative with Alzheimer's disease, have been shown to increase people's susceptibility to infectious diseases.

Coping with everyday stress

- Stress may stem from a wide variety of sources. Even positive events, such as the birth of a child or the marriage of a son or daughter can produce stress.
- Stress may lead to physical illness when a person undergoes several stressful events over a short period of time. The extent to which people become ill appears to depend on the extent to which they perceive a stressor as being a threat to their well-being and the extent to which they believe they can cope with that threat.
- Lazarus and Folkman have identified two types of coping. Problem-focused coping represents any attempt to reduce stress by attempting to change the event or situation producing the stress.
- Emotion-focused coping centres on changing one's personal reaction to the stressful event or situation. Emotion-focused coping may involve activities such as aerobic exercise, cognitive reappraisal, relaxation training and seeking social support.
- Meichenbaum's stress inoculation training programme is a problem-focused coping strategy that prepares people to cope with anticipated stressors. The programme involves three phases and seven goals. The first phase involves learning how to conceptualise the transactional nature of stress. The second phase entails learning coping skills specific to the stressors in their lives and practising or rehearsing these skills in hypothetical situations. The third phase involves preparing people to implement these coping skills in real-life situations. The seven goals of stress inoculation training focus on specific kinds of knowledge, behaviour and coping strategies central to preparing people to anticipate, confront and reduce the threat posed by stressful situations.
- Reviews of the benefits of psychological interventions in stress have produced mixed results; some interventions are modestly successful; others show no benefit.

Suggestions for further reading

Health psychology – general reading

Ogden, J. (2007) *Health Psychology* (4th edn). Open University Press.

Sarafino, E.P. (2008) *Health Psychology: Biopsychosocial interactions* (6th edn). Chichester: Wiley.

Psychoneuroimmunology and health

Kiecolt-Glaser, J.K., McGuire, L., Robles, T.F. and Glaser, R. (2002) Psychoneuroimmunology: Psychological influences on immune function and health. *Journal of Consulting and Clinical Psychology*, 70(3), 537–47.

Lekander, M. (2002) Ecological immunology: The role of the immune system in psychology and neuroscience. *European Psychologist*, 7(2), 98–115.

Sternberg, E.M. and Gold, P.W. (2001) The mind–body interaction in disease. *The Hidden Mind*. New York: Scientific American Library.

These recommendations provide different examples of interesting reading on health psychology issues.

Health psychology and specific behaviours and illnesses

Brandon, T.H. and Chassin, L. (2004) Motivational influences on cigarette smoking. *Annual Review of Psychology*, 55, 463–92.

Dubbert, P.M. (2002) Physical activity and exercise: Recent advances and current challenges. *Journal of Consulting and Clinical Psychology*, 70(3), 526–36.

Folkman, S. and Moskowitz, J.T. (2004) Coping: Pitfalls and promise. *Annual Review of Psychology*, 55, 74–7.

Kelly, J.A. and Kalichman, S.C. (2002) Behavioural research in HIV/AIDS primary and secondary prevention: Recent advances and future directions. *Journal of Consulting and Clinical Psychology*, 70(3), 626–39.

Niaura, R. and Abrams, D.B. (2002) Smoking cessation: Progress, priorities and prospectus. *Journal of Consulting and Clinical Psychology*, 70(3), 494–509.

Smith, T.W. and Ruiz, J.M. (2002) Psychosocial influences on the development and course of coronary heart disease: Current status and implications for research and practice. *Journal of Consulting and Clinical Psychology*, 70(3), 548–68.

Urry, H.L., Nitschke, J.B., Dolski, I., Jackson, D.C., Dalton, K.M., Mueller, C.J., Rosenkranz, M.A., Ryff, C.D., Singer, B.H. and Davidson, R.J. (2004) Making a life worth living: neural correlates of well-being. *Psychological Science*, 15, 6, 367–72.

Vitaliano, P.P., Young, H.M. and Zhang, J. (2004) Is caregiving a risk factor for illness? *Current Directions in Psychological Science*, 13, 1, 13–16.

A good selection of papers covering topics reviewed in the chapter.

Journals to consult

British Journal of Health Psychology

British Journal of Medical Psychology

British Medical Journal

Health Psychology

International Journal of Behavioural Medicine

International Journal of Stress

Journal of Abnormal Psychology

Journal of Community and Applied Psychology

Journal of Health Psychology

Journal of Occupational Health Psychology

Journal of Occupational Medicine

Journal of Occupational and Organisational Psychology

Journal of Personality and Social Psychology

Journal of Social and Occupational Medicine

New England Journal of Medicine

Psychology, Health and Medicine

Psychosomatic Medicine

Social Science and Medicine

Stress and Health

Stress Medicine

The Lancet

Work and Stress

Website addresses

http://www.psychology.org/links/Environment_Behavior_Relationships/Health/
A collection of health psychology links.

http://www.psychology.org/links/Environment_Behavior_Relationships/Health_Care/
A collection of links to sites about health management and prevention of ill health.

http://www.health-psychology.org.uk/menuItems/FAQs.php
A link to the British Psychological Society's Division of Health Psychology website.

http://www.dh.gov.uk/Home/fs/en
The UK Department of Health website.

http://www.who.int/en/
The World Health Organization website.

Abnormal psychology

CHAPTER 18

JK Rowling reveals her thoughts of suicide as a young single mother

Linda Johnston

While the 42-year-old author has spoken before of her battle with depression, it is the first time she has admitted that she considered ending her life.

At the time, she was living on state benefits after having separated from her then husband and was living in a cramped and unheated flat in Edinburgh with her baby daughter.

Rowling, whose Potter novels have sold more than 400 million copies, said: 'We're talking suicidal thoughts here, we're not talking "I'm a little bit miserable."'

'Two weeks later I had a phone call from my regular GP who had looked back over the notes . . . She called me back in and I got counselling through her. She absolutely saved me because I don't think I would have had the guts to do it twice.'

She said, 'I have never been remotely ashamed of having been depressed – never. What's to be ashamed of? I went through a really rough time and I am quite proud that I got out of that.'

Source: *The Herald*, 24 March 2008.

WHAT YOU SHOULD BE ABLE TO DO AFTER READING CHAPTER 18

- Define the term 'mental illness'.
- Explain the aim of classification of mental disorders and define mental abnormality.
- Describe the most important treatment approaches to mental disorders.
- Describe the symptoms and causes of major mental disorders.
- Evaluate theories of mental disorder.
- Evaluate treatment approaches to mental disorder.

QUESTIONS TO THINK ABOUT

- What makes an abnormal behaviour abnormal?
- Which term makes the best sense: mental disorder or mental illness?
- How, and in what ways, are mental illnesses different from 'physical' ones?
- Are mental illnesses categorical or do they fall along a continuum?
- Do all mental disorders have a biological basis?
- What are the best treatments for mental illness? Do you think some treatment approaches are more appropriate than others?

mypsychlab
where learning comes to life!

Explore the accompanying videos, simulations and animations on MyPsychLab. This chapter includes activities on: Perspectives on mental disorders • Hierarchy of anxiety • Genetic causes of schizophrenia • Mood disorders • Check your understanding and prepare for your exams using the multiple choice, short answer and essay practice tests also available.

Classification and diagnosis of mental disorders

Abnormal psychology is the area of psychology which studies and treats mental disorder. Mental disorders are disorders of thought, feeling or behaviour and are characterised by behaviourally deviant features. Their causes may be genetic, environmental, cognitive or neurobiological.

Some of these disorders you will be familiar with – depression and anxiety, for example. Others will not be so familiar, such as paraphilia and conversion disorder. Although the symptoms described for each disorder may apply to healthy individuals who exhibit a 'bad mood' or who are under stress, these disorders represent a severe impairment in functioning. Clinical depression is not the same as the 'low' we sometimes feel in life, and generalised anxiety disorder does not represent the stress we feel before an exam or speaking in public.

The term 'mental disorder' refers to a clinical impairment characterised by abnormal thought, feeling or behaviour. Some mental disorders, especially the less severe ones, appear to be caused by environmental factors or by a person's perception of these factors, such as stress or unhealthy family interactions. In contrast, many of the more severe mental disorders appear to be caused by hereditary and other biological factors that disrupt normal thought processes or produce inappropriate emotional reactions. The descriptions of mental disorders in this chapter necessarily make distinctions that are not always easy to make in real life; the essential features of the more important mental disorders are simplified here for the sake of clarity. In addition, many of the cases that clinicians encounter are less clear-cut than the ones included here and are thus not so easily classified.

To understand, diagnose and treat psychological disorders, some sort of classification system is needed. The need for a comprehensive classification system of psychological disorders was first recognised by Emil Kraepelin (1856–1926), who provided his version in a textbook of psychiatry published in 1883. The classification most widely used today still retains a number of Kraepelin's original categories.

What is 'abnormal'?

Mental disorders are characterised by abnormal behaviour, thoughts and feelings. The term 'abnormal' literally refers to any departure from the norm. Thus, a short or tall person is 'abnormal', and so is someone who is especially intelligent or talented. Albert Einstein was 'abnormal', as were Oscar Wilde and Pablo Picasso. The term 'abnormal' is often used pejoratively – it is used to refer to characteristics that are disliked or feared – but this is not the way in which it is used when describing mental illness. The most important feature of a mental disorder, however, may not be whether a person's behaviour is abnormal – different from that of most other people – but whether it is maladaptive. Mental disorders cause distress or discomfort and often interfere with people's ability to lead useful, productive lives. They often make it impossible for people to hold down jobs, raise families or relate to others socially.

The causes of mental disorders

What causes mental disorders? In general, they are caused by an interaction between hereditary, cognitive and environmental factors. In some cases, the genetic component is strong and the person is likely to develop a mental disorder even in a very supportive environment. In other cases, the cognitive and environmental components are strong. A complete understanding of mental disorders requires that scientists investigate genetic, cognitive and environmental factors. Once genetic factors are identified, the scientist faces the task of determining the physiological effects of the relevant genes and the consequences of these effects on a person's susceptibility to a mental disorder. Understanding the cognitive factors involved in mental disorders requires identification of the origins of distorted perceptions and maladaptive thought patterns. And environmental factors encompass more than simply a person's family history or present social interactions; they also include the effects of prenatal health and nutrition, childhood diseases and exposure to drugs and environmental toxins.

Different psychologists and other mental health professionals approach the study of mental disorders from different perspectives, each of which places more or less emphasis on these factors. The perspectives differ primarily in their explanation of the aetiology, or origin, of mental disorders. Some of these perspectives are described next.

The psychodynamic perspective

According to the psychodynamic perspective, based on Freud's early work described in Chapter 14, mental disorders originate in intrapsychic conflict produced by the three warring factions of the mind: the id, ego and superego. For some people, the conflict becomes so severe that the mind's defence mechanisms are ineffective, resulting in mental disorders that may involve, among other symptoms, extreme anxiety, obsessive thoughts and compulsive behaviour, depression, distorted perceptions and patterns of thinking, and paralysis or blindness for which there is no physical cause. As you saw in Chapter 14, the id, ego and superego are hypothetical constructs, not physical structures of the brain. But Freud and his followers often spoke as if these structures and their functions were real. Even today, psychodynamic theorists and practitioners approach mental disorders by emphasising the role of intrapsychic conflict in creating psychological distress and maladaptive behaviour.

The medical perspective

The medical perspective has its origins in the work of the ancient Greek physician Hippocrates. Hippocrates formulated the idea that excesses in the four humours (black bile, yellow bile, blood and phlegm) led to emotional problems. Other physicians, Greek and Roman, extended Hippocrates' ideas and developed the concept of mental illness – illnesses of the mind. Eventually, specialised institutions or asylums were established where people with mental disorders were confined. Early asylums were ill-run and the patients' problems were poorly understood and often mistreated. During the eighteenth and nineteenth centuries, massive reforms in the institutional care of people with mental disorders took place. The quality of the facilities and the amount of compassion for patients improved, and physicians, including neurosurgeons and psychiatrists, who were specifically trained in the medical treatment of mental disorders, were hired to care for these patients.

Today, the medical perspective is the dominant perspective in the treatment of mental disorders. Individuals with mental disorders are no longer confined to mental institutions. Instead, they are treated on an outpatient basis with drugs that are effective in abating the symptoms of mental disorders. Usually, only those people with very severe mental problems are institutionalised. The **medical model**, as the medical perspective is properly called, is based on the idea that mental disorders are caused by specific abnormalities of the brain and nervous system and that, in principle, they should be approached the same way as physical illnesses. As we shall see, several mental disorders, including schizophrenia, depression and bipolar disorder, are known to have specific biological causes and can be treated to some extent with drugs. We shall also see that genetics play a pivotal role in some of these disorders.

However, not all mental disorders can be traced so directly to physical causes. For that reason, other perspectives, which focus on the cognitive and environmental factors involved in mental disorders, have emerged.

The cognitive behavioural perspective

In contrast to the medical perspective, the cognitive behavioural perspective holds that mental disorders are learned maladaptive behaviour patterns that can best be understood by focusing on environmental factors and a person's perception of those factors. In this view, a mental disorder is not something that arises spontaneously within a person. Instead, it is caused by the person's interaction with their environment. For example, a person's excessive use of alcohol or other drugs may be negatively reinforced by the relief from tension or anxiety that often accompanies intoxication.

According to the cognitive behavioural perspective, it is not merely the environment that matters: what also counts is a person's ongoing subjective interpretation of the events taking place in their environment. Therapists operating from the cognitive behavioural perspective therefore encourage their clients to replace or substitute maladaptive thoughts and behaviours with more adaptive ones (Emmelkamp, 1994).

The humanistic and sociocultural perspective

As you saw in Chapter 14, proponents of the humanistic perspective argue that proper personality development occurs when people experience unconditional positive regard. According to this view, mental disorders arise when people perceive that they must earn the positive regard of others. Cultural variables influence the nature and extent to which people interpret their own behaviours as normal or abnormal. What is considered perfectly normal in one culture may be considered abnormal in another. Moreover, mental disorders exist that appear to occur only in certain cultures – a phenomenon called **culture-bound syndrome**. These are discussed in the International perspective section on pp. 780–82.

The diathesis-stress approach

None of the above perspectives is completely accurate in accounting for the origins of mental disorders. But elements of these perspectives may be combined to form a different, perhaps more comprehensive, perspective on mental disorders. The **diathesis-stress model** argues that the combination of a person's genetics and early learning experiences yields a predisposition (a diathesis) for a particular mental disorder. However, the mental disorder will develop only if that person is confronted with stressors that exceed their coping abilities. In other words, a person may be predisposed towards a mental disorder yet not develop it either because they have not encountered sufficient stressors to trigger its development or because they possess the cognitive behavioural coping skills needed to limit the negative effects of the stressor.

Classification of disorders

Mental disorders can be classified in many ways, but the two systems most commonly used in the world are those presented in the American Psychiatric Association's *Diagnostic and Statistical Manual (of Mental Disorders)* IV (DSM-IV TR)

(2000) and the World Health Organization's *International Classification of Diseases 10* (ICD-10). DSM-IV TR was originally devised by American psychologists for the classification of mental disorders, whereas ICD-10 was devised as an international classification system for all diseases. These two are more alike than different, although differences do exist (Andrews et al., 1999). Table 18.1 lists the classifications in DSM-IV TR, with several subclassifications omitted for the sake of simplicity.

Table 18.1 Summary of the DSM-IV classification scheme for axes I and II

Axis I – Major clinical syndromes

Disorders usually first appearing in infancy, childhood or adolescence	Any deviation from normal development, including mental retardation, autism, attention deficit disorder with hyperactivity, excessive fears, speech problems and highly aggressive behaviour
Delirium, dementia, amnestic and other cognitive disorders	Disorders due to deterioration of the brain because of ageing, disease (such as Alzheimer's disease, which was discussed in Chapter 11), or ingestion or exposure to drugs or toxic substances (such as lead)
Psychoactive substance abuse disorders	Psychological, social or physical problems related to abuse of alcohol or other drugs. (Psychoactive substance use and abuse was discussed in Chapters 3, 4 and 16 and is also discussed in this chapter)
Schizophrenia and other psychotic disorders	A group of disorders marked by loss of contact with reality, illogical thought, inappropriate displays of emotion, bizarre perceptions and usually some form of hallucinations or delusions
Mood disorders	Disorders involving extreme deviations from normal mood, including severe depression (major depression), excessive elation (mania), or alteration between severe depression and excessive elation (bipolar disorder)
Anxiety disorders	Excessive fear of specific objects (phobia); repetitive, persistent thoughts accompanied by ritualistic-like behaviour that reduces anxiety (obsessive–compulsive behaviour) panic attacks; generalised and intense feelings of anxiety; and feelings of dread caused by experiencing traumatic events such as natural disasters or combat
Somatoform disorders	Disorders involving pain, paralysis or blindness for which no physical cause can be found. Excessive concern for one's health, as is typical in persons with hypochondriasis
Factitious disorders	Fake mental disorders, such as Munchausen syndrome, in which the individual is frequently hospitalised because of their claims of illness
Dissociative disorders	Loss of personal identity and changes in normal consciousness, including amnesia and multiple personality disorder, in which there exists two or more independently functioning personality systems
Sexual and sex identity disorders	Disorders involving fetishes, sexual dysfunction (such as impotence or orgasmic dysfunctions), and problems of sexual identity (such as transsexualism)
Eating disorders	Disorders relating to excessive concern about one's body weight, such as anorexia nervosa (self-starvation) and bulimia (alternating periods of eating large amounts of food and vomiting). (Eating disorders were discussed in Chapter 13)
Sleep disorders	Disorders including severe insomnia, chronic sleepiness, sleepwalking, narcolepsy (suddenly falling asleep) and sleep apnoea. (Sleep disorders were discussed in Chapter 9)
Impulse control disorders	Disorders involving compulsive behaviours such as stealing, fire setting or gambling
Adjustment disorders	Disorders stemming from difficulties adjusting to significant life stressors, such as death of a loved one, loss of a job or financial difficulties, and family problems, including divorce. (Some adjustment disorders, as they pertain to difficulty in coping with life stressors, were discussed in Chapter 17)
Axis II – Personality disorders	Personality disorders are long-term, maladaptive and rigid personality traits that impair normal functioning and involve psychological stress. Two examples are antisocial personality disorder (lack of emphathy or care for others, lack of guilt for misdeeds, antisocial behaviour, and persistent lying, cheating and stealing) and narcissistic personality disorder (inflated sense of self-worth and importance and persistent seeking of attention)

DSM-IV TR classification

The DSM-IV TR is the latest version of a scheme that was devised to provide a reliable, universal set of diagnostic categories having criteria specified as explicitly as possible. The DSM-IV TR describes an individual's psychological condition using five different criteria, called **axes**. Individuals undergoing evaluation are assessed on each of the axes. Axis I contains information on major psychological disorders that require clinical attention, including disorders that may develop during childhood. Personality disorders are found on Axis II. Diagnoses can be made that include both Axis I and Axis II disorders, and multiple diagnoses can occur on either axis alone. For example, major depression and alcohol dependence are both Axis I disorders, and both disorders may characterise one individual at any one period of time. A person's psychological condition may be due to several different psychological disorders described in the DSM-IV TR, just as one person may suffer simultaneously from several different physical disorders.

Axes III through V provide information about the life of the individual in addition to the basic classification provided by Axes I and II. Axis III is used to describe any physical disorders, such as skin rashes or heightened blood pressure, accompanying the psychological disorder. Axis IV specifies the severity of stress that the person has experienced (usually within the last year). This axis details the source of stress (for example, family or work) and indicates its severity and approximate duration. Axis V describes the person's overall level of psychological, social or occupational functioning. The purpose of Axis V is to estimate the extent to which a person's quality of life has been diminished by the disorder. Ratings are made on a 100-point global assessment of functioning (GAF) scale, with 100 representing the absence or near absence of impaired functioning, 50 representing serious problems in functioning, and 10 representing impairment that may result in injury to the individual or to others.

The DSM-IV TR provides a systematic means of providing and evaluating a variety of personal and psychological information about any one specific individual. Alcohol dependence (Axis I) often leads to marital problems, which may also be partially associated with an antisocial personality disorder (Axis II). Marital problems may lead to a divorce and these problems and the divorce are themselves stressors (Axis IV) that may subsequently contribute to an episode of major depression (Axis I). Alcohol dependence may eventually lead to physical problems, such as cirrhosis of the liver (Axis III). These problems, now acting in concert, are likely to lead to an increased impairment in overall life functioning (Axis V) so that the individual has only a few friends, none of them close, and is unable to keep a job. The evaluation of this person might be summarised as follows:

Axis I: Alcohol dependence

Axis II: Antisocial personality disorder

Axis III: Alcoholic cirrhosis of the liver

Axis IV: Severe – divorce, loss of job

Axis V: GAF evaluation = 30 (a very serious impairment of functioning)

Controversies in Psychological Science – How valid and reliable is the DSM?

The issue

Although the DSM-IV TR is the most widely used classification system for mental disorders, it is not without its problems. Reflecting the fact that the DSM-IV TR has been strongly influenced by psychiatrists, the DSM-IV TR tends to be more consistent with the medical perspective on mental disorders. This means that diagnosis and treatment based on the DSM-IV TR emphasise biological factors, which, in turn, means that potential cognitive and environmental determinants may be overlooked.

The evidence

Another potential problem with the DSM-IV TR (and perhaps with any classification scheme) is questionable reliability. Reliability in this context means what it did in the context of psychological testing discussed in Chapter 2 – consistency across applications. If the DSM-IV TR was perfectly reliable, users would be able to diagnose each case in the same way. But evaluating psychological disorders is not so easy. Using the DSM-IV TR is not like using a recipe; it is more like navigating your way through an unfamiliar city using only a crude map. Using this map, you may or may not reach your destination. Mental disorders do not have distinct borders that allow a mental health professional to diagnose a disorder in a person with 100 per cent accuracy all of the time. Some critics argue, for example, that DSM encourages the making of false-positive judgements – claiming a disorder exists when there only exists a moderate, normal disruption in behaviour. For example, one in four cases of bereavement might be diagnosed as major depressive disorder when these people are undergoing a natural, event-specific change in mood (Wakefield *et al.*, 2007).

Personality disorder is one of the most commonly used diagnoses (Verheul and Widiger, 2004), but critics have highlighted

Controversies in Psychological Science – *Continued*

inconsistencies in how each type of personality disorder is rated – one type has five or eight criteria that have to be met but only two of the types have any published rationale for the criteria (Widiger and Trull, 2007). These authors also note that the approach to diagnosing personality disorders is now polythetic – that is, four out of five criteria need to be met, rather than all. Widiger and Trull suggest that each diagnostic category might be scored along a 5-point scale and this may be one solution.

This is why evidence suggests that actuarial (statistical) analysis of symptoms is better than clinical analysis (Meehl, 1954; Aegisdottir *et al.*, 2006). Specific indicators such as sex, age, test scores, medical history and so on (actuarial measures) are superior to expert 'experience' and knowledge of previous cases. You might guess that this name comes from the world of insurance (hence, actuary) and you'd be right: the actuarial method was used to assess how long a person would live (using statistics such as age, sex, height, weight, etc.) and to set levels of insurance.

Of course, not every individual will follow the pattern predicted by these statistics (not every overweight, short, old man will live longer than a slim, tall woman) but as a general guide they are a useful statistical predictor of groups of people's behaviour as a whole. In the clinical realm, aegisdottir *et al.* (2006)'s meta-analysis found that actuarial method was 13 per cent more accurate. Reasons for the success include its reliability – a decision is based on the same criteria and not based on the subjective impression of the clinician who may be influenced by irrelevant variables or not pay attention to relevant ones. Most clinicians, however, adopt the clinical method, despite the advantages of the actuarial method. As Chapter 2 showed, people are always more persuaded by the importance of narrative than the importance of statistics.

There will probably always be dangers in classifying mental disorders. No classification scheme is likely to be perfect, and no two people with the same diagnosis will behave in exactly the same way. Yet once people are labelled, they are likely to be perceived as having all the characteristics assumed to accompany that label; their behaviour will probably be perceived selectively and interpreted in terms of the diagnosis.

An experiment by Langer and Abelson (1974) illustrated how labelling can affect clinical judgements. A group of psychoanalysts were shown a videotape of a young man who was being interviewed. Half of the psychoanalysts were told that the man was a job applicant, while the other half were told that he was a patient. Although both groups of clinicians watched the same man exhibiting the same behaviour, those who were told that he was a patient rated him as being more disturbed, that is, less well adjusted.

It is easy to lapse into the mistaken belief that, somehow or other, labelling disorders explains why people are like they

are. Diagnosing a psychological disorder only describes the symptoms of the disorder; it does not explain its origins. To say that someone did something 'because he's schizophrenic' does not explain his behaviour. We need to be on guard against associating the names of disorders with people rather than with their symptoms. It is more appropriate to talk about 'someone who displays the characteristics of schizophrenia' than to say that 'he's a schizophrenic'.

According even to DSM-IV TR's defenders, 'the most ridiculed aspect of DSM classification system is its ever-expanding size' (Wakefield, 2001), and commentators have remarked that each new edition of the manual brings with it a new classification of a behaviour as a mental illness. Some view this enlargement as enlightenment and a recognition of a behaviour as a serious mental problem, illness or psychiatric condition. Others see the expansion as over-inclusive, over-eager and as inappropriately labelling odd or eccentric behaviour as deviant or as an illness without sufficient scientific evidence for doing so (Houts and Follette, 1998). New disorders are invented, according to critics, and previously accepted behaviours are labelled as disorders, in effect creating a 'social invention of mental disorders' (Houts, 2001).

Houts (2001), one of DSM's fiercest critics, refers to sleep disorders as an example of this invention and over-inclusiveness. Until DSM-III-R, sleep disorders were not considered mental disorders. 'It is as though sleep problems became mental disorders overnight sometime in 1987', he notes. Other behaviours which Houts argues are inappropriately classed as mental disorder include frotteurism (touching or rubbing up against another in a sexual way without consent), kleptomania (compulsive theft), dyscalculia (a disorder of mathematical thinking), pathological gambling and voyeurism. There is also the 'wastebasket' category of 'sexual disorder not otherwise specified' which represents exactly what it says: any sexual behaviour considered deviant by a psychiatrist that does not meet the criteria of the other disorders.

There are, therefore, some well-argued objections to the inclusion of these categories, and there are equally well-intentioned arguments for the inclusion of these and others.

Conclusion

DSM-V is being planned and professionals are currently being asked to comment on how it could be improved. One major theme that clinicians are being asked to explore is whether having categories of illness is now inappropriate and whether a more dimensional approach to diagnosis is better, i.e. is it better to view disorders as a dimension with major depression at one end and post-traumatic stress disorder (PTSD, described later on in the chapter) at the other, rather than as discrete disorders, independent of all others. Many clinicians are now

Controversies in Psychological Science – *Continued*

expressing frustration with the category approach (Widiger and Samuel, 2005). As Rounsaville *et al.* (2002: 12) argue:

> In the past 20 years . . . the disease entity assumption has been increasingly questioned as evidence has accumulated that prototypical mental disorders such as major depressive disorder, anxiety disorders, schizophrenia, and bipolar disorder seem to merge imperceptibly both into one another and into normality . . . with no demonstrable natural boundaries or zones of rarity in between.

This view has consequences that are practical and scientific: it asks us to re-evaluate how we view mental illness and, therefore, its causes and treatment. A recent discussion in the *Journal of Abnormal Psychology*, suggests that an overhaul of the approach to diagnosis is overdue, as long as the dimensional approach proposed is clinically useful and backed with clear evidence (Brown and Barlow, 2005; First, 2005; Watson, 2005).

The need for classification

Because labelling can have negative effects, some people, such as Szasz (1960, 1987), have suggested that we should abandon all attempts to classify and diagnose mental disorders. In fact, Szasz has argued that the concept of mental illness has done more harm than good because of the negative effects it has on those people who are said to be mentally ill. Szasz notes that labelling people as mentally ill places the responsibility for their care with the medical establishment, thereby relieving such people of responsibility for their mental states and for taking personal steps towards improvement. As you will see in the next section, the lay view of mental illness is not positive and almost consistently ill-informed. You saw in Chapter 1 how children's television programmes referred to unlikeable or eccentric characters using terms related to mental illness. A later section in this chapter on soldier's attitudes to seeking mental health help after a tour of duty cites a study which found that over 50 per cent of soldiers who meet screening criteria for various mental health problems said that their leadership/unit would have less confidence in them and that they would be seen as weak if they sought help (Hoge *et al.*, 2004). People who feel stigmatised by being labelled with the name of a mental illness feel more rejected, devalued and are up to seven times more likely to experience low self-esteem than are those who do not regard the diagnosis as a stigma (Link *et al.*, 2001; Perlick *et al.*, 2001).

However, proper classification has advantages for a patient. One advantage is that, with few exceptions, the recognition of a specific diagnostic category precedes the development of successful treatment for that disorder. Treatments for diseases such as diabetes, syphilis, tetanus and malaria were found only after the disorders could be reliably diagnosed. A patient may have a multitude of symptoms, but before the cause of the disorder (and hence its treatment) can be discovered, the primary symptoms must be identified. For example, Graves's disease is characterised by irritability, restlessness, confused and rapid thought processes and, occasionally, delusions and hallucinations. Little was known about the endocrine system during the nineteenth century when Robert Graves identified the disease, but we now know that this syndrome results from oversecretion of thyroxine, a hormone produced by the thyroid gland. Treatment involves prescription of antithyroid drugs or surgical removal of the thyroid gland, followed by administration of appropriate doses of thyroxine. Graves's classification scheme for the symptoms was devised many years before the

The boxer Frank Bruno's admission to a psychiatric hospital for depression was treated in two versions of the UK's best-selling daily newspaper, *The Sun*. This was the second edition, printed because of the complaints generated by the first in which the boxer was described as 'Bonkers Bruno'.

Source: The Sun/NI Syndication. Copyright© News Group Newspapers Ltd.

physiological basis of the disease could be understood. But once enough was known about the effects of thyroxine, physicians were able to treat Graves's disease and strike it off the roll of mental disorders.

On a less dramatic scale, different kinds of mental disorder have different causes, and they respond to different types of psychological treatment and drugs. If future research is to reveal more about causes and treatments of these disorders, we must be able to classify specific mental disorders reliably and accurately.

Another important reason for properly classifying mental disorders is prognosis. Some disorders have good prognoses; the patients are likely to improve soon and are unlikely to have a recurrence of their problems. Other disorders have progressive courses; patients are less likely to recover from these disorders. In the first case, patients can obtain reassurance about their futures; in the second case, patients' families can obtain assistance in making realistic plans.

Lay knowledge of mental illness

In 2000, a protest group in the US called StigmaBusters successfully lobbied the TV channel, ABC, to pull a show, *Wonderland*, which portrayed people with mental illness as being dangerous or unpredictable (Corrigan *et al.*, 2005). Lay understanding of mental illness is not good. Many people either know little or nothing about the symptoms or treatment of mental illness or misunderstand mental illness and assume that mentally ill people behave in ways that they, in reality, do not. Landlords who believe the stereotype of the mentally ill are less likely to offer accommodation or are more likely to offer poor accommodation (Page, 1995) and employers are likely to believe the mentally ill are incapable of working effectively (Page, 1995). Fear of mental illness also appears to have increased in the past 40 years (Phelan *et al.*, 2000), and this is the subject of the Controversies in Psychological Science section below.

Jorm (2000) found that members of the public had difficulty in recognising mental disorders correctly, with schizophrenia often mistaken for depression. Patients with depression are often incorrectly described as having a physical disorder (rather than a physiological one).

Misunderstanding of the term schizophrenia is probably the commonest, as a raft of European surveys has shown. Knowledge of aetiology is similarly questionable, with most people believing that depression and schizophrenia are caused by social or environmental stressors. These are important aetiological factors, Jorm argues, but environmental stressors in schizophrenia are triggers rather than causes. The public's view of the medication used to treat mental illness is almost uniformly negative, contrary to the views of clinicians and to evidence from randomised controlled trials showing the relative success of these drugs in reducing symptoms. When the public is asked why their views of drugs are negative, side effects and dependence on the drugs are usually cited. Natural remedies (such as vitamins) are regarded more positively.

Where the public gets information about mental illness is still something of a mystery. One study reported that 33 per cent of people obtained information from a close relative or friend with mental illness. Another study found that 32 per cent of people obtained such information from the media.

Compared with public efforts to improve the public's understanding of cancer and heart disease, information campaigns about mental illness have not been a resounding success or particularly numerous. Campaigns that are run show small but significant improvements in understanding but, as Jorm notes, they are not evaluated in a scientifically sound way. Jorm suggests, however, that targeted campaigns – aimed at specific groups – are quite successful. This provocative review suggests that we have a long way to go before the public's mental health literacy is improved. Educational strategies designed to teach people more about the reality of mental illness, via books, flyers, films and DVDs, for example, lead to short-term improvements in attitude but have no long-term effect (Corrigan *et al.*, 2001; Penn *et al.*, 1999). The greater the prejudice against the mentally ill, the more resistant people are to education. Face-to-face contact is slightly better. When people are confronted with the subject of their prejudice – and realise that they are not violent, unpredictable or inhuman – their attitude becomes more positive (Corrigan *et al.*, 2001). This attitude becomes even more positive when the stigmatized person has been moderately stereotyped (Reinke *et al.*, 2004).

Mental illness – An international perspective

The two manuals used by psychiatrists to diagnose mental disorder are the *Diagnostic and Statistical Manual of Mental Disorders* IV (DSM-IV TR; American Psychiatric Association, 1994) and *International Classification of Diseases* 10 (ICD-10; World Health Organization, 1992). Because these manuals are standard reference works for the diagnosis of mental illness, there is an implication that symptoms can be grouped together to form a disorder in any culture. The DSM-IV TR, for example, lists 350 disorders which should apply across cultures. In a survey of papers submitted to six prestigious

Mental illness – *Continued*

psychiatry journals over a three-year period only 6 per cent of papers came from areas outside Europe and America. This 6 per cent represents 90 per cent of the world's population. Could mental disorder be culture-dependent? Are these diagnostic manuals too Western-based? Might a mental disorder in one culture be classed as normal behaviour in another?

Some clinicians have argued that we cannot apply Western diagnostic criteria such as those in DSM to other cultures (Hinton and Kleinman, 1993). This cultural relativism argues that behaviour considered abnormal in one culture may be considered normal in another. In addition, a behaviour classed as one type of mental disorder in one culture may be classed as a different one in a different culture. These two problems are generic in diagnosing mental illness across cultures. The DSM-IV TR recognises the latter problem in its appendix which contains details of 25 culture-based syndromes. The authors responsible for the DSM and ICD have also attempted to address the problem of cultural relativism by conducting extensive cross-cultural investigations on the generalisability of mental disorder diagnosis. How culture-bound, therefore, are mental disorders? Tanaka-Matsumi and Draguns (1997) have found that depression, for example, is common across most cultures. A World Health Organization (WHO) study of depression in Switzerland, Canada, Japan and Iran (World Health Organization, 1983) found that 76 per cent of individuals diagnosed as depressed exhibited symptoms of sadness, joylessness, anxiety, tension and lack of energy. Levels of guilt, however, showed large variation between cultures. Iran reported the lowest levels (22 per cent of respondents), followed by Japan (45 per cent), Canada (58 per cent) and Switzerland (68 per cent). There was also within-culture variation. For example, the two Japanese cities studied (Nagasaki and Tokyo) showed different degrees of depression, with more core symptoms reported in Nagasaki.

A study of British and Turkish outpatients found that Turkish patients reported more somatic complaints (insomnia, hypochondria) whereas the British patients reported more psychological complaints such as guilt and pessimism (Ulusahin *et al.*, 1994).

Suicidal ideation (thoughts about suicide) and suicide are also symptoms of depression which show cultural variation. In a study of the suicide rates among 15–24-year-olds in a large number of countries including Egypt, Jordan, Kuwait, Syria, the Scandinavian countries, eastern Europe, Japan, Singapore and Sri Lanka, the Arabic states (Egypt, Jordan, etc.) had the lowest suicide rates whereas Scandinavia, eastern Europe and some Asian countries had the highest (Barraclough, 1988). The highest reported rates were for Sri Lanka (47 suicides per 100,000 of the population) and Hungary (38.6 per 100,000). The exact reasons for these high rates are unknown. Some have suggested that the weakening of family structure or religious

values is responsible; others suggest that endemic group violence is responsible in Sri Lanka and a fear of failure is responsible in Hungary, but these are vague, general reasons which could apply to other countries (Jilek-Aal, 1988). Paris (1991) has also cautioned that suicide and suicide attempts fluctuate across space and time and that such fluctuation may not be detected in epidemiological surveys of suicide.

Schizophrenia has been subject to three major cross-cultural studies over 25 years in 20 research centres from 17 countries. The aim of such exhaustive research has been to collect data, standardise the instruments used for measuring schizophrenic symptoms and conduct follow-up assessments (Jablensky, 1989). If different countries have different ways of measuring schizophrenia, for example, then a higher or lower incidence of the disorder may not reflect actual incidence but differences in the ways in which schizophrenia is diagnosed. The 1979 study conducted by the World Health Organization (1979) found that the prognosis (outcome) for schizophrenia was better in developing countries (Colombia, Nigeria, India) than in developed countries (USA, UK, Denmark). Schizophrenia was diagnosed as being more chronic in the most well-educated people, but only in developing countries. Later studies indicated that the outcome for schizophrenia was worse in countries such as India.

One of the most comprehensive cross-cultural studies examined 1,379 schizophrenic patients in 12 centres from 10 countries: Denmark (Aarhus), India (Agra and Chandigarh), Columbia (Cali), Ireland (Dublin), Nigeria (Fbadai), Russia (Moscow), the UK (Nottingham), Japan (Nagasaki), the Czech Republic (Prague) and the USA (Honolulu, Hawaii and Rochester, New York). In each of the countries, the incidence rates were comparable (Jablensky *et al.*, 1992).

A disorder which does present some cross-cultural problems is anxiety (Tseng *et al.*, 1990). Here, there is great cultural variability in terms of the degree of generalised anxiety reported. Tseng *et al.* (1986) asked psychiatrists in Beijing, Tokyo and Honolulu to diagnose the mental disorder of Chinese patients recorded on videotape. The Beijing psychiatrists diagnosed the patients as exhibiting neurasthenia; the others diagnosed adjustment reaction. When Japanese and American psychiatrists were asked to diagnose patients with social phobia, the Japanese psychiatrists showed greater agreement in their diagnosis of Japanese social phobics than did their American counterparts (Tseng *et al.*, 1990).

Results like these suggest that cultural variations exist in the diagnosis of some mental disorders. Perhaps because anxiety is a more vague syndrome than is depression or schizophrenia, it ought not to be surprising that great variation exists between cultures in diagnosing this disorder. When more specific anxiety disorders are examined, such as object phobia, some cross-cultural agreement occurs (Davey, 1992;

▶

Mental illness – *Continued*

Davey *et al.*, 1998). In their study of the nature of object phobia in Japanese, British, American, Scandinavian, Indian, Korean and Hong Kong individuals, Davey *et al.* (1998) reported that there was broad agreement on the stimuli considered phobia-related. This consistency suggests that, at least for some anxiety disorders, there is universality.

Slightly more problematical for diagnostic manuals such as the DSM and ICD are culture-bound syndromes (Simons and Hughes, 1985). Although the DSM-IV TR lists 25 of these, it does not provide any criteria for them. Anorexia, which is not explicitly defined as culture-bound in the DSM-IV TR, seems to predominate in Western countries although there are reports of the disorder appearing in Asia (Lee, 1995). Three culture-bound syndromes are Koro, Taijin Kyofusho and anthropophobia (Tanaka-Matsumi and Draguns, 1997). Koro is found in men in southern China or Southeast Asia and refers to a belief that genitals are withdrawn into the abdomen and a fear of death provoked by a female ghost (Tseng *et al.*, 1992). Taijin Kyofusho is a Japanese disorder similar to social phobia. However, individuals with this disorder have a specific fear of offending others by blushing, emitting offensive odours, staring inappropriately and presenting improper facial expressions (Tanaka-Matsumi, 1979). Anthropophobia seems to be the Chinese equivalent and involves the fear of being looked at.

It seems evident that although there is agreement between cultures about what constitutes a diagnosis for some mental disorders, there is clear variation for others. Anxiety, for example, seems to show the greatest variation, and depression and schizophrenia the least. Furthermore, there are some mental disorders which are culture-bound.

The treatment of mental disorders

The evolution of interventions

Mental disorder and its treatment has a long history. In the past, people suffering from mental disorder have been regarded with awe or fear; others whom we would now probably classify as paranoid schizophrenics were seen as instruments through whom gods or spirits were speaking. More often, they were considered to be occupied by devils or evil spirits and were made to suffer accordingly. The earliest known attempts to treat mental disorders involved trephining, or drilling holes in a person's skull. Presumably, the opening was made to permit evil spirits to leave the victim's head. In prehistoric times, this procedure was performed with a sharp-edged stone; later civilisations, such as the Egyptians, refined the practice. Signs of healing at the edges of the holes in prehistoric skulls indicate that some people survived these operations. An example is seen in Figure 18.1.

Many painful practices were directed at people's presumed possession by evil spirits. Individuals who were thought to be unwilling hosts for evil spirits were subjected to curses or insults designed to persuade the demons to leave. If this approach had no effect, exorcism was tried to make the person's body an unpleasant place for devils to reside. Other rituals included beatings, starving, near-drowning and the drinking of foul-tasting concoctions. The delusional schemes of psychotics often include beliefs of personal guilt and unworthiness. In a society that accepted the notion that there were witches and devils, these people were ready to imagine themselves as evil. They confessed to unspeakable acts of sorcery and welcomed their own persecution and punishment.

Until the eighteenth century, many Europeans accepted the idea that devils and spirits were responsible for peculiar behaviours in some people. But a few people believed

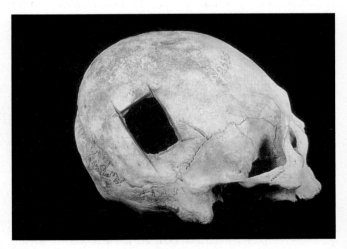

Figure 18.1 Among the earliest biological approaches to the treatment of mental disorders was the ancient practice of trephining, in which a hole was made in the skull to allow evil spirits to escape from the person's head.
Source: Loren McIntyre/Woodfin Camp & Associates, Inc.

that these disorders reflected diseases and that they should be treated medically, with compassion for the victim. Johann Wier, a sixteenth-century physician, was among the first to challenge the practice of witchcraft. He argued that most people who were being tortured and burned for practising witchcraft in fact suffered from mental illness. The Church condemned his writings as heretical and banned them. However, even within the Church some people began to realise that the prevailing beliefs and practices were wrong.

As belief in witchcraft and demonology waned, the clergy, the medical authorities and the general public began to regard people with mental disorders as ill. Torture and persecution eventually ceased. However, the lives of mentally ill people did not necessarily become better. The unfortunate ones were consigned to various asylums established for the care of the mentally ill. Most of these mental institutions were inhumane. Patients were often kept in chains and sometimes wallowed in their own excrement. Those who displayed bizarre catatonic postures or who had fanciful delusions were exhibited to the public for a fee. Many of the treatments designed to cure mental patients were little better than the tortures that had previously been used to drive out evil spirits. Patients were tied up, doused in cold water, bled, made to vomit, spun violently in a rotating chair, and otherwise assaulted. See Figure 18.2.

Mistreatment of the mentally ill did not go unnoticed by humanitarians. A famous and effective early reformer was Philippe Pinel (1745–1826), a French physician. In 1793, Pinel was appointed director of La Bicêtre, a mental hospital in Paris. Pinel believed that most mental patients would respond well to kind treatment. As an experiment, he removed the chains from some of the patients, took them out of dungeons and allowed them to walk about the hospital grounds. The experiment was a

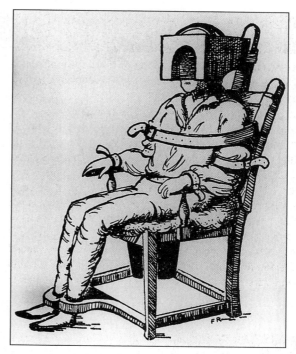

Figure 18.2 The 'tranquillising chair' devised by Benjamin Rush.
Source: © Bettman/Corbis.

remarkable success; an atmosphere of peace and quiet replaced the previous noise, stench and general aura of despair. Many patients were eventually discharged. Pinel's success at La Bicêtre was repeated when he was given charge of Salpêtrière Hospital. Some mentally ill people eventually recover – or at least get much better – without any treatment at all. But if a person was put in a mental institution that existed prior to Pinel's time, they had little chance to show improvement.

Controversies in Psychological Science – How violent are the mentally ill?

The issue

'On Sunday afternoon, September 3, 2006, Wayne Fenton, a prominent schizophrenia expert and an associate director at the National Institute of Mental Health (NIMH) [in the US] was found dead in his office. He had just seen a 19-year-old patient with schizophrenia who later admitted to the police that he had beaten Fenton with his fists'

Source: Friedman, 2006.

On the face of it, this extract from an article by Richard Friedman in the *New England Journal of Medicine* seems to confirm lay opinion: that people with certain types of mental illness are extremely violent. Friedman quotes a National Crime Victimization Survey for 1993 to 1999 showing that, in the US, non-fatal violence was meted out to 12.6 per 1,000 workers from various occupations. In physicians, the number rose to 21.9 per 1,000. In psychiatrists and mental health professionals, the figure was 68.2. The lay view seems to be accurate. But is it?

Controversies in Psychological Science – *Continued*

The evidence

In his review, Friedman cites evidence showing that violence is committed by the mentally ill, but it is rare, and rarer than that committed by those who use drugs and alcohol, for example. Another survey by the NIMH found that patients with schizophrenia, major depression or bipolar disorder were two to three times as likely to commit acts of violence involving physical assault (Swanson, 1994). The lifetime prevalence of violence in people who are seriously mentally ill was 16 per cent compared with 7 per cent for those without mental illness.

But the prevalence is only found in certain types of disorder – those who suffer anxiety rarely show aggression or acts of violence. One study has also found that the incidence of violence in schizophrenic patients discharged into the community and followed up over a year was no different from those with no psychiatric disorder (Steadman *et al.*, 1998).

Conclusion

What is important here is not the mental illness itself, but specific symptoms of that illness – schizophrenic individuals who are paranoid or hear voices commanding them to behave in a certain way are more likely to commit acts of violence than are those without these symptoms.

The development of modern treatment

The modern history of specific treatments for mental disorders probably began with Franz Anton Mesmer (1734–1815), an Austrian physician who practised in Paris in the late eighteenth and early nineteenth centuries. He devised a theory of 'magnetic fluxes', according to which he attempted to effect cures by manipulating iron rods and bottles of chemicals. In reality, he hypnotised his patients and thereby alleviated some of their symptoms. As a result, hypnosis was first known as mesmerism.

In 1815, there were approximately 2,000 individuals institutionalised in mental asylums in England. The number had increased a century later when one hundred or so asylums in England and Wales housed an average of 1,000 patients. In America, at the same time, the number housed was between 1,500 and 3,000. Dr William Black, a nineteenth-century English physician, kept a list of the causes of insanity of those individuals admitted to the Bethlem asylum, the largest madhouse in the UK at the time (it was also known as Bedlam). Figure 18.3 shows an example of one of these lists; it includes some unusual causes, such as 'sudden loss of several cows'.

A French neurologist, Jean Martin Charcot (1825–93), began his investigations of the therapeutic uses of hypnosis when one of his students hypnotised a woman and induced her to display the symptoms of a conversion reaction (hysteria). Charcot examined her and concluded that she was a hysterical patient. The student then woke the woman, and her symptoms vanished. Charcot had previously believed that hysteria had an organic basis, but this experience changed his opinion, and he began investigating its psychological causes.

Just before Freud began private practice, he studied with Charcot in Paris and observed the effects of hypnosis on hysteria. Freud's association with Charcot, and later with Breuer, started him on his life's study of the determinants of personality and the origins of mental illness. He created the practice of psychoanalysis. Some modern psychiatrists and psychologists still use some of his therapeutic methods to treat their clients.

Current treatments: the eclectic approach

Most therapists adopt a general, eclectic approach to the treatment of mental disorders. The **eclectic approach** (from the Greek *eklegein*, to 'single out') involves the therapist using whatever methods they feel will work best for a particular client at a particular time. Such therapists are not strongly wedded to particular theoretical orientations; instead, they seek the particular form of therapy that will best solve a particular client's problems. This often means combining aspects of several different treatment approaches according to a particular client's problem and personal circumstances. For example, Acierno *et al.* (1993) have shown that combinations of therapies are more effective in treating panic disorder than is any one alone.

see activity on mypsychlab

Causes, both Moral and Physical, ascertained in 249 cases.

MORAL		PHYSICAL	
Domestic Grief, Affliction, and Disappointment	7	Intemperance and Debauchery	57
Unfaithfulness, Unkindness, or Intemperance of Wife	6	Bad Company	1
Loss of Situation and Dread of Poverty	7	Masturbation	5
Want of Employment, and sufferings therefrom	6	Fatigue and Over-exertion	3
Reverse of Fortune, Loss of Property, &c.	12	Over-study	6
Loss of Wife or Children	3	Injury to Head	14
Disappointed Affection	3	Disease of Brain	2
Unhappiness at Home	1	Delirium Tremens	1
Erroneous Views in Religion	3	Fever – Typhus. Yellow. Erysipelas. Small-pox.	4
Sudden Shocks, Fright, &c.	29	Epilepsy	14
Jealousy	3	Paralysis	6
Pride	3	Chorea	2
Non-success in Business	1	Injury to Retina	1
Responsibility and over-anxiety	1	Disease of Lungs	3
Sudden Loss of Several Cows	1	⸻ Liver	1
Regret for a Theft	1	Old Age	4
Suicide of a Brother	1	Congenital Deficiency	16
Over-excitement at the Great Exhibition	1		140
	89		

Hereditary Predisposition assigned 20

Figure 18.3 William Black's (1810) list of the causes of insanity.

Types of treatment

Psychoanalysis and psychodynamic therapy

Sigmund Freud is given credit for developing **psychoanalysis** which, as you saw in Chapter 14, is a form of therapy aimed at providing the client with insight into their unconscious motivations and impulses. Freud's theory of personality suggests that unconscious conflicts based on the competing demands of the id (representing biological urges), the superego (representing the moral dictates of society), and the ego (representing reality) often lead to anxiety. The source of these conflicts, according to Freud, can usually be traced back to unacceptable, often sexually based, urges from early childhood: repressed impulses and feelings that lead to conscious anxiety. As Freud (1933, p. 26) explained:

> One of the tasks of psychoanalysis . . . is to lift the veil of amnesia which hides the earliest years of childhood and to bring to conscious memory the manifestations of early infantile sexual life which are contained in them.

The purpose of therapy is to create a setting in which clues about the origins of intrapsychic conflicts are most likely to be revealed by the client. These clues are revealed in clients' dreams, physical problems, memory (or failure to remember certain things), manner of speech, and cognitive and emotional reactions to therapy. Then, by exposing the client to these clues, they will gain insight into the problem.

While the psychoanalyst's primary role is interpretation, the client's main job is to provide the psychoanalyst with something to interpret: descriptions of their fears, anxieties, thoughts or repressed memories. This is not an easy task for the client to accomplish because the client unconsciously invokes one or more defence mechanisms, which, as you recall from Chapter 14, prevent anxiety-provoking memories and ideas from reaching conscious awareness. Together, the psychoanalyst and client work for insight into the client's problems.

Psychoanalytic techniques

Freud used **free association** to encourage the client to speak freely, without censoring possibly embarrassing or socially unacceptable thoughts. Freud achieved this goal in two ways. First, the client was encouraged to report any thoughts or images that came to mind, without worrying about their meaning. Secondly, Freud attempted to minimise any authoritative influence over the client's disclosures by eliminating eye contact. He usually sat in a chair at the head of a couch on which the client reclined.

Among the topics clients are encouraged to discuss are their dreams. Dream interpretation, the evaluation of the underlying meaning of dream content, is a hallmark of psychoanalysis (Freud, 1900). But even dream content is subject to some censoring, according to Freud, so that the analyst must be able to distinguish between the dream's manifest content (the actual images and events that occur within the dream) and latent content (the hidden meaning or significance of the dream). The manifest content masks the latent content because the latent content is anxiety-provoking and causes the person psychological discomfort.

Insight is not achieved quickly, nor do clients always find it easy to disclose private aspects of their personal lives. For example, a client may have to confront the reality of being abused as a child, or of being unloved, or of feeling peculiar, inferior or out of place. Although the client wishes to be cured, they do not look forward to the anxiety and apprehension that may result from recalling painful memories. The client often becomes defensive at some point during therapy, unconsciously attempting to halt further insight by censoring their true feelings: a process Freud called **resistance**.

Over a period of months or even years of therapy sessions taking place as often as several times a week, the client gradually becomes less inhibited, and the discussion begins to drift away from recent events to the more distant shores of early childhood. As the client relives aspects of childhood, they may begin to project powerful attitudes and emotions onto the therapist, a process called **transference**. The client may come to love or hate the therapist with the same intensity of the powerful emotions experienced in childhood towards parents or siblings.

Originally, Freud thought of transference as an impediment to therapy, a distraction from the real issues at hand. But he soon realised that the experience of transference was essential to the success of therapy (Erdelyi, 1985). Whereas free association uncovers many of the relevant events and facts of the client's life, transference provides the means for reliving significant early experiences. The therapist contributes to this experience by becoming a substitute for the real players in the client's life and so becomes a tool for illuminating the conflicts of the unconscious. Freud reasoned that the analyst, being human too, could just as easily project his or her emotions onto the client, a process he called **counter-transference**. Unlike transference, Freud believed counter-transference to be unhealthy and undesirable. To be effective, the analyst must remain emotionally detached and objective in their appraisal of the client's disclosures. For this reason, he argued that the analyst, in order to understand their own unconscious conflicts, should undergo complete analysis with another therapist.

Modern psychodynamic therapy

Psychoanalysis is now often referred to as **psychodynamic therapy** to reflect differences between modern psychoanalytic approaches and the original form of Freudian psychoanalysis. For example, although modern forms of psychodynamic therapies still focus on achieving insight into the unconscious, they tend to place less emphasis on sexual factors during development and more upon social and interpersonal experiences. Contemporary therapists also are more likely to address concerns and issues in the client's present life than to examine childhood experiences exclusively.

Modern psychodynamic therapists also view the ego as playing a more active role in influencing a person's thoughts and actions. Instead of viewing the ego as functioning merely to seek ways to satisfy the demands of the id and superego, they believe it to be a proactive component in one's overall psychological functioning. In other words, compared with Freud, modern psychodynamic therapists see the ego as having more control over the psyche. Thus, people receiving psychodynamic therapy are seen as being less constrained by the mind's unconscious forces than Freud thought them to be.

One modern form of psychodynamic therapy, time-limited therapy, takes 25–30 sessions with the therapist to complete (Strupp, 1993). The goal of time-limited therapy is to understand and improve the client's interpersonal skills through interpretation of transference processes. This therapy is based on Freud's belief that our early experiences with others influence the dynamics of our current relationships. Time-limited therapy focuses on the schemata that a client has about interpersonal relationships and attempts to modify those that are incorrect or that otherwise prevent the client from developing fulfilling relationships with others.

Evaluation

Evaluating the effectiveness of psychoanalysis or psychodynamic therapy is difficult because only a small proportion of people with mental disorders qualify for this method of treatment. To participate in this kind of therapy, a client must be intelligent, articulate and motivated enough to spend three or more hours a week working hard to uncover unconscious conflicts. In addition, they must be able to afford the therapist's fees, which are high. These qualifications rule out most psychotics, as well as people who lack the time or money to devote to such a long-term project. Furthermore, many people who enter this kind of therapy become dissatisfied with their progress and leave. In other cases, the therapist encourages a client to leave if they decide that the client is not cooperating fully. Thus, those who actually complete a course of therapy do not constitute a random sample, and we cannot conclude that this kind of therapy works just because a high percentage of this group is happy with the results. Those who have dropped out ought also to be counted.

Another problem in evaluating psychoanalysis and psychodynamic therapy is that therapists have a way to 'explain' their failures: they can blame them on the client (Eysenck, 1985). If the client appears to accept an insight into their behaviour but the behaviour does not change, the insight is said to be merely 'intellectual'. This escape clause makes the argument for the importance of insight completely circular and, therefore, illogical: if the client gets better, the improvement is due to insight; but if the client's behaviour remains unchanged, real (as opposed to 'intellectual') insight did not occur.

Humanistic therapies

Client-centred therapy

In the 1940s, Carl Rogers (1902–87) developed the first **humanistic therapy**, creating a major alternative to psychoanalysis. The aim of humanistic therapy is to provide the client with a greater understanding of their unique potential for personal growth and self-actualisation. Humanistic therapies proceed from the assumption that people are good and have innate worth. Psychological problems reflect some type of blocking of one's potential for personal growth; humanistic therapy aims to realise this potential.

Rogers found the formalism of psychoanalysis too confining and its emphasis on intrapsychic conflict too pessimistic (Tobin, 1991). His discontent led him to develop his own theory of personality, abnormal behaviour and therapy. His **client-centred therapy** is so named because of the respect given the client during therapy: the client decides what to talk about without direction or judgement from the therapist. The client takes ultimate responsibility for resolving the client's problems. The client, not a method or theory, is the focus of the therapy.

Rogers believed that the cause of many psychological problems can be traced to people's perceptions of themselves as they actually are (their real selves) as differing from the people they would like to be (their ideal selves). Rogers called this discrepancy between the real and the ideal perceptions of the self **incongruence**. The goal of client-centred therapy is to reduce incongruence by fostering experiences that will make attainment of the ideal self possible. Because the client's and not the therapist's thoughts direct the course of therapy, the therapist strives to make those thoughts, perceptions and feelings more noticeable to the client. This is frequently done through reflection, sensitive rephrasing or mirroring of the client's statements. For example:

> *Client*: I get so frustrated at my parents. They just don't understand how I feel. They don't know what it's like to be me.
>
> *Therapist*: You seem to be saying that the things that are important to you aren't very important to your parents. You'd like them now and then to see things from your perspective.

By reflecting the concerns of the client, the therapist demonstrates empathy, or the ability to perceive the world from another's viewpoint. The establishment of empathy is key in encouraging the client to deal with the incongruence between the real and the ideal selves.

For Rogers (1951), the 'worth and significance of the individual' is a basic ground rule of therapy. This theme is represented in therapy through **unconditional positive regard**, in which the therapist tries to convey to the client that his or her worth as a human being is not dependent on anything they think, do or feel.

In client-centred therapy, the therapist totally and unconditionally accepts the client and approves of them as a person so that the client can come to understand that their feelings are worthwhile and important. Once the client begins to pay attention to these feelings, a self-healing process begins. For example, a client usually has difficulty at first expressing feelings verbally. The therapist tries to understand the feelings underlying the client's confused state and to help them put those feelings into words. Through this process, the client learns to understand and heed their own drive towards self-actualisation. Consider the following example:

Alice: I was thinking about this business of standards. I somehow developed a sort of knack, I guess, of – well – habit – of trying to make people feel at ease around me, or to make things go along smoothly . . .

Counsellor: In other words, what you did was always in the direction of trying to keep things smooth and to make other people feel better and to smooth the situation.

A: Yes. I think that's what it was. Now the reason why I did it probably was – I mean, not that I was a good little Samaritan going around making other people happy, but that was probably the role that felt easiest for me to play. I'd been doing it around the home so much. I just didn't stand up for my own convictions, until I don't know whether I have any convictions to stand up for.

C: You feel that for a long time you've been playing the role of kind of smoothing out the frictions or differences or what not . . .

A: M-hum.

C: Rather than having any opinion or reaction of your own in the situation. Is that it?

A: That's it. Or that I haven't been really honestly being myself, or actually knowing what my real self is, and that I've been just playing a sort of false role. Whatever role no one else was playing, and that needed to be played at the time, I'd try to fill it in.

Source: Rogers (1951) pp. 152–3.

As this example illustrates, in Rogers's view, the therapist should not manipulate events but should create conditions under which the client can make their own decisions independently.

Evaluation

Unlike many other clinicians, who prefer to rely on their own judgements concerning the effectiveness of their techniques, Rogers himself stimulated a considerable amount of research on the effectiveness of client-centred therapy. He recorded therapeutic sessions so that various techniques could be evaluated. One researcher, Truax (1966), obtained permission from Rogers (and his clients) to record some therapy sessions, and he classified the statements made by the clients into several categories. One of the categories included statements of improving mental health, such as 'I'm feeling better lately' or 'I don't feel as depressed as I used to'. After each of the patients' statements, Truax noted Rogers's reaction to see whether he gave a positive response. Typical positive responses were 'Oh, really? Tell me more' or 'Uh-huh. That's nice' or just a friendly 'Mm'. Truax found that of the eight categories of client statements, only those that indicated progress were regularly followed by a positive response from Rogers. Not surprisingly, during their therapy, the clients made more and more statements indicating progress.

This study attests to the power of social reinforcement and its occurrence in unexpected places. Rogers was an effective and conscientious psychotherapist, but he had not intended to single out and reinforce his clients' realistic expressions of progress in therapy. (Of course, he did not uncritically reinforce exaggerated or unrealistic positive statements.) This finding does not discredit client-centred therapy. Rogers simply adopted a very effective strategy for altering a person's behaviour. He used to refer to his therapy as non-directive; however, when he realised that he was reinforcing positive statements, he stopped referring to it as non-directive because it obviously was not.

Gestalt therapy

The development of client-centred therapy owes much to its founder's disenchantment with classical psychoanalysis. For much the same reason, Fritz Perls (1893–1970), although trained in Freudian techniques, disengaged himself from orthodox psychoanalysis and founded gestalt therapy (Perls, 1969). **Gestalt therapy** emphasises the unity of mind and body by teaching the client to 'get in touch' with bodily sensations and emotional feelings long hidden from awareness. Gestalt therapy, which bears no relation to the perception school of the same name which we described in Chapter 6, places exclusive emphasis upon present experience – not on the past – and the gestalt therapist will often be quite confrontational, challenging the client to deal honestly with their emotions.

The therapist often uses the empty chair technique, in which the client imagines that they are talking to someone sitting in the chair beside them. For example, a woman may be asked to say the things that she had always wanted to say to her deceased father but did not while he was alive. The empty chair technique allows her to experience in the here and now the feelings and perceptions that she may have suppressed while her father was alive. It also allows her to express these feelings and to gain insight into how they have influenced her perception of herself and her world. This technique derives from Perls's belief that, for all of us, our memories, fears and feelings of guilt affect our relationships with others.

The gestalt therapist also encourages the client to gain a better understanding of their feelings by talking to their self (to different parts of their personality) and to inanimate objects. Any attempt by the client to avoid the reality of their situation is challenged by the therapist, who constantly attempts to keep the client's attention focused on present problems and tries to guide the client towards an honest confrontation with these problems. Perls argued, 'In the safe emergency of the therapeutic situation, the neurotic discovers that the world does not fall to pieces if he or she gets angry, sexy, joyous, mournful' (1967, p. 331).

Evaluation

Like psychoanalysis and client-centred therapy, gestalt therapy is inappropriate for serious problems such as psychoses. All three therapies are most effective for people who are motivated enough to want to change and who are intelligent enough to be able to gain some insight concerning their problems. Some of these problems include coping with everyday stressors as well as experiencing excessive anxiety and fear.

Behavioural and cognitive behavioural therapies

The fundamental assumption made by behavioural therapists is that people learn maladaptive or self-defeating behaviour in the same way as they learn adaptive behaviour. Undesirable behaviour, such as nail-biting or alcohol abuse, is the problem, not just a reflection of the problem. The methods that behavioural therapists use to induce behaviour change are extensions of classical and operant conditioning principles and work quite successfully.

Remember from Chapter 7 that, in classical conditioning, a previously neutral stimulus (ultimately the conditional stimulus, CS) comes to elicit the same response as a stimulus (unconditional stimulus, UCS) that naturally elicits that response because the CS reliably predicts the UCS. According to Joseph Wolpe (1958), one of the founders of behavioural therapy, many of our everyday fears and anxieties become associated with neutral stimuli through coincidence. Going to the dentist may evoke fear because the last time that you went you were not given enough anaesthetic and the drilling hurt. Although the dental surgery is usually not painful, you associate the dentist with pain because of your past experience. The next sections describe some of the more specific behavioural and cognitive behavioural approaches.

Systematic desensitisation

One behavioural therapy technique, developed by Wolpe, has been especially successful in eliminating some kinds of fear and phobia. This technique, called **systematic desensitisation**, is designed to remove the unpleasant emotional response produced by the feared object or situation and replace it with an incompatible one – relaxation.

The client is first trained to achieve complete relaxation. The essential task is to learn to respond quickly to suggestions to feel relaxed and peaceful so that these suggestions can elicit an immediate relaxation response. Next, client and therapist construct a hierarchy of anxiety-related stimuli.

Finally, the conditional stimuli (fear-eliciting situations) are paired with stimuli that elicit the learned relaxation response. For example, a person with a fear of spiders is instructed to relax and then to imagine hearing from a neighbour that she saw a spider in her garage. If the client reports no anxiety, they are instructed to move to the next item in the hierarchy and to imagine hearing a neighbour say that there is a tiny spider across the street; and so on. Whenever the client begins feeling anxious, they signal to the therapist with some predetermined gesture such as raising a finger. The therapist instructs the client to relax and, if necessary, describes a less threatening scene. The client is not permitted to feel severe anxiety at any time. Gradually, over a series of sessions (the average is 11), the client is able to get through the entire list, vicariously experiencing even the most feared encounters.

Scientific evaluations of systematic desensitisation have been positive, and several experiments have found that all elements of the procedure are necessary for its success (Emmelkamp, 1994). For example, a person will not get rid of a phobia merely by participating in relaxation training or by constructing hierarchies of fear-producing situations. Only pairings of the anxiety-producing stimuli with instructions to relax will reduce the fear.

Whereas practitioners of systematic desensitisation are careful not to permit their clients to become too anxious, practitioners of a procedure called **flooding** attempt to rid their clients of their fears by arousing them intensely until their responses diminish through habituation and they learn that nothing bad happens. The therapist describes, as graphically as possible, the most frightening encounters possible with the object of a client's phobia. The client tries to imagine the encounter and to experience intense fear (thereby 'flooding' the client's mind with anxious thoughts). In some cases, the client actually encounters the object of their fear, in which case the treatment is called *in vivo* (live) **implosion therapy**. Of course, the client is protected from any adverse effects of the encounter (or the encounter is imaginary), so there are no dangerous consequences. Eventually, the fear response begins to subside, and the client learns that even the worst imaginable encounter can become tolerable. In a sense, the client learns not to fear their own anxiety attack, and avoidance responses begin to extinguish.

Aversion therapy

In **aversion therapy**, a negative reaction to a neutral stimulus is caused by pairing it with an aversive stimulus (UCS). Aversion therapy attempts to establish an unpleasant response (such as a feeling of fear or disgust) to the object that produces the undesired behaviour. For example, a person with a fetish for women's shoes might be given painful electrical shocks while viewing colour slides of women's shoes. Aversion therapy has also been used to treat drinking, smoking, transvestism, exhibitionism and overeating. This technique has been shown to be moderately effective (Marshall *et al.*, 1991). However, because the method involves pain or nausea, the client's participation must be voluntary, and the method should be employed only if other approaches fail or are impractical.

The use of aversive methods raises ethical issues, particularly when the individual is so severely impaired that they are unable to give informed consent to a particular therapeutic procedure. It would seem reasonable that aversive methods involving stimuli such as electric shock should be used as the last resort. In a method called covert sensitisation, instead of experiencing a punishing stimulus after performing a behaviour, the client imagines that they are performing an undesirable behaviour and then imagines receiving an aversive stimulus.

Behaviour modification

Behaviour modification, a general term describing therapy based on operant conditioning principles (see Chapter 7), involves altering maladaptive behaviour by rearranging the contingencies between behaviour and its consequences. Increases in desirable behaviour can be brought about through either positive or negative reinforcement, and undesirable behaviour can be reduced through either extinction or punishment.

In its infancy, behaviour modification was applied chiefly to patients with schizophrenia (described in detail later) and the mentally retarded (Lindsley, 1956; Ayllon and Azrin, 1968; Neisworth and Madle, 1982). In the past three decades, however, use of operant conditioning principles has been extended to a wide array of behaviours and circumstances, for example weight management, anorexia nervosa, bed-wetting, smoking, and compliance with medical regimens (Kazdin, 1994).

Token economies

The behaviour-analytic approach has been used on a large scale in mental institutions with generally good success. Residents are often asked to do chores to engage them in active participation in their environment. In some instances, other specific behaviours are also targeted as desirable and therapeutic, such as helping residents who have more severe problems. To promote these social behaviours, therapists have designed **token economies**. A list of tasks is compiled, and residents receive tokens as rewards for performing the tasks; later, they can exchange these tokens for snacks, other desired articles or various privileges. The tokens become conditioned reinforcers for desirable and appropriate behaviours. The amount of time spent performing the desirable behaviours was high

when reinforcement contingencies were imposed and low when they were not.

Although token economies are based on a simple principle, they are very difficult to implement. A mental institution includes patients, caretakers, housekeeping staff and professional staff. If a token economy is to be effective, all staff members who deal with residents must learn how the system works; ideally, they should also understand and agree with its underlying principles. A token economy can easily be sabotaged by a few people who believe that the system is foolish, wrong or in some way threatening to themselves. If these obstacles can be overcome, token economies work very well.

Modelling

Humans (and many other animals) have the ability to learn without directly experiencing an event. People can imitate the behaviour of other people, watching what they do and, if the conditions are appropriate, performing the same behaviour. This capability provides the basis for the technique of **modelling**. Behaviour therapists have found that clients can make much better progress when they have access to a model providing examples of successful behaviours to imitate.

Social skills training

With social skills training, the client is taught to behave in a desirable and socially appropriate way. They might do this by engaging in **assertiveness training**, which teaches the client to be more direct about their feelings (Oltmans and Emery, 1998). A part of assertiveness training might be **role-playing**, in which the client is taught to act out or rehearse social skills by adopting the identity of another, socially skilled person.

Cognitive behavioural therapy

The first attempts at developing psychotherapies based on altering or manipulating cognitive processes emerged during the 1970s. These attempts were undertaken by behavioural therapists who suspected that maladaptive behaviour, or, for that matter, adaptive behaviour, could be due to more than only environmental variables. They began exploring how their clients' thoughts, perceptions, expectations and self-statements might interact with environmental factors in the development and maintenance of maladaptive behaviour.

The focus of **cognitive behavioural therapy** (CBT) is on changing the client's maladaptive thoughts, beliefs and perceptions. Like behaviour therapists – and unlike most insight psychotherapists – cognitive behaviour therapists are not particularly interested in events that occurred in the client's childhood. They are interested in the here and now and in altering the client's behaviour so that it becomes more functional. Although they employ many methods used by behavioural therapists, they believe that when behaviours change, they do so because of changes in cognitive processes.

There are many ways in which CBT can be applied to mental disorder. Attribution retraining, for example, involves retraining the client to alter their perception of causes of events or behaviour (attributions are perceived causes). One way in which this can be achieved is by requesting the client to adopt a more scientific approach to their beliefs. For example, it is common in depression for a depressed person to attribute causes for failure to themselves but to attribute successes to others. Attribution retraining should encourage the client to change these 'faulty' attributions and make them more realistic. One form of CBT designed to treat depression requires the patient to assess whether their view of themselves and others is distorted based on a considered analysis of their lives. This approach, based on the clinical work of Beck (1967, 1976; Beck and Emery, 1985), is considered in the section on depression below (see p. 827).

Another CBT approach, **rational-emotive therapy**, was developed in the 1950s by Albert Ellis, a clinical psychologist, and is based on the belief that psychological problems are caused by how people think about upsetting events and situations. In contrast to the other forms of CBT, rational-emotive therapy did not grow out of the tradition of behaviour therapy. Ellis asserts that psychological problems are the result of faulty cognitions; therapy is therefore aimed at changing people's beliefs. Rational-emotive therapy is highly directive and confrontational. The therapist tells their clients what they are doing wrong and how they should change.

According to Ellis and his followers, emotions are the products of cognition. A significant activating event (A) is followed by a highly charged emotional consequence (C), but it is not correct to say that A has caused C. Rather, C is a result of the person's belief system (B).

Therefore, inappropriate emotions (such as depression, guilt and anxiety) can be abolished only if a change occurs in the person's belief system. It is the task of the rational-emotive therapist to dispute the person's beliefs and to convince them that those beliefs are inappropriate. Ellis tries to show his clients that irrational beliefs are impossible to satisfy, that they make little logical sense, and that adhering to them creates needless anxiety, self-blame and self-doubt. The following are examples of the kinds of ideas that Ellis (1973), pp. 152–3 believes to be irrational:

> The idea that it is a necessity for an adult to be loved or approved by virtually every significant person in the community.

> The idea that one should be thoroughly competent, adequate, and goal-oriented in all possible respects if one is to consider oneself as having worth.

> The idea that human unhappiness is externally caused and that people have little or no ability to control their lives.

> The idea that one's past is an all-important determinant of one's present behaviour.

> The idea that there is invariably a right, precise, and perfect solution to human problems and that it is catastrophic if this perfect solution is not found.

In a review of research evaluating the effectiveness of rational-emotive therapy, Haaga and Davison (1989) concluded that the method has been shown to reduce general anxiety, test anxiety and unassertiveness. Rational-emotive therapy has appeal and potential usefulness for those who can enjoy and profit from intellectual teaching and argumentation. The people who are likely to benefit most from this form of therapy are those who are self-demanding and who feel guilty for not living up to their own standards of perfection. People with serious anxiety disorders or with severe thought disorders, such as schizophrenia and other psychoses, are unlikely to respond to an intellectual analysis of their problems.

Many therapists who adopt an eclectic approach use some of the techniques of rational-emotive therapy with some of their clients. In its advocacy of rationality and its eschewing of superstition, the therapy proposes a common-sense approach to living. However, many psychotherapists disagree with Ellis's denial of the importance of empathy in the relationship between therapist and client.

Of course, all of the treatments described here are examples of psychology 'in action'. However, two recent cognitive-behavioural approaches to treatment are novel enough to warrant some closer attention. One of these you will find in the section on phobia. The other is an approach designed to reduce trauma and this is the topic of the Psychology in Action section below.

Evaluation

Psychotherapists of traditional orientations have criticised behavioural therapy for its focus on the symptoms of a psychological problem to the exclusion of its root causes. Some psychoanalysts even argue that treatment of just the symptoms is dangerous. In their view, the removal of one symptom of an intrapsychic conflict will simply produce another, perhaps more serious, symptom through a process called **symptom substitution**.

There is little evidence that symptom substitution occurs. It is true that many people's behavioural problems are caused by conditions that existed in the past, and often these problems become self-perpetuating. Behavioural therapy can, in many cases, eliminate the problem behaviour without delving into the past. For example, a child may, for one reason or another, begin wetting the bed. The nightly awakening irritates the parents, who must change the bed sheets and the child's pyjamas. The disturbance often disrupts family relationships. The child develops feelings of guilt and insecurity and wets the bed more often. Instead of analysing the sources of family conflict, a therapist who uses behavioural therapy would install a device in the child's bed that rings a bell when they begin to urinate. The child awakens and goes to the bathroom to urinate and soon ceases to wet the bed. The elimination of bed-wetting causes rapid improvement in the child's self-esteem and in the entire family relationship. Symptom substitution does not appear to occur (Baker, 1969).

Although cognitive behavioural therapists believe in the importance of unobservable constructs such as feelings, thoughts and perceptions, they do not believe that good therapeutic results can be achieved by focusing on cognitions alone. They, like their behaviour-analytic colleagues, insist that it is not enough to have their clients introspect and analyse their thought patterns. Instead, therapists must help clients to change their behaviour. Behavioural changes can cause cognitive changes. For example, when a client observes that they are now engaging in fewer maladaptive behaviours and more adaptive behaviours, the client's self-perceptions and self-esteem are bound to change as a result. Therapy is more effective when attention is paid to cognitions as well as to behaviours.

Psychology in action – How instructions to express reduce distress

Imagine having experienced severe distress or trauma. You may have been physically attacked, robbed or sexually assaulted. Anecdotal evidence suggests that it is best to talk about these events to another person – this allows you to express your feelings about the event that you had previously kept to yourself. It is a form of catharsis, people will say. They might be right.

A novel medicine treatment for trauma has been emotional disclosure (ED) through expressive writing. ED involves asking an individual who has suffered severe trauma or distress to express how they feel about the distress or trauma by writing about it and to write or think about why they feel in the way that they do. This ostensibly simple technique has been found to improve coping, physical health, emotional health and immune system functioning in extremely distressed individuals (Smyth, 1998).

The pioneers of this technique, James Pennebaker and his colleagues (Pennebaker *et al.*, 1988; Pennebaker and Francis, 1996; Pennebaker, 1997), have published several studies showing that when distressed individuals are asked to write down their thoughts and express their emotions, these individuals required fewer visits from the doctor than did those who wrote about trivial topics. Individuals also showed an improvement in their immune system functioning. The participants in these studies were people suffering real distress – Holocaust survivors, the bereaved and the recently unemployed.

Replications by different groups are positive, but mixed. Some improvement in physical health beyond the 'treatment' period has been reported (Lepore, 1997) and survivors of trauma who create narratives about their distress feel better than those who do not (Foa *et al.*, 1995). Arthritic patients who wrote about the emotionally negative aspects of their illness saw an improvement in their condition (Kelley *et al.*, 1997). Sloan and Marx (2004) randomly assigned 49 women

who reported having experienced at least one traumatic event and who showed at least moderate levels of post-traumatic stress disorder to a disclosure condition – where they wrote about a traumatic event in prose as emotionally as possible – or a control condition where no writing occurred. Participants in the disclosure condition reported fewer psychological and physical symptoms a month after testing. The only improvement that was 'clinically' significant, however, was a reduction in depressive symptoms.

A study investigating the effects of ED in patients suffering serious illness found that it had little effect in reducing distress but patients who had little social contact with others or who found that the opportunities for expressing emotions to others were limited, benefited greatly from the process. Zakowski *et al.* (2004) randomly assigned 104 gynaecological and prostate cancer patients to an ED condition, where patients wrote about their trauma for 20 minutes a day for three days, or a non-ED condition (writing about a non-emotional topic). Those in the ED condition who had little opportunity for expressing emotion in social contexts benefited significantly from the ability to write about their illness. The lack of a reduction in stress is comparable to findings from studies of breast cancer which report similarly negative findings (Stanton and Danoff-Burg, 2002). The authors suggest that the benefits of writing in cancer patients might be better revealed in more objective, physical measures rather than subjective, self-report measures.

Some researchers have hypothesised that the benefits of expressive writing arise from the changes in thinking that such writing encourages (Pennebaker, 1997). When individuals write about cause and effect in their expressive writing and show insight into their distress, physical and psychological health improves – their thoughts become more methodically organised (Pennebaker *et al.*, 1997).

Psychology in action – *Continued*

Writing provides an outlet for the negative thoughts and feelings that the writer may be feeling but which they may want to inhibit. That such thoughts might impair day-to-day performance has been shown in some studies of working memory which, as you saw in Chapter 8, allows the brief storage of material for immediate manipulation. Working memory has a limited capacity – irrelevant events and stimuli can impair the action of working memory because attention has to be divided among different tasks. So, ignoring thoughts about a stressful or traumatic event requires paying attention to them in order to inhibit their appearance. The intrusive thoughts involve directing attention to them which takes away resources from other tasks that require working memory.

Research has found that undergraduates who wrote about their stressful thoughts and feelings on entering university showed significantly better working memory performance at the end of the experiment (Klein and Boals, 2001). More 'cognitive' than 'emotion' words were used at a later session (compared with earlier sessions). The researchers suggest that this supports Smyth's (1998) contention that if writing moderates health by changing cognition, changes in tests measuring cognition should be closely associated with the writing process. In a second experiment, students were asked to write about intrusive negative thoughts. They showed significant improvements in working memory than did those who wrote about a positive event or a trivial one.

This last finding suggests that the improvements may be due to the removal of intrusive negative thoughts, rather than intrusive thoughts per se (positive thoughts, for example, which may have been on people's minds, did not place significant strains on working memory). Of course, this study focused on one type of working memory task and did not measure health outcomes, but the authors hypothesise that the improvements in health as a result of expressive writing may be due to the improvements in working memory capacity.

Other forms of psychotherapy

Group therapy

Group psychotherapy, in which two or more clients meet simultaneously with a therapist to discuss problems, became common during the Second World War. The stresses of combat produced psychological problems in many members of the armed forces, and the demand for psychotherapists greatly exceeded the supply. What began as an economic necessity became an institution once the effectiveness of group treatment was recognised.

Because most psychological problems involve interactions with other people, treating these problems in a group setting may be worthwhile. Group therapy provides four advantages that are not found in individual therapy:

1 The group setting permits the therapist to observe and interpret actual interactions without having to rely on clients' descriptions, which may be selective or faulty.

2 A group can bring social pressure to bear on the behaviours of its members. If a person receives similar comments about their behaviour from all the members of a group, the message is often more convincing than if a psychotherapist delivers the same comments in a private session.

3 The process of seeing the causes of maladaptive behaviour in other people often helps a person to gain insight into their own problems. People can often learn from the mistakes of others.

4 Knowing that other people have problems similar to one's own can bring comfort and relief. People discover that they are not alone.

The structure of group therapy sessions can vary widely. Some sessions are little more than lectures, in which the therapist presents information about a problem common to all members of the group, followed by discussion. For example, in a case involving a person with severe mental or physical illness, the therapist explains to family members the nature, treatment and possible outcomes of the disorder. Then the therapist answers questions and allows people to share their feelings about what the illness has done to their family. Other groups are simply efficient ways to treat several clients at the same time. Most types of group therapy involve interactions among the participants.

Family therapy and couples therapy

In **family therapy**, a therapist meets with (usually) all the members of a client's family and analyses the ways in which individuals interact. The therapist attempts to get family members to talk to each other instead of addressing all comments and questions to them. As much as possible, the family therapist tries to collect data about the interactions – how individuals sit in relation to each other, who interrupts whom, who looks at whom before speaking – in order to infer the nature of interrelationships within the family. For example, there may be barriers between certain family members; perhaps a father is unable to communicate with one of his children. Or two or more family members may be so dependent on each other that they cannot function independently; they constantly seek each other's approval and, through overdependence, make each other miserable.

After inferring the family structure, the therapist attempts to restructure it by replacing maladaptive interactions with more effective, functional ones. The therapist suggests that perhaps all members of the family must change if the client is to make real improvement. They get family members to 'actualise' their transactional patterns – to act out their everyday relationships – so that the maladaptive interactions will show themselves. Restructuring techniques include forming temporary alliances between the therapist and one or more of the family members, increasing tension in order to trigger changes in unstable structures, assigning explicit tasks and homework to family members (for example, making them interact with other members), and providing general support, education and guidance. Sometimes, the therapist visits the family at home. For example, if a child in a family refuses to eat, the therapist will visit during a mealtime in order to see the problem acted out as explicitly as possible.

Behavioural therapists have also applied their methods of analysis and treatment to families. This approach focuses on the social environment provided by the family and on the ways in which family members reinforce or punish each other's behaviour. The strategy is to identify the maladaptive behaviours of the individuals and the ways these behaviours are inadvertently reinforced by the rest of the family. Then the therapist helps the family members find ways to increase positive exchanges and reinforce each other's adaptive behaviours. A careful analysis of the social dynamics of a family often reveals that changes need to be made not in the individual showing the most maladaptive behaviours but in the other members of the family.

All couples will find that they disagree on some important issues. These disagreements necessarily lead to conflicts. For example, they may have to decide whether to move to accommodate the career of one of the partners, they will have to decide how to spend their money, and they will have to decide how to allocate household chores. Their ability to resolve conflict is one of the most important factors affecting the quality and durability of their relationship (Schwartz and Schwartz, 1980).

Controversies in Psychological Science – Does psychotherapy work?

The issue

Evaluation of therapies and therapists is an important issue. It has received much attention, but almost everyone who is involved agrees that too little is known about the efficacy of psychotherapeutic methods, partly because psychotherapeutic effectiveness is difficult to study (Vervaeke and Emmelkamp, 1998). The most well-known psychotherapies, their goals and methods of intervention are summarised in Table 18.2. Given that there are at least 400 types of therapy and over 150 classified mental disorders (Garfield and Bergin, 1994), achieving some consistency across studies is difficult.

Several other factors make it extremely difficult to evaluate the effectiveness of a particular form of therapy or an individual therapist. These include measurement – there are no easily applied, commonly agreed criteria for mental health; and self-selection – clients choose whether to enter therapy, what type of therapy to engage in and how long to stay in therapy, which makes it nearly impossible to establish either a stable sample population or a control group. Self-selection means that certain kinds of people are more likely than others to enter a particular therapy and stick with it, which produces a biased sample. Lack of a stable sample and of a control group makes it difficult to compare the effectiveness of various kinds of therapy. Many patients change therapists or leave therapy altogether. What conclusions can we make about the effectiveness of a therapy by looking only at the progress made by the clients who remain with it?

Yet another problem with scientific evaluation of psychotherapy is the question of an appropriate control group. The effects of therapeutic drugs must be determined through comparison with the effects of placebos (innocuous pills that have no effects on people's thoughts and behaviour) to be sure that the improvement has not occurred merely because the patient thinks that a pill has done some good. Placebo effects can also occur in psychotherapy: people know that they are being treated and get better because they believe that the treatment should lead to improvement. Given these problems, what can we say about the efficacy of psychotherapy?

The evidence

In a pioneering, controversial paper on psychotherapeutic evaluation, Eysenck (1952) examined 19 studies assessing the effectiveness of psychotherapy. He reported that of the people who remained in psychoanalysis as long as their therapists thought they should, 66 per cent showed improvement. Similarly, 64 per cent of patients treated eclectically showed an improvement. However, 72 per cent of patients who were treated only custodially (receiving no psychotherapy) in institutions showed improvement. In other words, people got better just as fast by themselves as they did in therapy.

Subsequent studies were not much more supportive. Some investigators, including Eysenck, concluded that it was unethical to charge a person for psychotherapy because there was little scientific evidence for its effectiveness. Many forms of

Controversies in Psychological Science – *Continued*

Table 18.2 Summary of the basic assumptions, goals and methods involved in traditional forms of psychotherapy

Type of therapy	Basic assumptions	Primary goals	Typical method of analysis or intervention
Psychoanalysis	Behaviour is motivated by intrapsychic conflict and biological urges	To discover the sources of conflict and resolve them through insight	Free association, dream interpretation, interpretation of transference, resistance, memory, and manner of speech
Psychodynamic	Behaviour is motivated by both unconscious forces and interpersonal experiences	To understand and improve interpersonal skills	Interpretation of transference and modification of client's inappropriate schemata about interpersonal relationships
Humanistic and gestalt	People are good and have innate worth	To promote personal growth and self-actualisation and to enhance client's awareness of bodily sensations and feelings	Reduce incongruence through reflection, empathy, unconditional positive regard and techniques to enhance personal awareness and feelings of self-worth
Behavioural and cognitive behavioural	Behaviour is controlled largely by environmental contingencies, people's perception of them, or their combination	To change maladaptive behaviour and thinking patterns	Manipulate environmental variables, restructure thinking patterns and correct faulty thinking or irrational beliefs
Family/couples	Problems in relationships entail everybody involved in them	To discover how interactions influence problems in individual functioning	Analysis of patterns of family/couple's interaction and how others reinforce maladaptive and adaptive thinking and behaving

therapy have never been evaluated objectively because their practitioners are convinced that the method works and deem objective confirmation unnecessary.

Figure 18.4 summarises Smith *et al.*'s (1980) well-known meta-analysis of 475 studies comparing the outcome effectiveness of psychodynamic, gestalt, client-centred, systematic desensitisation, behaviour modification and cognitive behavioural therapies. Relative to no therapy, each of these therapies was shown to be superior in helping people with their problems. As you can see, behavioural and cognitive therapies tended to exceed others in effectiveness, although these differences were often small. More recent research has confirmed these results, indicating that almost all people who enter behavioural or cognitive behavioural therapy tend to improve with regard to the reason that brought them to therapy (Robinson *et al.*, 1990).

Several studies have suggested that the ability to form understanding, warm and empathetic relationships is one of the most important traits that distinguish an effective therapist from an ineffective one (Beutler *et al.*, 1994). For example,

Strupp and Hadley (1979) enlisted a group of lecturers on the basis of their reputation as warm, trustworthy, empathetic individuals. The lecturers (from the departments of English, history, mathematics and philosophy) were asked to hold weekly counselling sessions for students with psychological difficulties. Another group of students was assigned to professional psychotherapists, both psychologists and psychiatrists, and a third group received no treatment at all. Most of the students showed moderate depression or anxiety.

Although there was much variability, with some individual students showing substantial improvement, students who met with the lecturers did as well as those who met with the professional therapists. Both groups did significantly better than the control subjects who received no treatment. These results suggest that sympathy and understanding are the most important ingredients in the psychotherapeutic process, at least for treatment of mild anxiety or depression. In such cases, the therapists' theories of how mental disorders should be treated may be less important than their ability to establish warm, understanding relationships with their clients.

▶

Controversies in Psychological Science – *Continued*

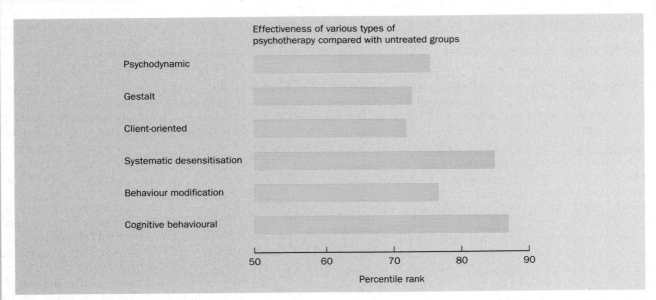

Figure 18.4 Effectiveness of psychotherapy. The results of Smith *et al.*'s meta-analysis comparing the effectiveness of different therapies.:

In one meta-analysis, Westen and Morrison (2001) scrutinised studies from nine clinical psychology and psychiatric journals published between 1990 and 1999. To be eligible for inclusion, studies had to test the efficacy of a specific psychosocial treatment against a waiting-list control group and an alternative therapy, had a follow-up of at least 12 months, had to include valid measures of outcome and had to be experimental in nature. Thirty-four studies met these inclusion criteria.

The authors found substantial improvement in mental health in up to half of the patients. The majority of patients, however, did not show sustained improvement at one to two years' follow-up, especially those who are depressed or generally anxious. Half of patients who complete a course of treatment will benefit from it, whereas the figure drops to 40 per cent if a patient simply enters treatment (but may not continue). The long-term treatment success for panic disorder is good, but the authors found that the depressed or anxious patient will maintain mild to significant levels of symptoms after treatment. The authors note that follow-up studies at two years were non-existent. In the four studies that did conduct such a follow-up, a quarter of depressed patients who did not abuse alcohol or drugs and were not suicidal will improve two years after treatment. Psychotherapy for panic disorder treatment was the most effective, with 46 per cent of patients showing sustained improvement.

The strict exclusion/inclusion criteria in the study is a plus and a negative. On the plus side, the studies reviewed are carefully selected and well-controlled experimental studies. On the negative side, few studies were included and complications such as co-morbidity (the appearance of one disorder with another) were not addressed because patients in the selected studies suffered exclusively from one disorder. The future should see the inclusion of studies employing other therapies.

Conclusion

The success of psychotherapy (which includes cognitive behavioural therapy as well as the other, humanistic therapies) rests on the type of therapy applied. There are some negative outcomes: an estimated 9–13 per cent of clients worsen after psychotherapy (Beutler and Clarkin, 1990). The application of psychotherapy to schizophrenia has been associated with a deterioration in the client's condition (Lambert and Bergin, 1994). Also, some problems may be inappropriate for psychotherapy: criminal or antisocial behaviour, for example. And some forms of psychotherapy appear to be ineffective in some contexts, such as influencing the survival rate from cancer (Coyne *et al.*, 2007; 2009). For some other problems, however, such as depression, psychotherapy may be quite effective when combined with other treatments.

Biological treatments

The most common biological treatment for mental illness is pharmacological. Psychopharmacological interventions are aimed at treating psychological problems by using chemical agents.

There are four major classes of drugs used to treat mental disorders: antipsychotic drugs, antidepressant drugs, anti-manic drugs and anti-anxiety drugs. We discuss the application and effectiveness of these drugs in the sections describing mental disorders.

Some people with depression do not respond to antidepressant drugs, but a substantial percentage of these people improve after a few sessions of **electroconvulsive therapy (ECT)** in which electrodes are applied to a person's head and a brief surge of electrical current is passed through them. Because antidepressant medications are generally slow-acting, taking ten days to two weeks for their therapeutic effects to begin, severe cases of depression are often treated with a brief course of ECT to reduce the symptoms immediately. These people are then maintained on an antidepressant drug.

There are several problems with ECT treatments. An excessive number of ECT treatments has been associated with permanent memory loss (Squire *et al.*, 1981) with little enduring effect on cognitive performance (Calev *et al.*, 1995; Barnes *et al.*, 1997). Nowadays, ECT is usually administered only to the right hemisphere, in order to minimise damage to people's verbal memories, and is used only when the patient's symptoms justify it. Because ECT undoubtedly achieves its effects through the biochemical consequences of the seizure, pharmacologists may discover new drugs that can produce rapid therapeutic effects without ECT's deleterious ones. Once this breakthrough occurs, ECT can be abandoned.

One other biological treatment for mental disorders is even more controversial than electroconvulsive therapy: psychosurgery or neurosurgery (Fenton, 1998). **Psychosurgery** involves the treatment of a mental disorder, in the absence of obvious organic damage, through brain surgery. In contrast, brain surgery to remove a tumour or diseased neural tissue or to repair a damaged blood vessel is not psychosurgery, and there is no controversy about these procedures.

Psychosurgery has its origins in the late 1930s when, at a conference at University College London, the results of frontal lobectomies on two chimpanzees, Becky and Lucy, were presented. The surgery resulted in an increase in calmness and passivity in the chimps. Egas Moniz, a 59-year-old Portuguese professor of neurology, one of the audience at the meeting, suggested that this technique might also be appropriate for humans. Late in 1935, the first frontal lobotomy operations were performed. While treating some symptoms, such as those in chronic schizo-phrenia, the prefrontal lobotomies were found to have serious side-effects, such as apathy and severe blunting of emotions, intellectual impairments, and deficits in judgement and planning ability. Nevertheless, the procedure was used for a variety of conditions, most of which were not improved by the surgery. Approximately 40,000 prefrontal lobotomies were performed in the USA alone, most of them from 1935 to 1955. A simple procedure, called 'ice pick' prefrontal lobotomy by its critics, was even performed on an outpatient basis, as seen in Figure 18.5. The development of antipsychotic drugs and the increasing attention paid to the serious side-effects of prefrontal lobotomy led to a sharp decline in the use of this procedure during the 1950s. Today it is no longer performed.

A few surgeons have continued to refine the technique of psychosurgery and now perform a procedure called a **cingulotomy**, which involves cutting the cingulum bundle, a small band of nerve fibres that connects the prefrontal cortex with parts of the limbic system (Ballantine *et al.*, 1987). Cingulotomies have been shown to be effective in helping some people who suffer from severe compulsions (Tippin and Henn, 1982). In a recent study, Baer *et al.* (1995) conducted a long-term follow-up study of 18 people who underwent cingulotomy for severe obsessive-compulsive disorder. For each of these people, other forms of therapy – drug therapy and behavioural therapy – had been unsuccessful in treating their symptoms. However, after their surgeries, the people in Baer's study showed marked improvements in their functioning, decreased symptoms of depression and anxiety, and few negative side-effects.

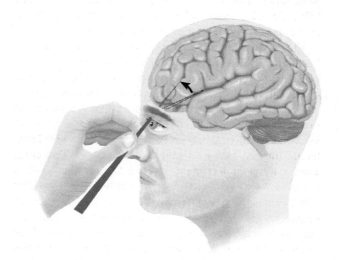

Figure 18.5 'Ice pick' prefrontal lobotomy. The sharp metal rod is inserted under the eyelid and just above the eye so that it pierces the skull and enters the base of the frontal lobe.

Source: Adapted with permission from Freeman, W., *Proceedings of the Royal Society of Medicine*, 1949, 42 (suppl.), 8–12. Reprinted by permission of The Royal Society of Medicine.

Table 18.3 Drugs commonly used to treat mental disorders

Therapeutic function	Class of drugs	Generic name	Trade name
Antipsychotic	Soporific	Chlorpromazine	Thorazine
	Non-soporific	Acetophenazine	Tindal
	Phenothiazines	Thioridazine	Mellaril
		Fluphenazine	Permitil
		Trifluoperazine	Stelazine
		Perphenazine	Trilafon
	Butyrophenones	Haloperidol	Haldol
Antidepressant	Tricyclics	Imipramine	Tofranil
	Monoamine oxidase inhibitors	Amitryptiline	Elavil
		Phenelzine	Nardil
	Serotonin reuptake inhibitors	Fluoxetine	Prozac
			Miltown
Anti-anxiety	Propanediols	Meprobamate	
	Benzodiazepines	Chlordiazepoxide	Librium
		Diazepam	Valium
Anti-manic	Lithium salts	Lithium carbonate	Eskalith

Drug therapy is the preferred biological treatment for mental disorders although it represents only a possible treatment, not a cure. Usually, the drugs are effective only to the extent that the people for whom they are prescribed actually use them. In some cases, people forget to take their drugs, only to have the disordered symptoms return. In other cases, people take their drugs, get better, and stop taking the drugs because they feel that they are no longer 'sick'. In this case, too, the symptoms soon return. For some people, this cycle repeats itself endlessly. Table 18.3 lists some of the drugs commonly used to treat mental disorders.

Mental disorders

The previous section described each of the major approaches to treating mental disorder. This section reviews some of the most important mental disorders. Each major class of disorder is described according to its symptoms, its possible causes and the current treatment approach.

suffer from delusions or severely disordered thought processes. Furthermore, they almost universally realise that they have a problem. Most neurotics are only too aware that their strategies for coping with the world are not working. Neurotic behaviour is usually characterised by avoidance rather than confrontation of problems.

Anxiety, somatoform and dissociative mental disorders

Anxiety, somatoform and dissociative mental disorders are often referred to as neuroses. Most neuroses are strategies of perception and behaviour that have become distorted or exaggerated. They are characterised by pathological increases in anxiety or by defence mechanisms applied too rigidly, resulting in mental processes that are maladaptive. Neurotic people are anxious, fearful, depressed and generally unhappy. However, unlike people who are afflicted with psychoses, they do not

Anxiety disorders

Several important types of mental disorders are classified as anxiety disorders, which have fear and anxiety as their most prominent symptoms. **Anxiety** is a sense of apprehension or doom that is accompanied by certain physiological reactions, such as accelerated heart rate, sweaty palms and tightness in the stomach. Anxiety disorders are the most common psychological disorders and the reported rate of anxiety disorder is twice as high in European women than in men (Weiller *et al.*, 1998). Five of the most important anxiety disorders are generalised anxiety disorder, panic disorder, phobic disorder, obsessive-compulsive disorder and post-traumatic stress disorder.

The most common of these are agoraphobia, panic disorder and generalised anxiety disorder, all of which are described next, together with possible aetiology. There seems to be national variation in the prevalence of these disorders. Generalised anxiety disorder is more frequent in cities such as Paris and Berlin, for example, whereas it is low in Manchester and Groningen (the Netherlands). Panic disorder appears to be more common in Manchester and agoraphobia in Groningen (Weiller *et al.*, 1998).

Generalised anxiety disorder (GAD)

Description

The principal characteristic of **generalised anxiety disorder (GAD)** is excessive worry about all matters relating to the individual's life: health, money, work, relationships and so on. According to DSM-IV TR, these worries must be present on most days and will have occurred over a period of at least six months. The anxious individual finds it difficult to control the worry and shows at least three symptoms out of the following: restlessness, being easily fatigued, difficulty concentrating, irritability, muscle tension and sleep disturbance. Around 12 per cent of anxiety disorders are GAD (American Psychiatric Association, 1994) and most individuals with GAD also experience depression which sometimes makes a clear-cut diagnosis of GAD difficult.

Anxious individuals spend considerably longer making decisions. For example, Tallis *et al.* (1991) asked a group of controls and clinically anxious individuals to respond if a target was present on a computer monitor. Although there was no difference between controls and anxious individuals when the target was present, the anxious group took significantly longer to make a decision when the target was absent. This finding demonstrates that anxious individuals seem to attend more to tasks that require them to make absolutely correct decisions.

Aetiology

Several models exist which try to explain GAD; some of these also apply to other mental disorders but this section limits itself to those which account for GAD explicitly. One explanation (Borkovec, 1994) suggests that GAD arises from the individual's drive to set and anticipate a set of goals that are desirable. In this context, the anxiety arises when a history of a frustrated failure to achieve affects the perception of cues associated with these goals. Anxiety is reflected in the individual's need to anticipate all possible outcomes, for fear of failing or not achieving.

Eysenck (1992) has argued that although Borkovec's model (described in full in Berkovec [1994] might explain pathological worry, it does not explain normal worry. Eysenck's model attempts to explain both by suggesting that worry or anxiety serves as an 'alarm function' which brings information concerning threat-related stimuli into awareness. In a sense, worry acts as a behaviour that will prepare an individual for future behaviour; it prompts the individual to anticipate future situations and their solutions.

Although older than Eysenck's, Gray's (1982) model suggests a similar mechanism but ties it to neurophysiology and certain brain systems. According to Gray, anxiety is evoked by signals of punishment, lack of reward, novel stimuli and innate fear stimuli. The individual detects such threats by means of a **behavioural inhibition system (BIS)** which also generates the anxiety. An important function of the BIS is that it helps the organism (Gray's theory applies to humans and other animals) to evaluate the threat content of a stimulus or event. The neurophysiology of the system is vast and complicated, involving neuroanatomical and neurochemical interaction between a number of brain regions. The BIS is thought to be represented by the septum and hippocampal formation.

Two-factor model

The two-factor model of anxiety suggests that individuals exhibit a vulnerability to anxiety owing to high trait anxiety and poor coping skills. There is a strong correlation between neuroticism and almost all major anxiety disorders (Andrews *et al.*, 1989; Andrews, 1991). There also seems to be a loss of control exhibited by anxious individuals and anxiety is often preceded by stressful life events (Last *et al.*, 1984), as Borkovec's model also suggests. Individuals with panic disorder and GAD have been found to rate their parents as less caring and as overprotective (Silove *et al.*, 1991), indicating perhaps one cause of the perceived lack of control. High trait anxiety individuals have been found to be very similar to clinically anxious patients in terms of their perception that events are out of their control and in terms of parental overprotection (Bennett and Stirling, 1998).

Information-processing models

A number of studies has suggested that individuals high in trait anxiety and those suffering GAD exhibit **attentional biases**. That is, they are significantly biased towards responding to threat- or anxiety-related material. Anxious people are more vigilant when reacting to threatening faces than non-threatening faces, for example (Bradley *et al.*, 1999). There are various ways of measuring this attentional bias and three of the most common measures are the dot probe, the emotional Stroop and the interpretation of ambiguous sentences (Eysenck *et al.*, 1991; Wells and Mathews, 1994).

The dot probe task involves the presentation of two words, one above the other, on a computer monitor. Individuals are asked to read aloud the word at the top; this word is either neutral or is an anxiety- or threat-related word. After a short pause, the individual is presented with either another pair of words or a dot where the top or bottom word appeared. The individual has to press a key when such a dot appears. MacLeod and his colleagues (MacLeod *et al.*, 1986; Matthews *et al.*, 1990) have reported that latencies are shorter for anxiety-related words in GAD patients.

Similar biases are reported for the emotional Stroop task. In this, individuals have to read the colour in which a word is written. These words are either neutral or anxiety-related. GAD patients and individuals high in trait anxiety exhibit a bias towards the anxiety-related words, although the effects found with the Stroop are not as robust as those seen in the dot probe (Williams *et al.*, 1996). Finally, anxious individuals have a tendency to interpret ambiguous sentences such as 'The two men watched as the chest was opened' as threatening, that is, they interpret the chest as being a person's torso rather than a large box (Eysenck *et al.*, 1991).

Each model of GAD has some merit; that Eysenck's and Gray's models flag anxiety as indicating an alarm system that prepares an individual for future action suggests that anxiety results from excessive monitoring for and detection of threat. The findings from attentional bias studies support this view. Why the anxiety should be produced by this appraisal in some individuals and not in others, however, is still unclear. Borkovec's model is useful in that it specifies previous non-reward and frustration as a cause of being unable to achieve goals. Gray's model is useful because it ties this appraisal down to one neuropsychological system.

Treatment

The most common form of treatment for GAD is psychopharmacological, with drug administration sometimes coupled with cognitive behavioural therapy. The drugs used to combat anxiety disorder are called **anti-anxiety drugs** or **anxiolytics**, and a list of the most common appears in Table 18.4.

The anxiolytics include barbiturates, benzodiazepines and antidepressants. Barbiturates are sedatives and include drugs such as Phenobarbital. However, because they are highly toxic and foster dependence, they are not widely used. Benzodiazepines are anticonvulsant and sedative drugs, and are the most widely prescribed. Two common benzodiazepines are chlordiazepoxide (Librium) and diazepam (Valium), both of which are low in toxicity.

Table 18.4 Some of the drugs used to treat anxiety

Substance	Generic name	Example
Benzodiazepines	Alprazolam	Xanax
	Chlordiazepoxide	Librium
	Clonazepam	Klonopin
	Clorazepate	Tranxene
	Diazepam	Valium
	Halazepam	Paxipam
	Lorazepam	Ativan
	Oxazepam	Serax, Zaxopam
	Prazepam	Centrax
Atypical agent	Buspirone	Buspar

Source: From Goodman and Gilman's *The Pharmacological Basis of Therapeutics*, 9th edn (Hardman, J.G. and Limberd, L.E., eds) 'Drugs and treatment of psychiatric disorders: psychosis and anxiety' (Baldessarini, R.J.). Copyright (1996) Reproduced with permission of The McGraw-Hill Companies, Inc.

A meta-analysis of 65 studies comparing CBT and/or pharmacological interventions with a control condition for the treatment of generalised anxiety disorder, found that CBT was a significantly better treatment than was no treatment (Mitte, 2005). When studies directly compare CBT with drug intervention, there was no significant difference in efficacy.

Panic disorder

Description

Panic has been described as a fear of fear (Foa *et al.*, 1984). Individuals who experience panic are threatened by the presence or the potential presence of fear-related physical states. People with **panic disorder** suffer from episodic attacks of acute anxiety – periods of acute and unremitting terror that grip them for lengths of time lasting from a few seconds to a few hours. The lifetime prevalence rate for panic disorder is estimated to be about 4 per cent (Katerndahl and Realini, 1993). Panic attacks (without agoraphobia, which is the anxiety disorder we discuss next) are equally likely to appear in men and women (Clarke, 1992). The disorder usually has its onset in young adulthood; it rarely begins after age 35 (Woodruff *et al.*, 1972).

Panic attacks include many physical symptoms, such as shortness of breath, sweating, racing heartbeat (trachycardia), physical tension, cognitive disorganisation, dizziness and fear of loss of support (jelly legs). The individual feels as if he or she is about to collapse and is on the point of death. Such catastrophic thoughts and feelings only exacerbate the physical symptoms and so the individual becomes involved in a self-fulfilling prophecy.

Between panic attacks, people with panic disorder tend to suffer from **anticipatory anxiety** – a fear of having a panic attack (Ottaviani and Beck, 1987). Because attacks can occur without apparent cause, these people anxiously worry about when the next one might strike them. Sometimes, a panic attack that occurs in a particular situation can cause the person to fear that situation. The anxiety we all feel from time to time is significantly different from the intense fear and terror experienced by a person gripped by a panic attack, as the case study below illustrates.

Aetiology

Genetic models

There seems to be a hereditary component to panic disorders: the concordance rate for the disorder is higher between identical twins than between fraternal twins (Torgerson, 1983). Almost 30 per cent of the first-degree relatives (parents, children and siblings) of a person with panic disorder also have panic disorder (Crowe *et al.*, 1983). According to Crowe *et al.*, the pattern of panic disorder within a family tree suggests that the disorder is caused by a single, dominant gene.

Panic attacks can be triggered in people with histories of panic disorder by giving them injections of lactic acid (a by-product of muscular activity) or by having them breathe air containing an elevated amount of carbon dioxide (Woods *et al.*, 1988; Cowley and Arana, 1990). People with family histories of panic attack are more likely to react to sodium lactate, even if they have never had a panic attack previously (Balon *et al.*, 1989). Some researchers believe that what is inherited is a tendency to react with alarm to bodily sensations that would not disturb most other people.

Clark's model

The most comprehensive (and cognitive) model of panic disorder is that proposed by David Clark. Clark (1986, 1988) argues that panic attacks are produced by the **catastrophic misinterpretation** of bodily events. Slight changes in bodily sensation are interpreted as symptomatic of a physical threat which makes the individual anxious. The more anxious the individual becomes, the more intense the bodily sensations become (the self-fulfilling prophecy referred to above). According to Clark's model, two processes contribute to the maintenance of this misinterpretation. The first is hypervigilance: the individual repeatedly checks for changes in bodily sensations; the second is avoidance strategies: the individual avoids those behaviours they feel will exacerbate the bodily sensations. For example, a person who is afraid that he is about to have a heart attack will avoid exercise (although this prevents the individual from discovering that exercise will not cause a heart attack).

Seligman (1988), however, has argued that the catastrophic misinterpretation theory is questionable on the grounds that the realisation that death will not accompany panic attacks will eventually dawn on these patients. Seligman suggests an alternative suggestion based on **evolutionary preparedness**, the notion that we are evolutionarily predisposed to respond in a specific way to some stimuli because it is to our advantage to do so (Seligman, 1971). Panic, in this context, is the individual's response to biologically prepared bodily sensations. However, as Power and Dalgleish (1997) argue, the failure to realise that death does not follow bodily sensations arises because individuals avoid situations and stimuli that would induce such bodily sensations in the first place. Seligman's formulation may not, therefore, be necessary (for the reason he suggests).

Interestingly, some patients maintain that they do not misinterpret their bodily sensations catastrophically and some are more difficult to convince that these sensations will not lead to death (McNally, 1990). These findings point to a degree of variation in panic disorder patients. The anxiety sensitivity hypothesis (Reiss and McNally, 1985), for example, suggests that some individuals are more anxiety-sensitive than others. The degree of sensitivity depends on pre-existing beliefs about the harmfulness of bodily sensations. These pre-existing beliefs predispose the individual to interpret bodily events negatively and erroneously. This leads to panic.

Treatment

Treatment for panic disorder can be both cognitive behavioural or pharmacological. Cognitive behavioural therapy, for example, is effective at reducing panic attacks. Such therapy would involve breathing and relaxation techniques, **cognitive restructuring** (altering misconceptions about the consequences of bodily sensations) and eliciting bodily sensations in the individual to demonstrate the non-harmful nature of such changes (Craske *et al.*, 1997). Antidepressants and anxiolytics are sometimes used to treat panic attacks with some success. Some individuals react badly to the drugs, however, and while they treat the anxiety generated during panic, they do not address the core problem of catastrophic misinterpretation.

Phobic disorders

Phobias – named after the Greek god Phobos, who frightened his enemies – are irrational fears of specific objects or situations. Because phobias can be highly specific, clinicians have coined a variety of inventive names, some of which are summarised in Table 18.5.

Table 18.5 Name and description of some common phobias

Name	Object or situation feared
Acrophobia	Heights
Agoraphobia	Open spaces
Ailurophobia	Cats
Algophobia	Pain
Astraphobia	Storms, thunder, lightning
Belonophobia	Needles
Claustrophobia	Enclosed spaces
Haematophobia	Blood
Monophobia	Being alone
Mysophobia	Contamination or germs
Nyctophobia	Darkness
Ochlophobia	Crowds
Pathophobia	Disease
Pyrophobia	Fire
Siderophobia	Railways
Syphilophobia	Syphilis
Taphophobia	Being buried alive
Triskaidekaphobia	Thirteen
Zoophobia	Animals, or a specific animal

Most individuals have one or more irrational fears of specific objects or situations, and it is difficult to draw a line between these fears and phobic disorders. If someone is afraid of spiders but manages to lead a normal life by avoiding them, it would seem inappropriate to say that the person has a mental disorder. Similarly, many otherwise normal people are afraid of speaking in public. The term 'phobic disorder' should be reserved for people whose fear makes their life difficult. The DSM-IV TR recognises three types of phobic disorder: agoraphobia, social phobia and simple phobia.

Agoraphobia

Agoraphobia (*agora* means 'marketplace' in Ancient Greek) is a fear of open spaces and is the most serious and common of the phobic disorders. It occurs in between 50 and 80 per cent of phobic disorders (Matthews *et al.*, 1981). It is reported three times as often in women as in men. Onset is sudden and individuals are usually in their early twenties (Clarke, 1992). The term was coined by Westphal in 1871 to describe four (male) cases who feared open spaces.

Most cases of agoraphobia are considered to be caused by panic attacks and are classified with them. Agoraphobia associated with panic attacks is defined as a fear of 'being in places or situations from which escape might be difficult (or embarrassing) or in which help might not be available in the event of a panic attack . . . As a result of this fear, the person either restricts travel or needs a companion when

away from home' (American Psychiatric Association, 1994). Agoraphobia can be severely disabling. Some people with this disorder have stayed inside their house for years, afraid to venture outside. Supermarkets and queuing are especially anxiety-provoking for agoraphobics. Features of supermarket layout such as stairways and diminished access, for example, are regarded as anxiety-provoking by agoraphobic individuals (Jones *et al.*, 1996).

Social phobia

Social phobia is an exaggerated 'fear of one or more situations . . . in which the person is exposed to possible scrutiny by others and fears that he or she may do something or act in a way that will be humiliating or embarrassing' (American Psychiatric Association, 1994). Most people with social phobia are only mildly impaired, but the situations in which they can operate may be severely curtailed. Social phobics, like patients with GAD, seem to bias their attention towards threat-related stimuli (Rapee and Heimberg, 1997).

At the core of the disorder seems to be conflict regarding the internal representation of their appearance and external indicators which evaluate them negatively. Rapee and Heimberg, therefore, proposed that socially phobic individuals allocate excessive attentional resources towards mental representations of how they are perceived by their audience. In a study in which high and low anxious social phobic individuals gave a five-minute speech in front of an audience that was behaving positively (smiling) or negatively (frowning), Veljaca and Rapee (1998) found that highly anxious individuals were better at detecting negative audience behaviours whereas the low anxiety individuals were better at detecting the positive behaviours. Social phobics also interpret ambiguous social events more negatively, and interpret mildly negative, unambiguous events more catastrophically than do people suffering from anxiety, or a group of healthy controls (Stopa and Clark, 2000).

Specific phobia

Specific phobia includes all other phobias, such as fear of snakes, darkness or heights. These phobias are often caused by a specific traumatic experience and are the easiest of all types of phobia to treat. The Epidemiological Catchment Area (ECA) Study found that insects, mice, snakes and bats were the more frequently cited feared/disgust-provoking stimuli (Robins and Regier, 1994). Animals are a common phobia. Davey (1992), for example, reported that one-third of women and one-quarter of men reported having a spider phobia.

The lifetime prevalence rate for simple phobia is estimated to be about 14 per cent for women and about

8 per cent for men (Robins and Regier, 1991), but approximately one-third of the population sometimes exhibit phobic symptoms (Goodwin and Guze, 1984).

Aetiology

Animal phobias are sometimes surprising because in Europe, for example, there are no indigenous lethally poisonous spiders, although spider phobias are common. One explanation for this anomaly is that we fear animals that have potentially lethal consequences; we are, therefore, predisposed to fear them. This is the preparedness hypothesis (Seligman, 1971) which we encountered in the section on panic disorder. Evidence for this hypothesis comes in the form of the deliberate conditioning of fear of spiders. These conditioning experiences are the most difficult to extinguish – more difficult than non-threatening stimuli (Ohman *et al.*, 1985; McNally, 1987).

However, Seligman's theory has its problems. For example, if we are adaptively predisposed to fear the stimuli producing simple phobias, what adaptive purpose does a fear of snails, moths and slugs serve? As McNally (1995) points out, we can ascribe adaptive significance to a fear of any object if we are creative enough. One theory suggests that phobias develop from a pairing of a phobic object with an aversive stimulus so that phobic stimuli become phobic by association. However, only 40–50 per cent of animal phobias appear to be accounted for in this way. Davey (1992) also reported that only 8 out of 118 spider phobics recall having a traumatic experience with spiders.

Matchett and Davey (1991) suggest an alternative explanation: that some stimuli become the object of phobia because of our inherent fear of contamination or disease. Animals (such as spiders, slugs, cockroaches) become feared because they seem disgusting and we would reject them as food on the basis of this disgust (although some individuals would be immune to such disgust responses; snails are considered a delicacy in certain parts of Europe). In fact, sensitivity to disgust may be an important determinant of the level of fear (Webb and Davey, 1993). To investigate whether some animal phobias were disgust- or fear-related, Davey *et al.* (1998) conducted a cross-cultural study of phobia in seven countries. An analysis of the data suggested that phobic stimuli could be divided into one of three categories: fear-irrelevant (for example, chicken, hamster, cow), fear-relevant (for example, lion, bear, alligator) and disgust-relevant (for example, cockroach, spider, maggot, worm). Disgust was consistent across cultures (although there were some cross-cultural differences with Indian respondents reporting lower levels of fear to the disgust stimuli and Japanese respondents showing higher levels of fear). This finding suggests that not all stimuli may be feared for the same reasons (perhaps the term 'simple phobia' is too simplistic, as Curtis *et al.* (1998) suggest).

Treatment

Phobias are sometimes treated by *systematic desensitisation* (described in the general section on treatment) or modelling. Bandura (1971), for example, has described a modelling session with people who had a phobic fear of snakes. The therapist himself performed the fearless behaviour at each step and gradually led participants into touching, stroking and then holding the snake's body with gloved and bare hands while the experimenter held the snake securely by head and tail. If a participant was unable to touch the snake following ample demonstration, they were asked to place their hand on the experimenter's and to move their own hand down gradually until it touched the snake's body. After participants no longer felt any apprehension about touching the snake under these secure conditions, anxieties about contact with the snake's head area and entwining tail were extinguished. The therapist again performed the tasks fearlessly, and then he and the participant performed the responses jointly. As participants became less fearful, the experimenter gradually

Cutting edge – Phobia reduction and cortisol

Although the release of the hormone cortisol is common during our response to stressful events and is also cued by exposure to phobic objects in phobic individuals, a group of researchers from Switzerland, Germany and the United States have reported that the administration of the chemical can reduce phobic symptoms (Soravia *et al.*, 2006). When glucocorticoid levels are high, memory can become impaired. The researchers reasoned that the administration of cortisol would lead to the inhibition of fear-related memory in phobia sufferers. This is

what they found, in a group of 20 people with social phobia and 20 people with spider phobia. Cortisone (25 mg) was administered orally one hour before participants were exposed to a social stressor or photograph of a spider (depending on the participant). Self-reported fear was significantly reduced in the cortisol group during the anticipation of the phobic stimulus, exposure to it and recovery from this exposure. Those in the placebo group did not produce this effect.

reduced his participation and control over the snake, until eventually participants were able to hold the snake in their lap without assistance, to let the snake loose in the room and retrieve it, and to let it crawl freely over their body. Progress through the graded approach tasks was paced according to the participants' apprehensiveness. When they reported being able to perform one activity with little or no fear, they were eased into a more difficult interaction. This treatment eliminated fear of snakes in 92 per cent of those who participated.

Modelling is successful for several reasons. Participants learn to make new responses by imitating those of the therapist and their behaviour in doing so is reinforced. When they observe a confident person approaching and touching a feared object without showing any signs of emotional distress, they probably experience a vicarious extinction of their own emotional responses. In fact, Bandura (1971, p. 684) reports that 'having successfully overcome a phobia that had plagued them for most of their lives, subjects reported increased confidence that they could cope effectively with other fear-provoking events', including encounters with other people.

Cognitive behavioural therapy has also been applied to agoraphobia (Ost *et al.*, 1993). In an experiment in which the effect of exposure (graded exposure to the phobic stimuli) was compared with exposure and CBT (combating negative thoughts and dysfunctional attitudes), Burke *et al.* (1997) found no difference in the effectiveness of the two therapies at six months following the therapy: both were equally effective. Similar combinations have also been found to be effective for social phobia (Scholing and Emmelkamp, 1996).

A recently developed treatment has taken the idea of exposure but added a technological element: virtual reality technology. This has many practical benefits. The fear of flying, for example, would be more efficiently treated using simulated or virtual stimuli rather than taking sufferers to airports. This approach is evaluated in the Psychology in Action section.

Psychology in action – Virtual planes can relieve real fear of flying

The fear may be more common than people imagine. According to one German study, 15 per cent of respondents reported having a fear of flying and around 60 per cent of those try to cope with this fear by drinking alcohol or taking tranquillisers (Wilhelm and Roth, 1997).

In many cases, treatment may take the form of cognitive behavioural therapy which exposes the patient to the fear-eliciting stressor with the aim of attenuating the fear that such stressors cause. For example, a patient may be exposed to real aeroplanes or may be walked around a stationary plane. Recently, however, psychologists have harnessed new technology to help people combat their fear of flying: virtual reality or VR (Klein, 1998). VR technology allows researchers to simulate events, locations or stimuli effectively using computer software. Consequently, it is a very convenient and inexpensive approach to treatment.

Rothbaum *et al.* (2000) randomly assigned 49 patients who expressed a fear of flying to one of three conditions: virtual reality (VR) training, standard exposure therapy or no therapy where patients were on a waiting list for treatment.

The VR training involved exposing the participant to a virtual aircraft (sitting in it while it took off and landed); standard exposure involved direct exposure to an airport and a stationary plane. Both experimental conditions were preceded by four sessions of anxiety management. Patients received treatment over eight weeks and a post-treatment flight was set up after this period to examine the efficacy of the VR treatment, as measured by willingness to fly and self-reported anxiety about the first flight.

Both VR and standard exposure treatments were better than the control condition in reducing fear of flying. The beneficial effects of exposure were still seen at a six-month follow-up. Ninety-three per cent of VR patients and 93 per cent of standard exposure patients had flown after treatment. The results show that VR may be an inexpensive and more convenient way of reducing the fear of flying than is actual exposure to real aeroplanes. If given the choice, patients indicated that they would opt for the VR treatment rather than real exposure.

Exposure to virtual reality also appears to be more effective at reducing flight anxiety than is relaxation therapy, a common

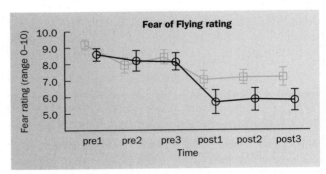

Figure 18.6 Fear of flying scores for people in the VR exposure group (black line) and the relaxation group (orange line).

Source: Muhlberger, A., Herrmann, M.J., Wiedemann, G., Ellgring, H. and Pauli, P., Repeated exposure of flight phobics to flights in virtual reality. *Behaviour Research and Therapy*, 2001, 39, 1033–1050. Copyright 2000, with permission from Elsevier.

Psychology in action – *Continued*

psychological intervention that some flyers adopt. Muhlberger *et al.* (2001) found that while exposure to VR flights increased feelings of fear, these feelings gradually attenuated and to a greater extent than they did in people undergoing relaxation training. Both approaches reduced flight anxiety, but VR was better, as Figure 18.6 shows.

Virtual reality technology of this kind has now been successfully used to treat arachnophobia (Carlin *et al.*, 1997) and claustrophobia (Botella *et al.*, 1998). As with all treatments, its success is measured by its long-term effects. A recent 12-month

follow-up study suggests that VR flight exposure has lasting effects on anxiety relief. Rothbaum's team followed up 24 patients who were either exposed to actual planes and an airport or to VR flying. As you saw in the section at the beginning, both interventions were successful at the first testing point. The follow-up study showed that the initial improvements were maintained. The results suggest that a very short-term treatment that imposes fewer practical demands than real exposure to planes and airports can have sustainable benefits.

Post-traumatic stress disorder (PTSD)

Description

Post-traumatic stress disorder (PTSD) is a relatively new anxiety disorder (it made its first appearance in DSM-III in 1980) and refers to anxiety that follows a traumatic event. This event poses a threat to the individual's life or the lives of others. Symptoms of the disorder include the re-experiencing of feelings related to the event (such as intrusive memories, thoughts and images related to the event), avoidant behaviour (such as denial and emotional numbing) and arousal (such as hypervigilance for trauma-related information). Sadness, guilt and anger are also associated with the disorder (Shore *et al.*, 1989). These latter symptoms are important because PTSD seldom appears alone but with other disorders or additional diagnoses (McFarlane, 1992; Bleich *et al.*, 1997). PTSD is a controversial inclusion in DSM-IV TR because its validity has been challenged. Some researchers point to the ease with which PTSD symptoms can easily be faked (Burges and McMillan, 2001).

The prevalence rate is around 25–30 per cent in the general population, and rape is associated with the greatest prevalence (Green, 1994). Other events which can produce PTSD are road traffic accidents (Stallard *et al.*, 1998; Murray *et al.*, 2002), bank robberies (Kamphuis and Emmelkamp, 1998), war (Fontana and Rosenheck, 1993), and natural or human-made disasters (Freedy *et al.*, 1994). Onset of the disorder may be delayed by many years (Blank, 1993). As with generalised anxiety disorder and panic disorder, there is a greater Stroop interference for words related to the trauma (Thrasher *et al.*, 1994).

The emergency services, especially its members who respond to disasters, may be more prone to developing the disorder because of the type of work they engage in. In the UK, ambulance drivers answer more calls than do the police and fire service combined. It might be expected, therefore, that the incidence of PTSD is high. In fact, the prevalence lies between 10 and 20 per cent. Clohessy and Ehlers (1999) asked 56 ambulance drivers in the UK to describe the most distressing aspects of their work and administered questionnaires which tapped their ability to cope with this distress and the degree to which the thoughts about the distress were intrusive. They found that 21 per cent of the sample met the criteria set by the DSM-IV TR for PTSD. Predictors of the severity of the post-traumatic stress were poor coping strategy, efforts to suppress intrusive thoughts and dwelling on previous distressing events.

In a study of 96 victims of physical or sexual assault, Dunmore *et al.* (1999) found that some factors were common to both onset and maintenance whereas others were specific to onset. Factors associated with both were appraising the event and the consequences of the event (dwelling on the assault and its aftermath) and adopting poor coping strategies (such as avoidance). Factors which were related to onset were feeling detached during the assault and being unable to perceive positive responses from others. The researchers suggest that these cognitive factors may contribute to PTSD in a number of ways. They may prevent recovery by encouraging poor coping strategy or by generating a sense of immediate threat.

Aetiology

Horowitz's (1979, 1986) model suggests that information about the trauma in PTSD is processed because of a mechanism called *completion tendency*. Completion tendency refers to the need for new information to be integrated into existing patterns of thought and memory. Power and Dalgleish (1997) describe how there is first a stunned reaction to the traumatic event and then a feeling of information overload as the individual realises the enormity of the trauma. Such information cannot be accommodated by existing mental schemata, and defence mechanisms, such as denial and numbing, provide a means of coping with this lack of accommodation. Completion tendency, however, insists on keeping the memory of the event alive (Horowitz calls this 'active memory') through flashbacks and nightmares. The anxiety results from the vacillation between these two processes: defence mechanisms and completion tendency. Although an honourable attempt at explaining PTSD, Power and Dalgleish (1997) query whether the model explains some features of the disorder. Why do only some individuals develop PTSD, for example? And why is PTSD delayed in some individuals?

An alternative model suggests that in PTSD the individual's beliefs about the world have been shattered. According to the model, the individual is assumed to view themselves as personally invulnerable, that the world is meaningful and comprehensible, and that the individual views themselves positively (Janoff-Bulman, 1989, 1992). These assumptions provide the bedrock of our life and give it structure. This structure is shattered after the traumatic event which gives rise to PTSD. The process by which this structure breakdown occurs, however, is not explained by the model.

Treatment

Various forms of treatment have been attempted with PTSD with varying success (Shalev *et al.*, 1996; Foa and Meadows, 1997). Debriefing appears to be ineffective (Deahl *et al.*, 1994) but drug treatment meets with mixed success (O'Brien and Nutt, 1998). Treatment based on exposure seems to be effective (Foa and Meadows, 1997).

Obsessive-compulsive disorder

Description

Individuals with **obsessive-compulsive disorder** (OCD) suffer from **obsessions** – thoughts that will not leave them – and **compulsions** – behaviours that they cannot keep from performing. In one study, impaired control of mental activities, checking, urges involving loss of motor control, and feeling contaminated were found to be the major classes of obsession and compulsion among a large sample of American college students (Sternberger and Burns, 1990). The lifetime prevalence rate is estimated to be about 2.5 per cent (Robins and Regier, 1991; Bebbington, 1998).

Unlike people with panic disorder, people with obsessive-compulsive disorder have a defence against anxiety – their compulsive behaviour. Unfortunately, the need to perform this compulsive behaviour often becomes more and more demanding of their time until it interferes with their daily life. Obsessions are seen in many mental disorders, including schizophrenia. However, unlike persons with schizophrenia, people with obsessive-compulsive disorder recognise that their thoughts and behaviours are senseless and wish that they would go away. The types of obsession and compulsion seen in these individuals are summarised in Table 18.6.

Table 18.6 The number and percentage of obsessive and compulsive symptoms reported by 70 children and adolescents diagnosed with obsessive-compulsive disorder

	Reported symptom at initial interview	
Obsessions	**Number**	**%**
Concern with dirt, germs or environmental toxins	28	40
Something terrible happening (fire, death or illness of self or loved one)	17	24
Symmetry, order or exactness	12	17
Scrupulosity (religious obsessions)	9	13
Concern or disgust with bodily wastes or secretions (urine, stools, saliva)	6	8
Lucky or unlucky numbers	6	8
Forbidden, aggressive or perverse sexual thoughts, images or impulses	3	4
Fear might harm others or oneself	3	4
Concern with household items	2	3
Intrusive nonsense sounds, words or music	1	1
Compulsions	**Number**	**%**
Excessive or ritualised handwashing, showering, bathing, toothbrushing or grooming	60	85
Repeating rituals (going in or out of a door, up or down from a chair)	36	51
Checking (doors, locks, cooker, appliances, emergency brake on car, homework)	32	46
Rituals to remove contact with contaminants	16	23
Touching	14	20
Measures to prevent harm to self or others	11	16
Ordering or arranging	12	17
Counting	13	18
Hoarding or collecting rituals	8	11
Rituals of cleaning household or inanimate objects	4	6
Miscellaneous rituals (such as writing, moving, speaking)	18	26

Consider the case of Sergei, a 17-year-old ex-student:

> Only a year ago, Sergei seemed to be a normal adolescent with many talents and interests. Then, almost overnight he was transformed into a lonely outsider, excluded from social life by his psychological disabilities. Specifically, he was unable to stop washing. Haunted by the notion that he was dirty – in spite of the contrary evidence of the senses – he began to spend more and more of his time cleansing himself of imaginary dirt. At first his ritual ablutions were confined to weekends and evenings and he was able to stay in school while keeping them up, but soon they began to consume all his time, forcing him to drop out of school, a victim of his inability to feel clean enough.
>
> *Source*: Rapoport (1989) p. 63.

Women are slightly more likely than men to have this diagnosis. Like panic disorder, obsessive-compulsive disorder most commonly begins in young adulthood (Robbins *et al.*, 1984). People with this disorder are unlikely to marry, perhaps because of the common obsessional fear of dirt and contamination or because the shame associated with the rituals they are compelled to perform causes them to avoid social contact (Turner *et al.*, 1985).

There are two principal kinds of obsession: obsessive doubt or uncertainty, and obsessive fear of doing something prohibited (Salkovskis *et al.*, 1998). Uncertainties, both trivial and important, preoccupy some people with obsessive-compulsive disorder almost completely. Others are plagued with the fear that they will do something terrible – swear aloud in church, urinate in someone's living room, kill themselves or a loved one, or jump off a bridge – although they seldom actually do anything antisocial. And even though they are often obsessed with thoughts of killing themselves, fewer than 1 per cent of them actually attempt suicide.

Most compulsions fall into one of four categories: counting, checking, cleaning and avoidance. For example, people might repeatedly check burners on the stove to see that they are off and windows and doors to be sure that they are locked. Some people wash their hands hundreds of times a day, even when they become covered with painful sores. Other people meticulously clean their homes or endlessly wash, dry and fold their clothes. Some become afraid to leave home because they fear contamination and refuse to touch other members of their families. If they do accidentally become 'contaminated', they usually have lengthy purification rituals.

Aetiology

Several possible causes have been suggested for obsessive-compulsive disorder. Unlike simple anxiety states, this disorder can be understood in terms of defence mechanisms. Some cognitive investigators have suggested that obsessions serve as devices to occupy the mind and displace painful thoughts.

Cognitive researchers also point out that persons with obsessive-compulsive disorder believe that they should be competent at all times, avoid any kind of criticism at all costs, and worry about being punished by others for behaviour that is less than perfect (Sarason and Sarason, 1993). Thus, one reason people who have obsessive-compulsive disorder may engage in checking behaviour is to reduce the anxiety caused by fear of being perceived by others as incompetent or to avoid others' criticism that they have done something less than perfectly.

If painful, anxiety-producing thoughts become frequent, and if turning to alternative patterns of thought reduces anxiety, then the principle of reinforcement predicts that the person will turn to these patterns more frequently. Just as an animal learns to jump a hurdle to escape a painful foot shock, a person can learn to think about a 'safe topic' in order to avoid painful thoughts. If the habit becomes firmly established, the obsessive thoughts may persist even when the original reason for turning to them – the situation that produced the anxiety-arousing thoughts – no longer exists. A habit can thus outlast its original causes.

Family studies have found that obsessive-compulsive disorder is associated with a neurological disorder called **Gilles de la Tourette's syndrome**, which appears during childhood (Janowic, 1993). Gilles de la Tourette's syndrome is characterised by muscular and vocal tics, including making facial grimaces, squatting, pacing, twirling, barking, sniffing, coughing, grunting or repeating specific words (especially vulgarities). It is not clear why some people with the faulty gene develop Gilles de la Tourette's syndrome early in childhood and others develop obsessive-compulsive disorder later in life.

Treatment

There are usually two forms of treatment employed in obsessive-compulsive disorder. The first is behavioural therapy in which the individual may be exposed to the object, situation or event that provokes the ritualistic behaviour (Emmelkamp, 1993). One example may be to deliberately dirty the hands of an individual who ritualistically washes their hands 20 or 30 times a day and not allow them to wash their hands (Rapoport, 1989). This type of therapy has met with some success in serious cases of obsessive-compulsive disorder. However, behavioural treatment appears to be more successful at eliminating compulsive than obsessive behaviour (Emmelkamp, 1993). Drug treatment appears to eliminate both successfully. These drugs are two serotonin-specific reuptake inhibitors (described in more detail in the section on depression below) and act by increasing the amount of the neurotransmitter, serotonin, in the brain.

Somatoform disorders

The primary symptoms of **somatoform disorder** are a bodily or physical (*soma* means 'body') problem for which there is no physiological basis. The two most important somatoform disorders are somatisation disorder and conversion disorder.

Somatisation disorder

Description

Somatisation disorder occurs mostly among women and involves complaints of wide-ranging physical ailments for which there is no apparent biological basis (the complaints must include at least 13 symptoms from a list of 35, which fall into the following categories: gastrointestinal symptoms, pain symptoms, cardiopulmonary symptoms, pseudoneurological symptoms, sexual symptoms, and female reproductive symptoms). This disorder used to be called hysteria. The older term derives from the Greek word *hysteria*, meaning 'uterus', because of the ancient belief that various emotional and physical ailments in women could be caused by the uterus wandering around inside the body, searching for a baby.

It is true that somatisation disorder is seen almost exclusively in women; however, modern use of the term 'hysteria' does not imply any gynaecological problems. Moreover, this disorder is rare even among women: Regier *et al.* (1988) found that the incidence of somatisation disorder in a sample of over 18,000 people was less than 1 per cent in women and non-existent in men. Somatisation disorder is often chronic, lasting for decades.

Aetiology

Somatisation disorder is most common in poorly educated women of low socio-economic status (Guze *et al.*, 1971). The disorder also runs in families. Coryell (1980) found that approximately 20 per cent of first-degree female relatives of people with somatisation disorder also had the disorder. In addition, many studies have shown that somatisation disorder is closely associated with antisocial personality disorder. First-degree male relatives of women with somatisation disorder have an increased incidence of alcoholism or antisocial behaviour, and first-degree female relatives of convicted male criminals have an increased incidence of somatisation disorder (Guze *et al.*, 1967; Woerner and Guze, 1968). These findings suggest that a particular environmental or genetic history leads to different pathological manifestations in men and women.

Conversion disorder

Description

Conversion disorder is characterised by physical complaints that resemble neurological disorders but have no underlying organic pathological basis. The symptoms include blindness, deafness, loss of feeling, and paralysis. According to the DSM-IV TR, a conversion disorder must have some apparent psychological reason for the symptoms; the symptoms must occur in response to an environmental stimulus that produces a psychological conflict, or they must permit the person to avoid an unpleasant activity or to receive support and sympathy. Unlike somatisation disorder, conversion disorder can afflict both men and women.

The term 'conversion', when applied to a mental disorder, derives from psychoanalytical theory, which states that the energy of an unresolved intrapsychic conflict is converted into a physical symptom. Hofling (1963, pp. 315–16) described one such case:

> The patient had taken the day off from work to be at home with his wife and [newborn] baby. During the afternoon, he had felt somewhat nervous and tense, but had passed off these feelings as normal for a new father . . .
>
> . . . The baby awoke and cried. Mrs L. said that she would nurse him . . . As she put the baby to her breast, the patient became aware of a smarting sensation in his eyes. He had been smoking heavily and attributed the irritation to the room's being filled with smoke. He got up and opened a window. When the smarting sensation became worse he went to the washstand and applied a cold cloth to his eyes. On removing the cloth, he found that he was completely blind . . . Psychotherapy was instituted . . . The visual symptoms disappeared rather promptly, with only very mild and fleeting exacerbations during the next several months . . .
>
> . . . He had been jealous of the baby – this was a difficult admission to make – and jealous on two distinct counts. One feeling was, in essence, a sexual jealousy, accentuated by his own sexual deprivation during the last weeks of the pregnancy. The other was . . . a jealousy of the maternal solicitude shown the infant by its mother.

Although the sensory deficits or paralyses of people with conversion disorders are not caused by damage to the nervous system, these people are not faking their illnesses. People who deliberately pretend they are sick in order to gain some advantage (such as avoiding work) are said to be malingering. Malingering is not defined as a mental disorder by the DSM-IV TR. Although it is not always easy to distinguish malingering from a conversion disorder, two criteria are useful. First, people with conversion disorders are usually delighted to talk about their symptoms in great detail, whereas malingerers are reluctant to do so for fear of having their deception discovered. Secondly, people with conversion disorders usually describe the symptoms with great drama and flair but do not appear to be upset about them.

Somatisation disorder consists of complaints of medical problems, but the examining physician is unable to see any signs that would indicate physical illness. In contrast, a patient with conversion disorder gives the appearance of having a neurological disorder such as blindness or paralysis. Psychophysiological disorders (also called psychosomatic disorders) are not the result of fictitious or imaginary symptoms; they are real, organic illnesses caused or made worse by psychological factors. For example, stress can cause gastric ulcers, asthma or other physical symptoms; ulcers caused by stress are real, not imaginary. Successful therapy would thus require reduction of the person's level of stress as well as surgical or medical treatment of the lesions in the stomach.

Aetiology

Psychoanalytical theory suggests that the psychic energy of unresolved conflicts (especially those involving sexual desires the patient is unwilling or unable to admit to having) becomes displaced into physical symptoms. In other words, psychoanalysts regard conversion disorders as primarily sexual in origin.

In contrast, behaviour analysts have suggested that conversion disorders can be learned for many reasons. This assertion gains support from the finding that people with these disorders usually suffer from physical symptoms of diseases with which they are already familiar (Ullman and Krasner, 1969). A patient often mimics the symptoms of a friend. Furthermore, the patient must receive some kind of reinforcement for having the disability: they must derive some benefit from it.

Treatment

Early treatment of somatoform disorders had concentrated on allowing the patient to explore past or previous traumas, although there was no evidence that this helped to treat the disorder. A method that seems to meet with some success is behavioural therapy. This may be especially relevant to those experiencing pain or sickness. The treatment involves not rewarding those behaviours which reinforce expressions of illness and pain, and rewarding ways of adapting to life and coping with it.

Dissociative disorders

In somatoform disorders, anxiety is avoided by the appearance of the symptoms of serious physical disorders. In **dissociative disorders**, anxiety is reduced by a sudden disruption in consciousness, which in turn produces changes in one's sense of identity.

Description

Like conversion disorder, the term 'dissociative disorder' comes from Freud. According to psychoanalytical theory, a person develops a dissociative disorder when a massive repression fails to keep a strong sexual desire from consciousness. As a result, the person resorts to dissociating one part of their mind from the rest.

The most common dissociative disorder is **psychogenic amnesia**, in which a person 'forgets' all their past life, along with the conflicts that were present, and begins a new one. The term 'psychogenic' means 'produced by the mind'. Because amnesia can also be produced by physical means – such as epilepsy, drug or alcohol intoxication, and brain damage – clinicians must be careful to distinguish between amnesias of organic and psychogenic origin.

A **psychogenic fugue** is a special form of amnesia in which a person deliberately leaves home and starts a new life elsewhere (fugue means 'flight'). You read about this in the memory at the movies section in Chapter 8.

Dissociative identity disorder is a very rare, but very striking, dissociative disorder that is marked by the presence of two or more separate personalities within the individual, either of which may be dominant at any given time. Only about 100 cases of dissociative identity disorder have been documented, and some investigators believe that many, if not most of them, are simulations, not actual mental disorders.

An interesting example of dissociative identity disorder is the case of Billy Milligan as told in the book *The Minds of Billy Milligan* (Keyes, 1981). Milligan was accused of rape and kidnapping but was deemed not guilty by reason of insanity. His psychiatric examination showed him to have 24 different personalities. Two were women and one was a young girl. There was a Briton, an Australian and a Yugoslav. One woman, a lesbian, was a poet, while the Yugoslav was an expert on weapons and munitions, and the Briton and Australian were minor criminals. Dissociative identity disorder has received much attention; people find it fascinating to contemplate several different personalities, most of whom are unaware of each other, existing within the same individual. Bliss (1980) suggests that dissociative identity disorder is a form of self-hypnosis, established early in life and motivated by painful experiences. In fact, the overwhelming majority of people diagnosed as having multiple personality disorder report having been physically abused when they were a child (Kluft, 1984).

Aetiology

Dissociative disorders are usually explained as responses to severe conflicts resulting from intolerable impulses or as responses to guilt stemming from an actual misdeed. Partly because they are rare, dissociative disorders are among the least understood of the mental disorders. In general, the dissociation is advantageous to the person. Amnesia enables the person to forget about a painful or unpleasant life. A person with fugue not only forgets but also leaves the area to start a new existence. And a dissociative identity disorder allows a person to do things that they would really like to do but cannot because of the strong guilt feelings that would ensue. The alternative personality can be one with a very weak conscience.

Treatment

Like early treatment for the somatoform disorders, early treatment for the dissociative disorders involved the patient recounting past and present traumas. It is assumed that the disorder arises from a failure to accept these traumas and the pain they caused. Acknowledging and expressing the trauma, therefore, is a means of accepting it and avoiding the need to dissociate (Oltmans and Emery, 1998). There is little evidence to suggest that the treatment is successful. Anti-anxiety drugs may also be prescribed to alleviate the patients' distress.

Personality disorders

see activity on mypsychlab

The DSM-IV TR classifies abnormalities in behaviour that impair social or occupational functioning as **personality disorders**. There are several types of personality disorder which the DSM has grouped into three clusters. Cluster A, for example, refers to the 'eccentric cluster' of schizotypal and paranoid personality disorder; Cluster B (the dramatic cluster) includes the narcissistic and antisocial personality disorders; and Cluster C (the anxious cluster) includes avoidant and dependent personality disorders (Van

Velzen and Emmelkamp, 1996). Another general cluster accounts for other personality disorders not covered by these clusters. Because there are so many personality disorders, this chapter focuses on just one in depth: antisocial personality disorder. Table 18.7 provides a description of the several other personality disorders.

Antisocial personality disorder and psycopathy

Antisocial personality disorder refers to a failure to conform to standards of decency, repeated lying and stealing, a failure to sustain long-lasting and loving relationships, low tolerance of boredom and a complete lack of guilt. Prichard (1835) used the term 'moral insanity' to describe people whose intellect was normal but in whom the 'moral and active principles of the mind are strongly perverted and depraved . . . and the individual is found to be incapable . . . of conducting himself with decency and propriety'. Koch (1889) introduced the term 'psychopathic inferiority', which soon became simply psychopathy; a person who displayed the disorder was called a psychopath. The first edition of the DSM used the term 'sociopathic personality disturbance', which was subsequently replaced by the present term, 'antisocial personality disorder'. Most clinicians still refer to such people as psychopaths or sociopaths but this is probably incorrect. There is good evidence, for example, that antisocial personality disorder/sociopathy and psychopathy are different disorders; the former is characterised by antisocial behaviour, usually criminal, whereas the latter is characterised by these antisocial activities plus other, more emotive factors such as lack of empathy for others, remorselessness and manipulativeness.

Description

People with antisocial personality disorder cause a considerable amount of distress in society. Many criminals can be diagnosed as psychopaths, and most psychopaths have a record of criminal behaviour. The offending psychopath commits more offences than the average criminal (Hare, 1981; Kosson *et al.*, 1990) and is significantly more violent. Hare and McPherson (1984) report that psychopaths are convicted of three-and-a-half times more violent crime than are non-psychopathic criminals. Because of data such as these, psychologists have made attempts to identify the chronic psychopathic offender early on in life. However, these studies have met with mixed success (Lynam, 1996; Raine *et al.*, 1996).

The diagnostic criteria of the DSM-IV TR include evidence of at least three types of antisocial behaviour before age 15 and at least four after age 18. The adult forms of antisocial behaviour include inability to sustain

Table 18.7 Descriptions of various personality disorders

Personality disorder	Description
Paranoid	Suspiciousness and extreme mistrust of others; enchanced perception of being under attack by others
Schizoid	Difficulty in social functioning – poor ability and little desire to become attached to others
Schizotypal	Unusual thought patterns and perceptions; poor communication and social skills
Histrionic	Attention-seeking; preoccupation with personal attractiveness; prone to anger when attempts at attracting attention fail
Narcissistic	Self-promoting; lack of empathy for others; attention-seeking; grandiosity
Borderline	Lack of impulse control; drastic mood swings; inappropriate anger; becomes bored easily and for prolonged periods; suicidal
Avoidant	Oversensitivity to rejection; little confidence in initiating or maintaining social relationships
Dependent	Uncomfortable being alone or in terminating relationships; places others' needs above one's own in order to preserve the relationship; indecisive
Obsessive-compulsive	Preoccupation with rules and order; tendency towards perfectionism; difficulty relaxing or enjoying life
Passive-aggressive	Negative attitudes; negativity is expressed through passive means; complaining, expressing envy and resentment towards others who are more fortunate
Depressive	Pervasive depressive cognitions and self-criticism; persistent unhappiness; feelings of guilt and inadequacy

Note: The anti social personality disorder, not listed here, is described in detail in the text.

Source: Adapted from Carson, R.C., et al., *Abnormal Psychology and Modern Life*, 10th edn. Published by Allyn & Bacon, Boston, MA. Copyright © 1996 by Pearson Education. By permission of the publisher.

consistent work behaviour; lack of ability to function as a responsible parent; repeated criminal activity, such as theft, pimping or prostitution; inability to maintain enduring attachment to a sexual partner; irritability and aggressiveness, including fights or assault; failure to honour financial obligations; impulsiveness and failure to plan ahead; habitual lying or use of aliases; and consistently reckless or drunken driving. In addition to meeting at least four of these criteria, the person must have displayed a 'pattern of continuous antisocial behaviour in which the rights of others are violated, with no intervening period of at least five years without antisocial behaviour'. The lifetime prevalence rate for antisocial personality disorder is estimated to be about 3.5 per cent (Robins and Regier, 1994), although estimates of prevalence reported in the DSM-IV TR are lower: about 3 per cent for men and less than 1 per cent for women.

Cleckley (1976) has listed 16 characteristics of antisocial personality disorder, seen in Table 18.8. Cleckley's list of features provides a good picture of what most psychopaths are like. They are unconcerned for other people's feelings and suffer no remorse or guilt if their actions hurt others. Although they may be superficially charming, they do not form real friendships; thus, they often become swindlers or confidence artists. Both male and female psychopaths are sexually promiscuous from an early age, but these encounters do not seem to mean much to them. Female psychopaths tend to marry early, to be unfaithful to their husbands, and soon become separated or divorced.

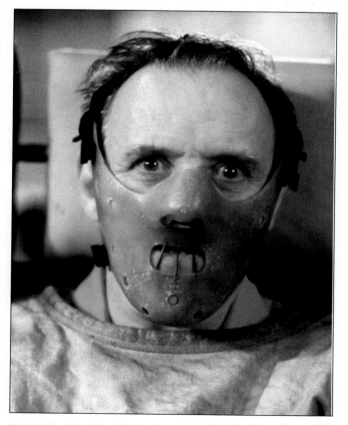

Not a typical psychopath.
Source: Everett Collection/Rex Features.

Table 18.8 Cleckley's primary characteristics of antisocial personality disorder

1   Superficial charm and good 'intelligence'
2   Absence of delusions and other signs of irrational thinking
3   Absence of 'nervousness'
4   Unreliability
5   Untruthfulness and insincerity
6   Lack of remorse or shame
7   Inadequately motivated antisocial behaviour
8   Poor judgement and failure to learn by experience
9   Pathological egocentricity and incapacity for love
10 General poverty in major affective reactions
11 Specific loss of insight
12 Unresponsiveness in general interpersonal relations
13 Fantastic and uninviting behaviour
14 Suicide rarely carried out
15 Sex life impersonal, trivial and poorly integrated
16 Failure to follow any life plan

Source: Cleckley, H., *The Mask of Sanity*, pp. 337–8. St Louis: C.V. Mosby, 1976. Reprinted with permission.

They tend to marry other psychopaths, so their husbands' behaviour is often similar to their own. Psychopaths habitually tell lies, even when there is no apparent reason for doing so and even when the lie is likely to be discovered. They steal things they do not need or even appear to want. When confronted with evidence of having lied or cheated, psychopaths do not act ashamed or embarrassed and usually shrug the incident off as a joke.

Psychopaths do not easily learn from experience; they tend to continue committing behaviours that get them into trouble. They also do not appear to be driven to perform their antisocial behaviours; instead, they usually give the impression that they are acting on whims. When someone commits a heinous crime such as a brutal murder, normal people expect that the criminal had a reason for doing so. However, criminal psychopaths are typically unable to supply a reason more compelling than 'I just felt like it'. They do not show much excitement or enthusiasm about what they are doing and do not appear to derive much pleasure from life.

Serial killers (clockwise): Ian Brady; Myra Hindley; Dennis Nielsen; Donald Nielsen, John George Haigh; Thomas Hamilton; Robert Black; Fred and Rosemary West.

Source: Press Association Images and Greater Manchester Police.

Aetiology

Cleckley (1976, p. 371) suggested that the psychopath's defect 'consists of an unawareness and a persistent lack of ability to become aware of what the most important experiences of life mean to others . . . The major emotional accompaniments are absent or so attenuated as to count for little.' Some investigators have hypothesised that this lack of involvement is caused by an unresponsive autonomic nervous system. If a person feels no anticipatory fear of punishment, they are perhaps more likely to commit acts that normal people would be afraid to commit. Similarly, if a person feels little or no emotional response to other people and to their joys and sorrows, they are unlikely to establish close relationships with them.

Many experiments have found that psychopaths do show less reactivity in situations involving punishment. For example, Hare (1965) demonstrated that psychopaths show fewer signs of anticipatory fear. All participants in Hare's study watched the numerals 1 through 12 appear in sequential order in the window of a device used to present visual stimuli. They were told that they would receive a very painful shock when the numeral 8 appeared. Psychopathic subjects showed much less anticipatory responsiveness than did normal control subjects or non-psychopathic criminals.

Psychopaths appear to be selectively aroused by some emotions. When viewing slides of facial expression of distress or threat, psychopaths are less responsive than a control group to the distress faces but are no different from controls when responding to the threatening faces (Blair *et al.*, 1997). Psychopaths also appear to respond differently to emotional words when these are presented to the left (analytical) or right (emotional) hemisphere. Psychopaths do not show the right-hemisphere advantage for recognising emotion (Day and Wong, 1996).

The quality of parenting is strongly related to the development of antisocial personality disorder. In particular, children whose parents ignore them or who leave them unsupervised for prolonged periods, often develop patterns of misconduct and delinquency (Lynam, 1996). When the parents do pay attention to their children, it tends to be in the form of harsh punishment or verbal abuse in response to their misdeeds. Thus, the children of these parents live in an environment that ranges from no attention at all to attention in the form of physical punishment and scoldings. In response, the children develop a pattern of behaviour that is characterised by increased aggression, distrust of others, concern only for themselves, and virtually no sense of right and wrong.

According to Hare (1996, p. 46), 'In some respects, it is as if psychopaths lack a central organiser to plan and keep track of what they think and say. The part of the brain that is more responsible than any other for monitoring, organising and integrating sensory input and behaviour, is the frontal cortex. People with damage to the frontal cortex have also been shown to exhibit irregularities in autonomic nervous system functioning such as a lack of heart rate responsiveness and galvanic skin response in contexts that require an assessment of risk.

Over many years, Adrian Raine and colleagues in the US have published controversial data linking frontal lobe dysfunction with psychopathic behaviour and antisocial personality disorder. In general, psychopaths tend to show less activity or less volume in this area, a region known to mediate some aspects of emotional and social behaviour, as you saw in Chapter 13. In what they describe as a study showing the 'first evidence for a structural brain deficit in antisocial personality disorder' (APD), Raine *et al.* (2000) compared the brain volume of 21 community volunteers with the DSM-IV TR ratified APD, with control groups and found that prefrontal brain volume of the APD group was 11 per cent less than other groups. They also showed little autonomic response when undertaking the social stressor task – they had their behaviour videotaped as they talked about their faults.

These findings are consistent with evidence from brain-damaged individuals showing that frontal patients have social problems and are unresponsive to threatening or risky behaviour when this response is measured autonomically. Commenting on Raine's findings, Damasio (2000) cautions against drawing too bold a conclusion from the study: 'One must be careful not to fall in the phrenological trap set behind every new identification of a brain area with some putative role', he says; 'the normal or pathologic effects associated with that certain area can be properly understood only in the context of multicomponent neural systems.'

To date, neuroimaging studies have focused on 'unsuccessful' psychopaths, i.e. those who have been caught and jailed. It has been suggested that successful psychopaths – those who are not caught and jailed – are behaviourally very similar to their incarcerated counterparts but are physiologically different (Widom, 1978). Ishikawa *et al.* (2001) recruited people from temporary employment agencies and administered the Hare Psychopathy Checklist to determine the degree of psychopathy in the sample. On the basis of individuals' responses, those scoring in the top (most psychopathic) and bottom third were selected. The top third were divided into those who had been convicted of a crime and those who had not. Heart rate and electrodermal response were measured.

The researchers found that, when compared with the control group, the successful psychopaths showed heightened heart rate activity and performed better than the unsuccessful psychopaths at a test of frontal lobe function. The authors suggest that this reactivity reflects the successful psychopath's greater awareness of changes in the social environment – they are better than unsuccessful psychopaths at assessing or making risky decisions; unsuccessful psychopaths show little autonomic nervous system (ANS) reaction to risk and it may be this lack of feedback from the ANS that leads to their slipping up.

Treatment

There is no standard, effective treatment for antisocial personality disorder or psychopathy and the treatments used have normally been designed for other purposes such as anger management or reducing deviant sexual behaviour (Oltmans and Emery, 1998). Whereas evidence suggests that there is some temporary effect on the behaviour, the effect does not generalise to other settings in the long term. One predictor of success, when it does happen, is a person's adherence to a treatment programme: the more successful complete the programme (Reid and Gacono, 2000).

Schizophrenic disorders

Schizophrenia, the most common psychosis, includes several types, each with a distinctive set of symptoms. There is some controversy over whether schizophrenia is a unitary disorder with various sub-types or whether each sub-type constitutes a distinct disorder. Because the prognosis differs for the various sub-types of schizophrenia, each would appear to differ at least in severity. An individual may, at different times, meet the criteria for different sub-types, although the diagnosis of schizophrenia seems valid and reliable (Mason *et al.*, 1997).

Description

Schizophrenia refers to a group of psychological disorders involving distortions of thought, perception and emotion, bizarre behaviour and social withdrawal. Around 8 to 40 cases per 1,000 are reported per year worldwide and the disorder appears to recognise no cultural or international boundaries. It is higher in urban areas and there is a lifetime risk of 0.7 per cent of developing the illness (and this is greater in men). It is highest in people of lowest socio-economic status, has its onset in adolescence or early adulthood, and genetic factors account for 80 per cent of the disorder's appearance (Tandon *et al.*, 2008a). Schizophrenia is probably the most serious of the mental disorders.

Descriptions of symptoms in ancient writings indicate that the disorder has been around for thousands of years (Jeste *et al.*, 1985). The word 'schizophrenia' literally means 'split mind', although it is commonly misinterpreted as 'split personality'. The schizophrenic does not suffer from split personality or multiple personality (those are other mental disorders) but from disordered thought and affect. The man who invented the term, Eugen Bleuler (in 1911), intended it to refer to a break with reality caused by such disorganisation of the various functions of the mind that thoughts and feelings no longer worked together normally.

Many studies of people who become schizophrenics in adulthood have found that they were different from others even in childhood. One study obtained home movies of people with adult-onset schizophrenia that showed them and their siblings when they were children (Walker and Lewine, 1990). Although the schizophrenia did not manifest itself until adulthood, viewers of the films (six graduate students and one professional clinical psychologist) did an excellent job of identifying the children who were to become schizophrenic. The viewers commented on the children's poor eye contact, relative lack of responsiveness and positive affect, and generally poor motor coordination.

There are also degrees of cognitive impairment seen in schizophrenia. Verbal fluency – the ability to name as many objects beginning with a particular letter or belonging to the same category – appears to be impaired in schizophrenic individuals (Gruzelier *et al.*, 1988), although the category version of this test appears to be better performed (Joyce *et al.*, 1996). Semantic memory and performance on 'frontal lobe' tasks is also impaired in schizophrenic individuals (Shallice *et al.*, 1991; Tamlyn *et al.*, 1992).

The prognosis for schizophrenia is described by the 'law of thirds'. Approximately one-third of the people who are diagnosed as having it will require institutionalisation for the rest of their lives. About one-third show remission of symptoms and may be said to be cured of the disorder. The final third are occasionally symptom-free (sometimes for many years) only to have the symptoms return, requiring more treatment and perhaps even institutionalisation.

Schizophrenia is characterised by two categories of symptoms: positive and negative. **Positive symptoms** include thought disorders, hallucinations and delusions. A **thought disorder** – a pattern of disorganised, irrational thinking – is probably the most pronounced symptom of schizophrenia. People with schizophrenia have great difficulty arranging their thoughts logically and sorting out plausible conclusions from absurd ones. In conversation, they jump from one topic to another as new associations come up. Sometimes, they utter meaningless words or choose words for their rhyme rather than for their meaning. **Delusions** are beliefs that are obviously contrary to fact. **Delusions of persecution** are false beliefs that others are plotting and conspiring against oneself. **Delusions of grandeur** are false beliefs in one's power and importance, such as a conviction that one has god-like powers or has special knowledge that no one else possesses. **Delusions of control** are related to delusions of persecution; the person believes, for example, that they are being controlled by others through such means as radar or tiny radio receivers implanted in their brain.

The third positive symptom of schizophrenia is **hallucinations**, which are perceptions of stimuli that are not actually present. The most common schizophrenic hallucinations are auditory, but such hallucinations can also involve any of the other senses. The typical schizophrenic hallucination consists of voices talking to the person. Sometimes, they order the person to act; sometimes, they scold the person for their unworthiness; sometimes, they just utter meaningless phrases. Sometimes, those with schizophrenia may also hear a voice that keeps a running commentary on their behaviour, or they hear two or more voices.

In contrast to the positive symptoms, the **negative symptoms** of schizophrenia are known by the absence of normal behaviours: flattened emotional response, poverty of speech, lack of initiative and persistence, inability to experience pleasure, and social withdrawal (Crow, 1980; Frith, 1987).

Types of schizophrenia

The DSM-IV TR identifies four types of schizophrenia: undifferentiated, catatonic, paranoid and disorganised. Most cases of schizophrenia, however, do not fit exactly into one of these categories. Many individuals are diagnosed with **undifferentiated schizophrenia**, that is, the patients have delusions, hallucinations and disorganised behaviour but do not meet the criteria for catatonic, paranoid or disorganised schizophrenia. In addition, some patients' symptoms change after an initial diagnosis, and their classification changes accordingly.

Catatonic schizophrenia (from the Greek *katateinein*, meaning 'to stretch or draw tight') is characterised by various motor disturbances, including catatonic postures – bizarre, stationary poses maintained for many hours – and waxy flexibility, in which the person's limbs can be moulded into new positions, which are then maintained. Catatonic schizophrenics are often aware of all that goes on about them and will talk about what happened after the episode of catatonia subsides.

The pre-eminent symptoms of **paranoid schizophrenia** are delusions of persecution, grandeur or control. The word 'paranoid' has become so widely used in ordinary language that it has come to mean 'suspicious'. However, not all paranoid schizophrenics believe that they are being persecuted. Some believe that they hold special powers that can save the world or that they are Christ, or Napoleon or the president of the USA.

Paranoid schizophrenics are among the most intelligent of psychotic patients, so, not surprisingly, they often build up delusional structures incorporating a wealth of detail. Even the most trivial event is interpreted in terms of a grand scheme, whether it is a delusion of persecution or one of grandeur. The way a person walks, a particular facial expression or movement, or even the shapes of clouds can acquire special significance. An example of a case study of paranoid schizophrenia appears in the Psychology in Action section.

Disorganised schizophrenia is a serious progressive and irreversible disorder characterised primarily by disturbances of thought. People with disorganised schizophrenia often display signs of emotion, especially silly laughter, that are inappropriate to the circumstances. Also, their speech tends to be a jumble of words: 'I came to the hospital to play, gay, way, lay, day, bray, donkey, monkey' (Snyder, 1974, p. 132). This sort of speech is often referred to as a word salad.

Psychology in action – Treating paranoid schizophrenia

Bill McClary, a 25-year-old unemployed man, did not go to the therapist willingly. His sister Coleen, with whom he had been living for 18 months, suggested that Bill receive professional help for behaviour that had become increasingly unusual. He would spend most of his time in social isolation, daydreaming, talking to himself and saying things that did not make sense. Although most people engage in such behaviour at some time, Bill's was constant and this is what worried his sister.

On seeking professional help, Bill appeared quiet and hesitant. During therapy, he was friendly but shy and ill-at-ease. It was only later that his therapist learned of even stranger and unusual behaviour reported by Bill's brother Roger.

It transpired that Bill had had occasional but not long-lasting heterosexual and homosexual relationships. After moving in with his sister, he became convinced that people were talking about him, especially about his sexuality. He came to believe that a group of conspirators had implanted microphones and cameras in the house to spy on his sexual encounters with men. These recordings were released as a film which Bill believed had grossed $50 million at the box office; this money was used to fund the activity of the Irish Republican Army in Northern Ireland and he would often feel deeply guilty and responsible for the deaths there because his money was used to buy arms and ammunition.

Bill also heard voices discussing his sexual behaviour in unpleasant terms. Often, these discussions would involve an element of punishment, such as 'He's a faggot; we've got to kill him'. The successfully released film was called *Honour Thy*

▶

Psychology in action – *Continued*

Father and Bill's name in the film was Gay Talese. Although Bill did not acknowledge the fact, this name actually belonged to a real novelist who wrote about organised crime. He maintained that his photograph had appeared on the cover of *Time* magazine in the previous year with the name Gay Talese printed clearly on it.

Bill was the youngest of four children born to Irish-American parents. He was very close to his mother and his father blamed him for the break-up of his marriage; he was often excluded from his father's activities. At the age of 12, Bill's father fell ill and Bill remembered wanting to see him dead. His school work was good and he eventually became a bank clerk – a stop-gap job while he thought of which career to pursue. He was quiet and polite but eccentric; he resigned after two years to become a lift operator, a job which afforded even more thinking time, but he was sacked after a year for being disorganised. He moved in with his mother shortly after this but because each made the other anxious, he moved out and moved in with his sister, her husband and their three children. It was at this point that Bill's unusual behaviour became noticeable.

Bill did not seem to enjoy life very much – he did not like interacting with others, was ambivalent about relationships and described sex in very impersonal terms. Initial therapy sessions targeted Bill's indifference and time-keeping and his sister was advised to ignore inappropriate behaviour. If he missed break-fast, then he would not have a snack cooked for him at eleven, as had previously happened. This strategy and others like it resulted in Bill keeping time and domestic appointments. He enjoyed helping his niece with her homework and so this pleasant activity was encouraged. Eventually, his schedule approached those of the house and he began to help more with domestic chores. Mumbling and lack of social contact was tackled next. The therapist advised Bill to move to one area of the house whenever he felt the need to mumble and talk to himself. This was partly but not totally successful. His shyness with other people was tackled by asking Bill to rehearse mentally conversations that might occur with other people.

When the 'film fantasy' was made aware to the therapist, however, Bill was prescribed thioridazine, a standard antipsychotic medication. This was successful in reducing the self-talk but his delusions remained. To try and eliminate these delusions, Bill was told to visit a local library and find the cover of *Time* with his photograph on. This he did and obviously did not find such a cover. However, he believed that the covers had been switched by conspirators. He was told to go to two more libraries but he was still convinced that the covers had been switched. Over the next few weeks, he began to believe that he might just have imagined the *Time* incident and his delusions managed to recede a little.

Source: Oltmans *et al.* (1995).

Aetiology

Research into the causes of all kinds and forms of schizophrenia throughout this century and the last reflects the challenge that psychologists face in attempting to understand how psychological and biological factors interact to influence behaviour. The diathesis-stress model of mental disorders, discussed earlier in the chapter, appears to describe accurately the causes of schizophrenia: schizophrenia appears to result from one or more inherited, biological predispositions that are activated by environmental stress. In fact, this is currently the predominant view of schizophrenia.

Genetic causes

The heritability of schizophrenia, or more precisely the heritability of a tendency towards schizophrenia, has now been firmly established by both twin studies and adoption studies. Identical (monozygotic) twins are much more likely to be concordant for schizophrenia than are fraternal (dizygotic) twins, and the children of parents with schizophrenia are more likely themselves to become schizophrenic, even if they were adopted and raised by non-schizophrenic parents (Kety *et al.*, 1968; Farmer *et al.*, 1987). Twin studies of schizophrenia compare the concordance rates of monozygotic twins with the concordance rates of siblings of different genetic relatedness who were reared either together or apart. The risk of one MZ twin developing the disorder if the other has it is between 50 and 70 per cent; in DZ twins, this is between 9 and 18 per cent. If both of a child's parents are affected, it has a 40–60 per cent of chance of developing the illness (Tanda *et al.*, 2008b).

If a person has been diagnosed with schizophrenia, there exists the possibility that other family members have the disorder, too. It is important to note that although the likelihood of developing schizophrenia increases if a person has schizophrenic relatives, this disorder is not a simple trait, like eye colour, that is inherited. Even if both parents are schizophrenic, the probability that their child will develop schizophrenia is 30 per cent or less.

Current findings provide strong evidence that schizophrenia is heritable, and they also support the conclusion that carrying a 'schizophrenia gene' does not mean that a person will necessarily become schizophrenic (see Figure 18.7).

These figures suggest that the environment may be an important trigger for the activation of the biological predisposition.

Several chromosomal regions have been identified as being involved in schizophrenia, around 20 (Lewis *et al.*, 2003), and the total number of genes linked with the disorder is 4,000, a quarter of all known genes (Keshavan *et al.*, 2008). The specific genes involved are likely to be *Sp21–22* and *22q 11–12*.

Neurochemical causes

Two classes of drug have been found to affect the symptoms of schizophrenia. Cocaine and amphetamine can cause symptoms of schizophrenia, both in schizophrenics and in non-schizophrenics; antipsychotic drugs, on the other hand, can reduce them. Because both types of drug affect neural communication in which dopamine serves as a transmitter substance, investigators have hypothesised that abnormal activity of these neurons is the primary cause of schizophrenia. That is, the **dopamine hypothesis** states that the positive symptoms of schizophrenia are produced by overactivity of synapses that use dopamine as a transmitter substance.

Amphetamine and related substances make naturally occurring schizophrenia worse: paranoids become more suspicious, disorganised schizophrenics become sillier, and catatonics become more rigid or hyperactive. Davis (1974) injected an amphetamine-like drug into schizophrenic patients whose symptoms had abated. Within one minute, each patient's condition changed 'from a mild schizophrenia into a wild and very florid schizophrenia'.

Chlorpromazine and other antipsychotic drugs are remarkably effective in alleviating the positive symptoms of schizophrenia but produce little consistemt improvement in the negative symptoms. Hallucinations diminish or disappear, delusions become less striking or cease altogether, and the patient's thought processes become more coherent. These drugs are not merely tranquillisers; for example, they cause a patient with catatonic immobility to begin moving again as well as cause an excited patient to quieten down. In contrast, true tranquillisers such as Librium or Valium only make a schizophrenic patient slow-moving and lethargic.

Amphetamine, cocaine and the antipsychotic drugs act on synapses – the junctions between nerve cells – in the brain. One neuron passes on excitatory or inhibitory messages to another by releasing a small amount of transmitter substance from its terminal button into the synaptic cleft. The chemical activates receptors on the surface of the receiving neuron, and the activated receptors either excite or inhibit the receiving neuron. Drugs such as amphetamine and cocaine cause the stimulation of receptors for dopamine. In contrast, antipsychotic drugs block dopamine receptors and prevent them from becoming stimulated. The focus of the drugs appears to be the D2 receptor in the striatum: around 70 per cent of these receptors are occupied by antipsychotic medication which blocks their action (Lidow *et al.*, 1998). Cocaine, conversely, activates this receptor.

Neurological causes

Ventricular enlargement/tissue loss

Weinberger and Wyatt (1982) found that the ventricles in the brains of schizophrenic patients were, on average, twice as large as those of normal subjects. This enlargement has been confirmed in 50 studies (Lewis, 1990); MRI studies further indicate that the medial temporal lobes may be affected (Chua and McKenna, 1995), although there appears to be a reduction in whole-brain size together with an increase in the occipital areas of the ventricles (Lawrie and Abukmeil, 1998). The most consistent finding is a reduction in the lateral or third ventricle (Tanda *et al.*, 2008a; Keshavan *et al.*, 2008).

There is a loss of total brain volume as well as reduced grey matter in the temporal lobe, the prefrontal cortex and the thalamus (Keshavan *et al.*, 2008). The caudate nucleus is larger in those who respond to treatment (Keshavan *et al.*, 2008). Loss of brain tissue, as assessed by CT scans, appears to be related to negative symptoms of schizophrenia but not to positive ones (Johnstone *et al.*, 1978). In

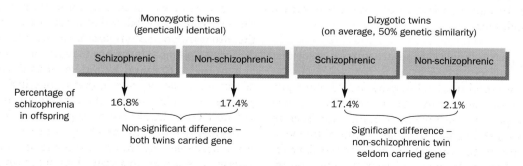

Figure 18.7 Heritability of schizophrenia. An explanation for evidence that people can have an unexpressed 'schizophrenia gene'.

addition, patients with loss of brain tissue respond poorly to antipsychotic drugs (Weinberger *et al.*, 1980). These studies suggest that positive and negative symptoms of schizophrenia have different causes: positive symptoms are a result of overactivity of dopamine synapses, whereas negative symptoms are produced by actual loss of brain tissue.

The prefrontal cortex

Metabolism in the prefrontal cortex is reduced in schizophrenia, a condition called hypofrontality (Kindermann *et al.*, 1997; Pae *et al.*, 2004) and which appears regardless of the patient's drug-taking status (Andreasen *et al.*, 1997).

PET studies of schizophrenic patients suggest that there is a decrease in dopamine receptors in the prefrontal cortex (Okubo *et al.*, 1997) and a decrease of N-acetyl aspartate in the frontal and temporal lobe (Keshavan *et al.*, 2008). There is also evidence that the neuronal density in the prefrontal cortex is 17 per cent higher compared with patients with Huntington's chorea and patients with schizophrenia-related disorders (Selemon *et al.*, 1995). These researchers suggested that this 'squashing' of neurons results from abnormal brain development and may account for the frontal lobe deficits. Keefe *et al.* (1995) found that schizophrenic patients performed poorly at keeping information in working memory over 30-second and 60-second delay periods, a frontal lobe function. Executive function and episodic memory performance, in general, is poor (Reichenberg and Harvey, 2007). These abnormalities are milder in the relatives of schizophrenic patients (Reichenberg and Harvey, 2007).

Crow (1998, 2002) has controversially suggested that a deficit in the functional lateralisation of the brain, especially the lateralisation of language, may be the cause of schizophrenia, although the evidence for this is mixed. A recent study found a significant reduction in the superior (top) part of the left temporal lobe in schizophrenic patients as well as a general reduction in the size of the temporal lobe, although this last finding was not statistically significant (Highley *et al.*, 1999). The researchers also found a relationship between this asymmetrical reduction and the time of onset of the disorder: the later the onset, the greater the reduction. Another study, this time of frontal lobe asymmetry, found that the planum temporale and Sylvian fissure were less lateralised in schizophrenic patients (Sommer *et al.*, 2001). As you saw in Chapter 10, asymmetry of these structures is associated with language processing.

Finally, Gray and colleagues have proposed that schizophrenia may be the result of abnormal connections between the limbic forebrain (especially the hippocampal formation) and the basal ganglia, the region of the brain implicated in the regulation of movement (Gray *et al.*, 1991; Gray, 1995). These neuroanatomical abnormalities correspond to increases in dopamine in a part of the basal ganglia called the nucleus accumbens. A disruption in these connections means that steps in a motor programme are not confirmed by the brain, leading to the expected outcome of each step being perceived as novel or unexpected.

Neurodevelopmental impairment

Various neurodevelopmental factors have been implicated in schizophrenia from cannabis use to obstetric complications (Keshavan *et al.*, 2008). Another possible neurological cause of schizophrenia is interference with normal prenatal brain development (Weinberger, 1996; Hultman *et al.*, 1997). Several studies have shown that people born during the winter months are more likely to develop schizophrenia later in life. Torrey *et al.* (1977) suggest that the causal factor could be seasonal variations in nutritional factors, or, more likely, variations in toxins or infectious agents in air, water or food. Several diseases known to be caused by viruses, such as measles, German measles and chicken pox, show a similar seasonality effect. The seasonality effect is seen most strongly in poor, urban locations, where people are at greater risk of viral infections (Machon *et al.*, 1983).

A seasonally related virus could affect either a pregnant woman or her newborn infant. Two pieces of evidence suggest that the damage is done prenatally. First, brain development is more susceptible to disruption prenatally than post-natally. Secondly, a study of the offspring of women who were pregnant during an epidemic of type A2 influenza in Finland occurring in 1957 showed an elevated incidence of schizophrenia (Mednick *et al.*, 1990). The increased incidence was seen only in the children of women who were in the second term of their pregnancy when the epidemic occurred. Presumably, the viral infection produced toxins that interfered with the brain development of some of the foetuses, resulting in the development of schizophrenia later in life. Weinberger (1996) has explicitly stated the neurodevelopmental hypothesis as follows: 'Schizophrenia is related to a defect in brain development. This defect predisposes to a characteristic pattern of brain malfunction in early adult life and to symptoms that respond to antidopaminergic drugs.' In a review of the evidence to suggest that this malfunction does occur and does have the consequences the hypothesis states, he suggests that the hypothesis is broadly supported although it has provoked more questions than answers.

Related to the viral hypotheses of schizophrenia are obstetric complications. Complications at birth have been associated with later development of schizophrenia (Hultman *et al.*, 1999) and infants who experience these complications are twice as likely to develop schizophrenia than is a control group (Geddes and Lawrie, 1995). Hultman *et al.*'s Swedish study of birth records of schizophrenic and control group infants report the same pattern: increased risk of schizophrenia is associated with complications during pregnancy and birth, especially in boys (Hultman *et al.*, 1997). Why these complications should be a risk factor, however, is unclear.

Cognitive and environmental causes

Family and expressed emotion

A study carried out in Finland has suggested that being raised by a 'mentally healthy' family helps to protect against the development of schizophrenia (Tienari *et al.*, 1987). The researchers examined the children of schizophrenic mothers who had been adopted away early in life. Following interviews and psychological tests, the families who adopted the children were classified as well-adjusted, moderately maladjusted or severely maladjusted. The children adopted by the well-adjusted families were least likely to show signs of mental disturbance, including schizophrenia. These findings suggest that the environment may be either an important cause or mediator of schizophrenia.

The personality and communicative abilities of either or both parents appear to play an influential role in the development of schizophrenic symptoms in children. Several studies have shown that children raised by parents who are dominating, overprotective, rigid and insensitive to the needs of others later develop schizophrenia (Roff and Knight, 1981). In many cases, a parent may be verbally accepting of the child yet in other ways reject them, which establishes a conflict for the child called a **double-bind**. For example, a mother may encourage her son to become emotionally dependent on her yet continually reject him when he tries to hug her or sit on her lap.

Schizophrenia also seems to occur at a higher than average rate among children who were reared in families characterised by verbal violence and disharmony. In a study of 14 schizophrenic individuals, Lidz *et al.* (1965) found that each of these individuals had a family that underwent either chronic discord in which the integrity of the parents' marriage was perpetually threatened, or marital problems in which the bizarre behaviour of one family member was tolerated by the other members. Children in families in which parents treat them with hostility or in which parents present confusing communication to them are at risk of developing schizophrenia. However, it is unclear whether marital discord, family hostility, and confusing communications are a cause or an effect of children's schizophrenia.

Another environmental factor which could account for the development of schizophrenia is **expressed emotion** or EE (Hooley *et al.*, 1996). Brown *et al.* (1966; Brown, 1985) identified a category of behaviours of families of individuals recovering from schizophrenia that seemed to be related to the patients' rates of recovery. They labelled

this variable expressed emotion, which consists of expressions of criticism, hostility and emotional over-involvement by the family members towards the patient. Patients living in a family environment in which the level of expressed emotion was low were more likely to recover, whereas those in families in which it was high were likely to continue to exhibit schizophrenic symptoms. The finding that low EE is associated with better outcome has since been replicated (Strachan *et al.*, 1989). Perceived criticism also appears to be important: in depressed patients, perceived criticism predicted a relapse in the mental disorder more reliably than did actual criticism (Hooley and Teasdale, 1989); mood disorder patients with high-EE families appear to be more non-verbally negative than patients from low-EE families (Simoneau *et al.*, 1998).

Jenkins and Karno (1992) report that in the past decade over 100 studies have investigated expressed emotion in countries ranging from North America, England, Denmark, and Italy to France, Spain, Germany, Taiwan, India, Egypt and Australia. Despite differences in the ways that people of different cultures perceive mental illness and express themselves, expressed emotion does not seem to be culture-bound. Two elements appear to be common to all cultures: critical comments and emotional over-involvement. If these elements are present in families of schizophrenics at low levels, patients are likely to recover quickly; if they are present at high levels, patients are less likely to recover quickly.

Jenkins and Karno also found that expressed emotion tends to be higher in industrialised cultures than in non-industrialised cultures. In other words, people in non-industrialised countries are more supportive of family members with schizophrenia than are people in industrialised countries. The reasons for this difference are many and appear to focus on the role that individuals play in the two environments.

Treatment

see activity on mypsychlab

The commonest form of treatment for schizophrenia is psychopharmacological. The only effective means of treating the disorder is by D2 antagonists. These **antipsychotic drugs** help to reduce the effects of schizophrenia apparently by blocking dopamine receptors in the brain. Presumably, overactivity of dopamine synapses is responsible for the positive symptoms of schizophrenia, which is why treatment is effective at combating the positive symptoms but has limited success in combating the negative symptoms (Keshavan *et al.*, 2008). Although dopamine-secreting neurons are located in several parts of the brain, most researchers believe that the ones involved in the symptoms of schizophrenia are located in the cerebral cortex and parts of the limbic system near the front of the brain. There is evidence that the education of the family/patient about the disorder reduces the likelihood of a relapse and that social skills training also improves outcome (Keshavan *et al.*, 2008).

A different system of dopamine-secreting neurons in the brain is involved in the control of movement. Occasionally, this system of neurons degenerates in older people, producing Parkinson's disease. Symptoms of this disorder include tremors, muscular rigidity, loss of balance, difficulty in initiating movement, and impaired breathing that makes speech indistinct. In severe cases the person is bedridden.

The major problem with antipsychotic drugs is that they do not discriminate between these two systems of dopamine-secreting neurons. The drugs interfere with the activity of both the circuits involved in the symptoms of schizophrenia and the circuits involved in the control of movements. Consequently, when a person with schizophrenia begins taking an antipsychotic drug, they often exhibit a movement disorder. Fortunately, the disorder is usually temporary and soon disappears.

However, after taking the antipsychotic drug for several years, some people develop a different, more serious, movement disorder known as **tardive dyskinesia** (tardive means late developing; dyskinesia refers to a disturbance in movement), an often irreversible and untreatable syndrome characterised by continual involuntary lip smacking, grimacing and drooling (Cummings and Wirshing, 1989). Severely affected people have difficulty talking, and occasionally the movements interfere with breathing. The risk of developing this syndrome increases with age, dose and duration of use (Hughes and Pierattini, 1992). For example, approximately 20 per cent of older people develop tardive dyskinesia. The symptoms can be alleviated temporarily by increasing the dose of the antipsychotic drug, but doing so only serves to increase and perpetuate the person's dependence on the medication (Baldessarini and Tarsy, 1980).

Clozapine, an anti-schizophrenic drug, is more effective than other antipsychotic drugs in helping cases of almost untreatable schizophrenia (Kane *et al.*, 1988). It improves the symptoms of about 30–50 per cent of those people who have not responded to traditional antipsychotic drugs. Because about 2 per cent of those taking clozapine suffer an inhibition of white blood cell production, which can be fatal, weekly blood tests have to be conducted. People with schizophrenia have not yet received clozapine for a long enough time for researchers to be sure that the drug will not eventually produce tardive dyskinesia.

Mood disorders

Everyone experiences moods varying from sadness to happiness to elation. We are excited when our team wins a game, saddened to learn

Stephen Fry, who has publicly discussed his bipolar disorder.
Source: Getty Images/Tim Whitby

that a friend's father has had a heart attack, thrilled at news of a higher than expected grade in an exam, and devastated by the death of a loved one. Some people, though, experience more dramatic mood changes than these. Significant shifts or disturbances in mood that affect normal perception, thought and behaviour are called mood disorders. They may be characterised by a deep, foreboding depression or by a combination of depression and euphoria.

Mood disorders are primarily disorders of emotion. The most severe mood disorders are bipolar disorder and major depression. **Bipolar disorder** is characterised by alternating periods of mania (wild excitement) and depression. **Major depression** involves persistent and severe feelings of sadness and worthlessness accompanied by changes in appetite, sleeping and behaviour. The lifetime prevalence rates for major depression are about 13 per cent for males and about 21 per cent for females (Kessler *et al.*, 1994a).

A less severe form of depression is called **dysthymic disorder**. The term comes from the Greek words *dus*, 'bad' and *thymos*, 'spirit'. The primary difference between this disorder and major depression is its relatively low severity. Similarly, **cyclothymic disorder** resembles bipolar disorder but is much less severe.

Mania

Mania (the Greek word for madness) is characterised by wild, exuberant, unrealistic activity unprecipitated by environmental events. During manic episodes, people are usually elated and self-confident; however, contradiction or interference tends to make them very angry. Their speech (and, presumably, their thought processes) becomes very rapid. They tend to flit from topic to topic and are full of

Author, creativity researcher and manic-depressive, Kay Jamison
Source: Getty Images

grandiose plans, but their thoughts are not as disorganised as those of people with schizophrenia. Manic patients also tend to be restless and hyperactive, often pacing around ceaselessly. They often have delusions and hallucinations, typically of a nature that fits their exuberant mood. Impairments in 'frontal lobe' function such as set-shifting, verbal memory and sustained attention have been reported (Clark *et al*., 2002), and the experience of the disorder has been related to an oversensitive frontal cortex (Harmon-Jones *et al*., 2002).

The usual response that manic speech and behaviour evokes in another person is one of sympathetic amusement. In fact, when an experienced clinician starts to become amused by a patient, the clinician begins to suspect the presence of mania. Because very few patients exhibit only mania, the DSM-IV TR classifies all cases in which mania occurs as bipolar disorder. Patients with bipolar disorder usually experience alternate periods of mania and depression. Each of these periods lasts from a few days to a few weeks, usually with several days of relatively normal behaviour between. Around 40 per cent of bipolar disorder patients will have been diagnosed with major depression previously (Bowden, 2001). Even according to DSM-IV TR, 'the specific diagnostic categories are meant to serve as guidelines to be informed by clinical judgement and are not meant to be used in a cookbook fashion'. Many therapists have observed that there is often something brittle and unnatural about the happiness during the manic phase, as though the patient

is making themselves be happy to ward off an attack of depression. Indeed, some manic patients are simply hyperactive and irritable rather than euphoric.

Depression

Description

> It was the worst experience of my life. More terrible even than watching my wife die of cancer. I am ashamed to admit that my depression felt worse than her death but it's true. I was in a state that bears no resemblance to anything I had experienced before. I was not just feeling very low. I was seriously ill. I was totally self-involved, negative and thought about suicide most of the time. I could not think properly let alone work, and wanted to remain curled up in bed all day.

These were the opening words of Professor Lewis Wolpert, Professor of Developmental Biology at University College London in his book, *Malignant Sadness*. Depressed people are extremely sad and are usually full of self-directed guilt, but not because of any particular environmental event. Depressed people cannot always state why they are depressed. Around 17 per cent of people will experience a major episode of depression at some point in their lives (Kessler *et al*., 1994b) and a similar percentage experiences disability at work due to the illness (Goldberg and Steury, 2001). Beck (1967) identified five cardinal symptoms of depression: (1) a sad and apathetic mood; (2) feelings of worthlessness and hopelessness; (3) a desire to withdraw from other people; (4) sleeplessness and loss of appetite and sexual desire; and (5) change in activity level, to either lethargy or agitation. Major depression must be distinguished from grief, such as that caused by the death of a loved one. People who are grieving feel sad and depressed but do not fear losing their minds or have thoughts of self-harm. Because many people who do suffer from major depression or the depressed phase of bipolar disorder commit suicide, these disorders are potentially fatal. The fatality rate by suicide for major depression is estimated at 15 per cent (Guze and Robins, 1970). According to Elizabeth Wurtzel, author of *Prozac Nation*:

> one day, you realise that your entire life is just awful, not worth living, a horror and a black blot on the white terrain of human existence. One morning, you wake up afraid you are going to live . . . for all intents and purposes, the deeply depressed are just the walking, waking dead.

Depression knows no social or intellectual barriers. Lewis Wolpert, Professor of Developmental Biology, Winston Churchill, British Prime Minister (both pictured here) and the late Stuart Sutherland, Professor of Psychology, have all suffered from major depression or bipolar disorder.

Sources: Courtesy Lewis Wolpert, Press Association Images.

The 'walking, waking dead', according to the World Health Organization (2002b), account for 4.4 per cent of the world's disease burden, a percentage similar to that for ischaemic heart disease and asthma and pulmonary disease combined. According to one study, depressive disorders are likely to be the second most common diseases by the year 2020 (Brown, 2001). Successful treatment, therefore, is vital. Interventions can reduce the burden of depression by as much as 10–30 per cent (Chisholm *et al.*, 2004).

The UK Office for National Statistics estimates that 2.6 million people suffered depression in England in 2000 (Thomas and Morris, 2003), 72 per cent of whom were girls/women and 20 per cent of whom were aged between 35 and 44 years. The direct cost to the National Health Service was estimated at almost £370 million. The total cost, which includes economic costs such as days taken off work and disability benefit, was estimated to be £9 billion. The cost of treatment, therefore, was a drop in the ocean compared to the other costs involved. Some 109.7 million working days were lost through depression and 2,615 deaths resulted from the disorder.

A Canadian study of 1,281 employees who had claimed depression-related absences from work found that 60 per cent who claimed disability benefit took antidepressants. Those who took the recommended drugs and at the right

dosage were less likely to claim long-term disability benefits or to leave work completely. The researchers estimated that early intervention would reduce the appearance of depression by three weeks, representing a financial saving of $3,500 per person. If early intervention had occurred in people who started taking the drugs 30 days after the start of the first episode of depression, savings of around $539,000 could have been made.

Of course, perhaps more important than the financial cost is the human, psychological cost. As Thomas and Morris (2003) conclude (p. 518), 'the intangible elements of pain and suffering of people with depressive disorders and their families and the effects on quality of life cannot be quantified in monetary terms'.

Aetiology

Cognitive causes

People with mood disorders do not have the same outlook on life as others. Specifically, they make negative statements about themselves and their abilities: 'Nobody likes me', 'I'm not good at anything', 'What's the point in even trying, I'll just mess it up anyway'. Because they are so negative about themselves, depressed people are particularly unpleasant to be around. The problem is that the depressed individual is caught in a vicious circle: negative statements strain interpersonal relationships, which result in others withdrawing or failing to initiate social support, which, in turn, reinforces the depressed individual's negative statements (Klerman and Weissman, 1986).

Beck (1967, 1991) suggested that the changes in affect seen in depression are not primary but instead are secondary to changes in cognition. That is, the primary disturbance is a distortion in the person's view of reality. For example, a depressed person may see a scratch on the surface of their car and conclude that the car is ruined; or a person whose recipe fails may see the unappetising dish as proof of their unworthiness; or a nasty letter from a creditor is seen as a serious and personal condemnation. According to Beck, depressed people's thinking is characterised by self-blame (things that go wrong are always their fault), overemphasis on the negative aspects of life (small problems are blown out of proportion), and failure to appreciate positive experiences (pessimism). This kind of pessimistic thinking involves negative thoughts about the self, about the present and about the future, which Beck collectively referred to as the **cognitive triad**. In short, depressed people blame their present miserable situation on their inadequacies and a lack of hope for improving the situation in the future.

The negative view of the self and events, however, seems to be time-specific. Depressed individuals who are asked to describe themselves 'right now' use negative terms, but use less negative terms when they describe how they usually feel (Brewin et al., 1992). Depressed patients are also likely to be negative when discussing things globally but not when discussing specific issues (Wycherley, 1995).

Beck's original model argued that cognition caused the emotional disorder, but his later reformulation of the theory suggested that cognition is part of a set of interacting mechanisms that include biological, psychological and social factors (Kovacs and Beck, 1978). In the reformulation, Beck argued that people might be predisposed to develop depression under certain circumstances. He called this a diathesis-stress theory. Central to the theory is that there is a set of schema – a stored collection of knowledge that affects encoding and understanding of all other processed information – which, when activated, sets off a series of negative thoughts and experiences. If the schema is depressogenic – characterised by depressive features – then an event which might activate these schemata leads to the person processing information very negatively. However, if a person is not exposed to these triggers, they will think or behave no more depressively than a person who does not possess depressogenic schemata. A study of undergraduates found that students with dysfunctional attitudes – those who were identified as having depressogenic schemata – felt more depressed after learning they had been refused a place at a univer-

sity of their choice than when learning that they had, a pattern not seen in students whose attitudes were not dysfunctional (Abela and D'Allessandro, 2002).

Beck also distinguished between two types of depression: sociotropic depression in which the abnormal belief derived from a dependence on others, and autonomous depression in which the individual was goal-oriented and relied little on others. The evidence for these two types as distinct varieties of depression, however, is mixed (Power and Dalgleish, 1997).

Another causal factor in depression appears to involve the attributional style of the depressed person (Abramson et al., 1978, 1989). According to this idea, it is not merely experiencing negative events that causes people to become depressed: what is more important are the attributions people make about why those events occur. People who are most likely to become depressed are those who attribute negative events and experiences to their own shortcomings and who believe that their life situations are never going to get any better. A person's attributional style, then, serves as a predisposition or diathesis for depression. In other words, people prone to depression tend to have a hopeless outlook on their life: 'I am not good at anything I try to do and it will never get any better. I am always going to be a useless person.' According to this view, depression is most likely when people with pessimistic attributional styles encounter significant or frequent life stressors (Abramson et al., 1989). The pessimistic attributions are then generalised to other, perhaps smaller, stressors, and eventually a deep sense of hopelessness and despair sets in. Thus, the original formulation of the theory was called the helplessness theory whereas the later reformulation became known as the hopelessness theory.

Such people also appear to suffer a double dose of hopelessness. Not only do they perceive negative outcomes as being their own fault, but they also perceive positive outcomes as being due to circumstance or to luck. In addition, they apply pessimistic attributions to a wide range of events and experiences and apply positive attributions only to a very narrow range of events and experiences, if any.

However, there is mixed evidence for a strong version of the hopelessness attribution theory. Swendsen (1998) reported that attributional style did not predict immediate depressed or anxious mood in a group of 91 individuals who were asked to report negative events, cognitions, anxiety and depression five times a day for one week. However, attributional style did predict 'individual' specific causal attributions made to negative events. Similar findings have been reported in other studies (Kapci, 1998). Lynd-Stevenson (1996, 1997) reports that hopelessness does not mediate the relationship between attributional style and depression but that there is a mediating effect when measures of hopelessness are relevant to the individual's ongoing life (in Lynd-Stevenson's sample's case, hopelessness related to unemployment). Attributional style, therefore, seems to apply only in certain, relevant contexts.

Genetic causes

Like schizophrenia, the mood disorders appear to have a genetic component. People who have first-degree relatives with a serious mood disorder are ten times more likely to develop these disorders than are people without afflicted relatives (Rosenthal, 1970). Furthermore, the concordance rate for bipolar disorder is 72 per cent for monozygotic twins, compared with 14 per cent for dizygotic twins. For major depression, the figures are 40 per cent and 11 per cent, respectively (Allen, 1976). Thus, bipolar disorder appears to be more heritable than major depression, and the two disorders appear to have different genetic causes. Recent studies, however, have cast doubt on the heritability of major depressive disorder (Andrew *et al.*, 1998).

Neurochemical causes

Drug treatments for depression (which are described in detail below) have shed some light on the biochemical causes of schizophrenia. Antidepressants such as imipramine, for example, stimulate synapses that use two transmitter substances, norepinephrine and serotonin. Other drugs such as reserpine, which is used to treat high blood pressure, can cause episodes of depression. Reserpine lowers blood pressure by blocking the release of norepinephrine in muscles in the walls of blood vessels, thus causing the muscles to relax. However, because the drug also blocks the release of norepinephrine and serotonin in the brain, a common side-effect is depression. This side-effect strengthens the argument that biochemical factors in the brain play an important role in depression.

Such data have suggested a biological amine theory of depression: depression results from a depletion in the monoamines, dopamine, norepinephrine or serotonin. The serotonin hypothesis is a variant of this general theory. The serotonin hypothesis suggests that this neurotransmitter (the lack of it) may be more involved in depression because blocking reuptake of serotonin is more effective than blocking norepinephrine. Given that most antidepressants augment serotonin (perhaps by different mechanisms), perhaps the involvement of other neurotransmitters is peripheral.

In addition to the amines, levels of the neurotransmitter Gamma amino byturic acid (GABA) have been found to be lower in the cerebrospinal fluid and plasma of individuals with unipolar depression (Brambila *et al.*, 2003). When depressed individuals are given drugs which increase the level of serotonin at serotonergic neurons or are given

ECT, the decrease in GABA concentration seen in the occipital cortex is reversed (Sanacora *et al.*, 2002, 2004). The roles of the two classes of GABA (the a and b classes) in depression, however, is unclear.

Neuropathological causes

In a neuroimaging study, activity in the prefrontal cortex near the top of the corpus callosum was reduced in individuals with unipolar and bipolar depression (Drevets *et al.*, 1997). This part of the prefrontal cortex is called the anterior cingulate cortex and a specific region within the cingulate – which has been called subgenual region sg24 – is less active in people with mood disorder, as Figure 18.8 shows.

Drevets *et al.* found that the volume of this region was lateralised to the left hemisphere, which is consistent with

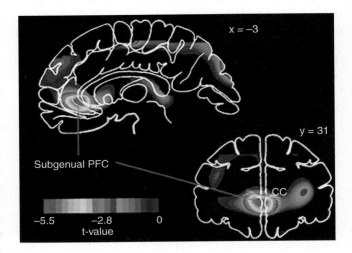

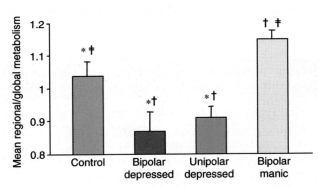

Figure 18.8 Decreases in activation in the prefrontal cortex seen in individuals with mood disorders.

Source: Drevets, W.C., Neuroimaging and neuropathological studies of depression: Implications for the cognitive-emotional features of mood disorders. *Current Opinion in Neurobiology*, 2001, 11, 240–49. Copyright 2001, with permission from Elsevier.

the data and model of normal emotion described in Chapter 13. These findings were subsequently replicated in a group of people with severe mood disorder (Hirayasu *et al.*, 1999).

When Drevets and his colleagues went on to explore the cellular nature of this region in people with mood disorder, they found the typical reduction in sg24 but also a reduction in the density of cells and in the number of glial cells (see Ongur *et al.*, 1998). A further study, using a larger sample, found that same pattern of cell reduction in a group of individuals with major and bipolar depression but only in a subset with a family history of the disorder (Torrey *et al.*, 2000). These cells carry neurotransmitter receptors and help to transport neurotransmitters, which may explain why their reduction is associated with depression; the reduction might also explain why this area is seen as smaller in people with depression and bipolar depression.

Studies have also implicated a dysfunction in the functioning of the hypothalamus (Bao *et al.*, 2008; Swaab and Bar 2005). For example, cortisol levels (the glucocorticoid you read about in the stress section of Chapter 17) are thought to be worse in the morning than in the afternoon (and depressed people are at their worst in the morning). Levels of cortisol are higher in depressed individuals than controls and an increase in the number of neurons in the hypothalamus that release corticotrophin-releasing hormone is found in these patients; the levels of CRH in cerebrospinal fluid is also higher and people on cortisol-increasing drugs report symptoms of depression. Serotonin is reduced in the presence of CRH and as the principal action of antidepressants is to make more serotonin available in the brain, these two factors may be linked.

Geography

Some studies suggest that depression and psychosis are more common in urban than rural areas but others report no such difference. To attempt to determine whether such a difference was real and consistent, Sundquist *et al.* (2004) followed up the entire Swedish population aged between 25 and 64 years who had been admitted to hospital with a diagnosis of depression and psychosis. Level of urbanisation was defined by population density.

They found that those patients who lived in the most densely populated areas were 68–77 per cent more likely to be at risk of developing psychosis and 12–20 per cent more likely to be at risk of developing depression than were patients who lived in the least densely populated areas.

Why such a difference should emerge is unknown. It may be that living in densely populated areas produces more adverse living circumstances, such as stressful events and little social support.

Cutting edge – Cold summers, depressed Swedes and antidepressants

Working on the hypothesis that restricted leisure activities of an outdoor nature would lead to increased stress and unhappiness, researchers at Uppsala and California Universities investigated the use of antidepressants during unseasonable cold summer weather in Sweden that would inhibit normal outdoor activity (Hartig *et al.*, 2007). In total, prescriptions administered between 1991 and 1998 were examined. More antidepressants were dispensed during cold Julys to men and women.

Suicide – An international perspective

Migration, low intelligence and substance use may separately be important risk factors for depression and suicide. In some countries, suicide rates have increase by over 60 per cent in the past five decades and you can see this pattern and the international incidence in Figure 18.9 a and b.

A study of immigration into Estonia, which had been part of the Soviet Union until independence in 1991 and had, therefore, a significant Russian population (about 30 per cent of the population were Russians in 1989), found that while the rate of suicide was lower in the Russian minority during Soviet rule, this pattern changed during the period of stabilisation following independence (Varnik *et al.*, 2005). The rate was higher than that found in Estonians in Estonia or in Russians in Russia, reflecting a change in status from privileged minority to non-privileged minority. The rates converged in 1998, suggesting to the authors that this may reflect the efforts by the Estonian government to integrate the Russian minority.

In a separate study of Swedish servicemen, Gunnell *et al.* (2005) found that of 987,308 Swedish men followed up for up to 26 years risk of suicide was 2–3 times higher in men with the lowest cognitive test scores compared to those with the highest. The greatest suicide risk emerged from the test of logic – this was the test correlating most significantly with suicide. Perhaps this reflects an inability to solve problems in real life; problems which, if left unresolved, lead to self-harm and death.

Suicide – *Continued*

Suicide attempts in adolescence are associated with heavy or frequent drinking and illegal drug-taking (Shaffer and Pfeffer, 2001; Gould *et al.*, 2003). A group of Norwegian researchers monitored the correlation between substance use and suicide in two surveys (in 1992 and 2002) of 23,000 13–19-year-olds (Rossow *et al.*, 2005). There was a significant relationship between increased substance use and suicide, but only in girls. For boys, the effect of substance use seemed to be less pronounced in 2002 than in 1992. For both sexes, the substance most significantly associated with suicide attempts was alcohol.

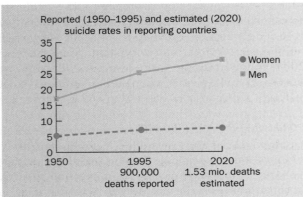

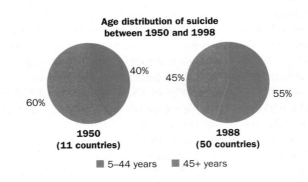

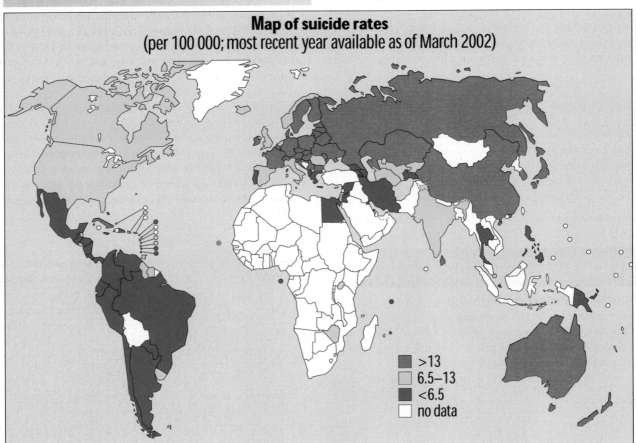

Figure 18.9 World Health Organisation statistics for suicide rates across the world

Source: World Health Organisation

Treatment

The two principal treatments for clinical depression are cognitive therapy and antidepressant medication.

Cognitive (behavioural) therapy

Beck's cognitive therapy begins by arguing that the negative beliefs held by depressed individuals are seen as conclusions based on faulty logic (Beck, 1967). A depressed person concludes that they are 'deprived, frustrated, humiliated, rejected or punished' (Beck et al., 1979, p. 120). Beck views the cognitions of the depressed individual in terms of a cognitive triad: a negative view of the self ('I am worthless'), of the outside world ('The world makes impossible demands on me'), and of the future ('Things are never going to get better').

Even when confronted with evidence that contradicts their negative beliefs, depressed individuals often find an illogical means of interpreting good news as bad news (Lewinsohn et al., 1980). For example, a student who receives an A grade on an exam might attribute the high grade to an easy, unchallenging exam rather than to their own mastery of the material. The fact that few others in the class received a high grade does little to convince the depressed person that they deserve congratulations for having done well. The depressed student goes on believing, against contrary evidence, that the good grade was not really deserved.

Once the faulty logic is recognised for what it is, therapy entails exploring means for correcting the distortions. The therapist does not accept the client's conclusions and inferences at their face value. Instead, those conclusions resulting from faulty logic are discussed so that the client may understand them from another perspective, changing their behaviour as a result.

Meta-analyses suggest that CBT can be a very effective means of combating depression and may even be more effective than tricyclic antidepressants (see below) in the long term (Hensley et al., 2004).

Antidepressant drugs

Tricyclic antidepressants

Antidepressant drugs are a class of drugs used to treat the symptoms of major depression and the most common of these are listed in Table 18.9. **Antimanic drugs** are used to treat the symptoms of bipolar disorder and mania. The earliest used antidepressant drugs were derived from the family of chemicals known as **tricyclics**, which refers to their 'three-ring' chemical structure (Lickey and Gordon, 1983).

Although the biology of depression is not well understood, the most widely accepted theory is that depression may result from a deficiency of the catecholamine neurotransmitters norepinephrine and serotonin. Each of these neurotransmitters may be involved in different types of depression, although researchers are not sure how. Antidepressant drugs seem to slow down the reuptake of these neurotransmitters by presynaptic axons. Although tricyclic antidepressants do not work for all people, about 60–80 per cent of those whose depression has brought despair to their lives gradually return to normal after having been placed on tricyclics for 2–6 weeks (Hughes and Pierattini, 1992). Unfortunately, tricyclics have many side-effects, including dizziness, sweating, weight gain, constipation, increased heart rate, poor concentration and dry mouth.

Monoamine oxidase inhibitors

Another class of antidepressants, introduced in the late 1950s, is the **monoamine oxidase inhibitors** (**MAOIs**), which take 1–3 weeks to begin alleviating depression. MAOIs prevent enzymes in the synaptic gap from destroying dopamine, norepinephrine and serotonin that have been released by presynaptic neurons. These drugs can have many side-effects, many of them fatal. The **tyramine cheese reaction**, for example, arises from the eating of foods containing tyramine such as some wines, milk products, coffee and chocolate. Because the monoamine oxidase does not oxidise tyramine, tyramine displaces epinephrine at epinephrine receptors. This produces severe hypertension and blurred vision, impotence, insomnia and nausea. It can also be fatal if leading to a haemorrhage. MAOIs also have been shown to be more effective in treating atypical depressions such as those involving hypersomnia (too much sleep) or mood swings (Hughes and Pierattini, 1992).

Serotonin-specific reuptake inhibitors

A relatively new class of drugs is **serotonin-specific reuptake inhibitors** (**SSRIs**), which, as their name suggests, block the reuptake of serotonin in nerve cells. As a result, the common feature of all SSRIs is that they enhance the transmission of serotonin. Perhaps the most common SSRI is fluoxetine (Prozac), first authorised for medical use in 1988. Fluoxetine inhibits the reuptake of serotonin, leaving more of that neurotransmitter in the synaptic cleft to stimulate post-synaptic receptors, and is the drug of first choice when tricyclic drug treatment has failed. SSRIs produce fewer negative side-effects than do tricyclics and the MAOIs, although some individuals do experience headache, gastrointestinal discomfort, insomnia, tremor and sexual dysfunction.

Table 18.9 Some of the drugs used to treat depression

Substance	Generic name	Example
Norepinephrine-reuptake inhibitors (Tertiary amine tricyclics)	Amitriptyline	Elavil
	Clomipramine	Anafranil
	Doxepin	Adapin, Sinequa
	Imipramine	Tofranil
	Trimipramine	Surmontil
Norepinephrine-reuptake inhibitors (Secondary amine tricyclics)	Amoxapine	Asendin
	Desipramine	Norpramin, Pertofrane
	Maprotiline	Ludiomil
	Nortriptyline	Pamelor
	Protriptyline	Vivactil
Serotonin-reuptake inhibitors	Fluoxetine	Prozac
	Fluvoxamine	Luvox
	Paroxetine	Paxil
	Sertraline	Zoloft
	Venlafaxine	Effexor
Atypical antidepressants	Bupropion	Wellbutrin
	Nefazodone	Serzone
	Trazodone	Desyrel
Monoamine oxidase inhibitors	Phenelzine	Nardil
	Tranylcypromine	Parnate
	Selegiline	Eldepryl

Source: From Goodman and Gilman's *The Pharmacological Basis of Therapeutics*, 9th edn (Hardman, J.G. and Limberd, L.E., eds), 'Drugs and the treatment of psychiatric disorders: psychosis and anxiety' (Baldessarini, R.J.). Reproduced with permission of The McGraw-Hill Companies.

Recent pharmacological treatments

Two developments in the psychopharmacology of depression have been second generation (atypical) depressants which block either norepinephrine reuptake or dopamine reuptake, and **dual-action antidepressants** which block certain serotonin receptors while inhibiting its reuptake. An example of the former, nefazdone, was released in 1995; an example of the latter, mirtazapine, was released in 1997. Neither type of drug has been authorised in all European countries and, because of their youth, little research is available evaluating their long-term efficacy.

The important factor in assessing the effect of antidepressant medication is the maintenance phase of the treatment. In the initial period of drug-taking, there is an acute phase in which the acute symptoms begin to stabilise. This period can last up to three months (Hirschfeld, 2001). The next period extends between the end of the acute period and the end of the depression itself, a period that can take up to 6 to 12 months. The danger is that if patients had stabilised in the acute phase, then they would have medication withdrawn. According to Hirschfeld (2001), however, around one-third to one-half of people who successfully stabilise in the acute phase, will relapse if medication is not sustained, hence the importance of monitoring behaviour closely during this period.

Lithium carbonate

Lithium carbonate is most effective in the treatment of bipolar disorders or simple mania (Young and Newham, 2006). People's manic symptoms usually decrease as soon as their blood level of lithium reaches a sufficiently high level (Gerbino *et al.*, 1978). In bipolar disorder, once the manic phase is eliminated, the depressed phase does not return. People with bipolar disorder have remained free of their symptoms for years as long as they have continued taking lithium carbonate. This drug can have some side-effects, such as a fine tremor or excessive urine production; but in general, the benefits far outweigh the adverse symptoms. However, an overdose of lithium is toxic, which means that the person's blood level of lithium must be monitored regularly. Psychotherapy has also been associated with some benefits, but this treatment is more successful for depression than mania (Scott, 2006).

The major difficulty with treating bipolar disorder is that people with this disorder often miss their 'high'.

The Blue Room at the Dana Centre in the Science Museum, London.

Source: Science and Society Picture Library.

When medication is effective, the mania subsides along with the depression. But most people enjoy at least the initial phase of their manic periods, and some believe that they are more creative at that time. In addition, many of these people say that they resent having to depend on a chemical 'crutch'. As a consequence, many people suffering from bipolar disorder stop taking their medication. Not taking their medication endangers the lives of these people because the risk of death by suicide is particularly high during the depressive phase of bipolar disorder.

Seasonal affective disorder (SAD)

Some people become depressed during the winter season, when days are short and nights are long. The symptoms of this form of depression, called **seasonal affective disorder**, are slightly different from those of major depression (Rosenthal *et al.*, 1984). Both forms include lowered mood, lethargy and sleep disturbances, but seasonal depression includes a craving for carbohydrates and an accompanying weight gain.

The original study of SAD found a pattern of depression during winter and hypomania during the spring/summer in 29 individuals (Rosenthal *et al.*, 1984). A high percentage of these individuals exhibited bipolar disorder (92 per cent). Similar percentages have been reported elsewhere (Thompson, 1989). Although various mechanisms have been advanced, the most interesting has been the proposal that the light-sensitive hormone mela-

tonin is dysfunctional in individuals with SAD. Seasonal affective disorder can be treated by exposing people to bright light for several hours a day, for example, or early in the morning (Rosenthal *et al.*, 1985; Thompson *et al.*, 1997). The direct evidence for the role of melatonin, however, appears to be inconclusive (Rosenthal and Wehr, 1992; Dalgleish *et al.*, 1996).

Sexual dysfunctions

The DSM-IV TR lists a number of sex-related disorders which have severe psychological consequences and causes. **Male sexual dysfunction**, for example, refers to the man's inability to achieve an erection, in the absence of impaired sexual desire – the desire is there, but the erection is not. Some authors have argued that this failure to achieve erection is due to some form of performance anxiety and that combating this anxiety will eliminate the problem; there is some evidence for this view (Munjack *et al.*, 1984). **Female sexual dysfunction** – the inability of the woman to achieve orgasm although the desire for orgasm is present – is sometimes treated by systematic desensitisation or masturbation training and both have been successful (Emmelkamp, 1994). Other disorders classified as sexual dysfunctions are the paraphilias.

Paraphilia

According to the DSM-IV TR, **paraphilia** constitutes a mental or behavioural disorder that has a sexual content. The individuals must be distressed by the urges or behaviour they exhibit and social or occupational functioning must be impaired. The paraphilias include: **fetishism** (the use of non-living objects for sexual excitement), **transvestic fetishism** (cross-dressing), **paedophilia** (sex with pre-pubescent children), **voyeurism** (looking at people without their knowledge while they are undressing/having sex), **sexual masochism** (the individual derives sexual gratification from being made to suffer), **sexual sadism** (the individual derives sexual gratification from inflicting suffering), **exhibitionism** (exposure of genitalia in public), **frotteurism** (rubbing against a person in public) and paraphilias not otherwise specified. The Psychology in Action section highlights just one of these paraphilias and shows how clinical psychologists can help treat the disorders.

Psychology in action – Treating exhibitionism

'Steve', a 34-year-old married man, was arrested for sexually assaulting a woman after attempting to help her fix her broken-down car. He fixed the woman's fan belt, pulled her to him and began fondling her buttocks. She pushed him away, but he exposed himself and began masturbating. After the woman contacted the police, Steve was arrested and charged.

Psychiatric assessment determined that Steve had a history of exhibitionism and frottage. As an adolescent, he would rub up against women in crowded places and, when he obtained his driver's licence, he used to park in car parks, watch women and covertly masturbate. When he was 16 years old, Steve remembered watching football in a park while sitting next to a female acquaintance. As he sat next to her, he began masturbating, eventually ejaculating. At the age of 13, he remembered playing with three young women and had an orgasm while wrestling with one of them when rubbing against her buttocks. He would repeat the behaviour with his 8-year-old sister, rubbing her buttocks until he orgasmed. When his sister threatened to tell their mother, he would masturbate to fantasies of buttock rubbing. After this, he would expose himself about 15 to 20 times a year, especially during times of stress. His sexual fantasy involved a woman catching him masturbating; the woman would be aroused by his erect state. This, however, never happened in real life. At the age of 24, he married Helen, a secretary. She gave birth to a son, who was 5 years old at the time of his father's arrest.

Steve's family history is a complex affair. His father changed jobs often and so the family moved frequently. Such frequent movement meant that Steve formed very few lasting relationships or friendships. He felt rejected by his father and clung to his mother, who was smothering and overprotective. She bathed him up until the age of 15. She would clean his penis by stroking it with a wet bar of soap and would enjoy seeing the erection this produced.

After the arrest, his wife complained of his lack of affection and of their poor sexual relations, but she knew nothing of his deviance. He did minimal parenting or household duties and his wife had little respect for him. Steve's treatment was initially aimed at stopping public masturbation and frottage. These behaviours were linked to car parks, shopping centres and subways; he was, therefore, told to avoid these places. He abstained for two months, but he still experienced urges to exhibit. To combat these urges, he was instructed to distract himself whenever he felt them – by imagining himself on a beach, feeling drowsy and soaking up the sun.

To change his fantasies and improve sexual relations with his wife, Steve was instructed to masturbate only while fantasising about intercourse. When he could not do this, he was told to masturbate while fantasising about frottage but at the point of orgasm, he should switch his fantasy to intercourse. This fantasy was then encouraged to appear earlier on during masturbation. By the fourth week of therapy, he could masturbate without having deviant fantasies. He was still turned on by seeing women's buttocks in tight jeans, however, and so was asked to imagine a non-sexual fantasy when seeing these, such as thinking about the woman's occupation or looking at her face instead.

During marital therapy, he was shocked that his wife viewed him so negatively. So shocked was he that he began to help more around the house and got a new job as a camera salesman. The usual foreplay (rubbing his wife's buttocks) was replaced with manual or oral stimulation and his sexual relations with his wife improved. Although Steve's deviant behaviour had not been 'cured', it had been contained.

Source: Oltmans *et al.* (1995).

Chapter review

Classification and diagnosis of mental disorders

- Psychologists and other mental health professionals view the causes of mental disorders from several different perspectives:
  - The psychodynamic perspective argues that mental disorders arise from intrapsychic conflict that overwhelms the mind's defence mechanisms.
  - The medical perspective asserts that mental disorders have an organic basis, as physical illnesses do.
  - The cognitive behavioural perspective maintains that mental disorders are learned patterns of maladaptive thinking and behaving.
  - The humanistic perspective suggests that mental disorders arise from an oversensitivity to the demands of others and because positive regard from others is conditional on meeting those demands.
  - The sociocultural perspective focuses on how cultural variables influence the development of mental disorders and people's subjective reactions to them.
- Many elements of these perspectives are integrated into the diathesis-stress model of mental disorders which suggests that biological inheritance and early learning experiences predispose us to develop mental disorders; these disorders are

expressed only if we encounter stressors that overwhelm our capacity to cope with them.

- The two major manuals for diagnostic mental disorder are the *Diagnostic and Statistical Manual of Mental Disorders* IV (American Psychiatric Association, 1994) and the *International Classification of Diseases* 10 (World Health Organization, 1992).
- There is strong cross-cultural agreement for the diagnosis of disorder such as schizophrenia, although anxiety and social phobia are not as uniformly diagnosed; there are also culture-bound disorders which are not universal.
- Research indicates that lay people continue to show poor understanding of the symptoms, possible causes and treatment of mental illness.

Treatment of mental disorders

- Historically, people suffering from emotional or behavioural problems were believed to be possessed by demons or were accused of being witches. They were often subjected to torture, including trephining, in which a small hole was punctured in the skull of the afflicted person to allow demonic spirits to escape. Mental patients in sixteenth- and seventeenth-century asylums encountered abject humiliation. Philippe Pinel, a French physician, is often credited with changing the asylum environment in the late eighteenth century.
- Modern therapy adopts an eclectic approach – the borrowing of methods from different treatments and blending them in a way that will work best in treating the patient's problem. There are, however, different types of treatment approaches that have specific characteristics.
- Insight psychotherapy is based primarily on conversation between therapist and client. The oldest form of insight psychotherapy, psychoanalysis, was devised by Freud.
- Psychoanalysis attempts to discover the forces that are warring in the client's psyche and to resolve these inner conflicts by bringing to consciousness the client's unconscious drives and the defences that have been established against them. Insight is believed to be the primary source of healing.
- Humanistic therapy emphasises conscious, deliberate mental processes.
- Client-centred therapy is based on the premise that people are healthy and good and that their problems result from faulty thinking. Instead of evaluating themselves in terms of their own self-concepts, they judge themselves by other people's standards. This tendency is rectified by providing an environment of unconditional positive regard in which clients can find their own way to good mental health.
- Gestalt therapy focuses on convincing clients that they must deal honestly with their present feelings in order to become more mentally healthy. According to gestalt therapists, the key to becoming happier is to confront one's fears and guilt and to keep one's emotions in proper perspective.
- The range of people that may benefit from insight therapy is limited and narrow. In general, those most likely to benefit are those who are intelligent and able to articulate their problems.

Insight psychotherapies are not effective with persons with serious mental disorders such as schizophrenia. There are also difficulties with evaluating their effectiveness.

- Behavioural therapists attempt to use the principles of classical and operant conditioning to modify behaviour – fears are eliminated or maladaptive behaviours are replaced with adaptive ones.
- Systematic desensitisation uses classical conditioning procedures to condition relaxation to stimuli that were previously producing fear. In contrast, implosion therapy attempts to extinguish fear and avoidance responses. Aversion therapy attempts to condition an unpleasant response to a stimulus with which the client is preoccupied, such as a fetish.
- The most formal system of therapy based on operant conditioning involves token economies, which arrange contingencies in the environment of people who reside in institutions.
- Some operant treatment is vicarious – people can imagine their own behaviour with its consequent reinforcement or punishment.
- Modelling involves using others as role models for behaviour.
- The major problem with behaviour therapy is the failure of patients to transfer behaviour outside the therapy setting. Techniques to promote generalisation include the use of intermittent reinforcement and recruitment of family and friends as adjunct therapists.
- Cognitive behavioural therapies attempt to change overt behaviour and unobservable cognitive processes.
- Rational-emotive therapy is based on the assumption that people's psychological problems stem from faulty cognitions. Its practitioners use many forms of persuasion, including confrontation, to encourage people to abandon faulty cognitions in favour of logical and healthy ones.
- Beck has developed ways to help depressed people correct errors of cognition that perpetuate self-defeating thoughts.
- Group therapy is based on the belief that certain problems can be treated more efficiently and more effectively in group settings.
- Practitioners of family therapy, couples therapy and some forms of group behaviour therapy observe people's interactions with others and attempt to help them learn how to establish more effective patterns of behaviour. Treatment of groups, including families and couples, permits the therapist to observe clients' social behaviours, and it uses social pressures to help convince clients of the necessity for behavioural change. It permits clients to learn from the mistakes of others and to observe that other people have similar problems, which often provides reassurance.
- The effectiveness of psychotherapeutic methods is difficult to assess: outcomes are difficult to measure objectively, ethical considerations make it hard to establish control groups for some types of disorder, and self-selection and drop-outs make it impossible to compare randomly selected groups of participants. Research suggests that behavioural therapy and cognitive behavioural therapy are effective.
- Biological treatments for mental disorders include drugs, electroconvulsive therapy and psychosurgery.

- Research has shown that treatment of the positive symptoms of schizophrenia with antipsychotic drugs, of major depression with antidepressant drugs, and of bipolar disorder with lithium carbonate are the most effective ways to alleviate the symptoms of these disorders.
- Tricyclic antidepressant drugs can also alleviate severe anxiety that occurs during panic attacks and agoraphobia and can reduce the severity of obsessive-compulsive disorder.
- Although electroconvulsive therapy is an effective treatment for depression, its use is reserved for cases in which rapid relief is critical because the seizures may produce brain damage.
- The most controversial treatment, psychosurgery, is rarely performed today. Its only accepted use, in the form of cingulotomy, is for treatment of crippling compulsions that cannot be reduced by more conventional means.

Mental disorders

Anxiety, somatoform and dissociative mental disorders

- Anxiety disorders refer to mental disorders which are characterised by excessive worry or fear and include generalised anxiety disorder, panic disorder, simple phobia, obsessive-compulsive disorder and post-traumatic stress disorder.
- Generalised anxiety disorder is characterised by excessive worry about all aspects of life; the most explanatory models suggest that anxiety serves as an alarm function preparing an organism for future action. It is best treated by anxiolytic (anti-anxiety) drugs.
- Panic disorder results from a fear of fear. A patient misinterprets bodily sensations catastrophically.
- Cognitive behavioural therapy and anti-anxiety drugs are effective treatments.
- Social phobia refers to an excessive pathological fear of speaking or performing in public.
- Agoraphobia, the most common phobia, is the fear of open spaces. Simple phobia is a fear of specific stimuli such as spiders and snakes.
- Recent research has applied virtual reality technology (exposure to computer-simulated events, objects or locations) to the treatment of the fear of flying and fear of spiders, with long-term success.
- Post-traumatic stress disorder refers to anxiety generated by an astonishing event or trauma (such as natural catastrophe, war or rape).
- Somatoform disorders include somatisation disorder and conversion disorder.
- Somatisation disorder refers to complaints of symptoms of illness without underlying physiological causes. Almost all people with this disorder are women.
- Conversion disorder involves specific neurological symptoms, such as paralysis or sensory disturbance, that are not produced by a physiological disorder.
- Dissociative disorders include psychogenic amnesia (with or without fugue) – a withdrawal from a painful situation or from intolerable guilt; multiple personalities – the adoption of several distinct and complete personalities.

Personality disorders

- Antisocial personality disorder refers to a pathological impairment in social and personal behaviour. It is also known as psychopathy or sociopathy, but antisocial personality is qualitatively different from psychopathy. Psychopaths are indifferent to the effects of their behaviour on other people, are impulsive, fail to learn from experience, are sexually promiscuous, lack commitment to a partner and are habitual liars. Some psychopaths are superficially charming and psychopathy tends to run in families.
- Evidence suggests that the frontal lobe is either dysfunctional or smaller in psychopaths.
- There is a significant association between psychopathy and alcohol abuse.

Schizophrenic disorders

- Schizophrenia is a mental illness characterised by distortions of thought, perception and emotion.
- The main positive symptoms of schizophrenia include thought disorders; delusions of persecution, grandeur and control; and hallucinations. The main negative symptoms include withdrawal, apathy and poverty of speech.
- DSM-IV TR classifies schizophrenia into several sub-types, including undifferentiated, catatonic, paranoid and disorganised.
- The diathesis-stress model suggests that some people seem to inherit a predisposition for the disorder, which is expressed when environmental stressors outweigh the person's attempts to cope with them.
- Recent research suggests that a low level of expressed emotion (including critical comments and emotional over-involvement) by family members facilitates the recovery of a patient with schizophrenia.
- Positive symptoms of schizophrenia can be made worse in schizophrenic patients by drugs that stimulate dopamine synapses (cocaine and amphetamine) and can be reduced or eliminated by drugs that block dopamine receptors (antipsychotic drugs).
- These findings have led to the dopamine hypothesis, which states that schizophrenia is caused by an inherited biochemical defect that causes dopamine neurons to be overactive.
- Enlargement of the ventricles is a consistent finding in schizophrenic patients and is unrelated to drug use; there is also evidence of reduced frontal lobe activation.
- Some researchers have suggested that lateralisation of function does not occur normally in schizophrenia.
- More recent studies indicate that schizophrenia can best be conceived of as two different disorders.
- The positive symptoms are produced by overactivity of dopamine neurons and can be treated with antipsychotic drugs. These positive symptoms are associated with limbic and sublimbic neural activation during verbal hallucination and verbal disorganisation.

- The negative symptoms, which do not respond to these drugs, are caused by brain abnormality. Investigators have found direct evidence of brain damage by inspecting CT scans of living patients' brains.
- Researchers have suggested three possible causes of the brain abnormality: a virus that triggers an autoimmune disease, which causes brain damage later in life; a virus that damages the brain early in life; and obstetric complications.

Mood disorders

- Mood disorders refer to a severe disturbance in emotion.
- Bipolar disorder consists of alternating periods of mania and depression; major depression consists of depression alone.
- Beck has noted that although mood disorders involve emotional reactions, these reactions may be, at least in part, based on faulty and negative cognition. Others such as

Abramson and co-workers suggest that depressed individuals are characterised by a negative attributional style which promotes helplessness and hopelessness.
- Heritability studies strongly suggest a biological component to mood disorders. This possibility receives support from the finding that biological treatments effectively reduce the symptoms of these disorders, while reserpine, a drug used to treat hypertension, can cause depression.
- Biological treatments include lithium carbonate for bipolar disorder and electroconvulsive therapy and antidepressant drugs (including monoamine oxidase inhibitors and tricyclic antidepressants) for depression.
- Neuroimaging research has shown that an area in the frontal cortex, sg24, is smaller in people suffering from depression.
- Recently developed drugs for depression, called serotonin-specific reuptake inhibitors, act by preventing reuptake of serotonin and blocking serotonin receptors.

Suggestions for further reading

Abnormal psychology – general reading

Bentall, R.P. and Beck, A.T. (2004) *Madness Explained: Psychosis and human nature*. New York: Penguin.

Carson, R.C., Butcher, J.N., Mineka, S. and Hooley, J.M. (2003) *Abnormal Psychology and Modern Life* (12th edn). New York: HarperCollins.

Davison, G.C. and Neale, J.M. (2006) *Abnormal Psychology* (10th edn). Chichester: Wiley.

Kramer, G.P., Bernstein, D.S. and Phares, V. (2009) *Introduction to Clinical Psychology* (7th edn). Boston: Prentice Hall.

Nevid, J. (2006) *Abnormal Psychology in a Changing World* (6th edn). Boston: Allyn & Bacon.

Oltmans, T.F. and Emery, R.E. (2010) *Abnormal Psychology* (6th edn). Upper Saddle River, NJ: Prentice Hall.

Abnormal psychology is one of the most popular areas of study in psychology. As a result, there are many good textbooks which are in their fourth editions (and beyond). The books listed here are very good introductions to the general area of mental disorder and are recommended for more information on topics covered in this chapter.

Specific mental illnesses

Arkowitz, H. and Lillienfeld, S.O. (2007) The best medicine? *Scientific American Mind*, 18, 5, 80–3.

Bentall, R. (2004) *Models of Madness: Psychologial, social and biological approaches to schizophrenia*. New York: Brunner-Routledge.

Brewin, C.R. (2001) A cognitive neuroscience account of posttraumatic stress disorder and its treatment. *Behaviour Research and Therapy*, 39, 373–93.

Cannistraro, P.A. and Rauch, S.L. (2003) Neural circuitry of anxiety: evidence from structural and functional neuroimaging studies. *Psychopharmacology Bulletin*, 37, 4, 8–25.

Cottraux, J. (2004) Recent developments in the research on generalized anxiety disorder. *Current Opinion in Psychiatry*, 17, 49–52.

Deacon, B.J. and Abramowitz, J.S. (2004) Cognitive and behavioural treatments for anxiety disorders: A review of meta-analytic findings. *Journal of Clinical Psychology*, 60, 4, 429–41.

Dobbs, D. (2006) Turning off depression. *Scientific American Mind*, 17, 4, 26–31.

Keshavan, M.S., Tandon, R., Boutros, N.N. and Nasrallah, H.A. (2008) Schizophrenia, 'Just the facts': What we know in 2008, Part 3: Neurobiology. *Schizophrenia Research*, 100, 89–107.

Tandon, R., Keshavan, M.S. and Nasrallah, H.A. (2008) Schizophrenia, 'Just the facts': What we know in 2008, Part 1: Overview. *Schizophrenia Research*, 100, 4–19.

Tandon, R., Keshavan, M.S. and Nasrallah, H.A. (2008). Schizophrenia, 'Just the facts': What we know in 2008, Part 2; Epidemiology and etiology. *Schizophrenia Research*, 100, 1–18.

Walker, E., Kestler, L., Bollini, A. and Hochman, K.M. (2004) Schizophrenia: Etiology and course. *Annual Review of Psychology*, 55, 401–30.

Special issue of *Cognition and Emotion* on cognitive biases in anxiety and depression (2002) 16, 3.

A number of books treat mental disorders separately, and the texts and papers here are some of the best covering anxiety, depression and schizophrenia.

Case studies and papers in mental illness

Jamison, K.R. (1993) *Touched with Fire*. New York: Free Press.

Jamison, K.R. (1995) *The Unquiet Mind*. London: Picador.

Jamison, K.R. (2004) *Exuberance*. New York: Knopf.

Meyer, R.G., Chapman, L.K. and Weaver, C.M. (2009) *Case Studies in Abnormal Behaviour* (8th edn). Boston: Allyn & Bacon.

ter, the mean is used to calculate other important statistics and has special mathematical properties that often make it more useful than the median.

Measures of variability

Many experiments produce two sets of numbers, one consisting of the experimental group's scores and one of the control group's scores. If the mean scores of these two groups differ, the experimenter can conclude that the independent variable had an effect. However, the experimenter must decide whether the difference between the two groups is larger than what would probably occur by chance. To make this decision, the experimenter calculates a **measure of variability**, a statistic that describes the degree to which scores in a set of numbers differ from each other. This measure can be used as a basis for comparing the means of the two groups.

Two sets of numbers can have the same mean or median and still be very different. For example, the mean and median of both sets of numbers listed in Table A.2 are the same, but the numbers are clearly different. The variability of the scores in set B is greater.

One way of stating the difference between the two sets of numbers in Table A.2 is to say that the numbers in set A range from 8 to 12 and the numbers in set B **range** from 0 to 20. The range of a set of numbers is simply the largest number minus the smallest. Thus, the range of set A is 4 and the range of set B is 20.

The range is not commonly used to describe the results of psychological experiments because another measure of variability – the standard deviation – has more useful mathematical properties. To calculate the standard deviation of a set of numbers, you first calculate the mean and then find the difference between each number and the mean. These difference scores are squared (that is, multiplied by themselves) and then summed. The mean of this total is called the **variance**; the **standard deviation** is the square root of the variance. The more different the numbers are from each other, the larger the standard deviation will be. This can be seen from the workings illustrated in Table A.3.

Measurement of relations

In correlational studies, the investigator measures the degree to which two variables are related. For example, suppose that a psychologist has developed a new aptitude test and wants to sell the test to university admissions committees for screening applicants. Before the committees will consider buying the test, the psychologist must show that a person's score on the test is related to their subsequent success at university. To do so, the psychologist will give the test to a group of first-year undergraduates entering university and later obtain their average course grades. The psychologist will then measure the relation between test scores and grades.

Imagine that we give the test to ten students entering university and later obtain their average grades. We will have two scores for each person. We can examine the relation between these variables by plotting the scores on

Table A.2 Two sets of numbers having the same mean and median but different ranges

Sample A	Sample B
8	0
9	5
10 Median	10 Median
11	15
12	20
Total 50	Total 50
Mean 50/5 = 10	Mean 50/5 = 10
Range 12 – 8 = 4	Range 20 – 0 = 20

Table A.3 Calculation of the variance and standard deviation of two sets of numbers having the same mean

Sample A			Sample B		
Score	Difference between score and mean	Difference squared	Score	Difference between score and mean	Difference squared
8	10 – 8 = 2	4	0	10 – 0 = 10	100
9	10 – 9 = 1	1	5	10 – 5 = 5	25
10	10 – 10 = 0	0	10	10 – 10 = 0	0
11	11 – 10 = 1	1	15	15 – 10 = 5	25
12	12 – 10 = 2	4	20	20 – 10 = 10	100
Total 50		Total 10	Total 50		Total 250
Mean 50/5 = 10		Mean (variance) 10/5 = 2	Mean 50/5 = 10		Mean (variance) 250/5 = 25
		Square root (standard deviation) 1.41			Square root (standard deviation) 5

a graph. For example, student R.J. received a test score of 14 and earned an average grade of 3.0 (corresponding to a good class of degree). We can represent this student's score as a point on the graph shown in Figure A.1.

The horizontal axis represents the test score, and the vertical axis represents the average grade. We put a point on the graph that corresponds to R.J.'s score on both of these measures.

We do this for each of the remaining students and then look at the graph, called a **scatterplot**, to determine whether the two variables are related. When we examine the scatterplot, we see that the points tend to be located along a diagonal line that runs from the lower left to the upper right, indicating that a rather strong relationship

exists between a student's test score and average grade, as seen in Figure A.1. High scores are associated with good grades, low scores with poor grades.

Although scatterplots are useful, we need a more convenient way to communicate the results to others, so we calculate the **correlation coefficient**, a number that expresses the strength of a relation. Calculating this statistic for the two sets of scores gives a correlation of +0.9 between the two variables.

The size of a correlation coefficient can vary from 0 (no relation) to 1.0 (perfect relation). A perfect relation means that if we know the value of a person's score on one measure, then we can predict exactly what his or her score will be on the other. Thus, a correlation of +0.9 is very close to perfect; our hypothetical aptitude test is an excellent predictor of how well a student will do at university.

Correlations can be negative as well as positive. A negative correlation indicates that high values on one measure are associated with low values on the other and vice versa. An example of a negative correlation is the relation between people's mathematical ability and the amount of time it would take them to solve a series of maths problems. People with the highest level of ability will take the least amount of time to solve the problems. For purposes of prediction, a negative correlation is just as good as a positive one. A correlation of −0.9 is an almost perfect relation, but in this case high scores on one measure predict low scores on the other. Examples of scatterplots illustrating high and low correlations, both positive and negative, are shown in Figure A.2.

If the points in a scatterplot fall along a line, the relation is said to be linear. But many relations are non-linear. For example, consider the relation between level of illumination and reading speed. Obviously, it is impossible to read in the dark. As the light level increases, people's reading speed will increase, but once an adequate amount of light falls on a page, further increases in light will have no effect. Finally, the light becomes so bright and dazzling that people's reading speed will decline, as seen in Figure A.3.

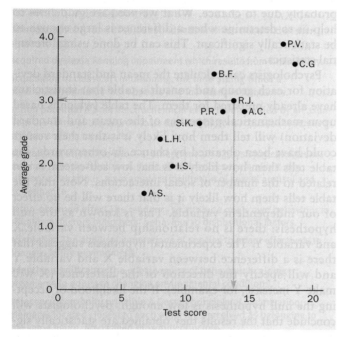

Figure A.1 A scatterplot of the test scores and average grades of ten students. An example of graphing one data point (student R.J.) is shown.

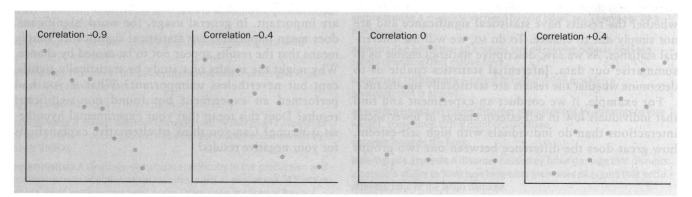

Figure A.2 Scatterplots of variables having several different levels of correlation.

covert sensitisation A method used by behavioural therapists in which a client imagines the aversive consequences of their inappropriate behaviour.

cranial nerve A bundle of nerve fibres attached to the base of the brain; conveys sensory information from the face and head and carries messages to muscles and glands.

creativity A process through which end products are created, usually in novel, unusual or unexpected ways.

cri-du-chat syndrome A genetic disorder arising from partial deletion of chromosome 5 which is associated with mental retardation and mewing sounds (hence cri-du-chat).

critical period A specific time in development during which certain experiences must occur for normal development to occur.

cross-cultural psychology The branch of psychology that studies and compares the effects of culture on behaviour.

crowd A group event involving a large number of people in the same place at the same time acting in a collective fashion.

CS pre-exposure effect The name given to the effect seen in latent inhibition – the phenomenon whereby a novel object is more successfully paired with a familiar one in conditioning.

cultural evolution The adaptive changes of cultures in response to environmental changes over time.

cultural psychology The branch of psychology which studies variations in behaviour within, but not necessarily across, cultures.

culture-bound syndrome Highly unusual mental disorders, similar in nature to non-psychotic mental disorders, that appear to be specific to only one or a few cultures.

cumulative recorder A mechanical device connected to an operant chamber for the purpose of recording operant responses as they occur in time.

cyclothymic disorder A less severe form of bipolar disorder.

cytoskeleton The skeletal structure of neurons.

dark adaptation The process by which the eye becomes capable of distinguishing dimly illuminated objects after going from a bright area to a dark one.

debriefing Full disclosure to research participants of the true nature and purpose of a research project after its completion.

deductive reasoning Inferring specific instances from general principles or rules.

deep dyslexia A severe inability to read; common words are sometimes read but are often replaced by semantically similar words.

deep processing The analysis of the complex characteristics of a stimulus, such as its meaning or its relationship to other stimuli.

defence mechanisms Mental systems that become active whenever unconscious instinctual drives of the id come into conflict with internalised prohibitions of the superego.

deferred imitation A child's ability to imitate the actions they have observed others perform. Piaget believed deferred imitation to result from the child's increasing ability to form mental representations of behaviour performed by others.

deferred imitation paradigm A child is exposed to an adult who is performing actions with a set of novel stimuli; after a delay, the child is then allowed to manipulate objects used by the experimenter. Identical use indicates a degree of imitation and learning.

deindividuation The loss of one's individuality and sense of personal responsibility in collective events.

delta activity The rhythmical activity of the electroencephalogram, having a frequency of less than 3.5 Hz, indicating deep (slow-wave) sleep.

delusions Beliefs that are obviously contrary to fact.

delusions of control The false belief that one's thoughts and actions are being controlled by other people or forces.

delusions of grandeur The false belief that one is famous, powerful or important.

delusions of persecution The false belief that other people are plotting against one.

dementia Cognitive deterioration associated with degenerative brain disorders.

dementia of the Alzheimer type (DAT) Cognitive impairment that arises from Alzheimer's disease.

dendrite A tree-like part of a neuron on which the terminal buttons of other neurons form synapses.

dependent variable The event whose value is measured in an experiment. Manipulation of independent variables demonstrates whether they affect the value of dependent variables.

depersonalisation The perception and treatment of self and others not as unique individual persons but as prototypical embodiments of a social group.

descriptive statistics Mathematical procedures for organising collections of data, such as determining the mean, the median, the range, the variance and the correlation coefficient.

detector In a regulatory process, a mechanism that signals when the system variable deviates from its set point.

determinant See causal event.

deuteranopia A form of hereditary anomalous colour vision; caused by defective 'green' cones in the retina.

developmental dyslexia A difficulty in learning to read despite adequate intelligence and appropriate educational opportunity.

developmental psychology The branch of psychology that studies the changes in behavioural, perceptual and cognitive capacities of organisms as a function of age and experience.

deviation IQ A procedure for computing the intelligence quotient; compares a child's score with those received by other children of the same chronological age.

Diagnostic and Statistical Manual IV **(DSM-IV TR)** A widely used manual for classifying psychological disorders.

diathesis model The notion that asymmetrical frontal cortex activation may predispose individuals to react negatively or positively to emotional stimuli.

diathesis-stress model A causal account of mental disorders based on the idea that mental disorders develop when a person possesses a predisposition for a disorder and faces stressors that exceed their abilities to cope with them.

dichotic listening A task that requires a person to listen to one of two different messages being presented simultaneously, one to each ear, through headphones.

dichromacy A deficit in colour vision in which a photopigment is missing.

difference threshold An alternative name for just-noticeable difference (jnd).

diffusion of responsibility An explanation of the failure of bystander intervention stating that, when several bystanders are present, no one person assumes responsibility for helping.

discourse analysis Qualitative method of analysis which involves the identification of themes, thoughts and ideas from transcripts of conversations or discussions.

discrimination (1) In operant conditioning, responding only when a specific discriminative stimulus is present but not when similar stimuli are present. (2) The differential treatment of people based on their membership in a particular group – discrimination is typically 'against' an out-group and in favour of the in-group. (3) In classical conditioning, the appearance of a conditioned response (CR) when one stimulus is presented (the CS+) but not another (the CS–).

discriminative stimulus In operant conditioning, the stimulus that sets the occasion for responding because, in the past, a behaviour has produced certain consequences in the presence of that stimulus.

disorganised schizophrenia A type of schizophrenia characterised primarily by disturbances of thought and a flattened or silly affect.

display rule A culturally determined rule that prescribes the expression of emotions in particular situations.

dispositional factors Individual personality characteristics that affect a person's behaviour.

dissociative disorders A class of disorders in which anxiety is reduced by a sudden disruption in consciousness, which in turn produces changes in one's sense of identity.

dissociative identity disorder A rare dissociative disorder in which two or more distinct personalities exist within the same person; each personality dominates in turn.

distinctive feature A physical characteristic of an object that helps distinguish it from other objects.

distinctiveness The extent to which a person engages in a particular behaviour in one situation but not in other situations.

divided attention Attention which is divided among two or more tasks.

dizygotic (DZ) twins Twins that are fertilised from different ova (and are, therefore, genetically different).

DNA 'Deoxyribonucleic acid'. The DNA structure resembles that of a twisted ladder. Strands of sugar and phosphates are connected by rungs made from adenine and thymine and guanine and cytosine.

doctrine of apperception The belief that we do not see objects as separate elements but as wholes.

doctrine of specific nerve energies Johannes Müller's observation that different nerve fibres convey specific information from one part of the body to the brain or from the brain to one part of the body.

doctrine of the association of ideas The belief that various associations are made between events and ideas, which allow meaningful thought to occur.

dominant allele The form of the gene that controls the expression of a trait. When a gene pair contains two dominant alleles or when it contains both a dominant and a recessive allele, the trait regulated by the dominant gene will be expressed.

door-in-the-face tactic Multiple-request technique to gain compliance, in which the focal request is preceded by a larger request that is bound to be refused.

dopamine hypothesis The hypothesis that the positive symptoms of schizophrenia are caused by overactivity of synapses in the brain that use dopamine.

double-aspect theory The belief that mental and physical events are characteristics of the same underlying entity.

double-bind The conflict caused for a child when they are given inconsistent messages or cues from a parent.

double-blind study An experiment in which neither the subject nor the experimenter knows the value of the independent variable.

Down syndrome A genetic disorder caused by a chromosomal aberration resulting in an extra twenty-first chromosome. People having Down syndrome are generally short, have broad skulls and round faces, and suffer impairments in physical, psychomotor and cognitive development.

drive A condition, often caused by physiological changes or homeostatic disequilibrium, that energises an organism's behaviour.

drive reduction hypothesis The hypothesis that a drive (resulting from physiological need or deprivation) produces an unpleasant state that causes an organism to engage in motivated behaviours. Reduction of drive is assumed to be reinforcing.

DSM-IV TR *See Diagnostic and Statistical Manual* IV.

dual-action antidepressants Antidepressants which block certain serotonin receptors and inhibit its reuptake.

dual-route model of reading A model which proposes that there are two, non-semantic routes that take the reader from spelling to sound. The lexical route retrieves words from the mental lexicon; the sublexical route converts letters into sound using grapheme–phoneme correspondence rules.

dual-task methodology A protocol in attention research whereby the participant undertakes two tasks simultaneously in order to determine the degree to which the performance of one interferes with the other.

dualism or Cartesian dualism The philosophical belief that reality consists of mind and matter.

Duchenne smile The genuine smile of joy characterised by the activation of specific facial muscles.

dyslexia A disorder impaired reading ability.

dysthymic disorder A less severe form of depression.

echoic memory A form of sensory memory for sounds that have just been perceived.

eclectic approach A form of therapy in which the therapist uses whatever method they feel will work best for a particular client at a particular time.

educational psychology The branch of psychology which applies psychological principles to our understanding of the educational process and children's learning and adjustment in education.

effortful processing Practising or rehearsing information through either shallow or deep processing.

ego The self. The ego also serves as the general manager of personality, making decisions regarding the pleasures that will be pursued at the id's request and the moral dictates of the superego that will be followed.

egocentrism Self-centredness; preoperational children can see the world only from their own perspective.

ego-ideal The internalisation of what a person would like to be.

egoistic relative deprivation Sense of personally having less than one feels one is entitled to relative to one's aspirations or to other individuals.

intelligence A person's ability to learn and remember information, to recognise concepts and their relations, and to apply the information to their own behaviour in an adaptive way.

intelligence quotient (IQ) A simplified single measure of general intelligence; by definition, the ratio of a person's mental age to their chronological age, multiplied by 100; often derived by other formulas.

interactionism The view that the mind and body are separate physical entities which interact.

intergroup relations Relations between groups or between individuals who are members of different groups and who are interacting in terms of their respective group memberships.

intermanual conflict The effect sometimes seen after split-brain surgery whereby one hand appears to behave in a contradictory way to the other.

intermittent reinforcement The occasional reinforcement of a particular behaviour; produces responding that is more resistant to extinction.

International Classification of Disorders 10 (ICD-10) A manual similar to DSM.

interneuron A neuron located entirely within the central nervous system.

interpersonal attraction People's tendency to approach each other and to evaluate each other positively.

interpersonal distance The distance apart at which people feel most comfortable in interacting in different situations, relationships and cultures.

interposition A monocular cue of depth perception; an object that partially occludes another object is perceived as closer.

interrater reliability The degree to which two or more independent observers agree in their ratings of another organism's behaviour.

intervening variables In behaviourism, the variables that modify the relationship between stimulus and response.

intraspecific aggression The attack by one animal upon another member of its species.

introspection Literally, 'looking within', in an attempt to describe one's own memories, perceptions, cognitive processes or motivations.

introversion The tendency to avoid the company of other people, especially large groups of people; shyness.

ion A positively or negatively charged particle; produced when many substances dissolve in water.

ion channel A special protein molecule located in the membrane of a cell; controls the entry or exit of particular ions.

ion transporter A special protein molecule located in the membrane of a cell; actively transports ions into or out of the cell.

iris The pigmented muscle of the eye that controls the size of the pupil.

isolation aphasia A language disturbance that includes an inability to comprehend speech or to produce meaningful speech accompanied by the ability to repeat speech and to learn new sequences of words; caused by brain damage to the left temporal/parietal cortex that spares Wernicke's area.

James–Lange theory A theory of emotion that suggests that behaviours and physiological responses are directly elicited by situations and that feelings of emotions are produced by feedback from these behaviours and responses.

just-noticeable difference (jnd) The smallest difference between two similar stimuli that can be distinguished. Also called difference threshold.

kin selection A type of selection that favours altruistic acts aimed at individuals who share some of the altruist's genes, such as parents, siblings, grandparents, grandchildren and, under certain conditions, distant relatives.

language acquisition device A hypothetical brain function which all children are said to have and which embodies the rules of universal grammar.

latency period The fourth of Freud's psychosexual stages, between the phallic stage and the genital stages during which there are no unconscious sexual urges or intrapsychic conflicts.

latent content The hidden message of a dream, produced by the unconscious.

latent inhibition The phenomenon whereby a novel object is more successfully paired with a familiar one in conditioning.

lateralisation Phenomenon whereby a function is the predominant responsibility of one side or part of the body or brain (e.g. speech production is lateralised in the left hemisphere).

law of attraction Byrne's theory that attraction towards a person bears a linear relationship to the proportion of attitudes associated with the person – the more similar you are to someone the more you like them.

law of closure A Gestalt law of organisation; elements missing from the outline of a figure are 'filled in' by the visual system.

law of effect Thorndike's observation that stimuli that occur as a consequence of a response can increase or decrease the likelihood of making that response again.

leader–member exchange (LMX) theory Theory that effective leadership rests on leaders developing personalised relationships with individual followers.

leakage A sign of expression of an emotion that is being masked.

learned helplessness A response to exposure to an inescapable aversive stimulus, characterised by reduced ability to learn a solvable avoidance task; thought to play a role in the development of some psychological disturbances.

learning An adaptive process in which the tendency to perform a particular behaviour is changed by experience.

lens The transparent organ situated behind the iris of the eye; helps to focus an image on the retina.

leptin Protein which is secreted by fat cells that have absorbed a large amount of triglyceride.

lexical awareness The ability to understand that speech and writing are composed of different, distinct elements called words.

libido An insistent, instinctual force that is unresponsive to the demands of reality; the primary source of motivation.

liking A feeling of personal regard, intimacy and esteem towards another person.

limbic cortex The cerebral cortex located around the edge of the cerebral hemispheres where they join with the brain stem; part of the limbic system.

limbic system A set of interconnected structures of the brain important in emotional and species-typical behaviour; includes the amygdala, hippocampus and limbic cortex.

linear perspective A monocular cue of depth perception; the arrangement or drawing of objects on a flat surface such that parallel lines receding from the viewer are seen to converge at a point on the horizon.

linguistic intergroup bias The use of concrete language that simply describes events when talking about positive out-group (and negative in-group) characteristics, and more general and abstract terms that relate to enduring traits when talking about negative out-group (and positive in-group) characteristics.

linguistic relativity The hypothesis that the language a person speaks is related to their thoughts and perceptions.

linguistics The study of the rules of language and the nature and meaning of written and spoken language.

lithium carbonate Drug used to treat bipolar disorder.

localisation of function The notion that functions may be localised in the brain at the neural, chemical or anatomical level.

locus of control An individual's beliefs that the consequences of their actions are controlled by internal person variables or by external environmental variables.

long-term memory Memory in which information is represented on a permanent or near-permanent basis.

long-term potentiation In learning and memory research, the strengthening of connections between neurons via repeated stimulation.

loving A combination of liking and a deep sense of attachment to, intimacy with, and caring for another person.

low-ball tactic Technique for inducing compliance in which a person who agrees to a request can feel committed even after finding that there is a hidden cost.

magnetic resonance imaging (MRI) Neuroimaging technique which allows neuropsychologists to observe the structure of the living brain by measuring the reverberation of hydrogen molecules in the brain as a magnetic field is passed over the head.

magnetoencephalography (MEG) A technique for measuring brain activation by detecting the activity of magnetic fields from a large number of neurons.

maintenance rehearsal The rote repetition of information; repeating a given item over and over again.

major depression Persistent and severe feelings of sadness and worthlessness accompanied by changes in appetite, sleeping and behaviour.

male sexual dysfunction The inability to achieve an erection.

mania Excessive emotional arousal and wild, exuberant, unrealistic activity.

manifest content The apparent storyline of a dream.

masking Attempting to hide the expression of an emotion.

matching A systematic selection of participants in groups in an experiment or (more often) a correlational study to ensure that the mean values of important subject variables of the groups are similar.

materialism A philosophical belief that reality can be known only through an understanding of the physical world, of which the mind is a part.

maturation Any relatively stable change in thought, behaviour or physical growth that is due to the ageing process and not to experience.

mean A measure of central tendency; the sum of a group of values divided by their number; the arithmetical average.

means–ends analysis An approach to problem-solving in which a person should look for differences between the current state and the goal state and seek ways to reduce these differences.

measure of central tendency A statistical measure used to characterise the value of items in a sample of numbers.

measure of variability A statistical measure used to characterise the dispersion in values of items in a sample of numbers.

median A measure of central tendency; the midpoint of a group of values arranged numerically.

medical model A perspective on mental illness which regards mental disorder as caused by specific abnormalities of the brain and nervous system.

medulla The part of the brain stem closest to the spinal cord; controls vital functions such as heart rate and blood pressure.

MEG See magnetoencephalography.

meiosis The form of cell division by which new sperm and ova are formed. The chromosomes within the cell are randomly rearranged so that new sperm and ova contain 23 individual chromosomes, or half of that found in other bodily cells.

memory The cognitive processes of encoding, storing and retrieving information.

meninges The three-layered set of membranes that enclose the brain and spinal cord.

menopause In women, the alternation in the endocrine system which leads to the pituitary gland and the hypothalamus releasing hormones that prevent the ovaries from controlling menstruation.

menstrual synchrony The phenomenon whereby menstrual cycles of more than one female become synchronous.

mental age A measure of a person's intellectual development; the level of intellectual development that could be expected for an average child of a particular age.

mental lexicon Hypothetical cognitive store of words and their meanings.

mental model A mental construction based on physical reality that is used to solve problems of logical deduction.

mental space (M-space) A hypothetical construct in Case's model of cognitive development similar to working memory, whose primary function is to process information from the external world.

mere exposure effect The formation of a positive attitude towards a person, place or thing, based solely on repeated exposure to that person, place or thing.

mesmerism Another word for hypnosis, named after Franz Anton Mesmer, an Austrian physician.

meta-analysis A statistical procedure by which the results of many studies are combined to estimate the magnitude of a particular effect.

metamemory Knowledge of the knowledge acquisition process.

method of loci A mnemonic system in which items to be remembered are mentally associated with specific physical locations or landmarks.

oval window An opening in the bone surrounding the cochlea. The stirrup presses against a membrane behind the oval window and transmits sound vibrations into the fluid within the cochlea.

overextension The use of a word to denote a larger class of items than is appropriate, for example, referring to the moon as a ball.

overtone A component of a complex tone; one of a series of tones whose frequency is a multiple of the fundamental frequency.

Pacinian corpuscle A specialised, encapsulated somatosensory nerve ending, which detects mechanical stimuli, especially vibrations.

paedophilia Sex with pre-pubescent children.

paleoanthropology The study of human evolution through interpreting fossil remains.

panic A feeling of fear mixed with hopelessness or helplessness.

panic disorder Unpredictable attacks of acute anxiety that are accompanied by high levels of physiological arousal and that last from a few seconds to a few hours.

papilla A small bump on the tongue that contains a group of taste buds.

parallel distributed processing A connectionist model devised by Seidenberg and McClelland to read regular, exception and non-words.

parallel processor The notion that the brain is composed of different modules which allow us to work simultaneously on more than one task.

paranoid schizophrenia A form of schizophrenia in which the person suffers from delusions of persecution, grandeur or control.

paraphilia Mental or behavioural disorder that has a sexual content.

parasympathetic branch The portion of the autonomic nervous system that activates functions that occur during a relaxed state.

parental investment The resources, including time, physical effort and risks to life, that a parent spends in procreation and in the feeding, nurturing and protecting of offspring.

parietal lobe The region of the cerebral cortex behind the frontal lobe and above the temporal lobe; contains the somatosensory cortex; is involved in spatial perception and memory.

passionate love An emotional, intense desire for sexual union with another person. Also called romantic love.

Pavlovian conditioning Similar to classical conditioning – the process by which a response normally elicited by one stimulus (the UCS) comes to be controlled by another stimulus (the CS) as well.

peg-word method A mnemonic system in which items to be remembered are associated with a set of mental pegs that one already has in memory, such as key words of a rhyme.

perception (1) A rapid, automatic, unconscious process by which we recognise what is represented by the information provided by our sense organs. (2) The detection of the more complex properties of a stimulus, including its location and nature; involves learning.

perceptual disorders Disorders in perception that tend to leave elementary sensation unimpaired.

period of concrete operations The third period in Piaget's theory of cognitive development during which children come to understand the conservation principle and other concepts, such as categorisation.

period of formal operations The fourth period in Piaget's theory of cognitive development during which individuals first become capable of more formal kinds of abstract thinking and hypothetical reasoning.

peripheral nervous system The cranial and spinal nerves; that part of the nervous system peripheral to the brain and spinal cord.

perseverance The tendency to continue to perform a behaviour even when it is not being reinforced.

perseveration Responding in a manner that was previously correct but is now inappropriate.

person variables Individual differences in cognition, which, according to Mischel, include competences, encoding strategies and personal constructs, expectancies, subjective values, and self-regulatory systems and plans.

personal constructs Idiosyncratic and personal ways of characterising other people.

personality A particular pattern of behaviour and thinking prevailing across time and situations that differentiates one person from another.

personality disorders Abnormalities in behaviour which impair social or occupational function.

personality trait An enduring personal characteristic that reveals itself in a particular pattern of behaviour in a variety of situations.

personality types Different categories into which personality characteristics can be assigned based on factors such as developmental experiences or physical characteristics.

phallic stage The third of Freud's psychosexual stages. During this stage, the primary erogenous zone is the genital area. At this time, children not only wish to stimulate their genitalia but also become attached to the opposite-sex parent.

phantom limb Sensations that appear to originate in a limb that has been amputated.

phenotype The outward expression of an organism's genotype; an organism's physical appearance and behaviour.

phenylketonuria (PKU) A genetic disorder caused by a particular pair of homozygous recessive genes and characterised by the inability to break down phenylalanine, an amino acid found in many high protein foods. The resulting high blood levels of phenylalanine cause mental retardation.

pheromone A chemical secreted by the body which induces stereotypical behaviour in the perceiving organism.

phi phenomenon The perception of movement caused by the turning on of two or more lights, one at a time, in sequence; responsible for the apparent movement of images in movies and television.

phobia Unreasonable fear of specific objects or situations, such as insects, animals or enclosed spaces, learned through classical conditioning.

phoneme The minimum unit of sound that conveys meaning in a particular language, such as /p/.

phonetic reading Reading by decoding the phonetic significance of letter strings; 'sound reading'.

phonological awareness The capacity to appreciate the sounds of words and be able to identify letters with sounds.

phonological dyslexia A reading disorder in which people can read familiar words but have difficulty reading unfamiliar words or pronounceable non-words because they cannot sound out words.

phonological loop See articulatory loop.

photopigment A complex molecule found in photoreceptors; when struck by light, it splits apart and stimulates the membrane of the photoreceptor in which it resides.

photoreceptor A receptive cell for vision in the retina; a rod or a cone.

physiological psychology The branch of psychology that studies the physiological basis of behaviour.

pituitary gland An endocrine gland attached to the hypothalamus at the base of the brain.

place-dependent memory Description of greater success in retrieval of material when acquisition and retrieval of information occur in the same location.

placebo An inert substance that cannot be distinguished from a real medication by the patient or subject; used as the control substance in a single-blind or double-blind experiment.

planned behaviour (theory of) Modification by Ajzen of the theory of reasoned action. It suggests that predicting a behaviour from an attitude measure is improved if people believe that they have control over that behaviour.

planum temporale Structure found in the primary auditory cortex which seems to be larger in the left than right hemisphere.

pleasure principle The rule that the id obeys: obtain immediate gratification, whatever form it may take.

polyandry The mating of one female with more than one male.

polygynandry The mating of several females with several males.

polygyny The mating of one male with more than one female.

pons The part of the brain stem just anterior to the medulla; involved in control of sleep.

positive brain allometry An increase in brain size relative to body size

positive reinforcement An increase in the frequency of a response that is regularly and reliably followed by an appetitive stimulus.

positive symptoms Symptoms of schizophrenia that may include thought disorder, hallucinations or delusions.

positivism The school of thought which states that all meaningful ideas can be reduced to observable material.

positron emission tomography (PET) Technique used to measure the degree of blood flow or oxygen consumption in the living brain as it engages in activity.

postconventional level Kohlberg's third and final level of moral development, in which people come to understand that moral rules include principles that apply across all situations and societies.

posterior Towards the back.

posterior part of the parietal cortex (PPC) Part of the brain responsible for the ability to locate objects in space.

posthypnotic amnesia A failure to remember what occurred during hypnosis; induced by suggestions made during hypnosis.

posthypnotic suggestibility The tendency of a person to perform a behaviour suggested by the hypnotist some time after the person has left the hypnotic state.

postsynaptic neuron A neuron with which the terminal buttons of another neuron form synapses and that is excited or inhibited by that neuron.

post-traumatic stress disorder (PTSD) Anxiety which follows a traumatic event.

preconventional level Kohlberg's first level of moral development, which bases moral behaviour on external sanctions, such as authority and punishment.

prefrontal cortex The anterior part of the frontal lobe; contains the motor association cortex.

prejudice An attitude or evaluation, usually negative, towards a group of people defined by their racial, ethnic or religious heritage or by their gender, occupation, sexual orientation, level of education, place of residence or membership of a particular group.

premoral stage of moral development First of Piaget's stages of moral development in which the child shows little understanding of rules or principles governing moral behaviour or understanding.

prenatal period The nine months between conception and birth. This period is divided into three developmental stages: the zygote, the embryo and the foetal stages.

preoperational period The second of Piaget's periods, which represents a 4–5 year transitional period between first being able to think symbolically and then being able to think logically. During this stage, children become increasingly capable of speaking meaningful sentences.

preoptic area A region at the base of the brain just in front of the hypothalamus; contains neurons that appear to control the occurrence of slow-wave sleep.

presynaptic neuron A neuron whose terminal buttons form synapses with and excite or inhibit another neuron.

primacy effect (1) The tendency to remember initial information. In the memorisation of a list of words, the primacy effect is evidenced by better recall of the words early in the list. (2) The tendency to form impressions of people based on the first information we receive about them.

primary appraisal In anxiety research, the initial evaluation of the environment as neutral, positive or negative.

primary auditory cortex The region of the cerebral cortex that receives information directly from the auditory system; located in the temporal lobes.

primary motor cortex The region of the cerebral cortex that directly controls the movements of the body; located in the back part of the frontal lobes.

primary punisher A biologically significant aversive stimulus, such as pain.

primary reinforcer A biologically significant appetitive stimulus, such as food or water.

primary somatosensory cortex The region of the cerebral cortex that receives information directly from the somatosensory system (touch, pressure, vibration, pain and temperature); located in the front part of the parietal lobes.

primary visual cortex (V1) The region of the cerebral cortex that receives information directly from the visual system; located in the occipital lobes.

principle of common fate States that elements that move in the same direction will be perceived as belonging together and forming a figure.

prisoner's dilemma Two-person game in which both parties are torn between competition and cooperation and, depending on mutual choices, both can win or both can lose.

proactive interference Interference in recall that occurs when previously learned information disrupts our ability to remember newer information.

problem-focused coping Any coping behaviour that is directed at reducing or eliminating a stressor.

process schizophrenia According to Bleuler, a form of schizophrenia characterised by a gradual onset and a poor prognosis.

social markers Features of speech style that convey information about mood, context, status and group membership.

social norms Informal rules defining the expected and appropriate behaviour in specific situations.

social phobia A mental disorder characterised by an excessive and irrational fear of situations in which the person is observed by others.

social psychology The branch of psychology that studies our social behaviour – how the actual, imagined or implied presence of other people influences our thoughts, feelings and behaviours.

social representations Collectively elaborated explanations of unfamiliar and complex phenomena that transform them into a familiar and simple form.

sociobiology The study of the genetic bases of social behaviour; the branch of biology which seeks to explain behaviour in terms of adaptation and evolution.

soma A cell body; the largest part of a neuron.

somatic marker hypothesis The idea that the ability to make decisions leading to positive or potentially negative consequences depends on the activation of somatic (bodily) states.

somatisation disorder A class of somatoform disorder, occurring mostly among women, that involves complaints of wide-ranging physical ailments for which there is no apparent biological cause.

somatoform disorder A mental disorder involving a bodily or physical problem for which there is no physiological basis.

somatosense Bodily sensations; sensitivity to such stimuli as touch, pain and temperature.

source memory Recall of the context in which an event occurred, rather than of the content/knowledge of the event.

spatial neglect A perceptual disorder in which the patient neglects (or fails to attend to) one side of the body, usually the left.

species-typical behaviour A behaviour seen in all or most members of a species, such as nest building, special food-getting behaviours or reproductive behaviours.

specific language impairment Difficulty in producing or understanding spoken language in the absence of known brain injury.

specific phobia An excessive and irrational fear of specific things, such as snakes, darkness or heights.

speech accommodation theory Modification of speech style to the context (e.g. listener, situation) of a face-to-face inter-individual conversation.

speech style The way in which something is said (e.g. accent, language), rather than the content of what is said.

spinal cord A long, thin collection of nerve cells attached to the base of the brain and running the length of the spinal column.

split brain The consequence of surgical excision of the fibres connecting the two cerebral hemispheres of the brain.

split-brain surgery A surgical procedure that severs the corpus callosum, thus abolishing the direct connections between the cortex of the two cerebral hemispheres.

split-half reliability The degree to which two halves or portions of the same measure correlate.

spontaneous recovery After an interval of time, the reappearance of a response that had previously been extinguished.

sport and exercise psychology The branch of psychology concerned with studying the effect of sport and exercise on behaviour and with applying psychological principles to our understanding of sport-related behaviour.

standard deviation A statistic that expresses the variability of a measurement; square root of the sum of the squared deviations from the mean.

Stanford–Binet Scale An intelligence test that consists of various tasks grouped according to mental age; provides the standard measure of the intelligence quotient.

state-dependent memory The tendency to recall information better when our mental or emotional state at retrieval matches that during encoding.

statistical significance The likelihood that an observed relation or difference between two variables is not due to chance factors.

stereopsis A form of depth perception based on retinal disparity.

stereotaxic apparatus A device used to insert an electrode into a particular part of the brain for the purpose of recording electrical activity, stimulating the brain electrically, or producing localised damage.

stereotype A shared, often unfavourable, generalisation held by members of one group about members of another group.

stereotype threat Feeling that one will be judged and treated in terms of negative stereotypes of one's group, and that one will inadvertently confirm these stereotypes through one's behaviour.

stigma Possession of some attribute, or characteristic, which conveys a social identity that is devalued in a particular social context.

stimulus equivalence A type of learning in which stimuli become equivalent even though the organism has never observed a relation between them; may be involved in learning how to read and manipulate symbols.

storage The process of maintaining information in memory.

Strange Situation A test of attachment in which an infant is exposed to different stimuli that may be distressing.

stranger anxiety The wariness and fearful responses, such as crying and clinging to their carers, that the infant exhibits in the presence of strangers.

stress A pattern of physiological, behavioural and cognitive responses to stimuli (real or imagined) that are perceived as endangering one's well-being.

stress inoculation training The stress management programme developed by Meichenbaum for teaching people to develop coping skills that increase their resistance to the negative effects of stress.

stressors Stimuli that are perceived as endangering one's well-being.

striving for superiority The motivation to seek superiority. Adler argued that striving for superiority is born out of our need to compensate for our inferiorities.

stroke A cerebrovascular accident; damage to the brain caused by a blood clot in a cerebral artery or rupture of a cerebral blood vessel.

Stroop effect A phenomenon whereby a well-practised memory is difficult to suppress and is retrieved automatically (e.g., if participants are asked to name the colours of words and see the word red written in the colour blue, they are likely to say 'red' rather than 'blue').

structuralism Wundt's system of experimental psychology; it emphasised introspective analysis of sensation and perception.

structured interview Predefined format for interviewing participants in research which allows little deviation from the questions set.

subjective ethnolinguistic vitality Individual group members' representation of the objective ethnolinguistic vitality of their group.

sublimation A defence mechanism that involves redirecting pleasure-seeking or aggressive instincts towards socially acceptable goals.

subliminal perception The perception of a stimulus, as indicated by a change in behaviour, at an intensity insufficient to produce a conscious sensation.

subordinate concept A concept that refers to types of items within a basic-level category.

subvocal articulation Uttering words inaudibly.

superego The repository of an individual's moral values, divided into the conscience – the internalisation of a society's rules and regulations – and the ego-ideal – the internalisation of one's goals.

superordinate concept A concept that refers to collections of basic-level concepts.

superstitious behaviour A behaviour that occurs in response to the non-contingent occurrence of an appetitive stimulus; appears to cause a certain event but in reality does not.

supervisory attentional system (SAS) A cognitive system, proposed by Norman and Shallice, which is responsible for the conscious attentional control needed to regulate behaviour.

suprachiasmatic nucleus (SCN) Structures located in the posterior of the hypothalamus which are thought to regulate circadian rhythms.

surface dyslexia A reading disorder in which people can read words phonetically but have difficulty reading irregularly spelled words by the whole-word method.

symbolic play Name given by Piaget to a certain type of play because infants used objects to symbolise other objects or were used to symbolise other activities.

sympathetic branch The portion of the autonomic nervous system that activates functions that accompany arousal and expenditure of energy.

symptom substitution The Freudian notion that the removal of one symptom will lead to its replacement by another.

synaesthesia Phenomenon where the stimulus in one sensory modality evokes a sensation in another.

synaesthete A person who experiences synaesthesia.

synapse The junction between the terminal button of one neuron and the membrane of a muscle fibre, a gland or another neuron.

synaptic cleft A fluid-filled gap between the presynaptic and postsynaptic membranes; the terminal button releases transmitter substance into this space.

syntax Grammatical rules for combining words to form phrases, clauses and sentences.

system variable The variable controlled by a regulatory mechanism; for example, temperature in a heating system.

systematic desensitisation A method of treatment in which the client is trained to relax in the presence of increasingly fearful stimuli.

T lymphocytes Cells that develop in the thymus gland that produce antibodies which defend the body against fungi, viruses and multicellular parasites.

taboo A societal rule prohibiting the members of a given culture from engaging in specific behaviours.

tachistoscope A device that can present visual stimuli for controlled (usually very brief) durations of time.

tardive dyskinesia A serious movement disorder that can occur when a person has been treated with antipsychotic drugs for an extended period.

target cell A cell whose physiological processes are affected by a particular hormone; contains special receptor molecules that respond to the presence of the hormone.

taste bud A small organ on the tongue that contains a group of gustatory receptor cells.

tectorial membrane A membrane located above the basilar membrane; serves as a shelf against which the cilia of the auditory hair cells move.

template A hypothetical pattern that resides in the nervous system and is used to perceive objects or shapes by a process of comparison.

temporal coding A means by which the nervous system represents information; different features are coded by the pattern of activity of neurons.

temporal lobe The portion of the cerebral cortex below the frontal and parietal lobes and containing the auditory cortex.

teratogens Drugs or other substances that can cause birth defects.

terminal button The rounded swelling at the end of the axon of a neuron; releases transmitter substance.

test–retest reliability The degree to which scores on one test correlate with the same test undertaken on another occasion.

texture A monocular cue of depth perception; the fineness of detail present in the surfaces of objects or on the ground or floor of a scene.

thalamus A region of the brain near the centre of the cerebral hemispheres. All sensory information except smell is sent to the thalamus and then relayed to the cerebral cortex.

Thematic Apperception Test (TAT) A projective test in which a person is shown a series of ambiguous pictures that involve people. The person is asked to make up a story about what the people are doing or thinking. The person's responses are believed to reflect aspects of their personality.

theory A set of statements designed to explain a set of phenomena; more encompassing than a hypothesis.

theory of mind The understanding of others' mental events.

theory of reasoned action The notion that behaviour follows from an intention to act and that these intentions are based on beliefs, feelings and attitudes.

theta activity EEG activity of 3.5–7.5 Hz; occurs during the transition between sleep and wakefulness.

thought disorder A pattern of disorganised, illogical and irrational thought that often accompanies schizophrenia.

threat gesture A stereotyped gesture that signifies that one animal is likely to attack another member of the species.

three-term contingency The relation among discriminative stimuli, behaviour and the consequences of that behaviour. A motivated organism emits a specific response in the presence of a discriminative stimulus because, in the past, that response has been reinforced only when the discriminative stimulus is present.

threshold The point at which a stimulus, or a change in the value of a stimulus, can just be detected.

timbre A perceptual dimension of sound, determined by the complexity of the sound, for example as shown by a mathematical analysis of the sound wave.

tip-of-the-tongue phenomenon An occasional problem with retrieval of information that we are sure we know but cannot immediately remember.

token economy A programme often used in institutions in which a person's adaptive behaviour is reinforced with tokens that are exchangeable for desirable goods or special privileges.

tolerance The decreased sensitivity to a drug resulting from its continued use.

top-down processing A perception based on information provided by the context in which a particular stimulus is encountered.

transactional theories of leadership Theories that attribute effective leadership to mutually beneficial exchange relations between leaders and followers.

transactive memory Shared system for encoding, storing and retrieving information in a group.

transcranial magnetic stimulation (TMS) A technique which modulates cortical activity by passing alternating magnetic fields across the scalp. (rTMS = repetitive transcranial magnetic stimulation.)

transduction The conversion of physical stimuli into changes in the activity of receptor cells of sensory organs.

transference The process by which a client begins to project powerful attitudes and emotions onto the therapist.

transformational leadership Effective leaders' transactions with followers are characterised by charisma, inspirational motivation, intellectual stimulation, and individualised consideration, which motivate followers to work for group goals that transcend immediate self-interest.

transvestic fetishism Dressing in the clothes normally associated with the opposite sex.

triarchic theory A theory of intelligence which posits that intelligence is made of componential, experiential and contextual elements.

trichromatic theory The theory that colour vision is accomplished by three types of photoreceptor, each of which is maximally sensitive to a different wavelength of light.

tricyclic antidepressants The earliest known antidepressants, so called because of their chemical three-ring structure.

tritanopia A form of hereditary anomalous colour vision; caused by a lack of 'blue' cones in the retina.

Turner's syndrome Genetic disorder in which all or a part of the X chromosome is missing; intelligence is within the normal range but individuals have problems with social adjustment.

two-point discrimination threshold The minimum distance between two small points that can be detected as separate stimuli when pressed against a particular region of the skin.

type A pattern A behaviour pattern characterised by high levels of competitiveness and hostility, impatience and an intense disposition; supposedly associated with an increased risk of coronary heart disease.

type B pattern A behaviour pattern characterised by lower levels of competitiveness and hostility, patience and an easygoing disposition; supposedly associated with a decreased risk of coronary heart disease.

type C (cancer-prone) personality A behaviour pattern marked by cooperativeness, unassertiveness, patience, suppression of negative emotions, and acceptance of external authority; supposedly associated with an increased likelihood of cancer.

tyramine cheese reaction A potentially fatal reaction to eating certain foods in individuals taking MAOIs.

UCR See unconditional response.

UCS See unconditional stimulus.

UCS pre-exposure effect A phenomenon in which conditioning is weak because the organism has already been exposed to a novel UCS before it is used in the conditioning experiment.

ultimate attribution error The tendency to attribute in-group failures and out-group successes externally, and in-group successes and out-group failures internally.

ultimate causes Evolutionary conditions that have slowly shaped the behaviour of a species over generations.

unconditional positive regard According to Rogers, the therapeutic expression that a client's worth as a human being is not dependent on anything that they do, say, feel or think.

unconditional response (UCR) In classical conditioning, a response, such as salivation, that is naturally elicited by the UCS.

unconditional stimulus (UCS) In classical conditioning, a stimulus, such as food, that naturally elicits a reflexive response, such as salivation.

unconscious The inaccessible part of the mind.

unconscious inference A mental computation of which we are unaware that plays a role in perception.

underextension The use of a word to denote a smaller class of items than is appropriate, for example referring only to one particular animal as a dog.

undifferentiated schizophrenia A type of schizophrenia characterised by fragments of the symptoms of different types of schizophrenia.

validity The degree to which the operational definition of a variable accurately reflects the variable it is designed to measure or manipulate.

variable A measure capable of assuming any of several values.

variable error An error caused by random differences in experimental conditions, such as the subject's mood or changes in the environment.

variable-interval schedule A schedule of reinforcement similar to a fixed-interval schedule but characterised by a variable time requirement having a particular mean.

variable-ratio schedule A schedule of reinforcement similar to a fixed-ratio schedule but characterised by a variable response requirement having a particular mean.

variance The square of the standard deviation.

variation The differences found across individuals of any given species in terms of their genetic, biological (size, strength, physiology) and psychological (intelligence, sociability, behaviour) characteristics.

vertebrae Bones that encase the spinal cord and constitute the vertebral column.

vestibular apparatus The receptive organs of the inner ear that contribute to balance and perception of head movement.

vestibular sac One of a set of two receptor organs in each inner ear that detect changes in the tilt of the head.

visual agnosia The inability of a person who is not blind to recognise the identity or use of an object by means of vision; usually caused by damage to the brain.

visuospatial scratchpad The component of working memory that stores visuospatial information.

voice onset time The delay between the initial sound of a voiced consonant (such as the puffing sound of the phoneme /p/) and the onset of vibration of the vocal cords.

volumetric thirst Thirst provoked by a reduction in the volume of blood plasma.

voyeurism Looking at people while they are undressing or having sex, without their knowledge.

waist-to-chest ratio In men, the ratio between size of waist and chest, which determines attractiveness

waist-to-hip ratio In women, the ratio between size of hips and waist, which determines attractiveness

wavelength The distance between adjacent waves of radiant energy; in vision, most closely associated with the perceptual dimension of hue.

Weber fraction The ratio between a just-noticeable difference and the magnitude of a stimulus; reasonably constant over the middle range of most stimulus intensities.

Wechsler Adult Intelligence Scale (WAIS) An intelligence test for adults devised by David Wechsler; contains eleven subtests divided into the categories of verbal and performance.

Wechsler Intelligence Scale for Children (WISC) An intelligence test for children devised by David Wechsler; similar in form to the Wechsler Adult Intelligence Scale.

Wernicke's aphasia A disorder caused by damage to the left temporal and parietal cortex, including Wernicke's area; characterised by deficits in the perception of speech and by the production of fluent but rather meaningless speech.

Wernicke's area A region of auditory association cortex located in the upper part of the left temporal lobe; involved in the recognition of spoken words.

white matter The portions of the central nervous system that are abundant in axons rather than cell bodies of neurons. The colour derives from the presence of the axons' myelin sheaths.

whole-word reading Reading by recognising a word as a whole; 'sight reading'.

withdrawal symptom An effect produced by discontinuance of use of a drug after a period of continued use; generally opposite to the drug's primary effects.

within-groups design See repeated measures design.

working memory A short-term memory system which allows the retention and processing of information concurrently.

zone of proximal (or potential) development According to Vygotsky, the range of tasks or skills that a child is unable to master alone but can with the assistance of adults or their peers.

zygote stage The first stage of prenatal development, during which the zygote divides many times and the internal organs begin to form.

Artmann, H., Grau, H., Adelman, M. and Schleiffer, R. (1985) Reversible and non-reversible enlargement of cerebrospinal fluid spaces in anorexia nervosa. *Neuroradiology*, 27, 103–12.

Asch, S.E. (1946) Forming impressions of personality. *Journal of Abnormal and Social Psychology*, 41, 258–90.

Asch, S.E. (1951) Effects of group pressure upon the modification and distortion of judgment. In H. Guetzkow (ed.) *Groups, Leadership, and Men*. Pittsburgh: Carnegie.

Asch, S.E. (1952) *Social Psychology*. New York: Prentice Hall.

Asch, S.E. (1955) Opinions and social pressure. *Scientific American Mind*, 193, 31–5.

Ashby, F.G., Isen, A.M. and Turken, A.U. (1999) A neuropsychological theory of positive affect and its influence on cognition. *Psychological Review*, 106(3), 529–50.

Ashcraft, M.H. and Kirk, E.P. (2001) The relationship among working memory, math anxiety and performance. *Journal of Experimental Psychology (General)*, 130, 224–37.

Ashmore, R.D. and Jussim, L. (1997) Towards a second century of the scientific analysis of self and identity. In R. Ashmore and L. Jussim (eds) *Self and Identity: Fundamental issues*. New York: Oxford University Press, pp. 3–19.

Ashton, C.H. (2001) Pharmacology and effects of cannabis: a brief review. *British Journal of Psychiatry*, 178, 101–6.

Asperger, H. (1944) Die autistischen Psychopathen im Kindesalter. *Archiv für Psychiatrie und Nervenkrankheiten*, 117, 76–136.

Aspinwall, L.G. and Taylor, S.E. (1992) Individual differences, coping, and psychological adjustment: A longitudinal study of college adjustment and performance. *Journal of Personality and Social Psychology*, 63, 989–1003.

Astin, J.A. (1998) Why patients use alternative medicine: results of a national study. *Journal of the American Medical Association*, 279, 1548–1553.

Astin, J.A., Marie, A., Pelletier, K.R., Hansen, E. and Haskell, W.L. (1998) A review of the incorporation of complementary and alternative medicine by mainstream physicians. *Archives of Internal Medicine*, 158, 2303–2310.

Astley, S.J., Clarren, S.K., Little, R.E., Sampson, P.D. and Daling, J.R. (1992) Analysis of facial shape in children gestationally exposed to marijuana, alcohol, or cocaine. *Pediatrics*, 89, 67–77.

Atkinson, R.C. and Shiffrin, R.M. (1968) Human memory: A proposed system and its control processes. In K.W. Spence and J.T. Spence (eds) *The Psychology of Learning and Motivation: Advances in research and theory*, Vol. 2. New York: Academic Press.

Au, T.K., Sidle, A.L. and Rollins, K.B. (1993) Developing an intuitive understanding of conservation and contamination: Invisible particles as a plausible mechanism. *Developmental Psychology*, 29, 286–99.

Augoustinos, M. and Walker, I. (1995) *Social Cognition: An integrated introduction*. London: Sage.

Augustin, M.D., Leder, H., Hutzler, F. and Carbon, C-C. (2008) Style follows content: On the microgenesis of art perception. *Acta Psychologia*, 128, 127–38.

Auyeung, B., Baron-Cohen, S., Ashwin, E., Knickmeyer, R., Taylor, K. and Hackett, G. (2009) Fetal testosterone and autistic traits. *British Journal of Psychology*, 100, 1–22.

Awh, E., Jonides, J., Smith, E.E., Schumacher, E.H., Koeppe, R.A. and Katz, S. (1996) Dissociation of storage and rehearsal in verbal working memory. *Psychological Science*, 7, 25–31.

Axel, R. (1995) The molecular logic of smell. *Scientific American Mind*, 273, 154–9.

Axelrod, R. and Hamilton, W.D. (1981) The evolution of cooperation. *Science*, 211, 1390–1396.

Ayabe-Kanamura, S., Schicker, I., Laska, M., Hudson, R., Distel, H., Kobayakawa, T. and Saito, S. (1998) Differences in perception of everyday odors: a Japanese–German cross-cultural study. *Chemical Senses*, 23, 31–8.

Ayllon, T. and Azrin, N.H. (1968) *The Token Economy: A motivational system for therapy and rehabilitation*. New York: Appleton-Century-Crofts.

Aylward, E.H. *et al.* (2003) Instructional treatment associated with changes in brain activation in children with dyslexia. *Neurology*, 61, 212–19.

Ayoko, B.O., Hartel, C.E., and Callan, V.J. (2002) Resolving the puzzle of productive and destructive conflict in culturally heterogeneous workgroups: A communication accommodation theory approach. *International Journal of Conflict Management*, 13, 165–95.

Azzopardi, P. and Cowey, A. (2001) Motion discrimination in cortically blind patients. *Brain*, 124, 30–46.

Baars, B.J. (1988) *A Cognitive Theory of Consciousness*. Cambridge: Cambridge University Press.

Baars, B.J., Newman, J. and Taylor, J.G. (1998) Neuronal mechanisms of consciousness: A relational global-workspace framework. In S.R. Hameroff, A.W. Kaszniak and A.C. Scott (eds) *Towards a Science of Consciousness II*. Cambridge, MA: MIT Press.

Babad, E., Darley, J.M. and Kaplowitz, H. (1999) Developmental aspects in students' course selection. *Journal of Educational Psychology*, 91(1), 157–68.

Babkin, B.P. (1949) *Pavlov: A biography*. Chicago: University of Chicago Press.

Back, M.D., Schmukle, S.C. and Egloff, B. (2006) Who is late and who is early? Big Five personality factors and punctuality in attending psychological experiments. *Journal of Research in Personality*, 40, 841–8.

Back, M.D., Schmukle, S.C. and Egloff, B. (2008) How extraverted is honey.bunny77@hotmail.de? Inferring personality from email addresses. *Journal of Research in Personality*, 42, 1116–1122.

Badcock, C. (1991) *Evolution and Individual Behavior: An introduction to human sociobiology*. Cambridge, MA: Blackwell.

Baddeley, A.D. (1982) Domains of recollection. *Psychological Review*, 89, 708–29.

Baddeley, A.D. (1986) *Working Memory*. Oxford: Clarendon Press.

Baddeley, A.D. (1992) Implicit memory and errorless learning: A link between cognitive theory and neuropsychological rehabilitation. In L.R. Squire and N. Butters (eds) *Neuropscyhology of Memory* (2nd edn). New York: Guilford Press.

Baddeley, A.D. (1996) *Human Memory: Theory and practice* (2nd edn). Hove: Psychology Press.

Baddeley, A.D., Baddeley, H.A., Bucks, R.S. and Wilcock, G.K. (2001) Attentional control in Alzheimer's disease. *Brain*, 124, 1492–1508.

Baddeley, A.D., DellaSala, S. and Spinnler, H. (1991) The two-component hypothesis of memory deficit in Alzheimer's disease. *Journal of Clinical and Experimental Neuropsychology*, 13, 372–80.

Baddeley, A.D. and Hitch, G.J. (1974) Working memory. In G.H. Bower (ed.) *The Psychology of Learning and Motivation: Advances in research and theory*, Vol. 8. New York: Academic Press.

Baddeley, A.D. and Hitch, G.J. (1977) Recency examined. In S. Dornic (ed.) *Attention and Performance*, Vol. 6. Hillsdale, NJ: Lawrence Erlbaum Associates.

Baddeley, A.D. and Logie, R.H. (1992) Auditory imagery and working memory. In R.S. Nickerson (ed.) *Attention and Performance*, Vol. 8. Hillsdale, NJ: Lawrence Erlbaum Associates.

Baddeley, A.D., Thomson, N. and Buchanan, M. (1975) Word length and the structure of short-term memory. *Journal of Verbal Learning and Verbal Behaviour*, 14, 575–89.

Baenninger, M.A. (1994) The development of face recognition: featural or configurational processing? *Journal of Experimental Child Psychology*, 57, 377–96.

Baenninger, M.A., Baenninger, R. and Houle, D. (1993) Attractiveness, attentiveness, and perceived male shortage: Their influence on the perceptions of other females. *Ethology and Sociobiology*, 14, 293–304.

Baer, D.M., Peterson, R.F. and Sherman, J.A. (1967) Development of imitation by reinforcing behavioral similarity to a model. *Journal of the Experimental Analysis of Behavior*, 10, 405–16.

Baer, L., Rauch, S.L., Ballantine, T.J., Martuza, R., Cosgrove, R., Casem, E., Giriona, L., Manzo, P.A., Dimino, C. and Jenike, M.A. (1995) Cingulotomy for intractable compulsive-obsessive disorder. *Archives of General Psychiatry*, 52, 384–92.

Bagwell, C.L., Newcomb, A.F. and Bukowski, W.M. (1998) Preadolescent friendship and peer rejection as predictors of adult adjustment. *Child Development*, 69, 1, 140–53.

Bahrick, H.P. (1984) Semantic memory content in permastore: Fifty years of memory for Spanish learned in school. *Journal of Experimental Psychology: General*, 113, 1–29.

Bahrick, H.P. (1992) Stabilized memory of unrehearsed knowledge. *Journal of Experimental Psychology: General*, 121(1), 112–13.

Bahrick, H.P., Bahrick, P.O. and Wittlinger, R.P. (1975) Fifty years of memories for names and faces: A cross-sectional approach. *Journal of Experimental Psychology: General*, 104, 54–75.

Bahrick, H.P., Hall, L.K. and da Costa, L.A. (2008) Fifty years of memory of college grades: Accuracy and distortions. *Emotion*, 8, 1.

Bai, D.L. and Bertenthal, B.I. (1992) Locomotor status and the development of spatial search skills. *Child Development*, 63, 215–26.

Bailey, A., Lecouteur, A., Gottesman, I., Bolton, P., Simonoff, E., Yuzda, E. and Rutter, M. (1995) Autism as a strongly genetic disorder: Evidence from a British twin study. *Psychological Medicine*, 25, 63–78.

Bailey, A., Phillips, W. and Rutter, M. (1996) Autism: Towards an integration of clinical, genetic, neuropsychological and neurobiological perspectives. *Journal of Child Psychology and Psychiatry*, 37(1), 89–126.

Bailey, J.M. and Pillard, R.C. (1991) A genetic study of male sexual orientation. *Archives of General Psychiatry*, 48, 1089–1096.

Bailey, J.M., Pillard, R.C., Neale, M.C. and Agyei, Y. (1993) Heritable factors influence sexual orientation in women. *Archives of General Psychiatry*, 50, 217–23.

Baillieux, H., Vandervliet, E.J.M., Manto, M., Parizel, P.M., Deyn, P.P. and Marien, P. (2009) Developmental dyslexia and widespread activation across the cerebellar hemispheres. *Brain and Language*, 108, 122–32.

Bain, J., Langevin, R., Dickey, R. and Ben-Aron, M. (1987) Sex hormones in murderers and assaulters. *Behavioural Science and the Law*, 5, 95–101.

Baker, B.L. (1969) Symptom treatment and symptom substitution in enuresis. *Journal of Abnormal Psychology*, 74, 42–9.

Baker, S.C., Rogers, R.D., Owen, A.M., Frith, C.D., Dolan, R.J., Frackowiak, R.S.J. and Robbins, T.W. (1996) Neural systems engaged by planning: A PET study of the Tower of London task. *Neuropsychologia*, 34(6), 515–26.

Baker, T.B., Japuntich, S.J., Hogle, J.M., McCarthy, D.E. and Curtin, J.J. (2006) Pharmacologic and behavioural withdrawal from addictive drugs. *Current Directions in Psychological Science*, 15, 5, 232–6.

Bakker, D.J. (1992) Neuropsychological classification and treatment of dyslexia. *Journal of Learning Disabilities*, 25(2), 102–9.

Baldessarini, R.J. (1996) Drugs and the treatment of psychiatric disorders: depression and mania. In J.G. Hardman and L.E. Limbird (eds) *Goodman and Gilman's The Pharmacological Basis of Therapeutics* (9th edn). New York: McGraw-Hill.

Baldessarini, R.J. and Tarsy, D. (1980) Dopamine and the pathophysiology of dyskinesias induced by antipsychotic drugs. *Annual Review of Neuroscience*, 3, 23–41.

Baldwin, J.D. and Baldwin, J.I. (1998) *Behavior Principles in Everyday Life* (3rd edn). Hillsdale, NJ: Prentice Hall.

Balkin, T.J., Braun, A.R., Wesensten, N.J., Jeffries, K., Varga, M., Baldwin, P., Belenky, G. and Herscovitch, P. (2002) The process of awakening: a PET study of regional brain activity patterns mediating the re-establishment of alertness and consciousness. *Brain*, 125, 2308–2319.

Ball, K. and Sekuler, R. (1982) A specific and enduring improvement in visual motion discrimination. *Science*, 218, 697–8.

Ballantine, H.T., Bouckoms, A.J., Thomas, E.K. and Giriunas, I.E. (1987) Treatment of psychiatric illness by stereotactic cingulotomy. *Biological Psychiatry*, 22, 807–19.

Balon, R., Jordan, M., Pohl, R. and Yeragani, V.K. (1989) Family history of anxiety disorders in control subjects with lactate-induced panic attacks. *American Journal of Psychiatry*, 146, 1304–1306.

Balota, D.A. and Faust, M.E. (2001) Attention in dementia of the Alzheimer type. In F. Boller and S.F. Cappa (eds), *Handbook of neuropsychology*, 2nd edition. Amsterdam: Elsevier Science.

Baltes, P.B. and Lindenberger, U. (1997) Emergence of a powerful connection between sensory and cognitive functions across the adult life span: A new window at the study of cognitive aging? *Psychology and Aging*, 12, 12–21.

Banbury, S. and Berry, D.C. (1998) Disruption of office-related tasks by speech and office noise. *British Journal of Psychology*, 89, 499–517.

Bandura, A. (1971) Psychotherapy based upon modeling principles. In A.E. Bergin and S.L. Garfield (eds) *Handbook of Psychotherapy and Behavior Change*. New York: Wiley.

Bandura, A. (1973) *Aggression: A social learning analysis*. Englewood Cliffs, NJ: Prentice Hall.

Bandura, A. (1977) *Social Learning Theory*. Upper Saddle River, NJ: Prentice Hall.

Bandura, A. (1978) The self system in reciprocal determinism. *American Psychologist*, 33, 344–58.

Bandura, A. (1982) Self-efficacy mechanism in human agency. *American Psychologist*, 37, 122–47.

Bandura, A. (1986) *Social Foundations of Thought and Action: A social–cognitive theory*. Englewood Cliffs, NJ: Prentice Hall.

Bandura, A. and Menlove, F.L. (1968) Factors determining vicarious extinction of avoidance behavior through symbolic modeling. *Journal of Personality and Social Psychology*, 8, 99–108.

Bangalore, S.S., Prasad, K.M.R., Montrose, D.M., Goradia, D.D., Diwadkar, V.A. and Keshavan, M.S. (2008) Cannabis use and brain structural alterations in first episode schizophrenia. *Schizophrenia Research*, 99, 1–6.

Banich, M.T. (1995) Interhemispheric processing: Theoretical considerations and empirical approaches. In R.J. Davidson and K. Hugdahl (eds) *Brain Asymmetry*. Cambridge, MA: MIT Press.

Blair, C., Gamson, D., Thorne, S. and Baker, D. (2005) Rising mean IQ: Cognitive demand of mathematics education for young children, population exposure to formal schooling, and the neurobiology of the prefrontal cortex. *Intelligence*, 33, 93–106.

Blair, R.J.R., Jones, L., Clark, F. and Smith, M. (1997) The psychopathic individual: A lack of responsiveness to distress cues? *Psychophysiology*, 34, 192–652.

Blair, I.V., Judd, C.M. and Chapleau, K.M. (2004) The influence of Afrocentric facial features in criminal sentencing. *Psychological Science*, 15, 674–9.

Blair, R.J.R., Morris, J.S., Frith, C.D., Perrett, D.I. and Dolan, R.J. (1999) Dissociable neural responses to facial expressions of sadness and anger. *Brain*, 122, 883–93.

Blakemore, C. and Mitchell, D.E. (1973) Environmental modification of the visual cortex and the neural basis of learning and memory. *Nature*, 241, 467–8.

Blanchard, R. (2004) Quantitative and theoretical analyses of the relation between older brothers and homosexuality in men. *Journal of Theoretical Biology*, 230, 173–87.

Blanchard, R., Cantor, J.M., Bogaert, A.F., Breedlove, S.M. and Ellis, L. (2006) Interaction of fraternal birth order and handedness in the development of male homosexuality. *Hormones and Behavior*, 49, 405–14.

Blank, A.S. (1993) The longitudinal course of post-traumatic stress disorder. In J.R.T. Davidson and E.B. Foa (eds) *Posttraumatic Stress Disorder: DSM-IV and beyond*. Washington, DC: Amercian Psychiatric Press.

Blanke, O., Ortigue, S. and Landis, T. (2003) Colour neglect in an artist. *The Lancet*, 361, 264.

Blankfield, R.P. (1991) Suggestion, relaxation, and hypnosis as adjuncts in the care of surgery patients: A review of the literature. *American Journal of Clinical Hypnosis*, 33, 172–86.

Blansjaar, B.A. *et al.* (2000) Prevalence of dementia in centenarians. *International Journal of Geriatric Psychiatry*, 15, 219–25.

Blass, T. (2000) The Milgram paradigm after 35 years: Some things we now know about obedience to authority. In T. Blass (Ed), *Obedience to Authority: Current perspectives on the Milgram experiment*. Hillsdale, NJ: Erlbaum.

Blass, T. (2009) From new haven to Santa Clara: A historical perspective on the Milgram obedience experiments. *American Psychologist*, 64, 1, 37–45.

Bleich, A., Koslowsky, M., Dolev, A. and Lerer, B. (1997) Post-traumatic stress disorder and depression. *British Journal of Psychiatry*, 170, 479–82.

Bliss, E.L. (1980) Multiple personalities: A report of 14 cases with implications for schizophrenia and hysteria. *Archives of General Psychiatry*, 37, 1388–1397.

Bliss, T. and Gardner-Medwin, A. (1973) Long-lasting potentiation of synaptic transmission in the dendate area of unanaesthetised rabbit following stimulation of the perforant path. *Journal of Physiology*, 232, 357–74.

Block, N., Flanagan, O. and Guzeldere, G. (1997) *The Nature of Consciousness*. Cambridge, MA: MIT Press.

Bloom, L. (1970) *Language Development: Form and function in emerging grammars*. Cambridge, MA: MIT Press.

Blount, C., Evans, C., Birch, S., Warren, F. and Norton, K. (2002) The properties of self-report research measures: Beyond psychometrics. *Psychology and Psychotherapy: Theory, Research and Practice*, 75, 151–64.

Blum, S.H. and Blum, L.H. (1974) Do's and don'ts: An informal study of some prevailing superstitions. *Psychological Reports*, 35, 567–71.

Blythe, I.M., Kennard, C. and Ruddock, K.H. (1987) Residual vision in patients with retinogeniculate lesions of the visual path. *Brain*, 110, 887–905.

Boaz, N.T. (1993) Origins of Hominidae. In A.J. Manyak and A. Manyak (eds) *Milestones in Human Evolution*. Prospect Heights, IL: Waveland Press.

Bochner, S. and Insko, C.A. (1966) Communicator discrepancy, source credibility, and opinion change. *Journal of Personality and Social Psychology*, 4, 614–21.

Bogen, J.E. (1993) The callosal syndromes. In K.M. Heilman and E. Valenstein (eds) *Clinical Neuropsychology*. New York: Academic Press.

Bogg, T. and Roberts, B.W. (2004) Conscientiousness and health-related behaviours: A meta-analysis of the leading behavioural contributors to mortality. *Psychological Bulletin*, 130, 6, 887–919.

Bohannon, J.N. (1988) Flashbulb memories for the space shuttle disaster: A tale of two theories. *Cognition*, 29, 179–96.

Bohannon, J.N. (1993) Theoretical approaches to language acquisition. In J.B. Gleason (ed.) *The Development of Language*. New York: Macmillan.

Bohannon, J.N. and Stanowicz, L. (1988) The issue of negative evidence: Adult responses to children's language errors. *Developmental Psychology*, 24, 684–89.

Bohn, A. and Berntsen, D. (2007) Pleasantness bias in flashbulb memories: positive and negative flashbulb memories of the fall of the Berlin Wall among East and West Germans. *Memory and Cognition*, 35, 3, 565–77.

Bohner, G., Moskowitz, G.B. and Chaiken, S. (1995) The interplay of heuristic and systematic processing of social information. *European Review of Social Psychology*, 6, 33–68.

Boles, D.B. (1984) Sex in lateralised tachistoscopic word recognition. *Brain and Language*, 23, 2, 307–17.

Boller, F. and Dennis, M. (1979) *Auditory Comprehension: Clinical and experimental studies with the token test*. New York: Academic Press.

Bolles, R.C. (1970) Species-specific defense reactions and avoidance learning. *Psychological Review*, 77, 32–48.

Bolles, R.C. (1979) *Learning Theory*. New York: Holt, Rinehart & Winston.

Bonvillian, J., Nelson, K.E. and Charrow, V. (1976) Languages and language-related skills in deaf and hearing children. *Sign Language Studies*, 12, 211–50.

Booth, A., Johnson, D.R. and Granger, D.A. (1999) Testosterone and men's depression: The role of social behaviour. *Journal of Health and Social Behaviour*, 40, 130–40.

Boothroyd, L.G., Jones, B.C., Burt, D.M. and Perrett, D.I. (2007) Partner characteristics associated with masculinity, health and maturity in male faces. *Personality and Individual Differences*, 43, 1161–1173.

Borgida, E. and Nisbett, R.E. (1977) The differential viewpoint of abstract vs. concrete information on decisions. *Journal of Applied Social Psychology*, 7, 258–71.

Boring, E.G. (1923) Intelligence as the tests test it. *The New Republic*, June, 35–7.

Boring, E.G. (1953) A history of introspection. *Psychological Bulletin*, 50, 169–89.

Borkovec, T.D. (1994) The nature, function and origins of worry. In G. Davey and F. Tallis (eds) *Worrying: Perspectives on theory, assessment and treatment*. Chichester: Wiley.

Born, J. *et al.* (2006) Sleep to remember. *Neuroscientist*, 12, 410–24.

Borovsky, D. and Rovee-Collier, C. (1989) Contextual restraints on memory retrieval at 6 months. *Child Development*, 61, 1569–1583.

Botella, C., Banos, R.M., Perpina, C., Villa, H., Alcaniz, M. and Rey, A. (1998) Virtual reality treatment of claustrophobia: A case report. *Behaviour Research and Therapy*, 36, 239–46.

Botez, M.I., Oliver, M., Vezina, J-L., Botez, T. and Kaufman, B. (1985) Defective revisualization: Dissociation between cognitive and imagistic thought. Case report and short review of the literature. *Cortex*, 21, 375–89.

Bottini, G., Corcoran, R., Sterzi, R., Paulesu, E., Schenone, P., Scarpa, P., Frackowiak, R.S.J. and Frith, C.D. (1994) The role of the right hemisphere in the integration of figurative aspects of language. *Brain*, 117, 1241–1253.

Bouchard, T. J. and Propping, P. (1993) *Twins as a Tool of Behavior Genetics*. Chichester: Wiley.

Boulton, M.J. (1997) Teachers' views on bullying definitions, attitudes and ability to cope. *British Journal of Educational Psychology*, 67, 223–33.

Bourgeois, M.J., Horowitz, I.A., ForsterLee, L. and Grahe, J. (1995) Nominal and interactive groups-effects of preinstruction and deliberations on decisions and evidence recall in complex trials. *Journal of Applied Psychology*, 80, 58–67.

Bourhis, R.Y. (1984) *Conflict and Language Planning in Quebec*. Clevedon: Multilingual Matters.

Bourtchouladze, R., Abel, T., Berman, N., Gordon, R., Lapidus, K. and Kandel, E.R. (1998) Different training procedures recruit either one or two critical periods for contextual memory consolidation, each of which requires protein synthesis and PKA. *Learning and Memory*, 5, 365–74.

Boutelle, K.N., Kirschenbaum, D.S., Baker, R.C. and Mitchell, M.E. (1999) How can obese weight controllers minimize weight gain during the high risk holiday season? By self-monitoring very consistently. *Health Psychology*, 18(4), 364–8.

Bowden, C.L. (2001) Strategies to reduce misdiagnosis of bipolar depression. *Psychiatric Services*, 52(1), 51–5.

Bower, G.H. (1981) Mood and memory. *American Psychologist*, 36, 129–48.

Bower, G.H. (1987) Commentary on mood and memory. *Behaviour Research and Therapy*, 25, 443–56.

Bower, G.H. and Clark, M.C. (1969) Narrative stories as mediators for serial learning. *Psychonomic Science*, 14, 181–2.

Bower, G.H. and Cohen, P.R. (1982) Emotional influences on memory and thinking: Data and theory. In S. Fiske and M. Clark (eds) *Affect and Cognition*. Hillsdale, NJ: Lawrence Erlbaum.

Bower, G.H. and Mayer, J.D. (1989) In search of mood-dependent retrieval. *Journal of Social Behaviour and Personality*, 4, 133–68.

Bower, T.G.R. (1972) *Perception in Infancy* (2nd edn). San Francisco: W.H. Freeman.

Bowlby, J. (1969) *Attachment*. New York: Basic Books.

Bowlby, J. (1973) *Separation: Anxiety and Anger*. New York: Basic Books.

Bowles, N.L. and Poon, L.W. (1985) Aging and retrieval of words in semantic memory. *Journal of Gerontology*, 40, 71–7.

Bowling, A. and Dieppe, P. (2005) What is successful ageing and who should define it? *British Medical Journal*, 331, 1548–1551.

Boynton, R.M. (1979) *Human Color Vision*. New York: Holt, Rinehart & Winston.

Boysson-Bardies, B., Sagart, L. and Durand, C. (1984) Discernible differences in the babbling of infants according to target language. *Journal of Child Language*, 11, 1–15.

Bradley, B.P., Mogg, K., Groom, C., deBono, J. and White, J. (1999) Attentional bias for emotional faces in generalized anxiety disorder. *British Journal of Clinical Psychology*, 38, 267–77.

Bradley, L. and Bryant, P. (1983) Categorising sounds and learning to read – a causal connection. *Nature*, 301, 419–21.

Brain, P. (1984) Biological explanations of human aggression and the resulting therapies offered by such approaches: A critical evaluation. In R. Blanchard and D. Blanchard (eds) *Advances in the Study of Aggression*. New York: Academic Press.

Brain, P. (1994) Hormonal aspects of aggression and violence. In A. Reiss, K. Micek and J. Roth (eds) *Understanding and Preventing Violence*, Vol. 2. New York: National Academic Press.

Brambila, P. *et al.* (2003) GABAergic dysfunction in mood disorders. *Molecular Psychiatry*, 8, 721–37.

Brandt, B. and Kvande, E. (1998) Masculinity and child care: the reconstruction of fathering. *Sociological Review*, 46(2), 293–313.

Branscombe, N.R., Wann, D.L., Noel, J.G. and Coleman, J. (1993) In-group or out-group extremity: Importance of threatened social identity. *Personality and Social Psychology Bulletin*, 19, 381–418.

Bransford, J.D. and Johnson, M.K. (1972) Contextual prerequisites for understanding: Some investigations of comprehension and recall. *Journal of Verbal Learning and Verbal Behavior*, 11, 717–26.

Bray, G.A. (1998) *Contemporary Diagnosis and Management of Obesity*. Newton, PA: Handbooks in Health Care.

Brazzelli, M., Colombo, N., Della Salla, S. and Spinnler, H. (1994) Spared and impaired cognitive abilities after bilateral frontal damage. *Cortex*, 30, 27–51.

Breillmann, R.S., Saling, M.M., Connell, A.B., Waites, A.B., Abbott, D.F. and Jackson, G.D. (2004) A high-field functional MRI study of quadri-lingual subjects. *Brain and Language*, 89, 531–42.

Breitmeyer, B.G. (1980) *Visual Masking: An integrative approach*. New York: Oxford University Press.

Brennan, W.M., Ames, E.W. and Moore, R. (1966) Age differences in infants' attention to patterns of different complexities. *Science*, 151, 354–6.

Brewer, J.B., Zhao, Z., Desmond, J.E., Glover, G.H. and Gabrieli, J.D.E. (1998) Making memories: Brain activity that predicts how well visual experience will be remembered. *Science*, 281, 1185–1187.

Brewer, M.B. and Caporael, L.R. (1990) Selfish genes versus selfish people: Sociobiology as origin myth. *Motivation and Emotion*, 14, 237–43.

Brewer, M.B and Gardner, W. (1996) Who is this 'we'? Levels of collective identity and self-representation. *Journal of Personality and Social Psychology*, 71, 83–93.

Brewer, M.B. and Kramer, R.M. (1986) Choice behavior in social dilemmas: Effects of social identity, group size, and decision framing. *Journal of Personality and Social Psychology*, 50, 543–9.

Brewer, M.B. and Miller, N. (1984) Beyond the contact hypothesis: Theoretical perspectives on desegregation. In N. Miller and M.B. Brewer (eds) *Groups in Contact: The psychology of desegregation*. New York: Academic Press, pp. 281–302.

Brewin, C.R., Smith, A.J., Power, M.J. and Furnham, A. (1992) State and trait differences in the depressive self-schema. *Behaviour Research and Therapy*, 30, 555–7.

Brickman, P. and Campbell, D.T. (1971) Hedonic relativism and planning the good society. In M.H. Appley (ed.), *Adaptation Level Theory: A symposium*. New York: Academic Press.

Bridges, A.M. and Jones, D.M. (1996) Word-dose in the disruption of serial recall by irrelevant speech: Phonological confusions or changing state? *Quarterly Journal of Experimental Psychology*, 49A, 919–39.

Briem, V. and Hedman, L.R. (1995) Behavioural effects of mobile telephone task on driver behaviour in a car following situation. *Accident Analysis and Prevention*, 27, 707–15.

Briggs, S.R. (1988) Shyness: introversion or neuroticism? *Journal of Research in Personality*, 22, 290–307.

Brissette, I., Scheier, M.F. and Carver, C.S. (2002) The role of optimism in social network development, coping and psychological adjustment

Cabeza, R., Grady, C.L., Nyberg, L., McIntosh, A.R., Tulving, E., Kapur, S., Jennings, J.M., Houle, S. and Craik, F.I.M. (1997) Age-related differences in neural activity during memory encoding and retrieval: A positron emission tomography study. *Journal of Neuroscience*, 17(1), 391–400.

Cabeza, R. and Nyberg, L. (2000) Imaging cognition II: Empirical review of 275 PET and fMRI studies. *Journal of Cognitive Neuroscience*, 12(1), 1–47.

Caccappoulo-van Vliet, E., Miozzo, M. and Stern, Y. (2004) Phonological dyslexia: A test case for reading models. *Psychological Science*, 15, 9, 583–90.

Calabrese, P., Markowitsch, H.J., Harders, A.G., Scholz, M. and Gehlen, W. (1995) Fornix damage and memory: A case report. *Cortex*, 31, 555–64.

Calder, A.J., Young, A.W., Rowland, D., Perrett, D.I., Hodges, J.R. and Etcoff, N.L. (1996) Facial emotion recognition after bilateral amygdala damage: Differentially severe impairment of fear. *Cognitive Neuropsychology*, 13, 699–745.

Calev, A., Gaudino, E.A., Squires, N.K. *et al.* (1995) ECT and non-memory cognition: A review. *British Journal of Clinical Psychology*, 34, 505–16.

Calvin, W.H. and Ojemann, G.A. (1994) *Conversations with Neil's Brain*. New York: Addison-Wesley.

Cameron, I., Curran, S., Newton, P. *et al.* (2000) Use of donepezil for the treatment of mild–moderate Alzheimer's disease: an audit of the assessment and treatment of patients in routine clinical practice. *International Journal of Geriatric Psychiatry*, 15, 887–91.

Campbell, A., Shirley, L., Heywood, C. and Crook, C. (2000) Infants' visual preference for sex-congruent babies, children, toys and activities: A longitudinal study. *British Journal of Developmental Psychology*, 18, 479–98.

Campbell, A., Shirley, L. and Caygill, L. (2002) Sex-typed preferences in three domains: Do two-year-olds need cognitive variables? *British Journal of Psychology*, 93.

Campbell, F.A., Pungello, E.P., Miller-Johnson, S., Burchinal, M. and Ramey, C.T. (2001) The development of cognitive and academic abilities: Growth curves from an early childhood educational experiment. *Developmental Psychology*, 37(2), 231–42.

Campfield, L.A., Smith, F.J., Guisez, Y., Devos, R. and Burn, P. (1995) Recombinant mouse OB protein: evidence for a peripheral signal linking adiposity and central neural networks. *Science*, 269, 546–9.

Cancer Research UK (2006) Smoking and cancer risk. http://info.cancerresearchuk.org/cancerstats/causes/lifestyle/tobacco/.

Canli, T. (2006) *Biology of Personality and Individual Difference*. New York: The Guilford Press.

Canli, T., Sivers, H., Whitfield, S.L., Gotlib, I.H. and Gabrieli, J.D.E. (2002) Amygdala response to happy faces as a function of extraversion. *Science*, 296, 2191.

Canli, T., Zhao, Z., Desmond, J.E., Kang, E., Gross, J. and Gabrieli, J.D.E. (2001) An fMRI study of personality influences on brain reactivity to emotional stimuli. *Behavioural Neuroscience*, 115, 1, 33–42.

Cann, A. and Ross, D.A. (1989) Olfactory stimuli as context cues in human memory. *American Journal of Psychology*, 102, 91–102.

Cannon, W.B. (1927) The James–Lange theory of emotions: A critical examination and an alternative theory. *American Journal of Psychology*, 39, 106–24.

Cannon, W.B. (1931) James–Lange and the thalamic theories of emotion. *Psychological Review*, 38, 281–95.

Cannon, W.B. and Washburn, A.L. (1912) An explanation of hunger. *American Journal of Physiology*, 29, 444–54.

Cantagallo, A. and Della Sala, S. (1998) Preserved insight in an artist with extrapersonal spatial neglect. *Cortex*, 34, 163–89.

Canter, D. (1989) Offender profiles. *The Psychologist*, 2, 12–16.

Canter, D. (1994) *Criminal Shadows: Inside the mind of a serial killer*. London: HarperCollins.

Canter, D. (2000) Offender profiling and criminal differentiation. *Legal and Criminological Psychology*, 5, 23–46.

Cantor, N. and Mischel, W. (1979) Prototypes in person perception. In L. Berkowitz (ed.) *Advances in Experimental Social Psychology*, Vol. 12. New York: Academic Press, pp. 3–52.

Cappa, S.E., Perani, D., Grassi, E., Bressi, S., Albertoni, M. and Franceschi, M. (1997) A PET follow-up study of recovery after stroke in acute aphasics. *Brain and Language*, 56, 55–67.

Caprara, G.V. and Perugini, M. (1994) Personality described by adjectives: Generalizability of the Big Five to the Italian lexical context. *European Journal of Personality*, 8, 357–69.

Carey, S. and Bartlett, E. (1978) Acquiring a single new word. *Proceedings of the Stanford Child Language Conference*, 15, 17–29.

Carey, S. and Diamond, R. (1977) From piecemeal to configurational representation of faces. *Science*, 195, 312–14.

Carli, L.L. (1990) Gender, language, and influence. *Journal of Personality and Social Psychology*, 59, 941–51.

Carlin, A.S., Hoffman, H.G. and Weghorst, S. (1997) Virtual reality and tactile augmentation in the treatment of spider phobia: A case study. *Behaviour Research and Therapy*, 35, 153–8.

Carlson, E.A. (1998) A prospective longitudinal study of attachment disorganization/disorientation. *Child Development*, 69(4), 1107–1128.

Carlson, K.A. and Russo, J.E. (2001) Biased interpretation of evidence by mock jurors. *Journal of Experimental Psychology: Applied*, 7(2), 91–103.

Carlson, N.R. (2001) *Foundations of Physical Psychology* (5th edn). Boston: Allyn & Bacon.

Carlsson, K., Petrovic, P., Skare, S., Petersson, K.M. and Ingvar, M. (2000) Tickling expectations: neural processing in anticipation of a sensory stimulus. *Journal of Cognitive Neuroscience*, 12, 691–703.

Carmody, D.P. and Lewis, M. (2006) Brain activation when hearing one's own and others' names. *Brain Research*, 1116, 153–8.

Carpenter, P.A. and Just, M.A. (1983) What your eyes do while your mind is reading. In K. Rayner (ed.) *Eye Movements in Reading: Perceptual and language processes*. New York: Academic Press.

Carpenter, P.A., Miyake, A. and Just, M.A. (1995) Language comprehension: Sentence and discourse processing. *Annual Review of Psychology*, 46, 91–120.

Carr-Chellman, A. and Duchastel, P. (2000) The ideal online course. *British Journal of Educational Technology*, 31, 3, 229–41.

Carr, E.G. and Lovaas, O.J.C. (1983) Contingent electric shock as a treatment for severe behavior problems. In S. Axelrod and J. Apsche (eds) *The Effect of Punishment on Human Behavior*. New York: Academic Press.

Carson, R.C., Butcher, J.N. and Mineka, S. (1996) *Abnormal Psychology and Modern Life* (10th edn). Boston, MA: Allyn & Bacon.

Carver, C.S. and Harmon-Jones, E. (2009) Anger is an approach-related affect: Evidence and implications. *Psychological Bulletin*, 135, 2, 183–204.

Carver, C.S. and Scheier, M.F. (1981) *Attention and Self-regulation: A control theory approach to human behavior*. New York: Springer-Verlag.

Carver, C.S. and Scheier, M.F. (1992) *Perspectives on Personality* (2nd edn). Boston: Allyn & Bacon.

Carver, C.S. and Scheier, M.F. (1999) Optimism. In C.R. Snyder (ed.) *Coping: The psychology of what works*. New York: Oxford University Press.

Carver, C.S., Smith, R.G., Antoni, M.H., Petronis, V.M., Weiss, S. and Derhagopian, R.P. (2005) Optimistic personality and psychosocial well-being during treatment predict psychosocial well-being among long-term survivors of breast cancer. *Health Psychology*, 24, 5, 508–16.

Case, L. and Smith, T.B. (2000) Ethnic representation in a sample of the literature of applied psychology. *Journal of Consulting and Clinical Psychology*, 68(6), 1107–1110.

Case, R. (1985) *Intellectual Development: A systematic reinterpretation*. New York: Academic Press.

Case, R. (1992) *The Mind's Staircase*. Hillsdale, NJ: Lawrence Erlbaum Associates.

Casey, B.J., Cohen, J.D., O'Craven, K., Davidson, R.J., Irwin, W., Nelson, C.A., Noll, D.C., Hu, X., Lowe, M.J., Rosen, B.R., Truwitt, C.L. and Turski, P.A. (1998) Reproducibility of fMRI results across four institutions using a spatial working memory task. *Neuroimage*, 8, 249–61.

Cash, T.F., Morrow, J.A., Hrabosky, J.I. and Perry, A.A. (2004) How has body image changed? A cross-sectional investigation of college women and men from 1983 to 2001. *Journal of Consulting and Clinical Psychology*, 72, 6, 1081–1089.

Caspi, A. (2000) The child is father of the man: Personality continuities from childhood to adulthood. *Journal of Personality and Social Psychology*, 78(1), 158–72.

Castro-Caldas, A., Petersson, K.M., Reis, A., Stone-Elander, S. and Ingvar, M. (1998) The illiterate brain: Learning to read and write during childhood influences the functional organization of the adult brain. *Brain*, 121, 1053–1063.

Catania, J.A., Kegeles, S.M. and Coates, T.J. (1990) Towards an understanding of risk behaviour: An AIDS Risk Reduction Model (ARRM). *Health Education Quarterly*, 17, 53–72.

Cavanaugh, J.C. (1990) *Adult Development and Aging*. Belmont, CA: Wadsworth.

Cerruti, D. (1990) Discrimination theory of rule-governed behavior. *Journal of the Experimental Analysis of Behavior*, 54, 129–53.

Chafin, S., Roy, M., Gerin, W. and Christenfeld, N. (2004) Music can facilitate blood pressure recovery from stress. *British Journal of Health Psychology*, 9, 393–403.

Chaiken, S. (1979) Communicator's physical attractiveness and persuasion. *Journal of Personality and Social Psychology*, 37, 1387–1397.

Chalmers, B. and Meyer, D. (1996) What men say about pregnancy, birth and parenthood. *Journal of Psychosomatic Obstetrics and Gynaecology*, 17, 47–52.

Chalmers, D.J. (1995) Facing up to the problems of consciousness. *Journal of Consciousness Studies*, 2(3), 200–219.

Chalmers, D.J. (1998) On the search for the neural correlate of consciousness. In S.R. Hameroff, A.W. Kaszniak and A.C. Scott (eds) *Towards a Science of Consciousness II*. Cambridge, MA: MIT Press.

Chamorro-Premuzic, T. and Furnham, A. (2007) Personality and music: Can traits explain how people use music in everyday life? *British Journal of Psychology*, 98, 175–85.

Chamorro-Premuzic, T., Furnham, A., Christopher, A.N., Garwood, J. and Martin, G.N. (2007) Birds of a feather: Students' preferences for lecturers' personalities by their own personality and learning approaches. *Personality and Individual Differences*.

Chance, S.A., Esiri, M.M. and Crow, T.J. (2002) Amygdala volume in schizophrenia: Post-mortem study and review of magnetic resonance imaging findings. *British Journal of Psychiatry*, 180, 331–338.

Chao, L.L., Haxby, J.V. and Martin, A. (1999) Attribute-based neural substrates in temporal cortex for perceiving and knowing about objects. *Nature Neuroscience*, 2, 913–19.

Chapin, F.S. (1938) Design for social experiments. *American Sociological Review*, 3, 786–800.

Chapman, K.L., Leonard, L.B. and Mervis, C.B. (1986) The effect of feedback on young children's inappropriate word usage. *Journal of Child Language*, 13, 101–17.

Charmaz, C. (1990) Discovering chronic illness: Using grounded theory. *Social Science and Medicine*, 30(11), 1161–1172.

Charmaz, K. and Henwood, K. (2008) Grounded theory. In C. Willig, and W. Stainton-Rogers (Eds). *The Sage Handbook of Qualitative Research in Psychology*. London: Sage.

Chasdi, E.H. (1994) *Culture and Human Development: The selected papers of John Whiting*. New York: Cambridge University Press.

Chassin, L., Presson, C.C., Rose, J.S. and Sherman, S.J. (1996) The natural history of cigarette smoking from adolescence to adulthood: Demographic predictors of continuity and change. *Health Psychology*, 15(6), 478–84.

Chatterjee, A. (2004) Neuropsychology of art. *Neuropsychologia*, 42, 1568–1583.

Chaves, J.F. (1989) Hypnotic control of clinical pain. In N.P. Spanos and J.F. Chaves (eds) *Hypnosis: The cognitive-behavioural perspective*. Buffalo, NY: Prometheus.

Chee, M.W.L., Chuah, L.Y.M., Venkatraman, V., Chan, W.Y., Philip, P. and Dinges, D.F. (2006) Functional imaging of working memory following normal sleep and after 24 and 35 h of sleep deprivation: Correlations of fronto-parietal activation with performance. *Neuroimage*, 31, 419–28.

Chee. M.W., Tan, E.W. and Thiel, T. (1999) Mandarin and English single word processing studied with functional magnetic resonance imaging. *Journal of Neuroscience*, 19, 3050–3056.

Chen, R., Classen, J., Gerloff, C., Celnik, P., Wassermann, E.M., Hallett, M. and Cohen, L.G. (1997) Depression of motor cortex excitability by low-frequency transcranial magnetic stimulation. *Neurology*, 48, 1398–1403.

Chen, Y.R., Brockner, J. and Katz, T. (1998) Toward an explanation of cultural differences in in-group favouritism: the role of individual versus collective primacy. *Journal of Personality and Social Psychology*, 75, 1490–502.

Cherkas, L.F., Aviv, A., Valdes, A.M., Hunkin, J.L., Gardner, J.P., Surdulescu, G.L. *et al.* (2006) The effects of social status on biological aging as measured by white-blood cell telomere length. *Aging Cell*, 5, 361–5.

Cherny, S.S., Fulker, D.W., Emde, R.N., Robinson, J., Corley, R.P., Reznick, J.S., Plomin, R. and DeFries, J.C. (1994) A developmental–genetic analysis of continuity and change in the Bayley Mental Development Index from 14 to 24 months: The MacArthur Longitudinal Twin Study. *Psychological Science*, 5, 354–360.

Cherry, E.C. (1953) Some experiments on the recognition of speech, with one and with two ears. *Journal of the Acoustical Society of America*, 25, 975–9.

Chida, Y. and Steptoe, A. (2009) Cortisol awakening response and psychosocial factors: A systematic review and meta-analysis. *Biological Psychology*, 80, 265–78.

Chiesa, M. and Hobbs, S. (2008) Making sense of social research: How useful is the Hawthorne effect? *European Journal of Social Psychology*, 38, 67–74.

Chipuer, H.M., Rovine, M.J. and Plomin, R. (1990) LISREL modelling: Genetic and environmental influences on IQ revisited. *Intelligence*, 14, 11–29.

Da Costa Pinto, A. (1991) Reading rates and digit span in bilinguals: The superiority of mother tongue. *International Journal of Psychology*, 26, 471–83.

D'Agincourt-Canning, L. (2006) Genetic testing for hereditary breast and ovarian cancer: Responsibility and choice. *Qualitative Health Research*, 16, 97–118.

Dalgleish, T., Rosen, K. and Marks, M. (1996) Rhythm and blues: The assessment and treatment of seasonal affective disorder. *British Journal of Clinical Psychology*, 35, 163–82.

Daly, J.J. and Wolpaw, J.R. (2008) Brain-computer interfaces in neurological rehabilitation. *Lancet Neurology*, 7, 1032–43.

Daly, M. and Wilson, M. (1978) *Sex, Evolution, and Behavior*. North Scituate, MA: Duxbury Press.

Daly, M. and Wilson, M. (1988) *Homicide*. New York: Aldine de Gruyter.

Daly, M. and Wilson, M. (1996) Violence against stepchildren. *Current Directions in Psychological Science*, 5, 77–81.

Damasio, A.R. (1995) Toward a neurobiology of emotion and feeling: Operational concepts and hypotheses. *The Neuroscientist*, 1, 19–25.

Damasio, A.R. (2000) A neural basis for sociopathy. *Archives of General Psychiatry*, 57, 128–9.

Damasio, A.R., Yamada, T., Damasio, H., Corbett, J. and McKee, J. (1980) Central achromatopsia: Behavioural, autonomic and physiologic aspects. *Neurology*, 30, 1064–1071.

Damasio, H. (1989) Neuroimaging contributions to the understanding of aphasia. In F. Boller and J. Grafman (eds) *Handbook of Neuropsychology*, Vol. 2. Amsterdam: Elsevier.

Damasio, H., Grabowski, T., Frank, R., Galaburda, A.M. and Damasio, A.R. (1994) The return of Phineas Gage: Clues about the brain from the skull of a famous patient. *Science*, 264, 1102–1105.

Damasio, H., Grabowski, T.J., Tranel, D., Hichwa, R.D. and Damasio, A.R. (1996) A neural basis for lexical retrieval. *Nature*, 380, 499–505.

Damjanovic, A.K., Yang, Y., Glaser, R., Kiecolt-Glaser, J.K., Nguyen, H., Laskowski, B. *et al.* (2007) Accelerated telomere erosion is associated with a declining immune function of caregivers of Alzheimer's disease patients. *Journal of Immunology*, 179, 4249–4254.

Damon, W. (1977) *The Social World of the Child*. San Francisco: Jossey-Bass.

Damon, W. (1980) Patterns of change in children's social reasoning: A two-year longitudinal study. *Child Development*, 51, 1010–1017.

Dan, A.J. and Bernhard, L.A. (1989) Menopause and other health issues for midlife women. In S. Hunter and M. Sundel (eds) *Midlife Myths: Issues, findings and practice implications*. California: Sage.

Daneman, M. and Carpenter, P.A. (1980) Individual differences in working memory and reading. *Journal of Verbal Learning and Verbal Behaviour*, 19, 450–66.

Daneman, M. and Hannon, B. (2001) Using working memory theory to investigate the construct validity of multiple-choice comprehension tests such as the SAT. *Journal of Experimental Psychology: General*, 130, 208–23.

Daniels, P. and Weingarten, K. (1982) *Sooner or Later: The timing of parenthood in adult lives*. New York: W.W. Norton.

Danner, D.D., Snowdon, D.A. and Friesen, W.V. (2001) Positive emotions in early life and longevity: Findings from the nun study. *Journal of Personality and Social Psychology*, 80, 5, 804–13.

Darbes, L.A. and Lewis, M.A. (2005) HIV-specific social support predicts less sexual risk behavior in gay male couples. *Health Psychology*, 24, 6, 617–22.

Darley, J.M. and Latané, B. (1968) Bystander intervention in emergencies: Diffusion of responsibility. *Journal of Personality and Social Psychology*, 8, 377–83.

Darwin, C. (1872) *The Expression of the Emotions in Man and Animals*. Reprinted in 1965 by University of Chicago Press, Chicago.

Darwin, C.J., Turvey, M.T. and Crowder, R.G. (1972) An auditory analogue of the Sperling partial report procedure: Evidence for brief auditory storage. *Cognitive Psychology*, 3, 255–67.

Darwin, F. (1887) *Charles Darwin's Autobiography*. Reprinted in 1950 by Henry Schuman, New York.

Davey, G.C.L. (1992) Characteristics of individuals with fear of spiders. *Anxiety Research*, 4, 299–314.

Davey, G.C.L., McDonald, A.S., Hirisave, U., Prabhu, C.G., Iwawaki, S., Jim, C.I., Mercklebach, H., de Jong, P.J., Leung, P.W.L. and Reimann, B.C. (1998) A cross-cultural study of animal fears. *Behaviour Research and Therapy*, 36, 735–50.

Davidoff, J. (1997) The neuropsychology of color. In C.L. Hardin and L. Maffi (eds) *Color Categories in Thought and Language*. New York: Cambridge University Press.

Davidson, A. R. and Jacard, J. (1979) Variables that moderate the attitude–behavior relation: Results of a longtitudinal survey. *Journal of Personality and Social Psychology*, 37, 1364–1376.

Davidson, J.E. and Sternberg, R.J. (1984) The role of insight in intellectual giftedness. *Gifted Child Quarterly*, 28, 58–64.

Davidson, J.M., Camargo, C.A. and Smith, E.R. (1979) Effects of androgen on sexual behavior in hypogonadal men. *Journal of Clinical Endocrinology and Metabolism*, 48, 955–8.

Davidson, R.J. (1992) Anterior cerebral asymmetry and the nature of emotion. *Brain and Cognition*, 20, 125–51.

Davidson, R.J. (1998) Anterior electrophysiological asymmetries, emotion and depression: Conceptual and methodological conundrums. *Psychophysiology*, 35, 607–14.

Davidson, R.J. and Fox, N.A. (1989) Frontal brain asymmetry predicts infants' response to maternal separation. *Journal of Abnormal Psychology*, 98(2), 127–31.

Davidson, R.J. and Hugdahl, K. (1995) *Brain Asymmetry*. Cambridge, MA: MIT Press.

Davidson, R.J. and Sutton, S.K. (1995) Affective neuroscience: The emergence of a discipline. *Current Opinion in Neurobiology*, 5(2), 217–24.

Davidson, R.J., Schwartz, G.E., Saron, C., Bennett, J. and Goleman, D.J. (1979) Frontal vs parietal EEG asymmetry during positive and negative affect. *Psychophysiology*, 16(2), 202–3.

Davies, G.M. and Patel, D. (2005) The influence of car and driver stereotypes on attributions of vehicle speed, position on the road and culpability in a road accident scenario. *Legal and Criminological Psychology*, 10, 45–62.

Davies, I.R.L., Laws, G., Corbett, G.G. and Jerrett, D.J. (1998) Cross-cultural differences in colour vision: Acquired 'colour blindness' in Africa. *Personality and Individual Differences*, 25, 1153–1162.

Davies, J.C. (1969) The J-curve of rising and declining satisfaction as a cause of some great revolutions and a contained rebellion. In H.D. Graham and T.R. Gurr (eds) *The History of Violence in America: Historical and comparative perspectives*. New York: Praeger, pp. 690–730.

Davies, N. (2008) *Flat Earth News*. London: Chatto & Windus.

Davis, J.D. and Campbell, C.S. (1973) Peripheral control of meal size in the rat: Effect of sham feeding on meal size and drinking rats. *Journal of Comparative and Physiological Psychology*, 83, 379–87.

Davis, J.H. (1973) Group decision and social interaction: A theory of social decision schemes. *Psychological Review*, 80, 97–125.

Davis, J.M. (1974) A two-factor theory of schizophrenia. *Journal of Psychiatric Research*, 11, 25–30.

Davis, W.L. and Phares, E.J. (1967) Internal–external control as a determinant of information-seeking in a social influence situation. *Journal of Personality*, 35, 547–61.

Davison, G.C. and Neale, J.M. (2006) *Abnormal Psychology* (10th edn). New York: Wiley.

Davitz, J.R. (1970) A dictionary and grammar of emotion. In M. Arnold (ed.) *Feelings and Emotions: The Loyola Symposium*. New York: Academic Press.

Dawes, R.M. (1991) Social dilemmas, economic self-interest, and evolutionary self-interest. In D.R. Brown and J.E. Keith-Smith (eds) *Frontiers of Mathematical Psychology: Essays in honour of Clyde Coombs*. New York: Springer-Verlag, pp. 53–79.

Dawkins, R. (1986) *The Blind Watchmaker*. London: Penguin.

Dawkins, R. (1996) *Climbing Mount Improbable*. New York: W.W. Norton.

Dawson, G., Frey, K., Panagiotides, H., Osterling, J. and Hessl, D. (1997) Infants of depressed mothers exhibit atypical frontal brain activity: A replication and extension of previous findings. *Journal of Child Psychology and Psychiatry*, 38(2), 179–86.

Day, R. and Wong, S. (1996) Anomalous perceptual asymmetries for negative emotional stimuli in the psychopath. *Journal of Abnormal Psychology*, 105, 648–52.

Deahl, M.P., Gillham, A.B., Thomas, J. *et al.* (1994) Psychological sequelae following the Gulf War. Factors associated with subsequent morbidity and the effectiveness of psychological debriefing. *British Journal of Psychiatry*, 165, 60–5.

De Araujo, I.E., Rolls, E.T., Velazco, M.I., Margot, C. and Cayeux, I. (2005) Cognitive modulation of olfactory processing. *Neuron*, 46, 671–9.

Deary, I.J., Batty, G.D., Pattie, A. and Gale, C.R. (2008) More intelligent, more dependable children live longer. *Psychological Science*, 19, 9, 874–80.

Deb, S. and Thompson, B. (1998) Neuroimaging in autism. *British Journal of Psychiatry*, 173, 299–302.

DeCasper, A.J. and Fifer, W.P. (1980) Of human bonding: Newborns prefer their mothers' voices. *Science*, 208, 1175–1176.

DeCasper, A.J. and Spence, M. (1986) Prenatal maternal speech influences newborns' perception of speech sounds. *Infant Behavior and Development*, 9, 133–50.

DeCasper, A.J., Lecanuet, J-P., Bunsel, M-C., Granier-Deferre, C. and Maugeais, R. (1994) Fetal reactions to recurrent maternal speech. *Infant Behaviour and Development*, 17, 159–64.

Decety, J., Grezes, J., Costes, N., Perani, D., Jeannerod, M., Procyk, E., Grassi, F. and Fazio, F. (1997) Brain activity during observation of actions. *Brain*, 120, 1763–1777.

deCharms, R.C., Maeda, F., Glover, G.H., Ludlow, D., Pauly, J.M., Soneji, D., Gabrieli, J.D.E. and Mackey, S.C. (2005) Control over brain activation and pain learned by using real-time functional MRI. *Proceedings of the National Academy of Sciences*, 102, 51, 18626–18631.

de Cremer, D. and van Vugt, M. (1999) Social identification effects in social dilemmas: A transformation of motives. *European Journal of Social Psychology*, 29, 871–93.

DeGrouchy, J. and Turleau, C. (1990) Autosomal disorders. In A.E.H. Emery and D.L. Rimoin (eds) *Principles and Practice in Medical Genetics*. Edinburgh: Churchill Livingstone.

Dehaene, S., Dupoux, E., Mehler, J, Cohen, L. and Paulesu, E. (1997) Anatomical variability in the cortical representation of first and second language. *NeuroReport*, 8, 3809–3815.

Delahanty, D.L., Dougall, A.L., Hawkes, L., Trakowski, J.H., Schmitz, J.B., Jenkins, F.J. and Baum, A. (1996) Time course of natural killer cell activity and lymphocyte proliferation in response to two acute stressors in healthy men. *Health Psychology*, 15, 48–55.

Delaunay-El Allam, M., Marlier, L. and Schaal, B. (2006) Learning at the breast: Preference formation for an artificial scent and its attraction against the odor of maternal milk. *Infant Behavior and Development*, 29, 308–21.

Del Boca, F.K., Darkes, J., Greenbaum, P.E. and Goldman, M.S. (2004) Up close and personal: Temporal variability in the drinking of individual college students during their first year. *Journal of Consulting and Clinical Psychology*, 72, 2, 155–64.

Deldin, P.J. and Levin, I.P. (1986) The effect of mood induction in a risky decision task. *Bulletin of the Psychonomic Society*, 24, 4–6.

Dell, G.S., Burger, L.K. and Svec, W.R. (1997) Language production and serial order: A functional analysis and a model. *Psychological Review*, 104(1), 123–47.

DeLoache, J.S. (1984) Oh where, oh where: memory-based searching by very young children. In C. Sophian (ed.) *Origins of Cognitive Skills*. Hillsdale, NJ: Lawrence Erlbaum Associates.

DeLongis, A., Folkman, S. and Lazarus, R.S. (1988) The impact of daily stress on health and mood: Psychological and social resources as mediators. *Journal of Personality and Social Psychology*, 54, 486–95.

Dement, W.C. (1974) *Some Must Watch While Some Must Sleep*. San Francisco: W.H. Freeman.

Demuth, J.P., Bie, T.D., Stajich, J.E., Cristiani, N. and Hahn, M.W. (2006) The evolution of mammalian gene families. *Plos ONE*, 1, e85.

Den Hartog, D.N., House, R.J., Hanges, P.J., Ruiz-Quintanilla, S.A. and Dorfman, P.W. (1999) Culture specific and cross-culturally generalizable implicit leadership theories: Are attributes of charismatic/transformational leadership universally endorsed? *Leadership Quarterly*, 10, 219–56.

Den Hartog, D.N. and Veburg, R.M. (1997) Charisma and rhetorics: Communicative techniques of international business leaders. *Leadership Quarterly*, 8(4), 355–91.

Dennett, D.D. (1991) *Consciousness Explained*. London: Penguin.

Dennis, M. and Whitaker, H.A. (1976) Language acquisition following hemidecortication: Linguistic superiority of the left over the right hemisphere. *Brain and Language*, 3, 404–33.

Dennis, T., Bendersky, M., Ramsay, D. and Lewis, M. (2006) Reactivity and regulation in children prenatally exposed to cocaine. *Developmental Psychology*, 42, 4, 688–97.

Dennison, C.D. and Coleman, J.C. (1998) Teenage motherhood: Experiences and relationships. In S. Clement (ed.) *Pregnancy and Childbirth*. Edinburgh: Churchill Livingstone.

DePaulo, B. and Friedman, H.S. (1998) Nonverbal communication. In D.T. Gilbert, S.T. Fiske and G. Lindzey (eds) *The Handbook of Social Psychology* (4th edn), Vol. 2. New York: McGraw-Hill, pp. 3–40.

DePaulo, B.M. and Pfeifer, R.L. (1986) On-the-job experience and skill at detecting deception. *Journal of Applied Social Psychology*, 16, 249–67.

DePue, R.A. and Monroe, S.M. (1986) Conceptualization and measurement of human disorder in life-stress research: The problem of chronic disturbance. *Psychological Bulletin*, 99, 36–51.

deQuervain, D.J-F. and Papassotiropoulos, A. (2006) Identification of a genetic cluster influencing memory performance and hippocampal activity in humans. *Proceedings of the National Academy of Sciences*, 103, 11, 4270–4274.

De Raad, B. (1998) Five big, Big Five issues: rationale, content, structure, status and crosscultural assessment. *European Psychologist*, 3(2), 113–24.

Deregowski, J.B., Muldrow, E.S. and Muldrow, W.F. (1972) Pictorial recognition in a remote Ethiopian village. *Perception*, 1, 417–25.

Fields, R.B. (1998) The dementias. In P.J. Snyder and P.D. Nussbaum (eds) *Clinical Neuropsychology*. Washington, DC: American Psychological Association.

Fiez, J.A., Raichle, M.E., Miezin, F.M., Petersen, S.E., Tallai, P. and Katz, W.F. (1995) PET studies of auditory and phonological processing: Effects of stimulus characteristics and task demands. *Journal of Cognitive Neuroscience*, 7(3), 357–75.

Fife-Shaw, C. (1997) Commentary on Joffe (1996) AIDS research and prevention: A social representational approach. *British Journal of Medical Psychology*, 70, 65–73.

Filsinger, E.E. and Monte, W.C. (1986) Sex history, menstrual cycle and psychophysical ratings of alpha androstenone: A possible human sex pheromone. *The Journal of Sex Research*, 22(2), 243–8.

Filsinger, E.E., Braun, J.J., Monte, W.C. and Linder, D.E. (1984) Human (*Homo sapiens*) responses to the pig (*Sus scrofa*) sex pheromone 5 alpha-androst-16-en-3-one. *Journal of Comparative Psychology*, 98(2), 219–22.

Fincham, F.D. (1998) Child development and marital relations. *Child Development*, 69(2), 543–74.

Fincham, F.D. and Bradbury, T.N. (1987) Cognitive processes and conflict in close relationships: An attribution–efficacy model. *Journal of Personality and Social Psychology*, 53, 1106–1118.

Fink, G.R., Halligan, P.W., Marshall, J.C., Frith, C.D., Frackowiak, R.S.J. and Dolan, R.J. (1996) Where in the brain does visual attention select the forest and the trees? *Nature*, 382, 626–8.

Finkel, D., Pedersen, N.L., McGue, M. and McClearn, G.E. (1995) Heritability of cognitive abilities in adult twins: Comparison and Minnesota and Swedish data. *Behaviour Genetics*, 25, 421–32.

Finkenauer, C., Luminet, O., Gisle, L., El-Ahmadi, A., van der Linden, M. and Philpot, P. (1998) Flashbulb memories of the underlying mechanisms of their formation: Toward an emotional-integrative model. *Memory and Cognition*, 26(3), 516–31.

Finlayson, C., Pacheco, F.G., Rodriguez-Vidal, J., Fa, D.A. *et al.* (2006) Late survival of Neanderthals at the southernmost extreme of Europe. *Nature*, 443, 850–3.

First, M.B. (2005) Clinical utility: A prerequisite for the adoption of a dimensional approach in DSM. *Journal of Abnormal Psychology*, 114, 4, 560–4.

Fischer, K.W. and Farrar, M.J. (1987) Generalizations about generalizations: How a theory of skill development explains both generality and specificity. *International Journal of Psychology*, 22, 643–77.

Fischer, K.W. and Pipp, S.L. (1984) Processes of cognitive development: Optimal level and skill development. In R. Sternberg (ed.) *Mechanisms of Cognitive Development*. New York: Freeman.

Fisher, J.D. and Fisher, W.A. (1992) Changing AIDS risk behaviour. *Psychological Bulletin*, 111, 455–74.

Fisher, R.P. and Geiselman, R.E. (1992) *Memory-enhancing Techniques for Investigative Interviewing*. Springfield, IL: Charles C. Thomas.

Fisher, R.P., Geiselman, R.E., Raymond, D.S., Jurkevich, L.M. and Warhaftig, M.L. (1987) Enhancing enhanced eyewitness testimony: Refining the cognitive interview. *Journal of Police Science and Administration*, 15, 291–7.

Fisher, S.E. (2005) On genes, speech and language. *New England Journal of Medicine*, 353, 16, 1655–1657.

Fiske, S.T. (1993) Controlling other people: The impact of power on stereotyping. *American Psychologist*, 48, 621–8.

Fiske, S.T. and Neuberg, S.L. (1990) A continuum of impression formation, from category-based to individuating processes: Influences of information and motivation on attention and interpretation.

In L. Berkowitz (ed.) *Advances in Experimental Social Psychology*, Vol. 23. New York: Academic Press, pp. 1–74.

Fiske, S.T. and Taylor, S.E. (1991) *Social Cognition* (2nd edn). New York: McGraw-Hill.

Fitzgerald, T.E., Tennen, H., Affleck, G. and Pransky, G.S. (1993) The relative importance of dispositional optimism and control appraisals in quality of life after coronary bypass surgery. *Journal of Behavioural Medicine*, 16, 25–43.

Fivush, R. (1984) Learning about school: The development of kindergartens' school scripts. *Child Development*, 55, 1697–1709.

Fivush, R., Gray, J.T. and Fromhoff, F.A. (1987) Two-year-olds talk about the past. *Cognitive Development*, 2, 393–410.

Flavell, J.H. (1992) Cognitive development: Past, present and future. *Developmental Psychology*, 28, 998–1005.

Flavell, J.H., Everett, B.H., Croft, K. and Flavell, E.R. (1981) Young children's knowledge about visual perception: Further evidence for the level 1–level 2 distinction. *Developmental Psychology*, 17, 99–103.

Flavell, J.H., Green, F.L. and Flavell, E.R. (1989) Young children's ability to differentiate appearance-reality and level 2 perspectives in the tactile modality. *Child Development*, 60, 201–13.

Flay, B.R., Ryan, K.B., Best, J.A., Brown, K.S., Kersell, M.W., d'Avernas, J.R. and Zanna, M.P. (1985) Are social-psychological smoking prevention programs effective? The Waterloo Study. *Journal of Behavioral Medicine*, 8, 37–59.

Flechtner-Mors, M., Ditschuneit, H.H., Johnson, T.D., Suchard, M.A. and Adler, G. (2000) Metabolic and weight loss effects of a long term dietary intervention in obese patients: A four year follow up. *Obesity Research*, 8, 399–402.

Fleischman, D.A. and Gabrieli, J.D.E. (1998) Repetition priming in healthy aging and Alzheimer's disease: A review of findings and theories. *Psychology and Aging*, 13, 88–119.

Fleischman, D.A. and Gabrieli, J.D.E. (1999) Long-term memory in Alzheimer's disease. *Current Opinion in Neurobiology*, 9, 240–4.

Fletcher, G.J.O. and Clark, M.S. (eds) (2001) *Blackwell Handbook of Social Psychology: Interpersonal processes*. Oxford: Blackwell.

Fletcher, P.C. and Henson, R.N.A. (2001) Frontal lobes and human memory. *Brain*, 849–81.

Fletcher, P.C., Shallice, T., Frith, C.D., Frackowiak, R.S. and Dolan, R.J. (1996) Brain activity during memory retrieval. The influence of imagery and semantic cueing. *Brain*, 119, 1587–1596.

Fletcher, P.C., Shallice, T. and Dolan, R.J. (1998a) The functional roles of prefrontal cortex in episodic memory. I. Encoding. *Brain*, 121, 1239–1248.

Fletcher, P.C., Shallice, T. and Dolan, R.J. (1998b) The functional roles of prefrontal cortex in episodic memory. II. Retrieval. *Brain*, 121, 1249–1256.

Fletcher, R. and Voke, J. (1985) *Defective Colour Vision: Fundamentals, diagnosis and management*. Bristol: Adam Hilger.

Flexser, A.J. and Tulving, E. (1978) Retrieval independence in recognition and recall. *Psychological Review*, 85, 153–71.

Flin, R.H. (1985) Development of face recognition: An encoding switch? *British Journal of Psychology*, 76, 125–34.

Flin, R. (1995) Children's testimony: Psychology on trial. In M. Zaragoza, I. Graham, G. Hall, R. Hirschman and Y. BenPorath (eds) *Memory and Testimony in the Child Witness*. Newbury Park, CA: Sage.

Flynn, J.M. and Rahbar, M.H. (1994) Prevalence of reading failure in boys compared with girls. *Psychology in Schools*, 31, 66–71.

Flynn, J.R. (1984) The mean of IQ of Americans: Massive gains 1932 to 1978. *Psychological Bulletin*, 99, 29–51.

Flynn, J.R. (1987) Massive IQ gains in 14 nations: What IQ tests really measure. *Psychological Bulletin*, 101, 171–91.

Flynn, J.R. (1999) Searching for justice: The discovery of IQ gains over time. *American Psychologist*, 54, 5–20.

Foa, E.B. and Meadows, E.A. (1997) Psychosocial treatments for post-traumatic stress disorder: A critical review. *Annual Review of Psychology*, 48, 449–80.

Foa, E.B., Steketee, G. and Young, M.C. (1984) Agoraphobia: Phenomenologic aspects, associated characteristics, and theoretical considerations. *Clinical Psychology Review*, 4, 431–57.

Foa, E.B., Molnar, C. and Cashman, L. (1995) Change in rape narratives during exposure therapy for post-traumatic stress disorder. *Journal of Traumatic Stress*, 8, 675–90.

Fodor, E.M. (1994) Subclinical manifestations of psychosis-proneness, ego strength, and creativity. *Personality and Individual Differences*, 18(5), 635–43.

Fodor, J. (1983) *The Modularity of Mind*. Cambridge, MA: MIT Press.

Fogel, A., Nelson-Goens, G.C., Hsu, H. and Shapiro, A.F. (2000) Do different infant smiles reflect different emotions? *Social Development*, 9, 497–522.

Folkman, S. and Lazarus, R.S. (1991) Coping and emotion. In A. Monat and R.S. Lazarus (eds) *Stress and Coping: An anthology*. New York: Columbia University Press.

Foltveld, P. (1995) Professional, psychology in Denmark. In A. Schorr and S. Saari (eds) *Psychology in Europe*. Gottingen: Hogrefe & Huber.

Fontana, A. and Rosenheck, R. (1993) A causal model of the etiology of war-related PTSD. *Journal of Traumatic Stress*, 6, 475–99.

Ford, T.E., Boxer, C.F., Armstrong, J. and Edel, J.R. (2008) More than 'just a joke': the prejudice-releasing function of sexist humor. *Personality and Social Psychology Bulletin*, 34, 2, 159–70.

Ford, T.E., Wentzel, E.R. and Lorion, J. (2001) Effects of exposure to sexist humor on perceptions of normative tolerance of sexism. *European Journal of Social Psychology*, 31, 677–91.

Foreyt, J. and Goodrick, G.D. (1993) Evidence for success of behaviour modification in weight loss and control. *Annals of Internal Medicine*, 119, 698–701.

Forgas, J.P. (2007) When sad is better than happy: Negative affect can improve the quality and effectiveness of persuasive messages and social influence strategies. *Journal of Experimental Social Psychology*, 43, 513–28.

Forgas, J.P., Goldenberg, L. and Unkelbach, C. (2009) Can bad weather improve your memory? *Journal of Experimental Social Psychology*, 45, 254–7.

Forsterling, F. (1988) *Attribution Theory in Clinical Psychology*. Chichester: Wiley.

Forsyth, D.R. (1990) *Group Dynamics*. Pacific Grove, CA: Brooks/Cole.

Fortin, S., Godbout, L. and Braun, C.M.J. (2003) Cognitive structure of executive deficits in frontally lesioned head trauma patients performing activities of daily living. *Cortex*, 39, 273–91.

Foster, J.J. and Parker, I. (1995) *Carrying out Investigations in Psychology*. Leicester: BPS Books.

Foster, J.K., Black, S.E., Buck, B.H. and Bronskill, M.J. (1997) Ageing and executive functions: A neuroimaging perspective. In P. Rabbitt (ed.) *Methodology of Frontal and Executive Function*. Hove: Psychology Press.

Foster, P.S. and Webster, D.G. (2001) Emotional memories: The relationship between age of memory and the corresponding psychophysiological responses. *International Journal Psychophysiology*, 41, 11–18.

Fouts, G. and Burggraf, K. (1999) Television situation comedies: Female body images and verbal reinforcement. *Sex Roles*, 40, 473–81.

Fouts, R.S. (1983) Chimpanzee language and elephant tails: A theoretical synthesis. In J. de Luce and H.T. Wilder (eds) *Language in Primates: Perspectives and implications*. New York: Springer-Verlag.

Fouts, R.S., Hirsch, A. and Fouts, D. (1983) Cultural transmission of a human language in a chimpanzee mother/infant relationship. In H.E. Fitzgerald, J.A. Mullins and P. Page (eds) *Psychological Perspectives, Child Nurturance Series*, Vol. 3. New York: Plenum Press.

Fowler, J.H. and Christakis, N.A. (2009) Dynamic spread of happiness in a large social network: longitudinal analysis over 20 years in Framingham Heart Study. *British Medical Journal*, 337, 1–9.

Fox, N.A. Rubin, K.H., Calkins, S.D., Marshall, T.R., Coplan, R.J., Porges, S.W., Long, J.M. and Stewart, S. (1995) Frontal activation asymmetry and social competence at four years of age. *Child Development*, 66, 1770–1784.

Fox, N.A., Henderson, H.A., Rubin, K.H., Calkins, S.D. and Schmidt, L.A. (2001) Continuity and discontinuity of behavioural inhibition and exuberance: Psychophysiological and behavioural influences across the first four years of life. *Child Development*, 72(1), 1–21.

Frackowiak, R.J.S., Friston, K.J., Frith, C.D., Dolan, R.J. and Mazziotta, J.C. (1997) *Human Brain Function*. Oxford: Academic Press.

Francis, S., Rolls, E.T., Bowtell, R., McGlone, F., O'Doherty, J., Browning, A., Clare, S. and Smith, E. (1999) The representation of pleasant touch in the brain and its relationship with taste and olfactory areas. *NeuroReport*, 10, 453–9.

Frankland, P.W., Bontempi, B., Talton, L.E., Kaczmarek, L. and Silva, A.J. (2004) The involvement of the anterior cingulated cortex in remote contextual fear memory. *Science*, 304, 881–3.

Franklin, S., Howard, D. and Patterson, K. (1994) Abstract word meaning deafness. *Cognitive Neuropsychology*, 11, 1–34.

Franks, N.P. and Lieb, W.R. (1998) The molecular basis of general anesthesia: current ideas. In S.R. Hameroff, A.W. Kaszniak and A.C. Scott (eds) *Towards a Science of Consciousness II*. Cambridge, MA: MIT Press.

Frederick, D.A., Peplau, L.A. and Lever, J. (2006) The swimsuit issue: Correlates of body image in a sample of 52, 677 heterosexual adults. *Body Image*, 3, 413–19.

Frederickson, B.L. and Roberts, T.A. (1997) Objectification theory: Towards understanding of women's lived experiences and mental health risks. *Psychology of Women Quarterly*, 21, 173–8.

Freedman, J.L. and Fraser, S.C. (1966) Compliance without pressure: The foot-in-the-door technique. *Journal of Personality and Social Psychology*, 4, 195–203.

Freedy, J.R., Saladin, M.E., Kilpatrick, D.G., Resnick, H.S. and Saunders, B.E. (1994) Understanding acute psychological distress following natural disaster. *Journal of Traumatic Stress*, 7, 257–73.

Freeman, R.C., Rodriguez, G.M. and French, J.F. (1996) Compliance with AZT treatment regimen of HIV-seropositive injection drug users: A neglected issue. *AIDS Education and Prevention*, 8, 58–71.

Fregni, F., Orsati, F., Pedrosa, W., Fecteau, S., Tome, F.A.M., Nitsche, M.A., Mecca, T., Macedo, E.C., Pascual-Leone, A. and Boggio, P.S. (2008) Transcranial direct current stimulation of the prefrontal cortex modulates the desire for specific foods. *Appetite*, 51, 34–41.

French, J.R.P. (1944) Organised and unorganised groups under fear and frustration. *University of Iowa Studies of Child Welfare*, 20, 231–308.

French, S.A., Hennrikus, D.J. and Jeffrey, R.W. (1996) Smoking status, dietary intake, and physical activity in a sample of working adults. *Health Psychology*, 15(6), 448–54.

Freud, S. (1900) *The Interpretation of Dreams*. London: George Allen & Unwin.

Goldberg, E. (1989) Gradiential approach to neocortical functional organization. *Journal of Clinical and Experimental Neuropsychology*, 11(4), 489–517.

Goldberg, L.R. (1993) The structure of phenotypic personality traits. *American Psychologist*, 48, 26–34.

Goldberg, R.J. and Steury, S. (2001) Depression in the workplace: Costs and barriers to treatment. *Psychiatric Services*, 52(12), 1639–1626.

Goldin-Meadow, S. and Feldman, H. (1977) The development of language-like communication without a language model. *Science*, 197, 401–3.

Goldman-Rakic, P.S. (1995) Cellular basis of working memory. *Neuron*, 14, 477–85.

Goldsmith, H.H. and Alansky, J.A. (1987) Maternal and infant predictors of attachment: A meta-analytic review. *Journal of Consulting and Clinical Psychology*, 55, 805–16.

Goldstein, D., Hahn, C.S., Hasher, L., Wiprzycka, U.J. and Zelazo, P.D. (2007) Time of day, intellectual performance, and behavioural problems in Morning versus Evening type adolescents: Is there a synchrony effect? *Personality and Individual Differences*, 42, 431–40.

Goldstein, D., Haldane, D. and Mitchell, C. (1990) Sex differences in visuo-spatial ability: The role of performance factors. *Memory and Cognition*, 18, 546–50.

Goldstein, E.B. (2007) *Sensation and Perception* (7th edn). California: Thompson.

Goldstone, R.L., Medink, D.L. and Gentner, D. (1991) Relational similarity and the nonindependence of features in similarity judgments. *Cognitive Psychology*, 23, 222–62.

Goleman, D. (1995) *Emotional Intelligence*. New York: Bantam Books.

Goleman, D. (1998) *Working with Emotional Intelligence*. New York: Bantam Books.

Goodale, M.A. and Milner, A.D. (1992) Separate visual pathways for perception and action. *Trends in Neurosciences*, 15, 2–25.

Goodale, M.A., Milner, A.D., Jakobson, L.S. and Carey, D.P. (1991) Perceiving the world and grasping it: A neurological dissociation. *Nature*, 349, 154–6.

Goodglass, H. (1976) Agrammatism. In H. Whitaker and H.A. Whitaker (eds) *Studies in Neurolinguistics*. New York: Academic Press.

Goodman, M.J., Tijerina, L., Bents, F.D. and Wierwille, W.W. (1999) Using cellular telephones in vehicles: Safe or unsafe? *Transportation Human Factors*, 1, 3–42.

Goodwin, D.W. and Guze, S.B. (1984) *Psychiatric Diagnosis* (3rd edn). New York: Oxford University Press.

Goodwin, F.K. and Jamison, K.R. (1990) *Manic-depressive Illness*. New York: Oxford University Press.

Gopnik, M. (1997) Language deficits and genetic factors. *Trends in Cognitive Neurosciences*, 1(1), 5–9.

Gorno-Tempini, M.L. and Price, C.J. (2001) Identification of famous faces and buildings: A functional neuroimaging study of semantically unique items. *Brain*, 124, 2087–2097.

Gorno-Tempini, M.L., Price, C.J., Josephs, O., Vandenberghe, R., Cappa, S.F., Kapur, N. and Frackowiak, R.S.J. (1998) The neural systems sustaining face and proper-name processing. *Brain*, 121, 2103–2118.

Gottesman, I.I. (1991) *Schizophrenia Genesis. The origins of madness*. New York: Freeman.

Gottesman, I.I. and Bertelsen, A. (1989) Confirming unexpressed genotypes for schizophrenia. *Archives of General Psychiatry*, 46, 867–72.

Gottesman, I.I. and Shields, J. (1982) *Schizophrenia: The epigenetic puzzle*. Cambridge: Cambridge University Press.

Gould, A. and Martin, G.N. (2001) 'A good odour to breathe?' The effect of pleasant ambient odour on human visual vigilance. *Applied Cognitive Psychology*, 15, 225–32.

Gould, M.S., Greenberg, T., Velting, D.M. and Shaffer, D. (2003) Youth suicide risk and preventive interventions: A review of the past 10 years. *Journal of the American Academy of Child and Adolescent Psychiatry*, 42, 386–405.

Gould, S.J. (1985) *The Flamingo's Smile*. New York: W.W. Norton.

Grabe, S., Hyde, J.S. and Ward, L.M. (2007) The role of the media in body image concerns among women: A meta-analysis of experimental and correlational studies. *Psychological Bulletin*, 134, 3, 460–76.

Grady, C.L., Springer, M.V., Hongwanishkul, D., McIntosh, A.R. and Winocur, G. (2006) Age-related changes in brain activity across the adult lifespan. *Journal of Cognitive Neuroscience*, 18, 2, 227–41.

Graen, G.B. and Uhl-Bien, M. (1995) Relationship-based approach to leadership: Development of leader–member exchange (LMX) theory of leadership over 25 years: Applying a multi-level multi-domain approach. *Leadership Quarterly*, 6, 219–47.

Graf, P. and Mandler, G. (1984) Activation makes words more accessible, but not necessarily more retrievable. *Journal of Verbal Learning and Verbal Behavior*, 23, 553–68.

Graf, P., Squire, L.R. and Mandler, G. (1984) The information that amnesic patients do not forget. *Journal of Experimental Psychology: Learning, Memory, and Cognition*, 10, 164–78.

Grafman, J., Livan, I., Massaquoi, S., Stewart, M., Sirigu, A. and Hallett, M. (1992) Cognitive planning deficit in patients with cerebellar atrophy. *Neurology*, 42, 1493–1496.

Grafton, S.T., Fadiga, L., Arbib, M.A. and Rizzolatti, G. (1997) Premotor cortex activation during observation and naming of familiar tools. *Neuroimage*, 6, 231–6.

Graham, C.A., Janssen, E. and Sanders, S.A. (2000) Effects of fragrance on female sexual arousal and mood across the menstrual cycle. *Psychophysiology*, 37, 76–84.

Graham, J.E., Rockwood, K., Beattie, B.L., Eastwood, R., Gauthier, S., Tuokko, H. and McDowell, I. (1997) Prevalence and severity of cognitive impairment with and without dementia in an elderly population. *Lancet*, 349, 1793–1796.

Graham, J.R. (1990) *MMPI-2: Assessing personality and psychopathology*. New York: Oxford University Press.

Graham, T.A. (2001) Teaching child development via the internet: opportunities and pitfalls. *Teaching of Psychology*, 28, 67–71.

Granhag, P.A. and Stromwall, L.A. (2001) Detection deception based on repeated interrogations. *Legal and Criminological Psychology*, 6, 85–101.

Grant, I., Marcotte, T.D., Heaton, R.K. and the HNRC Group (1999) Neurocognitive complications of HIV disease. *Psychological Science*, 10(3), 191–5.

Grant, P.R. (1986) *Ecology and Evolution of Darwin's Finches*. Princeton, NJ: Princeton University Press.

Grant, S., Contoreggi, C. and London, E.D. (2000) Drug abusers show impaired performance in a laboratory test of decision-making. *Neuropsychologia*, 38, 1180–1187.

Grant, V.J. and France, J.T. (2001) Dominance and testosterone in women. *Biological Psychology*, 58, 41–7.

Gray, J.A. (1971) The mind-brain identity theory as a scientific hypothesis. *Philosophical Quarterly*, 21, 247–54.

Gray, J.A. (1982) *The Neuropsychology of Anxiety*. Oxford: Oxford University Press.

Gray, J.A. (1987) *The Psychology of Fear and Stress* (2nd edn). Cambridge: Cambridge University Press.

Gray, J.A. (1995) A model of the limbic system and basal ganglia: Applications to anxiety and schizophrenia. In M.S. Gazzaniga (ed.) *The Cognitive Neurosciences*. Cambridge, MA: MIT Press.

Gray, J.A. (1998) Creeping up on the hard question of consciousness. In S.R. Hameroff, A.W. Kaszniak and A.C. Scott (eds) *Towards a Science of Consciousness II*. Cambridge, MA: MIT Press.

Gray, J.A., Feldon, J., Rawlins, J.N.P., Hemsley, D.R. and Smith, A.D. (1991) The neuropsychology of schizophrenia. *Behavioural and Brain Science*, 14, 1–84.

Gray, J.M., Young, A.W., Barker, W.A., Curtis, A. and Gibson, D. (1997) Impaired recognition of disgust in Huntington's disease gene carriers. *Brain*, 120, 2029–2038.

Gray, S.W., Ramsey, B.K. and Klaus, R.A. (1982) *From 3 to 20: The early training project*. Baltimore: University Park Press.

Gray, T. and Mill, D. (1990) Critical abilities, graduate education (Biology vs English), and belief in unsubstantiated phenomena. *Canadian Journal of Behavioural Science*, 22, 162–72.

Green, B.L. (1994) Psychosocial research in traumatic stress: An update. *Journal of Traumatic Stress*, 7, 341–62.

Green, D.M. and Swets, J.A. (1974) *Signal Detection Theory and Psychophysics*. New York: Krieger.

Greenberg, B.D., Li, Q., Lucas, F.R., Hu, S., Sirota, L.A. and Benjamin, J. (2000) Association between the serotonin transporter promoter polymorphism and personality traits in primarily a female population sample. *American Journal of Medical Genetics*, 96, 2, 202–16.

Greenberg, B.S., Eastin, M., Hofschire, L., Lachlan, K. and Brownell, K. (2003) Portrayals of overweight and obese individuals on commerical television. *American Journal of Public Heath*, 93, 1342–8.

Greenberg, D.L. (2004) President Bush's false 'flashbulb' memory of 9/11. *Applied Cognitive Psychology*, 18, 363–70.

Greenberg, L. and Barling, J. (1999) Predicting employee aggression against co-workers, subordinates and supervisors: The roles of person behaviours and perceived workplace factors. *Journal of Organizational Behaviour*, 20, 897–913.

Greenberg, R. and Pearlman, C.A. (1974) Cutting the REM nerve: An approach to the adaptive role of REM sleep. *Perspectives in Biology and Medicine*, 17, 513–21.

Greene, J.D.W. and Hodges, J.R. (1996a) Identification of famous faces and famous names in early Alzheimer's disease. *Brain*, 119, 111–28.

Greene, J.D.W. and Hodges, J.R. (1996b) Identification of remote memory: Evidence from a longitudinal study of dementia of the Alzheimer type. *Brain*, 119, 129–42.

Greenough, W.T. and Volkmar, F.R. (1973) Pattern of dendritic branching in occipital cortex of rats reared in complex environments. *Experimental Neurology*, 40, 491–504.

Greenwald, A.G., Banaji, M.R., Rudman, L.A., Farnham, S.D., Nosek, B.A. and Mellott, D.S. (2002) A unified theory of implicit attitudes, stereotypes, self-esteem, and self-concept. *Psychological Review*, 109, 3–25.

Greenwald, A.G., McGhee, D.E. and Schwartz, J.L.K. (1998) Measuring individual differences in implicit cognition: The implicit association test. *Journal of Personality and Social Psychology*, 74, 1464–1480.

Gregory, R.L. (1998) Mythical mechanisms (2): Is the brain a computer? *Perception*, 27, 127–8.

Greimel, E., Macht, M., Krumhuber, E. and Ellgring, H. (2006) Facial and affective reactions to tastes and their modulation by sadness and joy. *Physiology and Behavior*, 89, 261–9.

Gretton, H.M., Hare, R.D. and Catchpole, R.E.H. (2004) Psychopathy and offending from adolescence to adulthood: A 10-year follow-up. *Journal of Consulting and Clinical Psychology*, 72, 4, 636–45.

Grezes, J., Berthoz, S. and Passingham, R.E. (2006) Amygdala activation when one is the target of deceit: Did he lie to you or to someone else? *Neuroimage*, 30, 601–8.

Griffiths, M. and Payne, P.R. (1976) Energy expenditure in small children of obese and non-obese mothers. *Nature*, 260, 698–700.

Griffiths, R.R., Bigelow, G.E. and Henningfield, J.E. (1980) Similarities in animal and human drug-taking behavior. In N.K. Mello (ed.) *Advances in Substance Abuse, Vol. 1*. Greenwich, CT: JAI Press.

Griggs, R.A. and Cox, J.R. (1982) The elusive thematic-materials effect in Wason's selection task. *British Journal of Psychology*, 73, 407–20.

Grigorenko, E.L., Wood, F.B., Meyer, M.S. *et al.* (1997) Susceptibility loci for distinct components of developmental dyslexia on chromosomes 6 and 15. *American Journal of Human Genetics*, 60, 27–39.

Grimes, J. (1996) On the failure to detect changes in scenes across saccades. In K. Atkins (ed.), *Perception*, Vol 2, New York: Oxford University Press.

Griskevicius, V., Cialdini, R.B. and Kenrick, D.T. (2006) Peacocks, Picasso, and parental investment: The effects of romantic motives on creativity. *Journal of Personality and Social Psychology*, 91, 1, 63–76.

Groesz, L.M., Levine, M.P. and Murnen, S.K. (2002) The effect of experimental presentation of thin media images on body satisfaction: A meta-analytic review. *International Journal of Eating Disorders*, 31, 1–16.

Gross, M.U.M. (1993) *Exceptionally Gifted Children*. London: Routledge.

Grossenbacher, P.G. and Lovelace, C. (2001) Mechanisms of synaesthesia: Cognitive and physiological constraints. *Trends in Cognitive Science*, 5(1), 36–41.

Grossi, G., Semenza, C., Corazza, S. and Volterra, V. (1996) Hemisphere specialization for sign language. *Neuropsychologia*, 34, 7, 737–40.

Grossman, K., Grossman, K.E., Spangler, G., Suess, G. and Unzer, L. (1985) Maternal sensitivity and newborns' orientation responses as related to quality of attachment in Northern Germany. In I. Bretherton and E. Waters (eds) Growing points of attachment theory and research. *Monographs of the Society for Research in Child Development*, 50.

Groth-Marnat, G. (1997) *Handbook of Psychological Assessment* (3rd edn). New York: Wiley.

Gruter, T., Gruter, M. and Carbon, C-C. (2008) Neural and genetic foundations of face recognition and prosopagnosia. *Journal of Neuropsychology*, 2, 79–97.

Gruzelier, J., Seymour, K., Wilson, L., Idley, A. and Hirsch, S. (1988) Impairments on neuropsychological tests of temporohippocampal and frontohippocampal function and word fluency in remitting schizophrenia and affective disorders. *Archives of General Psychiatry*, 45, 623–9.

Guariglia, C., Padovani, A., Pantano, P. and Pizzamiglio, L. (1993) Unilateral neglect restricted to visual imagery. *Nature*, 364, 235–7.

Gudjonsson, G.H. (1994) Psychological evidence in court. In G.E. Lindzey and G.H. Powell (eds) *The Handbook of Adult Clinical Psychology*. London: Routledge.

Gudjonsson, G.H. (1996a) Forensic psychology in England: One practitioner's experience and viewpoint. *Legal and Criminological Psychology*, 1, 131–42.

Gudjonsson, G.H. (1996b) Psychological evidence in court. *The Psychologist*, May, 213–17.

Gudjonsson, G.H. (1997) The members of the BFMS, the accusers and their siblings. *The Psychologist*, March, 111–15.

Harmon-Jones, E., Abramson, L.Y., Sigelman, J., Bohlig, A., Hogan, M.E. and Harmon-Jones, C. (2002) Proneness to hypomania/mania symptoms or depression symptoms and asymmetrical frontal cortical responses to an anger-evoking event. *Journal of Personality and Social Psychology*, 82(4), 610–18.

Harré, R. and Secord, P. (1972) *The Explanation of Social Behaviour*. Oxford: Blackwell.

Harris, B. (1979) Whatever happened to Little Albert? *American Psychologist*, 34(2), 151–60.

Harris, C.R. (2002) Sexual and romantic jealousy in heterosexual and homosexual adults. *Psychological Science*, 13(1), 7–12.

Harris, G. and Booth, D.A. (1987) Infants' preference in food and previous dietary exposure in 6-month-old infants. *IRCS Medical Science*, 13, 1178–1179.

Harris, J.R. (1995) Where is the child's environment? A group socialization theory of development. *Psychological Review*, 102, 458–89.

Harris, M. (1991) *Cultural Anthropology* (3rd edn). New York: HarperCollins.

Harris, N.B. (1992) Sex, race, and experiences of aggression. *Aggressive Behavior*, 18, 201–17.

Harrison, D.A., Price, K.H., Gavin, J.H. and Florey, A. (2002) Time, teams, and task performance: changing effects of surface-and deep-level diversity on group functioning. *Academy of Management Journal*, 45, 1029–1045.

Harrison, J. and Baron-Cohen, S. (eds) (1996) *Synaesthesia: Classic and contemporary readings*. Oxford: Blackwell.

Harrison, L.K., Denning, S., Easton, H.L., Hall, J.C., Burns, V.E., Ring, C. and Carroll, D.G. (2001) The effects of competition and competitiveness on cardiovascular activity. *Psychophysiology*, 38, 601–6.

Harrison, Y. and Horne, J.A. (2000) Sleep loss and temporal memory. *The Quarterly Journal of Experimental Psychology*, 53A(1), 271–9.

Hartig, T., Catalanao, R. and Ong, M. (2007) Cold summer weather, constrained restoration, and the use of antidepressants in Sweden. *Journal of Environmental Psychology*, 27, 107–16.

Hartley, J. (1998) *Learning and Studying: A research perspective*. London: Routledge.

Hartshorne, H. and May, M.A. (1928) *Studies in Deceit*. New York: Macmillan.

Hartup, W.W. and Laursen, B. (1992) Conflict and context in peer relations. In C.H. Hart (ed.) *Children on Playgrounds: Research perspectives and applications*. Albany, NY: State University of New York Press.

Hartwig, M., Granhag, P.A., Stromwall, L.A. and Andersson, L.O. (2004) Suspicious minds: Criminals' ability to detect deception. *Psychology, Crime and Law*, 10, 1, 83–95.

Harwood, J., Giles, H. and Bourhis, R.Y. (1994) The genesis of vitality theory: Historical patterns and discoursal dimensions. *International Journal of the Sociology of Language*, 108, 167–206.

Haselton, M.G., Mortezaie, M., Pillsworth, E.G., Bleske-Rechek, A. and Frederick, D.A. (2007) Ovulatory shifts in human female ornamentation: Near ovulation, women dress to impress. *Hormones and Behavior*, 51, 40–5.

Hasher, L. and Zacks, R.T. (1988) Working memory, comprehension, and ageing: A review and a new view. In G.H. Bower (ed.) *The Psychology of Learning and Motivation*, Vol. 22. San Diego, CA: Academic Press.

Haslam, N., Rothschild, L. and Erbst, D. (1998) Essentialist beliefs about social categories. *British Journal of Social Psychology*, 39, 113–27.

Haste, H., Helkama, K. and Markoulis, D. (1998) Morality, wisdom and the life-span. In A. Demetriou, W. Doise and C.F.M. van Lieshout (eds) *Life-span Developmental Psychology*. Chichester: Wiley.

Hastie, R., Penrod, S.D. and Pennington, N. (1983) *Inside the Jury*. Cambridge, MA: Harvard University Press.

Hatcher, P.J., Hulme, C. and Snowling, M.J. (2004) Explicit phoneme training combined with phonic reading instruction helps young children at risk of reading failure. *Journal of Child Psychology and Psychiatry*, 45, 2, 338–58.

Hatfield, E. (1988) Passionate and compassionate love. In R.J. Sternberg and M.L. Barnes (eds) *The Psychology of Love*. New Haven, CT: Yale University Press.

Hatfield, E. and Sprecher, S. (1986) *Mirror, Mirror . . . The importance of looks in everyday life*. Albany, NY: SUNY Press.

Haward, L.R.C. (1979) The psychologist as expert witness. In D.P. Farrington, K. Hawkins and S.M.A. Lloyd-Bostock (eds) *Psychology, Law and Legal Processes*. London: Macmillan.

Haward, L.R.C. (1981) *Forensic Psychology*. London: Batsford.

Hawley, P.H. (1999) The ontogenesis of social dominance: A strategy-based evolutionary perspective. *Developmental Review*, 19, 97–132.

Haxby, J.V., Horwitz, B., Ungeldeider, L.G., Maisog, J.M. (1994) The functional organization of human extrastriate cortex: PET rCBF study of selective attention to faces and locations. *Journal of Neuroscience*, 14, 11, 1, 6336–6353.

Hayes, C. (1952) *The Ape in Our House*. London: Gollancz.

Hayes, N. (1997) *Doing Qualitative Analysis in Psychology*. Hove: Psychology Press.

Hayes, S.C. (1989) *Rule-governed Behavior: Cognition, contingencies, and instructional control*. New York: Plenum.

Health Education Authority (1991) *The Smoking Epidemic*. London: HEA.

Healy, A.F., Havas, D.A. and Parker, J.T. (2000) Comparing serial position effects in semantic and episodic memory using reconstruction of order tasks. *Journal of Memory and Language*, 42, 147–67.

Heap, M. and Dryden, W. (1991) *Hypnotherapy: A handbook*. Milton Keyes: Open University Press.

Hebb, D.O. (1949) *The Organization of Behaviour*. New York: Wiley/Interscience.

Hebb, D.O. (1955) Drives and the CNS (conceptual nervous system). *Psychological Review*, 62, 243–54.

Hebb, D.O., Lambert, W.E. and Tucker, G.R. (1973) A DMZ in the language war. *Psychology Today*, April, 55–62.

Hebert, L.E. *et al.* (1995) Age-specific incidence of Alzheimer's disease in a community population. *Journal of the American Medical Association*, 273, 1354–1359.

Heider, E.R. (1971) 'Focal' color areas and the development of color names. *Developmental Psychology*, 4, 447–55.

Heider, E.R. (1972) Universals in color naming and memory. *Journal of Experimental Psychology*, 93, 10–20.

Heider, F. (1958) *The Psychology of Interpersonal Relations*. New York: Wiley.

Heilman, M.E. and Stopeck, M.H. (1985) Attractiveness and corporate success: Different causal attributions for males and females. *Journal of Applied Psychology*, 70, 379–88.

Heim, N. and Hursch, C. (1979) Castration for sex offenders: Treatment or punishment? *Archives of Sexual Behaviour*, 8, 281–304.

Heine, S.J., Takemoto, T., Moskalenko, S., Lasaleta, J. and Henrich, J. (2008) Mirrors in the head: Cultural variation in objective self-awareness. *Personality and Social Psychology Bulletin*, 34, 7, 879–87.

Heinrich, H., Gevensleben, H., Freisleder, F.L., Moll, G.H. & Rothenberger, A. (2004) Training of slow cortical potentials in attention deficit/hyperactivty disorder: Evidence for positive behaviour and neurophysiological effects. *Biological Psychiatry*, 55, 772–5.

Helson, R. and Soto, C.J. (2005) Up and down in middle age: monotonic and nonmonotonic changes in roles, status and personality. *Journal of Personality and Social Psychology*, 89, 194–204.

Hendon, D.W., Roy, M.H and Ahmed, Z.U. (2003) Negotiation concession patterns: a multicountry, multiperiod study. *American Business Review*, 21, 75–81.

Hendry, L.B. and Kloep, M. (2002) *Lifespan Development: Resources, challenges, risks.* London: Thomson Learning.

Hendry, L.B., Kloep, M. and Olsson, S. (1998) Is there life beyond 'flow'? *Proceedings of 5th biennial conference of the EARA*, University of Liege.

Henke, P.G. (1982) The telencephalic limbic system and experimental gastric pathology: A review. *Neuroscience and Biobehavioral Reviews*, 6, 381–90.

Henkens, K., Sprengers, M. and Tazelaar, F. (1996) Unemployment and the older worker in the Netherlands: re-entry into the labour force or resignation. *Ageing and Society*, 16, 561–78.

Hensley, P.L., Nadiga, D. and Uhlenhuth, E.H. (2004) Long-term effectiveness of cognitive therapy in major depressive disorder. *Depression and Anxiety*, 20, 1–7.

Henss, R. (2000) Waist-to-hip ratio and female attractiveness: Evidence from photographic stimuli and methodological considerations. *Personality and Individual Differences*, 28, 501–13.

Hepper, P.G. (1994) Auditory learning in the human fetus. *Infant Behaviour and Development*, 17, 96.

Hepper, P.G. (1995) Human fetal 'olfactory' learning. *International Journal of Prenatal, Perinatal and Psychological Medicine*, 7, 147–51.

Herdt, G. and Lindenbaum, S. (eds) (1992) *Social Analyses in the Time of AIDS*. Newbury Park, CA: Sage.

Hermans, D., Pieters, G. and Eelen, P. (1998) Implicit and explicit memory for shape, body weight, and food-related words in patients with anorexia nervosa and nondieting controls. *Journal of Abnormal Psychology*, 107(2), 193–202.

Hermans, E.J., Putman, P. and van Honk, J. (2006) Testosterone administration reduces empathetic behavior: A facial mimicry study. *Psychoneuroendocrinology*, 31, 859–66.

Hermoye, L., Saint-Martin, C., Cosnard, G., Lee, S., Kim, J., Nassogne, M. *et al.* (2006) Pediatric diffusion tensor imaging: Normal database and observation of the white matter maturation in early childhood. *Neuroimage*, 29, 493–504.

Herrenkohl, R.C., Egolf, B.P. and Herrenkohl, E.C. (1997) Pre-school antecedents of adolescent assaultive behaviour: A longitudinal study. *American Journal of Orthopsychiatry*, 67, 422–33.

Herrnstein, R.J. and Murray, C. (1994) *The Bell Curve*. New York: Free Press.

Herrnstein, R.J., Nickerson, R.S., Sanchez, M. and Swets, J.A. (1986) Teaching thinking skills. *American Psychologist*, 41, 1279–1289.

Hertz-Pannier, L., Chiron, C., Van de Moortele, P-F., Bourgeois, M., Fohlen, M. and Dulac, O. (1999) Multi-task fMRI presurgical language mapping in children with cognitive impairment. *Neuroimage*, 9, S691.

Hertz-Pannier, L., Chiron, C., Jambaque, I., Renaux-Kieffer, V., Van de Moortele, P-F., Delalande, O., Fohlen, M., Brunelle, F. and Le Bihan, D. (2002) Late plasticity for language in a child's non-dominant hemisphere. *Brain*, 125, 361–72.

Herz, R.S. (1997) The effects of cue-distinctiveness on odor-based context dependent memory. *Memory and Cognition*, 25, 375–80.

Herz, R.S. and Cupchik, G.C. (1992) An experimental characterization of odor-evoked memories in humans. *Chemical Senses*, 17(5), 519–28.

Herz, R.S. and Engen, T. (1996) Odor memory: Review and analysis. *Psychonomic Bulletin Review*, 3(3), 300–13.

Hestbaek, A.D. (1998) Parenthood in the 1990s: Tradition and modernity in the parenthood of dual-earner couples with different lifemodes. *Childhood*, 5(4), 473–91.

Hewstone, M. (1989) *Causal Attribution: From cognitive processes to collective beliefs*. Oxford: Blackwell.

Hewstone, M. (1996) Contact and categorization: Social psychological interventions to change intergroup relations. In C.N. Macrae, C. Stangor and M. Hewstone (eds) *Stereotypes and Stereotyping*. New York: Guilford Press, pp. 323–68.

Hewstone, M. and Brown, R.J. (1986) *Causal Attribution: From cognitive processes to collective beliefs*. Oxford: Blackwell.

Hickok, G. and Poeppel, D. (2004) Dorsal and ventral streams: A framework for understanding aspects of the functional anatomy of language. *Cognition*, 92, 67–99.

Higgins, E.T. (1987) Self-discrepancy: A theory relating self and affect. *Psychological Review*, 94, 319–40.

Higgins, E.T. (1997) Beyond pleasure and pain. *American Psychologist*, 52, 1280–1300.

Higgins, E.T. (1998) Promotion and prevention: Regulatory focus as a motivational principle. *Advances in Experimental Social Psychology*, 30, 1–46.

Higgins, E.T. and Silberman, I. (1998) Development of regulatory focus: Promotion and prevention as ways of living. In J. Heckhausen and C.S. Dweck (eds) *Motivation and Self-regulation across the Lifespan*. New York: Cambridge University Press, pp. 78–113.

Higgins, E.T. and Tykocinski, O. (1992) Self-discrepancies and biographical memory: Personality and cognition at the level of psychological situation. *Personality and Social Psychology Bulletin*, 18, 527–35.

Higgins, E.T., Rholes, W.S. and Jones, C.R. (1977) Category accessibility and impression formation. *Journal of Experimental Social Psychology*, 13, 141–54.

Higgins, E.T. Roney, C., Crowe, E. and Hymes, C. (1994) Ideal versus ought predilections for approach and avoidance: Distinct self-regulatory systems. *Journal of Personality and Social Psychology*, 66, 276–86.

Higgins, S.T., Hughes, J.R. and Bickel, W.K. (1989) Effects of d-amphetamine on choice in social versus monetary reinforcement: A discrete trial test. *Pharmacology, Biochemistry, and Behavior*, 34, 297–301.

Higgins, S.T., Budney, A.J. and Bickel, W.K. (1994) Applying behavioral concepts and principles to the treatment of cocaine dependence. *Drug and Alcohol Dependence*, 7, 19–38.

Highley, J.R., McDonald, B., Walker, M.A., Esiri, M.M. and Crow, T.J. (1999) Schizophrenia and temporal lobe asymmetry. *British Journal of Psychology*, 175, 127–34.

Hilgard, E.R. (1978) States of consciousness in hypnosis: Divisions or levels? In F.H. Frankel and H.S. Zamansky (eds) *Hypnosis at its Bicentennial: Selected papers*. New York: Plenum Press.

Hilgard, E.R. (1986) *Divided Consciousness: Multiple controls in human thought and action*. New York: Wiley.

Hilgard, E.R. (1991) A neodissociation interpretation of hypnosis. In S.J. Lynn and J.H. Rhue (eds) *Theories of Hypnosis: Current models and perspectives*. New York: Guilford Press.

Hilgard, E.R. and Hilgard, J.R. (1994) *Hypnosis in the Relief of Pain*. New York: Brunner/Mazel.

Hill, H. and Bruce, V. (1996) Effects of lighting on the perception of facial surfaces. *Journal of Experimental Psychology: Human Perception and Performance*, 22(4), 986–1004.

Hill, R.A. and Barton, R.A. (2005) Red enhances human performance in contests. *Nature*, 435, 293.

Jockin, A., Arvey, R.D. and McGue, M. (2001) Perceived victimization moderates self-reports of workplace aggression and conflict. *Journal of Applied Psychology*, 86, 1262–1269.

Jodelet, D. (1991) *Madness and Social Representations*. Hemel Hempstead: Harvester Wheatsheaf.

Joffe, H. (1996) AIDS research and prevention: A social representational approach. *British Journal of Medical Psychology*, 69, 169–90.

Joffe, H. (1997) Juxtaposing positivist and non-positivist approaches to social scientific AIDS research: Reply to Fife-Shaw's commentary. *British Journal of Medical Psychology*, 70, 75–83.

Johansson, G. (1973) Visual perception of biological motion and a model for its analysis. *Perception and Psychophysics*, 14, 201–11.

Johnson, A.J. and Miles, C. (2008) Chewing gum and context-dependent memory: The independent roles of chewing gum and mint flavour. *British Journal of Psychology*, 99, 293–306.

Johnson, D.E. (1997) Medical issues in international adoption: factors that affect your child's pre-adoption health. *Adoptive Families*, 30, 18–20.

Johnson, D.E. (2000) Medical and developmental sequelae of early childhood institutionalization in international adoptees from Romania and the Russian Federation. In C.A. Nelson (ed.), *The Effects of Early Adversity on Neurobehavioural Development*. Mahwah, NJ: Erlbaum.

Johnson, D.L. and Walker, T. (1991) A follow-up evaluation of the Houston Parent–Child Development Centre: School performance. *Journal of Early Intervention*, 15, 226–36.

Johnson, J.H., Butcher, J.N., Null, C. and Johnson, K.N. (1984) Replicated item level factor analysis of the full MMPI. *Journal of Personality and Social Psychology*, 47, 105–14.

Johnson, J.S. and Newport, E.L. (1989) Critical period effects in second language learning: The influence of maturational state on the acquisition of English as a second language. *Cognitive Psychology*, 21, 60–99.

Johnson, M. (1998) The neural basis of cognitive development. In D. Kuhn and R.S. Siegler (eds) *Handbook of Child Psychology, Vol. 2: Cognition, perception and language*. New York: Wiley.

Johnson, M. and Johnson, M.H. (1991) CONSPEC and CONLERN: A two-process theory of infant face recognition. *Psychological Review*, 98, 164–81.

Johnson, M.K., Hashtroudi, S. and Lindsay, D.S. (1993) Source monitoring. *Psychological Bulletin*, 114, 3–28.

Johnson, S.A. *et al.* (2007) Beyond disgust: Impaired recognition of negative emotions prior to diagnosis in Huntington's disease. *Brain*, 130, 1732–1744.

Johnson-Laird, P.N. (1983) *Mental Models*. Cambridge, MA: Harvard University Press.

Johnson-Laird, P.N. (1985) Deductive reasoning ability. In R.J. Sternberg (ed.) *Human Abilities: An information-processing approach*. New York: W.H. Freeman.

Johnson-Laird, P.N. and Byrne, R.M.J. (1991) *Deduction*. Hillsdale, NJ: Lawrence Erlbaum Associates.

Johnson-Laird, P.N., Byrne, R.M.J. and Schaeken, W. (1992) Propositional reasoning by model. *Psychological Review*, 99, 418–39.

Johnston, V.S. (2006) Mate choice decisions: The role of facial beauty. *Trends in Cognitive Sciences*, 10, 1, 10–13.

Johnston, W.A. and Dark, V.J. (1986) Selective attention. *Annual Review of Psychology*, 37, 43–76.

Johnston, W.A. and Heinz, S.P. (1978) Flexibility and capacity demands of attention. *Journal of Experimental Psychology: General*, 107, 420–35.

Johnstone, E.C., Crow, T.J., Frith, C.D., Stevens, M., Kreel, L. and Husband, J. (1978) The dementia of dementia praecox. *Acta Psychiatrica Scandinavica*, 57, 305–24.

Jones, D. (1999) The cognitive psychology of auditory distraction: The 1997 BPS Broadbent Lecture. *British Journal of Psychology*, 90.

Jones, D.C. (1991) Friendship satisfaction and gender: An examination of sex differences in contributors to friendship satisfaction. *Journal of Social and Personal Relationships*, 8, 167–85.

Jones, D.C. (2004) Body image among adolescent girls and boys: A longitudinal study. *Developmental Psychology*, 40, 5, 823–35.

Jones, D.M. (1995) The fate of the unattended stimulus. Irrelevant speech and cognition. *Applied Cognitive Psychology*, 9, 23–38.

Jones, D.M., Madden, C. and Miles, C. (1992) Privileged access by irrelevant speech to short-term memory: The role of changing state. *Quarterly Journal of Experimental Psychology*, 44A, 645–59.

Jones, D.T. and Reed, R.R. (1989) Golf: An olfactory neuron specific-G protein involved in odorant signal transduction. *Science*, 244, 790–5.

Jones, E.E. (1990) *Interpersonal Perception*. New York: W.H. Freeman.

Jones, E.E. and Goethals, G.R. (1972) Order effects in impression formation: Attribution context and the nature of the entity. In E.E. Jones, D.E. Kanouse, H.H. Kelley, R.E. Nisbett, S. Valins and B. Weiner (eds) *Attribution: Perceiving the causes of behavior*. Morristown, NJ: General Learning Press, pp. 27–46.

Jones, E.E. and Harris, V.A. (1967) The attribution of attitudes. *Journal of Experimental Social Psychology*, 3, 1–24.

Jones, E.E. and Nisbett, R.E. (1971) The actor and observer: Divergent perceptions of the causes of behavior. In E.E. Jones, D.E. Kamouse, H.H. Kelley, R.E. Nisbett, S. Valins and B. Weiner (eds) *Attribution: Perceiving the causes of behavior*. Morristown, NJ: General Learning Press, pp. 79–94.

Jones, E.J.H. and Herbert, J.S. (2006) Exploring memory in infancy. *Infant and Child Development*, 15, 195–205.

Jones, G.V. (1989) Back to Woodworth: Role of interlopers in the tip-of-the-tongue phenomenon. *Memory and Cognition*, 17(1), 69–76.

Jones, G.V. and Martin, M. (1992) Conjunction in the language of emotions. *Cognition and Emotion*, 6, 369–86.

Jones, H.E. (1959) Intelligence and problem-solving. In J.E. Birren (ed.) *Handbook of Aging and the Individual*. Chicago: University of Chicago Press.

Jones, N.A., McFall, B.A. and Diego, M.A. (2004) Patterns of brain electrical activity in infants of depressed mothers who breastfeed and bottle feed: the mediating role of infant temperament. *Biological Psychology*, 67, 103–24.

Jones, R.B., Humphris, G. and Lewis, T. (1996) Do agoraphobics interpret the environment in large shops and supermarkets differently? *British Journal of Clinical Psychology*, 35, 635–7.

Jones, S.E. and Yarbrough, A.E. (1985) A naturalistic study of the meanings of touch. *Communication Monographs*, 52, 19–56.

Joormann, J. and Siemer, M. (2004) Memory accessibility, mood regulation, and dysphoria: Difficulties in repairing sad mood with happy memories? *Journal of Abnormal Psychology*, 113, 2, 179–88.

Jorm, A.F. (2000) Mental health literacy: Public knowledge and beliefs about mental disorders. *British Journal of Psychiatry*, 177, 396–401.

Joseph, S., Yule, W., Williams, R. and Hodgkinson, P. (1994) Correlates of post-traumatic stress at 30 months: the *Herald of Free Enterprise* disaster. *Behaviour Research and Therapy*, 32(5), 521–4.

Joseph, S., Dalgleish, T., Williams, R., Yule, W., Thrasher, S. and Hodgkinson, P. (1997) Attitudes towards emotional expression and post-traumatic stress in survivors of the *Herald of Free Enterprise* disaster. *British Journal of Clinical Psychology*, 36, 133–8.

Josephs, R.A., Sellers, J.G., Newman, M.L. and Mehta, P.H. (2006) The mismatch effect: When testosterone and status are at odds. *Journal of Personality and Social Psychology*, 90, 6, 999–1013.

Joslyn, S., Loftus, E., McNoughton, A. and Powers, J. (2001) Memory for memory. *Memory and Cognition*, 29(6), 789–97.

Jost, J.T. and Hunyadi, O. (2002) The psychology of system justification and the palliative function of ideology. *European Review of Social Psychology*, 13, 111–53.

Jourard, S.M. (1966) An exploratory study of body-accessibility. *British Journal of Social and Clinical Psychology*, 5, 221–31.

Jouvet, M. (1972) The role of monoamines and acetylcholine-containing neurons in the regulation of the sleep–waking cycle. *Ergebnisse der Physiologie*, 64, 166–307.

Joyce, E.M., Collinson, S.L. and Crichton, P. (1996) Verbal fluency in schizophrenia: Relationship with executive function, semantic memory and clinical alogia. *Psychological Medicine*, 26, 39–49.

Julesz, B. (1965) Texture and visual perception. *Scientific American Mind*, 212, 38–48.

Jung, R. (1974) Neuropsychologie und neurophysiologie des konturund formsehens in zeichnerei und malerei. In H. Weick (ed.) *Psychopathologie Mususcher Gestaltungen*, Stuttgart: F.K. Shattauer.

Jusczyk, P.W. and Hohne, E.A. (1997) Infants' memory for spoken words. *Science*, 277, 1984–1986.

Just, M.A. and Carpenter, P.A. (1980) A theory of reading: From eye fixations to comprehension. *Psychological Review*, 87, 329–54.

Just, M.A. and Carpenter, P.A. (1987) *The Psychology of Reading and Language Comprehension*. Boston: Allyn & Bacon.

Just, M.A., Carpenter, P.A. and Wu, R. (1983) *Eye Fixations in the Reading of Chinese Technical Text, Technical Report*. Pittsburgh: Carnegie-Mellon University.

Justus, T. (2004) The cerebellum and English grammatical morphology: Evidence from production, comprehension, and grammaticality judgments. *Journal of Cognitive Neuroscience*, 16, 7, 1115–1130.

Justus, T. and Ivry, R.B. (2001) The cognitive neuropsychology of the cerebellum. *International Review of Psychiatry*, 13, 276–82.

Kaas, J.H. and Hackett, T.A. (1999) 'What' and 'where' processing in auditory cortex, *Nature Neurocience*, 2, 1045–7.

Kaczmarek, B.L.J (1991) Aphasia in an artist: A disorder of symbolic processing. *Aphasiology*, 5, 361–71.

Kagan, J., Kearsley, R.B. and Zelazo, P.R. (1978) *Infancy: Its place in human development*. Cambridge, MA: Harvard University Press.

Kagan, J., Reznick, J.S. and Snidman, N. (1988) Biological bases of childhood shyness. *Science*, 240, 167–71.

Kageyama, T., Nishikido, N., Kobayashi, T., Kurokawa, Y. and Kabuto, M. (1997) Commuting, overtime, and cardiac autonomic activity in Tokyo. *Lancet*, 350, 639.

Kahkonen, M., Alitalo, T., Airaksinen, E., Matilamen, R., Laumiala, K., Auno, S. and Leisti, J. (1987) Prevalence of fragile X syndrome in four birth cohorts of children of school age. *Human Genetics*, 30, 234–8.

Kahneman, D. (1973) *Attention and Effort*. Englewood Cliffs, NJ: Prentice Hall.

Kahneman, D., Slovic, P. and Tversky, A. (1982) *Judgement Under Uncertainty: Heuristics and biases*. Cambridge: Cambridge University Press.

Kail, R. and Hall, L.K. (2001) Distinguishing short-term memory from working memory. *Memory and Cognition*, 29, 1–9.

Kajantie, E. and Phillips, D.I.W. (2006) The effects of sex and hormonal status on the physiological response to acute psychosocial stress. *Psychoneuroendocrinology*, 31, 151–78.

Kales, A., Scharf, M.B., Kales, J.D. and Soldatos, C.R. (1979) Rebound insomnia: A potential hazard following withdrawal of certain benzodiazepines. *Journal of the American Medical Association*, 241, 1692–1695.

Kalichman, S.C., Carey, M.P. and Johnson, B.T. (1996) Prevention of sexually transmitted HIV infection: a meta-analytic review of the behavioural outcome literature. *American Behavioral Medicine*, 18, 6–15.

Kalish, R.A. (1976) Death and dying in a social context. In R.H. Binstock and E. Shanas (eds) *Handbook of Aging and the Social Sciences*. New York: Van Nostrand Reinhold.

Kalivas, P.W. and Volko, N.D. (2005) The neural basis of addiction: A pathology of motivation and choice. *American Journal of Psychiatry*, 162, 1403–13.

Kamphuis, J.H. and Emmelkamp, P.M.G. (1998) Crime-related trauma: Psychological distress in victims of bankrobbery. *Journal of Anxiety Disorders*, 12(3), 199–208.

Kanazawa, H. and Loveday, L. (1988) The Japanese immigrant community in Brazil: Language contact and shift. *Journal of Multilingual and Multicultural Development*, 9, 423–35.

Kandel, E.R., Schwartz, J.H. and Jessell, T.M. (1995) *Essentials of Neural Science and Behaviour*. Englewood Cliffs, NJ: Prentice Hall.

Kane, J., Honigfeld, G., Singer, J., Meltzer, H. and the Clozaril Collaborative Study Group. (1988) Clozapine for the treatment-resistant schizophrenic: A double-blind comparison with chlorpromazine. *Archives of General Psychiatry*, 45, 789–96.

Kane, M.J., Bleckley, M.K., Conway, A.R.A. and Engle, R.W. (2001) A controlled-attention view of working memory capacity. *Journal of Experimental Psychology: General*, 130, 169–83.

Kanner, L. (1943) Autistic disturbances of affective contact. *Nervous Child*, 2, 217–50.

Kanwisher, N., McDermott, J. and Chun, M.M. (1997) The fusiform face area: A module in human extrastriate cortex specialised for face perception. *Journal of Neuroscience*, 17(1), 4302–4311.

Kanwisher, N., Stanley, D. and Harris, A. (1999) The fusiform face area is selective for faces not animals. *NeuroReport*, 10, 183–7.

Kanwisher, N., Tong, F. and Nakayama, K. (1998) The effect of face inversion on the human fusiform face area. *Cognition*, 68, B1–B11.

Kapci, E.G. (1998) Test of the hopelessness theory of depression drawing negative inference from negative life events. *Psychological Reports*, 82, 355–63.

Kaplan, E.L. and Kaplan, G.A. (1970) The prelinguistic child. In J. Eliot (ed.) *Human Development and Cognitive Processes*. New York: Holt, Rinehart & Winston.

Kapleau, P. (1980) *Three pillars of Zen: Teaching, practice and enlightenment*. Harden City, NY: Anchor Books.

Kapp, B.S., Gallagher, M., Applegate, C.D. and Frysinger, R.C. (1982) The amygdala central nucleus: Contributions to conditioned cardiovascular responding during aversive Pavlovian conditioning in the rabbit. In C.D. Woody (ed.) *Conditioning: Representation of involved neural functions*. New York: Plenum Press.

Karandashev, V. (2006) Teaching of undergraduate psychology in Russia. *International Journal of Psychology*, 41, 1, 58–64.

Karau, S.J. and Williams, K.D. (1993) Social loafing: A meta-analytic review and theoretical integration. *Journal of Personality and Social Psychology*, 65, 681–706.

Karau, S.J. and Williams, K.D. (1995) Social loafing: Research findings, implications, and future directions. *Current Directions in Psychological Science*, 4, 134–9.

Karbe, H., Herholz, K., Weber-Luxenburger, G., Ghaemi, M. and Heiss, W-D. (1998) Cerebral networks and functional brain asymmetry: Evidence from regional metabolic changes during word repetition. *Brain and Language*, 63, 108–21.

Karmiloff-Smith, A. (1988) The child is a theoretician, not an inductivist. *Mind and Language*, 3, 183–97.

Karmiloff-Smith, A. (1992) *Beyond Modularity: A developmental perspective on cognitive science*. Cambridge, MA: MIT Press.

Kashdan, T.B. and Fincham, F.D. (2002) Facilitating creativity by regulating curiosity. *American Psychologist*, 57, 373–4.

Kaski, D. (2002) Revision: Is visual perception a requisite for visual imagery? *Perception*, 31, 717–31.

Kassin, S.M. and Fong, C.T. (1999) 'I'm innocent!': Effects of training on judgements of truth and deception in the interrogation room. *Law and Human Behaviour*, 23, 499–516.

Kassin, S.M. and Kiechel, K.L. (1996) The social psychology of false confessions: Compliance, internalization and confabulation. *Psychological Science*, 7(3), 125–8.

Kassin, S.M., Ellsworth, P.C. and Smith, V.L. (1989) The 'general acceptance' of psychological research on eyewitness testimony: A survey of the experts. *American Psychologist*, 44, 1089–1098.

Kassin, S.M., Reddy, M.E. and Tulloch, W.F. (1990) Juror interpretations of ambiguous evidence: The need for cognition, presentation order, and persuasion. *Law and Human Behaviour*, 14, 43–55.

Kassin, S.M., Tubb, V.A., Hosch, H.M. and Memon, A. (2001) On the 'general acceptance' of eyewitness testimony research: A new survey of the experts. *American Psychologist*, 56, 405–16.

Katerndahl, D.A. and Realini, J.P. (1993) Lifetime prevalence rates of panic states. *American Journal of Psychiatry*, 150, 246–9.

Katz, D. (1935) *The World of Colour*. London: Kegan Paul, Trench, Trubner.

Kawakami, K., Dovidio, J.F., Moll, J., Hermsen, S. and Russin, A. (2000) Just say no (to stereotyping): Effects of training in the negation of stereotypic associations on stereotype activation. *Journal of Personality and Social Psychology*, 78, 871–88.

Kay, P. (1975) Synchronic variability and diachronic changes in basic color terms. *Language in Society*, 4, 257–70.

Kay, P. and Kempton, W. (1984) What is the Sapir–Whorf hypothesis? *American Anthropologist*, 86(1), 65–79.

Kay, P., Berlin, B. and Merrifield, W. (1991) Biocultural implications of systems of color naming. *Journal of Linguistic Anthropology*, 1(1), 12–25.

Kay, P., Berlin, B., Maffi, L. and Merrifield, W. (1997) Color naming across languages. In C.L. Hardin and L. Maffi (eds) *Color Categories in Thought and Language*. New York: Cambridge University Press.

Kaye, K. and Fogel, A. (1980) The temporal structure of face-to-face communication between mothers and infants. *Developmental Psychology*, 16, 454–64.

Kaye, W. (2008) Neurobiology of anorexia and bulimia nervosa. *Physiology and Behaviour*, 94, 121–35.

Kazdin, A.E. (1994) *Behavior Modification in Applied Settings*. Pacific Grove, CA: Brooks/Cole.

Keane, M.M., Gabrieli, J.D.E., Mapstone, H.C., Johnson, K.A. and Corkin, S. (1995) Double dissociation of memory capacities after bilateral occipital-lobe or medial temporal-lobe lesions. *Brain*, 118, 1129–1148.

Keating, D. (1979) Adolescent thinking. In J. Adelson (ed.) *Handbook of Adolescent Psychology*. New York: Wiley.

Kecklund, G. and Akerstedt, T. (2004) Apprehension of the subsequent working day is associated with a low amount of slow wave sleep. *Biological Psychology*, 66, 169–76.

Keefe, R.S.E., Roitman, S.E.C., Harvey, P.D. (1995) A pen-and-paper human analogue of a monkey prefrontal cortex activation task: Spatial working memory in patients with schizophenia. *Schizophenia Research*, 17, 25–33.

Keel, P.K., Dorer, D.J., Franko, D.L., Jackson, S.C. *et al.* (2005) Postremission predictors of relapse in women with eating disorders. *American Journal of Psychiatry*, 62, 2263–2268.

Keel, P.K., Heatherton, T.F., Dorer, D.J., Joiner, T.E. and Zalta, A.K. (2006) Point prevalence of bulimia nervosa in 1982, 1992 and 2002. *Psychological Medicine*, 36, 119–27.

Keel, P.K. and Klump, K.L. (2003) Are eating disorders culture-bound syndromes? Implications for conceptualizing their etiology. *Psychological Bulletin*, 129, 5, 747–69.

Keller, K.L., Steinmann, L., Nurse, R.J. and Tepper, B.J. (2002) Genetic taste sensitivity to 6-n-propylthiouracil influences food preference and reported intake in preschool children. *Appetite*, 38, 3–12.

Keller, K.L. and Tepper, B.J. (2004) Inherited taste sensitivity to 6-n-propylthiouracil in diet and body weight in children. *Obesity Research*, 12, 904–12.

Keller, M.C., Fredrickson, B.L., Ybarra, O., Cote, S., Johnson, K., Mikels, J., Conway, A. and Wager, T. (2005) A warm heart and a clear head: The contingent effect of weather on mood and cognition. *Psychological Science*, 16, 9, 724–31.

Keller, P.A. and Block, L.G. (1995) Increasing the persuasiveness of fear appeals: The effect of arousal and elaboration. *Journal of Consumer Research*, 22, 448–59.

Keller, S.E., Weiss, J.M., Schleifer, S.J., Miller, N.E. and Stein, M. (1983) Stress-induced suppression of immunity in adrenalectomized rats. *Science*, 221, 1301–1304.

Keller, T.A., Carpenter, P.A. and Just, M.A. (2003) Brain imaging of tongue-twister sentence comprehension: Twisting the tongue and the brain. *Brain and Language*, 84, 189–203.

Kelley, H.H. (1950) The warm–cold variable in first impressions of persons. *Journal of Personality*, 18, 431–9.

Kelley, H.H. (1967) Attribution theory in social psychology. In D. Levine (ed.) *Nebraska Symposium on Motivation*, Vol. 15. Lincoln: University of Nebraska Press.

Kelley, H.H. (1973) The process of causal attribution. *American Psychologist*, 28, 107–28.

Kelley, H.H. and Michela, J.L. (1980) Attribution theory and research. *Annual Review of Psychology*, 31, 457–501.

Kelley, J.E., Lumley, M.A. and Leisen, J.C. (1997) Health effects of emotional disclosure in rheumatoid arthritis patients. *Health Psychology*, 16, 331–40.

Kelly, G.A. (1955) *The Psychology of Personal Constructs*. New York: W.W. Norton.

Kelly, J.A. and Kalichman, S.C. (1998) Reinforcement value of unsafe sex as a predictor of condom use and continued HIV/AIDS risk behaviour among gay and bisexual men. *Health Psychology*, 17(4), 328–35.

Kelly, J.A., St Lawrence, J., Brasfield, T., Lemke, A., Amidei, T., Roffman, R., Hood, H., Smith, J., Kilgore, H. and McNeill, C. (1990) Psychological factors that predict AIDS high-risk versus AIDS precautionary behaviour. *Journal of Consulting and Clinical Psychology*, 58, 117–20.

Kelly, J.A., Otto-Salaj, L.L., Sikkema, K.J., Pinkerton, S.D. and Bloom, F.R. (1998) Implications of HIV treatment advances for behavioural research on AIDS: Protease inhibitors and new challenges in HIV secondary prevention. *Health Psychology*, 17(4), 310–19.

Kelly, S.D., Barr, D.J., Church, R.B. and Lynch, K. (1999) Offering a hand to pragmatic understanding: The role of speech and gesture comprehension and memory. *Journal of Memory and Language*, 40, 577–92.

Kemper, S. (1992) Language and aging. In F.I.M. Craik and T. Salthouse (eds) *The Handbook of Aging and Cognition*. Hillsdale, NJ: Lawrence Erlbaum Associates.

Kennedy, D.P. and Courchesne, E. (2007) The intrinsic functional organization of the brain in altered in autism. *Neuroimage*, 39, 1877–1885.

Kenny, P.J. (2007) Brain reward systems and compulsive drug use. *Trends in Pharmacological Sciences*, 28, 3, 135–41.

Kenny, P.J. *et al.* (2006) Conditioned withdrawal drives heroin consumption and decreased reward sensitivity. *Journal of Neuroscience*, 26, 5894–5900.

Kerns, K.A. and Barth, J.M. (1995) Attachment and play: Convergence across components of parent–child relationships and their relations to peer competence. *Journal of Social and Personal Relationships*, 12, 243–60.

Kerr, J.H. and van den Wollenberg, A.E. (1997) High and low intensity exercise and psychological mood states. *Psychology and Health*, 12, 603–18.

Kerr, N.L. (1978) Beautiful and blameless: Effects of victim attractiveness and responsibility on mock jurors' verdicts. *Personality and Social Psychology Bulletin*, 4, 479–82.

Kerr, N.L. (1992) Norms in social dilemmas. In D. Schroeder (ed.) *Social Dilemmas: Psychological perspectives*. New York: Praeger.

Kerr, N.L. and Park, E.S. (2001) Group performance in collaborative and social dilemma tasks: Progress and prospects. In M.A. Hogg and R.S. Tindale (eds) *Blackwell Handbook of Social Psychology: Group processes*. Oxford: Blackwell, pp. 107–38.

Kerstholt, J.H. and Jackson, J.L. (1998) Judicial decision making: Order of evidence presentation and availability of background information. *Applied Cognitive Psychology*, 12, 445–54.

Keshavan, M.S., Tandon, R., Boutros, N.N. and Nasrallah, H.A. (2008) Schizophrenia, 'Just the facts': What we know in 2008, Part 3: Neurobiology. *Schizophrenia Research*, 100, 89–107.

Kessel, R.G. and Kardon, R.H. (1979) *Tissues and Organs: A text-atlas of scanning electron microscopy*. San Francisco: W.H. Freeman.

Kessels, R.P.C., deHaan, E.H.F., Kappelle, L.J. and Postma, A. (2001) Varieties of human spatial memory: A meta-analysis on the effects of hippocampal lesions. *Brain Research Reviews*, 35, 295–303.

Kessler, R.C., McGonagle, K.A., Zhao, S., Nelson, C., Hughes, M., Eshleman, S., Wittchen, H. and Kendler, K. (1994a) Lifetime and 12–month prevalence of DSM-III-R psychiatric disorders in the United States. *Archives of General Psychiatry*, 51, 8–19.

Kessler, R.C., McGonagle, K.A., Zhao, S., Nelson, C., Hughes, M., Eshleman, S., Wittchen, H. and Kendler, K. (1994b) Lifetime and 12–month prevalence rates from the National Comorbidity Survey. *Archives of General Psychiatry*, 51, 8–19.

Kessler, R.C. *et al.* (2001) Mood disorders in children and adolescents: an epidemiologic perspective. *Biological Psychiatry*, 49, 1002–1014.

Kety, S.S., Rosenthal, D., Wender, P.H. and Schulsinger, F. (1968) The types and prevalence of mental illness in the biological and adoptive families of adopted schizophrenics. In D. Rosenthal and S.S. Kety (eds) *The Transmission of Schizophrenia*. Elmsford, NY: Pergamon Press.

Keyes, D. (1981) *The Minds of Billy Milligan*. New York: Bantam.

Kiang, N.Y-S. (1965) *Discharge Patterns of Single Nerve Fibers in the Cat's Auditory Nerve*. Cambridge, MA: MIT Press.

Kiecolt-Glaser, J.K., Malarkey, W.B., Chee, M., Newton, T., Caccioppo, J.T., Mao, H-Y. and Glaser, R. (1993) Negative behaviour during marital conflict is associated with immunological down-regulation. *Psychosomatic Medicine*, 55, 395–409.

Kiecolt-Glaser, J.K., Marucha, P.T., Malarkey, W.B., Mercado, A.M. and Glaser, R. (1995) Slowing of wound healing by psychological stress. *Lancet*, 346, 1194–1196.

Kiecolt-Glaser, J.K., Marucha, P.T., Atkinson, C. and Glaser, R. (2001) Hypnosis as a modulator of cellular immune dysregulation during acute stress. *Journal of Consulting and Clinical Psychology*, 69(4), 674–82.

Kilpatrick, L.A., Zald, D.H., Pardo, J.V. and Cahill, L.F. (2006) Sex-related differences in amygdala functional connectivity during resting conditions. *Neuroimage*, 30, 452–61.

Kim, J-Y., McHale, S.M., Osgood, D.W. and Crouter, A.C. (2006) Longitudinal course and family correlates of sibling relationships from childhood through adolescence. *Child Development*, 77, 6, 1746–1761.

Kim, K.H.S., Relkin, N.R., Lee, K-M. and Hirsch, J. (1997) Distinct cortical areas associated with native and second languages. *Nature*, 388, 171–4.

Kindermann, S.S., Karimi, A., Symonds, L., Brown, G.G. and Jeste, D.V. (1997) Review of functional magnetic resonance imaging in schizophrenia. *Schizophrenia Research*, 27, 2–3, 143–56.

King, J.A., Blair, R.J.R., Mitchell, D.G.V., Dolan, R.J. and Burgess, N. (2006) Doing the right thing: A common neural circuit for appropriate violent or compassionate behavior. *Neuroimage*, 30, 1069–1076.

King, M.C. and Wilson, A.C. (1975) Evolution at two levels in humans and chimpanzees. *Science*, 188, 4184, 107–16.

Kingma, A., Mooji, J.J., Metzemaekers, J.D. and Leeuw, J.A. (1994) Transient mutism and speech disorders after posterior fossa surgery in children with brain tumours. *Acta Neurochir (Wien)*, 131, 74–9.

Kinney, N.E. (2001) A guide to design and testing in online psychology courses. *Psychology Learning and Teaching*, 1, 1, 16–20.

Kinsey, A., Pomeroy, W.B. and Martin, C.E. (1948) *Sexual Behavior in the Human Male*. Philadelphia: Saunders.

Kinsey, A., Pomeroy, W.B., Martin, C.E. and Gebhard, P.H. (1953) *Sexual Behavior in the Human Female*. Philadelphia: Saunders.

Kirby, K.N., Petry, N.M. and Bickel, W.K. (1999) Heroin addicts have higher discount rates for delayed rewards than on-drug-using controls. *Journal of Experimental Psychology: General*, 128(1), 78–87.

Kircher, T.T.J., Senior, C., Phillips, M.L., Rabe-Hesketh, S., Benson, P.J., Bullmore, E.T., Brammer, M., Simmons, A., Bartels, M. and David, A.S. (2001) Recognizing one's own face. *Cognition*, 78, B1–B15.

Kirchner, T.R., Sayette, M.A., Cohn, J.F. and Moreland, R.L. (in press) Effects of alcohol on group formation among male social drinkers. *Journal of Studies on Alcohol*.

Kirk-Smith, M. and Booth, D.A. (1977) Effects of androstenol as sexual and other social attitudes. In Z. le Magnen and P. Macleod (eds) *Olfaction and Taste*. Vol. 6. London: IRL Press.

Kirk-Smith, M. and Booth, D.A. (1980) Effects of androstenone on choice of location in others' presence. In H. Van Der Starre (ed.) *Olfaction and Taste*, Vol. 2. London: IRL Press.

Kirk-Smith, M., Booth, D.A., Carroll, D. and Davies, P. (1978) Human social attitudes affected by androstenol. *Research and Communication in Psychology, Psychiatry and Behaviour*, 3, 379–84.

Kisilevsky, B.S. (1995) The influence of stimulus and subject variables on human fetal responses to sound and vibration. In J-P. Lecanuet, W.P. Fifer, N.A. Krasnegor and W.P. Smotherman (eds) *Fetal Development: A psychobiological perspective*. Hillsdale, NJ: Lawrence Erlbaum Associates.

Lambert, W.E. (1977) The effect of bilingualism on the individual: Cognitive and sociocultural consequences. In P.A. Hornby (ed.) *Bilingualism: Psychological, social and educational implications*. New York: Academic Press.

Lang, E.V., Benotsch, E.G., Flick, L.J., Lutgendorf, S., Berbaum, M.L., Berbaum, K.S., Logan, H. and Spiegel, D. (2000) Adjunctive non-pharmacological analgesia for invasive medical procedures: A randomised trial. *Lancet*, 355, 1486–1490.

Lang, P.J. (1979) A bio-informational theory of emotional imagery. *Psychophysiology*, 16, 495–512.

Lang, P.J. (1984) Cognition in emotion: Concept and action. In C.E. Izard, J. Kagan and R.B. Zajonc (eds) *Emotions, Cognition and Behaviour*. New York: Cambridge University Press.

Lange, C.G. (1887) *Über Gemüthsbewegungen*. Leipzig: T. Thomas.

Langer, E.J. and Abelson, R.P. (1974) A patient by any other name . . . Clinician group difference in labeling bias. *Journal of Consulting and Clinical Psychology*, 42, 4–9.

Langer, E.J., Bashner, R.S. and Chanowitz, B. (1985) Decreasing prejudice by increasing discrimination. *Journal of Personality and Social Psychology*, 49, 113–20.

Langeslag, S.J.E., Jansma, B.M., Franken, I.H.A. and van Strien, J.W. (2007) Event-related potential responses to love-related facial stimuli. *Biological Psychology*, 76, 109–15.

Langleben, D.D. (2008) Detection of deception with fMRI: are we there yet? *Legal and Criminological Psychology*, 13,1–9.

Langlois, J.H., Kalakanis, L., Rubenstein, A.J., Larson, A., Hallam, M. and Smoot, M. (2000) Maxims or myths of beauty? A meta-analytic and theoretical review. *Psychological Bulletin*, 126, 390–423.

Lankenau, H., Swigar, M.E., Bhimani, S., Luchins, S. and Quinlon, D.M. (1985) Cranial CT scans in eating disorder patients and controls. *Comprehensive Psychiatry*, 26, 136–47.

Lanzetta, J.T., Cartwright-Smith, J. and Kleck, R.E. (1976) Effects of nonverbal dissimulation on emotional experience and autonomic arousal. *Journal of Personality and Social Psychology*, 33, 354–70.

LaPiere, R.T. (1934) Attitudes and actions. *Social Forces*, 13, 230–7.

Larsen, J.T., Norris, C.J. and Cacioppo, J.T. (2003) Effects of positive and negative affect on electromyographic activity over zygomaticus major and corrugator supercilli. *Psychophysiology*, 40, 776–85.

LaRue, A. (1992) *Aging and Neuropsychological Assessment*. New York: Plenum Press.

Last, C.G., Barlow, D.H. and O'Brien, G.T. (1984) Precipitants of agoraphobia: Role of stressful life events. *Psychological Reports*, 54, 173–80.

Latané, B. and Darley, J.M. (1970) *The Unresponsive Bystander: Why doesn't he help?* New York: Appleton-Century-Crofts.

Lauer, R.H. (1989) *Social Problems and the Quality of Life*. Dubuque, IA: W.C. Brown.

Laughlin, P.R. and Ellis, A.L. (1986) Demonstrability and social combination processes on mathematical intellective tasks. *Journal of Experimental Social Psychology*, 22, 177–89.

Lavie, P., Pratt, H., Scharf, B., Peled, R. and Brown, J. (1984) Localized pontine lesion: Nearly total absence of REM sleep. *Neurology*, 34, 1118–1120.

Law, M.R. and Tang, J.L. (1995) An analysis of the effectiveness of intervention intended to help people stop smoking. *Archives of Internal Medicine*, 155, 1933–1941.

Lawrie, S.M. and Abukmeil, S.S. (1998) Brain abnormality in schizophrenia. *British Journal of Psychiatry*, 172, 110–20.

Lazarus, A.A. (1971) *Behavior Therapy and Beyond*. New York: McGraw-Hill.

Lazarus, R.S. (1966) *Psychological Stress and the Coping Process*. New York: McGraw-Hill.

Lazarus, R.S. (1984) Thoughts on the relations between emotion and cognition. In K.R. Scherer and P. Ekman (eds) *Approaches to Emotion*. Hillsdale, NJ: Lawrence Erlbaum Associates.

Lazarus, R.S. (1991) *Emotion and Adaptation*. New York: Oxford University Press.

Lazarus, R.S. and Folkman, S. (1984) *Stress, Appraisal, and Coping*. New York: Springer-Verlag.

Leahey, T.H. (2003) *A History of Psychology* (6th edn). Englewood Cliffs, NJ: Prentice Hall.

Leaper, C. and Ayres, M.M. (2007) A meta-analytic review of gender variations in adults' language use: Talkativeness, affiliative speech and assertive speech. *Personality and Social Psychology Review*, 11, 4, 328–63.

Leary, M.R., Tambor, E.S., Terdal, S.K. and Downs, D.L. (1995) Self-esteem as an interpersonal monitor: The sociometer hypothesis. *Journal of Personality and Social Psychology*, 68, 518–30.

LeBlanc, M.M. and Barling, J. (2004) Workplace aggression. *Current Directions in Psychological Science*, 13, 1, 9–12.

Lecanuet, J-P., Granier-Deferre, C. and Busnel, M-C. (1989) Differential fetal auditory reactiveness as a function of stimulus characteristics and state. *Seminars in Perinatology*, 13, 421–9.

Lecanuet, J-P., Granier-Deferre, C., Jacquet, A-Y. and Busnel, M-C. (1992) Decelerative cardiac responsiveness to acoustical stimulation in the near-term fetus. *Quarterly Journal of Experimental Psychology*, 44, 279–303.

Le Clec'H, G., Dehaene, S., Cohen, L., Mehler, J., Dupoux, E., Poline, J.B., Lehericy, S., van de Moortele, P.F. and Le Bihan, D. (2000) Distinct cortical areas for names of numbers and body parts independent of language and input modality. *Neuroimage*, 12, 381–91.

LeCompte, D.C., Neely, C.B. and Wilson, J.R. (1997) Irrelevant speech and irrelevant tones. *Journal of Experimental Psychology: Learning, Memory and Cognition*, 23, 472–83.

LeDoux, J.E. (1992) Brain mechanisms of emotion and emotional learning. *Current Opinion in Neurobiology*, 2, 191–7.

LeDoux, J.E. (1995a) Emotion: Clues from the brain. *Annual Review of Psychology*, 46, 209–35.

LeDoux, J.E. (1995b) In search of an emotional system in the brain: Leaping from fear to emotion and consciousness. In M.S. Gazzaniga (ed.) *The Cognitive Neurosciences*. Cambridge, MA: MIT Press.

LeDoux, J. (1996) *The Emotional Brain*. Englewood Cliffs, NJ: Simon & Schuster.

Lee, F., Hallahan, M. and Herzog, T. (1996) Explaining real-life events: How culture and domain shape attributions. *Personality and Social Psychology Bulletin*, 22, 732–41.

Lee, H-W., Rayner, K. and Pollatsek, A. (2001) The relative contribution of consonants and vowels to word identification during reading. *Journal of Memory and Language*, 44, 189–205.

Lee, K.H., Choi, Y.Y., Gray, J.R., Cho, S.H., Chae, J-H., Lee, S. and Kim, K. (2006) Neural correlates of superior intelligence; Stronger recruitment of posterior parietal cortex. *Neuroimage*, 29, 578–86.

Lee, J.L.C., Everitt, B.J. and Thomas, K.L. (2004) Independent cellular processes for hippocampal memory consolidation and reconsolidation. *Science*, 304, 839–43.

Lee, S. (1995) Self-starvation in context: Towards a culturally sensitive understanding of anorexia nervosa. *Social Science and Medicine*, 41, 25–36.

Lee, T.M.C., Liu, H-L., Tan, L-H., Chan, C.C.H., Mahankali, S., Feng, C-M, Hou, J., Fox, P.T. and Gao, J-H. (2002) Lie detection by functional magnetic resonance imaging. *Human Brain Mapping*, 15, 157–64.

Lee, T.M.C., Liu, H-L., Chan, C.C.H., Ng, Y-B., Fox, P.T. and Gao, J-H. (2005) Neural correlates of feigned memory impairment. *Neuroimage*, 28, 305–13.

Leenders, I. and Brugman, D. (2005) Moral/non-moral domain shift in young adolescents in relation to delinquent behaviour. *British Journal of Developmental Psychology*, 23, 1–6.

Lefcourt, H.M. and Martin, R.A. (1986) *Humor and Life Stress*. New York: Springer-Verlag.

Lefcourt, H.M., Davidson, K., Prkachin, K.M. and Mills, D.E. (1997) Humor as a stress moderator in the prediction of blood pressure obtained during five stressful tasks. *Journal of Research in Personality*, 31, 523–42.

Lefcourt, H.M., Davidson-Katz, K. and Kueneman, K. (1990) Humor and immune system functioning. *Humour: International Journal of Humor Research*, 3(3), 305–22.

Lefkowitz, M.M., Eron, L.D., Walder, L.O. and Huesmann, L.R. (1977) *Growing Up to Be Violent: A longitudinal study of the development of aggression*. New York: Pergamon Press.

Lefrancois, G.R. (1983) *Of Children, An Introduction to Child Development* (4th edn). Belmont, CA: Wadsworth.

LeGrand, R., Mondloch, C.J., Maurer, D. and Brent, H.P. (2004) Impairment in holistic face processing following early visual deprivation. *Psychological Science*, 15, 11, 762–8.

Lehrner, J., Eckersberger, C., Walla, P., Potsch, G. and Deecke, L. (2000) Ambient odor of orange in a dental office reduces anxiety and improves mood in female patients. *Physiology and Behaviour*, 71, 83–6.

Leibovici, D., Ritchie, K., Ledesert, B. *et al.* (1996) Does education level determine the course of cognitive decline? *Age and Ageing*, 25, 392–7.

Leinbach, M.D., Hort, B.E. and Fagot, B.I. (1997) Bears are for boys: Metaphorical associations in young children's gender stereotypes. *Cognitive Development*, 12, 107–30.

Lenneberg, E. (1967) *Biological Foundations of Language*. New York: Wiley.

Leonard, C., Eckert, M., Given, B., Virginia, B. and Eden, G. (2006) Individual differences in anatomy predict reading and oral language impairments in children. *Brain*, 129, 3329–3342.

Lepore, L. and Brown, R. (1997) Category and stereotype activation: Is prejudice inevitable? *Journal of Personality and Social Psychology*, 72, 275–87.

Lepore, S.J. (1997) Expressive writing moderates the relation between intrusive thoughts and depressive symptoms. *Journal of Personality and Social Psychology*, 73, 1030–1037.

Leppamaki, S., Partonen, T. and Lonnquist, J. (2002) Bright-light exposure combined with physical exercise elevates mood. *Journal of Affective Disorders*, 72, 139–44.

Leppamaki, S., Partonen, T., Piiroinen, P., Haukka, J. and Lonnquist, J. (2003) Timed bright-light exposure and complaints related to shift work among women. *Scandinavian Journal of Work, Environment and Health*, 29, 22–6.

Lerman, D.C. and Iwata, B.A. (1995) Prevalence of the extinction burst and its attenuation during treatment. *Journal of Applied Behaviour Analysis*, 28, 93–4.

Lerner, M.J. (1977) The justice motive: Some hypotheses as to its origins and forms. *Journal of Personality*, 45, 1–52.

Lesar, T.S., Briceland, L. and Stein, D.S. (1997) Factors related to errors in medication prescribing. *Journal of the American Medical Association*, 277, 312–17.

Lesch, K-P., Bengel, D., Heils, A., Sabol, S.Z., Greenberg, B.D. and Petri, S. (1996) Association of anxiety-related traits with a polymorphism in the serotonin transporter gene regulatory region. *Science*, 274, 1527–1531.

Leslie, A.M. (1987) Pretense and representation: The origins of 'theory of mind'. *Psychological Review*, 94, 412–26.

Lesne, S., Koh, M.T., Kotilinek, L., Kayed, R., Glabe, C.G., Yang, A., Gallagher, M. and Ashe, K.H. (2006) A specific amyloid-B protein assembly in the brain impairs memory. *Nature*, 440, 352–7.

LeVay, S. (1991) A difference in hypothalamic structure between heterosexual and homosexual men. *Science*, 253, 1034–1037.

Levelt, W. (1989) *Speaking: From intention to articulation*. Cambridge, MA: MIT Press.

Levenstein, S. (1998) Stress and peptic ulcer: Life beyond heliobacter. *British Medical Journal*, 316, 538–41.

Leventhal, H. and Scherer, K. (1987) The relationship of emotion to cognition: A functional approach to a semantic controversy. *Cognition and Emotion*, 1, 3–28.

Leventhal, H., Watts, J.C. and Pagano, R. (1967) Effects of fear and instructions on how to cope with danger. *Journal of Personality and Social Psychology*, 6, 313–21.

Levesque, M.J. and Vichesky, D.R. (2006) Raising the bar on the body beautiful: An analysis of the body image concerns of homosexual men. *Body Image*, 3, 45–55.

Levinger, G. (1980) Toward the analysis of close relationships. *Journal of Experimental Social Psychology*, 16, 510–44.

Levinson, D.J., Darrow, C.N., Klein, E.B., Levinson, M.H. and McKee, B. (1978) *The Seasons of a Man's Life*. New York: Alfred A. Knopf.

Levy, B. (1996) Improving memory in old age through implicit self-stereotyping. *Journal of Personality and Social Psychology*, 71, 1092–1106.

Levy, B., Ariely, D., Mazar, N., Chi, W., Lukas, S. and Elman, I. (2008) Gender differences in the motivational processing of facial beauty. *Learning and Motivation*, 39, 136–45.

Lewin, K. (1951) *Field Theory in Social Science*. New York: Harper.

Lewin, R. (1984) *Human Evolution: An illustrated introduction*. Cambridge, MA: Blackwell Scientific.

Lewinsohn, P.M., Mischel, W., Chaplin, W. and Barton, R. (1980) Social competence and depression: The role of illusory self-perceptions. *Journal of Abnormal Psychology*, 89, 194–202.

Lewis, C.A. (2001) Cultural stereotype of the effects of religion on mental health. *British Journal of Medical Psychology*, 74, 359–67.

Lewis, C.M., Levinson, D.F., Wise, L.H. *et al.* (2003) Genome scan meta-analysis of schizophrenia and bipolar disorder, part II. *American Journal of Human Genetics*, 73, 34–48.

Lewis, R.S., Weekes, N.Y. and Wand, T.H. (2007) The effect of a naturalistic stressor on frontal EEG asymmetry, stress and health. *Biological Psychology*, 75, 239–47.

Lewis, S.W. (1990) Computerised tomography in schizophrenia: 15 years on. *British Journal of Psychiatry*, 157 (suppl. 9), 16–24.

Leyens, J-P., Yzerbyt, V.Y. and Schadron, G. (1992) Stereotypes and social judgeability. *European Review of Social Psychology*, 3, 91–120.

Leyens, J-P., Yzerbyt, V.Y. and Schadron, G. (1994) *Stereotypes and Social Cognition*. London: Sage.

Lezak, M.D. (1995) *Neuropsychological Assessment*. New York: Oxford University Press.

Li, S-C., Lindenberger, U. and Sikstrom, S. (2001) Aging cognition: from neuromodulation to representation. *Trends in Cognitive Sciences*, 5(11), 479–86.

Li, W., Moallem, I., Paller, K.A. and Gottfriend, J.A. (2007) Subliminal smells can guide social preferences. *Psychological Science*, 18, 12, 1044–1049.

Liben, L.S., Susman, E.J., Finkelstein, J.W., Chinchilli, V.M., Kunselman, S., Schwab, J., Dubas, J.S., Demers, L.M., Lookingbill, G., D'Arcangelo, M.R., Krogh, H.R. and Kulin, H.E. (2002) The effects of sex steroids on spatial performance: A review and an experimental clinical investigation. *Developmental Psychology*, 38, 236–53.

Liberman, A.M., Cooper, F.S., Shankweiler, D.P. and Studdert-Kennedy, M. (1967) Perception of the speech code. *Psychological Review*, 74, 431–61.

Liberzon, J., Abelson, J.L., King, A. and Liberzon, I. (2008) Naturalistic stress and cortisol response to awakening: Adaptation to seafaring. *Psychoneuroendocrinology*, 33, 1023–1026.

Lickey, M.E. and Gordon, B. (1983) *Drugs for Mental Illness*. New York: W.H. Freeman.

Lidow, M.S., Williams, G.V. and Goldman-Rakic, P.S. (1998) The cerebral cortex: A case for a common site of action of antipsychotics. *Trends in Pharmacological Sciences*, 19, 136–40.

Lidz, T., Fleck, S. and Cornelison, A.R. (1965) *Schizophrenia and the Family*. New York: International Universities Press.

Lie, S.S., Malik, L. and Harris, D. (1994) *The Gender Gap in Higher Education: World yearbook of education*. London: Taylor and Francis.

Lieberman, I.Y., Mann, V.A., Shankweiler, D. and Werfelman, M. (1982) Children's memory for recurring linguistic and non-linguistic material in relation to reading ability. *Cortex*, 18, 367–75.

Liem, J.H. and Liem, G.R. (1990) Understanding the individual and family effects of unemployment. In J. Eckenrode and S. Gore (eds) *Stress Between Work and Family*. New York: Plenum Press.

Liggett, J. (1974) *The Human Face*. London: Constable.

Light, K.A. and Girdler, S.S. (1993) Cardiovascular health and women. In C.A Niven and D. Carroll (eds) *The Health Psychology of Women*. Chur, Switzerland: Harwood Press.

Likowski, K.U., Muhlberger, A., Seibt, B., Pauli, P. and Weyers, P. (2008) Modulation of facial mimicry by attitudes. *Journal of Experimental Social Psychology*, 44, 1065–1072.

Lilienfeld, S.O., Wood, J.W. and Garb, H.N. (2000) The scientific status of projective techniques. *Psychological Science in the Public Interest, 1*, 27–66.

Lilienfeld, S.O., Wood, J.W. and Garb, H.N. (2001) What's wrong with this picture? *Scientific American Mind*, May, 81–7.

Lindenberg, R., Fangerau, H. and Seitz, R.J. (2007) 'Broca's area' as a collective term? *Brain and Language*, 102, 22–9.

Lindsley, O.R. (1956) Operant conditioning methods applied to research in chronic schizophrenia. *Psychiatric Research Reports*, 24, 289–291.

Link, B.G., Struening, E.L., Neese-Todd, S., Asmussen, S. and Phelan, J.C. (2001) The consequences of stigma for the self-esteem of people with mental illnesses. *Psychiatric Services*, 52(12), 1621–1626.

Linn, M.C. and Petersen, A.C. (1985) Emergence and characterization of sex differences in spatial ability: A meta-analysis. *Child Development*, 56, 1479–1498.

Linsky, A.S., Bachman, R. and Straus, M.A. (1995) *Stress, Culture, and Aggression*. New Haven, CT: Yale University Press.

Linville, P.W. (1982) Affective consequences of complexity regarding the self and others. In M.S. Clark and S.T. Fiske (eds) *Affect and Cognition: The 17th annual Carnegie symposium on cognition*. Hillsdale, NJ: Lawrence Erlbaum Associates, pp. 79–109.

Linville, P.W., Fischer, G.W. and Salovey, P. (1989) Perceived distributions of the characteristics of in-group and out-group members: Empirical evidence and a computer simulation. *Journal of Personality and Social Psychology*, 57, 165–88.

Lisker, L. and Abramson, A. (1970) The voicing dimension: Some experiments in comparative phonetics. In *Proceedings of Sixth International Congress of Phonetic Sciences, Prague, 1967*. Prague: Academia.

Liston, C. and Kagan, J. (2002) Memory enhancement in early childhood. *Nature*, 419, 806.

Little, A.C., Jones, B.C., Burt, D.M. and Perrett, D.I. (2007) Preferences for symmetry in faces change across the menstrual cycle. *Biological Psychology*, 76, 209–16.

Liu, Y., Postupna, N., Falkenberg, J. and Anderson, M.E. (2008) High frequency deep brain stimulation: What are the therapeutic mechanisms. *Neuroscience and Biobehavioral Reviews, 32*, 343–51.

Lloyd, B. and Duveen, G. (1990) A semiotic analysis of the development of the social representation of gender. In G. Duveen and B. Lloyd (eds) *Social Representation and the Development of Knowledge*. Cambridge: Cambridge University Press.

Lloyd-Bostock, S.M.A. (1988) *Law in Practice: Applications of psychology to legal decision making and legal skills*. Leicester: BPS Books.

Lobo, A. *et al.* (2000) Prevalence of dementia and major subtypes in Europe. *Neurobiology of Aging*, 21, 49–55.

Lock, M. (1998) Menopause: lessons from anthropology. *Psychosomatic Medicine*, 60, 410–19.

Locke, J.L. (1993) *The Child's Path to Spoken Language*. Cambridge, MA: Harvard University Press.

Lockwood, P., Jordan, C.H. and Kunda, Z. (2002) Motivation by positive or negative role models: Regulatory focus determines who will best inspire us. *Journal of Personality and Social Psychology*, 83, 854–64.

Loeber, R. and Dishion, T.J. (1983) Early predictors of male delinquency: A review. *Psychological Bulletin*, 94, 68–99.

Loehlin, J.C. (1992) *Genes and Environment in Personality Development*. London: Sage.

Loehlin, J.C. and Nichols, R.C. (1976) *Heredity, Environment, and Personality*. Austin: University of Texas Press.

Loehlin, J.C., Lindzey, G. and Spuhler, J.N. (1975) *Race Differences in Intelligence*. San Fransisco: W.H. Freeman.

Loehlin, J.C., McCrae, R.R., Costa, P.T. and John, O.P. (1998) Heritabilities of common and measure-specific components of the Big Five personality factors. *Journal of Research in Personality*, 32, 431–53.

Loewen, L.J. and Suedfeld, P. (1992) Cognitive and arousal effects of masking office noise. *Environment and Behaviour*, 24, 381–95.

Loftus, E.F. (1986) Ten years in the life of an expert witness. *Law and Human Behaviour*, 10, 241–63.

Loftus, E.F. (1997) Creating false memories. *Scientific American Mind*, September, 50–5.

Loftus, E.F. and Palmer, J.C. (1974) Reconstruction of automobile destruction: An example of the interaction between language and memory. *Journal of Verbal Learning and Verbal Behavior*, 13, 585–9.

Loftus, E.F. and Zanni, G. (1975) Eyewitness testimony: The influence of the wording of a question. *Bulletin of the Psychonomic Society*, 5, 86–8.

Loftus, E.F., Miller, D.G. and Burns, H.J. (1978) Semantic integration of verbal information into a visual memory. *Journal of Experimental Psychology: Human Learning and Memory*, 4, 19–31.

Logie, R.H. (1995) *Visuo-spatial Working Memory*. Hove: Psychology Press.

Logie, R.H. (1996) The seven ages of working memory. In J.T.E. Richardson, R.W. Engle, L. Hasher, R.H. Logie, E.R. Stoltzfus and R.T. Zacks (eds) *Working Memory and Human Cognition*. Oxford: Oxford University Press.

Lomo, T. (1966) Frequency potentiation of excitatory synaptic activity in the dendate area of the hippocampal formation. *Acta Physiologica Scandinavica*, 68, 128.

LoPiccolo, J. and Friedman, J.M. (1985) Sex therapy: An integrated model. In S.J. Lynn and J.P. Garskee (eds) *Contemporary Psychotherapies: Models and methods*. New York: Merrill.

Lorenz, K. (1966) *On Aggression*. New York: Harcourt Brace Jovanovich.

Lorenzi-Cioldi, F. and Clémence, A. (2001) Group processes and the construction of social representations. In M.A. Hogg and R.S. Tindale (eds) *Blackwell Handbook of Social Psychology: Group processes*. Oxford: Blackwell, pp. 311–33.

Lorig, T.S. (1989) Human EEG and odor response. *Progress in Neurobiology*, 33, 387–98.

Lovell, D.M., Williams, J.M.G. and Hill, A.B. (1997) Selective processing of shape-related words in women with eating disorders, and those who have recovered. *British Journal of Clinical Psychology*, 36.

Lowden, A., Holmback, U., Akerstedt, T., Forslund, J., Lennernas, M. and Forslund, A. (2004) Performance and sleepiness during a 24 h wake in constant conditions are affected by diet. *Biological Psychology*, 65, 251–63.

Lowe, C. and Rabbitt, P. (1997) Cognitive models of ageing and frontal lobe deficits. In P. Rabbitt (ed.) *Methodology of Frontal and Executive Function*. Hove: Psychology Press.

Lowe, C.F. (1979) Determinants of human operant behavior. In M.D. Zeiler and P. Harzem (eds) *Advances in the Analysis of Behavior, Vol. 1: Reinforcement and the Organization of Behaviour*. Chichester: Wiley.

Lowe, C.F., Beasty, A. and Bentall, R.P. (1983) The role of verbal behavior in human learning: Infant performance on fixed-interval schedules. *Journal of the Experimental Analysis of Behavior*, 39, 157–64.

Lowe, L.P., Greenland, P., Ruth, K.J., Dyer, A.R., Stamler, R. and Stamler, J. (1998) Impact of major cardiovascular disease risk factors, particularly in combination, on 22-year mortality in women and men. *Archives of Internal Medicine*, 158, 2007–2014.

Lowenthal, K.M., Cinnirella, M., Evdoka, G. and Murphy, P. (2001) Faith conquers all? Beliefs about the role of religious factors in coping with depression among different cultural-religious groups in the UK. *British Journal of Medical Psychology*, 74, 293–303.

Lowin, A., Knapp, M.R.J. and McCrone, P. (2001) Alzheimer's disease in the UK: Comparative evidence on cost of illness and volume of health services research funding. *International Journal of Geriatric Psychiatry*, 16, 1143–1148.

Lubin, A., Hord, D., Tracy, M. and Johnson, L.C. (1976) Effects of exercise, bedrest and napping on performance decrement during 40 hours. *Psychophysiology*, 13, 334–9.

Lubow, R.E. (1989) *Latent Inhibition and Conditioned Attention Theory*. Cambridge: Cambridge University Press.

Lucas, K. and Lloyd, B. (1999) Starting smoking: Girls' explanations of the influence of peers. *Journal of Adolescence*, 22, 647–55.

Ludvigson, H.W. and Rottman, T.R. (1989) Effects of ambient odours of lavender and cloves on cognition, memory, affect and mood. *Chemical Senses*, 14, 525–36.

Ludwig, A.M. (1994) Mental illness and creative activity in female writers. *American Journal of Psychiatry*, 151, 1650–1656.

Lumeng, J.C., Cardinal, T.M., Sitto, J.R. and Kannan, S. (2008) Ability to taste 6-n-propylthiouracil and BMI in low-income preschool-aged children. *Obesity*, 16, 1522–1528.

Lundeberg, M.A., Fox, P.W., Brown, A.C. and Elbedour, S. (2000) Cultural influences on confidence: Country and gender. *Journal of Educational Psychology*, 92, 152–9.

Lundstrom, J.N., Goncalves, M., Esteves, F. and Olsson, M.J. (2003) Psychological effects of subthreshold exposure to the putative human pheromone 4, 16-androstadien-3-one. *Hormones and Behavior*, 44, 395–401.

Lundstrom, J.N., McClintock, M.K. and Olsson, M.J. (2006a) Effects of reproductive state on olfactory sensitivity suggest odor specificity. *Biological Psychology*, 71, 244–7.

Lundstrom, J.N., Olsson, M.J., Schaal, B. and Hummel, T. (2006b) A putative social chemosignal elicits faster cortical responses than perceptually similar odorants. *Neuroimage*, 30, 1340–1346.

Lundy, A.C. (1985) The reliability of the Thematic Apperception Test. *Journal of Personality Assessment*, 49, 141–5.

Lundy, A.C. (1988) Instructional set and thematic apperception test validity. *Journal of Personality Assessment*, 52, 309–20.

Lunt, I. (1995) Demographic trends in professional psychology in the United Kingdom. In A. Schorr and S. Saari (eds) *Psychology in Europe*. Göttingen: Hogrefe and Huber.

Lupfer, M.B., Clark, L.F. and Hutcherson, H.W. (1990) Impact of context on spontaneous trait and situational attributions. *Journal of Personality and Social Psychology*, 58, 239–49.

Lupien, S.J., Maheu, F., Tu, M., Fiocco, A. and Schramek, T.E. (2007) The effects of stress and stress hormones on human cognition: Implications for the field of brain and cognition. *Brain and Cognition*, 65, 209–37.

Luria, A.R. (1968) *The Mind of the Mnemonist*. London: Penguin.

Luria, A.R. (1972) *The Man With a Shattered World*. New York: Basic Books.

Lustig, C., May, C.P. and Hasher, L. (2001) Working memory span and the role of proactive interference. *Journal of Experimental Psychology: General*, 130, 199–207.

Lynam, D.R. (1996) Early identification of chronic offenders: Who is the fledgling psychopath? *Psychological Bulletin*, 120(2), 209–34.

Lynch, G., Muller, D., Seubert, P. and Larson, J. (1988) Long-term potentiation: Persisting problems and recent results. *Brain Research Bulletin*, 21, 363–72.

Lynd-Stevenson, R.M. (1996) A test of the hopelessness theory of depression in unemployed young adults. *British Journal of Clinical Psychology*, 35, 117–32.

Lynd-Stevenson, R.M. (1997) Generalized and event-specific hopelessness: Salvaging the mediation hypothesis of the hopelessness theory. *British Journal of Clinical Psychology*, 36, 73–83.

Lynn, R. (1991) Race differences in intelligence: A global perspective. *Mankind Quarterly*, 31, 255–96.

Lynn, R. (1993) Oriental Americans: Their IQ, educational attainment and socioeconomic status. *Personality and Individual Differences*, 15, 237–42.

Lynn, R. (1996) Racial and ethnic differences in intelligence in the United States on the Differential Ability Scale. *Personality and Individual Differences*, 20, 271–3.

Lynn, R. (1998) New data on black infant precocity. *Personality and Individual Differences*, 25, 801–4.

Lynn, R. and Harland, E.P. (1998) A positive effect of iron supplementation on the IQs of iron deficient children. *Personality and Individual Differences*, 24(6), 883–5.

McGue, M., Bacon, S. and Lykken, D.T. (1993) Personality stability and change in early adulthood: A behavior genetic analysis. *Developmental Psychology*, 29, 96–109.

McGue, M., Elkins, I., Walden, B. and Iacono, W.G. (2005) Perceptions of the parent–adolescent relationship: A longitudinal investigation. *Developmental Psychology*, 41, 6, 971–84.

McGuiness, D. and Morley, C. (1991) Sex differences in the development of visuo-spatial ability in pre-school children. *Journal of Mental Imagery*, 15, 143–50.

McGuire, P.K., Silbersweig, D.A., Wright, I., Murray, R.M., Frackowiak, R.S.J. and Frith, C.D. (1996) The neural correlates of inner speech and auditory verbal imagery in schizophrenia: Relationship to auditory verbal hallucinations. *British Journal of Psychiatry*, 169, 148–59.

McGuire, P.K., Quested, D.J., Spence, S.A., Murray, R.M., Frith, C.D. and Liddle, P.F. (1998) Pathophysiology of 'positive' thought disorder in schizoprenia. *British Journal of Psychiatry*, 173, 231–5.

McGuire, W.J. (1964) Inducing resistance to persuasion. In L. Berkowitz (ed.) *Advances in Experimental Social Psychology*, Vol. 1. New York: Academic Press, pp. 191–229.

McGuire, W.J. and Papageorgis, D. (1961) The relative efficacy of various types of prior belief-defence in producing immunity against persuasion. *Journal of Abnormal and Social Psychology*, 62, 327–37.

McKay, D.C. (1973) Aspects of the theory of comprehension, memory and attention. *Quarterly Journal of Experimental Psychology*, 25, 22–40.

McKeefry, D.J. and Zeki, S. (1997) The position and topography of the human colour centre as revealed by functional magnetic resonance imaging. *Brain*, 120, 2229–2242.

McKenna, D.D. and Farrell, B.D. (2006) Tropical forests are both evolutionary cradles and museums of leaf beetle diversity. *Proceedings of the National Academy of Science*, 103, 10947–10951.

McLellan, D.L. (1991) Functional recovery and the principles of disability medicine. In M. Swash and J. Oxbury (eds) *Clinical Neurology*. Edinburgh: Churchill Livingstone.

McManus, I.C. (1985) Handedness, language dominance and aphasia: A genetic model. *Psychological Medicine*, 8, 1–40.

McManus, I.C., Shergill, S. and Bryden, M.P. (1993) Annett's theory that individuals heterozygous for the right shift gene are intellectually advantaged: Theoretical and empirical problems. *British Journal of Psychology*, 84, 517–37.

McNally, R.J. (1987) Preparedness and phobias. *Psychological Bulletin*, 101, 283–303.

McNally, R.J. (1990) Psychological approaches to panic disorder: A review. *Psychological Bulletin*, 108, 403–19.

McNally, R.J. (1995) Preparedness, phobias, and the Panglossian paradigm. *Behavioural and Brain Sciences*, 18, 303–4.

McNamee, P., Bond, J. and Buck, D. (2001) Costs of dementia in England and Wales in the 21st century. *British Journal of Psychiatry*, 179, 261–6.

McNeill, D. (1970) *The Acquisition of Language: The study of developmental psycholinguistics*. New York: Harper & Row.

McReynolds, W.T. (1980) Learned helplessness as a schedule-shift effect. *Journal of Research in Personality*, 14, 139–57.

Mead, G.H. (1934) *Mind, self and society*. Chicago: University of Chicago Press.

Meador, K.J., Allen, M.E., Adams, R.J. and Loring, D.W. (1991) Allochiria vs allesthesia. Is there a misrepresentation? *Archives of Neurology*, 48, 546–9.

Mednick, S.A., Gabrielli, W.F. and Hutchings, B. (1983) Genetic influences in criminal behavior: Some evidence from an adoption cohort. In K.T.

VanDusen and S.A. Mednick (eds) *Prospective Studies of Crime and Delinquency*. Hingham, MA: Martinus Nijhoff.

Mednick, S.A., Machon, R.A. and Huttunen, M.O. (1990) An update on the Helsinki influenza project. *Archives of General Psychiatry*, 47, 292.

Meehl, P.E. (1956) Wanted – a good cookbook. *American Psychologist*, 11, 262–72.

Meehl, P.E. (1986) Causes and effects of my disturbing little book. *Journal of Personality Assessment*, 50, 370–5.

Meeter, M., Murre, J.M.J. and Janssen, S.M.J. (2005) Remembering the news: Modeling retention data from a study with 14,000 participants. *Memory and Cognition*, in press.

Mehler, J., Jusczyk, P., Lambertz, G., Halsted, N., Bertoncini, J. and Amiel-Tison, C. (1988) A precursor of language acquisition in young infants. *Cognition*, 29, 143–78.

Mehrabian, A. (1972) Nonverbal Communication. In J. Cole (ed.) *Nebraska Symposium on Motivation*, Vol. 19. Lincoln: University of Nebraska Press, pp. 107–62.

Meichenbaum, D. (1985) *Stress Inoculation Training*. New York: Pergamon Press.

Meichenbaum, D.H. (1977) *Cognitive-behavior Modification: An integrative approach*. New York: Plenum Press.

Meindl, J.R. and Lerner, M.J. (1985) Exacerbation of extreme responses to an out-group. *Journal of Personality and Social Psychology*, 47, 71–84.

Mejia-Arauz, R., Rogoff, B., Dexter, A. and Najafi, B. (2007) Cultural variation in children's social organization. *Child Development*, 78, 3, 1001–14.

Melamed, S., Shirom, A., Toker, S., Berliner, S. and Shapira, I. (2006) Burnout and risk of cardiovascular disease: Evidence, possible causal paths, and promising research directions. *Psychological Bulletin*, 132, 3, 327–53.

Melzak, R. (1992) Phantom limbs. *Scientific American Mind*, 266(4), 120–6.

Meltzoff, A.N. (1988) Infant imitation and memory: Nine-month-olds in immediate and deferred tests. *Child Development*, 59, 217–25.

Meltzoff, A.N. (1995) What infant memory tells us about infantile amnesia: Long-term recall and deferred imitation. *Journal of Experimental Child Psychology*, 59, 497–515.

Memon, A. and Higham, P.A. (1999) A review of the cognitive interview. *Psychology, Crime and Law*, 89, 265–83.

Memon, A. and Yarmey, A.D. (1999) Earwitness recall and identification: Comparison of the cognitive interview and the structured interview. *Perceptual and Motor Skills*, 88, 797–807.

Memon, A., Cronin, O., Eaves, R. and Bull, R. (1983) The cognitive interview and child witnesses. In N. Clark and G.M. Stephenson (eds) *Children, Evidence and Procedure*. Leicester: British Psychological Society.

Menn, L. and Stoel-Gammon, C. (1993) Phonological development: Learning sounds and sound patterns. In J.B. Gleason (ed.) *The Development of Language*. New York: Macmillan.

Menon, T., Morris, M.W., Chiu, C. and Hong, Y. (1999) Culture and the construal of agency: Attribution to individual versus group dispositions. *Journal of Personality and Social Psychology*, 76, 701–17.

Menon, V., Rivera, S.M., White, C.D., Glover, G.H. and Reiss, A.L. (2000) Dissociating prefrontal and parietal cortex activation during arithmetic processing. *Neuroimage*, 12, 357–65.

Merrens, M.R. and Richards, W.S. (1970) Acceptance of generalized bona fide personality interpretations. *Psychological Reports*, 27, 691–4.

Mervis, C.B. and Rosch, E. (1981) Categorization of natural objects. *Annual Review of Psychology*, 32, 89–116.

Mesoudi, A., Whiten, A. and Dunbar, R. (2006) A bias for social information in human cultural transmission. *British Journal of Psychology*, 97, 405–23.

Messinger, D.S., Fogel, A. and Dickson, K.L. (2001) All smiles are positive, but some smiles are more positive than others. *Developmental Psychology*, 37(5), 642–53.

Metalsky, G.I., Halberstadt, L.J. and Abramson, L.Y. (1987) Vulnerability to depressive mood reactions: Toward a more powerful test of the diathesis-stress and causal mediation components of the reformulated theory of depression. *Journal of Personality and Social Psychology*, 52, 386–93.

Meyer, P.A., Garrison, C.Z., Jackson, K.L. and Addy, C.L. (1993) Undesirable life events and depression in young adolescents. *Journal of Child and Family Studies*, 2, 47–60.

Miles, H.L. (1983) Apes and language: The search for communicative competence. In J. de Luce and H.T. Wilder (eds) *Language in Primates: Perspectives and implications*. New York: Springer-Verlag.

Miles, L.K. (2009) Who is approachable? *Journal of Experimental Social Psychology*, 45, 262–6.

Miles, M.B. and Huberman, A.M. (1994) *Qualitative Data Analysis: A sourcebook of new methods* (2nd edn). London: Sage.

Milgram, S. (1963) Behavioral study of obedience. *Journal of Abnormal and Social Psychology*, 67, 371–8.

Milgram, S. (1974) *Obedience to Authority*. London: Tavistock.

Miller, C.L. (1987) Qualitative differences among gender-stereotyped toys: Implications for cognitive and social development. *Sex Roles*, 16, 473–87.

Miller, D.T. and Porter, C.A. (1983) Self-blame in victims of violence. *Journal of Social Issues*, 39, 139–52.

Miller, G.A. (1956) The magical number seven plus or minus two: Some limits on our capacity for processing information. *Psychological Review*, 63, 81–97.

Miller, G.A. and Taylor, W.G. (1948) The perception of repeated bursts of noise. *Journal of the Acoustical Society of America*, 20, 171–82.

Miller, G.A., Heise, G. A. and Lichten, W. (1951) The intelligibility of speech as a function of the context of the test materials. *Journal of Experimental Psychology*, 41, 329–35.

Miller, G.A., Galanter, E. and Pribram, K. (1960) *Plans and the Structure of Behavior*. New York: Holt, Rinehart & Winston.

Miller, G.E. and Cohen, S. (2001) Psychological interventions and the immune system: A meta-analytic review and critique. *Health Psychology*, 20, 47–63.

Miller, J., Mckinstry, R, Phillip, J., Mukherjee, P. and Neil, J. (2003) Diffusion-tensor MR imaging of normal brain maturation: A guide of structural development and myelination. *American Journal of Radiology*, 180, 851–9.

Miller, J.D., Scott, E. and Okamoto, S. (2006) Public acceptance of evolution. *Science*, 313, 765–766.

Miller, J.G. (1997) Theoretical issues in cultural psychology. In J.W. Berry, Y.H. Poortinga and J. Pandey (eds) *Handbook of Cross-cultural Psychology: Theory and method*, Vol. 1. Boston: Allyn & Bacon.

Miller, J.N. and Ozonoff, S. (1997) Did Asperger's cases have Asperger disorder? A research note. *Journal of Child Psychology and Psychiatry*, 38(2), 247–51.

Miller, N.E. (1983) Behavioral medicine: Symbiosis between laboratory and clinic. *Annual Review of Psychology*, 34, 1–31.

Miller, R.J., Hennessy, R.T. and Leibowitz, H.W. (1973) The effect of hypnotic ablation of the background on the magnitude of the Ponzo perspective illusion. *International Journal of Clinical and Experimental Hypnosis*, 21, 180–91.

Milligan, K., Astington, J.W. and Dack, L.A. (2007) Language and theory of mind: Meta-analysis of the relation between language ability and false-belief understanding. *Child Development*, 78, 2, 622–46.

Milne, D. and Common, A. (1998) Delivering and evaluating psychological skills training for athletes and coaches. In H. Steinberg, I. Cockerill and A. Dewey (eds) *What Do Sport Psychologists Do?* Leicester: British Psychological Society.

Milner, A.D. (1998) Streams of consciousness: Visual awareness and the brain. *Trends in Cognitive Sciences*, 2(1), 25–30.

Milner, A.D. and Goodale, M.A. (1995) *The Visual Brain in Action*. Oxford: Oxford University Press.

Milner, A.D., Perrett, D.I., Johnston, R.S., Benson, P.I., Jordan, T.R. and Healey, D.W. (1991) Perception and action in 'visual form agnosia'. *Brain*, 114, 405–28.

Milner, B. (1964) Some effects of frontal lobotomy in man. In J.W. Warren and G. Akert (eds) *The Frontal Granular Cortex and Behaviour*. New York: McGraw-Hill.

Milner, B. (1970) Memory and the temporal regions of the brain. In K.H. Pribram and D.E. Broadbent (eds) *Biology of Memory*. New York: Academic Press.

Milner, B., Corkin, S. and Teuber, H-L. (1968) Further analysis of the hippocampal amnesic syndrome: 14 year follow-up study of HM. *Neuropsychologia*, 6, 217–24.

Mintun, M.A., LaRossa, G.N., Sheline, Y.I., Dence, C.S., Lee, S.Y., Mach, R.H. *et al* (2006) 11C PIB in a nondemented population: Potential antecedent marker of Alzheimer disease. *Neurology*, 67, 446–52.

Mirmiran, M. (1995) The function of fetal/neonatal rapid eye movement sleep. *Behavioural Brain Research*, 69, 13–22.

Mischel, W. (1968) *Personality and Assessment*. New York: Wiley.

Mischel, W. (1976) *Introduction to Personality* (2nd edn). New York: Holt, Rinehart & Winston.

Mischel, W. (1977) The interaction of person and situation. In D. Magnusson and N.S. Endler (eds) *Personality at the Crossroads: Current issues in interactional psychology*. Hillsdale, NJ: Lawrence Erlbaum Associates.

Mischel, W. (1979) On the interface of cognition and personality: Beyond the person–situation debate. *American Psychologist*, 34, 740–54.

Mischel, W. (1984) Convergences and challenges in the search for consistency. *American Psychologist*, 39, 351–64.

Mitte, K. (2005) Meta-analysis of cognitive-behavioural treatments for Generalized Anxiety Disorder: A comparison with pharmacotherapy. *Psychological Bulletin*, 131, 5, 785–95.

Mittenberg, W., Seidenberg, M., O'Leary, D.S. and DiGiulio, D. (1989) Changes in cerebral functioning associated with normal ageing. *Journal of Clinical and Experimental Neuropsychology*, 11(6), 918–32.

Miyake, A. (2001) Individual differences in working memory: Introduction to the special section. *Journal of Experimental Psychology: General*, 130(2), 163–8.

Miyake, K., Chen, S. and Campos, J.J. (1985) Infant temperament, mother's mode of interaction, and attachment in Japan: An interim report. In I. Bretherton and E. Waters (eds) *Growing points of attachment theory and research. Monographs of the Society for Research in Child Development*, 50.

Miyamoto, Y., Nisbett, R.E. and Masuda, T. (2006) Culture and physical environment: Holistic versus analytic perceptual affordances. *Psychological Science*, 17, 113–19.

Neisser, U. (1984) Interpreting Harry Bahrick's discovery: What confers immunity against forgetting? *Journal of Experimental Psychology: General*, 113, 32–5.

Neisser, U. and Becklen, R. (1975) Selective looking: Attending to visually significant events. *Cognitive Psychology*, 7, 480–94.

Neisser, U., Boodoo, G., Bouchard, T.J., Boykin, W.A., Brody, N., Ceci, S., Halpern, D.F., Loehlin, J.C., Perloff, R., Sternberg, R.J. and Urbina, S. (1996a) Intelligence: Knowns and unknowns. *American Psychologist*, 51(2), 77–101.

Neisser, U., Winograd, E., Bergman, E.T., Schreiber, C.A., Palmer, S.E. and Weldon, M.S. (1996b) Remembering the earthquake: Direct experience vs hearing the news. *Memory*, 4, 337–57.

Neisworth, J.T. and Madle, R.A. (1982) Retardation. In A.S. Bellack, M. Hersen and A.E. Kazdin (eds) *International Handbook of Behavior Modification and Therapy*. New York: Plenum Press.

Nelson, C.A. (1999) Neural plasticity and human development. *Current Directions in Psychological Science*, 8(2), 42–5.

Nelson, K. (1986) *Event Knowledge: Structure and function in development*. Hillsdale, NJ: Lawrence Erlbaum Associates.

Nelson, K. (1993) Events, narratives, memory: What develops? In M.E. Lamb and A.L. Brown (eds) *Memory and Affect in Development*. Hillsdale, NJ: Lawrence Erlbaum Associates.

Nelson, C.A. (2007) A neurobiological perspective on early human development. *Child Development Perspectives*, 1, 1, 13–18.

Nelson, L.D. and Simmons, J.P. (2007) Moniker maladies: When names sabotage success. *Psychological Science*, 18, 12, 1106–1112.

Nelson, M., Naismith, D.J., Burley, V., Gatenby, S. and Geddes, N. (1990) Nutrient intake vitamin/mineral supplementation and intelligence in British schoolchildren. *British Journal of Nutrition*, 64, 13–22.

Nemeth, C.J. and Ormiston, M. (2007) Creative idea generation: Harmony versus stimulation. *European Journal of Social Psychology*, 37, 524–35.

Nettle, D. (2007) Empathizing and systemizing: What are they, and what do they contribute to our understanding of psychological sex differences? *British Journal of Psychology*, 98, 237–55

Neubauer, V., Freudenthaler, H.H. and Pfurtscheller, G. (1995) Intelligence and spatiotemporal patterns of event-related desynchronization. *Intelligence*, 3, 249–66.

Neugarten, B.L. (1974) The roles we play. In *American Medical Association, Quality of Life: The middle years*. Acton, MA: Publishing Sciences Group.

Nevid, J.S., Art, R.J. and Moulton, J.L. (1996) Factors predicting participant attrition in a community-based, culturally specific smoking cessation program for Hispanic smokers. *Health Psychology*, 15(3), 226–9.

Neville, H.J., Bavelier, D., Corina, D., Rauschecker, J., Kami, A., Lalwani, A., Braun, A., Clark, V., Jezzard, P. and Turner, R. (1998) Cerebral organization for language in deaf and effects of experience. *Proceedings of the National Academy of Sciences of the USA*, 95(3), 922–9.

Nevin, J.A. (1988) Behavioral momentum and the partial reinforcement effect. *Psychological Bulletin*, 103, 44–56.

Newcomb, A.F. and Bagwell, C.L. (1995) Children's friendship relations: A meta-analytic review. *Psychological Bulletin*, 117, 306–47.

Newcombe, F., Mehta Z. and Deflaan, E.H.F. (1994) Category specificity in visual recognition. In M.J. Farah and G. Ratcliff (eds) *The Neuropsychology of High-level Vision*. Hove: Lawrence Erlbaum Associates.

Newcombe, N. and Huttenlocher, J. (1992) Children's early ability to solve perspective-taking problems. *Developmental Psychology*, 28, 635–43.

Newcombe, N., Huttenlocher, J., Drummey, A.B. and Wiley, J.G. (1998) The development of spatial location coding: Place learning and dead reckoning in the second and third years. *Cognitive Development*, 13, 185–200.

Newell, A. and Simon, H.A. (1972) *Human Problem Solving*. Englewood Cliffs, NJ: Prentice Hall.

Newport, E.L., Gleitman, H.R. and Gleitman, L. (1977) Mother I'd rather do it myself: Some effects and noneffects of maternal speech style. In C.E. Snow and C.A. Ferguson (eds) *Talking to Children: Language input and acquisition*. Cambridge: Cambridge University Press.

Newport, E.L. and Supalla, R. (1987) A critical period effect in the acquisition of a primary language. Unpublished manuscript cited by J.S. Johnson and E.L. Newport. Critical period effects in second language learning: The influence of maturational state on the acquisition of English as a second language. *Cognitive Psychology*, 21, 60–99.

Newson, J. and Newson, E. (1975) Intersubjectivity and the transmission of culture: On the social origins of symbolic functioning. *Bulletin of the British Psychological Society*, 28, 437–46.

Nezu, A.M., Nezu, C.M. and Blissett, S.E. (1988) Sense of humor as a moderator of the relation between stressful life events and psychological distress: A prospective analysis. *Journal of Personality and Social Psychology*, 54, 699–714.

Nicoll, C.S. and Russell, R.M. (1990) Analysis of animal rights literature reveals the underlying motives of the movement: Ammunition for counter-offensive by scientists. *Endocrinology*, 127, 985–9.

Nicholson, C.D. (1990) Pharmacology of nootropics and metabolically active compounds in relation to their use in dementia. *Psychopharmacology*, 101, 147–59.

Nicol, R. (1998) Conduct disorder. *Current Opinion in Psychiatry*, 11, 385–8.

Nicolaides, S., Toda, Y. and Smith, P.K. (2002) Knowledge and attitudes about school bullying in trainee teachers. *British Journal of Educational Psychology*, 72, 105–18.

Nicolaus, L.K. and Nellis, D.W. (1987) The first evaluation of the use of conditioned taste aversion to control predation by mongooses upon eggs. *Applied Animal Behaviour Science*, 17, 329–46.

Nicolaus, L.K., Hoffman, T.E. and Gustavson, C.R. (1982) Taste aversion conditioning in free ranging raccoons (*Procyon lotor*). *Northwest Science*, 56, 165–9.

Nicolson, R.I., Fawcett, A.J., Berry, E.L., Jenkins, I.H., Dean, P. and Brooks, D.J. (1999) Association of abnormal cerebellar activation with motor learning difficulties in dyslexic adults. *The Lancet*, 353, 1662–1667.

Nielsen, L.L. and Sarason, I.G. (1981) Emotion, personality, and selective attention. *Journal of Personality and Social Psychology*, 41, 945–60.

Nijboer, F., Fureda, A., Gunst, I. *et al.* (2008) An auditory brain-computer interface (BCI), *Journal of Neuroscience Methods*, 167, 43–50.

Nisbett, R.E. and Ross, L. (1980) *Human Inference: Strategies and shortcomings of social judgment*. Englewood Cliffs, NJ: Prentice Hall.

Nisbett, R.E. and Schachter, S. (1966) Cognitive manipulation of pain. *Journal of Experimental Social Psychology*, 2, 227–36.

Nisbett, R.E. and Wilson, T.D. (1977) Telling more than we can know: Verbal reports on mental processes. *Psychological Review*, 84, 231–59.

Nobre, A.C., Allison, T. and McCarthy, G. (1994) Word recognition in the human inferior temporal lobe. *Nature*, 372, 260–3.

Nochi, M. (1998) 'Loss of self' in the narratives of people with traumatic brain injury: A qualitative analysis. *Social Science and Medicine*, 46, 7, 869–78.

Noor, F. and Evans, D.C. (2003) The effect of facial symmetry on perceptions of personality and attractiveness. *Journal of Research in Personality*, 37, 339–47.

Norenzayan, A. and Heine, S.J. (2005) Psychological universals: What are they and how can we know? *Psychological Bulletin*, 131, 5, 763–84.

Norheim, A.J. and Fonnebo, V. (1998) Doctors' attitudes to acupuncture – a Norwegian study. *Social Science and Medicine*, 47(4), 519–23.

Norman, W.T. (1963) Toward an adequate taxonomy of personality attributes: Replicated factor structure in peer nomination personality ratings. *Journal of Abnormal and Social Psychology*, 66, 574–83.

North, T.C., McCullagh, P. and Tran, V. (1990) Effects of exercise on depression. *Exercise and Sport Sciences Reviews*, 18, 379–415.

Norton, L.S. and Crowley, C.M. (1995) Can students be helped to learn how to learn? An evaluation of an approaches to learning programme for first year students. *Higher Education*, 29, 307–28.

Nowak, M.A. and Sigmund, K. (1998) Evolution of indirect reciprocity by image scoring. *Nature*, 393, 573–7.

Nunez, J.M., Casey, B.J., Egner, T., Hare, T. and Hirsch, J. (2005) Intentional false responding shares neural substrates with response conflict and cognitive control. *Neuroimage*, 25, 267–77.

Nunn, C.L., Gittleman, J.L. and Antonovics, J. (2000) Promiscuity and the primate immune system. *Science*, 290, 1168–1170.

Nyberg, L., McIntosh, A.R., Cabeza, R., Habib, R., Houle, S. and Tulving, E. (1996) General and specific brain regions involved in encoding and retrieval of events: What, where and when. *Proceedings of the National Academy of Sciences*, USA, 93, 11280–11285.

O

Oakes, P.J., Haslam, S.A. and Turner, J.C. (1993) *Stereotyping and Social Reality*. Oxford: Blackwell.

Oakhill, J. and Garnham, A. (1988) *Becoming a Skilled Reader*. Oxford: Blackwell.

Oaksford, M., Morris, F., Grainger, B. and Williams, J.M.G. (1996) Mood, reasoning, and central executive processes. *Journal of Experimental Psychology: Learning, Memory and Cognition*, 22(2), 476–92.

Oatley, K. (1992) *Best Laid Schemes: The psychology of emotion*. Cambridge: Cambridge University Press.

Oatley, K. and Jenkins, J.M. (1996) *Understanding Emotion*. Oxford: Blackwell.

Oatley, K. and Johnson-Laird, P.N. (1987) Towards a cognitive theory of emotions. *Cognition and Emotion*, 1, 29–50.

O'Boyle, M.W., Cunnington, R., Silk, T.J., Vaughan, D., Jackson, G., Syngeniotis, A. and Egan, G.F. (2005) Mathematically gifted male adolescents activate a unique brain network during mental rotation. *Cognitive Brain Research*, 25, 583–7.

O'Brien, M. and Nutt, D. (1998) Loss of consciousness and post-traumatic stress disorder. *British Journal of Psychiatry*, 173, 102–4.

O'Carroll, R.E. (1995) The assessment of premorbid ability: A critical review. *Neurocase*, 1, 83–9.

Ochsner, K. and Lieberman, M. (2001) The emergence of social cognitive neuroscience. *American Psychologist*, 56, 717–34.

O'Connor, N. and Hermelin, B. (1988) Low intelligence and special abilities. *Journal of Child Psychology and Psychiatry*, 29, 391–6.

O'Connor, T.G. and Rutter, M. (2000) Attachment disorder behaviour following early severe deprivation: Extension and longitudinal follow-up. *Journal of the American Academy of Child and Adolescent Psychiatry*, 39, 703–12.

O'Craven and Kanwisher, N. (2000) Mental imagery of faces and places activates corresponding stimulus-specific brain regions. *Journal of Cognitive Neuroscience*, 12(6), 1013–1023.

Oddy, M. and Cogan, J. (2005) Coping with severe memory impairment. *Neuropsychological Rehabilitation*, 14, 5, 481494.

O'Doherty, J., Rolls, E.T., Francis, S., Bowtell, R., McGlone, F., Kobal, G., Renner, B. and Ahne, G. (2000) Sensory-specific satiety-related olfactory activation of the human orbitofrontal cortex. *NeuroReport*, 11, 399–403.

Offer, D. and Sabshin, M. (1984) *Normality and the Life Cycle: A critical integration*. New York: Basic Books.

Ohman, A., Dimberg, U. and Ost, L-G. (1985) Animal and social phobias: Biological constraints on learned fear responses. In S. Reiss and R. Bootzin (eds) *Theoretical Issues in Behaviour Therapy*. New York: Academic Press.

Ohnishi, T., Matsuda, H., Hashimoto, T., Kunihiro, T., Nishikawa, M., Uema, T. and Sasaki, M. (2000) Abnormal regional cerebral blood flow in childhood autism. *Brain*, 123, 1838–1844.

Okazaki, S. (2000) Asian American and White American differences on affective distress symptoms: Do symptom reports differ across reporting methods? *Journal of Cross-Cultural Psychology*, 31, 603625.

O'Keefe, J. and Nadel, L. (1978) *The Hippocampus as a Cognitive Map*. Oxford: Clarendon.

Okubo, Y., Suhara, T., Suzuki, K., Kobayashi, K., Inoue, O., Terasaki, O., Someya, Y., Sassa, T., Sudo, Y., Matsushima, E., Iyo, M., Tateno, Y. and Toru, M. (1997) Decreased prefrontal dopamine D1 receptors in schizophrenia revealed by PET. *Nature*, 385, 634–6.

Olds, J. and Milner, P.M. (1954) Positive reinforcement produced by electrical stimulation of septal area and other regions of the rat brain. *Journal of Comparative and Physiological Psychology*, 47, 419–27.

Olson, J.M., Vernon, P.A., Harris, J.A. and Jang, K.L. (2001) The heritability of attitudes: a study of twins. *Journal of Personality and Social Psychology*, 80(6), 845–60.

Oltmans, T.F. and Emery, R.E. (1998) *Abnormal Psychology* (2nd edn). Englewood Cliffs, NJ: Prentice Hall.

Oltmans, T.F., Neale, J.M. and Davison, G.C. (1995) *Case Studies in Abnormal Psychology*. New York: Wiley.

Olton, D.S., Becker, J.T and Handelsmann, G.E. (1979) Hippocampus, space and memory. *Behavioural and Brain Science*, 2, 313–65.

Olweus, D. (1993) *Bullying in Schools: What we know and what we can do*. Oxford: Blackwell.

O'Malley, P.M. and Johnston, L.D. (2002) Epidemiology of alcohol and other drug use among college students. *Journal of Studies on Alcohol*, Supplement No. 14, 23–39.

Omi, M. and Winant, H. (1994) *Racial Formation in the United States: From the 1960s to the 1980s*. New York: Routledge & Kegan Paul.

O'Neil, P.M., Smith, C.F., Foster, G.D. and Anderson, D.A. (2000) The perceived relative worth of reaching goal weight. *International Journal of Obesity*, 24, 1069–1076.

Ongur, D., Drevets, W.C. and Price, J.L. (1998) Gial reduction in the subgenual prefrontal cortex in mood disorders. *Proceedings of the National Academy of Sciences USA*, 95, 13290–13295.

O'Riordan, M. and Plaisted, K. (2001) Enhanced discrimination in autism. *Quarterly Journal of Experimental Psychology*, 54A(4), 961–79.

Orne, M.T. (1959) The nature of hypnosis: Artifact and essence. *Journal of Abnormal and Social Psychology*, 58, 277–99.

Orne, M.T. and Evans, F.J. (1965) Social control in the psychological experiment: Antisocial behavior and hypnosis. *Journal of Personality and Social Psychology*, 1, 189–200.

Ortigue, S., Bianchi-Demicheli, F., Hamilton, A.F. de C. and Grafton, S.T. (2007) The neural basis of love as a subliminal prime: an event-related functional Magnetic Resonance Imaging study. *Journal of Cognitive Neuroscience*, 19, 7, 1218–1230.

Plutchik, R. (1984) Emotions: A general psychoevolutionary theory. In K.R. Scherer and P. Ekman (eds) *Approaches to Emotion*. Hillsdale, NJ: Lawrence Erlbaum Associates.

Poggio, G.F. and Poggio, T. (1984) The analysis of stereopsis. *Annual Review of Neuroscience*, 7, 379–412.

Polich, J. and Kok, A. (1995) Cognitive and biological determinants of P300: An integrative overview. *Biological Psychology*, 41, 103–46.

Poline, J-B., Vandenberghe, R., Holmes, A.P., Friston, K.J. and Frackowiak, R.S.J. (1996) Reproducibility of PET activation studies: Lessons from a multi-center European experiment. *Neuroimage*, 4, 34–54.

Polk, T.A. and Farah, M.J. (2002) Functional MRI evidence for an abstract, not perceptual, word-form area. *Journal of Experimental Psychology: General*, 131(1), 65–72.

Pollack, I. and Pickett, J.M. (1964) Intelligibility of excerpts from fluent speech: Auditory vs structural context. *Journal of Verbal Learning and Verbal Behavior*, 3, 79–84.

Pollack, I.F., Polinko, P., Albright, A.L., Towbin, R. and Fitz, C. (1995) Mutism and pseudobulbar symptoms after resection of posterior fossa tumours in children: Incidence and pathophysiology. *Neurosurgery*, 37, 885–93.

Poole, D.A., Lindsay, D.S., Memon, A. and Bull, R. (1995) Psychotherapy and the recovery of memories of childhood sexual abuse: US and British practitioners' opinions, practices and experiences. *Journal of Consulting and Clinical Psychology*, 63(3), 426–37.

Popper, K.R. and Eccles, J. (1977) *The Self and its Brain: An argument for interactionism*. New York: Springer-Verlag.

Poropat, A.E. (2009) A meta-analysis of the five-factor model of personality and academic performance. *Psychological Bulletin*, 135, 2, 322–38.

Porter, J., Craven, B., Khan, R.M., Chang, S-J., Kang, I., Judkewicz, B., Volpe, J., Settles, G. and Sobel, N. (2007) Mechanisms of scent-tracking in humans. *Nature Neuroscience*, 10, 1, 27–9.

Porter, M., Penney, G.C., Russell, D., Russell, E. and Templeton, A. (1996) A population-based survey of women's experience of the menopause. *British Journal of Obstetrics and Gynaecology*, 103, 1025–1028.

Porter, S., Doucette, N.L., Woodworth, M., Earle, J. and MacNeil, B. (2008) Halfe the world knows not how the other halfe lies: Investigation of verbal and non-verbal signs of deception exhibited by criminal offenders and non-offenders. *Legal and Criminological Psychology*, 13, 27–38.

Porubska, K., Veit, R., Preissl, H., Fritsche, A. and Birbaumer, N. (2006) *Neuroimage*, 32, 1273–1280.

Posavac, H., Posavac, S. and Posavac, E. (1998) Exposure to media images of female attractiveness and concern with body weight images among young women. *Sex Roles*, 38, 187–201.

Posner, M. and Petersen, S.E. (1990) The attention system of the human brain. *Annual Review of Neuroscience*, 13, 25–42.

Posner, M.I., Snyder, C.R.R. and Davidson, B.J. (1980) Attention and the detection of signals. *Journal of Experimental Psychology: General*, 109, 160–74.

Post, F. (1994) Creativity and psychopathology: A study of 291 world-famous men. *British Journal of Psychiatry*, 165, 22–34.

Post, F. (1996) Verbal creativity, depression and alcoholism. *British Journal of Psychiatry*, 168, 545–55.

Postle, B.R., Berger, J.S. and D'Esposito, M. (1999) Functional neuroanatomical double dissociation of mnemonic and executive control processes contributing to working memory performance. *Proceedings of the National Academy of Sciences USA*, 96, 12959–12964.

Postman, L. and Phillips, L. (1965) Short-term temporal changes in free recall. *Quarterly Journal of Experimental Psychology*, 2, 509–22.

Postmes, T., Spears, R. and Lea, M. (1998) Breaching or building social boundaries? SIDE-effects of computer-mediated communication. *Communication Research*, 25, 689–715.

Postmes, T., Spears, R., Sakhel, K. and de-Groot, D. (2001) Social influence in computer-mediated communication: The effects of anonymity on group behavior. *Personality and Social Psychology Bulletin*, 27, 1243–1254.

Potter, J. and Wetherell, M. (1987) *Discourse and Social Psychology*. London: Sage.

Potter, J. and Wetherell, M. (1995) Discourse analysis. In J.A. Smith, R. Harré and L. vanLangenhove (eds) *Rethinking Research Methods in Psychology*. London: Sage.

Potts, G.R. (1972) Information processing strategies used in the encoding of linear orderings. *Journal of Verbal Learning and Verbal Behavior*, 11, 727–40.

Pound, N., Penton-Voak, I.S. and Brown, W.M. (2007) Facial symmetry is positively associated with self-reported extraversion. *Personality and Individual Differences*, 43, 1572–1582.

Powell, G.E. and Lindsay, S.J.E. (1994) An introduction to treatment. In S.J.E. Lindsay and G.E. Powell (eds) *The Handbook of Clinical Adult Psychology*. London: Routledge.

Powell, K.E., Thompson, P.D., Caspersen, C.J. and Kendrick, J.S. (1987) Physical activity and the incidence of coronary heart disease. *Annual Review of Public Health*, 8, 253–87.

Power, M. and Dalgleish, T. (1997) *Cognition and Emotion*. Hove: Psychology Press.

Prandini, C. and McCarthy, S. (2006) Teaching psychology as a science in Italy. *International Journal of Psychology*, 41, 1, 42–50.

Pratkanis, A.R., Breckler, S.H. and Greenwald, A.G. (1989) *Attitude Structure and Function*. Hillsdale, NJ: Lawrence Erlbaum Associates.

Pratto, F., Sidanius, J., Stallworth, L.M. and Malle, B.F. (1994) Social dominance orientation: A personality variable predicting social and political attitudes. *Journal of Personality and Social Psychology*, 67, 741–63.

Premack, D. (1976) Language and intelligence in ape and man. *American Scientist*, 64, 674–83.

Pressman, S.D., Cohen, S., Miller, G.E., Barkin, A., Rabin, B.S. and Treanor, J.J. (2005) Loneliness, social network size, and immune response to influenza vaccination in college freshmen. *Health Psychology*, 24, 3, 297–306.

Price, C.J., Gorno-Tempini, M.L., Graham, K.S., Biggio, N., Mechelli, A., Patterson, K. and Noppeney, U. (2003) Normal and pathological reading: Converging data from lesion and imaging studies. *Neuroimage*, 20, S30–S41.

Price, C.J. (2000) Functional imaging studies of aphasia. In J.C. Mazziotta, A.W. Toga and R.S.J. Frakowiak (eds), *Brain Mapping: The disorders*. San Diego: Academic Press.

Price, C.J., Wise, R.J.S., Watson, J.D.G., Patterson, K., Howard, D. and Frackowiak, R.S.J. (1994) Brain activity during reading: The effects of exposure duration and task. *Brain*, 117, 1255–1269.

Prichard, J. C. (1835) *A Treatise on Insanity and Other Disorders Affecting the Mind*. London: Sherwood, Gilbert & Piper.

Prigatano, G.P. (1992) Personality disturbances associated with traumatic brain injury. *Journal of Consulting and Clinical Psychology*, 60(3), 360–8.

Prince, R. (1985) The concept of the culture-bound syndromes: Anorexia nervosa and brain-fag. *Social Science and Medicine*, 21, 197–203.

Prior, M. (1992) Childhood autism. In S. Schwartz (ed.) *Case Studies in Abnormal Psychology*. New York: Wiley.

Prkachin, K.M., Mills, D.E., Zwaal, C. and Husted, J. (2001) Comparison of hemodynamic responses to social and nonsocial stress: Evaluation of an anger interview. *Psychophysiology*, 38, 879–85.

Proudfoot, J., Guest, D., Carson, J., Dunn, G. and Gray, J. (1997) Effect of cognitive-behavioural training on job-find among long-term unemployed people. *Lancet*, 350, 96–100.

Provins, K.A. (1997) Handedness and speech: A critical reappraisal of the role of genetic and environmental factors in the cerebral lateralization of function. *Psychological Review*, 104(3), 554–71.

Pugh, K.R., Mencl, W.E., Shaywitz, B.A., Shaywitz, S.E., Fulbright, R.K., Constable, R.T., Skudlarski, P., Marchione, K.E., Jenner, A.R., Fletcher, J.M., Lieberman, A.M., Shankweiler, D.P., Katz, L., Bronen, R.A., Lacadie, C. and Gore, J.C. (2000) The angular gyrus in developmental dyslexia: task-specific differences in functional connectivity within posterior cortex. *Psychological Science*, 11(1), 51–6.

Pugh, K.R., Shaywitz, B.A., Shaywitz, S.E., Constable, R.T., Skudlarski, P., Fulbright, R.K., Bronen, R.A., Shankweiler, D.P., Katz, L., Fletcher, J. and Gore, J.C. (1996) Cerebral organisation of component processes in reading. *Brain*, 119, 1221–1238.

Pulford, B.D. and Sohal, H. (2006) The influence of personality on HE students' confidence in their academic abilities. *Personality and Individual Differences*, 41, 1409–1419.

Putman, P.W. (2003) Ten-year research update review: child sexual abuse. *Journal of the American Academy of Child Adolescence and Psychiatry*, 42, 269–78.

Q

Quinones-Vidal E., Lopez-Garcia, J.J., Penaranda-Ortega, M. and Tortosa-Gil, F. (2004) The nature of social and personality psychology as reflected in JPSP, 1965–2000. *Journal of Personality and Social Psychology*, 86, 435–52.

R

Rabbitt, P., Maylor, E., McInnes, L., Bent, N. and Moore, B. (1995) What goods can self-assessment questionnaires deliver for cognitive gerontology? *Applied Cognitive Psychology*, 9, S127–S152.

Rabius, V., McAlister, A.L., Geiger, A., Huang, P. and Todd, R. (2004) Telephone counseling increases cessation rates among young adult smokers. *Health Psychology*, 23, 5, 539–41.

Radoeva, P.D., Prasad, S., Brainard, D.H. and Aguirre, G.K. (2008) Neural activity within area v1 reflects unconscious visual performance in a case of blindsight. *Journal of Cognitive Neuroscience*, 20, 11, 1927–1939.

Rae, C., Harasty, J.A., Dzendrowskyj, T.E., Talcott, J.B., Simpson, J.M., Blamire, A.M., Dixon, R.M., Lee, M.A., Thompson, C.H., Styles, P., Richardson, A.J. and Stein, J.F. (2002) Cerebellar morphology in developmental dyslexia. *Neuropsychologia*, 46, 1285–1292.

Rae, C., Lee, M.A., Dixon, R.M., Blamire, A.M., Thompson, C.H., Styles, P., Talcott, J., Richardson, A.J. and Stein, J.F. (1998) Metabolic anomalies in developmental dyslexia detected by 1H magnetic resonance spectroscopy. *Lancet*, 351, 1849–1852.

Raeside, J. (2007) The hard sell. *The Guardian Guide*, July, 14–20.

Ragland, D.R. and Brand, R.J. (1988) Type A behavior and mortality from coronary heart disease. *New England Journal of Medicine*, 318, 65–9.

Rahe, R.H. and Arthur, R.J. (1978) Life changes and illness reports. In K.E. Gunderson and R.H. Rahe (eds) *Life Stress and Illness*. Springfield, IL: Thomas.

Raine, A. (1997) *The Psychopathology of Crime* (2nd edn). New York: Academic Press.

Raine, A., Venables, P.H. and Williams, M. (1996) Better autonomic conditioning and faster electrodermal half-recovery time at age 15 years as possible protective factors against crime at age 29 years. *Developmental Psychology*, 32(4), 624–30.

Raine, A., Lencz, T., Bihrle, S., Lacasse, L. and Collenti, P. (2000) Reduced prefrontal gray matter volume and reduced autonomic activity in anti-social personality disorder. *Archives of General Psychiatry*, 57, 119–27.

Raine, A., Reynolds, C., Venables, P.H. and Mednick, S.A. (2002) Stimulation seeking and intelligence: A prospective longitudinal study. *Journal of Personality and Social Psychology*, 82, 663–74.

Rainville, P., Hofbauer, R.K., Bushnell, M.C., Duncan, G.H. and Price, D.D. (2002) Hypnosis modulates activity in brain structures involved in the regulation of consciousness. *Journal of Cognitive Neuroscience*, 14(6), 887–901.

Rajecki, D.J. (1989) *Attitudes* (2nd edn). Sunderland, MA: Sinauer Associates.

Ramus, P. (2006) Genes, brain and cognition. *Cognition*, 101, 247–69.

Randel, A.E. (2003) The salience of culture in multinational teams and its relation to team citizenship behaviour. *International Journal of Cross-Cultural Management*, 3, 27–44.

Randich, A. and LoLordo, V.M. (1979) Preconditioning exposure to the unconditioned stimulus affects the acquisition of the conditioned emotional response. *Learning and Motivation*, 10, 245–75.

Rao, S.M. (1986) Neuropsychology of multiple sclerosis: a critical review. *Journal of Clinical and Experimental Neuropsychology*, 8, 503.

Rapee, R.M. and Heimberg, R.G. (1997) A cognitive-behavioural model of anxiety in social phobia. *Behaviour Research and Therapy*, 35, 741–56.

Rapin, I. (1997) Autism. *New England Journal of Medicine*, 337(2), 97–104.

Rapoport, A. (1976) *Experimental Games and their Uses in Psychology*. Morristown, NJ: General Learning Press.

Rapoport, J.L. (1989) The biology of obsessions and compulsions. *Scientific American Mind*, March, 62–9.

Rasmussen, T. and Milner, B. (1977) The role of early left brain injury in determining lateralization of cerebral speech functions. *Annals of the New York Academy of Sciences*, 299, 355–69.

Rattner, A. (1988) Convicted but innocent: Wrongful conviction and the criminal justice system. *Law and Human Behaviour*, 12, 283–93.

Rauschecker, J.P. and Shannon, R.V. (2002) Sending sound to the brain. *Science*, 295, 1025–1029.

Ravaja, N., Turpeinen, M., Saari, T., Puttonen, S and Keltikangas-Jarvinen, L. (2008) The psychology of James Bond: Phasic emotional responses to violent video game events. *Emotion*, 8, 1.

Rawlings, D. (1985) Psychoticism, creativity and dichotic shadowing. *Personality and Individual Differences*, 6, 737–42.

Raynauld, R., Larivee, S. and Dionne, J. (1999) Peut-on ameliorer le judgement moral d'eleves de 10–12 ans? *Psychologie and Education*, 36, 55–78.

Rayner, K. and Pollatsek, A. (1989) *The Psychology of Reading*. Englewood Cliffs, NJ: Prentice Hall.

Reber, A.A. and Allen, R. (1978) Analogical and abstraction strategies in synthetic grammar learning: A functionalist interpretation. *Cognition*, 6, 189–221.

Reber, A.S. (1992) The cognitive unconscious: An evolutionary perspective. *Consciousness and Cognition*, 1, 93–133.

Schmitt, D.P., Realo, A., Voracek, M. and Allik, J. (2008) Why can't a man be more like a woman? Sex differences in Big Five personality traits across 55 cultures. *Journal of Personality and Social Psychology*, 94, 1, 168–82.

Schmolck, H., Buffalo, E.A. and Squire, L.R. (2000) Memory distortions develop over time: Recollections of the O.J. Simpson trial verdict after 15 and 32 months. *Psychological Science*, 11(1), 39–45.

Schneider, G.E. (1969) Two visual systems. *Science*, 163, 895–902.

Schoenthaler, S. (1991) *Improve Your Child's IQ and Behaviour*. London: BBC Books.

Schoenthaler, S., Amos, S.P., Doraz, W.E., Kelly, M.A. and Wakefield, J. (1991a) Controlled trial of vitamin–mineral supplementation: Effects on intelligence and brain function. *Personality and Individual Differences*, 12, 343–50.

Schoenthaler, S., Amos, S.P., Eysenck, H.J., Peritz, E. and Yudkin, J. (1991b) Controlled trial of vitamin–mineral supplementation: Effects on intelligence and performance. *Personality and Individual Differences*, 12, 351–62.

Scholing, A. and Emmelkamp, P.M.G. (1996) Treatment of generalized social phobia: Results at long-term follow-up. *Behaviour Research and Therapy*, 34(5/6), 447–52.

Schoning, S. *et al.* (2007) Functional anatomy of visuo-spatial working memory during mental rotation is influenced by sex, menstrual cycle, and sex steroid hormones. *Neuropsychologia*, 45, 3203–3214.

Schopler, E. (1996) Are autism and Asperger syndrome different labels or different disabilities? *Journal of Autism and Developmental Disorders*, 26, 109–10.

Schorr, A. (1995) German psychology after unification. In A. Schorr and S. Saari (eds) *Psychology in Europe*. Göttingen: Hogrefe & Huber.

Schouten, A.P., Valkenburg, P.M. and Peter, J. (2007) Precursors and underlying processes of adolescents' online self-disclosure: Developing and testing an 'Internet-attribute-perception' model. *Media Psychology*, 10, 292–314.

Schuchts, R.A. and Witkin, S.L. (1989) Assessing marital change during the transition to parenthood. *Social Casework: The Journal of Contemporary Social Work*, 70(2), 67–75.

Schul, Y. (1983) Integration and abstraction in impression formation. *Journal of Personality and Social Psychology*, 44, 45–54.

Schultz, W. (2007) Behavioral dopamine signals. *Trends in Neurosciences*, 30, 5, 201–10.

Schwartz, D., Dodge, K.A., Petit, G.S. and Bates, J.E. (2000) Friendship as a moderating factor in the pathway between early harsh home environment and later victimization in the peer group. *Developmental Psychology*, 36, 646–62.

Schwartz, G.E., Brown, S.L. and Ahern, G.L. (1980) Facial muscle patterning and subjective experience during affective imagery: sex differences. *Psychophysiology*, 17, 75–82.

Schwartz, M.F., Saffran, E.M. and Marin, O.S.M. (1980) The word order problem in agrammatism. I. Comprehension. *Brain and Language*, 10, 249–62.

Schwartz, N. (1999) Self-reports: How the questions shape the answers. *American Psychologist*, 54(2), 93–105.

Schwartz, R. and Schwartz, L.J. (1980) *Becoming a Couple*. Englewood Cliffs, NJ: Prentice Hall.

Schweizer, H. (1999) *Designing and Teaching an On-line Course: Spinning your web classroom*. Boston: Allyn & Bacon.

Scollon, C.N., Diener, E., Oishi, S. and Biswas-Diener, R. (2004) Emotions across cultures and methods. *Journal of Cross-Cultural Psychology*, 35, 3, 304–26.

Scollon, C.N., Diener, E., Oishi, S. and Biswas-Diener, R. (2005) An experience sampling and cross-cultural investigation of the relation between pleasant and unpleasant affect. *Cognition and Emotion*, 19, 1, 27–52.

Scott, E.C. and Matzke, N.J. (2007) Biological design in the classroom. *Proceedings of the National Academy of Science*, 104, 1, 8669–8676.

Scott, J. (2006) Psychotherapy for bipolar disorders – efficacy and effectiveness. *Journal of Psychopharmacology*, 20, 2, 46–50.

Scott, S.K., Young, A.W., Calder, A.J., Hellawell, D.J., Aggleton, J.P. and Johnson, M. (1997) Impaired auditory recognition of fear and anger following bilateral amygdala lesions. *Nature*, 385, 254–57.

Scoville, W.B. and Milner, B. (1957) Loss of recent memory after bilateral hippocampal lesions. *Journal of Neurology, Neurosurgery and Psychiatry*, 20, 11–21.

Scribner, S. (1977) Modes of thinking and ways of speaking: Culture and logic reconsidered. In P.N. Johnson-Laird and P.C. Wason (eds) *Thinking: Readings in cognitive science*. Cambridge: Cambridge University Press.

Scully, D., Kremer, J., Meade, M.M., Graham, R. and Dudgeon, K. (1998) Physical exercise and psychological well-being: A critical review. *British Journal of Sports Medicine*, 32, 111–20.

Searleman, A. (1977) A review of right hemisphere linguistic abilitites. *Psychological Bulletin*, 84, 503–28.

Sedikides, C. (1993) Assessment, enhancement, and verification determinants of the self-evaluation process. *Journal of Personality and Social Psychology*, 65, 317–38.

Sedikides, C. and Brewer, M.B. (eds) (2001) *Individual Self, Relational Self, and Collective Self*. Philadelphia, PA: Psychology Press.

Sedikides, C. and Gregg, A.P. (2003) Portraits of the self. In M.A. Hogg and J. Cooper (eds) *The Sage Handbook of Social Psychology*. London: Sage, pp. 110–38.

Seepersad, S. (2004) Coping with loneliness: Adolescent online and offline behavior. *CyberPsychology and Behavior*, 7, 35–9.

Segall, M.H., Campbell, D.T. and Herskovits, M.J. (1966) *The Influence of Culture on Visual Perception*. Indianapolis, Bobbs-Merrill.

Segall, M.H., Lonner, W.J. and Berry, J.W. (1998) Cross-cultural psychology as a scholarly discipline. *American Psychologist*, 53(10), 1101–1110.

Segalowitz, S.J. and Bryden, M.P. (1983) Individual differences in hemispheric representation of language. In S.J. Segalowitz (ed.) *Language Functions and Brain Organization*. New York: Academic Press.

Segerstrom, S.C., Tayor, S.E., Kemeny, M.E. and Fahey, J.L. (1998) Optimism is associated with mood, coping and immune change in response to stress. *Journal of Personality and Social Psychology*, 74(6), 1646–1655.

Sehulster, J.R. (1989) Content and temporal structure of autobiographical knowledge: Remembering twenty-five seasons at the Metropolitan Opera. *Memory and Cognition*, 17, 590–606.

Seidenberg, M.S. and McClelland, J.L. (1989) A distributed, developmental model of word recognition and naming. *Psychological Review*, 96, 523–68.

Select Committee on Science and Technology (1999) *Sixth report*. London: HMSO.

Selemon, L.D., Rajkowska, G. and Goldman-Rakic, P.S. (1995) Abnormally high neuronal density in the schizophrenic cortex. A morphometric analysis of prefrontal area 9 and occipital area 17. *Archives of General Psychiatry*, 52, 805–18.

Selfridge, O.G. (1959) *Pandemonium: A paradigm for learning. The Mechanisation of Thought Process*. London: HMSO.

Selfridge, O.G. and Neisser, U. (1960) Pattern recognition by machine. *Scientific American Mind*, 203, 60–8.

Seligman, M.E.P. (1971) Phobias and preparedness. *Behavior Therapy*, 2, 307–20.

Seligman, M.E.P. (1975) *Helplessness*. San Francisco: W.H. Freeman.

Seligman, M.E.P. (1988) Competing theories of panic. In S. Rachman and J.D. Maser (eds) *Panic: Psychological perspectives*. Hillsdale, NJ: Lawrence Erlbaum Associates.

Seligman, M.E.P. and Schulman, P. (1986) Explanatory style as a predictor of productivity and quitting among life insurance sales agents. *Journal of Personality and Social Psychology*, 50, 832–8.

Selye, H. (1956) *The Stress of Life*. New York: McGraw-Hill.

Selye, H. (1976) *Stress without Distress*. New York: Harper & Row.

Selye, H. (1991) History and present status of the stress concept. In A. Monat and R.S. Lazarus (eds) *Stress and Coping*. New York: Columbia University Press.

Selye, H. and Tuchweber, B. (1976) Stress in relation to aging and disease. In A. Everitt and J. Burgess (eds) *Hypothalamus, Pituitary and Aging*. Springfield, IL: Charles C. Thomas.

Semendeferi, K. and Damasio, H. (2000) The brain and its main anatomical subdivisions in living hominoids using magnetic resonance imaging. *Journal of Human Evolution*, 38, 317–32.

Semendeferi, K., Damasio, H., Frank, R. and Van Hoesen, G.W. (1997) The evolution of the frontal lobes: a volumetric analysis based on three-dimensional reconstructions of magnetic resonance scans of human and ape brains. *Journal of Human Evolution*, 32, 375–88.

Sergent, J. (1987) A new look at the human split brain. *Brain*, 110, 1375–1392.

Sergent, J. (1990) Furtive incursions into bicameral minds: Integrative and co-ordinating role of the subcortical structures. *Brain*, 113, 537–68.

Sergent, J. (1991) Processing of spatial relations within and between the disconnected cerebral hemispheres. *Brain*, 114, 1025–1043.

Sergent, J., Ohta, S. and Macdonald, B. (1992) Functional neuroanatomy of face and object processing: A PET study. *Brain*, 115, 15–36.

Sergerie, K., Chochol, C. and Armony, J.L. (2008) The role of the amygdala in emotional processing: A quantitative meta-analysis of functional neuroimaging studies. *Neuroscience and Biobehavioral Reviews*, 32, 811–30.

Seubert, J., Rea, A.F., Loughead, J. and Habel, U. (2008) Mood induction with olfactory stimuli reveals differential affective responses in males and females. *Chemical Senses*, in press.

Seymour, S.E., Reuter-Lorenz, P.A. and Gazzaniga, M.S. (1994) The disconnection syndrome: Basic findings reaffirmed. *Brain*, 117, 105–15.

Shackel, B. (1996) Ergonomics: Scope, contribution and future possibilities. *The Psychologist*, July, 304–8.

Shackelford, T.K. (2001) Partner-killing by women in cohabiting relationships and marital relationships. *Homicide Studies*, 5, 253–66.

Shackelford, T.K. and Buss, D.M. (2000) Marital satisfaction and spousal cost-infliction. *Personality and Individual Differences*, 28, 917–28.

Shackelford, T.K., Buss, D.M. and Bennett, K. (2002) Forgiveness or breakup: Sex differences in responses to a partner's infidelity. *Cognition and Emotion*, 16, 299–307.

Shaffer, D. and Pfeffer, C.R. (2001) Practice parameter for the assessment and treatment of children and adolescents with suicidal behaviour. *Journal of the American Academy of Child and Adolescent Psychiatry*, 40, 24S–51S.

Shaffer, L.H. (1975) Multiple attention in continuous verbal tasks. In S. Dornic (ed.) *Attention and Performance*, Vol. 5. New York: Academic Press.

Shafir, E., Simonson, I. and Tversky, A. (1993) Reason-based choice. *Cognition*, 49, 11–36.

Shah, J., Higgins, E.T. and Friedman, R.S. (1998) Performance incentives and means: How regulatory focus influences goal attainment. *Journal of Personality and Social Psychology*, 74, 285–93.

Shah, M., French, S.A., Jeffrey, R.W., McGovern, P.G., Forster, J.L. and Lando, H.A. (1993) Correlates of high fat/calorie food intake in a worksite population: The Healthy Worker Project. *Addictive Behaviours*, 18, 583–94.

Shah, P. and Miyake, A. (1996) The separability of working memory resources for spatial thinking and language processing: An individual differences approach. *Journal of Experimental Psychology: General*, 125, 4–27.

Shahidullah, S. and Hepper, P. (1993) The developmental origins of fetal responsiveness to an acoustic stimulus. *Journal of Reproductive and Infant Psychology*, 11, 135–42.

Shalev, A.Y., Bonne, O. and Eth, S. (1996) Treatment of the post-traumatic stress disorder. *Psychosomatic Medicine*, 58, 165–82.

Shallice, T. (1988) *From Neuropsychology to Mental Structure*. Cambridge: Cambridge University Press.

Shallice, T. and Burgess, P.W. (1991) Deficits in strategy application following frontal lobe damage in man. *Brain*, 114, 727–41.

Shalom, D.B. and Poeppel, D. (2008) Functional anatomic models of language: Assembling the pieces. *Neuroscientist*, 14, 1, 119–27.

Shams, L., Kamitani, Y. and Shimojo, S. (2000) What you see is what you hear. *Nature*, 408, 788.

Shanon, B. (1990) Consciousness. *Journal of Mind and Behaviour*, 11, 137–52.

Shanon, B. (1998) What is the function of consciousness? *Journal of Consciousness Studies*, 5(3), 295–308.

Shapiro, A.H. (1975) Behaviour of Kibbutz and urban children receiving an injection. *Psychophysiology*, 12, 79–82.

Shapiro, K.A., Pascual-Leone, A., Mottaghy, F.M. Gangitano, M. and Caramazza, A. (2001) Grammatical distinctions in the left frontal cortex. *Journal of Cognitive Neuroscience*, 13, 713–20.

Shapiro, L.R. and Solity, J. (2008) Delivering phonological and phonics training within whole-class teaching. *British Journal of Educational Psychology*, 78, 597–620.

Shapiro, P.J. and Weisberg, R.W. (1999) Creativity and bipolar diathesis: Common behavioural and cognitive components. *Cognition and Emotion*, 13(6), 741–62.

Sharma, U. (1992) *Complementary Medicine Today: Practitioners and patients*. London: Routledge.

Shatz, M. and Gelman, R. (1973) The development of communication skills: Modifications in the speech of young children as a function of listener. *Monographs of the Society for Research in Child Development*, 38 (Serial No. 152).

Shaver, P.R., Shaver, W.S. and Schwartz, J.C. (1992) Cross-cultural similarities and differences in emotion and its representation: A prototype approach. In M.S. Clark (ed.) *Review of Personality and Social Psychology*, Vol. 13. Newbury Park, CA: Sage.

Shavit, Y., Lewis, J.W., Terman, G.W., Gale, R.P. and Liebeskind, J.C. (1984) Opioid peptides mediate the suppressive effect of stress on natural killer cell cytotoxicity. *Science*, 223, 188–90.

Shavit, Y., Depaulis, A., Martin, F.C., Terman, G.W., Pechnick, R.N., Zane, C.J., Gale, R.P. and Liebeskind, J.C. (1986) Involvement of brain opiate receptors in the immune-suppressive effect of morphine. *Proceedings of the National Academy of Sciences*, USA, 83, 7114–7117.

In M.P. Zanna (ed.) *Advances in Experimental Social Psychology*, Vol. 34. San Diego: Academic Press, pp. 379–440.

Steele, R.J. and Morris, R.G. (1999) Delay-dependent impairment of a matching-to-place task with chronic and intrahippocampal infusion of the NMDA-antagonist D-AP5. *Hippocampus*, 9, 118–36.

Steen, S.N., Oppliger, R.A. and Brownell, K.D. (1988) Metabolic effects of repeated weight loss and regain in adolescent wrestlers. *Journal of the American Medical Association*, 260, 47–50.

Steers, R.M. and Rhodes, S.R. (1984) Knowledge and speculation about absenteeism. In P. Goodman and R. Atkin (eds) *Absenteeism*. San Francisco: Jossey-Bass.

Steffenburg, S., Gillberg, C., Helgren, L., Anderson, L., Gillberg, L., Jakobsson, G. and Bohman, M. (1989) A twin study of autism in Denmark, Finland, Iceland, Norway and Sweden. *Journal of Child Psychology and Psychiatry*, 30, 405–16.

Stein, J.F. (1991) Visuospatial sense, hemispheric asymmetry and dyslexia. In J.F. Stein (ed.) *Vision and Visual Dyslexia*. London: Macmillan.

Stein, J.F. and Walsh, V. (1997) To see but not to read; the magnocellular theory of dyslexia. *Trends in Neurosciences*, 20(4), 147–52.

Steiner, I.D. (1972) *Group Process and Productivity*. New York: Academic Press.

Stenner, P., Dancey, C. and Watts, S. (2000) The understanding of their illness amongst people with irritable bowel syndrome: A Q methodological study. *Social Science and Medicine*, 51, 3, 439–52.

Stenner, P., Watts, S. and Worrell, M. (2008) Q methodology. In C. Willig and W. Stainton-Rogers (eds) *The Sage Handbook of Qualitative Research in Psychology*. London: Sage.

Stephan, W.G. and Stephan, C.W. (1985) Intergroup anxiety. *Journal of Social Issues*, 41, 157–75.

Stephan, W.G. and Stephan, C.W. (2000) An integrated threat theory of prejudice. In S. Oskamp (ed.) *Reducing Prejudice and Discrimination*. Mahwah, NJ: Erlbaum, pp. 23–46.

Steptoe, A., Wardle, J. and Marmot, M. (2005) Positive affect and health-related neuroendocrine, cardiovascular and inflammatory processes. *Proceedings of the National Academy of Sciences*, 102, 18, 6508–6512.

Steptoe, A., Wright, C., Kunz-Ebrecht, S.R. and Iliffe, S. (2006) Dispositional optimism and health behaviour in community-dwelling older people: Associations with healthy ageing. *British Journal of Health Psychology*, 11, 71–84.

Sterman, M.B. (1981) EEG biofeedback: Physiological behavior modification. *Neuroscience and Biobehavioural Reviews*, 5, 405–12.

Sterman, M.B. and Clemente, C.D. (1962) Forebrain inhibitory mechanisms: Cortical synchronization induced by basal forebrain stimulation. *Experimental Neurology*, 6, 91–102.

Stern, J.A., Brown, M., Ulett, G.A. and Sletten, I. (1977) A comparison of hypnosis, acupuncture, morphine, Valium, aspirin, and placebo in the management of experimentally induced pain. In W.E. Edmonston, Jr. (ed.) *Hypnosis and Relaxation: Modern verification of an old equation*. New York: Wiley/Interscience.

Stern, K. and McClintock, M.K. (1998) Regulation of ovulation by human pheromones. *Nature*, 392, 177–9.

Stern, W. (1914) *The Psychological Methods of Testing Intelligence*. Baltimore: Warwick & York.

Sternberg, R.J. (1985) *Beyond IQ: A triarchic theory of human intelligence*. Cambridge: Cambridge University Press.

Sternberg, R.J. (1988a) *The Psychologist's Companion*. Leicester: BPS.

Sternberg, R.J. (1988b) *The Triangle of Love*. New York: Basic Books.

Sternberg, R.J. (2001) What is the common thread of creativity? *American Psychologist*, 56, 360–2.

Sternberg, R.J. (2002) Creativity as a decision. *American Psychologist*, 376.

Sternberg, R.J. and Davidson, J. (1996) *The Nature of Insight*. Cambridge, MA: MIT Press.

Sternberg, R.J. and Dess, N.K. (2001) Creativity for the new millennium. *American Psychologist*, 56, 332.

Sternberg, R.J. and Detterman, D.K. (1986) *What is Intelligence? Contemporary viewpoints on its nature and definition*. New Jersey: Norwood.

Sternberg, R.J. and Grigorenko, E. (1997) *Intelligence, Heredity and Environment*. New York: Cambridge University Press.

Sternberg, R.J. and Lubart, T.I. (1991) An investment theory of creativity and its development. *Human Development*, 32, 1–31.

Sternberg, R.J. and Lubart, T.I. (1995) *Defying the Crowd: Cultivating creativity in a culture of conformity*. New York: Free Press.

Sternberg, R.J. and Wagner, R.K. (1986) *Practical Intelligence: Nature and origins of competence in the everyday world*. New York: Cambridge University Press.

Sternberger, L.G. and Burns, G.L. (1990) Obsessions and compulsions: Psychometric properties of the Padua inventory with an American college population. *Behavior Research and Therapy*, 28, 341–5.

Stevenson, R.E., Schroer, R.J., Skinner, C., Fender, D. and Simensen, R.J. (1997) Autism and macroencephaly. *Lancet*, 349, 1744–1745.

Stewart, A.J. and Ostrove, J.M. (1998) Women's personality in middle age: gender, history and midcourse corrections. *American Psychologist*, 53(11), 1185–1194.

Stewart, F., Parkin, A.J. and Hunkin, N.M. (1992) Naming impairments following from herpes simplex encephalitis: category-specific? *Quarterly Journal of Experimental Psychology*, 44A, 261–84.

Stewart, L., Walsh, V., Frith, U and Rothwell, J. (2001) TMS produces two dissociable types of speech disruption. *Neuroimage*, 13, 472–8.

Stice, E., Shaw, H. and Marti, C.N. (2006) A meta-analytic review of obesity prevention programs for children and adolescents: the skinny on interventions that work. *Psychological Bulletin*, 132, 5, 667–91.

Stich, S.P. (1990) Rationality. In D.N. Osherson and E.E. Smith (eds) *An Invitation to Cognitive Science. Vol. 3: Thinking*. Cambridge, MA: MIT Press.

Stickgold, R. and Walker, M. P. (2007) Sleep-dependent memory consolidation and reconsolidation. *Sleep Medicine*, 8, 331–43.

Stine, E.L. and Bohannon, J.N. (1983) Imitations, interactions, and language acquisition. *Journal of Child Language*, 10, 589–603.

Stocks, J.T and Freddolino, P.P. (1998) Evaluation of a world wide web-based graduate social work research methods course. *Computers in Human Services*, 15, 51–69.

Stoddard, J.T. (1886) Composite portraiture. *Science*, 8, 89–91.

Stoerig, P. and Cowey, A. (1997) Blindsight in man and monkey. *Brain*, 120, 535–59.

Stoerig, P., Kleinschmidt, A. and Frahm, J. (1998) No visual responses in deenervated V1: High-resolution functional magnetic resonance imaging of a blindsight patient. *NeuroReport*, 9, 21–5.

Stokoe, W.C. (1983) Apes who sign and critics who don't. In J. de Luce and H.T. Wilder (eds) *Language in Primates: Perspectives and implications*. New York: Springer-Verlag.

Stone, A.A., Cox, D.S., Valdimarsdottir, H., Jandorf, L. and Neale, J.M. (1987) Evidence that secretory IgA antibody is associated with daily mood. *Journal of Personality and Social Psychology*, 52, 988–93.

Stone, V.E., Baron-Cohen, S. and Knight, R.T. (1998) Frontal lobe contributions to theory of mind. *Journal of Cognitive Neuroscience*, 10(5), 640–56.

Stoner, J.A.F. (1961) A comparison of individual and group decisions including risk. Unpublished Master's thesis, Massachusetts Institute of Technology, Boston.

Stoodley, C.J. and Schmahmann, J.D. (2009) Functional topography in the human cerebellum: A meta-analysis of neuroimging studies. *Neuroimage*, 44, 489–501.

Stopa, L. and Clark, D.M. (2000) Social phobia and interpretation of social events. *Behaviour Research and Therapy*, 38, 273–83.

Storandt, M. (2008) Cognitive deficits in the early stages of Alzheimer's disease. *Current Directions in Psychological Science*, 17, 3, 198–202.

Storandt, M., Grant, E.A., Miller, J.P. and Morris, J.C. (2006) Longitudinal course and neuropathological outcomes in original vs revised MCI and in preMCI. *Neurology*, 67, 467–73.

Stott, C.J. and Adang, O.M.J. (2004) 'Disorderly' conduct: social psychology and the control of football 'hooliganism' at 'Euro2004'. *The Psychologist*, 17, 318–19.

Stott, C., Hutchison, P. and Drury, J. (2001) 'Hooligans' abroad? Intergroup dynamics, social identity and participation in collective disorder at the 1998 World Cup finals. *British Journal of Social Psychology*, 40, 359–84.

Strachan, A.M., Feingold, D., Goldstein, M.J., Miklowitz, D.J. and Nuechterlein, K.H. (1989) Is expressed emotion an index of transactional process? II. Patient's coping style. *Family Process*, 28, 169–81.

Strack, F., Stepper, S. and Martin, L.L. (1988) Inhibiting and facilitating conditions of the human smile: A nonobtrusive test of the facial feedback hypothesis. *Journal of Personality and Social Psychology*, 54, 768–77.

Strahan, E.J., Wilson, A.E., Cressman, K.E. and Buote, V.M. (2006) Comparing to perfection: How cultural norms for appearance affect social comparisons and self-image. *Body Image*, 3, 211–27.

Strauss, A.L. and Corbin, J. (1990) *Basics of Qualitative Research: Grounded theory procedures and techniques*. Newbury Park, CA: Sage.

Strayer, D.L. and Johnston, W.A. (2001) Driven to distraction: Dual-task studies of simulated driving and conversing on a cellular telephone. *Psychological Science*, 12(6), 462–66.

Strenze, T. (2007) Intelligence and socioeconomic success: A meta-analytic review of longitudinal research. *Intelligence*, 35, 401–26.

Strick, M., Holland, R.W. and van Knippenberg, A. (2008) Seductive eyes: Attractiveness and direct gaze increase desire for associated objects. *Cognition*, 106, 1487–1496.

Strickland, B.R. (1979) Internal–external expectancies and cardiovascular functioning. In L.C. Perlmutter and R.A. Monty (eds) *Choice and Perceived Control*. Hillsdale, NJ: Lawrence Erlbaum Associates.

Stritzke, W.G.K., Lang, A.R. and Patrick, C.J. (1996) Beyond stress and arousal: A reconceptualization of alcohol–emotion relations with reference to psychophysiological methods. *Psychological Bulletin*, 120(3), 376–95.

Stroebe, W. and Diehl, M. (1994) Why groups are less effective than their members: On productivity losses in idea-generating groups. *European Review of Social Psychology*, 5, 271–303.

Stroebele, N. and de Castro, J.M. (2006) Listening to music while eating is related to increases in people's food intake and meal duration. *Appetite*, 47, 285–9.

Stroop, J.R. (1935) Studies of interference in serial verbal reactions. *Journal of Experimental Psychology*, 18, 743–62.

Stuart, G.W., McAnally, K.I., McKay, A., Johnston, M. and Castles, A. (2006) A test of the magnocellular deficit theory of dyslexia in an adult sample. *Cognitive Neuropsychology*, 23, 8, 1215–1229.

Strupp, H.H. (1993) The Vanderbilt psychotherapy studies: Synopsis. *Journal of Consulting and Clinical Psychology*, 61, 431–3.

Strupp, H.H. and Hadley, S.W. (1979) Specific vs. nonspecific factors in psychotherapy. *Archives of General Psychiatry*, 36, 1125–1136.

Studebaker, C.A. and Penrod, S.D. (1997) Pretrial publicity: The media, the law and common sense. *Psychology, Public Policy and Law*, 3(2/3), 428–60.

Stunkard, A.J., Sørenson, T.I., Harris, C., Teasdale, T.W., Chakraborty, R., Schull, W.J. and Schulsinger, F. (1986) An adoption study of human obesity. *New England Journal of Medicine*, 314, 193–8.

Sturr, J.F., Zhang, L., Taub, H.A., Hannon, D.J. and Jackowski, M.M. (1997) Psychophysical evidence for losses in rod sensitivity in the aging visual system. *Vision Research*, 37(4), 475–81.

Stuss, D.T., Gow, C.A. and Hetherington, C.R. (1992) 'No longer Gage': Frontal lobe dysfunction and emotional changes. *Journal of Consulting and Clinical Psychology*, 60(3), 349–59.

Stuss, D.T. and Levine, B. (1996) The dementias: Nosological and clinical factors related to diagnosis. *Brain and Cognition*, 31, 99–113.

Stuss, D.T., Gallup, G.G. and Alexander, M.P. (2001) The frontal lobes are necessary for 'theory of mind'. *Brain*, 124, 279–86.

Sugiyama, T., Takei, Y. and Abe, T. (1992) The prevalence of autism at Nagoya, Japan. In H. Naruse and E.M. Ornitz (eds) *Neurobiology of Infantile Autism*. Amsterdam: Excerpta Medica.

Sullivan, M.J. and Brender, W. (1986) Facial electromyography: A measure of affective processes during sexual arousal. *Psychophysiology*, 23, 182, 188.

Sullivan, M.W., Rovee-Collier, C. and Tynes, D.M. (1979) A conditioning analysis of infant long-term memory. *Child Development*, 50, 152–62.

Sullivan, R.M., Taborsky-Barba, S., Mendoza, R., Itano, A., Leon, M., Cotman, C.W., Payne, T.F. and Lott, I. (1991) Olfactory classical conditioning in neonates. *Pediatrics*, 87, 511–18.

Summala, H., Hakkanen, H., Mikkola, T. and Sinkkonen, J. (1999) Task effects on fatigue symptoms in overnight driving. *Ergonomics*, 42, 798–806.

Sundquist, K., Frank, G. and Sundquist, J. (2004) Urbanisation and incidence of psychosis and depression. *British Journal of Psychiatry*, 184, 293–8.

Sundstrom, E., Town, J.P. and Rice, R.W. (1994) Office noise, satisfaction and performance. *Environment and Behaviour*, 26, 195–222.

Sutherland, S. (1987) *Breakdown*. London: Wiedenfeld & Nicolson.

Sutton, J., Smith, P.K. and Swettenham, J. (1999) Social cognition and bullying: Social inadequacy or skilled manipulation? *British Journal of Developmental Psychology*, 17, 435–50.

Sutton, S.K. and Davidson, R.J. (2000) Prefrontal brain electrical asymmetry predicts the evaluation of affective stimuli. *Neuropsychologia*, 38, 1723–1733.

Suzdak, P.D., Glowa, J.R., Crawley, J.N., Schwartz, R.D., Skolnick, P. and Paul, S.M. (1986) A selective imidazobenzodiazepine antagonist of ethanol in the rat. *Science*, 234, 1243–1247.

Suzuki, L.A. and Valencia, R.R. (1997) Race-ethnicity and measured intelligence. *American Psychologist*, 52(10), 1103–1114.

Swaab, D.F., Bao, A-M. and Lucassen, P.J. (2005) The stress system in the human brain in depression and neurodegeneration. *Ageing Research Review*, 4, 141–94.

Tippin, J. and Henn, F.A. (1982) Modified leukotomy in the treatment of intractable obsessional neurosis. *American Journal of Psychiatry*, 139, 1601–1603.

Tobin, S.A. (1991) A comparison of psychoanalytic self-psychology and Carl Rogers's person-centered therapy. *Journal of Humanistic Psychology*, 31, 9–33.

Tolman, E.C., Ritchie, B.F. and Kalish, D. (1946) Studies in spatial learning: I. Orientation and the shortcut. *Journal of Experimental Psychology*, 36, 13–24.

Tomarken, A.J., Davidson, R.J. and Henriques, J.B. (1990) Resting frontal brain asymmetry predicts affective responses to films. *Journal of Personality and Social Psychology*, 59(4), 791–801.

Tomasello, M. and Farrar, J. (1986) Joint attention and early language. *Child Development*, 57, 1454–1463.

Tooby, J. and Cosmides, L. (1989) Evolutionary psychology and the generation of culture. Part I: Theoretical considerations. *Ethology and Sociobiology*, 10, 39–49.

Tooby, J. and Cosmides, L. (1990) On the universality of human nature and the uniqueness of the individual: The role of genetics and adaptation. *Journal of Personality*, 58, 17–67.

Tooby, J. and DeVore, I. (1987) The reconstruction of hominid behavioural evolution through strategic modelling. In G.W. Kinzey (ed.) *The Evolution of Human Behaviour: Primate models*. New York: SUNY Press.

Tootell, R.B., Reppas, J.B., Dale, A.M. and Look, R.B. (1995) Visual motion aftereffect in human cortical area MT revealed by functional magnetic resonance imaging. *Nature*, 375, 139–41.

Toplak, M.E., Connors, L., Shuster, J., Knezevic, B. and Parks, S. (2008) Review of cognitive, cognitive-behavioral, and neural-based interventions for Attention-Deficit/Hyperactivity Disorder. *Clinical Psychology Review*, 28, 801–23.

Topper, R., Mottaghy, F.M., Brugmann, M., Noth, J. and Huber, W. (1998) Facilitation of picture naming by focal transcranial magnetic stimulation of Wernicke's area. *Experimental Brain Research*, 121, 371–8.

Torgerson, S. (1983) Genetic factors in anxiety disorders. *Archives of General Psychiatry*, 40, 1085–1089.

Torrance, E.P. (1975) Creativity research in education: Still alive. In I.A. Taylor and J.W. Getzels (eds) *Perspectives in Creativity*. Chicago: Aldine.

Torrey, E.F., Torrey, B.B. and Peterson, M.R. (1977) Seasonality of schizophrenic births in the United States. *Archives of General Psychiatry*, 34, 1065–1070.

Torrey, E.F., Webster, M., Knable, M., Johnston, N. and Yolken, R.H. (2000) Foundation brain collection and Neuropathology Consortium. *Schizophrenia Research*, 44, 151–55.

Tourangeau, R. and Ellsworth, P.C. (1979) The role of facial response in the experience of emotion. *Journal of Personality and Social Psychology*, 37, 1519–1531.

Tourney, G. (1980) Hormones and homosexuality. In J. Marmor (ed.) *Homosexual Behavior*. New York: Basic Books.

Tovee, M.J. and Cornelissen, P.L. (2001) Female and male perceptions of female physical attractiveness in front-view and profile. *British Journal of Psychology*, 92, 391–402.

Trafimow, D., Triandis, H.C. and Goto, S.G. (1991) Some tests of the distinction between the private self and the collective self. *Journal of Personality and Social Psychology*, 60, 649–55.

Tramo, M.J. (2001) Music of the hemispheres. *Science*, 291, 54–6.

Tranel, D., Bechara, A. and Denburg, N.L. (2002) Asymmetric functional roles of right and left ventromedial prefrontal cortices in social conduct, decision-making, and emotional processing. *Cortex*, 38, 589–612.

Tranel, D. and Damasio, A.R. (1985) Knowledge without awareness: An autonomic index of facial recognition by prospopagnosics. *Science*, 30, 235–49.

Tranel, D., Damasio, A.R. and Damasio, H. (1988) Intact recognition of facial expression, gender and age in patients with impaired recognition of face identity. *Neurology*, 38, 690–6.

Tranel, D., Fowles, D.C., and Damasio, A.R. (1985) Electrodermal discrimination of familar and unfamiliar faces: A methodology. *Psychophysiology*, 22, 403–8.

Trapold, M.A. and Spence, K.W. (1960) Performance changes in eyelid conditioning as related to the motivational and reinforcing properties of the UCS. *Journal of Experimental Psychology*, 59, 212.

Travis, F. (1998) Cortical and cognitive development in 4th, 8th and 12th grade students. *Biological Psychology*, 48, 37–56.

Treffinger, D.J., Feldhusen, J.F. and Isaksen, S.G. (1990) Organization and structure of productive thinking. *Creative Learning Today*, 4(2), 6–8.

Treisman, A.M. (1960) Contextual cues in selective listening. *Quarterly Journal of Experimental Psychology*, 12, 242–8.

Treisman, A.M. (1964) Verbal cues, language, and meaning in selective attention. *American Journal of Psychology*, 77, 206–19.

Triandis, H.C. (1989) The self and social behavior in differing cultural contexts. *Psychological Review*, 96, 506–20.

Triandis, H.C., Leung, K., Villareal, M.J. and Clack, F.L. (1985) Allocentric versus idiocentric tendencies: Convergent and discriminant validation. *Journal of Research in Personality*, 19, 395–415.

Triplett, N. (1897) The dynamogenic factors in pacemaking and competition. *American Journal of Psychology*, 9, 507–533.

Trivers, R.L. (1971) The biology of reciprocal altruism. *Quarterly Review of Biology*, 46, 35–57.

Trivers, R L. (1972) Parental investment and sexual selection. In B. Campbell (ed.) *Sexual Selection and the Descent of Man*. Chicago: Aldine.

Troiano, R.P. and Flegal, K.M. (1998) Overweight children and adolescents: Description, epidemiology and demographics. *Pediatrics*, 101, 497–504.

Tronick, E., Als, H., Adamson, L., Wise, S. and Brazelton, T.B. (1978) The infant's response to entrapment between contradictory messages in face-to-face interaction. *Journal of the American Academy of Child Psychiatry*, 17, 1–13.

Trope, Y. (1986) Self-enhancement and self-assessment in achievement behavior. In R. Sorrentino and E.T. Higgins (eds) *Handbook of Motivation and Cognition*, Vol. 2. New York: Guilford Press, pp. 350–78.

Trope, Y. and Liberman, Y. (2003) Temporal construal. *Psychology Review*, 110, 403–21.

Trott, C.T., Friedman, D., Ritter, W. and Fabiani, M. (1997) Item and source memory: Differential age effects revealed by event-related potentials. *NeuroReport*, 8, 3373–3378.

Truax, C.B. (1966) Reinforcement and nonreinforcement in Rogerian psychotherapy. *Journal of Abnormal Psychology*, 71, 1–9.

Tryon, R. (1940) Genetic differences in maze-learning ability in rats. *Yearbook of the National Society for the Study of Education*, 39, 111–19.

Tseng, W.-S., Xu, N., Ebata, K., Hsu, J. and Cui, Y. (1986) Diagnostic pattern of neurosis among China, Japan and America. *American Journal of Psychiatry*, 143, 1010–1014.

Tseng, W.-S., Asai, M., Jiequi, L., Wibulswasd, P., Suryani, L.K., Wen, L-K., Brennan, J. and Hieby, E. (1990) Multicultural study of minor psychiatric disorders in Asia: Symptom manifestations. *International Journal of Social Psychiatry*, 36, 252–64.

Tseng, W.-S., Asai, M., Kitanishi, K., McLaughlin, D. and Kyomen, H. (1992) Diagnostic patterns of social phobia: Comparison in Tokyo and Hawaii. *Journal of Nervous and Mental Diseases*, 180, 380–5.

Tseng, W.-S., Lin, T.Y. and Yee, E. (1995) Concluding comments. In T.Y. Lin, W.-S. Tseng and E. Yee (eds) *Mental health in Chinese societies*. Hong Kong: Oxford University Press.

Tsukiura, T. and Cabeza, R. (2008) Orbitofrontal and hippocampal contributions to memory for face-name associations: The rewarding power of a smile. *Neuropsychologia*, 46, 2310–2319.

Tugade, M.M. and Fredrickson, B.L. (2004) Resilient individuals use positive emotions to bounce back from negative emotional experiences. *Journal of Personality and Social Psychology*, 86, 2, 320–33.

Tulving, E. (1972) Episodic and semantic memory. In E. Tulving and W. Donaldson (eds) *Organization of Memory*. New York: Academic Press.

Tulving, E. (1983) *Elements of Episodic Memory*. Oxford: Oxford University Press.

Tulving, E. (1984) Precis of 'Elements of Episodic Memory'. *The Behavioral and Brain Sciences*, 7, 223–68.

Tulving, E. and Arbuckle, T.Y. (1963) Sources of intratrial interference in immediate recall of paired associates. *Journal of Verbal Learning and Verbal Behaviour*, 1, 321–34.

Tulving, E., Kapur, S., Markowitsch, H.J., Craik, F.I. and Houle, S. (1994) Hemispheric encoding/retrieval asymmetry in episodic memory: positron emission tomography findings. *Proceedings of National Academy of Sciences* USA, 91, 2016–20.

Tung, H.H. and Carstensen, C.L. (2003) Sending memorable message to the old. *Journal of Personality and Social Psychology*, 85, 163–78.

Tupes, E.C. and Christal, R.E. (1961) Recurrent personality factors based on trait ratings. *USAF ASD Technical Report*, 61–97.

Turiel, E. (1998) The development of morality. In N. Eisenberg (ed.) *Handbook of Child Psychology, Vol. 3: Social, emotional and personality development*. New York: Wiley.

Turner, A.M. and Greenough, W.T. (1985) Differential rearing effects on rat visual cortex synapses. I. Synaptic and neuronal density and synapses per neuron. *Brain Research*, 329, 195–203.

Turner, J.C. (1991) *Social Influence*. Milton Keynes: Open University Press.

Turner, J.C., Hogg, M.A., Oakes, P.J., Reicher, S.D. and Wetherell, M.S. (1987) *Rediscovering the Social Group: A self-categorization theory*. Oxford: Blackwell.

Turner, J.C., Wetherell, M.S. and Hogg, M.A. (1989) Referent informational influence and group polarization. *British Journal of Social Psychology*, 28, 135–47.

Turner, J.R., Caroll, D. and Courtney, H. (1983) Cardiac and metabolic responses to 'Space Invaders': An instance of metabolically exaggerated cardiac adjustment? *Psychophysiology*, 20, 544–9.

Turner, P.J., Gervai, J. and Hinde, R.A. (1993) Gender-typing in young children: Preferences, behaviour and cultural differences. *British Journal of Developmental Psychology*, 11, 323–41.

Turner, S.M., Beidel, D.C. and Nathan, R.S. (1985) Biological factors in obsessive-compulsive disorders. *Psychological Bulletin*, 97, 430–50.

Tversky, A. and Kahneman, D. (1974) Judgment under uncertainty: Heuristics and biases. *Science*, 185, 1124–1131.

Tversky, A. and Kahneman, D. (1982) Judgment under uncertainty: Heuristics and biases. In D. Kahneman, P. Slovic and A. Tversky (eds) *Judgment under Uncertainty*. New York: Cambridge University Press.

Tversky, A. and Kahneman, D. (1983) Extensional versus intuitive reasoning: Conjunction fallacy in probability judgement. *Psychological Review*, 90, 293–315.

Twenge, J.M. (2001) Birth cohort changes in extraversion: A cross-temporal meta-analysis, 1966–1993. *Personality and Individual Differences*, 30, 735–48.

Tye-Murray, N., Spencer, L.and Woodworth, G.G. (1995) Acquisition of speech by children who have prolonged cochlear implant experience. *Journal of Speech and Hearing Research*, 38, 327–37.

Tyler, C.W. (1998) Painters centre one eye in portraits. *Nature*, 392, 877–8.

Tyler, T.R. and Smith, H.J. (1998) Social justice and social movements. In D.T. Gilbert, S.T. Fiske and G. Lindzey (eds) *The Handbook of Social Psychology* (4th edn), Vol. 2. New York: McGraw-Hill, pp. 595–632.

Tzeng, O.J.L. (1973) Positive recency effects in delayed free recall. *Journal of Verbal Learning and Verbal Behaviour*, 12, 436–9.

Udolf, R. (1983) *Forensic Hypnosis: Psychological and legal aspects*. Lexington, MA: Lexington Books.

Ueno, Y. (1993) Cross-cultural study of odor perception in Sherpa and Japanese people. *Chemical Senses*, 18, 352–3.

Uher, R., Brammer, M., Murphy, T., Campbell, I., Ng, V. Williams, S. *et al.* (2003) Recovery and chronicity in anorexia nervosa: brain activity associated with differential outcomes. *Biological Psychiatry*, 54, 934–42.

Ullian, E.M., Sapperstein, S.K., Christopherson, K.S. and Barres, B.A. (2001) Control of synapse number by glia. *Science*, 291, 657–60.

Ullman, L.P. and Krasner, L. (1969) *Psychological Approach to Abnormal Behavior*. Englewood Cliffs, NJ: Prentice Hall.

Ulusahin, A., Basoglu, M. and Paykel, E.S. (1994) A cross-cultural comparative study of depressive symptoms in British and Turkish clinical samples. *Social Psychiatry and Psychiatric Epidemiology*, 29, 31–9.

Umilta, C., Simion, F. and Valenza, E. (1996) Newborns' preference for faces. *European Psychologist*, 1(3), 200–5.

Ungerleider, L.G. and Mishkin, M. (1982) Two cortical visual systems. In D.J. Ingle, M.A. Goodale and R.J.W. Mansfield (eds) *Analysis of Visual Behavior*. Cambridge, MA: MIT Press.

United Nations Joint Programme on AIDS (1996) http://www.unaids.org/about/evaluation/files/EOI.doc

Uotinen, V. (1998) Age identification: A comparison between Finnish and North-American cultures. *International Journal of Aging and Human Development*, 46(2), 109–25.

Upton, D. and Cooper, C.D. (2001) Online health psychology: Do students need it, use it, like it and want it? *Psychology Learning and Teaching*, 3, 1, 27–35.

Urry, H.L., Nitschke, J.B., Dolski, I., Jackson, D.C., Dalton, K.M., Mueller, C.J., Rosenkranz, M.A., Ryff, C.D., Singer, B.H. and Davidson, R.J. (2004) Making a life worth living: neural correlates of well-being. *Psychological Science*, 15, 6, 367–72.

Utter, A.A. and Basso, M.A. (2008) The basal ganglia: An overview of circuits and function. *Neuroscience and Biobehavioural Reviews*, 32, 333–42.

US Bureau of Labor Statistics (1998) *National census of fatal occupational injuries, 1997 (USDL 98–336)* Washington, DC: Department of Labor.

Vaananen, A., Buunk, B.P., Kivimaki, M., Pentti, J. and Vahtera, J. (2005) When it is better to give than to receive: Long-term health effects of perceived reciprocity in support exchange. *Journal of Personality and Social Psychology*, 89, 2, 176–93.

Valenza, E., Simion, F., Cassia, V.M. and Umilta, C. (1996) Face preference at birth. *Journal of Experimental Psychology: Human Perception and Performance*, 27(4), 892–903.

Valins, S. and Nisbett, R.E. (1972) Attribution processes in the development and treatment of emotional disorders. In E.E. Jones, D.E. Kanouse, H.H. Kelley, R.E. Nisbett, S. Valins and B. Weiner (eds) *Attribution: Perceiving the causes of behavior*. Morristown, NJ: General Learning Press, pp. 137–50.

Valkenburg, P.M. and Peter, J. (2009) Social consequences of the internet for adolescents. *Current Directions in Psychological Science*, 18, 1, 1–5.

Vallar, G. (1998) Spatial hemineglect in humans. *Trends in Cognitive Sciences*, 2(3), 87–97.

Van Anders, S.M. and Watson, N.V. (2006) Testosterone levels in women and men who are single, in long-distance relationships, or same-city relationships. *Hormones and Behavior*, 51, 286–91.

Van Baal, G.C.M., van Beijsterveldt, C.E.M., Molenaar, P.C.M., Boomsma, D.I. and de Geus, E.J.C. (2001) A genetic perspective on the developing brain. *European Psychologist*, 6(4), 254–63.

Van Beek, Y., Hopkins, B. and Joeksma, J.B. (1994) Development of communicative behaviours in preterm infants: The effect of birthweight status and gestational age. *Infant Behavior and Development*, 17, 107–18.

Vandell, D.L. (2000) Parents, peer groups, and other socializing influences. *Developmental Psychology*, 36, 699–710.

Van den Eijnden, R.J.J.M., Meerkerk, G-J., Vermulst, A.A., Spijkerman, R. and Engels, R.C.M.E. (2008) Online communication, compulsive internet use, and psychosocial well-being among adolescents: A longitudinal study. *Developmental Psychology*, 44, 3, 655–65.

Vandenberghe, R., Duncan, J., Dupont, P., Ward, R (1997) Attention to 1 or 2 features in left or right visual field: A PET study. *Journal of Neuroscience*, 17, 10, 3739–50.

Vanderschuren, L.J. and Everitt, B.J. (2004) Drug seeking becomes compulsive after prolonged cocaine self-administration. *Science*, 305, 1017–1019.

van Dijk, T.A. (1987) *Communicating Racism: ethnic prejudice in thought and talk*. Newbury Park, CA: Sage.

Van Drunen, P. (1995) Professional psychology in The Netherlands. In A. Schorr and S. Saari (eds) *Psychology in Europe*. Göttingen: Hogrefe & Huber.

Van Goozen, S.H.M., Cohen-Kettenis, P.T., Gooren, L.J.G., Frijda, N.A. and Van De Poll, N.E. (1995) Gender differences in behaviour: Activating effects of cross-sex hormones. *Psychoneuroendocrinology*, 20, 343–63.

Van Herk, H., Poortinga, Y.H. and Verhallen, T.M.M. (2005) Response styles in rating scales: evidence of method bias in data from six EU countries. *Journal of Cross-Cultural Psychology*, 35, 3, 346–60.

van Knippenberg, B. and van Knippenberg, D. (2003) Leadership, identity, and influence: Relational concerns in the use of influence tactics. In D. van Knippenberg and M.A. Hogg (eds) *Leadership and Power: Identity processes in groups and organizations*. London: Sage, pp. 123–37.

Vanlancker-Sidtis, D. (2004) When only the right hemisphere is left: Studies in language and communication. *Brain and Language*, 91, 199–211.

Vanneman, R.D. and Pettigrew, T.F. (1972) Race and relative deprivation in the urban United States. *Race*, 13, 461–86.

Van Petten, C. and Kutas, M. (1990) Interaction between sentence context and word frequency in event-related brain potentials. *Memory and Cognition*, 18, 380–93.

Van Velzen, C.J.M. and Emmelkamp, P.M.G. (1996) The assessment of personality disorders: Implications for cognitive and behavior therapy. *Behaviour Research and Therapy*, 34(8), 655–68.

Van Wijnendaele, I. and Brysbaert, M. (2002) Visual word recognition in bilinguals: Phonological priming from the second to the first language. *Journal of Experimental Psychology: Human Perception and Performance*, 28(3), 616–27.

Vargha-Khadem, F., O'Gorman, A. and Watters, G. (1985) Aphasia and handedness in relation to hemispheric side, age at injury and severity of cerebral lesions during childhood. *Brain*, 108, 677–96.

Varnik, A., Kolves, K. and Wasserman, D. (2005) Suicide among Russians in Estonia: Database study before and after independence. *British Medical Journal*, 330, 176–7.

Vaughan, E. (1977) Misconceptions about psychology among psychology students. *Teaching of Psychology*, 4, 138–41.

Vaughan, T.M., McFarland, D.J., Schalk, G. *et al.* (2006) The Wadsworth BCI research and development program: at home with BCI. *IEEE Transactions of Neural Systems Rehabilitation Engineering*, 14, 229–33.

Vecera, S.P. and Farah, M.J. (1994) Does visual attention select objects or locations? *Journal of Experimental Psychology*, 123, 146–60.

Veljaca, V-A. and Rapee, R.M. (1998) Detection of negative and positive audience behaviours by socially anxious subjects. *Behaviour Research and Therapy*, 36, 311–21.

Venter, A., Lord, C. and Schopler, E. (1992) A follow-up study of high-functioning autistic children. *Journal of Child and Adolescent Psychiatry*, 33, 646–9.

Verheul, R. and Widiger, T.A. (2004) A meta-analysis of the prevalence and usage of the personality disorder not otherwise specified (PDNOS) diagnosis. *Journal of Personality Disorders*, 18, 309–19.

Verkuyten, M. (2001) National identification and intergroup evaluations in Dutch children. *British Journal of Developmental Psychology*, 19, 559–71.

Vernon, P.E. (1989) The nature–nurture problem in creativity. In J.A. Glover, R.R. Ronning and C.R. Reynolds (eds) *Handbook of Creativity*. New York: Plenum Press.

Vervaeke, G.A.C. and Emmelkamp, P.M.G. (1998) Treatment selection: What do we know? *European Journal of Psychological Assessment*, 14(1), 50–59.

Vescio, T.K., Gervais, S.J. Snyder, M. and Hoover, A. (2005) Power and the creation of patronizing environments: The stereotype-based behaviours of the powerful and their effects on female performance in masculine domains.

Vicari, S., Albertoni, A., Chilosi, A.M., Cipriani, P., Cioni, G. and Bates, E. (2000) Plasticity and reorganization during language development in children with early brain injury. *Cortex*, 36, 31–46.

Vidmar, N., Beale, S.S., Rose, M. and Donnelly, L.F. (1997) Should we rush to reform the criminal jury? Consider conviction rate data. *Judicature*, 80, 286–90.

Vidyasagar, T.R. and Pammer, K. (1999) Impaired visual search in dyslexia relates to the role of the magnocellular pathway in attention. *NeuroReport*, 10, 1283–1287.

Vignoles, V.L., Chryssochoou, X. and Breakwell, G.M. (2002) Evaluating models of identity motivation: Self-esteem is not the whole story. *Self and Identity*, 1, 3, 201–18.

Villemure, C. and Bushnell, M.C. (2007) The effects of the steroid androstadienone and pleasant odorants on the mood and the pain perception of men and women. *European Journal of Pain*, 11, 181–91.

Vincent, C. and Furnham, A. (1996) Why do patients turn to complementary medicine? An empirical study. *British Journal of Clinical Psychology*, 35, 37–48.

Visser, P.S. and Krosnick, J.A. (1998) Development of attitude strength over the life cycle: Surge and decline. *Journal of Personality and Social Psychology*, 75, 1389–1410.

Visser, G. and Peters, L. (1990) Alternative medicine and general practitioners in the Netherlands: Towards acceptance and integration. *Family Practitioner*, 7, 227–32.

Vitaliano, P.P., Zhang, J. and Scanlan, J.M. (2003) Is caregiving hazardous to one's physical health? A mata-analysis. *Psychological Bulletin*, 129, 6, 946–72.

Voets, N.L., Adcock, J.E., Flitney, D.E., Behrens, T.E.J., Hart, Y., Stacey, R., Carpenter, K. and Matthews, P.M. (2006) Distinct right frontal lobe activation in language processing following left hemisphere injury. *Brain*, 129, 754–66.

Vogel, J.L., Bowers, C.A. and Vogel, D.S. (2003) Cerebral lateralization of spatial abilities: A meta-analysis. *Brain and Cognition*, 52, 197–204.

von Békésy, G. (1960) *Experiments in Hearing*. New York: McGraw-Hill.

Von Cramon, D. and Kerkhoff, G. (1993) On the cerebral organization of elementary visuospatial perception. In B. Gulyas, D. Ottoson and P.E. Roland (eds) *Functional Organisation of the Human Visual Cortex*. Oxford: Pergamon Press.

Von Glinow, M., Shapiro, D.L. and Brett, J.M. (2004) Can we talk, and should we? Managing emotional conflict in multicultural teams. *Academy of Management Review*, 29, 578–92.

von Stumm, S., Chamorro-Premuzic, T. and Furnham, A. (2009) Decomposing self-estimates of intelligence: Structure and sex differences across 12 nations. *British Journal of Psychology*, 100, 429–42.

Von Wright, J.M., Anderson, K. and Stenman, U. (1975) Generalization of conditioned GSRs in dichotic listening. In P.M.A. Rabbitt and S. Dornic (eds) *Attention and Performance*, Vol. 5. London: Academic Press.

Vrij, A. (2000) *Detecting Lies and Deceit: The psychology of lying and the implications for professional practice*. Chichester: Wiley.

Vrij, A. (2001) Detecting the liars. *The Psychologist*, 14(11), 596–8.

Vrij, A. (2004a) Guidelines to catch a liar. In P-A. Granhag and L. Stromwall (eds), *The Detection of Deception in Forensic Contexts*. Cambridge: Cambridge University Press.

Vrij, A. (2004b) Why professionals fail to catch liars and how they can improve. *Legal and Criminological Psychology*, 9, 159–81.

Vrij, A. and Mann, S. (2001) Who killed my relative? Police officers' ability to detect real-life high stake lies. *Psychology, Crime and Law*, 7, 119–32.

Vul, E., Harris, C., Winkielman, P. and Pashler, H. (2009) Voodoo correlations in social neuroscience. *Perspectives in Psychological Science*, in press.

Vygotsky, L. (1976/1933) *Mind and Society: The development of higher mental processes*. Cambridge, MA: Harvard University Press.

Vygotsky, L. (1934/1962) *Thinking and Speaking*. Cambridge, MA: Harvard University Press.

Vygotsky, L.S. (1976) Play and its role in the mental development of the child. In J.S. Bruner, A. Jolly and K. Sylva (eds) *Play*. Harmondsworth: Penguin.

Vygotsky, L.S. (1987) Thinking and speech. In R.W. Rieber and A.S. Carton (eds) *The Collected Works of L.S. Vygotsky. Vol. 1: Problems of General Psychology* (N. Minick, trans.). New York: Plenum. Original work published in 1934.

 W

Wadden, T.A., Brownell, K.D. and Foster, G.D. (2002) Obesity: Responding to the growing epidemic. *Journal of Consulting and Clinical Psychology*, 70(3), 510–25.

Wade, G.N. and Gray, J.M. (1979) Gonadal effects on food intake and adiposity: A metabolic hypothesis. *Physiology and Behavior*, 22, 583–93.

Wade, T.J., Fuller, L., Bresnan, J., Schaefer, S. and Mlynarski, L. (2007) Weight halo effects: individual differences in personality evaluations and perceived life success of men as a function of weight. *Personality and Individual Differences*, 42, 317–24.

Wager, T.D., Rilling, J.K., Smith. E.E., Sokolik, A., Casey, K.L., Davidson, R.J., Kosslyn, S.M., Rose, R.M. and Cohen, J.D. (2004) Placebo-induced changes in fMRI in the anticipation and experience of pain. *Science*, 303, 5661, 1162–1167.

Wagner, A., Aizenstein, H., Mazurkewicz, L., Fudge, J., Frank, G.K., Putnam, K., Bailer, U.F., Fischer, L. and Kaye, W.H. (2008) Altered insula response to taste stimuli in individuals recovered from restricting-type anorexia nervosa. *Neuropsychopharmacology*, 33, 513–23.

Wagner, A.R., Siegal, S., Thomas, E. and Ellison, G.D. (1964) Reinforcement history and the extinction of a conditioned salivary response. *Journal of Comparative and Physiological Psychology*, 58, 354–8.

Wagstaff, G.F. (1987) Hypnotic induction, hypnotherapy and the placebo effect. *British Journal of Experimental and Clinical Hypnosis*, 4, 168–70.

Wagstaff, G.F. (1991) Compliance, belief and semantics in hypnosis: A nonstate, sociocognitive perspective. In S.J. Lynn and J.H. Rhue (eds) *Theories of Hypnosis: Current models and perspectives*. New York: Guilford Press.

Wagstaff, G.F. (1993) What expert witnesses can tell courts about hypnosis: A review of the association between hypnosis and the law. *Expert Evidence: The international digest of human behaviour science and law*, 2, 60–70.

Wagstaff, G.F. (1996) Methodological issues in hypnosis. In J. Haworth (ed.) *Psychological Research*. London: Routledge.

Wagstaff, G.F. and Royce, C. (1994) Hypnosis and the treatment of nailbiting: A preliminary trial. *Contemporary Hypnosis*, 11, 9–13.

Wakefield, J.C. (2001) The myth of DSM's invention of new categories of disorder: Houts's diagnostic discontinuity thesis disconfirmed. *Behaviour Research and Therapy*, 39, 575–624.

Walker, E. and Lewine, R.J. (1990) Prediction of adult-onset schizophrenia from childhood home movies of the patients. *American Journal of Psychiatry*, 147, 1052–1056.

Walker, L.J. (1989) A longitudinal study of moral reasoning. *Child Development*, 60, 157–66.

Walker, L.J., de Vries, B. and Trevethen, S.D. (1987) Moral stages and moral orientations in real-life and hypothetical dilemmas. *Child Development*, 58, 842–58.

Walker, M.P. *et al.* (2002) Practice with sleep makes perfect: sleep dependent motor skill learning. *Neuron*, 35, 205–11.

Walker, M.P. *et al* (2003) Sleep and the time course of motor skill learning. *Learning and Memory*, 10, 275–84.

Wallach, M. and Kogan, N. (1965) *Modes of Thinking in Young Children*. New York: Holt, Rinehart & Winston.

Wallen, K. (1990) Desire and ability: Hormones and the regulation of female sexual behavior. *Neuroscience and Biobehavioral Reviews*, 14, 233–41.

Wallen, K., Mann, D.R., Davis-DaSilva, M., Gaventa, S., Lovejoy, J.C. and Collins, D.C. (1986) Chronic gonadotropin-releasing hormone agonist treatment suppresses ovulation and sexual behavior in group-living female rhesus monkeys (*Macaca mulatta*). *Animal Behaviour*, 36, 369–75.

Wallentin, M. (2009) Putative sex differences in verbal abilities and language cortex: A critical review. *Brain and Language*, 108, 175–83.

Walsh, S. and Jackson, P.R. (1995) Partner support and gender: Contexts for coping with job loss. *Journal of Occupational and Organizational Psychology*, 68, 253–68.

Whitehead, R.G., Rowland, M.G.M., Hutton, M., Prentice, A.M., Müller, E. and Paul, A. (1978) Factors influencing lactation performance in rural Gambian mothers. *Lancet*, 2, 178–81.

Whiteman, M.C., Deary, I.J., Lee, A.J. and Fowkes, F.G.R. (1997) Submissiveness and protection from coronary heart disease in the general population: Edinburgh Artery Study. *Lancet*, 350, 541–5.

Whitney, I. and Smith, P.K. (1993) A survey of the nature and extent of bullying in junior/middle and secondary schools. *Educational Research*, 35, 3–25.

Whorf, B.L. (1956) Science and linguistics. In J.B. Carroll (ed.) *Language, Thought and Reality: Selected writings of Benjamin Lee Whorf*. Cambridge, MA: MIT Press.

Wichstrom, L. (1999) The emergence of gender difference in depressed mood during adolescence: The role of intensified gender socialization. *Developmental Psychology*, 35(1), 232–45.

Wicker, A.W. (1969) Attitudes versus actions: The relationship of verbal and overt behavioral responses to attitude objects. *Journal of Social Issues*, 25, 41–78.

Widaman, K.F. (2009) Phenylketonuria in children and mothers. *Current Directions in Psychological Science*, 18, 1, 48–52.

Widiger, T.A. and Samuel, D.B. (2005) Diagnostic categories or dimensions? A question for the Diagnostic and Statistical Manual of Mental Disorders, Fifth edn. *Journal of Abnormal Psychology*, 114, 5, 494–504.

Widiger, T.A. and Trull, T.J. (2007) Plate tectonics in the classification of personality disorder. *American Psychologist*, 62, 2, 71–83.

Widom, C.S. (1978) A methodology for studying non-institutionalized psychopaths. In R.D. Hare and D. Schalling (eds) *Psychopathic Behaviour: Approaches to research*. Chichester: Wiley.

Wiederman, M.W. (1997) Extramarital sex: Prevalence and correlates in a national survey. *Journal of Sex Research*, 34, 167–74.

Wieselquiest, J., Rusbult, C.E., Foster, C.A. and Agnew, C.R. (1999) Commitment, pro-relationship behavior, and trust in close relationships. *Journal of Personality and Social Psychology*, 77, 942–66.

Wilbanks, W. (1984) *Murder in Miami*. Lanham, MD: University Press of America.

Wilcoxon, H.C., Dragoin, W.B. and Kral, P.A. (1971) Illness-induced aversions in rat and quail: Relative salience of visual and gustatory cues. *Science*, 171, 826–8.

Wilensky, A.E., Schafe, G.E. and LeDoux, J.E. (1999) The amygdala modulates memory consolidation of fear-motivated inhibitory avoidance learning but not classicial fear conditioning. *Journal of Neuroscience*, 20, 7059–7066.

Wilhelm, F.H. and Roth, W.T. (1997) Clinical characteristics of flight phobia. *Journal of Anxiety Disorders*, 11, 241–61.

Wilhite, S.C. (1991) Evidence of a negative environmental reinstatement effect. *British Journal of Psychology*, 82, 325–42.

Wilkes, K.V. (1988) Information, physics, quantum: The search for links. In W. Zurek (ed.) *Complexity, Entropy and the Physics of Information*. Redwood City, CA: Addison-Wesley.

Wilkinson, S. and Kitzinger, C. (2008) Conversation analysis. In C. Willig and W. Stainton-Rogers (eds) *The Sage Handbook of Qualitative Research in Psychology*. London: Sage.

Will, J.A., Self, P.A. and Datan, N. (1976) Maternal behaviour and perceived sex of infant. *American Journal of Orthopsychiatry*, 46, 135–9.

Willemsen, M.C. and de Zwart, W.M. (1999) The effectiveness of policy and health education strategies for reducing adolescent smoking: A review of the evidence. *Journal of Adolescence*, 22, 587–99.

Williams, J.D., Rippon, G., Stone, B.M. and Annett, J. (1995) Psychophysiological correlates of dynamic imagery. *British Journal of Psychology*, 86(12), 283–300.

Williams, J.H. *et al.* (2004) A systematic review of action imitation in autistic spectrum disorder. *Journal of Autism and Developmental Disorders*, 34, 285–99.

Williams, J.M. and Dunlop, L.C. (1999) Pubertal timing and self-reported delinquency among male adolescents. *Journal of Adolescence*, 22, 157–71.

Williams, K.D. (2001) *Ostracism: The power of silence*. New York: Guilford Press.

Williams, K.D., Cheung, C.K.T. and Choi, W. (2000) Cyberostracism: Effects of being ignored over the internet. *Journal of Personality and Social Psychology*, 79, 748–62.

Williams, K.D., Harkins, S.G. and Karau, S.J. (2003) Social performance. In M.A. Hogg and J. Cooper (eds) *The Sage Handbook of Social Psychology*. London: Sage.

Williams, K.D., Harkins, S. and Latané, B. (1981) Identifiability as a deterrent to social loafing: Two cheering experiments. *Journal of Personality and Social Psychology*, 40, 303–11.

Williams, K.D., Karau, S.J. and Bourgeois, M. (1993) Working on collective tasks: Social loafing and social compensation. In M.A. Hogg and D. Abrams (eds) *Group Motivation: Social psychological perspectives*. London: Harvester Wheatsheaf, pp. 130–48.

Williams, K.D. and Sommer, K.L. (1997) Social ostracism by one's co-workers: Does rejection lead to loafing or compensation? *Personality and Social Psychology Bulletin*, 23, 693–706.

Williams, L.E. and Bargh, J.A. (2008) Keeping one's distance: The influence of spatial distance cues on affect and evaluation. *Psychological Science*, 19, 3, 302–8.

Williams, R.B., Hanel, T.L., Lee, K.L. and Kong, Y.H. (1980) Type A behavior, hostility, and coronary atherosclerosis. *Psychosomatic Medicine*, 42, 539–49.

Williams, W., Blythe, T., White, N., Li, J., Sternberg, R.J. and Gardner, H. (1996) *Practical Intelligence for School Handbook*. New York: HarperCollins.

Wills, G.I. (2003) Forty lives in the bebop business: Mental health in a group of eminent jazz musicians. *British Journal of Psychiatry*, 183, 255–9.

Wilson, A.E. and Ross, M. (2001) From chump to champ: People's appraisals of their earlier and present selves. *Journal of Personality and Social Psychology*, 80, 572–84.

Wilson, B.A. (1991) Long-term prognosis of patients with severe memory disorders. *Neuropsychological Rehabilitation*, 1, 117–34.

Wilson, B.A. (1995) Rehabilitation. In J.G. Beaumont, P.M. Kenealy and M.J.C. Rogers (eds) *Blackwell Dictionary of Neuropsychology*. Oxford: Blackwell.

Wilson, B.A., J.C. and Hughes, E. (1997) In A.J. Parkin (ed.) *Case Studies in the Neuropsychology of Memory*. Hove: Psychology Press.

Wilson, B.A. and Powell, G.E. (1994) Neurological problems: Treatment and rehabilitation. In S.J.E. Lindsey and G.E. Powell (eds) *Handbook of Clinical Adult Psychology*. London: Routledge.

Wilson, C., Nairn, R., Coverdale, J. and Panapa, A. (2000) How mental illness is portrayed in children's television. *British Journal of Psychiatry*, 176, 440–3.

Wilson, E.O. (1975) *Sociobiology: The new synthesis*. Cambridge, MA: Harvard University Press.

Wilson, E.O. (1978) *On Human Nature*. Cambridge, MA: Harvard University Press.

Wilson, M., Daly, M. and Wright, C. (1993) Uxoricide in Canada: demographic risk patterns. *Canadian Journal of Criminology*, 35, 263–91.

Wilson, M., Johnson, H. and Daly, M. (1995) Lethal and nonlethal violence against wives. *Canadian Journal of Criminology*, 37, 331–61.

Wilson, P. and Provost, S. (2006) Psychology in Australian universities. *International Journal of Psychology*, 41, 1, 3–9.

Wilson, P.N., Foreman, N. and Stanton, D. (1999) Improving spatial awareness in physically disabled children using virtual environments. *Engineering Science and Education Journal*, 8(5), 196–200.

Wilson, P.N., Foreman, N. and Tlauka, M. (1996a) Transfer of spatial information from a virtual to a real environment in able-bodied adults and disabled children. *Disability and Rehabilitation*, 18, 633–7.

Wilson, R.S., Sullivan, E.V., de Toledo-Morrell, L., Stebbins, G.T., Bennett, D.A. and Morrell, F. (1996) Association of memory and cognition in Alzheimer's disease with volumetric estimates of temporal lobe structures. *Neuropsychology*, 10, 459–63.

Winberg, J. and Porter, R.H. (1998) Olfaction and human neonatal behaviour: Clinical implications. *Acta Paediatrica*, 87, 6–10.

Winch, R. (1958) *Mate Selection: A study of complementary needs*. New York: Harper & Row.

Winchester, A.M. (1972) *Genetics: A survey of the principles of heredity*. Boston: Houghton Mifflin.

Windholz, G. (1997) Ivan P. Pavlov. *American Psychologist*, 52(9), 941–6.

Winefield, A.H. and Tiggemann, M. (1994) Affective reactions to employment and unemployment as a function of prior expectations and motivation. *Psychological Reports*, 75, 243–7.

Wing, R.R. (2002) Behavioural weight control. In T.A. Wadden and A.J. Stunkard (eds) *Handbook of Obesity Treatment*. New York: Guilford Press.

Winman, A. (2004) Do perfume additives termed human pheromones warrant being termed pheromones? *Physiology and Behavior*, 82, 697–701.

Winner, E. (1996) *Gifted Children: Myths and realities*. New York: Basic Books.

Winner, E. (1997) Exceptionally high intelligence and schooling. *American Psychologist*, 52(10), 1070–1081.

Winner, E., von Karolyi, C., Malinsky, D., French, L., Seliger, C., Ross, E. and Weber, C. (2001) Dyslexia and visual-spatial talents: Compensation vs deficit model. *Brain and Language*, 76, 81–110.

Winograd, E. and Killinger, W.A. (1983) Relating age at encoding in early childhood to adult recall: Development of flashbulb memories. *Journal of Experimental Psychology: General*, 112, 413–22.

Wise, R.J.S., Scott, S.K., Blank, C., Mummery, C.J., Murphy, K. and Warburton, E.A. (2001) Separate neural subsystems within 'Wernicke's area'. *Brain*, 124, 83–95.

Wiseman, R. and Watt, C. (2006) Belief in psychic ability and the misattribution hypothesis: A qualitative review. *British Journal of Psychology*, 97, 323–38.

Witelson, S.F., Glezer, I.I. and Kigar, D.L. (1995) Women have greater density of neurons in posterior temporal cortex. *Journal of Neuroscience*, 15, 3418–3428.

Witter, R.A., Stock, W.A., Okun, M.A. and Haring, M.J. (1985) Religion and subjective well-being in adulthood: a quantitative synthesis. *Review of Religious Research*, 26, 332–42.

Witvliet, C.V., Ludwig, T.E. and Vander Laan, K.L. (2001) Granting forgiveness or harbouring grudges: Implications for emotion, physiology and health. *Psychological Science*, 12(2), 117–23.

Woerner, P.L. and Guze, S.B. (1968) A family and marital study of hysteria. *British Journal of Psychiatry*, 114, 161–8.

Wolff, P.H. (1969) Crying and vocalization in early infancy. In B.M. Foss (ed.) *Determinants of Infant Behaviour*, Vol. 4. London: Methuen.

Wolpe, J. (1958) *Psychotherapy by Reciprocal Inhibition*. Stanford, CA: Stanford University Press.

Wood, C. and Cowan, N. (1995) The cocktail party phenomenon revisited: How frequent are attention shifts to one's name in an irrelevant auditory channel? *Journal of Experimental Psychology: Learning, Memory and Cognition*, 21, 255–60.

Wood, R.J., Rolls, B.J. and Ramsey, D.L. (1977) Drinking following intracarotid infusions of hypertonic solutions in dogs. *American Journal of Physiology*, 232, R88–R92.

Wood, R.L.I. and Rutterford, N.A. (2004) Relationships between measured cognitive ability and reported psychosocial activity after bilateral frontal lobe injury: An 18–year follow-up. *Neuropsychological Rehabilitation*, 14, 3, 329–50.

Wood, W. and Eagly, A.H. (2002) A cross-cultural analysis of the behaviour of women and men: Implications for the origins of sex differences. *Psychological Bulletin*, 128, 5, 699–727.

Woodall, K.L. and Matthews, K.A. (1993) Changes in and stability of hostile characteristics: Results from a 4–year longitudinal study of children. *Journal of Personality and Social Psychology*, 63, 491–9.

Woodcock, A. and Custovic, A. (1998) ABC of allergies: Avoiding exposure to indoor allergens. *British Medical Journal*, 316, 1075–1078.

Woodman, R.W. and Schoenfeldt, L.F. (1989) Individual differences in creativity: An interactionist perspective. In J.A. Glover, R.R. Ronning and C.R. Reynolds (eds) *Handbook of Creativity*. New York: Plenum Press.

Woodruff, R.A., Guze, S.B. and Clayton, P.J. (1972) Anxiety neurosis among psychiatric outpatients. *Comprehensive Psychiatry*, 13, 165–70.

Woodruff-Pak, D.S. (1997) *The Neuropsychology of Aging*. Oxford: Blackwell.

Woods, B.T. (1980) The restricted effects of right-hemisphere lesions after age one: Wechsler test data. *Neuropsychologia*, 18, 65–70.

Woods, R.T. (1994) Problems in the elderly. In S.J.E. Lindsey and G.E. Powell (eds) *Handbook of Clinical Adult Psychology*. London: Routledge.

Woods, S.C. *et al.* (2006) Pancreatic signals controlling food intake: insulin, glucagons and amylin. *Philosophical Transactions of the Royal Society of London B Biological Sciences*, 361, 1219–1235.

Woods, S.W., Charney, D.S., Goodman, W.K. and Heninger, G.R. (1988) Carbon dioxide-induced anxiety. *Archives of General Psychiatry*, 45, 43–52.

Woolley, J.D. (1997) Thinking about fantasy: Are children fundamentally different thinkers and believers from adults? *Child Development*, 68(6), 991–1011.

Worchel, F.F., Aaron, L.L. and Yates, D.F. (1990) Gender bias on the Thematic Apperception Test. *Journal of Personality Assessment*, 55, 593–602.

World Health Organization (1979) *Schizophrenia: An international follow-up study*. Geneva: WHO.

World Health Organization (1983) *Depressive disorders in different cultures: Report of the WHO collaborative study of standardised assessment of depressive disorders*. Geneva: WHO.

World Health Organization (1992) *The ICD-10 Classification of Mental and Behavioural Disorders: Clinical descriptions and diagnostic guidelines*. Geneva: WHO.

World Health Oganization (1998) *Obesity: Preventing and managing the global epidemic*. Geneva: WHO.

World Health Organization (2002a) *The Tobacco Atlas*. http://www.who.it/tobacco/statistics/tobacco_atlas/en/.

World Health Organization (2002b) *The World Health Report 2002: Reducing risks, promoting healthy life*. Geneva: WHO.

Wortman, C.B., Silver, R.C. and Kessler, R.C. (1993) The meaning of loss and adjustment to bereavement. In M.S. Stroebe, W. Stroebe and R.O. Hansson (eds) *Handbook of Bereavement: Theory, research and intervention*. Cambridge: Cambridge University Press.

Wright, B.A., Lombardino, L.J., King, W.M., Puranik, C.S., Leonard, C.M. and Merzenich, M.M. (1997) Deficits in auditory temporal and spectral resolution in language-impaired children. *Nature*, 387, 176–8.

Wright, D.B. (1993) Recall of the Hillsborough disaster over time: Systematic biases of 'flashbulb' memories. *Applied Cognitive Psychology*, 7, 129–38.

Wright, D.B., Gaskell, G.D. and O'Muircheartaigh, C.A. (1998) Flashbulb memory assumptions: Using national surveys to explore cognitive phenomena. *British Journal of Psychology*, 89, 103–22.

Wright, S.C., Aron, A., McLaughlin-Volpe, T. and Ropp, S.A. (1997) The extended contact effect: Knowledge of cross-group friendships and prejudice. *Journal of Personality and Social Psychology*, 73, 73–90.

Wycherley, R.J. (1995) Self-evaluation and self-reinforcement in depressed patients. *Clinical Psychology and Psychotherapy*, 2, 98–107.

Wynn, V.E. and Logie, R.H. (1998) The veracity of long-term memory: Did Bartlett get it right? *Applied Cognitive Psychology*, 12, 1–20.

Yabuta, N.H., Sawatari, A. and Callaway, E.M. (2001) Two functional channels from primary visual cortex to dorsal visual cortical areas. *Science*, 292, 297–300.

Yamagata, S., Suzuki, A., Ando, J., One, Y., Kijima, N., Yoshimura, K. *et al.* (2006) Is the genetic structure of human personality universal? A cross-cultural twin study from North American, Europe and Asia. *Journal of Personality and Social Psychology*, 90, 987–98.

Yanovski, S.Z. and Yanovski, J. (2002) Obesity. *New England Journal of Medicine*, 346, 591–602.

Yardley, L., McDermott, L., Pisarski, S., Duchaine, B. and Nakayama, K. (2008) Psychosocial consequences of developmental prosopagnosia: A problem of recognition. *Journal of Psychosomatic Research*, 65, 445–51.

Yates, W.R., Perry, P. and Murray, S. (1992) Aggression and hostility in anabolic steroid users. *Biological Psychiatry*, 31, 1232–1234.

Yu-Huan, H., Ying-Guan, Q. and Gui-Quing, Z. (1990) Crossed aphasia in Chinese: A clinical survey. *Brain and Language*, 39, 347–56.

Yossifova, M. and Loewenthal, K.M. (1999) Religion and the judgement of obsessionality. *Mental Health, Religion and Culture*, 2, 145–51.

Young, A., Stokes, M. and Crowe, M. (1984) Size and strength of the quadriceps muscles of old and young women. *European Journal of Clinical Investigation*, 14, 282–7.

Young, A.H. and Newham, J.I. (2006) Lithium in maintenance therapy for bipolar disorder. *Journal of Psychopharmacology*, 20, 2, 17–22.

Young, A.W., Newcombe, F., deHaan, E.H.F., Small, M. and Hau, D.C. (1993) Face perception after brain injury. *Brain*, 116, 941–59.

Young, L.J., Wang, Z. and Insel, T.R. (1998) Neuroendocrine bases of monogamy. *Trends in Neurosciences*, 21(2), 71–5.

Young, S.D., Adelstein, B.D. and Ellis, S.R. (2007) Demand characteristics in assessing motion sickness in a virtual environment: Or does taking a motion sickness questionnaire make you sick? *IEEE Transactions on Visualization and Computer Graphics*, 13, 422–8.

Youngston, R. (1998) *Scientific Blunders*. London: Robinson.

Youniss, J. and Smollar, J. (1985) *Adolescent Relations with Mothers, Fathers, and Friends*. Chicago: University of Chicago Press.

Yousem, D.M., Maldjian, J.A., Siddiqi, F., Hummel, T., Alsop, D.C., Geckle, R.J., Bilker, W.B. and Doty, R.L. (1999) Gender effects on odor-stimulated functional magnetic resonance imaging. *Brain Research*, 818, 480–7.

Yu, D.W. and Shepard, G.H. (1998) Is beauty in the eye of the beholder? *Nature*, 396, 321–2.

Yuki, M., Maddux, W.W., Brewer, M.B. and Takemura, K. (2005) Cross-cultural differences in relationship- and group-based trust. *Personality and Social Psychology Bulletin*, 31, 48–62.

Yuill, N. and Oakhill, J.V. (1991) *Children's Problems in Text Comprehension*. Cambridge: Cambridge University Press.

Yzerbyt, V.Y., Castano, E., Leyens, J-P. and Paladino, M-P. (2000) The primacy of the in-group: The interplay of entitativity and identification. *European Review of Social Psychology*, 11, 257–96.

Yzerbyt, V.Y., Coull, A.I. and Rocher, S. (1999) Fencing off the deviant: The role of cognitive resources in the maintenance of stereotypes. *Journal of Personality and Social Psychology*, 77, 448–62.

Zaccaro, S.J. (1984) Social loafing: The role of task attractiveness. *Personality and Social Psychology Bulletin*, 10, 99–106.

Zadro, L., Williams, K.D. and Richardson, R. (2005) Riding the 'O' train: Comparing the effects of ostracism and verbal dispute on targets and sources. *Group Processes and Intergroup Relations*, 8, 125–43.

Zagorsky, J.L. (2007) Do you have to be smart to be rich? The impact of IQ on wealth, income and financial distress. *Intelligence*, 35, 489–501.

Zaimov, K., Kitov, D. and Kolev, N. (1969) Aphasie chez un peintre. *Encephale*, 58, 377–417.

Zajonc, R.B. (1965) Social facilitation. *Science*, 149, 269–74.

Zajonc, R.B. (1968) Attitudinal effects of mere exposure. *Journal of Personality and Social Psychology*, Monograph Supplement, 9, 1–27.

Zajonc, R.B. (1984) On primacy of affect. In K.R. Scherer and P. Ekman (eds) *Approaches to Emotion*. Hillsdale, NJ: Lawrence Erlbaum Associates.

Zajonc, R.B. (1985) Emotion and facial efference: A theory reclaimed. *Science*, 228, 15–21.

Zak, P.J., Kurzban, R. and Matzner, W.T. (2005) Oxytocin is associated with human trustworthiness. *Hormones and Behavior*, 48, 522–7.

Zakowski, S.G., Ramati, A., Morton, C., Johnson, P. and Flanigan, R. (2004) Written emotional disclosure buffers the effects of social constraints on distress among cancer patients. *Health Psychology*, 23, 6, 555–63.

Zakzanis, K.K., Leach, L. and Kaplan, E. (1999) *Neuropsychological differential diagnosis*. Lisse: Swets & Zeitlinger.

Zaragoza, M.S. and Mitchell, K.J. (1996) Repeated suggestion and the creation of false memories. *Psychological Science*, 7, 294–300.

Zattore, R.J., Berlin, P. and Penhune, V.B. (2002) Structure and function of auditory cortex: Music and speech. *Trends in Cognitive Sciences*, 6(1), 37–46.

Zatorre, R.J., Evans, A.C., Meyer, E. and Gjedde, A. (1992) Lateralization of phonetic and pitch discrimination in speech processing. *Science*, 256, 846–9.

Zatorre, R.J., Meyer, E., Gjedde, A. and Evans, A.C. (1996) PET studies of phonetic processing of speech: Review, replication and reanalysis. *Cerebral Cortex*, 6(1), 21–30.

Zeanah, C.H., Boris, N.W. and Scheeringa, M.S. (1997) Psychopathology in infancy. *Journal of Child Psychology and Psychiatry*, 38(1), 81–99.

Zeanah, C.H., Nelson, CA., Fox, N.A., Smyke, A.T., Marshall, P., Parker, S.W. *et al* (2003) Designing research to study the effects of institutionalization on brain and behavioural development. *Development and Psychology*, 15, 885–907.

Zebrowitz, L.A. (1996) Physical appearance as a basis of stereotyping. In C.N. Macrae, C. Stangor and M. Hewstone (eds) *Stereotypes and Stereotyping*. New York: Guilford Press, pp. 79–120.

Zebrowitz, L.A. and Collins, M.A. (1997) Accurate social perception at zero acquaintance: The affordances of a Gibsonian approach. *Personality and Social Psychology Review*, 1, 204–23.

Zeegers, P. (2001) Approaches to learning in science: A longitudinal study. *British Journal of Educational Psychology*, 71, 115–132.

Zeidner, M. and Hammer, A.L. (1992) Coping with missile attack: Resources, strategies and outcomes. *Journal of Personality*, 60, 709–746.

Zeier, H., Brauchli, P. and Joller-Jemelka, H.I. (1996) Effects of work demands on immunoglobin A and cortisol in air-traffic controllers. *Biological Psychology*, 42, 413–23.

Zeisel, H. (1971) And then there was none: The diminution of federal jury. *University of Chicago Law Review*, 35, 228–41.

Zeki, S. (1993) *A Vision of the Brain*. Oxford: Blackwell Scientific.

Zeki, S. (1998) Art and the brain. *Daedalus*, 127(2), 71–103.

Zeki, S. and Ffytche, D.H. (1998) The Riddoch syndrome: Insights into the neurobiology of conscious vision. *Brain*, 121, 25–45.

Zelenski, J.M. and Larsen, R.J. (2000) The distribution of basic emotions in everyday life: A state and trait perspective from experience sampling data. *Journal of Research in Personality*, 34, 178–97.

Zelinsky, W. (1974) Selfward bound? Personal preference patterns and the changing map of American society. *Economic Geography*, 50, 144–79.

Zentner, M.R. (2005) Ideal mate personality concepts and compatibility in close relationships: A longitudinal analysis. *Journal of Personality and Social Psychology*, 89, 2, 242–56.

Zhang, H. and Xu, Y. (2006) Teaching of psychology to university students in China. *International Journal of Psychology*, 41, 1, 17–23.

Zhao, H. and Seibert, S.E. (2006) The Big Five personality dimensions and entrepreneurial status: A meta-analytical review. *Journal of Applied Psychology*, 91, 2, 259–71.

Zijlstra, F.R.H., Roe, A.E., Leonora, A.B. and Krediet, I. (1999) Temporal factors in mental work: Effects of interrupted activities. *Journal of Occupational and Organizational Psychology*, 72, 163–85.

Zilli, I., Giganti, F. and Salzarulo, P. (2007) Yawning in morning and evening types. *Physiology and Behavior*, 91, 218–22.

Zimbardo, P.G. (1970) The human choice: Individuation, reason, and order versus deindividuation, impulse, and chaos. In W.J. Arnold and D. Levine (eds) *Nebraska Symposium on Motivation*. Lincoln: University of Nebraska Press.

Zimbardo, P.G. (1982) Pathology of imprisonment. In D. Krebs (Ed), *Readings in Contemporary Social Psychology*. New York: Harper & Row.

Zisook, S., Schuchter, S.R., Irwin, M., Darko, D.F., Sledge, P. and Resovsky, K. (1994) Bereavement, depression and immune function. *Psychiatry Research*, 52, 1–10.

Zola, D. (1984) Redundancy and word perception during reading. *Perception and Psychophysics*, 36, 277–84.

Zorzi, M., Houghton, G. and Butterworth, B. (1998) Two routes or one in reading aloud? A connectionist dual-process model. *Journal of Experimental Psychology: Human Perception and Performance*, 24(4), 1131–1161.

Zuckerman, M. (1991) *Psychobiology of Personality*. Cambridge: Cambridge University Press.

Zuckerman, M. (2005) *Psychology of Personality* (2nd edn). Cambridge University Press.

Zukier, H. and Pepitone, A. (1984) Social roles and strategies in prediction: Some determinants of the use of base-rate information, *Journal of Personality and Social Psychology*, 47, 349–60.

Author Index

Subject Index

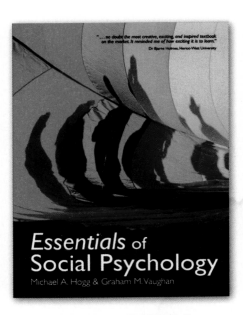